HALSBURY'S
Laws of England

FIFTH EDITION
2013

Volume 38A

This is volume 38A of the Fifth Edition of Halsbury's Laws of England, containing the third part of the title ELECTIONS AND REFERENDUMS.

The title ELECTIONS AND REFERENDUMS replaces the Fourth Edition title ELECTIONS AND REFERENDUMS, contained in vol 15(3) (2007 Reissue) and vol 15(4) (2007 Reissue). Both of those Fourth Edition volumes have been completely replaced and may now be archived.

For a full list of volumes comprised in a current set of Halsbury's Laws of England please see overleaf.

Fifth Edition volumes:

1 (2008), 2 (2008), 3 (2011), 4 (2011), 5 (2013), 6 (2011), 7 (2008), 8 (2010), 9 (2012), 10 (2012), 11 (2009), 12 (2009), 13 (2009), 14 (2009), 15 (2009), 16 (2011), 17 (2011), 18 (2009), 19 (2011), 21 (2011), 22 (2012), 23 (2013), 24 (2010), 25 (2010), 26 (2010), 27 (2010), 28 (2010), 30 (2012), 31 (2012), 32 (2012), 33 (2013), 34 (2011), 35 (2011), 36 (2011), 37 (2013), 38 (2013), 38A (2013), 39 (2009), 40 (2009), 41 (2009), 42 (2011), 43 (2011), 44 (2011), 45 (2010), 46 (2010), 48 (2008), 49 (2008), 50 (2008), 51 (2013), 52 (2009), 53 (2009), 54 (2008), 55 (2012), 56 (2011), 57 (2012), 60 (2011), 61 (2010), 62 (2012), 63 (2012), 64 (2012), 65 (2008), 66 (2009), 67 (2008), 68 (2008), 69 (2009), 70 (2012), 71 (2013), 72 (2009), 73 (2009), 74 (2011), 75 (2013), 76 (2013), 77 (2010), 78 (2010), 79 (2008), 80 (2013), 81 (2010), 82 (2010), 83 (2010), 84 (2013), 84A (2013), 85 (2012), 86 (2013), 87 (2012), 88 (2012), 88A (2013), 89 (2011), 90 (2011), 91 (2012), 92 (2010), 93 (2008), 94 (2008), 95 (2013), 96 (2012), 97 (2010), 98 (2013), 99 (2012), 100 (2009), 101 (2009), 102 (2010), 103 (2010)

Fourth Edition volumes (bold figures represent reissues):

1(1) (2001 Reissue), **8(1)** (2003 Reissue), 8(2), **12(1)**, **16(2)**, **17(2)**, **23(1)**, **23(2)**, **24**, **39(1B)**, 48 (2007 Reissue), 51, 52

Additional Materials:

Housing (*Housing Benefit*) containing vol **22** (2006 Reissue) paras 140–186; *Sentencing and Disposition of Offenders* (*Release and Recall of Prisoners*) containing vol **92** (2010) paras 761–820; *Tort* (*Conversion and Wrongful Interference with Goods*) containing vol **45(2)** (Reissue) paras 542–686

Fourth and Fifth Edition volumes:

2013 Consolidated Index (A–E), 2013 Consolidated Index (F–O), 2013 Consolidated Index (P–Z), 2014 Consolidated Table of Statutes, 2014 Consolidated Table of Statutory Instruments, etc, 2014 Consolidated Table of Cases (A–G), 2014 Consolidated Table of Cases (H–Q), 2014 Consolidated Table of Cases (R–Z, ECJ Cases)

Updating and ancillary materials:

2013 Annual Cumulative Supplement; Monthly Current Service; Annual Abridgments 1974–2012

December 2013

HALSBURY'S
Laws of England

FIFTH EDITION

LORD MACKAY OF CLASHFERN
Lord High Chancellor of Great Britain
1987–97

Volume 38A

2013

 LexisNexis®

Members of the LexisNexis Group worldwide

United Kingdom	LexisNexis, a Division of Reed Elsevier (UK) Ltd, Lexis House, 30 Farringdon Street, LONDON, EC4A 4HH, and London House, 20–22 East London Street, EDINBURGH, EH7 4BQ
Australia	LexisNexis Butterworths, Chatswood, New South Wales
Austria	LexisNexis Verlag ARD Orac GmbH & Co KG, Vienna
Benelux	LexisNexis Benelux, Amsterdam
Canada	LexisNexis Canada, Markham, Ontario
China	LexisNexis China, Beijing and Shanghai
France	LexisNexis SA, Paris
Germany	LexisNexis GmbH, Dusseldorf
Hong Kong	LexisNexis Hong Kong, Hong Kong
India	LexisNexis India, New Delhi
Italy	Giuffrè Editore, Milan
Japan	LexisNexis Japan, Tokyo
Malaysia	Malayan Law Journal Sdn Bhd, Kuala Lumpur
New Zealand	LexisNexis NZ Ltd, Wellington
Poland	Wydawnictwo Prawnicze LexisNexis Sp, Warsaw
Singapore	LexisNexis Singapore, Singapore
South Africa	LexisNexis Butterworths, Durban
USA	LexisNexis, Dayton, Ohio

FIRST EDITION	*Published in 31 volumes between 1907 and 1917*
SECOND EDITION	*Published in 37 volumes between 1931 and 1942*
THIRD EDITION	*Published in 43 volumes between 1952 and 1964*
FOURTH EDITION	*Published in 56 volumes between 1973 and 1987, with reissues between 1988 and 2008*
FIFTH EDITION	*Commenced in 2008*

A CIP Catalogue record for this book is available from the British Library.

ISBN 13 (complete set, standard binding): 9781405734394

ISBN 13: 9781405787772

ISBN 978-1-4057-8777-2

9 781405 787772

Typeset by Letterpart Limited, Caterham on the Hill, Surrey CR3 5XL
Printed and bound by CPI Group (UK) Ltd, Croydon, CR0 4YY
Visit LexisNexis at www.lexisnexis.co.uk

Editor in Chief

THE RIGHT HONOURABLE

LORD MACKAY OF CLASHFERN

LORD HIGH CHANCELLOR OF GREAT BRITAIN

1987–97

ELECTIONS AND REFERENDUMS

Consultant Editor

RICHARD PRICE, LLB, OBE, QC,

Bencher of the Honourable Society of Gray's Inn

The law stated in this volume is in general that in force on 1 November 2013, although subsequent changes have been included wherever possible.

Any future updating material will be found in the Current Service and annual Cumulative Supplement to Halsbury's Laws of England.

TABLE OF CONTENTS

Volume 37

ELECTIONS AND REFERENDUMS

Volume 38

Volume 38A

HOW TO USE HALSBURY'S LAWS OF ENGLAND

Volumes

Each text volume of Halsbury's Laws of England contains the law on the titles contained in it as at a date stated at the front of the volume (the operative date).

Information contained in Halsbury's Laws of England may be accessed in several ways.

First, by using the tables of contents.

Each volume contains both a general Table of Contents, and a specific Table of Contents for each title contained in it. From these tables you will be directed to the relevant part of the work.

Readers should note that the current arrangement of titles can be found in the Current Service.

Secondly, by using tables of statutes, statutory instruments, cases or other materials.

If you know the name of the Act, statutory instrument or case with which your research is concerned, you should consult the Consolidated Tables of statutes, cases and so on (published as separate volumes) which will direct you to the relevant volume and paragraph. The Consolidated Tables will indicate if the volume referred to is a Fifth Edition volume.

(Each individual text volume also includes tables of those materials used as authority in that volume.)

Thirdly, by using the indexes.

If you are uncertain of the general subject area of your research, you should go to the Consolidated Index (published as separate volumes) for reference to the relevant volume(s) and paragraph(s). The Consolidated Index will indicate if the volume referred to is a Fifth Edition volume.

(Each individual text volume also includes an index to the material contained therein.)

Additional Materials

The reorganisation of the title scheme of Halsbury's Laws for the Fifth Edition means that from time to time Fourth Edition volumes will be *partially* replaced by Fifth Edition volumes.

In certain instances an Additional Materials softbound book will be issued, in which will be reproduced material which has not yet been replaced by a Fifth Edition title. This will enable users to remove specific Fourth Edition volumes from the shelf and save valuable space pending the replacement of that material in the Fifth Edition. These softbound books are supplied to volumes subscribers free of charge. They continue to form part of the set of Halsbury's Laws Fourth Edition Reissue, and will be updated by the annual Cumulative Supplement and monthly Noter-Up in the usual way.

Updating publications

The text volumes of Halsbury's Laws should be used in conjunction with the annual Cumulative Supplement and the monthly Noter-Up.

The annual Cumulative Supplement

The Supplement gives details of all changes between the operative date of the text volume and the operative date of the Supplement. It is arranged in the same volume, title and paragraph order as the text volumes. Developments affecting particular points of law are noted to the relevant paragraph(s) of the text volumes. As from the commencement of the Fifth Edition, the Supplement will clearly distinguish between Fourth and Fifth Edition titles.

For narrative treatment of material noted in the Cumulative Supplement, go to the Annual Abridgment volume for the relevant year.

Destination Tables

In certain titles in the annual *Cumulative Supplement*, reference is made to Destination Tables showing the destination of consolidated legislation. Those Destination Tables are to be found either at the end of the titles within the annual *Cumulative Supplement*, or in a separate *Destination Tables* booklet provided from time to time with the *Cumulative Supplement*.

The Noter-Up

The Noter-Up is contained in the Current Service Noter-Up booklet, issued monthly and noting changes since the publication of the annual Cumulative Supplement. Also arranged in the same volume, title and paragraph order as the text volumes, the Noter-Up follows the style of the Cumulative Supplement. As from the commencement of the Fifth Edition, the Noter-Up will clearly distinguish between Fourth and Fifth Edition titles.

For narrative treatment of material noted in the Noter-Up, go to the relevant Monthly Review.

REFERENCES AND ABBREVIATIONS

ACT	Australian Capital Territory
A-G	Attorney General
Admin	Administrative Court
Admlty	Admiralty Court
Adv-Gen	Advocate General
affd	affirmed
affg	affirming
Alta	Alberta
App	Appendix
art	article
Aust	Australia
B	Baron
BC	British Columbia
C	Command Paper (of a series published before 1900)
c	chapter number of an Act
CA	Court of Appeal
CAC	Central Arbitration Committee
CA in Ch	Court of Appeal in Chancery
CB	Chief Baron
CCA	Court of Criminal Appeal
CCR	County Court Rules 1981 (SI 1981/1687) as subsequently amended
CCR	Court for Crown Cases Reserved
C-MAC	Courts-Martial Appeal Court
CO	Crown Office
COD	Crown Office Digest
CPR	Civil Procedure Rules 1998 (SI 1998/3132) as subsequently amended (see the Civil Court Practice)
Can	Canada
Cd	Command Paper (of the series published 1900–18)
Cf	compare
Ch	Chancery Division
ch	chapter
cl	clause

Cm	Command Paper (of the series published 1986 to date)
Cmd	Command Paper (of the series published 1919–56)
Cmnd	Command Paper (of the series published 1956–86)
Comm	Commercial Court
Comr.....................................	Commissioner
Court Forms (2nd Edn)..........	Atkin's Encyclopaedia of Court Forms in Civil Proceedings, 2nd Edn. See note 2 post.
Court Funds Rules 1987	Court Funds Rules 1987 (SI 1987/821) as subsequently amended
CrimPR	Criminal Procedure Rules 2010 (SI 2010/60) as subsequently amended
DC...	Divisional Court
DPP	Director of Public Prosecutions
EAT	Employment Appeal Tribunal
EC	European Community
ECJ..	Court of Justice of the European Community
EComHR................................	European Commission of Human Rights
ECSC......................................	European Coal and Steel Community
ECtHR Rules of Court...........	Rules of Court of the European Court of Human Rights
EEC.......................................	European Economic Community
EFTA	European Free Trade Association
EWCA Civ	Official neutral citation for judgments of the Court of Appeal (Civil Division)
EWCA Crim...........................	Official neutral citation for judgments of the Court of Appeal (Criminal Division)
EWHC....................................	Official neutral citation for judgments of the High Court
Edn..	Edition
Euratom	European Atomic Energy Community
Ex Ch....................................	Court of Exchequer Chamber
ex p	ex parte
Fam	Family Division
Fed	Federal
Forms & Precedents (5th Edn).......................................	Encyclopaedia of Forms and Precedents other than Court Forms, 5th Edn. See note 2 post.
GLC	Greater London Council
HC	High Court
HC	House of Commons
HK	Hong Kong
HL...	House of Lords

IAT	Immigration Appeal Tribunal
ILM	International Legal Materials
INLR	Immigration and Nationality Law Reports
IRC	Inland Revenue Commissioners
Ind	India
Int Rels	International Relations
Ir	Ireland
J	Justice
JA	Judge of Appeal
Kan	Kansas
LA	Lord Advocate
LC	Lord Chancellor
LCC	London County Council
LCJ	Lord Chief Justice
LJ	Lord Justice of Appeal
LoN	League of Nations
MR	Master of the Rolls
Man	Manitoba
n	note
NB	New Brunswick
NI	Northern Ireland
NS	Nova Scotia
NSW	New South Wales
NY	New York
NZ	New Zealand
OHIM	Office for Harmonisation in the Internal Market
OJ	The Official Journal of the European Community published by the Office for Official Publications of the European Community
Ont	Ontario
P	President
PC	Judicial Committee of the Privy Council
PEI	Prince Edward Island
Pat	Patents Court
q	question
QB	Queen's Bench Division
QBD	Queen's Bench Division of the High Court
Qld	Queensland
Que	Quebec
r	rule
RDC	Rural District Council
RPC	Restrictive Practices Court

RSC	Rules of the Supreme Court 1965 (SI 1965/1776) as subsequently amended
reg	regulation
Res	Resolution
revsd	reversed
Rly	Railway
s	section
SA	South Africa
S Aust	South Australia
SC	Supreme Court
SI	Statutory Instruments published by authority
SR & O	Statutory Rules and Orders published by authority
SR & O Rev 1904	Revised Edition comprising all Public and General Statutory Rules and Orders in force on 31 December 1903
SR & O Rev 1948	Revised Edition comprising all Public and General Statutory Rules and Orders and Statutory Instruments in force on 31 December 1948
SRNI	Statutory Rules of Northern Ireland
STI	Simon's Tax Intelligence (1973–1995); Simon's Weekly Tax Intelligence (1996-current)
Sask	Saskatchewan
Sch	Schedule
Sess	Session
Sing	Singapore
TCC	Technology and Construction Court
TS	Treaty Series
Tanz	Tanzania
Tas	Tasmania
UDC	Urban District Council
UKHL	Official neutral citation for judgments of the House of Lords
UKPC	Official neutral citation for judgments of the Privy Council
UN	United Nations
V-C	Vice-Chancellor
Vict	Victoria
W Aust	Western Australia
Zimb	Zimbabwe

NOTE 1. A general list of the abbreviations of law reports and other sources used in this work can be found at the beginning of the Consolidated Table of Cases.

NOTE 2. Where references are made to other publications, the volume number precedes and the page number follows the name of the publication; eg the reference '12 Forms & Precedents (5th Edn) 44' refers to volume 12 of the Encyclopaedia of Forms and Precedents, page 44.

NOTE 3. An English statute is cited by short title or, where there is no short title, by regnal year and chapter number together with the name by which it is commonly known or a description of its subject matter and date. In the case of a foreign statute, the mode of citation generally follows the style of citation in use in the country concerned with the addition, where necessary, of the name of the country in parentheses.

NOTE 4. A statutory instrument is cited by short title, if any, followed by the year and number, or, if unnumbered, the date.

TABLE OF STATUTES

TABLE OF STATUTORY INSTRUMENTS

H

L

TABLE OF CIVIL PROCEDURE

Practice Directions supplementing Civil Procedure Rules 1998, SI 1998/3132 (CPR)

TABLE OF EUROPEAN UNION LEGISLATION

TABLE OF CONVENTIONS ETC

TABLE OF CASES

PARA

Decisions of the European Court of Justice are listed below numerically. These decisions
are also included in the preceding alphabetical list.

ELECTIONS AND REFERENDUMS

VOLUME 37

VOLUME 38A

6. PROCEDURE FOR CONDUCTING REFERENDUMS

(1) GENERAL FRAMEWORK FOR THE CONDUCT OF NATIONAL AND REGIONAL REFERENDUMS

(i) In general

527. Referendums for which provision is made under the Political Parties, Elections and Referendums Act 2000. Part VII of the Political Parties, Elections and Referendums Act 2000[1] applies to any referendum held throughout: (1) the United Kingdom[2]; or (2) one or more of England[3], Scotland, Wales[4] and Northern Ireland[5]. For these purposes, 'referendum' means a referendum or other poll held, in pursuance of any provision made by or under an Act of Parliament[6], on one or more questions[7] specified in or in accordance with any such provision[8]. The referendum period in such a case is such period as is provided for by or under that Act[9]; and where the date of the poll in the case of any such referendum falls to be fixed under any provision made by or under that Act, the date so fixed must not be earlier than 28 days after the end of the period of 14 days within which the Electoral Commission must determine an application for designation[10] made by a permitted participant[11].

1 Ie the Political Parties, Elections and Referendums Act 2000 Pt VII (ss 101–129).
2 Political Parties, Elections and Referendums Act 2000 s 101(1)(a). As to the meaning of 'United Kingdom' see PARA 1 note 1.
3 As to the meaning of 'England' see PARA 1 note 1. The Political Parties, Elections and Referendums Act 2000 s 101(1)(c) provides that Pt VII also applies to any referendum held throughout any region in England specified in the Regional Development Agencies Act 1998 Sch 1, but Sch 1 was repealed by the Public Bodies Act 2011 Sch 6.
4 As to the meaning of 'Wales' see PARA 1 note 1. However, a poll held under the Government of Wales Act 2006 s 64 (poll held to ascertain views about whether or how any of the functions of the Welsh Ministers should be exercised: see PARA 662) is not to be taken to be a referendum to which the Political Parties, Elections and Referendums Act 2000 Pt VII applies: s 101(3) (amended by SI 2007/1338).
5 Political Parties, Elections and Referendums Act 2000 s 101(1)(b).
6 See eg the Regional Assemblies (Preparations) Act 2003 (repealed); and PARAS 4, 14. If the Secretary of State by order so provides, the Political Parties, Elections and Referendums Act 2000 s 101(2) applies to any specified Bill which has been introduced into Parliament before the making of the order as if it were an Act (s 101(4)(a)); and any specified provisions of Pt VII apply, subject to any specified modifications, in relation to any specified referendum for which provision is made by the Bill (s 101(4)(b)). In s 101(4), 'specified' means specified in the order under s 101(4): s 101(5). At the date at which this volume states the law, no such order had been made. As to the meaning of 'modification' see PARA 44 note 9. As to the Secretary of State see PARA 2. As to the conduct of local referendums and polls, which fall outside the scope of the definition of 'referendum' given in s 101(2), see PARA 555 et seq.
7 In the Political Parties, Elections and Referendums Act 2000 Pt VII, 'question' includes proposition (and 'answer' accordingly includes response): s 101(2)(b). As to the setting and approval of referendum questions see PARA 528.
8 Political Parties, Elections and Referendums Act 2000 s 101(2)(a). In connection with the national and regional referendums to which these provisions are applicable see further PARA 14. The Electoral Commission must, after each such referendum, prepare and publish, in such manner as the Commission may determine, a report on the administration of the referendum: see PARA 51. As to the Electoral Commission see PARA 34 et seq.
9 Political Parties, Elections and Referendums Act 2000 s 102(1), (3). However, in the case of a referendum to which an order under s 101(4) applies (see note 6), the referendum period is such period, not exceeding six months, as may be specified in the order (s 102(4)) unless the referendum period in such a case would end after the date of the poll, in which case it ends instead on that date (s 102(5)).

10 Ie, subject to the Political Parties, Elections and Referendums Act 2000 s 103(2), the period of 14 days mentioned in s 109(3) (see PARA 530). As to designation of permitted participants as organisations to whom assistance is available see PARA 530 et seq. As to the meaning of 'permitted participant' see PARA 529.

    If an order applies to the referendum under s 109(6) (Secretary of State may specify different periods of time in relation to applications for designation: see PARA 530), this period of 14 days must be read as referring to the period which is to apply instead: s 103(2).

11 Political Parties, Elections and Referendums Act 2000 s 103(1).

(ii) Referendum Questions

528. Wording of referendum questions. Where a Bill is introduced into Parliament which provides for the holding of a poll that would be a referendum[1] to which the general framework provisions apply[2] and the Bill specifies the wording of the referendum question[3], the Electoral Commission[4] must consider the wording of the question[5], and must publish a statement of any views of the Commission as to the intelligibility of that question as soon as reasonably practicable after the Bill is introduced[6] and in such manner as it may determine[7].

Where the wording of such a question falls to be specified in subordinate legislation[8] then, if a draft of the instrument in question is to be laid before Parliament for approval by each House, the Secretary of State[9] must consult the Commission on the wording of the referendum question[10] before any such draft is so laid[11] and he must, at the time when any such draft is so laid, lay before each House a report stating any views as to the intelligibility of that question which the Commission has expressed in response to that consultation[12]. If the instrument in question is to be subject to annulment in pursuance of a resolution of either House of Parliament, the Secretary of State must consult the Commission on the wording of the referendum question[13] before making the instrument[14] and he must, at the time when the instrument is laid before Parliament, lay before each House a report stating any views as to the intelligibility of that question which the Commission has expressed in response to that consultation[15].

1 As to the meaning of 'referendum' see PARA 527.
2 Political Parties, Elections and Referendums Act 2000 s 104(1)(a). The reference in the text is to a referendum to which the general framework provisions for the holding of referendums contained in Pt VII (ss 101–129) apply: see PARA 527.
3 Political Parties, Elections and Referendums Act 2000 s 104(1)(b). For these purposes, the 'referendum question' means the question or questions to be included in the ballot paper at the referendum: s 104(7). As to the meaning of 'question' see PARA 527 note 7.
4 As to the Electoral Commission see PARA 34 et seq.
5 Where any such Bill specifies not only the referendum question but also any statement which is to precede that question on the ballot paper at the referendum, any reference to the referendum question must be read as a reference to that question and that statement taken together: Political Parties, Elections and Referendums Act 2000 s 104(6).
6 Political Parties, Elections and Referendums Act 2000 s 104(2)(a).
7 Political Parties, Elections and Referendums Act 2000 ss 104(2)(b), 160(1).
8 Political Parties, Elections and Referendums Act 2000 s 104(3). The text refers to subordinate legislation within the meaning of the Interpretation Act 1978 (see STATUTES AND LEGISLATIVE PROCESS vol 96 (2012) PARA 608).
9 Political Parties, Elections and Referendums Act 2000 s 104(4). As to the Secretary of State see PARA 2.
10 Where any such draft instrument specifies not only the referendum question but also any statement which is to precede that question on the ballot paper at the referendum, any reference to the referendum question must be read as a reference to that question and that statement taken together: Political Parties, Elections and Referendums Act 2000 s 104(6).
11 Political Parties, Elections and Referendums Act 2000 s 104(4)(a).
12 Political Parties, Elections and Referendums Act 2000 s 104(4)(b).

13 Where any instrument to which the Political Parties, Elections and Referendums Act 2000
   s 104(5) applies specifies not only the referendum question but also any statement which is to
   precede that question on the ballot paper at the referendum, any reference to the referendum
   question must be read as a reference to that question and that statement taken together:
   s 104(6).
14 Political Parties, Elections and Referendums Act 2000 s 104(5)(a).
15 Political Parties, Elections and Referendums Act 2000 s 104(5)(b).

(iii) Permitted Participants

529. Meaning of 'permitted participant'. In relation to a particular
referendum[1] to which the general framework provisions apply[2], a 'permitted
participant' means[3]: (1) a registered party[4] by whom a declaration has been
made to the Electoral Commission[5] in relation to the referendum[6]; or (2) any of
the following by whom a notification has been given to the Commission[7] in
relation to the referendum, namely[8]: (a) any individual resident in the United
Kingdom[9] or registered in an electoral register[10]; or (b) one of the 'permissible
donors' for party funding purposes[11].

For these purposes, a registered party makes a declaration to the Commission
if the party makes a declaration to the Commission which identifies the
referendum to which it relates[12] and the outcome or outcomes[13] for which the
party proposes to campaign[14]. Such a declaration must be signed by the
responsible officers of the party[15] and, if made by a minor party[16], must be
accompanied by a notification which states the name of the person who will be
responsible for compliance on the part of the party with the financial controls
which operate during a referendum[17]. For these purposes, an individual or
body[18] gives a notification to the Commission if he or it gives the Commission a
notification which identifies the referendum to which it relates[19] and the
outcome or outcomes for which the giver of the notification proposes to
campaign[20]. Such a notification: (i) if given by an individual, must state his full
name[21] and his home address in the United Kingdom (or, if he has no such
address in the United Kingdom, his home address elsewhere)[22] and must be
signed by him[23]; or (ii) if given by one of the permissible donors[24], must state all
such details in respect of the body as are required[25] to be given in respect of such
a body as the donor of a recordable donation[26] and the name of the person or
officer who will be responsible for compliance on the part of the body with the
financial controls which operate during a referendum[27], and must be signed by
the body's secretary or a person who acts in a similar capacity in relation to the
body[28]. If at any time before the end of the compliance period[29] any of the
statements which are contained in a notification[30] (as it has effect for the time
being) ceases to be accurate, the permitted participant by whom the notification
was given must give the Commission a notification (a 'notification of alteration')
indicating that that statement is replaced by some other statement contained in
the notification of alteration[31] and conforming with the provision under which
the original notification was given[32].

The Commission must maintain a register of all declarations made to it by a
registered party[33] and of all notifications given to it by an individual or body[34].
The register must be maintained by the Commission in such form as it may
determine and must contain, in the case of each such declaration or notification,
all of the information supplied to the Commission in connection with it[35]. Where
any such declaration or notification is made or given to the Commission[36], it
must cause all the information contained therein to be entered in the register (or,
in the case of a notification of alteration, any change required as a consequence

of the notification to be made in the register) as soon as is reasonably practicable[37]; but the information which is to be so entered in the register in respect of a permitted participant who is an individual must not include his home address[38]. The Commission must make a copy of the register so kept by it[39] available for public inspection during ordinary office hours, either at the Commission's offices or at some convenient place appointed by it[40], although the Commission may make other arrangements for members of the public to have access to the register's contents[41]. If requested to do so by any person, the Commission must supply him with a copy of the register or any part of it[42] and the Commission may charge such reasonable fee as it may determine in respect of any inspection or access so allowed or any copy so supplied[43]. Where any such register is held by the Commission in electronic form, any copy so made available for public inspection or so supplied must be made available, or (as the case may be) supplied, in a legible form[44].

1   As to the meaning of 'referendum' see PARA 527.
2   Ie the Political Parties, Elections and Referendums Act 2000 Pt VII (ss 101–129).
3   Political Parties, Elections and Referendums Act 2000 s 105(1).
4   As to the meaning of 'registered party' see PARA 35 note 3.
5   Ie a declaration made under the Political Parties, Elections and Referendums Act 2000 s 106 (see the text and notes 12–17). As to the Electoral Commission see PARA 34 et seq.
6   Political Parties, Elections and Referendums Act 2000 s 105(1)(a).
7   Ie a notification made under the Political Parties, Elections and Referendums Act 2000 s 106 (see the text and notes 18–32).
8   Political Parties, Elections and Referendums Act 2000 s 105(1)(b).
9   As to the meaning of 'United Kingdom' see PARA 1 note 1.
10 Political Parties, Elections and Referendums Act 2000 s 105(1)(b)(i). The text refers to an electoral register as defined by s 54(8) (see PARA 288).
11 Ie: (1) a company registered under the Companies Act 2006 and incorporated within the United Kingdom or another member state which carries on business in the United Kingdom (Political Parties, Elections and Referendums Act 2000 ss 54(2)(b), 105(1)(b)(ii) (s 54(2)(b) amended by SI 2009/1941)); (2) a trade union entered in the list kept under the Trade Union and Labour Relations (Consolidation) Act 1992 (Political Parties, Elections and Referendums Act 2000 s 54(2)(d)); (3) a building society within the meaning of the Building Societies Act 1986 (see FINANCIAL SERVICES AND INSTITUTIONS vol 50 (2008) PARA 1856) (Political Parties, Elections and Referendums Act 2000 s 54(2)(e)); (4) a limited liability partnership registered under the Limited Liability Partnerships Act 2000 (see PARTNERSHIP vol 79 (2008) PARA 234 et seq) which carries on business in the United Kingdom (Political Parties, Elections and Referendums Act 2000 s 54(2)(f)); (5) a friendly society registered under the Friendly Societies Act 1974 (see FINANCIAL SERVICES AND INSTITUTIONS vol 50 (2008) PARA 2084 et seq) or a society registered (or deemed to be registered) under the Industrial and Provident Societies Act 1965 (see FINANCIAL SERVICES AND INSTITUTIONS vol 50 (2008) PARAS 2394, 2410 et seq) (Political Parties, Elections and Referendums Act 2000 s 54(2)(g)); and (6) any unincorporated association of two or more persons which does not fall within any of heads (1) to (5) above but which carries on business or other activities wholly or mainly in the United Kingdom and whose main office is there (s 54(2)(h)). As to the registration and incorporation of companies see COMPANIES vol 14 (2009) PARA 24 et seq; and as to the control of contributions and other donations made by companies generally to registered parties and other European Union political organisations, and European Union political expenditure incurred by companies, see the Companies Act 1985 Pt XA (ss 347A–347K); and COMPANIES vol 14 (2009) PARA 688 et seq. As to the list of trades unions referred to in the text see EMPLOYMENT vol 40 (2009) PARA 855. Unless certain conditions are met, the funds of a trade union may not be applied in the furtherance of certain political objects: see the Trade Union and Labour Relations (Consolidation) Act 1992 Pt I Ch VI (ss 71–96); and EMPLOYMENT vol 40 (2009) PARA 924 et seq.
12 Political Parties, Elections and Referendums Act 2000 ss 106(1)(a), 160(1).
13 For the purposes of the Political Parties, Elections and Referendums Act 2000 ss 107–109, 'outcome', in the case of a referendum, means a particular outcome in relation to any question asked in the referendum: s 106(7). As to the meaning of 'question' see PARA 527 note 7.
14 Political Parties, Elections and Referendums Act 2000 s 106(1)(b).

15 Political Parties, Elections and Referendums Act 2000 s 106(2)(a). The text refers to the 'responsible officers' of the party within the meaning of s 64 (see PARA 311 note 26).

16 As to the meaning of 'minor party' see PARA 253 note 8.

17 Political Parties, Elections and Referendums Act 2000 s 106(2)(b). The text refers to the provisions of Pt VII Ch II (ss 111–124) (see PARA 535 et seq). For the purposes of Pt VII, 'responsible person' means, if the permitted participant is a registered party, the treasurer of the party or, in the case of a minor party, the person for the time being notified to the Commission by the party in accordance with s 106(2)(b): s 105(2)(a). As to the treasurer of a registered party see PARA 253.

18 As to the meaning of 'body' see PARA 58 note 2.

19 Political Parties, Elections and Referendums Act 2000 ss 106(3)(a), 160(1). Any notification required to be given under the Political Parties, Elections and Referendums Act 2000 must be in writing: s 157(1).

20 Political Parties, Elections and Referendums Act 2000 s 106(3)(b).

21 Political Parties, Elections and Referendums Act 2000 s 106(4)(a)(i).

22 Political Parties, Elections and Referendums Act 2000 s 106(4)(a)(ii).

23 Political Parties, Elections and Referendums Act 2000 s 106(4)(a).

24 See note 11.

25 Ie by virtue of any of the provisions of the Political Parties, Elections and Referendums Act 2000 s 62(13), Sch 6 para 2(4), (6)–(10) (quarterly donation reports: see CONSTITUTIONAL LAW AND HUMAN RIGHTS).

26 Political Parties, Elections and Referendums Act 2000 s 106(4)(b)(i). As to the meaning of 'recordable donation' see PARA 311 note 14.

27 Political Parties, Elections and Referendums Act 2000 s 106(4)(b)(ii). The text refers to the provisions of Pt VII Ch II (see PARA 535 et seq). For the purposes of Pt VII, 'responsible person' means, if the permitted participant is an individual, that individual (s 105(2)(b)) and, otherwise, the person or officer for the time being notified to the Commission by the permitted participant in accordance with s 106(4)(b)(ii) (s 105(2)(c)).

28 Political Parties, Elections and Referendums Act 2000 s 106(4)(b).

29 For these purposes, the 'compliance period' is the period during which any provisions of the Political Parties, Elections and Referendums Act 2000 Pt VII Ch II (see PARA 535 et seq) remain to be complied with on the part of the permitted participant: s 106(6)(a).

30 Ie in accordance with any provision of the Political Parties, Elections and Referendums Act 2000 s 106(2) (see the text and notes 15–17) or s 106(4) (see the text and notes 21–28).

31 Political Parties, Elections and Referendums Act 2000 s 106(5)(a).

32 Political Parties, Elections and Referendums Act 2000 s 106(5)(b), (6)(b). The text refers to the notification conforming with either s 106(2) (see the text and notes 15–17) or s 106(4) (see the text and notes 21–28), whichever is appropriate.

33 Political Parties, Elections and Referendums Act 2000 ss 107(1)(a), 160(1). The text refers to declarations made under s 106 (see the text and notes 12–17).

34 Political Parties, Elections and Referendums Act 2000 s 107(1)(b). The text refers to notifications made under s 106 (see the text and notes 18–32).

35 Political Parties, Elections and Referendums Act 2000 s 107(2). The text refers to the information supplied to the Commission in connection with each such declaration or notification in pursuance of s 106 (see the text and notes 12–32).

36 Ie under the Political Parties, Elections and Referendums Act 2000 s 106 (see the text and notes 12–32).

37 Political Parties, Elections and Referendums Act 2000 s 107(3).

38 Political Parties, Elections and Referendums Act 2000 s 107(4).

39 Ie under the Political Parties, Elections and Referendums Act 2000 s 107 (see the text and notes 33–38).

40 Political Parties, Elections and Referendums Act 2000 s 149(1)(d), (2).

41 Political Parties, Elections and Referendums Act 2000 s 149(1)(d), (3).

42 Political Parties, Elections and Referendums Act 2000 s 149(1)(d), (4).

43 Political Parties, Elections and Referendums Act 2000 s 149(1)(d), (5).

44 Political Parties, Elections and Referendums Act 2000 s 149(1)(d), (7).

530. Power of Electoral Commission to designate permitted participants for assistance. In respect of any referendum[1] to which the general framework provisions apply[2], the Electoral Commission[3] may designate permitted participants[4] as organisations[5] to whom assistance is available[6]. Where there are only two possible outcomes[7] in the case of such a referendum, the Commission may, in relation to each of those outcomes, designate one permitted participant as representing those campaigning for the outcome in question[8]; but the Commission otherwise must not make any designation in respect of the referendum[9]. Where there are more than two possible outcomes in the case of such a referendum, the Secretary of State[10] may, after consulting the Commission, by order specify the possible outcomes in relation to which permitted participants may be designated[11]. In such a case the Commission may, in relation to each of two or more outcomes specified in any such order, designate one permitted participant as representing those campaigning for the outcome in question[12]; but the Commission otherwise must not make any designation in respect of the referendum[13].

A permitted participant seeking to be designated in this way must make an application for the purpose to the Electoral Commission[14]. An application for designation[15] must be accompanied by information or statements designed to show that the applicant adequately represents those campaigning for the outcome at the referendum in relation to which the applicant seeks to be designated[16] and it must be made within the period of 28 days[17] beginning with the first day of the referendum period[18]. Where an application for designation has been so made to the Commission, the application must be determined by the Commission within the period of 14 days which begins with the day after the end of the period of 28 days[19] beginning with the first day of the referendum period[20]. If there is only one application in relation to a particular outcome at the referendum, the Commission must designate the applicant unless[21]: (1) it is not satisfied that the applicant adequately represents those campaigning for that outcome[22]; or (2) it is prevented from making any designation[23] in respect of the referendum[24]. If there is more than one application in relation to a particular outcome at the referendum, the Commission must designate whichever of the applicants appears to it to represent to the greatest extent those campaigning for that outcome unless[25]: (a) it is not satisfied that any of the applicants adequately represents those campaigning for that outcome[26]; or (b) it is prevented from making any designation[27] in respect of the referendum[28].

1   As to the meaning of 'referendum' see PARA 527.
2   Ie the Political Parties, Elections and Referendums Act 2000 Pt VII (ss 101–129).
3   As to the Electoral Commission see PARA 34 et seq.
4   As to the meaning of 'permitted participant' see PARA 529.
5   As to the meaning of 'organisation' see PARA 53 note 26.
6   Political Parties, Elections and Referendums Act 2000 ss 108(1), 160(1). The text refers to the assistance that is available in accordance with s 110 (see PARA 531).
7   As to the meaning of 'outcome' see PARA 529 note 13.
8   Political Parties, Elections and Referendums Act 2000 s 108(2)(a).
9   Political Parties, Elections and Referendums Act 2000 s 108(2)(b).
10 As to the Secretary of State see PARA 2.
11 Political Parties, Elections and Referendums Act 2000 s 108(3). At the date at which this volume states the law, no such order had been made.
12 Political Parties, Elections and Referendums Act 2000 s 108(4)(a).
13 Political Parties, Elections and Referendums Act 2000 s 108(4)(b).
14 Political Parties, Elections and Referendums Act 2000 ss 109(1), 160(1). Any application required to be made under the Political Parties, Elections and Referendums Act 2000 must be in writing: s 157(1).
15 For these purposes, in relation to a referendum, any reference to designation is to designation in respect of the referendum under the Political Parties, Elections and Referendums Act 2000 s 108 (see the text and notes 1–13): s 109(7).
16 Political Parties, Elections and Referendums Act 2000 s 109(2)(a).

17 The Secretary of State may, in the case of any referendum to which the Political Parties, Elections and Referendums Act 2000 Part VII applies, by order provide for s 109 to have effect as if the period of 28 days referred to in s 109(2) was instead such shorter or longer period as is specified in the order: s 109(6). See the Regional Assembly and Local Government Referendums (Date of Referendums, Referendum Question and Explanatory Material) (North East Region) Order 2004, SI 2004/1963, art 6(1) (which modified the period of 28 days referred to in the Political Parties, Elections and Referendums Act 2000 s 109(2) to have effect, in relation to a referendum held in the North East region about the establishment of an elected assembly for that region, as if it were a period of 42 days); and the National Assembly for Wales Referendum (Assembly Act Provisions) (Limit on Referendum Expenses Etc) Order 2010, SI 2010/2985, art 3 (which modified the period of 28 days referred to in the Political Parties, Elections and Referendums Act 2000 s 109(2)(b) to have effect, in relation to the referendum held under the Government of Wales Act 2006 s 103 in accordance with the National Assembly for Wales Referendum (Assembly Act Provisions) (Referendum Question, Date of Referendum Etc) Order 2010, SI 2010/2837, as if it were a period of 35 days).

18 Political Parties, Elections and Referendums Act 2000 s 109(2)(b). As to the referendum period see PARA 527.

19 The Secretary of State may, in the case of any referendum to which the Political Parties, Elections and Referendums Act 2000 Part VII applies, by order provide for s 109 to have effect as if each, or either, of the periods of 28 and 14 days referred to in s 109(3) was instead such shorter or longer period as is specified in the order: s 109(6). See the Regional Assembly and Local Government Referendums (Date of Referendums, Referendum Question and Explanatory Material) (North East Region) Order 2004, SI 2004/1963, art 6(1) (which modified the period of 28 days referred to in the Political Parties, Elections and Referendums Act 2000 s 109(3) to have effect, in relation to a referendum held in the North East region about the establishment of an elected assembly for that region, as if it were a period of 42 days); and the National Assembly for Wales Referendum (Assembly Act Provisions) (Limit on Referendum Expenses Etc) Order 2010, SI 2010/2985, art 3 (which modified the period of 28 days referred to in the Political Parties, Elections and Referendums Act 2000 s 109(3) to have effect, in relation to the referendum held under the Government of Wales Act 2006 s 103 in accordance with the National Assembly for Wales Referendum (Assembly Act Provisions) (Referendum Question, Date of Referendum Etc) Order 2010, SI 2010/2837, as if it were a period of 35 days).

20 Political Parties, Elections and Referendums Act 2000 s 109(2)(b), (3).

21 Political Parties, Elections and Referendums Act 2000 s 109(4).

22 Political Parties, Elections and Referendums Act 2000 s 109(4)(a).

23 Ie by virtue of the Political Parties, Elections and Referendums Act 2000 s 108(2)(b) (see the text and note 9) or s 108(4)(b) (see the text and note 13).

24 Political Parties, Elections and Referendums Act 2000 s 109(4)(b).

25 Political Parties, Elections and Referendums Act 2000 s 109(5).

26 Political Parties, Elections and Referendums Act 2000 s 109(5)(a).

27 See note 23.

28 Political Parties, Elections and Referendums Act 2000 s 109(5)(b).

531. Assistance available to designated organisations. Where the Electoral Commission[1] has made any designations[2] in respect of a referendum[3], assistance is available to the organisations[4] so designated[5]. The Commission must make to each designated organisation a grant of the same amount, which must be an amount not exceeding £600,000 determined by the Commission[6]. Such a grant may be made subject to such conditions[7] as the Commission considers appropriate[8]. Each designated organisation (or, as the case may be, person authorised by the organisation) has rights conferred[9] as to: (1) the sending of referendum addresses free of charge[10]; (2) the use of rooms free of charge for holding public meetings[11]; and (3) referendum campaign broadcasts[12].

1   As to the Electoral Commission see PARA 34 et seq.

2   As to the meaning of references to designations see PARA 530 note 15. See further the National Assembly for Wales Referendum (Assembly Act Provisions) (Limit on Referendum Expenses Etc) Order 2010, SI 2010/2985, art 3; and PARA 530.

3   As to the meaning of 'referendum' see PARA 527.

4   As to the meaning of 'organisation' see PARA 53 note 26.

5   Political Parties, Elections and Referendums Act 2000 ss 110(1), 160(1). For the purposes of
    s 110 and Sch 12, 'designated organisation', in relation to a referendum, means a person or
    body designated by the Commission under s 108 (see PARA 530) in respect of that referendum:
    s 110(5). As to the meaning of 'body' see PARA 58 note 2.
6   Political Parties, Elections and Referendums Act 2000 s 110(2). The Secretary of State may by
    order vary the sum for the time being specified in s 110(2): see s 155; and PARA 299 note 36. At
    the date at which this volume states the law, no such order had been made.
7   As to the meaning of references to 'conditions' see PARA 60 note 15.
8   Political Parties, Elections and Referendums Act 2000 s 110(3).
9   Ie by or by virtue of the Political Parties, Elections and Referendums Act 2000 Sch 12 (see PARAS
    532–534).
10 Political Parties, Elections and Referendums Act 2000 s 110(4)(a). See PARA 532.
11 Political Parties, Elections and Referendums Act 2000 s 110(4)(b). See PARA 533.
12 Political Parties, Elections and Referendums Act 2000 s 110(4)(c). See PARA 534.

532.   Right of designated organisations to send referendum address post free.
Subject to such reasonable terms and conditions as the universal service
provider[1] concerned may specify[2], a designated organisation[3] is entitled to send
free of any charge for postage which would otherwise be made by a universal
service provider[4] either: (1) one unaddressed postal communication, containing
matter relating to the referendum[5] only and not exceeding 60 grammes in
weight, to each place in the referendum area[6] which, in accordance with those
terms and conditions, constitutes a delivery point for these purposes[7]; or (2) one
such postal communication addressed to each person entitled to vote at the
referendum[8]. A designated organisation is also, subject as mentioned above,
entitled to send free of any such charge for postage to each person entered in the
list of proxies for the referendum one such postal communication for each
appointment in respect of which that person is so entered[9].

1   For these purposes, 'universal service provider' has the same meaning as in the Postal Services
    Act 2011 Pt 3 (ss 27–67) (see POSTAL SERVICES vol 85 (2012) PARA 243): Political Parties,
    Elections and Referendums Act 2000 Sch 12 para 1(4) (amended by the Postal Services Act 2011
    Sch 12 para 158).
2   As to schemes as to terms and conditions for the provision of a universal postal service see the
    Postal Services Act 2000 s 89; and POSTAL SERVICES vol 85 (2012) PARA 272.
3   As to the meaning of 'designated organisation' see PARA 531 note 5.
4   Political Parties, Elections and Referendums Act 2000 Sch 12 para 1(1). Where any postal
    services are provided without charge by a universal postal service provider in pursuance of
    Sch 12 para 1, the universal postal service provider is entitled to be remunerated for having
    provided the services at the rate fixed in relation to them by virtue of a scheme under the Postal
    Services Act 2000 s 89 (schemes as to terms and conditions for provision of a universal postal
    service: see POSTAL SERVICES vol 85 (2012) PARA 272): Representation of the People Act 1983
    s 200A(1), (2) (s 200A added by the Postal Services Act 2000 Sch 8 para 18; Representation of
    the People Act 1983 s 200A(1)–(3) amended, s 200A(4) substituted, by the Postal Services
    Act 2011 Sch 12 para 119); Political Parties, Elections and Referendums Act 2000 Sch 12
    para 1(3). A sum which a universal postal service provider is entitled to receive in this way is
    charged on and issued out of the Consolidated Fund: Representation of the People Act 1983
    s 200A(3) (as so amended). For these purposes, 'postal services' has the same meanings as in the
    Postal Services Act 2011 s 27 (see POSTAL SERVICES vol 85 (2012) PARA 243): Representation of
    the People Act 1983 s 200A(4) (as so added). As to the Consolidated Fund see CONSTITUTIONAL
    LAW AND HUMAN RIGHTS vol 8(2) (Reissue) PARA 711 et seq; PARLIAMENT vol 78 (2010) PARAS
    1028–1031.
5   As to the meaning of 'referendum' see PARA 527.
6   For these purposes, the 'referendum area' means the area throughout which the referendum is
    being held: Political Parties, Elections and Referendums Act 2000 Sch 12 para 1(4).
7   Political Parties, Elections and Referendums Act 2000 Sch 12 para 1(1)(a).
8   Political Parties, Elections and Referendums Act 2000 Sch 12 para 1(1)(b). As to persons
    entitled to vote in a referendum under the Political Parties, Elections and Referendums Act 2000
    see PARA 103.
9   Political Parties, Elections and Referendums Act 2000 Sch 12 para 1(2).

533. Schools and rooms available to designated organisations for meetings at referendums. Persons authorised by a designated organisation[1] are entitled, for the purpose of holding public meetings in furtherance of the organisation's referendum campaign[2] to the use free of charge of certain rooms at reasonable times during the period of 28 days ending with the day before the date of the poll[3].

Such a person is entitled to the use of a suitable room[4] in the premises of a community, foundation or voluntary school[5] whose premises are situated in the referendum area[6]. However, a person is not entitled to exercise the right so conferred except on reasonable notice; and the right does not authorise any interference with the hours during which a room in school premises is used for educational purposes[7].

Such a person is also entitled to the use free of charge of any meeting room[8] situated in the referendum area the expense of maintaining which is payable wholly or mainly out of public funds[9] or by any local authority, or by a body whose expenses are so payable[10]. However, a person is not entitled to exercise the right so conferred except on reasonable notice; and the right does not authorise any interference with the use of a meeting room either for the purposes of the person maintaining it or under a prior agreement for its letting for any purpose[11].

Where a room is used for a meeting in pursuance of the rights so conferred, the person by whom or on whose behalf the meeting is convened must: (1) defray any expenses incurred in preparing, warming, lighting and cleaning the room and providing attendance for the meeting and restoring the room to its usual condition after the meeting[12]; and (2) defray the cost of repairing any damage done to the room or the premises in which it is situated, or to the furniture, fittings or apparatus in the room or premises[13].

1   As to the meaning of 'designated organisation' see PARA 531 note 5. As to the meaning of 'organisation' see PARA 53 note 26.

2   As to the meaning of 'referendum campaign' see PARA 535 note 4.

3   Political Parties, Elections and Referendums Act 2000 Sch 12 para 2(1).

4   For these purposes, 'room' includes a hall, gallery or gymnasium: Political Parties, Elections and Referendums Act 2000 Sch 12 para 2(6).

5   For these purposes, except those of the Political Parties, Elections and Referendums Act 2000 Sch 12 para 2(4)(b) (see the text and note 13), the premises of a school is not to be taken to include any private dwelling, where 'dwelling' includes any part of a building where that part is occupied separately as a dwelling: Sch 12 para 2(6). As to community, foundation and voluntary schools see EDUCATION vol 35 (2011) PARA 106 et seq.

6   Political Parties, Elections and Referendums Act 2000 Sch 12 para 2(1)(a), (2)(a). For this purpose, the 'referendum area' means the area throughout which the referendum is being held: Sch 12 para 2(7).

     Any arrangements for the use of a room in school premises must be made with the local authority maintaining the school or, in the case of a room in the premises of a foundation or voluntary aided school, with the governing body of the school: Sch 12 para 3(1), (2) (Sch 12 para 3(2) amended, Sch 12 para 3(5) added, by SI 2010/1158). Any question as to the rooms in school premises which a person authorised by a designated organisation is entitled to use, or as to the times at which he is entitled to use them, or as to the notice which is reasonable, must be determined by the Secretary of State: Political Parties, Elections and Referendums Act 2000 Sch 12 para 3(1), (3). Any person authorised by a designated organisation is entitled at all reasonable hours to inspect any lists prepared in pursuance of the Representation of the People Act 1983 s 95(6), Sch 5 para 4 (use of rooms for parliamentary election meetings: see PARA 336) or a copy of any such lists, in connection with exercising the rights conferred by the Political Parties, Elections and Referendums Act 2000 Sch 12 para 2: Sch 12 para 3(1), (4). As to the meaning of 'local education authority' see the Education Act 1996 s 579(1); and EDUCATION vol 35 (2011) PARA 58 (definition applied by the Political Parties, Elections and Referendums Act 2000 Sch 12 para 3(5) (as so added)). As to the Secretary of State see PARA 2.

7   Political Parties, Elections and Referendums Act 2000 Sch 12 para 2(5).
8   'Meeting room' means any room which it is the practice to let for public meetings: Political
     Parties, Elections and Referendums Act 2000 Sch 12 para 2(6).
9   As to references to payments out of public funds see PARA 299 note 21.
10   Political Parties, Elections and Referendums Act 2000 Sch 12 para 2(1)(b), (3). As to the
     meaning of 'body' see PARA 58 note 2.
11   Political Parties, Elections and Referendums Act 2000 Sch 12 para 2(5).
12   Political Parties, Elections and Referendums Act 2000 Sch 12 para 2(4)(a).
13   Political Parties, Elections and Referendums Act 2000 Sch 12 para 2(4)(b).

534.   Broadcasting during referendum period.   The British Broadcasting
Corporation ('the BBC')[1] must have regard, in determining its policy with respect
to referendum campaign broadcasts[2] by designated organisations[3], to any views
expressed by the Electoral Commission[4] for these purposes[5].

1   As to the BBC see BROADCASTING vol 4 (2011) PARA 603 et seq.
2   For these purposes, 'referendum campaign broadcast' has the same meaning as in the Political
     Parties, Elections and Referendums Act 2000 s 127 (see PARA 552): Sch 12 para 4(7).
3   As to the meaning of 'designated organisation' see PARA 531 note 5. As to the meaning of
     'organisation' see PARA 53 note 26.
4   As to the Electoral Commission see PARA 34 et seq.
5   Political Parties, Elections and Referendums Act 2000 Sch 12 para 4(6) (amended by the
     Communications Act 2003 Sch 17 para 167(1), (3)).

(iv) The Campaign

A. CONTROLS ON REFERENDUM EXPENSES

(A) In general

535.   Meaning of 'referendum expenses'.   In relation to a referendum[1] to
which the general framework provisions apply[2], 'referendum expenses' means
expenses incurred by or on behalf of any individual or body[3] which are expenses
incurred for referendum purposes[4] in respect of any of the matters set out in the
following list[5]:
  (1)   referendum campaign broadcasts, including agency fees, design costs
         and other costs in connection with preparing or producing such
         broadcasts[6];
  (2)   advertising of any nature (whatever the medium used), including agency
         fees, design costs and other costs in connection with preparing,
         producing, distributing or otherwise disseminating such advertising or
         anything incorporating such advertising and intended to be distributed
         for the purpose of disseminating it[7];
  (3)   unsolicited material addressed to electors (whether addressed to them by
         name or intended for delivery to households within any particular area
         or areas), including design costs and other costs in connection with
         preparing, producing or distributing such material (including the cost of
         postage)[8];
  (4)   any promotional material or other document providing information
         about the referendum or the issues or arguments[9] involved, including
         design costs and other costs in connection with preparing or producing
         or distributing or otherwise disseminating any such document[10];
  (5)   market research or canvassing conducted for the purpose of ascertaining
         polling intentions[11];

(6)   the provision of any services or facilities in connection with press conferences or other dealings with the media[12];

(7)   the transport (by any means) of persons to any place or places with a view to obtaining publicity in connection with a referendum campaign, including the costs of hiring a particular means of transport for the whole or part of the period during which the referendum campaign is being conducted[13];

(8)   rallies and other events, including public meetings (but not annual or other party conferences) organised so as to obtain publicity in connection with a referendum campaign or for other purposes connected with a referendum campaign, including costs incurred in connection with the attendance of persons at such events, the hire of premises for the purposes of such events or the provision of goods, services or facilities at them[14].

Nothing in heads (1) to (8) above is to be taken as extending to any expenses:

(a)   in respect of any property[15], services or facilities so far as those expenses fall to be met out of public funds[16];

(b)   incurred in respect of the remuneration or allowances payable to any member of the staff (whether permanent or otherwise) of the campaign organiser[17];

(c)   incurred in respect of an individual by way of travelling expenses (by any means of transport) or in providing for his accommodation or other personal needs to the extent that the expenses are paid by the individual from his own resources and are not reimbursed to him[18]; or

(d)   certain expenses incurred in connection with the Welsh Referendum[19].

Where, in the case of any individual or body, either: (i) property is transferred to the individual or body[20]; or (ii) property, services or facilities is or are provided for the use or benefit of the individual or body[21], either free of charge or at a discount of more than 10 per cent[22], and the property, services or facilities is or are made use of by or on behalf of the individual or body in circumstances such that, if any expenses were to be (or are) actually incurred by or on behalf of the individual or body in respect of that use, they would be (or are) referendum expenses actually incurred by or on behalf of the individual or body[23], an amount of referendum expenses (the 'appropriate amount') is treated, for the purposes of the statutory provisions which govern the control of referendum expenses, as incurred by the individual or body during the period for which the property, services or facilities is or are so made use of[24]. Where the whole or part of any such period falls within any period which is, in relation to the referendum to which the expenses relate, the referendum period[25], then such proportion of the appropriate amount[26] as reasonably represents the use made of the property, services or facilities during the referendum period is treated as incurred by or on behalf of the individual or body during the referendum period[27] and, if a return falls to be prepared[28] in respect of referendum expenses incurred by or on behalf of the individual or body during that period, the responsible person[29] must make a declaration of that amount[30], unless that amount is not more than £200[31]. Where head (i) above applies, the appropriate amount is determined as being such proportion of either the market value of the property (where the property is transferred free of charge)[32] or the difference between the market value of the property and the amount of expenses actually incurred by or on behalf of the individual or body in respect of the property (where the property is transferred at a discount)[33], as is reasonably attributable to the use made of the property[34].

Where head (ii) above applies, the appropriate amount is determined as being such proportion of either the commercial rate for the use of the property or the provision of the services or facilities (where the property, services or facilities is or are provided free of charge)[35] or the difference between that commercial rate and the amount of expenses actually incurred by or on behalf of the individual or body in respect of the use of the property or the provision of the services or facilities (where the property, services or facilities is or are provided at a discount)[36] as is reasonably attributable to the use made of the property, services or facilities[37]. However, no amount of referendum expenses is to be regarded as so incurred in respect of: (A) the transmission by a broadcaster[38] of a referendum campaign broadcast[39]; (B) the provision of any rights to assistance conferred[40] on a designated organisation (or persons authorised by such an organisation)[41]; or (C) the provision by any individual of his own services which he provides voluntarily in his own time and free of charge[42].

The Electoral Commission[43] may prepare, and from time to time revise, a code of practice giving guidance as to the kinds of expenses which do, or do not, fall within the matters specified either in heads (1) to (8) above or heads (a) to (c) above[44]. Once the Commission has prepared a draft of such a code, it must submit it to the Secretary of State for his approval[45]; and he may approve a draft code either without modification or with such modifications as he may determine[46]. The Secretary of State may also by order make such amendments to the matters specified either in heads (1) to (8) above or heads (a) to (c) above as he considers appropriate[47]; and he may make such an order either where the order gives effect to a recommendation of the Electoral Commission[48] or after consultation with the Electoral Commission[49].

1   As to the meaning of 'referendum' see PARA 527.
2   Ie the Political Parties, Elections and Referendums Act 2000 Pt VII (ss 101–129).
3   As to the meaning of 'body' see PARA 58 note 2. 'Campaign organiser', in relation to referendum expenses, means the individual or body by whom or on whose behalf the expenses are incurred: Political Parties, Elections and Referendums Act 2000 s 111(1), (4).
4   Political Parties, Elections and Referendums Act 2000 s 111(1), (2). 'For referendum purposes' means: (1) in connection with the conduct or management of any campaign conducted with a view to promoting or procuring a particular outcome in relation to any question asked in the referendum (s 111(1), (3)(a)); or (2) otherwise in connection with promoting or procuring any such outcome (s 111(1), (3)(b)). 'Referendum campaign' means a campaign such as is mentioned in head (1) above: s 111(1), (4). As to the meaning of 'question' see PARA 527 note 7; and as to the meaning of 'outcome' see PARA 529 note 13.
5   Ie expenses falling within the Political Parties, Elections and Referendums Act 2000 s 111(1), (2), Sch 13 paras 1–2 (see heads (1)–(8) and (a)–(c) in the text): Sch 13 para 1.
6   Political Parties, Elections and Referendums Act 2000 Sch 13 para 1(1). As to referendum campaign broadcasts generally see PARA 552.
7   Political Parties, Elections and Referendums Act 2000 Sch 13 para 1(2).
8   Political Parties, Elections and Referendums Act 2000 Sch 13 para 1(3). As to a designated organisation's right to send referendum addresses to electors generally see PARA 532.
9   Ie material to which the Political Parties, Elections and Referendums Act 2000 s 125 applies (see PARA 551).
10 Political Parties, Elections and Referendums Act 2000 Sch 13 para 1(4).
11 Political Parties, Elections and Referendums Act 2000 Sch 13 para 1(5).
12 Political Parties, Elections and Referendums Act 2000 Sch 13 para 1(6).
13 Political Parties, Elections and Referendums Act 2000 Sch 13 para 1(7).
14 Political Parties, Elections and Referendums Act 2000 Sch 13 para 1(8).
15 As to the meaning of 'property' see PARA 34 note 8.
16 Political Parties, Elections and Referendums Act 2000 Sch 13 para 2(a). As to references to payments out of public funds see PARA 299 note 21.
17 Political Parties, Elections and Referendums Act 2000 Sch 13 para 2(b).
18 Political Parties, Elections and Referendums Act 2000 Sch 13 para 2(c).

19 See the National Assembly for Wales Referendum (Assembly Act Provisions) (Limit on Referendum Expenses Etc) Order 2010, SI 2010/2985, art 5, which provides that expenses incurred in respect of the publication of any matter relating to the referendum held under the Government of Wales Act 2006 s 103 other than an advertisement in a newspaper or periodical, a broadcast made by the British Broadcasting Corporation or Sianel Pedwar Cymru, or a programme included in any service licensed under the Broadcasting Act 1990 Pt 1 or Pt 3 (ss 3–71, 85–126: see BROADCASTING) or the Broadcasting Act 1996 Pt 1 or Pt 2 (ss 1–39, 40–72: see BROADCASTING), are not referendum expenses for these purposes.

20 Political Parties, Elections and Referendums Act 2000 s 112(1)(a)(i). Any property given or transferred to any officer, member, trustee or agent of an individual or body in his capacity as such (and not for his own use or benefit) is to be regarded as given or transferred to the individual or body (and references to donations received by an individual or body accordingly include donations so given or transferred) (s 112(1), Sch 15 para 2(5)); and any reference to property being given or transferred to an individual or body is a reference to its being so given or transferred either directly or indirectly through any third person (Sch 15 para 2(6)(a)).

21 Political Parties, Elections and Referendums Act 2000 s 112(1)(a)(ii).

22 Political Parties, Elections and Referendums Act 2000 s 112(1)(a)(i), (ii). The discount referred to in the text is a discount of more than 10% of: (1) the market value of the property, in the case of head (i) in the text; or (2) the commercial rate for the use of the property or for the provision of the services or facilities, in the case of head (ii) in the text. As to the meaning of 'market value' see PARA 299 note 26. Where the services of an employee are made available by his employer for the use or benefit of an individual or body, then for the purposes of determining referendum expenses, the amount which is to be taken as constituting the commercial rate for the provision of those services is the amount of the remuneration or allowances payable to the employee by his employer in respect of the period for which his services are so made available (but do not include any amount in respect of any contributions or other payments for which the employer is liable in respect of the employee): s 112(5).

23 Political Parties, Elections and Referendums Act 2000 s 112(1)(b).

24 Political Parties, Elections and Referendums Act 2000 s 112(2). This provision has effect subject to s 112(9) (see heads (A)–(C) in the text). The text refers to the use made of the property or goods as mentioned in s 112(1)(b) (see the text and note 23).

25 As to the referendum period see PARA 527.

26 Ie such proportion of the appropriate amount determined in accordance with the Political Parties, Elections and Referendums Act 2000 s 112(3), (4) (see the text and notes 32–37).

27 Political Parties, Elections and Referendums Act 2000 s 112(6)(a), (7).

28 Ie under the Political Parties, Elections and Referendums Act 2000 s 120 (see PARA 542).

29 As to the meaning of 'responsible person' in relation to an individual or body which is not a registered party see PARA 529 note 27.

30 Political Parties, Elections and Referendums Act 2000 s 112(6)(b). A person commits an offence if he knowingly or recklessly makes such a declaration which is false: see s 112(8); and PARA 751.

31 Political Parties, Elections and Referendums Act 2000 s 112(6). The Secretary of State may by order vary the sum for the time being specified in s 112(6): see s 155; and PARA 299 note 36. At the date at which this volume states the law, no such order had been made. As to the Secretary of State see PARA 2.

32 Political Parties, Elections and Referendums Act 2000 s 112(3)(a).

33 Political Parties, Elections and Referendums Act 2000 s 112(3)(b).

34 Political Parties, Elections and Referendums Act 2000 s 112(3). The text refers to the use made of the property as mentioned in s 112(1)(b) (see the text and note 23).

35 Political Parties, Elections and Referendums Act 2000 s 112(4)(a).

36 Political Parties, Elections and Referendums Act 2000 s 112(4)(b).

37 Political Parties, Elections and Referendums Act 2000 s 112(4). The text refers to the use made of the property as mentioned in s 112(1)(b) (see the text and note 23).

38 As to the meaning of 'broadcaster' see PARA 299 note 43.

39 Political Parties, Elections and Referendums Act 2000 s 112(9)(a). The text refers to referendum campaign broadcasts within the meaning of s 127 (see PARA 552): s 112(9)(a).

40 Ie by virtue of the Political Parties, Elections and Referendums Act 2000 s 110(4), Sch 12 (see PARAS 531–534).

41 Political Parties, Elections and Referendums Act 2000 s 112(9)(b).

42 Political Parties, Elections and Referendums Act 2000 s 112(9)(c).

43 As to the Electoral Commission see PARA 34 et seq.

44 Political Parties, Elections and Referendums Act 2000 s 160(1), Sch 13 para 3(1).

45 Political Parties, Elections and Referendums Act 2000 s 160(1), Sch 13 para 3(2).

46 Political Parties, Elections and Referendums Act 2000 Sch 13 para 3(3). For these purposes, references to a draft code include a revised draft code: Sch 13 para 3(10). Once the Secretary of State has approved a draft code he must lay a copy of the draft, whether in its original form or in a form which incorporates any modifications determined under Sch 13 para 3(3), before each House of Parliament: Sch 13 para 3(4). As to the meaning of 'modification' see PARA 44 note 9. If the draft incorporates any such modifications, the Secretary of State must at the same time lay before each House a statement of his reasons for making them: Sch 13 para 3(5). If, within the 40-day period, either House resolves not to approve the draft, the Secretary of State must take no further steps in relation to the draft code (Sch 13 para 3(6)); but if no such resolution is made within the 40-day period, the Secretary of State must issue the code in the form of the draft laid before Parliament, and the code is to come into force on such date as the Secretary of State may by order appoint (Sch 13 para 3(7)). The Commission must arrange for the code to be published in such manner as it thinks appropriate: Sch 13 para 3(7). The prohibition in Sch 13 para 3(6) from taking further action in relation to a draft code does not prevent a new draft code from being laid before Parliament: Sch 13 para 3(8). For these purposes, the '40-day period', in relation to a draft code, means, if the draft is laid before one House on a day later than the day on which it is laid before the other House, the period of 40 days beginning with the later of the two days, and, in any other case, the period of 40 days beginning with the day on which the draft is laid before each House: Sch 13 para 3(8). In calculating this period, no account is taken of any period during which Parliament is dissolved or prorogued or during which both Houses are adjourned for more than four days: Sch 13 para 3(9).

47 Political Parties, Elections and Referendums Act 2000 Sch 13 para 4(1). At the date at which this volume states the law, no such order had been made.

48 Political Parties, Elections and Referendums Act 2000 Sch 13 para 4(2)(a).

49 Political Parties, Elections and Referendums Act 2000 Sch 13 para 4(2)(b).

536. Restriction on incurring referendum expenses without authority. For the purposes of controlling referendum expenses[1] incurred for referendum purposes[2], no amount of referendum expenses may be incurred by or on behalf of a permitted participant[3] unless it is incurred with the authority of either: (1) the responsible person[4]; or (2) a person authorised in writing by the responsible person[5]. Where any expenses are incurred in contravention of this restriction by a permitted participant that is a registered party[6], the expenses do not count as referendum expenses incurred by or on behalf of the permitted participant either for the purposes of the statutory provisions which impose financial limits on such expenditure[7] or for the purposes of the statutory provisions which require returns as to such expenditure[8].

A person commits an offence if, without reasonable excuse, he incurs any expenses in contravention of the restriction on incurring referendum expenses[9].

1 As to the meaning of 'referendum expenses' see PARA 535.
2 As to the meaning of 'for referendum purposes' see PARA 535 note 4.
3 As to the meaning of 'permitted participant' see PARA 529.
4 Political Parties, Elections and Referendums Act 2000 s 113(1)(a). As to the meaning of 'responsible person' in relation to a registered party see PARA 529 note 17; and as to the meaning of 'responsible person' in relation to an individual or body which is not a registered party see PARA 529 note 27.
5 Political Parties, Elections and Referendums Act 2000 s 113(1)(b). As to the limit on expenses incurred during the Welsh referendum held under the Government of Wales Act 2006 (see PARA 530) see the National Assembly for Wales Referendum (Assembly Act Provisions) (Limit on Referendum Expenses Etc) Order 2010, SI 2010/2985, art 4.
6 As to the meaning of 'registered party' see PARA 35 note 3.
7 Ie the Political Parties, Elections and Referendums Act 2000 ss 117–119 (see PARAS 540–541).
8 Political Parties, Elections and Referendums Act 2000 s 113(3). The text refers to the statutory provisions in ss 120–123 (see PARAS 542–544).
9 See the Political Parties, Elections and Referendums Act 2000 s 113(2); and PARA 751.

537. Restrictions on payments in respect of referendum expenses. For the purposes of controlling referendum expenses[1] incurred for referendum purposes[2], no payment (of whatever nature) may be made in respect of any referendum expenses incurred or to be incurred by or on behalf of a permitted participant[3] unless it is made by: (1) the responsible person[4]; or (2) a person authorised in writing by the responsible person[5]. Any payment made in respect of any such expenses by a person within head (1) or head (2) above must be supported by an invoice or a receipt unless it is not more than £200[6]; and where any such payment is made by a person within head (2) above, he must deliver to the responsible person both notification that he has made the payment[7] and the supporting invoice or receipt[8] as soon as possible after making the payment[9].

A person commits an offence if, without reasonable excuse, he makes any payment in contravention of the restriction on payments made in respect of referendum expenses or if he is a person within head (2) above who contravenes the requirements imposed on such a person regarding the delivery of notification and evidence[10].

1   As to the meaning of 'referendum expenses' see PARA 535.
2   As to the meaning of 'for referendum purposes' see PARA 535 note 4.
3   As to the meaning of 'permitted participant' see PARA 529.
4   Political Parties, Elections and Referendums Act 2000 s 114(1)(a). As to the meaning of 'responsible person' in relation to a registered party see PARA 529 note 17; and as to the meaning of 'responsible person' in relation to an individual or body which is not a registered party see PARA 529 note 27.
5   Political Parties, Elections and Referendums Act 2000 s 114(1)(b).
6   Political Parties, Elections and Referendums Act 2000 s 114(2). The Secretary of State may by order vary the sum for the time being specified in s 114(2): see s 155; and PARA 299 note 36. At the date at which this volume states the law, no such order had been made.
7   Political Parties, Elections and Referendums Act 2000 s 114(3)(a). Any notification required to be given under the Political Parties, Elections and Referendums Act 2000 must be in writing: s 157(1).
8   Political Parties, Elections and Referendums Act 2000 s 114(3)(b).
9   Political Parties, Elections and Referendums Act 2000 s 114(3).
10 See the Political Parties, Elections and Referendums Act 2000 s 114(4); and PARA 751.

538.   Claims in respect of referendum expenses.   For the purposes of controlling referendum expenses[1] incurred for referendum purposes[2], a claim for payment in respect of referendum expenses incurred by or on behalf of a permitted participant[3] during a referendum period[4] is not payable unless the claim is sent[5] to the responsible person[6], or any other person authorised[7] to incur the expenses[8], not later than 30 days[9] after the end of the referendum period[10]. Any claim so sent must be paid not later than 60 days after the end of the referendum period[11]; but this is without prejudice to any rights of a creditor of a permitted participant to obtain payment before the end of the period so allowed[12].

A person commits an offence if, without reasonable excuse, he pays any claim for payment in respect of referendum expenses which by virtue of being statute-barred[13] is not payable or if he makes any payment in respect of a claim after the end of the period allowed for the payment of claims[14].

If the responsible person or other person to whom a claim for payment in respect of referendum expenses is sent fails or refuses to pay the claim within the period allowed[15], where the claim[16] is sent to the responsible person[17] or to any other person with whose authority it is alleged that the expenditure was incurred[18] within the period allowed before such claims are barred[19], the claim is deemed to be a disputed claim[20]. The person by whom the disputed claim is made may bring an action for a disputed claim, and any sum paid in pursuance of a court's judgment or order so made in the proceedings is not deemed to be in contravention of the statutory provision forbidding payment of referendum expenses later than 42 days after the end of the referendum period[21].

1   As to the meaning of 'referendum expenses' see PARA 535.
2   As to the meaning of 'for referendum purposes' see PARA 535 note 4.
3   As to the meaning of 'permitted participant' see PARA 529.
4   As to the referendum period see PARA 527.
5   Political Parties, Elections and Referendums Act 2000 s 115(1).
6   Political Parties, Elections and Referendums Act 2000 s 115(1)(a). As to the meaning of 'responsible person' in relation to a registered party see PARA 529 note 17; and as to the meaning of 'responsible person' in relation to an individual or body which is not a registered party see PARA 529 note 27.
7   Ie authorised in writing by the responsible person under the Political Parties, Elections and Referendums Act 2000 s 113 (see PARA 536).
8   Political Parties, Elections and Referendums Act 2000 s 115(1)(b).
9   Where, in the case of any referendum expenses, the period allowed under the Political Parties, Elections and Referendums Act 2000 s 115(1) or s 115(2) (see the text and note 11) would otherwise end on: (1) a Saturday or Sunday, Christmas Eve, Christmas Day or Good Friday (s 77(9)(a) (amended by the Electoral Administration Act 2006 ss 20, 74(2), Sch 1 paras 49, 54, Sch 2); applied by the Political Parties, Elections and Referendums Act 2000 s 115(7)); (2) a bank holiday (s 77(9)(b)); or (3) a day appointed for public thanksgiving or mourning (s 77(9)(c)), the period instead ends on the first day following that day which is not one of those days (s 77(9)). For the purposes of head (2) above, 'bank holiday' means a day which is a bank holiday under the Banking and Financial Dealings Act 1971 (see TIME vol 97 (2010) PARA 321) in any part of the United Kingdom: (a) in which is situated the office of the responsible person in relation to the permitted participant or (as the case may be) other authorised person to whom the claim is sent pursuant to the Political Parties, Elections and Referendums Act 2000 s 115(1) (s 77(10)(a); applied by 115(7)); or (b) in which the person providing the property, services or facilities to which the expenses relate conducts his business (s 77(10)(b)); or (c) (if he conducts his business in more than one part of the United Kingdom) in which is situated the office from which dealings relating to the expenses were conducted (s 77(10)(c)). For these purposes, the address of the responsible person in relation to the permitted participant is to be regarded as being the registered address of the permitted participant: s 74(10)(a); applied by 115(7). 'Business' includes every trade, profession and occupation: s 160(1). As to the meaning of 'United Kingdom' see PARA 1 note 1. As to the meaning of 'property' see PARA 34 note 8.
10 Political Parties, Elections and Referendums Act 2000 s 115(1) (amended by the Electoral Administration Act 2006 s 65(3)(a)).
11 Political Parties, Elections and Referendums Act 2000 s 115(2) (amended by the Electoral Administration Act 2006 s 65(3)(b)).
12 Political Parties, Elections and Referendums Act 2000 s 115(6).
13 Ie by virtue of the Political Parties, Elections and Referendums Act 2000 s 115(1) (see the text and notes 1–10).
14 See the Political Parties, Elections and Referendums Act 2000 s 115(3); and PARA 751. The text refers to payment in respect of a claim after the end of the period allowed under s 115(2) (see the text and note 11).
15 Political Parties, Elections and Referendums Act 2000 s 116(1)(b). The text refers to the period allowed under s 115(2) (see the text and note 11), which is without prejudice to any rights of a creditor of a registered party to obtain payment before the end of the period so allowed (s 115(6)).
16 Ie the claim for payment in respect of referendum expenses incurred by or on behalf of a permitted participant as mentioned in the Political Parties, Elections and Referendums Act 2000 s 115(1) (see the text and notes 1–10).
17 Political Parties, Elections and Referendums Act 2000 s 116(1)(a)(i).
18 Political Parties, Elections and Referendums Act 2000 s 116(1)(a)(ii).
19 Political Parties, Elections and Referendums Act 2000 s 116(1)(a). The text refers to the period allowed under s 115(1) (see the text and notes 1–10).
20 Political Parties, Elections and Referendums Act 2000 s 116(1). As to the power to apply to the court for leave to pay a disputed claim see PARA 539; and as to the returns of disputed claims see PARA 542.
21 Political Parties, Elections and Referendums Act 2000 s 116(2). The text refers to the restriction otherwise contained in s 115(2) (see the text and note 11).

539. Application for leave to pay claims in respect of referendum expenses.
For the purposes of controlling referendum expenses[1] incurred for referendum purposes[2], the person making a claim for payment in respect of referendum expenses incurred by or on behalf of a permitted participant[3] during a referendum period[4], or the person with whose authority the expenses in question were incurred[5], may apply to the High Court or to the county court for leave to pay such a claim (even if it is sent in after the statutory period allowed of 30 days[6]) or may apply to the High Court or to the county court for leave to pay a disputed claim[7]. The court, if satisfied that for any special reason it is appropriate to do so, may by order grant the leave[8]. Any sum paid in pursuance of such an order of leave is not deemed to be a contravention of the provisions forbidding the making or payment of claims relating to referendum expenses later than the statutory period allowed[9].

1   As to the meaning of 'referendum expenses' see PARA 535.
2   As to the meaning of 'for referendum purposes' see PARA 535 note 4.
3   As to the meaning of 'permitted participant' see PARA 529.
4   Political Parties, Elections and Referendums Act 2000 s 115(4)(a). The text refers to a claim to which s 115(1) applies (see PARA 538). As to the referendum period see PARA 527.
5   Political Parties, Elections and Referendums Act 2000 s 115(4)(b). As to persons authorised to incur expenditure as mentioned in the text see s 113; and PARA 536.
6   Ie the period mentioned in the Political Parties, Elections and Referendums Act 2000 s 115(1) (see PARA 538).
7   Political Parties, Elections and Referendums Act 2000 ss 115(4), 116(3).
8   Political Parties, Elections and Referendums Act 2000 ss 115(4), 116(3).
9   Political Parties, Elections and Referendums Act 2000 ss 115(5), 116(3). The text refers to the period of 30 days within which a claim must be made under s 115(1) or the period of 60 days within which a claim must be paid under s 115(2) (see PARA 538). As to the returns of sums paid in pursuance of the leave see PARA 542.

(B) Financial Limits on Referendum Expenses

540. General restriction on referendum expenses for individual or body that is not a permitted participant. For the purposes of controlling referendum expenses[1] incurred for referendum purposes[2], the total referendum expenses incurred by or on behalf of any individual or body[3] during the referendum period[4] in the case of a particular referendum to which the general framework provisions apply[5] must not exceed £10,000[6] unless the individual or body is a permitted participant[7].

Where, at any time before the beginning of any referendum period, any expenses falling within the matters which qualify as referendum expenses[8] are incurred by or on behalf of an individual or body in respect of any property[9], services or facilities[10], but the property, services or facilities is or are made use of by or on behalf of the individual or body during the referendum period in circumstances such that, had any expenses been incurred in respect of that use during that period, they would[11] have constituted referendum expenses incurred by or on behalf of the individual or body during that period[12], the appropriate proportion of those expenses[13] is treated, for the purposes of imposing a general restriction on referendum expenses for an individual or body that is not a permitted participant[14], as referendum expenses incurred by or on behalf of the individual or body during that period[15].

Where, during the referendum period, any referendum expenses are incurred in excess of the general restriction imposed on such expenses by or on behalf of any individual or body who is not a permitted participant, any such individual or any person who authorised the expenses to be incurred by or on behalf of such a body is guilty of an offence if he knew or ought reasonably to have known that the expenditure would be incurred in excess of that limit; and the body in question is also guilty of an offence[16].

1   As to the meaning of 'referendum expenses' see PARA 535.
2   As to the meaning of 'for referendum purposes' see PARA 535 note 4.
3   As to the meaning of 'body' see PARA 58 note 2.
4   As to the referendum period see PARA 527.
5   Ie the Political Parties, Elections and Referendums Act 2000 Pt VII (ss 101–129).
6   The Secretary of State may by order vary the sum for the time being specified in the Political Parties, Elections and Referendums Act 2000 s 117(1): see s 155; and PARA 299 note 36. At the date at which this volume states the law, no such order had been made.
7   Political Parties, Elections and Referendums Act 2000 s 117(1). As to the meaning of 'permitted participant' see PARA 529.
8   Ie any expenses falling within the Political Parties, Elections and Referendums Act 2000 s 111(2) (see PARA 535).
9   As to the meaning of 'property' see PARA 34 note 8.
10 Political Parties, Elections and Referendums Act 2000 s 117(5)(a).
11 Ie by virtue of the Political Parties, Elections and Referendums Act 2000 s 111(2) (see PARA 535).
12 Political Parties, Elections and Referendums Act 2000 s 117(5)(b).
13 Ie the expenses mentioned in the Political Parties, Elections and Referendums Act 2000 s 117(5)(a) (see the text and notes 8–10). For these purposes, the appropriate proportion of the expenses mentioned in s 117(5)(a) is such proportion of those expenses as is reasonably attributable to the use made of the property, services or facilities as mentioned in s 117(5)(b) (see the text and notes 11–12): s 117(6).
14 Ie for the purposes of the Political Parties, Elections and Referendums Act 2000 s 117.
15 Political Parties, Elections and Referendums Act 2000 s 117(5).
16 See the Political Parties, Elections and Referendums Act 2000 s 117(2)–(4); and PARA 751.

541.   Special restrictions on referendum expenses for permitted participants. In relation to a referendum[1] held throughout the United Kingdom[2], the limit on referendum expenses[3] incurred by or on behalf of a permitted participant[4] during the referendum period[5] in the case of such a referendum is[6]:

(1)   £5 million in the case of a person or body designated for assistance[7];
(2)   in the case of a registered party[8] by which a declaration has been made in relation to the referendum[9] but which has not been designated for assistance[10]:
      (a)   £5 million, if the party's relevant percentage[11] exceeds 30 per cent[12];
      (b)   £4 million, if the party's relevant percentage is more than 20 per cent but not more than 30 per cent[13];
      (c)   £3 million, if the party's relevant percentage is more than 10 per cent but not more than 20 per cent[14];
      (d)   £2 million, if the party's relevant percentage is more than 5 per cent but not more than 10 per cent[15];
      (e)   £500,000, if the party's relevant percentage is not more than 5 per cent or if it has no relevant percentage[16]; and
(3)   £500,000 in the case of a person or body by whom a notification has been given in relation to the referendum[17] but who has not been designated for assistance[18].

In relation to a referendum which is not held throughout the United Kingdom[19], the limit on referendum expenses incurred by or on behalf of a permitted participant during the referendum period in the case of such a referendum is such amount as the Secretary of State[20] may by order prescribe[21]. Before making such an order, the Secretary of State must seek, and have regard to, the views of the Electoral Commission[22]; but where he proposes to make such an order otherwise than in accordance with the views of the Commission, he must on laying a draft of a statutory instrument containing the order before each House of Parliament also lay before each House a statement of his reasons for departing from the views of the Commission[23].

Where, at any time before the beginning of any referendum period, any expenses falling within the matters which qualify as referendum expenses[24] are incurred by or on behalf of an individual or body in respect of any property[25], services or facilities[26], but the property, services or facilities is or are made use of by or on behalf of the individual or body during the referendum period in circumstances such that, had any expenses been incurred in respect of that use during that period, they would[27] have constituted referendum expenses incurred by or on behalf of the individual or body during that period[28], the appropriate proportion of those expenses[29] is treated, for the purposes of imposing special restrictions on referendum expenses incurred by or on behalf of permitted participants[30], as referendum expenses incurred by or on behalf of the individual or body during that period[31].

Where, during the referendum period, any referendum expenses are incurred in excess of the special restrictions imposed on such expenses by or on behalf of any permitted participant, the permitted participant or other person who authorised the expenses is guilty of an offence if he knew or ought reasonably to have known that the expenditure would be incurred in excess of that limit; and the body or party in question is also guilty of an offence[32].

1   As to the meaning of 'referendum' see PARA 527.
2   Ie a referendum falling within the Political Parties, Elections and Referendums Act 2000 s 101(1)(a) (see PARA 527). As to the meaning of 'United Kingdom' see PARA 1 note 1.
3   As to the meaning of 'referendum expenses' see PARA 535.
4   As to the meaning of 'permitted participant' see PARA 529.
5   For the purposes of the Political Parties, Elections and Referendums Act 2000 ss 118, 120–123, Sch 14, any reference to referendum expenses incurred by or on behalf of a permitted participant during the referendum period includes any referendum expenses so incurred at any time before the individual or body became a permitted participant: s 118(5). As to the meaning of 'body' see PARA 58 note 2. As to the referendum period see PARA 527.
6   Political Parties, Elections and Referendums Act 2000 s 118(1), Sch 14 para 1(1), (2). The Secretary of State may by order vary the sum for the time being specified in Sch 14: see s 155; and PARA 299 note 36. At the date at which this volume states the law, no such order had been made.
7   Political Parties, Elections and Referendums Act 2000 Sch 14 para 1(2)(a). The text refers to a person or body designated under s 108 (see PARA 530).
8   As to the meaning of 'registered party' see PARA 35 note 3.
9   Ie which falls within the Political Parties, Elections and Referendums Act 2000 s 105(1)(a) (see PARA 529).
10 Political Parties, Elections and Referendums Act 2000 Sch 14 para 1(2)(b). The text refers to a registered party which has not been designated under s 108 (see PARA 530).
11 For these purposes: (1) a registered party has a relevant percentage in relation to a referendum if, at the last parliamentary general election taking place before the referendum, votes were cast for one or more candidates at the election authorised to use the party's registered name (Political Parties, Elections and Referendums Act 2000 Sch 14 para 1(3)(a)); and (2) the amount of its relevant percentage is equal to the percentage of the total number of votes cast for all candidates at that election which is represented by the total number of votes cast for the candidate or candidates mentioned in head (1) above (Sch 14 para 1(3)(b)). Where at any such general election a candidate was authorised to use the registered name of more than one registered party, then for the purposes of head (2) above as it applies in relation to each of those parties, the number of votes cast for the candidate must be taken to be the total number cast for him divided by the number of parties: Sch 14 para 1(4). As to parliamentary general elections see PARA 189 et seq.
12 Political Parties, Elections and Referendums Act 2000 Sch 14 para 1(2)(b)(i).

13 Political Parties, Elections and Referendums Act 2000 Sch 14 para 1(2)(b)(ii).
14 Political Parties, Elections and Referendums Act 2000 Sch 14 para 1(2)(b)(iii).
15 Political Parties, Elections and Referendums Act 2000 Sch 14 para 1(2)(b)(iv).
16 Political Parties, Elections and Referendums Act 2000 Sch 14 para 1(2)(b)(v).
17 Ie which falls within the Political Parties, Elections and Referendums Act 2000 s 105(1)(b) (see PARA 529).
18 Political Parties, Elections and Referendums Act 2000 Sch 14 para 1(2)(c). The text refers to a person or body who has not been designated under s 108 (see PARA 530).
19 Ie a referendum to which the Political Parties, Elections and Referendums Act 2000 Pt VII (ss 101–129) applies, other than one falling within s 101(1)(a) (see PARA 527).
20 As to the Secretary of State see PARA 2.
21 Political Parties, Elections and Referendums Act 2000 Sch 14 para 2(1), (2). Different amounts may be prescribed for different referendums or different categories of permitted participants: Sch 14 para 2(3). See the Regional Assembly and Local Government Referendums (Expenses Limits for Permitted Participants) Order 2004, SI 2004/1961; and the National Assembly for Wales Referendum (Assembly Act Provisions) (Limit on Referendum Expenses Etc) Order 2010, SI 2010/2985, art 4.
22 Political Parties, Elections and Referendums Act 2000 s 160(1), Sch 14 para 2(4). As to the Electoral Commission see PARA 34 et seq.
23 Political Parties, Elections and Referendums Act 2000 Sch 14 para 2(4).
24 Ie any expenses falling within the Political Parties, Elections and Referendums Act 2000 s 111(2) (see PARA 535).
25 As to the meaning of 'property' see PARA 34 note 8.
26 Political Parties, Elections and Referendums Act 2000 ss 117(5)(a), 118(4).
27 Ie by virtue of the Political Parties, Elections and Referendums Act 2000 s 111(2) (see PARA 535).
28 Political Parties, Elections and Referendums Act 2000 s 117(5)(b).
29 Ie the expenses mentioned in the Political Parties, Elections and Referendums Act 2000 s 117(5)(a) (see the text and notes 24–26). For these purposes, the appropriate proportion of the expenses mentioned in s 117(5)(a) is such proportion of those expenses as is reasonably attributable to the use made of the property, services or facilities as mentioned in s 117(5)(b) (see the text and notes 27–28): s 117(6).
30 Ie for the purposes of the Political Parties, Elections and Referendums Act 2000 s 118.
31 Political Parties, Elections and Referendums Act 2000 s 117(5).
32 See the Political Parties, Elections and Referendums Act 2000 s 118(2)–(3); and PARA 751.

(C) Returns as to Referendum Expenses

542. Returns as to referendum expenses. For the purposes of controlling referendum expenses[1] incurred for referendum purposes[2], where any referendum expenses are incurred by or on behalf of a permitted participant[3] during any referendum period[4] and that period ends[5], the responsible person[6] must make a return in respect of referendum expenses incurred by or on behalf of the permitted participant during that period[7].

Such a return must specify the referendum to which the expenditure relates, and must contain[8]:

(1) a statement of all payments made in respect of referendum expenses incurred by or on behalf of the permitted participant during the referendum period in question[9];

(2) a statement of all disputed claims[10];

(3) a statement of all the unpaid claims (if any) of which the responsible person is aware in respect of which an application has been made, or is about to be made, to a court for leave to pay the claim[11]; and

(4) in a case where the permitted participant either is not a registered party[12] or is a minor party[13], a statement of relevant donations[14] received in respect of the referendum which complies with the relevant requirements for such statements[15].

Such a return must be accompanied by:

(a)   all invoices or receipts relating to the payments mentioned in head (1) above[16]; and

(b)   in the case of any referendum expenses in relation to which an appropriate amount is treated as incurred by the permitted participant[17], any declaration falling to be made with respect to those expenses[18].

Where any referendum expenses are incurred at any time before the individual or body[19] became a permitted participant, the requirement to make such a return does not apply in relation to such expenses but the return must be accompanied by a declaration made by the responsible person of the total amount of such expenses incurred at any such time[20].

A report must be prepared by a qualified auditor[21] on such a return in respect of referendum expenses where, during any referendum period, the referendum expenses incurred by or on behalf of a permitted participant exceeds £250,000[22].

1   As to the meaning of 'referendum expenses' see PARA 535.

2   As to the meaning of 'for referendum purposes' see PARA 535 note 4.

3   As to the meaning of 'permitted participant' see PARA 529.

4   Political Parties, Elections and Referendums Act 2000 s 120(1)(a). The text refers to a referendum period within the meaning of s 102 (see PARA 527). As to the meaning of references, for these purposes, to referendum expenses incurred by or on behalf of a permitted participant during the referendum period see PARA 541 note 5.

5   Political Parties, Elections and Referendums Act 2000 s 120(1)(b).

6   As to the meaning of 'responsible person' in relation to a registered party see PARA 529 note 17; and as to the meaning of 'responsible person' in relation to an individual or body which is not a registered party see PARA 529 note 27.

7   Political Parties, Elections and Referendums Act 2000 s 120(1).

8   Political Parties, Elections and Referendums Act 2000 s 120(2). The Electoral Commission may by regulations prescribe a form of return which may be used for these purposes: ss 120(5), 160(1). Regulations made by the Electoral Commission are not statutory instruments and are not recorded in this work: see further PARA 47. As to the Electoral Commission see PARA 34 et seq.

9   Political Parties, Elections and Referendums Act 2000 s 120(2)(a).

10 Political Parties, Elections and Referendums Act 2000 s 120(2)(b). The text refers to all disputed claims within the meaning of s 116 (see PARA 538).

11 Political Parties, Elections and Referendums Act 2000 s 120(2)(c). The text refers to an application for leave to pay claims in respect of referendum expenses made under s 115(4) (see PARA 539).

12 As to the meaning of 'registered party' see PARA 35 note 3.

13 As to the meaning of 'minor party' see PARA 253 note 8.

14 For these purposes, 'relevant donation' has the same meaning as in the Political Parties, Elections and Referendums Act 2000 s 119, Sch 15 (see PARA 546): s 120(6).

15 Political Parties, Elections and Referendums Act 2000 s 120(2)(d). The text refers to the requirement for a statement of relevant donations to comply with Sch 15 paras 10–11 (see PARA 550).

16 Political Parties, Elections and Referendums Act 2000 s 120(3)(a).

17 Ie by virtue of the Political Parties, Elections and Referendums Act 2000 s 112 (see PARA 535).

18 Political Parties, Elections and Referendums Act 2000 s 120(3)(b). The text refers to a declaration falling to be made under s 112(6) (see PARA 535).

19 As to the meaning of 'body' see PARA 58 note 2.

20 Political Parties, Elections and Referendums Act 2000 s 120(4).

21 In relation to the appointment of an auditor to prepare a report under the Political Parties, Elections and Referendums Act 2000 s 121(1) (or, as the case may be, an auditor so appointed), s 43(6), (7) (regulations made by the Electoral Commission with respect to the appointment of auditors: see CONSTITUTIONAL LAW AND HUMAN RIGHTS) and s 44 (supplementary provisions about auditors: see CONSTITUTIONAL LAW AND HUMAN RIGHTS) apply as they apply in relation to the appointment of an auditor to carry out an audit under s 43 (annual audits: see CONSTITUTIONAL LAW AND HUMAN RIGHTS) (or, as the case may be, an auditor so appointed): s 121(2). As to the meaning of 'qualified auditor' see PARA 298 note 5. As to the general accounting requirements for permitted participants that are registered parties see PARA 298.

22 Political Parties, Elections and Referendums Act 2000 s 121(1). The Secretary of State may by
    order vary the sum for the time being specified in s 121(1): see s 155; and PARA 299 note 36. At
    the date at which this volume states the law, no such order had been made.

**543.   Delivery of returns as to referendum expenses to the Electoral
Commission.**   For the purposes of controlling referendum expenses[1] incurred for
referendum purposes[2], where any return as to referendum expenses falls to be
prepared[3] in respect of referendum expenses incurred by or on behalf of a
permitted participant[4], and an auditor's report on it falls to be prepared also[5],
the responsible person[6] must deliver the return to the Electoral Commission[7],
together with a copy of the auditor's report, within six months of the end of the
relevant referendum period[8]. In the case of any other such return which falls to
be prepared[9], the responsible person must deliver the return to the Commission
within three months of the end of the relevant referendum period[10].

Where, after the date on which a return is so delivered to the Commission,
leave is given by a court for any claim to be paid[11], the responsible person must,
within seven days after the payment, deliver to the Commission a return of any
sums paid in pursuance of the leave accompanied by a copy of the order of the
court giving the leave[12].

The responsible person commits an offence if, without reasonable excuse, he
fails to comply with the requirements as to any return or auditor's report[13].

1   As to the meaning of 'referendum expenses' see PARA 535.
2   As to the meaning of 'for referendum purposes' see PARA 535 note 4.
3   Ie under the Political Parties, Elections and Referendums Act 2000 s 120 (see PARA 542).
4   Political Parties, Elections and Referendums Act 2000 s 122(1)(a). As to the meaning of
    'permitted participant' see PARA 529. As to the meaning of references, for these purposes, to
    referendum expenses incurred by or on behalf of a permitted participant during the referendum
    period see PARA 541 note 5.
5   Political Parties, Elections and Referendums Act 2000 s 122(1)(b). The text refers to an auditor's
    report on a return as to campaign expenditure which falls to be prepared under s 121(1) (see
    PARA 542).
6   As to the meaning of 'responsible person' in relation to a registered party see PARA 529 note 17;
    and as to the meaning of 'responsible person' in relation to an individual or body which is not a
    registered party see PARA 529 note 27.
7   As to the Electoral Commission see PARA 34 et seq.
8   Political Parties, Elections and Referendums Act 2000 ss 122(1), 160(1). As to the referendum
    period see PARA 527.
9   Ie under the Political Parties, Elections and Referendums Act 2000 s 120 (see PARA 542).
10 Political Parties, Elections and Referendums Act 2000 s 122(2).
11 Ie leave to pay claims in respect of campaign expenditure given under the Political Parties,
    Elections and Referendums Act 2000 s 115(4) (see PARA 539).
12 Political Parties, Elections and Referendums Act 2000 s 122(3).
13 See the Political Parties, Elections and Referendums Act 2000 s 122(4); and PARA 751.

544.   Declaration made in relation to returns as to referendum expenses.   For
the purposes of controlling referendum expenses[1] incurred for referendum
purposes[2], each return[3] in respect of referendum expenses incurred by or on
behalf of a permitted participant[4] must be accompanied by a declaration which is
signed by the responsible person[5] and which must state that the responsible
person has examined the return in question[6] and that, to the best of his
knowledge and belief[7], it is a complete and correct return as required by law[8]
and all expenses shown in it as paid have been paid by him or by a person
authorised by him[9]. The declaration must also state, in a case where the
permitted participant either is not a registered party[10] or is a minor party[11], that
all relevant donations[12] recorded in the return as having been accepted by the

permitted participant are from permissible donors[13] and that no other relevant donations have been accepted by the permitted participant[14].

A person commits an offence if he knowingly or recklessly makes such a declaration falsely or if the requirements as to such a declaration are contravened at a time when he is the responsible person in the case of the permitted participant to which the return relates[15].

1　As to the meaning of 'referendum expenses' see PARA 535.
2　As to the meaning of 'for referendum purposes' see PARA 535 note 4.
3　Ie each return as to referendum expenses prepared under the Political Parties, Elections and Referendums Act 2000 s 120 (see PARA 542).
4　As to the meaning of 'permitted participant' see PARA 529. As to the meaning of references, for these purposes, to referendum expenses incurred by or on behalf of a permitted participant during the referendum period see PARA 541 note 5.
5　Political Parties, Elections and Referendums Act 2000 ss 123(1), 160(1). As to the meaning of 'responsible person' in relation to a registered party see PARA 529 note 17; and as to the meaning of 'responsible person' in relation to an individual or body which is not a registered party see PARA 529 note 27.
6　Political Parties, Elections and Referendums Act 2000 s 123(2)(a).
7　Political Parties, Elections and Referendums Act 2000 s 123(2)(b).
8　Political Parties, Elections and Referendums Act 2000 s 123(2)(b)(i).
9　Political Parties, Elections and Referendums Act 2000 s 123(2)(b)(ii). As to persons authorised to incur referendum expenses see PARA 536.
10　As to the meaning of 'registered party' see PARA 35 note 3.
11　As to the meaning of 'minor party' see PARA 253 note 8.
12　For these purposes, 'relevant donation' has the same meaning as in the Political Parties, Elections and Referendums Act 2000 s 119, Sch 15 (see PARA 546 note 12): s 123(5).
13　Political Parties, Elections and Referendums Act 2000 s 123(3)(a). As to the meaning of 'permissible donor' see PARA 529 note 11.
14　Political Parties, Elections and Referendums Act 2000 s 123(3)(b).
15　See the Political Parties, Elections and Referendums Act 2000 s 123(4); and PARA 751.

545. Public inspection of returns as to referendum expenses. For the purposes of controlling referendum expenses[1] incurred for referendum purposes[2], where the Electoral Commission[3] receives any return as to referendum expenses[4], it must[5], as soon as reasonably practicable after receiving the return, make a copy of the return, and of any documents accompanying it, available for public inspection[6] and keep any such copy available for public inspection for the period for which the return or other document is kept by it[7]. If the return contains a statement of relevant donations[8], the Commission must secure that the copy of the statement made available for public inspection does not include, in the case of any donation by an individual, the donor's address[9].

Where the Commission is for the time being required to make available for public inspection a copy of any document in this way, it must make the copy available for public inspection during ordinary office hours, either at the Commission's offices or at some convenient place appointed by it[10], although the Commission may make other arrangements for members of the public to have access to the document's contents[11]. If requested to do so by any person, the Commission must supply him with a copy of the document or any part of it[12]; and the Commission may charge such reasonable fee as it may determine in respect of any inspection or access so allowed or any copy so supplied[13]. Where any such document is held by the Commission in electronic form, any copy so made available for public inspection or so supplied must be made available, or (as the case may be) supplied, in a legible form[14].

At the end of the period of two years beginning with the date when any such return or other document is received by the Commission[15], it may cause the return or other document to be destroyed[16]; but, if requested to do so by the responsible person[17] in the case of the permitted participant concerned, it must arrange for the return or other document to be returned to that person[18].

1   As to the meaning of 'referendum expenses' see PARA 535.
2   As to the meaning of 'for referendum purposes' see PARA 535 note 4.
3   As to the Electoral Commission see PARA 34 et seq.
4   Ie any return as to referendum expenses prepared under the Political Parties, Elections and Referendums Act 2000 s 120 (see PARA 542). As to the delivery of returns to the Electoral Commission see PARA 543.
5   Political Parties, Elections and Referendums Act 2000 ss 124(1), 160(1).
6   Political Parties, Elections and Referendums Act 2000 s 124(1)(a).
7   Political Parties, Elections and Referendums Act 2000 s 124(1)(b).
8   Ie in accordance with the Political Parties, Elections and Referendums Act 2000 s 120(2)(d) (see PARA 542).
9   Political Parties, Elections and Referendums Act 2000 s 124(2).
10 Political Parties, Elections and Referendums Act 2000 s 149(2), (6)(d).
11 Political Parties, Elections and Referendums Act 2000 s 149(3), (6)(d).
12 Political Parties, Elections and Referendums Act 2000 s 149(4), (6)(d).
13 Political Parties, Elections and Referendums Act 2000 s 149(5), (6)(d).
14 Political Parties, Elections and Referendums Act 2000 s 149(7).
15 Political Parties, Elections and Referendums Act 2000 s 124(3).
16 Political Parties, Elections and Referendums Act 2000 s 124(3)(a).
17 As to the meaning of 'responsible person' in relation to a registered party see PARA 529 note 17; and as to the meaning of 'responsible person' in relation to an individual or body which is not a registered party see PARA 529 note 27.
18 Political Parties, Elections and Referendums Act 2000 s 124(3)(b).

B. CONTROLS ON DONATIONS RECEIVED BY CERTAIN PERMITTED PARTICIPANTS

546. Meaning of 'donation' in relation to certain permitted participants at a referendum. For the purposes of controlling donations at a referendum[1] to permitted participants[2] that either are not registered parties[3] or are minor parties[4], 'donation' means[5], in relation to a permitted participant[6]: (1) any gift[7] to the permitted participant[8] of money or other property[9]; (2) any sponsorship provided in relation to the permitted participant[10]; (3) any money spent (otherwise than by or on behalf of the permitted participant) in paying any referendum expenses[11] incurred by or on behalf of the permitted participant[12]; (4) any money lent to the permitted participant otherwise than on commercial terms[13]; (5) the provision otherwise than on commercial terms of any property, services or facilities for the use or benefit of the permitted participant (including the services of any person)[14]; (6) in the case of a permitted participant other than an individual, any subscription or other fee paid for affiliation to, or membership of, the permitted participant[15].

Where anything would be a donation both by virtue of head (2) above and by virtue of any other provision mentioned in head (1) or heads (3) to (6) above, head (2) above applies in relation to that donation to the exclusion of the other provision[16]. Any donation whose value is not more than £500 is disregarded[17]; and none of the following is to be regarded as a donation: (a) until a day to be appointed, any grant provided out of public funds[18], other than a grant provided to a designated organisation[19]; (b) the provision of any rights to assistance conferred on a designated organisation (or person authorised by a designated organisation)[20]; (c) the provision by an individual of his own services which he provides voluntarily in his own time and free of charge[21]; or (d) any interest accruing to a permitted participant in respect of any donation which is sent back by the permitted participant[22].

For these purposes, 'sponsorship' is provided in relation to a permitted participant if any money or other property is transferred to the permitted participant or to any person for the benefit of the permitted participant[23] and the purpose (or one of the purposes) of the transfer is, or must, having regard to all the circumstances, reasonably be assumed to be[24] either to help the permitted participant with meeting, or to meet, to any extent any defined expenses[25] incurred or to be incurred by or on behalf of the permitted participant[26] or to secure that to any extent any such expenses are not so incurred[27]. However, for these purposes: (i) the making of any payment in respect of any charge for admission to any conference, meeting or other event[28] or in respect of the purchase price of, or any other charge for access to, any publication[29]; or (ii) the making of any payment in respect of the inclusion of an advertisement in any publication where the payment is made at the commercial rate payable for the inclusion of such an advertisement in any such publication[30], do not constitute sponsorship[31].

1 As to the meaning of 'referendum expenses' see PARA 535.
2 As to the meaning of 'permitted participant' see PARA 529; but see also note 6.
3 As to the meaning of 'registered party' see PARA 35 note 3.
4 Political Parties, Elections and Referendums Act 2000 s 119, Sch 15 para 1(1). As to the meaning of 'minor party' see PARA 253 note 8.
5 Ie subject to the Political Parties, Elections and Referendums Act 2000 Sch 15 para 4 (see the text and notes 17–22). For these purposes, 'donation' must be construed in accordance with Sch 1 paras 2–4 (see the text and notes 6–31): Sch 15 para 1(5).
6 Political Parties, Elections and Referendums Act 2000 Sch 15 para 2(1). In accordance with Sch 15 para 1(1) (see the text and notes 1–4), 'permitted participant' does not for these purposes include a permitted participant which is a registered party other than a minor party: Sch 15 para 1(2), (3).
7 For these purposes, 'gift' includes bequest (and thus any form of testamentary disposition): Political Parties, Elections and Referendums Act 2000 s 160(1), Sch 15 para 2(6)(b).
8 For these purposes, any reference to anything being given or transferred to a permitted participant or any other person is a reference to its being given or transferred either directly or indirectly through any third person: Political Parties, Elections and Referendums Act 2000 Sch 15 para 2(6)(a). Anything given or transferred to any officer, member, trustee or agent of a permitted participant in his capacity as such (and not for his own use or benefit) is to be regarded as given or transferred to the permitted participant (and references to donations received by a permitted participant accordingly include donations so given or transferred): Sch 15 para 2(5).
9 Political Parties, Elections and Referendums Act 2000 Sch 15 para 2(1)(a). Where: (1) any money or other property is transferred to a permitted participant pursuant to any transaction or arrangement involving the provision by or on behalf of the permitted participant of any property, services or facilities or other consideration of monetary value (Sch 15 para 2(2)(a)); and (2) the total value in monetary terms of the consideration so provided by or on behalf of the permitted participant is less than the value of the money or (as the case may be) the market value of the property transferred (Sch 15 para 2(2)(b)), the transfer of the money or property constitutes a gift to the permitted participant for the purposes of Sch 15 para 2(1)(a), but subject to Sch 15 para 2(4) (see the text and note 16) (Sch 15 para 2(2)). The value of any donation falling within Sch 15 para 2(1)(a), other than money, must be taken to be the market value of the property in question: Sch 15 para 5(1). However, where Sch 15 para 2(1)(a) applies by virtue of Sch 15 para 2(2), the value of the donation must be taken to be the difference between: (a) the value of the money (or the market value of the property) in question (Sch 15 para 5(2)(a)); and (b) the total value in monetary terms of the consideration provided by or on behalf of the permitted participant (Sch 15 para 5(2)(b)). As to the meaning of 'market value' see PARA 299 note 26. As to the meaning of 'property' see PARA 34 note 8.
10 Political Parties, Elections and Referendums Act 2000 Sch 15 para 2(1)(b). For these purposes, sponsorship provided in relation to the permitted participant is defined by Sch 15 para 3 (see the text and notes 23–31): Sch 15 para 2(1)(b). The value of any donation falling within Sch 15 para 2(1)(b) is taken to be the value of the money or (as the case may be) the market value of the property, transferred as mentioned in Sch 15 para 3(1) (see the text and notes 23–27); and

accordingly any value in monetary terms of any benefit conferred on the person providing the sponsorship in question must be disregarded: Sch 15 para 5(3).

11 As to the meaning of 'referendum expenses' see PARA 535.

12 Political Parties, Elections and Referendums Act 2000 Sch 15 para 2(1)(c). As to the meaning of references to referendum expenses incurred by or on behalf of a permitted participant during the referendum period see PARA 541 note 5. In relation to a permitted participant at a referendum, a donation to the permitted participant for the purpose of meeting referendum expenses incurred by or on behalf of the permitted participant is referred to as a 'relevant donation': Sch 15 para 1(4).

13 Political Parties, Elections and Referendums Act 2000 Sch 15 para 2(1)(d). In determining, for these purposes, whether any money lent to a permitted participant is so lent otherwise than on commercial terms (Sch 15 para 2(3)(a)), regard must be had to the total value in monetary terms of the consideration provided by or on behalf of the permitted participant in respect of the loan or the provision of the property, services or facilities (Sch 15 para 2(3)). The value of any donation falling within Sch 15 para 2(1)(d) or Sch 15 para 2(1)(e) (see head (5) in the text) is taken to be the amount representing the difference between: (1) the total value in monetary terms of the consideration that would have had to be provided by or on behalf of the permitted participant in respect of the loan or the provision of the property, services or facilities if the loan had been made or the property, services or facilities had been provided, on commercial terms (Sch 15 para 5(4)(a)); and (2) the total value in monetary terms of the consideration, if any, actually so provided by or on behalf of the permitted participant (Sch 15 para 5(4)(b)). Where such a donation confers an enduring benefit on the donee over a particular period, the value of the donation is determined at the time when it is made, but must be so determined by reference to the total benefit accruing to the donee over that period: Sch 15 para 5(5).

14 Political Parties, Elections and Referendums Act 2000 Sch 15 para 2(1)(e). In determining, for these purposes, whether any property, services or facilities provided for the use or benefit of a permitted participant is or are so provided otherwise than on commercial terms (Sch 15 para 2(3)(b)), regard must be had to the total value in monetary terms of the consideration provided by or on behalf of the permitted participant in respect of the loan or the provision of the property, services or facilities (Sch 15 para 2(3)). See also note 13.

15 Political Parties, Elections and Referendums Act 2000 Sch 15 para 2(1)(f).

16 Political Parties, Elections and Referendums Act 2000 Sch 15 para 2(4). In the circumstances mentioned in the text, the general provisions as to sponsorship (see the text and notes 23–31) apply as well as the provision mentioned in head (2) in the text: Sch 15 para 2(4).

17 Political Parties, Elections and Referendums Act 2000 Sch 15 para 4(2) (amended by the Political Parties and Elections Act 2009 s 20(1)). The value is determined in accordance with the Political Parties, Elections and Referendums Act 2000 Sch 15 para 5 (see notes 9, 10, 13). The Secretary of State may by order vary the sum for the time being specified in Sch 15: see s 155; and PARA 299 note 36. At the date at which this volume states the law, no such order had been made.

18 As to references to payments out of public funds see PARA 299 note 21.

19 Political Parties, Elections and Referendums Act 2000 Sch 15 para 4(1)(a) (Sch 15 para 4(1)(a) prospectively repealed by the Political Parties and Elections Act 2009 Sch 6 para 30(1), (2)(a), Sch 17). At the date at which this volume states the law no day had been appointed for these purposes. As to the meaning of 'designated organisation' see PARA 531 note 5. The text refers to a grant other than a grant provided to a designated organisation by virtue of s 110(2) (see PARA 531).

20 Political Parties, Elections and Referendums Act 2000 Sch 15 para 4(1)(b). The text refers to any right conferred on a designated organisation by virtue of s 110(4), Sch 12 (see PARAS 531–534).

21 Political Parties, Elections and Referendums Act 2000 Sch 15 para 4(1)(c).

22 Political Parties, Elections and Referendums Act 2000 Sch 15 para 4(1)(d). The text refers to a donation which is dealt with by the permitted participant in accordance with s 56(2)(a), (b) (see PARA 548).

23 Political Parties, Elections and Referendums Act 2000 Sch 15 para 3(1)(a).

24 Political Parties, Elections and Referendums Act 2000 Sch 15 para 3(1)(b).

25 For this purpose, 'defined expenses' means expenses in connection with: (1) any conference, meeting or other event organised by or on behalf of the permitted participant (Political Parties, Elections and Referendums Act 2000 Sch 15 para 3(2)(a)); (2) the preparation, production or dissemination of any publication by or on behalf of the permitted participant (Sch 15 para 3(2)(b)); or (3) any study or research organised by or on behalf of the permitted participant (Sch 15 para 3(2)(c)). For this purpose, 'publication' means a publication made available in whatever form and by whatever means, whether or not to the public at large or any section of the public: Sch 15 para 3(5). The Secretary of State may by order made on the recommendation

of the Electoral Commission amend Sch 15 para 3(2) or Sch 15 para 3(3) (see the text and notes 28–31): Sch 15 para 3(4). At the date at which this volume states the law, no such order had been made. As to the Secretary of State see PARA 2; and as to the Electoral Commission see PARA 34 et seq.

26 Political Parties, Elections and Referendums Act 2000 Sch 15 para 3(1)(b)(i).
27 Political Parties, Elections and Referendums Act 2000 Sch 15 para 3(1)(b)(ii).
28 Political Parties, Elections and Referendums Act 2000 Sch 15 para 3(3)(a)(i). See note 25.
29 Political Parties, Elections and Referendums Act 2000 Sch 15 para 3(3)(a)(ii). See note 25.
30 Political Parties, Elections and Referendums Act 2000 Sch 15 para 3(3)(b). See note 25.
31 Political Parties, Elections and Referendums Act 2000 Sch 15 para 3(3). See note 25.

547.   Restrictions on permitted participants at a referendum accepting certain donations.   For the purposes of controlling donations[1] to permitted participants[2] at a referendum[3], a relevant donation[4] received by a permitted participant must not be accepted[5] if:

(1)   the person by whom the donation would be made is not, at the time of its receipt by the permitted participant, a permissible donor[6];

(2)   as from a day to be appointed, and until a day to be appointed, in the case of a donation of an amount exceeding £7,500, the permitted participant has not been given the required declaration[7];

(3)   as from the second appointed day referred to above, any declaration required to be made in respect of the donation[8] has not been received by the permitted participant[9]; or

(4)   the permitted participant is, whether because the donation is given anonymously or by reason of any deception or concealment or otherwise, unable to ascertain the identity of the person offering the donation[10].

Where any person (the 'principal donor') causes an amount (the 'principal donation') to be received by a permitted participant by way of a relevant donation either on behalf of himself and one or more other persons[11] or on behalf of two or more other persons[12], then for the purposes of the provisions relating to the controls on donations received by permitted participants at a referendum[13], each individual contribution by such person of more than £500 is treated as if it were a separate donation received from that person[14].

Where any person (the 'agent') causes an amount to be received by a permitted participant by way of a donation on behalf of another person (the 'donor')[15], and the amount of the donation is more than £500[16], the agent must ensure that, at the time when the donation is received by the permitted participant, the responsible person is given all such details in respect of the donor as are required to be included in donation reports[17].

A person commits an offence if, without reasonable excuse, he fails to comply with the provisions which impose controls on donations made through other persons or through agents[18].

1   As to the meaning of 'donation' see PARA 546.
2   As to the meaning of 'permitted participant' see PARA 529; but see also PARA 546 note 6.
3   Ie for the purposes of the Political Parties, Elections and Referendums Act 2000 s 119, Sch 15. As to the meaning of 'referendum' see PARA 527.
4   As to the meaning of 'relevant donation' see PARA 546 note 12.
5   Political Parties, Elections and Referendums Act 2000 Sch 15 para 6(1).
6   Political Parties, Elections and Referendums Act 2000 Sch 15 para 6(1)(a). As to the permissible donors for these purposes see s 54(2); and PARA 529 note 11. For these purposes, any payment received by a designated organisation by virtue of s 110(2) (see PARA 531) must be regarded as a donation received by the organisation from a permissible donor falling within s 54(2) (Sch 15 para 6(2)); and any relevant donation received by a permitted participant which is an exempt trust donation must be regarded as a relevant donation received by the permitted participant

from a permissible donor (Sch 15 para 6(3)). However, any relevant donation received by a permitted participant from a trustee of any property (in his capacity as such) is regarded as being from a person who is not such a permissible donor if that donation is not: (1) an exempt trust donation; or (2) a relevant donation transmitted by the trustee to the permitted participant on behalf of beneficiaries under the trust who are either persons who, at the time of its receipt by the permitted participant, are such permissible donors or the members of an unincorporated association which at that time is such a permissible donor: Sch 15 para 6(4). In relation to donations received by a permitted participant other than a designated organisation (within the meaning given by s 110(5): see PARA 531), references to a permissible donor falling within s 54(2) do not include a registered party: Sch 15 para 1(6). As to the meaning of 'registered party' see PARA 35 note 3; and as to the meaning of 'exempt trust donation' see PARA 288 note 7.

7 Political Parties, Elections and Referendums Act 2000 Sch 15 paras 6(1)(aa), 6A (Sch 15 paras 6(1)(aa), 6A, 6B prospectively added by the Political Parties and Elections Act 2009 Sch 3 para 7(1), (2), and Sch 15 para 6(1)(aa) prospectively substituted by Sch 4 para 7(1)). The required declaration is that referred to in the Political Parties, Elections and Referendums Act 2000 Sch 15 para 6A (prospectively added), which provides that where a person (P) causes an amount exceeding £7,500 to be received by a permitted participant by way of a donation, a written declaration must be given to the permitted participant by P, if P is an individual, or if not, by an individual authorised by P to make the declaration, stating, to the best of the individual's knowledge and belief, whether or not Sch 15 para 6A(2) applies to the donation (Sch 15 para 6A(1) (prospectively added)). Schedule 15 para 6A(2) applies if a person other than P has provided, or is expected to provide, money or any other benefit to P with a view to, or otherwise in connection with, the making of the donation, and the money, or the value of the benefit, is more than £7,500: Sch 15 para 6A(2) (prospectively added). Where a declaration under Sch 15 para 6A contains a statement to the effect that Sch 15 para 6A(2) applies to the donation, it must also state whether or not, in the opinion of the person making the declaration, Sch 15 para 6(5) or (7) (see the text and notes 11–17) applies to the donation and, if the person's opinion is that neither of those provisions apply to the donation, give the person's reasons for that opinion: Sch 15 para 6A(3) (prospectively added). The declaration must also state the full name and address of the person by whom it is made and, where the written declaration referred to in Sch 15 para 6A(1) is made by an individual authorised by P, state that the person is so authorised and describe the person's role or position in relation to P (Sch 15 para 6A(4) (prospectively added)). A person who knowingly or recklessly makes a false declaration Sch 15 para 6A commits an offence: see Sch 15 para 6A(5) (prospectively added); and PARA 752. Regulations made by the Secretary of State may make provision as to how the value of a benefit is to be calculated for the purposes of Sch 15 para 6A(2): Sch 15 para 6A(6) (prospectively added). At the date at which this volume states the law no such regulations had been made.

8 Ie any declaration required to be made in respect of the donation by the Political Parties, Elections and Referendums Act 2000 Sch 15 para 6A (see note 7) or Sch 15 para 6B (prospectively added: see note 7), which provides that an individual making to a permitted participant a donation in relation to which the condition set out in s 54(2ZA) (see CONSTITUTIONAL LAW AND HUMAN RIGHTS) applies must give to the permitted participant a declaration stating whether or not the individual satisfies that condition (Sch 15 para 6B(1) (prospectively added)). A declaration under Sch 15 para 6B must also state the individual's full name and address: Sch 15 para 6B(2) (prospectively added). A person who knowingly or recklessly makes a false declaration under Sch 15 para 6B commits an offence: see Sch 15 para 6B(3) (prospectively added); and PARA 752. The Secretary of State may by regulations make provision requiring a declaration under Sch 15 para 6B to be retained for a specified period: Sch 15 para 6B(4) (prospectively added). At the date at which this volume states the law no such regulations had been made.

9 Political Parties, Elections and Referendums Act 2000 Sch 15 paras 6(1)(aa) (prospectively substituted: see note 7).

10 Political Parties, Elections and Referendums Act 2000 Sch 15 para 6(1)(b).

11 Political Parties, Elections and Referendums Act 2000 Sch 15 para 6(5)(a).

12 Political Parties, Elections and Referendums Act 2000 Sch 15 para 6(5)(b).

13 Ie for the purposes of the Political Parties, Elections and Referendums Act 2000 Sch 15.

14 Political Parties, Elections and Referendums Act 2000 Sch 15 para 6(5) (Sch 15 para 6(5), (7)(b) amended by the Political Parties and Referendums Act 2009 s 20(1). In relation to each such separate donation, the principal donor must ensure that, at the time when the principal donation is received by the permitted participant, the responsible person is given, except in the case of a donation which the principal donor is treated as making, all such details in respect of the person treated as making the donation as are required by virtue of Sch 15 para 10(1)(c) (see PARA 550) and, in any case, all such details in respect of the donation as are required by virtue of Sch 15

para 10(1)(a) (see PARA 550): Sch 15 para 6(6). As to the meaning of 'responsible person' in relation to a registered party see PARA 529 note 17; and as to the meaning of 'responsible person' in relation to an individual or body which is not a registered party see PARA 529 note 27.

15 Political Parties, Elections and Referendums Act 2000 Sch 15 para 6(7)(a).
16 Political Parties, Elections and Referendums Act 2000 Sch 15 para 6(7)(b) (as amended: see note 14).
17 Political Parties, Elections and Referendums Act 2000 Sch 15 para 6(7) (as amended: see note 14). The text refers to the details in respect of the donor that are required to be reported by virtue of Sch 15 para 10(1)(c) (see PARA 550).
18 See the Political Parties, Elections and Referendums Act 2000 Sch 15 para 6(8); and PARA 752. The text refers to failure to comply with Sch 15 para 6(6), (7) (see the text and notes 14–17).

548. Acceptance or return of donations received by permitted participants at a referendum. The provisions which require a registered party[1] to: (1) take all reasonable steps to identify a donor in order to ascertain whether he is a permissible donor[2]; and (2) where a donor is unidentifiable or impermissible, to return the donation to its source or to send it to the Electoral Commission[3] or subject it to forfeiture on the application of the Commission[4], apply, subject to minor modification, for the purposes of controlling donations[5] to permitted participants[6] at a referendum[7] in relation to a permitted participant and any relevant donation[8] received by a permitted participant as they apply in relation to a registered party and a donation received by a registered party[9].

Accordingly, where a donation is received by a permitted participant[10] and it is not immediately decided that the permitted participant should (for whatever reason) refuse the donation[11], all reasonable steps must be taken forthwith by or on behalf of the permitted participant party to verify (or, so far as any of the following is not apparent, ascertain) the identity of the donor, whether he is a permissible donor, and (if that appears to be the case) all such details in respect of the donor as are required to be included in donation reports[12]. If a permitted participant receives a donation which it is prohibited from accepting[13], or which it is decided that the permitted participant should for any other reason refuse[14], then, within the period of 30 days beginning with the date when the donation is received by the permitted participant[15]:

(a)   the donation, or a payment of an equivalent amount, must be sent back to the person who made the donation or any person appearing to be acting on his behalf[16] (unless the permitted participant is unable to ascertain the identity of the person by whom the donation was made[17] (or, as from a day to be appointed, a required declaration has not been made[18]);

(b)   as from a day to be appointed, the donation, or a payment of an equivalent amount, must be sent back to the person appearing to be the donor[19]; and

(c)   the required steps[20] must[21] be taken in relation to the donation)[22].

Unless the donation is so returned or such steps are taken in relation to the donation within the period of 30 days so mentioned[23], and unless a record can be produced of the receipt of the donation and of the return of the donation or the equivalent amount (or of the required steps being taken in relation to the donation, as the case may be)[24] then, for these purposes, a donation received by a permitted participant is taken to have been accepted by the permitted participant[25].

In England and Wales[26], a magistrates' court may, on an application made by the Commission, order the forfeiture by the permitted participant of an amount equal to the value of any donation[27] received by a permitted participant which[28] the permitted participant is prohibited from accepting[29] but which has been accepted by the permitted participant[30]. The standard of proof in proceedings on such an application is that applicable to civil proceedings[31]; and such an order may be made whether or not proceedings are brought against any person for an offence connected with the donation[32]. Where such an order (a 'forfeiture order') is made by a magistrates' court[33], the permitted participant may, before the end of the period of 30 days beginning with the date on which any forfeiture order is made, appeal to the Crown Court[34]. Such an appeal is by way of a rehearing; and the court hearing such an appeal may make such order as it considers appropriate[35]. The standard of proof in relation to a rehearing on such an appeal remains that applicable to civil proceedings[36]; and an appropriate order may be made whether or not proceedings are brought against any person for an offence connected with the donation[37]. Any amount forfeited by an order made either on application or on appeal[38] must be paid into the Consolidated Fund[39], although this does not apply: (a) where an appeal is made[40], before the appeal is determined or otherwise disposed of[41]; and (b) in any other case, before the end of the period of 30 days beginning with the date on which any forfeiture order is made[42].

1   As to the meaning of 'registered party' see PARA 35 note 3.

2   Ie the Political Parties, Elections and Referendums Act 2000 s 56 (see the text and notes 10–25). Nothing in Pt IV (ss 50–71) affects minor parties (as to which see PARA 253 note 8). As to the meaning of 'permissible donor' see PARA 529 note 11.

3   Ie the Political Parties, Elections and Referendums Act 2000 s 57 (see note 20). See also note 2. As to the Electoral Commission see PARA 34 et seq.

4   Ie the Political Parties, Elections and Referendums Act 2000 s 58 (see the text and notes 26–32). The registered party may appeal against a forfeiture order (see s 59; and the text and notes 33–37); and rules of court under s 60 (see note 30; and the text and notes 38–42) may provide for the procedure on application or appeal under ss 58, 59. See also note 2.

5   As to the meaning of 'donation' see PARA 546.

6   As to the meaning of 'permitted participant' see PARA 529; but see also PARA 546 note 6.

7   Ie for the purposes of the Political Parties, Elections and Referendums Act 2000 s 119, Sch 15. As to the meaning of 'referendum' see PARA 527.

8   As to the meaning of 'relevant donation' see PARA 546 note 12.

9   Political Parties, Elections and Referendums Act 2000 Sch 15 para 7(1). Accordingly, in the application of ss 56–60 for these purposes: (1) s 56(1) has effect as if the reference to the particulars relating to a donor which would be required to be included in a donation report by virtue of ss 62, 63, Sch 6 para 2 (identity of donors (quarterly reports): see CONSTITUTIONAL LAW AND HUMAN RIGHTS), if the donation were a recordable donation within the meaning of Sch 6 (see CONSTITUTIONAL LAW AND HUMAN RIGHTS), were construed as a reference to the particulars which are required to be included in a return by virtue of Sch 15 para 10(1)(c) (see PARA 550) (Sch 15 para 7(2)(a)); (2) the provisions of s 56(3), (4) (or, as from a day to be appointed, s 56(3), (3B), (4)) have effect as if the reference to the treasurer of a registered party were construed as a reference to the responsible person in relation to the permitted participant (Sch 15 para 7(2)(b) (s 56(1A), (2)(aa), Sch 15 para 7(2)(aa) prospectively added, ss 56(2)(a), (b), (3B), (5)(a), (b), 58(1)(a), Sch 15 para 7(2)(b) prospectively amended, by the Political Parties and Elections Act 2009 ss 9(3), (4), 10(5), Sch 4 para 8, Sch 6 paras 15, 30(1), (4))); and (3) as from a day to be appointed, s 56(1A)(a) has effect as if the reference to a declaration under s 54B were a reference to a declaration under Sch 15 para 6B (see PARA 547 note 8) (Sch 15 para 7(2)(aa) (prospectively added)). As to the meaning of 'responsible person' in relation to a registered party see PARA 529 note 17; and as to the meaning of 'responsible person' in relation to an individual or body which is not a registered party see PARA 529 note 27.

10   Political Parties, Elections and Referendums Act 2000 s 56(1)(a) (as applied: see the text and notes 1–9).

11   Political Parties, Elections and Referendums Act 2000 s 56(1)(b) (as applied: see the text and notes 1–9). Where a donation is received by a permitted participant in the form of an amount paid into any account held by the permitted participant with a financial institution, it is taken

for these purposes to have been received by the permitted participant at the time when the permitted participant is notified in the usual way of the payment into the account: s 56(6) (as so applied).

12 Political Parties, Elections and Referendums Act 2000 s 56(1) (as applied and modified: see the text and notes 1–9). The text refers to the details in respect of the donor that are required to be reported by virtue of Sch 15 para 10(1)(c) (see PARA 550). As from a day to be appointed, in so far as s 56(1) requires steps to be taken to verify or ascertain whether an individual satisfies the condition set out in s 54(2ZA) (see CONSTITUTIONAL LAW AND HUMAN RIGHTS), the requirement is treated as having being complied with if the individual has given to the party a declaration under s Sch 15 para 6B (see PARA 547 note 8) stating that the individual satisfies that condition and the party had no reasonable grounds for thinking that the statement was incorrect: s 56(1A) (prospectively added (see note 9); as so applied).

13 Ie by virtue of the Political Parties, Elections and Referendums Act 2000 s 54(1), which is in similar terms to Sch 15 para 6(1) (see PARA 547).

14 Political Parties, Elections and Referendums Act 2000 s 56(2) (as applied: see the text and notes 1–9).

15 Political Parties, Elections and Referendums Act 2000 s 56(2) (as applied: see the text and notes 1–9).

16 Political Parties, Elections and Referendums Act 2000 s 56(2)(a) (prospectively amended and applied: see the text and notes 1–9). Where this provision applies in relation to a donation and the donation is not dealt with accordingly, the responsible person is guilty of an offence: see s 56(3) (as applied and modified); and PARA 752. Where a party or its treasurer is charged with an offence under s 56(3), it is a defence to prove that all reasonable steps were taken by or on behalf of the party to verify (or ascertain) whether the donor was a permissible donor, and as a result, the treasurer believed the donor to be a permissible donor: see s 56(3A) (added by the Political Parties and Referendums Act 2009 s 12); and PARA 752.

17 Ie unless the donation falls within the Political Parties, Elections and Referendums Act 2000 s 54(1)(b), which is in similar terms to Sch 15 para 6(1)(b) (see PARA 547).

18 Ie unless the donation falls within the Political Parties, Elections and Referendums Act 2000 s 54(1)(aa), which is in similar terms to Sch 15 para 6(1)(aa) (see PARA 547).

19 Political Parties, Elections and Referendums Act 2000 s 56(2)(aa) (prospectively added and applied: see the text and notes 1–9). This provision applies if the donation falls within s 54(1)(aa), which is in similar terms to Sch 15 para 6(1)(aa) (see PARA 547), but not s 54(1)(b), which is in similar terms to Sch 15 para 6(1)(b). As from a day to be appointed, where this provision applies in relation to a donation and the donation is not dealt with in accordance with s 56(2)(aa), the party and the treasurer of the party are each guilty of an offence: see s 56(3B) (prospectively added and applied); and PARA 752.

20 For these purposes, the required steps are as follows: (1) if the donation was transmitted by a person other than the donor, and the identity of that person is apparent, to return the donation to that person (Political Parties, Elections and Referendums Act 2000 s 57(1)(a) (as applied: see the text and notes 1–9)); (2) if head (1) above does not apply but it is apparent that the donor has, in connection with the donation, used any facility provided by an identifiable financial institution, to return the donation to that institution (s 57(1)(b) (as so applied)); and (3) in any other case, to send the donation to the Electoral Commission (s 57(1)(c) (as so applied); s 160(1)). Any reference to returning or sending a donation to any person or body includes a reference to sending a payment of an equivalent amount to that person or body (s 57(2) (as so applied)); and any amount sent to the Electoral Commission in pursuance of head (3) above must be paid by it into the Consolidated Fund (s 57(3) (as so applied); s 160(1)). As to the Consolidated Fund see CONSTITUTIONAL LAW AND HUMAN RIGHTS vol 8(2) (Reissue) PARA 711 et seq; PARLIAMENT vol 78 (2010) PARAS 1028–1031.

21 Ie if the donation falls within the Political Parties, Elections and Referendums Act 2000 s 54(1)(b) (see note 17).

22 Political Parties, Elections and Referendums Act 2000 s 56(2)(b) (prospectively added and applied: see the text and notes 1–9). Where this provision applies in relation to a donation and the donation is not dealt with accordingly, the responsible person is guilty of an offence: see s 56(4) (as applied and modified); and PARA 752.

23 Political Parties, Elections and Referendums Act 2000 s 56(5)(a) (prospectively amended and applied: see the text and notes 1–9).

24 Political Parties, Elections and Referendums Act 2000 s 56(5)(b) (prospectively amended and applied: see the text and notes 1–9).

25 Political Parties, Elections and Referendums Act 2000 s 56(5) (prospectively amended and applied: see the text and notes 1–9).

26 As to the meanings of 'England' and 'Wales' see PARA 1 note 1.

27 Political Parties, Elections and Referendums Act 2000 s 58(2), (5)(a) (as applied: see the text and notes 1–9).

28 Ie by virtue of the Political Parties, Elections and Referendums Act 2000 s 54(1)(a), (b) or, as from a day to be appointed, s 54(1)(a), (aa) or (b) (which are in similar terms to Sch 15 para 6(1)(a), (aa) and (b) (see PARA 547).

29 Political Parties, Elections and Referendums Act 2000 s 58(1)(a) (prospectively amended and applied: see the text and notes 1–9).

30 Political Parties, Elections and Referendums Act 2000 s 58(1)(b) (as applied: see the text and notes 1–9).

　　In relation to courts in any part of the United Kingdom, and without prejudice to the generality of any existing power to make rules, provision may be made by rules of court with respect to applications or appeals to any court under s 58 (as applied) or s 59 (as applied) (see the text and notes 1–9), for the giving of notice of such applications or appeals to persons affected, and generally with respect to the procedure under those statutory provisions before any court: s 60(1), (2) (s 60(1) amended by SI 2004/366; as so applied). In the case of a permitted participant which is not a body corporate: (1) proceedings under s 58 (as applied) or s 59 (as applied) must be brought against or by the party in its own name (and not in that of any of its members) (s 60(5)(a) (as so applied)); (2) for the purposes of any such proceedings any rules of court relating to the service of documents apply as if the permitted participant were a body corporate (s 60(5)(b) (as so applied)); and (3) any amount forfeited by an order under s 58 (as applied) or s 59 (as applied) must be paid out of the funds of the permitted participant (s 60(5)(c) (as so applied)). In Acts passed after 1889, in relation to any court, 'rules of court' means rules made by the authority having power to make rules or orders regulating the practice of that court: see the Interpretation Act 1978 Sch 1, Sch 2 para 4(1)(a); and STATUTES AND LEGISLATIVE PROCESS vol 96 (2012) PARA 1216.

31 Political Parties, Elections and Referendums Act 2000 s 58(3) (as applied: see the text and notes 1–9). See note 30.

32 Political Parties, Elections and Referendums Act 2000 s 58(4) (as applied: see the text and notes 1–9). See note 30.

33 Political Parties, Elections and Referendums Act 2000 s 59(1) (as applied: see the text and notes 1–9). See note 30.

34 Political Parties, Elections and Referendums Act 2000 s 59(2) (as applied: see the text and notes 1–9). See note 30.

35 Political Parties, Elections and Referendums Act 2000 s 59(3) (as applied: see the text and notes 1–9). See note 30.

36 Political Parties, Elections and Referendums Act 2000 ss 58(3), 59(4) (as applied: see the text and notes 1–9). See note 30.

37 Political Parties, Elections and Referendums Act 2000 ss 58(4), 59(4) (as applied: see the text and notes 1–9). See note 30.

38 Ie an order under the Political Parties, Elections and Referendums Act 2000 s 58 (as applied) (see the text and notes 26–32) or s 59 (as applied) (see the text and notes 33–37).

39 Political Parties, Elections and Referendums Act 2000 s 60(3) (as applied: see the text and notes 1–9).

40 Ie under the Political Parties, Elections and Referendums Act 2000 s 59(2) (as applied) (see the text and note 34).

41 Political Parties, Elections and Referendums Act 2000 s 60(4)(a) (as applied: see the text and notes 1–9).

42 Political Parties, Elections and Referendums Act 2000 ss 59(2), 60(4)(b) (as applied: see the text and notes 1–9).

549. Evasion of restrictions on donations received by permitted participants at a referendum. The provisions which create offences concerned with the evasion of restrictions on donations to a registered party[1] apply for the purposes of controlling relevant donations[2] received by permitted participants[3] at a referendum[4], subject to minor modification[5].

1 Ie the Political Parties, Elections and Referendums Act 2000 s 61 (see CONSTITUTIONAL LAW AND HUMAN RIGHTS). As to the meaning of 'registered party' see PARA 35 note 3.

2 As to the meaning of 'relevant donation' see PARA 546 note 12.

3 As to the meaning of 'permitted participant' see PARA 529; but see also PARA 546 note 6.

4   Ie for the purposes of the Political Parties, Elections and Referendums Act 2000 s 119, Sch 15. As to the meaning of 'referendum' see PARA 527.

5   See the Political Parties, Elections and Referendums Act 2000 Sch 15 para 8; and PARA 752.

550. Statement of relevant donations received by permitted participants at a referendum. For the purposes of controlling donations[1] to permitted participants[2] at a referendum[3], the responsible person[4] in relation to a permitted participant must include, in any return required to be prepared in respect of referendum expenses[5], a statement of relevant donations[6] which complies with the requirement to report any donations received from persons who are permissible donors as well as those received from persons who are not permissible donors[7].

Accordingly, in relation to each relevant donation accepted by the permitted participant where the value of the donation:

(1)   is more than £7,500[8]; or

(2)   when added to the value of any other donation or donations made by the same donor (whether or not falling within head (1) above), is more than that amount[9],

the statement must record[10]: (a) the amount of the donation (if a donation of money, in cash or otherwise) or (in any other case) the nature of the donation and its value[11]; (b) the date when the donation was accepted by the permitted participant[12]; (c) the information about the donor which is, in connection with recordable donations to registered parties, required to be recorded in donation reports[13]; (d) the total value of any relevant donations, other than those falling within head (1) or head (2) above, which are accepted by the permitted participant[14]; and (e) such other information as may be required by regulations made by the Electoral Commission[15]. As from a day to be appointed, where a declaration as to the course of a donation has been given[16], the statement must either state that no reason was found to think that the declaration was untruthful or inaccurate, or give details of any respects in which the declaration was found or suspected to be untruthful or inaccurate[17], and where a declaration as to whether an applicable condition has been satisfied has been given[18], the statement must either state that no reason was found for thinking that the declaration was incorrect, or give details of any respects in which the declaration was found or suspected to be incorrect[19].

Where a relevant donation has been received from a person who is not a permissible donor (an 'impermissible donor')[20], the statement must record: (i) the name and address of the donor[21]; (ii) the amount of the donation (if a donation of money, in cash or otherwise) or (in any other case) the nature of the donation and its value[22]; (iii) the date when the donation was received, and the date when, and the manner in which, it was dealt with in accordance with the provisions which regulate the handling of relevant donations made by impermissible donors[23]; (iv) such other information as is required by regulations made by the Commission[24]. Where a relevant donation has been received from a person whose identity cannot be ascertained[25], the statement must record: (A) details of the manner in which the donation was made[26]; (B) the amount of the donation (if a donation of money, in cash or otherwise) or (in any other case) the nature of the donation and its value[27]; (C) the date when the donation was received, and the date when and the manner in which it was dealt with in accordance with the provisions which regulate the handling of relevant donations made by persons whose identity cannot be ascertained[28]; and (D) such other information as is required by regulations made by the Commission[29]. As from a day to be appointed, where a relevant donation has been received without the required declaration[30], the statement must record: (aa) the name and address of the person appearing to be the donor[31]; (bb) the amount of the donation (if a donation of money, in cash or otherwise) or (in any other case) the nature of the donation and its value[32]; (cc) the date when the donation was received, and the date when, and the manner in which, it was dealt with in accordance with the provisions which regulate the handling of relevant donations made by impermissible donors[33]; (dd) such other information as is required by regulations made by the Commission[34].

1   As to the meaning of 'donation' see PARA 546.
2   As to the meaning of 'permitted participant' see PARA 529; but see also PARA 546 note 6.
3   Ie for the purposes of the Political Parties, Elections and Referendums Act 2000 s 119, Sch 15. As to the meaning of 'referendum' see PARA 527.
4   As to the meaning of 'responsible person' in relation to a registered party see PARA 529 note 17; and as to the meaning of 'responsible person' in relation to an individual or body which is not a registered party see PARA 529 note 27.
5   Ie any return required to be prepared under the Political Parties, Elections and Referendums Act 2000 s 120 (see PARA 542).
6   As to the meaning of 'relevant donation' see PARA 546 note 12.
7   Political Parties, Elections and Referendums Act 2000 Sch 15 para 9 (Sch 15 para 9A prospectively added, Sch 15 paras 9, 9A, 11(1), (2) prospectively amended, by the Political Parties and Referendums Act 2009 Sch 3 paras 8(1), 9(1), Sch 4 para 9). Until a day to be appointed the text refers to the requirement for a statement of relevant donations to comply with Sch 15 paras 10–11 (see the text and notes 8–15, 20–34); as from that day it refers to the requirement for a statement of relevant donations to comply with Sch 15 paras 9A–11 (see the text and notes 16–34): Sch 15 para 9 (prospectively amended). As to the meaning of 'permissible donor' see PARA 529 note 11.
8   Political Parties, Elections and Referendums Act 2000 Sch 15 para 10(1), (2)(a) (amended by the Political Parties and Referendums Act 2009 s 20(3)). The Secretary of State may by order vary the sum for the time being specified in Sch 15: see s 155; and PARA 299 note 36. At the date at which this volume states the law, no such order had been made. As to the Secretary of State see PARA 2.
9   Political Parties, Elections and Referendums Act 2000 Sch 15 para 10(1), (2)(b).
10 Political Parties, Elections and Referendums Act 2000 Sch 15 para 10(1).
11 Political Parties, Elections and Referendums Act 2000 Sch 15 para 10(1)(a). The value of the donation is determined in accordance with Sch 15 para 5 (see PARA 546).
12 Political Parties, Elections and Referendums Act 2000 Sch 15 para 10(1)(b). As to the acceptance of donations made to a permitted participant see PARA 548.
13 Political Parties, Elections and Referendums Act 2000 Sch 15 para 10(1)(c). The text refers to information about the donor which is required to be recorded in donation reports by virtue of ss 62, 63, Sch 6 para 2 (identity of donors (quarterly reports): see CONSTITUTIONAL LAW AND HUMAN RIGHTS). In the case of a donation made by an individual who has an anonymous entry in an electoral register (within the meaning of the Representation of the People Act 1983: see PARA 148), if the statement of relevant donations states that the permitted participant has seen evidence, of such description as is prescribed by the Secretary of State in regulations, that the individual donor has such an anonymous entry, the statement must be accompanied by a copy of the evidence: Political Parties, Elections and Referendums Act 2000 Sch 15 para 10(4) (added by the Electoral Administration Act 2006 s 10(2), Sch 1 paras 24, 30). The evidence prescribed for the purposes of the Political Parties, Elections and Referendums Act 2000 Sch 15 para 10(4) is a certificate of anonymous registration issued pursuant to the Representation of the People (England and Wales) Regulations 2001, SI 2001/341, reg 45G (see PARA 145): see the Political Donations and Regulated Transactions (Anonymous Electors) Regulations 2008, SI 2008/2869, reg 3. As to the making of regulations under the Political Parties, Elections and Referendums Act 2000 generally see PARA 34 note 2.
14 Political Parties, Elections and Referendums Act 2000 Sch 15 para 10(3)(a).
15 Political Parties, Elections and Referendums Act 2000 s 160(1), Sch 15 para 10(3)(b). Regulations made by the Electoral Commission are not statutory instruments and are not recorded in this work: see further PARA 47. As to the Electoral Commission see PARA 34 et seq.
16 Ie under the Political Parties, Elections and Referendums Act 2000 Sch 15 para 6A (see PARA 547).

17 Political Parties, Elections and Referendums Act 2000 Sch 15 para 9A(1) (prospectively added and amended: see note 7).

18 Ie under the Political Parties, Elections and Referendums Act 2000 Sch 15 para 6B (see PARA 547).

19 Political Parties, Elections and Referendums Act 2000 Sch 15 para 9A(2) (prospectively added and amended: see note 7).

20 Political Parties, Elections and Referendums Act 2000 Sch 15 para 11(1), (2). The text refers to the circumstance where Sch 15 para 6(1)(a) applies (see PARA 547).

21 Political Parties, Elections and Referendums Act 2000 Sch 15 para 11(2)(a).

22 Political Parties, Elections and Referendums Act 2000 Sch 15 para 11(2)(b). As to the ascertainment of value for these purposes see note 11.

23 Political Parties, Elections and Referendums Act 2000 Sch 15 para 11(2)(c), (3). The text refers to dealing with the donation in accordance with s 56(2)(a) (as applied): see PARA 548.

24 Political Parties, Elections and Referendums Act 2000 s 160(1), Sch 15 para 11(2)(d). As to the regulations referred to in the text see note 15.

25 Political Parties, Elections and Referendums Act 2000 Sch 15 para 11(3). The text refers to the circumstance where Sch 15 para 6(1)(b) applies (see PARA 547).

26 Political Parties, Elections and Referendums Act 2000 Sch 15 para 11(3)(a).

27 Political Parties, Elections and Referendums Act 2000 Sch 15 para 11(3)(b). As to the ascertainment of value for these purposes see note 11.

28 Political Parties, Elections and Referendums Act 2000 Sch 15 para 11(3)(c). The text refers to dealing with the donation in accordance with s 56(2)(b) (as applied): see PARA 548.

29 Political Parties, Elections and Referendums Act 2000 Sch 15 para 11(3)(d). As to the regulations referred to in the text see note 15.

30 Political Parties, Elections and Referendums Act 2000 Sch 15 para 11(1), (2) (prospectively amended: see note 7). The text refers to the circumstance where Sch 15 para 6(1)(aa) applies (see PARA 547).

31 Political Parties, Elections and Referendums Act 2000 Sch 15 para 11(2)(a) (prospectively amended: see note 7).

32 Political Parties, Elections and Referendums Act 2000 Sch 15 para 11(2)(b). As to the ascertainment of value for these purposes see note 11.

33 Political Parties, Elections and Referendums Act 2000 Sch 15 para 11(2)(c) (prospectively amended: see note 7). The text refers to dealing with the donation in accordance with s 56(2)(aa) (as applied): see PARA 548.

34 Political Parties, Elections and Referendums Act 2000 s 160(1), Sch 15 para 11(2)(d). As to the regulations referred to in the text see note 15.

C. PUBLICITY

551. Restriction on publication etc of promotional material by central and local government etc. No material which: (1) provides general information about a referendum[1] to which the general framework provisions[2] apply; (2) deals with any of the issues raised by any question[3] on which such a referendum is being held[4]; (3) puts any arguments for or against any particular answer[5] to any such question[6]; or (4) is designed to encourage voting at such a referendum[7], is to be published[8] during the period of 28 days ending with the date of the poll (the 'relevant period')[9] by or on behalf of any Minister of the Crown, government department or local authority[10] or any other person or body whose expenses are defrayed wholly or mainly out of public funds[11] or by any local authority[12]. However, this restriction on publication does not apply to: (a) material made available to persons in response to specific requests for information or to persons specifically seeking access to it[13]; (b) anything done by or on behalf of the Electoral Commission[14] or a designated person or body[15] to whom assistance is available[16]; (c) the publication of information relating to the holding of the poll[17]; or (d) the issue of press notices[18].

Material which relates to a referendum which is published during a referendum period must include certain information to help identify who is behind referendum publications (and therefore who has incurred referendum expenses)[19].

1   As to the meaning of 'referendum' see PARA 527.
2   Political Parties, Elections and Referendums Act 2000 s 125(1)(a). The text refers to the provisions of Pt VII (ss 101–129).
3   As to the meaning of 'question' see PARA 527 note 7.
4   Political Parties, Elections and Referendums Act 2000 s 125(1)(b).
5   As to the meaning of 'answer' see PARA 527 note 7.
6   Political Parties, Elections and Referendums Act 2000 s 125(1)(c).
7   Political Parties, Elections and Referendums Act 2000 s 125(1)(d).
8   For these purposes, 'publish' means make available to the public at large, or any section of the public, in whatever form and by whatever means (and 'publication' is to be construed accordingly): Political Parties, Elections and Referendums Act 2000 s 125(4)(a).
9   Political Parties, Elections and Referendums Act 2000 s 125(2), (4)(b).
10 Political Parties, Elections and Referendums Act 2000 s 125(2)(a).
11 As to references to payments out of public funds see PARA 299 note 21.
12 Political Parties, Elections and Referendums Act 2000 s 125(2)(b). This provision is not to be taken as applying to the British Broadcasting Corporation ('the BBC') or Sianel Pedwar Cymru: s 125(3). As to the BBC see BROADCASTING vol 4 (2011) PARA 603 et seq; and as to Sianel Pedwar Cymru see BROADCASTING vol 4 (2011) PARA 645.
13 Political Parties, Elections and Referendums Act 2000 s 125(3)(a).
14 As to the Electoral Commission see PARA 34 et seq.
15 As to the meaning of 'body' see PARA 58 note 2.
16 Political Parties, Elections and Referendums Act 2000 ss 125(3)(b), 160(1). The text refers to a person or body designated under s 108 (see PARA 530).
17 Political Parties, Elections and Referendums Act 2000 s 125(3)(c).
18 Political Parties, Elections and Referendums Act 2000 s 125(3)(d).
19 See the Political Parties, Elections and Referendums Act 2000 s 126; and PARA 750.

552.   Referendum campaign broadcasts.   A broadcaster[1] must not include in its broadcasting services any referendum campaign broadcast made on behalf of any person or body[2] other than one designated to receive assistance[3] in respect of the referendum[4] in question[5]. For these purposes, 'referendum campaign broadcast' means any broadcast whose purpose (or main purpose) is or may reasonably be assumed to be to further any campaign[6] conducted with a view to promoting or procuring a particular outcome[7] in relation to any question[8] asked in a referendum to which the general framework provisions[9] apply or otherwise to promote or procure any such outcome[10].

1   As to the meaning of 'broadcaster' see PARA 299 note 43.
2   As to the meaning of 'body' see PARA 58 note 2.
3   Ie a person or body designated under the Political Parties, Elections and Referendums Act 2000 s 108 (see PARA 530).
4   As to the meaning of 'referendum' see PARA 527.
5   Political Parties, Elections and Referendums Act 2000 s 127(1). Attempts to provide referendum broadcasts in the 1979 devolution referendums (the legal basis for which is cited in PARA 4) foundered following the decision in the case of *Wilson v Independent Broadcasting Authority* 1979 SC 351, 1979 SLT 279, Ct of Sess (regulator's decision to allocate a broadcast to each of the four Scottish parliamentary political parties, which divided three to one in favour of devolution, had acted in breach of its statutory duty to ensure that programmes broadcast on the subject of the referendum maintained a proper balance). As to the broadcaster's general duty of impartiality see BROADCASTING vol 4 (2011) PARA 895.
6   As to the meaning of 'referendum campaign' see PARA 535 note 4.
7   As to the meaning of 'outcome' see PARA 529 note 13.
8   As to the meaning of 'question' see PARA 527 note 7.
9   Ie the Political Parties, Elections and Referendums Act 2000 Pt VII (ss 101–129).
10 Political Parties, Elections and Referendums Act 2000 s 127(2).

(v) The Ballot

A. COUNTING OFFICERS

553. Chief counting officers and counting officers for referendums. In relation to any referendum[1] to which the general framework provisions apply[2], there must be a chief counting officer for the referendum, who is either the chairman of the Electoral Commission[3] or, if the chairman of the Commission appoints some other person to act as chief counting officer for the referendum, the person so appointed[4]. The chief counting officer for the referendum must appoint a counting officer for each relevant area in Great Britain[5]; and the local authority[6] in the case of each such area must place the services of its officers at the disposal of the counting officer for the area for the purpose of assisting him in the discharge of his functions[7].

Each counting officer must certify the number of ballot papers counted by him[8] and the number of votes cast in favour of each answer[9] to a question[10] asked in the referendum[11], as respects the votes cast in the area for which he is appointed[12]. The chief counting officer must certify the total number of ballot papers counted[13] and the total number of votes cast in favour of each answer to a question asked in the referendum[14], in the whole of the referendum area[15].

1   As to the meaning of 'referendum' see PARA 527.
2   Ie the Political Parties, Elections and Referendums Act 2000 Pt VII (ss 101–129).
3   Political Parties, Elections and Referendums Act 2000 ss 128(1), (2)(a), 160(1). As to the Electoral Commission see PARA 34 et seq; and as to the chairman of the Electoral Commission see PARA 35.
4   Political Parties, Elections and Referendums Act 2000 s 128(1), (2)(b).
5   Political Parties, Elections and Referendums Act 2000 s 128(1), (3). For these purposes, 'relevant area in Great Britain' means any of the following: (1) a district in England or a London borough (s 128(9)(a)(i)); (2) the City of London (including the Inner and Middle Temples), the Isle of Wight or the Isles of Scilly (s 128(9)(a)(ii)); or (3) a county or county borough in Wales (s 128(9)(a)(iv)), where it is comprised in the referendum area (s 128(9)(a)). 'Referendum area' means the parts or part of the United Kingdom, or (as the case may be) the region in England, throughout which the referendum is held as mentioned in s 101(1) (see PARA 527): s 128(9)(c). As to the meanings of 'Great Britain', 'United Kingdom', 'England' and 'Wales' see PARA 1 note 1. As to the Isles of Scilly and their council see PARA 11; and LOCAL GOVERNMENT vol 69 (2009) PARA 36. As to districts in England and their councils, and county or county boroughs in Wales and their councils, see LOCAL GOVERNMENT vol 69 (2009) PARA 22 et seq; and as to the London boroughs and the City of London (including the Temples) see LONDON GOVERNMENT vol 71 (2013) PARA 15 et seq.
6   For these purposes, 'local authority' means, in the case of a district in England or a London borough or a county or county borough in Wales, the council for that area (Political Parties, Elections and Referendums Act 2000 s 128(9)(b)(i)); and, in the case of the City of London (including the Inner and Middle Temples), the Isle of Wight or the Isles of Scilly, the Common Council of the City of London, the Council of the Isle of Wight or the Council of the Isles of Scilly, as the case may be (s 128(9)(b)(ii)). As to the Court of Common Council of the City of London see LONDON GOVERNMENT vol 71 (2013) PARA 34 et seq.
7   Political Parties, Elections and Referendums Act 2000 s 128(1), (4).
8   Political Parties, Elections and Referendums Act 2000 s 128(1), (5)(a). Where two or more forms of ballot paper are used in the referendum, a separate number must be certified under s 128(5)(a) in relation to each form of ballot paper so used: s 128(7).
9   As to the meaning of 'answer' see PARA 527 note 7.
10   As to the meaning of 'question' see PARA 527 note 7.
11   Political Parties, Elections and Referendums Act 2000 s 128(1), (5)(b).
12   Political Parties, Elections and Referendums Act 2000 s 128(1), (5).
13   Political Parties, Elections and Referendums Act 2000 s 128(1), (6)(a). Where two or more forms of ballot paper are used in the referendum, a separate number must be certified under s 128(6)(a) in relation to each form of ballot paper so used: s 128(7).

14 Political Parties, Elections and Referendums Act 2000 s 128(1), (6)(b).
15 Political Parties, Elections and Referendums Act 2000 s 128(1), (6).

B. POWER TO MAKE RULES FOR THE CONDUCT OF REFERENDUMS

554.   Orders regulating conduct of referendums. The Secretary of State[1] may by order[2] make such provision as he considers expedient for or in connection with regulating the conduct of referendums[3] to which the general framework provisions apply[4]. However, such an order does not apply in relation to any referendum in relation to which specific provision is made by any other enactment for or in connection with regulating any matters relating to the conduct of the referendum, except to such extent (if any) as may be provided by that enactment[5].

Before making such an order, the Secretary of State must consult the Electoral Commission[6].

1   As to the Secretary of State see PARA 2.
2   Such an order may, in particular, make provision for the creation of offences and apply (with or without modification) any provision of any enactment; and different provision may be so made in relation to different parts of the United Kingdom: Political Parties, Elections and Referendums Act 2000 s 129(2). See note 4. As to the meaning of 'United Kingdom' see PARA 1 note 1. As to the meaning of 'modification' see PARA 44 note 9; and as to the meaning of 'enactment' see PARA 53 note 2.
3   As to the meaning of 'referendum' see PARA 527.
4   Political Parties, Elections and Referendums Act 2000 s 129(1). The text refers to the provisions of Pt VII (ss 101–129). See the Regional Assembly and Local Government Referendums Order 2004, SI 2004/1962 (amended by SI 2010/1172; 2011/2085).
5   Political Parties, Elections and Referendums Act 2000 s 129(3).
6   Political Parties, Elections and Referendums Act 2000 ss 129(4), 160(1). As to the Electoral Commission see PARA 34 et seq.

(2) LOCAL REFERENDUMS AND POLLS

(i) Rules of Conduct for Local Referendums

555.   Conduct of a local authority referendum. For the purposes of conducting a referendum held by a local authority under the Local Government Act 2000 on proposals for the operation of executive arrangements involving certain forms of executive[1], certain of the following statutory provisions which apply for the purposes of elections are applied with modifications, namely: (1) the Representation of the People Act 1983[2]; (2) the Representation of the People Act 1985[3]; (3) the Representation of the People Act 2000[4]; (4) the Political Parties, Elections and Referendums Act 2000[5]; (5) the Electoral Administration Act 2006[6]; and (6) the Representation of the People (England and Wales) Regulations 2001[7].

Additional modifications to those provisions apply where the voting at such a referendum is to take place by post only[8].

1   Ie a referendum held under the Local Government Act 2000 Pt 1A (ss 9B–9R) (in relation to England) or Pt 2 (ss 10–48A) (in relation to Wales): see LOCAL GOVERNMENT vol 69 (2009) PARA 303 et seq).
2   See the Local Authorities (Conduct of Referendums) (Wales) Regulations 2008, SI 2008/1848, reg 8, Sch 4 Table 1; the Local Authorities (Conduct of Referendums) (England) Regulations 2012, SI 2012/323, regs 8, 11, 12, 13, Sch 4 Table 1; and PARA 15.
3   See the Local Authorities (Conduct of Referendums) (England) Regulations 2012, SI 2012/323, Sch 4 Table 2; and PARA 15.

4   Ie in relation to pilot schemes for voting and campaigning and in relation to absent voting provisions: see the Local Authorities (Conduct of Referendums) (Wales) Regulations 2008, SI 2008/1848, Sch 4 Table 2; the Local Authorities (Conduct of Referendums) (England) Regulations 2012, SI 2012/323, Sch 4 Table 3; and PARA 15.

5   See the Local Authorities (Conduct of Referendums) (Wales) Regulations 2008, SI 2008/1848, Sch 4 Table 3; the Local Authorities (Conduct of Referendums) (England) Regulations 2012, SI 2012/323, Sch 4 Table 4; and PARA 15.

6   See the Local Authorities (Conduct of Referendums) (Wales) Regulations 2008, SI 2008/1848, Sch 4 Table 4; the Local Authorities (Conduct of Referendums) (England) Regulations 2012, SI 2012/323, Sch 4 Table 5; and PARA 15.

7   Ie the Representation of the People (England and Wales) Regulations 2001, SI 2001/341, Pt IV (regs 50–63) (absent voters: see PARA 367 et seq) and Pt V (regs 64–91) (issue and receipt of postal ballot papers: see PARA 406 et seq): see the Local Authorities (Conduct of Referendums) (Wales) Regulations 2008, SI 2008/1848, Sch 4 Table 5; the Local Authorities (Conduct of Referendums) (England) Regulations 2012, SI 2012/323, Sch 4 Table 6; and PARA 15.

8   See the Local Authorities (Conduct of Referendums) (Wales) Regulations 2008, SI 2008/1848, Sch 4; the Local Authorities (Conduct of Referendums) (England) Regulations 2012, SI 2012/323, Sch 4; and PARA 590 et seq.

556.   Conduct of poll consequent on a parish or community meeting. A poll consequent on a parish or community meeting[1], taken on any question arising at the meeting[2], is conducted in accordance with rules made by the Secretary of State[3]. Subject to any adaptations, alterations or exceptions made by those rules, the provisions of the rules with respect to the elections of parish or community councillors[4], and certain provisions of the Representation of the People Act 1983[5], apply in the case of a poll so taken[6].

1   As to the constitution of, and procedure at, parish and community meetings see LOCAL GOVERNMENT vol 69 (2009) PARA 635 et seq.

2   As to when such a poll may be demanded see PARA 581. Where the question involves an appointment to office, the poll is akin to an election; the conduct of such polls is considered in this title alongside the conduct of other types of election: see PARA 200 et seq.

3   See the Local Government Act 1972 s 99, Sch 12 paras 18(5), 34(5); and LOCAL GOVERNMENT vol 69 (2009) PARA 638. As to the rules so made see the Parish and Community Meetings (Polls) Rules 1987, SI 1987/1.

4   Ie the Local Elections (Parishes and Communities) Rules 2006, SI 2006/3305 (which have replaced the Local Elections (Parishes and Communities) Rules 1986, SI 1986/2215 (revoked)): see PARA 383 et seq.

5   Ie the enactments mentioned in the Representation of the People Act 1983 s 187(1) (ie s 60 (see PARA 730), s 66 (see PARAS 739–743), Pt II (ss 67–119) (see PARA 231 et seq), Pt III (ss 120–186) (see PARA 761 et seq), and s 189 (see PARA 700)). Where the poll is to be taken on any question other than that of the election of the chairman of a parish meeting or of an appointment to any other office, the only provisions which apply are s 60, s 66, s 113 (see PARA 709), s 114 (see PARA 721), s 115 (see PARA 723), s 119 (see PARAS 230, 768), s 160(4), (5) (see PARA 905), s 168 (see PARA 887), s 169 (see PARAS 888, 890), s 173 (see PARA 905), s 174(5) (see PARA 910), s 176 (see PARA 883), s 177 (see PARA 884), s 179 (see PARA 891), s 180 (see PARAS 755, 886), s 181 (see PARAS 821, 877, 882), s 186 (see PARA 768), and s 189: Parish and Community Meetings (Polls) Rules 1987, SI 1987/1, r 6(a). References to the proper officer of the authority for which the election was held must be taken as references to the returning officer (r 6(b)); and references to an election under the local government Act are deemed to include a reference to a poll consequent on a parish or community meeting (r 6(g)). As to other modifications that apply in this case see r 6(d), (e). As to a poll taken on any appointment to office see PARA 200 et seq. As to the meaning of 'election under the local government Act' see PARA 11 note 2.

6   Parish and Community Meetings (Polls) Rules 1987, SI 1987/1, r 5. The Local Elections (Parishes and Communities) Rules 1986, SI 1986/2215, as they are applied and modified for the purposes of a poll consequent on a parish or community meeting, are set out in the Parish and Community Meetings (Polls) Rules 1987, SI 1987/1, r 5, Schedule (Schedule amended by SI 1987/262; SI 2005/2114; SI 2010/1172) and any such poll must be conducted in accordance with the rules set out therein: r 5.

557. Conduct of local poll under the Local Government Act 2003. A local authority[1] may conduct a poll[2] to ascertain the views of those polled about: (1) any matter relating to services provided in pursuance of the authority's functions or the authority's expenditure on such services[3]; or (2) any other matter if it is one relating to the authority's power[4] to promote the economic, social or environmental well-being of its area[5]. It is for the local authority concerned to decide who is to be polled and how the poll is to be conducted[6] but, in conducting such a poll, a local authority must have regard to any guidance issued by the appropriate person on facilitating participation in such a poll by such of those polled as are disabled people[7].

1 For these purposes, 'local authority' means: (1) in relation to England, a county council, a district council, a London borough council, the Greater London Authority, the Common Council of the City of London in its capacity as a local authority, the Council of the Isles of Scilly (Local Government Act 2003 s 116(5)(a)); and (2) in relation to Wales, a county council or a county borough council (s 116(5)(b)). As to districts and counties in England and county or county boroughs in Wales, and their councils, see LOCAL GOVERNMENT vol 69 (2009) PARA 24 et seq; as to the Council of the Isles of Scilly see LOCAL GOVERNMENT vol 69 (2009) PARA 36; as to the London boroughs and London borough councils see LONDON GOVERNMENT vol 71 (2013) PARA 20 et seq; as to the Court of Common Council of the City of London see LONDON GOVERNMENT vol 71 (2013) PARAS 34–38; and as to the Greater London Authority see LONDON GOVERNMENT vol 71 (2013) PARA 67 et seq.
2 The power to conduct a poll under the Local Government Act 2003 s 116 is without prejudice to any powers of a local authority exercisable otherwise than by virtue of s 116: s 116(4).
3 Local Government Act 2003 s 116(1)(a).
4 Ie the power under the Local Government Act 2000 s 2 (see LOCAL GOVERNMENT vol 69 (2009) PARA 463).
5 Local Government Act 2003 s 116(1)(b).
6 Local Government Act 2003 s 116(2).
7 Local Government Act 2003 s 116(3).

(ii) Preparing for the Referendum

A. LOCAL AUTHORITY REFERENDUM ON PROPOSALS FOR ARRANGEMENTS

(A) In general

558. Proposals for which a referendum is required. Under the Local Government Act 2000[1], local authorities[2] are able to make arrangements for the discharge of their functions by executives ('executive arrangements')[3]. Provision is made for the holding of a referendum where a change in governance arrangements is proposed[4].

1 Ie under the Local Government Act 2000 Pt 1A (ss 9B–9R) (in relation to England) and Pt 2 (ss 10–48A) (in relation to Wales): see LOCAL GOVERNMENT vol 69 (2009) PARA 303 et seq).
2 As to the meaning of 'local authority' for these purposes see LOCAL GOVERNMENT vol 69 (2009) PARA 23.
3 See the Local Government Act 2000 ss 9B(4), 10; and LOCAL GOVERNMENT vol 69 (2009) PARA 303. The executive must take one of the forms specified in s 9C(2), (3) or in regulations under s 9C(5) (in relation to England) or in s 11(2)–(4) or in regulations under s 11(5) (in relation to Wales): see LOCAL GOVERNMENT vol 69 (2009) PARA 327 et seq.
4 See the Local Government Act 2000 ss 9M–9MG (in relation to England), 25–30, 34–36 (in relation to Wales); see further PARA 559 et seq; and LOCAL GOVERNMENT.

(B) Petition to Local Authority calling for a Referendum to be held

559. Petitions calling for local authority referendum. An authority[1] must hold a referendum[2] where it receives a valid petition[3], but it is not required to hold such a referendum where it receives a petition which is not a valid petition[4]. A petition may be presented to a local authority either by properly addressing, pre-paying and posting it, or by delivering it, to any office of the authority (in relation to England) or to the authority's principal office (in relation to Wales)[5].

The Welsh Ministers (in relation to Wales) may, in the event of any failure by an authority to take any action which may or must be taken by the authority[6], itself take that action ('the default power')[7]; and the Secretary of State (in relation to England) may, in the event of any failure by an authority to take any action which may or must be taken by the authority[8], take that action ('the default power')[9].

1   As to local authorities see LOCAL GOVERNMENT vol 69 (2009) PARA 23 et seq.
2   Ie, in relation to Wales, by virtue of the Local Authorities (Referendums) (Petitions and Directions) (Wales) Regulations 2001, SI 2001/2292, Pt II (regs 3–17), or, in relation to England, by virtue of the Local Authorities (Referendums) (Petitions) (England) Regulations 2011, SI 2011/2914, Pt II (regs 3–17) (see PARAS 560–569).
3   For these purposes, 'valid petition' has the meaning given by the Local Authorities (Referendums) (Petitions and Directions) (Wales) Regulations 2001, SI 2001/2292, reg 9(1), in relation to Wales, and by the Local Authorities (Referendums) (Petitions) (England) Regulations 2011, SI 2011/2914, reg 9(1), in relation to England (see PARA 563): Local Authorities (Referendums) (Petitions and Directions) (Wales) Regulations 2001, SI 2001/2292, reg 3; Local Authorities (Referendums) (Petitions) (England) Regulations 2011, SI 2011/2914, reg 3.
4   Local Authorities (Referendums) (Petitions and Directions) (Wales) Regulations 2001, SI 2001/2292, reg 6(1); Local Authorities (Referendums) (Petitions) (England) Regulations 2011, SI 2011/2914, reg 6(1). The requirement set out in the text is, in relation to Wales, subject to the Local Authorities (Referendums) (Petitions and Directions) (Wales) Regulations 2001, SI 2001/2292, reg 7 (see PARA 561), reg 8(8) (see PARA 562) and reg 19 (see PARA 571), and, in relation to England, subject to the Local Authorities (Referendums) (Petitions) (England) Regulations 2011, SI 2011/2914, reg 7 (see PARA 561).
5   Local Authorities (Referendums) (Petitions and Directions) (Wales) Regulations 2001, SI 2001/2292, reg 6(2); Local Authorities (Referendums) (Petitions) (England) Regulations 2011, SI 2011/2914, reg 6(2).
6   Ie, in relation to Wales, under any of the Local Authorities (Referendums) (Petitions and Directions) (Wales) Regulations 2001, SI 2001/2292, Pt II (see PARAS 560–569), Pt III (regs 18–22) (directions and referendums: see PARAS 570–573) or Pt IV (regs 23–24) (action to be taken after referendums: see PARAS 653, 654).
7   Local Authorities (Referendums) (Petitions and Directions) (Wales) Regulations 2001, SI 2001/2292, reg 25.
8   Ie, in relation to England, under any of Local Authorities (Referendums) (Petitions) (England) Regulations 2011, SI 2011/2914, Pt 2 (see PARAS 560–569), and Pt 3 (regs 18, 19) (directions and referendums: see PARAS 653, 654).
9   Local Authorities (Referendums) (Petitions) (England) Regulations 2011, SI 2011/2914, reg 20.

560.   Verification number for petitions calling for local authority referendum.
In relation to England[1], in each year, the proper officer[2] of each authority[3] must, within the period of 14 days beginning with 15 February, publish the number that is equal to 5 per cent of the number of local government electors[4] for the authority's area shown in the revised version of the register or, as the case may be, the registers having effect for that area on that 15 February[5]. The number so published in each year is to be used for verification purposes[6] in relation to any petition presented to the authority in the period of 12 months beginning with 1 April in that year[7], unless the number published is less than the number published in the preceding year, in which case the number to be used for verification purposes, in relation to any petition presented to the authority in the period beginning on the date of publication of the lesser number and ending immediately before 1 April in that year, must be that lesser number[8]. As soon as reasonably practicable after the publication of the verification number, the

authority must publish in at least one newspaper circulating in its area a notice containing a statement[9]: (1) that the authority's proper officer has published the number that is equal to 5 per cent of the number of local government electors shown in the electoral register or registers having effect on 15 February in that year[10]; (2) of the number so published[11]; (3) that the number so published is to have effect for the purposes of determining the validity of petitions presented after 31 March in the year of publication and before 1 April in the following year, unless a different number has effect[12] because the number published is less than the number published in the preceding year[13]; (4) the effect of the provision[14] that applies where the number published is less than the number published in the preceding year[15]; and (5) of the address of the authority's principal office[16].

In relation to Wales[17], for the purposes of each petition period[18], the proper officer[19] of each authority must, within the period of 14 days beginning with the verification date[20], publish the number that is equal to 10 per cent of the number of local government electors for the authority's area shown in the revised version of the registers having effect for the area on the verification date[21]. The number so published is to be used for verification purposes[22] in relation to any petition presented to the authority during the petition period that is to commence seven months after the verification date to which that number relates[23]. As soon as reasonably practicable after the publication of a verification number, the authority must publish in at least one newspaper circulating in its area a notice containing a statement[24]: (a) that the authority's proper officer has published the number that is equal to 10 per cent of the number of local government electors shown in the electoral register or registers having effect for the authority's area on the date that[25] is the verification date[26]; (b) of the number so published[27]; (c) that the number so published will have effect for the purposes of determining the validity of petitions presented to the authority during the petition period for that authority that will commence seven months after the verification date referred to in head (a) above[28]; (d) of the dates on which that petition period for the authority will commence and end[29]; and (e) of the address of the authority's principal office[30].

1   As to the meaning of 'England' see PARA 1 note 1.
2   As to the meaning of 'proper officer' see PARA 140 note 2; definition applied by virtue of the Local Authorities (Referendums) (Petitions) (England) Regulations 2011, SI 2011/2914, reg 3.
3   As to the meaning of 'authority' in relation to England see LOCAL GOVERNMENT vol 69 (2009) PARA 23.
4   As to entitlement to vote as a local government elector see PARA 97 et seq. As to the meaning of 'local government election' see PARA 10 and as to the meaning of 'elector' see PARA 95 note 2.

5   Local Authorities (Referendums) (Petitions) (England) Regulations 2011, SI 2011/2914, reg 4(1). Where the whole of the period of 12 months beginning with 1 April in any year to which the Local Authorities (Referendums) (Petitions) (England) Regulations 2011, SI 2011/2914, reg 4(1) applies falls within a moratorium period, reg 4(1) does not apply as respects the years in which part of that period of 12 months falls: reg 4(2). For these purposes, 'moratorium period', in relation to a local authority's area and a petition in England, means the period of 9 years commencing with the day on which a referendum was last held under the Local Government Act 2000 Pt 1A (ss 9B–9R) (arrangements with respect to local authority governance in England: see LOCAL GOVERNMENT) in relation to that area, except where the referendum was held by virtue of an order under s 9N (see LOCAL GOVERNMENT), and the proposal for the authority to operate a mayor and cabinet executive was rejected: Local Authorities (Referendums) (Petitions) (England) Regulations 2011, SI 2011/2914, reg 3.
       In connection with the discharge of the duty imposed by reg 4(1), the proper officer may require an electoral registration officer to provide him with information relevant to the number that is to be so published; and an electoral registration officer who receives such a request must

comply with it within the period of seven days beginning with the day on which the request is received: reg 4(5). As to electoral registration officers see PARA 139 et seq.

6 In relation to England, 'verification purposes' means the purposes of establishing whether a petition is a valid petition by establishing the matters mentioned in the Local Authorities (Referendums) (Petitions) (England) Regulations 2011, SI 2011/2914, reg 8(3) (see PARA 562) or under reg 9(1)(a) (see PARA 563): reg 3. As to the meaning of 'valid petition' see PARA 559 note 3.

7 Local Authorities (Referendums) (Petitions) (England) Regulations 2011, SI 2011/2914, reg 4(3). 'Verification number', in relation to a petition, means the number to be used for verification purposes by virtue of reg 4(3) or (4), as the case may be: reg 3.

8 Local Authorities (Referendums) (Petitions) (England) Regulations 2011, SI 2011/2914, reg 4(4).

9 Local Authorities (Referendums) (Petitions) (England) Regulations 2011, SI 2011/2914, reg 5.

10 Local Authorities (Referendums) (Petitions) (England) Regulations 2011, SI 2011/2914, reg 5(a).

11 Local Authorities (Referendums) (Petitions) (England) Regulations 2011, SI 2011/2914, reg 5(b).

12 Ie by virtue of the Local Authorities (Referendums) (Petitions) (England) Regulations 2011, SI 2011/2914, reg 4(4) (see the text and note 8).

13 Local Authorities (Referendums) (Petitions) (England) Regulations 2011, SI 2011/2914, reg 5(c).

14 Ie the Local Authorities (Referendums) (Petitions) (England) Regulations 2011, SI 2011/2914, reg 4(4) (see the text and note 8).

15 Local Authorities (Referendums) (Petitions) (England) Regulations 2011, SI 2011/2914, reg 5(d).

16 Local Authorities (Referendums) (Petitions) (England) Regulations 2011, SI 2011/2914, reg 5(e).

17 As to the meaning of 'Wales' see PARA 1 note 1.

18 Ie subsequent to the first such period (as to which see the Local Authorities (Referendums) (Petitions and Directions) (Wales) Regulations 2001, SI 2001/2292, reg 4(1), (2) (reg 4 substituted by SI 2003/398)). For these purposes, 'petition period' has the meaning given by the Local Authorities (Referendums) (Petitions and Directions) (Wales) Regulations 2001, SI 2001/2292, reg 3A: reg 3 (definition added by SI 2003/398). Accordingly, the local government electorate for an authority's area in Wales may present petitions to that authority during a petition period, whose duration is six months: Local Authorities (Referendums) (Petitions and Directions) (Wales) Regulations 2001, SI 2001/2292, reg 3A(1), (2) (reg 3A added by SI 2003/398). Periods subsequent to the first (as to which see the Local Authorities (Referendums) (Petitions and Directions) (Wales) Regulations 2001, SI 2001/2292, reg 3A(3) (as so added)), commence on the date that is 12 months before the date on which each subsequent ordinary local government elections are to be held: reg 3A(4) (as so added). If part or the whole of one or more of an authority's petition periods as so determined are to fall within a moratorium period, that petition period, or those petition periods (which, for these purposes, are to be treated as a single petition period), commence on the date during that moratorium period that is 12 months before the earliest date on which a second (or subsequent) referendum may lawfully be held in the area of that authority: reg 3A(5) (as so added). Where an authority does not receive a valid petition during a petition period so determined, the date on which the next petition period for that authority commences is the date that is 12 months before the date on which the next ordinary local government elections are to be held: reg 3A(6) (as so added). However, this provision does not apply where part or the whole of a petition period determined in accordance with reg 3A(6) will fall within a year in which part or the whole of a petition period determined in accordance with reg 3A(5) falls: reg 3A(7) (as so added). Where an authority does not receive a valid petition during a petition period determined in accordance with reg 3A(5) and, by virtue of reg 3A(7), reg 3A(6) does not apply, the next petition period for that authority commences on the date that is 12 months before the date on which the ordinary local government elections which are subsequent to the next ordinary local government elections are to be held: reg 3A(8) (as so added). For these purposes, 'moratorium period', in relation to Wales, means the period of five years commencing on the date on which an authority holds a referendum under the Local Government Act 2000 Pt II (arrangements with respect to executives etc: see LOCAL GOVERNMENT vol 69 (2009) PARA 303 et seq): Local Authorities (Referendums) (Petitions and Directions) (Wales) Regulations 2001, SI 2001/2292, reg 3 (definition substituted by SI 2003/398). As to ordinary local government elections see PARA 197 et seq.

19 As to the meaning of 'proper officer' see PARA 140 note 2; definition applied by virtue of the Local Authorities (Referendums) (Petitions and Directions) (Wales) Regulations 2001, SI 2001/2292, reg 3.

20 In relation to Wales, 'verification date' means the date that is seven months before the commencement of a petition period: Local Authorities (Referendums) (Petitions and Directions) (Wales) Regulations 2001, SI 2001/2292, reg 3 (definition added by SI 2003/398).

21 Local Authorities (Referendums) (Petitions and Directions) (Wales) Regulations 2001, SI 2001/2292, reg 4(3) (as substituted: see note 18). The proper officer may, in connection with the discharge of the duty imposed by reg 4(3), make a request in writing to an electoral registration officer to provide the proper officer with information relevant to the number that is to be so published; and an electoral registration officer who receives such a request must comply with it within the period of seven days beginning with the day on which the request is received: reg 4(5).

22 In relation to Wales, 'verification purposes' means the purposes of establishing whether a petition is a valid petition: Local Authorities (Referendums) (Petitions and Directions) (Wales) Regulations 2001, SI 2001/2292, reg 3. As to the meaning of 'valid petition' see PARA 559 note 3.

23 Local Authorities (Referendums) (Petitions and Directions) (Wales) Regulations 2001, SI 2001/2292, reg 4(4) (as substituted: see note 18). 'Verification number', in relation to a petition, means the number to be used for verification purposes by virtue of reg 4(4): reg 3 (definition substituted by SI 2003/398).

24 Local Authorities (Referendums) (Petitions and Directions) (Wales) Regulations 2001, SI 2001/2292, reg 5 (reg 5 substituted by SI 2003/398).

25 Ie for the purposes of a petition period subsequent to the first (as to which see note 18).

26 Local Authorities (Referendums) (Petitions and Directions) (Wales) Regulations 2001, SI 2001/2292, reg 5(a) (as substituted: see note 24).

27 Local Authorities (Referendums) (Petitions and Directions) (Wales) Regulations 2001, SI 2001/2292, reg 5(b) (as substituted: see note 24).

28 Local Authorities (Referendums) (Petitions and Directions) (Wales) Regulations 2001, SI 2001/2292, reg 5(c) (as substituted: see note 24).

29 Local Authorities (Referendums) (Petitions and Directions) (Wales) Regulations 2001, SI 2001/2292, reg 5(d) (as substituted: see note 24).

30 Local Authorities (Referendums) (Petitions and Directions) (Wales) Regulations 2001, SI 2001/2292, reg 5(e) (as substituted: see note 24).

561. Post-announcement and post-direction petitions calling for local authority referendum. In relation to a petition received after an authority[1] has given notice of its intention to hold a referendum and of the date on which that referendum will be held[2] on proposals which involve a directly elected mayor, the authority is not required[3] to hold a referendum or to take any steps other than[4] steps to secure that the proper officer[5] as soon as reasonably practicable after the receipt of the petition notifies the petition organiser[6] and (in relation to Wales) the Welsh Ministers of the receipt of the petition, that the petition is a post-announcement petition[7] and (in relation to Wales) that the authority proposes to take no further action in relation to it and notifies the petition organiser that he may, within the period of two months beginning with the date of the notice, request the Welsh Ministers to consider the exercise of any power conferred in relation to referendums which follow a direction to the local authority from the Welsh Ministers[8].

In relation to Wales, where a petition is received by an authority after it has received a direction to hold a referendum[9] and before it has given notice of the date on which the referendum is to be held pursuant to the direction, and the constitutional change[10] proposed in the petition is the same as that in relation to which the direction requires the referendum to be held, the authority must take no further action in relation to the petition and must as soon as reasonably practicable[11] notify the Welsh Ministers and the petition organiser: (1) of the receipt of the petition[12]; and (2) that it proposes to take no further action in relation to the petition because it proposes the same constitutional change as that in relation to which the referendum is to be held pursuant to the direction[13].

Where a petition is received by an authority after it has received a direction to hold a referendum[14] and before it has given notice of the date on which the referendum is to be held pursuant to the direction[15] and the constitutional change proposed in the petition is not the same as that in relation to which the direction requires the referendum to be held[16], the authority must secure that the proper officer determines[17] whether the petition is a valid petition[18]. Where the proper officer determines that a petition of such a description is not a valid petition, the proper officer must publicise the invalid petition[19] but, subject to that, the authority must take no further action in relation to the petition[20] and the date of the direction is to be[21] the date of the proper officer's determination[22].

1   As to the meaning of 'authority' see LOCAL GOVERNMENT vol 69 (2009) PARA 23.
2   Ie, in relation to Wales, whether pursuant to the Local Authorities (Referendums) (Petitions and Directions) (Wales) Regulations 2001, SI 2001/2292, Pt II (regs 3–17) or a direction under reg 18 (see PARA 570), or, in relation to England, pursuant to the Local Authorities (Referendums) (Petitions) (England) Regulations 2011, SI 2011/2914, Pt II (regs 3–17), or, in either case, pursuant to the Local Government Act 2000 s 27 (referendum in case of proposals involving elected mayor: see LOCAL GOVERNMENT vol 69 (2009) PARA 314).
3   Ie by anything, in relation to Wales, in the Local Authorities (Referendums) (Petitions and Directions) (Wales) Regulations 2001, SI 2001/2292, Pt II, or, in relation to England, in the Local Authorities (Referendums) (Petitions) (England) Regulations 2011, SI 2011/2914, Pt II.
4   Local Authorities (Referendums) (Petitions and Directions) (Wales) Regulations 2001, SI 2001/2292, reg 7(1); Local Authorities (Referendums) (Petitions) (England) Regulations 2011, SI 2011/2914, reg 7(1). As well as the steps set out in the text and notes 5–8, the authority is also required to take the steps specified, in relation to Wales, by the Local Authorities (Referendums) (Petitions and Directions) (Wales) Regulations 2001, SI 2001/2292, reg 12, and, in relation to England, by the Local Authorities (Referendums) (Petitions) (England) Regulations 2011, SI 2011/2914, reg 12 (public inspection of petitions: see PARA 565).
5   As to the meaning of 'proper officer' see PARA 140 note 2 (definition applied, in relation to Wales, by virtue of the Local Authorities (Referendums) (Petitions and Directions) (Wales) Regulations 2001, SI 2001/2292, reg 3, and, in relation to England, by virtue of the Local Authorities (Referendums) (Petitions) (England) Regulations 2011, SI 2011/2914, reg 3).
6   'Petition organiser', in relation to constituent petitions amalgamated in accordance with the Local Authorities (Referendums) (Petitions and Directions) (Wales) Regulations 2001, SI 2001/2292, reg 8(1), or the Local Authorities (Referendums) (Petitions) (England) Regulations 2011, SI 2011/2914, reg 8(1) (see PARA 562), means the person determined in accordance with the Local Authorities (Referendums) (Petitions and Directions) (Wales) Regulations 2001, SI 2001/2292, reg 10(5) or the Local Authorities (Referendums) (Petitions) (England) Regulations 2011, SI 2011/2914, reg 10(5) (see PARA 563) and, in any other case, has the meaning given by the Local Authorities (Referendums) (Petitions and Directions) (Wales) Regulations 2001, SI 2001/2292, reg 10(4) or the Local Authorities (Referendums) (Petitions) (England) Regulations 2011, SI 2011/2914, reg 10(4) (see PARA 563): Local Authorities (Referendums) (Petitions and Directions) (Wales) Regulations 2001, SI 2001/2292, reg 3; Local Authorities (Referendums) (Petitions) (England) Regulations 2011, SI 2011/2914, reg 3.
7   'Post-announcement petition' means a petition received in the circumstances mentioned in the Local Authorities (Referendums) (Petitions and Directions) (Wales) Regulations 2001, SI 2001/2292, reg 7(1) or the Local Authorities (Referendums) (Petitions) (England) Regulations 2011, SI 2011/2914, reg 7(1): Local Authorities (Referendums) (Petitions and Directions) (Wales) Regulations 2001, SI 2001/2292, reg 3; Local Authorities (Referendums) (Petitions) (England) Regulations 2011, SI 2011/2914, reg 3.
8   Local Authorities (Referendums) (Petitions and Directions) (Wales) Regulations 2001, SI 2001/2292, reg 7(2); Local Authorities (Referendums) (Petitions) (England) Regulations 2011, SI 2011/2914, reg 7(2). The text refers to any power conferred on the Welsh Ministers by the Local Authorities (Referendums) (Petitions and Directions) (Wales) Regulations 2001, SI 2001/2292, Pt III (regs 18–22) (see PARA 570 et seq).
9   Ie under the Local Authorities (Referendums) (Petitions and Directions) (Wales) Regulations 2001, SI 2001/2292, reg 18(1) (see PARA 570).
10 'Constitutional change' means: (1) unless a local authority is operating executive arrangements which involve an elected mayor, a proposal that the authority should operate executive arrangements: (a) under which the executive takes the form specified in the Local Government

Act 2000 s 11(2), (4) (see LOCAL GOVERNMENT vol 69 (2009) PARA 327) or otherwise involves an elected mayor; or (b) in a form that is not specified in the proposal (Local Authorities (Referendums) (Petitions and Directions) (Wales) Regulations 2001, SI 2001/2292, reg 3); or (2) where a local authority is operating executive arrangements which involve an elected mayor ('existing executive arrangements'), a proposal that the authority should operate executive arrangements under which the executive takes a form which is specified in the proposal, involves an elected mayor, and differs from the form of executive under the existing executive arrangements (reg 3). For these purposes, in relation to a direction under the Local Authorities (Referendums) (Petitions and Directions) (Wales) Regulations 2001, SI 2001/2292, reg 18(1) (see PARA 570) that requires an authority to hold a referendum on a form of executive that includes an elected mayor, a petition received subsequently by that authority in which the form of executive is not specified must be treated as proposing the same constitutional change; and other constitutional changes must be treated as the same if they propose executive arrangements under which the executive takes the same form: Local Authorities (Referendums) (Petitions and Directions) (Wales) Regulations 2001, SI 2001/2292, reg 7(7).

11 Local Authorities (Referendums) (Petitions and Directions) (Wales) Regulations 2001, SI 2001/2292, reg 7(3).
12 Local Authorities (Referendums) (Petitions and Directions) (Wales) Regulations 2001, SI 2001/2292, reg 7(4)(a).
13 Local Authorities (Referendums) (Petitions and Directions) (Wales) Regulations 2001, SI 2001/2292, reg 7(4)(b).
14 See note 9.
15 Local Authorities (Referendums) (Petitions and Directions) (Wales) Regulations 2001, SI 2001/2292, reg 7(5)(a).
16 Local Authorities (Referendums) (Petitions and Directions) (Wales) Regulations 2001, SI 2001/2292, reg 7(5)(b).
17 Ie in accordance with the Local Authorities (Referendums) (Petitions and Directions) (Wales) Regulations 2001, SI 2001/2292, Pt II.
18 Local Authorities (Referendums) (Petitions and Directions) (Wales) Regulations 2001, SI 2001/2292, reg 7(5).
19 Ie in compliance with the Local Authorities (Referendums) (Petitions and Directions) (Wales) Regulations 2001, SI 2001/2292, reg 14(1) (see PARA 566).
20 Local Authorities (Referendums) (Petitions and Directions) (Wales) Regulations 2001, SI 2001/2292, reg 7(6)(a).
21 Ie in accordance with the Local Authorities (Referendums) (Petitions and Directions) (Wales) Regulations 2001, SI 2001/2292, reg 21 (see PARA 572).
22 Local Authorities (Referendums) (Petitions and Directions) (Wales) Regulations 2001, SI 2001/2292, reg 7(6)(b).

562. Amalgamation of petitions calling for local authority referendum.
Where more than one petition relating to the same area has been prepared, those petitions may, at any time before their presentation to the authority[1], be amalgamated; and those petitions must then be treated for all other purposes related to such petitions[2] as a single petition[3].

In relation to England, where an authority receive more than one petition relating to the same area, the proper officer[4] must, if satisfied as to their validity[5], amalgamate those petitions[6]; and those petitions must then be treated for all other purposes[7] as a single petition[8]. The proper officer must not amalgamate petitions: (1) if he or she is satisfied that the first petition received by the authority[9] contains a number of signatures of local government electors for the authority's area that equals or exceeds the verification number[10] and is, in other respects, a valid petition[11]; (2) if he or she is satisfied that the first and other amalgamated constituent petitions[12] contain numbers of signatures of local government electors for the authority's area that in aggregate equal or exceed the verification number and are, in other respects, valid petitions[13]; or (3) that do not propose the same constitutional change[14].

In relation to Wales, where constituent petitions amalgamated in this way do not propose the same constitutional change[15], the amalgamated petition must not be entertained by the authority unless it is accompanied by a statement, signed by the petition organiser[16] in relation to the amalgamated petition, that the amalgamated petition is presented with the agreement of the petition organiser of each of the constituent petitions[17]. Where an authority receives more than one petition relating to the same area, the proper officer[18] must, if satisfied as to their validity[19], amalgamate those petitions[20]; and those petitions must then be treated[21] as a single petition[22]. However, the proper officer must not amalgamate petitions if he is satisfied that the first petition received by the authority[23] contains a number of signatures of local government electors for the authority's area that equals or exceeds the verification number[24] and is, in other respects, a valid petition[25]. The proper officer: (a) must not amalgamate petitions that do not propose the same constitutional change unless the proper officer has obtained in writing the agreement of the petition organiser of each petition that would, after amalgamation, be a constituent petition[26]; and (b) must inform each petition organiser whose agreement is required for the purposes of head (b) above of the consequences of amalgamation[27]. Where an authority receives more than one petition on the same day and those petitions each contain a number of signatures of local government electors for the authority's area that equals or exceeds the verification number[28] and are, in other respects, valid petitions and those petitions do not propose the same constitutional change, that authority must make a determination as to the petition in relation to which it will hold a referendum[29]. Before making such a determination the authority must take into account the outcome of any prior consultation undertaken by it[30] and, if the authority considers it necessary, undertake further consultation with the local government electors for, and other interested persons in, the authority's area[31]. Where an amalgamated petition results from the combination of constituent petitions which do not propose the same constitutional change, the amalgamated petition must be treated[32] as proposing that the authority should operate executive arrangements under which the proposed form of executive is not specified[33].

1   As to the meaning of 'authority' see LOCAL GOVERNMENT vol 69 (2009) PARA 23.

2   Ie, in relation to Wales, for the purposes of the Local Authorities (Referendums) (Petitions and Directions) (Wales) Regulations 2001, SI 2001/2292, Pt II (regs 3–17), or, in relation to England, for the purposes of the Local Authorities (Referendums) (Petitions) (England) Regulations 2011, SI 2011/2914, Pt II (regs 3–17).

3   Local Authorities (Referendums) (Petitions and Directions) (Wales) Regulations 2001, SI 2001/2292, reg 8(1); Local Authorities (Referendums) (Petitions) (England) Regulations 2011, SI 2011/2914, reg 8(1). 'Petition', unless the context otherwise requires, includes an amalgamated petition (see note 6): Local Authorities (Referendums) (Petitions and Directions) (Wales) Regulations 2001, SI 2001/2292, reg 3; Local Authorities (Referendums) (Petitions) (England) Regulations 2011, SI 2011/2914, reg 3. In England, petitions must be amalgamated in the order in which they are received except that, where more than one petition is received on the same day: (1) the petition that contains the greatest number of signatures must be treated as the first to be received (Local Authorities (Referendums) (Petitions) (England) Regulations 2011, SI 2011/2914, reg 8(4)(a)); and (2) any other petitions must be treated in the following order: (a) the petition that contains the greatest number of signatures (reg 8(4)(b)(i)); and (b) the petition that contains the next greatest number of signatures; and so on (reg 8(4)(b)(ii)). In relation to Wales, petitions must be amalgamated in the order in which they are received except that, where more than one petition is received on the same day: (i) the petition that contains the greatest number of signatures must be treated as the first to be received (Local Authorities (Referendums) (Petitions and Directions) (Wales) Regulations 2001, SI 2001/2292, reg 8(7)(a)); (ii) the petition that proposes the same constitutional change as that proposed in the petition identified in accordance with head (i) above must be treated as the second to be received and, if there is more than one such petition, those petitions must be treated as received in sequence, beginning with the petition that contains the greater number of

signatures (reg 8(7)(b)); and (iii) any other petitions must be treated as received in the following order: (A) the petition that contains the greatest number of signatures (reg 8(7)(c)(i)); (B) the petition, if any, that proposes the same constitutional change as the petition identified in accordance with head (A) above (reg 8(7)(c)(ii)); (C) the petition that contains the next greatest number of signatures (reg 8(7)(c)(iii)); (D) the petition, if any, that proposes the same constitutional change as the petition identified in accordance with head (C) above (reg 8(7)(c)(iv)); (E) the petition that contains the next greatest number of signatures, and so on (reg 8(7)(c)(v)).

4   As to the meaning of 'proper officer' see PARA 140 note 2 (definition applied by virtue of the Local Authorities (Referendums) (Petitions) (England) Regulations 2011, SI 2011/2914, reg 3).

5   Ie if satisfied as to their validity in every respect other than that mentioned in the Local Authorities (Referendums) (Petitions) (England) Regulations 2011, SI 2011/2914, reg 9(1)(a) (see PARA 563).

6   Ie in accordance with the Local Authorities (Referendums) (Petitions) (England) Regulations 2011, SI 2011/2914, reg 8(4) (see the text and notes 23–25).

7   Ie for all other purposes of the Local Authorities (Referendums) (Petitions) (England) Regulations 2011, SI 2011/2914, Pt II.

8   Local Authorities (Referendums) (Petitions) (England) Regulations 2011, SI 2011/2914, reg 8(2).

9   Ie including constituent petitions amalgamated in accordance with the Local Authorities (Referendums) (Petitions) (England) Regulations 2011, SI 2011/2914, reg 8(1) (see the text and notes 1–3).

10 As to the meaning of 'verification number' see PARA 560 note 7.

11 Local Authorities (Referendums) (Petitions) (England) Regulations 2011, SI 2011/2914, reg 8(3)(a). As to the meaning of 'valid petition' see PARA 559 note 3.

12 Ie amalgamated in accordance with the Local Authorities (Referendums) (Petitions) (England) Regulations 2011, SI 2011/2914, reg 8(2) (see the text and notes 4–8). 'Constituent petitions' means petitions which have been amalgamated; and 'amalgamated petition' means the single petition resulting from an amalgamation of petitions in accordance with reg 8(1), (2): reg 3.

13 Local Authorities (Referendums) (Petitions) (England) Regulations 2011, SI 2011/2914, reg 8(3)(b).

14 Local Authorities (Referendums) (Petitions) (England) Regulations 2011, SI 2011/2914, reg 8(3)(c). 'Constitutional change': (1) in relation to an authority which are operating a leader and cabinet executive (England), means a proposal that the authority should start to operate a mayor and cabinet executive or the committee system instead; (2) in relation to an authority which are operating a mayor and cabinet executive, means a proposal that the authority should start to operate a leader and cabinet executive (England) or the committee system instead; and (3) in relation to an authority which are operating the committee system, means a proposal that the authority should start to operate a mayor and cabinet executive or a leader and cabinet executive (England) instead: reg 3.

15 As to the meaning of 'constitutional change' see PARA 561 note 10. For these purposes, constitutional changes must be treated as the same if they propose executive arrangements under which the executive takes the same form or if the proposed form of executive is not specified: Local Authorities (Referendums) (Petitions and Directions) (Wales) Regulations 2001, SI 2001/2292, reg 8(11).

16 As to the meaning of 'petition organiser' see PARA 561 note 6.

17 Local Authorities (Referendums) (Petitions and Directions) (Wales) Regulations 2001, SI 2001/2292, reg 8(2). For these purposes, 'constituent petitions' means petitions that have been amalgamated; and 'amalgamated petition' means the single petition resulting from an amalgamation of petitions in accordance with reg 8(1), (2): reg 3.

18 As to the meaning of 'proper officer' see PARA 140 note 2 (definition applied by virtue of the Local Authorities (Referendums) (Petitions and Directions) (Wales) Regulations 2001, SI 2001/2292, reg 3).

19 Ie in every respect other than that mentioned in the Local Authorities (Referendums) (Petitions and Directions) (Wales) Regulations 2001, SI 2001/2292, reg 9(1)(a) (see PARA 563).

20 Ie in compliance with the Local Authorities (Referendums) (Petitions and Directions) (Wales) Regulations 2001, SI 2001/2292, reg 8(7) (see note 3).

21 Ie for the purposes of the Local Authorities (Referendums) (Petitions and Directions) (Wales) Regulations 2001, SI 2001/2292, Pt II.

22 Local Authorities (Referendums) (Petitions and Directions) (Wales) Regulations 2001, SI 2001/2292, reg 8(3).

23 Ie including constituent petitions amalgamated in compliance with the Local Authorities (Referendums) (Petitions and Directions) (Wales) Regulations 2001, SI 2001/2292, reg 8(1) (see the text and notes 1–3).

24 As to entitlement to vote as a local government elector see PARA 97 et seq; and as to the verification number see PARA 560.

25 Local Authorities (Referendums) (Petitions and Directions) (Wales) Regulations 2001, SI 2001/2292, reg 8(4). Once a petition amalgamated in accordance with the Local Authorities (Referendums) (Petitions and Directions) (Wales) Regulations 2001, SI 2001/2292, reg 8(3) (see the text and notes 18–22) contains a number of signatures of local government electors for the authority's area that in aggregate equals or exceeds the verification number and is, in other respects, a valid petition, the proper officer must not amalgamate any other petition with that amalgamated petition: reg 8(5).

26 Local Authorities (Referendums) (Petitions and Directions) (Wales) Regulations 2001, SI 2001/2292, reg 8(6)(a).

27 Local Authorities (Referendums) (Petitions and Directions) (Wales) Regulations 2001, SI 2001/2292, reg 8(6)(b). The text refers to the consequence of amalgamation specified in the text and notes 32–33.

28 As to the meaning of 'verification number' see PARA 560 note 23.

29 Local Authorities (Referendums) (Petitions and Directions) (Wales) Regulations 2001, SI 2001/2292, reg 8(8).

30 Local Authorities (Referendums) (Petitions and Directions) (Wales) Regulations 2001, SI 2001/2292, reg 8(9)(a). The text refers to prior consultation undertaken in pursuance of the Local Government Act 2000 s 25 (see LOCAL GOVERNMENT vol 69 (2009) PARA 312) or s 31 (see LOCAL GOVERNMENT vol 69 (2009) PARA 365) or in pursuance of the Local Authorities (Referendums) (Petitions and Directions) (Wales) Regulations 2001, SI 2001/2292, reg 17 (see PARA 568) or reg 19 (see PARA 571).

31 Local Authorities (Referendums) (Petitions and Directions) (Wales) Regulations 2001, SI 2001/2292, reg 8(9)(b).

32 Ie for the purposes of the Local Authorities (Referendums) (Petitions and Directions) (Wales) Regulations 2001, SI 2001/2292, Pt II.

33 Local Authorities (Referendums) (Petitions and Directions) (Wales) Regulations 2001, SI 2001/2292, reg 8(10).

563. Formalities and validity of petitions calling for local authority referendum. A petition[1] is a valid petition if: (1) it is signed by not less than the verification number[2]; (2) it satisfies the requirements as to formalities[3]; and (3) it is presented to the authority[4] to which it is addressed on a day other than one that falls within a moratorium period (in relation to England)[5] or (in relation to Wales) on a day that falls within a petition period[6] for that authority[7]. In determining whether the petition satisfies the requirements of head (1) above: (a) where a person signs a petition but the information regarding his name and address[8] is not included, or is not included in a legible form, that person's signature must be disregarded[9]; (b) if a person signs a petition more than once, that person's second or subsequent signature must be disregarded[10]; and (c) any signature on a petition which bears a date earlier than twelve months (in relation to England) or six months (in relation to Wales) before the petition date[11] must be disregarded[12]. A petition is not invalid by reason only of a failure to satisfy any requirement as is mentioned in head (2) above if the constitutional change[13] in relation to which the referendum is sought can be ascertained[14].

A petition must on each sheet state the name of the authority to whom it is addressed[15] and the constitutional change in relation to which the referendum is sought[16], as well as containing a statement in the prescribed terms[17] or in terms to similar effect[18]. In relation to each person who signs a petition, the following information must be given: (i) that person's first name and surname and address[19]; and (ii) the date on which that person signs the petition[20]. A petition must contain, or must be accompanied by a statement that contains, the name and full address of the person (the 'petition organiser'[21]) to whom correspondence relating to the petition is to be sent[22]. Where petitions are amalgamated before they are presented to the authority, the petition organiser of each of the constituent petitions must determine the identity of the person (whether or not that person is the petition organiser of any of the constituent petitions) who is to be the petition organiser for the purposes of the amalgamated petition[23]; and the petition organiser of the amalgamated petition must notify the authority of his name and full address[24].

1 As to the meaning of 'petition' see PARA 562 note 3.

2 Local Authorities (Referendums) (Petitions and Directions) (Wales) Regulations 2001, SI 2001/2292, reg 9(1)(a); Local Authorities (Referendums) (Petitions) (England) Regulations 2011, SI 2011/2914, reg 9(1)(a) (referring to not less than the number of local government electors for the authority's area this is the verification number). As to the verification number see PARA 560.

3 Local Authorities (Referendums) (Petitions and Directions) (Wales) Regulations 2001, SI 2001/2292, reg 9(1)(b); Local Authorities (Referendums) (Petitions) (England) Regulations 2011, SI 2011/2914, reg 9(1)(b). The text refers to the requirements of the Local Authorities (Referendums) (Petitions and Directions) (Wales) Regulations 2001, SI 2001/2292, reg 10 (in relation to Wales) or the Local Authorities (Referendums) (Petitions) (England) Regulations 2011, SI 2011/2914, reg 10 (in relation to England) (see the text and notes 15–24).

4 As to the meaning of 'authority' see LOCAL GOVERNMENT vol 69 (2009) PARA 23.

5 Local Authorities (Referendums) (Petitions) (England) Regulations 2011, SI 2011/2914, reg 9(1)(c). As to the meaning of 'moratorium period' see PARA 560 note 5.

6 As to the meaning of 'petition period' see PARA 560 note 18.

7 Local Authorities (Referendums) (Petitions and Directions) (Wales) Regulations 2001, SI 2001/2292, reg 9(1)(c) (substituted by SI 2003/398).

8 Ie the information referred to in the Local Authorities (Referendums) (Petitions and Directions) (Wales) Regulations 2001, SI 2001/2292, reg 10(3)(a) (in relation to Wales) or the Local Authorities (Referendums) (Petitions) (England) Regulations 2011, SI 2011/2914, reg 10(3)(a) (in relation to England) (see head (i) in the text).

9 Local Authorities (Referendums) (Petitions and Directions) (Wales) Regulations 2001, SI 2001/2292, reg 9(3); Local Authorities (Referendums) (Petitions) (England) Regulations 2011, SI 2011/2914, reg 9(3).

10 Local Authorities (Referendums) (Petitions and Directions) (Wales) Regulations 2001, SI 2001/2292, reg 9(4); Local Authorities (Referendums) (Petitions) (England) Regulations 2011, SI 2011/2914, reg 9(4).

11 In relation to England, 'petition date' means (by virtue of the Local Authorities (Referendums) (Petitions) (England) Regulations 2011, SI 2011/2914, reg 3): (1) in relation to a petition submitted prior to the publication of the verification number in accordance with reg 4(1) (see PARA 560), the date on which that verification number is published; (2) subject to head (4) below, in relation to constituent petitions amalgamated in accordance with reg 8(2) (see PARA 562), the latest date on which any of the petitions amalgamated was received by the authority; (3) subject to head (4) below, in relation to any other petition, the date on which it was received by the authority; and (4) in relation to a petition received within the period of six months beginning with the date that is 12 months before the earliest date on which a second (or subsequent) referendum may lawfully be held in the area of the authority to whom the petition is addressed, the date on which that period of six months ends. In relation to Wales, 'petition date' means (by virtue of the Local Authorities (Referendums) (Petitions and Directions) (Wales) Regulations 2001, SI 2001/2292, reg 3 (amended by SI 2003/398)), in relation to constituent petitions amalgamated in accordance with reg 8(3) (see PARA 562), the latest date on which a constituent petition was received by the authority; and, in relation to any other petition, the date on which it was received by the authority. As to the meanings of 'amalgamated petition' and 'constituent petition' see PARA 562 notes 12, 17.

12 Local Authorities (Referendums) (Petitions and Directions) (Wales) Regulations 2001, SI 2001/2292, reg 9(5) (amended by SI 2003/398); Local Authorities (Referendums) (Petitions) (England) Regulations 2011, SI 2011/2914, reg 9(5).

13 As to the meaning of 'constitutional change' see PARAS 561 note 10, 562 note 14.

14 Local Authorities (Referendums) (Petitions and Directions) (Wales) Regulations 2001, SI 2001/2292, reg 9(2); Local Authorities (Referendums) (Petitions) (England) Regulations 2011, SI 2011/2914, reg 9(2).

15 Local Authorities (Referendums) (Petitions and Directions) (Wales) Regulations 2001, SI 2001/2292, reg 10(1)(a); Local Authorities (Referendums) (Petitions) (England) Regulations 2011, SI 2011/2914, reg 10(1)(a).

16 Local Authorities (Referendums) (Petitions and Directions) (Wales) Regulations 2001, SI 2001/2292, reg 10(1)(b); Local Authorities (Referendums) (Petitions) (England) Regulations 2011, SI 2011/2914, reg 10(1)(b).

17 Ie in the term set out, in relation to Wales, in the Local Authorities (Referendums) (Petitions and Directions) (Wales) Regulations 2001, SI 2001/2292, reg 10(2), Sch 1 (petition statement) and, in relation to England, in the Local Authorities (Referendums) (Petitions) (England) Regulations 2011, SI 2011/2914, reg 10(2), Sch 1 (petition statement).

18 Local Authorities (Referendums) (Petitions and Directions) (Wales) Regulations 2001, SI 2001/2292, reg 10(2); Local Authorities (Referendums) (Petitions) (England) Regulations 2011, SI 2011/2914, reg 10(2).

19 Local Authorities (Referendums) (Petitions and Directions) (Wales) Regulations 2001, SI 2001/2292, reg 10(3)(a); Local Authorities (Referendums) (Petitions) (England) Regulations 2011, SI 2011/2914, reg 10(3)(a).

20 Local Authorities (Referendums) (Petitions and Directions) (Wales) Regulations 2001, SI 2001/2292, reg 10(3)(b); Local Authorities (Referendums) (Petitions) (England) Regulations 2011, SI 2011/2914, reg 10(3)(b).

21 As to the meaning of 'petition organiser' see PARA 561 note 6.

22 Local Authorities (Referendums) (Petitions and Directions) (Wales) Regulations 2001, SI 2001/2292, reg 10(4); Local Authorities (Referendums) (Petitions) (England) Regulations 2011, SI 2011/2914, reg 10(4).

23 Local Authorities (Referendums) (Petitions and Directions) (Wales) Regulations 2001, SI 2001/2292, reg 10(5)(a); Local Authorities (Referendums) (Petitions) (England) Regulations 2011, SI 2011/2914, reg 10(5)(a).

24 Local Authorities (Referendums) (Petitions and Directions) (Wales) Regulations 2001, SI 2001/2292, reg 10(5)(b); Local Authorities (Referendums) (Petitions) (England) Regulations 2011, SI 2011/2914, reg 10(5)(b).

564. Procedure on receipt of petitions calling for local authority referendum.
As soon as reasonably practicable after receipt of a petition[1], the proper officer[2] must, if he has amalgamated the petition[3], notify the petition organiser[4] of each of the constituent petitions[5] of the petition date[6] of the amalgamated petition[7] or, in any other case, notify the petition organiser of the petition date[8]. As soon as reasonably practicable after receipt of a petition, and not later than the end of the notice period[9], the proper officer must determine the validity of the petition[10].

Where the petition is a second or subsequent petition ('later petition') which cannot lawfully be amalgamated with an earlier petition[11], the proper officer must[12], within the notice period, notify the petition organiser and (in relation to Wales) the Welsh Ministers: (1) of the receipt of the petition and of its petition date[13]; (2) of the receipt of every earlier petition and of its petition date[14]; (3) of the reason why the later petition cannot be amalgamated with any earlier petition[15]; and (4) that, by reason of the receipt of an earlier valid petition[16], the proper officer proposes to take no further action in relation to the later petition[17]. In relation to Wales, the proper officer must also notify the petition organiser that the petition organiser may, within the period of two months beginning with the date of the notice, request the Welsh Ministers to consider the exercise of any power[18] to require a referendum to be held following a direction to the authority[19], and must take such other steps as the Welsh Ministers may direct[20].

1 As to the meaning of 'petition' see PARA 562 note 3.

2 As to the meaning of 'proper officer' see PARA 140 note 2 (definition applied, in relation to Wales, by virtue of the Local Authorities (Referendums) (Petitions and Directions) (Wales) Regulations 2001, SI 2001/2292, reg 3, and, in relation to England, by virtue of the Local Authorities (Referendums) (Petitions) (England) Regulations 2011, SI 2011/2914, reg 3).

3 Ie, in relation to Wales, if the Local Authorities (Referendums) (Petitions and Directions) (Wales) Regulations 2001, SI 2001/2292, reg 8(3) applies in relation to the petition, or, in relation to England, if the Local Authorities (Referendums) (Petitions) (England) Regulations 2011, SI 2011/2914, reg 8(2) applies in relation to the petition (see PARA 562).

4 As to the meaning of 'petition organiser' see PARA 561 note 6.

5 As to the meaning of 'constituent petition' see PARA 562 notes 12, 17.

6 As to the meaning of 'petition date' see PARA 563 note 11.

7 Local Authorities (Referendums) (Petitions and Directions) (Wales) Regulations 2001, SI 2001/2292, reg 11(1)(a); Local Authorities (Referendums) (Petitions) (England) Regulations 2011, SI 2011/2914, reg 11(1)(a). As to the meaning of 'amalgamated petition' see PARA 562 notes 12, 17.

8 Local Authorities (Referendums) (Petitions and Directions) (Wales) Regulations 2001, SI 2001/2292, reg 11(1)(b); Local Authorities (Referendums) (Petitions) (England) Regulations 2011, SI 2011/2914, reg 11(1)(b).

9 For these purposes, 'notice period', in relation to a petition, means the period of one month beginning with the petition date: Local Authorities (Referendums) (Petitions and Directions) (Wales) Regulations 2001, SI 2001/2292, reg 3; Local Authorities (Referendums) (Petitions) (England) Regulations 2011, SI 2011/2914, reg 3.

10 Local Authorities (Referendums) (Petitions and Directions) (Wales) Regulations 2001, SI 2001/2292, reg 11(2); Local Authorities (Referendums) (Petitions) (England) Regulations 2011, SI 2011/2914, reg 11(2). As to the validity of petitions see PARA 563.

11 Ie for a reason mentioned in the Local Authorities (Referendums) (Petitions and Directions) (Wales) Regulations 2001, SI 2001/2292, reg 8(4)–(6) (in relation to Wales) or in the Local Authorities (Referendums) (Petitions) (England) Regulations 2011, SI 2011/2914, reg 8(3) (in relation to England) (see PARA 562).

12 Local Authorities (Referendums) (Petitions and Directions) (Wales) Regulations 2001, SI 2001/2292, reg 11(3); Local Authorities (Referendums) (Petitions) (England) Regulations 2011, SI 2011/2914, reg 11(3).

13 Local Authorities (Referendums) (Petitions and Directions) (Wales) Regulations 2001, SI 2001/2292, reg 11(4)(a)(i); Local Authorities (Referendums) (Petitions) (England) Regulations 2011, SI 2011/2914, reg 11(4)(a).

14 Local Authorities (Referendums) (Petitions and Directions) (Wales) Regulations 2001, SI 2001/2292, reg 11(4)(a)(ii); Local Authorities (Referendums) (Petitions) (England) Regulations 2011, SI 2011/2914, reg 11(4)(b).

15 Local Authorities (Referendums) (Petitions and Directions) (Wales) Regulations 2001, SI 2001/2292, reg 11(4)(a)(iii); Local Authorities (Referendums) (Petitions) (England) Regulations 2011, SI 2011/2914, reg 11(4)(c).

16 As to the meaning of 'valid petition' see PARA 559 note 3.

17 Local Authorities (Referendums) (Petitions and Directions) (Wales) Regulations 2001, SI 2001/2292, reg 11(4)(a)(iv); Local Authorities (Referendums) (Petitions) (England) Regulations 2011, SI 2011/2914, reg 11(4)(d).

18 Ie any power conferred on the Welsh Ministers by the Local Authorities (Referendums) (Petitions and Directions) (Wales) Regulations 2001, SI 2001/2292, reg 18 (see PARA 570 et seq).

19 Local Authorities (Referendums) (Petitions and Directions) (Wales) Regulations 2001, SI 2001/2292, reg 11(4)(b). As to the meaning of 'authority' see LOCAL GOVERNMENT vol 69 (2009) PARA 23.

20 Local Authorities (Referendums) (Petitions and Directions) (Wales) Regulations 2001, SI 2001/2292, reg 11(3).

565. Public inspection of petitions calling for local authority referendum. The authority[1] must secure that, for the period of six years beginning with the petition date[2], a petition[3] is available at its principal office for inspection by members of the public at all reasonable times and free of charge[4].

1 As to the meaning of 'authority' see LOCAL GOVERNMENT vol 69 (2009) PARA 23.

2 As to the meaning of 'petition date' see PARA 563 note 11.

3 As to the meaning of 'petition' see PARA 562 note 3.

4 Local Authorities (Referendums) (Petitions and Directions) (Wales) Regulations 2001, SI 2001/2292, reg 12; Local Authorities (Referendums) (Petitions) (England) Regulations 2011, SI 2011/2914, reg 12.

566. Publicity for petitions calling for local authority referendum. Where the proper officer[1] is satisfied that a petition[2] is valid[3], he must, within the notice period[4], notify the petition organiser[5] and (in relation to Wales) the Welsh Ministers: (1) of the proper officer's conclusion[6]; and (2) that a referendum is to be held[7]. In such a case, the authority[8] must publish in at least one newspaper circulating in its area a notice which contains a statement[9]: (a) that a valid petition[10] has been received[11]; (b) of the constitutional change[12] sought (or, in relation to Wales, as the case may be, treated as sought) by the petition[13]; (c) of the petition date[14]; (d) that the petition is available at the authority's principal office for inspection by members of the public at all reasonable times and free of charge[15]; (e) of the address of the authority's principal office[16]; and (f) that a referendum is to be held[17].

Where the proper officer is satisfied that a petition is not a valid petition, he must, within the notice period[18], notify the petition organiser (if any) and (in relation to Wales) the Welsh Ministers of his determination and of the reasons for that determination[19]. In such a case, the authority must publish in at least one newspaper circulating in its area a notice which contains a statement[20]: (i) that a petition has been received which has been determined to be an invalid petition[21]; (ii) of the reasons for that determination[22]; (iii) of the constitutional change sought (or, in relation to Wales, as the case may be, treated as sought) by the petition[23]; (iv) of the petition date[24]; (v) that the petition is available at the authority's principal office for inspection by members of the public at all reasonable times and free of charge[25]; and (vi) of the address of the authority's principal office[26]. Where a petition is invalid only because it does not comply with the requirement that it be signed by not less than the verification number[27], the notification of invalidity[28] and the associated statement to be published by the authority containing the information set out in heads (i) to (vi) above must also include a statement that the invalid petition may be amalgamated with any subsequent petitions which are submitted to the authority[29].

1   As to the meaning of 'proper officer' see PARA 140 note 2 (definition applied, in relation to England, by virtue of the Local Authorities (Referendums) (Petitions) (England) Regulations 2011, SI 2011/2914, reg 3; and, in relation to Wales, by virtue of the Local Authorities (Referendums) (Petitions and Directions) (Wales) Regulations 2001, SI 2001/2292, reg 3).

2   As to the meaning of 'petition' see PARA 562 note 3.

3   As to the validity of petitions see PARA 563.

4   As to the meaning of 'notice period' see PARA 564 note 9.

5   As to the meaning of 'petition organiser' see PARA 561 note 6. In relation to Wales, it is specified that, where the petition has been amalgamated in accordance with the Local Authorities (Referendums) (Petitions and Directions) (Wales) Regulations 2001, SI 2001/2292, reg 8(3) (see PARA 562), the petition organiser of each of the constituent petitions must be notified: see reg 13(1). As to the meaning of 'constituent petition' see PARA 562 notes 12, 17.

6   Local Authorities (Referendums) (Petitions and Directions) (Wales) Regulations 2001, SI 2001/2292, reg 13(1)(a); Local Authorities (Referendums) (Petitions) (England) Regulations 2011, SI 2011/2914, reg 13(1)(a).

7   Local Authorities (Referendums) (Petitions and Directions) (Wales) Regulations 2001, SI 2001/2292, reg 13(1)(b); Local Authorities (Referendums) (Petitions) (England) Regulations 2011, SI 2011/2914, reg 13(1)(b).

8   As to the meaning of 'authority' see LOCAL GOVERNMENT vol 69 (2009) PARA 23.

9   Local Authorities (Referendums) (Petitions and Directions) (Wales) Regulations 2001, SI 2001/2292, reg 13(2); Local Authorities (Referendums) (Petitions) (England) Regulations 2011, SI 2011/2914, reg 13(2).

10 As to the meaning of 'valid petition' see PARA 559 note 3.

11 Local Authorities (Referendums) (Petitions and Directions) (Wales) Regulations 2001, SI 2001/2292, reg 13(2)(a); Local Authorities (Referendums) (Petitions) (England) Regulations 2011, SI 2011/2914, reg 13(2)(a).

12 As to the meaning of 'constitutional change' see PARAS 561 note 10, 562 note 14.

13 Local Authorities (Referendums) (Petitions and Directions) (Wales) Regulations 2001, SI 2001/2292, reg 13(2)(b); Local Authorities (Referendums) (Petitions) (England) Regulations 2011, SI 2011/2914, reg 13(2)(b).

14 Local Authorities (Referendums) (Petitions and Directions) (Wales) Regulations 2001, SI 2001/2292, reg 13(2)(c); Local Authorities (Referendums) (Petitions) (England) Regulations 2011, SI 2011/2914, reg 13(2)(c). As to the meaning of 'petition date' see PARA 563 note 11.

15 Local Authorities (Referendums) (Petitions and Directions) (Wales) Regulations 2001, SI 2001/2292, reg 13(2)(d); Local Authorities (Referendums) (Petitions) (England) Regulations 2011, SI 2011/2914, reg 13(2)(d). See PARA 565.

16 Local Authorities (Referendums) (Petitions and Directions) (Wales) Regulations 2001, SI 2001/2292, reg 13(2)(e); Local Authorities (Referendums) (Petitions) (England) Regulations 2011, SI 2011/2914, reg 13(2)(e).

17 Local Authorities (Referendums) (Petitions and Directions) (Wales) Regulations 2001, SI 2001/2292, reg 13(2)(f); Local Authorities (Referendums) (Petitions) (England) Regulations 2011, SI 2011/2914, reg 13(2)(f).

18 In relation to Wales, the proper officer must, if possible, make the notification within the petition period, where the petition satisfies the requirements of the Local Authorities (Referendums) (Petitions and Directions) (Wales) Regulations 2001, SI 2001/2292, reg 9(1)(c) (see PARA 563): reg 14(1) (amended by SI 2003/398). As to the meaning of 'petition period' see PARA 560 note 18.

19 Local Authorities (Referendums) (Petitions and Directions) (Wales) Regulations 2001, SI 2001/2292, reg 14(1); Local Authorities (Referendums) (Petitions) (England) Regulations 2011, SI 2011/2914, reg 14(1). In relation to Wales, where the authority has made a determination under reg 8(8) (see PARA 562), the proper officer must, within the notice period, notify the National Assembly for Wales and the petition organiser of the authority's determination and the reasons for that determination: reg 14(2). In such a case, the authority must publish in at least one newspaper circulating in its area a notice which contains a statement: (1) that a valid petition has been received (reg 14(5)(a)); (2) that the authority will not take any action in relation to that petition on account of its having made a determination under reg 8(8) (reg 14(5)(b)); (3) of the reasons for that determination (reg 14(5)(c)); (4) of the constitutional change sought by the petition (reg 14(5)(d)); (5) of the petition date (reg 14(5)(e)); (6) that the petition is available at the authority's principal office for inspection by members of the public at all reasonable times and free of charge (reg 14(5)(f)); and (7) of the address of the authority's principal office (reg 14(5)(g)).

20 Local Authorities (Referendums) (Petitions and Directions) (Wales) Regulations 2001, SI 2001/2292, reg 14(3) (amended by SI 2003/398); Local Authorities (Referendums) (Petitions) (England) Regulations 2011, SI 2011/2914, reg 14(2). In relation to Wales, where a petition in relation to which a notice is to be published in accordance with the Local Authorities (Referendums) (Petitions and Directions) (Wales) Regulations 2001, SI 2001/2292, reg 14(3) satisfies the requirements of reg 9(1)(c) (see PARA 563), the authority must, if possible, publish that notice within the petition period and within the notice period: reg 14(3A) (added by SI 2003/398).

21 Local Authorities (Referendums) (Petitions and Directions) (Wales) Regulations 2001, SI 2001/2292, reg 14(3)(a); Local Authorities (Referendums) (Petitions) (England) Regulations 2011, SI 2011/2914, reg 14(2)(a).

22 Local Authorities (Referendums) (Petitions and Directions) (Wales) Regulations 2001, SI 2001/2292, reg 14(3)(b); Local Authorities (Referendums) (Petitions) (England) Regulations 2011, SI 2011/2914, reg 14(2)(b).

23 Local Authorities (Referendums) (Petitions and Directions) (Wales) Regulations 2001, SI 2001/2292, reg 14(3)(c); Local Authorities (Referendums) (Petitions) (England) Regulations 2011, SI 2011/2914, reg 14(2)(c).

24 Local Authorities (Referendums) (Petitions and Directions) (Wales) Regulations 2001, SI 2001/2292, reg 14(3)(d); Local Authorities (Referendums) (Petitions) (England) Regulations 2011, SI 2011/2914, reg 14(2)(d).

25 Local Authorities (Referendums) (Petitions and Directions) (Wales) Regulations 2001, SI 2001/2292, reg 14(3)(e); Local Authorities (Referendums) (Petitions) (England) Regulations 2011, SI 2011/2914, reg 14(2)(e).

26 Local Authorities (Referendums) (Petitions and Directions) (Wales) Regulations 2001, SI 2001/2292, reg 14(3)(f); Local Authorities (Referendums) (Petitions) (England) Regulations 2011, SI 2011/2914, reg 14(2)(f).

27 Ie where the petition does not comply with the Local Authorities (Referendums) (Petitions and Directions) (Wales) Regulations 2001, SI 2001/2292, reg 9(1)(a) (in relation to Wales) or with the Local Authorities (Referendums) (Petitions) (England) Regulations 2011, SI 2011/2914, reg 9(1)(a) (in relation to England) (see PARA 563). As to the verification number see PARA 560.
28 Ie the notification under the Local Authorities (Referendums) (Petitions and Directions) (Wales) Regulations 2001, SI 2001/2292, reg 14(1) (in relation to Wales) or under the Local Authorities (Referendums) (Petitions) (England) Regulations 2011, SI 2011/2914, reg 14(1) (in relation to England) (see the text and notes 18–19).
29 Local Authorities (Referendums) (Petitions and Directions) (Wales) Regulations 2001, SI 2001/2292, reg 14(4); Local Authorities (Referendums) (Petitions) (England) Regulations 2011, SI 2011/2914, reg 14(3).

567. Timing of local authority referendum in consequence of a valid petition.
In relation to England, except where the Secretary of State holds a referendum in exercise of the default power[1], a referendum in consequence of a valid petition[2] must be held[3] no later than the end of the nest ordinary day of election[4] after the petition date[5]. In relation to Wales, except where the Welsh Ministers hold a referendum in exercise of the default power[6], a referendum in consequence of a valid petition must be held[7] not later than[8] the end of the period of six months beginning with the petition date[9]; and a referendum must not be held before the end of the period of two months beginning with the date on which proposals for the operation of executive arrangements (including the fall-back provisions) and the accompanying statement are sent to the Welsh Ministers[10].

Such a referendum[11] may not be held on: (1) a Saturday or Sunday[12]; (2) Christmas Eve, Christmas Day, Maundy Thursday, Good Friday or a day which is a bank holiday[13]; or (3) any day appointed as a day of public thanksgiving or mourning[14].

1 Local Authorities (Referendums) (Petitions) (England) Regulations 2011, SI 2011/2914, reg 16(3). The text refers to the circumstances where the Secretary of State exercises the power conferred by reg 20 (see PARA 559).
2 As to the meaning of 'valid petition' see PARA 559 note 3.
3 Ie subject to the Local Authorities (Referendums) (Petitions) (England) Regulations 2011, SI 2011/2914, reg 16(2), (3) (see the text and notes 1, 5).
4 As to the meaning of 'ordinary day of election' see the Representation of the People Act 1983 s 37; and PARA 206 (definition applied by the Local Authorities (Referendums) (Petitions) (England) Regulations 2011, SI 2011/2914, reg 3).
5 Local Authorities (Referendums) (Petitions) (England) Regulations 2011, SI 2011/2914, reg 16(1). As to the meaning of 'petition date' see PARA 563 note 11. Regulation 16(1) does not apply where the petition date falls 4 months or less before the next ordinary day of election or the next ordinary day of election falls within the period of 6 months beginning with the date that is 6 months before the earliest date on which a second (or subsequent) referendum may lawfully be held in the area of the authority to whom the petition is addressed, and, in such a case, a referendum in consequence of a valid petition must be held no later than the end of the period of 6 months beginning with the petition date: reg 16(2).
6 Local Authorities (Referendums) (Petitions and Directions) (Wales) Regulations 2001, SI 2001/2292, reg 16(3). The text refers to the circumstances where the Welsh Ministers exercise the power conferred by the Local Authorities (Referendums) (Petitions and Directions) (Wales) Regulations 2001, SI 2001/2292, reg 25 (see PARA 559).
7 Ie subject to the Local Authorities (Referendums) (Petitions and Directions) (Wales) Regulations 2001, SI 2001/2292, reg 16(1A), (2), (3) (see the text and notes 6, 9, 10) and reg 21 (see PARA 572).
8 Local Authorities (Referendums) (Petitions and Directions) (Wales) Regulations 2001, SI 2001/2292, reg 16(1) (amended by SI 2003/398).
9 Local Authorities (Referendums) (Petitions and Directions) (Wales) Regulations 2001, SI 2001/2292, reg 16(1)(a) (amended by SI 2003/398). Provision is also made, in relation to Wales, for a referendum as mentioned in the text to be held not later than the end of the period of two months beginning with the date on which regulations under the Local Government Act 2000 s 45 (see LOCAL GOVERNMENT vol 69 (2009) PARA 319) come into force, if this is

later: Local Authorities (Referendums) (Petitions and Directions) (Wales) Regulations 2001, SI 2001/2292, reg 16(1)(b). As to the regulations so made see the Local Authorities (Conduct of Referendums) (Wales) Regulations 2004, SI 2004/870. As to the provisions that are so applied and modified see PARA 15.

In relation to Wales, where an authority's petition period commences, by virtue of the Local Authorities (Referendums) (Petitions and Directions) (Wales) Regulations 2001, SI 2001/2292, reg 3A(5) (see PARA 560), on the date that is 12 months before the earliest date on which that authority may hold a second (or subsequent) referendum and a valid petition is presented to that authority within that petition period, that authority must hold a referendum on the earliest date on which it may lawfully hold a second (or subsequent) referendum: reg 16(1A) (added by SI 2003/398). As to the meaning of 'authority' see LOCAL GOVERNMENT vol 69 (2009) PARA 23; and as to the meaning of 'petition period' see PARA 560 note 18.

10 Local Authorities (Referendums) (Petitions and Directions) (Wales) Regulations 2001, SI 2001/2292, reg 16(2). The text refers to proposals sent to the Welsh Ministers in accordance with reg 17(9) (see PARA 568).

11 Ie a referendum held following a petition under the Local Authorities (Referendums) (Petitions and Directions) (Wales) Regulations 2001, SI 2001/2292, Pt II (regs 3–17) (in relation to Wales) and under the Local Authorities (Referendums) (Petitions) (England) Regulations 2011, SI 2011/2914, Pt II (regs 3–17) (in relation to England) (see PARA 559 et seq).

12 Local Authorities (Referendums) (Petitions and Directions) (Wales) Regulations 2001, SI 2001/2292, reg 16(4)(a); Local Authorities (Referendums) (Petitions) (England) Regulations 2011, SI 2011/2914, reg 16(4)(a).

13 Local Authorities (Referendums) (Petitions and Directions) (Wales) Regulations 2001, SI 2001/2292, reg 16(4)(b); Local Authorities (Referendums) (Petitions) (England) Regulations 2011, SI 2011/2914, reg 16(4)(b). The text refers to a bank holiday under the Banking and Financial Dealings Act 1971 in England or in Wales (as the case may be): see TIME vol 97 (2010) PARA 321.

14 Local Authorities (Referendums) (Petitions and Directions) (Wales) Regulations 2001, SI 2001/2292, reg 16(4)(c); Local Authorities (Referendums) (Petitions) (England) Regulations 2011, SI 2011/2914, reg 16(4)(c).

568. Action taken before local authority referendum in consequence of a valid petition. In relation to England, before the holding of a referendum following a petition[1], the authority[2] must decide the extent to which a function which may be the responsibility of an executive of the authority under executive arrangements[3] are to be the responsibility of the executive (if applicable) should the form of governance that is the constitutional change[4] proposed in the petition be approved[5], and must draw up proposals for the operation of the form of governance that is the constitutional change proposed in the petition[6].

In relation to Wales, before the holding of such a referendum[7], the authority[8]must: (1) where the petition does not specify, or is treated as not specifying, the form proposed for the authority's executive[9], decide which form the executive is to take[10] and decide the extent to which specified functions[11] are to be the responsibility of the executive[12]; or (2) where the petition specifies the form proposed for the authority's executive, decide the extent to which the specified functions are to be the responsibility of the executive[13]. Before holding such a referendum, the authority must also: (a) draw up proposals for the operation of executive arrangements[14]; and (b) draw up outline fall-back proposals[15]. Before drawing up proposals under head (a) or head (b) above, the authority must take reasonable steps to consult the local government electors[16] for, and other interested persons in, the authority's area[17]. The authority's proposals under head (a) above must include such details of the executive arrangements as the Welsh Ministers may direct[18], a timetable with respect to the implementation of the proposals[19], and details of any transitional arrangements which are necessary for the implementation of the proposals[20]. In drawing up proposals under head (a) above, the authority must consider the extent to which the proposals, if implemented, are likely to assist in securing continuous improvement in the way in which the authority's functions are exercised, having regard to a combination of economy, efficiency and effectiveness[21]. The authority's proposals under head (b) above, where the authority is not then operating executive arrangements or alternative arrangements[22], must include such details of the executive arrangements or alternative arrangements to which they relate as the Welsh Ministers may direct[23], and a timetable with respect to the implementation of detailed fall-back proposals which are based on the outline fall-back proposals in the event that the proposals that are to be the subject of the referendum are rejected[24]; and the authority's proposals may include, as outline fall-back proposals, any proposals[25] approved by the Welsh Ministers[26]. Where the authority is then operating executive arrangements or alternative arrangements, the proposals under head (b) above are to consist of a summary of those arrangements[27]. Not later than two months before the date on which the referendum is to be held, the authority must send to the Welsh Ministers a copy of the proposals drawn up under heads (a) and (b) above[28] and a statement which describes the steps which the authority took to consult the local government electors for, and other interested persons in, the authority's area and the outcome of that consultation and the extent to which that outcome is reflected in the proposals[29].

1   Ie a referendum following a petition under the Local Authorities (Referendums) (Petitions) (England) Regulations 2011, SI 2011/2914, Pt II (regs 3–17) (see PARA 559 et seq).
2   As to the meaning of 'authority' see LOCAL GOVERNMENT vol 69 (2009) PARA 23.
3   Ie the functions specified in regulations under the Local Government Act 2000 s 9D(3)(b) (see LOCAL GOVERNMENT).
4   As to the meaning of 'constitutional change' see PARA 562 note 14.
5   Local Authorities (Referendums) (Petitions) (England) Regulations 2011, SI 2011/2914, reg 17(1).
6   Local Authorities (Referendums) (Petitions) (England) Regulations 2011, SI 2011/2914, reg 17(2). In drawing up such proposals the authority must have regard to any guidance for the time being issued by the Secretary of State under the Local Government Act 2000 s 9Q (see LOCAL GOVERNMENT): Local Authorities (Referendums) (Petitions) (England) Regulations 2011, SI 2011/2914, reg 17(3).
7   Ie a referendum following a petition under the Local Authorities (Referendums) (Petitions and Directions) (Wales) Regulations 2001, SI 2001/2292, Pt II (regs 3–17) (see PARA 559 et seq).
8   The authority must comply with any directions given for these purposes by the Welsh Ministers: Local Authorities (Referendums) (Petitions and Directions) (Wales) Regulations 2001, SI 2001/2292, reg 17(10).
9   As to the proposed forms of executive for which a referendum is required see PARA 558.
10 Local Authorities (Referendums) (Petitions and Directions) (Wales) Regulations 2001, SI 2001/2292, reg 17(1)(a)(i). The form of executive determined as mentioned in the text must include an elected mayor: reg 17(2). As to the meaning of 'elected mayor' see LOCAL GOVERNMENT vol 69 (2009) PARA 320.
11 Ie the functions specified in regulations under the Local Government Act 2000 s 13(3)(b) (see LOCAL GOVERNMENT vol 69 (2009) PARA 324).
12 Local Authorities (Referendums) (Petitions and Directions) (Wales) Regulations 2001, SI 2001/2292, reg 17(1)(a)(ii).
13 Local Authorities (Referendums) (Petitions and Directions) (Wales) Regulations 2001, SI 2001/2292, reg 17(1)(b).
14 Local Authorities (Referendums) (Petitions and Directions) (Wales) Regulations 2001, SI 2001/2292, reg 17(3)(a). As to executive arrangements see PARA 558; and LOCAL GOVERNMENT vol 69 (2009) PARA 303 et seq.
15 Local Authorities (Referendums) (Petitions and Directions) (Wales) Regulations 2001, SI 2001/2292, reg 17(3)(b). For these purposes, 'outline fall-back proposals' means an outline of the proposals that a local authority intends to implement if proposals that are to be the subject of a referendum under Pt II or Pt III (regs 18–22) (see PARAS 570–573) are rejected in that referendum: reg 2(1). As to fall-back proposals see also LOCAL GOVERNMENT vol 69 (2009) PARA 315.

16 As to entitlement to vote as a local government elector see PARA 97 et seq. As to the meaning of 'elector' see PARA 95 note 2.

17 Local Authorities (Referendums) (Petitions and Directions) (Wales) Regulations 2001, SI 2001/2292, reg 17(4). In drawing up proposals under head (a) or head (b) in the text, the authority must also have regard to any guidance for the time being issued by the Welsh Ministers under the Local Government Act 2000 s 38 (see LOCAL GOVERNMENT vol 69 (2009) PARA 305): Local Authorities (Referendums) (Petitions and Directions) (Wales) Regulations 2001, SI 2001/2292, reg 17(8).

18 Local Authorities (Referendums) (Petitions and Directions) (Wales) Regulations 2001, SI 2001/2292, reg 17(5)(a).

19 Local Authorities (Referendums) (Petitions and Directions) (Wales) Regulations 2001, SI 2001/2292, reg 17(5)(b).

20 Local Authorities (Referendums) (Petitions and Directions) (Wales) Regulations 2001, SI 2001/2292, reg 17(5)(c).

21 Local Authorities (Referendums) (Petitions and Directions) (Wales) Regulations 2001, SI 2001/2292, reg 17(6).

22 Ie arrangements specified in regulations made by the Welsh Ministers under the Local Government Act 2000 s 32(1) (alternative arrangements: see LOCAL GOVERNMENT vol 69 (2009) PARA 364): Local Authorities (Referendums) (Petitions and Directions) (Wales) Regulations 2001, SI 2001/2292, reg 3. As to the operation of alternative arrangements see LOCAL GOVERNMENT vol 69 (2009) PARA 364 et seq.

23 Local Authorities (Referendums) (Petitions and Directions) (Wales) Regulations 2001, SI 2001/2292, reg 17(7)(a)(i).

24 Local Authorities (Referendums) (Petitions and Directions) (Wales) Regulations 2001, SI 2001/2292, reg 17(7)(a)(ii).

25 Ie proposals under the Local Government Act 2000 s 28(1) (approval of outline fall-back proposals: see LOCAL GOVERNMENT vol 69 (2009) PARA 315).

26 Local Authorities (Referendums) (Petitions and Directions) (Wales) Regulations 2001, SI 2001/2292, reg 17(7)(a)(iii).

27 Local Authorities (Referendums) (Petitions and Directions) (Wales) Regulations 2001, SI 2001/2292, reg 17(7)(b).

28 Local Authorities (Referendums) (Petitions and Directions) (Wales) Regulations 2001, SI 2001/2292, reg 17(9)(a).

29 Local Authorities (Referendums) (Petitions and Directions) (Wales) Regulations 2001, SI 2001/2292, reg 17(9)(b).

569. Restrictions relating to publicity for local authority referendums held in consequence of a valid petition. An authority[1] must not incur any expenditure for the purpose of: (1) publishing any material which, in whole or in part, appears designed to influence local government electors[2] in deciding whether or not to sign a petition requesting a local authority referendum[3]; (2) assisting any person to publish any such material[4]; or (3) influencing or assisting any person to influence, by any other means, local government electors in deciding whether or not to sign a petition requesting a local authority referendum[5]. However, these restrictions are not to be taken as preventing an authority from incurring expenditure on publishing or otherwise providing to any person (whether or not in pursuance of any duty to do so) any factual information so far as it is presented fairly[6].

1 As to the meaning of 'authority' see LOCAL GOVERNMENT vol 69 (2009) PARA 23.

2 As to registration as a local government elector see PARA 113.

3 Local Authorities (Referendums) (Petitions and Directions) (Wales) Regulations 2001, SI 2001/2292, reg 15(1)(a); Local Authorities (Referendums) (Petitions) (England) Regulations 2011, SI 2011/2914, reg 15(1)(a). The text refers to a petition under the Local Authorities (Referendums) (Petitions and Directions) (Wales) Regulations 2001, SI 2001/2292, Pt II (regs 3–17) (in relation to Wales) or under the Local Authorities (Referendums) (Petitions) (England) Regulations 2011, SI 2011/2914, Pt II (regs 3–17) (in relation to England) (see PARA 559 et seq).

4   Local Authorities (Referendums) (Petitions and Directions) (Wales) Regulations 2001, SI 2001/2292, reg 15(1)(b); Local Authorities (Referendums) (Petitions) (England) Regulations 2011, SI 2011/2914, reg 15(1)(b).
5   Local Authorities (Referendums) (Petitions and Directions) (Wales) Regulations 2001, SI 2001/2292, reg 15(1)(c); Local Authorities (Referendums) (Petitions) (England) Regulations 2011, SI 2011/2914, reg 15(1)(c).
6   Local Authorities (Referendums) (Petitions and Directions) (Wales) Regulations 2001, SI 2001/2292, reg 15(2); Local Authorities (Referendums) (Petitions) (England) Regulations 2011, SI 2011/2914, reg 15(2). In determining for these purposes whether any information is presented fairly, regard must be had to any guidance for the time being issued by the Secretary of State under the Local Government Act 2000 s 38 (see LOCAL GOVERNMENT vol 69 (2009) PARA 305) (in relation to England) or by the Welsh Ministers under s 38 (see LOCAL GOVERNMENT vol 69 (2009) PARA 305) (in relation to Wales): Local Authorities (Referendums) (Petitions and Directions) (Wales) Regulations 2001, SI 2001/2292, reg 15(3); Local Authorities (Referendums) (Petitions) (England) Regulations 2011, SI 2011/2914, reg 15(3).

(C) Direction to Local Authority in Wales requiring a Referendum to be held

570.   Circumstances in which Welsh Ministers may require local authority referendum to be held.   The Welsh Ministers may by a direction in writing to the authority[1] require the authority to hold a referendum on whether it should operate executive arrangements[2] involving an executive which takes such permitted form[3] as may be specified in the direction[4]: (1) where it appears to them that specified circumstances have arisen[5]; (2) where they have rejected an authority's application for approval of outline fall-back proposals[6]; (3) where it appears to them that a direction is necessary to further compliance with best value requirements[7]; (4) if an authority requests them to do so[8]; or (5) if a petition organiser[9] requests them to do so[10].

Where a direction is given pursuant to head (1) above, the Welsh Ministers may specify in the direction[11]: (a) the form of executive to be included in proposals for the operation of executive arrangements[12]; (b) details (whether or not in the form of proposals that are to be the subject of the referendum) of the executive arrangements and their operation and any transitional arrangements necessary for the implementation of the proposals on which the referendum is to be held[13]; (c) a timetable with respect to the implementation of the proposals[14]; (d) the principles or matters to which the authority is to have regard in drawing up the proposals[15]; (e) except in a case where details in the form of proposals are specified pursuant to head (b) above, in relation to the consultation to be undertaken in drawing up those proposals, the persons with whom consultation is required, the manner of the consultation and the matters about which those persons are to be consulted[16]; (f) the outline fall-back proposals[17]; (g) details (whether or not in the form of proposals) of the detailed fall-back proposals that are to be implemented if the proposals that are to be the subject of the referendum are rejected[18].

1   As to the meaning of 'authority' see LOCAL GOVERNMENT vol 69 (2009) PARA 23.
2   As to the operation of executive arrangements see LOCAL GOVERNMENT vol 69 (2009) PARA 303 et seq.
3   Ie the form permitted by or under the Local Government Act 2000 s 11 (see LOCAL GOVERNMENT vol 69 (2009) PARA 327 et seq).
4   Local Authorities (Referendums) (Petitions and Directions) (Wales) Regulations 2001, SI 2001/2292, reg 18(1).
5   Local Authorities (Referendums) (Petitions and Directions) (Wales) Regulations 2001, SI 2001/2292, reg 18(1)(a). The text refers to the circumstances that are mentioned in any of the provisions of Sch 2 Pt I paras 1–6. Where a form of executive involving an elected mayor is specified in a petition in consequence of which proposals are drawn up under reg 17(3) (see

PARA 568), a direction given pursuant to head (1) in the text in respect of those proposals does not require the authority to hold a referendum on proposals involving any other form of executive: reg 18(4).

6	Local Authorities (Referendums) (Petitions and Directions) (Wales) Regulations 2001, SI 2001/2292, reg 18(1)(b). The text refers to proposals rejected under the Local Government Act 2000 s 28 (approval of outline fall-back proposals: see LOCAL GOVERNMENT vol 69 (2009) PARA 315). As to the meaning of 'outline fall-back proposals' see PARA 568 note 15.

7	Local Authorities (Referendums) (Petitions and Directions) (Wales) Regulations 2001, SI 2001/2292, reg 18(1)(c). The text refers to further compliance with the requirements of the Local Government Act 1999 Pt I (ss 1–29) (see LOCAL GOVERNMENT vol 69 (2009) PARA 688 et seq).

8	Local Authorities (Referendums) (Petitions and Directions) (Wales) Regulations 2001, SI 2001/2292, reg 18(1)(d).

9	As to the meaning of 'petition organiser' see PARA 561 note 6.

10	Local Authorities (Referendums) (Petitions and Directions) (Wales) Regulations 2001, SI 2001/2292, reg 18(1)(e). Where a form of executive involving an elected mayor is specified in a petition, a direction given in response to the request of the person who is the petition organiser in relation to that petition does not require the authority to hold a referendum on proposals involving any other form of executive: reg 18(3).

11	Local Authorities (Referendums) (Petitions and Directions) (Wales) Regulations 2001, SI 2001/2292, reg 18(2).

12	Local Authorities (Referendums) (Petitions and Directions) (Wales) Regulations 2001, SI 2001/2292, reg 18(2)(a). The text refers to proposals drawn up under reg 19(1)(c) (see PARA 571).

13	Local Authorities (Referendums) (Petitions and Directions) (Wales) Regulations 2001, SI 2001/2292, reg 18(2)(b).

14	Local Authorities (Referendums) (Petitions and Directions) (Wales) Regulations 2001, SI 2001/2292, reg 18(2)(c).

15	Local Authorities (Referendums) (Petitions and Directions) (Wales) Regulations 2001, SI 2001/2292, reg 18(2)(d).

16	Local Authorities (Referendums) (Petitions and Directions) (Wales) Regulations 2001, SI 2001/2292, reg 18(2)(e).

17	Local Authorities (Referendums) (Petitions and Directions) (Wales) Regulations 2001, SI 2001/2292, reg 18(2)(f).

18	Local Authorities (Referendums) (Petitions and Directions) (Wales) Regulations 2001, SI 2001/2292, reg 18(2)(g).

**571.	Action following receipt of direction to hold local authority referendum.**
On receipt of a direction to hold a local authority referendum[1] from the Welsh Ministers in which a relevant matter is specified[2], the authority[3] to which the direction is given must immediately[4]: (1) abandon any arrangements made for the holding of a referendum, whether in consequence of a petition[5] or an earlier direction by the Welsh Ministers to the extent that those arrangements are inconsistent with the arrangements necessary to conduct the referendum required by the direction[6]; (2) abandon all action in respect of any petition received on or before the day on which it receives the direction[7]; (3) draw up[8] proposals for the operation of executive arrangements[9]; (4) draw up[10] outline fall-back proposals[11]; and (5) make arrangements for the holding of a referendum on the proposals drawn up in accordance with head (3) above, to the extent required to supplement any arrangements that may continue by virtue of head (1) above[12].

Where, on the day on which the direction is received, the authority is in possession of the first petition submitted[13] to it[14] and has not complied with the requirement as to validity[15] in relation to it[16], the authority must satisfy itself as to the validity of the petition[17] and, subject to head (b) below, the direction is of no further effect[18]. Where, in a case to which these circumstances apply: (a) the authority is satisfied that the petition is valid, it must publicise the petition in accordance with the requirements as to valid petitions[19] and the direction[20] must be treated as revoked with effect from the date on which the required notice is so given[21]; (b) the authority is satisfied that the petition is invalid, it must publicise the petition in accordance with the requirements as to invalid petitions[22] and the direction[23] must be treated as effective from the date on which the required notice is so given[24]. On receipt of a direction[25] in which either the outline fall-back proposals[26] or the detailed fall-back proposals[27] are specified, the authority to which the direction is given must immediately take the steps necessary to give effect to the direction[28].

Where the authority to which a direction[29] has been given receives a petition submitted[30] to it[31], the petition is received before it has given notice of the date on which the referendum is to be held pursuant to the direction[32], the petition proposes a constitutional change[33] different from that in relation to which the direction requires a referendum to be held[34] and the proper officer determines[35] that the petition is a valid petition[36], the direction must be treated as revoked with effect from the date of the proper officer's determination[37]. In such a case, the authority must notify the Welsh Ministers and the petition organiser[38] of the date of the proper officer's determination[39].

In drawing up proposals for the operation of executive arrangements under head (3) above, the authority must: (i) where the direction specifies details, a form of executive or a timetable, include those details, that form of executive or that timetable[40]; (ii) where the direction requires regard to be had to principles or matters, have regard to those principles or matters[41]; (iii) where the direction requires consultation with specified persons, or in a specified manner or about specified matters, consult those persons, in that manner or about those matters, as the case may be[42]; (iv) consider the extent to which its proposals, if implemented, are likely to assist in securing continuous improvement in the way in which its functions are exercised, having regard to a combination of economy, efficiency and effectiveness[43]; (v) subject to heads (i) to (iv) above, decide which form the executive is to take[44], decide the extent to which the specified functions[45] are to be the responsibility of the executive[46] and take reasonable steps to consult the local government electors for, and other interested persons in, the authority's area[47].

The authority's outline fall-back proposals under head (4) above, where the authority is not then operating executive arrangements or alternative arrangements: (A) may not be drawn up before the authority has taken reasonable steps to consult the local government electors for, and other interested persons in, its area[48]; (B) must include such details of the executive arrangements or alternative arrangements to which they relate as the Welsh Ministers may direct[49]; (C) must include a timetable with respect to the implementation of the detailed fall-back proposals in the event that the proposals that are to be the subject of the referendum are rejected[50]; and (D) may include, as the authority's outline fall-back proposals, any proposals approved[51] by the Welsh Ministers[52]. Where the authority is then operating executive arrangements or alternative arrangements, the authority's outline fall-back proposals under head (4) above are to consist of a summary of those arrangements[53].

In drawing-up proposals under either head (3) or head (4) above, an authority must comply with any directions given by the Welsh Ministers[54] and must have regard to any guidance for the time being issued by them[55].

Not later than two months before the date on which the referendum is to be held, the authority must send to the Welsh Ministers a copy of the proposals drawn up under heads (3) and (4) above[56] and a statement which describes the steps which the authority took to consult the local government electors for, and other interested persons in, the authority's area and the outcome of that consultation and the extent to which that outcome is reflected in the proposals[57].

1 Ie under the Local Authorities (Referendums) (Petitions and Directions) (Wales) Regulations 2001, SI 2001/2292, reg 18 (see PARA 570).
2 Ie a matter referred to in any of the provisions of the Local Authorities (Referendums) (Petitions and Directions) (Wales) Regulations 2001, SI 2001/2292, reg 18(2)(a)–(e) (see PARA 570).
3 As to the meaning of 'authority' see LOCAL GOVERNMENT vol 69 (2009) PARA 23.
4 Local Authorities (Referendums) (Petitions and Directions) (Wales) Regulations 2001, SI 2001/2292, reg 19(1).
5 As to referendums held in consequence of a petition see PARA 559 et seq.
6 Local Authorities (Referendums) (Petitions and Directions) (Wales) Regulations 2001, SI 2001/2292, reg 19(1)(a).
7 Local Authorities (Referendums) (Petitions and Directions) (Wales) Regulations 2001, SI 2001/2292, reg 19(1)(b).
8 Ie in accordance with the Local Authorities (Referendums) (Petitions and Directions) (Wales) Regulations 2001, SI 2001/2292, reg 20(1), (2), (4) (see the text and notes 40–47, 54–55).
9 Local Authorities (Referendums) (Petitions and Directions) (Wales) Regulations 2001, SI 2001/2292, reg 19(1)(c).
10 Ie in accordance with the Local Authorities (Referendums) (Petitions and Directions) (Wales) Regulations 2001, SI 2001/2292, reg 20(3), (4) (see the text and notes 48–55).
11 Local Authorities (Referendums) (Petitions and Directions) (Wales) Regulations 2001, SI 2001/2292, reg 19(1)(d). As to the meaning of 'outline fall-back proposals' see PARA 568 note 15.
12 Local Authorities (Referendums) (Petitions and Directions) (Wales) Regulations 2001, SI 2001/2292, reg 19(1)(e).
13 Ie under the Local Authorities (Referendums) (Petitions and Directions) (Wales) Regulations 2001, SI 2001/2292, Pt II (regs 3–17) (see PARA 559 et seq), and including the single petition resulting from an amalgamation of petitions in accordance with reg 8(1) (see PARA 562).
14 Local Authorities (Referendums) (Petitions and Directions) (Wales) Regulations 2001, SI 2001/2292, reg 19(2)(a).
15 Ie compliance with the Local Authorities (Referendums) (Petitions and Directions) (Wales) Regulations 2001, SI 2001/2292, reg 11(2) (see PARA 564).
16 Local Authorities (Referendums) (Petitions and Directions) (Wales) Regulations 2001, SI 2001/2292, reg 19(2)(b).
17 Ie in accordance with the Local Authorities (Referendums) (Petitions and Directions) (Wales) Regulations 2001, SI 2001/2292, Pt II (see PARA 559 et seq).
18 Local Authorities (Referendums) (Petitions and Directions) (Wales) Regulations 2001, SI 2001/2292, reg 19(2).
19 Ie the authority must comply with the Local Authorities (Referendums) (Petitions and Directions) (Wales) Regulations 2001, SI 2001/2292, reg 13 (see PARA 566).
20 See note 1.
21 Local Authorities (Referendums) (Petitions and Directions) (Wales) Regulations 2001, SI 2001/2292, reg 19(3)(a). The text refers to the notice given under reg 13(1) (see PARA 566).
22 Ie the authority must comply with the Local Authorities (Referendums) (Petitions and Directions) (Wales) Regulations 2001, SI 2001/2292, reg 14 (see PARA 566).
23 See note 1.
24 Local Authorities (Referendums) (Petitions and Directions) (Wales) Regulations 2001, SI 2001/2292, reg 19(3)(b). The text refers to the notice given under reg 14(1) (see PARA 566).
25 See note 1.
26 Ie a matter specified in the Local Authorities (Referendums) (Petitions and Directions) (Wales) Regulations 2001, SI 2001/2292, reg 18(2)(f) (see PARA 570).
27 Ie a matter specified in the Local Authorities (Referendums) (Petitions and Directions) (Wales) Regulations 2001, SI 2001/2292, reg 18(2)(g) (see PARA 570).
28 Local Authorities (Referendums) (Petitions and Directions) (England) Regulations 2000, SI 2000/2852, reg 19(4).
29 See note 1.
30 See note 13.
31 Local Authorities (Referendums) (Petitions and Directions) (Wales) Regulations 2001, SI 2001/2292, reg 19(5)(a).
32 Local Authorities (Referendums) (Petitions and Directions) (Wales) Regulations 2001, SI 2001/2292, reg 19(5)(b).

33 As to the meaning of 'constitutional change' see PARA 561 note 10.

34 Local Authorities (Referendums) (Petitions and Directions) (Wales) Regulations 2001, SI 2001/2292, reg 19(5)(c).

35 Ie in accordance with the Local Authorities (Referendums) (Petitions and Directions) (Wales) Regulations 2001, SI 2001/2292, Pt II (see PARA 559 et seq). As to the meaning of 'proper officer' see PARA 140 note 2 (definition applied by virtue of reg 3).

36 Local Authorities (Referendums) (Petitions and Directions) (Wales) Regulations 2001, SI 2001/2292, reg 19(5)(d). As to the meaning of 'valid petition' see PARA 559 note 3.

37 Local Authorities (Referendums) (Petitions and Directions) (Wales) Regulations 2001, SI 2001/2292, reg 19(5).

38 As to the meaning of 'petition organiser' see PARA 561 note 6.

39 Local Authorities (Referendums) (Petitions and Directions) (Wales) Regulations 2001, SI 2001/2292, reg 19(6). The authority must include the notification referred to in the text in the notice required by reg 13(1) (see PARA 566).

40 Local Authorities (Referendums) (Petitions and Directions) (Wales) Regulations 2001, SI 2001/2292, reg 20(1)(a). Without prejudice to head (i) in the text, proposals under head (3) in the text must include such details of the executive arrangements as the Welsh Ministers may direct, a timetable with respect to the implementation of the proposals and details of any transitional arrangements which are necessary for the implementation of the proposals: reg 20(2).

41 Local Authorities (Referendums) (Petitions and Directions) (Wales) Regulations 2001, SI 2001/2292, reg 20(1)(b).

42 Local Authorities (Referendums) (Petitions and Directions) (Wales) Regulations 2001, SI 2001/2292, reg 20(1)(c).

43 Local Authorities (Referendums) (Petitions and Directions) (Wales) Regulations 2001, SI 2001/2292, reg 20(1)(d).

44 Local Authorities (Referendums) (Petitions and Directions) (Wales) Regulations 2001, SI 2001/2292, reg 20(1)(e)(i).

45 Ie the functions specified in regulations under the Local Government Act 2000 s 13(3)(b) (see LOCAL GOVERNMENT vol 69 (2009) PARA 324).

46 Local Authorities (Referendums) (Petitions and Directions) (Wales) Regulations 2001, SI 2001/2292, reg 20(1)(e)(ii).

47 Local Authorities (Referendums) (Petitions and Directions) (Wales) Regulations 2001, SI 2001/2292, reg 20(1)(e)(iii).

48 Local Authorities (Referendums) (Petitions and Directions) (Wales) Regulations 2001, SI 2001/2292, reg 20(3)(a)(i).

49 Local Authorities (Referendums) (Petitions and Directions) (Wales) Regulations 2001, SI 2001/2292, reg 20(3)(a)(ii).

50 Local Authorities (Referendums) (Petitions and Directions) (Wales) Regulations 2001, SI 2001/2292, reg 20(3)(a)(iii).

51 Ie under the Local Government Act 2000 s 28(1) (approval of outline fall-back proposals: see LOCAL GOVERNMENT vol 69 (2009) PARA 315).

52 Local Authorities (Referendums) (Petitions and Directions) (Wales) Regulations 2001, SI 2001/2292, reg 20(3)(a)(iv).

53 Local Authorities (Referendums) (Petitions and Directions) (Wales) Regulations 2001, SI 2001/2292, reg 20(3)(b).

54 Local Authorities (Referendums) (Petitions and Directions) (Wales) Regulations 2001, SI 2001/2292, reg 20(4)(a).

55 Local Authorities (Referendums) (Petitions and Directions) (Wales) Regulations 2001, SI 2001/2292, reg 20(4)(b). The text refers to guidance for the time being issued by the Welsh Ministers under the Local Government Act 2000 s 38 (see LOCAL GOVERNMENT vol 69 (2009) PARA 305).

56 Local Authorities (Referendums) (Petitions and Directions) (Wales) Regulations 2001, SI 2001/2292, reg 20(5)(a).

57 Local Authorities (Referendums) (Petitions and Directions) (Wales) Regulations 2001, SI 2001/2292, reg 20(5)(b).

572. Time for holding referendum required by direction. Except where the Welsh Ministers hold a referendum in exercise of the default power[1], a referendum required by a direction[2] must be held[3] not later than the end of the period of six months beginning with the date of the direction or the date that is treated[4] as the date of the direction[5]; and a referendum must not be held before the end of the period of two months beginning with the date on which proposals are sent[6] to Welsh Ministers[7]. Where the Welsh Ministers, in exercise of the default power[8], draw up outline fall-back proposals or proposals for the operation of executive arrangements[9] and direct an authority to hold a referendum on those proposals[10], the authority must hold the referendum not later than the end of the period of two months beginning with the date of the direction[11].

Such a referendum[12] may not be held on: (1) a Saturday or Sunday[13]; (2) Christmas Eve, Christmas Day, Maundy Thursday, Good Friday or a day which is a bank holiday[14]; or (3) any day appointed as a day of public thanksgiving or mourning[15].

1 Local Authorities (Referendums) (Petitions and Directions) (Wales) Regulations 2001, SI 2001/2292, reg 21(4). The text refers to the circumstances where the Welsh Ministers exercise the power conferred by reg 25 (see PARA 559).
2 Ie a direction under the Local Authorities (Referendums) (Petitions and Directions) (Wales) Regulations 2001, SI 2001/2292, reg 18 (see PARA 570).
3 Ie subject to the Local Authorities (Referendums) (Petitions and Directions) (Wales) Regulations 2001, SI 2001/2292, reg 21(2)–(4) (see the text and notes 1, 6–7, 12–15).
4 Ie in accordance with the Local Authorities (Referendums) (Petitions and Directions) (Wales) Regulations 2001, SI 2001/2292, reg 7(6) (see PARA 561), in a case to which that provision applies.
5 Local Authorities (Referendums) (Petitions and Directions) (Wales) Regulations 2001, SI 2001/2292, reg 21(1).
6 Ie in accordance with the Local Authorities (Referendums) (Petitions and Directions) (Wales) Regulations 2001, SI 2001/2292, reg 20(5) (see PARA 571).
7 Local Authorities (Referendums) (Petitions and Directions) (Wales) Regulations 2001, SI 2001/2292, reg 21(2).
8 See note 1.
9 Local Authorities (Referendums) (Petitions and Directions) (Wales) Regulations 2001, SI 2001/2292, reg 21(5)(a). As to the meaning of 'outline fall-back proposals' see PARA 568 note 15.
10 Local Authorities (Referendums) (Petitions and Directions) (Wales) Regulations 2001, SI 2001/2292, reg 21(5)(b).
11 Local Authorities (Referendums) (Petitions and Directions) (Wales) Regulations 2001, SI 2001/2292, reg 21(5).
12 Ie under the Local Authorities (Referendums) (Petitions and Directions) (Wales) Regulations 2001, SI 2001/2292, Pt III (regs 18–22) (see PARA 570 et seq).
13 Local Authorities (Referendums) (Petitions and Directions) (Wales) Regulations 2001, SI 2001/2292, reg 21(3)(a).
14 Local Authorities (Referendums) (Petitions and Directions) (Wales) Regulations 2001, SI 2001/2292, reg 21(3)(b). The text refers to a bank holiday under the Banking and Financial Dealings Act 1971 in Wales: see TIME vol 97 (2010) PARA 321.
15 Local Authorities (Referendums) (Petitions and Directions) (Wales) Regulations 2001, SI 2001/2292, reg 21(3)(c).

573. Publicity for local authority referendum required to be held by direction. The authority[1] to which a direction requiring a referendum to be held is given[2] must, not later than one month after the date of the direction, publish in at least one newspaper circulating in its area a notice which[3]: (1) sets out the terms of the direction[4]; and (2) contains a statement[5]: (a) that a direction in the terms set out in the notice has been given by the Welsh Ministers requiring a referendum to be held[6]; (b) of the form of executive to be included in the proposals that are to be the subject of the referendum[7]; and (c) that a referendum is to be held[8]. An authority may include in the notice to be so published, or may otherwise provide to any person (whether or not in pursuance of any duty to do so), any other factual information relating to the direction so far as it is presented fairly[9].

1 As to the meaning of 'authority' see LOCAL GOVERNMENT vol 69 (2009) PARA 23.
2 Ie under the Local Authorities (Referendums) (Petitions and Directions) (Wales) Regulations 2001, SI 2001/2292, reg 18 (see PARA 570).
3 Local Authorities (Referendums) (Petitions and Directions) (Wales) Regulations 2001, SI 2001/2292, reg 22(1).
4 Local Authorities (Referendums) (Petitions and Directions) (Wales) Regulations 2001, SI 2001/2292, reg 22(1)(a).
5 Local Authorities (Referendums) (Petitions and Directions) (Wales) Regulations 2001, SI 2001/2292, reg 22(1)(b).
6 Local Authorities (Referendums) (Petitions and Directions) (Wales) Regulations 2001, SI 2001/2292, reg 22(1)(b)(i).
7 Local Authorities (Referendums) (Petitions and Directions) (Wales) Regulations 2001, SI 2001/2292, reg 22(1)(b)(ii).
8 Local Authorities (Referendums) (Petitions and Directions) (Wales) Regulations 2001, SI 2001/2292, reg 22(1)(b)(iii).
9 Local Authorities (Referendums) (Petitions and Directions) (Wales) Regulations 2001, SI 2001/2292, reg 22(2). In determining for these purposes whether any information is presented fairly, regard must be had to any guidance for the time being issued by the Welsh Ministers under the Local Government Act 2000 s 38 (see LOCAL GOVERNMENT vol 69 (2009) PARA 305): Local Authorities (Referendums) (Petitions and Directions) (Wales) Regulations 2001, SI 2001/2292, reg 22(3).

(D) Campaign to Promote a Particular Result in a Local Authority Referendum

(a) Notices etc of Local Authority Referendum

574. Public notice of local authority referendum and proposals. In relation to England, the proper officer[1] must, not fewer than 56 days before the date on which a referendum[2] will[3] be held (the 'notification date'), publish in such a manner as he considers likely to bring to the attention of persons who live in the local authority area a notice which contains:

(1)   a statement that referendum proposals[4] have been drawn up[5];
(2)   a description of the main features of any proposals[6]; and
(3)   a statement outlining the procedure and administration of the referendum[7],

and at least 14 days before the day on which the proper officer of an authority publishes a notice in accordance with those requirements he must, by notice in writing, advise the proper officers of affected councils[8] that he intends to publish the notice and the date of the referendum to be held in the area[9]. It is then the duty of each proper officer to whom such notice has been given and whose council are considering the holding of a referendum in their area to consider whether it would be practicable to combine that referendum with the one of which such notice has been given[10]. Provision is made for the publicising of referendum proposals in England[11].

In relation to Wales, the proper officer[12] must, as soon as practicable after the proposals date[13], publish in at least one newspaper circulating in the local authority's area a notice which contains:

(a)   a statement that referendum proposals[14] have been sent to the Welsh Ministers[15];
(b)   a description of the main features of the proposals and of the outline fall-back proposals[16]; and
(c)   a statement outlining the procedure and administration of the referendum[17].

Provision is made for the publicising of referendum proposals in Wales[18].

1   As to the meaning of 'proper officer' see the Local Government Act 1972 s 270(3); and PARA 140 note 2 (definition applied, in relation to England, by virtue of the Local Authorities (Conduct of Referendums) (England) Regulations 2012, SI 2012/323, reg 2(1); and, in relation to Wales, by virtue of the Local Authorities (Conduct of Referendums) (Wales) Regulations 2008, SI 2008/1848, reg 2(1)).

2   In relation to England, 'referendum' means a referendum held under the Local Government Act 2000 s 9M (cases in which change is subject to approval in a referendum etc: see LOCAL GOVERNMENT), or by virtue of regulations or order made under any provision of Pt 1A (ss 9B–9R) (arrangements with respect to local authority governance in England: see LOCAL GOVERNMENT): Local Authorities (Conduct of Referendums) (England) Regulations 2012, SI 2012/323, reg 2(1).

3   Ie in accordance with the Local Authorities (Conduct of Referendums) (England) Regulations 2012, SI 2012/323, reg 4(1)(c)(ii); Local Authorities (Conduct of Referendums) (Wales) Regulations 2008, SI 2008/1848, reg 2(1).

4   Ie proposals drawn up under the Local Government Act 2000 s 9MA (referendum: proposals by local authority: see LOCAL GOVERNMENT), proposals drawn up under the Local Authorities (Referendums) (Petitions) (England) Regulations 2011, SI 2011/2914, reg 17(2) (see PARA 568), or any proposals required under an order under the Local Government Act 2000 s 9ME (see LOCAL GOVERNMENT) or s 9N (see LOCAL GOVERNMENT), as the case may be: Local Authorities (Conduct of Referendums) (England) Regulations 2012, SI 2012/323, reg 4(1)(a).

5   Local Authorities (Conduct of Referendums) (England) Regulations 2012, SI 2012/323, reg 4(1)(a), (9).

6   Local Authorities (Conduct of Referendums) (England) Regulations 2012, SI 2012/323, reg 4(1)(b).

7   Ie a statement: (1) that a referendum will be held (Local Authorities (Conduct of Referendums) (England) Regulations 2012, SI 2012/323, reg 4(1)(c)(i)); (2) of the date on which the referendum will be held (reg 4(1)(c)(ii)); (3) in a case to which reg 10(1) or (5) applies (see PARA 27), that the poll in the referendum will be taken together with the poll or polls in an election or elections of a description which is to be specified in the statement (reg 4(1)(c)(iii)); (4) of the question to be asked in the referendum (reg 4(1)(c)(iv)); (5) that the referendum will be conducted in accordance with procedures similar to those used at local government elections (reg 4(1)(c)(v)); (6) of the referendum expenses limit (as defined in 6(1): see PARA 578) that will apply in relation to the referendum and the number of local government electors by reference to which that limit has been calculated (reg 4(1)(c)(vi)); (7) of the address and times at which a copy of any proposals may be inspected (reg 4(1)(c)(vii)); (8) of the procedures for obtaining a copy of any proposals (reg 4(1)(c)(viii)); and (9) if the proper officer then knows that the poll in the referendum (whether or not it is to be taken together with the poll in an election) will be taken together with the poll in a referendum for another area, that the polls will be taken together for the two (or more) areas, which are to be specified in the statement (reg 4(1)(c)(ix)). As to the question to be asked in the referendum see PARA 575. As to the meaning of 'local government election' see the Representation of the People Act 1983 s 203(1); and PARA 11 (definition applied by the Local Authorities (Conduct of Referendums) (England) Regulations 2012, SI 2012/323, reg 2(1)).
     Unless this notice ('the first notice') is published fewer than 74 days before the date of the referendum, the proper officer must publish a second notice containing the particulars specified in reg 4(1)(c)(i)–(viii) and, if reg 4(1)(c)(ix) applies (whether or not it applied in relation to the first notice, if any), the particulars specified therein: reg 4(4). The second notice is to be published in the same manner as was used for the publication of the first notice and not more than 55 days and not fewer than 28 days before the date of the referendum: reg 4(5).

8   Ie the proper officer of the council of each district comprised in the county (if the proper officer of the authority which publishes the notice is the proper officer of a county council), or the proper officer of the council of the county in which the district lies and each of the district councils in that county (if the proper officer of the authority which publishes the notice is the proper officer of a district council comprised in an area for which there is a county council): Local Authorities (Conduct of Referendums) (England) Regulations 2012, SI 2012/323, reg 4(2)(a), (b). As to local authorities in England see LOCAL GOVERNMENT vol 69 (2009) PARA 24 et seq.

9   Local Authorities (Conduct of Referendums) (England) Regulations 2012, SI 2012/323, reg 4(2).

10   Local Authorities (Conduct of Referendums) (England) Regulations 2012, SI 2012/323, reg 4(3). Each such officer must reply to the notice within 7 days of its receipt, indicating whether that proper officer's authority wish to combine their referendum with that to which the notice refers: reg 4(3).

11   The authority must make available for inspection throughout the referendum period, at the address and times stated in the notice, and free of charge, a copy of any proposals, and must secure that sufficient copies are available for persons who wish to obtain copies (Local Authorities (Conduct of Referendums) (England) Regulations 2012, SI 2012/323, reg 4(6)) and may provide (whether or not in pursuance of any duty to do so) any other factual information relating to any proposals or the referendum so far as it is presented fairly (reg 4(7): in determining for the purposes of reg 4(7) whether any information is presented fairly, regard is, in accordance with the Local Government Act 2000 9Q (see LOCAL GOVERNMENT), to be had to any guidance for the time being issued by the Secretary of State thereunder (Local Authorities (Conduct of Referendums) (England) Regulations 2012, SI 2012/323, reg 4(8)). 'Referendum period', in relation to a referendum (including a further referendum), means the period beginning with the notification date and ending on the date of the referendum; 'further referendum' means a referendum held in pursuance of an order under reg 17(5) (see PARA 866): reg 2(1).

12   See note 1.

13   'Proposals date': (1) in relation to a referendum, other than a further referendum, means the date on which proposals under the Local Government Act 2000 s 25 (see LOCAL GOVERNMENT vol 69 (2009) PARA 312) which involve a form of executive for which a referendum is required, proposals under the Local Authorities (Referendums) (Petitions and Directions) (Wales) Regulations 2001, SI 2001/2292, reg 17 (see PARA 568) or reg 19 (see PARA 571), proposals under an order under the Local Government Act 2000 s 36 (see LOCAL GOVERNMENT vol 69 (2009) PARA 318), or proposals under regulations under the Local Government Act 2000 s 30 (see LOCAL GOVERNMENT vol 69 (2009) PARA 311) or s 33 (see LOCAL GOVERNMENT vol 69 (2009) PARA 366), are sent to the Welsh Ministers; and (2) in relation to a further referendum, means the day which falls two months before the day on which the poll at the further referendum is held: Local Authorities (Referendums) (Petitions and Directions) (Wales) Regulations 2001, SI 2001/2292, reg 2(1). 'Referendum' means a referendum held under the Local Government Act 2000 s 27 (referendum in case of proposals involving elected mayor: see LOCAL GOVERNMENT vol 69 (2009) PARAS 314–315), or by virtue of regulations or an order made under any provision of Pt II (ss 10–48A) (arrangements with respect to executives etc: see LOCAL GOVERNMENT vol 69 (2009) PARA 303 et seq); and 'further referendum' means a referendum held in pursuance of an order under the Local Authorities (Conduct of Referendums) (Wales) Regulations 2008, SI 2008/1848, reg 13(3): reg 2(1).

14   Ie proposals under the Local Government Act 2000 s 25 involving a form of executive for which a referendum is required, proposals under the Local Authorities (Referendums) (Petitions and Directions) (Wales) Regulations 2001, SI 2001/2292, reg 17(3) or 19(1), proposals under an order under the Local Government Act 2000 s 36, or proposals under regulations under s 30 or s 33, as the case may be: Local Authorities (Conduct of Referendums) (Wales) Regulations 2008, SI 2008/1848, reg 4(1)(a).

15   Local Authorities (Conduct of Referendums) (Wales) Regulations 2008, SI 2008/1848, reg 4(1)(a).

16   Local Authorities (Conduct of Referendums) (Wales) Regulations 2008, SI 2008/1848, reg 4(1)(b). 'Outline fall-back proposals': (1) in relation to proposals under the Local Government Act 2000 s 25, means an outline of the proposals that a local authority intend to implement if their proposals under s 25 are rejected in a referendum; (2) in relation to proposals under the Local Authorities (Referendums) (Petitions and Directions) (Wales) Regulations 2001, SI 2001/2292 reg 17 or reg 19, means an outline of the proposals that a local authority intend to implement if proposals that are to be the subject of a referendum under the Local Government Act 2000 Pt II (ss 10–48A: see LOCAL GOVERNMENT vol 69 (2009) PARA 303 et seq) or Pt III (ss 49–83: see LOCAL GOVERNMENT vol 69 (2009) PARA 232 et seq) are rejected in that referendum; (3) in relation to proposals under an order under s 36, means (a) if the local authority are then operating executive or alternative arrangements, a summary of those arrangements, and (b) in any other case, an outline of the proposals specified in the order that the local authority intend to implement if proposals that are to be the subject of a referendum are rejected in that referendum; and (4) in relation to proposals under regulations under s 30 or s 33, means a summary of the local authority's existing executive arrangements or existing alternative arrangements (as the case may be): Local Authorities (Conduct of Referendums) (Wales) Regulations 2008, SI 2008/1848, reg 2(1).

17   Ie a statement: (1) that a referendum will be held (Local Authorities (Conduct of Referendums) (Wales) Regulations 2008, SI 2008/1848, reg 4(1)(c)(i)); (2) of the date on which the referendum will be held (reg 4(1)(c)(ii)); (3) of the question to be asked in the referendum (reg 4(1)(c)(iii)); (4) that the referendum will be conducted in accordance with procedures similar to those used at local government elections (reg 4(1)(c)(iv)); (5) of the referendum expenses limit (as defined in

reg 6(1): see PARA 578) that will apply in relation to the referendum and the number of local government electors by reference to which that limit has been calculated (reg 4(1)(c)(v)); (6) of the address and times at which a copy of the proposals, and of the local authority's outline fall-back proposals, may be inspected (reg 4(1)(c)(vi)); and (7) of the procedures for obtaining a copy of the proposals and outline fall-back proposals (reg 4(1)(c)(vii)). As to the question to be asked in the referendum see PARA 575. As to the meaning of 'local government election' see the Representation of the People Act 1983 s 203(1); and PARA 11 (definition applied by the Local Authorities (Conduct of Referendums) (Wales) Regulations 2008, SI 2008/1848, reg 2(1)).

Unless this notice ('the first notice') is published fewer than 56 days before the date of the referendum, the proper officer must publish a second notice containing the particulars specified in reg 4(1)(c)(i)–(vii): reg 4(2). The second notice is to be published in the same newspaper or newspapers as were used for the publication of the first notice and no more than 55 days and no less than 28 days before the date of the referendum: reg 4(3).

18 The local authority must make available for inspection throughout the referendum period, at the address and times stated in the notice, and free of charge, a copy of their proposals and outline fall-back proposals, and must secure that sufficient copies are available for persons who wish to obtain copies (Local Authorities (Conduct of Referendums) (Wales) Regulations 2008, SI 2008/1848, reg 4(4)) and may provide (whether or not in pursuance of any duty to do so) any other factual information relating to the proposals, the outline fall-back proposals or the referendum so far as it is presented fairly (reg 4(5)). In determining for the purposes of reg 4(5) whether any information is presented fairly, regard is, in accordance with the Local Government Act 2000 s 38 (see LOCAL GOVERNMENT vol 69 (2009) PARA 305), to be had to any guidance for the time being issued by the Welsh Ministers under s 38: Local Authorities (Conduct of Referendums) (Wales) Regulations 2008, SI 2008/1848, reg 4(6). 'Referendum period', in relation to a referendum (including a further referendum), means the period beginning with 25 July 1998 (ie the date on which Local Authorities (Conduct of Referendums) (Wales) Regulations 2008, SI 2008/1848, were brought into force in accordance with reg 1) (where the proposals date precedes that date) or the proposals date (in any other case), and ending on the date of the referendum: reg 2(1).

575. The question to be asked at a local authority referendum. In relation to England, the question to be asked in a local authority referendum must be in the prescribed form, which differs according to whether the proposals in relation to which a referendum is to be held are for the authority to operate a mayor and cabinet executive[1], a leader and cabinet executive[2], or a committee system[3]. In relation to Wales, the question to be asked in a local authority referendum differs according to whether the proposals in relation to which the referendum is to be held involve a mayor and cabinet executive[4], a mayor and council manager executive[5], or a leader and cabinet executive[6].

1   As to the question to be asked where the proposals in relation to which a referendum is to be held in England are for the authority to operate a mayor and cabinet executive see the Local Authorities (Conduct of Referendums) (England) Regulations 2012, SI 2012/323, reg 3(a), Sch 1 paras 1, 2. As to the meaning of 'mayor and cabinet executive' see LOCAL GOVERNMENT vol 69 (2009) PARA 327.

2   As to the question to be asked where the proposals in relation to which a referendum is to be held in England are for the authority to operate a leader and cabinet executive see the Local Authorities (Conduct of Referendums) (England) Regulations 2012, SI 2012/323, reg 3(b), Sch 1 paras 3, 4. As to the meaning of 'leader and cabinet executive' see LOCAL GOVERNMENT vol 69 (2009) PARA 327.

3   As to the question to be asked where the proposals in relation to which a referendum is to be held in England are for the authority to operate committee system see the Local Authorities (Conduct of Referendums) (England) Regulations 2012, SI 2012/323, reg 3(c), Sch 1 paras 5, 6.

4   As to the question to be asked where the proposals in relation to which a referendum is to be held in Wales involve a mayor and cabinet executive see the Local Authorities (Conduct of Referendums) (Wales) Regulations 2008, SI 2008/1848, reg 3(a), Sch 1 para 1.

5   As to the question to be asked where the proposals in relation to which a referendum is to be held in Wales involve a mayor and council manager executive see the Local Authorities (Conduct of Referendums) (Wales) Regulations 2008, SI 2008/1848, reg 3(b), Sch 1 para 2. As to the meaning of 'mayor and council manager executive' see LOCAL GOVERNMENT vol 69 (2009) PARA 327.

6   As to the question to be asked where the proposals in relation to which a referendum is to be
     held in Wales involve a leader and cabinet executive see the Local Authorities (Conduct of
     Referendums) (Wales) Regulations 2008, SI 2008/1848, reg 3(c), Sch 1 para 3.

576.   Notice of date etc of local authority referendum.   In relation to both
England and Wales, the counting officer[1] must publish notice of the referendum[2],
stating the date of the poll[3]. The notice of referendum must state the date by
which applications to vote by post or by proxy and other applications and
notices about postal or proxy voting must reach the registration officer in order
that they may be effective for the referendum[4].

1   'Counting officer' means a person referred to in the Local Authorities (Conduct of Referendums)
     (Wales) Regulations 2008, SI 2008/1848, reg 9, or in the Local Authorities (Conduct of
     Referendums) (England) Regulations 2012, SI 2012/323, reg 9, as the case may be (see PARA
     586): Local Authorities (Conduct of Referendums) (Wales) Regulations 2008, SI 2008/1848,
     reg 2(1); Local Authorities (Conduct of Referendums) (England) Regulations 2012,
     SI 2012/323, reg 2(1).
2   As to the meaning of 'referendum' see PARA 574 notes 2, 13.
3   Local Authorities (Conduct of Referendums) (Wales) Regulations 2008, SI 2008/1848, Sch 3
     r 5(1); Local Authorities (Conduct of Referendums) (England) Regulations 2012, SI 2012/323,
     Sch 3 r 5(1).
4   Local Authorities (Conduct of Referendums) (Wales) Regulations 2008, SI 2008/1848, Sch 3
     r 5(2); Local Authorities (Conduct of Referendums) (England) Regulations 2012, SI 2012/323,
     Sch 3 r 5(2).

(b) Referendum Expenses

**577.   Definition of 'referendum expenses' for purposes of local authority
referendum.**   In relation to a local authority referendum[1], 'referendum expenses'
means the expenses incurred by or on behalf of any individual or body during
the referendum period[2] for referendum purposes[3] in respect of any of the matters
set out in the following list[4]:
   (1)   advertising of any nature (whatever the medium used), including agency
          fees, design costs and other costs in connection with preparing,
          producing, distributing or otherwise disseminating such advertising or
          anything incorporating such advertising and intended to be distributed
          for the purpose of disseminating it[5];
   (2)   unsolicited material addressed to electors (whether addressed to them by
          name or intended for delivery to households within any particular area
          or areas), including design costs and other costs in connection with
          preparing, producing or distributing such material (including the cost of
          postage)[6];
   (3)   any published promotional material or other document providing
          information about the referendum or the issues or arguments[7];
   (4)   market research or canvassing conducted for the purpose of ascertaining
          voting intentions[8];
   (5)   the provision of any services or facilities in connection with press
          conferences or other dealings with the media[9];
   (6)   the transport (by any means) of persons to any place or places with a
          view to obtaining publicity in connection with a referendum campaign,
          including the costs of hiring a particular means of transport for the
          whole or part of the referendum period[10]; and
   (7)   rallies and other events, including public meetings organised so as to
          obtain publicity in connection with a referendum campaign or for other
          purposes connected with a referendum campaign, including costs

incurred in connection with the attendance of persons at such events, the hire of premises for the purposes of such events or the provision of goods, services or facilities at them[11].

Nothing in heads (1) to (7) above is to be taken as extending to any expenses:

(a)   in respect of any property, services or facilities so far as those expenses fall to be met out of public funds[12];

(b)   incurred in respect of the remuneration or allowances payable to any member of the staff of the campaign organiser[13]; or

(c)   incurred in respect of an individual by way of travelling expenses (by any means of transport) or in providing for his accommodation or other personal needs to the extent that the expenses are paid by the individual from his own resources and are not reimbursed to him[14].

Where property, services or facilities is or are provided for the use or benefit of any person, either free of charge or at a discount of more than 10 per cent of the commercial rate for the use of the property or for the provision of the services or facilities[15], and the property, services or facilities is or are made use of by or on behalf of that person in circumstances such that, if any expenses were to be (or are) actually incurred by him or on his behalf in respect of that use, they would be (or are) referendum expenses actually incurred by him or on his behalf[16], an amount of referendum expenses (the 'appropriate amount') is treated, for the purposes of the statutory provisions which govern the control of referendum expenses, as incurred by that person during the period for which the property, services or facilities is or are made so use of, unless that amount is not more than £200[17]. For these purposes, the appropriate amount is determined as being such proportion of either the commercial rate for the use of the property or the provision of the services or facilities (where the property, services or facilities is or are provided free of charge)[18] or the difference between that commercial rate and the amount of expenses actually incurred by or on behalf of the person or body in respect of the use of the property or the provision of the services or facilities (where the property, services or facilities is or are provided at a discount)[19], as is reasonably attributable to the use made of the property, services or facilities[20]. However, no amount of referendum expenses is to be regarded as so incurred in respect of the provision by any individual of his own services which he provides voluntarily in his own time and free of charge[21].

1   As to the meaning of 'referendum' see PARA 574 notes 2, 13.
2   As to the meaning of 'referendum period' see PARA 574 notes 11, 18.
3   'For referendum purposes' means: (1) in connection with the conduct or management of any campaign conducted with a view to promoting or procuring a particular outcome in relation to the question asked in the referendum; or (2) otherwise in connection with promoting or procuring any such outcome: Local Authorities (Conduct of Referendums) (Wales) Regulations 2008, SI 2008/1848, reg 6(1); Local Authorities (Conduct of Referendums) (England) Regulations 2012, SI 2012/323, reg 6(1).
4   Local Authorities (Conduct of Referendums) (Wales) Regulations 2008, SI 2008/1848, reg 6(1); Local Authorities (Conduct of Referendums) (England) Regulations 2012, SI 2012/323, reg 6(1).
5   Local Authorities (Conduct of Referendums) (Wales) Regulations 2008, SI 2008/1848, Sch 2 para 1; Local Authorities (Conduct of Referendums) (England) Regulations 2012, SI 2012/323, Sch 2 para 1.
6   Local Authorities (Conduct of Referendums) (Wales) Regulations 2008, SI 2008/1848, Sch 2 para 2; Local Authorities (Conduct of Referendums) (England) Regulations 2012, SI 2012/323, Sch 2 para 2.
7   Local Authorities (Conduct of Referendums) (Wales) Regulations 2008, SI 2008/1848, Sch 2 para 3; Local Authorities (Conduct of Referendums) (England) Regulations 2012, SI 2012/323, Sch 2 para 3. The text refers to material of a description referred to the Local Authorities

(Conduct of Referendums) (Wales) Regulations 2008, SI 2008/1848, reg 5(1) or the Local Authorities (Conduct of Referendums) (England) Regulations 2012, SI 2012/323, reg 5(1) (restriction on publication etc of promotional materials: see PARA 579).

8   Local Authorities (Conduct of Referendums) (Wales) Regulations 2008, SI 2008/1848, Sch 2 para 4; Local Authorities (Conduct of Referendums) (England) Regulations 2012, SI 2012/323, Sch 2 para 4.

9   Local Authorities (Conduct of Referendums) (Wales) Regulations 2008, SI 2008/1848, Sch 2 para 5; Local Authorities (Conduct of Referendums) (England) Regulations 2012, SI 2012/323, Sch 2 para 5.

10 Local Authorities (Conduct of Referendums) (Wales) Regulations 2008, SI 2008/1848, Sch 2 para 6; Local Authorities (Conduct of Referendums) (England) Regulations 2012, SI 2012/323, Sch 2 para 6. 'Referendum campaign' means a campaign conducted with a view to promoting or procuring a particular outcome in relation to the question to be asked in a referendum: Local Authorities (Conduct of Referendums) (Wales) Regulations 2008, SI 2008/1848, reg 6(1); Local Authorities (Conduct of Referendums) (England) Regulations 2012, SI 2012/323, reg 6(1).

11 Local Authorities (Conduct of Referendums) (Wales) Regulations 2008, SI 2008/1848, Sch 2 para 7; Local Authorities (Conduct of Referendums) (England) Regulations 2012, SI 2012/323, Sch 2 para 7.

12 Local Authorities (Conduct of Referendums) (Wales) Regulations 2008, SI 2008/1848, Sch 2 para 8(a); Local Authorities (Conduct of Referendums) (England) Regulations 2012, SI 2012/323, Sch 2 para 8(a).

13 Local Authorities (Conduct of Referendums) (Wales) Regulations 2008, SI 2008/1848, Sch 2 para 8(b); Local Authorities (Conduct of Referendums) (England) Regulations 2012, SI 2012/323, Sch 2 para 8(b). 'Campaign organiser' means the individual or body by whom, or on whose behalf, referendum expenses are incurred (including expenses treated as incurred) in connection with a referendum campaign: Local Authorities (Conduct of Referendums) (Wales) Regulations 2008, SI 2008/1848, reg 6(1); Local Authorities (Conduct of Referendums) (England) Regulations 2012, SI 2012/323, reg 6(1).

14 Local Authorities (Conduct of Referendums) (Wales) Regulations 2008, SI 2008/1848, Sch 2 para 8(c); Local Authorities (Conduct of Referendums) (England) Regulations 2012, SI 2012/323, Sch 2 para 8(c).

15 Local Authorities (Conduct of Referendums) (Wales) Regulations 2008, SI 2008/1848, reg 7(1)(a); Local Authorities (Conduct of Referendums) (England) Regulations 2012, SI 2012/323, reg 7(1)(a). Where the services of an employee are made available by his employer for the use or benefit of a person, the amount which is to be taken as constituting the commercial rate for the provision of those services is the amount of the remuneration or allowances payable to the employee by his employer in respect of the period for which his services are so made available (but do not include any amount in respect of any contributions or other payments for which the employer is liable in respect of the employee): Local Authorities (Conduct of Referendums) (Wales) Regulations 2008, SI 2008/1848, reg 7(4); Local Authorities (Conduct of Referendums) (England) Regulations 2012, SI 2012/323, reg 7(4).

16 Local Authorities (Conduct of Referendums) (Wales) Regulations 2008, SI 2008/1848, reg 7(1)(b); Local Authorities (Conduct of Referendums) (England) Regulations 2012, SI 2012/323, reg 7(1)(b).

17 Local Authorities (Conduct of Referendums) (Wales) Regulations 2008, SI 2008/1848, reg 7(2); Local Authorities (Conduct of Referendums) (England) Regulations 2012, SI 2012/323, reg 7(2).

18 Local Authorities (Conduct of Referendums) (Wales) Regulations 2008, SI 2008/1848, reg 7(3)(a); Local Authorities (Conduct of Referendums) (England) Regulations 2012, SI 2012/323, reg 7(3)(a).

19 Local Authorities (Conduct of Referendums) (Wales) Regulations 2008, SI 2008/1848, reg 7(3)(b); Local Authorities (Conduct of Referendums) (England) Regulations 2012, SI 2012/323, reg 7(3)(b).

20 Local Authorities (Conduct of Referendums) (Wales) Regulations 2008, SI 2008/1848, reg 7(3); Local Authorities (Conduct of Referendums) (England) Regulations 2012, SI 2012/323, reg 7(3).

21 Local Authorities (Conduct of Referendums) (Wales) Regulations 2008, SI 2008/1848, reg 7(5); Local Authorities (Conduct of Referendums) (England) Regulations 2012, SI 2012/323, reg 7(5).

578. General restriction on local authority referendum expenses. The total referendum expenses[1] incurred or treated as incurred[2] by or on behalf of any individual or body must not exceed the referendum expenses limit[3], which is defined as the aggregate of £2,362 and such amount as is found by multiplying by 5.9 pence the number of entries in the relevant register[4].

Where any referendum expenses are incurred in excess of the referendum expenses limit, a person who knew or reasonably ought to have known that that limit would be exceeded, or who, without reasonable excuse, authorises another person to exceed that limit, is guilty of an offence[5].

1　As to the meaning of 'referendum expenses' for these purposes see PARA 577; and as to the meaning of 'referendum' for these purposes see PARA 574 notes 2, 13.
2　Ie in accordance with the Local Authorities (Conduct of Referendums) (Wales) Regulations 2008, SI 2008/1848, reg 7 (in relation to Wales) or the Local Authorities (Conduct of Referendums) (England) Regulations 2012, SI 2012/323, reg 7 (in relation to England).
3　Local Authorities (Conduct of Referendums) (Wales) Regulations 2008, SI 2008/1848, reg 6(2); Local Authorities (Conduct of Referendums) (England) Regulations 2012, SI 2012/323, reg 6(2). However, this provision does not affect the right of any creditor who, when the expenses were incurred, was ignorant of that expense being in contravention of the restriction on referendum expenses: Local Authorities (Conduct of Referendums) (Wales) Regulations 2008, SI 2008/1848, reg 6(8); Local Authorities (Conduct of Referendums) (England) Regulations 2012, SI 2012/323, reg 6(8).
4　Local Authorities (Conduct of Referendums) (Wales) Regulations 2008, SI 2008/1848, reg 6(1); Local Authorities (Conduct of Referendums) (England) Regulations 2012, SI 2012/323, reg 6(1).
5　Local Authorities (Conduct of Referendums) (Wales) Regulations 2008, SI 2008/1848, reg 6(3)–(7); Local Authorities (Conduct of Referendums) (England) Regulations 2012, SI 2012/323, reg 6(3)–(7); and PARA 751. For these purposes the 'relevant register' means the register (or registers) of local government electors published under the Representation of the People Act 1983 s 13 (publication of registers: see PARA 165) after the conclusion of the canvass conducted under s 10 (maintenance of registers (annual canvass): see PARA 151) in the year immediately preceding that in which the referendum is held, which has (or have) effect in the area of the local authority by which, or as regards which, the referendum is held (whether or not the persons to whom those entries relate are entitled to vote in the referendum): Local Authorities (Conduct of Referendums) (Wales) Regulations 2008, SI 2008/1848, reg 6(1); Local Authorities (Conduct of Referendums) (England) Regulations 2012, SI 2012/323, reg 6(1).

(c) Publicity

579. Restriction on publication etc of promotional material regarding local authority referendum. No material which: (1) provides general information about the local authority referendum[1]; (2) deals with any of the issues raised by the question[2] to be asked in the referendum[3]; or (3) puts any arguments for or against a particular answer to that question[4], is to be published[5] by or on behalf of a local authority during the period of 28 days ending with the date of the poll at the referendum[6]. However, this restriction on publication does not apply to: (a) material made available to persons in response to specific requests for information or to persons specifically seeking access to it[7]; (b) the publication of information relating to the holding of the poll at the referendum[8]; or (c) the publication of press notices containing factual information where the sole purpose of publication is to refute or correct any inaccuracy in material published by a person other than the local authority[9].

1　Local Authorities (Conduct of Referendums) (Wales) Regulations 2008, SI 2008/1848, reg 5(1)(a); Local Authorities (Conduct of Referendums) (England) Regulations 2012, SI 2012/323, reg 5(1)(a). As to the meaning of 'referendum' for these purposes see PARA 574 notes 2, 13.
2　As to the form of the question to be asked at a local authority referendum see PARA 575.
3　Local Authorities (Conduct of Referendums) (Wales) Regulations 2008, SI 2008/1848, reg 5(1)(b); Local Authorities (Conduct of Referendums) (England) Regulations 2012, SI 2012/323, reg 5(1)(b).

4   Local Authorities (Conduct of Referendums) (Wales) Regulations 2008, SI 2008/1848, reg 5(1)(c); Local Authorities (Conduct of Referendums) (England) Regulations 2012, SI 2012/323, reg 5(1)(c).

5   For these purposes, 'publish' means make available to the public at large, or to any section of the public, in whatever form and by whatever means including, in particular, by inclusion in any programme included in a programme service within the meaning of the Broadcasting Act 1990 (see BROADCASTING vol 4 (2011) PARA 507); and 'publication' is to be construed accordingly: Local Authorities (Conduct of Referendums) (Wales) Regulations 2008, SI 2008/1848, reg 5(4); Local Authorities (Conduct of Referendums) (England) Regulations 2012, SI 2012/323, reg 5(4).

6   Local Authorities (Conduct of Referendums) (Wales) Regulations 2008, SI 2008/1848, reg 5(2); Local Authorities (Conduct of Referendums) (England) Regulations 2012, SI 2012/323, reg 5(2).

7   Local Authorities (Conduct of Referendums) (Wales) Regulations 2008, SI 2008/1848, reg 5(3)(a); Local Authorities (Conduct of Referendums) (England) Regulations 2012, SI 2012/323, reg 5(3)(a).

8   Local Authorities (Conduct of Referendums) (Wales) Regulations 2008, SI 2008/1848, reg 5(3)(b); Local Authorities (Conduct of Referendums) (England) Regulations 2012, SI 2012/323, reg 5(3)(b).

9   Local Authorities (Conduct of Referendums) (Wales) Regulations 2008, SI 2008/1848, reg 5(3)(c); Local Authorities (Conduct of Referendums) (England) Regulations 2012, SI 2012/323, reg 5(3)(c).

580. Control of advertisements relating specifically to a local authority referendum. In general, the consent of the local planning authority, the Secretary of State or (as the case may be) the Welsh Ministers must be obtained before any advertisement may be displayed[1]. However, the display on any site in a voting area[2] of an advertisement[3] relating specifically to a local authority referendum does not in general require either express consent or deemed consent[4] provided that the advertisement is removed within 14 days after the close of the poll in the referendum to which it relates[5].

1   See the Town and Country Planning (Control of Advertisements) (England) Regulations 2007, SI 2007/783 (in relation to England); the Town and Country Planning (Control of Advertisements) Regulations 1992, SI 1992/666 (in relation to Wales); and PLANNING vol 82 (2010) PARA 956 et seq.

2   For these purposes, 'voting area' means the area in which a referendum is held: Local Authorities (Conduct of Referendums) (England) Regulations 2012, SI 2012/323, reg 2(1); Local Authorities (Conduct of Referendums) (Wales) Regulations 2008, SI 2008/1848, reg 2(1). As to the meaning of 'referendum' for these purposes see PARA 574 notes 2, 13.

3   As to the meaning of 'advertisement' see PLANNING vol 82 (2010) PARA 957.

4   As to the meanings of 'express consent' and 'deemed consent' see PLANNING vol 82 (2010) PARAS 976, 1006.

5   See the Town and Country Planning (Control of Advertisements) (England) Regulations 2007, SI 2007/783, Sch 1 Class E (applied and modified by the Local Authorities (Conduct of Referendums) (England) Regulations 2012, SI 2012/323, reg 19) (in relation to England); the Town and Country Planning (Control of Advertisements) Regulations 1992, SI 1992/666, Sch 2 Class F (applied and modified by the Local Authorities (Conduct of Referendums) (Wales) Regulations 2008, SI 2008/1848, reg 15) (in relation to Wales); and PLANNING vol 82 (2010) PARA 970.

B. POLLS CONSEQUENT ON PARISH OR COMMUNITY MEETINGS

581. How polls consequent on a parish or community meeting come about. A poll may be demanded before the conclusion of a parish or community meeting[1] on any question arising at the meeting, although no such poll may be taken unless either the person presiding at the meeting consents, or the poll is demanded by not less than ten, or one-third, of the local government electors present at the meeting, whichever is the less[2]. A poll consequent on a parish or community meeting is a poll of those entitled to attend the meeting as local government electors, and must be taken by ballot in accordance with rules made by the Secretary of State or, as the case may be, the Welsh Ministers[3].

1 As to parish or community meetings see LOCAL GOVERNMENT vol 69 (2009) PARA 635 et seq.
2 See the Local Government Act 1972 Sch 12 paras 18(4), 34(4); and LOCAL GOVERNMENT vol 69 (2009) PARA 638.
3 See the Local Government Act 1972 Sch 12 paras 18(5), 34(5); and LOCAL GOVERNMENT vol 69 (2009) PARA 638. As to the rules that have been made see the Parish and Community Meetings (Polls) Rules 1987, SI 1987/1; and PARA 383. As to expenses incurred in taking a poll consequent on a parish or community meeting see PARA 589.

582.   Day of poll consequent on a parish or community meeting taken on any question.   The day of a poll consequent on a parish or community meeting[1] must be fixed by the returning officer[2] and must not be earlier than the fourteenth day or later than the twenty-fifth day after the day on which the poll was demanded[3].

1 As to how polls consequent on a parish or community meeting come about see PARA 581.
2 As to returning officers at polls consequent on a parish or community meeting see PARA 588.
3 Parish and Community Meetings (Polls) Rules 1987, SI 1987/1, r 5, Schedule r 1. As to the computation of time in relation to a poll consequent on a parish or community meeting see PARA 212 note 5.

583.   Notification to council of poll consequent on a parish or community meeting taken on any question.   If a poll consequent on a parish or community meeting is required to be taken[1], the chairman of the meeting must notify the council of the area[2] in which the parish or community is situate of the fact[3]; and the chairman of the meeting must give the returning officer[4] such particulars as will enable him to give notice of the poll[5].

1 As to how polls consequent on a parish or community meeting come about see PARA 581.
2 Ie the district council in England and, by virtue of the Local Government (Wales) Act 1994 s 17, the county or county borough council in Wales. As to the meanings of 'England' and 'Wales' see PARA 1 note 1. As to districts in England, and their councils, see LOCAL GOVERNMENT vol 69 (2009) PARA 24 et seq; and as to counties and county boroughs in Wales, and their councils, see LOCAL GOVERNMENT vol 69 (2009) PARA 37 et seq.
3 Parish and Community Meetings (Polls) Rules 1987, SI 1987/1, r 4(1). As to parishes generally see LOCAL GOVERNMENT vol 69 (2009) PARA 27 et seq; and as to communities generally see LOCAL GOVERNMENT vol 69 (2009) PARA 41 et seq.
4 As to returning officers at polls consequent on a parish or community meeting see PARA 588.
5 Parish and Community Meetings (Polls) Rules 1987, SI 1987/1, r 4(2). As to the giving of public notice by a returning officer see PARA 588; and as to the notice of poll see PARA 608.

(iii) The Referendum

A. POLLING DISTRICTS AND POLLING PLACES

584.   Polling districts and stations at local authority referendum.   For referendums[1] by or in respect of a county in England[2] or a county or county borough in Wales[3], the council may divide a voting area[4] into polling districts, and may alter any polling district; and for referendums held by or in respect of a London borough or a district[5], the London borough or the district council may divide the London borough or the district or any voting area thereof into polling districts, and may alter any polling district[6].

Any power to constitute polling districts for the purpose of referendums must be exercised so that electors from any parliamentary polling district[7] wholly or partly within the voting area can, in the absence of special circumstances, be allotted to a polling station within the parliamentary polling place for that district unless the parliamentary polling place is outside the voting area[8].

1   As to the meaning of 'referendum' for these purposes see PARA 574 notes 2, 13.
2   As to the meaning of 'England' see PARA 1 note 1. As to counties in England, and their councils, see LOCAL GOVERNMENT vol 69 (2009) PARA 24 et seq.
3   As to the meaning of 'Wales' see PARA 1 note 1. As to counties and county boroughs in Wales, and their councils, see LOCAL GOVERNMENT vol 69 (2009) PARA 37 et seq.
4   As to the meaning of 'voting area' see PARA 580 note 2.
5   As to the London boroughs and their councils see LONDON GOVERNMENT vol 71 (2013) PARA 20 et seq. As to districts and their councils see LOCAL GOVERNMENT vol 69 (2009) PARA 24 et seq.
6   Representation of the People Act 1983 s 31(1), (1A) (s 31(1) amended, s 31(1A) added, by the Local Government (Wales) Act 1994 Sch 16 para 68(6)). The provisions of the Representation of the People Act 1983 s 31(1), (1A), (3) are applied and modified in relation to England and Wales by the Local Authorities (Conduct of Referendums) (Wales) Regulations 2008, SI 2008/1848, Sch 4 Table 1 and the Local Authorities (Conduct of Referendums) (England) Regulations 2012, SI 2012/323, Sch 4 Table 1. As to the provisions that are so applied and modified see PARA 15.
7   As to parliamentary polling districts and places see PARA 343 et seq.
8   Representation of the People Act 1983 s 31(3) (as applied and modified: see note 6).

585.   Extent of poll consequent on a parish or community meeting.   A poll consequent on a parish or community meeting which is required to be taken on a question not involving any appointment to office[1], may be held in part only of a parish or community[2], but any reference in the rules of conduct[3] to a parish or community must then be construed as reference to a part of a parish or part of a community, as the case may be[4].

1   As to how polls consequent on a parish or community meeting come about see PARA 581.
2   As to parishes generally see LOCAL GOVERNMENT vol 69 (2009) PARA 27 et seq; and as to communities generally see LOCAL GOVERNMENT vol 69 (2009) PARA 41 et seq.
3   As to the rules of conduct for a poll consequent on a parish or community meeting see PARA 556.
4   Parish and Community Meetings (Polls) Rules 1987, SI 1987/1, r 5, Schedule r 38(1).

B.   COUNTING OFFICERS AND RETURNING OFFICERS

(A)   Counting Officers at Local Authority Referendum

586.   Counting officer's functions, and assistance for counting officers at local authority referendum.   Functions conferred for the purposes of local authority referendums[1] on the counting officer[2] must be exercised in each voting area[3] by the person who is for the time being the returning officer at local government elections of councillors for that area under the Representation of the People Act 1983[4]. It is the counting officer's general duty at the referendum to do all such acts and things as may be necessary for effectually conducting the referendum in the manner provided by the rules[5]. The counting officer must also appoint and pay such persons as may be necessary for the purpose of the counting of the votes[6], and may by writing under his hand appoint one or more persons to discharge all or any of his functions[7].

1   Ie, in relation to Wales, by the Local Authorities (Conduct of Referendums) (Wales) Regulations 2008, SI 2008/1848, and, in relation to England, by the Local Authorities (Conduct of Referendums) (England) Regulations 2012, SI 2012/323. As to the meaning of 'referendum' for these purposes see PARA 574 notes 2, 13.
2   As to the meaning of 'counting officer' see PARA 576 note 1.

3 As to the meaning of 'voting area' see PARA 580 note 2.

4 Local Authorities (Conduct of Referendums) (Wales) Regulations 2008, SI 2008/1848, reg 9(1); Local Authorities (Conduct of Referendums) (England) Regulations 2012, SI 2012/323, reg 9(1). The text refers to the returning officer appointed, in relation to England, under the Representation of the People Act 1983 s 35(1) or (3) (see PARA 354) and, in relation to Wales, under s 35(1A)(a) (see PARA 354).

5 Local Authorities (Conduct of Referendums) (Wales) Regulations 2008, SI 2008/1848, reg 9(2); Local Authorities (Conduct of Referendums) (England) Regulations 2012, SI 2012/323, reg 9(2). The text refers to the rules of conduct provided, in relation to Wales, by the Local Authorities (Conduct of Referendums) (Wales) Regulations 2008, SI 2008/1848, and, in relation to England, by the Local Authorities (Conduct of Referendums) (England) Regulations 2012, SI 2012/323. As to the rules of conduct for a local authority referendum see PARA 555.

6 Local Authorities (Conduct of Referendums) (Wales) Regulations 2008, SI 2008/1848, reg 9(3); Local Authorities (Conduct of Referendums) (England) Regulations 2012, SI 2012/323, reg 9(3).

7 See the Representation of the People Act 1983 s 35(4) (amended by the Education Reform Act 1988 Sch 12 para 50; applied, in relation to Wales, by the Local Authorities (Conduct of Referendums) (Wales) Regulations 2008, SI 2008/1848, Sch 4 Table 1, and applied, in relation to England, by the Local Authorities (Conduct of Referendums) (England) Regulations 2012, SI 2012/323, Sch 4 Table 1). As to the provisions that are so applied and (where applicable) modified see PARA 15.

587. Counting officer's expenses at local authority referendum. All expenditure properly incurred by the counting officer[1] for a voting area[2] in relation to the holding of a referendum[3] must be paid by the council for that area in so far as that expenditure does not, in cases where there is a scale fixed for the purpose by the council, exceed that scale[4].

Before a poll is taken at such a referendum, the authority which appointed the returning officer[5] must, at the request of the counting officer or of any person acting as counting officer, advance to him such reasonable sum in respect of his expenses at the referendum as he may require[6].

1 As to the meaning of 'counting officer' see PARA 576 note 1.
2 As to the meaning of 'voting area' see PARA 580 note 2.
3 As to the meaning of 'referendum' for these purposes see PARA 574 notes 2, 13.
4 Representation of the People Act 1983 s 36(4) (s 36(4) amended by the Local Government (Wales) Act 1994 Sch 16 para 68(9); Representation of the People Act 1983 s 36(4), (6) applied and modified, in relation to Wales, by the Local Authorities (Conduct of Referendums) (Wales) Regulations 2008, SI 2008/1848, Sch 4 Table 1, and applied, in relation to England, by the Local Authorities (Conduct of Referendums) (England) Regulations 2012, SI 2012/323, Sch 4 Table 1). As to the provisions that are so applied and modified see PARA 15.
5 As to the designation of returning officers at local government elections see PARA 354.
6 Representation of the People Act 1983 s 36(6) (as applied and modified: see note 4).

(B) Returning Officers at Poll consequent on a Parish or Community Meeting

588. Returning officer and appointment of office at a poll consequent on parish or community meeting. If a poll consequent on a parish or community meeting is required to be taken on a question not involving any appointment to office[1], the chairman of the meeting must notify the council of the area[2] in which the parish or community[3] is situated and the council must appoint an officer of the council to be returning officer[4]. The returning officer must appoint an office for the purpose of the poll[5].

Any public notice required to be given by a returning officer for these purposes must be given by the notice being posted in some conspicuous place or places in the parish or community, and may also be given in such other manner as the returning officer thinks desirable for publicising it[6].

1   As to when a poll is required to be taken see PARA 582.
2   Ie the district council in England and, by virtue of the Local Government (Wales) Act 1994 s 17, the county or county borough council in Wales. As to the meanings of 'England' and 'Wales' see PARA 1 note 1. As to districts in England, and their councils, see LOCAL GOVERNMENT vol 69 (2009) PARA 24 et seq; and as to counties and county boroughs in Wales, and their councils, see LOCAL GOVERNMENT vol 69 (2009) PARA 37 et seq.
3   As to parishes generally see LOCAL GOVERNMENT vol 69 (2009) PARA 27 et seq; and as to communities generally see LOCAL GOVERNMENT vol 69 (2009) PARA 41 et seq.
4   Parish and Community Meetings (Polls) Rules 1987, SI 1987/1, r 4(1).
5   Parish and Community Meetings (Polls) Rules 1987, SI 1987/1, r 4(3).
6   Parish and Community Meetings (Polls) Rules 1987, SI 1987/1, r 5, Schedule r 38(2). Where the poll is held in part only of a parish or community, any reference to a parish or community in the rules is to be construed as a reference to part of the parish or community: Schedule r 38(1).

589.   Expenses incurred in taking a poll consequent on a parish or community meeting. The expenditure incurred in taking a poll consequent upon a parish or community meeting[1] falls upon the parish or community[2].

1   As to how polls consequent on a parish or community meeting come about see PARA 581.
2   See the Local Government Act 1972 s 150; and LOCAL GOVERNMENT FINANCE vol 70 (2012) PARA 9.

C.   MANNER OF VOTING AT REFERENDUM OR POLL

(A)   Voting Options

590.   Manner of voting at a local authority referendum. A person entitled to vote as an elector at a referendum[1] may vote in person at the polling station allotted to him under the appropriate rules[2], unless he is entitled as an elector to an absent vote at the referendum[3]. If he is entitled as an elector to vote by post at the referendum, he may vote by post[4]. If he is entitled to vote by proxy at the referendum, he may so vote unless, before a ballot paper has been issued for him to vote by proxy, he applies at the polling station allotted to him under the appropriate rules for a ballot paper for the purpose of voting in person, in which case he may vote in person there[5]. If he is not entitled as an elector to an absent vote at the referendum[6] but he cannot reasonably be expected to go in person to the polling station allotted to him under the appropriate rules by reason of the particular circumstances of his employment, either as a constable or by the counting officer[7], on the date of the poll for a purpose connected with the referendum[8], he may vote in person at any polling station in the voting area[9].

1   As to the meaning of 'referendum' see PARA 574 notes 2, 13; definition applied by virtue of the Representation of the People Act 2000 s 12, Sch 4 para 1 (Sch 4 applied and modified in relation to Wales, by the Local Authorities (Conduct of Referendums) (Wales) Regulations 2008, SI 2008/1848, Sch 4 Table 2, and applied, in relation to England, by the Local Authorities (Conduct of Referendums) (England) Regulations 2012, SI 2012/323, Sch 4 Table 3). As to the provisions that are so applied and modified see PARA 15.
2   The 'appropriate rules', in the case of a referendum, means the Local Government Act Referendums Rules within the meaning of, in relation to Wales, the Local Authorities (Conduct of Referendums) (Wales) Regulations 2008, SI 2008/1848 (see Sch 3), and, in relation to England, the Local Authorities (Conduct of Referendums) (England) Regulations 2012, SI 2012/323 (see Sch 3): Representation of the People Act 2000 Sch 4 para 1 (as applied and modified: see note 1).
3   Representation of the People Act 2000 Sch 4 para 2(1), (2), (6A) (Sch 4 para 2(5A), (6A) added, Sch 4 para 2(7) amended, Sch 4 para 2(8), (9) added, by the Electoral Administration Act 2006 ss 35(1), (2), (4), 38(6), Sch 1 para 137(1), (3); as applied and modified (see note 1)). For the purposes of the Representation of the People Act 2000 Sch 4 and the Representation of the People Act 1983, so far as it has effect in relation to England and Wales, a person entitled to vote at a referendum is entitled as an elector to vote by post or entitled to vote by proxy at the

referendum if he is shown in the absent voters list for the referendum as so entitled: see the Representation of the People Act 2000 Sch 4 para 2(7)–(9) (as so amended, added, applied and modified). For these purposes, the 'absent voters list' means the list kept under Sch 4 para 5(1) (see PARA 596): see Sch 4 para 1(1) (as so applied and modified). However, nothing in Sch 4 para 2(1)–(5) (as applied and modified) (see the text and notes 4–9) applies to a person to whom the Representation of the People Act 1983 s 7A (deemed residence for persons on remand: see PARA 120) applies, whether he is registered by virtue of that provision or not; and such a person may only vote by post or by proxy (where he is entitled as an elector to vote by post or, as the case may be, by proxy at the referendum): see the Representation of the People Act 2000 Sch 4 para 2(6)(b) (as so applied and modified). Provision is also made in connection with the voting rights of persons detained in mental hospitals: see Sch 4 para 2(5A) (as so added, applied and modified). As to applications to vote by proxy see PARA 592 et seq.

4	Representation of the People Act 2000 Sch 4 para 2(1), (3) (as applied and modified: see note 1).
5	Representation of the People Act 2000 Sch 4 para 2(1), (4) (as applied and modified: see note 1).
6	Representation of the People Act 2000 Sch 4 para 2(1), (5)(a) (as applied and modified: see note 1).
7	As to the meaning of 'counting officer' see PARA 576 note 1.
8	Representation of the People Act 2000 Sch 4 para 2(1), (5)(b) (as applied and modified: see note 1).
9	Representation of the People Act 2000 Sch 4 para 2(1), (5) (as applied and modified: see note 1). As to the meaning of 'voting area' see PARA 580 note 2.

**591.	Manner of voting at a poll consequent on a parish or community meeting.** A poll consequent on a parish or community meeting[1] is a poll of those entitled to attend the meeting as local government electors, and must be taken by ballot in accordance with rules made by the Secretary of State[2].

1	As to how polls consequent on a parish or community meeting come about see PARA 581.
2	See the Local Government Act 1972 s 99, Sch 12 paras 18(5), 34(5); and PARA 581. As to the rules that have been made see the Parish and Community Meetings (Polls) Rules 1987, SI 1987/1; and PARA 383. Those rules make no provision for postal voting in relation to a poll consequent on a parish or community meeting.

## (B)	Absent Voting at a Local Authority Referendum

### (a)	Applications relating to a Particular Period or an Indefinite Period

**592.	Application for absent vote at referendums for a particular period or for an indefinite period.** Where a person applies to the registration officer[1] to vote by post at a local authority referendum[2] (whether for an indefinite period or for a particular period specified in his application), the registration officer must grant the application[3] if he is satisfied that the applicant is or will be registered in the register of local government electors[4] and if the application contains the applicant's signature and date of birth and meets the prescribed requirements[5].

Where a person applies to the registration officer to vote by proxy[6] at referendums (whether for an indefinite period or for a particular period specified in his application), the registration officer must grant the application[7] if he is satisfied that the applicant is eligible to vote by proxy at referendums to which the application relates[8], if he is satisfied that the applicant is or will be registered in the register of local government electors[9], and if the application meets the prescribed requirements[10]. For these purposes, a person is eligible to vote by proxy at referendums:

(1)	if he is or will be registered as a service voter[11];
(2)	if he has an anonymous entry in the register of electors[12];
(3)	if he cannot reasonably be expected to go in person to the polling

station allotted or likely to be allotted to him under the appropriate rules[13] or to vote unaided there[14], by reason of blindness or other disability[15];

(4)   if he cannot reasonably be expected to go in person to that polling station by reason of the general nature of his occupation, service or employment or that of his spouse or civil partner, or by reason of his or his spouse's or his civil partner's attendance on a course provided by an educational institution[16]; or

(5)   if he cannot go in person from his qualifying address to that polling station without making a journey by air or sea[17].

Such an application[18] must state: (a) the full name of the applicant[19]; (b) the address in respect of which the applicant is registered or has applied to be (or is treated as having applied to be) registered in the register[20]; (c) in the case of such an application, the proxy's address, together with the name of the elector for whom he will act as proxy and the elector's address[21]; (d) in the case of a person applying to vote by post, the address to which the ballot paper should be sent[22]; (e) in the case of an application to vote by proxy, the grounds on which the elector claims to be entitled to an absent vote[23]; (f) in the case of a person who is unable to provide a signature, the reasons for his request for waiver of any requirement[24] to provide a signature and the name and address of any person who has assisted him to complete his application[25]; and (g) where the applicant has, or has applied for, an anonymous entry, that fact[26]. The application must be made in writing and must be signed and dated by the applicant[27]. Such an application which is made for an indefinite period or the period specified in the application must state that it is so made[28] and must specify all or any of the referendums or elections in respect of which it is made[29]. Where an application is made by an elector to vote by proxy, it must include an application for the appointment of a proxy which meets the prescribed requirements[30].

Where the registration officer grants an application to vote by post, he must notify the applicant of his decision[31]; and where he refuses an application, he must notify the applicant of his decision and of the reason for it[32].

1   For these purposes, a reference to the registration officer, in relation to a district or a London borough or a local authority in Wales, is a reference to the relevant registration officer appointed under the Representation of the People Act 1983 s 8 (see PARA 139); and for the purpose of the exercise of a registration officer's functions in relation to the referendum, s 52(1)–(4) (discharge of registration duties: see PARAS 140–143) and s 54(1), (3), (4) (payment of expenses of registration: see PARA 144) have effect: Local Authorities (Conduct of Referendums) (Wales) Regulations 2008, SI 2008/1848, Sch 4 para 1(2)(m); Local Authorities (Conduct of Referendums) (England) Regulations 2012, SI 2012/323, Sch 4 para 1(2)(m).

2   As to the meaning of 'referendum' see PARA 574 notes 2, 13; definition applied by virtue of the Representation of the People Act 2000 s 12, Sch 4 para 1 (Sch 4 applied and modified, in relation to Wales, by the Local Authorities (Conduct of Referendums) (Wales) Regulations 2008, SI 2008/1848, Sch 4 Table 2, and, in relation to England, by the Local Authorities (Conduct of Referendums) (England) Regulations 2012, SI 2012/323, Sch 4 Table 3). As to the provisions that are so applied and modified see PARA 15.

3   Representation of the People Act 2000 Sch 4 para 3(1) (Sch 4 para 3(1), (2)(c), (3)(b) amended, Sch 4 paras 3(3)(aa), (8)–(10), 7C, 7D added, by the Electoral Administration Act 2006 s 14(1), (4), (8), Sch 1 paras 20, 137; as applied and modified (see note 2)). Such an application must be disregarded for the purposes of any particular referendum if it is received by the registration officer after 5 pm on the eleventh day before the date of the poll at that referendum; and where a registration officer disregards an application for the purposes of any particular referendum, he must notify the applicant of this: Representation of the People (England and Wales) Regulations 2001, SI 2001/341, regs 56(1), 57(5) (regs 51(2)(b), 56(1), (2), 57(5) amended, reg 51A added, by SI 2006/752; provisions of those regulations applied and modified, in relation to Wales, by the Local Authorities (Conduct of Referendums) (Wales)

Regulations 2008, SI 2008/1848, Sch 4 Table 5, and, in relation to England, by the Local Authorities (Conduct of Referendums) (England) Regulations 2012, SI 2012/323, Sch 4 Table 6). Records of applications which have been granted must be kept: see the Representation of the People Act 2000 Sch 4 paras 3(9), (10), 7C, 7D (as so added, applied and modified); and the Representation of the People (England and Wales) Regulations 2001, SI 2001/341, regs 51(3A), (3B), 61B (regs 5, 6 amended, regs 51(2)(f), (g), (3A), (3B), 61B added, regs 51(3), 51A substituted, by SI 2006/2910; as so applied and modified).

4 Representation of the People Act 2000 Sch 4 para 3(1)(a) (as applied and modified: see note 2). As to the register of local government electors see PARA 145 et seq.

5 Representation of the People Act 2000 Sch 4 para 3(1)(b) (as amended, applied and modified: see note 2). The requirement to provide a signature may in some circumstances be dispensed with: see Sch 4 para 3(8) (as so added, applied and modified). For these purposes, a reference to anything being prescribed must be construed as a reference to its being provided for by a provision of subordinate legislation applied, in relation to Wales, by the Local Authorities (Conduct of Referendums) (Wales) Regulations 2004, SI 2004/870, and, in relation to England, by the Local Authorities (Conduct of Referendums) (England) Regulations 2001, SI 2001/1298: Local Authorities (Conduct of Referendums) (Wales) Regulations 2008, SI 2008/1848, Sch 4 para 1(2)(k); Local Authorities (Conduct of Referendums) (England) Regulations 2012, SI 2012/323, Sch 4 para 1(2)(k).

6 As to voting by proxy for an elector at a referendum see PARA 597 et seq.

7 Representation of the People Act 2000 Sch 4 para 3(2) (as applied and modified: see note 2). Such an application must be disregarded for the purposes of a particular referendum if it is received by the registration officer after 5 pm on the sixth day before the date of the poll at that referendum: Representation of the People (England and Wales) Regulations 2001, SI 2001/341, reg 56(2) (as amended, applied and modified: see note 3). Where a registration officer disregards an application for the purposes of any particular referendum, he must notify the applicant of this: reg 57(5) (as so applied and modified). See also reg 8; and PARA 141 note 5.

8 Representation of the People Act 2000 Sch 4 para 3(2)(a) (as applied and modified: see note 2).

9 Representation of the People Act 2000 Sch 4 para 3(2)(b) (as applied and modified: see note 2).

10 Representation of the People Act 2000 Sch 4 para 3(2)(c) (as amended, applied and modified: see note 2). As to the prescribed requirements see note 5. As to applications made by an elector to appoint a person as proxy to vote for him see PARA 597 et seq.

11 Representation of the People Act 2000 Sch 4 para 3(3)(a) (as applied and modified: see note 2). As to registration as a service voter see PARA 125 et seq.

12 Representation of the People Act 2000 Sch 4 para 3(3)(aa) (as added, applied and modified: see note 2).

13 Representation of the People Act 2000 Sch 4 para 3(3)(b)(i) (as amended, applied and modified: see note 2). As to the meaning of the 'appropriate rules' see PARA 590 note 2.

14 Representation of the People Act 2000 Sch 4 para 3(3)(b)(ii) (as amended, applied and modified: see note 2).

15 Representation of the People Act 2000 Sch 4 para 3(3)(b) (as amended, applied and modified: see note 2).

16 Representation of the People Act 2000 Sch 4 para 3(3)(c) (amended by the Civil Partnership Act 2004 Sch 27 para 164; as applied and modified (see note 2)).

17 Representation of the People Act 2000 Sch 4 para 3(3)(d) (as applied and modified: see note 2).

18 Applications relating to absent voting must comply with such requirements as are relevant to the application: Representation of the People (England and Wales) Regulations 2001, SI 2001/341, reg 51(1) (as applied and modified: see note 3). For detailed provision in connection with signatures and dates of birth see reg 51(3A), (3B) (as so added, applied and modified).

19 Representation of the People (England and Wales) Regulations 2001, SI 2001/341, reg 51(2)(a) (as applied and modified: see note 3).

20 Representation of the People (England and Wales) Regulations 2001, SI 2001/341, reg 51(2)(b) (as amended, applied and modified: see note 3).

21 Representation of the People (England and Wales) Regulations 2001, SI 2001/341, reg 51(2)(c) (as applied and modified: see note 3).

22 Representation of the People (England and Wales) Regulations 2001, SI 2001/341, reg 51(2)(d) (as applied and modified: see note 3).

23 Representation of the People (England and Wales) Regulations 2001, SI 2001/341, reg 51(2)(e) (as applied and modified: see note 3). For these purposes, a reference to a person voting as an elector is to be construed as a reference to a person voting on their own behalf; and a reference to a person's entitlement as an elector to an absent vote is to be construed as a reference to a person's entitlement to vote by post on their own behalf or to vote by proxy: Local Authorities

(Conduct of Referendums) (Wales) Regulations 2008, SI 2008/1848, Sch 4 para 1(2)(h), (i); Local Authorities (Conduct of Referendums) (England) Regulations 2012, SI 2012/323, Sch 4 para 1(2)(h), (i).
24　Ie under the Representation of the People Act 2000 Sch 4 para 3, 4, or 7 (as applied and modified) (see note 2; and PARAS 594, 600 et seq).
25　See the Representation of the People (England and Wales) Regulations 2001, SI 2001/341, reg 51(2)(f) (as added, applied and modified: see note 3).
26　Representation of the People (England and Wales) Regulations 2001, SI 2001/341, reg 51(2)(g) (as added, applied and modified: see note 3).
27　Representation of the People (England and Wales) Regulations 2001, SI 2001/341, reg 51(3) (as substituted, applied and modified: see note 3). The requirement in the Representation of the People (England and Wales) Regulations 2001, SI 2001/341 that any application, notice or objection should be in writing is satisfied where (apart from the usual meaning of that expression) the text of it is transmitted by electronic means, is received in legible form, and is capable of being used for subsequent reference: see reg 5 (as so amended, applied and modified). A requirement in the Representation of the People (England and Wales) Regulations 2001, SI 2001/341, for an application, notice or objection to be signed is satisfied (as an alternative to the signature given by hand) where there is both an electronic signature incorporated into or logically associated with a particular electronic communication and the certification by any person of such a signature: reg 6 (as so amended, applied and modified).
　　In relation to England only, the registration officer may satisfy himself that an application for an absent vote meets the requirement that it has been signed by the applicant by referring to any signature previously provided by the applicant to the registration officer or the counting officer: reg 51A (as so added, substituted and applied). As to the meaning of 'counting officer' see PARA 576 note 1.
28　Representation of the People (England and Wales) Regulations 2001, SI 2001/341, reg 51(4)(a) (as applied and modified: see note 3).
29　Representation of the People (England and Wales) Regulations 2001, SI 2001/341, reg 51(4)(b) (as applied and modified: see note 3).
30　Representation of the People (England and Wales) Regulations 2001, SI 2001/341, regs 51(6), 52 (as applied and modified: see note 3).
31　Representation of the People (England and Wales) Regulations 2001, SI 2001/341, reg 57(1) (as applied and modified: see note 3).
32　Representation of the People (England and Wales) Regulations 2001, SI 2001/341, reg 57(4) (as applied and modified: see note 3). In the context of elections, a right of appeal lies to the county court from certain decisions of the registration officer disallowing a person's application to vote by proxy or by post as elector: see PARA 172 et seq.

593.　Record of those entitled to an absent vote at referendums for a definite period or for an indefinite period. The registration officer[1] must keep a record of those whose applications for an absent vote at referendums[2] for a definite period or for an indefinite period[3] have been granted showing[4]: (1) whether their applications were to vote by post or proxy for an indefinite or a particular period (specifying that period)[5]; (2) whether their applications were in respect of referendums and elections[6]; (3) in the case of those who may vote by post, the addresses provided by them in their applications as the addresses to which their ballot papers are to be sent[7]; and (4) in the case of those who may vote by proxy, the names and addresses of those appointed as their proxies[8].

The registration officer must remove a person from the record: (a) if he applies to the registration officer to be removed[9]; (b) in the case of a person who is eligible to vote by proxy by virtue of having an anonymous entry, if he ceases to have an anonymous entry[10]; (c) in the case of any registered person, if he ceases to be registered or registered at the same qualifying address or ceases to be, or becomes, registered in pursuance of[11] a service declaration[12], a declaration of local connection[13] or an overseas elector's declaration[14]; (d) in the case of any person shown in the record as voting by proxy, if the registration officer gives notice that he has reason to believe there has been a material change of circumstances[15]; or (e) in the case of a person who applied to vote by post or proxy for a particular period, once that period has expired[16]. Where a person is removed from the record under any of heads (a) to (e) above, the registration officer must notify him of this and the reason for it[17].

A person shown in the record as voting by post may subsequently alter his choice by applying to the registration officer to vote by proxy instead (whether for an indefinite period or for a particular period specified in his application); and, if the registration officer would be required to grant that application to vote by proxy[18], the registration officer must amend the record accordingly[19]. Equally, a person shown in the record as voting by proxy may subsequently alter his choice by applying to the registration officer to vote by post instead (whether for an indefinite period or for a particular period specified in his application); and, if the application meets the prescribed requirements, the registration officer must amend the record accordingly[20].

1   As to the meaning of references to the registration officer for these purposes see PARA 592 note 1.

2   As to the meaning of 'referendum' see PARA 574 notes 2, 13; definition applied by virtue of the Representation of the People Act 2000 s 12, Sch 4 para 1 (Sch 4 applied and modified, in relation to Wales, by the Local Authorities (Conduct of Referendums) (Wales) Regulations 2008, SI 2008/1848, Sch 4 Table 2, and, in relation to England, by the Local Authorities (Conduct of Referendums) (England) Regulations 2012, SI 2012/323, Sch 4 Table 3). As to the provisions that are so applied and modified see PARA 15. As to the meaning of references to a person's entitlement as an elector to an absent vote see PARA 592 note 23.

3   Ie applications for the purposes of a local authority referendum under the Representation of the People Act 2000 Sch 4 para 3 (as amended, applied and modified) (see PARA 592).

4   Representation of the People Act 2000 Sch 4 para 3(4) (as applied and modified: see note 2). In connection with persons on the record under Sch 4 para 3(4), provision is made for the purpose of securing the provision of fresh signatures to the registration officer: see Sch 4 paras 7A, 7B (Sch 4 paras 3(5)(aa), 7A, 7B added by the Electoral Administration Act 2006 s 14(4), (8), Sch 1 para 20; as so applied and modified).

5   Representation of the People Act 2000 Sch 4 para 3(4)(a)(ii) (as applied and modified: see note 2).

6   Representation of the People Act 2000 Sch 4 para 3(4)(a)(i) (as applied and modified: see note 2).

7   Representation of the People Act 2000 Sch 4 para 3(4)(b) (as applied and modified: see note 2).

8   Representation of the People Act 2000 Sch 4 para 3(4)(c) (as applied and modified: see note 2). As to the appointment of proxies see PARA 597 et seq.

9   Representation of the People Act 2000 Sch 4 para 3(5)(a) (as applied and modified: see note 2). Such an application by an elector to be removed from the record must be disregarded for the purposes of a particular referendum if it is received by the registration officer after 5 pm on the eleventh day before the date of the poll at that referendum (Representation of the People (England and Wales) Regulations 2001, SI 2001/341, reg 56(5) (regs 56(5), 57(5) amended by SI 2001/1700; provisions of those regulations applied and modified, in relation to Wales, by the Local Authorities (Conduct of Referendums) (Wales) Regulations 2008, SI 2008/1848, Sch 4 Table 5, and, in relation to England, by the Local Authorities (Conduct of Referendums) (England) Regulations 2012, SI 2012/323, Sch 4 Table 6); and where a registration officer disregards an application for the purposes of any particular referendum, he must notify the applicant of this (see reg 57(5) (as so applied and modified)).

10 Representation of the People Act 2000 Sch 4 para 3(5)(aa) (as added, applied and modified: see notes 2, 4).

11 Representation of the People Act 2000 Sch 4 para 3(5)(b) (as applied and modified: see note 2).

12 Representation of the People Act 2000 Sch 4 para 3(5)(b)(i) (as applied and modified: see note 2). As to registration in pursuance of a service declaration see PARA 125 et seq.

13 Representation of the People Act 2000 Sch 4 para 3(5)(b)(ii) (as applied and modified: see note 2). As to registration in pursuance of a declaration of local connection see PARA 121 et seq.

14 Representation of the People Act 2000 Sch 4 para 3(5)(b)(iii) (as applied and modified: see note 2).

15 Representation of the People Act 2000 Sch 4 para 3(5)(c) (as applied and modified: see note 2).

16 Representation of the People Act 2000 Sch 4 para 3(5)(d) (as applied and modified: see note 2).

17 Representation of the People (England and Wales) Regulations 2001, SI 2001/341, reg 57(4B) (added and amended by SI 2006/2910; as applied and modified (see note 9)).

18 Ie if it were one that had been made for the purposes of a local authority referendum under the Representation of the People Act 2000 Sch 4 para 3(2) (see PARA 592).

19 Representation of the People Act 2000 Sch 4 para 3(6) (as applied and modified: see note 2). Such an application must be disregarded for the purposes of a particular referendum if it is received by the registration officer after 5 pm on the eleventh day before the date of the poll at that referendum: see the Representation of the People (England and Wales) Regulations 2001, SI 2001/341, reg 56(1) (amended by SI 2006/752; as applied and modified (see note 9)). Where a registration officer disregards an application for the purposes of any particular referendum, he must notify the applicant of this: reg 57(5) (as amended (see note 9); as so applied and modified).

20 Representation of the People Act 2000 Sch 4 para 3(7) (as applied and modified: see note 2). As to references to anything being prescribed see PARA 592 note 5: accordingly, the text refers to the requirements set out in the Representation of the People (England and Wales) Regulations 2001, SI 2001/341, Pt IV (regs 50–63A) (as applied and modified: see note 9; and PARA 15. An application under the Representation of the People Act 2000 Sch 4 para 3(7) (as applied and modified) must be disregarded for the purposes of a particular referendum if it is received by the registration officer after 5 pm on the eleventh day before the date of the poll at that referendum: see the Representation of the People (England and Wales) Regulations 2001, SI 2001/341, reg 56(1) (as so applied and modified). Where a registration officer disregards an application for the purposes of any particular referendum, he must notify the applicant of this: see reg 57(5) (as amended (see note 9); as so applied and modified).

(b) Applications relating to a Particular Referendum

594. Applications for absent vote at particular referendum. Where a person applies to the registration officer[1] to vote by post at a particular referendum[2], the registration officer must grant the application[3] if he is satisfied that the applicant is or will be registered in the register of local government electors[4] and if the application contains the applicant's signature and date of birth and meets the prescribed requirements[5]. Where a person applies to the registration officer to vote by proxy[6] at a particular referendum, the registration officer must grant the application[7] if: (1) he is satisfied that the applicant's circumstances on the date of the poll will be or are likely to be such that he cannot reasonably be expected to vote in person at the polling station allotted or likely to be allotted to him under the appropriate rules[8]; (2) he is satisfied that the applicant is or will be registered in the register of local government electors[9]; and (3) the application contains the applicant's signature and date of birth and meets the prescribed requirements[10]. Where a person who has an anonymous entry in the register of electors applies to the registration officer to vote by proxy the registration officer must grant the application if it meets the prescribed requirements[11].

A person who is included in the record kept of those entitled to an absent vote in respect of referendums either for a particular period or for an indefinite period[12], may, in respect of a particular referendum, apply to the registration officer[13] for his ballot paper to be sent to a different address from that shown in the record[14] or to vote by proxy[15], if he is shown in the record so kept as voting by post at referendums of the kind in question[16]; and the registration officer must grant such an application if[17], in the case of any application, it meets the prescribed requirements[18] and, in the case of an application to vote by proxy, the registration officer is satisfied that the applicant's circumstances on the date of the poll will be or are likely to be such that he cannot reasonably be expected to vote in person at the polling station allotted or likely to be allotted to him under the appropriate rules[19].

Such an application[20] must state: (a) the full name of the applicant[21]; (b) the address in respect of which the applicant is registered or has applied to be (or is treated as having applied to be) registered in the register[22]; (c) in the case of such an application, the proxy's address, together with the name of the elector for whom he will act as proxy and the elector's address[23]; (d) in the case of a person applying to vote by post, the address to which the ballot paper should be sent[24]; (e) in the case of an application to vote by proxy, the grounds on which the elector claims to be entitled to an absent vote[25]; (f) in the case of a person who is unable to provide a signature, the reasons for his request for waiver of any requirement[26] to provide a signature and the name and address of any person who has assisted him to complete his application[27]; and (g) where the applicant has, or has applied for, an anonymous entry, that fact[28]. Additionally, in relation to England, an application for a ballot paper to be sent to a different address from that shown in the record must set out why the applicant's circumstances will be or are likely to be such that he requires his ballot paper to be sent to that address[29]. Such an application which is made for a particular referendum must identify the referendum in question[30] and must state that it is made for a particular referendum[31]. The application must be made in writing and must be signed and dated by the applicant[32]. Where an application is made by an elector to vote by proxy, it must include an application for the appointment of a proxy which meets the prescribed requirements[33].

Where the registration officer grants an application to vote by post, he must notify the applicant of his decision[34]; and where he refuses an application, he must notify the applicant of his decision[35].

1   As to the meaning of references to the registration officer for these purposes see PARA 592 note 1. The registration officer must supply free of charge as many forms for use in connection with applications made under the provisions relating to absent voting as appear to that officer reasonable in the circumstances to any person who satisfies that officer of his intention to use the forms in connection with a referendum or referendums: see the Representation of the People (England and Wales) Regulations 2001, SI 2001/341, reg 4(1) (provisions of those regulations applied and modified, in relation to Wales, by the Local Authorities (Conduct of Referendums) (Wales) Regulations 2008, SI 2008/1848, Sch 4 Table 5, and, in relation to England, by the Local Authorities (Conduct of Referendums) (England) Regulations 2012, SI 2012/323, Sch 4 Table 6). As to the provisions that are so applied and modified see PARA 15.

2   As to the meaning of 'referendum' see PARA 574 notes 2, 13; definition applied by virtue of the Representation of the People Act 2000 Sch 4 para 1 (Sch 4 applied and modified, in relation to Wales, by the Local Authorities (Conduct of Referendums) (Wales) Regulations 2008, SI 2008/1848, Sch 4 Table 2, and, in relation to England, by the Local Authorities (Conduct of Referendums) (England) Regulations 2012, SI 2012/323, Sch 4 Table 3). As to the provisions that are so applied and modified see PARA 15. As to the meaning of references to a person's entitlement as an elector to an absent vote see PARA 592 note 23.

3   Representation of the People Act 2000 Sch 4 para 4(1) (Sch 4 para 4(1), (2) amended, Sch 4 paras 4(2A), (5)–(7), 7C, 7D added, by the Electoral Administration Act 2006 s 14(2), (4), (8), Sch 1 para 21; as applied and modified (see note 2)). Such an application must be refused if it is received by the registration officer after 5 pm on the eleventh day before the date of the poll at the referendum for which it is made; and where a registration officer disregards such an application for the purposes of any particular referendum, he must notify the applicant of this: see the Representation of the People (England and Wales) Regulations 2001, SI 2001/341, regs 56(4), 57(5) (regs 51(2)(b), 56(1), (4), 57(1), (5) amended, reg 56(3) substituted, regs 51A, 51B, 56(3A), 57(4A) added, by SI 2006/752; as applied and modified (see note 1)). Records of applications which have been granted must be kept: see the Representation of the People Act 2000 Sch 4 paras 4(6), (7), 7C, 7D (as so added, applied and modified); and the Representation of the People (England and Wales) Regulations 2001, SI 2001/341, reg 61B (regs 51(2)(d), 51B amended, reg 51(2)(f), (g), (3A), (3B), 61B added, regs 51A, 51(3), 56(3A) substituted, by SI 2006/2910; as so applied and modified).

4   Representation of the People Act 2000 Sch 4 para 4(1)(a) (as applied and modified: see note 2). As to the registers of electors see PARA 145 et seq.

5   Representation of the People Act 2000 Sch 4 para 4(1)(b) (as amended, applied and modified: see notes 2, 3). The requirement to provide a signature may in some circumstances be dispensed with: see Sch 4 para 4(5) (as so added, applied and modified). As to references to anything being prescribed see PARA 592 note 5: accordingly, the text refers to the requirements set out in the Representation of the People (England and Wales) Regulations 2001, SI 2001/341, Pt IV (regs 50–63A) (as applied and modified: see note 1; and PARA 15). For detailed provision in connection with signatures and dates of birth see reg 51(3A), (3B) (as so added, applied and modified).

6   As to voting by proxy at a referendum see PARA 597 et seq.

7   Representation of the People Act 2000 Sch 4 para 4(2) (as amended, applied and modified: see notes 2, 3). Such an application must be refused if it is received by the registration officer after 5 pm on the sixth day before the date of the poll at the referendum for which it is made: Representation of the People (England and Wales) Regulations 2001, SI 2001/341, reg 56(3) (as substituted, applied and modified: see notes 1, 3). Where an application under the Representation of the People Act 2000 Sch 4 para 4(2) is made on the grounds of the applicant's physical incapacity, and the applicant became physically incapacitated after 5 pm on the sixth day before the date of the poll at the referendum for which it is made, the application must be refused if it is received after 5 pm on the day of the poll at the referendum for which it is made: Representation of the People (England and Wales) Regulations 2001, SI 2001/341, reg 56(3A) (as so added, substituted, applied and modified). Where a registration officer disregards such an application for the purposes of any particular referendum, he must notify the applicant of this: reg 57(5) (as so applied and modified). This restriction applies also to applications made under the Representation of the People Act 2000 Sch 4 para 6(8) (as so applied and modified) made by virtue of an application under Sch 4 para 4(2) (as so amended, applied and modified: see notes 2, 3).

8   Representation of the People Act 2000 Sch 4 para 4(2)(a) (as amended, applied and modified: see notes 2, 3). As to the meaning of 'appropriate rules' see PARA 590 note 2.

9   Representation of the People Act 2000 Sch 4 para 4(2)(b) (as amended, applied and modified: see notes 2, 3).

10   Representation of the People Act 2000 Sch 4 para 4(2)(c) (as amended, applied and modified: see notes 2, 3). As to references to anything being prescribed see PARA 592 note 5: accordingly, the text refers to the requirements set out in the Representation of the People (England and Wales) Regulations 2001, SI 2001/341, Pt IV (regs 50–63A) (as applied and modified: see note 1; and PARA 15). As to additional requirements to be included in applications to vote by proxy at a particular referendum see PARA 595.

11   Representation of the People Act 2000 Sch 4 para 4(2A) (as added, applied and modified: see notes 2, 3).

12   Ie the record kept under the Representation of the People Act 2000 Sch 4 para 3 (as applied and modified) (see PARA 593).

13   Representation of the People Act 2000 Sch 4 para 4(3) (as applied and modified: see note 2).

14   Representation of the People Act 2000 Sch 4 para 4(3)(a) (as applied and modified: see note 2). Where the registration officer grants an application under Sch 4 para 4(3)(a) by the person shown as voting by post in the record kept under Sch 4 para 3(4) (see PARA 593), he must notify the applicant of this: Representation of the People (England and Wales) Regulations 2001, SI 2001/341, reg 57(4A)(a) (as added, applied and modified: see notes 1, 3).

15   Representation of the People Act 2000 Sch 4 para 4(3)(b) (as applied and modified: see note 2).

16   Representation of the People Act 2000 Sch 4 para 4(3) (as applied and modified: see note 2). Such an application must be refused for the purposes of any particular referendum if it is received by the registration officer after 5 pm on the eleventh day before the date of the poll at that referendum: Representation of the People (England and Wales) Regulations 2001, SI 2001/341, reg 56(1) (as amended, applied and modified: see notes 1, 3). Where a registration officer disregards such an application for the purposes of any particular referendum, he must notify the applicant of this: reg 57(5) (as so amended, applied and modified).

17   Representation of the People Act 2000 Sch 4 para 4(4) (as applied and modified: see note 2). Where the registration officer grants such an application made by a person shown as voting by post, he must notify the applicant of this: Representation of the People (England and Wales) Regulations 2001, SI 2001/341, reg 57(4A) (as added, applied and modified: see notes 1, 3).

18   Representation of the People Act 2000 Sch 4 para 4(4)(a) (as applied and modified: see note 2). As to references to anything being prescribed see PARA 592 note 5: accordingly, the text refers to the requirements set out in the Representation of the People (England and Wales) Regulations 2001, SI 2001/341, Pt IV (regs 50–63A) (as applied and modified: see note 1; and PARA 15).

19   Representation of the People Act 2000 Sch 4 para 4(4)(b) (as applied and modified: see note 2).

20 Applications relating to absent voting must comply with such requirements as are relevant to the application: Representation of the People (England and Wales) Regulations 2001, SI 2001/341, reg 51(1) (as applied and modified: see note 1).

21 Representation of the People (England and Wales) Regulations 2001, SI 2001/341, reg 51(2)(a) (as applied and modified: see note 1).

22 Representation of the People (England and Wales) Regulations 2001, SI 2001/341, reg 51(2)(b) (as amended, applied and modified: see notes 1, 3).

23 Representation of the People (England and Wales) Regulations 2001, SI 2001/341, reg 51(2)(c) (as applied and modified: see note 1).

24 Representation of the People (England and Wales) Regulations 2001, SI 2001/341, reg 51(2)(d) (as amended, applied and modified: see notes 1, 3).

25 Representation of the People (England and Wales) Regulations 2001, SI 2001/341, reg 51(2)(e) (as applied and modified: see note 1).

26 Ie under the Representation of the People Act 2000 Sch 4 para 3, 4, or 7 (as applied and modified) (see note 2; and PARAS 592, 600 et seq).

27 Representation of the People (England and Wales) Regulations 2001, SI 2001/341, reg 51(2)(f) (as added, applied and modified: see notes 1, 3).

28 Representation of the People (England and Wales) Regulations 2001, SI 2001/341, reg 51(2)(g) (as added, applied and modified: see notes 1, 3).

29 Representation of the People (England and Wales) Regulations 2001, SI 2001/341, reg 51B (as added, amended, applied and modified: see notes 1, 3).

30 Representation of the People (England and Wales) Regulations 2001, SI 2001/341, reg 51(5)(b) (as applied and modified: see note 1).

31 Representation of the People (England and Wales) Regulations 2001, SI 2001/341, reg 51(5)(a) (as applied and modified: see note 1). However, where the poll at one election or referendum falls on the same day as the poll at another election or referendum (as to which see PARA 20), the same application may be used for both: see reg 51(5) (as so applied and modified); and PARAS 371, 375, 378, 380.

32 Representation of the People (England and Wales) Regulations 2001, SI 2001/341, reg 51(3) (as substituted, applied and modified: see notes 1, 3). In relation to England, the registration officer may satisfy himself that an application for an absent vote meets the requirement that it has been signed by the applicant by referring to any signature previously provided by the applicant to the registration officer or the counting officer: reg 51A (as so added, substituted, applied and modified). As to the meaning of 'counting officer' see PARA 576 note 1. As to the requirements for documents to be in writing and signed see PARA 592 note 27.

33 Representation of the People (England and Wales) Regulations 2001, SI 2001/341, regs 51(6), 52 (as applied and modified: see note 1).

34 Representation of the People (England and Wales) Regulations 2001, SI 2001/341, reg 57(1) (as amended, applied and modified: see notes 1, 3).

35 Representation of the People (England and Wales) Regulations 2001, SI 2001/341, reg 57(4) (as applied and modified: see note 1). In the context of elections, a right of appeal lies to the county court only from certain decisions of the registration officer disallowing a person's application to vote by proxy or by post as elector: see PARA 172 et seq.

595.   Additional requirements for applications for a proxy vote at a particular referendum. An application to vote by proxy at a particular referendum[1] must set out why the applicant's circumstances on the date of the poll for that referendum will be or are likely to be such that he cannot reasonably be expected to vote in person at his allotted polling station[2]. Where such an application is made on the grounds of the applicant's disability[3] and is made after 5 pm on the sixth day before the date of the poll at the referendum for which it is made[4], such an application must be attested and signed by[5]:

(1)   a registered medical practitioner[6];

(2)   a nurse registered on the register maintained by the Nursing and Midwifery Council[7] by virtue of qualifications in nursing[8];

(3)   a registered dentist[9];

(4)   a registered dispensing optician or a registered optometrist[10];

(5)   a registered pharmacist[11];

(6)   a registered osteopath or chiropractor[12];

(7)   a Christian Science practitioner[13];

(8)   a registered health or social work practitioner[14];

(9)   a person carrying on a registered[15] care home[16];

(10)   the warden of premises forming one of a group of premises provided for persons of pensionable age or disabled persons for which there is a resident warden, where the applicant states that he resides in such premises[17];

(11)   a manager[18] of a registered mental health establishment, or on behalf of such a manager[19]; or

(12)   a person registered in the register[20] for social workers[21].

A person who qualifies by virtue of heads (1) to (8) above may not attest an application for this purpose unless he is treating the applicant for the disability specified in the application, the applicant is receiving care from him in respect of that disability, or the person is a social worker who qualifies by virtue of head (8) above and has arranged care or assistance for the applicant in respect of that disability[22]. A person who qualifies by virtue of head (12) above may not attest the application for this purpose unless he is treating the applicant for the disability specified in the application, the applicant is receiving care from him in respect of that disability, or he has arranged acre or assistance for the person in respect of their disability[23]. The person attesting the application must state: (a) his name and address and the qualification by virtue of which he attests the application[24]; (b) where the person who attests the application is a person who qualifies by virtue of heads (1) to (8) above, that he is treating the applicant for the disability specified in the application or the applicant is receiving care from him in respect of that disability[25]; (c) where the person who attests the application is a person who qualifies by virtue of head (12) above, that he is treating the applicant for the disability specified in the application, the applicant is receiving care from him in respect of the disability, or he has arranged care or assistance for the applicant in respect of that disability[26]; (d) that, to the best of his knowledge and belief, the applicant has the disability specified in the application and that he cannot reasonably be expected to go in person to his allotted polling station or to vote unaided there by reason of that disability[27]; and (e) that, to the best of his knowledge and belief, the disability specified in the application is likely to continue either indefinitely or for a period specified by the person attesting the application[28]. In addition[29], the person who attests the application must state, to the best of his knowledge and belief, the date upon which the applicant became disabled[30].

However, the provisions as to attestation[31] do not apply where the application is based on the applicant's blindness and the applicant is registered as a blind person by the local authority[32] which is specified in the application[33] or where the application states that the applicant is in receipt of the higher rate of the mobility component of a disability living allowance[34] or the enhanced rate of the mobility component of personal independence payment[35] because of the physical incapacity specified in the application[36].

1   Ie an application under the Representation of the People Act 2000 s 12, Sch 4 para 4(2) (as applied and modified) (see PARA 594). As to the meaning of 'referendum' see PARA 574 notes 2, 13; definition applied by virtue of Sch 4 para 1 (Sch 4 applied and modified, in relation to Wales, by the Local Authorities (Conduct of Referendums) (Wales) Regulations 2008, SI 2008/1848, Sch 4 Table 2, and, in relation to England, by the Local Authorities (Conduct of Referendums) (England) Regulations 2012, SI 2012/323, Sch 4 Table 3). As to the provisions that are so applied and modified see PARA 15. As to the meaning of references to a person's entitlement as an elector to an absent vote at a referendum see PARA 592 note 23.

2   Representation of the People (England and Wales) Regulations 2001, SI 2001/341, reg 55(1) (reg 55 substituted by SI 2006/752) (provisions of those regulations applied and modified, in relation to Wales, by the Local Authorities (Conduct of Referendums) (Wales) Regulations 2008, SI 2008/1848, Sch 4 Table 5, and, in relation to England, by the Local Authorities (Conduct of Referendums) (England) Regulations 2012, SI 2012/323, Sch 4 Table 6). This does not apply where the applicant has an anonymous entry: see the Representation of the People (England and Wales) Regulations 2001, SI 2001/341, reg 55(1A) (reg 53(2)–(4) substituted, regs 53(5A), 55(1A) added, regs 53(5)(b), 55(2)(a), (3) amended, by SI 2006/2910; as so applied and modified). As to the provisions that are so applied and modified see PARA 15. As to the meaning of 'his allotted polling station' in relation to an elector see PARA 368 note 32; definition applied by virtue of the Representation of the People (England and Wales) Regulations 2001, SI 2001/341, reg 50 (as so applied and modified). The application referred to in the text must also satisfy the general requirements of absent voting applications (as to which see PARA 594). As to the offence in respect of false statements see PARA 735.

3   Representation of the People (England and Wales) Regulations 2001, SI 2001/341, reg 55(2)(a) (as substituted, amended, applied and modified: see note 2).

4   Representation of the People (England and Wales) Regulations 2001, SI 2001/341, reg 55(2)(b) (as substituted, applied and modified: see note 2).

5   As to the offence of attesting such an application when not authorised to do so see PARA 735.

6   Representation of the People (England and Wales) Regulations 2001, SI 2001/341, reg 53(2)(a) (as substituted, applied and modified: see note 2).

7   Ie the register maintained under the Nursing and Midwifery Order 2001, SI 2002/253, art 5 (see MEDICAL PROFESSIONS vol 74 (2011) PARA 713).

8   Representation of the People (England and Wales) Regulations 2001, SI 2001/341, regs 53(2)(b) (substituted, applied and modified: see note 2).

9   Representation of the People (England and Wales) Regulations 2001, SI 2001/341, reg 53(2)(c) (as substituted, applied and modified: see note 2). A registered dentist is a registered dentist as defined by the Dentists Act 1984 s 53(1) (see MEDICAL PROFESSIONS vol 74 (2011) PARA 442).

10   Representation of the People (England and Wales) Regulations 2001, SI 2001/341, reg 53(2)(d) (as substituted, applied and modified: see note 2). The reference to registered dispensing optician and a registered optometrist is a reference to a registered dispensing optician or a registered optometrist within the meaning of the Opticians Act 1989 (see MEDICAL PROFESSIONS vol 74 (2011) PARA 317).

11   Representation of the People (England and Wales) Regulations 2001, SI 2001/341, reg 53(2)(e) (as substituted (see note 2); further substituted by SI 2010/231; as so applied and modified). The reference to registered pharmacist is a reference to a registered pharmacist as defined by the Pharmacy Order 2010, SI 2010/231, art 3(1) (see MEDICAL PROFESSIONS vol 74 (2011) PARA 784).

12   Representation of the People (England and Wales) Regulations 2001, SI 2001/341, reg 53(2)(f), (g) (as substituted, applied and modified: see note 2). The reference to registered osteopath or chiropractor is a reference to a registered osteopath or chiropractor as defined by the Osteopaths Act 1993 or the Chiropractors Act 1994 (see MEDICAL PROFESSIONS vol 74 (2011) PARAS 525, 603).

13   Representation of the People (England and Wales) Regulations 2001, SI 2001/341, reg 53(2)(h) (as substituted, applied and modified: see note 2).

14   Ie a person registered as a member of a profession to which the Health and Social Work Professions Order 2001, SI 2002/254 (see MEDICAL PROFESSIONS vol 74 (2011) PARA 916 et seq): Representation of the People (England and Wales) Regulations 2001, SI 2001/341, reg 53(2)(j) (as substituted (see note 2); amended by SI 2012/1479; as so applied and modified).

15   Ie a care home registered under the Care Standards Act 2000 Pt 2 (ss 11–42) (see SOCIAL SERVICES AND COMMUNITY CARE).

16   Representation of the People (England and Wales) Regulations 2001, SI 2001/341, reg 53(2)(k) (as substituted, applied and modified: see note 2).

17   Representation of the People (England and Wales) Regulations 2001, SI 2001/341, reg 53(2)(l) (as substituted, applied and modified: see note 2).

18   Ie within the meaning of the Mental Health Act 1983 s 145(1) (see MENTAL HEALTH AND CAPACITY vol 75 (2013) PARA 778).

19   Representation of the People (England and Wales) Regulations 2001, SI 2001/341, reg 53(2)(m) (as substituted, applied and modified: see note 2).

20   Ie the register maintained in accordance with the Care Standards Act 2000 s 56 (see SOCIAL SERVICES AND COMMUNITY CARE).

21   Representation of the People (England and Wales) Regulations 2001, SI 2001/341, reg 53(2)(n) (as substituted, applied and modified: see note 2).

22 Representation of the People (England and Wales) Regulations 2001, SI 2001/341, reg 53(3)(a) (as substituted (see note 2); amended by SI 2012/1479; as so applied and modified).
23 Representation of the People (England and Wales) Regulations 2001, SI 2001/341, reg 53(3)(b) (as substituted, applied and modified: see note 2).
24 Representation of the People (England and Wales) Regulations 2001, SI 2001/341, reg 53(4)(a) (as substituted, applied and modified: see note 2). A person who qualifies by virtue of reg 53(2)(m) (see head (11) in the text) must, instead of the matters specified in reg 53(4)(a), state in the attestation his name, his position in the hospital at which the applicant is liable to be detained or at which he is receiving treatment, that he is a person authorised to make the attestation, and, in the case of an applicant who is liable to be detained in hospital, the statutory provision under which the applicant is liable to be so detained: reg 53(5A) (as so added, applied and modified).
25 Representation of the People (England and Wales) Regulations 2001, SI 2001/341, reg 53(4)(b) (as substituted, applied and modified: see note 2).
26 Representation of the People (England and Wales) Regulations 2001, SI 2001/341, reg 53(4)(c) (as substituted, applied and modified: see note 2).
27 Representation of the People (England and Wales) Regulations 2001, SI 2001/341, reg 53(4)(d) (as substituted, applied and modified: see note 2). For these purposes, 'his allotted polling station', in relation to an elector, means the polling station allotted or likely to be allotted to him under the appropriate rules: see reg 53(7) (as so applied and modified). As to the meaning of the 'appropriate rules' see PARA 590 note 2.
28 Representation of the People (England and Wales) Regulations 2001, SI 2001/341, reg 53(4)(e) (as substituted, applied and modified: see note 2).
29 Ie in addition to those matters specified in the Representation of the People (England and Wales) Regulations 2001, SI 2001/341, reg 53(4) (see the text and notes 24–28).
30 Representation of the People (England and Wales) Regulations 2001, SI 2001/341, reg 55(3) (as substituted, amended, applied and modified: see note 2).
31 Ie the Representation of the People (England and Wales) Regulations 2001, SI 2001/341, reg 53(2)–(4) (see the text and notes 6–28).
32 Ie the local authority which has made arrangements for compiling and maintaining classified registers of persons who are blind, etc under the National Assistance Act 1948 s 29(4)(g) (see SOCIAL SERVICES AND COMMUNITY CARE vol 44(2) (Reissue) PARA 1021).
33 Representation of the People (England and Wales) Regulations 2001, SI 2001/341, reg 53(5)(a) (as applied and modified: see note 2). The fact that an applicant is registered with a local authority under the National Assistance Act 1948 s 29(4)(g) (see SOCIAL SERVICES AND COMMUNITY CARE vol 44(2) (Reissue) PARA 1021) is deemed sufficient evidence that he is eligible to vote by proxy on grounds of the applicant's physical incapacity: Representation of the People (England and Wales) Regulations 2001, SI 2001/341, reg 53(6) (as applied and modified: see note 2);.
34 Ie payable under the Social Security Contributions and Benefits Act 1992 ss 71, 73 (see SOCIAL SECURITY AND PENSIONS vol 44(2) (Reissue) PARA 102 et seq).
35 Ie payable under the Welfare Reform Act 2012 s 79(2) (see SOCIAL SECURITY AND PENSIONS).
35 Representation of the People (England and Wales) Regulations 2001, SI 2001/341, reg 53(5)(b) (as amended (see note 2); further amended by SI 2013/388; as so applied and modified).

596.   Absent voters list at a local authority referendum. In respect of each local authority referendum[1], the registration officer[2] must keep a special list (called the 'absent voters list') which consists of two lists[3]. The first is a list[4] of: (1) those whose applications to vote by post at that particular referendum[5] have been granted, together with the addresses provided by them in their applications as the addresses to which their ballot papers are to be sent[6]; and (2) those who are for the time being shown in the record kept of those entitled to an absent vote at referendums either for a particular period or for an indefinite period[7] as voting by post at particular referendums of the kind in question[8], together with the addresses provided by them in their applications[9] as the addresses to which their ballot papers are to be sent[10]. The second is a list[11] of: (a) those whose applications to vote by proxy at that particular referendum[12] have been granted[13]; and (b) those who are for the time being shown in the record kept of those entitled to an absent vote at referendums either for a particular period or for an indefinite period[14] as voting by proxy at particular referendums of the kind in question[15], together with (in each case) the names and addresses of those appointed as their proxies[16]. In the case of a person who has an anonymous entry in a register the postal voters list or list of proxies (as the case may be) must show in relation to the person only his electoral number and the period for which the anonymous entry has effect[17].

1   As to the meaning of 'referendum' see PARA 574 notes 2, 13; definition applied by virtue of the Representation of the People Act 2000 Sch 4 para 1 (Sch 4 applied and modified, in relation to Wales, by the Local Authorities (Conduct of Referendums) (Wales) Regulations 2008, SI 2008/1848, Sch 4 Table 2, and, in relation to England, by the Local Authorities (Conduct of Referendums) (England) Regulations 2012, SI 2012/323, Sch 4 Table 3). As to the provisions that are so applied and modified see PARA 15. As to the meaning of references to a person's entitlement as an elector to an absent vote at a referendum see PARA 592 note 23.
2   As to the meaning of references to the registration officer for these purposes see PARA 592 note 1.
3   Representation of the People Act 2000 Sch 4 para 5(1) (Sch 4 para 5(1), (2) amended, Sch 1 para 5(4) added, by the Electoral Administration Act 2006 Sch 1 paras 22, 137) (as applied and modified: see note 1).
4   Representation of the People Act 2000 Sch 4 para 5(2) (as amended, applied and modified: see notes 1, 3).
5   Ie applications made under the Representation of the People Act 2000 Sch 4 para 4(1) (as applied and modified) (see PARA 594).
6   Representation of the People Act 2000 Sch 4 para 5(2)(a) (as amended, applied and modified: see notes 1, 3).
7   Ie the record kept under the Representation of the People Act 2000 Sch 4 para 3 (as applied and modified) (see PARA 593).
8   Ie excluding those so shown whose applications to vote by proxy at the referendum under the Representation of the People Act 2000 Sch 4 para 4(3)(b) (as applied and modified) have been granted (see PARA 594).
9   Ie the applications made under the Representation of the People Act 2000 Sch 4 para 3 (as applied and modified) (see PARA 592) or, as the case may be, under Sch 4 para 4(3)(a) (as applied and modified) (see PARA 594).
10 Representation of the People Act 2000 Sch 4 para 5(2)(b) (as amended, applied and modified: see notes 1, 3).
11 Representation of the People Act 2000 Sch 4 para 5(3) (as applied and modified: see note 1).
12 Ie the applications made under the Representation of the People Act 2000 Sch 4 para 4(2), (3) (as applied and modified) (see PARA 594).
13 Representation of the People Act 2000 Sch 4 para 5(3)(a) (as applied and modified: see note 1).
14 See note 7.
15 Representation of the People Act 2000 Sch 4 para 5(3)(b) (as applied and modified: see note 1).
16 Representation of the People Act 2000 Sch 4 para 5(3) (as applied and modified: see note 1).
17 Representation of the People Act 2000 Sch 4 para 5(4) (as added, applied and modified: see notes 1, 3).

(c) Voting as Proxy at a Referendum

597.   Capacity of person to act as proxy for an elector at a referendum. Any person is capable of being appointed proxy to vote for another[1] at any local authority referendum[2] and he may vote in pursuance of the appointment[3]. However, the elector[4] cannot have more than one person at a time appointed as proxy to vote for him at referendums held in the same voting area[5]; and a person is not capable of being appointed to vote or voting as proxy if he is subject to any legal incapacity[6] (age apart[7]) to vote at that referendum as elector[8] or if he is neither a Commonwealth citizen[9] nor a citizen of the Republic of Ireland[10] nor a relevant citizen of the Union[11].

A person is not capable of voting as proxy at any local authority referendum unless on the date of the poll he has attained the age of 18[12]. A person is not entitled to vote as proxy at the same referendum held in any voting area on behalf of more than two electors of whom that person is not the spouse, civil partner, parent, grandparent, brother, sister, child or grandchild[13].

1   Ie subject to the restrictions contained in the Representation of the People Act 2000 s 12, Sch 4 para 6 (see the text and notes 2–13). As to applications made by an elector to vote by proxy at referendums for a particular period or for an indefinite period see PARA 592 et seq; and as to such applications made in relation to a particular referendum see PARA 594 et seq.

2   As to the meaning of 'referendum' see PARA 574 notes 2, 13; definition applied by virtue of the Representation of the People Act 2000 Sch 4 para 1 (Sch 4 applied and modified, in relation to Wales, by the Local Authorities (Conduct of Referendums) (Wales) Regulations 2008, SI 2008/1848, Sch 4 Table 2, and, in relation to England, by the Local Authorities (Conduct of Referendums) (England) Regulations 2012, SI 2012/323, Sch 4 Table 3). As to the provisions that are so applied and modified see PARA 15.

3   Representation of the People Act 2000 Sch 4 para 6(1) (as applied and modified: see note 2).

4   For these purposes, the term 'elector' refers to a person for whom a proxy is appointed: Representation of the People Act 2000 Sch 4 para 6(1) (as applied and modified: see note 2).

5   Representation of the People Act 2000 Sch 4 para 6(2)(b) (as applied and modified: see note 2). As to the meaning of 'voting area' see PARA 580 note 2.

6   As to the meaning of 'legal incapacity' for these purposes see PARA 95 note 8.

7   'Voting age' for a local government elector means 18 years or over: see PARA 97 note 14. See the text and note 12.

8   Representation of the People Act 2000 Sch 4 para 6(4)(a) (as applied and modified: see note 2).

9   As to who are Commonwealth citizens see BRITISH NATIONALITY vol 4 (2011) PARA 409.

10   As to who are citizens of the Republic of Ireland see BRITISH NATIONALITY vol 4 (2011) PARA 410.

11   Representation of the People Act 2000 Sch 4 para 6(4)(b) (as applied and modified: see note 2). As to the meaning of 'relevant citizen of the Union' see PARA 97 note 13.

12   Representation of the People Act 2000 Sch 4 para 6(5) (as applied and modified: see note 2).

13   Representation of the People Act 2000 Sch 4 para 6(6) (amended by the Civil Partnership Act 2004 Sch 27 para 164) (as applied and modified: see note 2).

598.   Applications for appointment to vote as proxy at a referendum.   Where the elector[1] applies to the registration officer[2] for the appointment of a proxy to vote for him at a local authority referendum[3] (whether for an indefinite period or for a particular period specified in his application[4]), the registration officer must make the appointment if the application meets the prescribed requirements[5] and he is satisfied that the elector is or will be[6] registered in the register of local government electors[7] and shown in the record kept of those entitled to an absent vote at referendums either for a particular period or for an indefinite period[8] as voting by proxy at such referendums[9], and that the proxy is capable of being, and willing to be, appointed to vote as proxy at such referendums[10].

Where the elector applies to the registration officer for the appointment of a proxy to vote for him at a particular referendum[11], the registration officer must make the appointment if the application meets the prescribed requirements[12] and he is satisfied that the elector[13] is or will be registered in the register of local government electors[14] and is or will be entitled to vote by proxy at that referendum by virtue of that application[15], and that the proxy is capable of being, and willing to be, appointed[16].

Such an application[17] must state: (a) the full name of the applicant[18]; (b) the address in respect of which the applicant is registered or has applied to be (or is treated as having applied to be) registered in the register[19]; (c) in the case of such an application, the proxy's address, together with the name of the elector for whom he will act as proxy and the elector's address[20]; (d) in the case of a person applying to vote by post, the address to which the ballot paper should be sent[21]; (e) in the case of an application to vote by proxy, the grounds on which the elector claims to be entitled to an absent vote[22]; (f) in the case of a person who is unable to provide a signature, the reasons for his request for waiver of any requirement[23] to provide a signature and the name and address of any person who has assisted him to complete his application[24]; and (g) where the applicant has, or has applied for, an anonymous entry, that fact[25]. The application must be made in writing and must be signed and dated by the applicant[26]. An application which is made for an indefinite period or the period specified in the application must identify those elections or referendums in respect of which it is made[27] and must state that it is made for an indefinite period or for a period specified in the application[28]. An application which is made for a particular referendum must identify the referendum in question[29] and must state that it is so made[30]. Where the poll at one election or referendum falls on the same day as the poll at another election or referendum, the same application may be used for both[31]. An application for the appointment of a proxy must state also the full name and address of the person whom the applicant wishes to appoint as his proxy, together with his family relationship, if any, with the applicant[32]. If the application is signed only by the applicant, it must contain a statement by him that he has consulted the person so named and that the person is capable of being and willing to be appointed to vote as his proxy[33]. If the application is signed also by the person to be appointed, it must contain a statement by that person that he is capable of being and willing to be appointed to vote as the applicant's proxy[34].

The appointment of a proxy is to be made by means of a proxy paper in the prescribed form issued by the registration officer[35].

Where the registration officer grants an application for the appointment of a proxy, he must confirm in writing to the elector that the proxy has been appointed, his name and address, and the duration of the appointment[36]. Where he refuses an application, he must notify the applicant of his decision and of the reason for it[37].

1   As to the meaning of 'elector' in this context see PARA 597 note 4.
2   As to the meaning of references to the registration officer for these purposes see PARA 592 note 1. The registration officer must supply free of charge as many forms for use in connection with applications made under the provisions relating to absent voting as appear to that officer reasonable in the circumstances to any person who satisfies that officer of his intention to use the forms in connection with a referendum or referendums: Representation of the People (England and Wales) Regulations 2001, SI 2001/341, reg 4(1) (provisions of those regulations applied and modified, in relation to Wales, by the Local Authorities (Conduct of Referendums) (Wales) Regulations 2008, SI 2008/1848, Sch 4 Table 5, and, in relation to England, by the Local Authorities (Conduct of Referendums) (England) Regulations 2012, SI 2012/323, Sch 4 Table 6). As to the provisions that are so applied and modified see PARA 15.
3   As to the meaning of 'referendum' see PARA 574 notes 2, 13; definition applied by virtue of the Representation of the People Act 2000 Sch 4 para 1 (Sch 4 applied and modified, in relation to Wales, by the Local Authorities (Conduct of Referendums) (Wales) Regulations 2008, SI 2008/1848, Sch 4 Table 2, and, in relation to England, by the Local Authorities (Conduct of Referendums) (England) Regulations 2012, SI 2012/323, Sch 4 Table 3). As to the provisions that are so applied and modified see PARA 15.
4   As to applications made by an elector to vote by proxy at referendums for a particular period or for an indefinite period see PARA 592 et seq.
5   As to references to anything being prescribed see PARA 592 note 5: accordingly, the text refers to the requirements set out in the Representation of the People (England and Wales) Regulations 2001, SI 2001/341, Pt IV (regs 50–63A) (as applied and modified). An application referred to in the text must be disregarded for the purposes of a particular referendum if it is received by the registration officer after 5 pm on the sixth day before the date of the poll at that referendum; and where a registration officer disregards an application for the purposes of any particular referendum, he must notify the applicant of this: see regs 56(2), 57(5) (regs 51(2)(b), 56(2), 57(5) amended, reg 56(3) substituted, regs 51A, 56(3A) added, by SI 2006/752) (as applied and modified: see note 2).

6   Representation of the People Act 2000 Sch 4 para 6(7) (as applied and modified: see note 3).
7   Representation of the People Act 2000 Sch 4 para 6(7)(a) (as applied and modified: see note 3). As to the registers of electors see PARA 145 et seq.
8   Ie the record kept for the purposes under the Representation of the People Act 2000 Sch 4 para 3 (as applied and modified) (see PARA 593).
9   Representation of the People Act 2000 Sch 4 para 6(7)(b) (as applied and modified: see note 3).
10 Representation of the People Act 2000 Sch 4 para 6(7) (as applied and modified: see note 3).
11 As to such applications see PARA 594.
12 As to the statutory requirements see note 5; and as to the requirements that have been prescribed see PARA 594. An application must be refused if it is received by the registration officer after 5 pm on the sixth day before the date of the poll at the referendum for which it is made: see the Representation of the People (England and Wales) Regulations 2001, SI 2001/341, reg 56(3) (as substituted, applied and modified: see notes 2, 5). Where a registration officer disregards such an application for the purposes of any particular referendum, he must notify the applicant of this: see reg 57(5) (as so amended, applied and modified).
13 Representation of the People Act 2000 Sch 4 para 6(8) (as applied and modified: see note 3).
14 Representation of the People Act 2000 Sch 4 para 6(8)(a) (as applied and modified: see note 3).
15 Representation of the People Act 2000 Sch 4 para 6(8)(b) (as applied and modified: see note 3). The text refers to entitlement to vote by virtue of an application under Sch 4 para 4(2), (3) (as applied and modified) (see PARA 594). Where an application under Sch 4 para 4(2) (as applied and modified) is made on the grounds of the applicant's physical incapacity and the applicant became physically incapacitated after 5 pm on the sixth day before the date of the poll at the referendum for which it is made, an application under Sch 4 para 6(8) (as applied and modified) made by virtue of that application must be refused if it is received after 5 pm on the day of the poll at the referendum for which it is made: see the Representation of the People (England and Wales) Regulations 2001, SI 2001/341, reg 56(3A) (as added, applied and modified: see notes 2, 5). Where a registration officer disregards such an application for the purposes of any particular referendum, he must notify the applicant of this: see reg 57(5) (as so amended, applied and modified).
16 Representation of the People Act 2000 Sch 4 para 6(8) (as applied and modified: see note 3).
17 Applications relating to absent voting must comply with such requirements as are relevant to the application: Representation of the People (England and Wales) Regulations 2001, SI 2001/341, reg 51(1) (as applied and modified: see note 2). For detailed provision in connection with signatures and dates of birth see reg 51(3A), (3B) (reg 51(2)(f), (g), (3A), (3B) added, regs 51(3), 51A substituted, by SI 2006/2910) (as so applied and modified).
18 Representation of the People (England and Wales) Regulations 2001, SI 2001/341, reg 51(2)(a) (as applied and modified: see note 2).
19 Representation of the People (England and Wales) Regulations 2001, SI 2001/341, reg 51(2)(b) (as amended, applied and modified: see note 2).
20 Representation of the People (England and Wales) Regulations 2001, SI 2001/341, reg 51(2)(c) (as applied and modified: see note 2).
21 Representation of the People (England and Wales) Regulations 2001, SI 2001/341, reg 51(2)(d) (as applied and modified: see note 2).
22 Representation of the People (England and Wales) Regulations 2001, SI 2001/341, reg 51(2)(e) (as applied and modified: see note 2).
23 Ie under the Representation of the People Act 2000 Sch 4 para 3, 4, or 7 (as applied and modified) (see PARAS 592, 594, 600 et seq).
24 Representation of the People (England and Wales) Regulations 2001, SI 2001/341, reg 51(2)(f) (as added, applied and modified: see notes 2, 17).
25 Representation of the People (England and Wales) Regulations 2001, SI 2001/341, reg 51(2)(g) (as added, applied and modified: see notes 2, 17).
26 Representation of the People (England and Wales) Regulations 2001, SI 2001/341, reg 51(3) (as substituted, applied and modified: see notes 2, 17). In relation to England, the registration officer may satisfy himself that an application for an absent vote meets the requirement that it has been signed by the applicant by referring to any signature previously provided by the applicant to the registration officer or the counting officer: see reg 51A (as added, substituted, applied and modified: see notes 2, 5, 17). As to the meaning of 'counting officer' see PARA 576 note 1. As to the requirements for documents to be in writing and signed see PARA 592 note 27.
27 Representation of the People (England and Wales) Regulations 2001, SI 2001/341, reg 51(4)(b) (as applied and modified: see note 2).
28 Representation of the People (England and Wales) Regulations 2001, SI 2001/341, reg 51(4)(a) (as applied and modified: see note 2).

29 Representation of the People (England and Wales) Regulations 2001, SI 2001/341, reg 51(5)(b) (as applied and modified: see note 2).

30 Representation of the People (England and Wales) Regulations 2001, SI 2001/341, reg 51(5)(a) (as applied and modified: see note 2).

31 Representation of the People (England and Wales) Regulations 2001, SI 2001/341, reg 51(5) (as applied and modified: see note 2).

32 Representation of the People (England and Wales) Regulations 2001, SI 2001/341, regs 51(6), 52 (as applied and modified: see note 2).

33 Representation of the People (England and Wales) Regulations 2001, SI 2001/341, reg 52(a) (as applied and modified: see note 2). As to capacity to act as proxy at a referendum see PARA 597.

34 Representation of the People (England and Wales) Regulations 2001, SI 2001/341, reg 52(b) (as applied and modified: see note 2).

35 Representation of the People Act 2000 Sch 4 para 6(9) (as applied and modified: see note 3). As to forms generally see note 2. As to the prescribed form of proxy paper for these purposes see the Representation of the People (England and Wales) Regulations 2001, SI 2001/341, reg 57(3), Sch 3 (Form E: proxy paper) (as applied and modified: see note 2). The prescribed form or a form substantially to the like effect may be used with such variations as the circumstances may require: see reg 4(2) (as so applied and modified).

36 Representation of the People (England and Wales) Regulations 2001, SI 2001/341, reg 57(2) (as applied and modified: see note 2).

37 Representation of the People (England and Wales) Regulations 2001, SI 2001/341, reg 57(4) (as applied and modified: see note 2). In the context of elections, a right of appeal lies to the county court only from certain decisions of the registration officer disallowing a person's application to vote by proxy or by post as elector: see PARA 172 et seq.

599.   Duration of appointment to vote as proxy at a referendum.   The appointment of a proxy at a local authority referendum[1] may be cancelled by the elector[2] giving notice to the registration officer[3]. The appointment also ceases to be in force[4]:

(1)   on the issue of a proxy paper appointing a different person to vote for him at a referendum or referendums, whether in the same voting area[5] or elsewhere[6]; and

(2)   where the appointment was for a particular period, once that period expires[7].

The appointment otherwise remains in force for the particular referendum for which the appointment was made[8] or, where the appointment was made for a particular period or for an indefinite period, while the elector is shown as voting by proxy in the record kept of those entitled to an absent vote at referendums either for a particular period or for an indefinite period[9], in pursuance of the same application[10] in respect of which he was included in that record[11].

Where the appointment of a proxy is cancelled by the elector or otherwise ceases to be in force, the registration officer must notify the elector that the appointment has been cancelled or, as the case may be, notify him that the appointment has ceased and the reason for it[12]. Where the appointment of a proxy is cancelled by notice given to the registration officer[13] or ceases to be in force[14] or is no longer in force for a particular period or for an indefinite period[15], the registration officer[16] must notify the person whose appointment as proxy has been cancelled, expired, ceases to be or is no longer in force (unless the registration officer has previously been notified by that person that he no longer wishes to act as proxy)[17] and must remove his name from the record of names and addresses of those appointed as proxies[18].

1   As to the meaning of 'referendum' see PARA 574 notes 2, 13; definition applied by virtue of the Representation of the People Act 2000 Sch 4 para 1 (Sch 4 applied and modified, in relation to Wales, by the Local Authorities (Conduct of Referendums) (Wales) Regulations 2008, SI 2008/1848, Sch 4 Table 2, and, in relation to England, by the Local Authorities (Conduct of

Referendums) (England) Regulations 2012, SI 2012/323, Sch 4 Table 3). As to the provisions that are so applied and modified see PARA 15. As to applications for the appointment of a proxy at a referendum see PARA 598.

2   As to the meaning of 'elector' in this context see PARA 597 note 4.

3   Representation of the People Act 2000 Sch 4 para 6(10) (as applied and modified: see note 1). However, such a notice must be disregarded for the purposes of a particular referendum if it is received by the registration officer after 5 pm on the eleventh day before the date of the poll at that referendum (see the Representation of the People (England and Wales) Regulations 2001, SI 2001/341, reg 56(5) (amended by SI 2001/1700) (provisions of those regulations applied and modified, in relation to Wales, by the Local Authorities (Conduct of Referendums) (Wales) Regulations 2008, SI 2008/1848, Sch 4 Table 5, and, in relation to England, by the Local Authorities (Conduct of Referendums) (England) Regulations 2012, SI 2012/323, Sch 4 Table 6)); and where a registration officer disregards an application for the purposes of any particular referendum, he must notify the applicant of this (see the Representation of the People (England and Wales) Regulations 2001, SI 2001/341, reg 57(5) (as so applied and modified)). As to the meaning of references to the registration officer for these purposes see PARA 592 note 1. As to the provisions that are so applied and modified see PARA 15.

4   Representation of the People Act 2000 Sch 4 para 6(10) (as applied and modified: see note 1).

5   As to the meaning of 'voting area' see PARA 580 note 2.

6   Representation of the People Act 2000 Sch 4 para 6(10)(b) (as applied and modified: see note 1).

7   Representation of the People Act 2000 Sch 4 para 6(10)(c) (as applied and modified: see note 1).

8   Representation of the People Act 2000 Sch 4 para 6(11)(a) (as applied and modified: see note 1).

9   Ie the record kept under the Representation of the People Act 2000 Sch 4 para 3 (as applied and modified) (see PARA 593).

10 Ie under the Representation of the People Act 2000 Sch 4 para 3 (as applied and modified) (see PARA 592).

11 Representation of the People Act 2000 Sch 4 para 6(11)(b) (as applied and modified: see note 1).

12 Representation of the People (England and Wales) Regulations 2001, SI 2001/341, reg 57(4C) (added by SI 2006/752; amended by SI 2006/2910) (as applied and modified: see note 3).

13 Ie under the Representation of the People Act 2000 Sch 4 para 6(10) (as applied and modified) (see the text and notes 1–3).

14 Ie under the Representation of the People Act 2000 Sch 4 para 6(10) (as applied and modified) (see the text and notes 4–7).

15 Ie under the Representation of the People Act 2000 Sch 4 para 6(11)(b) (as applied and modified) (see the text and notes 9–11).

16 Representation of the People (England and Wales) Regulations 2001, SI 2001/341, reg 59 (as applied and modified: see note 3).

17 Representation of the People (England and Wales) Regulations 2001, SI 2001/341, reg 59(a) (as applied and modified: see note 3).

18 Representation of the People (England and Wales) Regulations 2001, SI 2001/341, reg 59(b) (as applied and modified: see note 3). The text refers to the record kept under the Representation of the People Act 2000 Sch 4 para 3(4)(c) (as applied and modified) (see PARA 593).

600.   Voting in person as proxy at referendum.   A person entitled to vote as proxy at a referendum[1] may do so in person at the polling station allotted to the elector[2] under the appropriate rules[3]. Where a person is entitled to vote by post as proxy for the elector at any referendum[4], the elector may not apply for a ballot paper for the purpose of voting in person at the referendum[5]. To indicate that an elector or his proxy is entitled to vote by post and is for that reason not entitled to vote in person, the letter 'A' is placed against the name of that elector in any copy of the register, or part of it, provided for a polling station[6].

1   As to the meaning of 'referendum' see PARA 574 notes 2, 13; definition applied by virtue of the Representation of the People Act 2000 Sch 4 para 1 (Sch 4 applied and modified, in relation to Wales, by the Local Authorities (Conduct of Referendums) (Wales) Regulations 2008, SI 2008/1848, Sch 4 Table 2, and, in relation to England, by the Local Authorities (Conduct of Referendums) (England) Regulations 2012, SI 2012/323, Sch 4 Table 3). As to the provisions that are so applied and modified see PARA 15. As to applications for the appointment of a proxy at a referendum see PARA 598.

2   As to the meaning of 'elector' in this context see PARA 597 note 4.

3   Representation of the People Act 2000 Sch 4 para 7(1) (as applied and modified: see note 1).

4　As to applications to vote by post as proxy at referendum see PARA 601 et seq.
5　Representation of the People Act 2000 Sch 4 para 7(2) (as applied and modified: see note 1).
6　Representation of the People (England and Wales) Regulations 2001, SI 2001/341, reg 62 (amended by SI 2006/2910) (provisions of those regulations applied and modified, in relation to Wales, by the Local Authorities (Conduct of Referendums) (Wales) Regulations 2008, SI 2008/1848, Sch 4 Table 5, and, in relation to England, by the Local Authorities (Conduct of Referendums) (England) Regulations 2012, SI 2012/323, Sch 4 Table 6).

601. Application by person to vote by post as proxy at referendum. Where a person applies to the registration officer[1] to vote by post either as proxy at local authority referendums[2] (whether for an indefinite period or for a particular period specified in his application)[3] or as proxy at a particular referendum[4], the registration officer must grant the application[5] if: (1) the registration officer is satisfied that the elector[6] is or will be registered in the register of local government electors[7]; and (2) there is in force an appointment of the applicant as the elector's proxy to vote for him at referendums of the kind in question or, as the case may be, the referendum concerned[8]; and (3) the application contains the applicant's signature and date of birth and meets the prescribed requirements[9].

Such an application[10] must state: (a) the full name of the applicant[11]; (b) the address in respect of which the applicant is registered or has applied to be (or is treated as having applied to be) registered in the register[12]; (c) in the case of such an application, the proxy's address, together with the name of the elector for whom he will act as proxy and the elector's address[13]; (d) in the case of a person applying to vote by post, the address to which the ballot paper should be sent[14]; (e) in the case of an application to vote by proxy, the grounds on which the elector claims to be entitled to an absent vote[15]; (f) in the case of a person who is unable to provide a signature, the reasons for his request for waiver of any requirement[16] to provide a signature and the name and address of any person who has assisted him to complete his application[17]; and (g) where the applicant has, or has applied for, an anonymous entry, that fact[18]. The application must be made in writing and must be signed and dated by the applicant[19]. An application which is made for an indefinite period or the period specified in the application must state that it is so made[20] and must specify all or any of the elections or referendums in respect of which it is made[21]. An application which is made for a particular referendum must state that it is so made[22] and must identify the referendum in question[23]. Where the poll at one election or referendum falls on the same day as the poll at another election or referendum, the same application may be used for both[24].

Where the registration officer grants an application to vote by post, he must notify the applicant of his decision[25]; and where he refuses an application, he must notify the applicant of his decision and give the reason for it[26].

1　As to the meaning of references to the registration officer for these purposes see PARA 592 note 1.
2　As to the meaning of 'referendum' see PARA 574 notes 2, 13; definition applied by virtue of the Representation of the People Act 2000 Sch 4 para 1 (Sch 4 applied and modified, in relation to Wales, by the Local Authorities (Conduct of Referendums) (Wales) Regulations 2008, SI 2008/1848, Sch 4 Table 2, and, in relation to England, by the Local Authorities (Conduct of Referendums) (England) Regulations 2012, SI 2012/323, Sch 4 Table 3). As to the provisions that are so applied and modified see PARA 15. As to applications for the appointment of a proxy at a referendum see PARA 598.
3　Representation of the People Act 2000 Sch 4 para 7(4)(a) (as applied and modified: see note 2). As to applications so made see PARA 592.
4　Representation of the People Act 2000 Sch 4 para 7(4)(b) (as applied and modified: see note 2). As to applications so made see PARA 594.

5   Representation of the People Act 2000 Sch 4 para 7(4) (as applied and modified: see note 2). Such an application must be disregarded for the purposes of any particular referendum if it is received by the registration officer after 5 pm on the eleventh day before the date of the poll at that referendum; and where a registration officer disregards an application for the purposes of any particular referendum, he must notify the applicant of this: see the Representation of the People (England and Wales) Regulations 2001, SI 2001/341, regs 56(1), 57(5) (regs 51(2)(b), 56(1), 57(1), (5) amended, reg 51A added, by SI 2006/752) (provisions of those regulations applied and modified, in relation to Wales, by the Local Authorities (Conduct of Referendums) (Wales) Regulations 2008, SI 2008/1848, Sch 4 Table 5, and, in relation to England, by the Local Authorities (Conduct of Referendums) (England) Regulations 2012, SI 2012/323, Sch 4 Table 6.
    The registration officer must keep a record in relation to those whose applications under the Representation of the People Act 2000 Sch 4 para 7(4)(a) or (b) have been granted showing their dates of birth and signatures (unless the registration officer in pursuance of Sch 4 para 7(11) has dispensed with the requirement to provide a signature): Sch 4 para 7(12) (Sch 4 para 7(12), (13) added by the Electoral Administration Act 2006 s 14(3), (4), (8)) (as so applied and modified). Such record must be retained by the registration officer for the prescribed period: see the Representation of the People Act 2000 Sch 4 paras 7(13), 7C, 7D (as so added, applied and modified).
6   As to the meaning of 'elector' in this context see PARA 597 note 4.
7   Representation of the People Act 2000 Sch 4 para 7(5)(a) (as applied and modified: see note 2). As to the registers of electors see PARA 145 et seq.
8   Representation of the People Act 2000 Sch 4 para 7(5)(b) (as applied and modified: see note 2). As to the appointment of a proxy see PARA 598 et seq.
9   Representation of the People Act 2000 Sch 4 para 7(5)(c) (Sch 4 para 7(5)(c) amended, Sch 4 para 7(11) added, by the Electoral Administration Act 2006 s 14(3), (8)) (as applied and modified: see note 2). As to references to anything being prescribed see PARA 592 note 5: accordingly, the text refers to the requirements set out in the Representation of the People (England and Wales) Regulations 2001, SI 2001/341, Pt IV (regs 50–63) (as amended, applied and modified).
    The registration officer may dispense with the requirement under the Representation of the People Act 2000 Sch 4 para 7(5)(c) for the applicant to provide a signature if he is satisfied that the applicant is unable to provide a signature because of any disability the applicant has, to provide a signature because the applicant is unable to read or write, or to sign in a consistent and distinctive way because of any such disability or inability: Sch 4 para 7(11) (as so added, applied and modified).
10 Applications relating to absent voting must comply with such requirements as are relevant to the application: Representation of the People (England and Wales) Regulations 2001, SI 2001/341, reg 51(1) (as applied and modified: see note 5). For detailed provision in connection with signatures and dates of birth see reg 51(3A), (3B) (reg 51(2)(d) amended, reg 51(2)(f), (g), (3A), (3B) added, regs 51(3), 51A substituted, by SI 2006/2910) (as so applied and modified).
11 Representation of the People (England and Wales) Regulations 2001, SI 2001/341, reg 51(2)(a) (as applied and modified: see note 5).
12 Representation of the People (England and Wales) Regulations 2001, SI 2001/341, reg 51(2)(b) (as amended, applied and modified: see note 5).
13 Representation of the People (England and Wales) Regulations 2001, SI 2001/341, reg 51(2)(c) (as applied and modified: see note 5).
14 Representation of the People (England and Wales) Regulations 2001, SI 2001/341, reg 51(2)(d) (as amended, applied and modified: see notes 5, 10).
15 Representation of the People (England and Wales) Regulations 2001, SI 2001/341, reg 51(2)(e) (as applied and modified: see note 5).
16 Ie under the Representation of the People Act 2000 Sch 4 para 3, 4, or 7 (as applied and modified) (see PARAS 592, 594, 600 et seq).
17 Representation of the People (England and Wales) Regulations 2001, SI 2001/341, reg 51(2)(f) (as added, applied and modified: see notes 5, 10).
18 Representation of the People (England and Wales) Regulations 2001, SI 2001/341, reg 51(2)(g) (as added, applied and modified: see notes 5, 10).
19 Representation of the People (England and Wales) Regulations 2001, SI 2001/341, reg 51(3) (as substituted, applied and modified: see notes 5, 10). In relation to England, the registration officer may satisfy himself that an application for an absent vote meets the requirement that it has been signed by the applicant by referring to any signature previously provided by the applicant to the registration officer or the counting officer: see reg 51A (as so added, substituted,

applied and modified). As to the meaning of 'counting officer' see PARA 576 note 1. As to the requirements for documents to be in writing and signed see PARA 592 note 27.

20 Representation of the People (England and Wales) Regulations 2001, SI 2001/341, reg 51(4)(a) (as applied and modified: see note 5).

21 Representation of the People (England and Wales) Regulations 2001, SI 2001/341, reg 51(4)(b) (as applied and modified: see note 5).

22 Representation of the People (England and Wales) Regulations 2001, SI 2001/341, reg 51(5)(a) (as applied and modified: see note 5).

23 Representation of the People (England and Wales) Regulations 2001, SI 2001/341, reg 51(5)(b) (as applied and modified: see note 5).

24 Representation of the People (England and Wales) Regulations 2001, SI 2001/341, reg 51(5) (as applied and modified: see note 5).

25 Representation of the People (England and Wales) Regulations 2001, SI 2001/341, reg 57(1) (as amended, applied and modified: see note 5).

26 Representation of the People (England and Wales) Regulations 2001, SI 2001/341, reg 57(4) (as applied and modified: see note 5). In the context of elections, a right of appeal lies to the county court only from certain decisions of the registration officer disallowing a person's application to vote by proxy or by post as elector: see PARA 172 et seq.

602. Record of persons entitled to vote by post as proxy at a referendum. The registration officer[1] must keep a record of those whose applications to vote by post as proxy at local authority referendums[2] (whether for an indefinite period or for a particular period specified in the application)[3] have been granted showing[4]: (1) whether their applications were to vote by post as proxy for an indefinite or a particular period (specifying that period)[5]; (2) whether the applications were in respect of referendums[6]; and (3) the addresses provided by them in their applications as the addresses to which their ballot papers are to be sent[7].

The registration officer must remove a person from the record so kept[8]: (a) if he applies to the registration officer to be removed[9], (b) if the elector[10] ceases to be registered in the register of local government electors[11][3]; (c) if the appointment of the person concerned as the elector's proxy ceases to be in force (whether or not he is re-appointed)[12]; or (d) in the case of a person who applied to vote by post as proxy for a particular period, once that period expires[13]. Where a person is removed from the record under any of heads (a) to (d) above, the registration officer must notify him of this and the reason for it[16].

1 As to the meaning of references to the registration officer for these purposes see PARA 592 note 1.

2 As to the meaning of 'referendum' see PARA 574 notes 2, 13; definition applied by virtue of the Representation of the People Act 2000 Sch 4 para 1 (Sch 4 applied and modified, in relation to Wales, by the Local Authorities (Conduct of Referendums) (Wales) Regulations 2008, SI 2008/1848, Sch 4 Table 2, and, in relation to England, by the Local Authorities (Conduct of Referendums) (England) Regulations 2012, SI 2012/323, Sch 4 Table 3). As to the provisions that are so applied and modified see PARA 15.

3 Ie a record of those whose applications have been granted under the Representation of the People Act 2000 Sch 4 para 7(4)(a) (as applied and modified) (see PARA 601). In connection with persons on the record under Sch 4 para 7(6), provision is made for the purpose of securing the provision of fresh signatures to the registration officer: see Sch 4 paras 7A, 7B (added by the Electoral Administration Act 2006 s 14(4), (8); as so applied and modified).

4 Representation of the People Act 2000 Sch 4 para 7(6) (as applied and modified: see note 2); Representation of the People (England and Wales) Regulations 2001, SI 2001/341, reg 61B (reg 57(4B) amended, reg 61B added, by SI 2006/2910) (provisions of those regulations applied and modified, in relation to Wales, by the Local Authorities (Conduct of Referendums) (Wales) Regulations 2008, SI 2008/1848, Sch 4 Table 5, and, in relation to England, by the Local Authorities (Conduct of Referendums) (England) Regulations 2012, SI 2012/323, Sch 4 Table 6). In connection with persons on the record under the Representation of the People

Act 2000 Sch 4 para 7(6)), provision is made for the purpose of securing the provision of fresh signatures to the registration officer: see Sch 4 paras 7A, 7B (as added, applied and modified: see notes 2, 3).

5   Representation of the People Act 2000 Sch 4 para 7(6)(a)(ii) (as applied and modified: see note 2).

6   Representation of the People Act 2000 Sch 4 para 7(6)(a)(i) (as applied and modified: see note 2).

7   Representation of the People Act 2000 Sch 4 para 7(6)(b) (as applied and modified: see note 2).

8   Representation of the People Act 2000 Sch 4 para 7(9) (as applied and modified: see note 2).

9   Representation of the People Act 2000 Sch 4 para 7(9)(a) (as applied and modified: see note 2). Such an application by a proxy to be removed from the record so kept must be disregarded for the purposes of a particular referendum if it is received by the registration officer after 5 pm on the eleventh day before the date of the poll at that referendum (Representation of the People (England and Wales) Regulations 2001, SI 2001/341, reg 56(5) (amended by SI 2001/1700; as applied and modified (see note 4)); and where a registration officer disregards an application for the purposes of any particular referendum, he must notify the applicant of this (see reg 57(5) (reg 57(4B) added, reg 57(5) amended, by SI 2006/752; as so applied and modified)).

10 As to the meaning of 'elector' in this context see PARA 597 note 4.

11 Representation of the People Act 2000 Sch 4 para 7(9)(b) (as applied and modified: see note 2). The text refers to registration as mentioned in Sch 4 para 7(5)(a) (as applied and modified) (see PARA 601).

12 Representation of the People Act 2000 Sch 4 para 7(9)(c) (as applied and modified: see note 2).

13 Representation of the People Act 2000 Sch 4 para 7(9)(d) (as applied and modified: see note 2).

16 Representation of the People (England and Wales) Regulations 2001, SI 2001/341, reg 57(4B) (as added, amended, applied and modified: see notes 4, 9).

603.   Application in respect of a particular referendum by a proxy entitled to vote by post for an indefinite period or for a particular period.   Where a person, who is included in the record kept of those entitled to vote by post as proxy either for an indefinite period or for a particular period[1] in respect of local authority referendums[2], applies to the registration officer[3] for his ballot paper in relation to a particular referendum to be sent to a different address from that shown in the record, the registration officer must grant the application if it meets the prescribed requirements[4].

Such an application[5] must state: (1) the full name of the applicant[6]; (2) the address in respect of which the applicant is registered or has applied to be (or is treated as having applied to be) registered in the register[7]; (3) in the case of such an application, the proxy's address, together with the name of the elector for whom he will act as proxy and the elector's address[8]; (4) in the case of a person applying to vote by post, the address to which the ballot paper should be sent[9]; (5) in the case of an application to vote by proxy, the grounds on which the elector claims to be entitled to an absent vote[10]; (6) in the case of a person who is unable to provide a signature, the reasons for his request for waiver of any requirement[11] to provide a signature and the name and address of any person who has assisted him to complete his application[12]; and (7) where the applicant has, or has applied for, an anonymous entry, that fact[13]. In relation to England, an application must also set out why the applicant's circumstances will be or are likely to be such that he requires his ballot paper to be sent to a different address from that shown in the record[14]. An application must identify the referendum in question[15] and must state that it is made for a particular referendum[16]. The application must be made in writing and must be signed and dated by the applicant[17]. Where the poll at one election or referendum falls on the same day as the poll at another election or referendum, the same application may be used for both[18].

Where the registration officer grants an application to vote by post, he must notify the applicant of his decision[19]; and where he refuses an application, he must notify the applicant of his decision and of the reason for it[20].

1   Ie a record kept under the Representation of the People Act 2000 s 12, Sch 4 para 7(6) (as applied and modified) (see PARA 602).

2   As to the meaning of 'referendum' see PARA 574 notes 2, 13; definition applied by virtue of the Representation of the People Act 2000 Sch 4 para 1 (Sch 4 applied and modified, in relation to Wales, by the Local Authorities (Conduct of Referendums) (Wales) Regulations 2008, SI 2008/1848, Sch 4 Table 2, and, in relation to England, by the Local Authorities (Conduct of Referendums) (England) Regulations 2012, SI 2012/323, Sch 4 Table 3). As to the provisions that are so applied and modified see PARA 15.

3   As to the meaning of references to the registration officer for these purposes see PARA 592 note 1.

4   Representation of the People Act 2000 Sch 4 para 7(7) (as applied and modified: see note 2). As to references to anything being prescribed see PARA 592 note 5: accordingly, the text refers to the requirements set out in the Representation of the People (England and Wales) Regulations 2001, SI 2001/341, Pt IV (regs 50–63) (provisions of those regulations applied and modified, in relation to Wales, by the Local Authorities (Conduct of Referendums) (Wales) Regulations 2008, SI 2008/1848, Sch 4 Table 5, and, in relation to England, by the Local Authorities (Conduct of Referendums) (England) Regulations 2012, SI 2012/323, Sch 4 Table 6). An application under the Representation of the People Act 2000 Sch 4 para 7(7) (as applied and modified) must be refused if it is received by the registration officer after 5 pm on the eleventh day before the date of the poll at the referendum for which it is made; and where a registration officer disregards such an application for the purposes of any particular referendum, he must notify the applicant of this: Representation of the People (England and Wales) Regulations 2001, SI 2001/341, regs 56(4), 57(5) (regs 51(2)(b), 56(4), 57(5) amended, regs 51A, 51B, 57(4A) added, by SI 2006/752; as so applied and modified). Where the registration officer grants an application under the Representation of the People Act 2000 Sch 4 para 7(7) by the person shown as voting by post in the record kept under Sch 4 para 7(6) (see PARA 602), he must notify the applicant of this: Representation of the People (England and Wales) Regulations 2001, SI 2001/341, reg 57(4A)(b) (as so added, applied and modified).

5   Applications relating to absent voting must comply with such requirements as are relevant to the application: Representation of the People (England and Wales) Regulations 2001, SI 2001/341, reg 51(1) (as applied and modified: see note 4). For detailed provision in connection with signatures and dates of birth see reg 51(3A), (3B) (regs 51(2)(d), 51B amended, reg 51(2)(f), (g), (3A), (3B) added, regs 51(3), 51A substituted, by SI 2006/2910; as so applied and modified).

6   Representation of the People (England and Wales) Regulations 2001, SI 2001/341, reg 51(2)(a) (as applied and modified: see note 4).

7   Representation of the People (England and Wales) Regulations 2001, SI 2001/341, reg 51(2)(b) (as amended, applied and modified: see note 4).

8   Representation of the People (England and Wales) Regulations 2001, SI 2001/341, reg 51(2)(c) (as applied and modified: see note 4).

9   Representation of the People (England and Wales) Regulations 2001, SI 2001/341, reg 51(2)(d) (as amended, applied and modified: see notes 4, 5).

10   Representation of the People (England and Wales) Regulations 2001, SI 2001/341, reg 51(2)(e) (as applied and modified: see note 4).

11   Ie under the Representation of the People Act 2000 Sch 4 para 3, 4, or 7 (as applied and modified) (see PARAS 592, 594, 600 et seq).

12   Representation of the People (England and Wales) Regulations 2001, SI 2001/341, reg 51(2)(f) (as added, applied and modified: see notes 4, 5).

13   Representation of the People (England and Wales) Regulations 2001, SI 2001/341, reg 51(2)(g) (as added, applied and modified: see notes 4, 5).

14   Representation of the People (England and Wales) Regulations 2001, SI 2001/341, reg 51B (as added, amended, applied and modified: see notes 4, 5).

15   Representation of the People (England and Wales) Regulations 2001, SI 2001/341, reg 51(5)(b) (as applied and modified: see note 4).

16   Representation of the People (England and Wales) Regulations 2001, SI 2001/341, reg 51(5)(a) (as applied and modified: see note 4).

17   Representation of the People (England and Wales) Regulations 2001, SI 2001/341, reg 51(3) (as substituted, applied and modified: see notes 4, 5). In relation to England, the registration officer may satisfy himself that an application for an absent vote meets the requirement that it has been

signed by the applicant by referring to any signature previously provided by the applicant to the registration officer or the counting officer: see reg 51A (as added, substituted, applied and modified: see notes 4, 5). As to the meaning of 'counting officer' see PARA 576 note 1. As to the requirements for documents to be in writing and signed see PARA 592 note 27.

18   Representation of the People (England and Wales) Regulations 2001, SI 2001/341, reg 51(5) (as applied and modified: see note 4).

19   Representation of the People (England and Wales) Regulations 2001, SI 2001/341, reg 57(4A) (as added, applied and modified: see note 4).

20   Representation of the People (England and Wales) Regulations 2001, SI 2001/341, reg 57(4) (as applied and modified: see note 4). In the context of elections, a right of appeal lies to the county court only from certain decisions of the registration officer disallowing a person's application to vote by proxy or by post as elector: see PARA 172 et seq.

604.   List of postal proxy voters at a referendum. The registration officer[1] must, in respect of each local authority referendum[2], keep a special list[3]: (1) of those who are for the time being included in the record kept of persons entitled to vote by post as proxy either for an indefinite period or for a particular period[4] in respect of referendums of the kind in question, together with the addresses provided by them in their applications[5] as the addresses to which their ballot papers are to be sent[6]; and (2) of those whose applications to vote by post as proxy at a particular referendum[7] have been granted in respect of the referendum concerned, together with the addresses provided by them in their applications as the addresses to which their ballot papers are to be sent[8]. In the case of a person who has an anonymous entry in a register the special list must contain only his electoral number and the period for which the anonymous entry has effect[9].

As soon as practicable after 5 pm on the sixth day before the day of the poll at a referendum, the registration officer must publish the list of postal proxy voters by making a copy of it available for inspection at his office[10] and any person may make a copy (whether handwritten or by other means) of the whole or any part of it[11].

1   As to the meaning of references to the registration officer for these purposes see PARA 592 note 1.

2   As to the meaning of 'referendum' see PARA 574 notes 2, 13; definition applied by virtue of the Representation of the People Act 2000 Sch 4 para 1 (Sch 4 applied and modified, in relation to Wales, by the Local Authorities (Conduct of Referendums) (Wales) Regulations 2008, SI 2008/1848, Sch 4 Table 2, and, in relation to England, by the Local Authorities (Conduct of Referendums) (England) Regulations 2012, SI 2012/323, Sch 4 Table 3). As to the provisions that are so applied and modified see PARA 15.

3   Representation of the People Act 2000 Sch 4 para 7(8) (Sch 4 para 7(8) amended, Sch 4 para 7(8A) added, by the Electoral Administration Act 2006 Sch 1 paras 23, 137) (as applied and modified: see note 2).

4   Ie a record kept under the Representation of the People Act 2000 Sch 4 para 7(6) (as applied and modified) (see PARA 602).

5   Ie applications made under the Representation of the People Act 2000 Sch 4 para 7(4)(a) (as applied and modified) (see PARA 601) or, as the case may be, under Sch 4 para 7(7) (as applied and modified) (see PARA 603).

6   Representation of the People Act 2000 Sch 4 para 7(8)(a) (as amended, applied and modified: see notes 2, 3).

7   Ie a record of those whose applications have been granted under the Representation of the People Act 2000 Sch 4 para 7(4)(b) (as applied and modified) (see PARA 601).

8   Representation of the People Act 2000 Sch 4 para 7(8)(b) (as amended, applied and modified: see notes 2, 3).

9   Representation of the People Act 2000 Sch 4 para 7(8A) (as added, applied and modified: see notes 2, 3).

10   Representation of the People (England and Wales) Regulations 2001, SI 2001/341, reg 61(6)(a) (reg 61 substituted by SI 2006/2910) (provisions of those regulations applied and modified, in relation to Wales, by the Local Authorities (Conduct of Referendums) (Wales) Regulations 2008,

SI 2008/1848, Sch 4 Table 5, and, in relation to England, by the Local Authorities (Conduct of Referendums) (England) Regulations 2012, SI 2012/323, Sch 4 Table 6).

11 Representation of the People (England and Wales) Regulations 2001, SI 2001/341, reg 7(1) (renumbered by SI 2002/1871) (as applied and modified: see note 10).

605. Voting by post as proxy at referendum. If a person is entitled to vote as proxy at a local authority referendum[1] (by being included in the relevant list[2] in respect of that referendum) he may vote by post[3]. Where a person is entitled to vote by post as proxy for the elector[4] at any referendum, the elector may not apply for a ballot paper for the purpose of voting in person at the referendum[5].

2 As to the meaning of 'referendum' see PARA 574 notes 2, 13; definition applied by virtue of the Representation of the People Act 2000 Sch 4 para 1 (Sch 4 applied and modified, in relation to Wales, by the Local Authorities (Conduct of Referendums) (Wales) Regulations 2008, SI 2008/1848, Sch 4 Table 2, and, in relation to England, by the Local Authorities (Conduct of Referendums) (England) Regulations 2012, SI 2012/323, Sch 4 Table 3). As to the provisions that are so applied and modified see PARA 15. As to the entitlement to vote as proxy at a local authority referendum see PARA 597 et seq.

2 Ie the list kept under the Representation of the People Act 2000 Sch 4 para 7(8) (as applied and modified) (see PARA 604).

3 Representation of the People Act 2000 Sch 4 para 7(1), (3) (as applied and modified: see note 1).

4 As to the meaning of 'elector' in this context see PARA 597 note 4.

5 Representation of the People Act 2000 Sch 4 para 7(2) (as applied and modified: see note 1). To indicate that an elector or his proxy is entitled to vote by post and is for that reason not entitled to vote in person, the letter 'A' is placed against the name of that elector in any copy of the register, or part of it, provided for a polling station: Representation of the People (England and Wales) Regulations 2001, SI 2001/341, reg 62 (amended by SI 2006/2910) (provisions of those regulations applied and modified, in relation to Wales, by the Local Authorities (Conduct of Referendums) (Wales) Regulations 2008, SI 2008/1848, Sch 4 Table 5, and, in relation to England, by the Local Authorities (Conduct of Referendums) (England) Regulations 2012, SI 2012/323, Sch 4 Table 6).

D. POLLING

(A) In general

606. Poll at referendum or poll to be taken by secret ballot. The votes at a local authority referendum[1] or at a poll consequent on a parish or community meeting[2] must be given by ballot[3]. A person who has voted at the poll is not required, in any legal proceedings to question the poll, to state how or for whom he has voted[4].

The counting officer at a local authority referendum[5] or the returning officer at a poll consequent on a parish or community meeting[6] must make such arrangements as he thinks fit to ensure that: (1) every person attending at a polling station (otherwise than for the purpose of voting or assisting a blind voter to vote[7] or as a constable on duty there)[8]; and (2) every person attending at the counting of the votes (otherwise than as a constable on duty at the counting)[9], has been given a copy in writing of the statutory provisions relating to the requirement of secrecy that apply to attendance at a polling station or at the counting of votes (as the case may be)[10].

1 As to the meaning of 'referendum' for these purposes see PARA 574 notes 2, 13.

2 As to how polls consequent on a parish or community meeting come about see PARA 581.

3 See the Local Government Act 1972 Sch 12 paras 18(5), 34(5); and LOCAL GOVERNMENT vol 69 (2009) PARA 638.

4 Parish and Community Meetings (Polls) Rules 1987, SI 1987/1, r 5, Schedule r 6; Local Authorities (Conduct of Referendums) (Wales) Regulations 2008, SI 2008/1848, Sch 3 r 10; Local Authorities (Conduct of Referendums) (England) Regulations 2012, SI 2012/323, Sch 3 r 10.

5   As to the meaning of 'counting officer' see PARA 576 note 1.
6   As to returning officers at polls consequent on a parish or community meeting see PARA 588.
7   As to persons assisting voters on the grounds of blindness or other physical incapacity see PARA 623.
8   Parish and Community Meetings (Polls) Rules 1987, SI 1987/1, Schedule r 13(a); Local Authorities (Conduct of Referendums) (Wales) Regulations 2008, SI 2008/1848, Sch 3 r 19(a); Local Authorities (Conduct of Referendums) (England) Regulations 2012, SI 2012/323, Sch 3 r 19(a). As to constables on duty see PARA 618.
9   Parish and Community Meetings (Polls) Rules 1987, SI 1987/1, Schedule r 13(b); Local Authorities (Conduct of Referendums) (Wales) Regulations 2008, SI 2008/1848, Sch 3 r 19(b); Local Authorities (Conduct of Referendums) (England) Regulations 2012, SI 2012/323, Sch 3 r 19(b).
10 Parish and Community Meetings (Polls) Rules 1987, SI 1987/1, Schedule r 13(a), (b); Local Authorities (Conduct of Referendums) (Wales) Regulations 2008, SI 2008/1848, Sch 3 r 19(a), (b); Local Authorities (Conduct of Referendums) (England) Regulations 2012, SI 2012/323, Sch 3 r 19(a), (b). The text refers to: (1) for the purposes of those attending at a polling station, the requirement of secrecy set out in the Representation of the People Act 1983 s 66(1), (3), (6) (see PARAS 739, 741); and (2) for the purposes of those attending the counting of the votes, the requirement of secrecy set out in s 66(2), (6) (see PARA 740). At a poll consequent on a parish or community meeting, the provisions relating to the requirement of secrecy are subject to the adaptations, alterations and exceptions in the Parish and Community Meetings (Polls) Rules 1987, SI 1987/1, r 6(e) (Schedule r 13(a)); and in relation to a local authority referendum those provisions are subject to the adaptations, alterations and exceptions in the Local Authorities (Conduct of Referendums) (Wales) Regulations 2008, SI 2008/1848, Sch 4 Table 1, or in the Local Authorities (Conduct of Referendums) (England) Regulations 2012, SI 2012/323, Sch 4 Table 1, as the case may be (Local Authorities (Conduct of Referendums) (Wales) Regulations 2008, SI 2008/1848, Sch 3 r 19; Local Authorities (Conduct of Referendums) (England) Regulations 2012, SI 2012/323, Sch 3 r 19).

607.   The ballot papers and the official mark used at referendum or poll.   The ballot of every voter at a local authority referendum[1] or at a poll consequent on a parish or community meeting[2] consists of a ballot paper, which must be in the prescribed form[3]. Every such ballot paper: (1) must be capable of being folded up[4]; and (2) must have a number printed on the back[5]. Ballot papers must be security marked[6].

1   As to the meaning of 'referendum' for these purposes see PARA 574 notes 2, 13.
2   As to how polls consequent on a parish or community meeting come about see PARA 581.
3   Parish and Community Meetings (Polls) Rules 1987, SI 1987/1, r 5, Schedule r 4(1), (2); Local Authorities (Conduct of Referendums) (Wales) Regulations 2008, SI 2008/1848, Sch 3 r 7(1); Local Authorities (Conduct of Referendums) (England) Regulations 2012, SI 2012/323, Sch 3 r 7(1).
      As to the form of ballot paper appropriate to a poll consequent on a parish or community meeting as mentioned in the text see the Parish and Community Meetings (Polls) Rules 1987, SI 1987/1, Schedule Appendix of Forms (Form of ballot papers on a question other than that of appointment to an office). Where such a poll is taken on any question other than appointment to any office, every ballot paper must state the question or questions on which the poll is to be taken: Schedule r 4(2)(b). The question or questions must appear in the space indicated in the form set out in Schedule Appendix (Form of ballot papers on a question other than that of appointment to an office). The ballot papers at such a poll must be printed in accordance with the prescribed directions: Schedule r 4(2). As to the directions so prescribed see Schedule Appendix of Forms (Directions as to printing the ballot paper). Where a poll on the question of appointment to any office and a poll on any other question are taken together, ballot papers of a different colour must be used for each poll: Schedule r 4(3). As to polls consequent on a parish meeting involving a question of appointment to any office see PARA 200.
4   Parish and Community Meetings (Polls) Rules 1987, SI 1987/1, r 5, Schedule r 4(2)(c); Local Authorities (Conduct of Referendums) (Wales) Regulations 2008, SI 2008/1848, Sch 3 r 7(3)(a); Local Authorities (Conduct of Referendums) (England) Regulations 2012, SI 2012/323, Sch 3 r 7(3)(a).
5   Parish and Community Meetings (Polls) Rules 1987, SI 1987/1, r 5, Schedule r 4(2)(d); Local Authorities (Conduct of Referendums) (Wales) Regulations 2008, SI 2008/1848, Sch 3 r 7(3)(b); Local Authorities (Conduct of Referendums) (England) Regulations 2012, SI 2012/323, Sch 3

r 7(3)(b). Where the poll is governed by the Local Authorities (Conduct of Referendums) (Wales) Regulations 2008, SI 2008/1848, or the Local Authorities (Conduct of Referendums) (England) Regulations 2012, SI 2012/323, the ballot paper must also have another unique identifying mark printed on the back along with the number: Local Authorities (Conduct of Referendums) (Wales) Regulations 2008, SI 2008/1848, Sch 3 r 7(3)(b); Local Authorities (Conduct of Referendums) (England) Regulations 2012, SI 2012/323, Sch 3 r 7(3)(b). Where the poll is governed by the Parish and Community Meetings (Polls) Rules 1987, SI 1987/1, the ballot paper must also have attached a counterfoil with the number printed on it: Schedule r 4(2)(e)).

6   See the Parish and Community Meetings (Polls) Rules 1987, SI 1987/1, Schedule r 5; the Local Authorities (Conduct of Referendums) (Wales) Regulations 2008, SI 2008/1848, Sch 3 r 9; and the Local Authorities (Conduct of Referendums) (England) Regulations 2012, SI 2012/323, Sch 3 r 9.

608.   Notice of poll at referendum or poll.   Not later than the sixth day before the date of the local authority referendum[1] and not later than the fifth day before the day of the poll at a poll consequent on a parish or community meeting[2], the returning officer at such a poll[3] or the counting officer at such a referendum[4] must give public notice of the poll[5] which states[6]: (1) the day and hours fixed for the poll[7]; (2) the question to be asked (and, where applicable, particulars relating to the candidate or office)[8]; and (3) the situation of each polling station and the description of the persons entitled to vote there[9].

1   As to the meaning of 'referendum' for these purposes see PARA 574 notes 2, 13.

2   Parish and Community Meetings (Polls) Rules 1987, SI 1987/1, r 5, Schedule r 1. As to the computation of any period of time for these purposes see PARA 212 note 5. As to how polls consequent on a parish or community meeting come about see PARA 581.

3   As to returning officers at polls consequent on a parish or community meeting see PARA 588.

4   As to the meaning of 'counting officer' see PARA 576 note 1.

5   At a poll consequent on a parish or community meeting, the notice referred to in the text must refer to the parish or community meeting at which a poll was demanded: Parish and Community Meetings (Polls) Rules 1987, SI 1987/1, Schedule r 8.

6   Parish and Community Meetings (Polls) Rules 1987, SI 1987/1, Schedule r 8; Local Authorities (Conduct of Referendums) (Wales) Regulations 2008, SI 2008/1848, Sch 3 r 12(1), (2); Local Authorities (Conduct of Referendums) (England) Regulations 2012, SI 2012/323, Sch 3 r 12(1), (2).

7   Parish and Community Meetings (Polls) Rules 1987, SI 1987/1, Schedule r 8(a); Local Authorities (Conduct of Referendums) (Wales) Regulations 2008, SI 2008/1848, Sch 3 r 12(1)(a); Local Authorities (Conduct of Referendums) (England) Regulations 2012, SI 2012/323, Sch 3 r 12(1)(a). As to the date of a local authority referendum see PARA 576; and as to the day of a poll consequent on a parish or community meeting taken on any question see PARA 582.

8   Parish and Community Meetings (Polls) Rules 1987, SI 1987/1, Schedule r 8(b), (c); Local Authorities (Conduct of Referendums) (Wales) Regulations 2008, SI 2008/1848, Sch 3 r 12(1)(b); Local Authorities (Conduct of Referendums) (England) Regulations 2012, SI 2012/323, Sch 3 r 12(1)(b). At a poll consequent on a parish or community meeting, head (2) in the text applies only if the poll is taken on any question other than appointment to any office; and, in such a case, the name and address of the proposer of the resolution in respect of which the poll is being taken must be specified along with the particulars of the question: Parish and Community Meetings (Polls) Rules 1987, SI 1987/1, Schedule r 8(c). As to polls consequent on a parish meeting involving a question of appointment to any office see PARA 200.

9   Parish and Community Meetings (Polls) Rules 1987, SI 1987/1, Schedule r 8(d); Local Authorities (Conduct of Referendums) (Wales) Regulations 2008, SI 2008/1848, Sch 3 r 12(3); Local Authorities (Conduct of Referendums) (England) Regulations 2012, SI 2012/323, Sch 3 r 12(3).

609.   Issue of official poll cards at referendum.   The counting officer at a local authority referendum[1] must, as soon as practicable after the publication of the notice of the referendum, send to electors and their proxies an official poll card[2].

The official poll card must be sent or delivered to the voter's[3] qualifying address (in the case of a voter) and to the proxy's address as shown in the list of proxies (in the case of a proxy)[4].

1   As to the meaning of 'counting officer' see PARA 576 note 1; and as to the meaning of 'referendum' for these purposes see PARA 574 notes 2, 13.

2   Local Authorities (Conduct of Referendums) (Wales) Regulations 2008, SI 2008/1848, Sch 3 r 16(1); Local Authorities (Conduct of Referendums) (England) Regulations 2012, SI 2012/323, Sch 3 r 16(1). The official poll card must be in the appropriate form in the Local Authorities (Conduct of Referendums) (Wales) Regulations 2008, SI 2008/1848, Sch 3 Appendix, or in the Local Authorities (Conduct of Referendums) (England) Regulations 2012, SI 2012/323, Sch 3 Appendix, as the case may be, or a form to the like effect, and must set out the name of the council and of the voting area, the name of the voter, the voter's qualifying address and number on the register, the date and hours of the poll and the situation of the voter's polling station (or, in the case of a voter who has an anonymous entry in the register, such matter as is specified in the appropriate form in the Local Authorities (Conduct of Referendums) (Wales) Regulations 2008, SI 2008/1848, Sch 3 Appendix, or in the Local Authorities (Conduct of Referendums) (England) Regulations 2012, SI 2012/323, Sch 3 Appendix, as the case may be), and such other information as the counting officer thinks appropriate (and that other information may be provided to different voters or to different descriptions of voter): Local Authorities (Conduct of Referendums) (Wales) Regulations 2008, SI 2008/1848, Sch 3 r 16(3), (4); Local Authorities (Conduct of Referendums) (England) Regulations 2012, SI 2012/323, Sch 3 r 16(3), (4). As to publication of the notice of the referendum see PARA 576. There is no provision for poll cards to be issued for the purposes of a poll consequent on a parish or community meeting (as to which see generally PARA 581 et seq).

3   In the Local Authorities (Conduct of Referendums) (Wales) Regulations 2008, SI 2008/1848, Sch 3 r 16, and the Local Authorities (Conduct of Referendums) (England) Regulations 2012, SI 2012/323, Sch 3 r 16, references to a voter are to a person who is registered in the register of local government electors for the voting area in question on the last day for the publication of notice of the referendum and include a person then shown in the register as below voting age if (but only if) it appears from the register that the person will be of voting age on the day fixed for the poll: Local Authorities (Conduct of Referendums) (Wales) Regulations 2008, SI 2008/1848, Sch 3 r 16(5); Local Authorities (Conduct of Referendums) (England) Regulations 2012, SI 2012/323, Sch 3 r 16(5). As to the register of local government electors see PARA 145 et seq.

4   Local Authorities (Conduct of Referendums) (Wales) Regulations 2008, SI 2008/1848, Sch 3 r 16(2); Local Authorities (Conduct of Referendums) (England) Regulations 2012, SI 2012/323, Sch 3 r 16(2).

(B) Votes given for Referendum or Poll at Polling Station

610. Provision and allotment of polling stations for use at referendum or poll.
The counting officer at a local authority referendum[1] or the returning officer at a poll consequent on a parish or community meeting[2] must provide a sufficient number of polling stations[3] and allot the electors or voters to the polling stations in such manner as he thinks most convenient, subject to the following requirements[4]. The polling station allotted to electors from any parliamentary polling district[5] wholly or partly within the electoral area[6] (in the case of such a referendum) or within the parish or community[7] (in the case of such a poll) must, in the absence of special circumstances, be in the parliamentary polling place for that district[8]. One or more polling stations may be provided in the same room[9]. However, the counting officer or returning officer (as the case may be) must also provide each polling station with such number of compartments as may be necessary in which the voters can mark their votes screened from observation[10].

The counting officer or returning officer (as the case may be) may use free of charge for the purpose of taking the poll or counting the votes: (1) a room in a school maintained or assisted by a local education authority[11] or a school in respect of which grants are made out of moneys provided by Parliament (or, as the case may be, the Welsh Ministers), to the person or body of persons responsible for the management of the school[12]; or (2) a room the expense of maintaining which is payable out of any rate[13]. The counting officer or returning officer (as the case may be) must make good any damage done to, and defray any expense incurred by the persons having control over, any such room by reason of its being used for the purpose of taking the poll or counting the votes[14].

1　As to the meaning of 'counting officer' see PARA 576 note 1; and as to the meaning of 'referendum' for these purposes see PARA 574 notes 2, 13.
2　As to how polls consequent on a parish or community meeting come about see PARA 581; and as to returning officers appointed at polls consequent on a parish or community meeting see PARA 588.
3　Ie, at a poll consequent on a parish or community meeting, if more than one polling station is provided: Parish and Community Meetings (Polls) Rules 1987, SI 1987/1, r 5, Schedule r 9(1).
4　Parish and Community Meetings (Polls) Rules 1987, SI 1987/1, Schedule r 9(1); Local Authorities (Conduct of Referendums) (Wales) Regulations 2008, SI 2008/1848, Sch 3 r 14(1); Local Authorities (Conduct of Referendums) (England) Regulations 2012, SI 2012/323, Sch 3 r 14(1).
5　As to parliamentary polling districts see PARA 343 et seq.
6　As to the meaning of 'electoral area' see PARA 11.
7　As to parishes generally see LOCAL GOVERNMENT vol 69 (2009) PARA 27 et seq; and as to communities generally see LOCAL GOVERNMENT vol 69 (2009) PARA 41 et seq.
8　Parish and Community Meetings (Polls) Rules 1987, SI 1987/1, Schedule r 9(3); Local Authorities (Conduct of Referendums) (Wales) Regulations 2008, SI 2008/1848, Sch 3 r 14(3); Local Authorities (Conduct of Referendums) (England) Regulations 2012, SI 2012/323, Sch 3 r 14(3).
9　Parish and Community Meetings (Polls) Rules 1987, SI 1987/1, Schedule r 9(2); Local Authorities (Conduct of Referendums) (Wales) Regulations 2008, SI 2008/1848, Sch 3 r 14(2); Local Authorities (Conduct of Referendums) (England) Regulations 2012, SI 2012/323, Sch 3 r 14(2).
10　Parish and Community Meetings (Polls) Rules 1987, SI 1987/1, Schedule r 9(4); Local Authorities (Conduct of Referendums) (Wales) Regulations 2008, SI 2008/1848, Sch 3 r 14(4); Local Authorities (Conduct of Referendums) (England) Regulations 2012, SI 2012/323, Sch 3 r 14(4).
11　As to local education authorities see EDUCATION vol 35 (2011) PARA 24 et seq.
12　Parish and Community Meetings (Polls) Rules 1987, SI 1987/1, Schedule r 7(1)(a); Local Authorities (Conduct of Referendums) (Wales) Regulations 2008, SI 2008/1848, Sch 3 r 11(1)(a); Local Authorities (Conduct of Referendums) (England) Regulations 2012, SI 2012/323, Sch 3 r 11(1)(a).
13　Parish and Community Meetings (Polls) Rules 1987, SI 1987/1, Schedule r 7(1)(b); Local Authorities (Conduct of Referendums) (Wales) Regulations 2008, SI 2008/1848, Sch 3 r 11(1)(b); Local Authorities (Conduct of Referendums) (England) Regulations 2012, SI 2012/323, Sch 3 r 11(1)(b). For the purposes of a poll consequent on a parish or community meeting the use of a room in an unoccupied house for any of these purposes does not render a person liable to be rated or to pay any rate for the house: Parish and Community Meetings (Polls) Rules 1987, SI 1987/1, Schedule r 7(3).
14　Parish and Community Meetings (Polls) Rules 1987, SI 1987/1, Schedule r 7(2); Local Authorities (Conduct of Referendums) (Wales) Regulations 2008, SI 2008/1848, Sch 3 r 11(2); Local Authorities (Conduct of Referendums) (England) Regulations 2012, SI 2012/323, Sch 3 r 11(2).

611.　Equipment of polling stations. The counting officer at a local authority referendum[1] or the returning officer at a poll consequent on a parish or community meeting[2] must provide each presiding officer[3] with such number of ballot boxes and ballot papers as in the counting officer's or returning officer's opinion (as the case may be) may be necessary[4]. Every ballot box must be so constructed that the ballot papers can be put in it, but cannot be withdrawn from it, without the box being unlocked (or, in the case of a local authority referendum, where the box has no lock, without the seal being broken)[5].

The counting officer or returning officer (as the case may be) also must provide each polling station[6] with:

(1)   materials to enable voters (and, in the case of a local authority referendum, proxies) to mark the ballot papers[7];

(2)   in the case of a parish or community poll, instruments for stamping on them the official mark[8];

(3)   copies of the register of electors for the electoral area[9] (in the case of such a referendum) or for the parish or community[10] (in the case of such a poll) or such part of it as contains the names of the electors allotted to the station[11]; and

(4)   (in the case of a referendum) the parts of any special lists[12] prepared for the referendum corresponding to the register of electors or the part of it provided under head (3) above[13].

A notice in the specified form, giving directions for the guidance of the voters (and, in the case of a local authority referendum, proxies) in voting[14], must be printed in conspicuous characters and exhibited inside and outside every polling station[15]. In the case of a referendum, there must also be in each polling station: (a) at least one large version of the ballot paper, provided by the presiding officer and displayed for the assistance of voters and proxies who are partially-sighted[16]; (b) a device for enabling voters and proxies who are blind or partially sighted to vote without any need for assistance from the presiding officer or any companion[17]; and (c) in every compartment of every polling station[18] there must be exhibited a notice which instructs voters on the voting procedure[19].

1   As to the meaning of 'counting officer' see PARA 576 note 1; and as to the meaning of 'referendum' for these purposes see PARA 574 notes 2, 13.

2   As to how polls consequent on a parish or community meeting come about see PARA 581; and as to returning officers appointed at polls consequent on a parish or community meeting see PARA 588.

3   As to the appointment of presiding officers and their clerks see PARA 613.

4   Parish and Community Meetings (Polls) Rules 1987, SI 1987/1, Schedule r 11(1); Local Authorities (Conduct of Referendums) (Wales) Regulations 2008, SI 2008/1848, Sch 3 r 17(1); Local Authorities (Conduct of Referendums) (England) Regulations 2012, SI 2012/323, Sch 3 r 17(1).

       The counting officer must prepare a list containing the numbers and other unique identifying marks of all of the ballot papers to be provided by the counting officer in pursuance of the Local Authorities (Conduct of Referendums) (Wales) Regulations 2008, SI 2008/1848, Sch 3 r 17(1), or the Local Authorities (Conduct of Referendums) (England) Regulations 2012, SI 2012/323, Sch 3 r 17(1), as the case may be, and the list must be in the appropriate form or a form to like effect: Local Authorities (Conduct of Referendums) (Wales) Regulations 2008, SI 2008/1848, Sch 3 r 8(1), (2); Local Authorities (Conduct of Referendums) (England) Regulations 2012, SI 2012/323, Sch 3 r 8(1), (2). As to the appropriate form see the Local Authorities (Conduct of Referendums) (Wales) Regulations 2008, SI 2008/1848, Pt 8 Appendix of Forms (Corresponding Number List L1), and the Local Authorities (Conduct of Referendums) (England) Regulations 2012, SI 2012/323, Pt 8 Appendix of Forms (Corresponding Number List L1). The presiding officer must keep a list of persons to whom ballot papers are delivered in consequence of an alteration to the register made by virtue of the Representation of the People Act 1983 s 13B(3B) or s 13(3D) (notices specifying appropriate alterations to the register: see PARA 168) (applied and modified, in relation to Wales, by the Local Authorities (Conduct of Referendums) (Wales) Regulations 2008, SI 2008/1848, Sch 4 Table 1, and, in relation to England, by the Local Authorities (Conduct of Referendums) (England) Regulations 2012, SI 2012/323, Sch 4 Table 1: see PARA 15) which takes effect on the day of the poll: Local Authorities (Conduct of Referendums) (Wales) Regulations 2008, SI 2008/1848, Sch 3 r 32; Local Authorities (Conduct of Referendums) (England) Regulations 2012, SI 2012/323, Sch 3 r 32.

5   Parish and Community Meetings (Polls) Rules 1987, SI 1987/1, Schedule r 11(2); Local Authorities (Conduct of Referendums) (Wales) Regulations 2008, SI 2008/1848, Sch 3 r 17(2); Local Authorities (Conduct of Referendums) (England) Regulations 2012, SI 2012/323, Sch 3 r 17(2).

6   As to the provision and allotment of polling stations see PARA 610.
7   Parish and Community Meetings (Polls) Rules 1987, SI 1987/1, Schedule r 11(3)(a); Local
     Authorities (Conduct of Referendums) (Wales) Regulations 2008, SI 2008/1848, Sch 3
     r 17(3)(a); Local Authorities (Conduct of Referendums) (England) Regulations 2012,
     SI 2012/323, Sch 3 r 17(3)(a).
8   Parish and Community Meetings (Polls) Rules 1987, SI 1987/1, Schedule r 11(3)(b).
9   As to the meaning of 'electoral area' see PARA 11.
10   As to parishes generally see LOCAL GOVERNMENT vol 69 (2009) PARA 27 et seq; and as to
     communities generally see LOCAL GOVERNMENT vol 69 (2009) PARA 41 et seq.
11   Parish and Community Meetings (Polls) Rules 1987, SI 1987/1, Schedule r 11(3)(c); Local
     Authorities (Conduct of Referendums) (Wales) Regulations 2008, SI 2008/1848, Sch 3
     r 17(3)(b), (4); Local Authorities (Conduct of Referendums) (England) Regulations 2012,
     SI 2012/323, Sch 3 r 17(3)(b), (4).
12   As to the special lists referred to in the text see PARA 596.
13   Local Authorities (Conduct of Referendums) (Wales) Regulations 2008, SI 2008/1848, Sch 3
     r 17(3)(c), (d); Local Authorities (Conduct of Referendums) (England) Regulations 2012,
     SI 2012/323, Sch 3 r 17(3)(c), (d).
14   As to the form giving directions for the guidance of the voters in voting see the Parish and
     Community Meetings (Polls) Rules 1987, SI 1987/1, Schedule Appendix; Local Authorities
     (Conduct of Referendums) (Wales) Regulations 2008, SI 2008/1848, Sch 3 Appendix; Local
     Authorities (Conduct of Referendums) (England) Regulations 2012, SI 2012/323, Sch 3
     Appendix.
15   Parish and Community Meetings (Polls) Rules 1987, SI 1987/1, Schedule r 11(4); Local
     Authorities (Conduct of Referendums) (Wales) Regulations 2008, SI 2008/1848, Sch 3 r 17(6);
     Local Authorities (Conduct of Referendums) (England) Regulations 2012, SI 2012/323, Sch 3
     r 17(6). In the case of a referendum, provision is made for this form to be translated or produced
     in Braille: see the Local Authorities (Conduct of Referendums) (Wales) Regulations 2008,
     SI 2008/1848, Sch 3 r 17(7); and the Local Authorities (Conduct of Referendums) (England)
     Regulations 2012, SI 2012/323, Sch 3 r 17(7).
16   Local Authorities (Conduct of Referendums) (Wales) Regulations 2008, SI 2008/1848, Sch 3
     r 17(5)(a); Local Authorities (Conduct of Referendums) (England) Regulations 2012,
     SI 2012/323, Sch 3 r 17(5)(a).
17   See the Local Authorities (Conduct of Referendums) (Wales) Regulations 2008, SI 2008/1848,
     Sch 3 r 17(5)(b), (9); and the Local Authorities (Conduct of Referendums) (England)
     Regulations 2012, SI 2012/323, Sch 3 r 17(5)(b), (9).
18   As to the provision of compartments in polling stations see PARA 610.
19   See the Local Authorities (Conduct of Referendums) (Wales) Regulations 2008, SI 2008/1848,
     Sch 3 r 17(8); and the Local Authorities (Conduct of Referendums) (England) Regulations 2012,
     SI 2012/323, Sch 3 r 17(8).

612.   Loan of equipment provided for referendum or poll.   Any ballot boxes,
fittings and compartments provided for parliamentary elections[1] out of money
provided by Parliament may, on request, be lent to: (1) the counting officer at a
local authority referendum[2]; or (2) the returning officer at a poll consequent on a
parish or community meeting[3], on such terms and conditions as the Secretary of
State (or, as from a day to be appointed, the Electoral Commission) may
determine[4]. Any ballot boxes, fittings and compartments provided by, or
belonging to, a local authority within the meaning of the Local Government
Act 1972[5], must, on request, and if not required for immediate use by that
authority, be lent to such a counting officer or such a returning officer (as the
case may be) on such terms and conditions as may be agreed[6].

1   As to the equipment of polling stations for parliamentary elections see PARA 391.
2   As to the meaning of 'counting officer' see PARA 576 note 1; and as to the meaning of
     'referendum' for these purposes see PARA 574 notes 2, 13.
3   As to how polls consequent on a parish or community meeting come about see PARA 581; and as
     to returning officers appointed at polls consequent on a parish or community meeting see PARA
     588.
4   Local Government Act 1972 Sch 12 para 21(1); Representation of the People Act 1983 s 47(1)
     (amended by the Political Parties, Elections and Referendums Act 2000 Sch 21 para 6; and

SI 1991/1728). The provisions of the Representation of the People Act 1983 s 47(1) are applied and modified, in relation to Wales, by the Local Authorities (Conduct of Referendums) (Wales) Regulations 2008, SI 2008/1848, Sch 4 Table 1, and, in relation to England, by the Local Authorities (Conduct of Referendums) (England) Regulations 2012, SI 2012/323, Sch 4 Table 1. As to the provisions that are so applied and modified see PARA 15. As to the Secretary of State see PARA 2.

5   As to the meaning of 'local authority' for these purposes see LOCAL GOVERNMENT vol 69 (2009) PARA 23.

6   Local Government Act 1972 Sch 12 para 21(2) (as applied and modified: see note 4); Representation of the People Act 1983 s 47(2) (amended by the Local Government Act 1985 Sch 9 para 1(7)) (as so applied and modified).

613.   Appointment of presiding officers and clerks at referendum or poll.   The counting officer at a local authority referendum[1] or the returning officer at a poll consequent on a parish or community meeting[2] must appoint and pay[3] a presiding officer to attend at each polling station[4]. He must also appoint and pay such clerks as may be necessary for the purposes of the poll or referendum[5]. The counting officer or returning officer (as the case may be) may, if he thinks fit, preside at a polling station[6].

A presiding officer may do, by the clerks appointed to assist him, any act (including the asking of questions) which he is required or authorised to do at a polling station except order the arrest, exclusion or removal of any person from the polling station[7].

1   As to the meaning of 'counting officer' see PARA 576 note 1; and as to the meaning of 'referendum' for these purposes see PARA 574 notes 2, 13.

2   As to how polls consequent on a parish or community meeting come about see PARA 581; and as to returning officers appointed at polls consequent on a parish or community meeting see PARA 588.

3   At a poll consequent on a parish or community meeting, the remuneration of a presiding officer and clerks is discretionary: Parish and Community Meetings (Polls) Rules 1987, SI 1987/1, Schedule r 10(1).

4   Parish and Community Meetings (Polls) Rules 1987, SI 1987/1, Schedule r 10(1); Local Authorities (Conduct of Referendums) (Wales) Regulations 2008, SI 2008/1848, Sch 3 r 15(1); Local Authorities (Conduct of Referendums) (England) Regulations 2012, SI 2012/323, Sch 3 r 15(1).

5   Parish and Community Meetings (Polls) Rules 1987, SI 1987/1, Schedule r 10(1); Local Authorities (Conduct of Referendums) (Wales) Regulations 2008, SI 2008/1848, Sch 3 r 15(1); Local Authorities (Conduct of Referendums) (England) Regulations 2012, SI 2012/323, Sch 3 r 15(1).

6   Parish and Community Meetings (Polls) Rules 1987, SI 1987/1, Schedule r 10(2); Local Authorities (Conduct of Referendums) (Wales) Regulations 2008, SI 2008/1848, Sch 3 r 15(2); Local Authorities (Conduct of Referendums) (England) Regulations 2012, SI 2012/323, Sch 3 r 15(2). The provisions relating to a presiding officer apply to a counting officer or returning officer (as the case may be) so presiding with the necessary modifications as to things to be done by the counting officer or returning officer to the presiding officer or by the presiding officer to the counting officer or returning officer: Parish and Community Meetings (Polls) Rules 1987, SI 1987/1, Schedule r 10(2); Local Authorities (Conduct of Referendums) (Wales) Regulations 2008, SI 2008/1848, Sch 3 r 15(2); Local Authorities (Conduct of Referendums) (England) Regulations 2012, SI 2012/323, Sch 3 r 15(2).

7   Parish and Community Meetings (Polls) Rules 1987, SI 1987/1, Schedule r 10(3); Local Authorities (Conduct of Referendums) (Wales) Regulations 2008, SI 2008/1848, Sch 3 r 15(3); Local Authorities (Conduct of Referendums) (England) Regulations 2012, SI 2012/323, Sch 3 r 15(3).

614.   Appointments for the counting of votes at referendum or poll.   The counting officer at a local authority referendum[1] may appoint persons to attend at polling stations for the purpose of detecting personation ('polling observers')[2] and must appoint persons to observe the counting of the votes and the verification of the ballot paper account ('counting observers')[3]. For the purpose of assisting the counting officer in the discharge of the his functions relating to the appointment of counting observers[4], a petition organiser[5] may nominate persons who in the opinion of the petition organiser are suitable for appointment as counting observers[6]. The counting officer must not, without good cause, decline to appoint as a counting observer a person nominated[7] by a petition organiser[8], although he may, within restrictions, limit the number of observers so appointed[9]. Where a counting observer appointed on the nomination of a petition organiser dies or becomes incapable of acting, the petition organiser who made the nomination may nominate another person to be appointed as a counting observer in that person's place by giving notice in writing to the counting officer[10].

Any notice required to be given by the counting officer to a counting observer appointed on the nomination of a petition organiser may be delivered at, or sent by post to, the address stated in the notice of nomination[11]. A petition organiser may do any act or thing which any counting observer is authorised to do, or may assist any counting observer appointed on that person's nomination in doing any such act or thing[12]. Where any act or thing is required or authorised to be done[13] in the presence of the polling observers or counting observers, the non-attendance of any such person at the time and place appointed for the purpose does not, if the act or thing is otherwise duly done, invalidate the act or thing done[14].

1 As to the meaning of 'counting officer' see PARA 576 note 1; and as to the meaning of 'referendum' for these purposes see PARA 574 notes 2, 13. As to the facility afforded to candidates to appoint counting agents at a poll consequent on a parish meeting on a question of appointment to any office see the Parish and Community Meetings (Polls) Rules 1987, SI 1987/1, r 5, Schedule r 12; and PARA 394.

2 Local Authorities (Conduct of Referendums) (Wales) Regulations 2008, SI 2008/1848, Sch 3 r 18(1); Local Authorities (Conduct of Referendums) (England) Regulations 2012, SI 2012/323, Sch 3 r 18(1).

3 Local Authorities (Conduct of Referendums) (Wales) Regulations 2008, SI 2008/1848, Sch 3 r 18(2); Local Authorities (Conduct of Referendums) (England) Regulations 2012, SI 2012/323, Sch 3 r 18(2).

4 Ie his functions under the Local Authorities (Conduct of Referendums) (Wales) Regulations 2008, SI 2008/1848, Sch 3 r 18(2), and the Local Authorities (Conduct of Referendums) (England) Regulations 2012, SI 2012/323, Sch 3 r 18(2).

5 'Petition organiser', in relation to a referendum, means a person who is treated, in relation to Wales, by virtue of the Local Authorities (Referendums) (Petitions and Directions) (Wales) Regulations 2001, SI 2001/2292, reg 10(4) or (5), or for the purpose of the Local Authorities (Referendums) (Petitions) (England) Regulations 2011, SI 2011/2914, reg 19(4) or (5) (formalities of petition: see PARA 563), as the petition organiser of any valid petition (whether an amalgamated petition, a constituent petition or a post-announcement petition) received by the local authority by or in respect of which a referendum is held: Local Authorities (Conduct of Referendums) (Wales) Regulations 2008, SI 2008/1848, reg 2(1); Local Authorities (Conduct of Referendums) (England) Regulations 2012, SI 2012/323, reg 2(1). As to the meaning of 'valid petition' see PARA 559 note 3; as to the meanings of 'amalgamated petition' and 'constituent petition' see PARA 562 notes 12, 17; as to the meaning of 'post-announcement petition' see PARA 561 note 7.

6 Local Authorities (Conduct of Referendums) (Wales) Regulations 2008, SI 2008/1848, Sch 3 r 18(3); Local Authorities (Conduct of Referendums) (England) Regulations 2012, SI 2012/323, Sch 3 r 18(3). Such a nomination must be made by notice in writing to the counting officer not later than the fifth day before the poll (disregarding any day which is to be disregarded by virtue of the Local Authorities (Conduct of Referendums) (Wales) Regulations 2008, SI 2008/1848, Sch 3 r 4, or the Local Authorities (Conduct of Referendums) (England) Regulations 2012, SI 2012/323, Sch 3 r 4, and the notice must contain the address of each nominee: Local

Authorities (Conduct of Referendums) (Wales) Regulations 2008, SI 2008/1848, Sch 3 r 18(4); Local Authorities (Conduct of Referendums) (England) Regulations 2012, SI 2012/323, Sch 3 r 18(4).

In computing any period of time for the purposes of the Timetable the days mentioned in the Local Authorities (Conduct of Referendums) (Wales) Regulations 2008, SI 2008/1848, reg 14(2)(a)–(c), or in the Local Authorities (Conduct of Referendums) (England) Regulations 2012, SI 2012/323, reg 18(2)(a)–(c), as the case may be, must be disregarded, and any such day must not be treated as a day for the purpose of any proceedings up to the completion of the poll nor is the counting officer obliged to proceed with the counting of the votes on such a day: Local Authorities (Conduct of Referendums) (Wales) Regulations 2008, SI 2008/1848, Sch 3 r 4; Local Authorities (Conduct of Referendums) (England) Regulations 2012, SI 2012/323, Sch 3 r 4. The days mentioned in the Local Authorities (Conduct of Referendums) (Wales) Regulations 2008, SI 2008/1848, reg 14(2), and in the Local Authorities (Conduct of Referendums) (England) Regulations 2012, SI 2012/323, reg 18, are:

(1)   a Saturday or Sunday (Local Authorities (Conduct of Referendums) (Wales) Regulations 2008, SI 2008/1848, reg 14(2)(a); Local Authorities (Conduct of Referendums) (England) Regulations 2012, SI 2012/323, reg 18(2)(a));

(2)   Christmas Eve, Christmas Day, Good Friday or a day which is a bank holiday under the Banking and Financial Dealings Act 1971 in England or in Wales (as the case may be) (see TIME vol 97 (2010) PARA 321) (Local Authorities (Conduct of Referendums) (Wales) Regulations 2008, SI 2008/1848, reg 14(2)(b); Local Authorities (Conduct of Referendums) (England) Regulations 2012, SI 2012/323, reg 18(2)(b)); and

(3)   any day appointed as a day of public thanksgiving or mourning (Local Authorities (Conduct of Referendums) (Wales) Regulations 2008, SI 2008/1848, reg 14(2)(c); Local Authorities (Conduct of Referendums) (England) Regulations 2012, SI 2012/323, reg 18(2)(c)).

7   Ie nominated under the Local Authorities (Conduct of Referendums) (Wales) Regulations 2008, SI 2008/1848, Sch 3 r 18(3), or under the Local Authorities (Conduct of Referendums) (England) Regulations 2012, SI 2012/323, Sch 3 r 18(3) (see the text and notes 4–6).

8   Local Authorities (Conduct of Referendums) (Wales) Regulations 2008, SI 2008/1848, Sch 3 r 18(5); Local Authorities (Conduct of Referendums) (England) Regulations 2012, SI 2012/323, Sch 3 r 18(5).

9   The counting officer may limit the number of counting observers, so however that the number must be the same in the case of each petition organiser and the number allowed to a petition organiser must not (except in special circumstances) be fewer than the number obtained by dividing the number of clerks employed on the counting by the number of petition organisers: Local Authorities (Conduct of Referendums) (Wales) Regulations 2008, SI 2008/1848, Sch 3 r 18(6); Local Authorities (Conduct of Referendums) (England) Regulations 2012, SI 2012/323, Sch 3 r 18(6). For the purposes of the calculations required by these provisions, a counting observer who has been appointed on the nomination of more than one petition organiser is a separate counting observer for each of the petition organisers by whom the counting observer has been nominated: Local Authorities (Conduct of Referendums) (Wales) Regulations 2008, SI 2008/1848, Sch 3 r 18(6); Local Authorities (Conduct of Referendums) (England) Regulations 2012, SI 2012/323, Sch 3 r 18(6).

10 Local Authorities (Conduct of Referendums) (Wales) Regulations 2008, SI 2008/1848, Sch 3 r 18(7); Local Authorities (Conduct of Referendums) (England) Regulations 2012, SI 2012/323, Sch 3 r 18(7). Such a nomination must be made by notice in writing to the counting officer not later than the final day before the poll (disregarding any day which is to be disregarded by virtue of the Local Authorities (Conduct of Referendums) (Wales) Regulations 2008, SI 2008/1848, Sch 3 r 4, or the Local Authorities (Conduct of Referendums) (England) Regulations 2012, SI 2012/323, Sch 3 r 4 (), and the notice must contain the address of each nominee: Local Authorities (Conduct of Referendums) (Wales) Regulations 2008, SI 2008/1848, Sch 3 r 18(4), (8); Local Authorities (Conduct of Referendums) (England) Regulations 2012, SI 2012/323, Sch 3 r 18(4), (8). The counting officer must not, without good cause, decline to appoint as a counting observer a person nominated under the Local Authorities (Conduct of Referendums) (Wales) Regulations 2008, SI 2008/1848, Sch 3 r 18(7) or under the Local Authorities (Conduct of Referendums) (England) Regulations 2012, SI 2012/323, Sch 3 r 18(7) (Local Authorities (Conduct of Referendums) (Wales) Regulations 2008, SI 2008/1848, Sch 3 r 18(5), (8); Local Authorities (Conduct of Referendums) (England) Regulations 2012, SI 2012/323, Sch 3 r 18(5), (8)), although he may limit the number of counting observers, so however that the number must be the same in the case of each petition organiser and the number allowed to a petition organiser must not (except in special circumstances) be fewer than the number obtained by dividing the number of clerks employed on the counting by the number of

petition organisers (Local Authorities (Conduct of Referendums) (Wales) Regulations 2008, SI 2008/1848, Sch 3 r 18(6), (8); Local Authorities (Conduct of Referendums) (England) Regulations 2012, SI 2012/323, Sch 3 r 18(6), (8)). For the purposes of the calculations required by these provisions, a counting observer who has been appointed on the nomination of more than one petition organiser is a separate counting observer for each of the petition organisers by whom the counting observer has been nominated: Local Authorities (Conduct of Referendums) (Wales) Regulations 2008, SI 2008/1848, Sch 3 r 18(6), (8); Local Authorities (Conduct of Referendums) (England) Regulations 2012, SI 2012/323, Sch 3 r 18(6), (8).

11 Local Authorities (Conduct of Referendums) (Wales) Regulations 2008, SI 2008/1848, Sch 3 r 18(10); Local Authorities (Conduct of Referendums) (England) Regulations 2012, SI 2012/323, Sch 3 r 18(10). In the Local Authorities (Conduct of Referendums) (Wales) Regulations 2008, SI 2008/1848, Sch 3 r 18(10)–(12), and in the Local Authorities (Conduct of Referendums) (England) Regulations 2012, SI 2012/323, Sch 3 r 18(10)–(12), references to polling observers and counting observers are to be taken as references to polling observers and counting observers whose appointments have been duly made: Local Authorities (Conduct of Referendums) (Wales) Regulations 2008, SI 2008/1848, Sch 3 r 18(9); Local Authorities (Conduct of Referendums) (England) Regulations 2012, SI 2012/323, Sch 3 r 18(9).

12 Local Authorities (Conduct of Referendums) (Wales) Regulations 2008, SI 2008/1848, Sch 3 r 18(11); Local Authorities (Conduct of Referendums) (England) Regulations 2012, SI 2012/323, Sch 3 r 18(11). See note 11.

13 Ie by the Local Authorities (Conduct of Referendums) (Wales) Regulations 2008, SI 2008/1848, or the Local Authorities (Conduct of Referendums) (England) Regulations 2012, SI 2012/323.

14 Local Authorities (Conduct of Referendums) (Wales) Regulations 2008, SI 2008/1848, Sch 3 r 18(12); Local Authorities (Conduct of Referendums) (England) Regulations 2012, SI 2012/323, Sch 3 r 18(12). See note 11.

615.   Hours of polling at a referendum or poll. The hours of polling at a local authority referendum[1] must be between seven in the morning and ten in the evening on the day of the referendum[2]. Polling at a poll consequent on a parish or community meeting[3] takes place between the hours of four in the afternoon and nine at night on the day fixed for the poll[4].

1 As to the meaning of 'referendum' for these purposes see PARA 574 notes 2, 13.
2 Local Authorities (Conduct of Referendums) (Wales) Regulations 2008, SI 2008/1848, Sch 3 r 3; Local Authorities (Conduct of Referendums) (England) Regulations 2012, SI 2012/323, Sch 3 r 3.
3 As to how polls consequent on a parish or community meeting come about see PARA 581.
4 Parish and Community Meetings (Polls) Rules 1987, SI 1987/1, r 5, Schedule r 1.

616.   Sealing of ballot boxes at referendum or poll. Immediately before the commencement of the poll, the presiding officer[1] must show the ballot box empty to such persons, if any, as are present in the polling station, so that they may see that it is empty, and must then lock it up and place his seal on it in such manner as to prevent its being opened without breaking the seal, and must place it in his view for the receipt of ballot papers, and keep it so locked and sealed[2].

1 As to the appointment of presiding officers and clerks at a referendum or poll see PARA 613.
2 Parish and Community Meetings (Polls) Rules 1987, SI 1987/1, r 5, Schedule r 16; Local Authorities (Conduct of Referendums) (Wales) Regulations 2008, SI 2008/1848, Sch 3 r 23; Local Authorities (Conduct of Referendums) (England) Regulations 2012, SI 2012/323, Sch 3 r 23.

617.   Keeping of order at referendum or poll; adjournment in case of riot. It is the duty of the presiding officer[1] to keep order at his polling station[2]. If a person misconducts himself in the polling station, or fails to obey the lawful orders of the presiding officer, he may immediately, by order of the presiding officer, be removed from the polling station by a constable in or near that station, or by any other person authorised in writing by the counting officer (in relation to a local authority referendum)[3] or by the returning officer (in relation to a poll consequent on a parish or community meeting)[4] to remove him; and the person so removed may not, without the permission of the presiding officer, again enter the polling station during the day[5]. Any person so removed, may, if charged with the commission in the polling station of an offence, be dealt with as a person taken into custody by a constable for an offence without a warrant[6]. However, the powers of keeping order so conferred are not to be exercised so as to prevent a voter who is otherwise entitled to vote at a polling station from having an opportunity of voting at that station[7].

Where the proceedings at any polling station are interrupted or obstructed by riot or open violence, the presiding officer must adjourn the proceedings until the following day and forthwith give notice to the counting officer or to the returning officer (as the case may be)[8]. The hours of the poll on the day to which it is adjourned are the same as for the original day and references to the close of the poll are to be construed accordingly[9].

1   As to the appointment of presiding officers and clerks at a referendum or poll see PARA 613.
2   Parish and Community Meetings (Polls) Rules 1987, SI 1987/1, r 5, Schedule r 15(1); Local Authorities (Conduct of Referendums) (Wales) Regulations 2008, SI 2008/1848, Sch 3 r 22(1); Local Authorities (Conduct of Referendums) (England) Regulations 2012, SI 2012/323, Sch 3 r 22(1).
3   As to the meaning of 'counting officer' see PARA 576 note 1; and as to the meaning of 'referendum' for these purposes see PARA 574 notes 2, 13.
4   As to how polls consequent on a parish or community meeting come about see PARA 581; and as to returning officers appointed at polls consequent on a parish or community meeting see PARA 588.
5   Parish and Community Meetings (Polls) Rules 1987, SI 1987/1, Schedule r 15(2); Local Authorities (Conduct of Referendums) (Wales) Regulations 2008, SI 2008/1848, Sch 3 r 22(2); Local Authorities (Conduct of Referendums) (England) Regulations 2012, SI 2012/323, Sch 3 r 22(2).
6   Parish and Community Meetings (Polls) Rules 1987, SI 1987/1, Schedule r 15(3); Local Authorities (Conduct of Referendums) (Wales) Regulations 2008, SI 2008/1848, Sch 3 r 22(3); Local Authorities (Conduct of Referendums) (England) Regulations 2012, SI 2012/323, Sch 3 r 22(3).
7   Parish and Community Meetings (Polls) Rules 1987, SI 1987/1, Schedule r 15(4); Local Authorities (Conduct of Referendums) (Wales) Regulations 2008, SI 2008/1848, Sch 3 r 22(4); Local Authorities (Conduct of Referendums) (England) Regulations 2012, SI 2012/323, Sch 3 r 22(4).
8   Parish and Community Meetings (Polls) Rules 1987, SI 1987/1, Schedule r 24(1); Local Authorities (Conduct of Referendums) (Wales) Regulations 2008, SI 2008/1848, Sch 3 r 33(1); Local Authorities (Conduct of Referendums) (England) Regulations 2012, SI 2012/323, Sch 3 r 33(1).
9   Parish and Community Meetings (Polls) Rules 1987, SI 1987/1, Schedule r 24(2); Local Authorities (Conduct of Referendums) (Wales) Regulations 2008, SI 2008/1848, Sch 3 r 33(2); Local Authorities (Conduct of Referendums) (England) Regulations 2012, SI 2012/323, Sch 3 r 33(2).

618.   Admission to polling station at referendum or poll. At a poll consequent on a parish or community meeting[1] the presiding officer[2] must regulate the number of voters to be admitted to the polling station at the same time[3]. He must exclude all other persons except[3]:

(1)   where the poll is taken on the question of appointment to any office, the candidates and their spouses and civil partners[4];

(2)   where the poll is taken on any other question, the proposer of the resolution in respect of which the poll is taken[5];

(3)   the polling agents appointed to attend at the polling station[6];

(4)   the clerks appointed to attend at the polling station[7];

(5)   the constables on duty[8]; and

(6)   the companions of blind voters[9].

At a local authority referendum[10] the presiding officer must exclude all persons from the polling station except:

(a)   voters and proxies[11];

(b)   persons under the age of 18 who accompany voters and proxies to the polling station[12];

(c)   the polling observers appointed to attend at the polling station[13];

(d)   the clerks appointed to attend at the polling station[14];

(e)   persons who are entitled to attend[15] as observers[16];

(f)   the constables on duty[17];

(g)   the companions of voters and proxies with disabilities[18];

(h)   the elected mayor, if any, of the council in respect of which the referendum is held[19]; and

(i)   any petition organiser[20].

At a local authority referendum, the presiding officer must regulate the total number of voters, proxies and persons under the age of 18 who accompany them to be admitted to the polling station at the same time[21]. A constable or person employed by a counting officer[22] must not be admitted to vote in person elsewhere than at his or her own polling station allotted to him or her, except on production and surrender of a certificate as to his or her employment[23].

1   As to how polls consequent on a parish or community meeting come about see PARA 581; and as to returning officers appointed at polls consequent on a parish or community meeting see PARA 588.

2   As to the appointment of presiding officers and clerks at a referendum or poll see PARA 613.

3   Parish and Community Meetings (Polls) Rules 1987, SI 1987/1, r 5, Schedule r 14.

4   Parish and Community Meetings (Polls) Rules 1987, SI 1987/1, Schedule r 14(a) (amended by SI 2005/2114).

5   Parish and Community Meetings (Polls) Rules 1987, SI 1987/1, Schedule r 14(b).

6   Parish and Community Meetings (Polls) Rules 1987, SI 1987/1, Schedule r 14(c).

7   Parish and Community Meetings (Polls) Rules 1987, SI 1987/1, Schedule r 14(d).

8   Parish and Community Meetings (Polls) Rules 1987, SI 1987/1, Schedule r 14(e).

9   Parish and Community Meetings (Polls) Rules 1987, SI 1987/1, Schedule r 14(f).

10   As to the meaning of 'referendum' for these purposes see PARA 574 notes 2, 13.

11   Local Authorities (Conduct of Referendums) (Wales) Regulations 2008, SI 2008/1848, Sch 3 r 21(1)(a); Local Authorities (Conduct of Referendums) (England) Regulations 2012, SI 2012/323, Sch 3 r 21(1)(a).

12   Local Authorities (Conduct of Referendums) (Wales) Regulations 2008, SI 2008/1848, Sch 3 r 21(1)(b); Local Authorities (Conduct of Referendums) (England) Regulations 2012, SI 2012/323, Sch 3 r 21(1)(b).

13   Local Authorities (Conduct of Referendums) (Wales) Regulations 2008, SI 2008/1848, Sch 3 r 21(1)(c); Local Authorities (Conduct of Referendums) (England) Regulations 2012, SI 2012/323, Sch 3 r 21(1)(c).

14   Local Authorities (Conduct of Referendums) (Wales) Regulations 2008, SI 2008/1848, Sch 3 r 21(1)(d); Local Authorities (Conduct of Referendums) (England) Regulations 2012, SI 2012/323, Sch 3 r 21(1)(d).

15   Ie by virtue of any of the Political Parties, Elections and Referendums Act 2000 ss 6A–6D (applied and modified, in relation to Wales, by the Local Authorities (Conduct of Referendums) (Wales) Regulations 2008, SI 2008/1848, Sch 4 Table 3, and, in relation to England, by the Local Authorities (Conduct of Referendums) (England) Regulations 2012, SI 2012/323, Sch 4 Table 4). As to the provisions that are so applied and modified see PARA 15.

16   Local Authorities (Conduct of Referendums) (Wales) Regulations 2008, SI 2008/1848, Sch 3 r 21(1)(e); Local Authorities (Conduct of Referendums) (England) Regulations 2012, SI 2012/323, Sch 3 r 21(1)(e).

17   Local Authorities (Conduct of Referendums) (Wales) Regulations 2008, SI 2008/1848, Sch 3 r 21(1)(f); Local Authorities (Conduct of Referendums) (England) Regulations 2012, SI 2012/323, Sch 3 r 21(1)(f).

18   Local Authorities (Conduct of Referendums) (Wales) Regulations 2008, SI 2008/1848, Sch 3 r 21(1)(g); Local Authorities (Conduct of Referendums) (England) Regulations 2012, SI 2012/323, Sch 3 r 21(1)(g).

19   Local Authorities (Conduct of Referendums) (Wales) Regulations 2008, SI 2008/1848, Sch 3 r 21(1)(h); Local Authorities (Conduct of Referendums) (England) Regulations 2012, SI 2012/323, Sch 3 r 21(1)(h). As to the meaning of 'elected mayor' see PARA 98 note 2.

20   Local Authorities (Conduct of Referendums) (Wales) Regulations 2008, SI 2008/1848, Sch 3 r 21(1)(i); Local Authorities (Conduct of Referendums) (England) Regulations 2012, SI 2012/323, Sch 3 r 21(1)(i). As to the meaning of 'petition organiser' see PARA 561 note 6.

21   Local Authorities (Conduct of Referendums) (Wales) Regulations 2008, SI 2008/1848, Sch 3 r 21(2); Local Authorities (Conduct of Referendums) (England) Regulations 2012, SI 2012/323, Sch 3 r 21(2).

22   As to the meaning of 'counting officer' see PARA 576 note 1.

23   Local Authorities (Conduct of Referendums) (Wales) Regulations 2008, SI 2008/1848, Sch 3 r 21(3); Local Authorities (Conduct of Referendums) (England) Regulations 2012, SI 2012/323, Sch 3 r 21(3). The certificate must be in the form set out in the Local Authorities (Conduct of Referendums) (Wales) Regulations 2008, SI 2008/1848, Sch 3 Appendix, or in the Local Authorities (Conduct of Referendums) (England) Regulations 2012, SI 2012/323, Sch 3 Appendix (as the case may be), or a form to the like effect, and signed by an officer of police of or above the rank of inspector or by the counting officer, as the case may be: Local Authorities (Conduct of Referendums) (Wales) Regulations 2008, SI 2008/1848, Sch 3 r 21(3); Local Authorities (Conduct of Referendums) (England) Regulations 2012, SI 2012/323, Sch 3 r 21(3). Any certificate surrendered under these provisions must forthwith be cancelled: Local Authorities (Conduct of Referendums) (Wales) Regulations 2008, SI 2008/1848, Sch 3 r 21(4); Local Authorities (Conduct of Referendums) (England) Regulations 2012, SI 2012/323, Sch 3 r 21(4).

619. Questions to be put to voters at a referendum or poll. At a local authority referendum[1] or at a poll consequent on a parish or community meeting[2], the presiding officer[3] may put to any person applying for a ballot paper at the time of his application, but not afterwards, any of the prescribed questions[4]. At a local authority referendum certain of the prescribed questions are required to be put[5]. A ballot paper must not be delivered to any person required to answer any of the prescribed questions unless he has answered the questions or question satisfactorily[6]. No inquiry, except as so authorised, is permitted as to the right of any person to vote[7].

If any person knowingly and wilfully makes a false answer to any of the prescribed questions, he is guilty of an indictable offence and may be punished accordingly[8].

1   As to the meaning of 'referendum' for these purposes see PARA 574 notes 2, 13.

2   As to how polls consequent on a parish or community meeting come about see PARA 581.

3   As to the appointment of presiding officers and clerks at a referendum or poll see PARA 613.

4   Parish and Community Meetings (Polls) Rules 1987, SI 1987/1, Schedule r 17(1); Local Authorities (Conduct of Referendums) (Wales) Regulations 2008, SI 2008/1848, Sch 3 r 24(1)(a); Local Authorities (Conduct of Referendums) (England) Regulations 2012, SI 2012/323, Sch 3 r 24(1)(a). In relation to a poll consequent on a parish or community meeting on a question not involving appointment to office, the prescribed questions are set out in the Parish and Community Meetings (Polls) Rules 1987, SI 1987/1, Schedule r 17(1); and in relation to a local authority referendum, the prescribed questions are set out in the Local Authorities (Conduct of Referendums) (Wales) Regulations 2008, SI 2008/1848, Sch 3 r 24(1), (2), and in the Local Authorities (Conduct of Referendums) (England) Regulations 2012, SI 2012/323, Sch 3 r 24(1), (2). The function set out in the text may be discharged by a clerk appointed to assist the presiding officer: see PARA 613.

5   Local Authorities (Conduct of Referendums) (Wales) Regulations 2008, SI 2008/1848, Sch 3 r 24(1)(b); Local Authorities (Conduct of Referendums) (England) Regulations 2012, SI 2012/323, Sch 3 r 24(1)(b).

6   Parish and Community Meetings (Polls) Rules 1987, SI 1987/1, Schedule r 17(2); Local
     Authorities (Conduct of Referendums) (Wales) Regulations 2008, SI 2008/1848, Sch 3 r 24(3);
     Local Authorities (Conduct of Referendums) (England) Regulations 2012, SI 2012/323, Sch 3
     r 24(3).
7   Parish and Community Meetings (Polls) Rules 1987, SI 1987/1, Schedule r 17(3); Local
     Authorities (Conduct of Referendums) (Wales) Regulations 2008, SI 2008/1848, Sch 3 r 24(4);
     Local Authorities (Conduct of Referendums) (England) Regulations 2012, SI 2012/323, Sch 3
     r 24(4).
8   See the Perjury Act 1911 s 5 (false statutory declarations and other false statements without
     oath); and CRIMINAL LAW vol 26 (2010) PARA 673.

620.   Voting procedure at a referendum or poll.   At a poll consequent on a
parish or community meeting[1] a ballot paper must be delivered to a voter who
applies for one and, immediately before delivery:

(1)   the ballot paper must be stamped with the official mark[2];
(2)   the number and name of the elector as stated in the copy of the register
       of electors must be called out[3];
(3)   the number of the elector must be marked on the counterfoil[4]; and
(4)   a mark must be placed in the register of electors against the number of
       the elector to denote that a ballot paper has been received but without
       showing the particular ballot paper which has been received[5].

At a local authority referendum[6] a ballot paper must be delivered to a voter or
proxy who applies for one, and immediately before delivery:

(a)   the number and name of the voter as stated in the copy of the register of
       electors must be called out[7];
(b)   the number of the voter as stated in the register must be marked on the
       list of numbers[8] beside the number of the ballot paper to be issued to
       the voter[9];
(c)   a mark must be placed in the copy of the register of electors against the
       number of the voter to note that a ballot paper has been received but
       without showing the particular ballot paper which has been received[10];
       and
(d)   in the case of a person applying for a ballot paper as proxy, a mark must
       also be placed against that person's name in the list of proxies[11].

At any such poll or referendum, on receiving the ballot paper, the voter or
proxy must forthwith proceed into one of the compartments in the polling
station and there secretly mark his paper[12]. The voter or proxy must then fold
his paper up in such a way as to conceal his vote and he must then show to the
presiding officer the back of the paper, so as to disclose the official mark, and put
the ballot paper so folded up in the ballot box in the presence of the presiding
officer[13]. The voter must vote without undue delay and must leave the polling
station as soon as he has put his ballot paper into the ballot box[14].

It is an offence to interfere or attempt to interfere with a voter when he is
recording his vote[15].

1   As to how polls consequent on a parish or community meeting come about see PARA 581.
2   Parish and Community Meetings (Polls) Rules 1987, SI 1987/1, Schedule r 19(1)(a).
3   Parish and Community Meetings (Polls) Rules 1987, SI 1987/1, Schedule r 19(1)(b).
4   Parish and Community Meetings (Polls) Rules 1987, SI 1987/1, Schedule r 19(1)(c).
5   Parish and Community Meetings (Polls) Rules 1987, SI 1987/1, Schedule r 19(1)(d).
6   As to the meaning of 'referendum' for these purposes see PARA 574 notes 2, 13.
7   Local Authorities (Conduct of Referendums) (Wales) Regulations 2008, SI 2008/1848, Sch 3
     r 26(1)(a); Local Authorities (Conduct of Referendums) (England) Regulations 2012,
     SI 2012/323, Sch 3 r 26(1)(a). In the case of a voter who has an anonymous entry, that person
     must show the presiding officer his or her official poll card and only his or her number need be

called out in pursuance of these requirements: Local Authorities (Conduct of Referendums) (Wales) Regulations 2008, SI 2008/1848, Sch 3 r 26(2); Local Authorities (Conduct of Referendums) (England) Regulations 2012, SI 2012/323, Sch 3 r 26(2). This provision is modified where a voter has been added to the register pursuant to the Representation of the People Act 1983 s 13B (applied and modified, in relation to Wales, by the Local Authorities (Conduct of Referendums) (Wales) Regulations 2008, SI 2008/1848, Sch 4 Table 1, and, in relation to England, by the Local Authorities (Conduct of Referendums) (England) Regulations 2012, SI 2012/323, Sch 4 Table 1): see the Local Authorities (Conduct of Referendums) (Wales) Regulations 2008, SI 2008/1848, Sch 3 r 26(3)(a); and the Local Authorities (Conduct of Referendums) (England) Regulations 2012, SI 2012/323, Sch 3 r 26(3)(a). As to the provisions that are so applied and modified see PARA 15.

8 Ie the list mentioned in the Local Authorities (Conduct of Referendums) (Wales) Regulations 2008, SI 2008/1848, Sch 3 r 17(3)(d), or in the Local Authorities (Conduct of Referendums) (England) Regulations 2012, SI 2012/323, Sch 3 r 17(3)(d), as the case may be (see PARA 611).

9 Local Authorities (Conduct of Referendums) (Wales) Regulations 2008, SI 2008/1848, Sch 3 r 26(1)(b); Local Authorities (Conduct of Referendums) (England) Regulations 2012, SI 2012/323, Sch 3 r 26(1)(b). This provision is modified where a voter has been added to the register pursuant to the Representation of the People Act 1983 s 13B (as applied and modified: see note 7): see the Local Authorities (Conduct of Referendums) (England) Regulations 2012, SI 2012/323, Sch 3 r 26(3)(b); and the Local Authorities (Conduct of Referendums) (Wales) Regulations 2008, SI 2008/1848, Sch 3 r 26(3)(b).

10 Local Authorities (Conduct of Referendums) (England) Regulations 2012, SI 2012/323, Sch 3 r 26(1)(c); Local Authorities (Conduct of Referendums) (Wales) Regulations 2008, SI 2008/1848, Sch 3 r 26(1)(c). This provision is modified where a voter has been added to the register pursuant to the Representation of the People Act 1983 s 13B (as applied and modified: see note 7): see the Local Authorities (Conduct of Referendums) (Wales) Regulations 2008, SI 2008/1848, Sch 3 r 26(3)(c); and the Local Authorities (Conduct of Referendums) (England) Regulations 2012, SI 2012/323, Sch 3 r 26(3)(c).

11 Local Authorities (Conduct of Referendums) (Wales) Regulations 2008, SI 2008/1848, Sch 3 r 26(1)(d); Local Authorities (Conduct of Referendums) (England) Regulations 2012, SI 2012/323, Sch 3 r 26(1)(d).

12 Parish and Community Meetings (Polls) Rules 1987, SI 1987/1, Schedule r 19(2); Local Authorities (Conduct of Referendums) (Wales) Regulations 2008, SI 2008/1848, Sch 3 r 26(4); Local Authorities (Conduct of Referendums) (England) Regulations 2012, SI 2012/323, Sch 3 r 26(4).

13 Parish and Community Meetings (Polls) Rules 1987, SI 1987/1, Schedule r 19(2); Local Authorities (Conduct of Referendums) (Wales) Regulations 2008, SI 2008/1848, Sch 3 r 26(4); Local Authorities (Conduct of Referendums) (England) Regulations 2012, SI 2012/323, Sch 3 r 26(4).

14 Parish and Community Meetings (Polls) Rules 1987, SI 1987/1, Schedule r 19(3); Local Authorities (Conduct of Referendums) (Wales) Regulations 2008, SI 2008/1848, Sch 3 r 26(5); Local Authorities (Conduct of Referendums) (England) Regulations 2012, SI 2012/323, Sch 3 r 26(5).

15 See PARA 741.

621. Challenge of voter at a referendum or poll. If, at a poll consequent on a parish or community meeting[1], at the time a person applies for a ballot paper for the purpose of voting in person or after he has applied for a ballot paper for that purpose and before he has left the polling station, a candidate or his polling agent declares to the presiding officer[2] that he has reasonable cause to believe that the applicant has committed an offence of personation[3] and undertakes to substantiate the charge in a court of law[4], the presiding officer may order a constable to arrest the applicant, and the order of the presiding officer is sufficient authority for the constable so to do[5]. The person against whom such a declaration is made must not by reason of it be prevented from voting[6].

A person must not be prevented from voting at a local authority referendum[7] by reason only that:

(1)   any petition organiser[8] or polling observer[9] permitted to be present[10]

declares that he or she has reasonable cause to believe that the person has committed an offence of personation[11]; or

(2)   the person is arrested on the grounds that he or she is suspected of committing or of being about to commit such an offence[12].

1 As to how polls consequent on a parish or community meeting come about see PARA 581.
2 As to the appointment of presiding officers and clerks at a referendum or poll see PARA 613.
3 Parish and Community Meetings (Polls) Rules 1987, SI 1987/1, Schedule r 18(1)(a). As to the offence of personation see PARA 730.
4 Parish and Community Meetings (Polls) Rules 1987, SI 1987/1, Schedule r 18(1)(a).
5 Parish and Community Meetings (Polls) Rules 1987, SI 1987/1, Schedule r 18(1). A person arrested under these provisions must be dealt with as a person taken into custody by a constable for an offence without a warrant: Schedule r 18(3).
6 Parish and Community Meetings (Polls) Rules 1987, SI 1987/1, Schedule r 18(2).
7 As to the meaning of 'referendum' for these purposes see PARA 574 notes 2, 13.
8 As to the meaning of 'petition organiser' see PARA 614 note 5.
9 As to the appointment of polling observers at a referendum see PARA 614.
10 Ie in accordance with the Local Authorities (Conduct of Referendums) (Wales) Regulations 2008, SI 2008/1848, Sch 3 r 21(1), or the Local Authorities (Conduct of Referendums) (England) Regulations 2012, SI 2012/323, Sch 3 r 21(1), as the case may be (see PARA 618).
11 Local Authorities (Conduct of Referendums) (Wales) Regulations 2008, SI 2008/1848, Sch 3 r 25(a); Local Authorities (Conduct of Referendums) (England) Regulations 2012, SI 2012/323, Sch 3 r 25(a).
12 Local Authorities (Conduct of Referendums) (Wales) Regulations 2008, SI 2008/1848, Sch 3 r 25(b); Local Authorities (Conduct of Referendums) (England) Regulations 2012, SI 2012/323, Sch 3 r 25(b).

622.   Ballot papers marked by presiding officer at a referendum or poll. At a local authority referendum[1] or at a poll consequent on a parish or community meeting[2], on the application of a voter who is incapacitated by blindness or other physical cause from voting in the manner directed by the rules[3], or who declares orally that he is unable to read, the presiding officer[4] must, in the presence of the polling observers (if any)[5], cause the vote of the voter to be marked on a ballot paper in manner directed by the voter, and the ballot paper to be placed in the ballot box[6].

The name and number[7] on the register of electors of every voter whose vote is marked in pursuance of this rule, and the reason why it is so marked, must be entered on a list which is called the 'list of votes marked by the presiding officer'[8].

1 As to the meaning of 'referendum' for these purposes see PARA 574 notes 2, 13.
2 As to how polls consequent on a parish or community meeting come about see PARA 581.
3 Ie, in relation to a local authority referendum, by the Local Authorities (Conduct of Referendums) (England) Regulations 2012, SI 2012/323, or the Local Authorities (Conduct of Referendums) (Wales) Regulations 2008, SI 2008/1848, or, at a poll consequent on a parish or community meeting, by the Parish and Community Meetings (Polls) Rules 1987, SI 1987/1, r 5, Schedule (as to which see PARA 556).
4 As to the appointment of presiding officers and clerks at a referendum or poll see PARA 613.
5 As to the appointment of polling observers at a referendum see PARA 614.
6 Parish and Community Meetings (Polls) Rules 1987, SI 1987/1, Schedule r 20(1); Local Authorities (Conduct of Referendums) (Wales) Regulations 2008, SI 2008/1848, Sch 3 r 27(1); Local Authorities (Conduct of Referendums) (England) Regulations 2012, SI 2012/323, Sch 3 r 27(1).
7 As to the number of an elector see PARA 145.
8 Parish and Community Meetings (Polls) Rules 1987, SI 1987/1, Schedule r 20(2); Local Authorities (Conduct of Referendums) (Wales) Regulations 2008, SI 2008/1848, Sch 3 r 27(2); Local Authorities (Conduct of Referendums) (England) Regulations 2012, SI 2012/323, Sch 3 r 27(2). As to voting by proxy at a referendum see PARA 597 et seq. In the case of a person voting as proxy for a voter at a local authority referendum, the number to be entered together

with the proxy's name is to be the number in the register of the voter: Local Authorities (Conduct of Referendums) (Wales) Regulations 2008, SI 2008/1848, Sch 3 r 27(2); Local Authorities (Conduct of Referendums) (England) Regulations 2012, SI 2012/323, Sch 3 r 27(2). In relation to a local authority referendum this provision is modified where a voter has been added to the register pursuant to the Representation of the People Act 1983 s 13B (applied and modified, in relation to Wales, by the Local Authorities (Conduct of Referendums) (Wales) Regulations 2008, SI 2008/1848, Sch 4 Table 1, and, in relation to England, by the Local Authorities (Conduct of Referendums) (England) Regulations 2012, SI 2012/323, Sch 4 Table 1): see the Local Authorities (Conduct of Referendums) (Wales) Regulations 2008, SI 2008/1848, Sch 3 r 27(3); and the Local Authorities (Conduct of Referendums) (England) Regulations 2012, SI 2012/323, Sch 3 r 27(3). As to the provisions that are so applied and modified see PARA 15.

623. Voting at a referendum or poll by persons with disabilities. At a local authority referendum[1] or at a poll consequent on a parish or community meeting[2], if a voter (or, in the case of a local authority referendum, a proxy) makes an application to the presiding officer[3] to be allowed, on the ground of blindness (or, in the case of a local authority referendum, another disability or the inability to read, to vote with the assistance of another person by whom he is accompanied (called the 'companion'), the presiding officer must require the voter or proxy to declare (in the case of a local authority referendum, orally or in writing), whether he is so incapacitated by his blindness or other disability, or by his inability to read, as to be unable to vote without assistance[4].

If the presiding officer is satisfied that the voter (or proxy) is so incapacitated, and is also satisfied by a written declaration made by the companion of the voter or proxy with disabilities[5] that the companion is a qualified person and has not previously assisted more than one voter or proxy with disabilities to vote at the referendum or poll, he must grant the application, and then anything required to be done to or by the voter or proxy in connection with the giving of his vote may be done to, or with the assistance of, the companion[6]. The name and number in the register of electors[7] of every voter whose vote is given by a companion, and the name and address of the companion[8], must be entered on a list (which is called the 'list of voters or proxies with disabilities assisted by companions' in the case of a local authority referendum or the 'list of blind voters assisted by companions' in the case of a poll consequent on a parish or community meeting)[9]. The declaration made by the companion must be in the prescribed form[10] and must be made before the presiding officer at the time when the voter applies to vote with the assistance of a companion and must forthwith be given to the presiding officer who must attest and retain it[11]. No fee or other payment may be charged in respect of the declaration[12].

1   As to the meaning of 'referendum' for these purposes see PARA 574 notes 2, 13.
2   As to how polls consequent on a parish or community meeting come about see PARA 581.
3   As to the appointment of presiding officers and clerks at a referendum or poll see PARA 613.
4   Parish and Community Meetings (Polls) Rules 1987, SI 1987/1, Schedule r 21(1); Local Authorities (Conduct of Referendums) (Wales) Regulations 2008, SI 2008/1848, Sch 3 r 28(1); Local Authorities (Conduct of Referendums) (England) Regulations 2012, SI 2012/323, Sch 3 r 28(1).
5   For the purposes of a local authority referendum, a person is a voter or proxy with disabilities if he has made such a declaration as is mentioned in the text; and a person is qualified to assist a voter or proxy with disabilities to vote if that person is a person who is entitled to vote as an elector at the referendum or is the father, mother, brother, sister, spouse, civil partner, son or daughter of the voter and has attained the age of 18 years: Local Authorities (Conduct of Referendums) (Wales) Regulations 2008, SI 2008/1848, Sch 3 r 28(3); Local Authorities (Conduct of Referendums) (England) Regulations 2012, SI 2012/323, Sch 3 r 28(3). For the purposes of a poll consequent on a parish or community meeting on a question not involving appointment to office, a person is qualified to assist a blind voter to vote if that person is either

a person who is entitled to vote at the poll or the father, mother, brother, sister, spouse, civil partner, son or daughter of the blind voter and has attained the age of 18 years: Parish and Community Meetings (Polls) Rules 1987, SI 1987/1, Schedule r 21(3) (amended by SI 2005/2114).

6   Parish and Community Meetings (Polls) Rules 1987, SI 1987/1, Schedule r 21(2); Local Authorities (Conduct of Referendums) (Wales) Regulations 2008, SI 2008/1848, Sch 3 r 28(2); Local Authorities (Conduct of Referendums) (England) Regulations 2012, SI 2012/323, Sch 3 r 28(2).

7   As to the registers of electors and the number of an elector see PARA 145.

8   In the case of a person voting as proxy for an elector, the number to be entered together with the name of the voter must be the number of the elector: Local Authorities (Conduct of Referendums) (Wales) Regulations 2008, SI 2008/1848, Sch 3 r 28(4); Local Authorities (Conduct of Referendums) (England) Regulations 2012, SI 2012/323, Sch 3 r 28(4).

9   Parish and Community Meetings (Polls) Rules 1987, SI 1987/1, Schedule r 21(4); Local Authorities (Conduct of Referendums) (Wales) Regulations 2008, SI 2008/1848, Sch 3 r 28(4); Local Authorities (Conduct of Referendums) (England) Regulations 2012, SI 2012/323, Sch 3 r 28(4). In relation to a local authority referendum this provision is modified where a voter has been added to the register pursuant to the Representation of the People Act 1983 s 13B (applied and modified, in relation to Wales, by the Local Authorities (Conduct of Referendums) (Wales) Regulations 2008, SI 2008/1848, Sch 4 Table 1, and, in relation to England, by the Local Authorities (Conduct of Referendums) (England) Regulations 2012, SI 2012/323, Sch 4 Table 1): see the Local Authorities (Conduct of Referendums) (Wales) Regulations 2008, SI 2008/1848, Sch 3 r 28(5); and the Local Authorities (Conduct of Referendums) (England) Regulations 2012, SI 2012/323, Sch 3 r 28(5). As to the provisions that are so applied and modified see PARA 15.

10 The prescribed form is set out, in relation to a poll consequent on a parish or community meeting, in the Parish and Community Meetings (Polls) Rules 1987, SI 1987/1, Schedule Appendix of Forms (amended by SI 1987/262), and in relation to a local authority referendum in the Local Authorities (Conduct of Referendums) (Wales) Regulations 2008, SI 2008/1848, Sch 3 Appendix of Forms, or in the Local Authorities (Conduct of Referendums) (England) Regulations 2012, SI 2012/323, Sch 3 Appendix of Forms, as the case may be.

11 Parish and Community Meetings (Polls) Rules 1987, SI 1987/1, Schedule r 21(5); Local Authorities (Conduct of Referendums) (Wales) Regulations 2008, SI 2008/1848, Sch 3 r 28(6); Local Authorities (Conduct of Referendums) (England) Regulations 2012, SI 2012/323, Sch 3 r 28(6).

12 Parish and Community Meetings (Polls) Rules 1987, SI 1987/1, Schedule r 21(6); Local Authorities (Conduct of Referendums) (Wales) Regulations 2008, SI 2008/1848, Sch 3 r 28(7); Local Authorities (Conduct of Referendums) (England) Regulations 2012, SI 2012/323, Sch 3 r 28(7).

624.   Tendered ballot papers at a referendum or poll.   At a poll consequent on a parish or community meeting[1], if a person who represents himself to be a particular elector named on the register[2] applies for a ballot paper after another person has voted in person either as the elector, the applicant, on satisfactorily answering the questions permitted by law to be asked at the poll[3], is entitled to mark a ballot paper (called a 'tendered ballot paper') in the same manner as any other voter[4].

At a local authority referendum[5], if a person, representing themselves to be a particular voter named on the register and not named in the absent voters list[6], or a particular person named in the list of proxies as proxy for a voter and not entitled to vote by post as proxy, applies for a ballot paper after another person has voted in person either as the voter or the voter's proxy, the applicant is entitled, on satisfactorily answering the questions permitted by law to be asked at the poll, to mark a ballot paper (called a 'tendered ballot paper') in the same manner as any other voter or proxy[7]. If, at a local authority referendum:

(1)   a person applies for a ballot paper representing themselves to be a particular voter named on the register, the person is also named in the

postal voters list, and the person claims not to have made an application to vote by post at the referendum[8]; or

(2)   a person applies for a ballot paper representing themselves to be a particular person named as a proxy in the list of proxies, the person is also named in the proxy postal voters list, and the person claims not to have made an application to vote by post as proxy[9],

the person is entitled, on satisfactorily answering the questions permitted by law to be asked at the poll, to mark a ballot paper (called a 'tendered ballot paper') in the same manner as any other voter or proxy[10].

If, at a local authority referendum, before the close of the poll but after the last time at which a person may apply for a replacement postal ballot paper, a person represents themselves to be a particular voter named on the register who is also named in the postal voters list, or a particular person named as a proxy in the list of proxies and who is also named in the proxy postal voters list, and claims to have lost or not received their postal ballot paper[11], the person is entitled, on satisfactorily answering the questions permitted by law to be asked at the poll, to mark a ballot paper (called a 'tendered ballot paper') in the same manner as any other voter or proxy[12].

In either case, a tendered ballot paper must be of a colour differing from the other ballot papers and, instead of being put into the ballot box, it must be given to the presiding officer[13] and endorsed by him with the name of the voter and his number in the register of electors[14], and set aside in a separate packet[15]. The name of the voter and his number on the register of electors must be entered on a list (called the 'tendered votes list')[16].

In relation to a local authority referendum, these provisions are modified where a voter has been added to the register[17], and in the case of a voter who has an anonymous entry[18].

1   As to how polls consequent on a parish or community meeting come about see PARA 581.
2   As to the registers of electors see PARA 145 et seq.
3   As to the questions that may be put to person applying for a ballot paper see PARA 619.
4   Parish and Community Meetings (Polls) Rules 1987, SI 1987/1, Schedule r 22(1). As to the provisions relating to ballot papers generally see PARA 607.
5   As to the meaning of 'referendum' for these purposes see PARA 574 notes 2, 13.
6   As to the absent voters list and the list of proxies see PARA 596; and as to the entitlement to vote by post as proxy see PARA 590.
7   Local Authorities (Conduct of Referendums) (Wales) Regulations 2008, SI 2008/1848, Sch 3 r 29(1); Local Authorities (Conduct of Referendums) (England) Regulations 2012, SI 2012/323, Sch 3 r 29(1). This is subject to the provisions of the Local Authorities (Conduct of Referendums) (Wales) Regulations 2008, SI 2008/1848, Sch 3 r 30, or the Local Authorities (Conduct of Referendums) (England) Regulations 2012, SI 2012/323, Sch 3 r 30, as the case may be (see the text and notes 13–18): Local Authorities (Conduct of Referendums) (Wales) Regulations 2008, SI 2008/1848, Sch 3 r 29(1); Local Authorities (Conduct of Referendums) (England) Regulations 2012, SI 2012/323, Sch 3 r 29(1).
8   Local Authorities (Conduct of Referendums) (Wales) Regulations 2008, SI 2008/1848, Sch 3 r 29(2); Local Authorities (Conduct of Referendums) (England) Regulations 2012, SI 2012/323, Sch 3 r 29(2).
9   Local Authorities (Conduct of Referendums) (Wales) Regulations 2008, SI 2008/1848, Sch 3 r 29(3); Local Authorities (Conduct of Referendums) (England) Regulations 2012, SI 2012/323, Sch 3 r 29(3).
10   Local Authorities (Conduct of Referendums) (Wales) Regulations 2008, SI 2008/1848, Sch 3 r 29(4); Local Authorities (Conduct of Referendums) (England) Regulations 2012, SI 2012/323, Sch 3 r 29(4). This is subject to the provisions of the Local Authorities (Conduct of Referendums) (Wales) Regulations 2008, SI 2008/1848, Sch 3 r 30, or the Local Authorities (Conduct of Referendums) (England) Regulations 2012, SI 2012/323, Sch 3 r 30, as the case may be (see the text and notes 13–18): Local Authorities (Conduct of Referendums) (Wales)

Regulations 2008, SI 2008/1848, Sch 3 r 29(4); Local Authorities (Conduct of Referendums) (England) Regulations 2012, SI 2012/323, Sch 3 r 29(4).

11 Local Authorities (Conduct of Referendums) (Wales) Regulations 2008, SI 2008/1848, Sch 3 r 29(5); Local Authorities (Conduct of Referendums) (England) Regulations 2012, SI 2012/323, Sch 3 r 29(5).

12 Local Authorities (Conduct of Referendums) (Wales) Regulations 2008, SI 2008/1848, Sch 3 r 29(6); Local Authorities (Conduct of Referendums) (England) Regulations 2012, SI 2012/323, Sch 3 r 29(6). This is subject to the provisions of the Local Authorities (Conduct of Referendums) (Wales) Regulations 2008, SI 2008/1848, Sch 3 r 30, or the Local Authorities (Conduct of Referendums) (England) Regulations 2012, SI 2012/323, Sch 3 r 30, as the case may be (see the text and notes 13–18): Local Authorities (Conduct of Referendums) (Wales) Regulations 2008, SI 2008/1848, Sch 3 r 29(6); Local Authorities (Conduct of Referendums) (England) Regulations 2012, SI 2012/323, Sch 3 r 29(6).

13 As to the appointment of presiding officers and clerks at a referendum or poll see PARA 613.

14 As to the number of an elector see PARA 145.

15 Parish and Community Meetings (Polls) Rules 1987, SI 1987/1, Schedule r 22(2); Local Authorities (Conduct of Referendums) (Wales) Regulations 2008, SI 2008/1848, Sch 3 r 30(1); Local Authorities (Conduct of Referendums) (England) Regulations 2012, SI 2012/323, Sch 3 r 30(1). In the case of a person voting as proxy for a voter at a local authority referendum, the number to be endorsed or entered together with the proxy's name must be the number in the register of the voter: Local Authorities (Conduct of Referendums) (Wales) Regulations 2008, SI 2008/1848, Sch 3 r 30(3); Local Authorities (Conduct of Referendums) (England) Regulations 2012, SI 2012/323, Sch 3 r 30(3).

16 Parish and Community Meetings (Polls) Rules 1987, SI 1987/1, Schedule r 22(3); Local Authorities (Conduct of Referendums) (Wales) Regulations 2008, SI 2008/1848, Sch 3 r 30(2); Local Authorities (Conduct of Referendums) (England) Regulations 2012, SI 2012/323, Sch 3 r 30(2).

17 Ie pursuant to the Representation of the People Act 1983 s 13B (applied and modified, in relation to Wales, by the Local Authorities (Conduct of Referendums) (Wales) Regulations 2008, SI 2008/1848, Sch 4 Table 1, and, in relation to England, by the Local Authorities (Conduct of Referendums) (England) Regulations 2012, SI 2012/323, Sch 4 Table 1): see the Local Authorities (Conduct of Referendums) (Wales) Regulations 2008, SI 2008/1848, Sch 3 r 26(5); and the Local Authorities (Conduct of Referendums) (England) Regulations 2012, SI 2012/323, Sch 3 r 26(5). As to the provisions that are so applied and modified see PARA 15.

18 See the Local Authorities (Conduct of Referendums) (Wales) Regulations 2008, SI 2008/1848, Sch 3 r 30(4); and the Local Authorities (Conduct of Referendums) (England) Regulations 2012, SI 2012/323, Sch 3 r 30(4).

625.   Inadvertently spoilt ballot papers at a referendum or poll.   At a local authority referendum[1] or at a poll consequent on a parish or community meeting[2], a voter (or, in the case of a local authority referendum, a proxy) who has inadvertently dealt with his ballot paper in such manner that it cannot be conveniently used as a ballot paper may, on delivering it to the presiding officer[3] and proving to his satisfaction the fact of the inadvertence, obtain another ballot paper in place of the ballot paper so delivered (the 'spoilt ballot paper')[4]. The spoilt ballot paper must be immediately cancelled[5].

1   As to the meaning of 'referendum' for these purposes see PARA 574 notes 2, 13.

2   As to how polls consequent on a parish or community meeting come about see PARA 581.

3   As to the appointment of presiding officers and clerks at a referendum or poll see PARA 613.

4   Parish and Community Meetings (Polls) Rules 1987, SI 1987/1, Schedule r 23; Local Authorities (Conduct of Referendums) (Wales) Regulations 2008, SI 2008/1848, Sch 3 r 31; Local Authorities (Conduct of Referendums) (England) Regulations 2012, SI 2012/323, Sch 3 r 31.

626.   Procedure on close of poll at a referendum or poll.   As soon as practicable after the close of the poll consequent on a parish or community meeting[1], the presiding officer[2] must, in the presence of the polling agents, make up into separate packets, sealed with his own seal and the seals of such polling agents as desire to affix their seals:

(1)   each ballot box in use at his station, sealed so as to prevent the introduction of additional ballot papers and unopened (but with the key attached)[3];

(2)   the unused and spoilt ballot papers, placed together[4];

(3)   the tendered ballot papers[5];

(4)   the marked copies of the register of electors[6];

(5)   the counterfoils of the used ballot papers[7]; and

(6)   the tendered votes list[8], the list of blind voters assisted by companions[9], the list of votes marked by the presiding officer[10], a statement of the number of voters whose votes are so marked by the presiding officer under the heads 'physical incapacity' and 'unable to read', and the declarations made by the companions of blind voters[11].

As soon as practicable after the close of the poll at a local authority referendum[12], the presiding officer must, in the presence of the polling observers[13] (if any), make up into separate packets, sealed with his or her own seal and the seals of such polling observers as desire to affix their seals:

(a)   each ballot box in use at the station, sealed so as to prevent the introduction of additional ballot papers and unopened, but with the key, if any, attached[14];

(b)   the unused and spoilt ballot papers placed together[15];

(c)   the tendered ballot papers[16];

(d)   the marked copies of the register of electors[17] and of the list of proxies[18];

(e)   the corresponding number list[19];

(f)   the certificates as to employment on duty on the day of the poll[20];

(g)   the tendered votes list, the list of voters and proxies with disabilities assisted by companions[21], the list of votes marked by the presiding officer, a statement of the number of voters and proxies whose votes are so marked by the presiding officer under the heads 'disability' and 'unable to read', the relating to the correction of errors[22] list maintained, and the declarations made by the companions of voters and proxies with disabilities[23].

In either case the presiding officer must deliver the packets or cause them to be delivered to the returning or counting officer[24] to be taken charge of by that person; but if the packets are not delivered by the presiding officer personally to the returning or counting officer, the arrangements for their delivery must require the counting officer's approval[25]. The packets must be accompanied by a statement (referred to as 'the ballot paper account') made by the presiding officer showing the number of ballot papers entrusted to him or her, and accounting for them under the heads of ballot papers issued and not otherwise accounted for, unused, spoilt and tendered ballot papers[26].

1   As to how polls consequent on a parish or community meeting come about see PARA 581.

2   As to the appointment of presiding officers and clerks at a referendum or poll see PARA 613.

3   Parish and Community Meetings (Polls) Rules 1987, SI 1987/1, Schedule r 25(1)(a).

4   Parish and Community Meetings (Polls) Rules 1987, SI 1987/1, Schedule r 25(1)(b).

5   Parish and Community Meetings (Polls) Rules 1987, SI 1987/1, Schedule r 25(1)(c).

6   Parish and Community Meetings (Polls) Rules 1987, SI 1987/1, Schedule r 25(1)(d). The marked copies of the register of electors must not be in the same packet as the counterfoils of the used ballot papers: Schedule r 25(2).

7   Parish and Community Meetings (Polls) Rules 1987, SI 1987/1, Schedule r 25(1)(e).

8   As to the tendered votes list see PARA 624.

9   As to the list of voters with disabilities assisted by companions see PARA 623.

10   As to the list of votes marked by the presiding officer see PARA 622.

11 Parish and Community Meetings (Polls) Rules 1987, SI 1987/1, Schedule r 25(1)(f).

12 As to the meaning of 'referendum' for these purposes see PARA 574 notes 2, 13.

13 As to the appointment of polling observers at a referendum see PARA 614.

14 Local Authorities (Conduct of Referendums) (Wales) Regulations 2008, SI 2008/1848, Sch 3 r 34(1)(a); Local Authorities (Conduct of Referendums) (England) Regulations 2012, SI 2012/323, Sch 3 r 34(1)(a).

15 Local Authorities (Conduct of Referendums) (Wales) Regulations 2008, SI 2008/1848, Sch 3 r 34(1)(b); Local Authorities (Conduct of Referendums) (England) Regulations 2012, SI 2012/323, Sch 3 r 34(1)(b).

16 Local Authorities (Conduct of Referendums) (Wales) Regulations 2008, SI 2008/1848, Sch 3 r 34(1)(c); Local Authorities (Conduct of Referendums) (England) Regulations 2012, SI 2012/323, Sch 3 r 34(1)(c).

17 Ie including any marked copy notices issued under the Representation of the People Act 1983 s 13B(3B) or (3D) (notices specifying appropriate alterations to the register: see PARA 168) (applied and modified, in relation to Wales, by the Local Authorities (Conduct of Referendums) (Wales) Regulations 2008, SI 2008/1848, Sch 4 Table 1, and, in relation to England, by the Local Authorities (Conduct of Referendums) (England) Regulations 2012, SI 2012/323, Sch 4 Table 1: see PARA 15): see the Local Authorities (Conduct of Referendums) (Wales) Regulations 2008, SI 2008/1848, Sch 3 r 34(1)(d); and the Local Authorities (Conduct of Referendums) (England) Regulations 2012, SI 2012/323, Sch 3 r 34(1)(d).

   The presiding officer must keep a list of persons to whom ballot papers are delivered in consequence of an alteration to the register made by virtue of the Representation of the People Act 1983 s 13B(3B) or s 13(3D) which takes effect on the day of the poll: see the Local Authorities (Conduct of Referendums) (Wales) Regulations 2008, SI 2008/1848, Sch 3 r 32; the Local Authorities (Conduct of Referendums) (England) Regulations 2012, SI 2012/323, Sch 3 r 32; and PARA 611 note 4.

18 Local Authorities (Conduct of Referendums) (Wales) Regulations 2008, SI 2008/1848, Sch 3 r 34(1)(d); Local Authorities (Conduct of Referendums) (England) Regulations 2012, SI 2012/323, Sch 3 r 34(1)(d). The marked copies of the register of electors and of the list of proxies must be in one packet but must not be in the same packet as the completed corresponding number lists or the certificates as to employment on duty on the day of the poll: Local Authorities (Conduct of Referendums) (Wales) Regulations 2008, SI 2008/1848, Sch 3 r 34(2); Local Authorities (Conduct of Referendums) (England) Regulations 2012, SI 2012/323, Sch 3 r 34(2).

19 Ie the lists prepared under the Local Authorities (Conduct of Referendums) (Wales) Regulations 2008, SI 2008/1848, Sch 3 r 8, or under the Local Authorities (Conduct of Referendums) (England) Regulations 2012, SI 2012/323, Sch 3 r 8, as the case may be (see PARAS 611 note 4, 627 note 5), including the parts which were completed in accordance with the Local Authorities (Conduct of Referendums) (Wales) Regulations 2008, SI 2008/1848, Sch 3 r 26(1)(b), or the Local Authorities (Conduct of Referendums) (England) Regulations 2012, SI 2012/323, Sch 3 r 26(1)(b), as the case may be (together referred to in these Rules as 'the completed corresponding number lists'): Local Authorities (Conduct of Referendums) (Wales) Regulations 2008, SI 2008/1848, Sch 3 r 34(1)(e); Local Authorities (Conduct of Referendums) (England) Regulations 2012, SI 2012/323, Sch 3 r 34(1)(e).

20 Local Authorities (Conduct of Referendums) (Wales) Regulations 2008, SI 2008/1848, Sch 3 r 34(1)(f); Local Authorities (Conduct of Referendums) (England) Regulations 2012, SI 2012/323, Sch 3 r 34(1)(f).

21 As to this list see PARA 623.

22 Ie the list maintained under the Local Authorities (Conduct of Referendums) (Wales) Regulations 2008, SI 2008/1848, Sch 3 r 32, or under the Local Authorities (Conduct of Referendums) (England) Regulations 2012, SI 2012/323, Sch 3 r 32, as the case may be (see PARA 611 note 4).

23 Local Authorities (Conduct of Referendums) (Wales) Regulations 2008, SI 2008/1848, Sch 3 r 34(1)(g); Local Authorities (Conduct of Referendums) (England) Regulations 2012, SI 2012/323, Sch 3 r 34(1)(g).

24 As to returning officers at polls consequent on a parish or community meeting see PARA 588. As to the meaning of 'counting officer' see PARA 576 note 1.

25 Parish and Community Meetings (Polls) Rules 1987, SI 1987/1, Schedule r 25(1); Local Authorities (Conduct of Referendums) (Wales) Regulations 2008, SI 2008/1848, Sch 3 r 34(1); Local Authorities (Conduct of Referendums) (England) Regulations 2012, SI 2012/323, Sch 3 r 34(1).

26 Parish and Community Meetings (Polls) Rules 1987, SI 1987/1, Schedule r 25(3); Local
Authorities (Conduct of Referendums) (Wales) Regulations 2008, SI 2008/1848, Sch 3 r 34(3);
Local Authorities (Conduct of Referendums) (England) Regulations 2012, SI 2012/323, Sch 3
r 34(3).

(C) Votes given by Postal Ballot at a Local Authority Referendum

(a) Issue of Postal Ballot Papers at a Local Authority Referendum

**627. Counting officer's duty to issue postal ballot papers, etc at local authority
referendum.** At a local authority referendum[1], the counting officer[2] must issue
to those entitled to vote by post[3] a postal ballot paper and a postal voting
statement[4], together with such envelopes for their return (whether free of charge
or otherwise) as may be so prescribed[5]. The counting officer must also issue to
those entitled to vote by post such information as he or she thinks appropriate
about how to obtain translations into languages other than English of any
directions to or guidance for voters and proxies sent with the ballot paper[6], a
translation into Braille of such directions or guidance[7], graphical representations
of such directions or guidance[8], and the directions or guidance in any other form
(including any audible form)[9]. The postal voting statement must include
provision for the form to be signed and for stating the date of birth of the voter
or proxy[10]. In the case of a ballot paper issued to a person at an address in the
United Kingdom, the counting officer must ensure that the return of the ballot
paper and postal voting statement is free of charge to the voter or proxy[11].

1   As to the meaning of 'referendum' for these purposes see PARA 574 notes 2, 13.
2   As to the meaning of 'counting officer' see PARA 576 note 1.
3   As to applications made for absent voting see PARA 592 et seq.
4   Ie a statement in the appropriate form in the Local Authorities (Conduct of Referendums)
    (Wales) Regulations 2008, SI 2008/1848, Sch 3 Appendix of Forms, or in the Local Authorities
    (Conduct of Referendums) (England) Regulations 2012, SI 2012/323, Sch 3 Appendix of Forms,
    or a form to like effect.
5   Local Authorities (Conduct of Referendums) (Wales) Regulations 2008, SI 2008/1848, Sch 3
    r 13(1); Local Authorities (Conduct of Referendums) (England) Regulations 2012, SI 2012/323,
    Sch 3 r 13(1).
      The counting officer must prepare a list containing the numbers and other unique identifying
    marks of all of the ballot papers to be issued by the counting officer in pursuance of the Local
    Authorities (Conduct of Referendums) (Wales) Regulations 2008, SI 2008/1848, Sch 3 r 13(1),
    or the Local Authorities (Conduct of Referendums) (England) Regulations 2012, SI 2012/323,
    Sch 3 r 13(1), as the case may be, and the list must be in the appropriate form or a form to like
    effect: Local Authorities (Conduct of Referendums) (Wales) Regulations 2008, SI 2008/1848,
    Sch 3 r 8(1), (2); Local Authorities (Conduct of Referendums) (England) Regulations 2012,
    SI 2012/323, Sch 3 r 8(1), (2). As to the appropriate form see the Local Authorities (Conduct of
    Referendums) (Wales) Regulations 2008, SI 2008/1848, Pt 8 Appendix of Forms
    (Corresponding Number List L1), and the Local Authorities (Conduct of Referendums)
    (England) Regulations 2012, SI 2012/323, Pt 8 Appendix of Forms (Corresponding Number
    List L1).
6   Local Authorities (Conduct of Referendums) (Wales) Regulations 2008, SI 2008/1848, Sch 3
    r 13(2)(a); Local Authorities (Conduct of Referendums) (England) Regulations 2012,
    SI 2012/323, Sch 3 r 13(2)(a).
7   Local Authorities (Conduct of Referendums) (Wales) Regulations 2008, SI 2008/1848, Sch 3
    r 13(2)(b); Local Authorities (Conduct of Referendums) (England) Regulations 2012,
    SI 2012/323, Sch 3 r 13(2)(b).
8   Local Authorities (Conduct of Referendums) (Wales) Regulations 2008, SI 2008/1848, Sch 3
    r 13(2)(c); Local Authorities (Conduct of Referendums) (England) Regulations 2012,
    SI 2012/323, Sch 3 r 13(2)(c).
9   Local Authorities (Conduct of Referendums) (Wales) Regulations 2008, SI 2008/1848, Sch 3
    r 13(2)(d); Local Authorities (Conduct of Referendums) (England) Regulations 2012,
    SI 2012/323, Sch 3 r 13(2)(d).

10 Local Authorities (Conduct of Referendums) (Wales) Regulations 2008, SI 2008/1848, Sch 3 r 13(2)(3); Local Authorities (Conduct of Referendums) (England) Regulations 2012, SI 2012/323, Sch 3 r 13(3).
11 Local Authorities (Conduct of Referendums) (Wales) Regulations 2008, SI 2008/1848, Sch 3 r 13(2)(4); Local Authorities (Conduct of Referendums) (England) Regulations 2012, SI 2012/323, Sch 3 r 13(4).

628.   Notification of requirement of secrecy at proceedings relating to the issue of postal ballot papers at local authority referendum.   The counting officer[1] at a local authority referendum[2] must make such arrangements as he thinks fit to ensure that every person attending the proceedings in connection with the issue[3] of postal ballot papers[4] has been given a copy in writing of the statutory provisions relating to the requirement of secrecy that apply to those proceedings[5].

1   As to the meaning of 'counting officer' see PARA 576 note 1.
2   As to the meaning of 'referendum' for these purposes see PARA 574 notes 2, 13.
3   As to proceedings on the issue of postal ballot papers see PARA 630.
4   As to the meaning of 'postal ballot paper' see the Representation of the People (England and Wales) Regulations 2001, SI 2001/341, reg 64; and PARA 407 note 1 (provisions of those regulations applied and modified, in relation to Wales, by the Local Authorities (Conduct of Referendums) (Wales) Regulations 2008, SI 2008/1848, Sch 4 Table 5, and, in relation to England, by the Local Authorities (Conduct of Referendums) (England) Regulations 2012, SI 2012/323, Sch 4 Table 6). As to the provisions that are so applied and modified see PARA 15.
5   Representation of the People (England and Wales) Regulations 2001, SI 2001/341, reg 70 (as applied and modified: see note 4). The text refers to the requirement of secrecy set out in the Representation of the People Act 1983 s 66(4), (6) (applied and modified, in relation to Wales, by the Local Authorities (Conduct of Referendums) (Wales) Regulations 2008, SI 2008/1848, Sch 4 Table 1, and, in relation to England, by the Local Authorities (Conduct of Referendums) (England) Regulations 2012, SI 2012/323, Sch 4 Table 1 (see PARA 742)).

629.   Time of issue of postal ballot papers, etc at local authority referendum.   At a local authority referendum[1], the postal ballot paper[2] and postal voting statement must be issued by the counting officer[3] as soon as practicable after the registration officer[4] has granted the application to vote by post[5], except where a person is shown in the records kept of those entitled (for a defined period or for an indefinite period) to an absent vote at referendums[6] or to vote by post as proxy at referendums[7], in which two cases no postal ballot paper and declaration of identity may be issued until after 5 pm on the eleventh day before the date of the poll[8].

1   As to the meaning of 'referendum' for these purposes see PARA 574 notes 2, 13.
2   As to the meaning of 'postal ballot paper' see PARA 628 note 4.
3   As to the meaning of 'counting officer' see PARA 576 note 1. As to the counting officer's duty to issue postal ballot papers, etc see PARA 627.
4   As to the meaning of 'registration officer' see the Representation of the People (England and Wales) Regulations 2001, SI 2001/341, reg 3(1); and PARA 139 note 1 (provisions of those regulations applied and modified, in relation to Wales, by the Local Authorities (Conduct of Referendums) (Wales) Regulations 2008, SI 2008/1848, Sch 4 Table 5, and, in relation to England, by the Local Authorities (Conduct of Referendums) (England) Regulations 2012, SI 2012/323, Sch 4 Table 6). As to the provisions that are so applied and modified see PARA 15.
5   Representation of the People (England and Wales) Regulations 2001, SI 2001/341; reg 71(2) (reg 71(1), (2) amended by SI 2006/2910) (as applied and modified: see note 4). As to applications to vote by post see PARA 592.
6   Ie the record kept under the Representation of the People Act 2000 Sch 4 para 3(4) (as applied and modified) (see PARA 593).
7   Ie the record kept under the Representation of the People Act 2000 Sch 4 para 7(6) (as applied and modified) (see PARA 602).

8   Representation of the People (England and Wales) Regulations 2001, SI 2001/341, reg 71(1) (as amended, applied and modified: see notes 4, 5). As to the computation of time for these purposes see PARA 592 note 7.

630. Proceedings on the issue of postal ballot papers at local authority referendum. At a local authority referendum[1], no person may be present at the proceedings on the issue of postal ballot papers[2] other than the counting officer[3] and his clerks[4]. The following procedure must be followed:

(1)   the number of the elector[5] as stated in the register must be marked on the corresponding number list, next to the number and unique identifying mark of the ballot paper issued to that elector[6];

(2)   a mark must be placed in the postal voters list[7] or the list of proxy postal voters list[8] against the number of the elector to denote that a ballot paper has been issued to the elector or his proxy, but without showing the particular ballot paper issued[9]; and

(3)   the number of a postal ballot paper must be marked on the postal voting statement sent with that paper[10].

Where the poll at a referendum is taken with the poll at another election or referendum, special provision is made for the issue of postal ballot papers[11].

1   As to the meaning of 'referendum' for these purposes see PARA 574 notes 2, 13.
2   As to the meaning of 'postal ballot paper' see PARA 628 note 4.
3   As to the meaning of 'counting officer' see PARA 576 note 1.
4   Representation of the People (England and Wales) Regulations 2001, SI 2001/341, reg 67 (regs 67, 72(2)–(6) amended by SI 2006/2910) (provisions of those regulations applied and modified, in relation to Wales, by the Local Authorities (Conduct of Referendums) (Wales) Regulations 2008, SI 2008/1848, Sch 4 Table 5, and, in relation to England, by the Local Authorities (Conduct of Referendums) (England) Regulations 2012, SI 2012/323, Sch 4 Table 6). As to the provisions that are so applied and modified see PARA 15. This is without prejudice to the provisions of the Political Parties, Elections and Referendums Act 2000 ss 6A–6E (as to which see PARA 53): Representation of the People (England and Wales) Regulations 2001, SI 2001/341, reg 67 (as so amended, applied and modified).
5   As to the number of an elector see PARA 145.
6   Representation of the People (England and Wales) Regulations 2001, SI 2001/341, reg 72(2) (as amended, applied and modified: see note 4).
7   As to the meaning of 'postal voters list' see PARA 373 note 7.
8   As to the meaning of 'proxy postal voters list' see PARA 381 note 6.
9   Representation of the People (England and Wales) Regulations 2001, SI 2001/341, reg 72(3) (as amended, applied and modified: see note 4).
10   Representation of the People (England and Wales) Regulations 2001, SI 2001/341, reg 72(4) (as amended, applied and modified: see note 4).
11   Representation of the People (England and Wales) Regulations 2001, SI 2001/341, reg 72(5), (6) (as amended, applied and modified: see note 4).

631. Refusal to issue more than one postal ballot paper at local authority referendum. At a local authority referendum[1], where the counting officer[2] is satisfied that two or more entries in either the postal voters list[3] or the proxy postal voters list[4] or in each of those lists relate to the same elector, he must not issue more than one ballot paper in respect of the same elector in respect of any one referendum[5].

1   As to the meaning of 'referendum' for these purposes see PARA 574 notes 2, 13.
2   As to the meaning of 'counting officer' see PARA 576 note 1.
3   As to the postal voters list see PARA 373.
4   As to the proxy postal voters list see PARA 381.
5   Representation of the People (England and Wales) Regulations 2001, SI 2001/341, reg 73 (amended by SI 2006/2910) (provisions of those regulations applied and modified, in relation to Wales, by the Local Authorities (Conduct of Referendums) (Wales) Regulations 2008,

SI 2008/1848, Sch 4 Table 5, and, in relation to England, by the Local Authorities (Conduct of Referendums) (England) Regulations 2012, SI 2012/323, Sch 4 Table 6). As to the provisions that are so applied and modified see PARA 15.

632. Envelopes issued to postal voter at local authority referendum. At a local authority referendum[1], an envelope marked with the letter 'B' (a 'covering envelope'[2]) must be issued to a postal voter[3] by the counting officer[4] for the return of the postal ballot paper (or ballot papers, as the case may be)[5] and the postal voting statement also issued to him[6]. The counting officer must also issue to a postal voter a smaller envelope (a 'ballot paper envelope'[7]) which must be marked with the letter 'A', the words 'ballot paper envelope' and (unless the envelope has a window through which the number on the ballot paper or papers can be displayed), the number of the ballot paper or, as the case may be, ballot papers[8].

The address to which the postal ballot paper, the postal voting statement and the envelopes are to be sent is, in the case of an elector, the address shown in the postal voters list[9] or, in the case of a proxy, the address shown in the list of proxy postal voters list[10].

1   As to the meaning of 'referendum' for these purposes see PARA 574 notes 2, 13.
2   As to the meaning of 'covering envelope' see the Representation of the People (England and Wales) Regulations 2001, SI 2001/341, reg 64 (provisions of those regulations applied and modified, in relation to Wales, by the Local Authorities (Conduct of Referendums) (Wales) Regulations 2008, SI 2008/1848, Sch 4 Table 5, and, in relation to England, by the Local Authorities (Conduct of Referendums) (England) Regulations 2012, SI 2012/323, Sch 4 Table 6); and PARA 410 note 6. As to the provisions that are so applied and modified see PARA 15.
3   As to the meaning of 'postal voter' see the Representation of the People (England and Wales) Regulations 2001, SI 2001/341, reg 64 (as applied and modified: see note 2); and PARA 407 note 1.
4   As to the meaning of 'counting officer' see PARA 576 note 1.
5   As to the meaning of 'postal ballot paper' see PARA 628 note 4. There will be more than one ballot paper when the proceedings on the issue and receipt of postal ballot papers at more than one referendum or election have been taken together (as to which see PARA 20); as to special provision made for the marking of the envelopes used where the poll at one referendum or election is taken with the poll at another referendum or election Representation of the People (England and Wales) Regulations 2001, SI 2001/341, reg 74(4) (as applied and modified: see note 2).
6   Representation of the People (England and Wales) Regulations 2001, SI 2001/341, reg 74(1), (2) (reg 74(1)–(3) amended by SI 2006/2910) (as applied and modified: see note 2).
7   As to the meaning of 'ballot paper envelope' see the Representation of the People (England and Wales) Regulations 2001, SI 2001/341, reg 64 (as applied and modified: see note 2); and PARA 410.
8   Representation of the People (England and Wales) Regulations 2001, SI 2001/341, reg 74(3) (as amended, applied and modified: see notes 2, 6).
9   As to the meaning of 'postal voters list' see PARA 373 note 7.
10   Representation of the People (England and Wales) Regulations 2001, SI 2001/341, reg 72(7) (as applied and modified: see note 2). As to the meaning of 'proxy postal voters list' see PARA 381 note 6. These provisions are modified where a person has an anonymous entry in the register: see reg 72(8) (as so applied and modified).

633. Delivery of postal ballot papers at local authority referendum. At a local authority referendum[1], for the purposes of delivering postal ballot papers[2], the counting officer[3] may use: (1) a universal postal service provider[4]; (2) a commercial delivery firm[5]; or (3) clerks appointed by a counting officer to aid a presiding officer[6]. Except where head (3) above applies, postage must be pre-paid on the envelopes addressed to the postal voters[7]; and where the address provided by the postal voter for the receipt of the postal ballot paper is within the United Kingdom[8], return postage must be pre-paid on all covering envelopes also[9]. Where the services of a universal postal service provider or commercial delivery firm are to be used, envelopes addressed to postal voters must be counted and delivered by the counting officer with such form of receipt to be endorsed by that provider or firm as may be arranged[10].

1   As to the meaning of 'referendum' for these purposes see PARA 574 notes 2, 13.
2   As to the meaning of 'postal ballot paper' see PARA 628 note 4. There will be more than one ballot paper when the proceedings on the issue and receipt of postal ballot papers at more than one referendum or election have been taken together (as to which see PARA 20).
3   As to the meaning of 'counting officer' see PARA 576 note 1.
4   Representation of the People (England and Wales) Regulations 2001, SI 2001/341, reg 76(1)(a) (provisions of those regulations applied and modified, in relation to Wales, by the Local Authorities (Conduct of Referendums) (Wales) Regulations 2008, SI 2008/1848, Sch 4 Table 5, and, in relation to England, by the Local Authorities (Conduct of Referendums) (England) Regulations 2012, SI 2012/323, Sch 4 Table 6). As to the provisions that are so applied and modified see PARA 15. As to the meaning of 'universal postal service provider' see the Representation of the People (England and Wales) Regulations 2001, SI 2001/341, reg 64 (as so applied and modified); and PARA 411 note 4.
5   Representation of the People (England and Wales) Regulations 2001, SI 2001/341, reg 76(1)(b) (as applied and modified: see note 4).
6   Representation of the People (England and Wales) Regulations 2001, SI 2001/341, reg 76(1)(c) (as applied and modified: see note 4).
7   Representation of the People (England and Wales) Regulations 2001, SI 2001/341, reg 76(3) (as applied and modified: see note 4). As to the meaning of 'postal voter' see PARA 632 note 3.
8   As to the meaning of 'United Kingdom' see PARA 1 note 1.
9   Representation of the People (England and Wales) Regulations 2001, SI 2001/341, reg 76(4) (as applied and modified: see note 4).
10 Representation of the People (England and Wales) Regulations 2001, SI 2001/341, reg 76(2) (as applied and modified: see note 4).

634.   Sealing up of completed corresponding number lists and security of special lists at local authority referendum.   At a local authority referendum[1], as soon as practicable after the issue of each batch of postal ballot papers[2], the counting officer[3] must make up into a packet the completed corresponding number lists of those ballot papers which have been issued and he must seal the packet[4]. The returning officer is also required[5] to take proper precautions for the security of the marked copy of the postal voters list[6] and the proxy postal voters list[7].

1   As to the meaning of 'referendum' for these purposes see PARA 574 notes 2, 13.
2   As to the meaning of 'postal ballot paper' see PARA 628 note 4. There will be more than one ballot paper when the proceedings on the issue and receipt of postal ballot papers at more than one referendum or election have been taken together (as to which see PARA 20).
3   As to the meaning of 'counting officer' see PARA 576 note 1.
4   Representation of the People (England and Wales) Regulations 2001, SI 2001/341, reg 75(1) (reg 75(1), (2) amended by SI 2006/2910) (provisions of those regulations applied and modified, in relation to Wales, by the Local Authorities (Conduct of Referendums) (Wales) Regulations 2008, SI 2008/1848, Sch 4 Table 5, and, in relation to England, by the Local Authorities (Conduct of Referendums) (England) Regulations 2012, SI 2012/323, Sch 4 Table 6). As to the provisions that are so applied and modified see PARA 15.
5   Ie until the time referred to in the Representation of the People (England and Wales) Regulations 2001, SI 2001/341, reg 84(9) (see PARA 421).
6   As to the meaning of 'postal voters list' see PARA 373 note 7.
7   Representation of the People (England and Wales) Regulations 2001, SI 2001/341, reg 75(2) (as applied and modified: see note 4). As to the meaning of 'proxy postal voters list' see PARA 381 note 6.

635.   Spoilt postal ballot papers at local authority referendum.   At a local authority referendum[1], if a postal voter[2] has inadvertently dealt with his postal

ballot paper[3] or postal voting statement in such manner that it cannot
conveniently be used as a ballot paper (ie a 'spoilt ballot paper') or, as the case
may be, a postal voting statement (ie a 'spoilt postal voting statement'), he may
return the spoilt ballot paper[4] or voting statement either by hand or by post to
the counting officer[5]. On receipt of any such documents, the counting officer
must issue another postal ballot paper (or, as the case may be, ballot papers)
except where those documents are received after 5 pm on the day of the poll[6], in
which case he may only issue another postal ballot paper (or, as the case may be,
ballot papers) if the postal voter returned the documents by hand[7]. Any such
postal ballot paper or postal voting statement, whether spoilt or not, which has
been returned must be immediately cancelled[8]; and, as soon as practicable after
cancelling those documents, the counting officer must make up those documents
in a separate packet and he must seal the packet[9]. If, on any subsequent
occasion, documents are cancelled in this way, the sealed packet must be opened
and the additional cancelled documents included in it and the packet must be
again made up and sealed[10].

The counting officer must enter in a list kept for the purpose (the 'list of spoilt
postal ballot papers'): (1) the name and number of the elector as stated in the
register (or, in the case of an elector who has an anonymous entry, his electoral
number alone)[11]; (2) the number of the replacement postal ballot paper (or
papers) issued[12]; and (3) where the postal voter whose ballot paper is spoilt is a
proxy[13], his name and address[14].

1   As to the meaning of 'referendum' for these purposes see PARA 574 notes 2, 13.
2   As to the meaning of 'postal voter' see PARA 632 note 3.
3   As to the meaning of 'postal ballot paper' see PARA 628 note 4. There will be more than one
    ballot paper when the proceedings on the issue and receipt of postal ballot papers at more than
    one referendum or election have been taken together (as to which see PARA 20); and as to special
    provision made for spoilt ballot papers when the polls at more than one referendum or election
    have been taken together see the Representation of the People (England and Wales)
    Regulations 2001, SI 2001/341, reg 77(2) (reg 77(1), (2) substituted by SI 2006/752;
    Representation of the People (England and Wales) Regulations 2001, SI 2001/341,
    reg 77(1), (2), (8)(a) amended by SI 2006/2910) (provisions of those regulations applied and
    modified, in relation to Wales, by the Local Authorities (Conduct of Referendums) (Wales)
    Regulations 2008, SI 2008/1848, Sch 4 Table 5, and, in relation to England, by the Local
    Authorities (Conduct of Referendums) (England) Regulations 2012, SI 2012/323, Sch 4
    Table 6). As to the provisions that are so applied and modified see PARA 15.
4   As to the meaning of 'spoilt ballot paper' see the Representation of the People (England and
    Wales) Regulations 2001, SI 2001/341, reg 64 (as applied and modified: see note 3); and PARA
    414 note 3.
5   Representation of the People (England and Wales) Regulations 2001, SI 2001/341, reg 77(1) (as
    substituted, amended, applied and modified: see note 3). As to the meaning of 'counting officer'
    see PARA 576 note 1.
6   Representation of the People (England and Wales) Regulations 2001, SI 2001/341, reg 77(3)
    (reg 77(3) amended, reg 77(3A) added, reg 77(5), (7) substituted, by SI 2006/752) (as applied
    and modified: see note 3). Certain provisions as to the issue of postal ballot papers, namely the
    Representation of the People (England and Wales) Regulations 2001, SI 2001/341, reg 72 (as
    applied and modified) (except reg 72(3) (as applied and modified)) (see PARA 630) and, subject
    to reg 77(7) (as applied and modified) (see note 7), regs 74–76 (as applied and modified) (see
    PARAS 632–634), apply to the issue of replacement postal ballot papers: see reg 77(4) (as so
    applied and modified).
7   Representation of the People (England and Wales) Regulations 2001, SI 2001/341, reg 77(3A)
    (as added, applied and modified: see notes 3, 6). The counting officer may hand a replacement
    postal ballot paper to a postal voter who applies in person by 5 pm on the day before the day of
    the poll (and he may only hand a replacement postal ballot paper to a postal voter who applies
    in person after 5 pm on the day before the day of the poll) instead of delivering it in accordance
    with the statutory scheme (as to which see PARA 633): Representation of the People (England
    and Wales) Regulations 2001, SI 2001/341, reg 77(7) (as so substituted, applied and modified).

8 Representation of the People (England and Wales) Regulations 2001, SI 2001/341, reg 77(5) (as substituted, applied and modified: see notes 3, 6).
9 Representation of the People (England and Wales) Regulations 2001, SI 2001/341, reg 77(6) (as applied and modified: see note 3).
10 Representation of the People (England and Wales) Regulations 2001, SI 2001/341, reg 77(6) (as applied and modified: see note 3).
11 Representation of the People (England and Wales) Regulations 2001, SI 2001/341, reg 77(8)(a) (as amended, applied and modified: see note 3).
12 Representation of the People (England and Wales) Regulations 2001, SI 2001/341, reg 77(8)(b) (as applied and modified: see note 3).
13 As to applications to vote by proxy see PARA 592 et seq.
14 Representation of the People (England and Wales) Regulations 2001, SI 2001/341, reg 77(8)(c) (as applied and modified: see note 3).

636.   Lost postal ballot papers at local authority referendum.   At a local authority referendum[1], where a postal voter[2], by the fourth day before the day of the poll, claims either to have lost or not to have received his postal ballot paper[3], the postal voting statement[4] or one or more of the envelopes supplied for their return[5], he may apply (whether or not in person) to the counting officer[6] for a replacement ballot paper[7]. The voter must include evidence of his identity with any such application[8].

Where a postal voter exercises his entitlement to a replacement ballot paper, he must return the other documents which he has received and which have not been lost[9]. Any such postal ballot paper or postal voting statement which has been returned must be immediately cancelled[10]; and, as soon as practicable after cancelling those documents, the counting officer must make up those documents in a separate packet and he must seal the packet[11]. If, on any subsequent occasion, documents are cancelled in this way, the sealed packet must be opened and the additional cancelled documents included in it and the packet must be again made up and sealed[12].

Where the application for a replacement ballot paper is received by the counting officer before 5 pm on the day of the poll and the counting officer is satisfied as to the voter's identity and he has no reason to doubt that the postal voter has either lost or has not received the original postal ballot paper (or the postal voting statement or one or more of the envelopes provided for their return), he must issue another postal ballot paper or, as the case may be, postal ballot papers[13]. However where the application is received by the counting officer after 5 pm on the day before the day of the poll, he may only issue another postal ballot paper or, as the case may be, other ballot papers if the postal voter applied in person[14].

The counting officer must enter in a list kept for the purpose (the 'list of lost postal ballot papers'): (1) the name and number of the elector[15] as stated in the register (or, in the case of an elector who has an anonymous entry, his electoral number alone)[16]; (2) the number of the replacement postal ballot paper issued[17]; and (3) where the postal voter whose ballot paper is lost is a proxy[18], his name and address[19].

1 As to the meaning of 'referendum' for these purposes see PARA 574 notes 2, 13.
2 As to the meaning of 'postal voter' see PARA 632 note 3.
3 Representation of the People (England and Wales) Regulations 2001, SI 2001/341, reg 78(1)(a) (reg 78(1), (4)(c), (6) substituted, reg 78(2A)–(2C), (3A) added, reg 78(3) amended, by SI 2006/752; Representation of the People (England and Wales) Regulations 2001, SI 2001/341, regs 78(1), (2B), (3), (4)(a) amended by SI 2006/2910) (provisions of those regulations applied and modified, in relation to Wales, by the Local Authorities (Conduct of Referendums) (Wales) Regulations 2008, SI 2008/1848, Sch 4 Table 5, and, in relation to England, by the Local

Authorities (Conduct of Referendums) (England) Regulations 2012, SI 2012/323, Sch 4 Table 6). As to the provisions that are so applied and modified see PARA 15. As to the meaning of 'postal ballot paper' see PARA 628 note 4.

4   Representation of the People (England and Wales) Regulations 2001, SI 2001/341, reg 78(1)(b) (as substituted, amended, applied and modified: see note 3).

5   Representation of the People (England and Wales) Regulations 2001, SI 2001/341, reg 78(1)(c) (as substituted, amended, applied and modified: see note 3). As to the envelopes provided for use in postal voting see PARA 632.

6   As to the meaning of 'counting officer' see PARA 576 note 1.

7   Representation of the People (England and Wales) Regulations 2001, SI 2001/341, reg 78(1) (as substituted, amended, applied and modified: see note 3).

8   Representation of the People (England and Wales) Regulations 2001, SI 2001/341, reg 78(2) (as applied and modified: see note 3).

9   Representation of the People (England and Wales) Regulations 2001, SI 2001/341, reg 78(2A) (as added, applied and modified: see note 3). As to special provision made for lost ballot papers when the polls at more than one referendum or election have been taken together (as to which see PARA 20) see the Representation of the People (England and Wales) Regulations 2001, SI 2001/341, reg 78(2A)(b) (as so applied and modified).

10 Representation of the People (England and Wales) Regulations 2001, SI 2001/341, reg 78(2B) (as added, amended, applied and modified: see note 3).

11 Representation of the People (England and Wales) Regulations 2001, SI 2001/341, reg 78(2C) (as added, applied and modified: see note 3).

12 Representation of the People (England and Wales) Regulations 2001, SI 2001/341, reg 78(2C) (as added, applied and modified: see note 3).

13 Representation of the People (England and Wales) Regulations 2001, SI 2001/341, reg 78(3) (as amended, applied and modified: see note 3). There may be more than one ballot paper when the polls at more than one referendum or election have been taken together (as to which see PARA 20). Certain provisions as to the issue of postal ballot papers, namely reg 72 (as applied and modified) (except reg 72(3) (as applied and modified)) (see PARA 630) and, subject to reg 78(6) (as applied and modified) (see note 14), regs 74–76 (as applied and modified) (see PARAS 632–634), apply to the issue of replacement postal ballot papers: see reg 78(5) (as applied and modified).

14 Representation of the People (England and Wales) Regulations 2001, SI 2001/341, reg 78(3A) (as added, applied and modified: see note 3). Instead of delivering a replacement postal ballot paper in accordance with the statutory scheme (as to which see PARA 633), the counting officer may hand such a replacement to a postal voter who applies in person by 5 pm on the day before the day of the poll (and he may only hand a replacement postal ballot paper to a postal voter who applies in person after 5 pm on the day before the day of the poll): see reg 78(6) (as so substituted, applied and modified).

15 As to the number of an elector see PARA 145.

16 Representation of the People (England and Wales) Regulations 2001, SI 2001/341, reg 78(4)(a) (as amended, applied and modified: see note 3).

17 Representation of the People (England and Wales) Regulations 2001, SI 2001/341, reg 78(4)(b) (as applied and modified: see note 3).

18 As to applications to vote by proxy see PARA 592 et seq.

19 Representation of the People (England and Wales) Regulations 2001, SI 2001/341, reg 78(4)(c) (as substituted, applied and modified: see note 3).

(b) Receipt of Postal Ballot Papers at a Local Authority Referendum

637.   Attendance at proceedings on receipt of postal ballot papers at local authority referendum.   At a local authority referendum[1], no person may be present at the proceedings on the receipt of postal ballot papers[2] other than: (1) the counting officer[3] and his clerks[4]; and (2) persons who are entitled to attend[5] at the counting of the votes[6]. Each candidate may appoint one or more agents to attend the proceedings on the receipt of the postal ballot papers up to the number he may be authorised by the counting officer to appoint[7]. If an agent dies or becomes incapable of acting, the candidate may appoint another agent in his place[8]. Agents may be appointed and notice of appointment given to the returning officer by the candidate's election agent instead of by the candidate[9].

1   As to the meaning of 'referendum' for these purposes see PARA 574 notes 2, 13.
2   As to the meaning of 'postal voter' see PARA 632 note 3.
3   As to the meaning of 'counting officer' see PARA 576 note 1.
4   Representation of the People (England and Wales) Regulations 2001, SI 2001/341, reg 68(a) (provisions of those regulations applied and modified, in relation to Wales, by the Local Authorities (Conduct of Referendums) (Wales) Regulations 2008, SI 2008/1848, Sch 4 Table 5, and, in relation to England, by the Local Authorities (Conduct of Referendums) (England) Regulations 2012, SI 2012/323, Sch 4 Table 6). As to the provisions that are so applied and modified see PARA 15. As to the appointment of counting officer's clerks for counting purposes see PARA 614.
5   Ie in accordance with the Local Authorities (Conduct of Referendums) (Wales) Regulations 2008, SI 2008/1848, Sch 3 r 35(2)(a)–(e) (in relation to Wales), or in accordance with the Local Authorities (Conduct of Referendums) (England) Regulations 2012, SI 2012/323, Sch 3 r 35(2)(a)–(e) (in relation to England) (see PARA 646).
6   Representation of the People (England and Wales) Regulations 2001, SI 2001/341, reg 68(b) (as applied and modified: see note 4). This is without prejudice to the provisions of the Political Parties, Elections and Referendums Act 2000 ss 6A–6E (as to which see PARA 53): see the Representation of the People (England and Wales) Regulations 2001, SI 2001/341, reg 68 (amended by SI 2006/2910; as so applied and modified). Where in Pt V (regs 64–91) (as so applied and modified) any act or thing is required or authorised to be done in the presence of persons entitled to be present by virtue of reg 68, the non-attendance of any such persons or person at the time and place appointed for the purpose does not, if the act or thing is otherwise duly done, invalidate the act or thing done: see reg 69(8) (as so applied and modified).
7   Representation of the People (England and Wales) Regulations 2001, SI 2001/341, reg 69(1) (as applied and modified: see note 4). The number authorised must be the same in the case of each candidate: reg 69(1) (as so applied and modified). Notice in writing of the appointment stating the names and addresses of the persons appointed must be given by the candidate to the returning officer before the time fixed for the opening of the postal voters' ballot box: reg 69(2) (as so applied and modified). Where postal ballot papers for more than one election are issued together under reg 65 (see PARA 20), the returning officer to whom notice must be given under reg 69(2) and reg 69(4), (5) (see the text and notes 8–9) is the returning officer who issues the postal ballot papers: reg 69(3) (as so applied and modified).
     References to agents in Pt V (as so applied and modified) must be taken as references to agents whose appointments have been duly made and notified and, in the case of agents appointed under reg 69(1), who are within the number authorised by the counting officer: reg 69(6) (as so applied and modified). A candidate may himself do any act or thing which any agent of his, if appointed, would have been authorised to do, or may assist his agent in doing any such act or thing: reg 69(7) (as so applied and modified).
8   Representation of the People (England and Wales) Regulations 2001, SI 2001/341, reg 69(4) (as applied and modified: see note 4). The candidate must forthwith give to the returning officer notice in writing of the name and address of the agent so appointed: reg 69(4) (as so applied and modified). In connection with this notice see note 7.
9   Representation of the People (England and Wales) Regulations 2001, SI 2001/341, reg 69(5) (as applied and modified: see note 4). In connection with the notice required to be given see note 7.

638. Notification of requirement of secrecy at proceedings relating to the receipt of postal ballot papers at local authority referendum. The counting officer[1] at a local authority referendum[2] must make such arrangements as he thinks fit to ensure that every person attending the proceedings in connection with the receipt[3] of postal ballot papers[4] has been given a copy in writing of the statutory provisions relating to the requirement of secrecy that apply to those proceedings[5].

1   As to the meaning of 'counting officer' see PARA 576 note 1.
2   As to the meaning of 'referendum' for these purposes see PARA 574 notes 2, 13.
3   As to proceedings on the receipt of postal ballot papers see PARA 637.
4   As to the meaning of 'postal ballot paper' see PARA 628 note 4.
5   Representation of the People (England and Wales) Regulations 2001, SI 2001/341, reg 70 (provisions of those regulations applied and modified, in relation to Wales, by the Local Authorities (Conduct of Referendums) (Wales) Regulations 2008, SI 2008/1848, Sch 4 Table 5, and, in relation to England, by the Local Authorities (Conduct of Referendums) (England)

Regulations 2012, SI 2012/323, Sch 4 Table 6). As to the provisions that are so applied and modified see PARA 15. The text refers to the requirement of secrecy set out in the Representation of the People Act 1983 s 66(4), (6) (as applied and modified) (see PARA 742).

639. Provision of postal ballot boxes and receptacles at local authority referendum. The counting officer[1] at a local authority referendum[2] must provide a separate ballot box for: (1) the reception of the covering envelopes[3] when returned by the postal voters[4] (the 'postal voters' ballot box')[5]; and (2) the reception of postal ballot papers[6] (the 'postal ballot box')[7]. Each such ballot box must be marked 'postal voters' ballot box' or 'postal ballot box', as the case may be, and with the name of the voting area for which the referendum or referendums are held[8]. The postal ballot box must be shown to those present on the occasion of opening the first postal voters' ballot box as being empty[9] and must then be locked by the counting officer and sealed with his seal and the seals of such of those present as desire to affix their seals in such manner as to prevent the box being opened without breaking the seal[10]. The counting officer must also provide: (a) the receptacle for rejected votes[11]; (b) the receptacle for declarations of identity[12]; (c) the receptacle for ballot paper envelopes[13]; (d) the receptacle for rejected ballot paper envelopes[14]; (e) the receptacle for rejected votes (verification procedure)[15]; and (f) the receptacle for postal voting statements (verification procedure)[16].

The counting officer must take proper precautions for the safe custody of every such ballot box and receptacle[17].

1 As to the meaning of 'counting officer' see PARA 576 note 1.
2 As to the meaning of 'referendum' for these purposes see PARA 574 notes 2, 13.
3 As to the meaning of 'covering envelope' see PARA 410 note 6.
4 As to the meaning of 'postal voter' see PARA 632 note 3.
5 Representation of the People (England and Wales) Regulations 2001, SI 2001/341, reg 81(1)(a) (provisions of those regulations applied and modified, in relation to Wales, by the Local Authorities (Conduct of Referendums) (Wales) Regulations 2008, SI 2008/1848, Sch 4 Table 5, and, in relation to England, by the Local Authorities (Conduct of Referendums) (England) Regulations 2012, SI 2012/323, Sch 4 Table 6). As to the provisions that are so applied and modified see PARA 15.
6 As to the meaning of 'postal ballot paper' see PARA 628 note 4. As to the issue of postal ballot papers see PARA 627 et seq.
7 Representation of the People (England and Wales) Regulations 2001, SI 2001/341, reg 81(1)(b) (as applied and modified: see note 5).
8 Representation of the People (England and Wales) Regulations 2001, SI 2001/341, reg 81(2) (as applied and modified: see note 5). There will be more than one referendum where the polls at more than one referendum in England have been taken together (as to which see PARA 20).
9 Representation of the People (England and Wales) Regulations 2001, SI 2001/341, reg 81(3) (as applied and modified: see note 5).
10 Representation of the People (England and Wales) Regulations 2001, SI 2001/341, reg 81(4) (as applied and modified: see note 5).
11 Representation of the People (England and Wales) Regulations 2001, SI 2001/341, regs 64, 81(5)(a) (as applied and modified: see note 5).
12 Representation of the People (England and Wales) Regulations 2001, SI 2001/341, reg 81(5)(b) (reg 81(5)(b), (c) amended, reg 81(5)(e), (f) added, by SI 2006/2910) (as applied and modified: see note 5).
13 Representation of the People (England and Wales) Regulations 2001, SI 2001/341, reg 81(5)(c) (as amended, applied and modified: see notes 5, 12).
14 Representation of the People (England and Wales) Regulations 2001, SI 2001/341, reg 81(5)(d) (as applied and modified: see note 5).
15 Representation of the People (England and Wales) Regulations 2001, SI 2001/341, reg 81(5)(e) (as added, applied and modified: see notes 5, 12).
16 Representation of the People (England and Wales) Regulations 2001, SI 2001/341, reg 81(5)(f) (as added, applied and modified: see notes 5, 12).

17 Representation of the People (England and Wales) Regulations 2001, SI 2001/341, reg 81(6) (as applied and modified: see note 5).

640.   Return of postal ballot papers, etc to counting officer at local authority referendum.   At a local authority referendum[1], the manner in which any postal ballot paper[2] or postal voting statement may be returned to the counting officer[3] is by hand or by post and to a polling station it is by hand[4]. Where a covering envelope[5] (or an envelope which is stated to include a postal vote) is received by a counting officer (whether by hand or by post) before the close of the poll he must, immediately on receipt, place it unopened in a postal voters' ballot box[6]. Where an envelope, other than a covering envelope issued by the counting officer, has been opened and it contains a ballot paper envelope[7], postal voting statement or ballot paper, the first-mentioned envelope, together with its contents, must be placed in a postal voters' ballot box[8].

Where a postal ballot paper or postal voting statement has been returned to a polling station, the presiding officer[9] of that station must deliver, or cause to be delivered, any such paper or declaration to the counting officer in the same manner and at the same time as he delivers, or causes to be delivered, the packets of ballot papers and other documents which he is required to prepare on the close of poll at a polling station[10]. However, the counting officer may collect, or cause to be collected, any postal ballot paper or postal voting statement which the presiding officer of a polling station would otherwise be required in this way to deliver or cause to be delivered to him[11]; and where the counting officer collects, or causes to be collected, any postal ballot paper or postal voting statement in this way the presiding officer must first make it (or them) up into a packet (or packets) sealed with his own seal and the seals of such of those as are present and desire to affix their seals[12].

1   As to the meaning of 'referendum' for these purposes see PARA 574 notes 2, 13.
2   As to the meaning of 'postal ballot paper' see PARA 628 note 4. As to the issue of postal ballot papers see PARA 627 et seq.
3   As to the meaning of 'counting officer' see PARA 576 note 1.
4   Representation of the People (England and Wales) Regulations 2001, SI 2001/341, reg 79(1), (2) (regs 79(1)–(5), 82(2) amended by SI 2006/2910) (provisions of those regulations applied and modified, in relation to Wales, by the Local Authorities (Conduct of Referendums) (Wales) Regulations 2008, SI 2008/1848, Sch 4 Table 5, and, in relation to England, by the Local Authorities (Conduct of Referendums) (England) Regulations 2012, SI 2012/323, Sch 4 Table 6). As to the provisions that are so applied and modified see PARA 15.
5   As to the meaning of 'covering envelope' see PARA 410 note 6.
6   Representation of the People (England and Wales) Regulations 2001, SI 2001/341, reg 82(1) (as applied and modified: see note 4). As to the postal voters' ballot box see PARA 639.
7   As to the meaning of 'ballot paper envelope' see the Representation of the People (England and Wales) Regulations 2001, SI 2001/341, reg 64 (as applied and modified: see note 4); and PARA 410 note 8.
8   Representation of the People (England and Wales) Regulations 2001, SI 2001/341, reg 82(2) (as amended, applied and modified: see note 4).
9   As to the appointment of presiding officers and their clerks see PARA 613.
10 Representation of the People (England and Wales) Regulations 2001, SI 2001/341, reg 79(3) (reg 79(3) amended, reg 79(4), (5) added, by SI 2006/752; as amended, applied and modified (see note 4)). As to the procedure on the close of poll at a polling station see PARA 626.
11 Representation of the People (England and Wales) Regulations 2001, SI 2001/341, reg 79(4) (as added, amended, applied and modified: see notes 4, 10).
12 Representation of the People (England and Wales) Regulations 2001, SI 2001/341, reg 79(5) (as added, amended, applied and modified: see notes 4, 10).

641.   Notice of opening of postal voters' ballot box and covering envelopes at local authority referendum.   The counting officer[1] at a local authority referendum[2] must give to those persons who are entitled to attend[3] at the counting of the votes not less than 48 hours' notice in writing of each occasion on which a postal voters' ballot box[4] and the envelopes contained in it is to be opened[5]. Such a notice must specify the time and place at which such an opening is to take place[6].

1 As to the meaning of 'counting officer' see PARA 576 note 1.
2 As to the meaning of 'referendum' for these purposes see PARA 574 notes 2, 13.
3 Ie in accordance with the Local Authorities (Conduct of Referendums) (Wales) Regulations 2008, SI 2008/1848, Sch 3 r 35(2)(a)–(e) (in relation to Wales), or in accordance with the Local Authorities (Conduct of Referendums) (England) Regulations 2012, SI 2012/323, Sch 3 r 35(2)(a)–(e) (in relation to England) (see PARA 646).
4 As to the postal voters' ballot box see PARA 639.
5 Representation of the People (England and Wales) Regulations 2001, SI 2001/341, reg 80(1) (provisions of those regulations applied and modified, in relation to Wales, by the Local Authorities (Conduct of Referendums) (Wales) Regulations 2008, SI 2008/1848, Sch 4 Table 5, and, in relation to England, by the Local Authorities (Conduct of Referendums) (England) Regulations 2012, SI 2012/323, Sch 4 Table 6). As to the provisions that are so applied and modified see PARA 15.
6 Representation of the People (England and Wales) Regulations 2001, SI 2001/341, reg 80(2) (as applied and modified: see note 5).

642. Opening of postal voters' ballot box at local authority referendum. At a local authority referendum[1], each postal voters' ballot box[2] must be opened by the counting officer[3] in the presence of the counting observers[4], if in attendance[5]. So long as the counting officer ensures that there is at least one sealed postal voters' ballot box for the reception of covering envelopes[6] up to the time of the close of the poll, the other postal voters' ballot boxes may previously be opened by him[7]. The last postal voters' ballot box and the postal ballot box[8] must be opened at the counting of the votes[9].

1 As to the meaning of 'referendum' for these purposes see PARA 574 notes 2, 13.
2 As to the postal voters' ballot box see PARA 639.
3 As to the meaning of 'counting officer' see PARA 576 note 1.
4 As to the appointment of counting observers see PARA 614.
5 Representation of the People (England and Wales) Regulations 2001, SI 2001/341, reg 83(1) (provisions of those regulations applied and modified, in relation to Wales, by the Local Authorities (Conduct of Referendums) (Wales) Regulations 2008, SI 2008/1848, Sch 4 Table 5, and, in relation to England, by the Local Authorities (Conduct of Referendums) (England) Regulations 2012, SI 2012/323, Sch 4 Table 6). As to the provisions that are so applied and modified see PARA 15.
6 As to the meaning of 'covering envelope' see PARA 410 note 6.
7 Representation of the People (England and Wales) Regulations 2001, SI 2001/341, reg 83(2) (as applied and modified: see note 5).
8 As to the postal ballot box see PARA 639.
9 Representation of the People (England and Wales) Regulations 2001, SI 2001/341, reg 83(3) (as applied and modified: see note 5). As to the counting of votes at a local authority referendum see PARA 646 et seq.

643. Opening of covering envelopes at local authority referendum. At a local authority referendum[1], when a postal voters' ballot box[2] is opened, the counting officer[3] must count and record the number of covering envelopes[4] and then open separately each covering envelope (including any other envelope[5] which has been found to contain a ballot paper envelope[6], postal voting statement or ballot papers)[7], set aside for personal identifier verification a percentage, not less than 20 per cent, of the envelopes recorded on that occasion[8], and open separately each covering envelope[9]. Where the covering envelope does not contain the postal voting statement separately, the counting officer must open the ballot paper envelope to ascertain whether the postal voting statement is inside[10].

Where a covering envelope does not contain both a postal voting statement (whether separately or not) and a ballot paper envelope (or, if there is no ballot paper envelope, a ballot paper or ballot papers), the counting officer must mark the covering envelope 'provisionally rejected', attach its contents (if any) and place it in the receptacle for rejected votes[11].

An elector or a proxy voter who is shown in the postal voters list[12] or proxy postal voters list[13] may make a request, at any time between the first issue of postal ballots[14] and the close of the poll, that the returning officer confirm whether a mark is shown in the marked copy of the postal voters list or proxy postal voters list in a place corresponding to the number of the elector to denote that a postal vote has been returned and whether the number of the ballot paper issued to the elector or his proxy has been recorded on either of the lists of provisionally rejected votes kept[15] by the returning officer[16].

1   As to the meaning of 'referendum' for these purposes see PARA 574 notes 2, 13.
2   As to the postal voters' ballot box see PARA 639.
3   As to the meaning of 'counting officer' see PARA 576 note 1.
4   As to the meaning of 'covering envelope' see PARA 410 note 6.
5   Ie as described in the Representation of the People (England and Wales) Regulations 2001, SI 2001/341, reg 82(2) (as applied and modified) (see PARA 640).
6   As to the meaning of 'ballot paper envelope' see PARA 410 note 8.
7   Representation of the People (England and Wales) Regulations 2001, SI 2001/341, reg 84(1) (regs 84(1), 85(1) substituted, regs 84(1A), (1B), 84A, 85(1A), 85A added, regs 84(3), (4), 85(2)–(7) amended, by SI 2006/2910) (provisions of those regulations applied and modified, in relation to Wales, by the Local Authorities (Conduct of Referendums) (Wales) Regulations 2008, SI 2008/1848, Sch 4 Table 5, and, in relation to England, by the Local Authorities (Conduct of Referendums) (England) Regulations 2012, SI 2012/323, Sch 4 Table 6). As to the provisions that are so applied and modified see PARA 15.
8   Representation of the People (England and Wales) Regulations 2001, SI 2001/341, reg 84(1A) (as added, applied and modified: see note 7).
    Where any postal voting statement contained in an envelope has been set aside for personal identifier verification in accordance with reg 84(1A) or (5) the counting officer must satisfy himself that the postal voting statement is duly completed and as part of that process must compare the date of birth and the signature on the postal voting statement against the date of birth and signature contained in the personal identifier record relating to the person to whom the postal ballot paper was addressed: reg 85A(1) (as so added, applied and modified). Where the counting officer is not so satisfied, he must mark the statement 'rejected', attach to it the ballot paper envelope, or if there is no such envelope, the ballot paper, and, (after showing it to the counting observers or agents or both (as the case may be) and permitting them to view the entries in the personal identifiers record which relate to the person to whom the postal ballot paper was addressed), place it in the receptacle for rejected votes (verification procedure) (if any of the counting observers or agents object to the counting officer's decision, he must add the words 'rejection objected to': reg 85A(3), (4) (as so added, applied and modified). The counting officer must then examine the number on the postal voting statement against the number on the ballot paper envelope and, where they are the same, must place the statement and the ballot paper envelope respectively in the receptacle for postal voting statements (verification procedure) and the receptacle for ballot paper envelopes: reg 85A(5) (as so added, applied and modified). Where the number on a valid postal voting statement is not the same as the number on the ballot paper envelope or that envelope has no number on it (or only one number when the postal voting statement has more than one), the counting officer must open the envelope: reg 85A(6) (as so added, applied and modified). Where there is a valid postal voting statement but no ballot paper envelope, or the ballot paper envelope has been opened under reg 84(3) or reg 85A(6), the returning officer must place in the postal ballot box, any ballot paper the number on which is the same as the number on the valid postal voting statement (reg 85A(7), (8)(a) (as so added, applied and modified)), in the receptacle for rejected votes (verification procedure), any other ballot paper, with the valid postal voting statement attached and marked 'provisionally rejected' (reg 85A(8)(b) (as so added, applied and modified)), in the receptacle for rejected votes (verification procedure), any valid postal voting statement marked 'provisionally rejected' where there is no ballot paper, or in the case of a statement on which the number of more than one ballot paper appears, there is not a sufficient number of ballot papers

(in which case he must mark the statement to indicate which ballot paper is missing) (reg 85A(8)(c) (as so added, applied and modified)), and in the receptacle for postal voting statements (verification procedure), any valid statement not disposed of under reg 85A(8)(b) or (c) (reg 85A(8)(d) (as so added, applied and modified)).

Where any postal voting statement contained in an envelope has not been set aside for personal identifier verification in accordance with reg 84(1A) or (5) the counting officer must satisfy himself that the postal voting statement is duly completed: reg 85(1), (1A) (as so substituted, added, applied and modified). Where the counting officer is not so satisfied, he must mark the statement 'rejected', attach to it the ballot paper envelope, or if there is no such envelope, the ballot paper (or ballot papers), and (after showing it to the counting observers or agents or both (as the case may be)) place it in the receptacle for rejected votes (if any of the counting observers or agents object to his decision, he must add the words 'rejection objected to'): reg 85(2), (3) (as so amended, applied and modified). The counting officer must then examine the number (or numbers) on the postal voting statement against the number (or numbers) on the ballot paper envelope and, where they are the same, he must place the statement and the ballot paper envelope respectively in the receptacle for postal voting statements and the receptacle for ballot paper envelopes: reg 85(4) (as so amended, applied and modified). Where the number (or numbers) on a valid postal voting statement is not the same as the number (or numbers) on the ballot paper envelope, or that envelope has no number on it (or only one number when the postal voting statement has more than one), the returning officer must open the envelope: reg 85(5) (reg 85(5)–(7) substituted by SI 2002/1871; as so amended, applied and modified). Where there is a valid postal voting statement but no ballot paper envelope or the ballot paper envelope has been opened under the Representation of the People (England and Wales) Regulations 2001, SI 2001/341, reg 84(3) or reg 85(5), the returning officer must place in the postal ballot box, any ballot paper the number on which is the same as the number (or one of the numbers) on the valid postal voting statement (reg 85(6), (7)(a) (as so substituted, amended, applied and modified)), in the receptacle for rejected votes, any other ballot paper, with the valid postal voting statement attached and marked 'provisionally rejected' (reg 85(7)(b) (as so substituted, amended, applied and modified)), in the receptacle for rejected votes, any valid postal voting statement marked 'provisionally rejected' where there is no ballot paper or (in the case of a statement on which the number of more than one ballot paper appears, there is not a sufficient number of ballot papers and, in such a case), must mark the statement to indicate which ballot paper is missing (reg 85(7)(c) (as so substituted, amended, applied and modified)), and in the receptacle for postal voting statements, any valid statement not disposed of under reg 85(7)(b) or (c) (reg 85(7)(d) (as so substituted, amended, applied and modified)).

9   Representation of the People (England and Wales) Regulations 2001, SI 2001/341, reg 84(1B) (as added, applied and modified: see note 7). This includes an envelope described in reg 82(2) (as applied and modified) (see PARA 640): see reg 84(1B) (as so added, applied and modified).

10 Representation of the People (England and Wales) Regulations 2001, SI 2001/341, reg 84(3) (as amended, applied and modified: see note 7).

11 Representation of the People (England and Wales) Regulations 2001, SI 2001/341, reg 84(4) (as applied and modified: see note 7). As to the receptacle for rejected votes see PARA 639.

12 As to the meaning of 'postal voters list' see PARA 373 note 7.

13 As to the meaning of 'proxy postal voters list' see PARA 381 note 6.

14 Ie under the Representation of the People (England and Wales) Regulations 2001, SI 2001/341, reg 71 (as applied and modified: see PARA 629).

15 Ie under the Representation of the People (England and Wales) Regulations 2001, SI 2001/341, reg 87(2), (3) (as applied and modified: see PARA 645).

16 Representation of the People (England and Wales) Regulations 2001, SI 2001/341, reg 84A(1) (as added, applied and modified: see note 7). Such a request must be made by any method specified and include any evidence of the voter's identity requested, by the returning officer: reg 84A(2) (as so added, applied and modified). Where a request is received in accordance with reg 84A(2) the returning officer must satisfy himself that the request has been made by the elector or their proxy and where he is so satisfied provide confirmation of the matters under reg 84A(1): reg 84A(3) (as so added, applied and modified).

644. Opening of ballot paper envelopes at local authority referendum. The counting officer[1] at a local authority referendum[2] must open separately each ballot paper envelope[3] placed in the receptacle for ballot paper envelopes[4]. He must place: (1) in the postal ballot box[5], any ballot paper the number on which is the same as the number (or one of the numbers) on the ballot paper envelope[6];

(2) in the receptacle for rejected votes[7], any other ballot paper which is marked 'provisionally rejected' with the ballot paper envelope attached[8]; and (3) in the receptacle for rejected ballot paper envelopes[9], any ballot paper envelope which is marked 'provisionally rejected' because it does not contain either a ballot paper or, where more than one number appears on the ballot paper envelope, a sufficient number of ballot papers (and indicating, in such a case, the missing ballot paper)[10].

1   As to the meaning of 'counting officer' see PARA 576 note 1.
2   As to the meaning of 'referendum' for these purposes see PARA 574 notes 2, 13.
3   As to the meaning of 'ballot paper envelope' see PARA 410 note 8.
4   Representation of the People (England and Wales) Regulations 2001, SI 2001/341, reg 86(1) (provisions of those regulations applied and modified, in relation to Wales, by the Local Authorities (Conduct of Referendums) (Wales) Regulations 2008, SI 2008/1848, Sch 4 Table 5, and, in relation to England, by the Local Authorities (Conduct of Referendums) (England) Regulations 2012, SI 2012/323, Sch 4 Table 6). As to the provisions that are so applied and modified see PARA 15. As to the receptacle for ballot paper envelopes see PARA 639.
5   As to the postal ballot box see PARA 639.
6   Representation of the People (England and Wales) Regulations 2001, SI 2001/341, reg 86(2)(a) (as applied and modified: see note 4). There may be more than one number on a ballot paper envelope when the polls at more than one referendum or election have been taken together (as to which see PARA 20).
7   As to the receptacle for rejected votes see PARA 639.
8   Representation of the People (England and Wales) Regulations 2001, SI 2001/341, reg 86(2)(b) (as applied and modified: see note 4).
9   As to the receptacle for rejected ballot paper envelopes see PARA 639.
10   Representation of the People (England and Wales) Regulations 2001, SI 2001/341, reg 86(2)(c) (as applied and modified: see note 4).

645. Conclusion of postal ballot procedure at local authority referendum. In respect of any local authority referendum[1], the counting officer[2] must keep two separate lists of rejected postal ballot papers[3]: (1) in the first list, he must record the ballot paper number of any postal ballot paper for which no valid postal voting statement was received with it[4]; (2) in the second list, he must record the ballot paper number of any postal ballot paper which is entered on a valid postal voting statement where that ballot paper is not received with the postal voting statement[5].

Where the counting officer receives a valid postal voting statement without the postal ballot paper (or papers or, as the case may be, all of the papers) to which it relates, he may, at any time prior to the close of the poll, check the list kept under head (1) above to see whether the number (or numbers) of a postal ballot paper to which the statement relates is entered in that list[6]. Where the counting officer receives a postal ballot paper without the postal voting statement to which it relates, he may, at any time prior to the close of the poll, check the list kept under head (2) above to see whether the number of that ballot paper is entered in that list[7]. The counting officer must conduct either such check as soon as practicable after the receipt of packets from every polling station in the voting area[8] in question following the close of poll[9]. Where the ballot paper number in the list matches that number on a valid postal voting statement or, as the case may be, the postal ballot paper, the counting officer must retrieve that statement or paper[10]. As soon as practicable after the completion of this procedure, the counting officer must make up into separate packets the contents of: (a) the receptacle of rejected votes[11]; (b) the receptacle of postal voting statements[12]; (c) the receptacle of rejected ballot paper envelopes[13]; (d) the lists of spoilt and lost postal ballot papers[14]; (e) the receptacle of rejected votes (verification procedure)[15]; and (f) the receptacle of postal voting statements (verification procedure)[16], and he must seal up the packets[17]. Any document in those packets marked 'provisionally rejected' must be deemed to be marked 'rejected'[18]. The counting officer must then take the appropriate steps under the provisions governing the receipt of postal ballot papers[19] as though any document earlier marked 'provisionally rejected' had not been so marked, and he must amend the document accordingly[20].

Where it appears to the counting officer that a cancelled postal ballot paper has been placed in a postal voters' ballot box, in the receptacle for ballot paper envelopes, or a postal ballot box he must, on at least one occasion on which a postal voters ballot box is opened[21], also open any postal ballot box and the receptacle for ballot paper envelopes and: (i) retrieve the cancelled ballot paper[22]; (ii) show the ballot paper number on the cancelled ballot paper to the counting observers or agents or both (as the case may be)[23]; (iii) retrieve the postal voting statement that relates to a cancelled ballot paper from the receptacle for postal voting statements[24]; (iv) attach any cancelled postal ballot paper to the postal voting statement to which it relates[25]; (v) place the cancelled documents in a separate packet and deal[26] with that packet[27]; and (vi) unless the postal ballot box has been opened for the purposes of the counting of votes[28], re-lock (if it has a lock) and re-seal the postal ballot box in the presence of the counting observers or agents or both (as the case may be)[29]. Whilst retrieving a cancelled ballot paper in accordance with these provisions the counting officer and his staff must keep the ballot papers face downwards and must take proper precautions for preventing any person seeing the votes made on the ballot papers, and must not be permitted to view the corresponding number list used at the issue of postal ballot papers[30].

1   As to the meaning of 'referendum' for these purposes see PARA 574 notes 2, 13.
2   As to the meaning of 'counting officer' see PARA 576 note 1.
3   Representation of the People (England and Wales) Regulations 2001, SI 2001/341, reg 87(1) (provisions of those regulations applied and modified, in relation to Wales, by the Local Authorities (Conduct of Referendums) (Wales) Regulations 2008, SI 2008/1848, Sch 4 Table 5, and, in relation to England, by the Local Authorities (Conduct of Referendums) (England) Regulations 2012, SI 2012/323, Sch 4 Table 6). As to the provisions that are so applied and modified see PARA 15. As to the meaning of 'postal ballot paper' see PARA 628 note 4. As to the issue of postal ballot papers see PARA 627 et seq; and as to the rejection of postal ballot papers see PARA 643 et seq.
4   Representation of the People (England and Wales) Regulations 2001, SI 2001/341, reg 87(2) (reg 86A, 89(1)(e), (f) added, regs 87(2), (3), 88(1), (2), (4), 89(1)(b) amended, by SI 2006/2910; as applied and modified (see note 3)).
5   Representation of the People (England and Wales) Regulations 2001, SI 2001/341, reg 87(3) (as amended, applied and modified: see notes 3, 4).
6   Representation of the People (England and Wales) Regulations 2001, SI 2001/341, reg 88(1) (as amended, applied and modified: see notes 3, 4). There may be more than one postal ballot paper and number on a ballot paper envelope when the polls at more than one referendum or election have been taken together (as to which see PARA 20).
7   Representation of the People (England and Wales) Regulations 2001, SI 2001/341, reg 88(2) (as amended, applied and modified: see notes 3, 4).
8   As to the meaning of 'voting area' see PARA 580 note 2; definition applied by virtue of the Representation of the People Act 2000 Sch 4 para 1 (Sch 4 applied and modified in relation to England, by the Local Authorities (Conduct of Referendums) (England) Regulations 2012, SI 2012/323, Sch 4 Table 3 and in relation to Wales by the Local Authorities (Conduct of Referendums) (Wales) Regulations 2008, SI 2008/1848, Sch 4 Table 2).
9   Representation of the People (England and Wales) Regulations 2001, SI 2001/341, reg 88(3) (as applied and modified: see note 3). The text refers to the receipt of packets of ballot papers and other documents which the presiding officer is required to prepare on the close of poll at a polling station: see PARA 626.

10 Representation of the People (England and Wales) Regulations 2001, SI 2001/341, reg 88(4) (as amended, applied and modified: see notes 3, 4).

11 Representation of the People (England and Wales) Regulations 2001, SI 2001/341, reg 89(1)(a) (as applied and modified: see note 3). As to the receptacle for rejected votes see PARA 639.

12 Representation of the People (England and Wales) Regulations 2001, SI 2001/341, reg 89(1)(b) (as amended, applied and modified: see notes 3, 4). As to the receptacle of declarations of identity see PARA 639.

13 Representation of the People (England and Wales) Regulations 2001, SI 2001/341, reg 89(1)(c) (as applied and modified: see note 3). As to the receptacle for rejected ballot paper envelopes see PARA 639.

14 Representation of the People (England and Wales) Regulations 2001, SI 2001/341, reg 89(1)(d) (as applied and modified: see note 3).

15 Representation of the People (England and Wales) Regulations 2001, SI 2001/341, reg 89(1)(e) (as added, applied and modified: see notes 3, 4).

16 Representation of the People (England and Wales) Regulations 2001, SI 2001/341, reg 89(1)(f) (as added, applied and modified: see notes 3, 4).

17 Representation of the People (England and Wales) Regulations 2001, SI 2001/341, reg 89(1) (as applied and modified: see note 3).

18 Representation of the People (England and Wales) Regulations 2001, SI 2001/341, reg 89(2) (as applied and modified: see note 3).

19 As to the provisions governing the receipt of postal ballot papers at a local authority referendum see PARA 643 et seq.

20 Representation of the People (England and Wales) Regulations 2001, SI 2001/341, reg 88(5) (as applied and modified: see note 3).

21 Ie in accordance with the Representation of the People (England and Wales) Regulations 2001, SI 2001/341, reg 83 (see PARA 642).

22 Representation of the People (England and Wales) Regulations 2001, SI 2001/341, reg 86A(1), (2)(a) (as added, applied and modified: see notes 3, 4).

23 Representation of the People (England and Wales) Regulations 2001, SI 2001/341, reg 86A(2)(b) (as added, applied and modified: see notes 3, 4).

24 Representation of the People (England and Wales) Regulations 2001, SI 2001/341, reg 86A(2)(c) (as added, applied and modified: see notes 3, 4).

25 Representation of the People (England and Wales) Regulations 2001, SI 2001/341, reg 86A(2)(d) (as added, applied and modified: see notes 3, 4).

26 Ie in the manner provided for by the Representation of the People (England and Wales) Regulations 2001, SI 2001/341, reg 77(6) (see PARA 635).

27 Representation of the People (England and Wales) Regulations 2001, SI 2001/341, reg 86A(2)(e) (as added, applied and modified: see notes 3, 4).

28 Ie under the Local Authorities (Conduct of Referendums) (England) Regulations 2012, SI 2012/323, Sch 3 r 45 or the Local Authorities (Conduct of Referendums) (Wales) Regulations 2008, SI 2008/1848, Sch 3 r 45 (see PARA 659).

29 Representation of the People (England and Wales) Regulations 2001, SI 2001/341, reg 86A(2)(f) (as added, applied and modified: see notes 3, 4).

30 Representation of the People (England and Wales) Regulations 2001, SI 2001/341, reg 86A(3) (as added, applied and modified: see notes 3, 4).

E. COUNTING OF THE VOTES AT REFERENDUM OR POLL

646. Attendance at counting of votes at a referendum or poll. As soon as practicable after the close of the poll, the counting officer[1] (in relation to a local authority referendum[2]) or to the returning officer[3] (in relation to a poll consequent on a parish or community meeting[4]) must make arrangements for counting the votes in the presence of the counting observers (if any)[5]; and he must give notice to them in writing of the time and place at which the count of the votes will begin[6].

In relation to a local authority referendum, no person may, unless permitted by the counting officer, attend the counting of votes for any voting area[7] unless he is[8]: (1) the counting officer and his or her clerks[9]; (2) the counting observers[10]; (3) the elected mayor[11], if any, of the council in respect of which the referendum is held[12]; (4) the petition organisers[13]; or (5) persons who are entitled[14] to attend[15]. In relation to a poll consequent on a parish or community meeting, no person other than: (a) the returning officer and his clerks[16]; (b) the candidates and their spouses or civil partners (where the poll is taken on the question of appointment to any office)[17]; (c) the proposer of the resolution in respect of which the poll is taken (where the poll is taken on any other question)[18]; and (d) the counting agents[19], may be present at the counting of the votes, unless permitted by the returning officer to attend[20]. The counting officer or the returning officer (as the case may be) must make such arrangements as he thinks fit to ensure that every person attending at the counting of the votes (other than any constable on duty at the counting) has been given a copy in writing of the statutory provisions relating to the requirement of secrecy that apply to such attendance[21].

The counting officer or the returning officer (as the case may be) must give the counting observers or agents all such reasonable facilities for overseeing the proceedings, and all such information with respect to them, as he can give them consistently with the orderly conduct of the proceedings and the discharge of his duties in connection with them[22].

1 As to the meaning of 'counting officer' see PARA 576 note 1.
2 As to the meaning of 'referendum' for these purposes see PARA 574 notes 2, 13.
3 As to returning officers at polls consequent on a parish or community meeting see PARA 588.
4 As to how polls consequent on a parish or community meeting come about see PARA 581.
5 As to the appointment of counting observers see PARA 614.
6 Parish and Community Meetings (Polls) Rules 1987, SI 1987/1, r 5, Schedule r 26(1); Local Authorities (Conduct of Referendums) (Wales) Regulations 2008, SI 2008/1848, Sch 3 r 35(1); Local Authorities (Conduct of Referendums) (England) Regulations 2012, SI 2012/323, Sch 3 r 35(1).
7 As to the meaning of 'voting area' see PARA 580 note 2.
8 Local Authorities (Conduct of Referendums) (Wales) Regulations 2008, SI 2008/1848, Sch 3 r 35(2); Local Authorities (Conduct of Referendums) (England) Regulations 2012, SI 2012/323, Sch 3 r 35(2).
9 Local Authorities (Conduct of Referendums) (Wales) Regulations 2008, SI 2008/1848, Sch 3 r 35(2)(a); Local Authorities (Conduct of Referendums) (England) Regulations 2012, SI 2012/323, Sch 3 r 35(2)(a).
10 Local Authorities (Conduct of Referendums) (Wales) Regulations 2008, SI 2008/1848, Sch 3 r 35(2)(b); Local Authorities (Conduct of Referendums) (England) Regulations 2012, SI 2012/323, Sch 3 r 35(2)(b).
11 As to the meaning of 'elected mayor' see PARA 98 note 2.
12 Local Authorities (Conduct of Referendums) (Wales) Regulations 2008, SI 2008/1848, Sch 3 r 35(2)(c); Local Authorities (Conduct of Referendums) (England) Regulations 2012, SI 2012/323, Sch 3 r 35(2)(c).
13 Local Authorities (Conduct of Referendums) (Wales) Regulations 2008, SI 2008/1848, Sch 3 r 35(2)(d); Local Authorities (Conduct of Referendums) (England) Regulations 2012, SI 2012/323, Sch 3 r 35(2)(d).
14 Ie by virtue of any of the Political Parties, Elections and Referendums Act 2000 ss 6A–6D (see PARA 53).
15 Local Authorities (Conduct of Referendums) (Wales) Regulations 2008, SI 2008/1848, Sch 3 r 35(2)(e); Local Authorities (Conduct of Referendums) (England) Regulations 2012, SI 2012/323, Sch 3 r 35(2)(e).
16 Parish and Community Meetings (Polls) Rules 1987, SI 1987/1, Schedule r 26(2)(a).
17 Parish and Community Meetings (Polls) Rules 1987, SI 1987/1, Schedule r 26(2)(b) (amended by SI 2005/2114).
18 Parish and Community Meetings (Polls) Rules 1987, SI 1987/1, Schedule r 26(2)(c).
19 Parish and Community Meetings (Polls) Rules 1987, SI 1987/1, Schedule r 26(2)(d).
20 Parish and Community Meetings (Polls) Rules 1987, SI 1987/1, Schedule r 26(2). A person not entitled to attend at the counting of the votes may not be permitted to do so by the returning officer unless he is satisfied that the efficient counting of the votes will not be impeded: Schedule r 26(3).

21 See PARAS 606, 739–743.
22 Parish and Community Meetings (Polls) Rules 1987, SI 1987/1, Schedule r 26(4); Local Authorities (Conduct of Referendums) (Wales) Regulations 2008, SI 2008/1848, Sch 3 r 35(4); Local Authorities (Conduct of Referendums) (England) Regulations 2012, SI 2012/323, Sch 3 r 35(4). In particular, in relation to a poll consequent on a parish or community meeting, where the votes are counted by sorting the ballot papers according to votes for or against the question and then counting the number of ballot papers in each category, the proposer of the resolution is entitled to satisfy himself that the ballot papers are correctly sorted: Parish and Community Meetings (Polls) Rules 1987, SI 1987/1, Schedule r 26(5).

647. The count at a referendum or poll. The returning officer at a poll consequent on a parish or community meeting[1] must:

(1) in the presence of the counting agents open each ballot box, count and record the number of ballot papers in it and verify each ballot paper account[2];

(2) where two polls have been taken together, separate the ballot papers relating to each poll and count and record the number of ballot papers relating to each poll[3]; and

(3) then mix together the whole of the ballot papers relating to the poll or each poll, as the case may be, which were contained in the ballot boxes[4].

The counting officer[5] at a local authority referendum[6] must:

(a) in the presence of the counting observers[7] open each ballot box and count and record the number of ballot papers in it[8];

(b) in the presence of the counting observers verify each ballot paper account[9]; and

(c) count such of the postal ballot papers as have been duly returned[10] and record the number counted[11],

and must not count the votes given on any ballot papers until in the case of postal ballot papers, they have been mixed with the ballot papers from at least one ballot box, and in the case of ballot papers from a ballot box, they have been mixed with the ballot papers from at least one other ballot box[12].

In either case the returning or counting officer must not count any tendered ballot paper[13], and while separating (where applicable), counting and recording the number of ballot papers and counting the votes, must keep the ballot papers with their faces upwards and take all proper precautions for preventing any person from seeing the numbers or other unique identifying marks printed on the back of the papers[14]. The officer must verify each ballot paper account by comparing it with the number of ballot papers recorded by him, and the unused and spoilt ballot papers in his possession and the tendered votes list (opening and resealing the packets containing the unused and spoilt ballot papers and the tendered votes list) and must draw up a statement as to the result of the verification, which any counting agent or observer may copy[15]. The officer must so far as practicable proceed continuously with counting the votes, allowing only time for refreshment, except that he may, in so far as he thinks necessary, exclude the hours between 7 in the evening and 9 on the following morning[16].

1 As to how polls consequent on a parish or community meeting come about see PARA 581. As to returning officers at polls consequent on a parish or community meeting see PARA 588.
2 Parish and Community Meetings (Polls) Rules 1987, SI 1987/1, r 5, Schedule r 27(1)(a).
3 Parish and Community Meetings (Polls) Rules 1987, SI 1987/1, Schedule r 27(1)(b).
4 Parish and Community Meetings (Polls) Rules 1987, SI 1987/1, Schedule r 27(1)(c).
5 As to the meaning of 'counting officer' see PARA 576 note 1.
6 As to the meaning of 'referendum' for these purposes see PARA 574 notes 2, 13.
7 As to the appointment of counting observers see PARA 614.

8　Local Authorities (Conduct of Referendums) (Wales) Regulations 2008, SI 2008/1848, Sch 3 r 36(1)(a); Local Authorities (Conduct of Referendums) (England) Regulations 2012, SI 2012/323, Sch 3 r 36(1)(a).

9　Local Authorities (Conduct of Referendums) (Wales) Regulations 2008, SI 2008/1848, Sch 3 r 36(1)(b); Local Authorities (Conduct of Referendums) (England) Regulations 2012, SI 2012/323, Sch 3 r 36(1)(b).

10　A postal ballot paper must not be taken to be duly returned unless:

　　(1)　it is returned in the manner set out in the Local Authorities (Conduct of Referendums) (Wales) Regulations 2008, SI 2008/1848, Sch 3 r 36(4), or in the manner set out in the Local Authorities (Conduct of Referendums) (England) Regulations 2012, SI 2012/323, Sch 3 r 36(4), as the case may be, and reaches the counting officer or any polling station in the voting area in question before the close of the poll (Local Authorities (Conduct of Referendums) (Wales) Regulations 2008, SI 2008/1848, Sch 3 r 36(3)(a); Local Authorities (Conduct of Referendums) (England) Regulations 2012, SI 2012/323, Sch 3 r 36(3)(a));

　　(2)　the postal voting statement, duly signed, is also returned in the manner set out in the Local Authorities (Conduct of Referendums) (Wales) Regulations 2008, SI 2008/1848, Sch 3 r 36(4), or in the manner set out in the Local Authorities (Conduct of Referendums) (England) Regulations 2012, SI 2012/323, Sch 3 r 36(4), as the case may be, and reaches the counting officer or such a polling station before that time (Local Authorities (Conduct of Referendums) (Wales) Regulations 2008, SI 2008/1848, Sch 3 r 36(3)(b); Local Authorities (Conduct of Referendums) (England) Regulations 2012, SI 2012/323, Sch 3 r 36(3)(b));

　　(3)　the postal voting statement also states the date of birth of a voter or proxy (Local Authorities (Conduct of Referendums) (Wales) Regulations 2008, SI 2008/1848, Sch 3 r 36(3)(c); Local Authorities (Conduct of Referendums) (England) Regulations 2012, SI 2012/323, Sch 3 r 36(3)(c)); and

　　(4)　in a case where steps for verifying the date of birth and signature of a voter or proxy have been prescribed by regulations made under the Representation of the People Act 1983, the counting officer (having taken such steps) verifies that date of birth and that signature (Local Authorities (Conduct of Referendums) (Wales) Regulations 2008, SI 2008/1848, Sch 3 r 36(3)(d); Local Authorities (Conduct of Referendums) (England) Regulations 2012, SI 2012/323, Sch 3 r 36(3)(d)).

The Local Authorities (Conduct of Referendums) (Wales) Regulations 2008, SI 2008/1848, Sch 3 r 36(4), and the Local Authorities (Conduct of Referendums) (England) Regulations 2012, SI 2012/323, Sch 3 r 36(4), provide that the manner in which any postal ballot paper or postal voting statement may be returned to the counting officer, is by hand or by post, and to a polling station, is by hand.

11　Local Authorities (Conduct of Referendums) (Wales) Regulations 2008, SI 2008/1848, Sch 3 r 36(1)(c); Local Authorities (Conduct of Referendums) (England) Regulations 2012, SI 2012/323, Sch 3 r 36(1)(c).

12　Local Authorities (Conduct of Referendums) (Wales) Regulations 2008, SI 2008/1848, Sch 3 r 36(2); Local Authorities (Conduct of Referendums) (England) Regulations 2012, SI 2012/323, Sch 3 r 36(2).

13　Parish and Community Meetings (Polls) Rules 1987, SI 1987/1, Schedule r 27(2); Local Authorities (Conduct of Referendums) (Wales) Regulations 2008, SI 2008/1848, Sch 3 r 36(5); Local Authorities (Conduct of Referendums) (England) Regulations 2012, SI 2012/323, Sch 3 r 36(5).

14　Parish and Community Meetings (Polls) Rules 1987, SI 1987/1, Schedule r 27(3); Local Authorities (Conduct of Referendums) (Wales) Regulations 2008, SI 2008/1848, Sch 3 r 36(6); Local Authorities (Conduct of Referendums) (England) Regulations 2012, SI 2012/323, Sch 3 r 36(6).

15　Parish and Community Meetings (Polls) Rules 1987, SI 1987/1, Schedule r 27(4); Local Authorities (Conduct of Referendums) (Wales) Regulations 2008, SI 2008/1848, Sch 3 r 36(7); Local Authorities (Conduct of Referendums) (England) Regulations 2012, SI 2012/323, Sch 3 r 36(7).

16　Parish and Community Meetings (Polls) Rules 1987, SI 1987/1, Schedule r 27(5); Local Authorities (Conduct of Referendums) (Wales) Regulations 2008, SI 2008/1848, Sch 3 r 36(8); Local Authorities (Conduct of Referendums) (England) Regulations 2012, SI 2012/323, Sch 3 r 36(8). During the time so excluded the officer must place the ballot papers and other documents relating to the poll under his own seal and the seals of such of the counting observers or agents as desire to affix their seals, and otherwise take proper precautions for the security of the papers and documents: Parish and Community Meetings (Polls) Rules 1987, SI 1987/1,

Schedule r 27(6); Local Authorities (Conduct of Referendums) (Wales) Regulations 2008, SI 2008/1848, Sch 3 r 36(9); Local Authorities (Conduct of Referendums) (England) Regulations 2012, SI 2012/323, Sch 3 r 36(9).

648. Rejected ballot papers at a referendum or poll. At a local authority referendum[1] or at a poll consequent on a parish or community meeting[2], any ballot paper: (1) which does not bear the official mark[3]; or (2) on which votes are given for more than one answer (at a referendum) or for more candidates than the voter is entitled to vote for or on which votes are given for and against the same question (at a poll)[4]; or (3) on which anything is written or marked by which the voter can be identified except the printed number or (where applicable) other unique identifying mark on the back[5]; or (4) which is unmarked or void for uncertainty[6], is void and not counted[7]. However, a ballot paper on which a vote is marked elsewhere than in the proper place[8], or otherwise than by means of a cross[9], or by more than one mark[10], is not for such reason deemed to be void (in the case of a poll, either wholly or as respects that vote) if an intention that a vote is for one only of the answers (at a referendum) or for one or another of the candidates or for and against any question (at a poll) clearly appears, and the way the paper is marked does not itself identify the voter (or, in the case of a referendum, proxy) and it is not shown that he can be identified by it[11].

The counting officer[12] at a local authority referendum or the returning officer at a poll consequent on a parish or community meeting[13] (as the case may be) must endorse the word 'rejected' on any ballot paper which is not to be counted and must add to the endorsement the words 'rejection objected to' if an objection is made by a counting observer[14] or agent to his decision[15]. The counting officer or the returning officer (as the case may be) must draw up a statement showing the number of ballot papers rejected under the several heads of: (a) want of official mark[16]; (b) voting for more than one answer (at a referendum) or for more candidates than the voter is entitled to or for voting for and against the same question (at a poll)[17]; (c) writing or mark by which the voter could be identified[18]; (d) unmarked or void for uncertainty[19].

1   As to the meaning of 'referendum' for these purposes see PARA 574 notes 2, 13.
2   As to how polls consequent on a parish or community meeting come about see PARA 581.

3   Parish and Community Meetings (Polls) Rules 1987, SI 1987/1, r 5, Schedule r 29(1)(a); Local Authorities (Conduct of Referendums) (Wales) Regulations 2008, SI 2008/1848, Sch 3 ·r 38(1)(a); Local Authorities (Conduct of Referendums) (England) Regulations 2012, SI 2012/323, Sch 3 r 38(1)(a). As to the official mark used at a referendum or poll see PARA 607.

4   Parish and Community Meetings (Polls) Rules 1987, SI 1987/1, r 5, Schedule r 29(1)(b Local Authorities (Conduct of Referendums) (Wales) Regulations 2008, SI 2008/1848, Sch 3 r 38(1)(b); Local Authorities (Conduct of Referendums) (England) Regulations 2012, SI 2012/323, Sch 3 r 38(1)(b). At a poll consequent on a parish or community meeting, it is provided that, where the voter is entitled to vote for more than one candidate or on more than one question, a ballot paper is not to be deemed to be void for uncertainty as respects any vote as to which no uncertainty arises and that vote is to be counted: Parish and Community Meetings (Polls) Rules 1987, SI 1987/1, r 5, Schedule r 29(2).

5   Parish and Community Meetings (Polls) Rules 1987, SI 1987/1, r 5, Schedule r 29(1)(c); Local Authorities (Conduct of Referendums) (Wales) Regulations 2008, SI 2008/1848, Sch 3 r 38(1)(c); Local Authorities (Conduct of Referendums) (England) Regulations 2012, SI 2012/323, Sch 3 r 38(1)(c). As to the printing of ballot papers see PARA 607.

6   Parish and Community Meetings (Polls) Rules 1987, SI 1987/1, r 5, Schedule r 29(1)(d); Local Authorities (Conduct of Referendums) (Wales) Regulations 2008, SI 2008/1848, Sch 3 r 38(1)(d); Local Authorities (Conduct of Referendums) (England) Regulations 2012, SI 2012/323, Sch 3 r 38(1)(d).

7   Parish and Community Meetings (Polls) Rules 1987, SI 1987/1, r 5, Schedule r 29(1); Local
     Authorities (Conduct of Referendums) (Wales) Regulations 2008, SI 2008/1848, Sch 3 r 38(1);
     Local Authorities (Conduct of Referendums) (England) Regulations 2012, SI 2012/323, Sch 3
     r 38(1).
8   Parish and Community Meetings (Polls) Rules 1987, SI 1987/1, r 5, Schedule r 29(3)(a); Local
     Authorities (Conduct of Referendums) (Wales) Regulations 2008, SI 2008/1848, Sch 3
     r 38(2)(a); Local Authorities (Conduct of Referendums) (England) Regulations 2012,
     SI 2012/323, Sch 3 r 38(2)(a).
9   Parish and Community Meetings (Polls) Rules 1987, SI 1987/1, r 5, Schedule r 29(3)(b); Local
     Authorities (Conduct of Referendums) (Wales) Regulations 2008, SI 2008/1848, Sch 3
     r 38(2)(b); Local Authorities (Conduct of Referendums) (England) Regulations 2012,
     SI 2012/323, Sch 3 r 38(2)(b).
10   Parish and Community Meetings (Polls) Rules 1987, SI 1987/1, r 5, Schedule r 29(3)(c); Local
     Authorities (Conduct of Referendums) (Wales) Regulations 2008, SI 2008/1848, Sch 3
     r 38(2)(c); Local Authorities (Conduct of Referendums) (England) Regulations 2012,
     SI 2012/323, Sch 3 r 38(2)(c).
11   Parish and Community Meetings (Polls) Rules 1987, SI 1987/1, r 5, Schedule r 29(3); Local
     Authorities (Conduct of Referendums) (Wales) Regulations 2008, SI 2008/1848, Sch 3 r 38(2);
     Local Authorities (Conduct of Referendums) (England) Regulations 2012, SI 2012/323, Sch 3
     r 38(2).
12   As to the meaning of 'counting officer' see PARA 576 note 1.
13   As to returning officers at polls consequent on a parish or community meeting see PARA 588.
14   As to the appointment of counting observers at a referendum see PARA 614.
15   Parish and Community Meetings (Polls) Rules 1987, SI 1987/1, r 5, Schedule r 29(4)(a); Local
     Authorities (Conduct of Referendums) (Wales) Regulations 2008, SI 2008/1848, Sch 3 r 38(3);
     Local Authorities (Conduct of Referendums) (England) Regulations 2012, SI 2012/323, Sch 3
     r 38(3). At a poll consequent on a parish or community meeting, it is provided that, where a
     ballot paper is void in part but on which any vote is counted under the Parish and Community
     Meetings (Polls) Rules 1987, SI 1987/1, r 29(2), the returning officer must endorse the words
     'rejected in part' on the ballot paper and indicate which vote or votes have been counted:
     r 29(4)(b). In connection with the notification of rejected ballots see the Representation of the
     People Act 2000 s 12, Sch 4 para 7E (added by the Electoral Registration and Administration
     Act 2013 s 22(1); applied and modified, in relation to Wales, by the Local Authorities (Conduct
     of Referendums) (Wales) Regulations 2008, SI 2008/1848, Sch 4 Table 2, and, in relation to
     England, by the Local Authorities (Conduct of Referendums) (England) Regulations 2012,
     SI 2012/323, Sch 4 Table 3). As to the provisions that are so applied and modified see PARA 15.
16   Parish and Community Meetings (Polls) Rules 1987, SI 1987/1, r 5, Schedule r 29(5)(a); Local
     Authorities (Conduct of Referendums) (Wales) Regulations 2008, SI 2008/1848, Sch 3
     r 38(4)(a); Local Authorities (Conduct of Referendums) (England) Regulations 2012,
     SI 2012/323, Sch 3 r 38(4)(a).
17   Parish and Community Meetings (Polls) Rules 1987, SI 1987/1, r 5, Schedule r 29(5)(b); Local
     Authorities (Conduct of Referendums) (Wales) Regulations 2008, SI 2008/1848, Sch 3
     r 38(4)(b); Local Authorities (Conduct of Referendums) (England) Regulations 2012,
     SI 2012/323, Sch 3 r 38(4)(b).
18   Parish and Community Meetings (Polls) Rules 1987, SI 1987/1, r 5, Schedule r 29(5)(c); Local
     Authorities (Conduct of Referendums) (Wales) Regulations 2008, SI 2008/1848, Sch 3
     r 38(4)(c); Local Authorities (Conduct of Referendums) (England) Regulations 2012,
     SI 2012/323, Sch 3 r 38(4)(c).
19   Parish and Community Meetings (Polls) Rules 1987, SI 1987/1, r 5, Schedule r 29(5)(d); Local
     Authorities (Conduct of Referendums) (Wales) Regulations 2008, SI 2008/1848, Sch 3
     r 38(4)(d); Local Authorities (Conduct of Referendums) (England) Regulations 2012,
     SI 2012/323, Sch 3 r 38(4)(d). In relation to a poll consequent on a parish or community
     meeting, it is provided that the statement referred to in the text must include the number of
     ballot papers rejected in part and must record that number: Parish and Community Meetings
     (Polls) Rules 1987, SI 1987/1, r 5, Schedule r 29(5).

**649.   Conclusiveness of decision as to ballot papers of counting officer at
referendum and returning officer at poll.** The decision of the counting officer[1] at
a local authority referendum[2] or the returning officer at a poll consequent on a
parish or community meeting[3] on any question arising in respect of a ballot
paper is final, but is subject to review on a petition[4].

1   As to the meaning of 'counting officer' see PARA 576 note 1.
2   As to the meaning of 'referendum' for these purposes see PARA 574 notes 2, 13.
3   As to how polls consequent on a parish or community meeting come about see PARA 581. As to returning officers at polls consequent on a parish or community meeting see PARA 588.

4   Parish and Community Meetings (Polls) Rules 1987, SI 1987/1, r 5, Schedule r 30; Local Authorities (Conduct of Referendums) (Wales) Regulations 2008, SI 2008/1848, Sch 3 r 39; Local Authorities (Conduct of Referendums) (England) Regulations 2012, SI 2012/323, Sch 3 r 39.

650. Recount at a referendum or poll. A petition organiser[1] at a local authority referendum[2] or a candidate at a poll consequent on a parish or community meeting[3] may, if present when the counting or any recount of the votes at a referendum or poll is completed[4], require the counting officer[5] or returning officer[6] (as the case may be) to have the votes recounted or again recounted, but the counting officer or the returning officer may refuse to do so if in his opinion the request is unreasonable[7]. No step may be taken on the completion of the counting or any recount of votes until such petition organisers or candidates as are present at its completion have been given reasonable opportunity to exercise the right of demanding a recount[8].

1   As to the meaning of 'petition organiser' for these purposes see PARA 614 note 4.
2   As to the meaning of 'referendum' for these purposes see PARA 574 notes 2, 13.
3   As to how polls consequent on a parish or community meeting come about see PARA 581.
4   As to the count see PARA 646 et seq.
5   As to the meaning of 'counting officer' see PARA 576 note 1.
6   As to returning officers at polls consequent on a parish or community meeting see PARA 588.

7   Parish and Community Meetings (Polls) Rules 1987, SI 1987/1, r 5, Schedule r 28(1); Local Authorities (Conduct of Referendums) (Wales) Regulations 2008, SI 2008/1848, Sch 3 r 37(1); Local Authorities (Conduct of Referendums) (England) Regulations 2012, SI 2012/323, Sch 3 r 37(1).

8   Parish and Community Meetings (Polls) Rules 1987, SI 1987/1, r 5, Schedule r 28(2); Local Authorities (Conduct of Referendums) (Wales) Regulations 2008, SI 2008/1848, Sch 3 r 37(2); Local Authorities (Conduct of Referendums) (England) Regulations 2012, SI 2012/323, Sch 3 r 37(2).

651. Equality of votes at a referendum or poll. Where, after the counting of the votes (including any recount) at a local authority referendum[1] is completed[2], an equality of 'yes' and 'no' votes is found to exist between the answers, the counting officer[3] must forthwith decide the referendum by lot[4].

Where, after the counting of the votes (including any recount) at a poll consequent on a parish or community meeting[5] is completed[6], an equality of votes is found to exist between any candidates or for and against any question, and the addition of a vote would entitle any of those candidates to be declared elected or would decide the question, the returning officer[7] must forthwith decide that question by lot, and proceed as if the answer in favour of or against the question on which the lot falls had received an additional vote[8].

1   As to the meaning of 'referendum' for these purposes see PARA 574 notes 2, 13.
2   As to the counting of the votes (including any recount) at a local authority referendum see PARA 646 et seq.
3   As to the meaning of 'counting officer' see PARA 576 note 1.

4   Local Authorities (Conduct of Referendums) (Wales) Regulations 2008, SI 2008/1848, Sch 3 r 40; Local Authorities (Conduct of Referendums) (England) Regulations 2012, SI 2012/323, Sch 3 r 40.

3   As to how polls consequent on a parish or community meeting come about see PARA 581.

6   As to the counting of the votes (including any recount) at a poll consequent on a parish or community meeting see PARA 646 et seq.

7   As to returning officers at polls consequent on a parish or community meeting see PARA 588.
8   Parish and Community Meetings (Polls) Rules 1987, SI 1987/1, r 5, Schedule r 31.

F. FINAL PROCEEDINGS FOR THE REFERENDUM OR POLL

(A) Following a Local Authority Referendum

652.   Declaration of result at local authority referendum. The counting officer[1] at a local authority referendum[2] must forthwith: (1) declare the result of the referendum[3]; (2) inform the proper officer[4] of the authority[5] by or in respect of which the referendum was held of the result of the referendum[6]; and (3) give public notice of the result of the referendum[7], the number of ballot papers counted[8], the total number of votes cast for each answer[9] and the number of rejected ballot papers under each head shown in the statement of rejected ballot papers[10].

1   As to the meaning of 'counting officer' see PARA 576 note 1.
2   As to the meaning of 'referendum' for these purposes see PARA 574 notes 2, 13.
3   Local Authorities (Conduct of Referendums) (Wales) Regulations 2008, SI 2008/1848, Sch 3 r 41(a); Local Authorities (Conduct of Referendums) (England) Regulations 2012, SI 2012/323, Sch 3 r 41(a).
        In relation to a referendum in England, if the majority of the votes cast in a referendum other than a further referendum are in favour of the authority operating arrangements which differ from its existing arrangements, the result of the referendum is: (1) for the purposes of the Local Government Act 2000 s 9MB(3) (requirement to hold and give effect to referendum: see LOCAL GOVERNMENT), to approve the authority's proposals under s 9MA (referendum proposals by local authority: see LOCAL GOVERNMENT) (Local Authorities (Conduct of Referendums) (England) Regulations 2012, SI 2012/323, reg 14(2)(a)); (2) for the purposes of the Local Authorities (Referendums) (Petitions) (England) Regulations 2011, SI 2011/2914, reg 18 (action where referendum proposals approved: see PARA 653), and in accordance with the Local Government Act 2000 s 9MF(4) (further provision with respect to referendums: see LOCAL GOVERNMENT), to approve the proposals drawn up under the Local Authorities (Referendums) (Petitions) (England) Regulations 2011, SI 2011/2914, reg 17(2) (see PARA 568) which were the subject of the referendum (Local Authorities (Conduct of Referendums) (England) Regulations 2012, SI 2012/323, reg 14(2)(b)); (3) for the purposes of an order made under the Local Government Act 2000 s 9N (requiring referendum on change to mayor and cabinet executive: see LOCAL GOVERNMENT), to require the authority to start to operate a mayor and cabinet executive (Local Authorities (Conduct of Referendums) (England) Regulations 2012, SI 2012/323, reg 14(2)(c)); and (4) for the purposes of an order made under the Local Government Act 2000 s 9ME (referendum following order: see LOCAL GOVERNMENT), and in accordance with s 9MF(4), to require the authority to start to operate the form of governance that was the subject of the referendum held in consequence of the order (Local Authorities (Conduct of Referendums) (England) Regulations 2012, SI 2012/323, reg 14(2)(d)). If the majority of the votes cast in a referendum other than a further referendum are in favour of the continuation of the authority's existing arrangements, the result of the referendum is: (a) for the purposes of the Local Government Act 2000 s 9MB(3), to reject the authority's proposals under s 9MA (Local Authorities (Conduct of Referendums) (England) Regulations 2012, SI 2012/323, reg 14(3)(a)); (b) for the purposes of the Local Authorities (Referendums) (Petitions) (England) Regulations 2011, SI 2011/2914, reg 19 (action where referendum proposals rejected: see PARA 654)), and in accordance with the Local Government Act 2000 s 9MF(5), to reject the proposals drawn up under the Local Authorities (Referendums) (Petitions) (England) Regulations 2011, SI 2011/2914, reg 17(2) which were the subject of the referendum (Local Authorities (Conduct of Referendums) (England) Regulations 2012, SI 2012/323, reg 14(3)(b)); (c) for the purposes of an order made under the Local Government Act 2000 s 9N, to reject the proposal that the authority start to operate a mayor and cabinet executive (Local Authorities (Conduct of Referendums) (England) Regulations 2012, SI 2012/323, reg 14(3)(c)); and (d) for the purposes of an order made under the Local Government Act 2000 s 9ME, and in accordance with s 9MF(5), to reject the proposal that the authority start to operate the form of governance that was the subject of the referendum held in consequence of that order (Local Authorities (Conduct of Referendums) (England) Regulations 2012, SI 2012/323, reg 14(3)(d)). If the majority of the

votes cast in a further referendum are in favour of the authority continuing to operate a mayor and cabinet executive, the result of the referendum is to require the authority to continue to operate those arrangements: Local Authorities (Conduct of Referendums) (England) Regulations 2012, SI 2012/323, reg 14(4). If the majority of the votes cast in a further referendum are in favour of the authority changing its governance arrangements to those it operated at the time of the tainted referendum, the result of the referendum is to require the authority to implement those arrangements: reg 14(5). These provisions are subject to regs 16, 17 (see PARAS 766, 866): reg 14(1).

In relation to a referendum in Wales, if the majority of the votes cast in a referendum other than a further referendum are 'yes' votes, the result of the referendum is: (i) for the purposes of the Local Government Act 2000 s 27(7) (referendum in case of proposals involving elected mayor: see LOCAL GOVERNMENT vol 69 (2009) PARA 314), to approve the local authority's proposals under s 25 (see LOCAL GOVERNMENT vol 69 (2009) PARA 312) (Local Authorities (Conduct of Referendums) (Wales) Regulations 2008, SI 2008/1848, reg 10(2)(a)); and (ii) for the purposes of the Local Authorities (Referendums) (Petitions and Directions) (Wales) Regulations 2001, SI 2001/2292, reg 23 (action where referendum proposals approved: see PARA 653) or, as the case may be, the comparable provisions of any other regulations or order made under any provision of the Local Government Act 2000 Pt II (ss 10–48) (see LOCAL GOVERNMENT vol 69 (2009) PARA 314), to approve the proposals that were the subject of the referendum (Local Authorities (Conduct of Referendums) (Wales) Regulations 2008, SI 2008/1848, reg 10(2)(b)). If the majority of the votes cast in a referendum other than a further referendum are 'no' votes, the result of the referendum is: (aa) for the purposes of the Local Government Act 2000 s 27(8), to reject the local authority's proposals under s 25 (Local Authorities (Conduct of Referendums) (Wales) Regulations 2008, SI 2008/1848, reg 10(3)(a)); and (bb) for the purposes of the Local Authorities (Referendums) (Petitions and Directions) (Wales) Regulations 2001, SI 2001/2292, reg 24 (action where referendum proposals rejected: see PARA 654) or, as the case may be, the comparable provisions of any other regulations or order made under any provision of the Local Government Act 2000 Pt II, to reject the proposals that were the subject of the referendum (Local Authorities (Conduct of Referendums) (Wales) Regulations 2008, SI 2008/1848, reg 10(3)(b)). If the majority of the votes cast in a further referendum are 'yes' votes, the result of the referendum is to approve the continuation of the local authority's existing executive arrangements or their existing alternative arrangements (as the case may be): reg 10(4). If the majority of the votes cast in a further referendum are 'no' votes, the result of the referendum is to reject the continuation of the local authority's existing executive arrangements or their existing alternative arrangements (as the case may be): reg 10(5). In a case to which reg 10(5) applies, the Local Government Act 2000 s 27(8)–(12) is then to apply as if the result of the further referendum was the rejection of the local authority's proposals under s 25, but subject to specified modifications: see the Local Authorities (Conduct of Referendums) (Wales) Regulations 2008, SI 2008/1848, reg 10(6). These provisions are subject to regs 12, 13 (see PARAS 766, 866): reg 10(1).

4   As to the meaning of 'proper officer' see PARA 140 note 2 (definition applied, in relation to Wales, by virtue of the Local Authorities (Conduct of Referendums) (Wales) Regulations 2008, SI 2008/1848, reg 2(1), and, in relation to England, by virtue of the Local Authorities (Conduct of Referendums) (England) Regulations 2012, SI 2012/323, reg 2(1)).

5   As to the meaning of 'authority' see LOCAL GOVERNMENT vol 69 (2009) PARA 23.

6   Local Authorities (Conduct of Referendums) (Wales) Regulations 2008, SI 2008/1848, Sch 3 r 41(b); Local Authorities (Conduct of Referendums) (England) Regulations 2012, SI 2012/323, Sch 3 r 41(b).

7   Local Authorities (Conduct of Referendums) (Wales) Regulations 2008, SI 2008/1848, Sch 3 r 41(c)(i); Local Authorities (Conduct of Referendums) (England) Regulations 2012, SI 2012/323, Sch 3 r 41(c)(i).

8   Local Authorities (Conduct of Referendums) (Wales) Regulations 2008, SI 2008/1848, Sch 3 r 41(c)(ii); Local Authorities (Conduct of Referendums) (England) Regulations 2012, SI 2012/323, Sch 3 r 41(c)(ii). As to the counting of the votes (including any recount) at a local authority referendum see PARA 646 et seq.

9   Local Authorities (Conduct of Referendums) (Wales) Regulations 2008, SI 2008/1848, Sch 3 r 41(c)(iii); Local Authorities (Conduct of Referendums) (England) Regulations 2012, SI 2012/323, Sch 3 r 41(c)(iii).

10 Local Authorities (Conduct of Referendums) (Wales) Regulations 2008, SI 2008/1848, Sch 3 r 41(c)(iv); Local Authorities (Conduct of Referendums) (England) Regulations 2012, SI 2012/323, Sch 3 r 41(c)(iv). As to the statement of rejected ballot papers see PARA 648.

653. Action to be taken where proposals at local authority referendum are approved. If the result of a referendum held in England or Wales following a petition[1], or a referendum held in Wales in pursuance of a direction[2], is to approve the proposals that were the subject of the referendum, the authority[3] must implement the proposals that were the subject of the referendum[4]. In relation to a referendum in Wales, where the authority is then operating executive arrangements that take a form that differs from those that were the subject of the referendum, the provisions relating to the operation of, and publicity for, executive arrangements[5] apply for the purpose of enabling the authority to operate the executive arrangements that were the subject of the referendum as it applies for the purpose of enabling an authority to operate executive arrangements in other circumstances, subject to modifications[6].

1   Ie, in relation to England, under the Local Authorities (Referendums) (Petitions) (England) Regulations 2011, SI 2011/2914, Pt II (regs 3–17) and, in relation to Wales, under the Local Authorities (Referendums) (Petitions and Directions) (Wales) Regulations 2001, SI 2001/2292, Pt II (regs 3–17) (see PARA 559 et seq).
2   Ie under the Local Authorities (Referendums) (Petitions and Directions) (Wales) Regulations 2001, SI 2001/2292, Pt III (regs 18–22) (see PARA 570 et seq).
3   As to the meaning of 'authority' see LOCAL GOVERNMENT vol 69 (2009) PARA 23.
4   Local Authorities (Referendums) (Petitions and Directions) (Wales) Regulations 2001, SI 2001/2292, reg 23(a); Local Authorities (Referendums) (Petitions) (England) Regulations 2011, SI 2011/2914, reg 18. In relation to a referendum in Wales the implementation must be in accordance with the timetable included in the proposals under the Local Authorities (Referendums) (Petitions and Directions) (Wales) Regulations 2001, SI 2001/2292, reg 17(3)(a) (see PARA 568) or, as the case may be, reg 19(1)(c) (see PARA 571): see reg 23(a).
5   Ie the Local Government Act 2000 s 29 (see LOCAL GOVERNMENT vol 69 (2009) PARA 309).
6   See the Local Authorities (Referendums) (Petitions and Directions) (Wales) Regulations 2001, SI 2001/2292, reg 23(b).

654. Action where proposals at local authority referendum are rejected. If the result of a referendum held in England following a petition[1] is to reject the proposals that were the subject of the referendum the authority[2] may not implement those proposals and must continue to operate their existing form of governance arrangements[3].

If the result of a referendum held in Wales following a petition[4] or in pursuance of a direction[5] is to reject the proposals that were the subject of the referendum: (1) the authority may not implement those proposals[6]; and (2) if the authority is not then operating alternative arrangements or executive arrangements[7], it must draw up detailed fall-back proposals which are based on its outline fall-back proposals[8]. Detailed fall-back proposals must comprise the details (if any) specified in a direction[9] and such other details of the executive arrangements or alternative arrangements to which they relate as the Welsh Ministers may direct[10] as well as details of any transitional arrangements which are necessary for the implementation of the fall-back proposals[11]. In drawing up detailed fall-back proposals, the authority must comply with any directions given by the Welsh Ministers[12]; and, where those proposals involve executive arrangements, the authority must, unless a direction has been given in relation to that matter, decide the extent to which the specified functions[13] are to be the responsibility of the executive[14]. Except to the extent that detailed fall-back proposals involving executive arrangements or alternative arrangements are specified in a direction[15], the authority must: (a) before drawing up proposals in accordance with head (2) above, take reasonable steps to consult the local government electors[16] for, and other interested persons in, the authority's area[17];

and (b) in drawing up those proposals, consider the extent to which the proposals, if implemented, are likely to assist in securing continuous improvement in the way in which the authority's functions are exercised, having regard to a combination of economy, efficiency and effectiveness[18]. Where detailed fall-back proposals are drawn up in accordance with head (2) above, the authority must send a copy of them to the Welsh Ministers[19].

If, when the referendum results in a rejection of the proposals that were the subject of the referendum, the authority is then operating executive arrangements, it must continue to operate those arrangements until it is authorised or required to operate different executive arrangements or authorised to operate alternative arrangements in place of its existing executive arrangements[20]; and, if the authority is then operating alternative arrangements, it must continue to operate those arrangements until it is authorised to operate different alternative arrangements or authorised or required to operate executive arrangements in place of its existing alternative arrangements[21].

The authority must implement detailed fall-back proposals in accordance with the timetable[22].

1 Ie under the Local Authorities (Referendums) (Petitions) (England) Regulations 2011, SI 2011/2914, Pt II (regs 3–17) (see PARA 559 et seq).
2 As to the meaning of 'authority' see LOCAL GOVERNMENT vol 69 (2009) PARA 23.
3 Local Authorities (Referendums) (Petitions) (England) Regulations 2011, SI 2011/2914, reg 19.
4 Ie under the Local Authorities (Referendums) (Petitions and Directions) (Wales) Regulations 2001, SI 2001/2292, Pt II (regs 3–17) (see PARA 559 et seq).
5 Ie under the Local Authorities (Referendums) (Petitions and Directions) (Wales) Regulations 2001, SI 2001/2292, Pt III (regs 18–22) (see PARA 570 et seq).
6 Local Authorities (Referendums) (Petitions and Directions) (Wales) Regulations 2001, SI 2001/2292, reg 24(1)(a).
7 As to the operation of executive arrangements see LOCAL GOVERNMENT vol 69 (2009) PARA 303 et seq; and as to the operation of alternative arrangements see LOCAL GOVERNMENT vol 69 (2009) PARA 364 et seq.
8 Local Authorities (Referendums) (Petitions and Directions) (Wales) Regulations 2001, SI 2001/2292, reg 24(1)(b). As to the meaning of 'outline fall-back proposals' see PARA 568 note 15.
9 Local Authorities (Referendums) (Petitions and Directions) (Wales) Regulations 2001, SI 2001/2292, reg 24(2)(a). The text refers to the details (if any) specified in a direction under reg 18(1) (see PARA 570).
10 Local Authorities (Referendums) (Petitions and Directions) (Wales) Regulations 2001, SI 2001/2292, reg 24(2)(b).
11 Local Authorities (Referendums) (Petitions and Directions) (Wales) Regulations 2001, SI 2001/2292, reg 24(2)(c).
12 Local Authorities (Referendums) (Petitions and Directions) (Wales) Regulations 2001, SI 2001/2292, reg 24(3)(a).
13 Ie the functions specified in regulations under the Local Government Act 2000 s 13(3)(b) (see LOCAL GOVERNMENT vol 69 (2009) PARA 324).
14 Local Authorities (Referendums) (Petitions and Directions) (Wales) Regulations 2001, SI 2001/2292, reg 24(3)(b).
15 Ie specified in a direction under the Local Authorities (Referendums) (Petitions and Directions) (Wales) Regulations 2001, SI 2001/2292, reg 18(1) (see PARA 570).
16 As to entitlement to vote as a local government elector see PARA 97 et seq. As to the meaning of 'local government election' see PARA 11; and as to the meaning of 'elector' see PARA 95 note 2.
17 Local Authorities (Referendums) (Petitions and Directions) (Wales) Regulations 2001, SI 2001/2292, reg 24(4)(a).
18 Local Authorities (Referendums) (Petitions and Directions) (Wales) Regulations 2001, SI 2001/2292, reg 24(4)(b).
19 Local Authorities (Referendums) (Petitions and Directions) (Wales) Regulations 2001, SI 2001/2292, reg 24(5).
20 Local Authorities (Referendums) (Petitions and Directions) (Wales) Regulations 2001, SI 2001/2292, reg 24(1)(c).

21 Local Authorities (Referendums) (Petitions and Directions) (Wales) Regulations 2001, SI 2001/2292, reg 24(1)(d).
22 Local Authorities (Referendums) (Petitions and Directions) (Wales) Regulations 2001, SI 2001/2292, reg 24(6). The text refers to the timetable included in the proposals pursuant to reg 17(7)(a)(ii) (see PARA 568) or, as the case may be, reg 20(3)(a)(iii) (see PARA 571). Where detailed fall-back proposals are based on proposals approved under the Local Government Act 2000 s 28(1) (approval of outline fall-back proposals: see LOCAL GOVERNMENT vol 69 (2009) PARA 315), the timetable referred to in the text must be extended to the extent that there is any delay in making the necessary regulations under s 11(5) (forms of local authority executive: see LOCAL GOVERNMENT vol 69 (2009) PARA 327) or, as the case may be, under s 32 (alternative arrangements: see LOCAL GOVERNMENT vol 69 (2009) PARA 364).

(B) Following a Poll consequent on a Parish or Community Meeting

655. Declaration of result of poll consequent on a parish or community meeting. At a poll consequent on a parish or community meeting on any question other than a question of appointment to any office[1], when the result of the poll has been ascertained[2], the returning officer[3] must forthwith: (1) declare the number of votes given for and against the question and whether the proposal to which the question relates has been carried or not[4]; (2) give notice[5] of the result of the poll to the chairman of the meeting at which the poll was demanded[6]; and (3) give notice of the declaration as to the number of votes under head (1) above, together with the number of rejected ballot papers under each head shown in the statement of rejected ballot papers[7].

1 As to how polls consequent on a parish or community meeting come about see PARA 581.
2 As to the counting of the votes (including any recount) at a poll consequent on a parish or community meeting see PARA 646 et seq.
3 As to returning officers at polls consequent on a parish or community meeting see PARA 588.
4 Parish and Community Meetings (Polls) Rules 1987, SI 1987/1, r 5, Schedule r 32(b)(i).
5 As to the giving of notice by the returning officer at a poll consequent on a parish or community meeting see PARA 588.
6 Parish and Community Meetings (Polls) Rules 1987, SI 1987/1, Schedule r 32(b)(ii). As to the constitution of, and procedure at, parish and community meetings see LOCAL GOVERNMENT vol 69 (2009) PARA 635 et seq.
7 Parish and Community Meetings (Polls) Rules 1987, SI 1987/1, Schedule r 32(b)(iii). As to the statement of rejected ballot papers see PARA 648.

G. DISPOSAL OF DOCUMENTS FOLLOWING REFERENDUM OR POLL

656. Sealing up of ballot papers at a referendum or poll. At a local authority referendum[1] or at a poll consequent on a parish or community meeting[2], on the completion of the counting[3], the counting officer[4] (at a referendum) and the returning officer (at a poll)[5] must seal up in separate packets the counted and rejected ballot papers[6]. The sealed packets of tendered ballot papers[7] or of counterfoils[8] or of marked copies of the register of electors[9] must not be opened by the returning officer or the counting officer (as the case may be)[10].

Special provision is made for the sealing of the contents of receptacles used for the purposes of postal voting at a local authority referendum[11].

1 As to the meaning of 'referendum' for these purposes see PARA 574 notes 2, 13.
2 As to how polls consequent on a parish or community meeting come about see PARA 581.
3 As to the counting of the votes (including any recount) at a local authority referendum or poll consequent on a parish or community meeting see PARA 646 et seq.
4 As to the meaning of 'counting officer' see PARA 576 note 1.
5 As to returning officers at polls consequent on a parish or community meeting see PARA 588.
6 Parish and Community Meetings (Polls) Rules 1987, SI 1987/1, r 5, Schedule r 33(1); Local Authorities (Conduct of Referendums) (Wales) Regulations 2008, SI 2008/1848, Sch 3 r 42(1);

Local Authorities (Conduct of Referendums) (England) Regulations 2012, SI 2012/323, Sch 3 r 42(1). As to rejected ballot papers see PARA 648. In the case of a poll consequent on a parish or community meeting, the packet of rejected ballot papers must include those rejected in part also: Schedule r 33(1).

7 As to tendered ballot papers see PARA 624.
8 And, in the case of a local authority referendum, certificates of employment on duty on the day of the poll (as to which see PARA 618): Local Authorities (Conduct of Referendums) (Wales) Regulations 2008, SI 2008/1848, Sch 3 r 42(2)(c); Local Authorities (Conduct of Referendums) (England) Regulations 2012, SI 2012/323, Sch 3 r 42(2)(c).
9 And, in the case of a local authority referendum, marked copies of the register of electors, including any marked copy notices issued under the Representation of the People Act 1983 s 13B(3B) or (3D) (notices specifying appropriate alterations to the register: see PARA 168) (applied and modified, in relation to Wales, by the Local Authorities (Conduct of Referendums) (Wales) Regulations 2008, SI 2008/1848, Sch 4 Table 1, and, in relation to England, by the Local Authorities (Conduct of Referendums) (England) Regulations 2012, SI 2012/323, Sch 4 Table 1: see PARA 15), and lists of proxies: Local Authorities (Conduct of Referendums) (Wales) Regulations 2008, SI 2008/1848, Sch 3 r 42(2)(d); Local Authorities (Conduct of Referendums) (England) Regulations 2012, SI 2012/323, Sch 3 r 42(2)(d). As to the list of proxies see PARA 596; and as to the procedure for marking copies of voter records see PARA 620. The presiding officer must keep a list of persons to whom ballot papers are delivered in consequence of an alteration to the register made by virtue of the Representation of the People Act 1983 s 13B(3B) or s 13(3D) which takes effect on the day of the poll: see the Local Authorities (Conduct of Referendums) (Wales) Regulations 2008, SI 2008/1848, Sch 3 r 32; the Local Authorities (Conduct of Referendums) (England) Regulations 2012, SI 2012/323, Sch 3 r 32; and PARA 611 note 4.
10 Parish and Community Meetings (Polls) Rules 1987, SI 1987/1, r 5, Schedule r 33(2); Local Authorities (Conduct of Referendums) (Wales) Regulations 2008, SI 2008/1848, Sch 3 r 42(2); Local Authorities (Conduct of Referendums) (England) Regulations 2012, SI 2012/323, Sch 3 r 42(2).
11 See PARA 645.

657. Delivery of documents relating to a referendum or poll. The counting officer at a local authority referendum[1] and the returning officer at a poll consequent on a parish or community meeting[2], must, after sealing up the ballot papers[3], forward to the relevant registration officer[4] (in the case of a local authority referendum) or the proper officer of the council[5] of the district[6] in which the parish or community[7] is situate (in the case of a poll consequent on a parish or community meeting): (1) the packets of ballot papers in his possession[8]; (2) the ballot paper accounts[9], and the statements of rejected ballot papers[10] and of the result of the verification of the ballot paper accounts[11]; (3) the tendered votes lists[12], the lists of blind voters[13] (in the case of a poll consequent on a parish or community meeting) or voters and proxies with disabilities assisted by companions[14] (in the case of a local authority referendum), the lists of votes marked by the presiding officers and the statements relating to them[15], the lists of persons to whom ballot papers are delivered in consequence of an alteration to the register which takes effect on the day of the poll[16] (in the case of a local authority referendum), and the declarations made by the companions of blind voters (in the case of a poll consequent on a parish or community meeting) or of voters and proxies with disabilities (in the case of a local authority referendum)[17]; (4) the packets of counterfoils (in the case of a poll consequent on a parish or community meeting) or completed corresponding number lists (in the case of a local authority referendum)[18]; (5) the packets containing marked copies of the registers of electors (in the case of a poll consequent on a parish or community meeting) or certificates as to employment on duty on the day of the poll (in the case of a local authority referendum)[19]; and (6) (in the case of a local authority referendum) the packets containing marked copies of registers[20] and of the postal voters list, of the lists of proxies and of the proxy postal voters list[21], endorsing on each packet a description of its contents, the date of the referendum to which it relates and the name of the local authority by which or in respect of which the referendum was held.(in the case of a referendum) or the name of the parish or community for which the poll was held and the date of the poll to which the documents relate (in the case of a poll)[22].

1   As to the meaning of 'referendum' for these purposes see PARA 574 notes 2, 13; and as to the meaning of 'counting officer' see PARA 576 note 1.

2   As to how polls consequent on a parish or community meeting come about see PARA 581; and as to returning officers at polls consequent on a parish or community meeting see PARA 588.

3   As to the sealing up of ballot papers at a referendum or poll see PARA 656.

4   As to the meaning of 'registration officer' see the Representation of the People Act 1983 s 8; and PARA 139 (definition applied, in relation to Wales, by virtue of the Local Authorities (Conduct of Referendums) (Wales) Regulations 2008, SI 2008/1848, Sch 3 r 2(2), and, in relation to England, by virtue of the Local Authorities (Conduct of Referendums) (England) Regulations 2012, SI 2012/323, Sch 3 r 2(2)).

5   Ie any officer appointed for the purpose by the council: Parish and Community Meetings (Polls) Rules 1987, SI 1987/1, r 5, Schedule r 38(3).

6   As to counties and districts in England, and their councils, see LOCAL GOVERNMENT vol 69 (2009) PARA 24 et seq. As to counties and county boroughs in Wales, and their councils, see LOCAL GOVERNMENT vol 69 (2009) PARA 37 et seq.

7   As to parishes generally see LOCAL GOVERNMENT vol 69 (2009) PARA 27 et seq; and as to communities generally see LOCAL GOVERNMENT vol 69 (2009) PARA 41 et seq.

8   Parish and Community Meetings (Polls) Rules 1987, SI 1987/1, Schedule r 34(a); Local Authorities (Conduct of Referendums) (Wales) Regulations 2008, SI 2008/1848, Sch 3 r 43(1)(a); Local Authorities (Conduct of Referendums) (England) Regulations 2012, SI 2012/323, Sch 3 r 43(1)(a).

9   As to the ballot paper accounts see PARA 647.

10   As to the statement of rejected ballot papers see PARA 648.

11   Parish and Community Meetings (Polls) Rules 1987, SI 1987/1, Schedule r 34(b); Local Authorities (Conduct of Referendums) (Wales) Regulations 2008, SI 2008/1848, Sch 3 r 43(1)(b); Local Authorities (Conduct of Referendums) (England) Regulations 2012, SI 2012/323, Sch 3 r 43(1)(b).

12   As to the tendered votes list see PARA 624.

13   As to the list of blind voters see PARA 623.

14   As to the list of voters with disabilities assisted by companions see PARA 623.

15   As to the list of votes marked by the presiding officer see PARA 622.

16   Ie the list maintained under the Local Authorities (Conduct of Referendums) (Wales) Regulations 2008, SI 2008/1848, Sch 3 r 32, or under the Local Authorities (Conduct of Referendums) (England) Regulations 2012, SI 2012/323, Sch 3 r 32, as the case may be (see PARA 611 note 4).

17   Parish and Community Meetings (Polls) Rules 1987, SI 1987/1, Schedule r 34(c); Local Authorities (Conduct of Referendums) (Wales) Regulations 2008, SI 2008/1848, Sch 3 r 43(1)(c); Local Authorities (Conduct of Referendums) (England) Regulations 2012, SI 2012/323, Sch 3 r 43(1)(c). As to declarations made by the companions of voters with disabilities see PARA 623.

18   Parish and Community Meetings (Polls) Rules 1987, SI 1987/1, Schedule r 34(d); Local Authorities (Conduct of Referendums) (Wales) Regulations 2008, SI 2008/1848, Sch 3 r 43(1)(d); Local Authorities (Conduct of Referendums) (England) Regulations 2012, SI 2012/323, Sch 3 r 43(1)(d).

19   Parish and Community Meetings (Polls) Rules 1987, SI 1987/1, Schedule r 34(e); Local Authorities (Conduct of Referendums) (Wales) Regulations 2008, SI 2008/1848, Sch 3 r 43(1)(e); Local Authorities (Conduct of Referendums) (England) Regulations 2012, SI 2012/323, Sch 3 r 43(1)(e).

20   Ie including any marked copy notices issued under the Representation of the People Act 1983 s 13B(3B) or (3D) (notices specifying appropriate alterations to the register: see PARA 168) (applied and modified, in relation to Wales, by the Local Authorities (Conduct of Referendums) (Wales) Regulations 2008, SI 2008/1848, Sch 4 Table 1, and, in relation to England, by the Local Authorities (Conduct of Referendums) (England) Regulations 2012, SI 2012/323, Sch 4 Table 1: see PARA 15).

21 Local Authorities (Conduct of Referendums) (Wales) Regulations 2008, SI 2008/1848, Sch 3 r 43(1)(f); Local Authorities (Conduct of Referendums) (England) Regulations 2012, SI 2012/323, Sch 3 r 43(1)(f).

22 Parish and Community Meetings (Polls) Rules 1987, SI 1987/1, Schedule r 34; Local Authorities (Conduct of Referendums) (Wales) Regulations 2008, SI 2008/1848, Sch 3 r 43(1); Local Authorities (Conduct of Referendums) (England) Regulations 2012, SI 2012/323, Sch 3 r 43(1).

658. Forwarding of documents after postal voting at a local authority referendum. The counting officer[1] at a local authority referendum[2] must forward[3] to the relevant registration officer certain packets[4] containing documents relating to postal voting[5]. He must endorse on each packet a description of its contents, the date of the referendum to which it relates, and the name of the voting area[6] for which the referendum was held[7].

Where any covering envelopes[8] are received by the counting officer after the close of the poll[9] or where any envelopes addressed to postal voters[10] are returned as undelivered too late to be re-addressed, or where any spoilt postal ballot papers[11] are returned too late to enable other postal ballot papers to be issued, the counting officer must put them unopened into a separate packet, seal up the packet and endorse and forward it at a subsequent date in the same manner as the postal voting packets previously forwarded[12].

1 As to the meaning of 'counting officer' see PARA 576 note 1.
2 As to the meaning of 'referendum' for these purposes see PARA 574 notes 2, 13.
3 As to the sealing up of postal ballot papers at a referendum see PARA 645.
4 Ie the packets referred to in the Representation of the People (England and Wales) Regulations 2001, SI 2001/341, reg 75 (as applied and modified) (counterfoils and special lists: see PARA 634), reg 77(6) (as applied and modified) (spoilt postal ballot papers: see PARA 635), reg 78(2C) (as applied and modified) (cancelled postal ballot papers: see PARA 636) reg 84(9) (opening of covering envelopes: see PARA 421) and reg 89 (as applied and modified) (contents of receptacles: see PARA 645).
5 Representation of the People (England and Wales) Regulations 2001, SI 2001/341, reg 91(1)(a) (reg 91(1) amended by SI 2006/752; SI 2006/2910) (provisions of those regulations applied and modified, in relation to Wales, by the Local Authorities (Conduct of Referendums) (Wales) Regulations 2008, SI 2008/1848, Sch 4 Table 5, and, in relation to England, by the Local Authorities (Conduct of Referendums) (England) Regulations 2012, SI 2012/323, Sch 4 Table 6). As to the provisions that are so applied and modified see PARA 15.
6 As to the meaning of 'voting area' see PARA 580 note 2; definition applied by virtue of the Representation of the People Act 2000 Sch 4 para 1 (Sch 4 applied and modified, in relation to Wales, by the Local Authorities (Conduct of Referendums) (Wales) Regulations 2008, SI 2008/1848, Sch 4 Table 2, and, in relation to England, by the Local Authorities (Conduct of Referendums) (England) Regulations 2012, SI 2012/323, Sch 4 Table 3).
7 Representation of the People (England and Wales) Regulations 2001, SI 2001/341, reg 91(1)(a) (as amended, applied and modified: see note 5).
8 As to the meaning of 'covering envelope' see PARA 410 note 6.
9 Ie apart from those delivered by the presiding officer in accordance with the provisions of the Representation of the People (England and Wales) Regulations 2001, SI 2001/341, reg 79(3) (as applied and modified) (see PARA 640).
10 As to the meaning of 'postal voter' see PARA 632 note 3.
11 As to spoilt postal ballot papers see PARA 635.
12 Representation of the People (England and Wales) Regulations 2001, SI 2001/341, reg 91(3) (as applied and modified: see note 5).

659. Retention and public inspection of documents relating to a referendum or poll. Following a local authority referendum[1] the relevant registration officer[2] must retain for one year all documents relating to a referendum forwarded to him or her by a counting officer[3], and then, unless otherwise directed by an order of a county court, the Crown Court, a magistrates' court or an election court, must cause them to be destroyed[4]. An order for the inspection or production of any rejected ballot papers in the custody of the relevant registration officer, or for the opening of a sealed packet of the completed corresponding number lists or certificates as to employment on duty on the day of the poll or for the inspection of any counted ballot papers in the relevant registration officer's custody, may be made by a county court[5], if the court is satisfied by evidence on oath that the order is required for the purpose of instituting or maintaining a prosecution for an offence in relation to ballot papers, or for the purpose of a referendum petition[6]. An order for the opening of a sealed packet of the completed corresponding number lists or of certificates as to employment on duty on the day of the poll or for the inspection of any counted ballot papers in the custody of the relevant registration officer may be made by an election court[7]. An order under these provisions may be made subject to such conditions as to persons, time, place and mode of inspection, or production or opening, as the court making the order may think expedient[8]. In making and carrying into effect an order for the opening of a packet of the completed corresponding number lists or of certificates as to employment on duty on the day of the poll or for the inspection of counted ballot papers, care must be taken that the way in which the vote of any particular person has been given must not be disclosed until it has been proved that that person's vote was given and that the vote has been declared by a competent court to be invalid[9]. An appeal lies to the High Court from any order of a county court under these provisions[10].

Following a poll consequent on a parish or community meeting[11], the proper officer of the council of the district in which the parish or community is situate[12] must retain for six months among the records of the council all documents relating to a referendum or poll (as the case may be) which are forwarded to him by the returning officer[13], and then, unless otherwise directed by an order of the county court or election court, must cause them to be destroyed[14]. The documents forwarded to the proper officer (except ballot papers and counterfoils) must be open to public inspection at such time and in such manner as may be determined by the council of which he is an officer[15]. On request, the proper officer must supply copies of or extracts from the documents open to public inspection on payment of such fees, and subject to such conditions, as may be determined by the council of which he is an officer[16].

1   As to the meaning of 'referendum' for these purposes see PARA 574 notes 2, 13.
2   As to the meaning of 'registration officer' see the Representation of the People Act 1983 s 8; and PARA 139 (definition applied, in relation to Wales, by virtue of the Local Authorities (Conduct of Referendums) (Wales) Regulations 2008, SI 2008/1848, Sch 3 r 2(2), and, in relation to England, by virtue of the Local Authorities (Conduct of Referendums) (England) Regulations 2012, SI 2012/323, Sch 3 r 2(2)).
3   Ie pursuant to any provision of the Local Authorities (Conduct of Referendums) (Wales) Regulations 2008, SI 2008/1848, Sch 3, or of the Local Authorities (Conduct of Referendums) (England) Regulations 2012, SI 2012/323, Sch 3, as the case may be. As to the meaning of 'counting officer' see PARA 576 note 1.
4   Local Authorities (Conduct of Referendums) (England) Regulations 2012, SI 2012/323, Sch 3 r 45; Local Authorities (Conduct of Referendums) (Wales) Regulations 2008, SI 2008/1848, Sch 3 r 45.
5   As to the production and inspection of documents by order of the court see PARA 851. As to offences which relate to persons who interfere with access to or the control of referendum documents see PARA 745. Any power given under these provisions to a county court may be exercised by any judge of the court otherwise than in open court: Local Authorities (Conduct of Referendums) (Wales) Regulations 2008, SI 2008/1848, Sch 3 r 44(6); Local Authorities (Conduct of Referendums) (England) Regulations 2012, SI 2012/323, Sch 3 r 44(6).
6   Local Authorities (Conduct of Referendums) (Wales) Regulations 2008, SI 2008/1848, Sch 3 r 44(1); Local Authorities (Conduct of Referendums) (England) Regulations 2012, SI 2012/323, Sch 3 r 44(1). Where an order is made for the production by the relevant registration officer of

any document in his or her possession relating to any specified referendum the production by the relevant registration officer or his or her agent of the document ordered in such manner as may be directed by that order is conclusive evidence that the document relates to the specified referendum and any endorsement on any packet of ballot papers so produced is prima facie evidence that the ballot papers are what they are stated to be by the endorsement: Local Authorities (Conduct of Referendums) (Wales) Regulations 2008, SI 2008/1848, Sch 3 r 44(7); Local Authorities (Conduct of Referendums) (England) Regulations 2012, SI 2012/323, Sch 3 r 44(7). The production from proper custody of a ballot paper purporting to have been used at any referendum and a completed corresponding number list with a number marked in writing beside the number of the ballot paper, is prima facie evidence that the person whose vote was given by that ballot paper was the person whose entry in the register of electors or on a notice issued under the Representation of the People Act 1983 s 13B(3B) or (3D) (notices specifying appropriate alterations to the register: see PARA 168) (applied and modified, in relation to Wales, by the Local Authorities (Conduct of Referendums) (Wales) Regulations 2008, SI 2008/1848, Sch 4 Table 1, and, in relation to England, by the Local Authorities (Conduct of Referendums) (England) Regulations 2012, SI 2012/323, Sch 4 Table 1: see PARA 15) at the time of the referendum contained the same number as the number written as mentioned above: Local Authorities (Conduct of Referendums) (Wales) Regulations 2008, SI 2008/1848, Sch 3 r 44(8); Local Authorities (Conduct of Referendums) (England) Regulations 2012, SI 2012/323, Sch 3 r 44(8). Save as by these provisions provided, no person is allowed to inspect any rejected or counted ballot papers in the possession of the relevant registration officer or open any sealed packets of the completed corresponding number lists or of certificates as to employment on duty on the day of the poll: Local Authorities (Conduct of Referendums) (Wales) Regulations 2008, SI 2008/1848, Sch 3 r 44(9); Local Authorities (Conduct of Referendums) (England) Regulations 2012, SI 2012/323, Sch 3 r 44(9).

7   Local Authorities (Conduct of Referendums) (Wales) Regulations 2008, SI 2008/1848, Sch 3 r 44(2); Local Authorities (Conduct of Referendums) (England) Regulations 2012, SI 2012/323, Sch 3 r 44(2).

8   Local Authorities (Conduct of Referendums) (Wales) Regulations 2008, SI 2008/1848, Sch 3 r 44(3); Local Authorities (Conduct of Referendums) (England) Regulations 2012, SI 2012/323, Sch 3 r 44(3).

9   Local Authorities (Conduct of Referendums) (Wales) Regulations 2008, SI 2008/1848, Sch 3 r 44(4); Local Authorities (Conduct of Referendums) (England) Regulations 2012, SI 2012/323, Sch 3 r 44(4).

10   Local Authorities (Conduct of Referendums) (Wales) Regulations 2008, SI 2008/1848, Sch 3 r 44(5); Local Authorities (Conduct of Referendums) (England) Regulations 2012, SI 2012/323, Sch 3 r 44(5).

11   As to how polls consequent on a parish or community meeting come about see PARA 581.

12   As to the meanings of 'proper officer of the council', 'district' and 'parish or community' see PARA 657 notes 5–7.

13   As to returning officers at polls consequent on a parish or community meeting see PARA 588.

14   Parish and Community Meetings (Polls) Rules 1987, SI 1987/1, Schedule r 36(1).

15   Parish and Community Meetings (Polls) Rules 1987, SI 1987/1, Schedule r 36(2).

16   Parish and Community Meetings (Polls) Rules 1987, SI 1987/1, Schedule r 36(3).

H.   PILOT SCHEMES REGARDING VOTING AND CAMPAIGNING AT LOCAL AUTHORITY REFERENDUMS

660.   Pilot schemes submitted by principal councils regarding the conduct of a local authority referendum.   Where a relevant local authority[1] submits to the Secretary of State[2] proposals for a pilot scheme to apply to particular local authority referendums[3] held in the authority's area[4] and those proposals are approved by the Secretary of State, either without modification or with such modifications as, after consulting the authority, he considers appropriate[5], the Secretary of State must by order[6] make such provision for and in connection with the implementation of the scheme in relation to those referendums as he considers appropriate (which may include provision modifying or disapplying any enactment)[7]. Such a scheme may make, in relation to local authority referendums in the area of a relevant local authority, provision differing in any respect from that made under or by virtue of the Local Government Act 2000[8] as regards one or more of the following, namely: (1) when, where and how voting at the referendums is to take place[9]; (2) how the votes cast at the referendums are to be counted[10]; (3) the sending by any campaign organiser[11] of referendum communications free of charge for postage[12]. Without prejudice to the generality of these provisions, such a scheme may make provision: (a) for voting to take place on more than one day (whether each of those days is designated as a day of the poll or otherwise) and at places other than polling stations[13]; or (b) for postal charges incurred in respect of the sending of campaign organisers' referendum communications as mentioned in head (3) above to be paid by the authority concerned[14].

1   For these purposes, 'relevant local authority' means, as respects England, a county council, a district council or a London borough council and, as respects Wales, a county council or a county borough council: Representation of the People Act 2000 s 10(11) (s 10 applied and modified, in relation to Wales, by the Local Authorities (Conduct of Referendums) (Wales) Regulations 2008, SI 2008/1848, Sch 4 Table 2, and, in relation to England, by the Local Authorities (Conduct of Referendums) (England) Regulations 2012, SI 2012/323, Sch 4 Table 3). As to the provisions that are so applied and modified see PARA 15. As to counties and districts in England, and their councils, see LOCAL GOVERNMENT vol 69 (2009) PARA 24 et seq; as to counties and county boroughs in Wales, and their councils, see LOCAL GOVERNMENT vol 69 (2009) PARA 37 et seq; as to London boroughs, and their councils, see LONDON GOVERNMENT vol 71 (2013) PARAS 15; and as to the Greater London Authority see LONDON GOVERNMENT vol 71 (2013) PARA 67 et seq. A county council, a district council or a London borough council in England and a county council or a county borough council in Wales is referred to as a 'principal council': see LOCAL GOVERNMENT vol 69 (2009) PARA 23.
2   As to the Secretary of State see PARA 2.
3   Ie including any such proposals which are submitted by a relevant local authority jointly with the Electoral Commission, in which case references to the authority must be read as references to the authority and the Commission: Representation of the People Act 2000 s 10(1A) (s 10(1A), (6A) added by the Political Parties, Elections and Referendums Act 2000 Sch 21 para 16; as applied and modified (see note 1)). As to the Electoral Commission see PARA 34 et seq. As to the meaning of 'referendum' for these purposes see PARA 574 notes 2, 13.
4   Representation of the People Act 2000 s 10(1)(a) (as applied and modified: see note 1).
5   Representation of the People Act 2000 s 10(1)(b) (as applied and modified: see note 1).
6   Where the Secretary of State makes any such order he must send a copy of the order to the authority concerned and to the Electoral Commission, and that authority must publish the order in its area in such manner as it thinks fit: Representation of the People Act 2000 s 10(5) (as applied and modified: see note 1)). In a case where any proposals are not jointly submitted under s 10(1A) (see note 3), the Secretary of State must consult the Electoral Commission before making any such order: s 10(1A) (as so added, applied and modified).
7   Representation of the People Act 2000 s 10(1) (as applied and modified: see note 1).
8   As to schemes for the conduct of referendums under or by virtue of the Local Government Act 2000 see PARA 555 et seq.
9   Representation of the People Act 2000 s 10(2)(a) (as applied and modified: see note 1).
10   Representation of the People Act 2000 s 10(2)(b) (as applied and modified: see note 1).
11   Ie within the meaning of the Local Authorities (Conduct of Referendums) (Wales) Regulations 2008, SI 2008/1848, reg 6, or within the meaning of the Local Authorities (Conduct of Referendums) (England) Regulations 2012, SI 2012/323, reg 6, as the case may be (see PARA 577 note 13).
12   Representation of the People Act 2000 s 10(2)(c) (as applied and modified: see note 1).
13   Representation of the People Act 2000 s 10(3)(a) (as applied and modified: see note 1).
14   Representation of the People Act 2000 s 10(3)(b) (as applied and modified: see note 1). Where a scheme makes provision for postal charges incurred in respect of the sending of campaign organisers' referendum communications to be paid as is mentioned in head (b) in the text, the Secretary of State's order under s 10(1) (as applied and modified) (see the text and notes 1–7) may make provision for disapplying the Local Authorities (Conduct of Referendums) (Wales) Regulations 2008, SI 2008/1848, reg 6, or the Local Authorities (Conduct of Referendums) (England) Regulations 2012, SI 2012/323, reg 6, as the case may be, in relation to the payment of such charges by the authority: Representation of the People Act 2000 s 10(3) (as so applied and modified).

661. Evaluation by the Electoral Commission of pilot schemes relating to voting and campaigning at local authority referendums. Once any local authority referendums[1] have taken place in relation to which a pilot scheme order applied[2], the Electoral Commission[3] must prepare a report on the scheme[4]. Such a report must be prepared in consultation with the local authority concerned[5]; and that authority must provide the Commission with such assistance as it may reasonably require in connection with the preparation of the report (and such assistance may, in particular, include the making by the authority of arrangements for ascertaining the views of voters about the operation of the scheme)[6]. The report must, in particular, contain[7]: (1) a description of the scheme and of the respects in which the provision made by it differed from that made by or under the Local Government Act 2000[8]; (2) a copy of the order of the Secretary of State[9]; and (3) an assessment of the scheme's success or otherwise in facilitating voting at the referendums in question[10] and, if it made provision as respects the counting of votes cast at those referendums, the counting of votes, or in encouraging voting at the referendums in question or enabling voters to make informed decisions at those referendums[11]. If the Secretary of State so requests in writing, the report must also contain an assessment of such other matters relating to the scheme as are specified in his request[12]. Once the Commission has prepared the report, it must send a copy of it to the Secretary of State and to the authority concerned, and that authority must publish the report in its area, in such manner as it thinks fit, by the end of the period of three months beginning with the date of the declaration of the result of the referendums in question[13].

1   As to the meaning of 'referendum' for these purposes see PARA 574 notes 2, 13.
2   Ie in relation to which a scheme under the Representation of the People Act 2000 s 10(1) (as applied and modified) applied (see PARA 660).
3   As to the Electoral Commission see PARA 34 et seq.
4   Representation of the People Act 2000 s 10(6) (s 10(6), (7) amended, s 10(6A) added, s 10(10) substituted, by the Political Parties, Elections and Referendums Act 2000 Sch 21 para 16); Representation of the People Act 2000 s 10 applied and modified, in relation to Wales, by the Local Authorities (Conduct of Referendums) (Wales) Regulations 2008, SI 2008/1848, Sch 4 Table 2, and, in relation to England, by the Local Authorities (Conduct of Referendums) (England) Regulations 2012, SI 2012/323, Sch 4 Table 3). As to the provisions that are so applied and modified see PARA 15.
5   As to the local authorities which may propose such a scheme see PARA 660 note 1.
6   Representation of the People Act 2000 s 10(6A) (as added, applied and modified: see note 4).
7   Representation of the People Act 2000 s 10(7) (as amended, applied and modified: see note 4).
8   Representation of the People Act 2000 s 10(7)(a) (as applied and modified: see note 4). As to schemes for the conduct of referendums under or by virtue of the Local Government Act 2000 see PARA 555 et seq.
9   Representation of the People Act 2000 s 10(7)(b) (as applied and modified: see note 4). The text refers to the pilot scheme order made under s 10(1) (as applied and modified) (see PARA 660). As to the Secretary of State see PARA 2.
10 An assessment of the scheme's success or otherwise in facilitating voting at the referendums in question must include a statement by the authority concerned as to whether, in its opinion: (1) the turnout of voters was higher than it would have been if the scheme had not applied (Representation of the People Act 2000 s 10(8)(a) (as applied and modified: see note 4)); (2) voters found the procedures provided for their assistance by the scheme easy to use (s 10(8)(b) (as so applied and modified)); (3) the procedures provided for by the scheme led to any increase in personation or other electoral offences or in any other malpractice in connection with referendums (s 10(8)(c) (as so applied and modified)); (4) those procedures led to any increase in expenditure, or to any savings, by the authority (s 10(8)(d) (as so applied and modified)).
11 Representation of the People Act 2000 s 10(7)(c) (as applied and modified: see note 4).
12 Representation of the People Act 2000 s 10(9) (as applied and modified: see note 4).
13 Representation of the People Act 2000 s 10(10) (as substituted, applied and modified: see note 4). As to the declaration of results at a local authority referendum see PARA 652.

(iv) Poll regarding the Functions of the Welsh Ministers

662. Poll held to ascertain views about whether or how any of the functions of the Welsh Ministers should be exercised. The Welsh Ministers[1] may hold a poll in an area consisting of Wales[2] or any part (or parts) of Wales for the purpose of ascertaining the views of those polled about whether or how any of the functions of the Welsh Ministers[3] should be exercised[4].

1 As to the Welsh Ministers see CONSTITUTIONAL LAW AND HUMAN RIGHTS.
2 As to the meaning of 'Wales' see PARA 1 note 1.
3 Ie other than the function under the Government of Wales Act 2006 s 62 (see CONSTITUTIONAL LAW AND HUMAN RIGHTS).
4 Government of Wales Act 2006 s 64(1). In connection with the legislative powers of the Welsh Ministers and the National Assembly for Wales see further STATUTES AND LEGISLATIVE PROCESS vol 96 (2012) PARAS 602, 986 et seq.

663. Persons entitled to vote in a poll regarding the functions of the Welsh Ministers. The persons entitled to vote in a poll held in Wales to ascertain views about whether or how any of the functions of the Welsh Ministers should be exercised[1] are those who: (1) would be entitled to vote as electors at a local government election[2] in an electoral area[3] wholly or partly included in the area in which the poll is held[4]; and (2) are registered in the register of local government electors[5] at an address within the area in which the poll is held[6].

1 Ie a poll held under the Government of Wales Act 2006 s 64 (see PARA 662).
2 As to entitlement to vote as a local government elector see PARA 97 et seq. As to the meaning of 'local government election' see PARA 11; and as to the meaning of 'elector' for these purposes see PARA 95 note 2.
3 As to the meaning of 'electoral area' see PARA 11.
4 Government of Wales Act 2006 s 64(2)(a).
5 As to registration as a local government elector see PARA 113.
6 Government of Wales Act 2006 s 64(2)(b).

664. Provision as to the conduct of polls regarding the functions of the Welsh Ministers. The Welsh Ministers[1] may by order make provision as to the conduct of polls (or any poll) held in Wales to ascertain views about whether or how any of their functions should be exercised[2] or for the combination of such polls (or any such poll) with polls at any elections[3]. Such an order may apply or incorporate, with or without modifications or exceptions, any provision of or made under any enactment relating to elections or referendums; and the provision which may be made as to the conduct of polls (or any poll) includes, in particular, provision for disregarding alterations in a register of electors[4].

1 As to the Welsh Ministers see CONSTITUTIONAL LAW AND HUMAN RIGHTS.
2 Ie a poll held under the Government of Wales Act 2006 s 64 (see PARA 662).
3 Government of Wales Act 2006 s 64(3). A statutory instrument containing such an order is subject to annulment in pursuance of a resolution of the National Assembly for Wales: s 64(5).
4 Government of Wales Act 2006 s 64(4).

7. IRREGULARITIES, OFFENCES AND LEGAL PROCEEDINGS

(1) INJUNCTIONS AND ORDERS

665. Jurisdiction of court to grant injunction or order. The High Court has a general jurisdiction to grant an injunction (whether interim or final) in all cases in which it appears to the court to be just and convenient to do so; and any such order may be made unconditionally or upon such terms and conditions as the court thinks just[1]. However, this general power has been exercised rarely when called upon in cases relating to elections. For instance, the court has refused to grant injunctive relief where the administrative authority of a political party has intervened by the deselection of candidates and the imposition of new candidates at an election[2]; and the court declined to grant an injunction where a candidate broke his agreement with the other candidate not to use polling agents at the election[3].

Although jurisdiction is conferred on the High Court to make orders before an election in restraint of false statements made in relation to a candidate[4], the guiding principle otherwise is that the court should be extremely slow to intervene in the machinery of an election before it has taken place, and should do so only in exceptional circumstances[5]. Nevertheless, where a candidate was alleged to be telling untruths about himself in nomination papers so that he was in breach of the Representation of the People Act 1983[6], it was held that the court had jurisdiction to entertain proceedings for an injunction to restrain the breach[7].

1   See the Senior Courts Act 1981 s 37(1), (2); and CIVIL PROCEDURE vol 11 (2009) PARA 347.
2   *Choudhry v Triesman* [2003] EWHC 1203 (Ch), [2003] 22 LS Gaz R 29, (2003) Times, 2 May (candidates replaced after internal investigation by the Labour Party concluded that the selection procedures in the claimants' wards were 'unsound'; on the facts, the candidates failed to obtain injunctive relief in the form of a mandatory injunction and declaratory relief to the effect that their selections be allowed to stand and to ensure that their names were presented to the returning officer). It is possible that an injunction may be granted restraining a candidate who has not been regularly adopted by a local political association as its official candidate from acting as though he had been officially adopted and campaigning on that basis as the official candidate: see *Noonan v De Pinna* (1953) Times, 18 November (where the judge, after deciding that the meeting at which the candidate had been adopted had been irregularly convened, said that the question whether an injunction should be granted was one of convenience and decided not to grant an injunction).
3   See *Ainsworth v Lord Muncaster* (1885) 2 TLR 108 (in which Cave J stated that an injunction ought to be refused if only because the public had an interest in the proper conduct of elections). As to how far the public interest in the conduct of elections allows the court to intervene by way of injunction or order under general powers where allegedly-fraudulent devices are used see the text and notes 6–7; and PARA 723. As to the appointment of polling agents see PARA 394.
4   See PARA 666.
5   *R (on the application of Begum) v Tower Hamlets London Borough Council* [2006] EWCA Civ 733, [2006] LGR 674; revsg [2006] EWHC 1074 (Admin), [2006] All ER (D) 243 (Apr), [2006] 19 LS Gaz R 26. The principle set out in the text has been stated in the context of the court refusing applications for judicial review of a returning officer's decision to reject nomination papers: *R (on the application of Begum) v Tower Hamlets London Borough Council* at [20]–[22]; *R (on the application of De Beer) v Balabanoff* [2002] EWHC 670 (Admin) at [37]–[38], (2002) Times, 25 April at [37]–[38] (per curiam) (although judicial review does lie against a returning officer's decision regarding nomination papers, it is an area in which the courts should be extremely slow to interfere and the returning officer ordinarily should be left to conduct the election process as provided by Parliament).
6   Ie in breach of the Representation of the People Act 1983 s 115(2)(b) (undue influence (use of fraudulent devices): see PARA 723).

7   *Spencer v Huggett* [1997] 30 LS Gaz R 30 (court had jurisdiction to entertain proceedings for an
     injunction to restrain the breach, despite the fact that it constituted a crime, on the basis that the
     public wrong being alleged interfered with the claimant candidate's private right to stand at an
     election untainted by corruption or, alternatively, that the claimant would suffer special damage
     from such interference with that public right; application refused in this case). As to the general
     rule of procedural exclusivity and the distinction drawn between public law rights and private
     law rights see *Gouriet v Union of Post Office Workers* [1978] AC 435, [1977] 3 All ER 70, HL;
     and JUDICIAL REVIEW vol 61 (2010) PARA 661.

**666.   Interim or perpetual injunctions restraining false statements about
candidates before or during election.**   A person making or publishing any false
statement of fact before or during an election[1] in relation to a candidate's
personal character or conduct at an election[2] may be restrained by interim or
perpetual injunction by the High Court or the county court from any repetition
of that false statement or of a false statement of a similar character in relation to
the candidate[3]. The false statement of fact may or may not be such as would
sustain an action for defamation[4]. For the purpose of granting an interim
injunction, prima facie proof of the falsity of the statement is sufficient[5]; but an
interim injunction ought not to be granted where justification is pleaded in
answer to an action for libel, unless the court is satisfied that the defendants have
no reasonable prospect of success at the trial[6].

The public interest which limits the right of organs of central or local
government to sue for libel[7] is sufficiently strong to justify extending the
limitation to cover a political party and those putting themselves forward for
office or to govern[8].

1   Ie before or during a parliamentary, local government, Welsh Assembly (constituency or
     regional) or European parliamentary election. As to the meanings of 'Assembly election',
     'constituency election' and 'regional election' see PARA 3 note 2; as to the meaning of
     'parliamentary election' see PARA 9; and as to the meaning of 'local government election' see
     PARA 11. As to European parliamentary elections see PARA 217 et seq.
2   The making or publishing of such a statement is an illegal practice: see the Representation of the
     People Act 1983 s 106(1); and PARA 680.
3   Representation of the People Act 1983 s 106(3); European Parliamentary Elections
     Regulations 2004, SI 2004/293, reg 71(2); National Assembly for Wales (Representation of the
     People) Order 2007, SI 2007/236, art 73(4). The text refers to 'any false statement of fact as
     mentioned above' but it is not clear whether the phrase 'as mentioned above' attaches to those
     words which limit the false statement to having been made or published before or during an
     election for the purpose of affecting the return of any candidate at the election and/or the words
     which refer simply to false statements relating to personal character or conduct (illegal practice
     of making false statements: see PARA 680). In *Ellis v National Union of Conservative and
     Constitutional Associations, Middleton and Southall* (1900) 109 LT Jo 493, it was said that for
     an injunction to be granted the statement must be made before or during an election and for the
     purpose of affecting a candidate's return. In *Mills v Drummond* (1934) 78 Sol Jo 192, an
     injunction was granted restraining the defendants from issuing statements to the effect that the
     plaintiff was the sort of person to use or had used his position as chairman of a local authority's
     entertainments committee to further the showing or exploitation of wild animals at circuses of
     which the defendant strongly disapproved, whether or not the furtherance was for his own
     personal gain. In *Fairbairn v Scottish National Party* 1979 SC 393, an injunction was granted
     because the statement complained of was reasonably capable of bearing the innuendo that the
     candidate, who prior to the election was a member of Parliament, had failed to deal with
     correspondence and had thereby failed to perform his duties as such.
         The Representation of the People Act 1983 s 106(3) is notable for conferring an explicit
     power to take out an injunction while an election campaign is in progress; in practice, the court's
     general jurisdiction to grant an injunction has been exercised sparingly whilst an election
     campaign has been ongoing (see PARA 665). In the application of the European Parliamentary
     Elections Regulations 2004, SI 2004/293, reg 71(2) to Gibraltar, the reference to the county
     court should be read as a reference to the Gibraltar court: see reg 71(3). As to the establishment

of electoral regions (including the 'combined region', which includes Gibraltar) for the purpose of elections to the European Parliament see PARA 77.

4 *Louth Northern Division Case* (1911) 6 O'M & H 103 at 165. A statement, though false or unjustifiable or derogatory, is not prohibited by the Representation of the People Act 1983 s 106(1) (false statements as to candidates as an illegal practice: see PARA 680) if it simply deals with the political position or reputation of a candidate, and does not relate to his personal character or conduct; accordingly, a statement that a candidate is a communist was held not to be within the corresponding provision relating to municipal elections (*Burns v Associated Newspapers Ltd* (1925) 89 JP 205).

5 Representation of the People Act 1983 s 106(3); European Parliamentary Elections Regulations 2004, SI 2004/293, reg 71(2); National Assembly for Wales (Representation of the People) Order 2007, SI 2007/236, art 73(4). See eg *Bayley v Edmunds, Byron and Marshall* (1895) 11 TLR 537, CA.

6 *Burns v Associated Newspapers Ltd* (1925) 89 JP 205. As to whether statute bars a plea of qualified privilege as respects defamatory statements by or on behalf of a candidate at an election see the Defamation Act 1952 s 10; and PARA 330.

7 See *Derbyshire County Council v Times Newspapers Ltd* [1993] AC 534, [1993] 1 All ER 1011, HL (it would place an undesirable fetter on freedom of speech and be contrary to the public interest if organs of central or local government were favoured with the right to sue for libel).

8 *Goldsmith v Bhoyrul* [1998] QB 459, [1997] 4 All ER 268 (a political party, even when set up as a corporation, has no right at common law to maintain an action for defamation).

(2) IRREGULARITIES AND OFFENCES

(i) Validity of and Irregularities at Elections

667. Effect of breaches of election rules by returning officer. No election[1] is to be declared invalid by reason of any act or omission by the returning officer[2] or any other person in breach of his official duty in connection with the election or otherwise of the appropriate elections rules[3] if it appears to the tribunal having cognisance of the question that the election was so conducted as to be substantially in accordance with the law as to elections, and that the act or omission did not affect its result[4]. The function of the court in exercising this jurisdiction is not assisted by consideration of a standard of proof but, having regard to the consequences of declaring an election void, there must be a preponderance of evidence supporting any conclusion that the result was affected[5]. Where breaches of the elections rules, although trivial, have affected the result, that by itself is enough to compel the court to declare the election void even though it has been conducted substantially in accordance with the law as to elections[6]. Conversely, if the election was conducted so badly that it was not substantially in accordance with the law as to elections, the election is vitiated, irrespective of whether the result was affected or not[7].

If, owing to a mistake in the notice of election, some candidates are misled into delivering their nomination papers too late and they are rejected by the returning officer for being late, the election will be avoided[8]. On the other hand, failure to comply with the timetable as respects the publication of the notice of the election[9] does not render the election void if the result of the election has not been affected by it[10]. The wrongful rejection of the nomination of a candidate will avoid an election[11]. The inclusion on a ballot paper of the name of a candidate who has withdrawn will avoid an election if the number of votes given to that candidate might affect the result[12]. The marking of the faces of a number of ballot papers with the electors' numbers in the register before delivering them to the voters will not, if the result is unaffected, avoid the election[13]; but the marking in this way of all the ballot papers would avoid the election[14]. Failure to open or close the poll at a polling station at the correct time[15] will not avoid an election provided that it can be shown that the result was not affected[16]. Failure to count or record the number of ballot papers in each box or mix the whole of the ballot papers before counting[17], or failure to comply strictly with the provisions as to forwarding documents after the close of the poll[18], is not sufficient to avoid the election. The exposure of a few ballot papers by the voters themselves would not invalidate an election in the absence of a conspiracy to nullify the law relating to elections[19].

1   Ie no parliamentary or local government election (or other election under the Local Government Act 1972), and no Welsh Assembly (constituency or regional) or European parliamentary election. As to the meanings of 'Assembly election', 'constituency election' and 'regional election' see PARA 3 note 2; as to the meaning of 'parliamentary election' see PARA 9; as to the meaning of 'local government election' see PARA 11; and as to the meaning of 'election under the Local Government Act 1972' see PARA 11 note 2. As to European parliamentary elections see PARA 217 et seq.
2   As to returning officers see PARA 350 et seq.
3   As to the elections rules see PARA 383. See further *Akhtar v Jahan, Iqbal v Islam* [2005] All ER (D) 15 (Apr) at [536]–[548], Election Ct (decision revsd in part, but on a point of evidence, sub nom *R (on the application of Afzal) v Election Court* [2005] EWCA Civ 647, [2005] LGR 823).
4   See the Representation of the People Act 1983 ss 23(3), 48(1), 187(2); the European Parliamentary Elections Regulations 2004, SI 2004/293, reg 9(5); the National Assembly for Wales (Representation of the People) Order 2007, SI 2007/236, art 17(3); and PARAS 350, 354, 357, 360. Where votes were wrongly rejected and the inclusion of such votes would have resulted in a tie (which is then determined by the returning officer by lot: see PARA 434), such a tie is a 'result' for these purposes: *Ruffle v Rogers* [1982] QB 1220, [1982] 2 All ER 157, CA. The 'result' means the success of one candidate over another and not merely an alteration in the number of votes given to each candidate: *Clare, Eastern Division Case* (1892) 4 O'M & H 162 at 164; *Islington, West Division Case* (1901) 5 O'M & H 120.
5   *Edgell v Glover* [2003] EWHC 2566 (QB), [2003] All ER (D) 44 (Nov) (threshold was not so high as to exclude the court from concluding that the result was affected when there was evidence before the court that the result was affected, but where there was also evidence that if further enquiries were carried out there was a remote possibility the conclusion would be shown to be wrong). See also *Re Kensington North Parliamentary Election* [1960] 2 All ER 150 at 153, [1960] 1 WLR 762 at 766 per Streatfield J (it is for the court to make up its mind on the evidence as a whole whether there was a substantial compliance with the law as to elections or whether the act or omission affected the result), distinguishing *Islington, West Division Case* (1901) 5 O'M & H 120 at 130 (approving *Gribbin v Kirker* (1873) IR 7 CL 30), where it was stated that the onus rests on the respondent of proving that the result of the election was not affected by the transgression; and see *Levers v Morris* [1972] 1 QB 221, [1971] 3 All ER 1300, DC.
6   *Morgan v Simpson* [1975] QB 151, [1974] 3 All ER 722, CA (official mark not stamped to a total of 44 ballot papers; result affected); and see *Gunn v Sharpe* [1974] QB 808, [1974] 2 All ER 1058, DC (mistake in not stamping 102 ballot papers affected the result); *Considine v Didrichsen* [2004] EWHC 2711 (QB), [2004] All ER (D) 365 (Nov) (unascertained number of electors failed to receive proper ballot papers at an all-postal ballot; result presumed to be affected where winning margin was only seven votes). Cf *Woodward v Sarsons* (1875) LR 10 CP 733, explained in *Morgan v Simpson* (an election conducted substantially in accordance with the law as to elections is not vitiated by breaches of the elections rules or mistake at the polls provided that the result of the election not affected); *Islington, West Division Case* (1901) 5 O'M & H 120 (14 ballot papers issued after 8 pm; result of election not affected).
7   *Morgan v Simpson* [1975] QB 151 at 164, [1974] 3 All ER 722 at 728, CA, per Lord Denning MR, applying *Hackney Case* (1874) 2 O'M & H 77 (two polling stations closed all day; approximately 5,000 voters unable to vote). Intimidation that prevents free voting also avoids an election: *Dudley Case* (1874) 2 O'M & H 115 (riot in town). In *Akhtar v Jahan, Iqbal v Islam* [2005] All ER (D) 15 (Apr), Election Ct (decision revsd in part, but on a point of evidence, sub nom *R (on the application of Afzal) v Election Court* [2005] EWCA Civ 647, [2005] LGR 823) (cited in PARA 895), it was held that charges against the returning officer were not made out but it was observed that shortcomings in the conduct of the election invited the kind of abuses that led to the election being avoided due to extensive postal voting fraud.
8   *Howes v Turner* (1876) 1 CPD 670; *R v Glover* (1866) 15 LT 289.

9   As to publication of the notice of the election see PARA 196.

10 *Clare, Eastern Division Case* (1892) 4 O'M & H 162 at 164–166.

11 *Haverfordwest Case, Davies v Lord Kensington* (1874) LR 9 CP 720; *Mayo Case* (1874) 2 O'M & H 191.

12 *Wilson v Ingham* (1895) 64 LJQB 775, DC.

13 *Woodward v Sarsons* (1875) LR 10 CP 733, explained in *Morgan v Simpson* [1975] QB 151, [1974] 3 All ER 722, CA. Cf *Gunn v Sharpe* [1974] QB 808, [1974] 2 All ER 1058, DC (issue of 102 ballot papers not stamped with official mark affected result of election). See also the text and notes 6, 7.

14 *Deans v Stevenson* 1882 9 R (Ct of Sess) 1077 at 1088. As to the effect of the failure to mark the counterfoils of the ballot papers with the numbers in the register see *Pickering v Startin* (1873) 28 LT 111.

15 *Clare, Eastern Division Case* (1892) 4 O'M & H 162; *East Kerry Case* (1911) 6 O'M & H 58 at 85; *Drogheda Borough Case* (1874) 2 O'M & H 201; *Worcester Borough Case* (1880) 3 O'M & H 184.

16 *Islington, West Division Case* (1901) 5 O'M & H 120 at 130; *Latham v Glasgow Corpn* 1921 SC 694 at 706; *Gribbin v Kirker* (1873) IR 7 CL 30; *Hackney Case* (1874) 31 LT 69.

17 *Re Pembroke Election Petition* [1908] 2 IR 433.

18 *Horsham Second Case* (1848) 1 Pow R & D 240 (packets not duly sealed); *Kidderminster Borough Case* (1850) 1 Pow R & D 260 at 262 (packets not duly endorsed); *Barnstaple Borough Case* (1853) 2 Pow R & D 206 (covering letter from the returning officer to the Clerk of the Crown not duly sent).

19 *Louth, Northern Division Case* (1911) 6 O'M & H 103 at 139.

668.   Defect in title of returning officer.   An election[1] is not liable to be questioned by reason of a defect in the title, or want of title, of the person presiding at or conducting the election, if that person was then in actual possession of, or acting in, the office giving the right to preside at or conduct the election[2].

1   Ie a parliamentary or local government election, or Welsh Assembly (constituency or regional) or European parliamentary election. As to the meanings of 'Assembly election', 'constituency election' and 'regional election' see PARA 3 note 2; as to the meaning of 'parliamentary election' see PARA 9; and as to the meaning of 'local government election' see PARA 11. As to European parliamentary elections see PARA 217 et seq.

2   See the Representation of the People Act 1983 ss 24(2), 35(5); the European Parliamentary Elections Regulations 2004, SI 2004/293, reg 14; the National Assembly for Wales (Representation of the People) Order 2007, SI 2007/236, art 22(1); and PARAS 350, 354, 357, 360. As to returning officers see PARA 350 et seq.

669.   Validity of local government elections.   A local government election or other election under the Local Government Act 1972[1], unless questioned by election petition within the period fixed by law for those proceedings, is deemed to have been to all intents a good and valid election[2].

1   As to the meaning of 'local government election' see PARA 11; and as to the meaning of 'election under the Local Government Act 1972' see PARA 11 note 2.

2   Representation of the People Act 1983 ss 48(2), 187(2). As to petitions questioning local elections see PARA 762 et seq.

670.   Effect of failure to hold London borough election.   If a municipal election in a London borough[1] is not held on the appointed day or within the appointed time, or becomes void, the municipal corporation is not thereby dissolved or disabled from acting[2].

1   As to the London boroughs and their councils see LOCAL GOVERNMENT vol 69 (2009) PARA 35; LONDON GOVERNMENT vol 71 (2013) PARA 15 et seq.

2   Representation of the People Act 1983 s 39(9).

(ii) Illegal Practices

671. Practices which are illegal. Certain acts or omissions (mainly but not exclusively made by the candidate or election agent[1]) that contravene controls placed on the election campaign[2] constitute illegal practices; these include:

(1) meeting election expenses by accepting donations not provided to the candidate or election agent[3];

(2) knowingly incurring an expense in excess of the maximum amount of election expenses[4];

(3) paying election expenses otherwise than through the election agent[5];

(4) paying statute-barred claims for election expenses[6];

(5) paying election expenses out of time[7];

(6) failing to make the return or declaration as to election expenses[8];

(7) making an inaccurate return as to election expenses[9];

(8) failing to deliver or send the required returns or declarations of expenses authorised by the election agent[10];

(9) disturbing a meeting[11];

(10) making a false statement concerning the personal character or conduct of a candidate for the purpose of affecting the return of any candidate[12];

(11) knowingly publishing a false statement as to the withdrawal of a candidate for the purpose of promoting or procuring the election of another candidate[13];

(12) consenting to multiple nominations for candidacy at a European parliamentary election[14].

Some summary offences also constitute illegal practices[15]; and a candidate or election agent who is personally guilty of making an illegal payment or employment is guilty also of an illegal practice[16].

There is no statutory definition of the term 'illegal practices' and, although some kinds of electoral malpractice are expressly stated to be such, other kinds are stated to be 'corrupt practices' or simply criminalised without being allocated to either category[17]. Dishonest abuses of the franchise, including some illegal practices, have produced findings of general corruption and of personal corruption amounting to electoral fraud (although that term is not used in the legislation)[18].

1 As to the meaning of 'candidate' see PARA 230. As to the appointment of election agents generally see PARA 231 et seq.
2 See PARA 230 et seq.
3 See PARA 672.
4 See PARA 673. As to knowingly incurring expenses at elections under the Local Government Act 1972 where election agents are not required see PARA 678.
5 See PARA 674. As to paying expenses at elections under the Local Government Act 1972 where election agents are not required see PARA 678.
6 See PARA 675.
7 See PARA 675.
8 See PARA 676.
9 See PARA 676.
10 See PARA 677.
11 See PARA 679.
12 See PARA 680.
13 See PARA 680.
14 See PARA 681.
15 As to offences which also constitute illegal practices see PARA 699 et seq.

16 See PARA 682 et seq.
17 See *Re Central Ward, Slough Election Petition, Simmons v Khan* [2008] EWHC B4 (QB),
    Election   Ct,   at   [24]–[31]   per   Commissioner   Mawrey   QC.   In   that   case,
    Commissioner Mawrey QC approached the petition on the basis that, where the Representation
    of the People Act 1983 Act, or any related electoral statute, made conduct in relation to an
    election into a criminal offence, that conduct amounted to an illegal practice for the purposes of
    avoiding an election whether or not this was expressly spelled out in the provision concerned:
    see at [30] per Commissioner Mawrey QC. As to corrupt practices see PARA 704 et seq.
18 See PARA 754. As to avoidance of an election by reason of general corruption see PARA 895.

**672.   Meeting election expenses by accepting donations not provided to
candidate or election agent.**   In the case of any candidate[1] at an election[2], any
money or other property[3] provided (whether as a gift or loan) by any person
other than the candidate or his election agent[4], and for the purpose of meeting
election expenses[5] incurred by or on behalf of the candidate, must be provided to
the candidate or his election agent[6]; and any person who provides any money or
other property in contravention of this restriction is guilty of an illegal practice[7].

1   As to the meaning of 'candidate' generally see PARA 230. The reference in the text is to an
    'individual candidate' for the purposes of a European parliamentary election (see the European
    Parliamentary Elections Regulations 2004, SI 2004/293, reg 42(1); and PARA 286); and to either
    a 'constituency candidate' or an 'individual candidate' for the purposes of a Welsh Assembly
    election (constituency or regional) (see the National Assembly for Wales (Representation of the
    People) Order 2007, SI 2007/236, art 41(1); and PARA 286). As to the meanings of 'Assembly
    election', 'constituency election' and 'regional election' see PARA 3 note 2. As to the meanings of
    'candidate', 'constituency candidate' and 'individual candidate' in relation to a Welsh Assembly
    election see PARA 230 note 19; and as to the meaning of 'individual candidate' in relation to a
    European parliamentary election see PARA 230 note 32. As to European parliamentary elections
    see PARA 217 et seq.
2   Ie a parliamentary or local government election, or Welsh Assembly (constituency or regional)
    or European parliamentary election. As to the meaning of 'parliamentary election' see PARA 9;
    and as to the meaning of 'local government election' see PARA 11.
        The Representation of the People Act 1983 s 71A does not apply, however, at an election
    under the local government Act which is not a local government election (see the Representation
    of the People Act 1983 s 90(2); and PARA 678); and, in relation to an election of parish
    councillors in England or of community councillors in Wales, the provisions of s 90(1), Sch 4
    apply instead: see s 90(1)(b); and PARA 675. As to the meaning of 'election under the local
    government Act' see PARA 11 note 2. As to the meanings of 'England' and 'Wales' see PARA 1
    note 1. As to the election of parish and community councillors see PARA 200 et seq.
3   As to the meaning of 'property' for these purposes see PARA 286 note 3.
4   As to the appointment of election agents generally see PARA 231 et seq.
5   As to the meaning of 'election expenses' see PARA 269.
6   See, in relation to a parliamentary or local government election, the Representation of the
    People Act 1983 s 71A(1), in relation to a Welsh Assembly election, the National Assembly for
    Wales (Representation of the People) Order 2007, SI 2007/236, art 39(1) and, in relation to a
    European parliamentary election, the European Parliamentary Elections Regulations 2004,
    SI 2004/293, reg 42(1); and PARA 286.
7   Representation of the People Act 1983 s 71A(3) (s 71A added by the Political Parties, Elections
    and   Referendums   Act   2000   s   130(1),   (2),   (4)); European   Parliamentary   Elections
    Regulations 2004, SI 2004/293, reg 42(3); National Assembly for Wales (Representation of the
    People) Order 2007, SI 2007/236, art 41(3). As to excuses and the right to apply for relief see
    PARA 690 et seq; and as to the consequences of illegal practices see PARA 888 et seq.

**673.   Election expenses knowingly incurred by candidate or election agent in
excess of financial limits.**   Where any election expenses[1] are incurred in excess of
any maximum amount specified under the provisions which limit such expenses[2],
any candidate[3] or election agent[4] who incurred, or authorised the incurring of,
the election expenses, and who knew or ought reasonably to have known[5] that
the expenses would be incurred in excess of that maximum amount, is guilty of
an illegal practice[6].

1 As to the meaning of 'election expenses' see PARA 269.
2 Ie, in relation to a parliamentary or local government election, a maximum amount specified in the Representation of the People Act 1983 s 76(2), or prescribed by order under s 76(2A), or the permitted amount in s 76ZA(2), or, in relation to a European parliamentary election, a maximum amount specified in the European Parliamentary Elections Regulations 2004, SI 2004/293, reg 47(4), or, in relation to a Welsh Assembly election, the appropriate maximum amount specified in the National Assembly for Wales (Representation of the People) Order 2007, SI 2007/236, art 47(3) (see PARA 273). As to the meaning of 'parliamentary election' see PARA 9; and as to the meaning of 'local government election' see PARA 11. As to the meaning of 'Assembly election' see PARA 3 note 2. As to European parliamentary elections see PARA 217 et seq.

 The Representation of the People Act 1983 s 76 is applied and modified for the purpose of local authority mayoral elections in England and Wales by the Local Authorities (Mayoral Elections) (England and Wales) Regulations 2007, SI 2007/1024, reg 3(2)–(5), Sch 2 Table 1: see PARA 11 note 14. As to elections for the return of a local authority mayor see PARA 198.

3 As to the meaning of 'candidate' generally see PARA 230. At a European parliamentary election, the reference is to sums paid out and expenses incurred on behalf of an individual candidate at an election: see the European Parliamentary Elections Regulations 2004, SI 2004/293, reg 47(1); and PARA 273. As to the meaning of 'individual candidate' at a European parliamentary election see PARA 230 note 32. At a Welsh Assembly election, the reference to a candidate is to a constituency candidate at a Welsh Assembly constituency election, and to an individual candidate at a Welsh Assembly regional election: see the National Assembly for Wales (Representation of the People) Order 2007, SI 2007/236, art 47(1); and PARA 273. As to the meanings of 'constituency election' and 'regional election' see PARA 3 note 2. As to the meanings of 'constituency candidate' at a Welsh Assembly constituency election and 'individual candidate' at a Welsh Assembly regional election see PARA 230 note 19.

4 As to the appointment of election agents generally see PARA 231 et seq.
5 In previous enactments of the provision set out in the text, the word 'knowingly' was used and it was held that the word meant knowing at the time payment was made, or the expense incurred, that it was an election expense; and if, when the total of those expenses was added up, the total was in excess of the maximum, then the offence was complete; it was not necessary to prove that when a particular payment was made or expense incurred the candidate or election agent was aware that the maximum amount had been exceeded: *Northumberland, Berwick-upon-Tweed Division Case* (1923) 7 O'M & H 1 at 19–20; *Oxford Borough Case* (1924) 7 O'M & H 49 at 67.

6 Representation of the People Act 1983 s 76(1B) (added by the Political Parties, Elections and Referendums Act 2000 s 132(1), (4), (6); and amended by the Electoral Administration Act 2006 s 47, Sch 1 paras 69, 71); Representation of the People Act 1983 s 76ZA(5) (s 76ZA added by the Political Parties and Elections Act 2009 s 21(1)); European Parliamentary Elections Regulations 2004, SI 2004/293, reg 47(3); National Assembly for Wales (Representation of the People) Order 2007, SI 2007/236, art 47(2). As to excuses and the right to apply for relief see PARA 690 et seq; and as to the consequences of illegal practices see PARA 888 et seq.

 The Representation of the People Act 1983 s 76(1B) does not apply at an election under the local government Act which is not a local government election: see the Representation of the People Act 1983 s 90(2); and PARA 678. In relation to an election of parish councillors in England or of community councillors in Wales, where election agents are not required, s 76(1B) has effect as if for the references to an election agent there were substituted references to any agent of the candidate: s 90(1)(a) (amended by the Political Parties, Elections and Referendums Act 2000 s 138(1), Sch 18 paras 1, 11(a)). As to the meaning of 'election under the local government Act' see PARA 11 note 2. As to the meanings of 'England' and 'Wales' see PARA 1 note 1. As to the election of parish and community councillors see PARA 200 et seq.

674. Payment of election expenses otherwise than by or through candidate's election agent.
No payment[1], of whatever nature, may be made[2] either by a candidate[3] at an election[4] or by any other person, in respect of election expenses incurred by or on behalf of the candidate[5] unless it is made by or through the candidate's election agent[6]; and a person who makes any payment in contravention of this prohibition is guilty of an illegal practice[7].

1 As to the meaning of 'payment' see PARA 270 note 1.
2 Ie subject to exceptions set out, in relation to a parliamentary or local government election, in the Representation of the People Act 1983 s 73(5), or, in relation to a European parliamentary

election, in the European Parliamentary Elections Regulations 2004, SI 2004/293, reg 43(5), or, in relation to a Welsh Assembly election, in the National Assembly for Wales (Representation of the People) Order 2007, SI 2007/236, art 43(4) (see PARA 270). As to the meaning of 'parliamentary election' see PARA 9; and as to the meaning of 'local government election' see PARA 11. As to the meaning of 'Assembly election' see PARA 3 note 2. As to European parliamentary elections see PARA 217 et seq.

3   As to the meaning of 'candidate' generally see PARA 230. The reference in the text is to an 'individual candidate' for the purposes of a European parliamentary election: see the European Parliamentary Elections Regulations 2004, SI 2004/293, reg 43(1)(a); and PARA 270. As to the meaning of 'individual candidate' at a European parliamentary election see PARA 230 note 32. For the purposes of Welsh Assembly elections, the reference is to either a constituency candidate at a constituency election, or an individual candidate at a regional election: see the National Assembly for Wales (Representation of the People) Order 2007, SI 2007/236, art 43(1)(a); and PARA 270. As to the meanings of 'constituency election' and 'regional election' for the purposes of Welsh Assembly elections see PARA 3 note 2; and as to the meanings of 'constituency candidate' and 'individual candidate' see PARA 230 note 19.

4   The Representation of the People Act 1983 s 73 does not apply at an election under the local government Act which is not a local government election (see the Representation of the People Act 1983 s 90(2); and PARA 678); and, in relation to an election of parish councillors in England or of community councillors in Wales, the provisions of s 90(1), Sch 4 apply instead: see s 90(1)(b); and PARA 675. As to the meaning of 'election under the local government Act' see PARA 11 note 2. As to the meanings of 'England' and 'Wales' see PARA 1 note 1. As to the election of parish and community councillors see PARA 200 et seq.

5   As to the meaning of 'election expenses incurred by or on behalf of a candidate' see PARA 269 note 15.

6   See, in relation to a parliamentary or local government election, the Representation of the People Act 1983 s 73(1), or, in relation to a European parliamentary election, the European Parliamentary Elections Regulations 2004, SI 2004/293, reg 43(1), or, in relation to a Welsh Assembly election, the National Assembly for Wales (Representation of the People) Order 2007, SI 2007/236, art 43(1); and PARA 270. As to the appointment of election agents generally see PARA 231 et seq.

7   Representation of the People Act 1983 s 73(6) (amended by the Political Parties, Elections and Referendums Act 2000 ss 138, 158(2), (3)(a), Sch 18 paras 1, 3(1), (6), Sch 22); European Parliamentary Elections Regulations 2004, SI 2004/293, reg 43(6); National Assembly for Wales (Representation of the People) Order 2007, SI 2007/236, art 43(5). The making of such a payment remains an illegal practice even if the money is repaid: *York County, East Riding, Buckrose Division Case* (1886) 4 O'M & H 110 at 116. However, where a payment was made through a person other than the election agent by mistake and the money was returned and the transaction was genuine and honest, it was held that no offence had been committed: *Monmouth Boroughs Case* (1901) 5 O'M & H 166 at 170. As to excuses and the right to apply for relief see PARA 690 et seq; and as to the consequences of illegal practices see PARA 888 et seq.

675.   Payment of statute-barred claims for election expenses or of claims out of time.   An election agent[1] who pays a claim for election expenses[2] which is submitted to him later than 21 days after the day on which the result of the election is declared[3] or who makes a payment after the expiry of the 28 days limit[4] is guilty of an illegal practice[5]. However, except in the case of a European parliamentary election, if the election court reports that it has been proved to the court by the candidate that any payment was made by an election agent without the candidate's sanction or connivance[6], the candidate's election is not void, nor is he subject to any incapacity by reason only of that payment having been made in contravention of the prohibition on the payment of a claim that is statute-barred or out of time[7].

At an election of parish councillors in England or of community councillors in Wales[8], if any person makes a payment[9] in contravention of the provision which bars any claim against any person in respect of any election expenses incurred by or on behalf of a candidate which is not sent in[10] within 14 days after the day of election or the provision which bars the payment of any election expenses so incurred 21 days after the day of election[11], he is guilty of an illegal practice, but a candidate is not liable, nor is his election void, for any such illegal practice committed without his consent or connivance[12].

1 As to the appointment of election agents generally see PARA 231 et seq. At a European parliamentary election, the reference is to an individual candidate or his election agent: see the European Parliamentary Elections Regulations 2004, SI 2004/293, reg 48(1), (2); and PARA 276. As to the meaning of 'individual candidate' at a European parliamentary election see PARA 230 note 32. As to European parliamentary elections see PARA 217 et seq. As to the appointment of a sub-agent at a European parliamentary election see PARA 241 et seq. In the case of a Welsh Assembly election, the reference is to a candidate or his election agent at a constituency election, and to an individual candidate or his election agent at a regional election: see the National Assembly for Wales (Representation of the People) Order 2007, SI 2007/236, art 49(1); and PARA 276. As to the meanings of 'Assembly election', 'constituency election' and 'regional election' for these purposes see PARA 3 note 2. As to the meanings of 'candidate', 'constituency candidate' and 'individual candidate' see PARA 230 note 19.

2 As to the meaning of 'election expenses' see PARA 269.

3 Ie in contravention of, at a parliamentary or local government election, the Representation of the People Act 1983 s 78(1), or, at a European parliamentary election, the European Parliamentary Elections Regulations 2004, SI 2004/293, reg 48(1), or, at a Welsh Assembly election, the National Assembly for Wales (Representation of the People) Order 2007, SI 2007/236, art 49(1) (see PARA 276). As to the meaning of 'parliamentary election' see PARA 9; and as to the meaning of 'local government election' see PARA 11.

4 Ie in contravention of, at a parliamentary or local government election, the Representation of the People Act 1983 s 78(2), or, at a European parliamentary election, the European Parliamentary Elections Regulations 2004, SI 2004/293, reg 48(2), or, at a Welsh Assembly election, the National Assembly for Wales (Representation of the People) Order 2007, SI 2007/236, art 49(2) (see PARA 276).

5 Representation of the People Act 1983 s 78(3); European Parliamentary Elections Regulations 2004, SI 2004/293, reg 48(4); National Assembly for Wales (Representation of the People) Order 2007, SI 2007/236, art 49(3). As to excuses and the right to apply for relief see PARA 690 et seq; and as to the consequences of illegal practices see PARA 888 et seq.

     The Representation of the People Act 1983 s 78 does not apply at an election under the local government Act which is not a local government election: see the Representation of the People Act 1983 s 90(2); and PARA 678. As to the meaning of 'election under the local government Act' see PARA 11 note 2. As to the meanings of 'England' and 'Wales' see PARA 1 note 1. As to the election of parish and community councillors see PARA 200 et seq.

6 In the case of a Welsh Assembly election, the reference is to the sanction or connivance of a candidate at a constituency election or of an individual candidate at a regional election: see the National Assembly for Wales (Representation of the People) Order 2007, SI 2007/236, art 49(4).

7 Representation of the People Act 1983 s 78(3); National Assembly for Wales (Representation of the People) Order 2007, SI 2007/236, art 49(4).

8 Ie where election agents are not required. As to the election of parish and community councillors see PARA 200 et seq.

9 As to the meaning of 'payment' see PARA 270 note 2.

10 It is not clear whether the claim must be in the possession of the person within the 14 days or merely have been dispatched within that time. However, to the extent that 'send' is synonymous with 'transmit', the latter construction is the correct one: see *MacKinnon v Clark* [1898] 2 QB 251 at 257, CA, per A L Smith LJ.

11 See the Representation of the People Act 1983 s 90(1)(b), Sch 4 para 1(1); and PARA 294.

12 Representation of the People Act 1983 Sch 4 para 1(2).

676. Failure to make required financial returns or declarations as to election expenses. If a candidate[1] or election agent[2] fails to comply with the statutory requirements that govern returns as to election expenses[3], or declarations as to election expenses[4], he is guilty of an illegal practice[5]. A return which is defective, in that it omits certain election expenses or gives erroneous figures, also constitutes an illegal practice[6]. However, the delivery of the return and election agent's declaration separately and at different times but both within the prescribed period is apparently not an offence[7].

At an election of parish councillors in England or of community councillors in Wales[8], if the candidate fails to make the required return and declaration as to election expenses[9], he is guilty of an illegal practice[10].

1   Ie a candidate at a parliamentary or local government election, at a European parliamentary election, or at a Welsh Assembly election. As to the meaning of 'Assembly election' see PARA 3 note 2. As to the meaning of 'parliamentary election' see PARA 9; and as to the meaning of 'local government election' see PARA 11. As to European parliamentary elections see PARA 217 et seq. As to the meaning of 'candidate' generally see PARA 230.
     At a European parliamentary election, the reference is to an individual candidate: see the European Parliamentary Elections Regulations 2004, SI 2004/293, reg 56. As to the meaning of 'individual candidate' at a European parliamentary election see PARA 230 note 32. In the case of a Welsh Assembly election, the reference is to a candidate, being a reference to a constituency candidate at a constituency election, and to an individual candidate at a regional election: see the National Assembly for Wales (Representation of the People) Order 2007, SI 2007/236, art 56. As to the meanings of 'constituency election' and 'regional election' for these purposes see PARA 3 note 2. As to the meanings of 'candidate', 'constituency candidate' and 'individual candidate' for these purposes see PARA 230 note 19.
2   As to the appointment of election agents generally see PARA 231 et seq.
3   Ie, in relation to a parliamentary or local government election, under the Representation of the People Act 1983 s 81, or, in relation to a European parliamentary election, under the European Parliamentary Elections Regulations 2004, SI 2004/293, reg 51, or, in relation to a Welsh Assembly election, under the National Assembly for Wales (Representation of the People) Order 2007, SI 2007/236, art 52 (see PARA 280). As to the meaning of 'return as to election expenses' see PARA 281 note 1.
4   Ie, in relation to a parliamentary or local government election, under the Representation of the People Act 1983 s 82, or, in relation to a European parliamentary election, under the European Parliamentary Elections Regulations 2004, SI 2004/293, reg 52, or, in relation to a Welsh Assembly election, under the National Assembly for Wales (Representation of the People) Order 2007, SI 2007/236, arts 53, 54 (see PARA 281). As to the meaning of 'declaration as to election expenses' see PARA 281 note 3.
5   Representation of the People Act 1983 s 84; European Parliamentary Elections Regulations 2004, SI 2004/293, reg 54; National Assembly for Wales (Representation of the People) Order 2007, SI 2007/236, art 56. As to excuses and the right to apply for relief see PARA 690 et seq; and as to the consequences of illegal practices see PARA 888 et seq. If the candidate knowingly makes the accompanying declaration as to election expenses falsely, he is guilty of a corrupt practice: see PARA 708.
     The Representation of the People Act 1983 s 84 does not apply at an election under the local government Act which is not a local government election (see the Representation of the People Act 1983 s 90(2); and PARA 678). As to the meaning of 'election under the local government Act' see PARA 11 note 2. As to the meanings of 'England' and 'Wales' see PARA 1 note 1. As to the election of parish and community councillors see PARA 200 et seq.
6   *Cheltenham Case, Smythies and Claridge v Mathias, Davies' Case* (1911) 6 O'M & H 194; *Cork, Eastern Division Case* (1911) 6 O'M & H 318; *Northumberland, Berwick-upon-Tweed Division Case* (1923) 7 O'M & H 1; *Oxford Borough Case* (1924) 7 O'M & H 49.
7   *Re Ramsgate Town Council, ex p Hobbs* (1889) 5 TLR 272, DC.
8   Ie where election agents are not required: see PARA 295.
9   See the Representation of the People Act 1983 s 90(1)(b), Sch 4 para 3; and PARA 295.
10   Representation of the People Act 1983 Sch 4 para 5. If the candidate knowingly makes the accompanying declaration falsely, he is guilty of a corrupt practice: see Sch 4 para 5; and PARA 708.

677.   Failure to deliver or send returns or declarations of expenses authorised by election agent.   If a person fails to deliver or send any declaration or return, or a copy of it, as required by the statutory prohibitions on the incurring of election expenses[1] by any person other than the candidate[2], his election agent[3] and persons authorised in writing by the election agent[4], he is guilty of an illegal practice[5].

These provisions no longer apply for the purposes of a local authority mayoral election[6].

1 As to the meaning of 'election expenses' see PARA 269. As to the meaning of 'return as to election expenses' see PARA 281 note 1; and as to the meaning of 'declaration as to election expenses' see PARA 281 note 3.

2 Ie a candidate at a parliamentary or local government election, at a European parliamentary election, or at a Welsh Assembly election. As to the meaning of 'Assembly election' see PARA 3 note 2. As to the meaning of 'parliamentary election' see PARA 9; and as to the meaning of 'local government election' see PARA 11. As to European parliamentary elections see PARA 217 et seq. As to the meaning of 'candidate' generally see PARA 230. At a European parliamentary election, the reference is to an 'individual candidate': see the European Parliamentary Elections Regulations 2004, SI 2004/293, reg 46(1); and PARA 272. As to the meaning of 'individual candidate' in relation to a European parliamentary election see PARA 230 note 32. At a Welsh Assembly election, the reference in the text is to a constituency candidate at a constituency election, and to an individual candidate at a regional election: see the National Assembly for Wales (Representation of the People) Order 2007, SI 2007/236, art 46(1); and see PARA 272. As to the meanings of 'constituency election' and 'regional election' for these purposes see PARA 3 note 2. As to the meanings of 'candidate', 'constituency candidate' and 'individual candidate' for these purposes see PARA 230 note 19.

3 As to the appointment of election agents generally see PARA 231 et seq. In relation to a European parliamentary election, references to an election agent include a sub-agent: see the European Parliamentary Elections Regulations 2004, SI 2004/293, reg 46(7); and PARA 272 note 5. As to the appointment of a sub-agent at a European parliamentary election see PARA 241 et seq.

4 See, in relation to a parliamentary or local government election, the Representation of the People Act 1983 s 75(1), or, in relation to a European parliamentary election, the European Parliamentary Elections Regulations 2004, SI 2004/293, reg 46(1), or, in relation to a Welsh Assembly election, the National Assembly for Wales (Representation of the People) Order 2007, SI 2007/236, art 46(1); and see PARA 272.

5 Representation of the People Act 1983 s 75(5) (amended by the Representation of the People Act 1985 s 24, Sch 4 para 24); European Parliamentary Elections Regulations 2004, SI 2004/293, reg 46(5); National Assembly for Wales (Representation of the People) Order 2007, SI 2007/236, art 46(9). As to the liability of officers of associations or bodies which are guilty of an offence, the court's power to mitigate or remit any incapacity and the limitation of the liability of a candidate for an offence by an agent see PARA 687 et seq; and as to the consequences of illegal practices see PARA 888 et seq.

The Representation of the People Act 1983 s 75 does not apply at an election under the local government Act which is not a local government election (see the Representation of the People Act 1983 s 90(2); and PARA 678); and, in relation to an election of parish councillors in England or of community councillors in Wales, the provisions of s 90(1), Sch 4 apply instead: see s 90(1)(b); and PARA 675. As to elections in the City of London see PARA 33.

6 See the Local Authorities (Mayoral Elections) (England and Wales) Regulations 2002, SI 2002/185, reg 3(2), Sch 2 Table 1 (revoked), which applied the Representation of the People Act 1983 s 75, subject to modifications; and see now the Local Authorities (Mayoral Elections) (England and Wales) Regulations 2007, SI 2007/1024, reg 3(2)–(5), Sch 2 Table 1; and PARA 11 note 14.

678. Paying or incurring expenses at elections under the Local Government Act 1972 where election agent not required. At an election under the Local Government Act 1972[1] which is not a local government election[2], the general statutory provisions relating to election expenses[3] have no application[4]. If a candidate at such an election or any person on his behalf knowingly pays any sum or incurs any expense, whether before, during or after that election, on account of or in respect of the conduct or management of the election, he is guilty of an illegal practice[5].

1 See PARA 11 note 2. In the application of the Representation of the People Act 1983 Pt II (ss 67–119) to a poll consequent on a parish or community meeting, 'election under the local government Act' is deemed to include a reference to a poll consequent on a parish or community meeting (see PARA 200 et seq): Parish and Community Meetings (Polls) Rules 1987, SI 1987/1, r 6(g).

2 As to the meaning of 'local government election' see PARA 11.

3 Ie the Representation of the People Act 1983 ss 71A–89 (see PARA 269 et seq): see s 90(2) (amended by the Political Parties, Elections and Referendums Act 2000 s 138, Sch 18 paras 1, 11(d)).

4   See the Representation of the People Act 1983 s 90(2) (as amended: see note 3); and PARA 297.

5   Representation of the People Act 1983 s 90(2) (as amended: see note 3). As to the consequences of an illegal practice see PARA 888 et seq.

679. Disturbing election or referendum meetings. Any person who at certain lawful public meetings[1] acts, or incites others to act, in a disorderly manner for the purpose of preventing the transaction of the business for which the meeting was called together is guilty of an illegal practice[2]. If a constable reasonably suspects any person of committing such an offence, he may, if requested so to do by the chairman of the meeting, require that person to declare to him immediately his name and address[3]. If that person refuses or fails so to declare his name and address, or if he gives a false name and address, he is liable on summary conviction to a fine[4].

1   Ie certain political meetings held, in relation to a parliamentary election, in a parliamentary constituency, or held, in relation to a local government election, in the electoral area for that election, or held, in relation to a European Parliamentary election, in a European Parliamentary electoral region, or held, in relation to a Welsh Assembly constituency election, in the Assembly constituency, or, in relation to a Welsh Assembly regional election, in the Assembly electoral region, for which the election is held: see the Representation of the People Act 1983 s 97(2); the European Parliamentary Elections Regulations 2004, SI 2004/293, reg 68(2); the National Assembly for Wales (Representation of the People) Order 2007, SI 2007/236, art 70(2); and PARA 338. As to the meanings of 'constituency' for the purposes of parliamentary elections, and 'parliamentary election', see PARA 9. As to the meanings of 'electoral area' and 'local government election' see PARA 11. As to the meanings of 'Assembly election', 'Assembly constituency', Assembly electoral region', 'constituency election', and regional election' see PARA 3 note 2. As to electoral regions constituted for the purposes of European parliamentary elections (including the 'combined region' which includes Gibraltar) see PARA 77.

     The Representation of the People Act 1983 s 97 is applied and modified for the purpose of local authority mayoral elections in England and Wales by the Local Authorities (Mayoral Elections) (England and Wales) Regulations 2007, SI 2007/1024, reg 3(2)–(5), Sch 2 Table 1 (see PARA 11 note 14); and the Representation of the People Act 1983 s 97 has effect also for the purposes of local authority referendums, subject to the modifications specified, in relation to Wales, by the Local Authorities (Conduct of Referendums) (Wales) Regulations 2008, SI 2008/1848, reg 8(2), Sch 4 Table 1, and, in relation to England, by the Local Authorities (Conduct of Referendums) (England) Regulations 2012, SI 2012/323, regs 8(2), 11–13, Sch 4 Table 1 (see PARA 15 note 2). As to the meaning of 'referendum' see PARA 574 note 2.

2   Representation of the People Act 1983 s 97(1); European Parliamentary Elections Regulations 2004, SI 2004/293, reg 68(1); National Assembly for Wales (Representation of the People) Order 2007, SI 2007/236, art 70(1). As to the punishment and consequences of illegal practices see PARA 888 et seq.

3   Representation of the People Act 1983 s 97(3); European Parliamentary Elections Regulations 2004, SI 2004/293, reg 68(3); National Assembly for Wales (Representation of the People) Order 2007, SI 2007/236, art 70(3).

4   Representation of the People Act 1983 s 97(3) (amended by the Police and Criminal Evidence Act 1984 ss 26(1), 119, Sch 7 Pt I); European Parliamentary Elections Regulations 2004, SI 2004/293, reg 68(3); National Assembly for Wales (Representation of the People) Order 2007, SI 2007/236, art 70(3). The fine mentioned in the text is one not exceeding level 1 on the standard scale: see the Representation of the People Act 1983 s 97(3) (as so amended); the European Parliamentary Elections Regulations 2004, SI 2004/293, reg 68(3); and the National Assembly for Wales (Representation of the People) Order 2007, SI 2007/236, art 70(3). As to the standard scale see SENTENCING AND DISPOSITION OF OFFENDERS vol 92 (2010) PARA 142. As to the penalty that applies where such an offence is committed in relation to a meeting held, for the purposes of a European Parliamentary election, in Gibraltar see the European Parliamentary Elections Regulations 2004, SI 2004/293, reg 68(3).

680. False statements as to candidates. A person who[1]:

(1)   before or during an election[2];

(2)   for the purpose of affecting the return of any candidate at the election[3],

makes or publishes any false statement of fact in relation to the candidate's personal character or conduct[4] is guilty of an illegal practice, unless he can show that he had reasonable grounds for believing, and did believe[5], the statement to be true[6]. It is essential that the statement complained of should relate to the personal rather than the political character or conduct of the candidate[7]. Accordingly, the court has to make a plain decision as to whether any particular statement goes to the political conduct, character or position of a candidate, or to his personal character or conduct, because a statement cannot be of both types[8]. However, any court, in considering an alleged breach of the statute, is obliged to have regard to the fundamental right to freedom of expression that attaches to the maker or publisher, which is guaranteed under the Convention for the Protection of Human Rights and Fundamental Freedoms (1950)[9], as well as to the other Convention rights that have to be balanced with or against it[10], save that the Convention right to freedom of expression is not engaged in relation to statements made dishonestly[11]. The false statement of fact need not be defamatory at common law[12], so long as it is a statement which is calculated to influence the electors (as, for instance, a statement made in a hunting county that the candidate has shot a fox, or a statement made to promoters of total abstinence that the candidate has taken a glass of wine[13]). It is irrelevant whether the statement complained of has or has not been provoked by a statement of a similar character made on the part of an opponent[14]. The words of the statement will be interpreted according to their real and true meaning, and not necessarily according to their literal sense[15].

Other than at a European parliamentary election, a candidate is not liable, nor is his election to be avoided, for any illegal practice relating to such false statements committed by his agent other than his election agent[16], unless:

(a)   it can be shown that the candidate or his election agent has authorised or consented to the committing of the illegal practice by the other agent or has paid for the circulation of the false statement constituting the illegal practice[17], or

(b)   an election court finds and reports that the candidate's election was procured or materially assisted in consequence of the making or publishing of such a false statement[18].

Any person who before or during an election (other than a European parliamentary election) knowingly publishes a false statement of the withdrawal of any candidate at the election for the purpose of promoting or procuring the election of another candidate is guilty of an illegal practice[19]; but the candidate is not liable, nor may his election be avoided, for any such illegal practice committed by his agent other than his election agent[20].

1   Ie or any director of any body or association corporate which: see the Representation of the People Act 1983 s 106(1); the European Parliamentary Elections Regulations 2004, SI 2004/293, reg 71(1); and the National Assembly for Wales (Representation of the People) Order 2007, SI 2007/236, art 73(1).

2   Representation of the People Act 1983 s 106(1)(a); European Parliamentary Elections Regulations 2004, SI 2004/293, reg 71(1)(a); National Assembly for Wales (Representation of the People) Order 2007, SI 2007/236, art 73(1)(a). The election mentioned in the text may be a parliamentary or local government election, a European parliamentary election, or a Welsh Assembly election, as the case may be. As to the meaning of 'Assembly election' see PARA 3 note 2. As to the meaning of 'parliamentary election' see PARA 9; and as to the meaning of 'local government election' see PARA 11. As to European parliamentary elections see PARA 217 et seq.

3   Representation of the People Act 1983 s 106(1)(b); European Parliamentary Elections Regulations 2004, SI 2004/293, reg 71(1)(b); National Assembly for Wales (Representation of the People) Order 2007, SI 2007/236, art 73(1)(b). At a Welsh Assembly election, the purpose

expressed in head (2) in the text is the purpose of affecting how a vote is given at the election: see art 73(1)(b). As to the meaning of 'candidate' generally see PARA 230. At a European parliamentary election, the reference is to any registered party or individual candidate, and accordingly the statement (see the text and notes 4–6) may relate either to a candidate on the list of that party or to that individual candidate: see the European Parliamentary Elections Regulations 2004, SI 2004/293, reg 71(1). As to the meanings of 'registered party' and 'list' (submitted by a registered party) see PARA 230 note 29; and as to the meaning of 'individual candidate' see PARA 230 note 32.

4   The statement may be oral or written: *Cumberland, Cockermouth Division Case* (1901) 5 O'M & H 155. A person making or publishing any such false statement of fact may be restrained by interim or perpetual injunction from any repetition of that false statement (or from making a false statement of a similar character) and prima facie proof of falsity is sufficient for these purposes: see the Representation of the People Act 1983 s 106(3); the European Parliamentary Elections Regulations 2004, SI 2004/293, reg 71(2); the National Assembly for Wales (Representation of the People) Order 2007, SI 2007/236, art 73(4); and PARA 666.

5   The belief must in each case depend on the character and nature of the information given: *Sunderland Borough Case, Storey v Doxford* (1896) 5 O'M & H 53 at 65.

6   Representation of the People Act 1983 s 106(1); European Parliamentary Elections Regulations 2004, SI 2004/293, reg 71(1); National Assembly for Wales (Representation of the People) Order 2007, SI 2007/236, art 73(1). As to remedy by way of interim or perpetual injunction to restrain a person from any repetition of a false statement or of a false statement of a similar character in relation to the candidate see PARA 666.

7   *Cumberland, Cockermouth Division Case* (1901) 5 O'M & H 155 at 164; *Sheffield, Attercliffe Division Case* (1906) 5 O'M & H 218; *Fairbairn v Scottish National Party* 1979 SC 393 (every false statement in relation to the public character of a candidate may in one sense reflect upon the candidate's personal character, but, before there can be an illegal practice in terms of the statute, the false statement of fact must be directly related to the personal character of the candidate's conduct). Cf *Anon* (1897), reported in *Jelf's Corrupt and Illegal Practices Prevention Acts* (3rd Edn) p 215; but see also *Bayley v Edmunds, Byron and Marshall* (1895) 11 TLR 537, CA, where a charge that the candidate 'hypocritically feeling in his conscience that he was doing wrong for the purpose of making large profits for himself, locked out his workmen for a certain length of time, and that then, some time afterwards, he found that his conscience reproved him, and resolved he would starve them no longer', was held to be within the provision. A statement that a candidate would not pay his hotel bill or debts is within the provision: *Davies v Ward* (1910) Times, 18 January. On the other hand, a statement that a candidate is a communist is not within the provision: *Burns v Associated Newspapers Ltd* (1925) 89 JP 205. The words 'radical traitors' were held to be not within the provisions, as being a statement of opinion rather than of fact: *Ellis v National Union of Conservative and Constitutional Associations, Middleton and Southall* (1900) 44 Sol Jo 750. See also *Sunderland Borough Case* (1896) 5 O'M & H 53 at 62, where it was said that a mere argumentative statement of the conduct of a public man, even though in respect of his private life, is not always, and in many cases certainly would not be, within this provision; *DPP v Edwards* [2002] EWHC 636 (Admin), [2002] All ER (D) 314 (Mar) (the statement '[K] whilst sitting as chairman of housing hands his son-in-law's company a £125,000 building contract' clearly attributed personal and private motives to the decision to allocate the contract to the company and so did relate to the personal conduct of K; a distinction is made between an act of the authority through the committee assigning contracts, which was a public act, and the role that K might have had in the decision-making process that led to the allocation of the contract, which was not); and *R (on the application of Woolas) v Parliamentary Election Court* [2010] EWHC 3169 (Admin), [2012] QB 1, [2010] NLJR 1756, [2010] All ER (D) 60 (Dec) (statement that candidate was willing to condone threats of violence in pursuit of political advantage was a statement that went to his personal character).

8   *R (on the application of Woolas) v Parliamentary Election Court* [2010] EWHC 3169 (Admin), [2012] QB 1, [2010] NLJR 1756, [2010] All ER (D) 60 (Dec) (a statement about reneging on a promise to live in the constituency was a statement relating to the candidate's political position; other statements (about the petitioner seeking the electoral support of Muslims who advocated violence, in particular towards the claimant, and refusing to condemn extremists who advocated violence against the claimant) fell within the Representation of the People Act 1983 s 106(1), as being statements that related to the candidate's personal character, and the election court's findings of illegal practice could not be impugned). A false statement of fact relating to a candidate's personal conduct may be used for the purpose of representing a candidate as guilty of either private immorality or public immorality, political or otherwise, and it is in either case equally within the statutory provision: *Louth, Northern Division Case* (1911) 6 O'M & H 103.

9 Ie the Convention for the Protection of Human Rights and Fundamental Freedoms (Rome, 4 November 1950; TS 71 (1953); Cmd 8969) ('ECHR') art 10 (see RIGHTS AND FREEDOMS vol 88A (2013) PARA 398 et seq).

10 Ie including the candidate's right to the protection of his reputation under ECHR art 8 (ie the right to reputation as part of the right to respect for private and family life: see RIGHTS AND FREEDOMS vol 88A (2013) PARA 317 et seq), and the public's right to free elections guaranteed under the ECHR, First Protocol (Paris, 20 March 1952; TS 46; Cmnd 9221; Council of Europe, ETS no 9) art 3 (see RIGHTS AND FREEDOMS vol 88A (2013) PARAS 572–593): see *R (on the application of Woolas) v Parliamentary Election Court* [2010] EWHC 3169 (Admin), [2012] QB 1, [2010] NLJR 1756, [2010] All ER (D) 60 (Dec). As to reputation being disparaged by defamatory statements see also the text and notes 12–13.

11 *R (on the application of Woolas) v Parliamentary Election Court* [2010] EWHC 3169 (Admin), [2012] QB 1, [2010] NLJR 1756, [2010] All ER (D) 60 (Dec).

12 In some senses, the words of the provision are narrower and in some senses wider than is consistent with the law of libel: *St George's Division, Tower Hamlets, Case* (1895) 5 O'M & H 89 at 101, 103–104. As to whether statute bars a plea of qualified privilege as respects defamatory statements by or on behalf of a candidate at an election see the Defamation Act 1952 s 10; and PARA 330.

13 *Sunderland Borough Case, Storey v Doxford* (1896) 5 O'M & H 53 at 62 per Pollock B. This is not of course a decision that such words could not in any circumstances bear a defamatory meaning at common law, but that it is not necessary to give them such a defamatory meaning in order to bring them within the provision.

14 *Monmouth Boroughs Case* (1901) 5 O'M & H 166 at 173.

15 *Silver v Benn* (1896) 12 TLR 199 at 200, DC (where Kay LJ speaks of 'what the passage meant to convey'). The question to be determined is what in the circumstances is the true meaning which the reader would place upon the statements: *Louth, Northern Division Case* (1911) 6 O'M & H 103 at 154–157. The true meaning will depend on the occasion of the publication, the persons publishing, the person attacked and the readers intended to be addressed: *Louth, Northern Division Case* at 158; and see *Sheffield, Attercliffe Division Case* (1906) 5 O'M & H 218 at 223. This is inconsistent, however, with dicta in *Ellis v National Union of Conservative and Constitutional Associations, Middleton and Southall* (1900) 44 Sol Jo 750, where the published statement was construed literally and the question of innuendo was disregarded. But, in *Fairbairn v Scottish National Party* 1979 SC 393, Ct of Sess, the court took account of the innuendo that the words were reasonably capable of bearing.

16 As to the appointment of election agents generally see PARA 231 et seq. At a Welsh Assembly election, the reference is to:
   (1)   in the case of a constituency candidate or an individual candidate, his agent other than his election agent (National Assembly for Wales (Representation of the People) Order 2007, SI 2007/236, art 73(2)(a)); but
   (2)   in the case of a party list candidate, the agent of the registered political party on whose list he is a candidate other than that party's election agent in relation to that list (art 73(2)(b)).
   As to the meanings of 'candidate', 'constituency candidate' and 'individual candidate' for these purposes see PARA 230 note 19; and as to the meanings of 'party list', 'party list candidate' and 'registered political party' see PARA 230 note 23.
   Where the candidate is not required to have an election agent (see PARA 231 note 3), the reference to an illegal practice committed by an agent of the candidate is to be taken as a reference to an illegal practice committed without the candidate's knowledge and consent and the reference to the election agent is omitted: Representation of the People Act 1983 s 106(7).

17 Representation of the People Act 1983 s 106(2)(a); National Assembly for Wales (Representation of the People) Order 2007, SI 2007/236, art 73(3)(i). At a Welsh Assembly election, the reference to the candidate includes, in the case of a party list candidate, another candidate of the party on whose list he appears: see art 73(2)(i).

18 Representation of the People Act 1983 s 106(2)(b); National Assembly for Wales (Representation of the People) Order 2007, SI 2007/236, art 73(3)(ii).

19 Representation of the People Act 1983 s 106(5); National Assembly for Wales (Representation of the People) Order 2007, SI 2007/236, art 73(5). At a Welsh Assembly election, the purpose expressed in the text is the purpose of promoting or procuring a particular result at the election: see art 73(5).

20 Representation of the People Act 1983 s 106(6); National Assembly for Wales (Representation of the People) Order 2007, SI 2007/236, art 73(6). At a Welsh Assembly election, the reference is to:

(1)   in the case of a constituency candidate or an individual candidate, his agent other than his election agent (art 73(6)(a)); but

(2)   in the case of a party list candidate, the agent of the registered political party on whose list he is a candidate other than that party's election agent in relation to that list (art 73(6)(b)).

Where the candidate is not required to have an election agent (see PARA 231 note 3), the reference to an illegal practice committed by an agent of the candidate is to be taken as a reference to an illegal practice committed without the candidate's knowledge and consent and the reference to the election agent is omitted: see the Representation of the People Act 1983 s 106(7).

681.   Illegal practices connected with candidature at European parliamentary general election.   A person who, at a general election of members of the European Parliament ('MEPs')[1]:

(1)   consents to nomination as an individual candidate[2] in more than one electoral region[3];

(2)   consents to nomination as an individual candidate in an electoral region, and consents to being nominated in a list submitted by a registered party[4], whether in that region or some other[5];

(3)   consents to being nominated in the list submitted by more than one registered party in the same region[6]; or

(4)   consents to being nominated in the lists submitted by a registered party or parties for more than one region[7],

is guilty of an illegal practice[8].

If a person, on any occasion when[9] elections to the European Parliament are held in all member states, stands as a candidate at such an election in the United Kingdom and in any other member state, he is guilty of an offence[10]; and such an offence is an illegal practice[11].

1   As to European parliamentary general elections see PARA 217 et seq.
2   As to the requirement for a candidate to consent to nomination see PARA 258. As to the meaning of 'individual candidate' in the context of a European parliamentary election see PARA 230 note 32.
3   European Parliamentary Elections Regulations 2004, SI 2004/293, reg 28(2)(a). As to electoral regions constituted for the purposes of European parliamentary elections (including the 'combined region' which includes Gibraltar) see PARA 77.
4   As to the meanings of 'registered party' and 'list' (submitted by a registered party) see PARA 230 note 29.
5   European Parliamentary Elections Regulations 2004, SI 2004/293, reg 28(2)(b).
6   European Parliamentary Elections Regulations 2004, SI 2004/293, reg 28(2)(c).
7   European Parliamentary Elections Regulations 2004, SI 2004/293, reg 28(2)(d).
8   European Parliamentary Elections Regulations 2004, SI 2004/293, reg 28(2). As to the consequences of illegal practices see PARA 888 et seq.
9   Ie under the 1976 Act concerning the election of the representatives of the Assembly by direct universal suffrage (OJ L278, 08.10.76, p 5) (the '1976 Act') (amended and renumbered by Council Decision (EC and Euratom) 2002/772 (OJ L283, 21.10.2002, p 1)), annexed to Decision (ECSC, EEC and Euratom) 76/787 (OJ L278, 08.10.76, p 1)) (see PARA 6).
10   European Parliamentary Elections (Changes to the Franchise and Qualification of Representatives) Regulations 1994, SI 1994/342, reg 4(1) (amended by SI 2004/1374).
11   European Parliamentary Elections (Changes to the Franchise and Qualification of Representatives) Regulations 1994, SI 1994/342, reg 4(2). The text refers to an illegal practice within the meaning of the Representation of the People Act 1983, and the provisions of that Act which relate to illegal practices, as applied by regulations under the European Parliamentary Elections Act 2002, accordingly have effect in relation to any such offence: European Parliamentary Elections (Changes to the Franchise and Qualification of Representatives) Regulations 1994, SI 1994/342, reg 4(2); Interpretation Act 1978 s 17(2).

B. ILLEGAL PAYMENT, EMPLOYMENT OR HIRING

682. Illegal payment or employment by candidate or election agent. The following are illegal payments or employments:

(1)   payment to induce the corrupt withdrawal of a candidate[1];

(2)   payment to an elector or proxy for the exhibition of election notices[2];

(3)   the employment of a paid canvasser[3];

(4)   the provision of money for any prohibited payment[4];

(5)   the provision of money in excess of the maximum allowed for election expenses[5].

A person guilty of an offence of illegal payment or employment is liable, on summary conviction, to a fine[6]; but a candidate[7] or election agent[8] who is personally guilty of an offence of illegal payment or employment is guilty of an illegal practice[9].

1   See PARA 683.
2   See PARA 684.
3   See PARA 685.
4   See PARA 686.
5   See PARA 686.
6   See PARA 889. The penalty is a fine not exceeding level 5 on the standard scale: see PARA 889. As to the standard scale see SENTENCING AND DISPOSITION OF OFFENDERS vol 92 (2010) PARA 142.
7   As to the meaning of 'candidate' generally see PARA 230.
8   As to the appointment of election agents generally see PARA 231 et seq.
9   Representation of the People Act 1983 s 175(2) (amended by the Political Parties, Elections and Referendums Act 2000 s 158(1), Sch 21 para 6(1), (6)); European Parliamentary Elections Regulations 2004, SI 2004/293, reg 113(2); National Assembly for Wales (Representation of the People) Order 2007, SI 2007/236, art 127(2). If an offence of illegal payment or employment is committed with the candidate's knowledge and consent at an election where candidates are not required to have election agents (see PARA 231 note 3), the candidate is guilty of an illegal practice: see the Representation of the People Act 1983 s 175(2) (as so amended). As to the circumstances in which relief is available see PARA 687 et seq; and as to the consequences of illegal payment or employment see PARA 889.

683. Inducing or procuring corrupt withdrawal of candidate by illegal payment. Any person who corruptly induces or procures another person to withdraw from being a candidate[1] at an election[2], in consideration of any payment or promise of payment, and any person withdrawing in pursuance of the inducement or procurement, is guilty of an illegal payment[3].

1   As to the meaning of 'candidate' generally see PARA 230. At a European parliamentary election, the reference is to being an individual candidate at an election: see the European Parliamentary Elections Regulations 2004, SI 2004/293, reg 72. As to the meaning of 'individual candidate' in relation to a European parliamentary election see PARA 230 note 32. As to European parliamentary elections see PARA 217 et seq.
2   Ie at a parliamentary or local government election, a European parliamentary election, or a Welsh Assembly election, as the case may be. As to the meaning of 'Assembly election' see PARA 3 note 2. As to the meaning of 'parliamentary election' see PARA 9; and as to the meaning of 'local government election' see PARA 11.
3   Representation of the People Act 1983 s 107; European Parliamentary Elections Regulations 2004, SI 2004/293, reg 72; National Assembly for Wales (Representation of the People) Order 2007, SI 2007/236, art 74. A candidate or election agent who is personally guilty of the offence is guilty of an illegal practice: see PARA 682. As to the circumstances in which relief is available see PARA 687 et seq; and as to the consequences of illegal payment or employment see PARA 889.

684. Illegal payments for exhibition of election notices. For the purposes of promoting or procuring the election of a candidate[1] at an election[2], no payment or contract for payment may be made to an elector or proxy for an elector[3] on account of the exhibition of, or the use of any house, land, building or premises for the exhibition of, any address[4], bill or notice[5], unless:

(1) it is the ordinary business of the elector or proxy as an advertising agent[6] to exhibit for payment bills and advertisements[7]; and

(2) the payment or contract is made in the ordinary course of that business[8].

If any payment or contract for payment is knowingly made in contravention of this prohibition either before, during or after an election, the person making the payment or contract, and (if he knew it to be in contravention) any person receiving the payment or being a party to the contract, is guilty of an illegal practice[9].

1 As to the meaning of 'candidate' generally see PARA 230. At a European parliamentary election, the reference is to promoting or procuring the election of a registered party or an individual candidate: see the European Parliamentary Elections Regulations 2004, SI 2004/293, reg 73(1). As to the meaning of 'registered party' see PARA 230 note 29; and as to the meaning of 'individual candidate' see PARA 230 note 32. As to European parliamentary elections see PARA 217 et seq. At a Welsh Assembly election, the purpose expressed in the text is the purpose of promoting or procuring a particular result at an Assembly election: see the National Assembly for Wales (Representation of the People) Order 2007, SI 2007/236, art 75(1). As to the meaning of 'Assembly election' see PARA 3 note 2.

2 Ie at a parliamentary or local government election, a European parliamentary election, or a Welsh Assembly election, as the case may be. As to the meaning of 'parliamentary election' see PARA 9; and as to the meaning of 'local government election' see PARA 11. As to the meaning of references to promoting or procuring a candidate's election at an election see PARA 269 note 4.
  The Representation of the People Act 1983 s 109 has effect for the purposes of local authority referendums, subject to the modifications specified, in relation to Wales, by the Local Authorities (Conduct of Referendums) (Wales) Regulations 2008, SI 2008/1848, reg 8(2), Sch 4 Table 1, and, in relation to England, by the Local Authorities (Conduct of Referendums) (England) Regulations 2012, SI 2012/323, regs 8(2), 11–13, Sch 4 Table 1: see PARA 15 note 2. As to the meaning of 'referendum' see PARA 574 note 2.

3 As to the meaning of 'elector' in relation to a parliamentary or local government election see PARA 95 note 2; in relation to a European parliamentary election, see PARA 111 note 4; and, in relation to a Welsh Assembly election, see PARA 110 note 6. As to applications to vote by post or by proxy see PARA 367 et seq.

4 An address appears to cover anything which is in the nature of an appeal to a voter to vote for a particular candidate: *Exeter Case* (1911) 6 O'M & H 228 at 249. A special election edition of a local newspaper, designed to promote the election of a particular candidate and authorised by the candidate, was held to be an address: *Oxford Borough Case* (1924) 7 O'M & H 49 at 83. See also *Barrow-in-Furness Case* (1886) 4 O'M & H 76; *Stepney Division, Tower Hamlets Case* (1886) 4 O'M & H 34, 37.

5 Representation of the People Act 1983 s 109(1); European Parliamentary Elections Regulations 2004, SI 2004/293, reg 73(1); National Assembly for Wales (Representation of the People) Order 2007, SI 2007/236, art 75(1). As to what may constitute a bill see PARA 748 note 6.

6 See *Exeter Case* (1911) 6 O'M & H 228 at 242.

7 Representation of the People Act 1983 s 109(1)(a); European Parliamentary Elections Regulations 2004, SI 2004/293, reg 73(1)(a); National Assembly for Wales (Representation of the People) Order 2007, SI 2007/236, art 75(1)(a).

8 Representation of the People Act 1983 s 109(1)(b); European Parliamentary Elections Regulations 2004, SI 2004/293, reg 73(1)(b); National Assembly for Wales (Representation of the People) Order 2007, SI 2007/236, art 75(1)(b).

9 Representation of the People Act 1983 s 109(2); European Parliamentary Elections Regulations 2004, SI 2004/293, reg 73(2); National Assembly for Wales (Representation of the People) Order 2007, SI 2007/236, art 75(2). A candidate or election agent who is personally guilty of the offence is guilty of an illegal practice: see PARA 682. As to the liability of officers of associations or bodies which are guilty of an offence, the court's power to mitigate or remit any incapacity and the limitation of the liability of a candidate for an offence by an agent see PARA 687 et seq; and as to the consequences of illegal practices see PARA 888 et seq.

685. Illegal employment of paid canvassers. If, for the purpose of promoting or procuring a candidate's election[1], a person is, either before, during or after an election, engaged or employed for payment or promise of payment as a canvasser, the person so engaging or employing him, and the person so engaged or employed, are guilty of illegal employment[2].

A person who is lawfully engaged or employed for payment for some lawful purpose is not, however, deprived of the ordinary right of a citizen to canvass, and he may therefore canvass so long as it is not for his canvassing that he is paid[3]. Although the payment of canvassers is illegal, there is nothing illegal in the payment of the expenses of a canvass[4].

1 Ie at a parliamentary or local government election, a European parliamentary election, or a Welsh Assembly election, as the case may be. As to the meaning of 'Assembly election' see PARA 3 note 2. As to the meaning of 'parliamentary election' see PARA 9; and as to the meaning of 'local government election' see PARA 11. As to European parliamentary elections see PARA 217 et seq.

As to the meaning of 'candidate' generally see PARA 230. As to the meaning of references to promoting or procuring a candidate's election at an election see PARA 269 note 4. At a European parliamentary election, the reference is to promoting or procuring the election of a registered party or an individual candidate: see the European Parliamentary Elections Regulations 2004, SI 2004/293, reg 75. As to the meaning of 'registered party' see PARA 230 note 29; and as to the meaning of 'individual candidate' see PARA 230 note 32. At a Welsh Assembly election, the purpose expressed in the text is the purpose of promoting or procuring a particular result at an Assembly election: see the National Assembly for Wales (Representation of the People) Order 2007, SI 2007/236, art 77.

2 Representation of the People Act 1983 s 111; European Parliamentary Elections Regulations 2004, SI 2004/293, reg 75; National Assembly for Wales (Representation of the People) Order 2007, SI 2007/236, art 77. A candidate or election agent who is personally guilty of the offence is guilty of an illegal practice: see PARA 682. As to the circumstances in which relief is available see PARA 687 et seq; and as to the consequences of illegal payment or employment see PARA 889.

The Representation of the People Act 1983 s 111 has effect for the purposes of local authority referendums, subject to the modifications specified, in relation to Wales, by the Local Authorities (Conduct of Referendums) (Wales) Regulations 2008, SI 2008/1848, reg 8(2), Sch 4 Table 1, and, in relation to England, by the Local Authorities (Conduct of Referendums) (England) Regulations 2012, SI 2012/323, regs 8(2), 11–13, Sch 4 Table 1: see PARA 15 note 2. As to the meaning of 'referendum' see PARA 574 note 2.

3 *Stafford County, Lichfield Division Case* (1895) 5 O'M & H 27 at 28–29; cf *Elgin and Nairn Case* (1895) 5 O'M & H 1 at 13.

4 *Ipswich Case, Packard v Collings and West* (1886) 54 LT 619 at 625.

686. Providing money for prohibited payment or for expenses incurred in excess of the maximum amount. A person is guilty of an illegal payment if he knowingly provides money[1]:

(1)   for any payment which is contrary to the statutory provisions which govern elections[2]; or

(2)   for any expenses incurred in excess of the maximum amount so allowed[3]; or

(3)   for replacing any money expended in any such payment or expenses[4],

except where the payment or the incurring of the expenses may have been previously allowed[5] to be an exception[6].

1 See the Representation of the People Act 1983 s 112; the European Parliamentary Elections Regulations 2004, SI 2004/293, reg 76; and the National Assembly for Wales (Representation of the People) Order 2007, SI 2007/236, art 78. A candidate or election agent who is personally guilty of the offence is guilty of an illegal practice: see PARA 682. As to the circumstances in which relief is available see PARA 687 et seq; and as to the consequences of illegal payment or employment see PARA 889.

The Representation of the People Act 1983 s 112 has effect for the purposes of local authority referendums, subject to the modifications specified, in relation to Wales, by the Local Authorities (Conduct of Referendums) (Wales) Regulations 2008, SI 2008/1848, reg 8(2), Sch 4 Table 1, and, in relation to England, by the Local Authorities (Conduct of Referendums) (England) Regulations 2012, SI 2012/323, regs 8(2), 11–13, Sch 4 Table 1: see PARA 15 note 2. As to the meaning of 'referendum' see PARA 574 note 2.

2   Representation of the People Act 1983 s 112(a); European Parliamentary Elections Regulations 2004, SI 2004/293, reg 76(a); National Assembly for Wales (Representation of the People) Order 2007, SI 2007/236, art 78(a). Head (1) in the text refers to the provisions contained in the Representation of the People Act 1983, in relation to a parliamentary or local government election, or in the European Parliamentary Elections Regulations 2004, SI 2004/293, in relation to a European parliamentary election, or in the National Assembly for Wales (Representation of the People) Order 2007, SI 2007/236, in relation to a Welsh Assembly election (see PARA 383). As to the meaning of 'Assembly election' see PARA 3 note 2. As to the meaning of 'parliamentary election' see PARA 9; and as to the meaning of 'local government election' see PARA 11. As to European parliamentary elections see PARA 217 et seq.

It is thought that the prohibition in the Representation of the People Act 1983 s 75 (expenses incurred by outsiders in publicising a candidate or in promoting political debate at an election: see PARA 272) is not a prohibition on a payment of money.

3   Representation of the People Act 1983 s 112(b); European Parliamentary Elections Regulations 2004, SI 2004/293, reg 76(b); National Assembly for Wales (Representation of the People) Order 2007, SI 2007/236, art 78(b). As to the maximum amount so allowed as mentioned in head (2) in the text see PARA 273.

4   Representation of the People Act 1983 s 112(c); European Parliamentary Elections Regulations 2004, SI 2004/293, reg 76(c); National Assembly for Wales (Representation of the People) Order 2007, SI 2007/236, art 78(c).

5   Ie under mitigation (see PARA 690 et seq): see the Representation of the People Act 1983 s 112; the European Parliamentary Elections Regulations 2004, SI 2004/293, reg 76; and the National Assembly for Wales (Representation of the People) Order 2007, SI 2007/236, art 78.

6   See the Representation of the People Act 1983 s 112; the European Parliamentary Elections Regulations 2004, SI 2004/293, reg 76; and the National Assembly for Wales (Representation of the People) Order 2007, SI 2007/236, art 78.

C. RELIEF

687. Relief in respect of failure to deliver or send returns or declarations of expenses authorised by election agent. If a person fails to deliver or send any declaration or return as to election expenses[1] or a copy of it as required, he is guilty of an illegal practice[2]; except that:

(1)   the court before which a person is convicted may, if it thinks it just in the special circumstances of the case, mitigate or entirely remit any incapacity imposed by virtue of the conviction[3]; and

(2)   a candidate[4] is not liable, nor is his election to be avoided, for such an illegal practice committed by an agent without his consent or connivance[5].

Where any act or omission of an association or body of persons, corporate or unincorporate, is an offence declared to be an illegal practice in this way, any person who at the time of the act or omission was a director, general manager, secretary or other similar officer of the association or body, or who was purporting to act in any such capacity, is to be deemed to be guilty of that offence[6], unless he proves that: (a) the act or omission took place without his consent or connivance[7]; and (b) that he exercised all such diligence to prevent the commission of the offence as he ought to have exercised having regard to the nature of his functions in that capacity and to all the circumstances[8].

These provisions no longer apply for the purposes of a local authority mayoral election[9].

1   As to the meaning of 'election expenses' see PARA 269. As to the meaning of 'return as to election expenses' see PARA 281 note 1; and as to the meaning of 'declaration as to election expenses' see PARA 281 note 3.

2   See the Representation of the People Act 1983 s 75(5); the European Parliamentary Elections Regulations 2004, SI 2004/293, reg 46(5); the National Assembly for Wales (Representation of the People) Order 2007, SI 2007/236, art 46(9); and PARA 677. As to the punishment of illegal practices see PARA 888; as to the other consequences of illegal practices see PARA 905 et seq.

3   Representation of the People Act 1983 s 75(5)(i); European Parliamentary Elections Regulations 2004, SI 2004/293, reg 46(5); National Assembly for Wales (Representation of the People) Order 2007, SI 2007/236, art 46(10). As to personal incapacity incurred on proof of corrupt or illegal voting practices at a parliamentary, local government election or local authority referendum, see the Representation of the People Act 1983 ss 160(4), 173; and PARA 905. As to personal incapacity incurred on proof of corrupt or illegal voting practices at a Welsh Assembly election see the National Assembly for Wales (Representation of the People) Order 2007, SI 2007/236, arts 110, 111, 123; and PARA 907. As to personal incapacity incurred on conviction of corrupt or illegal voting practices at a European parliamentary election see the European Parliamentary Elections Regulations 2004, SI 2004/293, reg 107; and PARA 909. As to mitigation and remission of incapacities so imposed see PARA 910. As to the meaning of 'Assembly election' see PARA 3 note 2; as to the meaning of 'parliamentary election' see PARA 9; and as to the meaning of 'local government election' see PARA 11.

4   Ie a candidate at a parliamentary, local government, or Welsh Assembly election. As to the meaning of 'candidate' generally see PARA 230.

5   Representation of the People Act 1983 s 75(5)(ii); National Assembly for Wales (Representation of the People) Order 2007, SI 2007/236, art 46(11). As to the avoidance of elections see PARAS 894–896.

6   Representation of the People Act 1983 s 75(6); European Parliamentary Elections Regulations 2004, SI 2004/293, reg 46(6); National Assembly for Wales (Representation of the People) Order 2007, SI 2007/236, art 46(12).

7   Representation of the People Act 1983 s 75(6)(a); European Parliamentary Elections Regulations 2004, SI 2004/293, reg 46(6)(a); National Assembly for Wales (Representation of the People) Order 2007, SI 2007/236, art 46(12)(a).

8   Representation of the People Act 1983 s 75(6)(b); European Parliamentary Elections Regulations 2004, SI 2004/293, reg 46(6)(b); National Assembly for Wales (Representation of the People) Order 2007, SI 2007/236, art 46(12)(b).

9   See the Local Authorities (Mayoral Elections) (England and Wales) Regulations 2002, SI 2002/185, reg 3(2), Sch 2 Table 1 (revoked), which applied the Representation of the People Act 1983 s 75, subject to modifications; and see now the Local Authorities (Mayoral Elections) (England and Wales) Regulations 2007, SI 2007/1024, reg 3(2)–(5), Sch 2 Table 1; and PARA 11 note 14.

688. Relief in respect of returns or declarations as to election expenses. Either a candidate at an election[1], or his election agent[2], may apply for relief to the High Court, an election court or a county court[3], which may grant the relief sought[4]:

(1)   to a candidate, in respect of any failure to deliver the return and declarations as to election expenses[5], or any part of them, or in respect of any error or false statement in them[6]; or

(2)   to an election agent, in respect of the failure to deliver the return and declarations which he was required to deliver, or any part of them, or in respect of any error or false statement in them[7].

The candidate may apply for relief on the ground that the failure, error or false statement arose: (a) by reason of his illness[8]; (b) by reason of the absence, death, illness or misconduct of his election agent[9] or sub-agent, or of any clerk or officer of that agent[10]; or (c) by reason of inadvertence or any reasonable cause of a like nature[11], and not by reason of any want of good faith on the part of the applicant[12]. The election agent may apply for relief on the ground that the failure, error or false statement arose: (i) by reason of his illness[13]; or (ii) by reason of the death or illness of any prior election agent of the candidate, or by reason of the absence, death, illness or misconduct of any sub-agent, clerk or officer of an election agent of a candidate[14]; or (iii) by reason of inadvertence, or any reasonable cause of a like nature[15], and not by reason of any want of good faith on the part of the applicant[16].

Where a person makes such an application he must notify the Director of Public Prosecutions of it, who may attend the hearing of it and make representations at the hearing in respect of it[17].

After such further notice of an application[18] as the court considers fit, and on production of such evidence of the grounds stated in the application and of the good faith of the application, and otherwise, as the court considers fit, the court may make such order for allowing an authorised excuse for the failure, error or false statement as it considers just[19]. Where, on such an application, it appears to the court that any person who is or has been an election agent or sub-agent[20] has refused or failed to make such return or to supply such particulars as will enable the candidate and his election agent respectively[21] to comply with the requirements as to returns or declarations as to election expenses[22], the court, before making an order allowing an authorised excuse, must order that person to attend before it[23]. On the attendance of that person, the court must, unless he shows cause to the contrary, order him to make the return and declaration, or to deliver a statement of the particulars required to be contained in the return, as the court considers just, within such time, to such person and in such manner as it may direct, or may order him to be examined with respect to the particulars[24]. If a person fails to comply with any order of the court, it may order him to pay a fine[25].

An order allowing an authorised excuse may make the allowance conditional upon the making of the return and declaration in a modified form or within an extended time, and upon the compliance with such other terms as to the court seem best calculated for carrying into effect the objects of the statutory provisions relating to the matter[26]. Such an order relieves the applicant for the order from any liability or consequences under the provisions governing elections[27] in respect of the matter excused by the order[28]. Where, in the case of a parliamentary, local government or Welsh Assembly election, it is proved to the court by the candidate that any act or omission of the election agent in relation to the return and declarations was without the candidate's sanction or connivance, and that the candidate took all reasonable means for preventing the act or omission, the court must relieve the candidate from the consequences of his election agent's act or omission[29]. For the purposes of a parliamentary, local government or Welsh Assembly election, the date of the order, (or, if conditions and terms are to be complied with, the date at which the applicant fully complies with them) is called, 'the date of the allowance of the excuse'[30].

1   Ie a candidate at a parliamentary or local government election, a European parliamentary election, or a Welsh Assembly election, as the case may be. As to the meaning of 'Assembly election' see PARA 3 note 2. As to the meaning of 'parliamentary election' see PARA 9; and as to the meaning of 'local government election' see PARA 11. As to European parliamentary elections see PARA 217 et seq. As to the meaning of 'candidate' generally see PARA 230. As to the meaning of 'candidate' in relation to a Welsh Assembly election specifically see PARA 230 note 19. At a European parliamentary election, the reference is to an individual candidate: see the European Parliamentary Elections Regulations 2004, SI 2004/293, reg 55(1). As to the meaning of 'individual candidate' in relation to a European parliamentary election see PARA 230 note 32.

2   As to the appointment of election agents generally see PARA 231 et seq.

3   Representation of the People Act 1983 s 86(1); European Parliamentary Elections Regulations 2004, SI 2004/293, reg 55(1); National Assembly for Wales (Representation of the People) Order 2007, SI 2007/236, art 58(1). In the application of this provision to European

Parliamentary elections held in Gibraltar, the reference to a county court, must be read as a reference to the Gibraltar court: see the European Parliamentary Elections Regulations 2004, SI 2004/293, reg 55(8). As to electoral regions constituted for the purposes of European parliamentary elections (including the 'combined region' which includes Gibraltar) see PARA 77.

4   Representation of the People Act 1983 s 86(2); European Parliamentary Elections Regulations 2004, SI 2004/293, reg 55(3); National Assembly for Wales (Representation of the People) Order 2007, SI 2007/236, art 58(3).

5   As to the meaning of 'election expenses' see PARA 269. As to the meaning of 'return as to election expenses' see PARA 281 note 1; and as to the meaning of 'declaration as to election expenses' see PARA 281 note 3.

6   Representation of the People Act 1983 s 86(2)(a) (s 86(2)(a), (b) amended by the Representation of the People Act 1985 s 24, Sch 4 para 30); European Parliamentary Elections Regulations 2004, SI 2004/293, reg 55(3)(a); National Assembly for Wales (Representation of the People) Order 2007, SI 2007/236, art 58(3)(a). As to the requirement to prepare and send returns and declarations as to election expenses where the expenses are authorised by an election agent see PARA 279 et seq; and as to the requirement to prepare and send returns and declarations as to election expenses in relation to an election of parish or community councillors, at which an election agent is not required, see PARA 295. As to a failure to meet the requirements for such financial returns or declarations see PARA 676; and as to a failure to deliver or send such returns or declarations see PARA 677.

7   Representation of the People Act 1983 s 86(2)(b) (as amended: see note 6); European Parliamentary Elections Regulations 2004, SI 2004/293, reg 55(3)(b); National Assembly for Wales (Representation of the People) Order 2007, SI 2007/236, art 58(3)(b).

8   Representation of the People Act 1983 s 86(3)(a); European Parliamentary Elections Regulations 2004, SI 2004/293, reg 55(4)(a); National Assembly for Wales (Representation of the People) Order 2007, SI 2007/236, art 58(4)(a). For an instance see *Re Lloyd George's Application* (1932) 76 Sol Jo 166.

9   For instances of illness of an election agent see *Ipswich Case* (1887) 3 TLR 397, DC; *Re Walworth Election* (1911) Times, 9 February.

10 Representation of the People Act 1983 s 86(3)(b); European Parliamentary Elections Regulations 2004, SI 2004/293, reg 55(4)(b); National Assembly for Wales (Representation of the People) Order 2007, SI 2007/236, art 58(4)(b). As to the nomination of a sub-agent at certain parliamentary and local government elections see PARA 233; in relation to elections to the National Assembly for Wales see PARA 237; and in relation to European parliamentary elections see PARA 241.

11 Representation of the People Act 1983 s 86(3)(d); European Parliamentary Elections Regulations 2004, SI 2004/293, reg 55(4)(d); National Assembly for Wales (Representation of the People) Order 2007, SI 2007/236, art 58(4)(d). For consideration of the meaning of 'inadvertence' and 'reasonable cause of a like nature' see PARAS 691–692. For cases relating to returns and declarations in which relief has been granted see PARA 693.

12 Representation of the People Act 1983 s 86(3); European Parliamentary Elections Regulations 2004, SI 2004/293, reg 55(4); National Assembly for Wales (Representation of the People) Order 2007, SI 2007/236, art 58(4).

13 Representation of the People Act 1983 s 86(3)(a); European Parliamentary Elections Regulations 2004, SI 2004/293, reg 55(4)(a); National Assembly for Wales (Representation of the People) Order 2007, SI 2007/236, art 58(4)(a).

14 Representation of the People Act 1983 s 86(3)(c); European Parliamentary Elections Regulations 2004, SI 2004/293, reg 55(4)(c); National Assembly for Wales (Representation of the People) Order 2007, SI 2007/236, art 58(4)(c).

15 Representation of the People Act 1983 s 86(3)(d); European Parliamentary Elections Regulations 2004, SI 2004/293, reg 55(4)(d); National Assembly for Wales (Representation of the People) Order 2007, SI 2007/236, art 58(4)(d).

16 Representation of the People Act 1983 s 86(3); European Parliamentary Elections Regulations 2004, SI 2004/293, reg 55(4); National Assembly for Wales (Representation of the People) Order 2007, SI 2007/236, art 58(4).

17 Representation of the People Act 1983 s 86(1A) (added by the Representation of the People Act 1985 Sch 4 para 30(a); and amended by the Legal Services Act 2007 s 208(1), Sch 21 paras 48, 49(a)); European Parliamentary Elections Regulations 2004, SI 2004/293, reg 55(2); National Assembly for Wales (Representation of the People) Order 2007, SI 2007/236, art 58(2). In place of the Director of Public Prosecutions, his assistant or any barrister or solicitor (or, at a parliamentary election, authorised person) duly appointed as the Director's representative may attend the hearing and make representations: see the Representation of the People Act 1983 s 86(1A) (as so added and amended); the European Parliamentary Elections

Regulations 2004, SI 2004/293, reg 55(2); and the National Assembly for Wales (Representation of the People) Order 2007, SI 2007/236, art 58(2). For these purposes, 'authorised person' means a person (other than a barrister or solicitor) who, for the purposes of the Legal Services Act 2007, is an authorised person in relation to an activity which constitutes the exercise of a right of audience (within the meaning of that Act: see LEGAL PROFESSIONS vol 65 (2008) PARA 512): Representation of the People Act 1983 s 86(1B) (added by the Legal Services Act 2007 Sch 21 paras 48, 49(b)). Where a person makes an application to the Gibraltar court, references to the Director of Public Prosecutions must be construed as references to the Attorney General for Gibraltar: see the European Parliamentary Elections Regulations 2004, SI 2004/293, reg 55(9). As to the Director of Public Prosecutions see CRIMINAL PROCEDURE vol 27 (2010) PARAS 23, 33 et seq.

18 Ie in the parliamentary constituency or local government area, or in the Assembly constituency or electoral region, or in the European parliamentary electoral region (as the case may be), for which the election was held: see the Representation of the People Act 1983 s 86(4); the European Parliamentary Elections Regulations 2004, SI 2004/293, reg 55(5); and the National Assembly for Wales (Representation of the People) Order 2007, SI 2007/236, art 58(5). As to the meanings of 'Assembly constituency' and 'Assembly electoral region' see PARA 3 note 2; as to the meaning of 'parliamentary constituency' see PARA 9; and as to the meaning of 'local government area' see PARA 33 note 7.

19 Representation of the People Act 1983 s 86(4); European Parliamentary Elections Regulations 2004, SI 2004/293, reg 55(5); National Assembly for Wales (Representation of the People) Order 2007, SI 2007/236, art 58(5).

20 Ie of an individual candidate, for the purposes of a European parliamentary election: see the European Parliamentary Elections Regulations 2004, SI 2004/293, reg 56(1). References to the election agent or sub-agent include a person authorised in writing by the election agent or any sub-agent to incur election expenses: reg 56(4).

21 For the purposes of a Welsh Assembly election, the reference is to a candidate and his election agent at a constituency election or to an individual candidate and his election agent at a regional election: see the National Assembly for Wales (Representation of the People) Order 2007, SI 2007/236, art 59(1). As to the meaning of 'individual candidate' in relation to a Welsh Assembly election see PARA 230 note 19.

22 See note 5.

23 Representation of the People Act 1983 s 87(1); European Parliamentary Elections Regulations 2004, SI 2004/293, reg 56(1); National Assembly for Wales (Representation of the People) Order 2007, SI 2007/236, art 59(1).

24 Representation of the People Act 1983 s 87(2); European Parliamentary Elections Regulations 2004, SI 2004/293, reg 56(2); National Assembly for Wales (Representation of the People) Order 2007, SI 2007/236, art 59(2).

25 Representation of the People Act 1983 s 87(3) (amended by the Representation of the People Act 1985 Sch 4 para 31); European Parliamentary Elections Regulations 2004, SI 2004/293, reg 56(3); National Assembly for Wales (Representation of the People) Order 2007, SI 2007/236, art 59(3). The penalty is a fine not exceeding the amount of the maximum fine to which he would be liable if at the time the order is made he were convicted of a summary offence on conviction of which he was liable to a fine of level 5 on the standard scale: see the Representation of the People Act 1983 s 87(3) (as so amended); the European Parliamentary Elections Regulations 2004, SI 2004/293, reg 56(3); and the National Assembly for Wales (Representation of the People) Order 2007, SI 2007/236, art 59(3). As to the standard scale see SENTENCING AND DISPOSITION OF OFFENDERS vol 92 (2010) PARA 142.

26 Representation of the People Act 1983 s 86(6); European Parliamentary Elections Regulations 2004, SI 2004/293, reg 55(6); National Assembly for Wales (Representation of the People) Order 2007, SI 2007/236, art 58(7). The text refers to the objects of, in relation to a parliamentary or local government election, the Representation of the People Act 1983 Pt II (ss 67–119) (election campaign), or, in relation to a European parliamentary election, the European Parliamentary Elections Regulations 2004, SI 2004/293, Pt 2 (regs 31–81) (election campaign), or, in relation to a Welsh Assembly election, the National Assembly for Wales (Representation of the People) Order 2007, SI 2007/236, Pt 3 (arts 37–85) (election campaign) (see PARA 231 et seq): see the Representation of the People Act 1983 s 86(6); the European Parliamentary Elections Regulations 2004, SI 2004/293, reg 55(6); and the National Assembly for Wales (Representation of the People) Order 2007, SI 2007/236, art 58(7).

27 Ie, in relation to a parliamentary or local government election, the Representation of the People Act 1983, or, in relation to a European parliamentary election, the European Parliamentary Elections Regulations 2004, SI 2004/293, or, in relation to a Welsh Assembly election, the National Assembly for Wales (Representation of the People) Order 2007, SI 2007/236 (see PARA

383): see the Representation of the People Act 1983 s 86(7); the European Parliamentary Elections Regulations 2004, SI 2004/293, reg 55(7); and the National Assembly for Wales (Representation of the People) Order 2007, SI 2007/236, art 58(8).
28 Representation of the People Act 1983 s 86(7); European Parliamentary Elections Regulations 2004, SI 2004/293, reg 55(7); National Assembly for Wales (Representation of the People) Order 2007, SI 2007/236, art 58(8).
29 Representation of the People Act 1983 s 86(5); National Assembly for Wales (Representation of the People) Order 2007, SI 2007/236, art 58(6). As to what those consequences might otherwise be see PARA 901 et seq.
30 Representation of the People Act 1983 s 86(8); National Assembly for Wales (Representation of the People) Order 2007, SI 2007/236, art 58(9). 'Date of the allowance of an authorised excuse' has the meaning given by the Representation of the People Act 1983 s 86(8), or the National Assembly for Wales (Representation of the People) Order 2007, SI 2007/236, art 58(9), accordingly: see the Representation of the People Act 1983 s 118; and the National Assembly for Wales (Representation of the People) Order 2007, SI 2007/236, art 84(1).

689. Relief in respect of returns or declarations as to election expenses at parish or community council elections. If the candidate at an election of parish or community councillors[1] applies to the High Court, an election court or the county court[2] and shows that any failure to make the required return and declaration as to election expenses[3] or either of them, or any error or false statement in them, has arisen by reason of[4]:

(1)   his illness or absence[5]; or

(2)   the absence, death, illness or misconduct of any agent, clerk or officer[6]; or

(3)   inadvertence or any reasonable cause of a like nature[7],

and not by reason of any want of good faith on his part[8], then, after such notice of the application as the court considers fit[9], and on production of such evidence of the grounds stated in the application and of the good faith of the applicant and otherwise, as it considers fit[10], the court may make such order allowing the authorised excuse for the failure, error or false statement as it considers just[11]. An appeal lies to the High Court from any such order made by a county court[12].

1   As to the election of parish or community councillors see PARA 200 et seq. As to elections in the City of London see PARA 33.
2   The jurisdiction vested in the county court as mentioned in the text may be exercised otherwise than in open court: see the Representation of the People Act 1983 s 90(1)(b), Sch 4 para 9(a).
3   As to the duty to make such return and declaration see PARA 295.
4   Representation of the People Act 1983 Sch 4 para 7(1).
5   Representation of the People Act 1983 Sch 4 para 7(1)(a). See also PARA 688.
6   Representation of the People Act 1983 Sch 4 para 7(1)(b).
7   Representation of the People Act 1983 Sch 4 para 7(1)(c). For consideration of the meaning of 'inadvertence' and 'reasonable cause of a like nature' see PARAS 691–692. For cases relating to returns and declarations in which relief has been granted see PARA 693.
8   Representation of the People Act 1983 Sch 4 para 7(1).
9   Representation of the People Act 1983 Sch 4 para 7(1)(i).
10 Representation of the People Act 1983 Sch 4 para 7(1)(ii).
11 Representation of the People Act 1983 Sch 4 para 7(1). The order may make the allowance conditional on compliance with such terms as to the court seem best calculated for carrying into effect the objects of Sch 4 (see PARA 294), and the order relieves the applicant from any liability or consequence under the Representation of the People Act 1983 in respect of the matters excused by the order: Sch 4 para 7(2). The date of the order, or if conditions and terms are to be complied with, the date on which the applicant fully complies with them, is called for this purpose 'the date of the allowance of the excuse': (Sch 4 para 7(3)); and the 'date of the allowance of an authorised excuse' has the meaning given by Sch 4 para 7 accordingly (see s 118).
12 Representation of the People Act 1983 Sch 4 para 9(b). As to appeals to the High Court generally see CIVIL PROCEDURE vol 12 (2009) PARA 1657.

690. Relief in respect of illegal practice, payment, employment or hiring. If any act or omission of any person is likely to constitute an illegal practice, payment, employment or hiring[1], an application for relief may be made in all cases to an election court or to the High Court[2], although an application for relief in respect of payment of a claim for election expenses sent in late, or the payment of such expenses after time[3], may be made to a county court[4].

An applicant for such relief must show to the court by such evidence as to the court seems sufficient[5]:

(1)   that any act or omission of any person otherwise would be, by reason of being in contravention of the provisions that govern elections[6], an illegal practice, payment, employment or hiring[7];

(2)   that the act or omission arose from inadvertence[8], or from accidental miscalculation or from some other reasonable cause[9] of a like nature, and in any case did not arise from any want of good faith[10]; and

(3)   that such notice of the application has been given[11], as to the court seems fit[12].

Where a person makes such an application he must notify the Director of Public Prosecutions of it, and the Director or his assistant or representative may attend at the hearing and make representations at the hearing in respect of it[13]. If, under the circumstances, it seems to the court to be just that either the offender or any other person should not be subject to any of the consequences of the act or omission constituting the offence, the court may make an order allowing the act or omission to be an exception from the statutory provisions making it an illegal practice, payment, employment or hiring, and thereupon no person is subject to any of the consequences of the act or omission[14].

1   There is no relief under this provision in respect of any corrupt practice: *Norwich Case, Birbeck v Bullard* (1886) 4 O'M & H 84, 54 LT 625; *Cheltenham Case, Smythies and Claridge v Mathias, Davies' Case* (1911) 6 O'M & H 194 at 223. As to special provision for relief in the case of failure to make proper returns and declarations as to election expenses see PARA 688.

2   Representation of the People Act 1983 s 167(1); European Parliamentary Elections Regulations 2004, SI 2004/293, reg 108(1); National Assembly for Wales (Representation of the People) Order 2007, SI 2007/236, art 119(1).
     The Representation of the People Act 1983 s 167 has effect for the purposes of local authority referendums, subject to the modifications specified, in relation to Wales, by the Local Authorities (Conduct of Referendums) (Wales) Regulations 2008, SI 2008/1848, reg 8(2), Sch 4 Table 1, and, in relation to England, by the Local Authorities (Conduct of Referendums) (England) Regulations 2012, SI 2012/323, regs 8(2), 11–13, Sch 4 Table 1: see PARA 15 note 2. As to the meaning of 'referendum' see PARA 574 note 2.

3   Ie payments made in contravention of, in relation to a parliamentary or local government election, the Representation of the People Act 1983 s 78(1), (2), or, in relation to a parish or community council election, s 90, Sch 4 para 1, or, in relation to a European parliamentary election, the European Parliamentary Elections Regulations 2004, SI 2004/293, reg 48(1), (2), or, in relation to a Welsh Assembly election, the National Assembly for Wales (Representation of the People) Order 2007, SI 2007/236, art 49(1)–(3) (see PARA 276): see the Representation of the People Act 1983 s 167(1); the European Parliamentary Elections Regulations 2004, SI 2004/293, reg 108(1); and the National Assembly for Wales (Representation of the People) Order 2007, SI 2007/236, art 119(1). As to the meaning of 'Assembly election' see PARA 3 note 2. As to the meaning of 'parliamentary election' see PARA 9; and as to the meaning of 'local government election' see PARA 11. As to European parliamentary elections see PARA 217 et seq.

4   Representation of the People Act 1983 s 167(1); European Parliamentary Elections Regulations 2004, SI 2004/293, reg 108(1); National Assembly for Wales (Representation of the People) Order 2007, SI 2007/236, art 119(1). In the application of this provision to European Parliamentary elections held in Gibraltar, the reference to a county court, must be read as a reference to the Gibraltar court: see the European Parliamentary Elections Regulations 2004, SI 2004/293, reg 108(4)(a). As to electoral regions constituted for the purposes of European parliamentary elections (including the 'combined region' which includes Gibraltar) see PARA 77. As to the procedure on the application see PARAS 696–698.

5	Representation of the People Act 1983 s 167(2); European Parliamentary Elections Regulations 2004, SI 2004/293, reg 108(3); National Assembly for Wales (Representation of the People) Order 2007, SI 2007/236, art 119(3). Mere assertions are insufficient; evidence must be forthcoming: *Ex p Perry* (1884) 48 JP 824, DC; and see *Ex p Haseldine* (1895) 59 JP 71, DC.

6	Ie, in relation to a parliamentary or local government election, the Representation of the People Act 1983, or, in relation to a European parliamentary election, the European Parliamentary Elections Regulations 2004, SI 2004/293, or, in relation to a Welsh Assembly election, the National Assembly for Wales (Representation of the People) Order 2007, SI 2007/236 (see PARA 383): see the Representation of the People Act 1983 s 167(2)(a); the European Parliamentary Elections Regulations 2004, SI 2004/293, reg 108(3)(a); and the National Assembly for Wales (Representation of the People) Order 2007, SI 2007/236, art 119(3)(a).

7	Representation of the People Act 1983 s 167(2)(a); European Parliamentary Elections Regulations 2004, SI 2004/293, reg 108(3)(a); National Assembly for Wales (Representation of the People) Order 2007, SI 2007/236, art 119(3)(a). An application must not be made hypothetically in respect of certain matters if found by the court to be illegal: *Walsall Case* (1892) as cited in Day 76.

8	As to the meaning of 'inadvertence' see PARA 691.

9	For an example of what may constitute reasonable cause see PARA 692.

10	Representation of the People Act 1983 s 167(2)(b); European Parliamentary Elections Regulations 2004, SI 2004/293, reg 108(3)(b); National Assembly for Wales (Representation of the People) Order 2007, SI 2007/236, art 119(3)(b). As examples where an application for relief under the Representation of the People Act 1983 s 167 has been granted see *Re Terry* [2003] All ER (D) 404 (Jul) (although the applicant had made disclosure of all of his breaches only under pressure, relief was granted because the failures had been inadvertent and the court had noted the view of the Director of Public Prosecutions that the breaches had not resulted from any want of good faith); *Finch v Richardson* [2008] EWHC 3067 (QB), [2009] 1 WLR 1338, [2009] All ER (D) 01 (Jan) (evidence indicated that commission of illegal practices in the instant case had been inadvertent and there was no suggestion of any want of good faith).

11	Ie in the parliamentary constituency or area of the authority, in relation to a parliamentary or local government election, or in the European parliamentary electoral region, in relation to a European parliamentary election, or in the Assembly constituency or electoral region, in relation to a Welsh Assembly election, for which the election was held: see the Representation of the People Act 1983 s 167(2)(c); the European Parliamentary Elections Regulations 2004, SI 2004/293, reg 108(3)(c); and the National Assembly for Wales (Representation of the People) Order 2007, SI 2007/236, art 119(3)(c). As to the meaning of 'Assembly constituency' see PARA 3 note 2; and as to the meaning of 'parliamentary constituency' see PARA 9. As to the area of the authority for which a local government election is held see PARA 11.

12	Representation of the People Act 1983 s 167(2)(c); European Parliamentary Elections Regulations 2004, SI 2004/293, reg 108(3)(c); National Assembly for Wales (Representation of the People) Order 2007, SI 2007/236, art 119(3)(c). As to the notice of application for relief see further PARA 696.

13	Representation of the People Act 1983 s 167(1A) (added by the Representation of the People Act 1985 s 24, Sch 4 para 56); European Parliamentary Elections Regulations 2004, SI 2004/293, reg 108(2); National Assembly for Wales (Representation of the People) Order 2007, SI 2007/236, art 119(2). Where a person makes an application to the Gibraltar court, references to the Director of Public Prosecutions must be construed as references to the Attorney General for Gibraltar: see the European Parliamentary Elections Regulations 2004, SI 2004/293, reg 108(4)(b). As to the Director of Public Prosecutions see CRIMINAL PROCEDURE vol 27 (2010) PARAS 23, 33 et seq.

14	Representation of the People Act 1983 s 167(2); European Parliamentary Elections Regulations 2004, SI 2004/293, reg 108(3); National Assembly for Wales (Representation of the People) Order 2007, SI 2007/236, art 119(3). See also *Northumberland, Hexham Division Case, Hudspeth and Lyal v Clayton* (1892) 4 O'M & H 143 at 144.

691. Inadvertence as ground for relief in respect of illegal practice, etc.
'Inadvertence' means negligence or carelessness where the circumstances show an absence of bad faith[1]. Inadvertence may proceed from the applicant not knowing what was done or not knowing that it was wrong[2].

Ignorance of the law may in certain circumstances amount to inadvertence[3]. If a non-qualified person consults a legally qualified person and receives bad advice, he is not to be penalised on that account, but if he acts on the advice of non-qualified persons in the hope that his action is legal and it is not, he is liable to be refused relief for taking the risk[4]. Similarly, relief will be granted if a person is misled by a textbook on election law[5]. If any person, after reading the text of a statute or regulations, fails to understand an obscure or difficult point, he may be relieved, but not if the matter is set out clearly[6]; relief in such cases may be more readily granted where the legislation is new[7]. On the other hand relief granted to a candidate or other person on the ground of ignorance might be refused to an election agent on the ground that it was his duty to acquaint himself with the law[8]. Relief has been granted to an applicant who claimed that he had been misled by his parliamentary experience and had not appreciated that a difference existed between parliamentary and local government election law[9].

The fact that the election contest was severe is not a ground for allowing payments of expenses in excess of the maximum[10]. However, where inadvertence on the part of an election agent was caused mainly by the stressful and unpleasant media attention directed towards her as a result of allegations made against the candidate, relief was granted for a failure on the part of the agent to return a properly-witnessed declaration[11].

1   *Re County Councillors' Elections, De Wette's Case* (1889) 5 TLR 173, DC; *Re County Council Elections, ex p Lenanton, ex p Pierce* (1889) 53 JP 263, DC; *Re Bedwellty Constituency Parliamentary Election, ex p Finch* (1965) 109 Sol Jo 514, 63 LGR 406 (carelessness will not prevent relief being granted provided it does not approach recklessness). See also *Clark v Butcher* [2001] All ER (D) 396 (Nov), QBD (although it was not desirable simply to rely on a returning officer's circular as to the maximum expenses, and the applicants' approach to calculating the maximum expenses and apportionment had been somewhat lacking, the applicants' conduct amounted to nothing more than inadvertence and the respondents had failed to show that there had been a lack of good faith); and *Finch v Richardson* [2008] EWHC 3067 (QB), [2009] 1 WLR 1338, [2009] All ER (D) 01 (Jan) (on the evidence, the commission of the illegal practices in the instant case had been inadvertent and there was no suggestion of any want of good faith; if an illegal practice arose that could occur only as a result of a very high degree of carelessness or negligence, then that might lead to a conclusion that, if committed by professional men as distinguished and experienced as the claimants, then it could not have been by inadvertence, but that was an approach to the facts, not a proposition of law, and it was not the position in the instant case).

2   *Stepney Borough Case, Rushmere v Isaacson* (1892) as reported in 4 O'M & H 178 at 182, Day 116 at 120 per Cave J.

3   *Nichol v Fearby* [1923] 1 KB 480, a decision relating to a failure to make a return of election expenses (see PARA 677). In *Nichol v Fearby* at 498, McCardie J expressed the view that dicta must be deemed overruled which did not allow for ignorance of the law to fall within the word 'inadvertence' (he had earlier cited dicta to such effect in *Walsall Borough Case* (1892) 4 O'M & H 123 at 128 per Pollock B and at 129 per Hawkins J, and in *West Bromwich Case* (1911) 6 O'M & H 256 at 289 per Bucknill J). In *Nichol v Fearby* at 498–499, McCardie J found support for the preferred view that ignorance of the law may amount to inadvertence in *Stepney Borough Case, Rushmere v Isaacson* (1892) as reported in 4 O'M & H 178 at 182, Day 116 at 120 per Cave J; *Southampton Borough Case* (1895) 5 O'M & H 17 at 26 per Bruce J; *West Bromwich Case* at 287 per Ridley J; and *Ex p Caine* (1922) 39 TLR 100, DC. See also *Worcester City Case, ex p Williamson* (1906) 51 Sol Jo 14; *Worcester Borough Case, ex p Caldicote* (1907) 51 Sol Jo 593; *Munro and M'Mullen v Mackintosh* 1920 SC 218; *Smith and Sloan v Mackenzie* 1919 SC 546.

4   *Re School Board Election, ex p Montefiore* (1888) 5 TLR 78, DC; *Re County Councils' Elections, Layton and Woodbridge's Case* (1889) 5 TLR 198, DC; *Re County Councillors Elections, Meason's Case* (1889) 5 TLR 220 at 221, DC; *Rotherhithe Divisional Case, ex p Payne* (1894) Times, 2 November; *Re Widnes Borough and Lancaster County Council Elections, Collins' Application* (1952) 96 Sol Jo 514, 50 LGR 655, DC. In *Re Berry* (1978) Times, 11 February, DC, a candidate at a local government election who had previously been an election agent at two parliamentary elections and had previously been a candidate at a local government election was refused relief for failing to include the name and address of the printer and publisher on election leaflets, but his election agent, who was not so experienced, was granted relief.

5   *Re County Councillors' Elections, Birley's Case* (1889) 5 TLR 220, DC; *Re Preston, Fishwick Ward Councillor, Re Hubberstey* (1899) 43 Sol Jo 826, DC.
6   *Re the Local Government Act 1888, Re the Municipal Elections (Corrupt and Illegal Practices) Act 1884, ex p Walker* (1889) 22 QBD 384, CA.
7   *Stepney Division, Tower Hamlets Case* (1886) 4 O'M & H 34, 37 at 53. See also *Ex p Matthews* (1886) 2 TLR 548, DC (failure to make return of election expenses: see PARAS 653, 660); and see *Shipston-on-Stour RDC Election* (1953) Times, 9 June, DC.
8   *Ex p Polson* (1923) 39 TLR 231; *Re Pole and Scanlon* 1921 SC 98 (cases relating to failure to make a return of election expenses: see PARAS 653, 660). On the other hand it has been stated that it is the candidate's duty to familiarise himself to some extent with election law and not to shut his eyes to it: *Cork, Eastern Division Case* (1911) 6 O'M & H 318 at 360.
9   *Cambridge Borough Case, ex p Hawkins and French* (1899) 44 Sol Jo 102, DC.
10 *Ex p Ayrton* (1885) 2 TLR 214, DC.
11 *Curran v Lord Advocate* 1999 SLT 332, OH.

692.   Other reasonable cause as ground for relief in respect of illegal practice, etc.   A candidate whose express instructions had been disregarded by his election agent has been excused in respect of an excessive expenditure beyond the authorised maximum[1]. Special statutory provision is made by which, in certain cases where there are joint candidates at a local government election, excess election expenses are to be deemed to have arisen from a reasonable cause[2].

1   *Ex p Stopes, Southwark Division Case* (1889) Times, 5 March.
2   See PARA 275.

693.   Applications for relief in respect of illegal practice, etc which have been granted.   Relief has been granted in respect of:
(1)   paid canvassers[1];
(2)   election documents not bearing the name and address of the printer and publisher[2];
(3)   the hiring of committee rooms in premises which are prohibited for the purpose[3]; and
(4)   certain other illegal payments[4].
Relief has also been granted in respect of election expenses incurred in excess of the authorised maximum[5], or paid otherwise than by or through the election agent[6]; in respect of failure to make returns and declarations as to election expenses[7] within the prescribed time[8]; in respect of returns of election expenses which were inaccurate or insufficient[9]; and in respect of failure to send documents required to accompany the return of election expenses[10].

1   *Re County Councillors' Elections, Birley's Case* (1889) 5 TLR 220, DC. Cf *Re County Council Elections, ex p Thomas* (1889) 5 TLR 198, DC; revsd on appeal (1889) 60 LT 728, 5 TLR 234, CA, but on grounds which would no longer apply.
2   *Re Liverpool, Toxteth Division, Election* (1950) Times, 8 March (where the omission of the publisher's name was said to be a venial offence for which relief was granted); *Re Shipston-on-Stour RDC Election* (1953) Times, 9 June; *Re Hambledon RDC Election* (1960) Times, 20 January, DC; *Re Liverpool City Council Election* (1964) Times, 16 May, DC. See also *Re Huntingdon Borough Municipal Election, ex p Clark* (1885) 52 LT 260, DC; *Re County Councillors Elections, Vickerman's Case* (1889) 5 TLR 220, DC; *Re North Camberwell Election* (1910) Times, 15 January; *Cumberland, Cockermouth Division Case* (1901) 5 O'M & H 155; *Re Farringdon Ward Election* (1912) Times, 30 January; *Re County Councillor Elections, Byrch's Case* (1889) 5 TLR 195, DC; *Re County Councillors' Elections, Earl Manvers' Case* (1889) 5 TLR 220, DC; *Re Hailsham Division of Norfolk Election of County Councillors, ex p Ives* (1888) 5 TLR 136, DC; *Ex p Jessel* (1910) Times, 21 January; *Bettesworth v Allingham* (1885) 16 QBD 44, DC. Relief can only be granted to the candidate or election agent and not to the printer or publisher: *Re County Councillors' Elections, De Wette's Case* (1889) 5 TLR 173, DC; *Re County Council Elections, ex p Lenanton, ex p Pierce* (1889) 53 JP 263, DC; but cf *Re Huntingdon Borough Municipal Election, ex p Clark*; *Re Hailsham Division of Norfolk Election of County Councillors, ex p Ives*; and see *Re Terry* [2003] All ER (D) 404 (Jul)

(candidate in a local election published a leaflet which did not display the name and address of the printer or publisher, claiming that the omission had been inadvertent and as a result of his photocopying machine breaking down).

3   *Re Hart* (1885) 2 TLR 24, DC; *Re Terry and Wharton* (1884) 1 TLR 183, DC; *Kesteven, Lincolnshire, Bennington Division Case, ex p Hutchinson* (1888) 5 TLR 136, DC; *Re Whitechapel Election* (1906) Times, 15 February; *Re County Council Elections, ex p Lenanton, ex p Pierce* (1889) 53 JP 263, DC; *Re County Councillors' Elections* (1889) 5 TLR 195, DC; *Ex p Kyd* (1887) 14 TLR 64, DC; *Ex p Hughes* (1900) 45 Sol Jo 79, DC. Relief was refused, however, in *Re School Board Election, ex p Montefiore* (1888) 5 TLR 78, DC; *West Bromwich Case* (1911) 6 O'M & H 256 at 286.

4   *Ex p Caine* (1922) 39 TLR 100; *Ex p Polson* (1923) 39 TLR 231.

5   *Re Wakefield Constituency Parliamentary Election, ex p Harrison* (1966) 110 Sol Jo 708, 64 LGR 383 (young voters not entitled to vote not excluded in computing maximum expenses; see now, however, PARA 273); *Re Bodmin Constituency Parliamentary Election, ex p Bessell* (1966) Times, 7 July (young voters and non-residents not excluded); *Re Bedwellty Constituency Parliamentary Election, ex p Finch* (1965) 109 Sol Jo 514 (number of electors miscalculated); *Re Bristol South East Constituency Parliamentary Election* (1964) Times, 11 December (maximum calculated on basis that it was a county constituency whereas it was in fact a borough constituency). See also *Ex p Ayrton* (1885) 2 TLR 214, DC; *Ex p De Lafontaine* (1914) 78 JP Jo 352, DC; *Ex p Touche* (1915) Times, 28 July, DC; *Ex p Hughes* (1897) 42 Sol Jo 163, DC; and see *Cheltenham Case, Smythies and Claridge v Mathias, Davies' Case* (1911) 6 O'M & H 194 at 199, 223.

6   *Worcester City Case, ex p Williamson* (1906) 51 Sol Jo 14; *Worcester Borough Case, ex p Caldicote* (1907) 51 Sol Jo 593.

7   As to special statutory provisions relating to the granting of relief in the case of such returns and declarations and for the conditions which may be imposed see PARAS 688–689.

8   *Wigan Case* (1885) 2 TLR 159, DC; *Ex p Matthews* (1886) 2 TLR 548, DC; *Ipswich Case* (1887) 3 TLR 397, DC; *Ex p Oake* (1904) Times, 10 August, DC; *Smith v Sloan and Mackenzie* 1919 SC 546; *Munro and M'Mullen v Mackintosh* 1920 SC 218; *Re Pole and Scanlon* 1921 SC 98; *Ex p Polson* (1923) 39 TLR 231 (but see PARA 691); *Nichol v Fearby* [1923] 1 KB 480. See also *Ex p Robson* (1886) 18 QBD 336; *Ex p Pennington* (1898) 46 WR 415, DC (cases where no expenses had been incurred and the candidate had omitted to make a nil return; in *Ex p Robson*, a return and declaration were ordered to be made as a condition of relief).

9   *Plymouth, Drake Division Case* (1929) 7 O'M & H 101 at 110, 129; *York County East Riding, Buckrose Division Case* (1886) 4 O'M & H 110 at 117–119; *Stepney Division, Tower Hamlets Case* (1886) 4 O'M & H 34, 37 at 53; *Norwich Case, Birbeck v Bullard* (1886) 4 O'M & H 84, 54 LT 625; *Finch v Richardson* [2008] EWHC 3067 (QB), [2009] 1 WLR 1338, [2009] All ER (D) 01 (Jan) (use of personal driver, supplied by candidate's employers, to perform tasks, including delivering election address documents to the electorate and a small number of letters, etc, should have been assessed and declared as part of the candidate's expenses return; but, on the evidence, the commission of the illegal practices had been inadvertent and there was no suggestion of any want of good faith).

10   *Clark v Sutherland* 1897 24 R (Ct of Sess) 821, 34 Sc LR 555.

694. Applications for relief in respect of illegal practice, etc which have been refused. Relief has been refused in respect of the payment of a voter's railway fare to enable him to go and vote[1]; in respect of a libellous placard containing an unjustifiable attack on the candidate's opponent[2]; and where the offence was conducted on a considerable scale or was likely to influence the election[3]. It is doubtful if relief would be refused merely because the applicant had committed more than one offence[4].

Relief has been refused where the applicant failed to convince the court that he and his agents had taken all reasonable steps to ensure a proper election campaign and to prevent the commission of illegal practices[5]; where there was a wholesale disregard of election law[6]; and where the evidence on the affidavits was conflicting[7].

1   *Southampton Borough Case* (1895) 5 O'M & H 17 at 25.

2 *Re County Councillors' Elections, De Wette's Case* (1889) 5 TLR 173, DC; and cf *Re County Councillors' Elections, Fenwick's Case* (1889) 5 TLR 220, DC (where a letter was alleged to be scurrilous but was found not to be so by the court and relief was granted).

3 *Re Warwick County, Dunchurch Division, ex p Darlington* (1889) 53 JP 71, DC; *Re Droitwich Elective Auditors' Case, ex p Tolley, ex p Slater* (1907) 71 JP 236, DC.

4 Relief was refused in *Re Ramsgate Town Council, ex p Hobbs* (1889) 5 TLR 272, DC (although this was not the only ground of refusal: see the text and note 7); but relief was allowed in *Stepney Borough Case, Rushmere v Isaacson* (1892) 4 O'M & H 178 at 181 and in *Ex p Polson* (1923) 39 TLR 231. See *West Ham, North Division Case* (1911) 6 O'M & H 392 at 394 per Ridley J ('An irregularity in an account—the court would probably relieve for it. Let it be two and they may relieve for them. But this is a case in which in almost every particular which has been given some error has been committed while other things have never been recognised or thought of at all').

5 *Rochester Borough Case* (1892) 4 O'M & H 156 at 160; *Southampton Borough Case* (1895) 5 O'M & H 17 at 22.

6 *Cork, Eastern Division Case* (1911) 6 O'M & H 318 at 360.

7 *Re Ramsgate Town Council, ex p Hobbs* (1889) 5 TLR 272, DC; *Re Hambleton* (1953) 103 L Jo 703, county court (where the Director of Public Prosecutions stated that there was no reported case of relief being granted if the evidence was contradictory).

695. Time of application for relief in respect of illegal practice, etc. An application for relief in respect of an illegal practice may be made at any time[1]. It may be made before the poll[2], or after the withdrawal of an election petition[3], or when an election petition is threatened[4], or after the issue of a writ claiming penalties[5]. The application must be made promptly after the discovery of the act or omission or it may be refused on the ground of delay[6]. If an election petition has been presented, the court will usually decline to adjudicate upon an application for relief by the successful candidate whose election is questioned by the petition, and the court may either refuse the application or adjourn the hearing until the petition has been heard[7]. In some cases, however, especially where the act complained of is trivial and not likely in itself to have affected the result of the election, the court will be prepared to adjudicate even though the result is that the grant of relief puts an end to the petition[8].

1 As to such applications see PARA 690 et seq.

2 *Ex p Kyd* (1897) 14 TLR 64, DC.

3 *Lichfield Case* (1892) as cited in Day 76.

4 *Re County Councillors' Elections, Stephens' Case* (1889) 5 TLR 203, DC.

5 *Nichol v Fearby* [1923] 1 KB 480.

6 *Re Pembroke County Council Case* (1889) 5 TLR 272, DC; on appeal sub nom *Re Local Government Act 1888, ex p Birtwhistle* (1889) 5 TLR 321, CA.

7 *Ex p Wilks* (1885) 16 QBD 114, DC; *Re County Councils' Elections, Evans' Case* (1889) 5 TLR 206 at 207, DC; *Re County Councillors' Elections, Hempson's Case* (1889) 5 TLR 220, DC.

8 *Ex p Forster* (1903) 89 LT 18, DC.

696. Notice of application for relief. A court may make an order granting relief only after such notice of the application is given as the court considers fit[1]. As well as notice being given to the Director of Public Prosecutions[2], notice should be given to each of the candidates and to the returning officer and there should be public advertisement in newspapers circulating in the area for which the election is held[3]. It is not necessary to give notice by posters[4] but the notice must be given a sufficient time before the application is intended to be made[5]. The notice must give sufficient information as to the relief sought[6]. Less notice is required when relief is asked during the trial of an election petition[7].

1 As to relief with reference to returns and declarations as to election expenses see PARAS 688–689; and as to relief in respect of illegal practice, payment, employment or hiring see PARA 690.

2   See PARA 690.
3   *Salop, Southern or Ludlow Division Case* (1886) 54 LT 129, DC; *Re County Councillors'*
    Elections, De Wette's Case (1889) 5 TLR 173, DC; *Re County Council Elections,*
    ex p Lenanton, ex p Pierce (1889) 53 JP 263, DC.
4   *Ex p Kyd* (1897) 14 TLR 154, DC; but see *Ex p Perry* (1884) 48 JP 824, DC.
5   *Re County Councillors' Elections* (1889) 5 TLR 195, DC.
6   *Ex p Graveson (Re Elections of County Councillors)* (1889) Times, 31 January. Where the
    notice of application given in an advertisement differed from the application itself, it was held
    that the difference did not matter and relief was allowed: *Re Wakefield Constituency*
    Parliamentary Election, ex p Harrison (1966) 110 Sol Jo 708, 64 LGR 383.
7   *Plymouth, Drake Division Case* (1929) 7 O'M & H 101 at 110; *Norwich Case, Birbeck v*
    Bullard (1886) 54 LT 625, 4 O'M & H 84; and see *Hexham Case* (1892) as cited in Day 76;
    Dorsetshire, Eastern Division Case (1911) 6 O'M & H 22 at 23, 28.

**697.   Supporting affidavits in respect of application for relief for illegal
practice, etc.**   Unless an application for relief is made to an election court[1], it
must be supported by affidavit[2]. If there is more than one applicant, there should
be a joint affidavit by all the applicants[3]. The evidence must bring the case
clearly within the statutory provisions[4]. The court will not act on an unsworn
medical certificate that a candidate is too ill to swear an affidavit[5]. A
corroborative affidavit in support of the applicant should also be obtained[6].

1   As to such applications see PARA 690 et seq.
2   *Re County Councillors' Elections, Macdona's Case* (1889) 5 TLR 220, DC. Where an affidavit
    contained errors, a corrected affidavit was required: *Re Wakefield Constituency Parliamentary*
    Election, ex p Harrison (1966) 110 Sol Jo 708, 64 LGR 383.
3   *Re Andrews, Re Streatham Vestry Election* (1899) 68 LJQB 683, DC.
4   *Re Huntingdon Borough Municipal Elections, ex p Clark* (1885) 52 LT 260, 1 TLR 243, DC.
5   *Re County Councillors' Elections, Lord Dinevor's Case* (1889) 5 TLR 220 at 221, DC (where
    the application was adjourned).
6   *Ex p Haseldine* (1895) 59 JP 71, DC.

**698.   Parties and costs in respect of application for relief for illegal practice,
etc.**   On an application for relief[1], a candidate[2], the returning officer[3], or an
elector[4] (or a committee of electors[5]) may appear to consent or oppose. If the
opposition is founded on facts not appearing on evidence filed in support of the
application, the parties opposing should be prepared with affidavits of such
facts[6].

The applicant will in general have to bear the cost of his application[7]. The
applicant may also be ordered to pay the costs of the opposition[8]. A returning
officer will not be awarded his costs if he appears unnecessarily[9].

1   As to such applications see PARA 690 et seq.
2   *Ex p Wilks* (1885) 16 QBD 114, DC.
3   *Essex, South Western Division Case* (1886) 2 TLR 388, DC; *Wigan Case* (1885) 2 TLR
    159, DC.
4   *Wigan Case* (1885) 2 TLR 159, DC; *Kesteven, Lincolnshire, Bennington Division Case,*
    ex p Hutchinson (1888) 5 TLR 136, DC.
5   *Re Ramsgate Town Council, ex p Hobbs* (1889) 5 TLR 272, DC.
6   *Ex p Wilks* (1885) 16 QBD 114, DC.
7   *Stepney Borough Case, Rushmere v Isaacson* (1892) 4 O'M & H 178 at 183. If the respondent
    to an election petition charging illegal practices delays notice of his application for relief until
    the charges have been established before the court, he may have to bear the costs of the trial of
    the charges even though he obtains relief: *Stepney Borough Case, Rushmere v Isaacson* at
    183–184. For a case where an applicant was granted relief by the Court of Appeal on the terms
    of paying the costs of the application to the Divisional Court and the appeal see *Ex p Walker*
    (1889) 22 QBD 384, CA. As to costs see further PARA 870 et seq.
8   Costs were ordered where the application was unduly wide (*Re County Councillors' Elections,*
    ex p Keatinge and Wynn's Case (1889) 5 TLR 195, DC), or where the opposition was in the

public interest (*Ex p Kyd* (1897) 14 TLR 154, DC; *Re Ramsgate Town Council, ex p Hobbs* (1889) 5 TLR 272, DC). See also *Re County Councillors' Elections, Fenwick's Case* (1889) 5 TLR 220, DC; *Re County Councillors' Elections, Gregory and Frost's Case* (1889) 5 TLR 220 at 221, DC; *Kesteven, Lincolnshire, Bennington Division Case, ex p Hutchinson* (1889) 5 TLR 136, DC (where costs were allowed); *Re Local Government Act 1888, ex p Birtwhistle* (1889) 5 TLR 321, CA (where costs were not allowed). Where at the time an application first came before the court it was opposed on the ground that proper notice had not been given but such notice was afterwards given, the court at a subsequent hearing allowed the application and granted costs to the party who had opposed the application at the earlier hearing and had subsequently withdrawn, but it made no other order for costs: *Re Warwick County, Dunchurch Division, ex p Darlington* (1889) 53 JP 71, DC. See also *Ex p Oake* (1904) Times, 10 August, DC (application for relief in proceedings for penalty).

9   *Ex p Stephens* (1889) Times, 2 February.

(iii) Offences which are also Illegal Practices

699.   Offences which also constitute illegal practices. The following summary offences are also deemed to be illegal practices[1]:

(1)   certain voting offences[2];

(2)   broadcasting from outside the United Kingdom with intent to influence a parliamentary, Welsh Assembly or European Parliamentary election[3];

(3)   publishing imitation poll cards at certain elections[4];

(4)   failure of a candidate or election agent to display relevant details on election publications[5].

Dishonest abuses of the franchise, including some illegal practices, have produced findings of general corruption and of personal corruption amounting to electoral fraud (although that term is not used in the legislation)[6].

1   As to abuses of the electoral system that are characterised as 'illegal practices' without being expressly criminalised see PARA 671 et seq.
2   See PARA 700.
3   See PARA 701.
4   See PARA 702.
5   See PARA 703.
6   See PARA 754. As to avoidance of an election by reason of general corruption see PARA 895.

700.   Voting offences which are illegal practices. A person is guilty of an offence constituting an illegal practice[1]:

(1)   if he votes[2] in person or by post, whether as an elector or as proxy, or applies to vote by proxy or by post as elector, at a parliamentary[3] or local government election[4], or elections, or at a Welsh Assembly election or elections, or at a European parliamentary election[5], knowing that he is subject to a legal incapacity[6] to vote at the election (or, as the case may be, at elections) of that kind[7];

(2)   if he applies for the appointment of a proxy to vote for him at any parliamentary or local government election, or elections, or at a Welsh Assembly election or elections, or at any European parliamentary election, knowing that he or the person to be appointed is subject to a legal incapacity to vote at the election (or, as the case may be, at elections) of that kind[8];

(3)   if he votes, whether in person or by post, as proxy for some other person at a parliamentary or local government election, or at a Welsh Assembly election, or at a European parliamentary election, knowing that that person is subject to a legal incapacity to vote[9];

(4)   if he votes as elector otherwise than by proxy: (a) more than once in the same constituency at any parliamentary election or more than once in

the same electoral area at any local government election[10], or more than once in the same Assembly constituency at any Welsh Assembly election, or more than once in the same electoral region[11] at any European Parliamentary election[12]; (b) in more than one constituency at a general election, or in more than one electoral area at an ordinary election of councillors for a local government area[13] which is not a single electoral area, or in more than one Assembly constituency at a Welsh Assembly general election, or in more than one electoral region at a European parliamentary election[14]; or (c) in any constituency at a parliamentary general election, or in any electoral area at an ordinary election of councillors for a local government area which is not a single electoral area, or in any Assembly constituency at a Welsh Assembly election, or in any electoral region at a European parliamentary election, when there is in force an appointment of a person to vote as his proxy at the election in some other such constituency or electoral area[15];

(5)   if he votes as elector in person either: (a) at a parliamentary or local government election, or Welsh Assembly election, or European parliamentary election at which he is entitled to vote by post[16]; or (b) at a parliamentary or local government election, or Welsh Assembly election, or European parliamentary election, knowing that a person appointed to vote as his proxy at the election either has already voted in person or is entitled to vote by post at that election[17];

(6)   if he applies for a person to be appointed as his proxy to vote for him at parliamentary elections in any constituency, or at Assembly elections in any Assembly constituency, or at European parliamentary elections in any electoral region, without applying for the cancellation of a previous appointment of a third person then in force in respect of that or another constituency or that or another electoral region or without withdrawing a pending application for such an appointment in respect of that or another constituency, or that or another electoral region[18];

(7)   if he votes as proxy for the same elector either: (a) more than once in the same constituency at any parliamentary election, or more than once in the same electoral area at any local government election, or more than once in the same Assembly constituency at any Welsh Assembly election, or more than once in the same electoral region at any European parliamentary election[19]; or (b) in more than one constituency at a parliamentary general election, or in more than one electoral area at an ordinary election of councillors for a local government area which is not a single electoral area, or in more than one Assembly constituency at a Welsh Assembly general election, or in more than one electoral region at a European parliamentary election[20];

(8)   if he votes in person as proxy for an elector at a parliamentary or local government, or Welsh Assembly, or European parliamentary election at which he is entitled to vote by post as proxy for that elector[21];

(9)   if he votes in person as proxy for an elector at a parliamentary or local government, or Welsh Assembly, or European parliamentary election knowing that the elector has already voted in person at the election[22];

(10)   if he votes[23] at a parliamentary election in any constituency or at a local government election in any electoral area, or at a Welsh Assembly election[24], or at a European parliamentary election in any electoral

region, as proxy for more than two persons of whom he is not the spouse, civil partner, parent, grandparent, brother, sister, child or grandchild[25];

(11) if he knowingly induces or procures some other person to do an act which is, or but for that other person's want of knowledge would be, an offence by that other person under any of heads (1) to (10) above[26].

The court before which a person is convicted of one of these offences may, however, if the court thinks it just in the special circumstances of the case, mitigate or entirely remit any incapacity for voting[27]. A candidate at a parliamentary, local government, or Welsh Assembly election is not liable, nor is his election avoided, for any such illegal practice of any agent of his other than an offence of knowingly inducing or procuring some other person to do an act which is, or but for that other person's want of knowledge would be, such an illegal practice[28].

If any person votes, or induces or procures any person to vote, at an election under the local government Act[29] which is not a local government election[30], knowing that he or that person is prohibited by any enactment from voting at that election, he is guilty of an illegal practice[31]. A candidate is not, however, liable nor is his election avoided for any such illegal practice committed without his knowledge or consent[32].

1   See the Representation of the People Act 1983 s 61(1), (7); the European Parliamentary Elections Regulations 2004, SI 2004/293, reg 24(1), (8); and the National Assembly for Wales (Representation of the People) Order 2007, SI 2007/236, art 31(2), (9). As to the punishment of illegal practices see PARA 888.
    The Representation of the People Act 1983 s 61 is applied and modified for the purpose of local authority mayoral elections in England and Wales by the Local Authorities (Mayoral Elections) (England and Wales) Regulations 2007, SI 2007/1024, reg 3(2)–(5), Sch 2 Table 1 (see PARA 11 note 14); and the Representation of the People Act 1983 s 61 has effect also for the purposes of local authority referendums, subject to the modifications specified, in relation to Wales, by the Local Authorities (Conduct of Referendums) (Wales) Regulations 2008, SI 2008/1848, reg 8(2), Sch 4 Table 1, and, in relation to England, by the Local Authorities (Conduct of Referendums) (England) Regulations 2012, SI 2012/323, regs 8(2), 11–13, Sch 4 Table 1 (see PARA 15 note 2). As to the meaning of 'referendum' see PARA 574 note 2. For the purposes of extending the rights of relevant citizens of the Union who (subject to the requirement of registration) may vote at European parliamentary elections, and of citizens and nationals of accession states who (subject to the requirement of registration) may vote at local government and European parliamentary elections, the Representation of the People Act 1983 s 61 is applied with modifications: see the Local and European Parliamentary Elections (Registration of Citizens of Accession States) Regulations 2003, SI 2003/1557, reg 2(1), (5). As to the meaning of 'relevant citizen of the Union' for these purposes see PARA 102 note 5.

2   For these purposes, a person who has applied for a ballot paper for the purpose of voting in person, or who has marked, whether validly or not, and returned a ballot paper issued for the purpose of voting by post, is deemed to have voted: Representation of the People Act 1983 s 61(6); European Parliamentary Elections Regulations 2004, SI 2004/293, reg 24(7); National Assembly for Wales (Representation of the People) Order 2007, SI 2007/236, art 31(1). Where, in relation to a Welsh Assembly election, a person is entitled to give two votes in an Assembly constituency (whether in person as elector or by proxy, or by post as elector or by proxy) he votes once in relation to each Assembly election for which his votes are given: art 31(10). As to the meanings of 'Assembly constituency' and 'Assembly election' see PARA 3 note 2. As to the meaning of 'elector' in relation to a parliamentary or local government election see PARA 95 note 2; in relation to a European parliamentary election, see PARA 111 note 4; and, in relation to a Welsh Assembly election, see PARA 110 note 6. As to applications to vote by post or by proxy see PARA 367 et seq.

3   As to the meaning of 'parliamentary election' see PARA 9.

4   As to the meaning of 'local government election' see PARA 11. As to elections in the City of London see PARA 33.

5   As to European parliamentary elections see PARA 217 et seq.

6   For these purposes, references to a person being subject to a legal incapacity to vote do not, in
     relation to things done before polling day at the election or first election for which they are
     done, include his being below voting age if he will be of voting age on that day: Representation
     of the People Act 1983 s 61(1); European Parliamentary Elections Regulations 2004,
     SI 2004/293, reg 24(1); National Assembly for Wales (Representation of the People)
     Order 2007, SI 2007/236, art 31(3). For this purpose, references to legal incapacity to vote at a
     European parliamentary election include incapacity to vote at the kind of election from which
     the entitlement to vote at a European parliamentary election derives: European Parliamentary
     Elections Regulations 2004, SI 2004/293, reg 24(2). 'Voting age' is currently 18 years for all
     purposes: see PARAS 95 note 2, 97 note 14, 102 note 10.
7   Representation of the People Act 1983 s 61(1)(a) (s 61(1), (2) amended by the Representation of
     the People Act 1985 ss 11, 28, Sch 2 para 2, Sch 5); European Parliamentary Elections
     Regulations 2004, SI 2004/293, reg 24(1)(a); National Assembly for Wales (Representation of
     the People) Order 2007, SI 2007/236, art 31(2)(a).
8   Representation of the People Act 1983 s 61(1)(b) (as amended: see note 7); European
     Parliamentary Elections Regulations 2004, SI 2004/293, reg 24(1)(b); National Assembly for
     Wales (Representation of the People) Order 2007, SI 2007/236, art 31(2)(b).
9   Representation of the People Act 1983 s 61(1)(c) (as amended: see note 7); European
     Parliamentary Elections Regulations 2004, SI 2004/293, reg 24(1)(c); National Assembly for
     Wales (Representation of the People) Order 2007, SI 2007/236, art 31(2)(c).
10   As to the meaning of 'parliamentary constituency' see PARA 9; and as to the meaning of
     'electoral area' see PARA 11.
11   As to electoral regions constituted for the purposes of European parliamentary elections
     (including the 'combined region' which includes Gibraltar) see PARA 77.
12   Representation of the People Act 1983 s 61(2)(a)(i); European Parliamentary Elections
     Regulations 2004, SI 2004/293, reg 24(3)(a)(i); National Assembly for Wales (Representation of
     the People) Order 2007, SI 2007/236, art 31(4)(a)(i).
        In the case of Authority elections, head (4) in the text does not have effect; but a person is
     guilty of an offence if he votes as an elector otherwise than by proxy:
     (1)   more than once at the same election of the Mayor of London (Representation of the
            People Act 1983 s 61(2A)(a) (s 61(2A) added by the Greater London Authority
            Act 1999 s 17, Sch 3 paras 1, 10(1), (2)));
     (2)   more than once at the same election of the London members of the London Assembly
            at an ordinary election (Representation of the People Act 1983 s 61(2A)(b) (as so
            added));
     (3)   more than once in the same Assembly constituency at the same election of a
            constituency member of the London Assembly (s 61(2A)(c) (as so added));
     (4)   in more than one Assembly constituency at the same ordinary election (s 61(2A)(d) (as
            so added)); or
     (5)   in any Assembly constituency at an ordinary election, or an election of the Mayor of
            London held under the Greater London Authority Act 1999 s 16 (filling a vacancy in
            the office of London Mayor: see PARA 204), when there is in force an appointment of a
            person to vote as his proxy at the election in some other Assembly constituency
            (Representation of the People Act 1983 s 61(2A)(e) (as so added)).
     As to the meanings of 'Authority constituency' and 'Authority election' see PARA 11.
        A person is guilty of an offence if, on any occasion when elections to the European
     Parliament are held in all the member states under the 1976 Act concerning the election of the
     representatives of the Assembly by direct universal suffrage (OJ L278, 08.10.76, p 5) (the '1976
     Act') (amended and renumbered by Council Decision (EC and Euratom) 2002/772 (OJ L283,
     21.10.2002, p 1)), annexed to Decision (ECSC, EEC and Euratom) 76/787 (OJ L278, 08.10.76,
     p 1)) (see PARA 6), he votes as an elector more than once in those elections, whether in the
     United Kingdom or elsewhere: European Parliamentary Elections Act 2002 s 9(1) (amended by
     SI 2004/1374). The European Parliamentary Elections Act 2002 s 9(1) is without prejudice to
     any enactment relating to voting offences, as applied by regulations under the European
     Parliamentary Elections Act 2002, to elections of members of the European Parliament ('MEPs')
     held in the United Kingdom and Gibraltar: s 9(2) (amended by SI 2004/366). Provisions of the
     Representation of the People Act 1983, as applied by regulations under the European
     Parliamentary Elections Act 2002, have effect in relation to an offence under s 9 as they have
     effect in relation to an offence under the Representation of the People Act 1983 s 61(2); in
     particular, s 61(7) (see the text and notes 27–28) and s 178 (prosecution of offences committed
     outside the United Kingdom: see PARA 885) apply: see the European Parliamentary Elections
     Act 2002 s 9(3), (4). As to the meaning of 'United Kingdom' see PARA 1 note 1.
13   As to the meaning of 'local government area' see PARA 33 note 7.

14 Representation of the People Act 1983 s 61(2)(a)(ii); European Parliamentary Elections Regulations 2004, SI 2004/293, reg 24(3)(a)(ii); National Assembly for Wales (Representation of the People) Order 2007, SI 2007/236, art 31(4)(a)(ii). In the case of Authority elections see note 12. As to Welsh Assembly general elections see PARA 12 et seq.

15 Representation of the People Act 1983 s 61(2)(a)(iii); European Parliamentary Elections Regulations 2004, SI 2004/293, reg 24(3)(a)(iii); National Assembly for Wales (Representation of the People) Order 2007, SI 2007/236, art 31(4)(a)(iii). In relation to European parliamentary elections, head (4)(c) in the text applies when there is in force an appointment of a person to vote as an elector's proxy at the election in respect of an address other than the address by virtue of which he votes as elector: see the European Parliamentary Elections Regulations 2004, SI 2004/293, reg 24(3)(a)(iii). In the case of Authority elections see note 12.

16 Representation of the People Act 1983 s 61(2)(b); European Parliamentary Elections Regulations 2004, SI 2004/293, reg 24(3)(b); National Assembly for Wales (Representation of the People) Order 2007, SI 2007/236, art 31(4)(b).

In relation to a parliamentary or local government election, a person is not guilty of an offence under head (5)(a) in the text only by reason of his having marked a tendered ballot paper in pursuance of the Representation of the People Act 1983 s 23(1), Sch 1 r 40(1ZC), (1ZE) (see PARA 403): see s 61(6A) (added by the Electoral Administration Act 2006 s 38(3)). In relation to a European parliamentary election, a person is not guilty of an offence under head (5)(a) in the text only by reason of his having marked a tendered ballot paper in pursuance of the European Parliamentary Elections Regulations 2004, SI 2004/293, reg 44(4) or reg 44(6) (see PARA 403): see reg 24(7A) (added by SI 2009/186). In relation to a Welsh Assembly election, a person is not guilty of an offence under head (5)(a) in the text only by reason of his having marked a tendered ballot paper in pursuance of the National Assembly for Wales (Representation of the People) Order 2007, SI 2007/236, Sch 5 para 49(4) or Sch 5 para 49(6) (see PARA 403): see art 31(8).

17 Representation of the People Act 1983 s 61(2)(c); European Parliamentary Elections Regulations 2004, SI 2004/293, reg 24(3)(c); National Assembly for Wales (Representation of the People) Order 2007, SI 2007/236, art 31(4)(c).

18 Representation of the People Act 1983 s 61(2)(d) (as amended: see note 7); European Parliamentary Elections Regulations 2004, SI 2004/293, reg 24(3)(d); National Assembly for Wales (Representation of the People) Order 2007, SI 2007/236, art 31(4)(d).

19 Representation of the People Act 1983 s 61(3)(a)(i); European Parliamentary Elections Regulations 2004, SI 2004/293, reg 24(4)(a)(i); National Assembly for Wales (Representation of the People) Order 2007, SI 2007/236, art 31(5)(a)(i).

In the case of Authority elections, head (7) in the text does not have effect; but a person is guilty of an offence if he votes as proxy for the same elector:

(1) more than once at the same election of the Mayor of London (Representation of the People Act 1983 s 61(3A)(a) (s 61(3A) added by the Greater London Authority Act 1999 Sch 3 paras 1, 10(1), (3)));

(2) more than once at the same election of the London members of the London Assembly at an ordinary election (Representation of the People Act 1983 s 61(3A)(b) (as so added));

(3) more than once in the same Assembly constituency at the same election of a constituency member of the London Assembly (s 61(3A)(c) (as so added)); or

(4) in more than one Assembly constituency at the same ordinary election (s 61(3A)(d) (as so added)).

20 Representation of the People Act 1983 s 61(3)(a)(ii); European Parliamentary Elections Regulations 2004, SI 2004/293, reg 24(4)(a)(ii); National Assembly for Wales (Representation of the People) Order 2007, SI 2007/236, art 31(5)(a)(ii). In the case of Authority elections see note 19.

21 Representation of the People Act 1983 s 61(3)(b); European Parliamentary Elections Regulations 2004, SI 2004/293, reg 24(4)(b); National Assembly for Wales (Representation of the People) Order 2007, SI 2007/236, art 31(5)(b).

In relation to a parliamentary or local government election, a person is not guilty of an offence under head (8) in the text only by reason of his having marked a tendered ballot paper in pursuance of Sch 1 r 40(1ZC), (1ZE) (see PARA 403): see s 61(6A) (as added: see note 16). In relation to a European parliamentary election, a person is not guilty of an offence under head (8) in the text only by reason of his having marked a tendered ballot paper in pursuance of the European Parliamentary Elections Regulations 2004, SI 2004/293, reg 44(4) or reg 44(6) (see PARA 403): see reg 24(7A) (as added: see note 16). In relation to a Welsh Assembly election, a person is not guilty of an offence under head (8) in the text only by reason of his having marked a tendered ballot paper in pursuance of the National Assembly for Wales (Representation of the People) Order 2007, SI 2007/236, Sch 5 para 49(4) or Sch 5 para 49(6) (see PARA 403): see art 31(8).

22   Representation of the People Act 1983 s 61(3)(d); European Parliamentary Elections Regulations 2004, SI 2004/293, reg 24(4)(c); National Assembly for Wales (Representation of the People) Order 2007, SI 2007/236, art 31(5)(c).

23   For the purposes of this offence, a previous application made in circumstances which entitle the applicant only to mark a tendered ballot paper must, if he does not exercise that right, be disregarded: see the Representation of the People Act 1983 s 61(6); European Parliamentary Elections Regulations 2004, SI 2004/293, reg 24(7); National Assembly for Wales (Representation of the People) Order 2007, SI 2007/236, art 31(1). As to the marking of tendered ballot papers see PARA 403.

24   Ie, in the case of a Welsh Assembly general election, at constituency elections in Assembly constituencies in an Assembly electoral region (or in one such election) or, in the case of a constituency election other than at an Assembly general election, at a constituency election, or at a regional election (whether or not at an Assembly general election): see the National Assembly for Wales (Representation of the People) Order 2007, SI 2007/236, art 31(6). As to the meanings of 'constituency election' and 'regional election' see PARA 3 note 2.

25   Representation of the People Act 1983 s 61(4) (amended by the Representation of the People Act 1985 Sch 2 para 2; and by the Civil Partnership Act 2004 s 261(1), Sch 27 para 83); European Parliamentary Elections Regulations 2004, SI 2004/293, reg 24(5) (amended by SI 2005/2114); National Assembly for Wales (Representation of the People) Order 2007, SI 2007/236, art 31(6).

26   Representation of the People Act 1983 s 61(5); European Parliamentary Elections Regulations 2004, SI 2004/293, reg 24(6); National Assembly for Wales (Representation of the People) Order 2007, SI 2007/236, art 31(7).

27   Representation of the People Act 1983 s 61(7)(a); European Parliamentary Elections Regulations 2004, SI 2004/293, reg 24(8); National Assembly for Wales (Representation of the People) Order 2007, SI 2007/236, art 31(9)(a). As to the incapacities imposed as mentioned in the text see PARAS 905–909; and as to mitigation and remission of incapacities so imposed see PARA 910.

28   Representation of the People Act 1983 s 61(7)(b); National Assembly for Wales (Representation of the People) Order 2007, SI 2007/236, art 31(9)(b). The text refers to an offence under head (11) in the text.

29   As to the meaning of 'election under the local government Act' see PARA 11 note 2.

30   An election under the local government Act which is not a local government election will include eg the election of the chairman of a county or district council. For this purpose it also includes a poll consequent on a parish or community meeting: Parish and Community Meetings (Polls) Rules 1987, SI 1987/1, r 6(a). See also PARA 10.

31   Representation of the People Act 1983 s 189(1).

32   Representation of the People Act 1983 s 189(2).

701.   Contravention of prohibition on broadcasting from outside United Kingdom with intent to influence certain elections.   An offence relating to the prohibition imposed on broadcasting from outside the United Kingdom with intent to influence elections[1] is an illegal practice[2]. The court before which a person is convicted of such an offence may, however, if it thinks it just in the special circumstances of the case, mitigate or entirely remit any incapacity which may be so imposed[3].

Where any act or omission of an association or body of persons, corporate or unincorporate, is an illegal practice under these provisions, any person who at the time of the act or omission was a director, general manager, secretary or other similar officer of the association or body, or was purporting to act in any such capacity, is deemed to be guilty of the illegal practice[4], unless he proves: (1) that the act or omission took place without his consent or connivance[5]; and (2) that he exercised all such diligence to prevent the commission of the illegal practice as he ought to have exercised having regard to the nature of his functions in that capacity and to all the circumstances[6].

1   Ie, in relation to a parliamentary election, under the Representation of the People Act 1983
    s 92(1), or, in relation to a European parliamentary election, under the European Parliamentary
    Elections Regulations 2004, SI 2004/293, reg 64(1), or, in relation to a Welsh Assembly election,
    under the National Assembly for Wales (Representation of the People) Order 2007,
    SI 2007/236, art 66(1) (see PARA 331): see the Representation of the People Act 1983 s 92(2);
    the European Parliamentary Elections Regulations 2004, SI 2004/293, reg 64(2); and the
    National Assembly for Wales (Representation of the People) Order 2007, SI 2007/236,
    art 66(2). As to the meaning of 'United Kingdom' see PARA 1 note 1. As to the meaning of
    'Assembly election' see PARA 3 note 2. As to the meaning of 'parliamentary election' see PARA 9;
    and as to the meaning of 'local government election' see PARA 11. As to European parliamentary
    elections see PARA 217 et seq. As to elections in the City of London see PARA 33.
        The Representation of the People Act 1983 s 92(2), (3) has effect for the purposes of local
    authority referendums, subject to the modifications specified, in relation to Wales, by the Local
    Authorities (Conduct of Referendums) (Wales) Regulations 2008, SI 2008/1848, reg 8(2), Sch 4
    Table 1, and, in relation to England, by the Local Authorities (Conduct of Referendums)
    (England) Regulations 2012, SI 2012/323, regs 8(2), 11–13, Sch 4 Table 1: see PARA 15 note 2.
    As to the meaning of 'referendum' see PARA 574 note 2.
2   Representation of the People Act 1983 s 92(2); European Parliamentary Elections
    Regulations 2004, SI 2004/293, reg 64(2); National Assembly for Wales (Representation of the
    People) Order 2007, SI 2007/236, art 66(2). As to the punishment of illegal practices see PARA
    888.
3   Representation of the People Act 1983 s 92(2); European Parliamentary Elections
    Regulations 2004, SI 2004/293, reg 64(2); National Assembly for Wales (Representation of the
    People) Order 2007, SI 2007/236, art 66(2). As to the incapacities which may be imposed see
    PARA 901 et seq. As to the court's general power to mitigate or remit incapacities see PARA 910.
4   Representation of the People Act 1983 s 92(3); European Parliamentary Elections
    Regulations 2004, SI 2004/293, reg 64(3); National Assembly for Wales (Representation of the
    People) Order 2007, SI 2007/236, art 66(3).
5   Representation of the People Act 1983 s 92(3)(a); European Parliamentary Elections
    Regulations 2004, SI 2004/293, reg 64(3)(a); National Assembly for Wales (Representation of
    the People) Order 2007, SI 2007/236, art 66(3)(a).
6   Representation of the People Act 1983 s 92(3)(b); European Parliamentary Elections
    Regulations 2004, SI 2004/293, reg 64(3)(b); National Assembly for Wales (Representation of
    the People) Order 2007, SI 2007/236, art 66(3)(b).

**702.   Contravention of prohibition on issuing imitation poll cards at certain
elections.**   No person, for the purpose of promoting or procuring the election of
any candidate[1] at a parliamentary[2], or European parliamentary[3], or Welsh
Assembly election[4], or at certain local government elections[5], may issue any poll
card or document so closely resembling an official poll card as to be calculated to
deceive[6]; and an offence under this provision is an illegal practice[7]. The court
before which a person is convicted of such an offence may, however, if it thinks it
just in the special circumstances of the case, mitigate or entirely remit any
incapacity which may be so imposed[8].

Where any act or omission of an association or body of persons, corporate or
unincorporate, is an illegal practice under these provisions, any person who at
the time of the act or omission was a director, general manager, secretary or
other similar officer of the association or body, or was purporting to act in any
such capacity, is deemed to be guilty of an illegal practice[9], unless he proves:
(1) that the act or omission took place without his consent or connivance[10]; and
(2) that he exercised all such diligence to prevent the commission of the illegal
practice as he ought to have exercised having regard to the nature of his
functions in that capacity and to all the circumstances[11].

1   As to the meaning of 'candidate' for this purpose see PARA 230. As to the meaning of references
    to promoting or procuring a candidate's election see PARA 269 note 4.
2   As to the meaning of 'parliamentary election' see PARA 9.
3   Ie for the purpose of promoting or procuring the election of a registered party or any individual
    candidate at a European parliamentary election: see the European Parliamentary Elections

Regulations 2004, SI 2004/293, reg 66. As to the meaning of 'registered party' see PARA 230 note 29; and as to the meaning of 'individual candidate' see PARA 230 note 32. As to European parliamentary elections see PARA 217 et seq.

4 Ie for the purpose of promoting or procuring a particular result at a Welsh Assembly election: see the National Assembly for Wales (Representation of the People) Order 2007, SI 2007/236, art 68. As to the meaning of 'Assembly election' see PARA 3 note 2.

5 The Representation of the People Act 1983 s 94 applies to any local government election in relation to which rules made under s 36 (see PARA 383) require an official poll card to be sent to electors in a form prescribed by the rules: s 94(2) (s 94(1) renumbered and amended, s 94(2) added, by the Representation of the People Act 1985 s 24, Sch 4 para 36). As to the issue of official poll cards for these purposes see PARA 389. As to the meaning of 'local government election' generally see PARA 11. As to elections in the City of London see PARA 33.

The Representation of the People Act 1983 s 94 is applied and modified for the purpose of local authority mayoral elections in England and Wales by the Local Authorities (Mayoral Elections) (England and Wales) Regulations 2007, SI 2007/1024, reg 3(2)–(5), Sch 2 Table 1 (see PARA 11 note 14); and the Representation of the People Act 1983 s 94 has effect for the purposes of local authority referendums, subject to the modifications specified, in relation to Wales, by the Local Authorities (Conduct of Referendums) (Wales) Regulations 2008, SI 2008/1848, reg 8(2), Sch 4 Table 1, and, in relation to England, by the Local Authorities (Conduct of Referendums) (England) Regulations 2012, SI 2012/323, regs 8(2), 11–13, Sch 4 Table 1 (see PARA 15 note 2). As to the meaning of 'referendum' see PARA 574 note 2.

6 Representation of the People Act 1983 s 94(1) (as renumbered and amended: see note 5); European Parliamentary Elections Regulations 2004, SI 2004/293, reg 66; National Assembly for Wales (Representation of the People) Order 2007, SI 2007/236, art 68.

7 Representation of the People Act 1983 s 92(2) (applied by s 94(1) (as renumbered and amended: see note 5)); European Parliamentary Elections Regulations 2004, SI 2004/293, reg 64(2) (applied by reg 66); National Assembly for Wales (Representation of the People) Order 2007, SI 2007/236, art 66(2) (applied by art 68). As to the consequences of illegal practices see PARA 888 et seq.

8 Representation of the People Act 1983 s 92(2) (applied by s 94(1) (as renumbered and amended: see note 5)); European Parliamentary Elections Regulations 2004, SI 2004/293, reg 64(2) (applied by reg 66); National Assembly for Wales (Representation of the People) Order 2007, SI 2007/236, art 66(2) (applied by art 68). As to those incapacities see PARA 901 et seq. As to the courts' power to mitigate or remit incapacities see PARA 910.

9 Representation of the People Act 1983 s 92(3) (applied by s 94(1) (as renumbered and amended: see note 5)); European Parliamentary Elections Regulations 2004, SI 2004/293, reg 64(3) (applied by reg 66); National Assembly for Wales (Representation of the People) Order 2007, SI 2007/236, art 66(3) (applied by art 68).

10 Representation of the People Act 1983 s 92(3)(a) (applied by s 94(1) (as renumbered and amended: see note 5)); European Parliamentary Elections Regulations 2004, SI 2004/293, reg 64(3)(a) (applied by reg 66); National Assembly for Wales (Representation of the People) Order 2007, SI 2007/236, art 66(3)(a) (applied by art 68).

11 Representation of the People Act 1983 s 92(3)(b) (applied by s 94(1) (as renumbered and amended: see note 5)); European Parliamentary Elections Regulations 2004, SI 2004/293, reg 64(3)(b) (applied by reg 66); National Assembly for Wales (Representation of the People) Order 2007, SI 2007/236, art 66(3)(b) (applied by art 68).

703. Failure of candidate or election agent to comply with requirements in relation to election publications. In relation to a parliamentary or local government election[1], where any material which can reasonably be regarded as intended to promote or procure[2] the election of a candidate[3] (whether or not it can be so regarded as intended to achieve any other purpose as well) is published in contravention of the requirements which apply to such material[4], a candidate or his election agent[5] who would otherwise be guilty of an offence[6] is guilty of an illegal practice instead[7].

Where a candidate or his election agent, either at a Welsh Assembly constituency or regional election[8], or at a European parliamentary election[9], contravenes the statutory requirement for relevant details to be included in published election material[10], he is guilty of an illegal practice[11].

1   As to the meaning of 'parliamentary election' see PARA 9; and as to the meaning of 'local government election' see PARA 11.
2   As to the meaning of the words 'promoting or procuring' see PARA 272 note 2.
3   As to the meaning of 'candidate' generally see PARA 230.
4   Ie in contravention of the restrictions contained in the Representation of the People Act 1983 s 110(2) (see PARA 748): see s 110(12) (s 110 substituted by the Political Parties, Elections and Referendums Act 2000 s 138, Sch 18 paras 1, 14).
    The Representation of the People Act 1983 s 110 is applied and modified for the purposes of local authority referendums, subject to the modifications specified, in relation to Wales, by the Local Authorities (Conduct of Referendums) (Wales) Regulations 2008, SI 2008/1848, reg 8(2), Sch 4 Table 1, and, in relation to England, by the Local Authorities (Conduct of Referendums) (England) Regulations 2012, SI 2012/323, regs 8(2), 11–13, Sch 4 Table 1: see PARA 15 note 2. As to the meaning of 'referendum' see PARA 574 note 2.
5   As to the appointment of an election agent for parliamentary and local government elections see PARA 231.
6   Ie who, apart from the Representation of the People Act 1983 s 110(12), would be guilty of an offence under s 110(9) as the promoter of the material, the person by whom the material is published or the printer of the material or under s 110(10) as the promoter of the material or the person by whom the material is published (see PARA 748): see s 110(12) (as substituted: see note 4).
7   Representation of the People Act 1983 s 110(12) (as substituted: see note 4). As to the effect of this provision see PARA 748. As to the consequences of illegal practices see PARA 888 et seq.
8   As to the meanings of 'constituency election' and 'regional election' see PARA 3 note 2. At a Welsh Assembly election, the reference is to:
    (1)   a constituency candidate, or an individual candidate, or his election agent (National Assembly for Wales (Representation of the People) Order 2007, SI 2007/236, art 76(12)(a));
    (2)   a party list candidate, or the election agent of the registered political party in relation to that party's list (art 76(12)(b)).
    As to the meanings of 'candidate', 'constituency candidate' and 'individual candidate' for these purposes see PARA 230 note 19; and as to the meanings of 'party list', 'party list candidate' and 'registered political party' see PARA 230 note 23. As to the appointment of an election agent for elections to the National Assembly for Wales see PARA 235.
9   As to European parliamentary elections see PARA 217 et seq; and as to the appointment of the election agent of a registered party or for an individual candidate at a European parliamentary election see PARA 239.
10 Ie, in relation to a European parliamentary election, the European Parliamentary Elections Regulations 2004, SI 2004/293, reg 74(7), or, in relation to a Welsh Assembly election, the National Assembly for Wales (Representation of the People) Order 2007, SI 2007/236, art 76(9), (10), contravention of which is an offence (see PARA 748): see the European Parliamentary Elections Regulations 2004, SI 2004/293, reg 74(9) (reg 74 substituted by SI 2009/186); and the National Assembly for Wales (Representation of the People) Order 2007, SI 2007/236, art 76(12).
11 European Parliamentary Elections Regulations 2004, SI 2004/293, reg 74(9) (as substituted: see note 10); National Assembly for Wales (Representation of the People) Order 2007, SI 2007/236, art 76(12).

(iv) Corrupt Practices

A. IN GENERAL

704. Practices which are corrupt. The following are corrupt practices[1]:
(1)   making false statements in support of the nomination of candidates at elections[2];
(2)   issuing false certificates authorising a description to be used by a candidate at an election[3];
(3)   incurring certain expenses without the authorisation of the election agent[4];
(4)   making a false declaration as to such expenses[5];
(5)   making a false declaration as to election expenses[6];

(6)   bribery[7];
(7)   treating[8];
(8)   undue influence[9].

Some indictable offences may also constitute corrupt practices[10].

The term 'corrupt practices' is not defined in the legislation, and must be construed as being confined to those practices which are expressly declared to be corrupt practices on the face of the statute[11]. Corrupt practices are the most serious electoral offences and the electoral consequences for a candidate or for others of being found guilty of corrupt practices are more significant than those relating to illegal practices[12]. Dishonest abuses of the franchise, including but not limited to corrupt practices, have produced findings of general corruption and of personal corruption amounting to electoral fraud[13].

1   As to the consequences of corrupt practices see PARA 887 et seq.
2   See PARA 705.
3   See PARA 706.
4   See PARA 707.
5   See PARA 707.
6   See PARA 708.
7   See PARA 709 et seq.
8   See PARAS 721–722.
9   See PARAS 723–728.
10 As to abuses of the electoral system which are expressly criminalised and also characterized as corrupt practices see PARA 729 et seq.
11 *Re Central Ward, Slough Election Petition, Simmons v Khan* [2008] EWHC B4 (QB), Election Ct, at [16]–[23] per Commissioner Mawrey QC.
12 *Re Central Ward, Slough Election Petition, Simmons v Khan* [2008] EWHC B4 (QB), Election Ct, at [16]–[23] per Commissioner Mawrey QC. As to illegal practices see PARA 671 et seq.
13 See PARA 754. As to avoidance of an election by reason of general corruption see PARA 895.

705.   Making false statements in connection with the nomination of candidates at elections.   A person is guilty of a corrupt practice[1] if, at any parliamentary election[2] or any local government election[3], or at any Welsh Assembly[4], or European parliamentary election[5], he causes or permits to be included in a document delivered or otherwise furnished to a returning officer[6] for use in connection with the election[7]:

(1)   a statement of the name or home address of a candidate[8] at the election which he knows to be false in any particular[9]; or

(2)   (except in the case of a European parliamentary election) anything which purports to be the signature of an elector[10] who proposes, seconds or assents to, the nomination of such a candidate, or a person who subscribes a nomination paper[11], as the case may be, but which he knows: (a) was not written by the elector or person by whom it purports to have been written[12]; or (b) if written by that elector or person, was not written by him for the purpose of signifying that he was proposing, seconding, or assenting to, that candidate's nomination, or, as the case may be, for the purpose of subscribing that nomination paper[13].

In relation to a parliamentary or Welsh Assembly election, a person is also guilty of a corrupt practice if he causes or permits to be included in a document delivered or otherwise furnished to a returning officer for use in connection with the election:

(i)   a certificate authorising[14] the use by a candidate[15] of a description if he knows that the candidate is standing in another election[16] in which the poll is to be held on the same day as the poll at the election to which the certificate relates[17]; or (ii)　in relation to a parliamentary election only, a statement in a home address form[18], regarding the constituency within which that address is situated (or, if that address is outside the United Kingdom[19], the country within which it is situated), which he knows to be false in any particular[20].

A person is guilty of a corrupt practice if he makes in any document in which he gives his consent to his nomination as a candidate[21]:

(A)　a statement of his date of birth[22]; or

(B)　a statement as to his qualification for being elected at that election[23]; or

(C)　a statement, except in the case of a European parliamentary election, that he is not a candidate at another election[24], the poll for which is to be held on the same day as the poll at the election to which the consent relates[25],

which he knows to be false in any particular[26].

1　As to the consequences of corrupt practices see PARA 887 et seq.

2　See the Representation of the People Act 1983 s 65A(2)(a) (s 65A added by the Representation of the People Act 2000 s 15(1), Sch 6 paras 3, 5). As to the meaning of 'parliamentary election' see PARA 9.

3　Ie, except for the purposes of the Representation of the People Act 1983 s 65A(1)(c) (see the text and notes 14–16) and s 65(1A)(c) (see the text and notes 24–25), any local government election in England and Wales: see s 65A(2)(b) (s 65A as added (see note 2); s 65A(2)(b) amended by the Electoral Administration Act 2006 s 23(1), (4)). As to the meanings of 'England' and 'Wales' see PARA 1 note 1. As to the meaning of 'local government election' generally see PARA 11. As to elections in the City of London see PARA 33.

4　As to the meaning of 'Assembly election' see PARA 3 note 2.

5　As to European parliamentary elections see PARA 217 et seq.

6　As to returning officers see PARA 350 et seq.

7　See the Representation of the People Act 1983 s 65A(1), (2) (as added: see note 2); European Parliamentary Elections Regulations 2004, SI 2004/293, reg 27; National Assembly for Wales (Representation of the People) Order 2007, SI 2007/236, art 34(1).

8　As to the meaning of 'candidate' generally see PARA 230. As to the meaning of 'candidate' in relation to a Welsh Assembly election specifically see PARA 230 note 19.

9　Representation of the People Act 1983 s 65A(1)(a) (as added: see note 2); European Parliamentary Elections Regulations 2004, SI 2004/293, reg 27; National Assembly for Wales (Representation of the People) Order 2007, SI 2007/236, art 34(1)(a).

　　In *R v Duffy* (1994) 15 Cr App Rep (S) 677, CA (which pre-dated the offence set out in the text), a failure to perfect the consent to nomination form was held to be essentially a technical offence and, even where that failure formed part of a reprehensible plan, the Court of Appeal declined to use it as a peg on which to criminalise the behaviour; the facts of the case disclosed that a candidate had arranged for a fellow candidate's nomination in order to split his opponent's vote but that the latter's consent to nomination form had contained defects which were not necessary to the mischievous purpose (the candidate's signature had not been witnessed properly and the address given had related to the accused rather than to the candidate); and it was held that the conduct, however reprehensible, was permissible under the law as it stood and that the judge at first instance had erred in giving a custodial sentence on the basis that the irregularity amounted to a fraud on the electorate when a substantial financial penalty would have been more appropriate.

10　As to the meaning of 'elector' in relation to a parliamentary or local government election see PARA 95 note 2; and, in relation to a Welsh Assembly election, see PARA 110 note 6.

11　Representation of the People Act 1983 s 65A(1)(b) (as added: see note 2); National Assembly for Wales (Representation of the People) Order 2007, SI 2007/236, art 34(1)(b). As to the nomination of candidates at parliamentary and local government elections see PARA 224 et seq.

12　Representation of the People Act 1983 s 65A(1)(b)(i) (as added: see note 2); National Assembly for Wales (Representation of the People) Order 2007, SI 2007/236, art 34(1)(b)(i).

13　Representation of the People Act 1983 s 65A(1)(b)(ii) (as added: see note 2); National Assembly for Wales (Representation of the People) Order 2007, SI 2007/236, art 34(1)(b)(ii).

14　Ie for the purposes of the Representation of the People Act 1983 s 23(1), Sch 1 r 6A, in relation to a parliamentary election, or for the purposes of the National Assembly for Wales (Representation of the People) Order 2007, SI 2007/236, Sch 5 para 5, in relation to a Welsh

Assembly constituency election, or Sch 5 para 8, in the case of a Welsh Assembly regional election (see PARAS 256, 706): see the Representation of the People Act 1983 s 65A(1)(c) (s 65A as added (see note 2); s 65A(1)(c) added by the Electoral Administration Act 2006 s 23(1), (2)); and the National Assembly for Wales (Representation of the People) Order 2007, SI 2007/236, art 34(1)(c), (d). As to the meanings of 'constituency election' and 'regional election' see PARA 3 note 2.

15 Ie the use by:
(1)   a candidate at a parliamentary election (see the Representation of the People Act 1983 s 65A(1)(c) (as added: see note 14));
(2)   a constituency candidate at an Assembly constituency election (see the National Assembly for Wales (Representation of the People) Order 2007, SI 2007/236, art 34(1)(c));
(3)   a registered political party at an Assembly regional election (see art 34(1)(d)).
As to the meanings of 'constituency candidate' and 'individual candidate' see PARA 230 note 19; and as to the meaning of 'registered political party' see PARA 230 note 23.

16 Ie if he knows that:
(1)   the candidate is standing at a parliamentary election in another constituency (see the Representation of the People Act 1983 s 65A(1)(c) (as added: see note 14));
(2)   the candidate is a candidate in another Assembly constituency election (see the National Assembly for Wales (Representation of the People) Order 2007, SI 2007/236, art 34(1)(c));
(3)   a candidate on that registered political party's list of candidates at an Assembly regional election is also an individual candidate or a party list candidate for another registered political party at that Assembly election or is a candidate in another Assembly election (see art 34(1)(d)).
As to the meaning of 'Assembly constituency' see PARA 3 note 2; and as to the meaning of 'constituency' in relation to a parliamentary election see PARA 9. As to the meanings of 'party list' and 'party list candidate' see PARA 230 note 23.

17 Representation of the People Act 1983 s 65A(1)(c) (as added: see note 14); National Assembly for Wales (Representation of the People) Order 2007, SI 2007/236, art 34(1)(c), (d). See note 3.

18 Ie a statement under the Representation of the People Act 1983 Sch 1 r 6(5)(b) (see PARAS 256, 706): see s 65A(1)(aa) (s 65A as added (see note 2); s 65A(1)(aa) added by the Political Parties and Elections Act 2009 s 39, Sch 6 para 4). As to the requirement for a nomination paper at a parliamentary election to be accompanied by a home address form see PARA 256.

19 As to the meaning of 'United Kingdom' see PARA 1 note 1.

20 Representation of the People Act 1983 s 65A(1)(aa) (as added: see note 18).

21 See the Representation of the People Act 1983 s 65A(1A), (2) (s 65A as added (see note 2); s 65A(1A), (1B) added by the Electoral Administration Act 2006 s 23(1), (3)); European Parliamentary Elections Regulations 2004, SI 2004/293, reg 28(3) (reg 28(3), (4) added by SI 2009/186); National Assembly for Wales (Representation of the People) Order 2007, SI 2007/236, art 34(2), (3), (4). As to the consent to nomination required of a candidate see PARA 258.

At a European parliamentary election, the reference to a candidate is to an individual candidate or a candidate being nominated in a list submitted by a registered party at such an election: see the European Parliamentary Elections Regulations 2004, SI 2004/293, reg 28(3) (as so added). As to the meanings of 'registered party' and 'list' (submitted by a registered party) see PARA 230 note 29; and as to the meaning of 'individual candidate' see PARA 230 note 32.

At a Welsh Assembly election, the reference in the text to a candidate is to a constituency candidate in the case of a constituency election, or to an individual candidate or a party list candidate at a regional election: see the National Assembly for Wales (Representation of the People) Order 2007, SI 2007/236, art 34(2), (3), (4).

22 Representation of the People Act 1983 s 65A(1A)(a) (as added: see note 21); European Parliamentary Elections Regulations 2004, SI 2004/293, reg 28(3)(a) (as added: see note 21); National Assembly for Wales (Representation of the People) Order 2007, SI 2007/236, art 34(2)(a), (3)(a), (4)(a).

23 Representation of the People Act 1983 s 65A(1A)(b) (as added: see note 21); European Parliamentary Elections Regulations 2004, SI 2004/293, reg 28(3)(b) (as added: see note 21); National Assembly for Wales (Representation of the People) Order 2007, SI 2007/236, art 34(2)(b), (3)(b), (4)(b). For these purposes, a statement as to a candidate's qualification is a statement that he is qualified for being elected, that he will be qualified for being elected, or that to the best of his knowledge and belief he is not disqualified for being elected: Representation of the People Act 1983 s 65A(1B) (as so added); European Parliamentary Elections

Regulations 2004, SI 2004/293, reg 28(4) (as so added); National Assembly for Wales (Representation of the People) Order 2007, SI 2007/236, art 34(5).

24 Ie that he is not:

(1) a candidate at a parliamentary or Assembly constituency election for any other constituency (see the Representation of the People Act 1983 s 65A(1A)(c) (as added: see note 21); and the National Assembly for Wales (Representation of the People) Order 2007, SI 2007/236, art 34(2)(c));

(2) if an individual candidate at an Assembly regional election, a party list candidate at that regional election nor a candidate in another Assembly election (see the National Assembly for Wales (Representation of the People) Order 2007, SI 2007/236, art 34(3)(c));

(3) if a party list candidate at an Assembly regional election, either an individual candidate or a candidate on the list submitted by another registered political party, or a candidate in another Assembly election (see art 34(4)(c)).

25 Representation of the People Act 1983 s 65A(1A)(c) (as added: see note 21); National Assembly for Wales (Representation of the People) Order 2007, SI 2007/236, art 34(2)(c), (3)(c), (4)(c).

26 See the Representation of the People Act 1983 s 65A(1A) (as added: see note 21); European Parliamentary Elections Regulations 2004, SI 2004/293, reg 28(3) (as added: see note 21); National Assembly for Wales (Representation of the People) Order 2007, SI 2007/236, art 34(2), (3), (4).

706. Issuing false certificate authorising a description to be used by candidate at an election. A person[1] is guilty of a corrupt practice[2] if he fraudulently purports to be authorised to issue a certificate[3], which authorises a description to be used by a candidate[4] at an election, on behalf of a registered political party's nominating officer[5].

1 As to the meaning of 'person' see PARA 95 note 1.
2 As to the consequences of corrupt practices see PARA 887 et seq.
3 Ie:

(1) issue a certificate under the Representation of the People Act 1983 s 23(1), Sch 1 r 6A(1), (1B), in relation to a parliamentary election (see PARA 256) (see Sch 1 r 6A(2) (added by the Registration of Political Parties Act 1998 s 13, Sch 2 para 2; and amended by the Electoral Administration Act 2006 s 74(1), Sch 1 paras 104, 129(1), (3)));

(2) issue a certificate under the European Parliamentary Elections Regulations 2004, SI 2004/293, Sch 1 r 5(2), (4), or make the statement required by Sch 1 r 6(6), in relation to a European parliamentary election (see PARA 256) (see Sch 1 rr 5(6), 6(8) (Sch 1 substituted by SI 2009/186));

(3) issue a certificate under the Local Elections (Principal Areas) (England and Wales) Rules 2006, SI 2006/3304, Sch 2 r 5(1), (3), in relation to a local government election for principal areas, or under the Local Elections (Parishes and Communities) (England and Wales) Rules 2006, SI 2006/3305, Sch 2 r 5(1), (3), in relation to a local government election for parishes or communities (see PARA 256) (see the Local Elections (Principal Areas) (England and Wales) Rules 2006, SI 2006/3304, Sch 2 r 5(5); and the Local Elections (Parishes and Communities) (England and Wales) Rules 2006, SI 2006/3305, Sch 2 r 5(5));

(4) issue a certificate under the National Assembly for Wales (Representation of the People) Order 2007, SI 2007/236, Sch 5 para 5(1), (3), in relation to a Welsh Assembly constituency election, or under Sch 5 para 8(1), in the case of a Welsh Assembly regional election (see Sch 5 paras 5(7), 8(4));

(5) issue a certificate under the Local Authorities (Mayoral Elections) (England and Wales) Regulations 2007, SI 2007/1024, Sch 1 r 7(1), (3), in relation to a local authority mayoral election (see PARA 256) (see Sch 1 r 7(5));

(6) issue a certificate under the Greater London Authority Elections Rules 2007, SI 2007/3541, Sch 1 r 6(5), (7), Sch 3 r 6(5), (7), or make the statement required by Sch 2 r 7(2)(b), in relation to a London Authority election (see PARA 256) (see Sch 1 r 6(9), Sch 2 r 7(4), Sch 3 r 6(9)).

As to the meaning of 'Assembly election' see PARA 3 note 2. As to the meaning of 'parliamentary election' see PARA 9. As to the meanings of 'Authority election' and 'local government election' see PARA 11. As to the election of councillors for local government principal areas see PARA 197 et seq; as to elections for the return of a local authority mayor see PARA 198; and as to the ordinary elections of parish or community councillors see PARA 200 et seq. As to European parliamentary elections see PARA 217 et seq.

4   As to the meaning of 'candidate' generally see PARA 230.

5   Representation of the People Act 1983 Sch 1 r 6A(2) (as added and amended: see note 3); European Parliamentary Elections Regulations 2004, SI 2004/293, Sch 1 rr 5(6), 6(8) (as substituted: see note 3); Local Elections (Principal Areas) (England and Wales) Rules 2006, SI 2006/3304, Sch 2 r 5(5); Local Elections (Parishes and Communities) (England and Wales) Rules 2006, SI 2006/3305, Sch 2 r 5(5); National Assembly for Wales (Representation of the People) Order 2007, SI 2007/236, Sch 5 paras 5(7), 8(4); Local Authorities (Mayoral Elections) (England and Wales) Regulations 2007, SI 2007/1024, Sch 1 r 7(5); Greater London Authority Elections Rules 2007, SI 2007/3541, Sch 1 r 6(9), Sch 2 r 7(4), Sch 3 r 6(9). As to a registered political party's nominating officer see PARA 253.

707.   Incurring third party election expenses without due authorisation or making false declaration as to such expenses.   If a person:

(1)   incurs (or aids, abets, counsels or procures any other person to incur) any election expenses[1] in publicising a candidate or in promoting political debate at an election in contravention of the statutory prohibition on the incurring of such expenses other than by the candidate[2], his election agent[3] and persons authorised in writing by the election agent[4]; or

(2)   knowingly makes the required declaration as to such expenses falsely[5],

he is guilty of a corrupt practice[6]; except that:

(a)   the court before which a person is convicted may, if the court thinks it just in the special circumstances of the case, mitigate or entirely remit any incapacity imposed by virtue of the conviction[7]; and

(b)   a candidate[8] is not liable, nor is his election to be avoided, for such a corrupt practice committed by an agent without his consent or connivance[9].

Where any act or omission of an association or body of persons, corporate or unincorporate, is an offence declared to be a corrupt practice in this way, any person who at the time of the act or omission was a director, general manager, secretary or other similar officer of the association or body, or who was purporting to act in any such capacity, is to be deemed to be guilty of that offence[10], unless he proves that: (i) the act or omission took place without his consent or connivance[11]; and (ii) that he exercised all such diligence to prevent the commission of the offence as he ought to have exercised having regard to the nature of his functions in that capacity and to all the circumstances[12].

These provisions no longer apply for the purposes of a local authority mayoral election[13].

1   As to the meaning of 'election expenses' see PARA 269.

2   As to the meaning of 'candidate' for these purposes see PARA 279 note 2. As to the meaning of 'candidate' generally see PARA 230. In relation to a European parliamentary election, the reference is specifically to an individual candidate: see the European Parliamentary Elections Regulations 2004, SI 2004/293, reg 46(1); and PARA 272. As to the meaning of 'individual candidate' in relation to a European parliamentary election see PARA 230 note 32. As to European parliamentary elections see PARA 217 et seq.

3   As to the appointment of an election agent generally see PARA 231 et seq. For the purposes of a European parliamentary election, references to an election agent include a sub-agent: see the European Parliamentary Elections Regulations 2004, SI 2004/293, reg 46(7); and PARA 272. As to the appointment of a sub-agent at a European parliamentary election see PARA 241 et seq.

4   Representation of the People Act 1983 s 75(5)(a); European Parliamentary Elections Regulations 2004, SI 2004/293, reg 46(5)(a); National Assembly for Wales (Representation of the People) Order 2007, SI 2007/236, art 46(8)(a).

Head (1) in the text refers to contravention of the Representation of the People Act 1983 s 75, in relation to a parliamentary or local government election, or the European Parliamentary Elections Regulations 2004, SI 2004/293, reg 46, in relation to a European parliamentary election, or the National Assembly for Wales (Representation of the People) Order 2007, SI 2007/236, art 46, in relation to a Welsh Assembly election (see PARA 272). As to the meaning of 'Assembly election' see PARA 3 note 2; as to the meaning of 'parliamentary election' see PARA 9; and as to the meaning of 'local government election' see PARA 11.

5   Representation of the People Act 1983 s 75(5)(b); European Parliamentary Elections Regulations 2004, SI 2004/293, reg 46(5)(b); National Assembly for Wales (Representation of the People) Order 2007, SI 2007/236, art 46(8)(b).

Head (2) in the text refers to the declaration required by the Representation of the People Act 1983 s 75(2), in relation to a parliamentary or local government election, or the European Parliamentary Elections Regulations 2004, SI 2004/293, reg 46(3), in relation to a European parliamentary election, or the National Assembly for Wales (Representation of the People) Order 2007, SI 2007/236, art 46(5), in relation to a Welsh Assembly election (see PARA 279).

6   Representation of the People Act 1983 s 75(5); European Parliamentary Elections Regulations 2004, SI 2004/293, reg 46(5); National Assembly for Wales (Representation of the People) Order 2007, SI 2007/236, art 46(8). As to the consequences of corrupt practices see PARA 887 et seq.

The Representation of the People Act 1983 s 75 does not apply at an election under the local government Act which is not a local government election (see the Representation of the People Act 1983 s 90(2); and PARA 678); and, in relation to an election of parish councillors in England or of community councillors in Wales, the provisions of s 90(1), Sch 4 apply instead: see s 90(1)(b); and PARA 675. As to the meaning of 'election under the local government Act' see PARA 11 note 2. As to elections in the City of London see PARA 33.

7   Representation of the People Act 1983 s 75(5)(i); European Parliamentary Elections Regulations 2004, SI 2004/293, reg 46(5); National Assembly for Wales (Representation of the People) Order 2007, SI 2007/236, art 46(10). As to personal incapacity incurred on proof of corrupt or illegal voting practices at a parliamentary, local government election or local authority referendum, see the Representation of the People Act 1983 ss 160(4), 173; and PARA 905. As to personal incapacity incurred on proof of corrupt or illegal voting practices at a Welsh Assembly election see the National Assembly for Wales (Representation of the People) Order 2007, SI 2007/236, arts 110, 111, 123; and PARA 907. As to personal incapacity incurred on conviction of corrupt or illegal voting practices at a European parliamentary election see the European Parliamentary Elections Regulations 2004, SI 2004/293, reg 107; and PARA 909. As to mitigation and remission of incapacities so imposed see PARA 910.

8   Ie a candidate at a parliamentary, local government, or Welsh Assembly election.

9   Representation of the People Act 1983 s 75(5)(ii); National Assembly for Wales (Representation of the People) Order 2007, SI 2007/236, art 46(11). As to the avoidance of elections see PARA 894–896.

10 Representation of the People Act 1983 s 75(6); European Parliamentary Elections Regulations 2004, SI 2004/293, reg 46(6); National Assembly for Wales (Representation of the People) Order 2007, SI 2007/236, art 46(12).

11 Representation of the People Act 1983 s 75(6)(a); European Parliamentary Elections Regulations 2004, SI 2004/293, reg 46(6)(a); National Assembly for Wales (Representation of the People) Order 2007, SI 2007/236, art 46(12)(a).

12 Representation of the People Act 1983 s 75(6)(b); European Parliamentary Elections Regulations 2004, SI 2004/293, reg 46(6)(b); National Assembly for Wales (Representation of the People) Order 2007, SI 2007/236, art 46(12)(b).

13 See the Local Authorities (Mayoral Elections) (England and Wales) Regulations 2002, SI 2002/185, reg 3(2), Sch 2 Table 1 (revoked), which applied the Representation of the People Act 1983 s 75, subject to modifications; and see now the Local Authorities (Mayoral Elections) (England and Wales) Regulations 2007, SI 2007/1024, reg 3(2)–(5), Sch 2 Table 1; and PARA 11 note 14.

708. False declarations or returns as to election expenses.

If a candidate[1] or election agent[2] at a parliamentary[3] or local government election[4], or at a Welsh Assembly, or European parliamentary election, knowingly[5] makes the required declaration as to election expenses (or return as to personal expenses)[6] falsely, he is guilty of a corrupt practice[7]. Before any defendant may be so convicted, the tribunal of fact must be satisfied:

(1)   that the defendant made a declaration as to election expenses as required[8];

(2)   that such declaration was false, in that expenses which should have been included were omitted or expenses which were included were understated, or both[9]; and

(3)   that the defendant knew such declaration to be false, either because the defendant knew that expenses which should have been included were omitted or because the defendant knew that expenses which were included were understated, or both[10].

1   As to the meaning of 'candidate' generally see PARA 230.
     In the case of a European parliamentary election, the reference to an individual candidate is implicit: see the European Parliamentary Elections Regulations 2004, SI 2004/293, reg 51(1); and PARA 280. As to the meaning of 'individual candidate' at a European parliamentary election see PARA 230 note 32. As to European parliamentary elections see PARA 217 et seq.
     In the case of a Welsh Assembly election, the candidate referred to in the text may be either a constituency candidate at a constituency election or an individual candidate at a regional election (see the National Assembly for Wales (Representation of the People) Order 2007, SI 2007/236, art 52(1); and PARA 280), or each candidate on a party list submitted by a registered political party at a regional election (see art 54(1); and PARA 281). As to the meanings of 'Assembly election', 'constituency election' and 'regional election' see PARA 3 note 2; as to the meanings of 'constituency candidate' and 'individual candidate' see PARA 230 note 19; and as to the meanings of 'party list', 'party list candidate' and 'registered political party' see PARA 230 note 23.
2   As to the appointment of an election agent generally see PARA 231 et seq.
3   As to the meaning of 'parliamentary election' see PARA 9.
4   As to the meaning of 'local government election' see PARA 11.
5   The word 'knowingly' is levelled at an offence based on moral turpitude, and guilt must be proved: see *Cork, Eastern Division Case* (1911) 6 O'M & H 318 at 347.
6   Ie:
     (1)   the declaration as to election expenses required, in relation to a parliamentary or local government election where election agents must be appointed, by the Representation of the People Act 1983 s 82 (see PARA 281) (see s 82(6)), or, in relation to an election of parish or community councillors (where election agents are not required), under s 90(1)(b), Sch 4 para 3 (see PARA 293) (see Sch 4 para 5);
     (2)   the declaration as to election expenses required, in relation to a European parliamentary election, by the European Parliamentary Elections Regulations 2004, SI 2004/293, reg 52 (see PARA 281) (see reg 52(6)), or the return as to personal expenses required by reg 53 (see PARA 280 note 29) (see reg 53(2));
     (3)   the declaration as to election expenses required, in relation to a Welsh Assembly election, under the National Assembly for Wales (Representation of the People) Order 2007, SI 2007/236, art 53 (constituency and individual candidates: see PARA 281) (see art 53(5)), or art 54 (party list candidates: see PARA 281) (art 54(3)).
     As to the meaning of 'declaration as to election expenses' see PARA 281 note 3.
7   Representation of the People Act 1983 s 82(6); Sch 4 para 5; European Parliamentary Elections Regulations 2004, SI 2004/293, regs 52(6), 53(2); National Assembly for Wales (Representation of the People) Order 2007, SI 2007/236, arts 53(5), 54(3). As to the consequences of a corrupt practice see PARA 887 et seq.
     A candidate or election agent who knowingly makes a false declaration as to election expenses is also guilty of an offence under the Perjury Act 1911: see s 5(b) (false statutory declarations: see CRIMINAL LAW vol 26 (2010) PARA 673) and s 16(1) (dual liability for making a false statement which is both an offence under the Perjury Act 1911, and a corrupt practice by virtue of some other Act: see CRIMINAL LAW vol 26 (2010) PARA 681).
8   *R v Jones, R v Whicher* [1999] 2 Cr App Rep 253 at 258, CA, per Lord Bingham CJ.
9   *R v Jones, R v Whicher* [1999] 2 Cr App Rep 253 at 258, CA, per Lord Bingham CJ.
10   *R v Jones, R v Whicher* [1999] 2 Cr App Rep 253 at 258, CA, per Lord Bingham CJ. The requirement in head (3) in the text is the nub of the offence and defines the dishonest knowledge which constitutes the mens rea of the crime: see *R v Jones, R v Whicher* at 259 per Lord Bingham CJ. Honest belief in the truth of the declaration, and thus in the completeness and accuracy of the figures disclosed, is a complete defence; but it is for the prosecution to prove lack of honest belief and not for the defendant to prove his honesty: see *R v Jones, R v Whicher*

at 259 per Lord Bingham CJ. Accordingly, the candidate is not required to perform the role of auditor to the agent: *Sharma v DPP* [2005] EWHC 902 (Admin), [2005] All ER (D) 214 (May) (where a candidate had conducted a superficial examination of the return, trusting that his agent had done his job properly, the candidate could state honestly that to the best of his knowledge and belief the return was complete and accurate).

B. BRIBERY

709. Bribery. A person[1] is guilty of a corrupt practice if he is guilty of bribery at an election[2]. A person is guilty of bribery if he, directly or indirectly, by himself[3] or by any other person on his behalf[4]:

(1) gives any money[5] or procures any office[6] to or for any voter[7], or to or for any other person[8] on behalf of any voter, or to or for any other person, in order to induce[9] any voter to vote or refrain from voting[10]; or

(2) corruptly[11] does any such act, as mentioned in head (1) above, on account of any voter having voted or refrained from voting[12]; or

(3) makes any such gift or procurement, as mentioned in heads (1) and (2) above, to or for any person in order to induce that person to procure, or endeavour to procure, the return of any person at an election[13] or the vote of any voter[14],

or if upon or in consequence of any such gift or procurement, as mentioned in heads (1) to (3) above, he procures or engages, promises or endeavours to procure the return of any person at an election[15] or the vote of any voter[16].

1 As to the meaning of 'person' see PARA 95 note 1.
2 Representation of the People Act 1983 s 113(1); European Parliamentary Elections Regulations 2004, SI 2004/293, reg 77(1); National Assembly for Wales (Representation of the People) Order 2007, SI 2007/236, art 79(1). As to votes struck off for bribery see PARA 842; and as to the consequence of a corrupt practice see PARA 887 et seq. Bribery at a parliamentary or local government election was an offence at common law but the offence is now covered in the express statutory provisions. As to the meaning of 'parliamentary election' see PARA 9; and as to the meaning of 'local government election' see PARA 11. As to the meaning of 'Assembly election' see PARA 3 note 2. As to European parliamentary elections see PARA 217 et seq.
    The Representation of the People Act 1983 s 113 is applied and modified for the purposes of local authority referendums, subject to the modifications specified, in relation to Wales, by the Local Authorities (Conduct of Referendums) (Wales) Regulations 2008, SI 2008/1848, reg 8(2), Sch 4 Table 1, and, in relation to England, by the Local Authorities (Conduct of Referendums) (England) Regulations 2012, SI 2012/323, regs 8(2), 11–13, Sch 4 Table 1: see PARA 15 note 2. As to the meaning of 'referendum' see PARA 574 note 2.
3 Personal corruption ought not to be charged except upon good grounds (*Tewkesbury Case, Collins v Price* (1880) 3 O'M & H 97 at 99; cf *Canterbury Borough Case* (1880) 3 O'M & H 103 at 104), otherwise the petitioner will be penalised in costs (*Salisbury Case, Rigden v Edwards and Grenfell* (1880) 44 LT 193, 3 O'M & H 130; *Sandwich Case* (1880) 3 O'M & H 158). Where a candidate in person gives tickets to voters, and the tickets are exchangeable for money when presented to that candidate's agent, the court may find the agent personally guilty of bribery: *Canterbury Case* (1853) 2 Pow R & D 14 at 15 (in this case each voter was allowed to name two others for coloured tickets, and the parliamentary committee avoided the election). Where the candidate has not appointed another person as election agent, it is the more easy to establish personal bribery against that candidate: *Cashel Borough Case* (1869) 1 O'M & H 286 at 288.
4 Representation of the People Act 1983 s 113(2); European Parliamentary Elections Regulations 2004, SI 2004/293, reg 77(2); National Assembly for Wales (Representation of the People) Order 2007, SI 2007/236, art 79(2). A corrupt act done with a view to the betrayal of the candidate on whose behalf it purports to be done is not bribery for which he can be held liable: *Stafford Borough Case* (1869) 21 LT 210 at 212, 1 O'M & H 228 at 231.
5 'Giving money' includes giving, lending, agreeing to give or lend, offering, promising or promising to procure or to endeavour to procure any money or valuable consideration: Representation of the People Act 1983 s 113(2)(i); European Parliamentary Elections

Regulations 2004, SI 2004/293, reg 77(2)(i); National Assembly for Wales (Representation of the People) Order 2007, SI 2007/236, art 79(3)(a). See further PARA 710.

6   'Procuring an office' includes giving, procuring, agreeing to give or procure, offering, promising or promising to procure or to endeavour to procure, any office, place or employment: Representation of the People Act 1983 s 113(2)(ii); European Parliamentary Elections Regulations 2004, SI 2004/293, reg 77(2)(ii); National Assembly for Wales (Representation of the People) Order 2007, SI 2007/236, art 79(3)(b). A seat on a town council may be the means of bribery within this provision, because it is an office of honour and dignity and the natural and fair object of reasonable ambition on the part of many electors: *Waterford Borough Case* (1870) 2 O'M & H 24 at 25; *Roberts v Hogg* 1971 SLT 78.

7   For this purpose, 'voter' also includes any person who has or claims to have a right to vote: Representation of the People Act 1983 s 113(7); European Parliamentary Elections Regulations 2004, SI 2004/293, reg 77(7); National Assembly for Wales (Representation of the People) Order 2007, SI 2007/236, art 79(8). The fact that the voter was ineligible for voting does not necessarily prevent it being bribery: *Lichfield Case, Anson v Dyott* (1869) 20 LT 11, 1 O'M & H 22; *Guildford Case* (1869) 19 LT 729, 1 O'M & H 13.

8   There must be distinct evidence that the gift was made to the third person with a view to bribing a particular voter: *Clare County Case* (1860) Wolf & B 138. Where money was alleged to have been distributed to non-voters in the expectation that they would spend it in drink at the public-houses and thus indirectly influence the votes of the publicans, O'Brien J said 'this was not contemplated as being within the Act': *Youghal Borough Case* (1869) 1 O'M & H 291 at 294.

9   If the act is done for the purpose of so inducing the voter, it is no answer to say that the bribe was unsuccessful: *Henslow v Fawcett* (1835) 3 Ad & El 51 at 58; *Harding v Stokes* (1837) 2 M & W 233 at 235; *Sulston v Norton* (1761) 3 Burr 1235.

10 Representation of the People Act 1983 s 113(2)(a); European Parliamentary Elections Regulations 2004, SI 2004/293, reg 77(2)(a); National Assembly for Wales (Representation of the People) Order 2007, SI 2007/236, art 79(2)(a). There must be an inducement to vote or to refrain from voting for a particular person: *Cooper v Slade* (1856) 6 E & B 447 at 456; revsd on the facts (1858) 6 HL Cas 746. See also *Oldham Case* (1869) 20 LT 302 at 311, 1 O'M & H 151 at 165; *Cork, Eastern Division Case* (1911) 6 O'M & H 318 at 363. As to whether paying a voter's travelling expenses may constitute bribery see PARA 711.

11 'Corruptly' imports intention: *Wallingford Case* (1869) 19 LT 766 at 767–768, 1 O'M & H 57 at 58. 'Corruptly' does not mean wickedly, immorally or dishonestly or anything of that sort (*Bewdley Case* (1869) 19 LT 676 at 678, 1 O'M & H 16 at 19), but doing something knowing that it is wrong (*Bradford Case (No 2)* (1869) 19 LT 723 at 724, 1 O'M & H 35 at 37), and doing it with the object and intention of doing that thing which the statute intended to forbid (*Norfolk, Northern Division Case* (1869) 21 LT 264 at 268, 1 O'M & H 236 at 242).

12 Representation of the People Act 1983 s 113(2)(b); European Parliamentary Elections Regulations 2004, SI 2004/293, reg 77(2)(b); National Assembly for Wales (Representation of the People) Order 2007, SI 2007/236, art 79(2)(b).

13 References to procuring the return of any person at an election include, in the case of an election of the London members of the London Assembly at an ordinary election, references to procuring the return of candidates on a list of candidates submitted by a registered political party for the purposes of that election: Representation of the People Act 1983 s 113(2)(iii) (added by the Greater London Authority Act 1999 s 17, Sch 3 paras 1, 30). As to the meaning of 'London member' see PARA 11 note 5. As to references to a registered political party submitting a list of candidates to be London members of the London Assembly at an ordinary election see PARA 230 note 14. As to London Assembly ordinary elections see PARA 199; and LONDON GOVERNMENT vol 71 (2013) PARA 76 et seq. At a European parliamentary election, the reference is to 'the return of any individual candidate or registered party' at such an election: see the European Parliamentary Elections Regulations 2004, SI 2004/293, reg 77(2)(c). As to the meaning of 'registered party' see PARA 230 note 29; and as to the meaning of 'individual candidate' see PARA 230 note 32. At a Welsh Assembly election, the reference is to inducing a person 'to procure, or endeavour to procure, a particular result at an Assembly election': see the National Assembly for Wales (Representation of the People) Order 2007, SI 2007/236, art 79(2)(c).

14 Representation of the People Act 1983 s 113(2)(c); European Parliamentary Elections Regulations 2004, SI 2004/293, reg 77(2)(c); National Assembly for Wales (Representation of the People) Order 2007, SI 2007/236, art 79(2)(c). This provision, originally enacted in 1854, was directed against any such extensive bribery as might amount to a purchase of a seat and against corrupt agreements with persons whose local influence would enable them to control the

return: *Coventry Case, Berry v Eaton and Hill* (1869) 1 O'M & H 97 at 102. Under the different conditions in which elections are now contested, this provision does not appear to be of much practical importance.

15 At a European parliamentary election, the reference is to 'the return of any person or registered party' at such an election: see the European Parliamentary Elections Regulations 2004, SI 2004/293, reg 77(2). At a Welsh Assembly election, the reference is to a person who 'procures or engages, promises or endeavours to procure, a particular result at an Assembly election': see the National Assembly for Wales (Representation of the People) Order 2007, SI 2007/236, art 79(2).

16 Representation of the People Act 1983 s 113(2); European Parliamentary Elections Regulations 2004, SI 2004/293, reg 77(2); National Assembly for Wales (Representation of the People) Order 2007, SI 2007/236, art 79(2). As to the offence of receipt of a bribe see PARA 719.

710. Consideration for a bribe. The consideration for a bribe need not be money; it may be any money or valuable consideration[1]. The gift or promise of refreshments may amount to both treating and bribery[2]. Treating, however, will not as a rule be regarded as bribery if it takes the form of refreshment to be consumed at the moment and not pocketed, reserved or promised for future enjoyment, although whether it is or is not to be regarded as bribery will depend on the circumstances[3].

Loans may be as much bribery as absolute gifts[4]. Excessive payments may amount to bribery[5]. An offer to bribe is as bad as actual bribery, but it is more difficult to prove[6]. Colourable employment of any person to render valueless services is bribery[7].

1 See PARA 709 note 5. Permission to shoot rabbits on the candidate's estate was held to be bribery in *Launceston Case* (1874) 30 LT 823 at 825 et seq, 2 O'M & H 129 at 133.

2 *Bodmin Case* (1869) 1 O'M & H 117 at 124; *Tynemouth Case* (1853) 21 LTOS 67; *Huddersfield Case, Priestley's Case* (1859) Wolf & B 28 at 36. As to the offence of bribery at elections see PARA 709; and as to treating at elections see PARAS 721–722.

3 *Bodmin Case* (1869) 1 O'M & H 117; *Youghal Borough Case* (1869) 1 O'M & H 291.

4 See the meaning of 'giving money' in PARA 709 note 5.

5 *Huddersfield Case, Priestley's Case* (1859) Wolf & B 28 at 36 (giving more for pigs than their real value); *St George's Division, Tower Hamlets, Case* (1895) 5 O'M & H 89 (giving more for services rendered than their real value); *Dartmouth Borough Case* (1859) Wolf & B 19 (payment without inquiry of more than a fair charge for a room for the candidate's wife to witness the election proceedings); *Hartlepools Case* (1910) 6 O'M & H 1 (where it was suggested that a legal expense may, if exaggerated, be turned into a bribe, eg where by the provision of unnecessarily costly arrangements for conveying speakers and others to a meeting the persons conveyed are bribed); *Sandwich Case* (1880) 3 O'M & H 158 (hiring rooms for no object).

6 *Coventry Case, Berry v Eaton and Hill* (1869) 1 O'M & H 97 at 107; and see the meanings of 'giving money' and 'procuring an office' in PARA 709 notes 5, 6.

7 *Boston Case, Buxton v Garfit* (1880) 44 LT 287, 3 O'M & H 150; *Gravesend Case* (1880) 44 LT 64 at 65–66, 3 O'M & H 81 at 84; *Boston Case, Tunnard v Ingram* (1880) 44 LT 287, 3 O'M & H 151; *Stroud Case, Baynes v Stanton* (1874) 2 O'M & H 181 at 183; *Penryn Case* (1869) 1 O'M & H 127 at 129; *Cambridge Borough Case* (1857) Wolf & D 28; *Oxford City Case* (1857) Wolf & D 106 at 109.

711. Travelling expenses may constitute bribery. The unconditional payment, or promise of payment, to a voter of his travelling expenses is not bribery[1], but the payment or promise of payment to a voter of his travelling expenses on the condition, express or implied, that he would vote for a particular candidate is bribery[2].

The mere payment of travelling expenses after the poll and without proof of any previous promise to a voter who has come of his own accord and voted is not bribery, although it is an illegal payment[3]. The payment of a sum of money ostensibly as travelling expenses but in excess of the mere travelling expenses may be bribery even though it is paid unconditionally[4]. The payment of a substitute to do the voter's work while he votes is bribery[5].

1   *Cooper v Slade* (1856) 6 E & B 447 (revsd on the facts (1858) 6 HL Cas 746); *Bolton Case* (1874) 2 O'M & H 138 at 144. As to the offence of bribery at elections see PARA 709.
2   *Cooper v Slade* (1858) 6 E & B 447; *Ipswich Case, Packard v Collings and West* (1886) 54 LT 619, 4 O'M & H 70; *Dublin City Case* (1869) 1 O'M & H 270; *Coventry Case, Berry v Eaton and Hill* (1869) 1 O'M & H 97; *Horsham Case, Aldridge v Hurst* (1876) 3 O'M & H 52.
3   *Harwich Borough Case* (1880) 3 O'M & H 61 at 67 (a case in which there was no doubt that the voter expected to be paid); *Maidstone Borough Case, Evans v Viscount Castlereagh* (1906) 5 O'M & H 200; cf *Horsham Case, Aldridge v Hurst* (1876) 3 O'M & H 52. See also *Wareham Case* (1857) Wolf & D 85 at 88, 29 LTOS 346 at 347.
4   *Stroud Case, Marling v Dorington* (1874) 2 O'M & H 103; *Louth, Northern Division Case* (1911) 6 O'M & H 103; cf *Salisbury Case, Rigden v Edwards and Grenfell* (1880) 44 LT 193 at 194, 3 O'M & H 130 at 133; *Maidstone Borough Case, Evans v Viscount Castlereagh* (1906) 5 O'M & H 200; *Carlisle Case* (1860) Wolf & B 90.
5   *Plymouth Case* (1880) 3 O'M & H 107. As to payments for loss of time while voting see PARA 712.

712.   Time off to allow for voting may constitute bribery.   Payments by an employer to his employees in respect of time lost while voting at elections have in certain cases been held to constitute bribery[1]. It is expressly provided, however, that nothing in the statutory provisions which govern the election campaign[2] makes it illegal for an employer to permit electors or their proxies[3] to absent themselves from his employment for a reasonable time[4] for the purpose of voting at the poll at a parliamentary election[5], or at a Welsh Assembly[6], or European parliamentary[7], election, without having any deduction from their salaries or wages on account of their absence[8], if the permission:

(1)   is (so far as practicable without injury to the employer's business) given equally to all persons alike who are at the time in his employment[9];

(2)   is not given with a view to inducing any person to give his vote in a particular way at the election[10]; and

(3)   is not refused to any person for the purpose of preventing him from giving his vote in a particular way at the election[11].

This provision must not be construed as making illegal any act which would not be illegal otherwise[12].

1   See *Staleybridge Case, Ogden, Woolley and Buckley v Sidebottom, Gilbert's Case* (1869) 20 LT 75, 1 O'M & H 66; *Gravesend Case* (1880) 44 LT 64, 3 O'M & H 81 (holiday with pay); *Simpson v Yeend* (1869) LR 4 QB 626. As to the offence of bribery at elections see PARA 709.
2   Ie, in relation to a parliamentary or local government election, the Representation of the People Act 1983 Pt II (ss 67–119) (see PARA 231 et seq), or, in relation to a European parliamentary election, the European Parliamentary Elections Regulations 2004, SI 2004/293, Pt 2 (regs 31–81) (see PARA 239 et seq), or, in relation to a Welsh Assembly election, the National Assembly for Wales (Representation of the People) Order 2007, SI 2007/236, Pt 3 (arts 37–85) (see PARA 235 et seq): see the Representation of the People Act 1983 s 117(2); the European Parliamentary Elections Regulations 2004, SI 2004/293, reg 81; and the National Assembly for Wales (Representation of the People) Order 2007, SI 2007/236, art 83(2).
3   As to the meaning of 'elector' in relation to a parliamentary or local government election see PARA 95 note 2; in relation to a European parliamentary election, see PARA 111 note 4; and, in relation to a Welsh Assembly election, see PARA 110 note 6. As to applications to vote by post or by proxy see PARA 367 et seq.
4   As to what is a reasonable time see *Aylesbury Case* (1886) 4 O'M & H 59 at 60–61.
5   As to the meaning of 'parliamentary election' see PARA 9.
6   As to the meaning of 'Assembly election' see PARA 3 note 2.
7   As to European parliamentary elections see PARA 217 et seq.
8   Representation of the People Act 1983 s 117(2); European Parliamentary Elections Regulations 2004, SI 2004/293, reg 81; National Assembly for Wales (Representation of the People) Order 2007, SI 2007/236, art 83(2).

9 Representation of the People Act 1983 s 117(2)(a); European Parliamentary Elections Regulations 2004, SI 2004/293, reg 81(a); National Assembly for Wales (Representation of the People) Order 2007, SI 2007/236, art 83(2)(a).

10 Representation of the People Act 1983 s 117(2)(b); European Parliamentary Elections Regulations 2004, SI 2004/293, reg 81(b); National Assembly for Wales (Representation of the People) Order 2007, SI 2007/236, art 83(2)(b). Head (2) in the text refers specifically:

    (1) at a parliamentary election, to inducing any person to record his vote for any particular candidate at the election (see the Representation of the People Act 1983 s 117(2)(b));

    (2) at a European parliamentary election, to inducing any person to record his vote for any particular registered party or individual candidate at the election (see the European Parliamentary Elections Regulations 2004, SI 2004/293, reg 81(b)).

As to the meaning of 'candidate' generally see PARA 230. As to the meaning of 'registered party' at a European parliamentary election see PARA 230 note 29; and as to the meaning of 'individual candidate' see PARA 230 note 32.

11 Representation of the People Act 1983 s 117(2)(c); European Parliamentary Elections Regulations 2004, SI 2004/293, reg 81(c); National Assembly for Wales (Representation of the People) Order 2007, SI 2007/236, art 83(2)(c). Head (3) in the text refers specifically to the purpose:

    (1) at a parliamentary election, of preventing any person from recording his vote for any particular candidate at the election (see the Representation of the People Act 1983 s 117(2)(c));

    (2) at a European parliamentary election, of preventing any person from recording his vote for any particular registered party or individual candidate at the election (see the European Parliamentary Elections Regulations 2004, SI 2004/293, reg 81(c)).

12 Representation of the People Act 1983 s 117(2); European Parliamentary Elections Regulations 2004, SI 2004/293, reg 81; National Assembly for Wales (Representation of the People) Order 2007, SI 2007/236, art 83(2).

713. Payments for past services may constitute bribery. Payments for past services may in special circumstances amount to bribery. Thus, payment on a balance due which had not been paid until an election occurred, and was then made by a person not liable for the debt and for the avowed purpose of inducing an elector to vote, was held to be bribery[1]. The promise of payment of an outstanding account on condition that the elector should forbear from voting for the opposing candidate as previously promised by him has been held to be bribery[2]. The payment of a just claim, however, will not lightly be taken to be bribery[3].

1 *Cambridge Borough Case* (1843) Bar & Arn 169. As to the offence of bribery at elections see PARA 709.
2 *Sligo Borough Case* (1853) 2 Pow R & D 256.
3 *Galway Borough Case* (1857) Wolf & D 136 at 142.

714. Charitable gifts may constitute bribery. The distribution of genuine charitable gifts to voters has always been allowed[1]. On the other hand, what are called 'charitable gifts' may be merely a specious and subtle form of bribery[2]. If a gift is charitable, it will not become bribery because of the use made of it, even if political capital is made out of the gift[3]; it is not possible by any subsequent act to make that which was legal at the time illegal and criminal[4].

The imminence of an election is an important factor to be taken into consideration in deciding whether a particular act of charity amounts to bribery. A charitable design may be unobjectionable so long as no election is in prospect, but if an election becomes imminent the danger of the gift being regarded as bribery is increased[5]. It has been said that charity at election times ought to be kept in the background by politicians[6].

The question is one of degree. An isolated small donation on the occasion of a birth or death may not be bribery although such gifts on an extensive scale would lead to the inference that they were given to influence voters[7]. It is legitimate for a member of Parliament to benefit his constituency and the court will not therefore draw any adverse inference from the fact that he confines his charity to his constituency[8]. The care with which charity is dispensed by a candidate or his agents is also likely to be a factor to be considered[9]. An agent may turn what was intended by the candidate to be a charitable gift into a corrupt gift, however[10].

1   *Maldon Case* (1857) Wolf & D 162 at 163, 30 LTOS 76.
2   *Plymouth Case* (1880) 3 O'M & H 107.
3   *Dorsetshire, Eastern Division Case* (1910) 6 O'M & H 22 at 42. In *Windsor Case, Herbert v Gardiner* (1874) 31 LT 133 at 135, 2 O'M & H 88 at 90, Bramwell B said that a man is not to refrain from doing that which he legitimately might have done on account of the existence of a motive which by itself would have been an illegitimate motive. It was similarly held in *Carrickfergus Borough Case* (1880) 3 O'M & H 90. In a later case, however, Pollock B and Bruce J disapproved of *Windsor Case, Herbert v Gardiner*, and said that the court must take all the facts into consideration and must then answer the question whether the motive of the act in question was true charity, or whether it was done in order to corrupt the minds of the voters: *St George's Division, Tower Hamlets, Case* (1895) 5 O'M & H 89 at 93–94. See also *Salisbury Case, Moore v Kennard* (1883) 4 O'M & H 21 at 29; *Nottingham Borough, East Division Case* (1911) 6 O'M & H 292 at 310; *King's Lynn Case, Flanders v Ingleby* (1911) 6 O'M & H 179 at 192. Subscriptions to charities stimulated by gratitude or hope of favours to come are not bribes: *Westbury Case, Laverton v Phipps, Harrop's Case* (1869) 1 O'M & H 47 at 49. As to the offence of bribery at elections see PARA 709.
4   *Stafford County, Lichfield Division Case* (1895) 5 O'M & H 27.
5   *Kingston-upon-Hull, Central Division Case* (1911) 6 O'M & H 372 at 374.
6   *Wigan Case, Spencer and Prestt v Powell* (1881) 4 O'M & H 1 at 14; *Kingston-upon-Hull, Central Division Case* (1911) 6 O'M & H 372 at 380.
7   *Windsor Case, Richardson-Gardner v Eykyn* (1869) 19 LT 613, 1 O'M & H 1.
8   *Plymouth Case* (1880) 3 O'M & H 107; *Nottingham Borough, East Division Case* (1911) 6 O'M & H 292.
9   *Nottingham Borough, East Division Case* (1911) 6 O'M & H 292 at 309, 311; *Kingston-upon-Hull, Central Division Case* (1911) 6 O'M & H 372 at 380, 383, 390; *Boston Borough Case, Malcolm v Parry* (1874) LR 9 CP 610; *Stafford Borough Case* (1869) 21 LT 210 at 211, 1 O'M & H 228 at 230.
10 *Boston Borough Case, Malcolm v Parry* (1874) LR 9 CP 610.

715.   Other instances of bribery.   Taking a burdensome share in a building society in order to relieve a voter and thereby to induce him to vote has been held to be bribery[1], as has a promise that the voter 'shall be no loser' by his coming to vote[2], paying a man's debts to release him from prison so that he could vote[3], and paying a man to personate a voter[4].

A corrupt agreement to vote for a certain candidate the benefit of which is afterwards taken over and adopted by another candidate has been held to be bribery for which the latter may be held liable[5].

An agreement to forgo payments of rent has been considered corrupt on the facts of the particular case[6].

1   *Bewdley Case, Spencer v Harrison* (1880) 44 LT 283, 3 O'M & H 145. As to the offence of bribery at elections see PARA 709.
2   *Staleybridge Case, Ogden, Woolley and Buckley v Sidebottom, Gilbert's Case* (1869) 20 LT 75 at 79, 1 O'M & H 66 at 67; but see PARA 711.
3   *Londonderry Borough Case* (1869) 1 O'M & H 274.
4   *Lisburn Case* (1863) Wolf & B 221 at 225. As to personation see PARA 730.
5   *Dover Case* (1860) Wolf & B 121 at 126–127.
6   *Ipswich Case* (1857) Wolf & D 173 at 178.

716.   Time of bribe.   In order to constitute the offence of bribery[1] it does not matter how long before an election a bribe is given provided the bribe is operative at the time of the election[2]. Time is, however, material when considering the question of evidence; it is obvious that where a considerable time elapses between a bribe and an election the difficulty of proving bribery is much increased. If the act of bribery is committed shortly before the poll, the act will be assumed to be bribery until the contrary is shown[3]. If the act of bribery is committed after the voter has voted, it must be shown to have been done corruptly and for this purpose it is at least important to see whether it was done in pursuance of an antecedent promise[4].

1   As to the offence of bribery at elections see PARA 709.
2   *Sligo Borough Case* (1869) 1 O'M & H 300; *Stroud Case* (1874) 2 O'M & H 181. See also *Windsor Case, Herbert v Gardiner* (1874) 31 LT 133 at 136, 2 O'M & H 88 at 91 per Bramwell B (the force of a bribe must be in existence, continuing till the time of the election, before it will avoid the election).
3   *Limerick Borough Case* (1869) 1 O'M & H 260.
4   Bribery after the election is a difficult charge to establish (*Norwich Case* (1859) Wolf & B 58 at 62), but if clearly made out it is sufficient to avoid the election (*Harwich Borough Case* (1880) 3 O'M & H 61 at 70). Where a corrupt expectation on the part of the voter was followed by payment on behalf of the candidate, that voter's vote was struck off by a parliamentary committee (*Dublin Case* (1836) Falc & Fitz 88 at 204); and 'head money', 'market money' and 'dinner money' paid after the election to voters in pursuance of an understanding avoided the election (*Newcastle-under-Lyme Case* (1842) Bar & Aust 436 at 453; *Durham City Case* (1843) Bar & Arn 201 at 215). Whether an antecedent promise must necessarily be proved was left undecided in *Northallerton Case* (1869) 1 O'M & H 167. In *Caldicott v Corrupt Practices Comrs* (1907) 21 Cox CC 404, the court declined to convict in the absence of an antecedent promise; but in *Cheltenham Case, Smythies and Claridge v Mathias, Davies' Case* (1911) 6 O'M & H 194 at 212, the court did not accept this view but agreed that it was important to see whether there was an antecedent promise or not. See also *Stroud Case* (1874) 2 O'M & H 181 at 184; *Cooper v Slade* (1858) 6 HL Cas 746 at 790.
    The time at which an alleged act of treating is done is also considered to be relevant to that particular offence: see PARA 722.

717.   Payments for expenditure in bribes.   A person is guilty of bribery if he advances or pays or causes to be paid any money to or to the use of any other person with the intent that that money or any part of it is to be expended in bribery at any election[1], or knowingly pays or causes to be paid any money to any person in discharge or repayment of any money wholly or in part expended in bribery at any such election[2]. It is not necessary that the person to whom the money is paid should be the person who is intended to expend it in bribery; the payment of money into a bank to be expended in bribery would come within this provision[3].

1   Ie at any parliamentary election, any local government election, any Welsh Assembly election, or any European parliamentary election. As to the meaning of 'Assembly election' see PARA 3 note 2; as to the meaning of 'parliamentary election' see PARA 9; and as to the meaning of 'local government election' see PARA 11. As to elections in the City of London see PARA 33; and as to European parliamentary elections see PARA 217 et seq.
    The Representation of the People Act 1983 s 113 is applied and modified for the purposes of local authority referendums, subject to the modifications specified, in relation to Wales, by the Local Authorities (Conduct of Referendums) (Wales) Regulations 2008, SI 2008/1848, reg 8(2), Sch 4 Table 1, and, in relation to England, by the Local Authorities (Conduct of Referendums) (England) Regulations 2012, SI 2012/323, regs 8(2), 11–13, Sch 4 Table 1: see PARA 15 note 2. As to the meaning of 'referendum' see PARA 574 note 2.
2   Representation of the People Act 1983 s 113(3); European Parliamentary Elections Regulations 2004, SI 2004/293, reg 77(3); National Assembly for Wales (Representation of the People) Order 2007, SI 2007/236, art 79(4).
3   *Aylesbury Case* (1804) 2 Peck 258 at 259; *Rye Case* (1848) 1 Pow R & D 112.

718.   Payment of legitimate expenses not to constitute bribery.   The provisions relating to the payment of bribes at an election[1] do not extend and must not be construed as extending to any money paid or agreed to be paid for or on account of any legal expenses incurred in good faith at or concerning such an election[2]. This has been interpreted as meaning that the provisions in question do not extend to any money paid or agreed to be paid for or on account of any expenses incurred in good faith at or concerning any election, provided those expenses are not illegal on some other ground. For instance, the payment of expenses of committee rooms and advertisements is not unlawful, even though they are incurred with a view to inducing the person receiving the payment to vote[3]. A public subscription for defraying a candidate's expenses is not illegal[4]; nor is it illegal for one candidate to pay the election expenses of another, unless the former intends by so doing to purchase any influence which the latter may have with the electors[5].

1 Ie, in relation to a parliamentary or local government election, the Representation of the People Act 1983 s 113(1)–(3), or, in relation to a European parliamentary election, the European Parliamentary Elections Regulations 2004, SI 2004/293, reg 77(1)–(3), or, in relation to a Welsh Assembly election, the National Assembly for Wales (Representation of the People) Order 2007, SI 2007/236, art 79(1)–(4) (see PARAS 709, 717): see the Representation of the People Act 1983 s 113(4); the European Parliamentary Elections Regulations 2004, SI 2004/293, reg 77(4); and the National Assembly for Wales (Representation of the People) Order 2007, SI 2007/236, art 79(5). As to the meaning of 'Assembly election' see PARA 3 note 2; as to the meaning of 'parliamentary election' see PARA 9; and as to the meaning of 'local government election' see PARA 11. As to elections in the City of London see PARA 33; and as to European parliamentary elections see PARA 217 et seq.
   The Representation of the People Act 1983 s 113 is applied and modified for the purposes of local authority referendums, subject to the modifications specified, in relation to Wales, by the Local Authorities (Conduct of Referendums) (Wales) Regulations 2008, SI 2008/1848, reg 8(2), Sch 4 Table 1, and, in relation to England, by the Local Authorities (Conduct of Referendums) (England) Regulations 2012, SI 2012/323, regs 8(2), 11–13, Sch 4 Table 1: see PARA 15 note 2. As to the meaning of 'referendum' see PARA 574 note 2.
2 Representation of the People Act 1983 s 113(4); European Parliamentary Elections Regulations 2004, SI 2004/293, reg 77(4); National Assembly for Wales (Representation of the People) Order 2007, SI 2007/236, art 79(5).
3 *Cooper v Slade* (1858) 6 HL Cas 746 at 766.
4 *Belfast Borough Case* (1869) 1 O'M & H 281 at 285.
5 *Coventry Case, Berry v Eaton and Hill* (1869) 1 O'M & H 97.

719. Offence of receiving bribe. A voter is guilty of bribery if:

(1) before or during an election[1], he directly or indirectly by himself or by any other person on his behalf receives, agrees or contracts for any money, gift, loan or valuable consideration, office, place or employment for himself or for any other person for voting or agreeing to vote or for refraining or agreeing to refrain from voting[2];

(2) after such an election, he directly or indirectly by himself or by any other person on his behalf receives any money or valuable consideration on account of any person having voted or refrained from voting or having induced any other person to vote or refrain from voting[3].

Merely asking for a bribe has been held not to constitute an offence under this prohibition[4].

The corrupt receipt of a bribe is a separate offence and distinct from that of which the briber is guilty[5].

1 Ie a parliamentary election, a local government election, a Welsh Assembly election, or a European parliamentary election. As to the meaning of 'Assembly election' see PARA 3 note 2; as to the meaning of 'parliamentary election' see PARA 9; and as to the meaning of 'local government election' see PARA 11. As to elections in the City of London see PARA 33; and as to European parliamentary elections see PARA 217 et seq.

The Representation of the People Act 1983 s 113 is applied and modified for the purposes of local authority referendums, subject to the modifications specified, in relation to Wales, by the Local Authorities (Conduct of Referendums) (Wales) Regulations 2008, SI 2008/1848, reg 8(2), Sch 4 Table 1, and, in relation to England, by the Local Authorities (Conduct of Referendums) (England) Regulations 2012, SI 2012/323, regs 8(2), 11–13, Sch 4 Table 1: see PARA 15 note 2. As to the meaning of 'referendum' see PARA 574 note 2.

2   Representation of the People Act 1983 s 113(5); European Parliamentary Elections Regulations 2004, SI 2004/293, reg 77(5); National Assembly for Wales (Representation of the People) Order 2007, SI 2007/236, art 79(6). This provision concerns voters who receive bribes before or during, but not after, an election. As to votes struck off for bribery see PARA 842.

3   Representation of the People Act 1983 s 113(6); European Parliamentary Elections Regulations 2004, SI 2004/293, reg 77(6); National Assembly for Wales (Representation of the People) Order 2007, SI 2007/236, art 79(7). This provision concerns voters and non-voters who receive bribes of money or valuable consideration, but not an office or employment, after an election. The provision has little practical significance now because it is unlikely to matter so much whether a particular person votes or abstains from voting since no constituency or electoral area consists of so few voters as was formerly the case.

4   *Mallow Borough Case* (1870) 2 O'M & H 18. See also *Ipswich Case* (1835) Kn & Omb 332.

5   *Boston Borough Case, Malcolm v Parry* (1874) LR 9 CP 610.

720.   Proof of bribery. Due proof of a single act of bribery by or with the knowledge and consent of the candidate or by his agents, however insignificant that act may be, is sufficient to invalidate the election[1]. The judges are not at liberty to weigh its importance[2], nor can they allow any excuse, whatever the circumstances may be, such as they can allow in certain conditions in cases of treating or undue influence by agents[3]. For this reason, clear and unequivocal proof is required before a case of bribery will be held to have been established; and suspicion is not sufficient[4]. The confession of the person alleged to have been bribed is not conclusive[5].

A corrupt motive must in all cases be strictly proved[6]. For this purpose, a corrupt motive in the mind of the person bribed alone is not enough; the question is as to the intention of the person who bribes him[7].

Where the evidence as to bribery consists merely of offers or proposals to bribe, stronger evidence will be required than in the case of a successful bribe because of the greater likelihood of there having been some misunderstanding[8]. A general conversation as to a candidate's wealth and liberality is not evidence of an offer to bribe[9]. General evidence may, however, be given to show what the character of particular acts has presumably been[10].

1   *Plymouth Case* (1880) 3 O'M & H 107 at 108.

2   *Shrewsbury Case* (1870) 2 O'M & H 36 at 37; *Norwich Case* (1871) 23 LT 701 at 704, 2 O'M & H 38 at 41.

3   See PARA 721 et seq.

4   *Lichfield Case, Anson v Dyott* (1869) 20 LT 11 at 13 et seq, 1 O'M & H 22 at 28. Clear evidence must also be given that the person bribing was the candidate's agent: see PARAS 245–246.

5   *Stroud Case, Baynes v Stanton and Dickinson* (1874) 2 O'M & H 107 at 108.

6   *Lichfield Case, Anson v Dyott* (1869) 20 LT 11, 1 O'M & H 22.

7   *Wallingford Case* (1869) 19 LT 766, 1 O'M & H 57; *Westminster Borough Case* (1869) 20 LT 238 at 245, 1 O'M & H 89 at 95.

8   *Cheltenham Case, Gardner v Samuelson* (1869) 1 O'M & H 62 at 64–65; *Mallow Borough Case* (1870) 2 O'M & H 18 at 22.

9   *Northallerton Case* (1869) 1 O'M & H 167 at 168.

10   *Beverley Case* (1869) 20 LT 792 at 795–796, 1 O'M & H 143 at 144–145.

C. TREATING

721. Treating. A person guilty of treating at an election[1] is guilty of a corrupt practice[2]. The following persons[3] are guilty of treating:

(1) any person who corruptly[4], by himself or by any other person, either before, during or after an election, directly or indirectly gives or provides, or pays wholly or in part the expense of giving or providing, any meat, drink, entertainment or provision to or for any person[5]: (a) for the purpose of corruptly influencing that person or any other person to vote or refrain from voting[6]; or (b) on account of that person or any other person having voted or refrained from voting, or being about to vote or refrain from voting[7];

(2) every elector or proxy for an elector who corruptly accepts or takes any such meat, drink, entertainment, or provision[8].

1 Ie at a parliamentary election, a local government election, a Welsh Assembly election, or at a European parliamentary election. As to the meaning of 'Assembly election' see PARA 3 note 2; as to the meaning of 'parliamentary election' see PARA 9; and as to the meaning of 'local government election' see PARA 11. As to elections in the City of London see PARA 33; and as to European parliamentary elections see PARA 217 et seq.
    The Representation of the People Act 1983 s 114 is applied and modified for the purposes of local authority referendums, subject to the modifications specified, in relation to Wales, by the Local Authorities (Conduct of Referendums) (Wales) Regulations 2008, SI 2008/1848, reg 8(2), Sch 4 Table 1, and, in relation to England, by the Local Authorities (Conduct of Referendums) (England) Regulations 2012, SI 2012/323, regs 8(2), 11–13, Sch 4 Table 1: see PARA 15 note 2. As to the meaning of 'referendum' see PARA 574 note 2.
2 Representation of the People Act 1983 s 114(1); European Parliamentary Elections Regulations 2004, SI 2004/293, reg 78(1); National Assembly for Wales (Representation of the People) Order 2007, SI 2007/236, art 80(1). As to the consequences of a corrupt practice see PARA 887 et seq. Prior to the enactment of statutory provisions, treating was an offence at common law.
3 'Person' includes a corporate body: see PARA 95 note 1.
4 As to the meaning of 'corrupt' see PARA 709 note 11; and as to what is regarded as corrupt in the context of treating see PARA 722. See also *Bradford Case (No 2)* (1869) 19 LT 723, 1 O'M & H 35; *Wigan Case, Spencer and Prestt v Powell* (1881) 4 O'M & H 1; *Ipswich Case, Packard v Collings and West* (1886) 54 LT 619, 4 O'M & H 70, which cases concern treating to secure general popularity and therefore to influence votes.
5 Representation of the People Act 1983 s 114(2); European Parliamentary Elections Regulations 2004, SI 2004/293, reg 78(2); National Assembly for Wales (Representation of the People) Order 2007, SI 2007/236, art 80(2).
6 Representation of the People Act 1983 s 114(2)(a); European Parliamentary Elections Regulations 2004, SI 2004/293, reg 78(2)(a); National Assembly for Wales (Representation of the People) Order 2007, SI 2007/236, art 80(2)(a).
7 Representation of the People Act 1983 s 114(2)(b); European Parliamentary Elections Regulations 2004, SI 2004/293, reg 78(2)(b); National Assembly for Wales (Representation of the People) Order 2007, SI 2007/236, art 80(2)(b).
8 Representation of the People Act 1983 s 114(3); European Parliamentary Elections Regulations 2004, SI 2004/293, reg 78(3); National Assembly for Wales (Representation of the People) Order 2007, SI 2007/236, art 80(3). As to votes struck off for treating see PARA 842.

722. Treating must be corrupt. The essence of the offence of treating is that it should be corrupt[1]. Treating, in fact, is often innocent; and *prima facie* it will be taken so to be[2]. The statutory provision against treating does not in general apply to mutual treating between equals or to treating in connection with business matters, but it applies to the treating of an inferior by a superior, otherwise than in return for services rendered, with a view to securing the goodwill of the particular person treated and to influencing the vote[3]. The alleged offender's previous and habitual conduct will be considered[4]. No man is bound to abstain from customary and harmless hospitality because an election is pending[5].

Where refreshments are a mere incident of a political meeting there is no offence, but if persons are gathered together merely to gratify their appetites and so influence their votes, then it is corrupt treating[6]. The gift or promise of refreshments may amount to both treating and bribery[7]. It is not necessarily corrupt, however, to attract people to meetings by offering refreshments of a moderate kind[8]. The giving of refreshments to persons employed at the election, if done honestly and in good faith, is not illegal[9].

The time at which the act is done is also a relevant consideration, for the treating must have reference to some election and must be for the purpose of influencing the vote of the person treated[10], and must have a continuing operation on the elector at the time of the election[11].

A candidate at a general election may be guilty of treating even though the treating took place before the dissolution of Parliament and consequently before he came within the statutory definition of 'candidate'[12]. A corrupt act is not the less corrupt because it is done a long time before the election, but in determining whether it is reasonable to conclude that an act is done with a view to influencing votes, the element of time becomes a very material one[13]. Treating after an election, to be illegal, must be done under such circumstances as to lead to the inference that it was done in pursuance of an antecedent agreement[14].

Custom is only relevant as having some bearing on the intent of a particular individual[15].

A candidate who is reported by an election court guilty by his agents of treating may be excused from the consequences in certain circumstances[16].

1   As to the statutory offence of treating see PARA 721.
2   *Aylesbury Case* (1886) 4 O'M & H 59 at 63; cf *Shoreditch, Haggerston Division Case, Cremer v Lowles* (1896) 5 O'M & H 68 at 72, where on the facts of the particular case the judges differed. But treating intended to secure general popularity, and so to influence votes, is corrupt treating: *Bradford Case (No 2)* (1869) 19 LT 723, 1 O'M & H 35; *Wigan Case, Spencer and Prestt v Powell* (1881) 4 O'M & H 1; *Ipswich Case* (1886) 54 LT 619, 2 TLR 477.
3   *Norwich Case, Birbeck v Bullard* (1886) 4 O'M & H 84, 54 LT 625.
4   *Aylesbury Case* (1886) 4 O'M & H 59 (school feast customarily given by respondent).
5   *Worcester Borough Case, Glaszard and Turner v Allsopp* (1892) Day 85 at 88.
6   *Rochester Borough Case* (1892) 4 O'M & H 156 at 157 (where a threepenny ticket entitled the holder to partake of food and various wines). The practice of political associations giving entertainments, picnics, suppers, teas, sports etc has been judicially described as 'a practice dangerously akin to corrupt treating', and one which, 'if indulged in by a candidate, would certainly amount to corrupt treating' (*Northumberland, Hexham Division Case, Hudspeth and Lyal v Clayton* (1892) 4 O'M & H 143 at 150); but this is 'not an intimation that any of the transactions referred to are to be taken alone as amounting to corrupt treating'. It is always a question of intention, and the court looks to the whole of the circumstances in each case: *Rochester Borough Case*.
    If you give drink to a man with the intention of confirming his vote and keeping up the party zeal of those believed to be already supporting your candidate, that is corrupt treating: *Cornwall, Bodmin Division Case* (1906) 5 O'M & H 225 at 231. Where a candidate is in the midst of people who are drinking and the worse for drink, it will not necessarily be inferred that because there was drinking there must have been treating: *Southampton Borough Case* (1895) 5 O'M & H 17.
7   *Bodmin Case* (1869) 1 O'M & H 117 at 124; *Tynemouth Case* (1853) 21 LTOS 67; *Huddersfield Case, Priestley's Case* (1859) Wolf & B 28 at 36. As to the offence of bribery see PARA 709 et seq.
8   *St George's Division, Tower Hamlets, Case* (1895) 5 O'M & H 89 at 99; *Great Yarmouth Borough Case* (1906) 5 O'M & H 176 at 194. The question of corrupt treating must be in each case a question of fact. If the refreshments provided were excessive, if the occasions were

numerous, and if there were other circumstances calculated to excite suspicion, a corrupt intention might be inferred: *St George's Division, Tower Hamlets, Case.*

9   *Westminster Borough Case* (1869) 20 LT 238, 1 O'M & H 89; *Bradford Case (No 2)* (1869) 19 LT 723, 1 O'M & H 35. See also *Barrow-in-Furness Case* (1886) 4 O'M & H 76, where non-workers participated in the refreshments.

10 *Norwich Case, Birbeck v Bullard* (1886) 4 O'M & H 84 at 91, 54 LT 625 at 627. Treating at a local government election held shortly before a parliamentary election and with a view to influencing the latter is treating at the parliamentary election: *Hastings Case, Calthorpe and Sutton v Brassey and North, Foster's Case* (1869) 21 LT 234, 1 O'M & H 217; and see *Great Yarmouth Borough Case* (1906) 5 O'M & H 176.

11 *Tamworth Case, Hill and Walton v Peel and Bulwer* (1869) 20 LT 181, 1 O'M & H 75; *Berwick-upon-Tweed Case* (1803) 1 Peck 401 at 402; *Northumberland, Hexham Division Case* (1892) 4 O'M & H 143, as explained in *Rochester Borough Case* (1892) 4 O'M & H 156; *St George's Division, Tower Hamlets, Case* (1896) 5 O'M & H 89; *Cornwall, Bodmin Division Case* (1896) 5 O'M & H 225.

12 *Norwich Case, Birkbeck v Bullard* (1886) 4 O'M & H 84 at 86 (cf the report in 54 LT 625 at 627); *Aylesbury Case* (1886) 4 O'M & H 59 at 63; *Montgomery Boroughs Case* (1892) 4 O'M & H 167 at 168; *Walsall Borough Case* (1892) as reported in Day 106 at 112, where it was said that the period in respect of which a candidate can be held responsible must be confined within reasonable limits; *Youghal Election Petition* (1869) IR 3 CL 530 (although it should be noted that the definition of treating in that case differed from the present definition (see PARA 721)). For the current statutory definition of 'candidate' see PARA 230; and see now the second regulated period (the 'long period') for pre-candidacy expenses that is provided for where Parliament is dissolved after a period of more than 55 months (cited in PARA 274).

13 *St George's Division, Tower Hamlets, Case* (1896) 5 O'M & H 89 at 100–101; cf *Lancaster County, Lancaster Division Case* (1896) 5 O'M & H 39 at 43, where, although the person who eventually became the election agent took part in an entertainment given by a political association, it was held that there had not in the circumstances been any corrupt treating for which his principal, the candidate, was responsible.

14 *Brecon Borough Case, Watkins and Watkins v Holford* (1871) 2 O'M & H 43; *Harwich Borough Case* (1880) 3 O'M & H 61; *Poole Case, Hurdle and Stark v Waring* (1874) 31 LT 171, 2 O'M & H 123; *Kidderminster Case* (1874) 2 O'M & H 170; *Salford Case* (1869) 20 LT 120, 1 O'M & H 133. The time at which an alleged act of bribery is done is also considered to be relevant to that particular offence: see PARA 716.

15 *Great Yarmouth Borough Case* (1906) 5 O'M & H 176 at 193 per Channell J (otherwise even bribery might be justified upon the ground that it was the custom to take a coin for a vote).

16 See PARA 901.

D. UNDUE INFLUENCE

723.   Undue influence.   A person guilty of undue influence at an election[1] is guilty of a corrupt practice[2]; and a person[3] is guilty of undue influence:

(1)   if he, directly or indirectly, by himself or by any other person on his behalf, makes use of or threatens to make use of any force, violence or restraint[4], or inflicts or threatens to inflict, by himself or by any other person, any temporal[5] or spiritual injury[6], damage, harm or loss upon or against any person in order to induce or compel that person to vote or refrain from voting, or on account of that person having voted or refrained from voting[7];

(2)   if, by abduction, duress or any fraudulent device or contrivance[8], he impedes or prevents[9], or intends to impede or prevent, the free exercise of the franchise of an elector (or proxy for an elector)[10], or so compels, induces or prevails upon, or intends so to compel, induce or prevail upon, an elector (or proxy for an elector) either to vote or to refrain from voting[11].

A candidate who is reported by an election court guilty by his agents of the corrupt practice of undue influence may be excused from the consequences in certain circumstances[12].

1   Ie at a parliamentary election, a local government election, a Welsh Assembly election, or at a
     European parliamentary election. As to the meaning of 'Assembly election' see PARA 3 note 2; as
     to the meaning of 'parliamentary election' see PARA 9; and as to the meaning of 'local
     government election' see PARA 11. As to elections in the City of London see PARA 33; and as to
     European parliamentary elections see PARA 217 et seq. A person in a position of authority and
     responsibility who, without being personally guilty of any overt act, nevertheless does nothing to
     prevent undue influence becomes responsible for the undue influence if it is clear that he could
     have prevented it if he had chosen to do so: see PARA 728.
         The Representation of the People Act 1983 s 115 is applied and modified for the purposes of
     local authority referendums, subject to the modifications specified, in relation to Wales, by the
     Local Authorities (Conduct of Referendums) (Wales) Regulations 2008, SI 2008/1848, reg 8(2),
     Sch 4 Table 1, and, in relation to England, by the Local Authorities (Conduct of Referendums)
     (England) Regulations 2012, SI 2012/323, regs 8(2), 11–13, Sch 4 Table 1: see PARA 15 note 2.
     As to the meaning of 'referendum' see PARA 574 note 2.

2   Representation of the People Act 1983 s 115(1); European Parliamentary Elections
     Regulations 2004, SI 2004/293, reg 79(1); National Assembly for Wales (Representation of the
     People) Order 2007, SI 2007/236, art 81(1). As to votes struck off for undue influence see PARA
     842; and as to the consequences of a corrupt practice see PARA 887 et seq. See also *East Kerry
     Case* (1910) 6 O'M & H 58; *R v Rowe, ex p Mainwaring* [1992] 4 All ER 821, [1992] 1 WLR
     1059, CA, at 829 and 1068 per Farquharson LJ, at 830 and 1069 per Nolan LJ and at 831 and
     1070 per Parker LJ (reference to a person being 'guilty' of corrupt practice connotes a criminal
     offence and, accordingly, a criminal standard of proof is to be applied in a civil court no less
     than in a criminal court); and see PARA 831 et seq. As to the standard of proof required for a
     vote to be avoided for personation see PARA 844.

3   'Person' includes a corporate body: see PARA 95 note 1. A corporation cannot be convicted of an
     offence involving personal violence: *R v Cory Bros & Co* [1927] 1 KB 810.

4   As to the use or threatened use of force, violence or restraint see PARA 724.

5   As to temporal influences see PARA 725.

6   As to spiritual influence see PARA 726.

7   Representation of the People Act 1983 s 115(2)(a); European Parliamentary Elections
     Regulations 2004, SI 2004/293, reg 79(2)(a); National Assembly for Wales (Representation of
     the People) Order 2007, SI 2007/236, art 81(2)(a).

8   As to what might constitute fraudulent device or contrivance see PARA 727.

9   See *R v Rowe, ex p Mainwaring* [1992] 4 All ER 821, [1992] 1 WLR 1059, CA, where the court
     refused to construe the words 'calculated to impede or prevent' from the Representation of the
     People Act 1983 s 115(2)(b) (as originally enacted) but advised its amendment by reference to
     the less blatant and less easily detected but no less effective methods of exerting influence which
     are available and are worthy of attracting a penalty. In *R v Rowe, ex p Mainwaring* at 826 and
     1064–1065, Farquharson LJ explained that the difference between 'impeding' and 'preventing'
     lies in the effect on the voter's choice of candidate and that the operative time for the offence is
     the moment of voting: an improper influence which is brought to bear on the mind of a voter
     and causes him to vote as the person exercising that improper influence intended (when
     otherwise he would not), 'prevents' the free exercise of his franchise; a voter who, though
     influenced by the impropriety, is not thereby caused to vote in the way intended (either because
     he was going to vote that way anyway, or because the device did not cause him to change his
     allegiance), is 'impeded' in the free exercise of his franchise. See further *R v Rowe,
     ex p Mainwaring* at 830 and 1068–1069 per Nolan LJ.

10   As to the meaning of 'elector' in relation to a parliamentary or local government election see
     PARA 95 note 2; in relation to a European parliamentary election, see PARA 111 note 4; and, in
     relation to a Welsh Assembly election, see PARA 110 note 6. As to applications to vote by post or
     by proxy see PARA 367 et seq.

11   Representation of the People Act 1983 s 115(2)(b) (amended by the Electoral Administration
     Act 2006 s 39(1), (2)); European Parliamentary Elections Regulations 2004, SI 2004/293,
     reg 79(2)(b) (substituted by SI 2009/186); National Assembly for Wales (Representation of the
     People) Order 2007, SI 2007/236, art 81(2)(b). In *Spencer v Huggett* [1997] 30 LS Gaz R 30
     (cited in PARA 665), it was held that the court had jurisdiction to grant an injunction to restrain
     a breach of the Representation of the People Act 1983 s 115(2)(b) (as originally enacted), where
     a candidate was alleged to be telling untruths about himself in nomination papers. See also
     note 8.

12   See PARA 901.

724. Use or threatened use of force, violence or restraint. It is the undue influence on individual voters and not general rioting or violence which constitutes the corrupt practice[1]. In order to constitute undue influence a threat must be serious and intended to influence the voter[2]. A threat may amount to undue influence even though the person using the threat has no power to carry it out[3]. An unsuccessful threat has been held to amount to undue influence[4]. It has been held to be an offence where a voter's sister was told that he would be hurt if she did not keep him at home[5].

1 *Cheltenham Case, Gardner v Samuelson* (1869) 1 O'M & H 62; *Nottingham Borough Case* (1869) 1 O'M & H 245. As to the offence of undue influence see PARA 723; and as to the consequences of a corrupt practice see PARA 887 et seq.
2 *North Norfolk Case* (1869) 1 O'M & H 236 at 240, 242. See also *Windsor Case, Herbert v Gardiner* (1874) 31 LT 133 at 136, 2 O'M & H 88 at 91 per Bramwell B (the force of a threat must be in existence, continuing till the time of the election, before it will avoid the election).
3 *Oldham Case* (1869) 20 LT 302, 1 O'M & H 151 at 162.
4 *Northallerton Case* (1869) 1 O'M & H 167; *Durham County, Northern Division Case (No 2)* (1874) 2 O'M & H 152.
5 *Louth, Northern Division Case* (1911) 6 O'M & H 103 at 140. There do not appear to be any cases of duress where the threat was directed not against the voter himself but against a relative or friend of the voter.

725. Temporal influence. The law cannot strike at the existence of influence; it cannot take away from a man who has property, or who can give employment, the influence he has over those whom he can benefit[1]. A landlord is therefore entitled to use influence with his tenants if he does so legitimately[2]. He has a perfect right to choose a tenant who agrees with him in politics rather than one who does not[3]. A suggestion to a tenant to vote for a particular candidate and a request that, if the voter could not do so, he should stay at home and not vote against that candidate, has been held not to exceed the bounds of legitimate influence[4]; but the threat of eviction of a tenant, who then votes under the influence of that threat, is undue influence[5].

If an employer dismisses an employee, he may be called upon to prove that he has good grounds for the dismissal apart from political grounds[6], and if the dismissal were for political reasons it would amount to undue influence[7].

Where workmen for political purposes ill-treated certain of their fellow workmen and expelled them from a common place of employment, they were guilty of undue influence[8].

It has been laid down that to withdraw, or to threaten to withdraw, one's custom in order to induce a voter to vote or to abstain from voting amounts to undue influence[9]. On the other hand, it has been said that it is open to a man to say that he chooses to deal with another, not in accordance with the merits of the commodities he sells, but according to his politics on one side or the other[10]. A letter written by a lady withdrawing her custom from a voter, who occasionally looked after puppies for her, on the ground of his political views, has been stated to be not sufficient to justify a criminal charge of undue influence[11]. It appears that the loss, or threat of loss, must be so serious that a judge could direct a jury in a criminal court to find the individual guilty of the statutory offence[12].

A promise to take no proceedings on a bill of sale if a voter voted as required might amount to undue influence[13].

1 *Lichfield Case, Anson v Dyott* (1869) 20 LT 11, 1 O'M & H 22. As to the statutory offence of undue influence at elections see PARA 723; and as to the consequences of a corrupt practice see PARA 887 et seq.
2 *Galway Borough Case* (1869) 22 LT 75 at 77, 1 O'M & H 303 at 306.

3　*Windsor Case, Herbert v Gardiner* (1874) 31 LT 133 at 137, 2 O'M & H 88 at 93 (where the eviction of tenants for the way they voted at the previous election was held not to be undue influence on the ground that the undue influence undoubtedly used at the previous election had not been repeated at the election under consideration and was not still operative).

4　*Galway County Case* (1872) 2 O'M & H 46 at 54.

5　*Windsor Case, Herbert v Gardiner* (1874) 31 LT 133, 2 O'M & H 88.

6　*Blackburn Case* (1869) 1 O'M & H 198; *Dorsetshire, Eastern Division Case* (1910) 6 O'M & H 22 at 31, 46.

7　*Westbury Case, Laverton v Phipps, Harrop's Case* (1869) 20 LT 16 at 22, 1 O'M & H 47 at 52; *Wareham Case* (1857) Wolf & D 85 at 90, 29 LTOS 346 at 347 (threatening to dismiss an employee unless he voted for the sitting member); *Harwich Case (No 2)* (1866) 14 LT 383.

8　See *Blackburn Case* (1869) 20 LT 823, 1 O'M & H 198.

9　*R v Barnwell* (1857) 29 LTOS 107; *R v Wilson* (1910) Times, 12 July.

10　*Durham County, Northern Division Case (No 2)* (1874) 2 O'M & H 152.

11　*R v Wilson* (1910) Times, 12 July.

12　*North Norfolk Case* (1869) 1 O'M & H 236 at 241–242.

13　*Cheltenham Case, Digby's Case* (1866) 14 LT 839 at 841.

726. Spiritual influence. Ministers of religion may legitimately address their congregations upon the candidates' conflicting claims, but, in this connection, must not hold out hopes of reward for the hereafter, or threaten to excommunicate or to withhold the sacraments, or denounce the voting for any particular candidate as a sin[1].

1　*Galway Borough Case* (1869) 22 LT 75, 1 O'M & H 303; *Longford Case* (1870) 2 O'M & H 6; *Tipperary Case* (1870) 2 O'M & H 31; *Meath, Southern Division Case* (1892) 4 O'M & H 130; *Meath, Northern Division Case* (1892) 4 O'M & H 185 at 188.

727. Fraudulent device or contrivance. A candidate who has adopted a name which closely resembles that of another candidate standing at the same election may be held to contravene the statutory provisions aimed at preventing undue influence[1].

It is not clear whether matters relating to the secrecy of the ballot come within the statutory provisions or not. In one case, a newspaper article distributed in a constituency alleged a plan by which it would be possible to ascertain after the election how each voter had voted; on a prosecution for undue influence, the judges were divided in opinion, the senior judge holding that it was not within the provisions because it was impossible to specify or ascertain the individuals affected by it, the junior judge holding that it was within the provisions because it was a contrivance interfering with the free exercise of the franchise[2]. Where a number of voters who could read and write had been induced to vote as illiterates, and so to disclose unnecessarily for whom they voted, the court held that, although the facts were suspicious and might be relevant on the question of intimidation, illegal intent had not been established and there was no proof of a contrivance[3].

A fraudulent scheme by which an elector is prevented from receiving a candidate's election literature may constitute undue influence, as his freedom of choice has been impeded[4].

Watching voters at polling stations in the hope that by so doing they might be induced to vote for a particular candidate, or at all events not to vote against him, has been held to be a legal, although an objectionable, practice[5].

An agreement by two voters to pair and not vote has in the absence of fraud been held not to come within the statutory provisions aimed at preventing undue influence even though one voter as the result of false information thought the other had voted and in consequence voted himself[6].

1   See *Lyell v Hayward (also known as Lyell)* (15 April 1997, unreported) (defendant's use of claimant's name on nomination papers was calculated to induce electors in the constituency to believe that he was in fact the claimant and constituted a fraudulent device or contrivance to impede or prevent the free exercise of the franchise of such electors). As to the statutory offence of undue influence see PARA 723.

A previous case of similar fact had been decided on the basis that the effect of a candidate adopting a name which was likely to mislead members of the electorate was an abuse of the electoral process and that this abuse allowed the court to exercise its powers to prevent an abuse of its own procedure: see *R v Returning Officer for the Parliamentary Constituency of Barnet and Finchley, ex p Bennett v Thatcher* (3 June 1983, unreported), CA (where a male candidate changed his name by deed poll to 'Margaret Thatcher' (who was then prime minister) and styled his address as 'Downing Street Mansions'; it was held that his nomination paper was designed to confuse the electorate and to make a farce of the electoral process and that, accordingly, his application for the discretionary remedy of judicial review of the returning officer's rejection of the nomination paper was refused without needing to determine whether or not the returning officer acted lawfully in so rejecting it). Where a nomination paper is an obvious unreality (eg if it purported to nominate a deceased Sovereign), it has been suggested, as an obiter dictum, that it ought to be rejected: *Harford v Linsksey* [1899] 1 QB 852 at 862, DC, per Wright J (but that case concerned the right of a validly nominated, but disqualified, candidate to bring an election petition). This suggestion was cited in *Hobbs v Morey* [1904] 1 KB 74 at 78, DC, but to support the proposition that, in the event of such a nomination being accepted, no notice of disqualification (see PARA 268) need be published by an opposing candidate.

2   *Down County Case* (1880) 3 O'M & H 115.

3   *Louth, Northern Division Case* (1911) 6 O'M & H 103 at 139.

4   *Roberts v Hogg* 1971 SLT 78 (the accused took possession of election literature of another party which was intended for distribution to the electors prior to a local government election; it was found that he took it, not to distribute it, but to destroy or suppress it, and he was convicted), cited with approval in *R v Rowe, ex p Mainwaring* [1992] 4 All ER 821, [1992] 1 WLR 1059, CA, to support the point that the Representation of the People Act 1983 s 115(2)(b) (see PARA 723) does not rely on intention only.

5   *Lichfield Borough Case* (1880) 3 O'M & H 136; *Dorsetshire, Eastern Division Case* (1910) 6 O'M & H 22 at 48.

6   *Northallerton Case* (1869) 1 O'M & H 167 at 169.

728.   Acquiescence by official in face of undue influence.   A mere passive outsider who owes no duty to interfere or prevent undue influence cannot be made responsible for it; but a person in a position of authority and responsibility who, without being personally guilty of any overt act, nevertheless does nothing to prevent the undue influence becomes responsible for the undue influence if it is clear that he could have prevented it if he had chosen to do so[1].

1   *Louth, Northern Division Case* (1911) 6 O'M & H 103 at 143.

(v)   Offences which are also Corrupt Practices

729.   Offences which also constitute corrupt practices.   The following indictable offences are also deemed to be corrupt practices[1]:
  (1)   personation[2];
  (2)   offences arising from false applications to vote by post or by proxy[3].
Dishonest abuses of the franchise, including but not limited to corrupt practices, have produced findings of general corruption and of personal corruption amounting to electoral fraud (although that term is not used in the legislation)[4].

1   As to the consequences of corrupt practices see PARA 887 et seq. As to abuses of the electoral system which are characterised as corrupt practices without being expressly criminalised see PARA 704 et seq.

2   See PARA 730.

3   See PARA 731.

4   See PARA 754. As to avoidance of an election by reason of general corruption see PARA 895.

730. Personation. A person[1] is guilty of a corrupt practice if he commits, or aids, abets, counsels or procures the commission of, the offence of personation[2]. A person is deemed to be guilty of personation at an election or referendum[3] if he[4]:

(1)	votes in person or by post as some other person, whether as an elector or as proxy[5], and whether that other person is living or dead or is a fictitious person[6]; or

(2)	votes in person or by post as proxy: (a) for a person whom he knows or has reasonable grounds for supposing to be dead or to be a fictitious person[7]; or (b) when he knows or has reasonable grounds for supposing that his appointment as proxy is no longer in force[8].

A person who has applied for a ballot paper for the purpose of voting in person or who has marked, whether validly or not, and returned a ballot paper issued for the purpose of voting by post, is deemed to have voted[9].

Mens rea is an essential ingredient in personation[10], and an agent who honestly believes that the person whom he is instigating to vote is the person whose name is on the register is not guilty of a corrupt practice, although the person whose vote is in question may know that he is not the person whose name is on the register[11]. On the same principle, if a person believes that he is entitled to vote in the name in which he votes but innocently votes in the name of another, this does not amount to personation[12]. However, using the name of a real person to register a name on the register when that person is not qualified by residence (or for some other reason) to vote in that constituency or ward, and then using that name to cast a vote, is as much personation as using the name of a fictitious person[13].

1	As to the meaning of 'person' see PARA 95 note 1.
2	Representation of the People Act 1983 s 60(1); European Parliamentary Elections Regulations 2004, SI 2004/293, reg 23(1); National Assembly for Wales (Representation of the People) Order 2007, SI 2007/236, art 30(1). As to an example of inducing a person to commit personation see *R v Hague* (1864) 4 B & S 715. As to striking off a vote for personation see PARA 844; as to the consequences of corrupt practices generally see PARA 887 et seq; and as to the avoidance of an election on report of a corrupt practice see PARA 894.
	The Representation of the People Act 1983 s 60 is applied for the purposes of a poll consequent on a parish or community meeting: see s 187(1) (amended by the Representation of the People Act 1985 ss 24, 28, Sch 4 para 64, Sch 5); and the Parish and Community Meetings (Polls) Rules 1987, SI 1987/1, r 6(a), (d). The Representation of the People Act 1983 s 60 also is applied and modified for the purposes of local authority referendums, subject to the modifications specified, in relation to Wales, by the Local Authorities (Conduct of Referendums) (Wales) Regulations 2008, SI 2008/1848, reg 8(2), Sch 4 Table 1, and, in relation to England, by the Local Authorities (Conduct of Referendums) (England) Regulations 2012, SI 2012/323, regs 8(2), 11–13, Sch 4 Table 1: see PARA 15 note 2. As to the meaning of 'referendum' see PARA 574 note 2.
3	Ie at a parliamentary election, a local government election, a Welsh Assembly election, or at a European parliamentary election. As to the meaning of 'Assembly election' see PARA 3 note 2; as to the meaning of 'parliamentary election' see PARA 9; and as to the meaning of 'local government election' see PARA 11. As to elections in the City of London see PARA 33; and as to European parliamentary elections see PARA 217 et seq.
4	See the Representation of the People Act 1983 s 60(2); the European Parliamentary Elections Regulations 2004, SI 2004/293, reg 23(2); and the National Assembly for Wales (Representation of the People) Order 2007, SI 2007/236, art 30(2). The Police and Criminal Evidence Act 1984 s 24A (arrest without warrant (other persons): see POLICE AND INVESTIGATORY POWERS vol 84A (2013) PARA 488) does not permit a person other than a constable to arrest inside a polling station a person who commits or is suspected of committing an offence under the Representation of the People Act 1983 s 60, in relation to a parliamentary or local government election, or under the National Assembly for Wales (Representation of the People) Order 2007, SI 2007/236, art 30(1)–(3), in relation to a Welsh Assembly election: Electoral Administration

Act 2006 s 71; National Assembly for Wales (Representation of the People) Order 2007, SI 2007/236, art 30(4). As to the challenge and arrest of a person suspected of personation see PARA 400.

5   As to the meaning of 'elector' in relation to a parliamentary or local government election see PARA 95 note 2; in relation to a European parliamentary election, see PARA 111 note 4; and, in relation to a Welsh Assembly election, see PARA 110 note 6. As to applications to vote by post or by proxy see PARA 367 et seq.

6   Representation of the People Act 1983 s 60(2)(a); European Parliamentary Elections Regulations 2004, SI 2004/293, reg 23(2)(a); National Assembly for Wales (Representation of the People) Order 2007, SI 2007/236, art 30(2)(a). If the name of the voter was placed on the register with the intention of enabling him to vote, he does not commit the offence by applying for a ballot paper in that name, even though the name is not his own: *R v Fox* (1887) 16 Cox CC 166; and see *Oldham Case* (1869) 1 O'M & H 151 at 152. See also the text and notes 10–13. As to the effect of misdescription in documents published by a registration officer see PARA 150.

7   Representation of the People Act 1983 s 60(2)(b)(i); European Parliamentary Elections Regulations 2004, SI 2004/293, reg 23(2)(b)(i); National Assembly for Wales (Representation of the People) Order 2007, SI 2007/236, art 30(2)(b)(i).

8   Representation of the People Act 1983 s 60(2)(b)(ii); European Parliamentary Elections Regulations 2004, SI 2004/293, reg 23(2)(b)(ii); National Assembly for Wales (Representation of the People) Order 2007, SI 2007/236, art 30(2)(b)(ii).

9   Representation of the People Act 1983 s 60(3); European Parliamentary Elections Regulations 2004, SI 2004/293, reg 23(3); National Assembly for Wales (Representation of the People) Order 2007, SI 2007/236, art 30(3).

10   *Gloucester Borough Case, Guise v Wait* (1873) 2 O'M & H 59 at 63–64; *Stepney Division, Tower Hamlets Case* (1886) 54 LT 684 at 685. A candidate is nevertheless liable to have his election avoided for corrupt practices (including procuring personation) committed by his agent even though the acts were unauthorised by him: see *Gloucester Borough Case*; and see also PARA 244.

11   *Gloucester Borough Case, Guise v Wait* (1873) 2 O'M & H 59 at 63. Conversely, the agent may be guilty although the voter may be innocent: *Hexham Case* (1892) cited in Day 68.

12   *Athlone Borough Case* (1880) 3 O'M & H 57 at 59 (where a son, who succeeded his father, having the same name, voted in the name of his father, who was in fact the person intended on the register). As to misdescription in documents published by a registration officer see note 6.

13   *Re Central Ward, Slough Election Petition, Simmons v Khan* [2008] EWHC B4 (QB), Election Ct. If the real person consents (*a fortiori* if he actually completes the offending documents), he is himself guilty of personation and those who induce him to commit that fraud are likewise guilty; but, if the name of the real person has not been used with his knowledge or consent, then that name is, to all intents and purposes, a fictitious name properly so called and thus expressly within the Representation of the People Act 1983 s 60: *Re Central Ward, Slough Election Petition, Simmons v Khan*.

731.   Offences which are corrupt practices arising from false applications to vote by post or by proxy.   A person[1] commits an offence if he[2]:

(1)   engages in any act specified in heads (a) to (d) below at an election[3]; and

(2)   intends, by doing so, to deprive another of an opportunity to vote or to make for himself or another a gain of a vote to which he or the other is not otherwise entitled or a gain of money or property[4].

The prohibited acts are:

(a)   applying for a postal or proxy vote[5] as some other person (whether that other person is living or dead or is a fictitious person)[6];

(b)   otherwise making a false statement in, or in connection with, an application for a postal or proxy vote[7];

(c)   inducing the registration officer[8] or returning officer[9] to send a postal ballot paper[10] or any communication relating to a postal or proxy vote to an address which has not been agreed to by the person entitled to the vote[11];

(d) causing a communication relating to a postal or proxy vote (or containing a postal ballot paper) not to be delivered to the intended recipient[12].

A person who commits such an offence or who aids, abets, counsels or procures the commission of such an offence is guilty of a corrupt practice[13].

1 As to the meaning of 'person' see PARA 95 note 1.
2 Representation of the People Act 1983 s 62A(1) (s 62A added by the Electoral Administration Act 2006 s 40); European Parliamentary Elections Regulations 2004, SI 2004/293, Sch 2 para 11(1) (Sch 2 substituted by SI 2009/186); National Assembly for Wales (Representation of the People) Order 2007, SI 2007/236, art 14(7).
  The Representation of the People Act 1983 s 62A applies at a poll consequent on a parish or community meeting by virtue of s 187(1) and the Local Government Act 1972 s 99, Sch 12 paras 18(5), 34(5): see PARA 383. The Representation of the People Act 1983 s 62A is also applied and modified for the purposes of local authority referendums, subject to the modifications specified, in relation to Wales, by the Local Authorities (Conduct of Referendums) (Wales) Regulations 2008, SI 2008/1848, reg 8(2), Sch 4 Table 1, and, in relation to England, by the Local Authorities (Conduct of Referendums) (England) Regulations 2012, SI 2012/323, regs 8(2), 11–13, Sch 4 Table 1: see PARA 15 note 2. As to the meaning of 'referendum' see PARA 574 note 2.
3 Representation of the People Act 1983 s 62A(1)(a) (as added: see note 2); European Parliamentary Elections Regulations 2004, SI 2004/293, Sch 2 para 11(1)(a) (as substituted: see note 2); National Assembly for Wales (Representation of the People) Order 2007, SI 2007/236, art 14(7)(a). The election referred to in the text may be a parliamentary election, a local government election, a Welsh Assembly election, or a European parliamentary election. As to the meaning of 'Assembly election' see PARA 3 note 2; as to the meaning of 'parliamentary election' see PARA 9; and as to the meaning of 'local government election' see PARA 11. As to elections in the City of London see PARA 33; and as to European parliamentary elections see PARA 217 et seq. The provision made by the Representation of the People Act 1983 s 62A covers some of the many and various kinds of abuse of electoral procedures that were found to have prevailed in *Akhtar v Jahan, Iqbal v Islam* [2005] All ER (D) 15 (Apr), Election Ct (decision revsd in part, but on a point of evidence, sub nom *R (on the application of Afzal) v Election Court* [2005] EWCA Civ 647, [2005] LGR 823); and in *Re Central Ward, Slough Election Petition, Simmons v Khan* [2008] EWHC B4 (QB), Election Ct. See further PARA 754 et seq.
4 Representation of the People Act 1983 s 62A(1)(b) (as added: see note 2); European Parliamentary Elections Regulations 2004, SI 2004/293, Sch 2 para 11(1)(b) (as substituted: see note 2); National Assembly for Wales (Representation of the People) Order 2007, SI 2007/236, art 14(7)(b). For this purpose, property includes any description of property: see the Representation of the People Act 1983 s 62A(3) (as so added); the European Parliamentary Elections Regulations 2004, SI 2004/293, Sch 2 para 11(3) (as so substituted); and the National Assembly for Wales (Representation of the People) Order 2007, SI 2007/236, art 14(9).
5 For these purposes, a reference to a postal vote includes a reference to a proxy postal vote: see the Representation of the People Act 1983 s 62A(4) (as added: see note 2); the European Parliamentary Elections Regulations 2004, SI 2004/293, Sch 2 para 11(4) (as substituted: see note 2); and the National Assembly for Wales (Representation of the People) Order 2007, SI 2007/236, art 14(10). As to applications to vote by post or by proxy see PARA 367 et seq.
6 Representation of the People Act 1983 s 62A(2)(a) (as added: see note 2); European Parliamentary Elections Regulations 2004, SI 2004/293, Sch 2 para 11(2)(a) (as substituted: see note 2); National Assembly for Wales (Representation of the People) Order 2007, SI 2007/236, art 14(8)(a). Using the name of a real person to register a name on the register and apply for a postal vote when that person is not qualified by residence (or for some other reason) to vote in that constituency or ward, would involve corrupt practices under the Representation of the People Act 1983 s 62A: *Re Central Ward, Slough Election Petition, Simmons v Khan* [2008] EWHC B4 (QB), Election Ct.
7 Representation of the People Act 1983 s 62A(2)(b) (as added: see note 2); European Parliamentary Elections Regulations 2004, SI 2004/293, Sch 2 para 11(2)(b) (as substituted: see note 2); National Assembly for Wales (Representation of the People) Order 2007, SI 2007/236, art 14(8)(b).
8 As to electoral registration officers see PARA 139 et seq.
9 In the case of a European parliamentary election, the reference is to a local returning officer: see the European Parliamentary Elections Regulations 2004, SI 2004/293, Sch 2 para 11(2)(c) (as substituted: see note 2). At a Welsh Assembly election, the reference is to the constituency

returning officer: see the National Assembly for Wales (Representation of the People) Order 2007, SI 2007/236, art 14(8)(c). As to the meaning of 'constituency returning officer' for this purpose see PARA 18 note 2. As to returning officers for parliamentary elections see PARA 350 et seq; as to returning officers for local government elections see PARA 354 et seq; and as to local returning officers appointed for the purposes of elections to the European Parliament see PARA 360.

10   For these purposes, a reference to a postal ballot paper includes a reference to a proxy postal ballot paper: see the Representation of the People Act 1983 s 62A(4) (as added: see note 2); the European Parliamentary Elections Regulations 2004, SI 2004/293, Sch 2 para 11(4) (as substituted: see note 2); and the National Assembly for Wales (Representation of the People) Order 2007, SI 2007/236, art 14(10).

11   Representation of the People Act 1983 s 62A(2)(c) (as added: see note 2); European Parliamentary Elections Regulations 2004, SI 2004/293, Sch 2 para 11(2)(c) (as substituted: see note 2); National Assembly for Wales (Representation of the People) Order 2007, SI 2007/236, art 14(8)(c).

12   Representation of the People Act 1983 s 62A(2)(d) (as added: see note 2); European Parliamentary Elections Regulations 2004, SI 2004/293, Sch 2 para 11(2)(d) (as substituted: see note 2); National Assembly for Wales (Representation of the People) Order 2007, SI 2007/236, art 14(8)(d).

13   Representation of the People Act 1983 s 62A(5) (as added: see note 2); European Parliamentary Elections Regulations 2004, SI 2004/293, Sch 2 para 11(5) (as substituted: see note 2); National Assembly for Wales (Representation of the People) Order 2007, SI 2007/236, art 14(11).

(vi)   Offences

732.   Offences.   The following are offences which do not constitute either a corrupt or illegal practice[1]:

(1)   interfering with or obstructing the registration officer's duty to maintain electoral registers[2];

(2)   interference with documents published or made available by the registration officer in pursuance of his duties[3];

(3)   unlawful disclosure of the full electoral register or its contents[4];

(4)   making a false statement in or irregular attestation of any declaration or form used in connection with absent voting[5];

(5)   making a false or irregular declaration of local connection, service declaration or overseas elector's declaration[6];

(6)   making a false statement in any application or declaration required for registration or nomination purposes by a relevant citizen of the Union[7];

(7)   breaches of official duty[8];

(8)   tampering with nomination or ballot papers[9];

(9)   contravening the requirement to keep the ballot secret[10];

(10)   publishing an exit poll before the poll is closed[11];

(11)   failure to comply with conditions on access to or control of election documents[12];

(12)   acting as a candidate's agent while an election official[13];

(13)   canvassing in the police area while a member of the police force[14];

(14)   failure to display required details on election or referendum publications[15];

(15)   contravening the controls imposed on expenditure incurred during election and referendum campaigns[16];

(16)   contravening the controls imposed on donations during election and referendum campaigns[17];

(17)   obstructing the Electoral Commission in its duties[18].

Although many kinds of electoral malpractice are made into criminal offences, there is no consistency in the treatment of those offences, especially in the way that some summary offences are expressly stated to be 'illegal practices', the more serious offences are stated to be 'corrupt practices', and those under heads (1) to (17) above are not characterised as either; a purposive construction of the legislation might allow any conduct that is made into a criminal offence under heads (1) to (17) above to be treated as an 'illegal practice' for the purposes of avoiding an election, whether or not this is expressly spelled out in the statutory provision concerned[19].

1   As to illegal practices see PARA 671 et seq; as to criminal offences that are also characterised as illegal practices see PARA 699 et seq; as to corrupt practices see PARA 704 et seq; and as to criminal offences that are also characterised as corrupt practices see PARA 729 et seq. As to the punishment of offences see PARA 882 et seq. See also the text and note 19.
2   See PARA 733.
3   See PARA 733.
4   See PARA 734.
5   See PARA 735.
6   See PARA 735.
7   See PARA 736.
8   See PARA 737.
9   See PARA 738.
10   See PARAS 739–743.
11   See PARA 744.
12   See PARA 745.
13   See PARA 746.
14   See PARA 747.
15   See PARAS 748–750.
16   See PARA 751.
17   See PARA 752.
18   See PARA 753.

19   *Re Central Ward, Slough Election Petition, Simmons v Khan* [2008] EWHC B4 (QB), Election Ct, at [24]–[31] per Commissioner Mawrey QC (in considering whether to avoid an election, the purpose of the misconduct found must always be to affect the result of the election to which it relates; if a candidate's election has been procured by the commission of criminal offences, Parliament cannot be saying that his election should stand merely because Parliament has omitted to write into the sections creating those offences words saying 'these are also illegal practices'). In that case, Commissioner Mawrey QC observed that, in an earlier case, he had treated an offence under the Representation of the People Act 2000 Sch 4 para 8 (see PARA 735) as an illegal practice, notwithstanding the absence of express words making it an 'illegal practice' in that part of the Act, a decision that was not challenged on appeal: see at [29] per Commissioner Mawrey QC; and as to the earlier proceedings cited see *Akhtar v Jahan, Iqbal v Islam* [2005] All ER (D) 15 (Apr), Election Ct (decision revsd in part, but on a point of evidence, sub nom *R (on the application of Afzal) v Election Court* [2005] EWCA Civ 647, [2005] LGR 823). In *Re Maybury and Sheerwater Ward of Woking Borough Council, Ali v Bashir* [2013] EWHC 2572 (QB), [2013] All ER (D) 24 (Nov), Commissioner Mawrey QC repeated and applied his treatment of misconduct amounting to a criminal offence as constituting an illegal practice, notwithstanding the absence of express words in the relevant statute making it an illegal practice, referring again to his previous rulings to that effect which had not been challenged.

733.   Interference with the duties of registration officer.   A person who for any purpose connected with the registration of electors[1] provides to a registration officer[2] any false information is guilty of an offence[3], and is liable on summary conviction to a fine, or to a term of imprisonment, or to both[4].

If any person fails to comply with any requisition of a registration officer[5] to give information, either for the purposes of that officer's duties in maintaining registers of parliamentary and local government electors[6], or for the purposes of that officer's duty under the Juries Act 1974[7], that person is liable on summary conviction to a fine[8].

If any person without lawful authority destroys, mutilates, defaces or removes any notice published by the registration officer in connection with his registration duties with regard to any parliamentary or local government election[9], any Welsh Assembly election[10], or any European parliamentary election[11], or any copies of a document which have been made available for inspection in pursuance of those duties, he is liable on summary conviction to a fine[12].

1   As to the registration of electors see PARA 142 et seq.

2   As to electoral registration officers see PARA 139 et seq.

3   Representation of the People Act 1983 s 13D(1) (s 13D added by the Electoral Fraud (Northern Ireland) Act 2002 s 7(1) in relation to Northern Ireland, and extended to the whole of the United Kingdom by virtue of the Electoral Administration Act 2006 s 15(8); Representation of the People Act 1983 s 13D(1) substituted by the Electoral Administration Act 2006 s 15(1), (2)). For these purposes, 'false information' means a signature which is not the usual signature of, or was written by a person other than, the person whose signature it purports to be: Representation of the People Act 1983 s 13D(3) (s 13D as so added; s 13D(3), (4) amended by the Electoral Administration Act 2006 s 15(1), (4), (5)). A person does not commit an offence, however, if he did not know, and had no reason to suspect, that the information was false: Representation of the People Act 1983 s 13D(4) (as so added and amended). Where sufficient evidence is adduced to raise an issue with respect to such a defence, the court must assume that the defence is satisfied unless the prosecution proves beyond reasonable doubt that it is not: s 13D(5) (as so added).

The Representation of the People Act 1983 s 13D is applied to the provision of false registration information for the registration of relevant citizens of the Union as European Parliamentary electors in connection with European parliamentary elections: see the European Parliamentary Elections (Franchise of Relevant Citizens of the Union) Regulations 2001, SI 2001/1184, reg 7; and PARA 736.

4   Representation of the People Act 1983 s 13D(6) (s 13D as added (see note 3); s 13D(6) amended, s 13D(8) added, by the Electoral Administration Act 2006 s 15(1), (6)–(7)). A person guilty of an offence under the Representation of the People Act 1983 s 13D(1) is liable on summary conviction to imprisonment for a term not exceeding 51 weeks, or to a fine not exceeding level 5 on the standard scale, or to both: see the Representation of the People Act 1983 s 13D(6) (s 13D as so added, s 13D(6) as so amended). In relation to an offence committed before the date of commencement of the Criminal Justice Act 2003 s 281(5) (not yet in force) (alteration of penalties for summary offences: see SENTENCING AND DISPOSITION OF OFFENDERS vol 92 (2010) PARA 374), the reference in the Representation of the People Act 1983 s 13D(6) to 51 weeks must be taken to be a reference to six months: s 13D(8) (as so added). As to the standard scale see SENTENCING AND DISPOSITION OF OFFENDERS vol 92 (2010) PARA 142. As to the application and modification of these provisions see note 3.

5   Ie any such requisition as is mentioned in the Representation of the People (England and Wales) Regulations 2001, SI 2001/341, reg 23 (see PARA 142): see reg 23(3) (amended by SI 2006/2910). By virtue of the Representation of the People (England and Wales) Regulations 2001, SI 2001/341, reg 13(6), (7), reg 23 applies to registration in pursuance of a European parliamentary overseas elector's declaration as it applies to registration in pursuance of an overseas elector's declaration: see PARA 101 note 7.

6   As to the duty of registration officers to maintain, prepare and publish registers of electors see PARA 143.

7   Ie to give information required for the purposes of a registration officer's duty under the Juries Act 1974 s 3(1) (electoral register as basis of jury selection: see JURIES vol 61 (2010) PARA 812): see the Representation of the People (England and Wales) Regulations 2001, SI 2001/341, reg 23(2); and PARA 142.

8   Representation of the People (England and Wales) Regulations 2001, SI 2001/341, reg 23(3) (as amended: see note 5). The penalty is a fine not exceeding level 3 on the standard scale: see reg 23(3) (as so amended). As to the standard scale see SENTENCING AND DISPOSITION OF OFFENDERS vol 92 (2010) PARA 142.

9   As to the meaning of 'parliamentary election' see PARA 9; and as to the meaning of 'local government election' see PARA 11. As to elections in the City of London see PARA 33.

10 As to the meaning of 'Assembly election' see PARA 3 note 2.

11 As to European parliamentary elections see PARA 217 et seq.

12　Representation of the People (England and Wales) Regulations 2001, SI 2001/341, reg 11; European Parliamentary Elections Regulations 2004, SI 2004/293, Sch 2 para 16 (Sch 2 substituted by SI 2009/186); National Assembly for Wales (Representation of the People) Order 2007, SI 2007/236, art 146. The penalty is a fine not exceeding level 3 on the standard scale: see the Representation of the People (England and Wales) Regulations 2001, SI 2001/341, reg 11; the European Parliamentary Elections Regulations 2004, SI 2004/293, Sch 2 para 16 (as so substituted); and the National Assembly for Wales (Representation of the People) Order 2007, SI 2007/236, art 146. Although the European Parliamentary Elections Regulations 2004, SI 2004/293, Sch 2 makes provision for the purposes of a European parliamentary election with respect to absent voting in particular, its general purpose is to make provision with respect to the manner of voting at such elections (see PARA 365 et seq) and the prohibition set out in Sch 2 para 13 appears to have a general effect.

　　The Representation of the People (England and Wales) Regulations 2001, SI 2001/341, reg 11 has been applied and modified for the purposes of a local authority referendum, in relation to Wales, by the Local Authorities (Conduct of Referendums) (Wales) Regulations 2008, SI 2008/1848, Sch 4 Table 5; and, in relation to England, by the Local Authorities (Conduct of Referendums) (England) Regulations 2012, SI 2012/323, Sch 4 Table 6. As to the meaning of 'referendum' see PARA 574 note 2. The Representation of the People (England and Wales) Regulations 2001, SI 2001/341, reg 11 also applies, by virtue of reg 13(6), (7), to a European parliamentary overseas elector's declaration and registration as it applies to an overseas elector's declaration and registration (see PARA 101 note 7) and, for the purposes of the registration of relevant citizens of the Union as European parliamentary electors, as it applies for the purposes of the registration of parliamentary and local government electors, subject to any modification and exceptions specified in relation to those provisions in the European Parliamentary Elections (Franchise of Relevant Citizens of the Union) Regulations 2001, SI 2001/1184, reg 9, Schedule (see PARA 102 note 6).

734.　Offences connected with supply and inspection of the full electoral register and associated records. A person who inspects the full register[1] and makes a copy of it or records any particulars included in it otherwise than by means of handwritten notes[2] is guilty of an offence and liable on summary conviction to a fine[3].

A person who inspects the copy of the full register that is held by the British Library[4] or by the National Library of Wales[5], as the case may be, or the copy that is supplied to the Statistics Board[6] or any copy that is supplied to a public library or a local authority archives service[7], or who inspects a copy of any information which would be included in the postal voters lists[8], the list of proxies[9] or the proxy postal voters lists[10] (whether a printed copy or in data form)[11], and who makes copies of any part, or records any particulars included therein, otherwise than by means of handwritten notes, is guilty of an offence[12] and is liable on summary conviction to a fine[13].

A person is guilty of an offence and liable on summary conviction to a fine if he contravenes any of the following provisions[14] relating to disclosure of the full register or associated records[15]:

(1)　a returning officer[16] or counting officer[17] to whom the registration officer[18] supplies, together with the copy of the register (or any part thereof), a copy of the record of anonymous entries[19] (or any part thereof) may not supply to any person a copy of the record or disclose information contained in it or make use of any such information, otherwise than for the purposes of an election or referendum[20];

(2)　each person who has been supplied with a copy of the record of anonymous entries in accordance with the Juries Act 1974[21] may not supply a copy of the record or disclose information contained in it or make use of any such information, otherwise than for the purpose of summoning jurors[22];

(3)　no person serving whether as a constable, officer or employee of any police force in Great Britain[23], the Police Information Technology Organisation[24], any body of constables established under an Act of Parliament or the National Crime Agency[25], to whom the registration officer has supplied a copy of the record of anonymous entries together with the register, may supply to any person a copy of the record, disclose any information contained in it or make use of any such information, otherwise than for the purposes of the prevention and detection of crime and the enforcement of the criminal law (whether in England and Wales or elsewhere) or the vetting of a relevant person for the purpose of safeguarding national security[26];

(4)   no person who obtains any information which would be included in the postal voters lists, the list of proxies or the proxy postal voters lists may use it for other than the permitted purposes[27] or in contravention of any restrictions which are specified or which would apply to the use of the full register under the provisions by virtue of which the information was supplied[28];

(5)   the processor[29] of registration data may not disclose the full register or the information contained in it except to the person who supplied it to the processor or an employee of that person or to a person who is entitled to obtain a copy of the full register or any employee of such a person[30];

(6)   the registration officer or a member of his staff[31] may not supply to any person a copy of the full register or disclose information contained in it (which is not contained in the edited register[32]) or make use of any such information, otherwise than in accordance with the statutory provisions[33];

(7)   any officer to whom copies of the register are delivered under the Juries Act 1974[34] and any other person to whom a copy of the full register has been supplied or to whom information contained in it has been disclosed for the purpose of summoning jurors may not supply a copy of the full register or disclose information contained in it (which is not contained in the edited register) or make use of any such information, otherwise than for the purpose of summoning jurors[35];

(8)   a person to whom a copy of the full register has been supplied for a permitted purpose (and any person who has obtained access to a copy of the full register or information contained in it by any other means) may not supply a copy of the full register or disclose information contained in it (and not contained in the edited register) or make use of any such information, other than for a permitted purpose[36];

(9)   a person employed by the British Library or by the National Library of Wales to whom a free copy of the full register has been supplied may not supply a copy of the full register other than to another such person or to a person using that library to inspect it under supervision, or disclose information contained in it (and not contained in the edited register) otherwise than by allowing a person using that library to inspect it under supervision or make use of any such information[37];

(10)   a person who obtains a copy of the full register (or to whom information contained in it that is not contained in the edited register is disclosed by a person employed by the British Library or by the National Library of Wales in circumstances where more than ten years have expired since that version of the register was first published and

the supply or disclosure is for research purposes in compliance with the relevant conditions[38]) may not supply a copy of it, or disclose any such information or make use of any such information, otherwise than for research purposes in compliance with the relevant conditions[39];

(11) a returning officer[40] to whom a copy of the register has been supplied for electoral purposes may not supply a copy of the full register or disclose any information contained in it (that is not contained in the edited register) or make use of any such information, other than for the purposes of an election[41];

(12) a person employed by the Statistics Board may not supply a copy of the full register other than to another such person or disclose any information contained in it (that is not contained in the edited register) otherwise than by allowing a person using the premises of that office to inspect it under supervision or by publishing information about electors which does not include the name or address of any elector or make use of any such information other than for statistical purposes[42];

(13) a person who obtains a copy of the full register (or to whom information contained in it that is not contained in the edited register is disclosed by a person employed by the Statistics Board in circumstances where more than ten years have expired since that version of the register was first published and the supply or disclosure is for research purposes in compliance with the relevant conditions) may not supply a copy of it, or disclose any such information or make use of any such information, otherwise than for research purposes in compliance with the relevant conditions[43];

(14) the Electoral Commissioners or any person employed by the Electoral Commission[44] may not supply a copy of the full register other than to an Electoral Commissioner or another such person, or disclose any information contained in it that is not contained in the edited register (otherwise than where necessary to carry out the Commission's duties in relation to the rules on permissible donors in the Political Parties, Elections and Referendums Act 2000, or by publishing information about electors which does not include the name or address of any elector), or make use of any such information otherwise than in connection with their functions under, or by virtue of, the Political Parties, Elections and Referendums Act 2000[45];

(15) a member of the Boundary Commission for England[46], or of the Boundary Commission for Wales[47], or of the Local Democracy and Boundary Commission for Wales[48], or a person appointed to assist the Commission in question to carry out its functions, or a person employed by the Commission in question, may not supply a copy of the full version of the register, other than to another relevant person, or disclose any information contained in it and not contained in the edited register (otherwise than by publishing information about electors which does not include the name and address of any elector), or process or make use of any such information, other than in connection with their statutory functions[49];

(16) an elected representative person who has been supplied with a copy of the register for electoral purposes may not supply a copy of the full register to any person or disclose any information contained in it that is not contained in the edited register or make use of any such

information, otherwise than for purposes in connection with the office by virtue of which he is entitled to the full register or for electoral purposes[50];

(17) the holder of a relevant elective office which is subject to the statutory controls relating to donations[51] or a candidate[52] for election at a parliamentary[53], local government[54] or Authority election[55] who has been supplied with a copy of the register may not supply a copy of the full register to any person, or disclose any information contained in it that is not contained in the edited register, or make use of any such information otherwise than for the purpose of complying with the controls on donations[56];

(18) any person nominated to act for a particular constituency by the registered nominating officer of a registered political party[57] who has been supplied with a copy of the register may not supply a copy of the full register to any person or disclose any information contained in it (that is not contained in the edited register) or make use of any such information, otherwise than for electoral purposes or the purposes of electoral registration[58];

(19) a person employed by, or assisting (whether or not for reward) a registered political party other than a minor party[59], or a recognised third party[60] other than a registered political party or a permitted participant[61] other than a registered political party, and to which a copy of the register has been supplied, may not supply a copy of the full register to any person or disclose any information contained in it (that is not contained in the edited register) or make use of any such information, otherwise than for electoral or referendum purposes or for the purpose of complying with the relevant controls on donations to registered parties or permitted participants (as the case may be)[62];

(20) a councillor or employee of a local authority by which the registration officer was appointed, or whose area falls wholly or partly within the registration area of that local authority, other than a parish council or community council falling within head (21) below, may not supply a copy of the full register to any person other than to another councillor of or employee of the same local authority or disclose any information contained in it that is not included in the edited register or make use of any such information, except where necessary for the discharge of a statutory function of the local authority or any other local authority relating to security, law enforcement and crime prevention or for the purposes of a local poll under the Local Government Act 2003[63] or for statistical purposes (in which case no information is to be disclosed which includes the name and address of any elector)[64];

(21) a parish or community councillor, or a person employed by or otherwise assisting (whether or not for reward) a parish or community council and to which a copy of the register has been supplied, may not supply a copy of the full register to any person or disclose any information contained in it that is not included in the edited register or make use of any such information, otherwise than for the purpose of establishing whether any person is entitled to attend and participate in a meeting of, or take any action on behalf of, the parish or community, as the case may be, or for the purposes of a local poll under the Local Government Act 2003[65];

(22) a candidate at a parliamentary or local government election, at a Welsh

Assembly election, or European parliamentary election, where any part of the area in respect of which the candidate stands for election includes the whole or part of a registration area to whom a copy of the register has been supplied, may not supply a copy of the full register to any person or disclose any information contained in it (that is not contained in the edited register) or make use of any such information, other than for electoral purposes[66];

(23)　a person authorised by a government department (other than the Security Service, the Government Communications Headquarters, and the Secret Intelligence Service)[67] to be supplied with a copy of the full register (or a person to whom he discloses information which is contained in the full register) may not disclose information contained in the full register except to any person falling within heads (16) to (22) above and for use for the purposes for which such a person could obtain a copy of the register under the provision concerned[68];

(24)　a person serving whether as a constable, officer or employee in specified police forces and organisations may not supply a copy of the full register to any person, or disclose any information contained in it (that is not contained in the edited register), or make use of any such information, otherwise than for the purposes of the prevention and detection of crime and the enforcement of the criminal law (whether in England and Wales or elsewhere) or for the vetting of a relevant person for the purpose of safeguarding national security[69];

(25)　a person employed by the public library or the local authority archives service may not supply a copy of the full register other than to another such person or to a person using the library or the archives service to inspect it under supervision, or disclose any information contained in it (that is not contained in the edited register) otherwise than by allowing a person using the library or the archives service to inspect it under supervision, or make use of any such information[70];

(26)　a person who obtains a copy of the full register (or to whom information contained in it that is not contained in the edited register is disclosed by a person employed by a public library or local authority archives service in circumstances where more than ten years have expired since that version of the register was first published and the supply or disclosure is for research purposes in compliance with the relevant conditions) may not supply a copy of it, or disclose any such information or make use of any such information, otherwise than for research purposes in compliance with the relevant conditions[71];

(27)　a person in a specified government department (or any body which carries out the vetting of any person for the purpose of safeguarding national security), or a credit reference agency, to which a copy of the register has been supplied (or a person to whom a copy of the full register is duly supplied or to whom information contained in it is duly disclosed) may not supply a copy of the full register to any person, or disclose any information contained in it (that is not contained in the edited register), or make use of any such information, other than for the purpose set out in the provision by virtue of which the full register has been supplied (the 'relevant restrictions')[72].

1　As to the meaning of 'full register' see PARA 167 notes 2, 9.

2   As to provision made for inspection of the full register see the Representation of the People (England and Wales) Regulations 2001, SI 2001/341, reg 7(2)–(5) (reg 7(2)–(5) added by SI 2002/1871); and PARA 167 note 9.

3   Representation of the People (England and Wales) Regulations 2001, SI 2001/341, reg 7(4) (as added: see note 2). The penalty is a fine not exceeding level 5 on the standard scale: see reg 7(4) (as so added). As to the standard scale see SENTENCING AND DISPOSITION OF OFFENDERS vol 92 (2010) PARA 142.

     By virtue of the Representation of the People (England and Wales) Regulations 2001, SI 2001/341, reg 13(6), (7), reg 7 is applied with modifications to registration in pursuance of a European parliamentary overseas elector's declaration as it applies to registration in pursuance of an overseas elector's declaration (see PARA 101 note 7); and for the purposes of extending the rights of relevant citizens of the Union who (subject to the requirements of registration) may vote at European parliamentary elections, reg 7 is applied with modifications (see the European Parliamentary Elections (Franchise of Relevant Citizens of the Union) Regulations 2001, SI 2001/1184, reg 9, Schedule; and PARA 102 note 6).

4   See the Representation of the People (England and Wales) Regulations 2001, SI 2001/341, reg 97(4); and PARA 180. As to the British Library see NATIONAL CULTURAL HERITAGE vol 77 (2010) PARA 906 et seq.

5   See the Representation of the People (England and Wales) Regulations 2001, SI 2001/341, reg 97A(6); and PARA 180. As to the National Library of Wales see NATIONAL CULTURAL HERITAGE vol 77 (2010) PARA 906 et seq.

6   See the Representation of the People (England and Wales) Regulations 2001, SI 2001/341, reg 99(5); and PARA 187. As to the Statistics Board see REGISTRATION CONCERNING THE INDIVIDUAL vol 88 (2012) PARA 334.

7   See the Representation of the People (England and Wales) Regulations 2001, SI 2001/341, reg 109A(8); and PARA 181. As to the meaning of 'public library' for these purposes see PARA 181 note 1; and as to the meaning of 'local authority archives service' for these purposes see PARA 181 note 2.

8   As to the meaning of 'postal voters lists' see PARA 373 note 7.

9   As to the meaning of 'list of proxies' see PARA 373 note 14.

10   As to the meaning of 'proxy postal voters lists' see PARA 381 note 6.

11   See the Representation of the People (England and Wales) Regulations 2001, SI 2001/341, reg 61(14); and PARA 185 note 11. As to the meaning of 'data form' see PARA 180 note 11.

12   Representation of the People (England and Wales) Regulations 2001, SI 2001/341, reg 115(1), (2) (reg 115 added by SI 2002/1871 and substituted by SI 2006/2910; the Representation of the People (England and Wales) Regulations 2001, SI 2001/341, reg 115(2) amended by the Counter-Terrorism Act 2008 ss 20(4), 99, Sch 1 para 2, Sch 9 Pt 2). A person is guilty of an offence:

     (1)   if he contravenes any of the provisions specified in the Representation of the People (England and Wales) Regulations 2001, SI 2001/341, reg 115(2) (see also the text and notes 4–11; and heads (1) to (27) in the text) (reg 115(1)(a) (as so added and substituted)); or

     (2)   if he is an appropriate supervisor of a person (P) who fails to comply with any of those provisions and he failed to take appropriate steps (reg 115(1)(b) (as so added and substituted)).

However, P is not guilty of an offence under reg 115(1):

     (a)   if he has an appropriate supervisor (reg 115(3)(a) (as so added and substituted)); and

     (b)   if he has complied with all the requirements imposed on him by his appropriate supervisor (reg 115(3)(b) (as so added and substituted)).

Nor is a person who is not P or an appropriate supervisor guilty of an offence under reg 115(1) if he takes all reasonable steps to ensure that he complies with the provisions specified in reg 115(2): see reg 115(4) (as so added and substituted). For these purposes, an 'appropriate supervisor' is a person who is a director of a company or concerned in the management of an organisation in which P is employed or under whose direction or control P is; and 'appropriate steps' are such steps as it was reasonable for the appropriate supervisor to take to secure the operation of procedures designed to prevent, so far as reasonably practicable, the occurrence of a failure to comply with the provisions in reg 115(2): see reg 115(5) (as so added and substituted).

13   Representation of the People (England and Wales) Regulations 2001, SI 2001/341, reg 115(6) (as added and substituted: see note 12). The penalty is a fine not exceeding level 5 on the standard scale: see reg 115(6) (as so added and substituted).

14   Ie if he contravenes any of the provisions described in heads (1) to (27) in the text, or if he is an appropriate supervisor of a person who fails to comply with any of the specified provisions and

he failed to take appropriate steps (see note 12): see the Representation of the People (England and Wales) Regulations 2001, SI 2001/341, reg 115(1), (2), (6) (reg 115 as added and substituted, reg 115(2) as amended: see note 12).

15 See the Representation of the People (England and Wales) Regulations 2001, SI 2001/341, reg 115(1), (2), (6) (reg 115 as added and substituted, reg 115(2) as amended: see note 12). The penalty is a fine not exceeding level 5 on the standard scale: see reg 115(1), (6) (as so added and substituted). As to defences see note 12.

16 As to returning officers for parliamentary elections see PARA 350 et seq; as to returning officers for local government elections see PARA 354 et seq; as to the returning officer at elections for the return of members of the National Assembly for Wales see PARA 357; and as to returning officers for European parliamentary elections see PARA 360 et seq.

17 As to the counting officer see PARA 576 note 1.

18 As to the registration officer see PARA 139.

19 As to the form and content of the record of anonymous entries see PARA 145.

20 Representation of the People (England and Wales) Regulations 2001, SI 2001/341, reg 115(2) (reg 115 as added and substituted, reg 115(2) as amended: see note 12). Head (1) in the text recites the prohibition that is contained in reg 45C(4) (see PARA 182).

21 Ie either in accordance with the Representation of the People (England and Wales) Regulations 2001, SI 2001/341, reg 45D (see PARA 179) or in accordance with the Juries Act 1974 s 3(1A) (see JURIES vol 61 (2010) PARA 801 et seq).

22 Representation of the People (England and Wales) Regulations 2001, SI 2001/341, reg 115(2) (reg 115 as added and substituted, reg 115(2) as amended: see note 12). Head (2) in the text recites the prohibition that is contained in reg 45D(4) (see PARA 179).

23 As to the administration of police areas and police forces in England and Wales see POLICE AND INVESTIGATORY POWERS vol 84 (2013) PARA 52 et seq.

24 The Police Information Technology Organisation was subsumed into the National Policing Improvement Agency (NPIA) on 1 April 2007, but the information and communications technology function of the NPIA has been transferred to the Police ICT company, which was incorporated in 2012 with the Home Office and Association of Chief Police Officers as joint owners: see POLICE AND INVESTIGATORY POWERS vol 84 (2013) PARA 160. At the date at which this volume states the law, the Police ICT company is not yet fully operational, however.

25 With effect from 1 October 2013, the Serious Organised Crime Agency was abolished and its operations merged into a larger National Crime Agency: see the Crime and Courts Act 2013 Pt 1 (ss 1–16); and POLICE AND INVESTIGATORY POWERS.

26 Representation of the People (England and Wales) Regulations 2001, SI 2001/341, reg 115(2) (reg 115 as added and substituted, reg 115(2) as amended: see note 12). Head (3) in the text recites the prohibition that is contained in reg 45F(3) (see PARA 186).

27 As to the meaning of 'permitted purpose' see PARA 179 note 18.

28 Representation of the People (England and Wales) Regulations 2001, SI 2001/341, reg 115(2) (reg 115 as added and substituted, reg 115(2) as amended: see note 12). Head (4) in the text recites the prohibition that is contained in reg 61(3) (see PARA 185 note 11).

29 As to the meaning of 'processor' see PARA 180 note 11.

30 Representation of the People (England and Wales) Regulations 2001, SI 2001/341, reg 115(2) (reg 115 as added and substituted, reg 115(2) as amended: see note 12). Head (5) in the text recites the prohibition that is contained in reg 92(9) and refers to persons entitled to obtain a copy of the full register under the Representation of the People (England and Wales) Regulations 2001, SI 2001/341 (see PARA 180 note 11).

31 As to the appointment of deputies and assistants to the registration officer see PARA 140.

32 As to the meaning of 'edited register' see PARA 167 note 4.

33 Representation of the People (England and Wales) Regulations 2001, SI 2001/341, reg 115(2) (reg 115 as added and substituted, reg 115(2) as amended: see note 12). Head (6) in the text recites the prohibition that is contained in reg 94(3) and refers to the statutory provisions contained in any enactment, including the Representation of the People (England and Wales) Regulations 2001, SI 2001/341 (see PARA 179). As to the meaning of 'enactment' for these purposes see PARA 179 note 8.

34 Ie under the Juries Act 1974 s 3(1) (electoral register as basis of jury selection: see JURIES vol 61 (2010) PARA 812).

35 Representation of the People (England and Wales) Regulations 2001, SI 2001/341, reg 115(2) (reg 115 as added and substituted, reg 115(2) as amended: see note 12). Head (7) in the text recites the prohibition that is contained in reg 95(2) (see PARA 179).

36 Representation of the People (England and Wales) Regulations 2001, SI 2001/341, reg 115(2) (reg 115 as added and substituted, reg 115(2) as amended: see note 12). Head (8) in the text recites the prohibition that is contained in reg 96(2) (see PARA 179).

37 Representation of the People (England and Wales) Regulations 2001, SI 2001/341, reg 115(2) (reg 115 as added and substituted, reg 115(2) as amended: see note 12). Head (9) in the text recites the prohibition that is contained, in relation to England, in reg 97(2) and, in relation to Wales, in reg 97A(4) (see PARA 180).

38 As to the meaning of 'relevant conditions' see PARA 180 note 11.

39 Representation of the People (England and Wales) Regulations 2001, SI 2001/341, reg 115(2) (reg 115 as added and substituted, reg 115(2) as amended: see note 12). Head (10) in the text recites the prohibition that is contained, in relation to England, in reg 97(6) and, in relation to Wales, in reg 97A(8) (see PARA 180).

40 Ie, for these purposes, the returning officer for a non-metropolitan county, the persons or officers who are the returning officers at an election of members of the London Assembly and of the Mayor of London or the returning officer appointed for elections to each parish or community council within the electoral area: see the Representation of the People (England and Wales) Regulations 2001, SI 2001/341, reg 98(2); and PARA 182.

41 Representation of the People (England and Wales) Regulations 2001, SI 2001/341, reg 115(2) (reg 115 as added and substituted, reg 115(2) as amended: see note 12). Head (11) in the text recites the prohibition that is contained in reg 98(9) (see PARA 182).

42 Representation of the People (England and Wales) Regulations 2001, SI 2001/341, reg 115(2) (reg 115 as added and substituted, reg 115(2) as amended: see note 12). Head (12) in the text recites the prohibition that is contained in reg 99(3) (see PARA 187).

43 Representation of the People (England and Wales) Regulations 2001, SI 2001/341, reg 115(2) (reg 115 as added and substituted, reg 115(2) as amended: see note 12). Head (13) in the text recites the prohibition that is contained in reg 99(7) (see PARA 187).

44 As to the Electoral Commission see PARA 34 et seq.

45 Representation of the People (England and Wales) Regulations 2001, SI 2001/341, reg 115(2) (reg 115 as added and substituted, reg 115(2) as amended: see note 12). Head (14) in the text recites the prohibitions contained in reg 100(3), (5) (see PARA 183).

46 As to the Boundary Commission for England see PARA 68.

47 As to the Boundary Commission for Wales see PARA 68.

48 The Local Democracy and Boundary Commission for Wales is the body formerly known as the Local Government Boundary Commission for Wales, which has been continued in existence and renamed, by the Local Government (Democracy) (Wales) Act 2013: see s 2; and PARA 72.

49 Representation of the People (England and Wales) Regulations 2001, SI 2001/341, reg 115(2) (reg 115 as added and substituted, reg 115(2) as amended: see note 12). Head (15) in the text recites the prohibition that is contained in reg 101(6) (see PARA 184).

50 Representation of the People (England and Wales) Regulations 2001, SI 2001/341, reg 115(2) (reg 115 as added and substituted, reg 115(2) as amended: see note 12). Head (16) in the text recites the prohibition that is contained in reg 103(3) (see PARA 185).

51 Ie the holder of a relevant elective office within the meaning of the Political Parties, Elections and Referendums Act 2000 s 71, Sch 7 para 1(8) (see CONSTITUTIONAL LAW AND HUMAN RIGHTS).

52 As to the meaning of 'candidate' for these purposes see PARA 185 note 20.

53 As to the meaning of 'parliamentary election' see PARA 9.

54 As to the meaning of 'local government election' see PARA 11.

55 As to the meaning of 'Authority election' see PARA 11.

56 Representation of the People (England and Wales) Regulations 2001, SI 2001/341, reg 115(2) (reg 115 as added and substituted, reg 115(2) as amended: see note 12). Head (17) in the text recites the prohibition that is contained in reg 104(3) (see PARA 185), which refers to the controls on donations contained in the Representation of the People Act 1983 s 71A, Sch 2A (see PARA 286 et seq) or in the Political Parties, Elections and Referendums Act 2000 Sch 7 (see CONSTITUTIONAL LAW AND HUMAN RIGHTS), as the case may be.

57 Ie within the meaning of the Political Parties, Elections Referendums Act 2000 s 24 (see CONSTITUTIONAL LAW AND HUMAN RIGHTS).

58 Representation of the People (England and Wales) Regulations 2001, SI 2001/341, reg 115(2) (reg 115 as added and substituted, reg 115(2) as amended: see note 12). Head (18) in the text recites the prohibition that is contained in reg 105(4) (see PARA 185).

59 Ie a registered political party other than a minor party within the meaning of the Political Parties, Elections and Referendums Act 2000 s 160(1) (see PARA 253 note 8).

60 Ie a recognised third party within the meaning of the Political Parties, Elections and Referendums Act 2000 s 85(5) (control of expenditure by third parties in national parliamentary election campaigns: see PARA 313).

61 Ie a permitted participant within the meaning of the Political Parties, Elections and Referendums Act 2000 s 105(1) (permitted participant for the purpose of referendums: see PARA 529).

62	Representation of the People (England and Wales) Regulations 2001, SI 2001/341, reg 115(2) (reg 115 as added and substituted, reg 115(2) as amended: see note 12). Head (19) in the text recites the prohibition that is contained in reg 106(3) (see PARA 185), which refers to purposes in connection with the campaign in respect of the referendum identified in the declaration made to the Electoral Commission by the participant under the Political Parties, Elections and Referendums Act 2000 s 106 (see PARA 529) and the controls on donations under Pt IV (ss 50–71) (control of donations to registered parties, individuals and members associations: see CONSTITUTIONAL LAW AND HUMAN RIGHTS) or under s 95, Sch 11 (control of donations to recognised third parties: see PARA 325 et seq) or under s 119, Sch 15 (control of donations to permitted participants: see PARA 546 et seq), as the case may be.

63	Ie a local poll under the Local Government Act 2003 s 116 (see PARA 557 et seq).

64	Representation of the People (England and Wales) Regulations 2001, SI 2001/341, reg 115(2) (reg 115 as added and substituted, reg 115(2) as amended: see note 12). Head (20) in the text recites the prohibition that is contained in reg 107(3) (see PARA 185).

65	Representation of the People (England and Wales) Regulations 2001, SI 2001/341, reg 115(2) (reg 115 as added and substituted, reg 115(2) as amended: see note 12). Head (21) in the text recites the prohibition that is contained in reg 107(8) (see PARA 185).

66	Representation of the People (England and Wales) Regulations 2001, SI 2001/341, reg 115(2) (reg 115 as added and substituted, reg 115(2) as amended: see note 12). Head (22) in the text recites the prohibition that is contained in reg 108(5) (see PARA 185).

67	As to the Security Service see CONSTITUTIONAL LAW AND HUMAN RIGHTS vol 8(2) (Reissue) PARA 471. As to the Secret Intelligence Service see CONSTITUTIONAL LAW AND HUMAN RIGHTS vol 8(2) (Reissue) PARA 472. As to the Government Communications Headquarters see CONSTITUTIONAL LAW AND HUMAN RIGHTS vol 8(2) (Reissue) PARA 473. As to the meaning of 'authorised person' for these purposes see PARA 188 note 32.

68	Representation of the People (England and Wales) Regulations 2001, SI 2001/341, reg 115(2) (reg 115 as added and substituted, reg 115(2) as amended: see note 12). Head (23) in the text recites the prohibition that is contained in reg 113(5), (6) (see PARA 188 note 32).

69	Representation of the People (England and Wales) Regulations 2001, SI 2001/341, reg 115(2) (reg 115 as added and substituted, reg 115(2) as amended: see note 12). Head (24) in the text recites the prohibition that is contained in reg 109(3) (see PARA 185).

70	Representation of the People (England and Wales) Regulations 2001, SI 2001/341, reg 115(2) (reg 115 as added and substituted, reg 115(2) as amended: see note 12). Head (25) in the text recites the prohibition that is contained in reg 109A(6) (see PARA 181).

71	Representation of the People (England and Wales) Regulations 2001, SI 2001/341, reg 115(2) (reg 115 as added and substituted, reg 115(2) as amended: see note 12). Head (26) in the text recites the prohibition that is contained in reg 109A(10) (see PARA 181).

72	Representation of the People (England and Wales) Regulations 2001, SI 2001/341, reg 115(2) (reg 115 as added and substituted, reg 115(2) as amended: see note 12). Head (27) in the text recites the prohibition that is contained in reg 112(4), (5) (see PARA 188).

735. Offences as to certain voting applications or declarations. A person who:

(1)	in any declaration or form used in connection with an application for absent voting[1], provides false information to a registration officer[2]; or

(2)	attests an application to vote by post or by proxy[3] when he knows he is not authorised to do so (or when he knows that it contains a statement which is false)[4],

is guilty of an offence and is liable on summary conviction to a fine (or to a term of imprisonment, or both, except in relation to a European parliamentary election)[5].

A person who:

(a)	makes a declaration of local connection or a service declaration when he is not authorised to do so[6], or (except in the case of a person who is permitted to make such a declaration notwithstanding the fact that by reason of age he is not yet entitled to vote[7]) when he knows that he is subject to a legal incapacity to vote[8], or when he knows that it contains a statement which is false[9]; or

(b)   attests a service declaration[10] when he knows that he is not authorised to do so, or when he knows that it contains a false statement as to any required particulars[11],

is guilty of an offence and is liable on summary conviction to a fine[12].

A person who makes a declaration for the purposes of an application for an anonymous entry in the register of electors[13]:

(i)   when he knows that he is subject to a legal incapacity to vote[14] (except as permitted by the Representation of the People Act 1983)[15]; or

(ii)   when he knows that it contains a statement which is false[16],

is guilty of an offence and is liable on summary conviction to a fine[17].

A person who makes an overseas elector's declaration[18] (or a declaration purporting to be such a declaration) when he knows that he is subject to a legal incapacity to vote at parliamentary elections (age apart), or when he knows that it contains a statement which is false, is guilty of an offence[19]. A person who attests an overseas elector's declaration[20] (or a declaration purporting to be such a declaration) when he knows that he is not authorised to attest such a declaration, or when he knows that it contains a statement which is false, is also guilty of an offence[21]. Either such offence is punishable on summary conviction by a fine[22].

1   Ie used for any of the purposes of the Representation of the People Act 2000 s 12, Sch 4 para 3(1), (2) (absent vote for a particular period or for an indefinite period: see PARA 367), or under Sch 4 para 4(1), (2) (absent vote at a particular election: see PARA 371), or under Sch 4 para 7 (voting as proxy for an indefinite period or for a particular period or at a particular election: see PARA 378), in relation to a parliamentary or local government election, or, in relation to a European parliamentary election, the European Parliamentary Elections Regulations 2004, SI 2004/293, Sch 2, or, in relation to a Welsh Assembly election, the National Assembly for Wales (Representation of the People) Order 2007, SI 2007/236, arts 8–9, 11–12 (see PARA 367 et seq): see the Representation of the People Act 1983 s 13D(1A) (s 13D added by the Electoral Fraud (Northern Ireland) Act 2002 s 7(1) in relation to Northern Ireland, and extended to the whole of the United Kingdom by virtue of the Electoral Administration Act 2006 s 15(8); Representation of the People Act 1983 s 13D(1A) added by the Electoral Administration Act 2006 s 15(1), (3)); the Representation of the People Act 2000 Sch 4 para 8(a); the European Parliamentary Elections Regulations 2004, SI 2004/293, Sch 2 para 10(a) (Sch 2 substituted by SI 2009/186); and the National Assembly for Wales (Representation of the People) Order 2007, SI 2007/236, art 14(1). As to the meaning of 'Assembly election' see PARA 3 note 2; as to the meaning of 'parliamentary election' see PARA 9; and as to the meaning of 'local government election' see PARA 11. As to elections in the City of London see PARA 33; and as to European parliamentary elections see PARA 217 et seq.

     The Representation of the People Act 2000 s 12, Sch 4 are applied and modified for the purpose of local authority mayoral elections in England and Wales by the Local Authorities (Mayoral Elections) (England and Wales) Regulations 2007, SI 2007/1024, reg 3(2)–(5), Sch 2 Table 3 (see PARA 11 note 14); and they have effect for the purposes of local authority referendums, subject to the modifications specified, in relation to Wales, by the Local Authorities (Conduct of Referendums) (Wales) Regulations 2008, SI 2008/1848, reg 8(2), Sch 4 Table 2, and, in relation to England, by the Local Authorities (Conduct of Referendums) (England) Regulations 2012, SI 2012/323, regs 8(2), 11–13, Sch 4 Table 3 (see PARA 15 note 2). The Representation of the People Act 1983 s 13D is applied to the provision of false registration information for the registration of relevant citizens of the Union as European Parliamentary electors in connection with European parliamentary elections: see the European Parliamentary Elections (Franchise of Relevant Citizens of the Union) Regulations 2001, SI 2001/1184, reg 7; and PARA 736.

2   Representation of the People Act 1983 s 13D(1A) (as added: see note 1); Representation of the People Act 2000 Sch 4 para 8(a); European Parliamentary Elections Regulations 2004, SI 2004/293, Sch 2 para 10(a) (as substituted: see note 1); National Assembly for Wales (Representation of the People) Order 2007, SI 2007/236, art 14(1). In the case of a European parliamentary election, the offence is worded as being to make 'a statement which [that person] knows to be false': see the European Parliamentary Elections Regulations 2004, SI 2004/293, Sch 2 para 10(a) (as so substituted). Accordingly, except in the case of a European parliamentary

election, 'false information' means a signature which is not the usual signature of, or was written by a person other than, the person whose signature it purports to be: Representation of the People Act 1983 s 13D(3) (s 13D as added (see note 1); s 13D(3), (4) amended by the Electoral Administration Act 2006 s 15(1), (4), (5)); National Assembly for Wales (Representation of the People) Order 2007, SI 2007/236, art 14(2). A person does not commit an offence, however, if he did not know, and had no reason to suspect, that the information was false: Representation of the People Act 1983 s 13D(4) (as so added and amended); National Assembly for Wales (Representation of the People) Order 2007, SI 2007/236, art 14(3). Where sufficient evidence is adduced to raise an issue with respect to such a defence, the court must assume that the defence is satisfied unless the prosecution proves beyond reasonable doubt that it is not: Representation of the People Act 1983 s 13D(5) (as so added and amended); National Assembly for Wales (Representation of the People) Order 2007, SI 2007/236, art 14(4).

3   Ie attests an application made for an absent vote, in relation to a parliamentary or local government election, under the Representation of the People Act 2000 Sch 4 para 3 for a particular period or for an indefinite period (see PARA 367), or under Sch 4 para 4 at a particular election (see PARA 371), or, in relation to a European parliamentary election, under the European Parliamentary Elections Regulations 2004, SI 2004/293, Sch 2 para 3 for a particular period or for an indefinite period (see PARA 367), or under Sch 2 para 4 at a particular election (see PARA 371), or, in relation to a Welsh Assembly election, under the National Assembly for Wales (Representation of the People) Order 2007, SI 2007/236, art 8 for a particular period or for an indefinite period (see PARA 367) or at a particular election under art 9 (see PARA 371): see the Representation of the People Act 1983 s 13D(1A) (as added: see note 1); the Representation of the People Act 2000 Sch 4 para 8(b); the European Parliamentary Elections Regulations 2004, SI 2004/293, Sch 2 para 10(b) (as substituted: see note 1); and the National Assembly for Wales (Representation of the People) Order 2007, SI 2007/236, art 14(1). See note 1.

4   Representation of the People Act 1983 s 13D(1A) (as added: see note 1); Representation of the People Act 2000 Sch 4 para 8(b); European Parliamentary Elections Regulations 2004, SI 2004/293, Sch 2 para 10(b) (as substituted: see note 1); National Assembly for Wales (Representation of the People) Order 2007, SI 2007/236, art 14(1). See note 2.

5   Representation of the People Act 1983 s 13D(1A), (6) (s 13D as added (see note 1); s 13D(6) amended, s 13D(8) added, by the Electoral Administration Act 2006 s 15(1), (6), (7)); Representation of the People Act 2000 Sch 4 para 8; European Parliamentary Elections Regulations 2004, SI 2004/293, Sch 2 para 10 (as substituted: see note 1); National Assembly for Wales (Representation of the People) Order 2007, SI 2007/236, art 14(1), (5). The penalty in respect of a European parliamentary election (or, in respect of a parliamentary election, under the Representation of the People Act 2000 Sch 4 para 8) is a fine not exceeding level 5 on the standard scale: see the Representation of the People Act 2000 Sch 4 para 8; and the European Parliamentary Elections Regulations 2004, SI 2004/293, Sch 2 para 10 (as so substituted). However, a person guilty of an offence under the Representation of the People Act 1983 s 13D(1A), or under the National Assembly for Wales (Representation of the People) Order 2007, SI 2007/236, art 14(1), is liable on summary conviction to imprisonment for a term not exceeding 51 weeks, or to a fine not exceeding level 5 on the standard scale, or to both: see the Representation of the People Act 1983 s 13D(6) (s 13D as so added, s 13D(6) as so amended); and the National Assembly for Wales (Representation of the People) Order 2007, SI 2007/236, art 14(5). In relation to an offence committed before the date of commencement of the Criminal Justice Act 2003 s 281(5) (not yet in force) (alteration of penalties for summary offences: see SENTENCING AND DISPOSITION OF OFFENDERS vol 92 (2010) PARA 374), the reference in the Representation of the People Act 1983 s 13D(6), and in the National Assembly for Wales (Representation of the People) Order 2007, SI 2007/236, art 14(5), to 51 weeks must be taken to be a reference to six months: Representation of the People Act 1983 s 13D(8) (as so added); National Assembly for Wales (Representation of the People) Order 2007, SI 2007/236, art 14(6). As to the standard scale see SENTENCING AND DISPOSITION OF OFFENDERS vol 92 (2010) PARA 142. As to the application and modification of these provisions see note 1.
   In *Re Central Ward, Slough Election Petition, Simmons v Khan* [2008] EWHC B4 (QB), Election Ct, Commissioner Mawrey QC observed that, in an earlier case, he had treated an offence under the Representation of the People Act 2000 Sch 4 para 8 as an illegal practice, notwithstanding the absence of express words making it an 'illegal practice' in that part of the Act, a decision that was not challenged on appeal: see at [29] per Commissioner Mawrey QC; and as to the earlier proceedings cited see *Akhtar v Jahan, Iqbal v Islam* [2005] All ER (D) 15 (Apr), Election Ct (decision revsd in part, but on a point of evidence, sub nom *R (on the*

application of Afzal) v Election Court [2005] EWCA Civ 647, [2005] LGR 823). As to illegal practices see PARA 671 et seq; and as to summary offences that are also illegal practices see PARA 699 et seq.

6 Ie not authorised, in the case of a declaration of local connection, by the Representation of the People Act 1983 s 7B(1) (see PARA 121) or, in the case of a service declaration, by s 15(1) (see PARA 126): see s 62(1)(a) (s 62(1) substituted by the Representation of the People Act 2000 s 8, Sch 1 paras 1, 17). As to declarations of local connection see PARA 121; and as to service declarations see PARA 125 et seq.

7 See, in the case of a declaration of local connection, the Representation of the People Act 1983 s 7B(1) (see PARA 121) and, in the case of a service declaration, s 15(1) (see PARA 126).

8 Where the declaration is available only for local government elections (see PARA 97 et seq), this means a legal incapacity to vote at local government elections: see the Representation of the People Act 1983 s 62(2) (amended by the Electoral Administration Act 2006 s 10(2), Sch 1 paras 2, 9(1), (3)). As to the meaning of 'legal incapacity' see PARA 95 note 8. As to the persons who have a service qualification see PARA 125; and as to the persons who have a declaration of local connection see PARA 121.

   The Representation of the People Act 1983 s 62 applies, as it applies to those who are registered as parliamentary and local government electors, in relation to relevant citizens of the Union who are registered as European parliamentary electors, subject to any modification and exceptions specified in the European Parliamentary Elections (Franchise of Relevant Citizens of the Union) Regulations 2001, SI 2001/1184, reg 9, Schedule: see PARA 102 note 6. As to the meaning of 'relevant citizen of the Union' for these purposes see PARA 102 note 5.

9 Representation of the People Act 1983 s 62(1)(a) (as substituted: see note 6). As to the application of this provision see note 8.

10 As to the attestation of a service declaration see PARA 127.

11 Representation of the People Act 1983 s 62(1)(b) (as substituted: see note 6). Head (b) in the text refers to the particulars required by regulations made under s 16 (see PARA 127): see s 62(1)(b) (as so substituted). As to the application of this provision see note 8.

12 Representation of the People Act 1983 s 62(1) (as substituted: see note 6). The penalty mentioned in the text is a fine not exceeding level 5 on the standard scale: see s 62(1) (as so substituted). As to the application of this provision see note 8.

13 Ie a declaration made under the Representation of the People Act 1983 s 9B(1)(b) (see PARA 147): see s 62(1A) (added by the Electoral Administration Act 2006 Sch 1 paras 2, 9(1), (2)). As to the meaning of 'anonymous entry' in relation to a register of electors see PARA 148.

   As from a day to be appointed under the Electoral Registration and Administration Act 2013 s 27(1), the reference in the Representation of the People Act 1983 s 62(1A) to s 9B(1)(b) is repealed, and a reference to s 9B(1A)(a) (not yet in force: see PARA 147) added: see s 62(1A) (as so added; prospectively amended by the Electoral Registration and Administration Act 2013 s 13(1), Sch 4 paras 1, 19). However, at the date at which this volume states the law, no such day had been appointed.

14 Where the declaration is available only for local government elections (see PARA 97 et seq), this means a legal incapacity to vote at local government elections: see the Representation of the People Act 1983 s 62(2) (as amended: see note 8). As to the application of this provision see note 8.

15 Representation of the People Act 1983 s 62(1A)(a) (as added: see note 13). As to the exception permitted by the Representation of the People Act 1983 that is referred to in head (i) in the text see PARA 95 et seq. As to the application of this provision see note 8.

16 Representation of the People Act 1983 s 62(1A)(b) (as added: see note 13). As to the application of this provision see note 8.

17 Representation of the People Act 1983 s 62(1A) (as added: see note 13). The penalty mentioned in the text is a fine not exceeding level 5 on the standard scale: see s 62(1A) (as so added). As to the application of these provisions see note 8.

18 As to overseas elector's declarations see PARA 114 et seq.

19 Representation of the People Act 1985 s 12(1). As to the application, with modifications, of s 12 in relation to peers who are registered to vote at a European parliamentary election see the Representation of the People (England and Wales) Regulations 2001, SI 2001/341, reg 13(4), Sch 4; and PARA 101 note 7.

20 As to the attestation of an overseas elector's declaration see PARA 134.

21 Representation of the People Act 1985 s 12(2). As to the application of this provision see note 19.

22 Representation of the People Act 1985 s 12(4). The penalty mentioned in the text is a fine not exceeding level 5 on the standard scale: see s 12(4). As to the application of this provision see note 19.

736. Offences as to applications or declarations made by a relevant citizen of the Union. A person who makes a statement which he knows to be false either in an application by a relevant citizen of the Union[1] for registration as a European parliamentary elector[2] or in a related declaration[3] is guilty of an offence and liable on summary conviction to a fine[4].

A person who makes a statement which he knows to be false, in the declaration required[5] before a relevant citizen of the Union[6] can be validly nominated[7] as an individual candidate[8] or as a candidate on a registered party's list[9], is guilty of an offence and liable on summary conviction to a fine[10].

1   As to the meaning of 'relevant citizen of the Union' for these purposes see PARA 102 note 5.
2   Ie in an application required by the European Parliamentary Elections (Franchise of Relevant Citizens of the Union) Regulations 2001, SI 2001/1184, reg 6(1) (see PARA 159): see reg 7(1).
3   Ie in a declaration required by the European Parliamentary Elections (Franchise of Relevant Citizens of the Union) Regulations 2001, SI 2001/1184, reg 6(2) (see PARA 159): see reg 7(1).
4   European Parliamentary Elections (Franchise of Relevant Citizens of the Union) Regulations 2001, SI 2001/1184, reg 7(1). The penalty mentioned in the text is a fine not exceeding level 3 on the standard scale: see reg 7(1). As to the standard scale see SENTENCING AND DISPOSITION OF OFFENDERS vol 92 (2010) PARA 142.
    The provisions of the Representation of the People Act 1983 Pt III (ss 120–186) (legal proceedings: see PARA 761 et seq) relating to the prosecution of offences, as applied by regulations made under the European Parliamentary Elections Act 2002 (see PARA 383), have effect in relation to such an offence as they have effect in relation to an offence under the Representation of the People Act 1983 as so applied: European Parliamentary Elections (Franchise of Relevant Citizens of the Union) Regulations 2001, SI 2001/1184, reg 7(2); Interpretation Act 1978 s 17(2).
5   Ie required by the European Parliamentary Elections Regulations 2004, SI 2004/293, Sch 1 para 9(2) (see PARA 229): see reg 28(1).
6   As to the meaning of 'relevant citizen of the Union' for these purposes see PARA 149 note 17.
7   As to the nomination of candidates at elections see PARA 255 et seq.
8   As to the meaning of 'individual candidate' for these purposes see PARA 230 note 32.
9   As to the meanings of 'registered party' and 'list' (submitted by a registered party) see PARA 230 note 29.
10 European Parliamentary Elections Regulations 2004, SI 2004/293, reg 28(1). The penalty mentioned in the text is a fine not exceeding level 3 on the standard scale (or, in Gibraltar, a fine not exceeding £1000): see reg 28(1). As to electoral regions constituted for the purposes of European parliamentary elections (including the 'combined region' which includes Gibraltar) see PARA 77.

737. Breaches of official duty. If any of the following persons is, without reasonable cause, guilty of any act or omission in breach of his official duty, he is liable on summary conviction to a fine[1]:

(1)   the Clerk of the Crown at a parliamentary election[2];
(2)   any registration officer[3], returning officer[4] or presiding officer[5];
(3)   any other person whose duty it is to be responsible after an election[6] for the used ballot papers and other documents[7] (including returns and declarations as to expenses)[8];
(4)   any official designated by a universal postal service provider[9]; and
(5)   any deputy of a person mentioned in any of heads (1) to (4) above, or any person appointed to assist, or in the course of his employment assisting[10], a person so mentioned in connection with his official duties[11].

'Official duty' is to be construed accordingly[12], but it does not include duties imposed otherwise than by the law relating to elections or to the registration of parliamentary or local government electors[13]. None of the persons mentioned in heads (1) to (5) above is liable for breach of his official duty to any penalty at common law, and no action for damages lies in respect of the breach by such a person of his official duty[14]. Where a returning officer[15] is guilty of an act or omission in breach of his official duty, but he remedies that act or omission in full by taking the steps allowed for the correction of procedural errors[16], he is deemed to be not guilty of that offence[17], except in relation to any conviction which takes place, or any penalty which is imposed, before the date on which the act or omission is remedied in full[18].

1   Representation of the People Act 1983 s 63(1) (s 63 substituted by the Representation of the People Act 1985 s 24, Sch 4 para 19); European Parliamentary Elections Regulations 2004, SI 2004/293, reg 25(1); National Assembly for Wales (Representation of the People) Order 2007, SI 2007/236, art 32(1). The penalty mentioned in the text is a fine not exceeding level 5 on the standard scale: see the Representation of the People Act 1983 s 63(1) (as so substituted); the European Parliamentary Elections Regulations 2004, SI 2004/293, reg 25(1); and the National Assembly for Wales (Representation of the People) Order 2007, SI 2007/236, art 32(1). As to the standard scale see SENTENCING AND DISPOSITION OF OFFENDERS vol 92 (2010) PARA 142.
    The Representation of the People Act 1983 s 63 is applied with modifications by the Representation of the People (England and Wales) Regulations 2001, SI 2001/341, reg 13(4), Sch 4, in relation to peers who are registered to vote at a European parliamentary election (see PARA 101 note 7) and by the European Parliamentary Elections (Franchise of Relevant Citizens of the Union) Regulations 2001, SI 2001/1184, reg 9, Schedule, in relation to relevant citizens of the Union who are registered to vote at a European parliamentary election (see PARA 102 note 6). The Representation of the People Act 1983 s 62A is also applied and modified for the purposes of local authority referendums, subject to the modifications specified, in relation to Wales, by the Local Authorities (Conduct of Referendums) (Wales) Regulations 2008, SI 2008/1848, reg 8(2), Sch 4 Table 1, and, in relation to England, by the Local Authorities (Conduct of Referendums) (England) Regulations 2012, SI 2012/323, regs 8(2), 11–13, Sch 4 Table 1: see PARA 15 note 2. As to the meaning of 'referendum' see PARA 574 note 2.

2   Representation of the People Act 1983 s 63(3)(a) (as substituted: see note 1). As to the meaning of 'parliamentary election' see PARA 9. 'Clerk of the Crown' means Clerk of the Crown in Chancery: see s 202(1). As to the Clerk of the Crown see CONSTITUTIONAL LAW AND HUMAN RIGHTS vol 8(2) (Reissue) PARA 921.

3   As to electoral registration officers see PARA 139 et seq.

4   Ie including, in relation to a European parliamentary election, a local returning officer: see the European Parliamentary Elections Regulations 2004, SI 2004/293, reg 25(3)(a). As to the designation of returning officers and local returning officers at European parliamentary elections see PARA 360 et seq. As to returning officers for parliamentary elections see PARA 350 et seq; as to returning officers for local government elections see PARA 354 et seq; and as to returning officers at Welsh Assembly elections see PARA 357 et seq. As to the meaning of 'Assembly election' see PARA 3 note 2; and as to the meaning of 'local government election' see PARA 11. As to European parliamentary elections see PARA 217 et seq.

5   Representation of the People Act 1983 s 63(3)(b) (s 63 as substituted (see note 1); s 63(3)(b) amended by the Political Parties and Elections Act 2009 ss 25(a), 39, Sch 7); European Parliamentary Elections Regulations 2004, SI 2004/293, reg 25(3)(a); National Assembly for Wales (Representation of the People) Order 2007, SI 2007/236, art 32(3)(a). As to the appointment of presiding officers and their clerks see PARA 393.

6   Ie a parliamentary or local government election, or a Welsh Assembly election, or a European parliamentary election: see the Representation of the People Act 1983 s 63(3)(c) (s 63 as substituted (see note 1); s 63(3)(c) amended by the Electoral Administration Act 2006 s 41(8)); the European Parliamentary Elections Regulations 2004, SI 2004/293, reg 25(3)(bb) (reg 25(3)(bb), (4), (5) added by SI 2009/186); and the National Assembly for Wales (Representation of the People) Order 2007, SI 2007/236, art 32(3)(b).
    The Representation of the People Act 1983 s 63 has effect as if any reference in it to a local government election included a reference to any other election under the Local Government Act 1972: Representation of the People Act 1983 s 187(2) (amended by the Representation of the People Act 1985 s 24, Sch 4 para 64(b)).

7   As to the sealing up and disposal etc of ballot papers etc on close of a poll see PARA 495 et seq,

8   Representation of the People Act 1983 s 63(3)(c) (s 63 as substituted (see note 1); s 63(3)(c) as amended (see note 6)); European Parliamentary Elections Regulations 2004, SI 2004/293, reg 25(3)(bb) (as added: see note 6); National Assembly for Wales (Representation of the People)

Order 2007, SI 2007/236, art 32(3)(b). As to the meaning of 'return as to election expenses' see PARA 281 note 1; and as to the meaning of 'declaration as to election expenses' see PARA 281 note 3.

9   Representation of the People Act 1983 s 63(3)(d) (s 63 as substituted (see note 1); s 63(3)(d) amended by SI 2001/1149); European Parliamentary Elections Regulations 2004, SI 2004/293, reg 25(3)(b) (amended by SI 2009/186); National Assembly for Wales (Representation of the People) Order 2007, SI 2007/236, art 32(3)(c). As to the meaning of 'universal postal service provider' see PARAS 330 note 1, 366 note 16.

10 As to local authority staff who may assist at an election see PARA 350 et seq.

11 Representation of the People Act 1983 s 63(3)(e) (as substituted: see note 1); European Parliamentary Elections Regulations 2004, SI 2004/293, reg 25(3)(c) (amended by SI 2009/186); National Assembly for Wales (Representation of the People) Order 2007, SI 2007/236, art 32(3)(d).

12 In so construing 'official duty', it is clear from the list of persons specified that duties after an election in connection with the retention of documents used at an election fall within the expression. Where there are gross discrepancies in the counting of the votes, the clerks responsible for them might be guilty, in the absence of reasonable cause, of a dereliction of duty and liable for the offence now set out in the Representation of the People Act 1983 s 63: see *McWhirter v Platten* [1970] 1 QB 508 at 516, [1969] 1 All ER 172 at 176, DC, per Lord Parker CJ. As to inspection of the ballot papers for the purposes of prosecution for such an offence see PARA 851.

13 Representation of the People Act 1983 s 63(3) (as substituted: see note 1); European Parliamentary Elections Regulations 2004, SI 2004/293, reg 25(3); National Assembly for Wales (Representation of the People) Order 2007, SI 2007/236, art 32(3). Certain peers resident outside the United Kingdom may be included in a register for use only at European parliamentary elections: see PARA 100.

14 Representation of the People Act 1983 s 63(2) (as substituted: see note 1); European Parliamentary Elections Regulations 2004, SI 2004/293, reg 25(2); National Assembly for Wales (Representation of the People) Order 2007, SI 2007/236, art 32(2). Unlike the provision which the Representation of the People Act 1983 s 63(2) replaced as respects parliamentary elections (ie s 63(2) as originally enacted), it provides no exemption from penalties under any enactment and accordingly the persons listed in the text could be prosecuted for statutory offences done in connection with the election (if any are relevant). The actions at common law in respect of which this provision provides protection were actions for damages against the returning officer: see *Ashby v White* (1704) 2 Ld Raym 938, HL. It is for consideration whether the Representation of the People Act 1983 s 63(2) provides protection in respect of the tort of misfeasance in public office, where there is a deliberate act or omission which is intended to harm the person at whom it is directed: see *Bourgoin SA v Ministry of Agriculture, Fisheries and Food* [1986] QB 716, [1985] 3 All ER 585, CA. In addition, a returning officer at a parliamentary election might be liable to be punished by the House of Commons if he acts corruptly or with partiality: see *Great Grimsby Case* (1803) 1 Peck 59 at 74; *Middlesex Case* (1804) 2 Peck 1 at 28. However, since those cases were decided, the jurisdiction in respect of controverted elections has been transferred from the House of Commons to the courts by the Parliamentary Elections Act 1868. Furthermore, detailed provision as to the conduct of elections is now made by legislation and breach of duty in connection therewith is an offence under the statutory provision set out in the text.

15 Ie, in relation to a European parliamentary election, a local returning officer to whom the European Parliamentary Elections Regulations 2004, SI 2004/293, reg 9 applies (see PARA 360): see reg 25(4) (as added: see note 6).

16 Ie by taking steps, in relation to a parliamentary election, under the Electoral Administration Act 2006 s 46(1) (see PARAS 530 note 26, 354 note 25), or, in relation to a European parliamentary election, under the European Parliamentary Elections Regulations 2004, SI 2004/293, reg 9(4A) (see PARA 360 note 26), or, in relation to an Assembly election, under the National Assembly for Wales (Representation of the People) Order 2007, SI 2007/236, art 21(1) (see PARA 357): see the Representation of the People Act 1983 s 63(4) (s 63(4), (5) added by the Electoral Administration Act 2006 s 46(6)); the European Parliamentary Elections Regulations 2004, SI 2004/293, reg 25(4) (as added: see note 6); and the National Assembly for Wales (Representation of the People) Order 2007, SI 2007/236, art 32(4).

17 Representation of the People Act 1983 s 63(4) (as added: see note 16); Electoral Administration Act 2006 s 46(3); European Parliamentary Elections Regulations 2004, SI 2004/293, reg 25(4) (as added: see note 6); National Assembly for Wales (Representation of the People) Order 2007, SI 2007/236, art 32(4).

18 Representation of the People Act 1983 s 63(5) (as added: see note 16); European Parliamentary
    Elections Regulations 2004, SI 2004/293, reg 25(5) (as added: see note 6); National Assembly
    for Wales (Representation of the People) Order 2007, SI 2007/236, art 32(5). The breach by an
    election professional of his or her relevant duty, resulting from carelessness or neglect rather
    than deliberate intent, may yet contribute to a finding of electoral fraud by an Election Court on
    grounds of electoral malpractice: see PARA 754 note 3.

738. Tampering with nomination and ballot papers. A person[1] is guilty of an
offence if, at an election[2], he:

(1)   fraudulently defaces or fraudulently destroys any nomination paper[3];
(2)   fraudulently defaces or fraudulently destroys any ballot paper, or the
       official mark on any ballot paper, or postal voting statement, or official
       envelope used in connection with voting by post[4];
(3)   without due authority supplies any ballot paper to any person[5];
(4)   fraudulently puts into any ballot box any paper other than the ballot
       paper which he is authorised by law to put in[6];
(5)   fraudulently takes out of the polling station any ballot paper[7];
(6)   without due authority destroys, takes, opens, or otherwise interferes
       with any ballot box or packet of ballot papers then in use for the
       purposes of the election[8]; or
(7)   fraudulently or without due authority, as the case may be, attempts to
       do any of the acts listed under heads (1) to (6) above[9].

If a returning officer[10], a presiding officer or a clerk appointed to assist[11] in
taking the poll, counting the votes, or assisting at the proceedings in connection
with the issue and receipt of postal ballot papers[12], is guilty of one of the
offences described under heads (1) to (7) above, he is liable on conviction to a
penalty[13]; and any other person who is guilty of such an offence is also liable to
a penalty[14].

If any person in a poll consequent on a parish or community meeting[15]:

(a)   fraudulently defaces or fraudulently destroys any ballot paper or the
       official mark[16];
(b)   without due authority supplies a ballot paper to any person[17];
(c)   fraudulently puts into a ballot box any paper other than the ballot paper
       which he is authorised by law to put in[18];
(d)   fraudulently takes out of the polling station any ballot paper[19]; or
(e)   without due authority destroys, takes, opens, or otherwise interferes
       with any ballot box or packet of ballot papers then in use for the
       purposes of the poll[20],

he is liable on conviction to a penalty[21].

1 As to the meaning of 'person' see PARA 95 note 1.
2 Representation of the People Act 1983 s 65(1); European Parliamentary Elections
   Regulations 2004, SI 2004/293, reg 26(1); National Assembly for Wales (Representation of the
   People) Order 2007, SI 2007/236, art 33(1). As to the meaning of 'Assembly election' see PARA 3
   note 2; as to the meaning of 'parliamentary election' see PARA 9; and as to the meaning of 'local
   government election' see PARA 11. As to elections in the City of London see PARA 33; and as to
   European parliamentary elections see PARA 217 et seq.
       The Representation of the People Act 1983 s 65 has been applied and modified for the
   purposes of local authority referendums, in relation to Wales, by the Local Authorities (Conduct
   of Referendums) (Wales) Regulations 2008, SI 2008/1848, Sch 4 Table 1; and, in relation to
   England, by the Local Authorities (Conduct of Referendums) (England) Regulations 2012,
   SI 2012/323, Sch 4 Table 1. As to the meaning of 'referendum' for these purposes see PARA 574
   note 2.
3 Representation of the People Act 1983 s 65(1)(a); European Parliamentary Elections
   Regulations 2004, SI 2004/293, reg 26(1)(a); National Assembly for Wales (Representation of
   the People) Order 2007, SI 2007/236, art 33(1)(a). As to nomination papers see PARA 255 et seq.

At a European parliamentary election, head (1) in the text refers to any nomination paper, and to the list of candidates submitted by a registered party: see the European Parliamentary Elections Regulations 2004, SI 2004/293, reg 26(1)(a). As to the meanings of 'registered party' and 'list' (submitted by a registered party) see PARA 230 note 29. At a Welsh Assembly election, the reference is to any constituency, individual, or party nomination paper: see the National Assembly for Wales (Representation of the People) Order 2007, SI 2007/236, art 33(1)(a). As to the meaning of 'party nomination paper' at a Welsh Assembly regional election see PARA 255; and as to the meanings of 'constituency nomination paper' and 'individual nomination paper' see PARA 256. As to the meanings of 'constituency election' and 'regional election' see PARA 3 note 2.

The forgery of signatures on a nomination paper has potential to constitute an offence under the Forgery and Counterfeiting Act 1981 and may contribute to a finding of general corruption and/or electoral fraud on an election petition: see PARA 754.

4   Representation of the People Act 1983 s 65(1)(b) (amended by the Electoral Administration Act 2006 s 47, Sch 1 paras 69, 72, 96); European Parliamentary Elections Regulations 2004, SI 2004/293, reg 26(1)(b) (amended by SI 2009/186); National Assembly for Wales (Representation of the People) Order 2007, SI 2007/236, art 33(1)(b). As to the manner of voting see PARA 363 et seq; as to ballot papers and the official mark see PARA 386 et seq; and as to the issue of postal voting statements see PARA 406. As to the inspection of other documents see PARAS 503–511. As to the inspection of the ballot papers for the purpose of initiating or maintaining a prosecution for an offence in relation to the ballot papers see PARA 851.

Forgery of a ballot paper, or of the official mark on a ballot paper, and forged or altered ballot papers, or postal voting statements, have potential to constitute an offence under the Forgery and Counterfeiting Act 1981 and may contribute to a finding of general corruption and/or electoral fraud on an election petition: see PARA 754.

5   Representation of the People Act 1983 s 65(1)(c); European Parliamentary Elections Regulations 2004, SI 2004/293, reg 26(1)(c); National Assembly for Wales (Representation of the People) Order 2007, SI 2007/236, art 33(1)(c).

6   Representation of the People Act 1983 s 65(1)(d); European Parliamentary Elections Regulations 2004, SI 2004/293, reg 26(1)(d); National Assembly for Wales (Representation of the People) Order 2007, SI 2007/236, art 33(1)(d).

7   Representation of the People Act 1983 s 65(1)(e); European Parliamentary Elections Regulations 2004, SI 2004/293, reg 26(1)(e); National Assembly for Wales (Representation of the People) Order 2007, SI 2007/236, art 33(1)(e). As to whether a voter who takes a ballot paper out of a station deciding not to vote commits an offence see *Re Derbyshire, North-Eastern, Case, Holmes v Lee and Cleaver* (1923) 39 TLR 423.

8   Representation of the People Act 1983 s 65(1)(f); European Parliamentary Elections Regulations 2004, SI 2004/293, reg 26(1)(f); National Assembly for Wales (Representation of the People) Order 2007, SI 2007/236, art 33(1)(f). Breaking a glass vessel containing a noxious fluid over the aperture of a ballot box has been held to be interference with the ballot box since interference with the ballot papers in the ballot box is equivalent to interference with the ballot box: *R v Chapin* (1909) 74 JP 71, 22 Cox CC 10.

9   Representation of the People Act 1983 s 65(1)(g); European Parliamentary Elections Regulations 2004, SI 2004/293, reg 26(1)(g); National Assembly for Wales (Representation of the People) Order 2007, SI 2007/236, art 33(1)(g).

10   As to returning officers for parliamentary elections see PARA 350 et seq; as to returning officers for local government elections see PARA 354 et seq; and as to returning officers at Welsh Assembly elections see PARA 357 et seq. At a European parliamentary election, both a returning officer and a local returning officer are specified for these purposes: see the European Parliamentary Elections Regulations 2004, SI 2004/293, reg 26(3). As to the designation of returning officers and local returning officers at European parliamentary elections see PARA 360 et seq.

11   As to the appointment of presiding officers and their clerks see PARA 393.

12   As to proceedings in connection with the issue and receipt of postal ballot papers see PARA 406 et seq.

13   Representation of the People Act 1983 s 65(3) (s 65(3), (4) substituted by the Representation of the People Act 1985 s 23, Sch 3 para 2); European Parliamentary Elections Regulations 2004, SI 2004/293, reg 26(3); National Assembly for Wales (Representation of the People) Order 2007, SI 2007/236, art 33(2). The penalty mentioned in the text is, on conviction on indictment, a fine, or imprisonment for a term not exceeding two years, or both, and the penalty on summary conviction is a fine not exceeding the statutory maximum, or imprisonment for a term not exceeding six months, or both: see the Representation of the People Act 1983 s 65(3) (as so substituted); the European Parliamentary Elections Regulations 2004, SI 2004/293,

reg 26(3); and the National Assembly for Wales (Representation of the People) Order 2007, SI 2007/236, art 33(2). In relation to an offence committed in relation to a Welsh Assembly election after the date of commencement of the Criminal Justice Act 2003 s 281(5) (not yet in force) (alteration of penalties for summary offences: see SENTENCING AND DISPOSITION OF OFFENDERS vol 92 (2010) PARA 374), the reference to six months must be taken to be a reference to 51 weeks: see the National Assembly for Wales (Representation of the People) Order 2007, SI 2007/236, art 33(4). As to the statutory maximum see SENTENCING AND DISPOSITION OF OFFENDERS vol 92 (2010) PARA 140; and as to the prescribed sum see SENTENCING AND DISPOSITION OF OFFENDERS vol 92 (2010) PARA 141.

14   Representation of the People Act 1983 s 65(4) (as substituted: see note 13); European Parliamentary Elections Regulations 2004, SI 2004/293, reg 26(4); National Assembly for Wales (Representation of the People) Order 2007, SI 2007/236, art 33(3). The penalty mentioned in the text is, on summary conviction, a fine not exceeding level 5 on the standard scale, or imprisonment for a term not exceeding six months, or both: see the Representation of the People Act 1983 s 65(4) (as so substituted); the European Parliamentary Elections Regulations 2004, SI 2004/293, reg 26(4); and the National Assembly for Wales (Representation of the People) Order 2007, SI 2007/236, art 33(3). In relation to an offence committed after the date of commencement of the Criminal Justice Act 2003 s 281(5) (not yet in force) (alteration of penalties for summary offences: see SENTENCING AND DISPOSITION OF OFFENDERS vol 92 (2010) PARA 374), the reference to six months must be taken to be a reference to 51 weeks: see the National Assembly for Wales (Representation of the People) Order 2007, SI 2007/236, art 33(4). As to the standard scale see SENTENCING AND DISPOSITION OF OFFENDERS vol 92 (2010) PARA 142.

15   As to polls consequent on a parish meeting on a question involving appointment to office see PARA 200 et seq; and as to polls consequent on a parish or community meeting on other questions see PARA 556 et seq.

16   Local Government Act 1972 Sch 12 paras 22(a), 38(a).

17   Local Government Act 1972 Sch 12 paras 22(b), 38(b).

18   Local Government Act 1972 Sch 12 paras 22(c), 38(c).

19   Local Government Act 1972 Sch 12 paras 22(d), 38(d).

20   Local Government Act 1972 Sch 12 paras 22(e), 38(e).

21   See the Local Government Act 1972 Sch 12 paras 22, 38. If he is a returning officer or an authorised person appointed to assist in taking the poll or counting the votes, the penalty on conviction on indictment is imprisonment for a term not exceeding two years (Sch 12 paras 22(i), 38(i)); in any other case, he is liable on conviction on indictment to imprisonment for a term not exceeding six months or to a fine or to both, or on summary conviction to imprisonment for a term not exceeding six months or to a fine not exceeding the prescribed sum or to both (Sch 12 paras 22(ii), 38(ii); Criminal Law Act 1977 s 32(1); Magistrates' Courts Act 1980 s 32(1)). As to the court's power to fine in lieu of or in addition to the power to sentence to imprisonment see SENTENCING AND DISPOSITION OF OFFENDERS vol 92 (2010) PARA 2. As to the returning officer at a poll consequent on a parish meeting on a question involving appointment to office see PARA 356; and as to the returning officer at a poll consequent on a parish or community meeting on other questions see PARA 588.

739.   Offence related to the requirement of secrecy. Every returning officer[1] and every presiding officer or clerk attending at a polling station[2], every candidate[3], election agent[4] or polling agent[5] so attending[6], and every representative of the Electoral Commission who is entitled[7] so to attend[8], must maintain, and aid in maintaining, the secrecy of voting and must not, except for some purpose authorised by law, communicate to any person[9] before the poll is closed any information as to[10]:

(1)   the name of any elector or proxy for an elector[11] who has or has not applied for a ballot paper or voted at a polling station[12];

(2)   the number on the register of electors of any elector who, or whose proxy, has or has not applied for a ballot paper or voted at a polling station[13]; or

(3)   the official mark on any ballot paper[14].

If a person acts in contravention of these requirements, he is liable on summary conviction to a penalty[15].

1 As to returning officers for parliamentary elections see PARA 350 et seq; as to returning officers for local government elections see PARA 354 et seq; and as to returning officers at Welsh Assembly elections see PARA 357 et seq. At a European parliamentary election, a local returning officer is specified for these purposes: see the European Parliamentary Elections Regulations 2004, SI 2004/293, reg 29(1)(a). As to the designation of local returning officers at European parliamentary elections see PARA 360 et seq. As to the meaning of 'Assembly election' see PARA 3 note 2; as to the meaning of 'parliamentary election' see PARA 9; and as to the meaning of 'local government election' see PARA 11. As to elections in the City of London see PARA 33; and as to European parliamentary elections see PARA 217 et seq.

2 Representation of the People Act 1983 s 66(1)(a); European Parliamentary Elections Regulations 2004, SI 2004/293, reg 29(1)(a); National Assembly for Wales (Representation of the People) Order 2007, SI 2007/236, art 35(1)(a), (b). As to the appointment of presiding officers and their clerks see PARA 393.

The Representation of the People Act 1983 s 66 applies at a poll consequent on a parish or community meeting by virtue of s 187(1) and the Local Government Act 1972 s 99, Sch 12 paras 18(5), 34(5): see PARA 383. See also the Parish and Community Meetings (Polls) Rules 1987, SI 1987/1, r 6(a). At such a poll, any reference to an election agent or the proxy for an elector is to be omitted: r 6(e). The Representation of the People Act 1983 s 66 also has been applied and modified for the purposes of local authority referendums, in relation to Wales, by the Local Authorities (Conduct of Referendums) (Wales) Regulations 2008, SI 2008/1848, Sch 4 Table 1; and, in relation to England, by the Local Authorities (Conduct of Referendums) (England) Regulations 2012, SI 2012/323, Sch 4 Table 1. As to the meaning of 'referendum' for these purposes see PARA 574 note 2.

3 As to the meaning of 'candidate' generally see PARA 230.

4 As to the appointment of an election agent for parliamentary and local government elections see PARA 231; as to the appointment of an election agent for elections to the National Assembly for Wales see PARA 235; and as to the appointment of the election agent of a registered party or for an individual candidate at a European parliamentary election see PARA 239.

5 As to the appointment of polling agents see PARA 394. In the case of a local authority referendum, the reference in the text is to every polling observer so attending: see the Representation of the People Act 1983 s 66(1)(b) (as applied and modified: see note 2). As to the appointment of counting observers at a referendum see PARA 586.

6 Representation of the People Act 1983 s 66(1)(b); European Parliamentary Elections Regulations 2004, SI 2004/293, reg 29(1)(b); National Assembly for Wales (Representation of the People) Order 2007, SI 2007/236, art 35(1)(c).

7 Ie by virtue of any of the Political Parties, Elections and Referendums Act 2000 ss 6A–6D (Electoral Commission representatives and accredited observers to attend electoral proceedings and observe working practices: see PARA 53): see the Representation of the People Act 1983 s 66(1)(c) (added by the Electoral Administration Act 2006 s 47, Sch 1 paras 69, 82); the European Parliamentary Elections Regulations 2004, SI 2004/293, reg 29(1)(c) (substituted by SI 2009/186); and the National Assembly for Wales (Representation of the People) Order 2007, SI 2007/236, art 35(1)(d). As to the Electoral Commission see PARA 34 et seq.

8 Representation of the People Act 1983 s 66(1)(c) (as added: see note 7); European Parliamentary Elections Regulations 2004, SI 2004/293, reg 29(1)(c) (as substituted: see note 7); National Assembly for Wales (Representation of the People) Order 2007, SI 2007/236, art 35(1)(d).

9 Where a polling agent left a marked copy of the register in the committee room of the candidate by whom he was employed, but there was no evidence that it was seen by anyone while it was in the room, it was held that no offence had been committed: *Stannanought v Hazeldine* (1879) 4 CPD 191. The mere communication by the returning officer of the numbers on the backs of ballot papers given out after the close of the poll so that there might be a record of such papers is not an offence if it does not in fact lead, and is not intended to lead, to any disclosures of the names of voters or of the persons for whom they voted: *Islington, West Division Case* (1901) 5 O'M & H 120 at 126. The admission of the defendant that he did disclose the information is sufficient evidence without showing that the voter in fact voted: *R v Unkles* (1874) IR 8 CL 50.

10 Representation of the People Act 1983 s 66(1); European Parliamentary Elections Regulations 2004, SI 2004/293, reg 29(1); National Assembly for Wales (Representation of the People) Order 2007, SI 2007/236, art 35(1). A communication by a polling agent as to the course of the poll will not avoid the election: *Bolton Case* (1874) 2 O'M & H 138 at 141, 143.

11 As to the meaning of 'elector' in relation to a parliamentary or local government election see PARA 95 note 2; in relation to a European parliamentary election, see PARA 111 note 4; and, in relation to a Welsh Assembly election, see PARA 110 note 6. As to applications to vote by post or by proxy see PARA 367 et seq.

12 Representation of the People Act 1983 s 66(1)(i); European Parliamentary Elections Regulations 2004, SI 2004/293, reg 29(1)(i); National Assembly for Wales (Representation of the People) Order 2007, SI 2007/236, art 35(1)(i).

13 Representation of the People Act 1983 s 66(1)(ii); European Parliamentary Elections Regulations 2004, SI 2004/293, reg 29(1)(ii); National Assembly for Wales (Representation of the People) Order 2007, SI 2007/236, art 35(1)(ii). As to the number of an elector see PARA 145; and as to the registers of electors see PARA 145 et seq.

14 Representation of the People Act 1983 s 66(1)(iii); European Parliamentary Elections Regulations 2004, SI 2004/293, reg 29(1)(iii); National Assembly for Wales (Representation of the People) Order 2007, SI 2007/236, art 35(1)(iii). As to ballot papers see PARA 386 et seq. As to security measures associated with the ballot paper see PARA 387.

15 Representation of the People Act 1983 s 66(6) (amended by the Representation of the People Act 1985 s 23, Sch 3 para 3); European Parliamentary Elections Regulations 2004, SI 2004/293, reg 29(7); National Assembly for Wales (Representation of the People) Order 2007, SI 2007/236, art 35(6). The penalty mentioned in the text is a fine not exceeding level 5 on the standard scale or imprisonment for a term not exceeding six months: see the Representation of the People Act 1983 s 66(6) (as so amended); the European Parliamentary Elections Regulations 2004, SI 2004/293, reg 29(7); and the National Assembly for Wales (Representation of the People) Order 2007, SI 2007/236, art 35(6). In relation to an offence committed after the date of commencement of the Criminal Justice Act 2003 s 281(5) (not yet in force) (alteration of penalties for summary offences: see SENTENCING AND DISPOSITION OF OFFENDERS vol 92 (2010) PARA 374), the reference to six months must be taken to be a reference to 51 weeks: see the National Assembly for Wales (Representation of the People) Order 2007, SI 2007/236, art 35(7). As to the standard scale see SENTENCING AND DISPOSITION OF OFFENDERS vol 92 (2010) PARA 142.

740. Contravention of requirement of secrecy at count and verification of ballot paper accounts. Every person attending at the counting of the votes at an election[1] must maintain, and aid in maintaining, the secrecy of voting[2]; and must not:

(1) ascertain or attempt to ascertain at the counting of the votes the number or other unique identifying mark on the back of any ballot paper[3]; or

(2) communicate any information obtained at the counting of the votes as to the way in which any vote is given on any particular ballot paper[4].

If a person acts in contravention of these requirements, he is liable on summary conviction to a penalty[5].

1 Ie or at the verification of the ballot paper accounts at a European parliamentary election (which procedure takes place separately from the counting of the votes: see PARA 465), except in relation to head (1) in the text: see the European Parliamentary Elections Regulations 2004, SI 2004/293, reg 29(2); and see further note 3. As to the meaning of 'Assembly election' see PARA 3 note 2; as to the meaning of 'parliamentary election' see PARA 9; and as to the meaning of 'local government election' see PARA 11. As to elections in the City of London see PARA 33; and as to European parliamentary elections see PARA 217 et seq. As to attendance at the counting of the votes at elections see PARA 424 et seq.

2 Representation of the People Act 1983 s 66(2); European Parliamentary Elections Regulations 2004, SI 2004/293, reg 29(2); National Assembly for Wales (Representation of the People) Order 2007, SI 2007/236, art 35(2). As to notification of the requirement of secrecy see PARA 385.
   The Representation of the People Act 1983 s 66 applies at a poll consequent on a parish or community meeting by virtue of s 187(1) and the Local Government Act 1972 s 99, Sch 12 paras 18(5), 34(5): see PARA 383. See also the Parish and Community Meetings (Polls) Rules 1987, SI 1987/1, r 6(a). At such a poll, the reference to the giving of votes is to the candidate for whom any vote is given: r 6(e). The Representation of the People Act 1983 s 66 also has been applied and modified for the purposes of local authority referendums, in relation to Wales, by the Local Authorities (Conduct of Referendums) (Wales) Regulations 2008, SI 2008/1848, Sch 4 Table 1; and, in relation to England, by the Local Authorities (Conduct of Referendums) (England) Regulations 2012, SI 2012/323, Sch 4 Table 1. As to the meaning of 'referendum' for these purposes see PARA 574 note 2.

3 Representation of the People Act 1983 s 66(2)(a) (amended by the Electoral Administration Act 2006 s 47, Sch 1 paras 69, 86(a), 96); European Parliamentary Elections Regulations 2004,

SI 2004/293, reg 29(2)(a) (amended by SI 2009/186); National Assembly for Wales (Representation of the People) Order 2007, SI 2007/236, art 35(2)(a). As to ballot papers see PARA 386 et seq. As to security measures associated with the ballot paper see PARA 387.

4   Representation of the People Act 1983 s 66(2)(b); European Parliamentary Elections Regulations 2004, SI 2004/293, reg 29(2)(b); National Assembly for Wales (Representation of the People) Order 2007, SI 2007/236, art 35(2)(b). At a parliamentary election, head (2) in the text refers to information obtained at the counting of the votes as to the candidate for whom any vote is given on any particular ballot paper: see the Representation of the People Act 1983 s 66(2)(b). In relation to an election of the London members of the London Assembly at an ordinary election, the reference to 'the candidate for whom any vote is given' must be read as 'the candidate for whom, or the registered political party towards the return of whose candidates, any vote is given' (s 66(7) (s 66(7), (8) added by the Greater London Authority Act 1999 s 17, Sch 3 paras 1, 11)); and any reference to the return of a registered political party's candidates is a reference to the return of candidates included in the list of candidates submitted by the registered political party for the purposes of the election (Representation of the People Act 1983 s 66(8) (as so added)). As to the meaning of 'London member' see PARA 11 note 5. As to the meaning of 'candidate' generally see PARA 230. As to references to a registered political party submitting a list of candidates to be London members of the London Assembly at an ordinary election see PARA 230 note 14. As to London Assembly ordinary elections see PARA 199; and LONDON GOVERNMENT vol 71 (2013) PARA 76 et seq.

At a European parliamentary election, head (2) in the text applies equally to the verification of the ballot paper accounts as to the counting of the votes (see note 1); and no person attending at the verification of the ballot paper accounts may express to any person an opinion based on information obtained at that verification as to the likely result of the election (European Parliamentary Elections Regulations 2004, SI 2004/293, reg 29(3)).

5   Representation of the People Act 1983 s 66(6) (amended by the Representation of the People Act 1985 s 23, Sch 3 para 3); European Parliamentary Elections Regulations 2004, SI 2004/293, reg 29(7); National Assembly for Wales (Representation of the People) Order 2007, SI 2007/236, art 35(6). The penalty mentioned in the text is a fine not exceeding level 5 on the standard scale or imprisonment for a term not exceeding six months: see the Representation of the People Act 1983 s 66(6) (as so amended); the European Parliamentary Elections Regulations 2004, SI 2004/293, reg 29(7); and the National Assembly for Wales (Representation of the People) Order 2007, SI 2007/236, art 35(6). In relation to an offence committed after the date of commencement of the Criminal Justice Act 2003 s 281(5) (not yet in force) (alteration of penalties for summary offences: see SENTENCING AND DISPOSITION OF OFFENDERS vol 92 (2010) PARA 374), the reference to six months must be taken to be a reference to 51 weeks: see the National Assembly for Wales (Representation of the People) Order 2007, SI 2007/236, art 35(7). As to the standard scale see SENTENCING AND DISPOSITION OF OFFENDERS vol 92 (2010) PARA 142.

741. Interference with voter.

No person may, at an election[1]:

(1)   interfere with or attempt to interfere with a voter when recording his vote[2];

(2)   otherwise obtain or attempt to obtain in a polling station information as to the way in which a voter in that station is about to vote or has voted[3];

(3)   communicate at any time to any person any information obtained in a polling station as to the way in which a voter in that station is about to vote or has voted, or as to the number or other unique identifying mark on the back of the ballot paper given to a voter at that station[4]; or

(4)   directly or indirectly induce a voter to display his ballot paper after he has marked it, so as to make known to any person the way in which he has voted[5].

If a person acts in contravention of these requirements, he is liable on summary conviction to a penalty[6].

1   Representation of the People Act 1983 s 66(3); European Parliamentary Elections Regulations 2004, SI 2004/293, reg 29(4); National Assembly for Wales (Representation of the People) Order 2007, SI 2007/236, art 35(3). As to the meaning of 'Assembly election' see PARA 3 note 2; as to the meaning of 'parliamentary election' see PARA 9; and as to the meaning of 'local

government election' see PARA 11. As to elections in the City of London see PARA 33; and as to European parliamentary elections see PARA 217 et seq.

The Representation of the People Act 1983 s 66 applies at a poll consequent on a parish or community meeting by virtue of s 187(1) and the Local Government Act 1972 s 99, Sch 12 paras 18(5), 34(5): see PARA 383. See also the Parish and Community Meetings (Polls) Rules 1987, SI 1987/1, r 6(a). At such a poll, the reference to the giving of votes is to the candidate for whom any vote is given: r 6(e). The Representation of the People Act 1983 s 66 also has been applied and modified for the purposes of local authority referendums, in relation to Wales, by the Local Authorities (Conduct of Referendums) (Wales) Regulations 2008, SI 2008/1848, Sch 4 Table 1; and, in relation to England, by the Local Authorities (Conduct of Referendums) (England) Regulations 2012, SI 2012/323, Sch 4 Table 1. As to the meaning of 'referendum' for these purposes see PARA 574 note 2.

2   Representation of the People Act 1983 s 66(3)(a); European Parliamentary Elections Regulations 2004, SI 2004/293, reg 29(4)(a); National Assembly for Wales (Representation of the People) Order 2007, SI 2007/236, art 35(3)(a).

3   Representation of the People Act 1983 s 66(3)(b); European Parliamentary Elections Regulations 2004, SI 2004/293, reg 29(4)(b); National Assembly for Wales (Representation of the People) Order 2007, SI 2007/236, art 35(3)(b). At a parliamentary election, head (2) in the text refers to information as to the candidate for whom a voter in that station is about to vote or has voted: see the Representation of the People Act 1983 s 66(3)(b). In relation to an election of the London members of the London Assembly at an ordinary election, the reference to 'the candidate for whom a voter in that station is about to vote or has voted' must be read as 'the candidate for whom, or the registered political party towards the return of whose candidates, a voter in that station is about to vote or has voted' (s 66(7) (s 66(7), (8) added by the Greater London Authority Act 1999 s 17, Sch 3 paras 1, 11)); and any reference to the return of a registered political party's candidates is a reference to the return of candidates included in the list of candidates submitted by the registered political party for the purposes of the election (Representation of the People Act 1983 s 66(8) (as so added)). As to the meaning of 'London member' see PARA 11 note 5. As to the meaning of 'candidate' generally see PARA 230. As to references to a registered political party submitting a list of candidates to be London members of the London Assembly at an ordinary election see PARA 230 note 14. As to London Assembly ordinary elections see PARA 199; and LONDON GOVERNMENT vol 71 (2013) PARA 76 et seq.

4   Representation of the People Act 1983 s 66(3)(c) (amended by the Electoral Administration Act 2006 s 47, Sch 1 paras 69, 86(b), 96); European Parliamentary Elections Regulations 2004, SI 2004/293, reg 29(4)(c) (amended by SI 2009/186); National Assembly for Wales (Representation of the People) Order 2007, SI 2007/236, art 35(3)(c). At a parliamentary election, head (3) in the text refers to information obtained in a polling station as to the candidate for whom a voter in that station is about to vote or has voted: see the Representation of the People Act 1983 s 66(3)(c) (as so amended); and see note 3. As to ballot papers see PARA 386 et seq. As to security measures associated with the ballot paper see PARA 387.

5   Representation of the People Act 1983 s 66(3)(d); European Parliamentary Elections Regulations 2004, SI 2004/293, reg 29(4)(d); National Assembly for Wales (Representation of the People) Order 2007, SI 2007/236, art 35(3)(d). At a parliamentary election, head (4) in the text refers to inducing voter to display his ballot paper after he has marked it so as to make known to any person the name of the candidate for whom he has or has not voted: see the Representation of the People Act 1983 s 66(3)(d); and see note 3.

6   Representation of the People Act 1983 s 66(6) (amended by the Representation of the People Act 1985 s 23, Sch 3 para 3); European Parliamentary Elections Regulations 2004, SI 2004/293, reg 29(7); National Assembly for Wales (Representation of the People) Order 2007, SI 2007/236, art 35(6). The penalty mentioned in the text is a fine not exceeding level 5 on the standard scale or imprisonment for a term not exceeding six months: see the Representation of the People Act 1983 s 66(6) (as so amended); the European Parliamentary Elections Regulations 2004, SI 2004/293, reg 29(7); and the National Assembly for Wales (Representation of the People) Order 2007, SI 2007/236, art 35(6). In relation to an offence committed after the date of commencement of the Criminal Justice Act 2003 s 281(5) (not yet in force) (alteration of penalties for summary offences: see SENTENCING AND DISPOSITION OF OFFENDERS vol 92 (2010) PARA 374), the reference to six months must be taken to be a reference to 51 weeks: see the National Assembly for Wales (Representation of the People) Order 2007, SI 2007/236, art 35(7). As to the standard scale see SENTENCING AND DISPOSITION OF OFFENDERS vol 92 (2010) PARA 142.

742. Contravention of requirement of secrecy at issue or receipt of postal ballot papers. Every person attending the proceedings in connection with the issue or the receipt of ballot papers for persons voting by post at an election[1] must maintain, and aid in maintaining, the secrecy of the voting[2]; and must not:

(1)   except for some purpose authorised by law communicate, before the poll is closed, to any person any information obtained at those proceedings as to the official mark[3];

(2)   except for some purpose authorised by law, communicate to any person at any time any information obtained at those proceedings as to the number or other unique identifying mark on the back of the ballot paper sent to any person[4];

(3)   except for some purpose authorised by law, attempt to ascertain at the proceedings in connection with the receipt of ballot papers the number or other unique identifying mark on the back of any ballot paper[5]; or

(4)   attempt to ascertain, at the proceedings in connection with the receipt of the ballot papers, the way in which any vote is given in any particular ballot paper, or communicate any information with respect thereto obtained at those proceedings[6].

If a person acts in contravention of these requirements, he is liable on summary conviction to a penalty[7].

1   As to proceedings in connection with the issue and receipt of postal ballot papers see PARA 406 et seq. As to the meaning of 'Assembly election' see PARA 3 note 2; as to the meaning of 'parliamentary election' see PARA 9; and as to the meaning of 'local government election' see PARA 11. As to elections in the City of London see PARA 33; and as to European parliamentary elections see PARA 217 et seq.

2   Representation of the People Act 1983 s 66(4); European Parliamentary Elections Regulations 2004, SI 2004/293, reg 29(5); National Assembly for Wales (Representation of the People) Order 2007, SI 2007/236, art 35(4).
     The Representation of the People Act 1983 s 66(4) does not apply at a poll consequent on a parish or community meeting: see s 187(1); the Local Government Act 1972 s 99, Sch 12 paras 18(5), 34(5): the Parish and Community Meetings (Polls) Rules 1987, SI 1987/1, r 6(a), (e); and see PARA 383. The Representation of the People Act 1983 s 66 has been applied and modified for the purposes of local authority referendums, however, in relation to Wales, by the Local Authorities (Conduct of Referendums) (Wales) Regulations 2008, SI 2008/1848, Sch 4 Table 1; and, in relation to England, by the Local Authorities (Conduct of Referendums) (England) Regulations 2012, SI 2012/323, Sch 4 Table 1. As to the meaning of 'referendum' for these purposes see PARA 574 note 2.

3   Representation of the People Act 1983 s 66(4)(a); European Parliamentary Elections Regulations 2004, SI 2004/293, reg 29(5)(a); National Assembly for Wales (Representation of the People) Order 2007, SI 2007/236, art 35(4)(a). As to ballot papers see PARA 386 et seq. As to security measures associated with the ballot paper see PARA 387.

4   Representation of the People Act 1983 s 66(4)(b) (s 66(4)(b), (c) amended by the Electoral Administration Act 2006 s 47, Sch 1 paras 69, 86(c), 96); European Parliamentary Elections Regulations 2004, SI 2004/293, reg 29(5)(b) (reg 29(5)(b), (c) amended by SI 2009/186); National Assembly for Wales (Representation of the People) Order 2007, SI 2007/236, art 35(4)(b). As to security measures associated with the ballot paper see PARA 387.

5   Representation of the People Act 1983 s 66(4)(c) (as amended: see note 4); European Parliamentary Elections Regulations 2004, SI 2004/293, reg 29(5)(c) (as amended: see note 4); National Assembly for Wales (Representation of the People) Order 2007, SI 2007/236, art 35(4)(c).

6   Representation of the People Act 1983 s 66(4)(d); European Parliamentary Elections Regulations 2004, SI 2004/293, reg 29(5)(d); National Assembly for Wales (Representation of the People) Order 2007, SI 2007/236, art 35(4)(d). At a parliamentary election, head (4) in the text refers to attempts to ascertain, at the proceedings in connection with the receipt of the ballot papers, the candidate for whom any vote is given in any particular ballot paper: see the Representation of the People Act 1983 s 66(3)(d). In relation to an election of the London members of the London Assembly at an ordinary election, the reference to 'the candidate for whom any vote is given in any particular ballot paper' must be read as 'the candidate for whom,

or the registered political party towards the return of whose candidates, any vote is given in any particular ballot paper' (s 66(7) (s 66(7), (8) added by the Greater London Authority Act 1999 s 17, Sch 3 paras 1, 11)); and any reference to the return of a registered political party's candidates is a reference to the return of candidates included in the list of candidates submitted by the registered political party for the purposes of the election (Representation of the People Act 1983 s 66(8) (as so added)). As to the meaning of 'London member' see PARA 11 note 5. As to the meaning of 'candidate' generally see PARA 230. As to references to a registered political party submitting a list of candidates to be London members of the London Assembly at an ordinary election see PARA 230 note 14. As to London Assembly ordinary elections see PARA 199; and LONDON GOVERNMENT vol 71 (2013) PARA 76 et seq.

7   Representation of the People Act 1983 s 66(6) (amended by the Representation of the People Act 1985 s 23, Sch 3 para 3); European Parliamentary Elections Regulations 2004, SI 2004/293, reg 29(7); National Assembly for Wales (Representation of the People) Order 2007, SI 2007/236, art 35(6). The penalty mentioned in the text is a fine not exceeding level 5 on the standard scale or imprisonment for a term not exceeding six months: see the Representation of the People Act 1983 s 66(6) (as so amended); the European Parliamentary Elections Regulations 2004, SI 2004/293, reg 29(7); and the National Assembly for Wales (Representation of the People) Order 2007, SI 2007/236, art 35(6). In relation to an offence committed after the date of commencement of the Criminal Justice Act 2003 s 281(5) (not yet in force) (alteration of penalties for summary offences: see SENTENCING AND DISPOSITION OF OFFENDERS vol 92 (2010) PARA 374), the reference to six months must be taken to be a reference to 51 weeks: see the National Assembly for Wales (Representation of the People) Order 2007, SI 2007/236, art 35(7). As to the standard scale see SENTENCING AND DISPOSITION OF OFFENDERS vol 92 (2010) PARA 142.

743.   Contravention of requirement of secrecy for persons having undertaken to assist a voter with disabilities. No person, having undertaken to assist a voter with disabilities to vote at an election[1], may communicate at any time to any person any information as to the way in which that voter intends to vote or has voted[2], or as to the number or other unique identifying mark on the back of the ballot paper given for the use of that voter[3]. If a person acts in contravention of these requirements he is liable on summary conviction to a penalty[4].

1   As to votes given by voters with disabilities assisted by companions see PARA 402. As to the meaning of 'Assembly election' see PARA 3 note 2; as to the meaning of 'parliamentary election' see PARA 9; and as to the meaning of 'local government election' see PARA 11. As to elections in the City of London see PARA 33; and as to European parliamentary elections see PARA 217 et seq.

2   At a parliamentary election, the reference is to a blind voter and any information as to the candidate for whom that voter intends to vote or has voted: see the Representation of the People Act 1983 s 66(5) (amended by the Electoral Administration Act 2006 s 47, Sch 1 paras 69, 86(d), 96). In relation to an election of the London members of the London Assembly at an ordinary election, the reference to 'the candidate for whom that voter intends to vote or has voted' must be read as 'the candidate for whom, or the registered political party towards the return of whose candidates, that voter intends to vote or has voted' (Representation of the People Act 1983 s 66(7) (s 66(7), (8) added by the Greater London Authority Act 1999 s 17, Sch 3 paras 1, 11)); and any reference to the return of a registered political party's candidates is a reference to the return of candidates included in the list of candidates submitted by the registered political party for the purposes of the election (Representation of the People Act 1983 s 66(8) (as so added)). As to the meaning of 'London member' see PARA 11 note 5. As to the meaning of 'candidate' generally see PARA 230. As to references to a registered political party submitting a list of candidates to be London members of the London Assembly at an ordinary election see PARA 199; and LONDON GOVERNMENT vol 71 (2013) PARA 76 et seq.

      The Representation of the People Act 1983 s 66 applies at a poll consequent on a parish or community meeting by virtue of s 187(1) and the Local Government Act 1972 s 99, Sch 12 paras 18(5), 34(5): see PARA 383. See also the Parish and Community Meetings (Polls) Rules 1987, SI 1987/1, r 6(a). At such a poll, the reference to the giving of votes is to the candidate for whom any vote is given: r 6(e). The Representation of the People Act 1983 s 66 also has been applied and modified for the purposes of local authority referendums, in relation to Wales, by the Local Authorities (Conduct of Referendums) (Wales) Regulations 2008,

SI 2008/1848, Sch 4 Table 1; and, in relation to England, by the Local Authorities (Conduct of Referendums) (England) Regulations 2012, SI 2012/323, Sch 4 Table 1. As to the meaning of 'referendum' for these purposes see PARA 574 note 2.

3 Representation of the People Act 1983 s 66(5) (as amended: see note 2); European Parliamentary Elections Regulations 2004, SI 2004/293, reg 29(6) (amended by SI 2009/186); National Assembly for Wales (Representation of the People) Order 2007, SI 2007/236, art 35(5). As to ballot papers see PARA 386 et seq. As to security measures associated with the ballot paper see PARA 387.

4 Representation of the People Act 1983 s 66(6) (amended by the Representation of the People Act 1985 s 23, Sch 3 para 3); European Parliamentary Elections Regulations 2004, SI 2004/293, reg 29(7); National Assembly for Wales (Representation of the People) Order 2007, SI 2007/236, art 35(6). The penalty mentioned in the text is a fine not exceeding level 5 on the standard scale or imprisonment for a term not exceeding six months: see the Representation of the People Act 1983 s 66(6) (as so amended); the European Parliamentary Elections Regulations 2004, SI 2004/293, reg 29(7); and the National Assembly for Wales (Representation of the People) Order 2007, SI 2007/236, art 35(6). In relation to an offence committed after the date of commencement of the Criminal Justice Act 2003 s 281(5) (not yet in force) (alteration of penalties for summary offences: see SENTENCING AND DISPOSITION OF OFFENDERS vol 92 (2010) PARA 374), the reference to six months must be taken to be a reference to 51 weeks: see the National Assembly for Wales (Representation of the People) Order 2007, SI 2007/236, art 35(7). As to the standard scale see SENTENCING AND DISPOSITION OF OFFENDERS vol 92 (2010) PARA 142.

744. Contravention of prohibition on publication of exit polls. No person may publish[1] before the poll at an election[2] is closed[3]:

(1) any statement relating to the way in which voters have voted at the election where that statement is (or might reasonably be taken to be) based on information given by voters after they have voted[4]; or

(2) any forecast[5] as to the result of the election[6] which is (or might reasonably be taken to be) based on information so given[7].

If a person acts in contravention of this prohibition, he is liable on summary conviction to a penalty[8].

1 For these purposes, 'publish' means make available to the public at large, or any section of the public, in whatever form and by whatever means: see the Representation of the People Act 1983 s 66A(4) (s 66A added by the Representation of the People Act 2000 s 15(1), Sch 6 paras 3, 6); the European Parliamentary Elections Regulations 2004, SI 2004/293, reg 30(3); and the National Assembly for Wales (Representation of the People) Order 2007, SI 2007/236, art 36(4).

2 Ie any parliamentary election, or any local government election, a Welsh Assembly election, or a European parliamentary election: see the Representation of the People Act 1983 s 66A(2) (as added: see note 1); the European Parliamentary Elections Regulations 2004, SI 2004/293, reg 30(1); and the National Assembly for Wales (Representation of the People) Order 2007, SI 2007/236, art 36(1). As to the meaning of 'Assembly election' see PARA 3 note 2; as to the meaning of 'parliamentary election' see PARA 9; and as to the meaning of 'local government election' see PARA 11. As to elections in the City of London see PARA 33; and as to European parliamentary elections see PARA 217 et seq.

The Representation of the People Act 1983 s 66A has been applied and modified for the purposes of local authority referendums, in relation to Wales, by the Local Authorities (Conduct of Referendums) (Wales) Regulations 2008, SI 2008/1848, Sch 4 Table 1; and, in relation to England, by the Local Authorities (Conduct of Referendums) (England) Regulations 2012, SI 2012/323, Sch 4 Table 1. As to the meaning of 'referendum' for these purposes see PARA 574 note 2.

3 Representation of the People Act 1983 s 66A(1), (2) (as added: see note 1); European Parliamentary Elections Regulations 2004, SI 2004/293, reg 30(1); National Assembly for Wales (Representation of the People) Order 2007, SI 2007/236, art 36(1). At a European parliamentary election, the reference is to the 'close of the poll' which means, in the case of a general election of members of the European Parliament ('MEPs'), the close of the polling in the member state whose electors are the last to vote in the election: see the European Parliamentary Elections Regulations 2004, SI 2004/293, reg 30(3). Under European Union legislation, elections to the European Parliament are held on the date and at the times fixed by each member state but

for all member states this date must fall within the same period starting on a Thursday morning and ending on the following Sunday: see PARA 222.

4   Representation of the People Act 1983 s 66A(1)(a) (as added: see note 1); European Parliamentary Elections Regulations 2004, SI 2004/293, reg 30(1)(a); National Assembly for Wales (Representation of the People) Order 2007, SI 2007/236, art 36(1)(a).

5   For these purposes, 'forecast' includes estimate: see the Representation of the People Act 1983 s 66A(4) (as added: see note 1); the European Parliamentary Elections Regulations 2004, SI 2004/293, reg 30(3); and the National Assembly for Wales (Representation of the People) Order 2007, SI 2007/236, art 36(4).

6   For these purposes, any reference to the result of an election is a reference to the result of the election either as a whole or so far as any particular candidate or candidates at the election is or are concerned: see the Representation of the People Act 1983 s 66A(4) (as added: see note 1); the European Parliamentary Elections Regulations 2004, SI 2004/293, reg 30(3); and the National Assembly for Wales (Representation of the People) Order 2007, SI 2007/236, art 36(4).

7   Representation of the People Act 1983 s 66A(1)(b) (as added: see note 1); European Parliamentary Elections Regulations 2004, SI 2004/293, reg 30(1)(b); National Assembly for Wales (Representation of the People) Order 2007, SI 2007/236, art 36(1)(b).

8   Representation of the People Act 1983 s 66A(3) (as added: see note 1); European Parliamentary Elections Regulations 2004, SI 2004/293, reg 30(2); National Assembly for Wales (Representation of the People) Order 2007, SI 2007/236, art 36(2). The penalty mentioned in the text is a fine not exceeding level 5 on the standard scale or imprisonment for a term not exceeding six months: see the Representation of the People Act 1983 s 66A(3) (as so added); the European Parliamentary Elections Regulations 2004, SI 2004/293, reg 30(2); and the National Assembly for Wales (Representation of the People) Order 2007, SI 2007/236, art 36(2). In relation to an offence committed after the date of commencement of the Criminal Justice Act 2003 s 281(5) (not yet in force) (alteration of penalties for summary offences: see SENTENCING AND DISPOSITION OF OFFENDERS vol 92 (2010) PARA 374), the reference to six months must be taken to be a reference to 51 weeks: see the National Assembly for Wales (Representation of the People) Order 2007, SI 2007/236, art 36(3). As to the standard scale see SENTENCING AND DISPOSITION OF OFFENDERS vol 92 (2010) PARA 142.

745.   Offences regarding access to or control of election or referendum documents.   A person is guilty of an offence:

(1)   if he fails to comply with any of the conditions imposed under the parliamentary election rules that govern the retention and public inspection of election documents[1], or in pursuance of regulations under the Electoral Administration Act 2006 that govern the inspection and supply of documents relating to an election other than a parliamentary election[2]; or

(2)   if he is an appropriate supervisor of a person (the 'supervised person')[3] who fails to comply with such a condition, and he failed to take appropriate steps[4].

A supervised person who has an appropriate supervisor and who has complied with all the requirements imposed on him by his appropriate supervisor is not guilty of such an offence, however[5]; and a person who is not a supervised person or an appropriate supervisor is not guilty of such an offence if he takes all reasonable steps to ensure that he complies with the conditions[6].

A person who is guilty of such an offence is liable on summary conviction to a penalty[7].

1   Ie conditions imposed in pursuance of regulations under the Representation of the People Act 1983 s 23(1), Sch 1 r 57, in relation to a parliamentary election (see PARA 503), or, in relation to a European parliamentary election, conditions imposed under the European Parliamentary Elections Regulations 2004, SI 2004/293, Sch 1 para 70 (see PARA 511): see the Representation of the People Act 1983 s 66B(1)(a) (s 66B added by the Electoral Administration Act 2006 s 41(9)); and the European Parliamentary Elections Regulations 2004, SI 2004/293, Sch 1 para 72(1)(a) (Sch 1 substituted by SI 2009/186). As to the meaning of 'parliamentary election' see PARA 9. As to European parliamentary elections see PARA 217 et seq.

2   Representation of the People Act 1983 s 66B(1)(a) (as added: see note 1); Electoral
     Administration Act 2006 s 43(1)(a); European Parliamentary Elections Regulations 2004,
     SI 2004/293, Sch 1 para 72(1)(a) (as substituted: see note 1). The reference in the text is to
     regulations under the Electoral Administration Act 2006 s 42 (see PARAS 505, 508, 510): see
     s 43(1)(a). As to the meaning of 'Assembly election' see PARA 3 note 2; and as to the meaning of
     'local government election' see PARA 11.
         The Electoral Administration Act 2006 s 43 has been applied and modified for the purposes
     of local authority referendums, in relation to Wales, by the Local Authorities (Conduct of
     Referendums) (Wales) Regulations 2008, SI 2008/1848, reg 8(2), Sch 4 Table 4; and, in relation
     to England, by the Local Authorities (Conduct of Referendums) (England) Regulations 2012,
     SI 2012/323, regs 8(2), 11–13, Sch 4 Table 5. As to the meaning of 'referendum' for these
     purposes see PARA 574 note 2.
3   For these purposes, an appropriate supervisor is a person who is a director of a company or who
     is concerned in the management of an organisation in which the supervised person is employed
     or under whose direction or control the supervised person is: Representation of the People
     Act 1983 s 66B(4)(a) (as added: see note 1); Electoral Administration Act 2006 s 43(4)(a);
     European Parliamentary Elections Regulations 2004, SI 2004/293, Sch 1 para 72(4)(a) (as
     substituted: see note 1).
4   Representation of the People Act 1983 s 66B(1)(b) (as added: see note 1); Electoral
     Administration Act 2006 s 43(1)(b); European Parliamentary Elections Regulations 2004,
     SI 2004/293, Sch 1 para 72(1)(b) (as substituted: see note 1). For these purposes, appropriate
     steps are such steps as it was reasonable for the appropriate supervisor to take to secure the
     operation of procedures designed to prevent, so far as reasonably practicable, the occurrence of
     a failure to comply with the conditions: Representation of the People Act 1983 s 66B(4)(b) (as
     so added); Electoral Administration Act 2006 s 43(4)(b); European Parliamentary Elections
     Regulations 2004, SI 2004/293, Sch 1 para 72(4)(b) (as substituted: see note 1).
5   Representation of the People Act 1983 s 66B(2) (as added: see note 1); Electoral Administration
     Act 2006 s 43(2); European Parliamentary Elections Regulations 2004, SI 2004/293, Sch 1
     para 72(2) (as substituted: see note 1).
6   Representation of the People Act 1983 s 66B(3) (as added: see note 1); Electoral Administration
     Act 2006 s 43(3); European Parliamentary Elections Regulations 2004, SI 2004/293, Sch 1
     para 72(3) (as substituted: see note 1).
7   Representation of the People Act 1983 s 66B(5) (as added: see note 1); Electoral Administration
     Act 2006 s 43(5); European Parliamentary Elections Regulations 2004, SI 2004/293, Sch 1
     para 72(5) (as substituted: see note 1). The penalty mentioned in the text is a fine not exceeding
     level 5 on the standard scale: see the Representation of the People Act 1983 s 66B(5) (as so
     added); the Electoral Administration Act 2006 s 43(5); and the European Parliamentary
     Elections Regulations 2004, SI 2004/293, Sch 1 para 72(5) (as so substituted). As to the
     standard scale see SENTENCING AND DISPOSITION OF OFFENDERS vol 92 (2010) PARA 142.

746.   Contravention of prohibition on officials acting as candidates' agents.   If:

(1)   any returning officer at an election[1]; or

(2)   any officer or clerk appointed under the elections rules[2]; or

(3)   any partner or clerk of any such person[3],

acts as an agent of a candidate[4] in the conduct or management of the election[5],
he is guilty of an offence[6], and is liable on summary conviction to a penalty[7].
This does not, however, prevent a candidate from acting as his own election
agent[8].

1   Representation of the People Act 1983 s 99(1)(a); European Parliamentary Elections
     Regulations 2004, SI 2004/293, reg 69(1)(a); National Assembly for Wales (Representation of
     the People) Order 2007, SI 2007/236, art 71(1)(a), (b), (c). Head (1) in the text refers to:
     (1)   any returning officer at a parliamentary or local government election (see the
            Representation of the People Act 1983 s 99(1)(a));
     (2)   any returning officer or local returning officer at a European parliamentary election (see
            the European Parliamentary Elections Regulations 2004, SI 2004/293, reg 69(1)(a));
     (3)   any constituency or regional returning officer at a Welsh Assembly constituency election
            (see the National Assembly for Wales (Representation of the People) Order 2007,
            SI 2007/236, art 71(1)(a));
     (4)   any constituency or regional returning officer at a Welsh Assembly regional election (see
            art 71(1)(b));

(5)   any person appointed under art 20(1) (ie one or more persons appointed to discharge the functions of either a constituency returning officer (whether at a constituency or regional Assembly election) or a regional returning officer at a regional Assembly election: see PARA 357) (see art 71(1)(c)).

As to the meanings of 'Assembly election', 'Assembly constituency election' and 'Assembly regional election' see PARA 3 note 2; as to the meaning of 'parliamentary election' see PARA 9; and as to the meaning of 'local government election' see PARA 11. As to elections in the City of London see PARA 33; and as to European parliamentary elections see PARA 217 et seq. As to the meanings of 'constituency returning officer' and 'regional returning officer' at a Welsh Assembly election see PARA 18 note 2. As to returning officers for parliamentary elections see PARA 350 et seq; as to returning officers for local government elections see PARA 354 et seq; and as to the designation of returning officers and local returning officers at European parliamentary elections see PARA 360 et seq.

The Representation of the People Act 1983 s 99 has been applied and modified for the purpose of local authority mayoral elections in England and Wales by the Local Authorities (Mayoral Elections) (England and Wales) Regulations 2007, SI 2007/1024, reg 3(2)–(5), Sch 2 Table 1: see PARA 11 note 14. The Representation of the People Act 1983 s 99 also has been applied to an election under the local government Act, where references to an election under the local government Act are deemed to include a reference to a poll consequent on a parish or community meeting: see the Parish and Community Meetings (Polls) Rules 1987, SI 1987/1, r 6(d), (g). See also the Representation of the People Act 1983 s 187(1); the Local Government Act 1972 s 99, Sch 12 paras 18(5), 34(5); and PARA 383. As to the returning officer at a poll consequent on a parish meeting on a question involving appointment to office see PARA 356; and as to the returning officer at a poll consequent on a parish or community meeting on any other question see PARA 588.

2   Representation of the People Act 1983 s 99(1)(b); European Parliamentary Elections Regulations 2004, SI 2004/293, reg 69(1)(b); National Assembly for Wales (Representation of the People) Order 2007, SI 2007/236, art 71(1)(d). Head (2) in the text refers to any officer or clerk appointed:

(1)   under the parliamentary elections rules, or the rules under the Representation of the People Act 1983 s 36 (appointment of presiding officers and their clerks by returning officer: see PARA 393) (see s 99(1)(b));

(2)   under the European parliamentary elections rules (see PARA 393) (see the European Parliamentary Elections Regulations 2004, SI 2004/293, reg 69(1)(b));

(3)   under the National Assembly for Wales (Representation of the People) Order 2007, SI 2007/236, Sch 5 (see PARA 393) (see art 71(1)(d)).

As to the meanings of 'European parliamentary elections rules' and 'parliamentary elections rules' see PARA 383.

3   Representation of the People Act 1983 s 99(1)(c); European Parliamentary Elections Regulations 2004, SI 2004/293, reg 69(1)(c); National Assembly for Wales (Representation of the People) Order 2007, SI 2007/236, art 71(1)(e).

4   As to the meaning of 'candidate' generally see PARA 230. As to the appointment of an election agent for parliamentary and local government elections see PARA 231; as to the appointment of an election agent for elections to the National Assembly for Wales see PARA 235; and as to the appointment of the election agent of a registered party or for an individual candidate at a European parliamentary election see PARA 239. At a European parliamentary election, the prohibition acts upon an agent of a registered party which has submitted a list, a candidate on that list or an individual candidate: see the European Parliamentary Elections Regulations 2004, SI 2004/293, reg 69(1). As to the meanings of 'registered party' and 'list' (submitted by a registered party) in relation to a European parliamentary election see PARA 230 note 29; and as to the meaning of 'individual candidate' for these purposes see PARA 230 note 32. At a Welsh Assembly election, the reference is to any candidate or registered political party which has submitted a list of candidates: see the National Assembly for Wales (Representation of the People) Order 2007, SI 2007/236, art 71(1). As to the meaning of 'candidate' (ie either a 'constituency candidate' or 'individual candidate') for these purposes see PARA 230 note 19; and as to the meanings of 'party list', 'party list candidate' and 'registered political party' see PARA 230 note 23.

5   It is not necessary that the agent should be an agent for the management of the whole election; it is sufficient if he is agent for part of the election. He must be not simply an agent who might be employed to such an extent as might make the candidate answerable for corrupt or illegal practices committed by him, but employed in the way of managing a portion of the election: *North Norfolk Case, Burton's Case* (1869) 1 O'M & H 236 at 239.

6 Representation of the People Act 1983 s 99(1); European Parliamentary Elections Regulations 2004, SI 2004/293, reg 69(1); National Assembly for Wales (Representation of the People) Order 2007, SI 2007/236, art 71(1).

7 Representation of the People Act 1983 s 99(2) (substituted by the Representation of the People Act 1985 s 23, Sch 3 para 4); European Parliamentary Elections Regulations 2004, SI 2004/293, reg 69(2); National Assembly for Wales (Representation of the People) Order 2007, SI 2007/236, art 71(2). The penalty mentioned in the text is a fine not exceeding level 4 on the standard scale: see the Representation of the People Act 1983 s 99(2) (as so substituted); the European Parliamentary Elections Regulations 2004, SI 2004/293, reg 69(2); and the National Assembly for Wales (Representation of the People) Order 2007, SI 2007/236, art 71(2). As to the standard scale see SENTENCING AND DISPOSITION OF OFFENDERS vol 92 (2010) PARA 142. In relation to a European parliamentary election held in Gibraltar, the fine must not exceed £2500: see the European Parliamentary Elections Regulations 2004, SI 2004/293, reg 69(2). As to the establishment of electoral regions (including the 'combined region', which includes Gibraltar) for the purpose of elections to the European Parliament see PARA 77.

8 See the Representation of the People Act 1983 s 99(1); the European Parliamentary Elections Regulations 2004, SI 2004/293, reg 69(1); and the National Assembly for Wales (Representation of the People) Order 2007, SI 2007/236, art 71(1). At a European parliamentary election, the reference in the text is to an individual candidate not being prevented from acting as his own election agent: see the European Parliamentary Elections Regulations 2004, SI 2004/293, reg 69(1). At a Welsh Assembly election, neither a constituency nor an individual candidate is prevented from acting as his own election agent. nor a party list candidate from acting as election agent for the registered political party on whose list he is a candidate: see the National Assembly for Wales (Representation of the People) Order 2007, SI 2007/236, art 71(1).

747. Illegal canvassing by police officers. No member of a police force[1] may by word, message, writing, or in any other manner, endeavour to persuade any person to give, or dissuade any person from giving, his vote, whether as an elector or as proxy[2]:

(1)   at any parliamentary election for a constituency[3];
(2)   at any local government election for any electoral area[4];
(3)   at any European parliamentary election for an electoral region[5];
(4)   at any constituency election for a Welsh Assembly constituency[6];
(5)   at any regional election for a Welsh Assembly electoral region[7].

which is either wholly or partly within the police area[8]. A person acting in contravention of this prohibition is liable on summary conviction to a penalty[9]. A member of a force, however, is not to be subjected to any such penalty for anything done in the discharge of his duty as a member of the force[10].

1 As to the administration of police areas and police forces in England and Wales see POLICE AND INVESTIGATORY POWERS vol 84 (2013) PARA 52 et seq.

2 See the Representation of the People Act 1983 s 100(1); the European Parliamentary Elections Regulations 2004, SI 2004/293, reg 70(1); and the National Assembly for Wales (Representation of the People) Order 2007, SI 2007/236, art 72(1). As to the meaning of 'elector' in relation to a parliamentary or local government election see PARA 95 note 2; in relation to a European parliamentary election, see PARA 111 note 4; and, in relation to a Welsh Assembly election, see PARA 110 note 6. As to applications to vote by post or by proxy see PARA 367 et seq.

The Representation of the People Act 1983 s 100 applies to a poll consequent on a parish or community meeting by virtue of s 187(1) and the Local Government Act 1972 s 99, Sch 12 paras 18(5), 34(5) (see PARA 383); and see the Parish and Community Meetings (Polls) Rules 1987, SI 1987/1, r 6. The Representation of the People Act 1983 s 100 also has been applied and modified for the purposes of local authority referendums, in relation to Wales, by the Local Authorities (Conduct of Referendums) (Wales) Regulations 2008, SI 2008/1848, Sch 4 Table 1; and, in relation to England, by the Local Authorities (Conduct of Referendums) (England) Regulations 2012, SI 2012/323, Sch 4 Table 1. As to the meaning of 'referendum' for these purposes see PARA 574 note 2.

3 Representation of the People Act 1983 s 100(1)(a). As to the meanings of 'parliamentary constituency' and 'parliamentary election' see PARA 9.

4 Representation of the People Act 1983 s 100(1)(b). As to the meanings of 'electoral area' and 'local government election' see PARA 11.

5   European Parliamentary Elections Regulations 2004, SI 2004/293, reg 70(1). As to the establishment of electoral regions (including the 'combined region', which includes Gibraltar) for the purpose of elections to the European Parliament see PARA 77; and as to European parliamentary elections see PARA 217 et seq.

6   National Assembly for Wales (Representation of the People) Order 2007, SI 2007/236, art 72(1)(a). As to the meanings of 'Assembly constituency' and 'constituency election' see PARA 3 note 2.

7   National Assembly for Wales (Representation of the People) Order 2007, SI 2007/236, art 72(1)(b). As to the meanings of 'Assembly electoral region' and 'regional election' see PARA 3 note 2.

8   See the Representation of the People Act 1983 s 100(1); the European Parliamentary Elections Regulations 2004, SI 2004/293, reg 70(1); and the National Assembly for Wales (Representation of the People) Order 2007, SI 2007/236, art 72(1). In relation to a European parliamentary election held in Gibraltar, the reference to the police area must be construed as a reference to Gibraltar itself: see the European Parliamentary Elections Regulations 2004, SI 2004/293, reg 70(3).

9   Representation of the People Act 1983 s 100(2) (amended by the Representation of the People Act 1985 s 23, Sch 3 para 5); European Parliamentary Elections Regulations 2004, SI 2004/293, reg 70(2); National Assembly for Wales (Representation of the People) Order 2007, SI 2007/236, art 72(2). The penalty mentioned in the text is a fine not exceeding level 3 on the standard scale: see the Representation of the People Act 1983 s 100(2) (as so amended); the European Parliamentary Elections Regulations 2004, SI 2004/293, reg 70(2); and the National Assembly for Wales (Representation of the People) Order 2007, SI 2007/236, art 72(2). As to the standard scale see SENTENCING AND DISPOSITION OF OFFENDERS vol 92 (2010) PARA 142. In relation to a European parliamentary election held in Gibraltar, the fine must not exceed £1000: see the European Parliamentary Elections Regulations 2004, SI 2004/293, reg 70(2).

10   Representation of the People Act 1983 s 100(2) (as amended: see note 9); European Parliamentary Elections Regulations 2004, SI 2004/293, reg 70(2); National Assembly for Wales (Representation of the People) Order 2007, SI 2007/236, art 72(2).

748.   Failure to display details on election publications.   No material which can reasonably be regarded as intended to promote or procure the election of a candidate[1] (whether or not it can be so regarded as intended to achieve any other purpose as well)[2] may be published[3] unless the following requirements are complied with[4]:

(1)   where the material is a document consisting (or consisting principally) of a single side of printed matter, the name and address of the printer[5] of the document[6], the name and address of the promoter[7] of the material[8], and the name and address of any person on behalf of whom the material is being published (and who is not the promoter)[9] (the 'relevant details'), must appear on the face of the document[10];

(2)   where the material is a printed document other than one to which head (1) above applies, the name and address of the printer of the document[11], the name and address of the promoter of the material[12] and the name and address of any person on behalf of whom the material is being published (and who is not the promoter)[13] (the 'relevant details'), must appear either on the first or the last page of the document[14];

(3)   where the material is an advertisement contained in a newspaper or periodical: (a) the name and address of the printer of the newspaper or periodical must appear either on its first or last page[15]; and (b) the name and address of the promoter of the material[16], and the name and address of any person on behalf of whom the material is being published (and who is not the promoter)[17], must be included in the advertisement[18];

(4)   in the case of any other material (except where it relates to a European parliamentary election), the name and address of the promoter of the

material[19], and the name and address of any person on behalf of whom the material is being published (and who is not the promoter)[20] must be included in the material in accordance with requirements imposed by regulations which may be made for these purposes by the Secretary of State after consulting the Electoral Commission[21].

Where any material is published in contravention of these requirements, the promoter of the material and any other person by whom the material is so published (and, in the case of material falling within heads (1) to (3) above, the printer of the material also) are guilty of an offence and liable on summary conviction to a penalty[22]. It is a defence for a person charged with such an offence to prove that the contravention of the requirements arose from circumstances beyond his control, and that he took all reasonable steps, and exercised all due diligence, to ensure that that contravention would not arise[23]. A candidate or his election agent[24] who would be guilty of such an offence is instead guilty of an illegal practice[25].

1 As to the meaning of 'candidate' generally see PARA 230. The text refers to the candidate at a parliamentary or local government election, an Assembly election, or a European parliamentary election. As to the meaning of 'Assembly election' see PARA 3 note 2; as to the meaning of 'parliamentary election' see PARA 9; and as to the meaning of 'local government election' see PARA 11. As to elections in the City of London see PARA 33; and as to European parliamentary elections see PARA 217 et seq. As to the meaning of 'promoting or procuring' for these purposes see PARA 272 note 2.

2 See the Representation of the People Act 1983 s 110(1) (s 110 substituted by the Political Parties, Elections and Referendums Act 2000 s 138, Sch 18 paras 1, 14); the European Parliamentary Elections Regulations 2004, SI 2004/293, reg 74(1) (substituted by SI 2009/186); and the National Assembly for Wales (Representation of the People) Order 2007, SI 2007/236, art 76(1). For the purpose of determining whether any material is material such as is mentioned in the text, it is immaterial that it does not expressly mention the name of any candidate: Representation of the People Act 1983 s 110(14) (as so substituted); European Parliamentary Elections Regulations 2004, SI 2004/293, reg74(11) (as so substituted); National Assembly for Wales (Representation of the People) Order 2007, SI 2007/236, art 76(14).

The Representation of the People Act 1983 s 110 has been applied and modified for the purposes of local authority referendums, in relation to Wales, by the Local Authorities (Conduct of Referendums) (Wales) Regulations 2008, SI 2008/1848, Sch 4 Table 1; and, in relation to England, by the Local Authorities (Conduct of Referendums) (England) Regulations 2012, SI 2012/323, Sch 4 Table 1. As to the meaning of 'referendum' for these purposes see PARA 574 note 2. The substitution made by the Political Parties, Elections and Referendums Act 2000 Sch 18 paras 1, 14 had no effect in relation to any election for which the date of the poll specified in the notice of election issued in relation to that election was on or before 2 May 2007, and, in relation to any such election, the Election Publications Act 2001 s 1(1), (2)(a) continued to have effect: see the Political Parties, Elections and Referendums Act 2000 (Commencement No 3 and Transitional Provisions) Order 2006, SI 2006/3416, arts 3(b), 4, 5. The Election Publications Act 2001 continued the Representation of the People Act 1983 s 110 in the form in which it had effect immediately before the day originally appointed for the Political Parties, Elections and Referendums Act 2000 Sch 18 paras 1, 14 to come into effect, ie 16 February 2001 (the 'commencement date': see the Political Parties, Elections and Referendums Act 2000 (Commencement No 1 and Transitional Provisions) Order 2001, SI 2001/222, art 2, Sch 1 Pt I). See further the Election Publications Act 2001 ss 1–3. As to the case law which attached to the previous form of wording of the Representation of the People Act 1983 s 110 see notes 3, 6, 7.

3 For these purposes, 'publish' means make available to the public at large, or any section of the public, in whatever form and by whatever means: see the Representation of the People Act 1983 s 110(13) (as substituted: see note 2); the European Parliamentary Elections Regulations 2004, SI 2004/293, reg74(10) (as substituted: see note 2); and the National Assembly for Wales (Representation of the People) Order 2007, SI 2007/236, art 76(15). Under case law which attached to the previous form of wording of the Representation of the People Act 1983 s 110 (see note 2), it had been argued that by the 'custom and comity of the printing trade' the name of a printer appearing on a placard means that he is also the publisher: *Re County Councillors' Elections* (1889) 5 TLR 195, DC. However, a distinct statement as to who is the publisher as

well as to who is the printer may be required: see *Re County Councillors' Elections*; *Ex p Jessel* (1910) Times, 21 January; *Re Berry* [1978] Crim LR 357 (name of printer and publisher not on election leaflets). The returning officer would presumably be the publisher of official notices (which would qualify as 'documents' for these purposes, although official poll cards would not). See also PUBLISHING vol 85 (2012) PARA 702.

4 See the Representation of the People Act 1983 s 110(2) (as substituted: see note 2); the European Parliamentary Elections Regulations 2004, SI 2004/293, reg74(2) (as substituted: see note 2); and the National Assembly for Wales (Representation of the People) Order 2007, SI 2007/236, art 76(2).

5 For these purposes, 'print' means print by whatever means; and 'printer' must be construed accordingly: see the Representation of the People Act 1983 s 110(13) (as substituted: see note 2); the European Parliamentary Elections Regulations 2004, SI 2004/293, reg74(10) (as substituted: see note 2); and the National Assembly for Wales (Representation of the People) Order 2007, SI 2007/236, art 76(15). See also note 3.

6 Representation of the People Act 1983 s 110(2)(a), (3)(a), (4) (as substituted: see note 2); European Parliamentary Elections Regulations 2004, SI 2004/293, reg74(2), (3)(a), (4) (as substituted: see note 2); National Assembly for Wales (Representation of the People) Order 2007, SI 2007/236, art 76(2)(a), (3)(a), (4).

Under case law which attached to the previous form of wording of the Representation of the People Act 1983 s 110 (see note 2), a duplicated personal letter was held to be a 'document': *Re Shipston-on-Stour RDC Election* (1953) Times, 9 June; *Re Liverpool City Council Election* (1964) Times, 16 May, DC. The previous wording of the Representation of the People Act 1983 s 110 attached to 'any bill, placard or poster having reference to an election', and authorities developed as to the classification of a document as a 'bill', 'placard' or 'poster': see *Re Essex County Councillors, Barstow Division, Election* (1888) 5 TLR 159, DC; *Barrow-in-Furness Case* (1886) 4 O'M & H 76; *Re Shrewsbury County Councillors' Election* (1888) 5 TLR 160, DC; *Re East Suffolk and Eye Borough County Councillors' Election* (1888) 5 TLR 170, DC; *Cheshire, Knutsford Division Case* (1888) 5 TLR 170: *Re Election of Common Councilmen for the Ward of Farringdon Without in the City of London* (1925) 161 LT Jo 26, DC. See also *Cumberland, Cockermouth Division Case* (1901) 5 O'M & H 155; *Alcott v Emden* (1904) 68 JP 434, DC (where a circular headed with the complainant's name and the words 'Shall he be our new Mayor' and sent to the complainant, the town clerk and four councillors in August 1903, it being known that the complainant intended to stand as candidate for that post at the next election on the following 9 November, was held to have reference to the election and to be a bill); and *Oxford Borough Case* (1924) 7 O'M & H 49 at 73, 84, 93 (postcards reading 'You did not forget me a year ago. I shall not forget you' held not to be bills, placards or posters). A poster is something that is stuck up: *Alcott v Emden* (1904) 68 JP 434.

7 For these purposes, the 'promoter', in relation to any material which can reasonably be regarded as intended to promote or procure the election of a candidate at an election (whether or not it can be so regarded as intended to achieve any other purpose as well), means the person causing the material to be published: see the Representation of the People Act 1983 s 110(13) (as substituted: see note 2); the European Parliamentary Elections Regulations 2004, SI 2004/293, reg74(10) (as substituted: see note 2); and the National Assembly for Wales (Representation of the People) Order 2007, SI 2007/236, art 76(15). Under case law which attached to the previous form of wording of the Representation of the People Act 1983 s 110 (see note 2), where a candidate's brother gave the instructions for the printing of an election address, not bearing the printer's name and address, to be done for the candidate, and the cost was debited to the candidate but not paid by him, it was held that the candidate had not been proved to have printed or caused to be printed the election address, even though the document purported to be signed by him: *Bettesworth v Allingham* (1885) 16 QBD 44, DC.

8 Representation of the People Act 1983 s 110(2)(a), (3)(b), (4) (as substituted: see note 2); European Parliamentary Elections Regulations 2004, SI 2004/293, reg74(2), (3)(b), (4) (as substituted: see note 2); National Assembly for Wales (Representation of the People) Order 2007, SI 2007/236, art 76(2)(a), (3)(b), (4).

9 Representation of the People Act 1983 s 110(2)(a), (3)(c), (4) (as substituted: see note 2); European Parliamentary Elections Regulations 2004, SI 2004/293, reg74(2), (3)(c), (4) (as substituted: see note 2); National Assembly for Wales (Representation of the People) Order 2007, SI 2007/236, art 76(2)(a), (3)(c), (4).

10 Representation of the People Act 1983 s 110(2)(a), (4) (as substituted: see note 2); European Parliamentary Elections Regulations 2004, SI 2004/293, reg74(2), (4) (as substituted: see note 2); National Assembly for Wales (Representation of the People) Order 2007, SI 2007/236, art 76(2)(a), (4).

11 Representation of the People Act 1983 s 110(2)(a), (3)(a), (5) (as substituted: see note 2); European Parliamentary Elections Regulations 2004, SI 2004/293, reg74(2), (3)(a), (5) (as substituted: see note 2); National Assembly for Wales (Representation of the People) Order 2007, SI 2007/236, art 76(2)(a), (3)(a), (5).

12 Representation of the People Act 1983 s 110(2)(a), (3)(b), (5) (as substituted: see note 2); European Parliamentary Elections Regulations 2004, SI 2004/293, reg74(2), (3)(b), (5) (as substituted: see note 2); National Assembly for Wales (Representation of the People) Order 2007, SI 2007/236, art 76(2)(a), (3)(b), (5).

13 Representation of the People Act 1983 s 110(2)(a), (3)(c), (5) (as substituted: see note 2); European Parliamentary Elections Regulations 2004, SI 2004/293, reg74(2), (3)(c), (5) (as substituted: see note 2); National Assembly for Wales (Representation of the People) Order 2007, SI 2007/236, art 76(2)(a), (3)(c), (5).

14 Representation of the People Act 1983 s 110(2)(a), (5) (as substituted: see note 2); European Parliamentary Elections Regulations 2004, SI 2004/293, reg74(2), (5) (as substituted: see note 2); National Assembly for Wales (Representation of the People) Order 2007, SI 2007/236, art 76(2)(a), (3)(a), (5).

15 Representation of the People Act 1983 s 110(2)(a), (6)(a) (as substituted: see note 2); European Parliamentary Elections Regulations 2004, SI 2004/293, reg74(2), (6)(a) (as substituted: see note 2); National Assembly for Wales (Representation of the People) Order 2007, SI 2007/236, art 76(2), (6)(a).

16 Representation of the People Act 1983 s 110(2)(a), (3)(b), (6)(b) (as substituted: see note 2); European Parliamentary Elections Regulations 2004, SI 2004/293, reg74(2), (3)(b), (6)(b) (as substituted: see note 2); National Assembly for Wales (Representation of the People) Order 2007, SI 2007/236, art 76(2)(a), (3)(b), (6)(b).

17 Representation of the People Act 1983 s 110(2)(a), (3)(c), (6)(b) (as substituted: see note 2); European Parliamentary Elections Regulations 2004, SI 2004/293, reg74(2), (3)(c), (6)(b) (as substituted: see note 2); National Assembly for Wales (Representation of the People) Order 2007, SI 2007/236, art 76(2)(a), (3)(c), (6)(b).

18 Representation of the People Act 1983 s 110(2)(a), (6)(b) (as substituted: see note 2); European Parliamentary Elections Regulations 2004, SI 2004/293, reg74(2), (6)(b) (as substituted: see note 2); National Assembly for Wales (Representation of the People) Order 2007, SI 2007/236, art 76(2)(a), (6)(b).

19 Representation of the People Act 1983 s 110(2)(b), (7)(a) (as substituted: see note 2); National Assembly for Wales (Representation of the People) Order 2007, SI 2007/236, art 76(2)(b), (7)(a).

20 Representation of the People Act 1983 s 110(2)(b), (7)(b) (as substituted: see note 2); National Assembly for Wales (Representation of the People) Order 2007, SI 2007/236, art 76(2)(b), (7)(b).

21 Representation of the People Act 1983 s 110(2)(b), (7) (as substituted: see note 2); National Assembly for Wales (Representation of the People) Order 2007, SI 2007/236, art 76(2)(b), (7). Such regulations may in particular specify:

  (1) the manner and form in which such details must be included in any such material for the purpose of complying with any such requirement (Representation of the People Act 1983 s 110(8)(a) (as so substituted); National Assembly for Wales (Representation of the People) Order 2007, SI 2007/236, art 76(8)(a));

  (2) circumstances in which any such requirement does not have to be complied with by a person of any description specified in the regulations, or in which a breach of any such requirement by a person of any description so specified is not to result in the commission of an offence under the Representation of the People Act 1983 s 110, or the National Assembly for Wales (Representation of the People) Order 2007, SI 2007/236, art 76, as the case may be (see the text and notes 24–25), by that person or by a person of any such description (Representation of the People Act 1983 s 110(8)(b) (as so substituted); National Assembly for Wales (Representation of the People) Order 2007, SI 2007/236, art 76(8)(b));

  (3) circumstances in which material is, or is not, to be taken for the purposes of the regulations to be published or (as the case may be) published by a person of any description so specified (Representation of the People Act 1983 s 110(8)(c) (as so substituted); National Assembly for Wales (Representation of the People) Order 2007, SI 2007/236, art 76(8)(c)).

The power to make such regulations for the purposes of a Welsh Assembly election is exercisable by statutory instrument which is subject to annulment in pursuance of a resolution of either House of Parliament: art 76(13). For the purposes of the Statutory Instruments Act 1946 s 1 (see STATUTES AND LEGISLATIVE PROCESS vol 96 (2012) PARA 1045), the National Assembly for

Wales (Representation of the People) Order 2007, SI 2007/236, art 76(13) has effect as if contained in an Act of Parliament: see art 76(13). At the date at which this volume states the law, no such regulations had been made under either the Representation of the People Act 1983 s 110 or the National Assembly for Wales (Representation of the People) Order 2007, SI 2007/236, art 76. As to the Secretary of State see PARA 2. As to the Electoral Commission see PARA 34 et seq.

22 See the Representation of the People Act 1983 s 110(9), (10) (as substituted: see note 2); European Parliamentary Elections Regulations 2004, SI 2004/293, reg74(7) (as substituted: see note 2); National Assembly for Wales (Representation of the People) Order 2007, SI 2007/236, art 76(9), (10). The penalty mentioned in the text is a fine not exceeding level 5 on the standard scale: see the Representation of the People Act 1983 s 110(9), (10) (as so substituted); the European Parliamentary Elections Regulations 2004, SI 2004/293, reg74(7) (as so substituted); and the National Assembly for Wales (Representation of the People) Order 2007, SI 2007/236, art 76(9), (10). As to the standard scale see SENTENCING AND DISPOSITION OF OFFENDERS vol 92 (2010) PARA 142. Liability for an offence which arises out of the requirement set out in head (4) in the text is subject to regulations made by virtue of the Representation of the People Act 1983 s 110(8)(b), or the National Assembly for Wales (Representation of the People) Order 2007, SI 2007/236, art 76(8)(b), as the case may be (see note 21): see the Representation of the People Act 1983 s 110(10) (as so substituted); and the National Assembly for Wales (Representation of the People) Order 2007, SI 2007/236, art 76(10).

23 See the Representation of the People Act 1983 s 110(11) (as substituted: see note 2); European Parliamentary Elections Regulations 2004, SI 2004/293, reg74(8) (as substituted: see note 2); National Assembly for Wales (Representation of the People) Order 2007, SI 2007/236, art 76(11). See *DPP v Edwards* [2002] EWHC 636 (Admin), [2002] All ER (D) 314 (Mar) (as it stood at the time of the offence, the Representation of the People Act 1983 s 110 was an absolute offence and so it could not be contended that the omission of details from election leaflets had been inadvertent and that the defendant had taken immediate steps to rectify the situation).

24 As to the appointment of an election agent for parliamentary and local government elections see PARA 231; and as to the appointment of the election agent of a registered party or for an individual candidate at a European parliamentary election see PARA 239. At a Welsh Assembly election, the reference is to:
 (1) a constituency candidate, or an individual candidate, or his election agent (see the National Assembly for Wales (Representation of the People) Order 2007, SI 2007/236, art 76(12)(a); and PARA 703);
 (2) a party list candidate, or the election agent of the registered political party in relation to that party's list (see art 76(12)(b); and PARA 703).
As to the meanings of 'candidate', 'constituency candidate' and 'individual candidate' for these purposes see PARA 230 note 19; and as to the meanings of 'party list', 'party list candidate' and 'registered political party' see PARA 230 note 23. As to the appointment of an election agent for elections to the National Assembly for Wales see PARA 235.

25 See the Representation of the People Act 1983 s 110(12) (as substituted: see note 2); the European Parliamentary Elections Regulations 2004, SI 2004/293, reg 74(9) (as substituted: see note 2); the National Assembly for Wales (Representation of the People) Order 2007, SI 2007/236, art 76(12); and PARA 703. As to the consequences of illegal practices see PARA 888 et seq.

749. Failure to display details on election material published by third parties in national election campaigns. No election material produced by third parties for national election campaigns[1] may be published[2] unless the following requirements are complied with[3]:
 (1) where the material is a document consisting (or consisting principally) of a single side of printed matter, the name and address of the printer[4] of the document[5], the name and address of the promoter[6] of the material[7], and the name and address of any person on behalf of whom the material is being published (and who is not the promoter)[8] (the 'relevant details'), must appear on the face of the document[9];
 (2) where the material is a printed document other than one to which head (1) above applies, the name and address of the printer of the document[10], the name and address of the promoter of the material[11],

and the name and address of any person on behalf of whom the material is being published (and who is not the promoter)[12] (the 'relevant details'), must appear either on the first or the last page of the document[13];

(3)   where the material is an advertisement contained in a newspaper or periodical: (a) the name and address of the printer of the newspaper or periodical must appear either on its first or last page[14]; and (b) the name and address of the promoter of the material[15], and the name and address of any person on behalf of whom the material is being published (and who is not the promoter)[16], must be included in the advertisement[17];

(4)   in the case of any other material, the name and address of the promoter of the material[18], and the name and address of any person on behalf of whom the material is being published (and who is not the promoter)[19], must be included in the material in accordance with requirements imposed by regulations which may be made for these purposes by the Secretary of State after consulting the Electoral Commission[20].

Where any material is published in contravention of these requirements, the promoter of the material, and any other person by whom the material is so published (and, in the case of material falling within heads (1) to (3) above, the printer of the material) are guilty of an offence[21] and liable on summary conviction to a penalty[22]. It is a defence for a person charged with such an offence to prove that the contravention of the requirements arose from circumstances beyond his control and that he took all reasonable steps, and exercised all due diligence, to ensure that that contravention would not arise[23].

1   For these purposes, 'election material' has the meaning given by the Political Parties, Elections and Referendums Act 2000 s 85(3) (controlled expenditure by third parties in national election campaigns: see PARA 313 note 4): see s 143(11).

      The Political Parties, Elections and Referendums Act 2000 s 143 had no effect in relation to any election for which the date of the poll specified in the notice of election issued in relation to that election was on or before 2 May 2007, and in relation to any such election the Election Publications Act 2001 s 1(1), (2)(a) continued to have effect: see the Political Parties, Elections and Referendums Act 2000 (Commencement No 3 and Transitional Provisions) Order 2006, SI 2006/3416, arts 3(a), 4, 5. Under the Election Publications Act 2001 the Political Parties, Elections and Referendums Act 2000 s 143 was deemed not to have come into force on the day originally appointed, ie 16 February 2001 (the 'commencement date': see the Political Parties, Elections and Referendums Act 2000 (Commencement No 1 and Transitional Provisions) Order 2001, SI 2001/222, art 2, Sch 1 Pt I). See further the Election Publications Act 2001 ss 1–3.

2   For these purposes, 'publish' means make available to the public at large, or any section of the public, in whatever form and by whatever means: see the Political Parties, Elections and Referendums Act 2000 s 143(11). See note 1. As to case law that attached to a similar form of wording that appeared in the Representation of the People Act 1983 s 110 (as originally enacted) see PARA 748.

3   Political Parties, Elections and Referendums Act 2000 s 143(1). See note 1.

4   For these purposes, 'print' means print by whatever means; and 'printer' must be construed accordingly: see the Political Parties, Elections and Referendums Act 2000 s 143(11). See note 1.

5   Political Parties, Elections and Referendums Act 2000 s 143(1)(a), (2)(a), (3). See note 1.

6   For these purposes, the 'promoter', in relation to any election material, means the person causing the material to be published: see the Political Parties, Elections and Referendums Act 2000 s 143(11). See note 1.

7   Political Parties, Elections and Referendums Act 2000 s 143(1)(a), (2)(b), (3). See note 1.

8   Political Parties, Elections and Referendums Act 2000 s 143(1)(a), (2)(c), (3). For the purposes of s 143(2)(c), election material which can be reasonably regarded as promoting, procuring or enhancing the electoral success or standing of two or more candidates standing in the name of a party or included in a list of candidates submitted by the party in connection with the election,

is not to be regarded as being published on behalf of a candidate merely because it can be regarded as promoting, procuring or enhancing his electoral success or standing, but it may be regarded as being published on behalf of the party: see s 143(2A), (2B) (s 143(2A), (2B) added by the Electoral Administration Act 2006 s 66(2)). Any amendment effected by the Electoral Administration Act 2006 s 66(2) has no effect in relation to an election for which the date of the poll specified in the notice of election issued in relation to that election is on or before 2 May 2007: see the Electoral Administration Act 2006 (Commencement No 2, Transitional and Savings Provisions) Order 2006, SI 2006/3412, art 6, Sch 2 para 1. See note 1.

9   Political Parties, Elections and Referendums Act 2000 s 143(1)(a), (3). See note 1.

10   Political Parties, Elections and Referendums Act 2000 s 143(1)(a), (2)(a), (4). See note 1.

11   Political Parties, Elections and Referendums Act 2000 s 143(1)(a), (2)(b), (4). See note 1.

12   Political Parties, Elections and Referendums Act 2000 s 143(1)(a), (2)(c), (4). See notes 1, 8.

13   Political Parties, Elections and Referendums Act 2000 s 143(1)(a), (4). See note 1.

14   Political Parties, Elections and Referendums Act 2000 s 143(1)(a), (5)(a). See note 1.

15   Political Parties, Elections and Referendums Act 2000 s 143(1)(a), (2)(b), (5)(b). See note 1.

16   Political Parties, Elections and Referendums Act 2000 s 143(1)(a), (2)(c), (5)(b). See notes 1, 8.

17   Political Parties, Elections and Referendums Act 2000 s 143(1)(a), (5)(b). See note 1.

18   Political Parties, Elections and Referendums Act 2000 s 143(1)(b), (6)(a). See note 1.

19   Political Parties, Elections and Referendums Act 2000 s 143(1)(b), (6)(b). See note 1.

20   Political Parties, Elections and Referendums Act 2000 s 143(1)(b), (6). Such regulations may in particular specify:

     (1)   the manner and form in which such details must be included in any such material for the purpose of complying with any such requirement (s 143(7)(a));

     (2)   circumstances in which any such requirement does not have to be complied with by a person of any description specified in the regulations, or in which a breach of any such requirement by a person of any description so specified is not to result in the commission of an offence under s 143 (see the text and note 21) by that person or by a person of any description (s 143(7)(b));

     (3)   circumstances in which material is, or is not, to be taken for the purposes of the regulations to be published or (as the case may be) published by a person of any description so specified (s 143(7)(c)).

     At the date at which this volume states the law, no such regulations had been made. As to the Secretary of State see PARA 2. As to the Electoral Commission see PARA 34 et seq.

21   See the Political Parties, Elections and Referendums Act 2000 s 143(8), (9). Liability for an offence which arises out of the requirement set out in head (4) in the text is subject to regulations made by virtue of s 143(7)(b) (see note 20): see s 143(9). See note 1. As to offences under the Political Parties, Elections and Referendums Act 2000 committed by bodies corporate or unincorporated associations see PARA 893.

22   See the Political Parties, Elections and Referendums Act 2000 s 150, Sch 20. The penalty mentioned in the text is a fine on summary conviction not exceeding level 5 on the standard scale: see s 150, Sch 20. As to summary proceedings for offences committed under the Political Parties, Elections and Referendums Act 2000 see PARA 892; and as to the Court's duty to report convictions for offences committed under the Political Parties, Elections and Referendums Act 2000 to the Electoral Commission see PARA 904. As to the Electoral Commission's powers to apply civil sanctions to offences and contraventions under the Political Parties, Elections and Referendums Act 2000 see PARA 757. As to the standard scale see SENTENCING AND DISPOSITION OF OFFENDERS vol 92 (2010) PARA 142.

23   See the Political Parties, Elections and Referendums Act 2000 s 143(10). See note 1.

750. Failure to display details on referendum material. No material wholly or mainly relating to a referendum[1] to which the general framework provisions apply[2] is to be published[3] during the referendum period[4] unless the following requirements are met:

     (1)   where the material is a document consisting (or consisting principally) of a single side of printed matter, the name and address of the printer[5] of the document[6], the name and address of the promoter[7] of the material[8], and the name and address of any person on behalf of whom the material is being published (and who is not the promoter)[9], must appear on the face of the document[10];

     (2)   where the material is a printed document other than one to which head

(1) above applies, the name and address of the printer of the document[11], the name and address of the promoter of the material[12], and the name and address of any person on behalf of whom the material is being published (and who is not the promoter)[13], must appear either on the first or the last page of the document[14];

(3) where the material is an advertisement contained in a newspaper or periodical: (a) the name and address of the printer of the newspaper or periodical must appear either on its first or last page[15]; and (b) the name and address of the promoter of the material[16], and the name and address of any person on behalf of whom the material is being published (and who is not the promoter)[17], must be included in the advertisement[18];

(4) in the case of any other material, the name and address of the promoter of the material[19] and the name and address of any person on behalf of whom the material is being published (and who is not the promoter)[20], must be included in the material in accordance with requirements imposed by regulations which may be made for these purposes by the Secretary of State after consulting the Electoral Commission[21].

Where, during the referendum period, any material is published in contravention of these requirements, the promoter of the material, and any other person by whom the material is so published (and, in the case of material falling within heads (1) to (3) above, the printer of the document) are guilty of an offence[22] and liable on summary conviction to a penalty[23]. It is a defence for a person charged with such an offence to prove that the contravention of the requirements arose from circumstances beyond his control, and that he took all reasonable steps, and exercised all due diligence, to ensure that that contravention would not arise[24].

1   As to the meaning of 'referendum' for these purposes see PARA 527.
2   Ie a referendum to which the Political Parties, Elections and Referendums Act 2000 Pt VII (ss 101–129) (see PARA 527 et seq) applies: see s 126(1).
3   For these purposes, 'publish' means make available to the public at large, or any section of the public, in whatever form and by whatever means: see the Political Parties, Elections and Referendums Act 2000 s 126(11). As to case law that attached to a similar form of wording that appeared in the Representation of the People Act 1983 s 110 (as originally enacted) in relation to election material see PARA 748.
4   See the Political Parties, Elections and Referendums Act 2000 s 126(1). As to the referendum period see PARA 527.
    The Political Parties, Elections and Referendums Act 2000 s 126(1) does not apply to any material published for the purposes of a referendum if the publication is required under or by virtue of any enactment: s 126(10A) (added by the Electoral Administration Act 2006 s 66(1)). As to the disapplication of the Political Parties, Elections and Referendums Act 2000 s 126 in relation to any material published for the purposes of a referendum held by virtue of the Government of Wales Act 2006 s 103(1) (see CONSTITUTIONAL LAW AND HUMAN RIGHTS), where the publication is required under the Order in Council that causes the referendum to be held, see s 103(7), Sch 6 para 9; and see the National Assembly for Wales Referendum (Assembly Act Provisions) (Referendum Question, Date of Referendum Etc) Order 2010, SI 2010/2837; and CONSTITUTIONAL LAW AND HUMAN RIGHTS.
5   For these purposes, 'print' means print by whatever means; and 'printer' must be construed accordingly: see the Political Parties, Elections and Referendums Act 2000 s 126(11).
6   Political Parties, Elections and Referendums Act 2000 s 126(1)(a), (2)(a), (3).
7   For these purposes, the 'promoter', in relation to any material falling within the Political Parties, Elections and Referendums Act 2000 s 126(1), means the person causing the material to be published: see s 126(11).
8   Political Parties, Elections and Referendums Act 2000 s 126(1)(a), (2)(b), (3).
9   Political Parties, Elections and Referendums Act 2000 s 126(1)(a), (2)(c), (3).
10 Political Parties, Elections and Referendums Act 2000 s 126(1)(a), (3).

11 Political Parties, Elections and Referendums Act 2000 s 126(1)(a), (2)(a), (4).
12 Political Parties, Elections and Referendums Act 2000 s 126(1)(a), (2)(b), (4).
13 Political Parties, Elections and Referendums Act 2000 s 126(1)(a), (2)(c), (4).
14 Political Parties, Elections and Referendums Act 2000 s 126(1)(a), (4).
15 Political Parties, Elections and Referendums Act 2000 s 126(1)(a), (5)(a).
16 Political Parties, Elections and Referendums Act 2000 s 126(1)(a), (2)(b), (5)(b).
17 Political Parties, Elections and Referendums Act 2000 s 126(1)(a), (2)(c), (5)(b).
18 Political Parties, Elections and Referendums Act 2000 s 126(1)(a), (5)(b).
19 Political Parties, Elections and Referendums Act 2000 s 126(1)(b), (6)(a).
20 Political Parties, Elections and Referendums Act 2000 s 126(1)(b), (6)(b).
21 Political Parties, Elections and Referendums Act 2000 s 126(1)(b), (6). Such regulations may in particular specify:
    (1) the manner and form in which such details must be included in any such material for the purpose of complying with any such requirement (s 126(7)(a));
    (2) circumstances in which any such requirement does not have to be complied with by a person of any description specified in the regulations, or in which a breach of any such requirement by a person of any description so specified is not to result in the commission of an offence under s 126 (see the text and note 22) by that person or by a person of any such description (s 126(7)(b));
    (3) circumstances in which material is, or is not, to be taken for the purposes of the regulations to be published or (as the case may be) published by a person of any description so specified (s 126(7)(c)).
    At the date at which this volume states the law, no such regulations had been made. As to the Secretary of State see PARA 2. As to the Electoral Commission see PARA 34 et seq.
22 See the Political Parties, Elections and Referendums Act 2000 s 126(8), (9). As to offences under the Political Parties, Elections and Referendums Act 2000 committed by bodies corporate or unincorporated associations see PARA 893.
23 See the Political Parties, Elections and Referendums Act 2000 s 150, Sch 20. The penalty mentioned in the text is a fine on summary conviction not exceeding level 5 on the standard scale: see s 150, Sch 20. As to summary proceedings for offences committed under the Political Parties, Elections and Referendums Act 2000 see PARA 892; and as to the Court's duty to report convictions for offences committed under the Political Parties, Elections and Referendums Act 2000 to the Electoral Commission see PARA 904. As to the Electoral Commission's powers to apply civil sanctions to offences and contraventions under the Political Parties, Elections and Referendums Act 2000 see PARA 757. As to the standard scale see SENTENCING AND DISPOSITION OF OFFENDERS vol 92 (2010) PARA 142.
24 See the Political Parties, Elections and Referendums Act 2000 s 126(10).

751. Offences related to contravention of the controls imposed on expenditure incurred during election and referendum campaigns. A person commits an offence:

(1) if he knowingly or recklessly makes a false declaration as to the value of notional election campaign expenditure[1] incurred by or on behalf of a registered party[2], or as to the value of notional controlled expenditure[3] incurred by or on behalf of a third party in a national election campaign[4], or as to the value of notional referendum expenses[5] incurred by or on behalf of an individual or body during the referendum period[6];

(2) if, without reasonable excuse and in contravention of the restrictions, he incurs any election campaign expenditure without authority by or on behalf of a registered party[7], or if he incurs any controlled expenditure without authority by or on behalf of a recognised third party[8], or if he incurs any referendum expenses without authority[9];

(3) if, without reasonable excuse, he makes any payment in contravention of the restrictions that apply in respect of payments made in relation to election campaign expenditure[10], in respect of controlled expenditure incurred by or on behalf of a third party[11], or in respect of referendum expenses[12], or if he contravenes the requirements imposed on such a person regarding delivery of notification and evidence[13];

(4) if, without reasonable excuse he pays any claim which by virtue of being statute-barred is not payable or if he makes any payment in respect of a claim after the end of the period allowed for the payment of claims in respect of election campaign expenditure[14], or in respect of controlled expenditure incurred by or on behalf of a recognised third party[15], or in respect of referendum expenses[16];

(5) if he, as treasurer or deputy treasurer of a registered party, authorised election campaign expenditure to be incurred by or on behalf of the party during the specified period, where he knew (or ought reasonably to have known) that the expenditure would be incurred in excess of the statutory limitation that applies during that period[17], or if he (or the responsible person, if the third party is not an individual) incurred controlled expenditure in the United Kingdom by or on behalf of a third party during a regulated period (whether that third party was a recognised third party[18] or not[19]) and he knew or ought reasonably to have known that the expenditure would be incurred in excess of the statutory limitation that applies during that period[20];

(6) where a permitted participant[21], or a body or individual who was not a permitted participant at a referendum, incurred referendum expenses during the referendum period, and he[22] knew, or ought reasonably to have known, that the expenses were being incurred or would be incurred in excess of the statutory limitation that applies during that period[23];

(7) where, at a local authority referendum, any referendum expenses are incurred in excess of the referendum expenses limit[24], and he knew or reasonably ought to have known that that limit would be exceeded, or if he, without reasonable excuse, authorised another person to exceed that limit[25];

(8) if, without reasonable excuse, he: (a) fails to deliver a required return as to expenditure to the Electoral Commission[26]; or (b) delivers such a return which does not comply with the requirements as to the statements contained therein or as to the accompanying evidence[27]; or (c) fails to report late payments[28], in respect of election campaign expenditure[29], or in respect of controlled expenditure incurred by or on behalf of a recognised third party[30], or in respect of referendum expenses incurred by or on behalf of a permitted participant[31];

(9) if he, as treasurer of a registered party, knowingly or recklessly makes a declaration as to election campaign expenditure falsely or if the requirements as to such a declaration are contravened at a time when he is treasurer of the registered party to which the return relates[32], or if he knowingly or recklessly makes a declaration as to controlled expenditure falsely or if the requirements as to such a declaration are contravened at a time when he is the responsible person in the case of the recognised third party to which the return relates[33], or if he knowingly or recklessly makes a declaration as to referendum expenses falsely or if the requirements as to such a declaration are contravened at a time when he is the responsible person in the case of the permitted participant to which the return relates[34].

A person guilty of such an offence is liable to a penalty[35].

A person also commits an offence if he accepts the office of deputy treasurer of a registered party when[36] he is not eligible to be so appointed[37]; and a person guilty of such an offence is liable to a penalty[38].

1   Ie under the Political Parties, Elections and Referendums Act 2000 s 73(6) (see PARA 299), as the treasurer or a deputy treasurer of a registered party appointed under s 74 (see PARA 300): see s 73(6), (8). As to the meaning of 'registered party' see PARA 35 note 3; and as to the meaning of 'campaign expenditure' see PARA 299. As to the treasurer of a registered party see PARA 253.

2   Political Parties, Elections and Referendums Act 2000 s 73(8).

3   Ie under the Political Parties, Elections and Referendums Act 2000 s 86(6) (see PARA 313), as the responsible person of the third party: see s 86(6), (8). As to the meaning of 'controlled expenditure' for these purposes see PARA 313; as to the meaning of 'third party' for these purposes see PARA 313 note 1; and as to the meaning of 'responsible person' for these purposes see PARA 313 note 15.

4   Political Parties, Elections and Referendums Act 2000 s 86(8).

5   Ie under the Political Parties, Elections and Referendums Act 2000 s 112(6) (see PARA 535): see s 112(8). As to the meaning of 'referendum expenses' see PARA 535.

6   Political Parties, Elections and Referendums Act 2000 s 112(8). As to the referendum period see PARA 527.

7   Political Parties, Elections and Referendums Act 2000 s 75(2). As to the restrictions mentioned in the text see PARA 301.

8   Political Parties, Elections and Referendums Act 2000 s 90(2). As to the restrictions mentioned in the text see PARA 315.

9   Political Parties, Elections and Referendums Act 2000 s 113(2). As to the restrictions mentioned in the text see PARA 536.

10   Political Parties, Elections and Referendums Act 2000 s 76(4). As to the restrictions mentioned in the text see PARA 302.

11   Political Parties, Elections and Referendums Act 2000 s 91(4). As to the restrictions mentioned in the text see PARA 316.

12   Political Parties, Elections and Referendums Act 2000 s 114(4). As to the restrictions mentioned in the text see PARA 537.

13   See the Political Parties, Elections and Referendums Act 2000 ss 76(4), 91(4), 114(4). As to the requirements mentioned in the text see PARAS 302, 316, 537.

14   Political Parties, Elections and Referendums Act 2000 s 77(3). As to the restrictions mentioned in the text see PARA 303.

15   Political Parties, Elections and Referendums Act 2000 s 92(3). As to the restrictions mentioned in the text see PARA 317.

16   Political Parties, Elections and Referendums Act 2000 s 115(3). As to the restrictions mentioned in the text see PARA 538.

17   Political Parties, Elections and Referendums Act 2000 s 79(2). As to the limitation mentioned in the text see PARA 305. In the circumstances set out in the text, the party is also guilty of an offence: see s 79(2). It is a defence for any person or registered party charged with an offence under s 79(2) to show that any code of practice for the time being issued under s 72(2), Sch 8 para 3 (see PARA 299) was complied with in determining the items and amounts of campaign expenditure to be entered in the relevant return as to campaign expenditure under s 80 (see PARA 307), and that the limit would not have been exceeded on the basis of the items and amounts entered in that return: see s 79(3).

18   As to the limits imposed on recognised third parties see the Political Parties, Elections and Referendums Act 2000 s 94(1), Sch 10; and PARA 319.

19   See the Political Parties, Elections and Referendums Act 2000 s 94(3). The limits imposed on third parties which are not recognised third parties are £10,000 for England, and £5,000 for Wales: see s 94(5). As to a recognised Gibraltar third party see s 94(5A), (11) (s 94(5A), (11) added y SI 2004/366).

20   See the Political Parties, Elections and Referendums Act 2000 s 94(2), (4). In the circumstances set out in the text, if the third party is not an individual, the third party is also guilty of an offence: see s 94(2), (4).

21   Ie a registered party falling within the Political Parties, Elections and Referendums Act 2000 s 105(1)(a) (see PARA 529) or an individual falling within s 105(1)(b) (see PARA 529) or a body falling within s 105(1)(b) (see PARA 529): see s 118(2). As to the meaning of 'permitted participant' see PARA 529.

22   Ie, in the case of a permitted participant, as the responsible person or any deputy treasurer of a registered party falling within the Political Parties, Elections and Referendums Act 2000

s 105(1)(a) (see PARA 529) or as an individual falling within s 105(1)(b) (see PARA 529) or as the responsible person of a body falling within s 105(1)(b) (see PARA 529) (see s 118(2)) and, in the case of an individual who was not a permitted participant, that individual (see s 117(2)) and, in the case of a body which was not a permitted participant, any person who authorised the expenses to be incurred by or on behalf of the body (see s 117(3)). As to the meaning of 'responsible person' in relation to a permitted participant which is a registered party see PARA 529 note 17; and as to the meaning of 'responsible person' in relation to a permitted participant which is an individual or body but which is not a registered party see PARA 529 note 27.

23 See the Political Parties, Elections and Referendums Act 2000 ss 117(2), (3), 118(2). As to the limits imposed on a body or individual who is not a permitted participant see PARA 540; and as to the limits imposed on permitted participants see PARA 541. Where the circumstances set out in the text apply to a body who was not a permitted participant, the body in question is also guilty of an offence (s 117(4)); where the circumstances set out in the text apply to a permitted participant who is a registered party falling within s 105(1)(a) (see PARA 529), the party is also guilty of an offence and, where the circumstances set out in the text apply to a permitted participant who is a body falling within s 105(1)(b) (see PARA 529), the body is also guilty of an offence (see s 118(2)). It is a defence for a permitted participant or other person charged with an offence under s 118(2) to show that any code of practice for the time being issued under s 111(1), (2), Sch 13 para 3 (see PARA 535) was complied with in determining the items and amounts of campaign expenditure to be entered in the relevant return as to referendum expenses under s 120 (see PARA 542), and to show that the limit would not have been exceeded on the basis of the items and amounts entered in that return: see s 118(3).

24 As to the limit referred to in the text see PARA 578.

25 Local Authorities (Conduct of Referendums) (Wales) Regulations 2008, SI 2008/1848, reg 6(3); Local Authorities (Conduct of Referendums) (England) Regulations 2012, SI 2012/323, reg 6(3). Where information is given to the Director of Public Prosecutions that an offence as set out under head (7) in the text has been committed, it is his duty to make such inquiries and institute such prosecutions as the circumstances of the case appear to him to require: Local Authorities (Conduct of Referendums) (Wales) Regulations 2008, SI 2008/1848, reg 6(4); Local Authorities (Conduct of Referendums) (England) Regulations 2012, SI 2012/323, reg 6(4). Where such an offence which has been committed by a body corporate is proved to have been committed with the consent or connivance of, or to have been attributable to any neglect on the part of, a director, manager, secretary or other similar officer of the body corporate, or any other person purporting to act in any such capacity, he, as well as the body corporate, is guilty of that offence and liable to be proceeded against and punished accordingly: Local Authorities (Conduct of Referendums) (Wales) Regulations 2008, SI 2008/1848, reg 6(5); Local Authorities (Conduct of Referendums) (England) Regulations 2012, SI 2012/323, reg 6(5). As to the Director of Public Prosecutions see CRIMINAL PROCEDURE vol 27 (2010) PARAS 23, 33 et seq.

26 Political Parties, Elections and Referendums Act 2000 ss 82(4)(a), 98(4)(a), 122(4)(a). As to the Electoral Commission see PARA 34 et seq.

27 Political Parties, Elections and Referendums Act 2000 ss 82(4)(b), 98(4)(b), 122(4)(b).

28 Political Parties, Elections and Referendums Act 2000 ss 82(4)(c), 98(4)(c), 122(4)(c).

29 Political Parties, Elections and Referendums Act 2000 s 82(4). The person liable for such an offence is the treasurer of a registered party: see s 82(4). As to the requirements that need to be met in the delivery of returns as to election campaign expenditure see PARA 308.

30 Political Parties, Elections and Referendums Act 2000 s 98(4). The person liable for such an offence is the responsible person in the case of a recognised third party: see s 98(4). As to the requirements that need to be met in the delivery of returns as to controlled expenditure see PARA 322.

31 Political Parties, Elections and Referendums Act 2000 s 122(4). The person liable for such an offence is the responsible person in the case of a permitted participant: s 122(4). As to the requirements that need to be met in the delivery of returns as to referendum expenses incurred by or on behalf of a permitted participant see PARA 543.

32 Political Parties, Elections and Referendums Act 2000 s 83(3). As to the declaration that is required as mentioned in the text see PARA 309.

33 Political Parties, Elections and Referendums Act 2000 s 99(4). As to the declaration that is required in respect of controlled expenditure as mentioned in the text see PARA 323.

34 Political Parties, Elections and Referendums Act 2000 s 123(4). As to the declaration that is required as mentioned in the text see PARA 544.

35 A person guilty of an offence:
    (1)   under head (1) in the text is liable, on conviction on indictment, to a fine or to imprisonment for a term not exceeding one year or, on summary conviction, to a fine

not exceeding the statutory maximum or to imprisonment for a term not exceeding six months (see the Political Parties, Elections and Referendums Act 2000 s 150, Sch 20);

(2)   under any of heads (2), (3), (4), (8)(a) or (8)(c) in the text is liable, on summary conviction, to a fine not exceeding level 5 on the standard scale (see s 150, Sch 20);

(3)   under head (5) in the text is liable, on conviction on indictment, to a fine or, on summary conviction, to a fine not exceeding the statutory maximum (see s 150, Sch 20);

(4)   under head (6) in the text is liable, on summary conviction, to a fine not exceeding the statutory maximum or, on conviction on indictment, to a fine (but a person who is guilty of an offence under head (6) in the text and who acted on behalf of a permitted participant or on behalf of a body which was not a permitted participant is liable, on conviction on indictment, to a fine or to imprisonment for a term not exceeding one year or, on summary conviction, to a fine not exceeding the statutory maximum or to imprisonment for a term not exceeding six months) (see s 150, Sch 20);

(5)   under head (7) in the text is liable, on summary conviction, to a fine not exceeding the statutory maximum or to a term of imprisonment not exceeding 12 months or both or, on conviction on indictment, to a fine or to a term of imprisonment not exceeding 12 months or both (Local Authorities (Conduct of Referendums) (Wales) Regulations 2008, SI 2008/1848, reg 6(6); Local Authorities (Conduct of Referendums) (England) Regulations 2012, SI 2012/323, reg 6(6));

(6)   under head (8)(b) or head (9) in the text is liable, on summary conviction, to a fine not exceeding the statutory maximum or to a term of imprisonment not exceeding six months or both or, on conviction on indictment, to a fine or to a term of imprisonment not exceeding one year or both (Political Parties, Elections and Referendums Act 2000 s 150, Sch 20).

In relation to an offence committed after the date of commencement of the Criminal Justice Act 2003 s 281(5) (not yet in force) (alteration of penalties for summary offences: see SENTENCING AND DISPOSITION OF OFFENDERS vol 92 (2010) PARA 374), the reference to six months must be taken to be a reference to 51 weeks: Political Parties, Elections and Referendums Act 2000 s 150(5) (added by SI 2008/1319). As to the statutory maximum see SENTENCING AND DISPOSITION OF OFFENDERS vol 92 (2010) PARA 140. As to summary proceedings for offences committed under the Political Parties, Elections and Referendums Act 2000 see PARA 892; as to offences under the Political Parties, Elections and Referendums Act 2000 committed by bodies corporate or unincorporated associations see PARA 893; and as to the Court's duty to report convictions for offences committed under the Political Parties, Elections and Referendums Act 2000 to the Electoral Commission see PARA 904. As to the Electoral Commission's powers to apply civil sanctions to offences and contraventions under the Political Parties, Elections and Referendums Act 2000 see PARA 757. As to the standard scale see SENTENCING AND DISPOSITION OF OFFENDERS vol 92 (2010) PARA 142.

36 Ie by virtue of the Political Parties, Elections and Referendums Act 2000 s 74(3) (see PARA 300): see s 74(4).

37 Political Parties, Elections and Referendums Act 2000 s 74(4).

38 See the Political Parties, Elections and Referendums Act 2000 s 150, Sch 20. Such a person is liable, on summary conviction, to a fine not exceeding level 5 on the standard scale: see s 150, Sch 20.

752.   Offences related to contravention of the controls imposed on donations during election and referendum campaigns. At an election[1], if a person without reasonable excuse fails to comply with the provisions which require principal donors[2], and agents acting on behalf of donors[3], to give the required details of each relevant donation[4] made to a candidate[5] or his election agent[6] or to a recognised third party[7], as the case may be, he commits an offence[8]. A person guilty of such an offence is liable to a penalty[9]. At a referendum[10], if a person without reasonable excuse fails to comply with the provisions which require principal donors[11] and agents acting on behalf of donors[12] to give the required details of each relevant donation[13] made to a permitted participant[14], he commits an offence[15]. A person guilty of such an offence is liable to a penalty[16].

At an election, if a donation made by a person who is not a permissible donor at the time of its receipt by a registered party[17] or by a recognised third party[18] (as the case may be) is not sent back as required, the candidate or his election agent (in relation to the registered party) or the responsible person or the party itself (in relation to the recognised third party) is each guilty of an offence[19]; and if the required steps are not taken in relation to a donation where the registered party[20] or recognised third party[21], as the case may be, is unable to ascertain the identity of the person offering it (whether because it is given anonymously or by reason of any deception or concealment or otherwise), the candidate or his election agent (in relation to the registered party) or the responsible person (in relation to the recognised third party) is each guilty of an offence[22]. In either case, a person found guilty of the offence is liable to a penalty[23]. At a referendum, if a donation made by a person who is not a permissible donor at the time of its receipt by a permitted participant[24] is not sent back as required, the responsible person in relation to the permitted participant is guilty of an offence[25]; and if the required steps are not taken in relation to a donation where the permitted participant is unable to ascertain the identity of the person offering it (whether because it is given anonymously or by reason of any deception or concealment or otherwise), the responsible person in relation to the permitted participant is guilty of an offence[26]. In either case, a person found guilty of the offence is liable to a penalty[27].

A person commits an offence if he knowingly enters into, or knowingly does any act in furtherance of, any arrangement which facilitates or is likely to facilitate, whether by means of any concealment or disguise or otherwise, the making of relevant donations to a candidate or his election agent or to a recognised third party (as the case may be) in relation to an election or to a permitted participant at a referendum by any person or body other than a permissible donor[28]. A person also commits an offence if he knowingly gives the candidate at an election or his election agent (or both) or the responsible person (in relation to a recognised third party at an election or a permitted participant at a referendum) any information relating to the amount of any donation made, or relating to the person or body making such a donation, which is false in a material particular or if, with intent to deceive, he withholds from them any material information relating to any such matter[29]. A person found guilty of any such offence is liable to a penalty[30].

1   Ie at a parliamentary or local government election, a Welsh Assembly election, or a European parliamentary election. As to the meaning of 'Assembly election' see PARA 3 note 2; as to the meaning of 'parliamentary election' see PARA 9; and as to the meaning of 'local government election' see PARA 11. As to elections in the City of London see PARA 33; and as to European parliamentary elections see PARA 217 et seq.

2   Ie, in the case of a parliamentary or local government election, the Representation of the People Act 1983 Sch 2A para 6(5), or, in the case of a European parliamentary election, the European Parliamentary Elections Regulations 2004, SI 2004/293, Sch 6 para 6(5), or, in the case of a Welsh Assembly election, the National Assembly for Wales (Representation of the People) Order 2007, SI 2007/236, Sch 6 para 6(5) (see PARA 288) or, in the case of donations made to recognised third parties, the Political Parties, Elections and Referendums Act 2000 Sch 11 para 6(5) (see PARA 326): see the Representation of the People Act 1983 Sch 2A para 6(7) (Sch 2A added by the Political Parties, Elections and Referendums Act 2000 s 130(1)–(4), Sch 16); the Political Parties, Elections and Referendums Act 2000 Sch 11 para 6(7); the European Parliamentary Elections Regulations 2004, SI 2004/293, Sch 6 para 6(7); and the National Assembly for Wales (Representation of the People) Order 2007, SI 2007/236, Sch 6 para 6(7).

3   Ie, in the case of a parliamentary or local government election, the Representation of the People Act 1983 Sch 2A para 6(6), or, in the case of a European parliamentary election, the European Parliamentary Elections Regulations 2004, SI 2004/293, Sch 6 para 6(6), or, in the case of a Welsh Assembly election, the National Assembly for Wales (Representation of the People) Order 2007, SI 2007/236, Sch 6 para 6(6) (see PARA 288) or, in the case of donations made to recognised third parties, the Political Parties, Elections and Referendums Act 2000 Sch 11

para 6(6) (see PARA 326): see the Representation of the People Act 1983 Sch 2A para 6(7) (as added: see note 2); the Political Parties, Elections and Referendums Act 2000 Sch 11 para 6(7); the European Parliamentary Elections Regulations 2004, SI 2004/293, Sch 6 para 6(7); and the National Assembly for Wales (Representation of the People) Order 2007, SI 2007/236, Sch 6 para 6(7).

4   As to the meanings of 'donation' and 'relevant donation' in relation to candidates at an election see PARA 287.

5   As to the meaning of 'candidate' generally see PARA 230. The reference in the text is to an 'individual candidate' for the purposes of a European parliamentary election. As to the meaning of 'individual candidate' in relation to a European parliamentary election see PARA 230 note 32.

6   As to the appointment of an election agent for parliamentary and local government elections see PARA 231; as to the appointment of an election agent for elections to the National Assembly for Wales see PARA 235; and as to the appointment of the election agent of a registered party or for an individual candidate at a European parliamentary election see PARA 239.

7   As to the meaning of 'recognised third party' see PARA 313 note 15; and for these purposes see PARA 325 note 3. As to the meanings of 'donation' and 'relevant donation' in relation to a recognised third party see PARA 325.

8   Representation of the People Act 1983 Sch 2A para 6(7) (as added: see note 2); Political Parties, Elections and Referendums Act 2000 Sch 11 para 6(7); European Parliamentary Elections Regulations 2004, SI 2004/293, Sch 6 para 6(7); National Assembly for Wales (Representation of the People) Order 2007, SI 2007/236, Sch 6 para 6(7).

As from a day to be appointed under the Political Parties and Elections Act 2009 s 43(1), a person who knowingly or recklessly makes a false written declaration, under the Political Parties, Elections and Referendums Act 2000 Sch 11 para 6A (not yet in force) (see PARA 326 note 5) as to the source of any amount exceeding £7,500 received by a recognised third party by way of a donation, or under Sch 11 para 6B stating whether or not the income tax liability of an individual making a donation to a recognised third party for the current tax year falls to be determined on the basis that the individual is resident, ordinarily resident and domiciled in the United Kingdom in that year, commits an offence: see Sch 11 paras 6A(5), 6B(3) (prospectively added by the Political Parties and Elections Act 2009 Sch 3 para 4(2), Sch 4 para 4(2)). However, at the date at which this volume states the law, no such day had been appointed in relation to any of these provisions.

9   Representation of the People Act 1983 Sch 2A para 6(8) (as added: see note 2); Political Parties, Elections and Referendums Act 2000 s 150, Sch 20; European Parliamentary Elections Regulations 2004, SI 2004/293, Sch 6 para 6(8); National Assembly for Wales (Representation of the People) Order 2007, SI 2007/236, Sch 6 para 6(8). Such a person is liable, on summary conviction, to a fine not exceeding the statutory maximum or to a term of imprisonment not exceeding six months or both or, on conviction on indictment, to a fine or to a term of imprisonment not exceeding one year or both: see the Representation of the People Act 1983 Sch 2A para 6(8) (as so added); the Political Parties, Elections and Referendums Act 2000 s 150, Sch 20; the European Parliamentary Elections Regulations 2004, SI 2004/293, Sch 6 para 6(8); and the National Assembly for Wales (Representation of the People) Order 2007, SI 2007/236, Sch 6 para 6(8). In relation to an offence committed after the date of commencement of the Criminal Justice Act 2003 s 281(5) (not yet in force) (alteration of penalties for summary offences: see SENTENCING AND DISPOSITION OF OFFENDERS vol 92 (2010) PARA 374), the reference to six months must be taken to be a reference to 51 weeks: Political Parties, Elections and Referendums Act 2000 s 150(5) (added by SI 2008/1319); European Parliamentary Elections Regulations 2004, SI 2004/293, Sch 6 para 6(8); National Assembly for Wales (Representation of the People) Order 2007, SI 2007/236, Sch 6 para 6 (9). As to summary proceedings for offences committed under the Political Parties, Elections and Referendums Act 2000 see PARA 892; and as to the Court's duty to report convictions for offences committed under the Political Parties, Elections and Referendums Act 2000 to the Electoral Commission see PARA 904. As to the Electoral Commission's powers to apply civil sanctions to offences and contraventions under the Political Parties, Elections and Referendums Act 2000 see PARA 757. As to the statutory maximum see SENTENCING AND DISPOSITION OF OFFENDERS vol 92 (2010) PARA 140.

As from a day to be appointed under the Political Parties and Elections Act 2009 s 43(1), a person who commits an offence under the Political Parties, Elections and Referendums Act 2000 Sch 11 para 6A(5) or Sch 11 para 6B(3) (not yet in force) (see note 8) is liable, on summary conviction, to a fine not exceeding the statutory maximum or to a term of imprisonment not exceeding 12 months or both or, on conviction on indictment, to a fine or to a term of imprisonment not exceeding one year or both: see s 150, Sch 20 (prospectively amended by the

Political Parties and Elections Act 2009 Sch 3 para 10, Sch 4 para 10). However, at the date at which this volume states the law, no such day had been appointed in relation to any of these provisions.

10 As to the meaning of 'referendum' for these purposes see PARA 527.

11 Ie the Political Parties, Elections and Referendums Act 2000 Sch 15 para 6(6) (see PARA 547): see Sch 15 para 6(8).

12 Ie the Political Parties, Elections and Referendums Act 2000 Sch 15 para 6(7) (see PARA 547): see Sch 15 para 6(8).

13 As to the meanings of 'donation' and 'relevant donation' for these purposes see PARA 546.

14 As to the meaning of 'permitted participant' see PARA 529; and see also PARA 546 note 6.

15 Political Parties, Elections and Referendums Act 2000 Sch 15 para 6(8). As to offences under the Political Parties, Elections and Referendums Act 2000 committed by bodies corporate or unincorporated associations see PARA 893.

As from a day to be appointed under the Political Parties and Elections Act 2009 s 43(1), a person who knowingly or recklessly makes a false written declaration, under the Political Parties, Elections and Referendums Act 2000 Sch 15 para 6A (not yet in force) (see PARA 547 note 7) as to the source of any amount exceeding £7,500 received by a permitted participant by way of a donation, or under Sch 15 para 6B stating whether or not the income tax liability of an individual making a donation to a permitted participant for the current tax year falls to be determined on the basis that the individual is resident, ordinarily resident and domiciled in the United Kingdom in that year, commits an offence: see Sch 15 paras 6A(5), 6B(3) (prospectively added by the Political Parties and Elections Act 2009 Sch 3 para 7(2), Sch 4 para 7(2)). However, at the date at which this volume states the law, no such day had been appointed in relation to any of these provisions.

16 Political Parties, Elections and Referendums Act 2000 s 150, Sch 20. Such a person is liable, on summary conviction, to a fine not exceeding the statutory maximum or to a term of imprisonment not exceeding six months or both or, on conviction on indictment, to a fine or to a term of imprisonment not exceeding one year or both: see s 150, Sch 20.

As from a day to be appointed under the Political Parties and Elections Act 2009 s 43(1), a person who commits an offence under the Political Parties, Elections and Referendums Act 2000 Sch 15 para 6A(5) or Sch 15 para 6B(3) (not yet in force) (see note 15) is liable, on summary conviction, to a fine not exceeding the statutory maximum or to a term of imprisonment not exceeding 12 months or both or, on conviction on indictment, to a fine or to a term of imprisonment not exceeding one year or both: see s 150, Sch 20 (prospectively amended by the Political Parties and Elections Act 2009 Sch 3 para 10, Sch 4 para 10). However, at the date at which this volume states the law, no such day had been appointed in relation to any of these provisions.

17 As to the acceptance or return of donations received by a candidate at an election see PARA 289.

18 As to the acceptance or return of donations made to a recognised third party at an election see PARA 327.

19 Political Parties, Elections and Referendums Act 2000 s 56(3) (s 56 applied and modified by the Representation of the People Act 1983 Sch 2A para 7 (as added: see note 2); the Political Parties, Elections and Referendums Act 2000 Sch 11 para 7; the European Parliamentary Elections Regulations 2004, SI 2004/293, Sch 6 para 7; and the National Assembly for Wales (Representation of the People) Order 2007, SI 2007/236, Sch 6 para 7(2)). As to the meaning of 'responsible person' in relation to a recognised third party see PARA 313 note 15.

As from a day to be appointed under the Political Parties and Elections Act 2009 s 43(1), the Political Parties, Elections and Referendums Act 2000 Sch 11 para 7 is amended so that it refers to the Political Parties, Elections and Referendums Act 2000 s 56(3), (3B), (4) (s 56(3B) not yet in force) (see Sch 11 para 7(2)(b) (prospectively amended by the Political Parties and Elections Act 2009 s 39, Sch 6 para 29(1), (4))); and a further modification is added for these purposes, namely that the Political Parties, Elections and Referendums Act 2000 s 56(1A)(a) (not yet in force) has effect as if the reference to a declaration under s 54B (not yet in force) (residence declaration) were construed as a reference to a declaration under Sch 11 para 6B (not yet in force) (see PARA 326 note 5) (see Sch 11 para 7(2)(aa) (prospectively added by the Political Parties and Elections Act 2009 s 10(8), Sch 4 para 5)). However, at the date at which this volume states the law, no such day had been appointed in relation to any of these provisions. See further PARA 327.

20 As to the steps required to be taken with regard to the acceptance or return of donations received by a candidate at an election see PARA 289.

21 As to the steps required to be taken with regard to the acceptance or return of donations made to a recognised third party at an election see PARA 327.

22 Political Parties, Elections and Referendums Act 2000 s 56(4) (as applied and modified: see note 19).
23 Political Parties, Elections and Referendums Act 2000 s 150, Sch 20. Such a person is liable, on summary conviction, to a fine not exceeding the statutory maximum or to a term of imprisonment not exceeding six months or both or, on conviction on indictment, to a fine or to a term of imprisonment not exceeding one year or both: see s 150, Sch 20.
24 As to the acceptance or return of donations received by permitted participants at a referendum see PARA 548.
25 Political Parties, Elections and Referendums Act 2000 s 56(3); applied and modified by s 118, Sch 15 para 7. As to the meaning of 'responsible person' in relation to a permitted participant which is a registered party see PARA 529 note 17; and as to the meaning of 'responsible person' in relation to a permitted participant which is an individual or body but which is not a registered party see PARA 529 note 27.
    As from a day to be appointed under the Political Parties and Elections Act 2009 s 43(1), the Political Parties, Elections and Referendums Act 2000 Sch 15 para 7 is amended so that it refers to the Political Parties, Elections and Referendums Act 2000 s 56(3), (3B), (4) (s 56(3B) not yet in force) (see Sch 15 para 7(2)(b) (prospectively amended by the Political Parties and Elections Act 2009 s 39, Sch 6 para 30(1), (4))); and a further modification is added for these purposes, namely that the Political Parties, Elections and Referendums Act 2000 s 56(1A)(a) (not yet in force) has effect as if the reference to a declaration under s 54B (not yet in force) (residence declaration) were construed as a reference to a declaration under Sch 15 para 6B (not yet in force) (see PARA 547 note 8) (see Sch 15 para 7(2)(aa) (prospectively added by the Political Parties and Elections Act 2009 s 10(8), Sch 4 para 8)). However, at the date at which this volume states the law, no such day had been appointed in relation to any of these provisions.
26 Political Parties, Elections and Referendums Act 2000 s 56(4); applied and modified by Sch 15 para 7 (see note 25).
27 Political Parties, Elections and Referendums Act 2000 s 150, Sch 20. Such a person is liable, on summary conviction, to a fine not exceeding the statutory maximum or to a term of imprisonment not exceeding six months or both or, on conviction on indictment, to a fine or to a term of imprisonment not exceeding one year or both: see s 150, Sch 20.
28 Political Parties, Elections and Referendums Act 2000 s 61(1) (s 61 applied and modified by the Representation of the People Act 1983 Sch 2A para 9 (as added: see note 2); the Political Parties, Elections and Referendums Act 2000 Sch 11 para 8, Sch 15 para 8; the European Parliamentary Elections Regulations 2004, SI 2004/293, Sch 6 para 9; and the National Assembly for Wales (Representation of the People) Order 2007, SI 2007/236, Sch 6 para 9). At a European parliamentary election, the reference is to the making of relevant donations to an individual candidate or his election agent: see the European Parliamentary Elections Regulations 2004, SI 2004/293, Sch 6 para 9(b).
29 Political Parties, Elections and Referendums Act 2000 s 61(2) (as applied and modified: see note 28).
30 Political Parties, Elections and Referendums Act 2000 s 150, Sch 20. Such a person is liable, on summary conviction, to a fine not exceeding the statutory maximum or to a term of imprisonment not exceeding six months or both or, on conviction on indictment, to a fine or to a term of imprisonment not exceeding one year or both: see s 150, Sch 20.

753.   Offences regarding obstruction of the Electoral Commission in its duties etc. A person commits an offence:

(1)   if he fails, without reasonable excuse, to comply with any requirement imposed under or by virtue of the provisions[1] that govern the Electoral Commission's investigatory powers[2];

(2)   if he intentionally obstructs a person authorised by or by virtue of those provisions[3] in the carrying out of that person's functions under the authorisation[4];

(3)   if he knowingly or recklessly provides false information in purported compliance with a requirement imposed under or by virtue of those provisions[5];

(4)   if he alters, suppresses, conceals or destroys (or if he causes or permits the alteration, suppression, concealment or destruction of) any book, record[6] or other document[7] which is or is liable to be required to be

produced for inspection under the Electoral Commission's investigatory powers[8], and does so with the intention of falsifying the document or enabling any person to evade any of the provisions of the Political Parties, Elections and Referendums Act 2000[9];

(5)　if he is the office-holder in circumstances where the relevant person[10] (in the case of a supervised organisation[11]), or a person acting on his behalf, requests a person holding an office in any such organisation (the 'office-holder') to supply the relevant person with any information which he reasonably requires for the purposes of any of the provisions of the Political Parties, Elections and Referendums Act 2000[12], and the office-holder: (a) without reasonable excuse, fails to supply the relevant person with that information as soon as is reasonably practicable[13]; or (b) in purporting to comply with the request, knowingly supplies the relevant person with any information which is false in a material particular[14];

(6)　if, with intent to deceive, he withholds: (a) from the relevant person (in the case of a supervised organisation)[15]; or (b) from a supervised individual[16], any information required by the relevant person or that individual for the purposes of any of the provisions of the Political Parties, Elections and Referendums Act 2000[17].

A person guilty of such an offence is liable to a penalty[18].

1　Ie imposed under or by virtue of the Political Parties, Elections and Referendums Act 2000 s 146, Sch 19B (see PARAS 64, 65): see Sch 19B para 13(1) (s 146 substituted, Sch 19B added, by the Political Parties and Elections Act 2009 s 2(1), (2), Sch 1).

2　See the Political Parties, Elections and Referendums Act 2000 Sch 19B para 13(1) (as added: see note 1). As to the establishment and constitution of the Electoral Commission see PARA 34 et seq; and as to the Electoral Commission's investigatory powers see PARAS 64, 65. As to the Commission's powers to apply civil sanctions to offences and contraventions under the Political Parties, Elections and Referendums Act 2000 see PARA 757.

3　Ie authorised by or by virtue of the Political Parties, Elections and Referendums Act 2000 Sch 19B (see PARAS 64, 65): see Sch 19B para 13(2) (as added: see note 1).

4　See the Political Parties, Elections and Referendums Act 2000 Sch 19B para 13(2) (as added: see note 1). As to the meaning of 'functions' see PARA 34 note 2.

5　See the Political Parties, Elections and Referendums Act 2000 Sch 19B para 13(3) (as added: see note 1). Head (3) in the text refers to purported compliance with a requirement imposed under or by virtue of Sch 19B (see PARAS 64, 65): see Sch 19B para 13(3) (as so added).

6　As to the meaning of 'record' see PARA 45 note 2.

7　As to the meaning of 'document' see PARA 48 note 1.

8　Ie under the Political Parties, Elections and Referendums Act 2000 Sch 19B para 1 (disclosure notices: see PARA 64) or Sch 19B para 3 (powers of production etc in relation to suspected offences or contraventions see PARA 65): see s 148(1) (amended by the Political Parties and Elections Act 2009 s 39, Sch 6 para 23).

9　Political Parties, Elections and Referendums Act 2000 s 148(1) (as amended: see note 8).

10　For these purposes, 'relevant person' means a person who is (or has been):

(1)　in relation to a registered party (other than a minor party) or the central organisation of such a party, the treasurer of the party (Political Parties, Elections and Referendums Act 2000 s 148(6)(c)(i));

(2)　in relation to any accounting unit of such a party, the registered treasurer of the unit (s 148(6)(c)(ii));

(3)　in relation to a regulated donee which is a members association, the responsible person for the purposes of s 71, Sch 7 (control of donations to individuals and members associations: see CONSTITUTIONAL LAW AND HUMAN RIGHTS) (s 148(6)(c)(iii));

(4)　in relation to a regulated participant which is a members association, the person responsible for the purposes of Sch 7A (control of loans and certain other transactions to individuals and members associations: see CONSTITUTIONAL LAW AND HUMAN RIGHTS) (s 148(6)(c)(iiia) (s 148(6)(c)(iiia), (6)(da) added by the Electoral Administration Act 2006 Sch 1 paras 138, 151(1), (4), (5)));

    (5)   in relation to a recognised third party, the responsible person for the purposes of the Political Parties, Elections and Referendums Act 2000 Pt VI (ss 85–100) (controls affecting expenditure by recognised third parties in national parliamentary election campaigns: see PARA 313 et seq) (s 148(6)(c)(iv));

    (6)   in relation to a permitted participant, the responsible person for the purposes of in Pt VII (ss 101–129) (referendums: see PARA 527 et seq) (s 148(6)(c)(v)).

'Regulated donee' and 'members association' have the same meanings as in Sch 7 (see s 148(6)(d)); 'regulated participant' has the same meaning as in Sch 7A (see (s 148(6)(da) (as so added)); 'recognised third party' has the same meaning as in Pt VI (see PARA 313 note 15) and 'permitted participant' has the same meaning as in Pt VII (see PARA 529) (see s 148(6)(e)). As to the meaning of 'responsible person' in relation to a recognised third party see PARA 313 note 15; as to the meaning of 'responsible person' in relation to a permitted participant which is a registered party see PARA 529 note 17; and as to the meaning of 'responsible person' in relation to a permitted participant which is an individual or body but which is not a registered party see PARA 529 note 27. As to the meaning of 'registered party' see PARA 35 note 3; as to the meaning of 'treasurer' see PARA 50 note 7; as to the meaning of 'minor party' see PARA 253 note 8; and as to the meanings of 'accounting units', 'central organisation' (in relation to a registered party) and 'party with accounting units' see PARA 253 note 15.

11 For these purposes, 'supervised organisation' means:

    (1)   a registered party or (in the case of such a party with accounting units) the central organisation of the party or any of its accounting units (Political Parties, Elections and Referendums Act 2000 s 148(6)(b)(i));

    (2)   a regulated donee which is a members association (s 148(6)(b)(ii));

    (3)   a regulated participant which is a members association (s 148(6)(b)(iia) (added by the Electoral Administration Act 2006 Sch 1 paras 138, 151(1), (3)));

    (4)   a recognised third party other than an individual (Political Parties, Elections and Referendums Act 2000 s 148(6)(b)(iii)); or

    (5)   a permitted participant other than an individual (s 148(6)(b)(iv)).

In s 146(1)–(3), any reference to a supervised organisation includes a reference to a former supervised organisation: see s 148(4).

12 Political Parties, Elections and Referendums Act 2000 s 148(2).

13 Political Parties, Elections and Referendums Act 2000 s 148(2)(a).

14 Political Parties, Elections and Referendums Act 2000 s 148(2)(b).

15 Political Parties, Elections and Referendums Act 2000 s 148(3)(a).

16 Political Parties, Elections and Referendums Act 2000 s 148(3)(b). For these purposes, 'supervised individual' means an individual who is a regulated donee, regulated participant, a recognised third party or a permitted participant: see s 148(6)(a) (definition amended by the Electoral Administration Act 2006 Sch 1 paras 138, 151(1), (2)). In the Political Parties, Elections and Referendums Act 2000 s 148(1)–(3), any reference to a supervised individual includes a reference to a former supervised individual (see s 148(4)); and s 148(1)–(3) applies in relation to a person who is (or has been) a candidate at an election, or the election agent for such a candidate, as it applies in relation to a supervised individual (or a former supervised individual), except that in its application in relation to any such person any reference to any of the provisions of the Political Parties, Elections and Referendums Act 2000 includes a reference to any other enactment imposing any restriction or other requirement falling within s 145(1)(b) (compliance with restrictions and other requirements imposed in relation to election expenses or donations: see PARA 62) (see s 148(5)). As to the meaning of 'election' see PARA 62 note 10; and as to the meaning of 'election agent' see PARA 62 note 11. As to the nomination of sub-agents see PARA 233 et seq.

17 Political Parties, Elections and Referendums Act 2000 s 148(3).

18 Political Parties, Elections and Referendums Act 2000 s 150, Sch 20 (Sch 20 amended by the Political Parties and Elections Act 2009 s 2(3)). A person guilty of an offence:

    (1)   under any of head (1), head (2) or head (5)(a) in the text is liable, on summary conviction, to a fine not exceeding level 5 on the standard scale (see the Political Parties, Elections and Referendums Act 2000 s 150, Sch 20 (Sch 20 as so amended));

    (2)   under head (3) above is punishable (on summary conviction) with a fine not exceeding the statutory maximum or with 12 months imprisonment or (on conviction on indictment) with a fine or with up to one year's imprisonment (see s 150, Sch 20 (Sch 20 as so amended));

    (3)   under any of head (4), head (5)(b) or head (6) in the text is liable, on summary conviction, to a fine not exceeding the statutory maximum or to a term of imprisonment not exceeding six months or both or, on conviction on indictment, to a fine or to a term of imprisonment not exceeding one year or both (see s 150, Sch 20).

In relation to an offence committed after the date of commencement of the Criminal Justice Act 2003 s 281(5) (not yet in force) (alteration of penalties for summary offences: see SENTENCING AND DISPOSITION OF OFFENDERS vol 92 (2010) PARA 374), the reference to six months must be taken to be a reference to 51 weeks: Political Parties, Elections and Referendums Act 2000 s 150(5) (added by SI 2008/1319). As to summary proceedings for offences committed under the Political Parties, Elections and Referendums Act 2000 see PARA 892; as to offences under the Political Parties, Elections and Referendums Act 2000 committed by bodies corporate or unincorporated associations see PARA 893; and as to the Court's duty to report convictions for offences committed under the Political Parties, Elections and Referendums Act 2000 to the Electoral Commission see PARA 904. As to the statutory maximum see SENTENCING AND DISPOSITION OF OFFENDERS vol 92 (2010) PARA 140. As to the standard scale see SENTENCING AND DISPOSITION OF OFFENDERS vol 92 (2010) PARA 142. As to the Commission's powers to apply civil sanctions to offences and contraventions under the Political Parties, Elections and Referendums Act 2000 see PARA 757.

(vii) Corrupt Practices, Offences and Illegal Practices amounting to Electoral Fraud

754. Electoral fraud. The term 'electoral fraud' does not appear in the legislation but it has currency as a term of art[1], used to describe deliberate abuses of the electoral process[2] that bear upon the individual will of voters, but which may be deployed so widely that the outcome of the election itself is influenced, if not dictated, by those abuses rather than by the collective will of the electorate[3]. Much of this activity may fall within the scope of the electoral legislation, and involve any, or any combination, of the following corrupt practices, offences, and illegal practices (a non-exclusive list):

(1)   bribery[4];
(2)   treating[5];
(3)   undue influence[6];
(4)   provision of false information in order to obtain registration[7];
(5)   provision of false information in order to obtain an absent vote (a postal or a proxy vote)[8];
(6)   personation and other voting offences (such as multiple voting)[9];
(7)   tampering with ballot papers[10];
(8)   breaches of the secrecy of the ballot[11].

As well as bearing upon a voter's will, electoral fraud may involve corrupt and illegal practices that vitiate a person's candidacy (such as the making of false statements, either before the campaign to obtain a nomination for candidacy[12], or during the campaign in an attempt to influence the electorate[13]). Further offences that fall outside the scope of the electoral legislation may be found from the same facts, such as (a non-exclusive list):

(a)   making a false statement under the Perjury Act 1911[14];
(b)   using a false instrument under the Forgery and Counterfeiting Act 1981[15];
(c)   theft (for example, theft of postal ballot papers)[16];
(d)   an offence under the Fraud Act 2006[17], or conspiracy to defraud at common law[18].

One distinction to be made between electoral offences and non-electoral offences is that criminal courts have a greater range of penalties available to them than an election court (which is also constrained to hear cases within the statutory time-frame)[19].

Electoral fraud, if found to be so widespread at an election that it may be reasonably supposed to have affected the result, will result in the election being declared void, by reason of an elected candidate or his agents being reported guilty of corrupt or illegal practices[20], or on the ground of general corruption[21]. The first case in which electoral fraud involving abuse of the postal voting system on a large scale had been proved involved findings that candidates and their supporters in various wards at a local government election had committed acts of bribery and undue influence, had unlawfully applied for and obtained blank ballot papers in order to personate true voters, had obtained unused postal voting packages either by unlawfully obtaining them from postmen, or by theft from electors' premises, and also that they altered completed ballot papers[22]; at a later date, another local government election was declared void after it was found that a candidate and his agent had made fraudulent applications to register to vote shortly before the election, had made false applications to vote by post, and had committed various personation offences[23].

1   Egregious examples of abuse, particularly involving the absent voting provisions (see PARA 363 et seq), notably came to light in court cases from 2005 onwards (see the text and notes 22–23), and the conclusions drawn in such cases, especially in *Akhtar v Jahan, Iqbal v Islam* [2005] All ER (D) 15 (Apr), Election Ct (see at [716] per Commissioner Mawrey QC: 'evidence of electoral fraud that would disgrace a banana republic'), started to arouse public concern. As part of its general remit, the Electoral Commission commenced a review of electoral fraud vulnerabilities to identify whether there are opportunities to improve confidence in the security of electoral processes in the United Kingdom, and as part of that process, has published *Electoral fraud in the UK: Evidence and issues paper* (May 2013). As to the establishment and constitution etc of the Electoral Commission see PARA 34 et seq.

2   Ie including (but not limited to) abuses of the franchise, electoral mechanisms and electoral procedures. The Electoral Commission has identified four main areas of vulnerability in the current system: (1) postal voting; (2) proxy voting; (3) voting at polling stations; and (4) electoral registration: see *Electoral fraud in the UK: Evidence and issues paper* (May 2013) para 4.4. The vulnerability listed under head (4) above is being addressed by the system of individual electoral registration which, at the date at which this volume states the law, is likely to provide the basis for the register in use at the 2015 general election and beyond (see PARA 152 et seq), but its effectiveness will be monitored by the Electoral Commission in the mean time.

3   The wording in the text follows *Electoral fraud in the UK: Evidence and issues paper* (May 2013), which suggests, as a working definition of electoral fraud: 'deliberate wrong-doing in the electoral process, which is intended to distort the individual or collective will of the electorate' (see *Appendix 1: working definitions of electoral fraud*). The Electoral Commission suggests two further definitions: (1) electoral malpractice ('the breach by an election professional of his or her relevant duty, resulting from carelessness or neglect rather than deliberate intent'); and (2) non-electoral fraud ('deliberate wrong-doing involving the electoral process, but which is intended to influence or defraud an individual or body unrelated to the electoral process'): see *Appendix 1: working definitions of electoral fraud*. Although head (1) above impinges upon this title (see especially PARA 737 (breaches of official duty)), the focus in the text is on electoral fraud (as defined), and especially on abuses that fall within the scope of current legislation.

4   See PARA 709 et seq (a corrupt practice).

5   See PARAS 721, 722 (a corrupt practice).

6   See PARA 723 et seq (a corrupt practice).

7   See PARAS 731 (an offence which is also a corrupt practice), 735 (a simple offence).

8   See PARAS 731 (an offence which is also a corrupt practice), 735 (a simple offence). Postal voting on demand had been introduced by the Representation of the People Act 2000: see PARA 363 et seq.

9   See PARAS 700 (an offence which is also an illegal practice), 730 (an offence which is also a corrupt practice).

10 See PARA 738 (a simple offence).

11 See PARA 739 (a simple offence).

12 See PARAS 705 (a corrupt practice), 738 (a simple offence).

13 See PARA 680 (an illegal practice).

14 See the Perjury Act 1911 s 5(b) (false statutory declarations: see CRIMINAL LAW vol 26 (2010) PARA 673) and s 16(1) (dual liability for making a false statement which is both an offence under the Perjury Act 1911, and a corrupt practice by virtue of some other Act: see CRIMINAL LAW vol 26 (2010) PARA 681).

15 Forgery of signatures on a nomination paper, applications to vote, or postal voting statements, forgery of a ballot paper (or the official mark on a ballot paper), or completed ballot papers that are proved to be forged or altered, might constitute an offence under the Forgery and Counterfeiting Act 1981 (see generally CRIMINAL LAW vol 25 (2010) PARA 339 et seq). See also PARAS 729 et seq, 735 et seq. As to the inspection of the ballot papers or counterfoils for the purpose of initiating or maintaining a prosecution for an offence in relation to the ballot papers see PARA 851.

16 See generally CRIMINAL LAW vol 25 (2010) PARA 278 et seq (although *quaere* whether such a charge would either be brought in isolation on the facts or otherwise reflect the *gravamen* of the case).

17 Ie dishonestly making a false representation, or dishonestly failing to disclose information under a legal duty (see CRIMINAL LAW vol 25 (2010) PARA 305 et seq). See also PARA 735 et seq.

18 See CRIMINAL LAW vol 25 (2010) PARA 80.

19 As to questioning elections and referendums see PARA 761 et seq. As to the sentencing powers of criminal courts generally see CRIMINAL LAW; and SENTENCING AND DISPOSITION OF OFFENDERS.

20 See PARA 894. Parties and witnesses who give evidence at the trial of an election petition can be prosecuted for perjury: see PARA 826.

21 See PARA 895.

22 See *Akhtar v Jahan, Iqbal v Islam* [2005] All ER (D) 15 (Apr), Election Ct; and *Re Maybury and Sheerwater Ward of Woking Borough Council, Ali v Bashir* [2013] EWHC 2572 (QB), [2013] All ER (D) 24 (Nov).

23 See *Re Central Ward, Slough Election Petition, Simmons v Khan* [2008] EWHC B4 (QB), Election Ct; and *Re Maybury and Sheerwater Ward of Woking Borough Council, Ali v Bashir* [2013] EWHC 2572 (QB), [2013] All ER (D) 24 (Nov).

(viii) Civil Liabilities

A. CIVIL SANCTIONS FOR FAILURE TO COMPLY WITH REQUIREMENTS OF THE REPRESENTATION OF THE PEOPLE ACT 1983

755. Financial penalty for sitting or voting in office where no financial returns or declarations are transmitted. If, in the case of any candidate at a parliamentary election[1], the return[2] and declarations[3] as to election expenses are not delivered before the expiration of the time limited for the purpose, that candidate must not after the expiration of that time sit or vote in the House of Commons as the member for the constituency[4] for which the election was held, until[5]:

(1) that return and those declarations have been delivered[6]; or

(2) the date of the allowance of an authorised excuse[7] for the failure to deliver the same[8];

and if he sits or votes in contravention of this restriction, he forfeits £100 for every day on which he so sits or votes[9].

Similarly a candidate at a local government election[10] must not, after the expiration of the expiration of the time limited for the purpose, sit or vote in the council for the local government area for which the election was held to which he has been elected until[11]:

(a) the appropriate return and declaration or declarations have been delivered[12]; or

(b) the date of the allowance of an authorised excuse[13],

and, if he does so, he forfeits £50 for every day on which he so sits or votes[14].

At a Welsh Assembly election[15], if the required return and declaration (or declarations)[16] are not delivered before the expiry of the time limited for the purpose, the candidate must not, after the expiry of that time, sit or vote in the National Assembly for Wales as member for the Assembly constituency or Assembly electoral region[17] for which the election was held[18] until:

(i)   that return and those declarations (or that declaration, as the case may be) have been delivered[19]; or

(ii)   the date of the allowance of an authorised excuse for the failure to deliver that return and those declarations (or, as the case may be, that declaration)[20],

and if he sits or votes in contravention of this restriction, he forfeits £100 for every day on which he so sits or votes[21].

Civil proceedings for a penalty under these provisions must be commenced within the period of one year beginning with the day in respect of which the penalty is alleged to have been incurred[22]. In respect of a candidate at a local government election[23], instead of civil proceedings for a penalty, summary proceedings may be instituted[24] in a magistrates' court and he is liable on conviction to a fine of an amount not exceeding the amount of the penalty that would be recoverable in civil proceedings[25].

1   As to the meaning of 'candidate' generally see PARA 230; and as to the meaning of 'parliamentary election' see PARA 9.

2   As to the meaning of 'return as to election expenses' see PARA 281 note 1. A return which has been duly delivered constitutes a good return for these purposes, even if there is an error in the return: *Mackinnon v Clark* [1898] 2 QB 251 at 257–258, CA, per A L Smith LJ.

3   As to the meaning of 'declaration as to election expenses' see PARA 281 note 3.

4   As to the meaning of 'constituency' see PARA 9.

5   See the Representation of the People Act 1983 s 85(1) (s 85(1), (1)(a), (1)(b) amended by the Representation of the People Act 1985 s 24, Sch 4 para 29(a)).

6   Representation of the People Act 1983 s 85(1)(a) (as amended: see note 5).

7   As to the meaning of the 'date of the allowance of an authorised excuse' for these purposes see PARA 688 note 30.

8   Representation of the People Act 1983 s 85(1)(b) (as amended: see note 5). The penalty belongs to the Crown: *Bradlaugh v Clarke* (1883) 8 App Cas 354, HL.

9   See the Representation of the People Act 1983 s 85(1).

10   As to the meaning of 'local government election' see PARA 11. The Representation of the People Act 1983 s 85(1), (2) does not apply in relation to a candidate in an election of the Mayor of London (for which separate provision is made by disqualification under s 85A: see PARA 906): s 85(2A)(a) (s 85(2A) added by the Greater London Authority Act 1999 s 17, Sch 3 paras 1, 25). Nor does the Representation of the People Act 1983 s 85 apply to an election of parish councillors in England or community councillors in Wales but provision is made in relation to a parish council in England and community council in Wales under Sch 4: see s 90(1)(b); and PARA 675. However, the Representation of the People Act 1983 s 85 has been applied and modified for the purpose of local authority mayoral elections in England and Wales by the Local Authorities (Mayoral Elections) (England and Wales) Regulations 2007, SI 2007/1024, reg 3(2)–(5), Sch 2 Table 1: see PARA 11 note 14.

11   See the Representation of the People Act 1983 s 85(1) (as amended: see note 5) (applied and modified by s 85(2)); Sch 4 para 4(1). As to the meaning of 'local government area' see PARA 33 note 7. As respects an Authority election, except an election of the Mayor of London, the reference to the council for the local government area for which the election was held must be taken as a reference to the London Assembly: s 85(2A)(b) (as so added). As to the meaning of 'Authority election' see PARA 11. As to elections in the City of London see PARA 33.

12   See the Representation of the People Act 1983 s 85(1)(a) (as amended: see note 5) (as applied and modified: see note 11). In the case of a candidate included in a list submitted by a registered political party under the Greater London Authority Act 1999 s 4(6), Sch 2 para 5(2) (election of London members of the London Assembly: see PARA 226), the references to returns and declarations in respect of election expenses are references to the declaration as to election expenses by the candidate: s 85(2A)(c) (as added: see note 10).

13   See the Representation of the People Act 1983 s 85(1)(b) (as amended: see note 5) (as applied and modified: see note 11). As to the meaning of 'date of the allowance of an authorised excuse' in relation to a parish or community council see PARA 689 note 11.

14   See the Representation of the People Act 1983 s 85(1) (as applied and modified: see note 11); and Sch 4 para 4(1)(a). This provision does not apply to sitting or voting at meetings of committees of the council: *Nichol v Fearby* [1923] 1 KB 480.

15 As to the meaning of 'Assembly election' see PARA 3 note 2.

16 Ie:

(1)   in the case of a constituency candidate or an individual candidate, the return and
      declarations as to election expenses (National Assembly for Wales (Representation of
      the People) Order 2007, SI 2007/236, art 57(1)(a)); or

(2)   in the case of a party list candidate, his declaration as to election expenses
      (art 57(1)(b)).

As to the meanings of 'candidate', 'constituency candidate' and 'individual candidate' for these
purposes see PARA 230 note 19; and as to the meanings of 'party list', 'party list candidate' and
'registered political party' see PARA 230 note 23.

17 As to the meanings of 'Assembly constituency' and 'Assembly electoral region' see PARA 3
    note 2.

18 See the National Assembly for Wales (Representation of the People) Order 2007, SI 2007/236,
    art 57(1).

19 See the National Assembly for Wales (Representation of the People) Order 2007, SI 2007/236,
    art 57(1)(i), (ii). Head (i) in the text refers to the delivery of:

(1)   in the case of a constituency candidate or an individual candidate, the return and
      declarations as to election expenses (art 57(1)(i)); or

(2)   in the case of a party list candidate, his declaration as to election expenses
      (art 57(1)(ii)).

20 National Assembly for Wales (Representation of the People) Order 2007, SI 2007/236,
    art 57(1)(iii). As to the meaning of the 'date of the allowance of an authorised excuse' for these
    purposes see PARA 688 note 30.

21 See the National Assembly for Wales (Representation of the People) Order 2007, SI 2007/236,
    art 57(2).

22 Representation of the People Act 1983 s 85(3) (substituted by the Representation of the People
    Act 1985 Sch 4 para 29(b)); Representation of the People Act 1983 Sch 4 para 4(2) (substituted
    by the Representation of the People Act 1985 Sch 4 para 89(b)); National Assembly for Wales
    (Representation of the People) Order 2007, SI 2007/236, art 57(3). For these purposes, where
    the service or execution of legal process on or against the alleged offender is prevented by the
    absconding or concealment or act of the alleged offender, the issue of legal process is deemed to
    be a commencement of a proceeding; but, where this does not apply, the service or execution of
    legal process on or against the alleged offender, and not its issue, is deemed to be the
    commencement of the proceeding: Representation of the People Act 1983 s 85(4) (amended by
    the Political Parties, Elections and Referendums Act 2000 s 138(1), Sch 18 para 1, 19(2));
    Representation of the People Act 1983 Sch 4 para 4(3) (amended by the Representation of the
    People Act 1985 Sch 4 para 89(b); and the Political Parties, Elections and Referendums
    Act 2000 Sch 18 para 1, 19(7)); National Assembly for Wales (Representation of the People)
    Order 2007, SI 2007/236, art 57(4). On any proceedings for a penalty under the Representation
    of the People Act 1983 s 85, or Sch 4 para 4, or under the National Assembly for Wales
    (Representation of the People) Order 2007, SI 2007/236, art 57, the certificate of the
    appropriate returning officer at an election, that the election mentioned in the certificate was
    duly held, and that the person named in the certificate was a candidate at the election, is
    sufficient evidence of the facts stated in it: see the Representation of the People Act 1983 s 180;
    and the National Assembly for Wales (Representation of the People) Order 2007, SI 2007/236,
    art 131. As to the meaning of 'appropriate returning officer' for the purposes of a Welsh
    Assembly election see PARA 18 note 2.

23 See note 10.

24 As to the time within which the proceedings must be instituted see PARA 883.

25 Representation of the People Act 1983 s 85(2)(b); Sch 4 para 4(1)(b).

**756.   Civil penalties for failure to make application for registration when
required by registration officer.** As from a day to be appointed[1], a registration
officer[2] who gives a person an invitation to apply for registration in a register
maintained by the officer[3] may subsequently require the person to make an
application for registration by a specified date[4]; and a registration officer may
impose a civil penalty on a person who fails to comply with a requirement
imposed by the officer in this way[5].

The amount of a civil penalty is to be specified in regulations[6]; and the
procedure for imposing a civil penalty on a person is to be set out in regulations[7].
Regulations also may:

(1) specify steps that a registration officer must take before imposing a civil penalty[8];

(2) give a person on whom a civil penalty is imposed a right to request a review of the decision to impose the penalty, and a right to appeal against the decision to the First-tier Tribunal[9];

(3) specify circumstances in which a civil penalty may not be imposed, or in which a civil penalty may be cancelled[10];

(4) impose duties on registration officers about the keeping of accounts and other records in connection with civil penalties[11];

(5) allow interest to be charged on a civil penalty that is paid late, and allow an additional penalty to be imposed for late payment[12];

(6) make provision about the recovery of civil penalties by registration officers[13]; and

(7) make further provision about civil penalties[14].

A civil penalty received by a registration officer must be paid into the Consolidated Fund[15].

1 The Representation of the People Act 1983 s 9E, Sch ZA1 is added by the Electoral Registration and Administration Act 2013 s 5(1), (2), Sch 3, as from a day to be appointed under s 27(1). At the date at which this volume states the law, no such day had been appointed.

2 As to registration officers see PARA 139.

3 As to the duty of registration officers to maintain, prepare and publish registers of electors see PARA 143.

4 See the Representation of the People Act 1983 s 9E(4) (prospectively added: see note 1); and PARA 155. Regulations may make provision about requirements under s 9E(4), including provision for them to be cancelled in specified circumstances, and may specify steps that a registration officer must take before imposing a requirement: see s 9E(6) (prospectively added); and PARA 155. As to the making of regulations under the Representation of the People Act 1983 generally see PARA 28 note 16.

5 See the Representation of the People Act 1983 s 9E(7) (prospectively added: see note 1); and PARA 155. The civil penalties that may be imposed for a failure to make an application for registration when required by the registration officer are set out in Sch ZA1: see s 9E(8), Sch ZA1 para 1 (prospectively added). For these purposes, 'civil penalty' includes any interest or additional penalty: Sch ZA1 para 9 (prospectively added).

6 Representation of the People Act 1983 Sch ZA1 para 2 (prospectively added: see note 1).

7 Representation of the People Act 1983 Sch ZA1 para 3(1) (prospectively added: see note 1). The regulations must, in particular, require the registration officer to give the person written notice specifying:
(1) the amount of the penalty (Sch ZA1 para 3(2)(a) (prospectively added));
(2) the reasons for imposing it (Sch ZA1 para 3(2)(b) (prospectively added)); and
(3) the date by which and manner in which it is to be paid (Sch ZA1 para 3(2)(c) (prospectively added)).

8 Representation of the People Act 1983 Sch ZA1 para 4 (prospectively added: see note 1).

9 Representation of the People Act 1983 Sch ZA1 para 5(1) (prospectively added: see note 1). Regulations under Sch ZA1 para 5 may, in particular:
(1) specify the grounds on which a person may request a review or appeal (Sch ZA1 para 5(2)(a) (prospectively added));
(2) specify the time within which a person must request a review or appeal (Sch ZA1 para 5(2)(b) (prospectively added));
(3) require a person to request a review before appealing (Sch ZA1 para 5(2)(c) (prospectively added));
(4) make provision about the procedure for a review (Sch ZA1 para 5(2)(d) (prospectively added));
(5) make further provision about reviews and appeals (including provision as to the powers available on a review or appeal) (Sch ZA1 para 5(2)(e) (prospectively added)).
As to the First-tier Tribunal see COURTS AND TRIBUNALS vol 24 (2010) PARA 876 et seq.

10 Representation of the People Act 1983 Sch ZA1 para 6 (prospectively added: see note 1).

11 Representation of the People Act 1983 Sch ZA1 para 7 (prospectively added: see note 1).

12 Representation of the People Act 1983 Sch ZA1 para 8 (prospectively added: see note 1).

13 Representation of the People Act 1983 Sch ZA1 para 10 (prospectively added: see note 1).
14 Representation of the People Act 1983 Sch ZA1 para 12 (prospectively added: see note 1).
15 Representation of the People Act 1983 Sch ZA1 para 11 (prospectively added: see note 1). As to the Consolidated Fund see CONSTITUTIONAL LAW AND HUMAN RIGHTS vol 8(2) (Reissue) PARA 711 et seq; PARLIAMENT vol 78 (2010) PARAS 1028–1031.

B. CIVIL SANCTIONS FOR FAILURE TO COMPLY WITH REQUIREMENTS OF THE POLITICAL PARTIES, ELECTIONS AND REFERENDUMS ACT 2000

757. Imposition of fixed monetary penalties. The Electoral Commission[1] may by notice impose a fixed monetary penalty[2] on:

(1)   a person[3]; or

(2)   a registered party[4]; or

(3)   a recognised third party[5]; or

(4)   a permitted participant[6],

if satisfied beyond reasonable doubt that the person mentioned in head (1) above, or a person holding an office within the party mentioned in head (2) above, or the responsible person in relation to the recognised third party mentioned in head (3) above[7], or the responsible person in relation to the permitted participant mentioned in head (4) above[8]:

(a)   has committed a prescribed offence under the Political Parties, Elections and Referendums Act 2000[9]; or

(b)   has (otherwise than by committing an offence under the Act) contravened a prescribed restriction or requirement imposed by or by virtue of the Political Parties, Elections and Referendums Act 2000[10].

Where the Commission proposes to impose a fixed monetary penalty on a person, it must serve on the person a notice of what is proposed[11], and such a notice must offer the person the opportunity to discharge his liability for the fixed monetary penalty by payment of a prescribed sum (which must be less than or equal to the amount of the penalty)[12]. Provision is made for the person to make representations and appeals if he does not discharge his liability in this way[13].

1   As to the establishment and constitution of the Electoral Commission see PARA 34 et seq.
2   For the purposes of the Political Parties, Elections and Referendums Act 2000 s 147, Sch 19C, a 'fixed monetary penalty' is a requirement to pay to the Commission a penalty of a prescribed amount: Sch 19C paras 1(5), 29 (s 147 substituted, Sch 19C added, by the Political Parties and Elections Act 2009 s 3(1), (2), Sch 2). The Political Parties, Elections and Referendums Act 2000 Sch 19C makes provision for civil sanctions in relation to the commission of offences under the Political Parties, Elections and Referendums Act 2000, and in relation to the contravention of restrictions or requirements imposed by or by virtue of the Political Parties, Elections and Referendums Act 2000: see s 147 (as so substituted). The Secretary of State may by order (a 'supplementary order') make provision (including transitional provision) supplementing that made by Sch 19C, and make provision that is consequential on or incidental to that made by Sch 19C: see Sch 19C para 16(1) (as so added). As to the power of the Secretary of State to make any order under the Political Parties, Elections and Referendums Act 2000 see PARA 34 note 2. As to the Secretary of State see PARA 2. As to the making of supplementary orders see further Sch 19C paras 16(2), (3), 17–21 (as so added). 'Prescribed' means prescribed in a supplementary order (which has the meaning given in Sch 19C para 16(1)): see Sch 19C para 29 (as so added). In exercise of the powers conferred by Sch 19C paras 1, 2, 5, 9, 10, 15, 16, 18, 19 and 21, the Lord President of the Council has made the Political Parties, Elections and Referendums (Civil Sanctions) Order 2010, SI 2010/2860. Accordingly, the amount prescribed for the purposes of the Political Parties, Elections and Referendums Act 2000 Sch 19C para 1(5) is £200: Political Parties, Elections and Referendums (Civil Sanctions) Order 2010, SI 2010/2860, Sch 1 para 1. The Commission may recover a fixed monetary penalty, or any interest or other financial penalty for late payment on the order of a court, as if payable under a court order: art 5(1). Any amount that is payable under the Political Parties, Elections and

Referendums Act 2000 Sch 19C by an unincorporated association must be paid out of the funds of the association: Sch 19C para 24 (as so added). A fixed monetary penalty received by the Commission (including interest or penalties for late payment) must be paid into the Consolidated Fund: see Sch 19C para 26 (as so added). As to the guidance that must be prepared and published by the Commission in relation to its powers of enforcement see Sch 19C para 25 (as so added). Each report by the Commission under Sch 1 para 20 (see PARA 46) must contain information about the use made by the Commission of their powers under Sch 19C during the year in question: see Sch 19C para 27 (as so added). As to the Consolidated Fund see CONSTITUTIONAL LAW AND HUMAN RIGHTS vol 8(2) (Reissue) PARA 711 et seq; PARLIAMENT vol 78 (2010) PARAS 1028–1031.

3   See the Political Parties, Elections and Referendums Act 2000 Sch 19C para 1(1) (as added: see note 2).

4   See the Political Parties, Elections and Referendums Act 2000 Sch 19C para 1(2) (as added: see note 2). As to the meaning of 'registered party' see PARA 35 note 3.

5   See the Political Parties, Elections and Referendums Act 2000 Sch 19C para 1(3) (as added: see note 2). For these purposes, 'recognised third party' has the meaning given in s 85(5) (control of expenditure by third parties in national parliamentary election campaigns: see PARA 313): see Sch 19C para 29 (as so added).

6   See the Political Parties, Elections and Referendums Act 2000 Sch 19C para 1(4) (as added: see note 2). For these purposes, 'permitted participant' has the meaning given in s 105(1) (permitted participant for the purpose of referendums: see PARA 529): see Sch 19C para 29 (as so added).

7   For these purposes, 'responsible person' in relation to a recognised third party has the meaning given in the Political Parties, Elections and Referendums Act 2000 s 85(7) (see PARA 313 note 15): see Sch 19C para 29 (as added: see note 2).

8   See the Political Parties, Elections and Referendums Act 2000 Sch 19C para 1(1)–(4) (as added: see note 2). For these purposes, 'responsible person' in relation to a permitted participant has the meaning given in s 105(2) (see PARA 529 note 17): see Sch 19C para 29 (as so added). The Commission must not take into account a statement made by a person in compliance with a requirement imposed under Sch 19B (Commission's investigatory powers: see PARAS 64, 65) in deciding whether to impose a fixed monetary penalty on the person, unless a penalty or requirement has been imposed in respect of an offence under Sch 19B para 13(3) (providing false information in purported compliance with a requirement: see PARA 753): Sch 19C para 23(1), (2) (as so added). As to disclosure to the Commission of information held by or on behalf of the Crown Prosecution Service, or a member of a police force in England and Wales, for the purpose of the exercise by the Commission of any powers conferred on them under or by virtue of Sch 19C see Sch 19C para 28 (as so added).

9   Political Parties, Elections and Referendums Act 2000 Sch 19C para 1(1)(a), (2)(a), (3)(a), (4)(a) (as added: see note 2). As to the offences prescribed for the purposes of Sch 19C para 1(1)(a) see the Political Parties, Elections and Referendums (Civil Sanctions) Order 2010, SI 2010/2860, art 4(1), Sch 2 Pt 1. In the case of a fixed monetary penalty imposed under the Political Parties, Elections and Referendums Act 2000 Sch 19C para 1(1)(a), (2)(a), (3)(a) or (4)(a), where the offence in question is triable summarily (whether or not it is also triable on indictment), and punishable on summary conviction by a fine (whether or not it is also punishable by a term of imprisonment), the amount of the penalty may not exceed the maximum amount of that fine: Sch 19C para 1(6) (as so added).

10   Political Parties, Elections and Referendums Act 2000 Sch 19C para 1(1)(b), (2)(b), (3)(b), (4)(b) (as added: see note 2). As to the restrictions and requirements prescribed for the purposes of Sch 19C para 1(1)(b) see the Political Parties, Elections and Referendums (Civil Sanctions) Order 2010, SI 2010/2860, art 4(2), Sch 2 Pt 2; and as to the restrictions and requirements prescribed for the purposes of the Political Parties, Elections and Referendums Act 2000 Sch 19C para 1(2)(b), (3)(b), (4)(b) see the Political Parties, Elections and Referendums (Civil Sanctions) Order 2010, SI 2010/2860, art 4(3), Sch 2 Pt 3.

11   See the Political Parties, Elections and Referendums Act 2000 Sch 19C para 2(1) (as added: see note 2). As to the contents of the notice under Sch 19C para 2(1) see further Sch 19C para 3(1), (2) (as so added). The Commission may not serve on a person a notice under Sch 19C para 2(1) in relation to any act or omission in relation to which a discretionary requirement has been imposed on that person (see PARA 758), or a stop notice has been served on that person (see PARA 759): Sch 19C para 22(1) (as so added).

Where a notice under Sch 19C para 2(1) is served on a person, no criminal proceedings for an offence under the Political Parties, Elections and Referendums Act 2000 may be instituted against the person in respect of the act or omission to which the notice relates before the end of the period within which the person's liability may be discharged as mentioned in Sch 19C para 2(2) (see the text and note 12), and, if the liability is so discharged, the person may not at any time be convicted of an offence under the Political Parties, Elections and Referendums Act 2000 in relation to that act or omission: see Sch 19C para 4(1) (as so added). A person on whom a fixed monetary penalty is imposed may not at any time be convicted of an offence under the Political Parties, Elections and Referendums Act 2000 in respect of the act or omission giving rise to the penalty: see Sch 19C para 4(2) (as so added).

12 See the Political Parties, Elections and Referendums Act 2000 Sch 19C para 2(2) (as added: see note 2). The amount prescribed for the purposes of Sch 19C para 2(2) is £200: Political Parties, Elections and Referendums (Civil Sanctions) Order 2010, SI 2010/2860, Sch 1 para 2. Any sum so received by the Commission must be paid into the Consolidated Fund: see the Political Parties, Elections and Referendums Act 2000 Sch 19C para 26 (as so added).

13 See the Political Parties, Elections and Referendums Act 2000 Sch 19C paras 2(3)–(7), 3(3) (as added: see note 2). As to appeals and dates fixed for the payment of penalties (including late payments) see the Political Parties, Elections and Referendums (Civil Sanctions) Order 2010, SI 2010/2860, art 7(1), Sch 1 paras 3, 4. As to the county court's powers on such an appeal see art 8(2).

As from a day to be appointed under the Crime and Courts Act 2013 s 61(3), the Political Parties, Elections and Referendums Act 2000 Sch 19C para 2(7) is amended by the Crime and Courts Act 2013 s 17(5), Sch 9 Pt 3 para 121(d). However, at the date at which this volume states the law, no such day had been appointed.

758. Imposition of discretionary requirements. The Electoral Commission[1] may impose one or more discretionary requirements[2] on:

(1)   a person[3]; or

(2)   a registered party[4]; or

(3)   a recognised third party[5]; or

(4)   a permitted participant[6],

if satisfied beyond reasonable doubt that the person mentioned in head (1) above, or a person holding an office within the party mentioned in head (2) above, or the responsible person in relation to the recognised third party mentioned in head (3) above[7], or the responsible person in relation to the permitted participant mentioned in head (4) above[8]:

(a)   has committed a prescribed offence under the Political Parties, Elections and Referendums Act 2000[9]; or

(b)   has (otherwise than by committing an offence under the Act) contravened a prescribed restriction or requirement imposed by or by virtue of the Political Parties, Elections and Referendums Act 2000[10].

Where the Commission proposes to impose a discretionary requirement on a person, it must serve on the person a notice of what is proposed[11]. Provision is made for the person served with such a notice to make written representations and objections to the Commission in relation to the proposed imposition of the discretionary requirement[12], and to appeal against any such requirement so imposed[13]. The Commission may by notice impose a monetary penalty (a 'non-compliance penalty') on a person for failing to comply with a non-monetary discretionary requirement imposed on the person[14].

1   As to the establishment and constitution of the Electoral Commission see PARA 34 et seq.

2   For the purposes of the Political Parties, Elections and Referendums Act 2000 s 147, Sch 19C, a 'discretionary requirement' is:

(1)   a requirement to pay a monetary penalty to the Commission of such amount as the Commission may determine (Sch 19C paras 5(5)(a), 29 (s 147 substituted, Sch 19C added, by the Political Parties and Elections Act 2009 s 3(1), (2), Sch 2)); or

(2)   a requirement to take such steps as the Commission may specify, within such period as they may specify, to secure that the offence or contravention does not continue or recur (Political Parties, Elections and Referendums Act 2000 Sch 19C paras 5(5)(b), 29 (as so added)); or

(3)   a requirement to take such steps as the Commission may specify, within such period as

they may specify, to secure that the position is, so far as possible, restored to what it would have been if the offence or contravention had not happened (Sch 19C paras 5(5)(c), 29 (as so added)).

Discretionary requirements may not be imposed on the same person on more than one occasion in relation to the same act or omission: Sch 19C para 5(6) (as so added). A requirement referred in head (1) above is a 'variable monetary penalty', and a requirement referred in head (2) or head (3) above is a 'non-monetary discretionary requirement': see Sch 19C paras 5(7), 29 (as so added). A notice imposing a requirement under head (2) above is known as a 'compliance notice'; and a notice imposing a requirement under head (3) above is known as a 'restoration notice': see the Political Parties, Elections and Referendums (Civil Sanctions) Order 2010, SI 2010/2860, art 2. The maximum amount that the Commission may impose as a variable monetary penalty is £20,000: Sch 1 para 5. The Commission may recover a variable monetary penalty, or any interest or other financial penalty for late payment on the order of a court, as if payable under a court order: art 5(1). Any amount that is payable under the Political Parties, Elections and Referendums Act 2000 Sch 19C by an unincorporated association must be paid out of the funds of the association: Sch 19C para 24 (as so added). A variable monetary penalty received by the Commission (including interest or penalties for late payment) must be paid into the Consolidated Fund: see Sch 19C para 26 (as so added). As to the guidance that must be prepared and published by the Commission in relation to its powers of enforcement see Sch 19C para 25 (as so added). Each report by the Commission under Sch 1 para 20 (see PARA 46) must contain information about the use made by the Commission of their powers under Sch 19C during the year in question: see Sch 19C para 27 (as so added). As to the scheme laid down in Sch 19C see PARA 757 note 2. As to the Consolidated Fund see CONSTITUTIONAL LAW AND HUMAN RIGHTS vol 8(2) (Reissue) PARA 711 et seq; PARLIAMENT vol 78 (2010) PARAS 1028–1031.

3 See the Political Parties, Elections and Referendums Act 2000 Sch 19C para 5(1) (as added: see note 2).

4 See the Political Parties, Elections and Referendums Act 2000 Sch 19C para 5(2) (as added: see note 2). As to the meaning of 'registered party' see PARA 35 note 3.

5 See the Political Parties, Elections and Referendums Act 2000 Sch 19C para 5(3) (as added: see note 2). As to the meaning of 'recognised third party' for these purposes see PARA 757 note 5.

6 See the Political Parties, Elections and Referendums Act 2000 Sch 19C para 5(4) (as added: see note 2). As to the meaning of 'permitted participant' for these purposes see PARA 757 note 6.

7 As to the meaning of 'responsible person' in relation to a recognised third party for these purposes see PARA 757 note 7.

8 See the Political Parties, Elections and Referendums Act 2000 Sch 19C para 5(1)–(4) (as added: see note 2). As to the meaning of 'responsible person' in relation to a permitted participant for these purposes see PARA 757 note 8. The Commission must not take into account a statement made by a person in compliance with a requirement imposed under Sch 19B (Commission's investigatory powers: see PARAS 64, 65) in deciding whether to impose a discretionary requirement on the person, unless a penalty or requirement was imposed in respect of an offence under Sch 19B para 13(3) (providing false information in purported compliance with a requirement: see PARA 753): Sch 19C para 23(1), (2) (as so added). As to disclosure to the Commission of information held by or on behalf of the Crown Prosecution Service, or a member of a police force in England and Wales, for the purpose of the exercise by the Commission of any powers conferred on them under or by virtue of Sch 19C see Sch 19C para 28 (as so added).

9 Political Parties, Elections and Referendums Act 2000 Sch 19C para 5(1)(a), (2)(a), (3)(a), (4)(a) (as added: see note 2). 'Prescribed' means prescribed in a supplementary order (which has the meaning given in Sch 19C para 16(1): see PARA 757 note 2): see Sch 19C para 29 (as so added). As to the offences prescribed for the purposes of Sch 19C para 5(1)(a) see the Political Parties, Elections and Referendums (Civil Sanctions) Order 2010, SI 2010/2860, art 4(1), Sch 2 Pt 1. In the case of a variable monetary penalty imposed under the Political Parties, Elections and Referendums Act 2000 Sch 19C para 5(1)(a), (2)(a), (3)(a) or (4)(a), where the offence in question is triable summarily only, and punishable on summary conviction by a fine (whether or not it is also punishable by a term of imprisonment), the amount of the penalty may not exceed the maximum amount of that fine: Sch 19C para 5(8) (as so added).

10 Political Parties, Elections and Referendums Act 2000 Sch 19C para 5(1)(b), (2)(b), (3)(b), (4)(b) (as added: see note 2). As to the restrictions and requirements prescribed for the purposes of Sch 19C para 5(1)(b) see the Political Parties, Elections and Referendums (Civil Sanctions) Order 2010, SI 2010/2860, art 4(2), Sch 2 Pt 2; and as to the restrictions and requirements prescribed for the purposes of the Political Parties, Elections and Referendums Act 2000 Sch 19C para 5(2)(b), (3)(b), (4)(b) see the Political Parties, Elections and Referendums (Civil Sanctions) Order 2010, SI 2010/2860, art 4(3), Sch 2 Pt 3.

11	See the Political Parties, Elections and Referendums Act 2000 Sch 19C para 6(1) (as added: see note 2). As to the contents of the notice under Sch 19C para 2(1) see further Sch 19C para 7(1), (2) (as so added). The Commission may not serve on a person a notice under Sch 19C para 6(1), or serve a stop notice on that person (see PARA 759), in relation to any act or omission in relation to which a fixed monetary penalty has been imposed on that person (see PARA 757), or in relation to which the person's liability for a fixed monetary penalty has been discharged as mentioned in Sch 19C para 2(2) (see PARA 757): Sch 19C para 22(2) (as so added).

12	See the Political Parties, Elections and Referendums Act 2000 Sch 19C para 6(2) (as added: see note 2).

13	See the Political Parties, Elections and Referendums Act 2000 Sch 19C paras 6(3)–(7), 7(3) (as added: see note 2). As to certification of completion of the steps required, appeals and dates fixed for the payment of penalties (including late payments) see the Political Parties, Elections and Referendums (Civil Sanctions) Order 2010, SI 2010/2860, art 7(1), Sch 1 paras 6–9. As to the county court's powers on such an appeal see art 8(2), (3). A person on whom a discretionary requirement is imposed may not at any time be convicted of an offence under the Political Parties, Elections and Referendums Act 2000 in respect of the act or omission giving rise to the requirement (Sch 19C para 8(1) (as so added)), except where a non-monetary discretionary requirement is imposed on the person, no variable monetary penalty is imposed on the person, and the person fails to comply with the non-monetary discretionary requirement (see Sch 19C para 8(2) (as so added)).

	As from a day to be appointed under the Crime and Courts Act 2013 s 61(3), the Political Parties, Elections and Referendums Act 2000 Sch 19C para 6(7) is amended by the Crime and Courts Act 2013 s 17(5), Sch 9 Pt 3 para 121(d). However, at the date at which this volume states the law, no such day had been appointed.

14	See the Political Parties, Elections and Referendums Act 2000 Sch 19C para 9(1) (as added: see note 2). 'Non-compliance penalty' has the meaning given in Sch 19C para 9(1): see Sch 19C para 29 (as so added). As to the contents of a notice imposing a non-compliance penalty see the Political Parties, Elections and Referendums (Civil Sanctions) Order 2010, SI 2010/2860, art 6(2). Subject to any prescribed criteria, or any prescribed maximum or minimum amounts, the amount of a non-compliance penalty is to be such as the Commission may determine: Political Parties, Elections and Referendums Act 2000 Sch 19C para 9(2) (as so added). Provision is made for the person to appeal against any such notice: see Sch 19C para 9(3), (4) (as so added). Such an appeal must be made within 28 days of the day on which the notice was received: Political Parties, Elections and Referendums (Civil Sanctions) Order 2010, SI 2010/2860, art 6(5). As to the county court's powers on such an appeal see art 8(2). The amount of a non-compliance penalty must be determined by the Commission having regard to all the circumstances of the case and must not be less than £500 nor more than £20,000: art 6(1). If the steps specified in the compliance notice or restoration notice are completed, and a certificate is issued by the Commission under Sch 1 para 6 (see note 13), within the period set for payment of the non-compliance penalty the Commission may by notice waive, or reduce the amount of, a non-compliance penalty, however: art 6(4). A non-compliance penalty must be paid to the Commission: art 6(3). A non-compliance penalty received by the Commission must be paid into the Consolidated Fund: see the Political Parties, Elections and Referendums Act 2000 Sch 19C para 26 (as so added).

	As from a day to be appointed under the Crime and Courts Act 2013 s 61(3), the Political Parties, Elections and Referendums Act 2000 Sch 19C para 9(4) is amended by the Crime and Courts Act 2013 s 17(5), Sch 9 Pt 3 para 121(d). However, at the date at which this volume states the law, no such day had been appointed.

759. Imposition of stop notices. The Electoral Commission[1] may serve on a person a notice (a 'stop notice')[2] prohibiting the person from carrying on an activity specified in the notice until the person has taken the steps specified in the notice[3]. This power applies where[4]:

(1)	the person is carrying on the activity[5] (or is likely to carry on the activity)[6];

(2)	the Commission reasonably believes that the activity as carried on by the person involves (or will involve) or is likely to involve (or will be likely to involve) the person[7]:

	(a)	committing a prescribed offence under the Political Parties, Elections and Referendums Act 2000[8]; or

    (b)   contravening (otherwise than by committing an offence under the Act) a prescribed restriction or requirement imposed by or by virtue of the Political Parties, Elections and Referendums Act 2000[9]; and

(3)   the Commission reasonably believes that the activity as carried on (or as likely to be carried on) by the person is seriously damaging (or will seriously damage) public confidence in the effectiveness of the controls in the Political Parties, Elections and Referendums Act 2000 on the income and expenditure of registered parties[10] and others, or presents (or will present) a significant risk of doing so[11].

Where, after the service of a stop notice on a person, the Commission is satisfied that the person has taken the steps specified in the notice, it must issue a certificate to that effect (a 'completion certificate')[12].

A person served with a stop notice who does not comply with it is guilty of an offence[13], and is liable to a penalty[14].

1   As to the establishment and constitution of the Electoral Commission see PARA 34 et seq.

2   For the purposes of the Political Parties, Elections and Referendums Act 2000 s 147, Sch 19C, 'stop notice' has the meaning given in Sch 19C para 10(1): see Sch 19C para 29 (s 147 substituted, Sch 19C added, by the Political Parties and Elections Act 2009 s 3(1), (2), Sch 2). A stop notice must include information as to the grounds for serving the notice, rights of appeal, and the consequences of not complying with the notice: Political Parties, Elections and Referendums Act 2000 Sch 19C para 11 (as so added). The Commission must not take into account a statement made by a person in compliance with a requirement imposed under Sch 19B (Commission's investigatory powers: see PARAS 64, 65) in deciding whether to serve a stop notice on the person: Sch 19C para 23(1) (as so added). As to disclosure to the Commission of information held by or on behalf of the Crown Prosecution Service, or a member of a police force in England and Wales, for the purpose of the exercise by the Commission of any powers conferred on them under or by virtue of Sch 19C see Sch 19C para 28 (as so added). As to the guidance that must be prepared and published by the Commission in relation to its powers of enforcement see the Political Parties, Elections and Referendums Act 2000 Sch 19C para 25 (as so added). Each report by the Commission under Sch 1 para 20 (see PARA 46) must contain information about the use made by the Commission of their powers under Sch 19C during the year in question: see Sch 19C para 27 (as so added). As to the scheme laid down in Sch 19C see PARA 757 note 2.

3   See the Political Parties, Elections and Referendums Act 2000 Sch 19C para 10(1) (as added: see note 2). The steps referred to in the text must be steps to secure that the activity is carried on or (as the case may be) will be carried on in a way that does not involve the person acting as mentioned in head (2) in the text: Sch 19C para 10(4) (as so added). A person served with a stop notice may appeal against the decision to serve it: see Sch 19C para 13(1), (3) (as so added). An appeal under Sch 19C para 13(1) against the decision to serve a stop notice must be made within 28 days of the day on which the notice was received: Political Parties, Elections and Referendums (Civil Sanctions) Order 2010, SI 2010/2860, Sch 1 para 12(1). Where an appeal under the Political Parties, Elections and Referendums Act 2000 Sch 19C para 13(1) is made, the stop notice is not suspended unless suspended or varied on the order of the county court: Political Parties, Elections and Referendums (Civil Sanctions) Order 2010, SI 2010/2860, art 8(1). As to the county court's powers on such an appeal see art 8(2). The Commission may by notice in writing at any time withdraw a stop notice (without prejudice to its power to serve another in respect of the activity specified in the withdrawn notice): art 7(2).

    As from a day to be appointed under the Crime and Courts Act 2013 s 61(3), the Political Parties, Elections and Referendums Act 2000 Sch 19C para 13(3) is amended by the Crime and Courts Act 2013 s 17(5), Sch 9 Pt 3 para 121(d). However, at the date at which this volume states the law, no such day had been appointed.

4   See the Political Parties, Elections and Referendums Act 2000 Sch 19C para 10(2), (3) (as added: see note 2).

5   Political Parties, Elections and Referendums Act 2000 Sch 19C para 10(2)(a) (as added: see note 2).

6   Political Parties, Elections and Referendums Act 2000 Sch 19C para 10(3)(a) (as added: see note 2).

7   See the Political Parties, Elections and Referendums Act 2000 Sch 19C para 10(2)(b), (3)(b) (as added: see note 2).

8   See the Political Parties, Elections and Referendums Act 2000 Sch 19C para 10(2)(b)(i), (3)(b)(i) (as added: see note 2). 'Prescribed' means prescribed in a supplementary order (which has the meaning given in Sch 19C para 16(1): see PARA 757 note 2): see Sch 19C para 29 (as so added). As to the offences prescribed for the purposes of Sch 19C para 10(2)(b)(i), (3)(b)(i) see the Political Parties, Elections and Referendums (Civil Sanctions) Order 2010, SI 2010/2860, art 4(1), Sch 2 Pt 1.

9   See the Political Parties, Elections and Referendums Act 2000 Sch 19C para 10(2)(b)(ii), (3)(b)(ii) (as added: see note 2). As to the restrictions and requirements prescribed for the purposes of Sch 19C para 10(2)(b)(ii), (3)(b)(ii) see the Political Parties, Elections and Referendums (Civil Sanctions) Order 2010, SI 2010/2860, art 4(2), Sch 2 Pt 2.

10 As to the meaning of 'registered party' see PARA 35 note 3.

11 See the Political Parties, Elections and Referendums Act 2000 Sch 19C para 10(2)(c), (3)(c) (as added: see note 2).

12 Political Parties, Elections and Referendums Act 2000 Sch 19C para 12(1) (as added: see note 2). 'Completion certificate' has the meaning given in Sch 19C para 12(1): see Sch 19C para 29 (as so added). A stop notice ceases to have effect on the issue of a completion certificate relating to that notice: Sch 19C para 12(2) (as so added). A person on whom a stop notice is served may at any time apply for a completion certificate; and the Commission must make a decision whether to issue a completion certificate within 14 days of the day on which it receives such an application: Sch 19C para 12(3) (as so added). A person served with a stop notice may appeal against a decision not to issue a completion certificate: see Sch 19C para 13(2), (3) (as so added). An appeal under Sch 19C para 13(2) against a decision not to issue a completion certificate must be made within 28 days of the day on which notification of the decision was received: Political Parties, Elections and Referendums (Civil Sanctions) Order 2010, SI 2010/2860, Sch 1 para 12(2). As to the county court's powers on such an appeal see art 8(3). Where an appeal under the Political Parties, Elections and Referendums Act 2000 Sch 19C para 13(2) is made, the stop notice is not suspended unless suspended or varied on the order of the county court: Political Parties, Elections and Referendums (Civil Sanctions) Order 2010, SI 2010/2860, art 8(1). As to applications for, and the Commission's powers to revoke, completion certificates see further Sch 1 paras 10–11.

    As from a day to be appointed under the Crime and Courts Act 2013 s 61(3), the Political Parties, Elections and Referendums Act 2000 Sch 19C para 13(3) is amended by the Crime and Courts Act 2013 s 17(5), Sch 9 Pt 3 para 121(d). However, at the date at which this volume states the law, no such day had been appointed.

13 Political Parties, Elections and Referendums Act 2000 Sch 19C para 14 (as added: see note 2).

14 Political Parties, Elections and Referendums Act 2000 s 150, Sch 20 (Sch 20 amended by the Political Parties and Elections Act 2009 s 3(3)). A person guilty of such an offence is liable, on summary conviction, to a fine not exceeding £20,000 or 12 months imprisonment, or both, and (on conviction on indictment) to a fine or up to two years imprisonment, or both: see the Political Parties, Elections and Referendums Act 2000 s 150, Sch 20 (Sch 20 as so amended). As to summary proceedings for offences committed under the Political Parties, Elections and Referendums Act 2000 see PARA 892; and as to offences under the Political Parties, Elections and Referendums Act 2000 committed by bodies corporate or unincorporated associations see PARA 893.

760.   Commission's power to accept enforcement undertakings.   Where:

(1)   the Electoral Commission[1] has reasonable grounds to suspect that a person[2]:

    (a)   has committed a prescribed offence under the Political Parties, Elections and Referendums Act 2000[3]; or

    (b)   has (otherwise than by committing an offence under the Act) contravened a prescribed restriction or requirement imposed by or by virtue of the Political Parties, Elections and Referendums Act 2000[4];

(2)   the person offers an undertaking (an 'enforcement undertaking') to take such action, within such period, as is specified in the undertaking[5];

(3)   the action so specified is:

    (a)   action to secure that the offence or contravention does not continue or recur[6];

    (b)   action to secure that the position is, so far as possible, restored to what it would have been if the offence or contravention had not happened[7]; or

    (c)   action of a prescribed description[8]; and

  (4)   the Commission accepts the undertaking[9],

then, unless the person has failed to comply with the undertaking or any part of it[10]:

    (i)   the person may not at any time be convicted of an offence under the Political Parties, Elections and Referendums Act 2000 in respect of the act or omission to which the undertaking relates[11];

    (ii)   the Commission may not impose on the person any fixed monetary penalty[12] that it would otherwise have power to impose[13] in respect of that act or omission[14];

    (iii)   the Commission may not impose on the person any discretionary requirement[15] that it would otherwise have power to impose[16] in respect of that act or omission[17].

Where, after accepting an enforcement undertaking from a person, the Commission is satisfied that the undertaking has been complied with in full it must issue a certificate to that effect[18].

1   As to the establishment and constitution of the Electoral Commission see PARA 34 et seq.

2   See the Political Parties, Elections and Referendums Act 2000 s 147, Sch 19C para 15(1) (s 147 substituted, Sch 19C added, by the Political Parties and Elections Act 2009 s 3(1), (2), Sch 2). As to disclosure to the Commission of information held by or on behalf of the Crown Prosecution Service, or a member of a police force in England and Wales, for the purpose of the exercise by the Commission of any powers conferred on them under or by virtue of the Political Parties, Elections and Referendums Act 2000 Sch 19C see Sch 19C para 28 (as so added). As to the scheme laid down in Sch 19C see PARA 757 note 2.

3   Political Parties, Elections and Referendums Act 2000 Sch 19C para 15(1)(a)(i) (as added: see note 2). 'Prescribed' means prescribed in a supplementary order (which has the meaning given in Sch 19C para 16(1): see PARA 757 note 2): see Sch 19C para 29 (as so added). As to the offences prescribed for the purposes of Sch 19C para 15(1)(a)(i) see the Political Parties, Elections and Referendums (Civil Sanctions) Order 2010, SI 2010/2860, art 4(1), Sch 2 Pt 1.

4   Political Parties, Elections and Referendums Act 2000 Sch 19C para 15(1)(a)(ii) (as added: see note 2). As to the restrictions and requirements prescribed for the purposes of Sch 19C para 15(1)(a)(ii) see the Political Parties, Elections and Referendums (Civil Sanctions) Order 2010, SI 2010/2860, art 4(2), Sch 2 Pt 2.

5   Political Parties, Elections and Referendums Act 2000 Sch 19C para 15(1)(b) (as added: see note 2). 'Enforcement undertaking' has the meaning given in Sch 19C para 15(1)(b): see Sch 19C para 29 (as so added). As to the contents of an enforcement undertaking see the Political Parties, Elections and Referendums (Civil Sanctions) Order 2010, SI 2010/2860, Sch 1 para 13. The Commission may publish any enforcement undertaking which it accepts in whatever manner it sees fit: Sch 1 para 14.

6   Political Parties, Elections and Referendums Act 2000 Sch 19C para 15(1)(c)(i) (as added: see note 2).

7   Political Parties, Elections and Referendums Act 2000 Sch 19C para 15(1)(c)(ii) (as added: see note 2).

8   Political Parties, Elections and Referendums Act 2000 Sch 19C para 15(1)(c)(iii) (as added: see note 2).

9   Political Parties, Elections and Referendums Act 2000 Sch 19C para 15(1)(d) (as added: see note 2).

10 See the Political Parties, Elections and Referendums Act 2000 Sch 19C para 15(2) (as added: see note 2).

11 Political Parties, Elections and Referendums Act 2000 Sch 19C para 15(2)(a) (as added: see note 2).

12 As to the meaning of 'fixed monetary penalty' for these purposes see PARA 757 note 2.

13 Ie by virtue of the Political Parties, Elections and Referendums Act 2000 Sch 19C para 1 (see PARA 757): see Sch 19C para 15(2)(b) (as added: see note 2).

14 Political Parties, Elections and Referendums Act 2000 Sch 19C para 15(2)(b) (as added: see note 2).

15 As to the meaning of 'discretionary requirement' for these purposes see PARA 758 note 2.

16 Ie by virtue of the Political Parties, Elections and Referendums Act 2000 Sch 19C para 5 (see PARA 758): see Sch 19C para 15(2)(c) (as added: see note 2).

17 Political Parties, Elections and Referendums Act 2000 Sch 19C para 15(2)(c) (as added: see note 2).

18 Political Parties, Elections and Referendums (Civil Sanctions) Order 2010, SI 2010/2860, Sch 1 para 15(1). An enforcement undertaking ceases to have effect on the issue of a certificate relating to that undertaking: Sch 1 para 15(2). A person who has given an enforcement undertaking may at any time apply for a certificate, and the Commission must make a decision whether to issue a certificate within 28 days of the day on which it receives such an application: Sch 1 para 15(3). As to such applications see further Sch 1 para 15(4), (5). The Commission may revoke a certificate if it was granted on the basis of inaccurate, incomplete or misleading information, and if the Commission revokes a certificate, the enforcement undertaking has effect as if the certificate had not been issued: Sch 1 para 15(6). A person who has given an enforcement undertaking may, within 28 days of the day on which notification of the decision was received, appeal to a county court against a decision not to issue a certificate under Sch 1 para 15: Sch 1 para 16(1), (2). As to the county court's powers on such an appeal see art 8(3). As to the guidance that must be prepared and published by the Commission in relation to its powers of enforcement see the Political Parties, Elections and Referendums Act 2000 Sch 19C para 25 (as added: see note 2). Each report by the Commission under Sch 1 para 20 (see PARA 46) must contain information about the use made by the Commission of their powers under Sch 19C during the year in question: see Sch 19C para 27 (as so added).

(3) QUESTIONING ELECTIONS AND REFERENDUMS

(i) Method and Regulation of Procedure

761. Questioning parliamentary elections. No parliamentary election[1] and no return to Parliament[2] may be questioned except by a petition (a 'parliamentary election petition')[3] complaining of an undue election or undue return, which is presented in accordance with the statutory provisions[4].

The Representation of the People Act 1983 does not define what is meant by an undue election or undue return, but a number of the provisions of that Act provide that a parliamentary election may be avoided for corrupt or illegal practices or similar offences[5]. The occurrence of these offences may form the ground for bringing an election petition. Further, certain persons are disqualified from being candidates at parliamentary elections[6], and if such a person is elected, his election can only be questioned by an election petition[7]. A returning officer's decision that a nomination paper is invalid can be questioned on an election petition[8]. Other objections to a candidate's nomination can also be considered on an election petition[9]. When the result of the poll has been ascertained it is the returning officer's duty forthwith to declare the candidate to whom the majority of votes have been given to be elected[10]. If it is alleged that there has been a miscount, a petition may be brought demanding a recount[11]; if it is contended that votes were wrongly admitted or rejected, a petition may claim the seat for an unsuccessful candidate on the ground that he had a majority of lawful votes[12]. No parliamentary election is to be declared invalid by reason of any act or omission by the returning officer or any other person in breach of his official duty in connection with the election or otherwise of the parliamentary elections rules if it appears to the tribunal having cognisance of the question that the election was so conducted as to be substantially in accordance with the law as to elections and the act or omission did not affect the result[13].

A petition complaining of no return is deemed to be a parliamentary election petition, and the High Court may make such order on the petition as it thinks expedient for compelling a return to be made or it may allow the petition to be heard by an election court[14] as provided with respect to ordinary election petitions[15].

1   As to the meaning of 'parliamentary election' see PARA 9.
2   The distinction drawn by the statute between a petition questioning a parliamentary election and one questioning a return to Parliament does not appear in relation to a petition questioning an election under the Local Government Act 1972: see PARA 762.
3   For these purposes, 'election petition' means a petition presented in pursuance of the Representation of the People Act 1983 Pt III (ss 120–186) (legal proceedings): s 202(1).
4   Representation of the People Act 1983 s 120(1). The text refers to the provisions of Pt III. As to the application of Pt III to other polls see PARA 763.
5   As to illegal practices (including those which are also offences) see PARA 671 et seq; as to corrupt practices (including those which are also offences) see PARA 704 et seq, and as to the consequences of such practices see PARA 887 et seq. As to corruption generally see PARA 895; and as to employment of a corrupt agent see PARA 896.
6   As to disqualification for membership of the House of Commons (and therefore for candidacy at parliamentary elections) see PARA 224.
7   See e g *Galway County Case* (1872) 2 O'M & H 46; *Tipperary County Case* (1875) 3 O'M & H 19. The returning officer cannot hold a nomination paper invalid on the ground of the candidate's disqualification unless the rules so provide: see PARA 263. As to votes regarded as thrown away see PARA 845.
8   See the Representation of the People Act 1983 s 23(1), Sch 1 r 12(6); and PARA 263. See also *R v Dublin Town Clerk* (1909) 43 ILT 169. A returning officer's decision that a nomination paper is valid is final: see the Representation of the People Act 1983 Sch 1 r 12(5); and PARA 263.
9   See the Representation of the People Act 1983 Sch 1 r 12(6); and PARA 263. Notwithstanding the different statutory wording on which the cases were decided, see *Monks v Jackson* (1876) 1 CPD 683; *Brown v Benn* (1889) 53 JP 167, DC; *Boyce v White* (1905) 92 LT 240, DC.
10   See the Representation of the People Act 1983 Sch 1 r 50(1); and PARA 479.
11   See e g *Renfrew County Case* (1874) 2 O'M & H 213; *Halifax Case* (1893) 9 TLR 563, 4 O'M & H 203; *Lancaster County, North Lonsdale Division Case* (1910) 6 O'M & H 97; *Wiltshire, North Western Chippenham Division Case* (1911) 6 O'M & H 99; *Mile End Division, Tower Hamlets, Case* (1911) 6 O'M & H 100; *Gloucester Borough Case, Lynch v Terrell* (1911) 6 O'M & H 101; *St Pancras, West Division Case* (1911) 6 O'M & H 102. As to applications for a recount see PARAS 855–856.
12   *Taunton Case, Williams and Mellor v Cox* (1869) 21 LT 169 at 173, 1 O'M & H 181 at 186; *York County West Riding, Southern Division Case* (1869) 1 O'M & H 213 at 215. As to the rejection of ballot papers see PARA 427 et seq.
13   See the Representation of the People Act 1983 s 23(3); and PARA 350.
14   For these purposes, 'election court' means, in relation to a parliamentary election petition, the judges presiding at the trial: Representation of the People Act 1983 s 202(1).
15   Representation of the People Act 1983 s 120(2).

762. Questioning local elections. An election under the Local Government Act 1972[1] may be questioned on the following grounds: (1) that the person whose election is questioned was, at the time of the election, disqualified[2]; or (2) that the person whose election is questioned was not duly elected[3]; or (3) that the election was avoided by corrupt or illegal practices[4]; or (4) that corrupt or illegal practices or illegal payments, employments or hirings, committed with reference to the election for the purpose of promoting or procuring the election of any person, have so extensively prevailed that they may be reasonably supposed to have affected the result[5]; or (5) that the candidate or his election agent personally engaged, as a canvasser or agent for the conduct or management of the election, any person whom he knew or had reasonable grounds for supposing to be subject to an incapacity to vote at the election by reason of his having been convicted of certain corrupt or illegal practices[6]. An election under the Local Government Act 1972 must not be questioned on any of these grounds except by an election petition[7]. A returning officer's decision that a nomination paper is invalid[8] can be questioned on an election petition[9]. Other objections to a candidate's nomination have also been considered on an election petition[10]. An election under the Local Government Act 1972 can be declared invalid on the ground of irregularities on the part of election officials if it appears to the court that the election was not so conducted as to be substantially in accordance with the law as to elections or that the irregularities affected the result[11].

1   As to the meaning of 'election under the Local Government Act 1972' see PARA 11 note 2. As to elections in the City of London see PARA 33. As to the application of the Representation of the People Act 1983 Pt III (ss 120–186) to other polls see PARA 763.
2   Representation of the People Act 1983 s 127(a). As to disqualification for being elected to local government office see LOCAL GOVERNMENT vol 69 (2009) PARA 119.
3   Representation of the People Act 1983 s 127(b). This covers claims for a scrutiny (see PARA 839 et seq) or for a recount (see PARAS 855–856): see *Greenock Case* (1892) Day 20.
4   Representation of the People Act 1983 s 127. As to the avoidance of elections where the elected candidate has been reported guilty of corrupt or illegal practices see PARA 894.
5   See the Representation of the People Act 1983 s 164; and PARA 895 (provisions applied by s 127).
6   See the Representation of the People Act 1983 s 165; and PARA 896 (provisions applied by s 127).
7   Representation of the People Act 1983 s 127; *R v Morton* [1892] 1 QB 39. The seat or office is, however, vacated if the successful candidate is convicted of a corrupt practice: see PARA 905.
8   As to questioning the validity of nomination papers see PARA 263.
9   See the Local Elections (Principal Areas) (England and Wales) Rules 2006, SI 2006/3304, r 3, Sch 2 r 8(8); the Local Elections (Parishes and Communities) (England and Wales) Rules 2006, SI 2006/3305, r 3, Sch 2 r 8(8); and PARA 263.
10   See *Brown v Benn* (1889) 53 JP 167; *Boyce v White* (1905) 92 LT 240, DC. The wording of the statutory provisions on which those cases were decided was, however, different from that of the current provisions (see note 9).
11   See the Representation of the People Act 1983 s 48(1); and PARA 354. See also *Morgan v Simpson* [1975] QB 151, [1974] 3 All ER 722, CA; *Ruffle v Rogers* [1982] QB 1220, [1982] 3 All ER 157, CA.

763.   Application of provisions relating to questioning parliamentary and local elections to other polls.   The statutory provisions relating to parliamentary and local election petitions[1], so far as they apply to the election of parish or community councillors or of the chairman of a parish or community council[2], have effect subject to such adaptations, modifications and exceptions as may be made by rules made by the Secretary of State[3]. The statutory provisions relating to the questioning of elections[4] apply also to the election of the chairman of a parish meeting, and to a poll consequent on a parish or community meeting relating to appointment to any other office, as though they were polls for elections of parish or community councillors, subject to certain modifications and adaptations[5].

No return of an elected mayor or elected executive member at an election[6] is to be questioned except by an election petition under the provisions of the Representation of the People Act 1983[7] as applied by or incorporated in regulations made for the purpose[8].

The provision made for the questioning of an election under the Local Government Act 1972 is applied and modified also for the purpose of questioning a local authority referendum[9].

1   Ie the provisions of the Representation of the People Act 1983 Pt III (ss 120–186) (legal proceedings).
2   As to the election of councillors for parish or community councils and of the chairman for parish meetings generally see PARA 200. As to parish meetings see further the text and notes 4–5. As to elections in the City of London see PARA 33.

3   Representation of the People Act 1983 s 187(1)(b) (amended by the Representation of the People Act 1985 s 24, Sch 4 para 64). As to the Secretary of State see PARA 2. The reference in the text is to rules under the Representation of the People Act 1983 s 36 (see PARA 383). The only modifications so made under the current rules are, in the case of parish or community elections, a reduction in the amount of the security which a petitioner must give for costs (see PARA 796) and the substitution of references to the returning officer for references to the proper officer of the authority: see the Local Elections (Parishes and Communities) (England and Wales) Rules 2006, SI 2006/3305, r 6. As to the returning officer at a parish or community council election see PARA 354.

4   See note 1.

5   Representation of the People Act 1983 s 187(1) (as amended: see note 3); Local Government Act 1972 s 99, Sch 12 paras 18(5), 34(5) (amended by the Representation of the People Act 1983 s 206, Sch 8 para 14); Parish and Community Meetings (Polls) Rules 1987, SI 1987/1, r 6. The provisions referred to in the Representation of the People Act 1983 s 187(1) are applied to such an election and to such polls as are mentioned in the text subject to the modifications that: (1) references to the proper officer of the authority for which the election was held are to be taken as references to the returning officer (Parish and Community Meetings (Polls) Rules 1987, SI 1987/1, r 6(b)); (2) references to the authority for which the election was held are to be taken as references to the parish and references to the area thereof are to be construed accordingly, except that in the Representation of the People Act 1983 s 130(6) (place of trial of petition: see PARA 806) for the words 'area of authority for which the election was held' there is to be substituted 'district in which the parish is situate' (Parish and Community Meetings (Polls) Rules 1987, SI 1987/1, r 6(c)); (3) the amount of security for costs is reduced (see PARA 796) (r 6(f)); and (4) references to an election under the local government Act are to be deemed to include a reference to a poll consequent on a parish or community meeting (r 6(g)). As to the rules for polls consequent on a parish or community meeting generally see PARA 383. As to the meaning of 'election under the local government Act' see PARA 11 note 2.

     Although all polls consequent on a parish or community meeting must be conducted by ballot (see the Local Government Act 1972 Sch 12 para 18(5), 34(5); and LOCAL GOVERNMENT vol 69 (2009) PARA 638), not all such polls relate to the election of officials, to which alone the statutory provisions as to the questioning of elections apply and the provisions do not apply to polls on a question other than a question of appointment to an office: Parish and Community Meetings (Polls) Rules 1987, SI 1987/1, r 6(a). As to the election of the chairman of a parish meeting see the Local Government Act 1972 ss 15(10), 88(3), Sch 12 paras 17, 33; and see PARA 200. Although Sch 12 para 17(3) refers to the appointment of the chairman of a parish meeting and Sch 12 para 17(2) to the chairman being chosen, it is submitted that it is not intended to draw a distinction between his election and his being appointed or chosen: see the Representation of the People Act 1983 s 187(1). A parish or community meeting may have the right to elect to other offices, such as that of a charity trustee: see CHARITIES vol 8 (2010) PARA 265.

6   As to the meanings of 'elected executive member' and 'elected mayor' see LOCAL GOVERNMENT vol 69 (2009) PARA 320. As to elections for the return of a local authority mayor see PARA 198 et seq. See also the Local Government Act 2000 s 9HE (added by the Localism Act 2011 s 21, Sch 2 Pt 1 para 1) under which regulations may make provision as to the conduct of elections for the return of elected mayors, and the questioning of elections for the return of elected mayors and the consequences of irregularities. At the date at which this volume states the law no such regulations had been made: see PARA 383. At the date at which this volume states the law, no provision had been made in relation to the return of executive members in England and Wales.

7   See note 1.

8   See the Local Government Act 2000 s 44(4); and LOCAL GOVERNMENT vol 69 (2009) PARA 320. Accordingly, for the purposes of s 44(4), the Representation of the People Act 1983 Pt III has effect in relation to the questioning of an election for the return of an elected mayor as it has effect in relation to the questioning of an election under the local government Act: Local Authorities (Mayoral Elections) (England and Wales) Regulations 2007, SI 2007/1024, reg 5.

9   See the Local Authorities (Conduct of Referendums) (Wales) Regulations 2008, SI 2008/1848, regs 8, 11(7), (8), Sch 4 Table 1, Sch 5; the Local Authorities (Conduct of Referendums) (England) Regulations 2012, SI 2012/323, regs 8, 15(7), (8), Sch 4 Table 1, Sch 6; and PARA 766.

764. Questioning Welsh Assembly elections.   No Welsh Assembly election[1] and no return[2] to the National Assembly for Wales may be questioned except by a petition complaining of an undue election or undue return (an 'Assembly election petition')[3] presented in accordance with the statutory provisions[4].

A petition complaining of no return is deemed to be an Assembly election petition and the High Court may make such order on the petition as it thinks expedient for compelling a return to be made[5] or may allow the petition to be heard by an election court[6] as provided with respect to ordinary Assembly election petitions[7]. A Welsh Assembly election can be declared invalid on the ground of irregularities on the part of election officials if it appears to the court that the election was not so conducted as to be substantially in accordance with the law as to elections or that the irregularities affected the result[8].

1   As to the meaning of 'Assembly election' in the context of Welsh Assembly elections see PARA 3 note 2.

2   For these purposes, the expression 'return' as the context requires refers to a return following an Assembly election and 'vacancy return' refers to a return in respect of a vacancy in an electoral region (see PARA 215): National Assembly for Wales (Representation of the People) Order 2007, SI 2007/236, art 86(3).

3   'Assembly election petition' includes a petition complaining of an undue return in respect of a vacancy in an electoral region (see PARA 215): National Assembly for Wales (Representation of the People) Order 2007, SI 2007/236, art 86(1).

4   National Assembly for Wales (Representation of the People) Order 2007, SI 2007/236, art 86(1). The text refers to the provisions of Pt 4 (arts 86–138) (see also PARA 767 et seq).

5   National Assembly for Wales (Representation of the People) Order 2007, SI 2007/236, art 86(2)(a).

6   For these purposes, 'election court' means the judges presiding at the trial of an Assembly election petition: National Assembly for Wales (Representation of the People) Order 2007, SI 2007/236, art 2(1).

7   National Assembly for Wales (Representation of the People) Order 2007, SI 2007/236, art 86(2)(b).

8   See the National Assembly for Wales (Representation of the People) Order 2007, SI 2007/236, art 17(3); and PARA 357.

765.   Questioning European parliamentary elections.   No European parliamentary election[1] and no declaration of the result by the returning officer[2] may be questioned except by a petition complaining of an undue election or undue declaration (a 'European parliamentary election petition') presented in accordance with the statutory provisions[3].

A petition complaining that no declaration of the result has been given by the returning officer is deemed to be a European parliamentary election petition and the High Court may make such order on the petition as it thinks expedient for compelling a declaration of the result to be made[4] or it may allow the petition to be heard by an election court as provided with respect to ordinary European parliamentary election petitions[5].

No European parliamentary election petition may be brought on the grounds of the commission of corrupt or illegal practices, except on grounds of personation or other voting offences[6], or where an application may be made[7] for a declaration that a person who purports to be a member of the European Parliament ('MEP') for a particular electoral region is disqualified or was so disqualified at the time when, or at some time since, he was returned as an MEP[8]. A European parliamentary election can be declared invalid on the ground of irregularities on the part of election officials if it appears to the court that the election was not so conducted as to be substantially in accordance with the law as to elections or that the irregularities affected the result[9].

1   As to European parliamentary elections see PARA 217 et seq.

2   Ie under the European Parliamentary Elections Regulations 2004, SI 2004/293, reg 9(1), Sch 1 para 56 (see PARA 470).
3   European Parliamentary Elections Regulations 2004, SI 2004/293, reg 88(1). The text refers to the provisions of Pt 4 (regs 86–122) (see PARA 767 et seq).
4   European Parliamentary Elections Regulations 2004, SI 2004/293, reg 88(2)(a).
5   European Parliamentary Elections Regulations 2004, SI 2004/293, reg 88(2)(b).
6   European Parliamentary Elections Regulations 2004, SI 2004/293, reg 88(3). The text refers to the grounds of the commission of corrupt or illegal practices set out in reg 23 (personation: see PARA 730) and reg 24 (voting offences which are illegal practices: see PARA 700).
7   Ie under the European Parliamentary Elections Act 2002 s 11 (see PARA 228).
8   European Parliamentary Elections Regulations 2004, SI 2004/293, reg 88(4).
9   See the European Parliamentary Elections Regulations 2004, SI 2004/293, reg 9(5); and PARA 360.

766.   Questioning local authority referendums. A local authority referendum[1] may be questioned by petition (a 'referendum petition'): (1) on the ground that the result of the referendum was not in accordance with the votes cast[2]; (2) on the ground that the referendum was avoided by corrupt or illegal practices[3]; (3) on the grounds that corrupt or illegal practices or illegal payments, employments or hirings, committed with reference to the referendum for the purpose of promoting or procuring a particular result in the referendum, have so extensively prevailed that they may be reasonably supposed to have affected the result[4]; or (4) subject to head (3) above, on the ground that a payment of money or other reward has been made or promised since the referendum in pursuance of a corrupt or illegal practice relevant to local authority referendums[5]. Certain provisions of the Representation of the People Act 1983[6] which apply to the questioning of an election under the Local Government Act 1972[7] have effect, subject to minor modification, in relation to the questioning of a local authority referendum[8].

Where a referendum petition is presented on any of the grounds specified in heads (1) to (3) above (or where leave is granted for the presentation of a referendum petition brought under the ground mentioned in head (4)) in relation to a local authority referendum at which the question asked relates to proposals involving governance arrangements[9] and in which the majority of the votes cast are in favour of the authority operating arrangements which differ from their existing arrangements[10], then: (a) if the petition is presented before the authority has passed the resolution required enabling it to operate the executive arrangements that were the subject of the referendum[11], the authority must take no further steps in consequence of the referendum until the election court has certified its determination in the matter of the referendum petition[12]; and (b) if the petition is presented after the authority has passed the resolution so required[13], the authority must continue to operate the arrangements that are the subject of that resolution[14].

Where a referendum petition is presented on any of the grounds specified in heads (1) to (3) above (or where leave is granted for the presentation of a referendum petition brought under the ground mentioned in head (4)) in relation to a local authority referendum at which the question asked relates to proposals involving either a mayor or elected councillors[15] and in which the majority of the votes cast are in favour of the authority operating arrangements which differ from their existing arrangements[16], and without an election for the return of an elected mayor having taken place in consequence of the referendum[17], the local authority must take no further steps in consequence of the referendum until the election court has certified its determination in the matter of the referendum petition[18]. Where leave is granted for the presentation of a referendum petition at which the question asked relates to proposals involving either a mayor or elected councillors[19] and in which the majority of the votes cast are in favour of the authority operating arrangements which differ from its existing arrangements[20], and after an election for the return of an elected mayor has taken place in consequence of the referendum[21], the elected mayor is to continue in office[22].

In relation to Wales only, where a referendum petition is presented on any of the grounds specified in heads (1) to (3) above (or where leave is granted for the presentation of a referendum petition brought under the ground mentioned in head (4)) in relation to a local authority referendum in which the majority of the votes cast are 'no' votes, and where the local authority's outline fall-back proposals[23] are based on the executive or alternative arrangements[24] which it was operating at the date of the referendum, it must continue to operate those arrangements[25]. However, where a referendum petition is presented on any of the grounds specified in heads (1) to (3) above (or where leave is granted for the presentation of a referendum petition) in relation to a referendum in which the majority of the votes cast are 'no' votes: (i) if the petition is presented before the local authority has passed the resolution required enabling it to operate either the executive arrangements that were the subject of the referendum[26] or the existing alternative arrangements[27], the local authority must take no further steps in consequence of the referendum until the election court has certified its determination in the matter of the referendum petition[28]; and (ii) if the petition is presented after the local authority has passed either such resolution[29], the local authority must continue to operate the executive arrangements or, as the case may be, the alternative arrangements that are the subject of that resolution[30].

1   Ie a referendum held, in relation to Wales, under the Local Authorities (Conduct of Referendums) (Wales) Regulations 2008, SI 2008/1848, or, in relation to England, under the Local Authorities (Conduct of Referendums) (England) Regulations 2012, SI 2012/323. As to the meaning of 'referendum' for these purposes see PARA 574 note 2.

2   Local Authorities (Conduct of Referendums) (Wales) Regulations 2008, SI 2008/1848, reg 11(1)(a); Local Authorities (Conduct of Referendums) (England) Regulations 2012, SI 2012/323, reg 15(1)(a).

3   Local Authorities (Conduct of Referendums) (Wales) Regulations 2008, SI 2008/1848, reg 11(1)(b); Local Authorities (Conduct of Referendums) (England) Regulations 2012, SI 2012/323, reg 15(1)(b). The text refers to such corrupt or illegal practices within the meaning of the Representation of the People Act 1983 as are relevant to referendums, in relation to Wales, by virtue of the Local Authorities (Conduct of Referendums) (Wales) Regulations 2008, SI 2008/1848, regs 8, 11(8), or, in relation to England, by virtue of the Local Authorities (Conduct of Referendums) (England) Regulations 2012, SI 2012/323, regs 8, 11, 13, 15(8) (see the text and notes 6–8).

4   Local Authorities (Conduct of Referendums) (Wales) Regulations 2008, SI 2008/1848, reg 11(1)(c); Local Authorities (Conduct of Referendums) (England) Regulations 2012, SI 2012/323, reg 15(1)(c). The text refers to the grounds provided by the Representation of the People Act 1983 s 164 (avoidance of election for general corruption etc: see PARA 895), as applied for these purposes, in relation to Wales, by the Local Authorities (Conduct of Referendums) (Wales) Regulations 2008, SI 2008/1848, reg 11(8), and, in relation to England, by the Local Authorities (Conduct of Referendums) (England) Regulations 2012, SI 2012/323, reg 15(8) (see the text and notes 6–8).

5   Local Authorities (Conduct of Referendums) (Wales) Regulations 2008, SI 2008/1848, reg 11(1)(d); Local Authorities (Conduct of Referendums) (England) Regulations 2012, SI 2012/323, reg 15(1)(d). The text refers to a corrupt or illegal practice relevant to referendums, in relation to Wales, by virtue of the Local Authorities (Conduct of Referendums) (Wales) Regulations 2008, SI 2008/1848, regs 8, 11(8), or, in relation to England, by virtue of the Local Authorities (Conduct of Referendums) (England) Regulations 2012, SI 2012/323, regs 8, 11, 13, 15(8) (see the text and notes 6–8).

6   Ie certain provisions of the Representation of the People Act 1983 Pt III (ss 120–186) (legal proceedings) as set out, in relation to Wales, in the Local Authorities (Conduct of Referendums)

(Wales) Regulations 2008, SI 2008/1848, reg 11(8), Sch 5, or, in relation to England, in the Local Authorities (Conduct of Referendums) (England) Regulations 2012, SI 2012/323, reg 15(8), Sch 6.

7   As to the questioning of an election under the Local Government Act 1972 see PARA 762. As to the meaning of 'election under the Local Government Act 1972' see PARA 11 note 2.

8   Local Authorities (Conduct of Referendums) (Wales) Regulations 2008, SI 2008/1848, reg 11(8), Sch 5; Local Authorities (Conduct of Referendums) (England) Regulations 2012, SI 2012/323, reg 15(8), Sch 6.

9   Ie if the question was in the form set out, in relation to England, in the Local Authorities (Conduct of Referendums) (England) Regulations 2012, SI 2012/323, Sch 1 para 3, 4, 5 or 6. In relation to Wales, the question asked relates to proposals involving a leader and cabinet executive in the form set out in the Local Authorities (Conduct of Referendums) (Wales) Regulations 2008, SI 2008/1848, Sch 1 para 3 (see PARA 575). As to the meaning of 'leader and cabinet executive' see LOCAL GOVERNMENT vol 69 (2009) PARA 327.

10 See the Local Authorities (Conduct of Referendums) (Wales) Regulations 2008, SI 2008/1848, reg 12(1)(a), (2)(a); and the Local Authorities (Conduct of Referendums) (England) Regulations 2012, SI 2012/323, reg 16(1)(a), (2)(a) (referred to as 'yes votes').

11 Local Authorities (Conduct of Referendums) (Wales) Regulations 2008, SI 2008/1848, reg 12(1)(b); Local Authorities (Conduct of Referendums) (England) Regulations 2012, SI 2012/323, reg 16(1)(b). The text refers to the resolution required, in relation to England under the Local Government Act 2000 s 9KC and, in relation to Wales under s 29 (see LOCAL GOVERNMENT vol 69 (2009) PARA 309): see PARA 653.

12 Local Authorities (Conduct of Referendums) (Wales) Regulations 2008, SI 2008/1848, reg 12(1); Local Authorities (Conduct of Referendums) (England) Regulations 2012, SI 2012/323, reg 16(1).

13 Local Authorities (Conduct of Referendums) (Wales) Regulations 2008, SI 2008/1848, reg 12(3)(b); Local Authorities (Conduct of Referendums) (England) Regulations 2012, SI 2012/323, reg 16(3)(b).

14 Local Authorities (Conduct of Referendums) (Wales) Regulations 2008, SI 2008/1848, reg 12(3); Local Authorities (Conduct of Referendums) (England) Regulations 2012, SI 2012/323, reg 16(3).

15 Ie, in relation to Wales, if the question asked relates to proposals involving either a mayor and cabinet executive or a mayor and council manager executive, in the form set out in the Local Authorities (Conduct of Referendums) (Wales) Regulations 2008, SI 2008/1848, Sch 1 para 1, 2, or, in relation to England, in the form set out in the Local Authorities (Conduct of Referendums) (England) Regulations 2012, SI 2012/323, Sch 1 para 1 or 2 (see PARA 575). As to the meaning of 'mayor and cabinet executive' see LOCAL GOVERNMENT vol 69 (2009) PARA 327.

16 Local Authorities (Conduct of Referendums) (Wales) Regulations 2008, SI 2008/1848, reg 12(4)(a); Local Authorities (Conduct of Referendums) (England) Regulations 2012, SI 2012/323, reg 16(4)(a) (referred to as 'yes votes').

17 Local Authorities (Conduct of Referendums) (Wales) Regulations 2008, SI 2008/1848, reg 12(4)(b); Local Authorities (Conduct of Referendums) (England) Regulations 2012, SI 2012/323, reg 16(4)(b).

18 Local Authorities (Conduct of Referendums) (Wales) Regulations 2008, SI 2008/1848, reg 12(4); Local Authorities (Conduct of Referendums) (England) Regulations 2012, SI 2012/323, reg 16(4).

19 See note 15.

20 Local Authorities (Conduct of Referendums) (Wales) Regulations 2008, SI 2008/1848, reg 12(8)(a); Local Authorities (Conduct of Referendums) (England) Regulations 2012, SI 2012/323, reg 16(5)(a).

21 Local Authorities (Conduct of Referendums) (Wales) Regulations 2008, SI 2008/1848, reg 12(8)(b); Local Authorities (Conduct of Referendums) (England) Regulations 2012, SI 2012/323, reg 16(5)(b).

22 Local Authorities (Conduct of Referendums) (Wales) Regulations 2008, SI 2008/1848, reg 12(8); Local Authorities (Conduct of Referendums) (England) Regulations 2012, SI 2012/323, reg 16(5).

23 As to the meaning of 'outline fall-back proposals' in relation to Wales see PARA 574 note 16.

24 As to the meaning of 'existing executive arrangements' see PARA 561 note 10. As to alternative arrangements see LOCAL GOVERNMENT vol 69 (2009) PARA 364.

25 Local Authorities (Conduct of Referendums) (Wales) Regulations 2008, SI 2008/1848, reg 12(5).

26 Ie the resolution required under the Local Government Act 2000 s 29 (see LOCAL GOVERNMENT vol 69 (2009) PARA 309): see PARA 653.

27 Ie the resolution required under the Local Government Act 2000 s 33: see LOCAL GOVERNMENT vol 69 (2009) PARA 366.

28 Local Authorities (Conduct of Referendums) (Wales) Regulations 2008, SI 2008/1848, reg 12(6).

29 See notes 26, 27.

30 Local Authorities (Conduct of Referendums) (Wales) Regulations 2008, SI 2008/1848, reg 12(7).

767. Election petition rules. The authority having power to make rules of court for the Senior Courts may make rules for the purposes of election petitions[1].

Subject to the provisions of the Representation of the People Act 1983[2] (and, in relation to a Welsh Assembly election, the rules provided as to the conduct of elections for the return of Assembly members[3] and, in relation to a European parliamentary election, the European parliamentary elections rules[4]) and subject to the rules governing the procedure for petitions[5], the practice and procedure of the High Court apply to a petition as if it were an ordinary claim within the High Court's jurisdiction, notwithstanding any different practice, principle or rule on which the committees of the House of Commons used to act in dealing with such petitions[6].

1 Representation of the People Act 1983 s 182(1) (amended by the Constitutional Reform Act 2005 s 59(5), Sch 11 para 28(1), (3)(a)); European Parliamentary Elections Regulations 2004, SI 2004/293, reg 120(1); National Assembly for Wales (Representation of the People) Order 2007, SI 2007/236, art 134(1). The rule-making power referred to in the text is exercisable by statutory instrument which is subject to annulment in pursuance of a resolution of either House of Parliament: Representation of the People Act 1983 s 182(2)(b); European Parliamentary Elections Regulations 2004, SI 2004/293, reg 120(2)(b); National Assembly for Wales (Representation of the People) Order 2007, SI 2007/236, art 134(2)(b). As respects parliamentary elections (see PARA 761) and elections under the Local Government Act 1972 (see PARA 762), the current rules are the Election Petition Rules 1960, SI 1960/543 (which have effect as if made under the Representation of the People Act 1983 s 182 by virtue of the Interpretation Act 1978 s 17(2)(b)). Those rules have effect in relation to a Welsh Assembly election petition (see PARA 764) as if made in the exercise of the power conferred by the National Assembly for Wales (Representation of the People) Order 2007, SI 2007/236, art 134(1), subject to the modifications set out in Sch 9: art 134(3). The Election Petition Rules 1960, SI 1960/543 also have effect in relation to a local authority referendum petition (see PARA 766) as they have effect in relation to a local election petition within the meaning of those rules subject to the modifications set out, in relation to Wales, in the Local Authorities (Conduct of Referendums) (Wales) Regulations 2008, SI 2008/1848, Sch 6 (see reg 11(9)), and, in relation to England, in the Local Authorities (Conduct of Referendums) (England) Regulations 2012, SI 2012/323, Sch 7 (see reg 15(9)). As respects European parliamentary elections (see PARA 765), the current rules are, by virtue of the Interpretation Act 1978 s 17(2)(b), the European Parliamentary Election Petition Rules 1979, SI 1979/521. For the purposes of the Statutory Instruments Act 1946 (see STATUTES AND LEGISLATIVE PROCESS vol 96 (2012) PARA 1045), this power is to be treated as if conferred on a minister of the Crown: Representation of the People Act 1983 s 182(2)(a); European Parliamentary Elections Regulations 2004, SI 2004/293, reg 120(2)(a); National Assembly for Wales (Representation of the People) Order 2007, SI 2007/236, art 134(2)(a). As to the application of the Representation of the People Act 1983 Pt III (ss 120–186) to other polls see PARA 763.

2 Ie including those provisions applied and modified for the purposes of a local authority referendum (see PARA 766).

3 Ie the National Assembly for Wales (Representation of the People) Order 2007, SI 2007/236 (see PARA 383).

4 As to the meaning of 'European parliamentary elections rules' see PARA 383.

5 See note 1.

6 Election Petition Rules 1960, SI 1960/543, r 2(4) (amended by SI 1999/1352); European Parliamentary Election Petition Rules 1979, SI 1979/521, r 2(3) (amended by SI 1999/1398; SI 2004/1415); and see note 3. As to the relevance of the principles, practice and rules on which committees of the House of Commons used to act see PARAS 771, 779, 817.

768. Mandatory time limits. Where the day or last day on which anything is required or permitted to be done by, or in pursuance of, the provisions governing the questioning of elections and referendums[1] is a Saturday or Sunday, Christmas Eve, Christmas Day, Good Friday, a bank holiday[2] or any day appointed for public thanksgiving or mourning, the requirement or permission is deemed to relate to the first day after that which is not one of those days[3]. In computing any period of not more than seven days, any of those days is to be disregarded[4].

Any period of time prescribed by the rules governing the procedure for petitions[5] for the purposes of: (1) applications made by the petitioner to fix the amount of security for costs which he is to give[6]; (2) service by the petitioner on the respondent[7] and on the Director of Public Prosecutions of a notice of the presentation of the petition and of the nature and amount of the security which he has given[8]; and (3) service by the respondent on the petitioner of any notice of his objection to a recognisance[9] and the issue and service on the petitioner of an application notice to determine the validity or otherwise of the objection[10], must be computed in accordance with the provisions set out above[11] and must not be varied by order or otherwise[12]. Accordingly, there is no scope available for a court to order service out of time under these provisions whose mandatory nature cannot be avoided[13] despite the draconian regime as regards time for service to which this gives rise[14].

Otherwise (that is, except for the purposes set out in heads (1) to (3) above) the relevant provisions of the Civil Procedure Rules[15] apply to any period of time prescribed by the rules which govern the procedure for petitions as if it were prescribed by the Civil Procedure Rules[16].

1 Ie, in relation to a parliamentary or local government election, the Representation of the People Act 1983 Pt III (ss 120–186) (including those provisions as applied and modified) or, in relation to a Welsh Assembly election, the National Assembly for Wales (Representation of the People) Order 2007, SI 2007/236, Pt 4 (arts 86–138) or, in relation to a European parliamentary election, the European Parliamentary Elections Regulations 2004, SI 2004/293, Pt 4 (regs 86–122).

2 As to the meaning of 'bank holiday' for these purposes see PARA 230 note 11.

3 Representation of the People Act 1983 s 186, applying s 119(1)(a), (2) (s 119(2) substituted by the Representation of the People Act 1985 s 19(4); and amended by the Electoral Administration Act 2006 ss 20, 74(2), Sch 1 paras 49, 51(1), Sch 2); in relation to a European parliamentary election, the European Parliamentary Elections Regulations 2004, SI 2004/293, reg 87, applying reg 32(1)(a), (2) (reg 32(2) amended by SI 2009/186), or, at a Welsh Assembly election, the National Assembly for Wales (Representation of the People) Order 2007, SI 2007/236, art 138, applying art 85(1)(a), (2). As to the application of the Representation of the People Act 1983 Pt III (ss 120–186) to other polls see PARA 763.

4 Representation of the People Act 1983 s 186, applying s 119(1)(b); European Parliamentary Elections Regulations 2004, SI 2004/293, reg 87, applying reg 32(1)(b); National Assembly for Wales (Representation of the People) Order 2007, SI 2007/236, art 138, applying art 85(1)(b); and see note 3.

5 As to the current rules see PARA 767 note 1.

6 Ie for the purposes of the Election Petition Rules 1960, SI 1960/543, r 5 or, in relation to a European parliamentary election, the European Parliamentary Election Petition Rules 1979, SI 1979/521, r 5 (see PARA 796). The text refers to the amount of security for costs which the petitioner is to give pursuant to the Representation of the People Act 1983 s 136, or, in relation to a European parliamentary election, the European Parliamentary Elections Regulations 2004, SI 2004/293, reg 94, or, in relation to a Welsh Assembly election, the National Assembly for Wales (Representation of the People) Order 2007, SI 2007/236, art 92 (see PARA 796).

7 Ie within the meaning of the Representation of the People Act 1983 s 121(2) (parliamentary election petition: see PARA 782) or s 128(2) (local election petition: see PARA 791) or, in relation to a European parliamentary election, the European Parliamentary Elections Regulations 2004, SI 2004/293, reg 89(2), or, in relation to a Welsh Assembly election, the National Assembly for Wales (Representation of the People) Order 2007, SI 2007/236, art 87(3), (4) (see PARA 782).

8   Ie for the purposes of the Election Petition Rules 1960, SI 1960/543, r 6 or, in relation to a
     European parliamentary election, the European Parliamentary Election Petition Rules 1979,
     SI 1979/521, r 6 (see PARA 798).
9   Ie on any ground mentioned in the Representation of the People Act 1983 s 136(4) or, in
     relation to a European parliamentary election, the European Parliamentary Elections
     Regulations 2004, SI 2004/293, reg 94(4), or, in relation to a Welsh Assembly election, the
     National Assembly for Wales (Representation of the People) Order 2007, SI 2007/236, art 92(4)
     (see PARA 799).
10   Ie for the purposes of the Election Petition Rules 1960, SI 1960/543, r 7 or, in relation to a
     European parliamentary election, the European Parliamentary Election Petition Rules 1979,
     SI 1979/521, r 7 (see PARA 799).
11   Ie in accordance with the Representation of the People Act 1983 s 119 or, in relation to a
     European parliamentary election, the European Parliamentary Elections Regulations 2004,
     SI 2004/293, reg 87.
12   Election Petition Rules 1960, SI 1960/543, r 19(1) (amended by SI 1985/1278; SI 1999/1352;
     SI 2003/972); European Parliamentary Election Petition Rules 1979, SI 1979/521, r 18(1)
     (amended by SI 1988/557; SI 1999/1398; SI 2003/971; SI 2004/1415). Where any period of time
     limited by the Representation of the People Act 1983 (or, in relation to a European
     parliamentary election, by the European parliamentary elections rules) for presenting a petition
     or filing any document expires on a day (not being a day mentioned in the Representation of the
     People Act 1983 s 119(2) or the European Parliamentary Elections Regulations 2004,
     SI 2004/293, reg 32(2), as the case may be) on which the election petitions office is closed, the
     petition or document is deemed to be duly presented or filed if it is placed in the letter box
     provided for the purpose at that office and an affidavit stating the time at which this was done
     is filed on the next day on which the office is open: Election Petition Rules 1960, SI 1960/543,
     r 19(2) (amended by SI 1985/1278); European Parliamentary Election Petition Rules 1979,
     SI 1979/521, r 18(2) (amended by SI 2004/1415). 'Election petitions office' means the office of
     the Queen's Bench Masters' Secretary's Department at the Central Office of the Royal Courts of
     Justice: Election Petition Rules 1960, SI 1960/543, r 2(2) (amended by SI 1985/1278); European
     Parliamentary Election Petition Rules 1979, SI 1979/521, r 2(1). As to the meaning of 'European
     parliamentary elections rules' see PARA 383. The Election Petition Rules 1960, SI 1960/543 have
     been applied for the purposes of Welsh Assembly election petitions and local authority
     referendum petitions: see PARA 767 note 1.
13   *Ahmed v Kennedy, Ullah v Pagel* [2002] EWCA Civ 1793, [2003] 2 All ER 440, [2003] 1 WLR
     1820. The prescribed time mentioned in the Representation of the People Act 1983 s 136(3) (see
     PARA 798) is that prescribed by the Election Petition Rules 1960, SI 1960/543, r 6 (see PARA
     798); and r 19 prohibits any enlargement of the time limit so prescribed (see head (2) in the
     text), the Election Petition Rules 1960, SI 1960/543, having primacy over the Civil Procedure
     Rules in this respect (see the text and notes 15–16): *Ahmed v Kennedy, Ullah v Pagel*, applying
     Williams v Tenby Corpn (1879) 5 CPD 135 (service of notice within the prescribed time was a
     condition precedent to the trial of an election petition) and approving *Absalom v Gillett* [1995]
     2 All ER 661, [1995] 1 WLR 128 (petition served in relation to a City of London election). In
     the latter case, Laws J at 670, 136–137 cited *Carter v Griffiths* (28 July 1981, unreported)
     (rejecting a submission that the predecessor provisions to the Representation of the People
     Act 1983 s 136 were directory only), and noted that Ralph Gibson J in *Carter v Griffiths* cited
     Devan Nair v Yong Kuan Teik [1967] 2 AC 31 at 44–45, [1967] 2 All ER 34 at 40, PC, in a case
     concerning similar rules in respect of election petitions in Malaysia, where *Williams v Tenby
     Corpn* was stated to be 'plainly rightly decided'. *Devan Nair v Yong Kuan Teik* was considered
     to be highly persuasive in *Ahmed v Kennedy, Ullah v Pagel*, which also overruled *Young v
     Figgins, The Shrewsbury Petition* (1869) 19 LT 499 (in which a failure to serve a respondent
     was characterised as a 'formal objection' to be ignored under a rule in the Election Petition
     Rules 1868 (no equivalent to which survives in the Election Petition Rules 1960, SI 1960/543)).
     See also PARA 798 note 5.
14   *Absalom v Gillett* [1995] 2 All ER 661 at 672, [1995] 1 WLR 128 at 138 per Laws J
     (incompetent petition served in relation to a City of London election could not be amended and
     served again out of time although the petitioner's case had at least arguable merits; the public
     interest in the speedy determination of election disputes was readily acknowledged). Where a
     notice has been timeously served by a petitioner but it does not satisfy all the requirements of the
     Representation of the People Act 1983 s 136(3) (see PARA 798), the court will regard it as a
     complete failure to give the required notice within the prescribed time, and the petition will be
     struck out as being a nullity: *Ahmed v Kennedy, Ullah v Pagel* [2002] EWCA Civ 1793, [2003]
     2 All ER 440, [2003] 1 WLR 1820, approving and applying *Absalom v Gillett*. Minor defects
     (such as those arising from typographical errors or mistakes in photocopying) might be

remediable but the question of which errors are fatal, and which are remediable, will depend on the facts of each case: see *Ahmed v Kennedy* at [28] per Simon Brown LJ (obiter). *Ahmed v Kennedy* was applied in *Saghir v Najib* [2005] EWHC 417 (QB), [2005] All ER (D) 353 (Mar), where the petitioners' failure to place an amended petition on the court file was held to constitute a failure properly to serve notice of the petition together with a copy, and their failure to state, in the notice as to the nature and amount of security, the date on which security had actually been given also constituted a failure properly to serve that notice. In *Hussein v Khan* [2006] EWHC 262 (QB), [2006] All ER (D) 348 (Feb), a request for an extension of time was determined by considering not only the reasons for the delay but also the strength and merit of the case which the petition disclosed, an approach which was justified on the basis that two competing public interests were considered to be in play: firstly, that of ensuring the propriety and freedom from corruption of elections; and, secondly, that of ensuring that election petitions were dealt with speedily. On the facts of the case, however, the application was dismissed as disclosing no cause of action and because, given the time the petitioners had already had, it would not have been appropriate to permit them even more time to produce an amended petition.

See, however, *Miller v Bull* [2009] EWHC 2640 (QB), [2010] 1 WLR 1861, [2010] PTSR 1737 (under previous authority and conventional statutory interpretation, the Election Petition Rules 1960, SI 1960/543, r 19(1) disapplied CPR 3.1(2)(a) in relation to an application under the Petition Rules 1960, SI 1960/543, r 6(1); however, where the petitioner failed to serve notice stating the amount and nature of security when all other requirements were met, the effect would be disproportionate and incompatible with the Convention for the Protection of Human Rights and Fundamental Freedoms (Rome, 4 November 1950; TS 71 (1953); Cmd 8969) ('the European Convention on Human Rights') art 6, and the First Protocol art 3 (see RIGHTS AND FREEDOMS vol 88A (2013) PARA 243); the Election Petition Rules 1960, SI 1960/543, r 19 should be read down to be subject to the court's power to give relief from sanctions) (*Ahmed v Kennedy, Ullah v Pagel* [2002] EWCA Civ 1793, [2002] All ER 440 not followed).

15   Ie CPR 2.8–2.11 (calculation of time for doing any act specified by the Civil Procedure Rules: see CIVIL PROCEDURE vol 11 (2009) PARAS 88–89, 248) and CPR 3.1(2)(a) (court's power to extend or shorten time for compliance: see CIVIL PROCEDURE vol 11 (2009) PARAS 247, 249; CIVIL PROCEDURE vol 12 (2009) PARA 1665).

16   Election Petition Rules 1960, SI 1960/543, r 19(1) (amended by SI 1999/1352; SI 2003/972); European Parliamentary Election Petition Rules 1979, SI 1979/521, r 18(1) (amended by SI 1999/1398; SI 2003/971); and see note 12.

(ii) Election Court

A. PARLIAMENTARY, EUROPEAN PARLIAMENTARY, AND WELSH ASSEMBLY ELECTIONS

769.   Constitution of the court. A parliamentary, Welsh Assembly or European parliamentary election petition[1] is tried by two judges on the rota for the trial of parliamentary election petitions[2]. The judges to be placed on this rota in each year are to be selected, in such manner as may be provided by rules of court, from the judges of the Queen's Bench Division of the High Court exclusive of any who are members of the House of Lords[3]. A judge on the rota is eligible again in the succeeding or any subsequent year[4]. Notwithstanding the expiry of the year for which a judge has been placed on the rota he may act as if that year had not expired for the purpose of continuing to deal with, giving judgment in, or dealing with any ancillary matter relating to, any case with which he may have been concerned during that year[5].

The judges for the time being on the rota try the election petitions standing for trial according to their seniority unless they otherwise agree[6].

The judges presiding at the trial of an election petition are called 'the election court'[7].

1   As to parliamentary election petitions see PARA 761; as to Welsh Assembly election petitions see PARA 764; and as to European Parliamentary election petitions see PARA 765.

2   Representation of the People Act 1983 s 123(1)(a); European Parliamentary Elections Regulations 2004, SI 2004/293, reg 91(1); National Assembly for Wales (Representation of the

People) Order 2007, SI 2007/236, art 89(1). As to the appointment of judges of the Supreme Court of Gibraltar for the trial of an election petition relating to the election of members of the European Parliament ('MEPs') in the combined region see the European Parliament (Representation) Act 2003 s 23. As to the combined region see PARA 77.

3   Senior Courts Act 1981 s 142(1) (amended by the Representation of the People Act 1983 s 206, Sch 8 para 26).
4   Senior Courts Act 1981 s 142(3).
5   Senior Courts Act 1981 s 142(2).
6   Representation of the People Act 1983 s 123(1)(a); European Parliamentary Elections Regulations 2004, SI 2004/293, reg 91(1); National Assembly for Wales (Representation of the People) Order 2007, SI 2007/236, art 89(1).
7   Representation of the People Act 1983 s 123(1); European Parliamentary Elections Regulations 2004, SI 2004/293, reg 91(1); National Assembly for Wales (Representation of the People) Order 2007, SI 2007/236, art 89(1).

770.   Appointment of masters.   The duties to be performed in relation to parliamentary, Welsh Assembly or European parliamentary elections[1] by the prescribed officer[2] are to be performed by such one or more masters of the Senior Courts (Queen's Bench Division) as the Lord Chief Justice may determine[3].

The master of the Queen's Bench division who is for the time being so nominated[4] as the prescribed officer in relation to parliamentary elections is also to be the prescribed officer in relation to elections under the local government Act[5] and in relation to European parliamentary elections[6].

1   As to the meaning of 'Assembly election' in the context of Welsh Assembly elections see PARA 3 note 2; and as to the meaning of 'parliamentary election' see PARA 9. As to European parliamentary elections see PARA 217 et seq.
2   Ie, in relation to a parliamentary election, under the Representation of the People Act 1983 Pt III (ss 120–186), or, in relation to a European parliamentary election, under the European Parliamentary Elections Regulations 2004, SI 2004/293, Pt 4 (regs 86–122), or, in relation to a Welsh Assembly election, under the National Assembly for Wales (Representation of the People) Order 2007, SI 2007/236, Pt 4 (arts 86–138) (see PARA 761 et seq).
3   Representation of the People Act 1983 s 157(4) (amended by the Constitutional Reform Act 2005 s 59(5), Sch 11 para 28(1), (2)(a)); Constitutional Reform Act 2005 Sch 11 para 1(2); European Parliamentary Elections Regulations 2004, SI 2004/293, reg 106(3); National Assembly for Wales (Representation of the People) Order 2007, SI 2007/236, art 107(4).
4   Ie under the Representation of the People Act 1983 s 157(4) (see the text and notes 1–3).
5   See PARA 792.
6   Election Petition Rules 1960, SI 1960/543, r 2(3) (amended by SI 1985/1278); European Parliamentary Election Petition Rules 1979, SI 1979/521, r 2(2) (amended by virtue of the European Communities (Amendment) Act 1986 s 3; and by SI 1988/557; SI 2004/1415). References to the prescribed officer in the rules governing the procedure for petitions are to be construed accordingly: Election Petition Rules 1960, SI 1960/543, r 2(3); European Parliamentary Election Petition Rules 1979, SI 1979/521, r 2(2). The Election Petition Rules 1960, SI 1960/543 have been applied for the purposes of Welsh Assembly election petitions: see PARA 767 note 1.

771.   Jurisdiction, status and practice of the election court.   Subject to the relevant provisions governing elections[1], the election court[2] has the same powers, jurisdiction and authority as a High Court judge; and the election court is a court of record[3]. Subject to those provisions and the rules made thereunder[4], the principles, practice and rules on which committees of the House of Commons used to act in dealing with election petitions are to be observed, so far as may be, by the High Court and election court in the case of parliamentary or Welsh Assembly election petitions[5].

Where the petition alleges the commission of corrupt or illegal practices, the election court has quasi-inquisitorial as well as judicial duties, as the court must investigate and report whether any corrupt or illegal practices have been committed by, or with the consent of, the candidate, or by any other person, or whether they have extensively prevailed[6].

1   Ie, in relation to a parliamentary election, the Representation of the People Act 1983, or, in relation to a European parliamentary election, the European Parliamentary Elections Regulations 2004, SI 2004/293, or, in relation to a Welsh Assembly election, the National Assembly for Wales (Representation of the People) Order 2007, SI 2007/236.
2   As to the meaning of 'election court' for these purposes see PARA 769.
3   Representation of the People Act 1983 s 123(2); European Parliamentary Elections Regulations 2004, SI 2004/293, reg 91(2); National Assembly for Wales (Representation of the People) Order 2007, SI 2007/236, art 89(2). Judicial review is available as respects the determination of an election court: see *R (on the application of Woolas) v Parliamentary Election Court* [2010] EWHC 3169 (Admin), [2012] QB 1, [2010] NLJR 1756, in which it was held that the relationship of a parliamentary election court to the High Court is such that it should be regarded as an inferior tribunal so that its actions can be the subject of judicial review (see at [54]); and it was further held that jurisdiction in judicial review is not confined to an excess of jurisdiction in the narrow sense but extends to correcting errors made in the law it has to apply (see at [58]). The decisions in *R v Cripps, ex p Muldoon* [1984] QB 68, [1983] 3 All ER 72, DC and in *R (on the application of Cart) v Upper Tribunal* [2010] EWCA Civ 859, [2011] QB 120, [2010] 4 All ER 714, [2010] STC 2556 were considered. See also PARA 779 note 3.
4   As to the current rules see PARA 767 note 1.
5   Representation of the People Act 1983 s 157(2); National Assembly for Wales (Representation of the People) Order 2007, SI 2007/236, art 107(2). As to parliamentary election petitions see PARA 761; and as to Welsh Assembly election petitions see PARA 764. There is no equivalent provision for the purposes of European parliamentary election petitions because corrupt and illegal practices may be cited in such petitions only when they are related to personation and other voting offences: see PARA 765.
6   See PARA 859.

772.   Jurisdiction of judges on rota and master.   An application for leave to pay claims for election expenses sent in too late[1], and an application for an injunction to restrain the publication of false statements about a candidate[2], must, in so far as application is made to the High Court, be heard by one of the judges on the rota or by a master[3]. An application to amend a parliamentary election petition[4] and an application for the remission of incapacities on the ground that the evidence was perjured[5] must be heard by one of the judges on the rota or by a master. Certain other matters may, in so far as application is made to the High Court[6], be heard only by one of the judges on the rota and not by a master. They are as follows: an application for relief in respect of failure to make the return and declaration as to election expenses[7]; and an application to except an innocent act from being an illegal practice, payment, employment or hiring[8]. In all the foregoing cases the jurisdiction is subject to rules of court[9].

If practicable, any jurisdiction conferred on a judge by the Election Petition Rules 1960[10] or the European Parliamentary Election Petition Rules 1979[11] is to be exercised by a rota judge, and, if not, by some other judge of the Queen's Bench Division[12], and any jurisdiction conferred by those rules on a master is to be exercised by the prescribed officer[13] or in his absence by some other master of the Queen's Bench Division[14]. If practicable, matters relating to the trial of a petition, and most questions of an interim nature, should be heard by one of the judges on the rota[15].

1   See PARA 277.
2   See PARA 666.
3   As to the rota see PARA 769. Application may be made to the county court instead: see PARAS 277, 666.
4   See PARA 794.
5   As to the mitigation and remission of incapacities see PARA 910.

6 As to applications to the county court in these matters see PARAS 688, 690.

7 See PARA 688.

8 See PARA 690.

9 Rules of court mean either election petition rules made or having effect as if made under the Representation of the People Act 1983 s 182 (see PARA 767), or rules of court made or having effect as if made under the Senior Courts Act 1981 s 84 (see COURTS AND TRIBUNALS vol 24 (2010) PARAS 861–862): see the Interpretation Act 1978 s 5, Sch 1. In relation to proceedings under the Representation of the People Acts (other than proceedings under the Representation of the People Act 1983 s 30 (see PARA 353)), the Civil Procedure Rules provide that the jurisdiction of the High Court in matters relating to Parliamentary and local government elections are to be exercised by the Divisional Court except that: (1) any jurisdiction, under a provision of any of those Acts, exercisable by a single judge is to be exercised by a single judge; (2) any jurisdiction, under any such provision, exercisable by a master is to be exercised by a master; and (3) where the court's jurisdiction in matters relating to Parliamentary elections is exercisable by a single judge, that jurisdiction in matters relating to local government elections is also exercisable by a single judge: CPR PD 8A—*Alternative Procedure for Claims* para 17A.

10 Ie the Election Petition Rules 1960, SI 1960/543.

11 Ie the European Parliamentary Election Petition Rules 1979, SI 1979/521.

12 Election Petition Rules 1960, SI 1960/543, r 3(1); European Parliamentary Election Petition Rules 1979, SI 1979/521, r 3(1). The Election Petition Rules 1960, SI 1960/543 have been applied for the purposes of Welsh Assembly election petitions and other petitions: see PARA 767.

13 As to the prescribed officer see PARA 770.

14 Election Petition Rules 1960, SI 1960/543, r 3(2) (amended by SI 1985/1278); European Parliamentary Election Petition Rules 1979, SI 1979/521, r 3(2) (amended by SI 1988/557); and see note 12.

15 See *Shaw v Reckitt (Pontefract Election Petition)* [1893] 1 QB 779; on appeal [1893] 2 QB 59, CA (parliamentary election petition). See also PARA 786 note 3.

773. Registrar. The rota judge[1] fixing the time and place of trial of a parliamentary, Welsh Assembly or European parliamentary election petition[2] must also appoint an officer of the Senior Courts to act as registrar of the election court[3] for the purposes of the trial[4].

1 As to the rota see PARA 769.

2 As to parliamentary election petitions see PARA 761; as to Welsh Assembly election petitions see PARA 764; and as to European parliamentary election petitions see PARA 765. As to the fixing of the time and place of trial see PARA 806.

3 As to the meaning of 'election court' for these purposes see PARA 769.

4 Election Petition Rules 1960, SI 1960/543, r 9(5) (amended by SI 1985/1278); European Parliamentary Election Petition Rules 1979, SI 1979/521, r 9(4). The Election Petition Rules 1960, SI 1960/543 have been applied for the purposes of Welsh Assembly election petitions and other petitions: see PARA 767.

774. Payment of expenses. The travelling and other expenses of the judges trying a parliamentary, Welsh Assembly or European parliamentary election petition[1], and all expenses properly incurred in providing them with necessary accommodation and with a proper court, are defrayed by the Treasury[2] (or, in the case of a Welsh Assembly election, the Secretary of State[3]) out of money provided by Parliament[4].

1 As to parliamentary election petitions see PARA 761; as to Welsh Assembly election petitions see PARA 764; and as to European parliamentary election petitions see PARA 765. As to the fixing of the time and place of trial see PARA 806.

2 As to the Treasury see CONSTITUTIONAL LAW AND HUMAN RIGHTS vol 8(2) (Reissue) PARAS 512–517.

3 As to the Secretary of State see PARA 2.

4 Representation of the People Act 1983 s 124 (amended by the Representation of the People Act 1985 ss 24, 28, Sch 4 para 45, Sch 5); European Parliamentary Elections Regulations 2004, SI 2004/293, reg 92; National Assembly for Wales (Representation of the People) Order 2007, SI 2007/236, art 90.

B. LOCAL GOVERNMENT ELECTIONS AND LOCAL AUTHORITY REFERENDUMS

775.   Constitution of the court.   A petition questioning a local authority referendum[1] or an election under the Local Government Act 1972[2] is tried by an election court consisting of a person qualified and appointed as follows[3].

A person is not qualified to constitute an election court[4]: (1) unless he satisfies the judicial-appointment eligibility condition on a 7-year basis[5]; or (2) if the court is for the trial of an election or referendum petition (as the case may be) relating to any local government area[6] in which he resides[7].

The judges for the time being on the rota for the trial of parliamentary election petitions[8], or any two of those judges[9]: (a) may annually appoint as many qualified persons, not exceeding five, as they may think necessary as commissioners for the trial of petitions questioning a local authority referendum or elections under the Local Government Act 1972 (as the case may be)[10]; and (b) must from time to time assign the petitions to be tried by each commissioner[11].

If a commissioner to whom the trial of a petition is assigned dies, or becomes incapable of acting or declines to act, the rota judges (or two of them) may assign the trial to be conducted or continued by another of the commissioners so appointed[12].

1   Ie a referendum, in relation to England, under the Local Authorities (Conduct of Referendums) (England) Regulations 2012, SI 2012/323, and, in relation to Wales, under the Local Authorities (Conduct of Referendums) (Wales) Regulations 2008, SI 2008/1848. As to the meaning of 'referendum' for these purposes see PARA 574 note 2. Provision is made for questioning a local authority referendum by applying and modifying the provision made for questioning an election under the Local Government Act 1972: see PARA 766. As to the meaning of 'election under the Local Government Act 1972' see PARA 11 note 2. As to the application of the Representation of the People Act 1983 Pt III (ss 120–186) to other polls see PARA 763.
2   As to the questioning of an election in England and Wales under the Local Government Act 1972 see PARA 762.
3   Representation of the People Act 1983 s 130(1) (amended by the Courts and Legal Services Act 1990 s 71(2), Sch 10 para 50); Local Authorities (Conduct of Referendums) (Wales) Regulations 2008, SI 2008/1848, reg 11(7); Local Authorities (Conduct of Referendums) (England) Regulations 2012, SI 2012/323, reg 15(7).
4   Representation of the People Act 1983 s 130(2) (amended by the Courts and Legal Services Act 1990 Sch 10 para 50); and see note 3.
5   Representation of the People Act 1983 s 130(2)(a) (substituted by the Tribunals, Courts and Enforcement Act 2007 s 50, Sch 10 Pt 1 para 14); and see note 3. As to the judicial-appointment eligibility condition see COURTS AND TRIBUNALS vol 24 (2010) PARA 645.
6   As to the meaning of 'local government area' see PARA 33 note 7.
7   Representation of the People Act 1983 s 130(2)(b) (amended by the Political Parties, Elections and Referendums Act 2000 s 137(a), Sch 17 paras 1, 2); and see note 3.
8   As to the rota for the trial of parliamentary election petitions see PARA 769.
9   Representation of the People Act 1983 s 130(3); and see note 3.
10 Representation of the People Act 1983 s 130(3)(a) (amended by the Courts and Legal Services Act 1990 Sch 10 para 50); and see note 3.
11 Representation of the People Act 1983 s 130(3)(b); and see note 3.
12 Representation of the People Act 1983 s 130(4); and see note 3.

776.   Court officers.   The election court may employ officers and clerks as prescribed[1]. The rota judge fixing the time and place of trial of a petition questioning a local authority referendum[2] or an election under the Local Government Act 1972[3] must appoint an officer of the Senior Courts to act as registrar of the election court for the purposes of the trial[4].

A shorthand writer must also attend the trial of a local election or local authority referendum petition[5]. This officer is appointed by the commissioner to whom the trial is assigned and he is entitled to be paid expenses on the same scale as a shorthand writer attending the trial of an action in the Queen's Bench Division[6]. The commissioner may also appoint a proper person to act as his clerk for the purposes of the trial[7].

1   Representation of the People Act 1983 s 131(2); and see note 2. 'Prescribed' means prescribed by rules of court: s 185. As to the current rules see PARA 767 note 1.
2   Ie a referendum, in relation to England, under the Local Authorities (Conduct of Referendums) (England) Regulations 2012, SI 2012/323, and, in relation to Wales, under the Local Authorities (Conduct of Referendums) (Wales) Regulations 2008, SI 2008/1848. As to the meaning of 'referendum' for these purposes see PARA 574 note 2. Provision is made for questioning a local authority referendum by applying and modifying the provision made for questioning an election under the Local Government Act 1972: see PARA 766. As to the meaning of 'election under the Local Government Act 1972' see PARA 11 note 2. As to the rota see PARA 769. As to the application of the Representation of the People Act 1983 Pt III (ss 120–186) to other polls see PARA 763.
3   As to the questioning of an election in England and Wales under the Local Government Act 1972 see PARA 762.
4   Election Petition Rules 1960, SI 1960/543, r 9(5) (amended by SI 1985/1278). The Election Petition Rules 1960, SI 1960/543 have been applied and modified for the purposes of a local authority referendum petition: see PARA 767 note 1. The Election Petition Rules 1960, SI 1960/543 are also applied for the purposes of other election petitions: see PARA 767.
5   Representation of the People Act 1983 s 131(3); and see note 2. As to the shorthand writer's expenses see PARA 778; and as to his duties see PARA 818.
6   Election Petition Rules 1960, SI 1960/543, r 18(1) (amended by SI 1985/1278); and see note 4.
7   Election Petition Rules 1960, SI 1960/543, r 18(2); and see note 4.

777.   Court accommodation and attendance; repayment of expenses.   The proper officer[1] of the authority for which the local government election[2] or local authority referendum[3] was held (or, in the case of a parish or community election, the returning officer at that election[4]) must provide suitable accommodation for holding the election court[5], and any expenses incurred by him for this purpose must be paid by that authority[6].

The election court appointed for the trial of a petition questioning a local authority referendum or an election under the Local Government Act 1972[7] may, in its discretion, order that the expenses incurred by the proper officer of the authority in receiving the election court, be repaid wholly or in part to the proper officer[8]: (1) by the petitioner, if in the opinion of the election court the petition is frivolous and vexatious[9]; or (2) by the respondent, when in the opinion of the election court he has been personally guilty of corrupt practices at the election or referendum (as the case may be)[10]. Such an order may be enforced as an order for payment of costs[11], but a deposit made or a security given[12] is not to be applied for any such repayment to the proper officer until all costs and expenses payable by the petitioner or respondent to any party to the petition have been satisfied[13].

All constables and bailiffs must give their assistance to the court in the execution of its duties[14].

1   As to the meaning of 'proper officer' see PARA 140 note 2.
2   As to the meaning of 'local government election' see PARA 11.
3   As to the meaning of 'referendum' for these purposes see PARA 574 note 2. Provision is made for questioning a local authority referendum by applying and modifying the provision made for questioning an election under the Local Government Act 1972: see PARA 766. As to the meaning of 'election under the Local Government Act 1972' see PARA 11 note 2. As to the application of the Representation of the People Act 1983 Pt III (ss 120–186) to other polls see PARA 763.
4   See the Local Elections (Parishes and Communities) (England and Wales) Rules 2006, SI 2006/3305, r 6(a). The returning officer at a parish or community election is an officer of the council of the district in which the parish or community is situated (see PARA 354), but it is

submitted that this does not result in a shift of the financial burden of the expenses from the parish or community to the district. As to the application of the provisions questioning local elections to parish or community elections see PARA 763.

5   Ie as constituted under the Representation of the People Act 1983 s 130 (see PARA 775), including that provision as applied (see note 3).
6   Representation of the People Act 1983 s 131(1); and see note 3.
7   As to the questioning of an election in England and Wales under the Local Government Act 1972 see PARA 762.
8   Representation of the People Act 1983 s 133(1); and see note 3.
9   Representation of the People Act 1983 s 133(1)(i); and see note 3.
10 Representation of the People Act 1983 s 133(1)(ii); and see note 3.
11 Representation of the People Act 1983 s 133(2); and see note 3. As to the recovery of costs see PARA 880.
12 As to the making of deposits or the giving of security for costs see PARAS 796–798.
13 Representation of the People Act 1983 s 133(2); and see note 3.
14 Representation of the People Act 1983 s 131(2); and see note 3.

778.   Remuneration of commissioner and staff; repayment of expenses.   The remuneration and allowances to be paid to the commissioner for his services in respect of the trial of a petition questioning a local authority referendum[1] or an election under the Local Government Act 1972[2], and to any officers, clerks or shorthand writers[3] employed in relation to the trial, are fixed by a scale, which is made and may be varied by the judges on the rota for the trial of parliamentary election petitions[4], with Treasury approval[5]. The remuneration and allowances are paid in the first instance by the Treasury, but they must be repaid to the Treasury on its certificate by the authority for which the election or referendum (as the case may be) was held[6].

The election court appointed for the trial of a petition questioning a local authority referendum or an election under the Local Government Act 1972[7] may, in its discretion, order that the remuneration and allowances payable to the commissioner in respect of the trial of an election or referendum petition (as the case may be), and to any officers, clerks or shorthand writers be repaid wholly or in part to the Treasury[8]: (1) by the petitioner, if in the opinion of the election court the petition is frivolous and vexatious[9]; or (2) by the respondent, when in the opinion of the election court he has been personally guilty of corrupt practices at the election or referendum (as the case may be)[10]. Such an order may be enforced as an order for payment of costs[11], but a deposit made or a security given[12] is not to be applied for any such repayment to the Treasury until all costs and expenses payable by the petitioner or respondent to any party to the petition have been satisfied[13].

1   Ie a referendum, in relation to England, under the Local Authorities (Conduct of Referendums) (England) Regulations 2012, SI 2012/323, and, in relation to Wales, under the Local Authorities (Conduct of Referendums) (Wales) Regulations 2008, SI 2008/1848. As to the meaning of 'referendum' for these purposes see PARA 574 note 2. Provision is made for questioning a local authority referendum by applying and modifying the provision made for questioning an election under the Local Government Act 1972: see PARA 766. As to the meaning of 'election under the Local Government Act 1972' see PARA 11 note 2. As to the application of the Representation of the People Act 1983 Pt III (ss 120–186) to other polls see PARA 763.
2   As to the questioning of an election in England and Wales under the Local Government Act 1972 see PARA 762.
3   As to the appointment of the shorthand writer see PARA 776. His expenses are treated as part of the expenses in receiving the election court: Representation of the People Act 1983 s 131(3); and see note 1.
4   As to the rota for the trial of parliamentary election petitions see PARA 769.
5   Representation of the People Act 1983 s 132(1); and see note 1. As to the Treasury see CONSTITUTIONAL LAW AND HUMAN RIGHTS vol 8(2) (Reissue) PARAS 512–517.

6 Representation of the People Act 1983 s 132(2); and see note 1. Application is made to the Treasury Commissioners and should be accompanied by an account setting out the remuneration earned.

7 As to the constitution of the court see PARA 775.

8 Representation of the People Act 1983 s 133(1); and see note 1.

9 Representation of the People Act 1983 s 133(1)(i); and see note 1.

10 Representation of the People Act 1983 s 133(1)(ii); and see note 1.

11 Representation of the People Act 1983 s 133(2); and see note 1. As to the recovery of costs see PARA 880.

12 As to the making of deposits or the giving of security for costs see PARAS 796–798.

13 Representation of the People Act 1983 s 133(2); and see note 1.

779. Election court's jurisdiction. For the purposes of the trial of a petition questioning a local authority referendum[1] or an election under the Local Government Act 1972[2], the election court has the same powers and privileges as a judge on the trial of a parliamentary election petition[3]. However, it is probable that these powers are inapplicable once the trial has been concluded[4].

Where the petition alleges the commission of corrupt or illegal practices, the election court has quasi-inquisitorial, as well as judicial, duties, as the court must investigate and report whether any corrupt or illegal practices have been committed (and by whom) or whether they have extensively prevailed[5].

Any jurisdiction conferred on a judge by the Election Petition Rules 1960[6] should, where practicable, be exercised by a judge on the rota for the trial of parliamentary election petitions[7] and, if not, by some other judge of the Queen's Bench Division[8]. Any such jurisdiction conferred by those rules on a master is exercised by the prescribed officer[9] or, in his absence, by some other master of the Queen's Bench Division[10].

Subject to the provisions of the Representation of the People Act 1983 and of the rules made under it[11], the principles, practice and rules on which committees of the House of Commons used to act in dealing with election petitions must be observed, so far as may be, by the High Court and election court in the case of petitions questioning elections under the Local Government Act 1972[12].

1 Ie a referendum, in relation to England, under the Local Authorities (Conduct of Referendums) (England) Regulations 2012, SI 2012/323, and, in relation to Wales, under the Local Authorities (Conduct of Referendums) (Wales) Regulations 2008, SI 2008/1848. As to the meaning of 'referendum' for these purposes see PARA 574 note 2. Provision is made for questioning a local authority referendum by applying and modifying the provision made for questioning an election under the Local Government Act 1972: see PARA 766. As to the meaning of 'election under the Local Government Act 1972' see PARA 11 note 2. As to the application of the Representation of the People Act 1983 Pt III (ss 120–186) to other polls see PARA 763.

2 As to the questioning of an election in England and Wales under the Local Government Act 1972 see PARA 762.

3 Representation of the People Act 1983 s 130(5); and see note 1. As to the trial of parliamentary election petitions see PARA 769 et seq. It was on the basis of this provision in an earlier enactment that it was held that the local election court was a court of record: *R v Maidenhead Corpn* (1882) 9 QBD 494 at 500, CA, per Jessell MR. That case was not referred to in the judgment in *R v Cripps, ex p Muldoon* [1984] QB 68, [1983] 2 All ER 72, DC, where it was held that the election court was an inferior court subject to judicial review by the High Court; however, on appeal, this point was left open since, on the facts of the case, the High Court could exercise jurisdiction anyway in respect of an order as to costs, and it was said that it was 'unnecessary to reach any decision as to the jurisdiction of the Divisional Court in relation to the work of a local election court. That jurisdiction depends on the local election court being an 'inferior court' and not a 'superior court of record' (see [1984] QB 686 at 698, [1984] 2 All ER 705 at 712, CA, per Sir John Donaldson MR). More recently, it has become accepted that the decision of an election commissioner sitting as a local election court is susceptible to judicial review: see eg *R v Rowe, ex p Mainwaring* [1992] 4 All ER 821, [1992] 1 WLR 1059, CA (a case on appeal from the Divisional Court which had judicially reviewed the decision of an

election commissioner); and see *R (on the application of Afzal) v Election Court* [2005] EWCA Civ 647, [2005] LGR 823. See also *R (on the application of Woolas) v Parliamentary Election Court* [2010] EWHC 3169 (Admin), [2012] QB 1, [2010] NLJR 1756; and PARA 771 note 3.

4   *R v Cripps, ex p Muldoon* [1984] QB 686 at 697, [1984] 2 All ER 705 at 712, CA, per Sir John Donaldson MR. These remarks were in the context of the exercise of the 'slip rule' power of the High Court which, in the view of the Court of Appeal, had been imported by virtue of the Representation of the People Act 1983 s 130(5). But the variation in the order as to costs which the commissioner had purported to make after the trial of the local election petition in that case had been concluded did not in any event fall within the slip rule because it made a substantial alteration and did not correct an ambiguity. The Court of Appeal pointed to a judge's power to reconsider or vary prior to the conclusion of a trial apart from the slip rule: *R v Cripps, ex p Muldoon* at 695 and 710 per Sir John Donaldson MR. However, 'once the order has been perfected the trial judge is *functus officio* and in his capacity as the trial judge has no further power to reconsider or vary his decision whether under the slip rule or otherwise': *R v Cripps, ex p Muldoon* at 695 and 710 per Sir John Donaldson MR. The decision in *R v Cripps, ex p Muldoon* was approved and applied by the Court of Appeal in *Conservative and Unionist Party v Election Comr* [2010] EWCA Civ 1332, [2011] PTSR 416, [2010] All ER (D) 241 (Nov) (see PARA 871 note 3).

5   See PARAS 820, 862.

6   Ie the Election Petition Rules 1960, SI 1960/543.

7   As to the rota for the trial of parliamentary election petitions see PARA 767.

8   Election Petition Rules 1960, SI 1960/543, rr 2(2), 3(1). The Election Petition Rules 1960, SI 1960/543 have been applied and modified for the purposes of a local authority referendum petition: see PARA 767 note 1. The Election Petition Rules 1960, SI 1960/543, are also applied for the purposes of other petitions: see PARA 767.

9   As to the prescribed officer see PARA 770.

10   Election Petition Rules 1960, SI 1960/543, r 3(2) (amended by SI 1985/1278); and see note 8.

11   Ie the Election Petition Rules 1960, SI 1960/543 (see PARA 767), including those rules as applied (see note 8). As to practice and procedure on the hearing see further PARA 817.

12   Representation of the People Act 1983 s 157(2); and see note 1.

(iii) Petitions

A. PARLIAMENTARY, EUROPEAN PARLIAMENTARY, AND WELSH ASSEMBLY ELECTIONS

780. Form and contents of election petition. A parliamentary, Welsh Assembly or European parliamentary election petition[1] must be in the prescribed form[2], and must state: (1) in which capacity the petitioner or each of the petitioners presents the petition[3]; (2) the date and result of the election to which the petition relates, and, in the case of a parliamentary or Welsh Assembly election petition, the date on which the return was made to the Clerk of the Crown of the member declared to have been elected[4]; (3) in the case of a petition alleging corrupt or illegal practices[5], the date from which the time for the presentation of the petition is to be calculated[6]; and (4) the grounds on which relief is sought, setting out with sufficient particularity the facts relied on but not the evidence by which they are to be proved[7]. It is sufficient for the petition to allege the grounds generally, and a petition alleging that the respondent and his agents are charged with bribery, corruption and undue influence, and also with illegal practices, would in form be sufficient[8]. A general allegation in a petition must not, however, be so worded as effectively to include acts not committed until after the presentation of the petition, and if the petitioner proposes to proceed upon charges of any such acts, he must amend the petition[9]. The petition must conclude with a prayer setting out particulars of the relief claimed[10], and must be signed by the petitioner or all the petitioners if more than one[11].

1   As to parliamentary election petitions see PARA 761; as to Welsh Assembly election petitions see PARA 764; and as to European parliamentary election petitions see PARA 765.

2   Representation of the People Act 1983 s 121(3); European Parliamentary Elections
     Regulations 2004, SI 2004/293, reg 89(3); National Assembly for Wales (Representation of the
     People) Order 2007, SI 2007/236, art 87(5). In the case of a parliamentary election, the petition
     must be in the form set out in the Election Petition Rules 1960, SI 1960/543, Schedule (amended
     by SI 1985/1278), or a form to the like effect with such variations as the circumstances may
     require: Election Petition Rules 1960, SI 1960/543, r 4(1). In the case of a European
     parliamentary election, the petition must be in the form set out in the European Parliamentary
     Election Petition Rules 1979, SI 1979/521, Schedule (amended by SI 2004/1415), or a form to
     the like effect with such variations as the circumstances may require: European Parliamentary
     Election Petition Rules 1979, SI 1979/521, r 4(1). The Election Petition Rules 1960, SI 1960/543
     have been applied for the purposes of Welsh Assembly election petitions and other petitions: see
     PARA 767.
          See *Scarth v Amin* [2008] EWHC 2886 (QB), [2009] PTSR 827, [2008] All ER (D) 265
     (Nov) (the Election Petition Rules 1960, SI 1960/543, r 4(1) did not require a petition to state all
     the matters of which the Local Elections (Principal Areas) (England and Wales) Rules 2006,
     SI 2006/3304, r 50 required the returning officer to give notice at the time when the result of a
     poll on a contested election had been ascertained (see PARA 482); it would be wrong in principle
     to adopt an interpretation of the 1960 Rules which placed conditions upon the presentation of
     valid petitions which were more restrictive than necessary to achieve the certainty that was
     required, and which obstructed the determination of what opinion the people had expressed).
     See also *Ali v Bashir* [2012] EWHC 3007 (QB) at [27], [2012] All ER (D) 70 (Nov) at [27] (the
     Election Petition Rules 1960, SI 1960/543, r 4(1) did not contemplate slavish adherence to the
     form of the Schedule; it permitted a form 'to like effect'). See further *Miller v Bull* [2009] EWHC
     2640 (QB), [2010] 1 WLR 1861, [2010] PTSR 1737 (see PARA 768); *Saghir v Najib* [2005]
     EWHC 417 (QB), [2005] All ER (D) 353 (Mar); *Ahmed v Kennedy* [2002] EWCA Civ 1793,
     [2003] 2 All ER 440, [2003] 1 WLR 1820; *Hussein v Khan* [2006] EWHC 262 (QB), [2006] All
     ER (D) 348 (Feb); *Pilling v Reynolds* [2008] EWHC 316 (QB), [2009] 1 All ER 163.

3   Election Petition Rules 1960, SI 1960/543, r 4(1)(a) (amended by SI 1985/1278); European
     Parliamentary Election Petition Rules 1979, SI 1979/521, r 4(1)(a) (amended by SI 2004/1415);
     and see note 2. As to the persons who may present a petition see PARA 781.

4   Election Petition Rules 1960, SI 1960/543, r 4(1)(b); European Parliamentary Election Petition
     Rules 1979, SI 1979/521, r 4(1)(b); and see note 2. In the case of a Welsh Assembly election,
     provision is made also for a petition relating to a return in respect of an electoral region vacancy
     (see PARA 215), in which case the date on which the person was treated as declared to be
     returned as an Assembly member must be specified: Election Petition Rules 1960, SI 1960/543,
     r 4(1)(ba); National Assembly for Wales (Representation of the People) Order 2007,
     SI 2007/236, Sch 9 para 4 (see note 2). As to the making of the return to the Clerk of the Crown
     see PARA 480.

5   Ie a petition mentioned in the Representation of the People Act 1983 s 122(2), (3) (see PARA
     785). There is no provision equivalent to head (3) in the text for the purposes of European
     parliamentary election petitions because corrupt and illegal practices may be cited in such
     petitions only when they are related to personation and other voting offences: see PARA 765.

6   Election Petition Rules 1960, SI 1960/543, r 4(1)(c) (amended by SI 1985/1278); and see note 2.
     As to the time for the presentation of an election petition in such a case see PARA 785.

7   Election Petition Rules 1960, SI 1960/543, r 4(1)(d); European Parliamentary Election Petition
     Rules 1979, SI 1979/521, r 4(1)(d); and see note 2. As to the ordering of particulars see PARAS
     808–810.

8   *Beal v Smith* (1869) LR 4 CP 145; *Greenock Election Petition* (1868) reported in footnote to
     Beal v Smith at 150; *Lancaster County, Lancaster Division Case* (1896) 5 O'M & H 39 at 41
     per Bruce J, who at 41–42 expressed an opinion in favour of the general character of the
     offences charged being set out in separate paragraphs instead of a general allegation of corrupt
     and illegal practices. Such a form has the advantage of not affording occasion for an order for
     the immediate service of particulars.

9   *Cremer v Lowles* [1896] 1 QB 504, CA; and see PARA 786 note 13.

10   Election Petition Rules 1960, SI 1960/543, r 4(1); European Parliamentary Election Petition
     Rules 1979, SI 1979/521, r 4(1); and see note 2.

11   Representation of the People Act 1983 s 121(3); European Parliamentary Elections
     Regulations 2004, SI 2004/293, reg 89(3); National Assembly for Wales (Representation of the
     People) Order 2007, SI 2007/236, art 87(5).

781.   Who may present an election petition. A parliamentary, Welsh Assembly
or European parliamentary election petition[1] may be presented by any one or

more of the following persons: (1) a person who voted as an elector, or who had a right so to vote, at the election to which the petition relates[2]; or (2) a person claiming to have had a right to be returned or elected at the election[3]; or (3) a person alleging himself to have been a candidate at the election[4].

1 As to parliamentary election petitions see PARA 761; as to Welsh Assembly election petitions see PARA 764; and as to European parliamentary election petitions see PARA 765.

2 Representation of the People Act 1983 s 121(1)(a); European Parliamentary Elections Regulations 2004, SI 2004/293, reg 89(1)(a); National Assembly for Wales (Representation of the People) Order 2007, SI 2007/236, art 87(1)(a). The reference to a person who voted as an elector or who had the right so to vote does not include a person who had an anonymous entry in the register of electors: Representation of the People Act 1983 s 121(1A) (added by the Electoral Administration Act 2006 s 10(2), Sch 1 paras 2, 11); European Parliamentary Elections Regulations 2004, SI 2004/293, reg 89(1A) (added by SI 2009/186); National Assembly for Wales (Representation of the People) Order 2007, SI 2007/236, art 87(2). As to the meaning of 'anonymous entry' in relation to a register of electors see PARA 148.
   The words set out in head (1) in the text prima facie include a person who has voted without being entitled to do so. In *Harford v Linskey* [1899] 1 QB 852, DC, at 859 and 862, Wright J (quoting the Municipal Corporations Act 1882 s 88 (repealed), the words of which are, as regards this point, substantially the same) expressed the view that those words would cover the case of a voter who had no right to vote. The point seems never to have been decided. The fact of the mention of the alternative in the provision tends to show that such a case is included, as otherwise, it is submitted, it would have been sufficient to say merely 'some person who had a right to vote'. The question was raised but not decided in *Walsall Case* (1892) cited in Day 1.

3 Representation of the People Act 1983 s 121(1)(b); European Parliamentary Elections Regulations 2004, SI 2004/293, reg 89(1)(b); National Assembly for Wales (Representation of the People) Order 2007, SI 2007/236, art 87(1)(b). A person who is incapable of being duly elected because he is too young could not be a person claiming the right to be elected for the purposes of this provision: *Hobson v Fishburn* (1988) Times, 21 November, DC (but see note 4). In relation to a Welsh Assembly election, it is provided that a person claiming to have had a right to be returned in an electoral region vacancy (see PARA 215) also may present a petition: National Assembly for Wales (Representation of the People) Order 2007, SI 2007/236, art 87(1)(d).

4 Representation of the People Act 1983 s 121(1)(c); European Parliamentary Elections Regulations 2004, SI 2004/293, reg 89(1)(c); National Assembly for Wales (Representation of the People) Order 2007, SI 2007/236, art 87(1)(c). As to the meaning of 'candidate' see PARA 230. As to the nomination of a candidate see PARA 255 et seq. In *Hobson v Fishburn* (1988) Times, 21 November, DC, a person who was too young to be duly elected but who had been nominated as a candidate could have brought an election petition under the provision set out in head (3) in the text (but see note 3). See also *Harford v Linskey* [1899] 1 QB 852 at 859 per Wright J (who said, quoting the Municipal Corporations Act 1882 s 88 (repealed) (the words of which are, as regards this point, substantially the same), that the words of the statute seem designed to express something wider than absolutely valid candidature).

782. Respondent. The respondent to a parliamentary, Welsh Assembly or European parliamentary election petition[1] is the member of Parliament or Welsh Assembly member or member of the European Parliament ('MEP') whose election or return is complained of[2]. Where, however, a parliamentary or Welsh Assembly election petition complains of the conduct of a returning officer[3], he is deemed to be a respondent for the purposes of the provisions[4] as to election petitions[5]. The allegation against the returning officer need not necessarily be one of wilful misconduct, and he may be joined as a respondent where the acts or omissions or negligence complained of are not personal but are those of his subordinates[6].

An unsuccessful candidate cannot be made a respondent to an election petition against his will[7]. However, a petition may be presented complaining of the election or return of a member who has since died[8].

1   As to parliamentary election petitions see PARA 761; as to Welsh Assembly election petitions see PARA 764; and as to European parliamentary election petitions see PARA 765.

2   Representation of the People Act 1983 s 121(2); European Parliamentary Elections Regulations 2004, SI 2004/293, reg 89(2); National Assembly for Wales (Representation of the People) Order 2007, SI 2007/236, art 87(3).

3   As to returning officers for parliamentary elections see PARA 350 et seq. In relation to a European parliamentary election, the returning officer and any local returning officer are both specified and, accordingly, subsequent references to the 'officer' or to the 'respondent' are taken to be references to the 'officer (or officers) in question' and the 'respondent (or respondents)' respectively: see the European Parliamentary Elections Regulations 2004, SI 2004/293, reg 89(2). As to the designation of returning officers and local returning officers at European parliamentary elections see PARA 360 et seq. For the purposes of Welsh Assembly elections, the reference, in relation to a constituency election, is to a constituency returning officer and, in relation to a regional election, is to a regional returning officer (see PARA 18 note 2): see the National Assembly for Wales (Representation of the People) Order 2007, SI 2007/236, art 87(3). For these purposes, art 86(2) also applies if the petition complains of the conduct of a constituency returning officer in the exercise of his functions in relation to a regional election: art 87(4). As to the meanings of 'constituency election' and 'regional election' in the context of Welsh Assembly elections see PARA 3 note 2.

4   Ie, in relation to a parliamentary election, under the Representation of the People Act 1983 Pt III (ss 120–186), or, in relation to a European parliamentary election, under the European Parliamentary Elections Regulations 2004, SI 2004/293, Pt 4 (regs 86–122), or, in relation to a Welsh Assembly election, under the National Assembly for Wales (Representation of the People) Order 2007, SI 2007/236, Pt 4 (arts 86–138) (see PARA 761 et seq).

5   Representation of the People Act 1983 s 121(2); European Parliamentary Elections Regulations 2004, SI 2004/293, reg 89(2); National Assembly for Wales (Representation of the People) Order 2007, SI 2007/236, art 87(3). If it is proposed to give evidence at the hearing of an election petition to implicate the returning officer, he should be made a respondent: Tamworth Case, Hill and Walton v Peel and Bulwer (1869) 20 LT 181, 1 O'M & H 75 (it being proposed to offer evidence implicating the returning officer, Willes J refused leave to have him called as a witness, as no charge had been made against him in the petition). It seems that a returning officer who is so deemed to be a respondent is entitled to the same notices as to presentation of the petition, the proposed security, etc, as an ordinary respondent: see Young v Figgins (1868) 19 LT 499.

6   Islington, West Division Case (1901) 5 O'M & H 120; Drogheda Borough Case (1874) 2 O'M & H 201; Warrington Case, Crozier v Rylands (1869) 19 LT 812, 1 O'M & H 42; but see, contra, Harmon v Park (1880) 6 QBD 323, CA; Cirencester Case (1893) cited in Day 3. In the latter case, on a summons being taken out by a respondent for leave to serve the petition on the returning officer, Mathew J refused it on the ground that it was unnecessary, as by the fact of the returning officer's conduct being complained of he was already deemed to be a respondent; but on a summons being subsequently taken out by the returning officer for particulars of the charges against him, Cave J held that he was not a party, as wilful misconduct was not alleged against him. It is submitted that the view expressed by Mathew J is the correct view of the position of a returning officer against whose conduct of the election complaint is made in the petition. Cf the judgment of Lord Selbourne LC in Harmon v Park at 328–329; and see Haverfordwest Case, Davies v Lord Kensington (1874) LR 9 CP 720, DC; Athlone Borough Election Petition (1874) 2 O'M & H 186; Clare, Eastern Division Case (1892) 4 O'M & H 162.

7   Maidenhead Case, Lovering v Dawson (1875) LR 10 CP 711, DC. See also Yates v Leach (1874) LR 9 CP 605, DC.

8   Tipperary County Case (1875) IR 9 CL 173; Mitchell's Case (1696) cited in 1 Lud EC 456; Peterborough City Case (1728) 21 Commons Journals 162; Durham City Case (1853) 108 Commons Journals 562, 596. The reason for this is that the proceeding is not of a personal nature against a dead man. It is the assertion of a right in rem: Tipperary County Case. Where it is alleged that the votes given for the successful candidate were votes thrown away (see PARA 845), there might be advantages in proceeding with the petition.

783. Notice of respondent's intention not to oppose. Not less than seven days before the day fixed for the trial[1], a respondent who does not intend to oppose a parliamentary, Welsh Assembly or European parliamentary election petition[2] must serve notice to that effect on the petitioner and the Director of Public

Prosecutions[3]. The giving of notice by a respondent of his intention not to oppose the petition does not of itself cause him to cease to be a respondent[4].

1   As to the computation of this period see PARA 768; and as the fixing of the time and place of trial see PARA 806.
2   As to parliamentary election petitions see PARA 761; as to Welsh Assembly election petitions see PARA 764; and as to European parliamentary election petitions see PARA 765.
3   Election Petition Rules 1960, SI 1960/543, r 15; European Parliamentary Election Petition Rules 1979, SI 1979/521, r 15. The Election Petition Rules 1960, SI 1960/543 have been applied for the purposes of Welsh Assembly election petitions and other petitions: see PARA 767.
4   *Yates v Leach* (1874) LR 9 CP 605.

784. Mode of presentation of election petition. A parliamentary, Welsh Assembly or European parliamentary election petition[1] must be presented to the High Court if the constituency[2] or the electoral region[3] to which it relates is in England or Wales[4]. The petition is presented by delivering it to the prescribed officer[5] or otherwise by dealing with it in the prescribed manner[6], that is by filing it in the election petitions office[7] and at the same time leaving three copies there[8]. It is the duty of the prescribed officer to send a copy of the election petition to the returning officer of the constituency or electoral region (as the case may be) to which the petition relates[9], and the returning officer must forthwith publish it in that constituency or electoral region[10].

1   As to parliamentary election petitions see PARA 761; as to Welsh Assembly election petitions see PARA 764; and as to European parliamentary election petitions see PARA 765.
2   Ie the parliamentary constituency in the case of a parliamentary election or the Assembly constituency in the case of a Welsh Assembly constituency election. As to the meanings of 'Assembly constituency election' and 'Assembly constituency' in the context of Welsh Assembly elections see PARA 3 note 2; and as to the meanings of 'parliamentary election', and 'constituency' in relation to a parliamentary election, see PARA 9.
3   Ie the Assembly electoral region in the case of a Welsh Assembly regional election, or the combined region or any European parliamentary electoral region wholly in England and Wales in the case of a European parliamentary election. As to the meanings of 'Assembly electoral region' and 'Assembly regional election' in the context of Welsh Assembly elections see PARA 3 note 2. As to European parliamentary elections see PARA 217 et seq; and as to the establishment of electoral regions for the purpose of elections to the European Parliament (including the combined region) see PARA 77.
4   Representation of the People Act 1983 s 121(3); European Parliamentary Elections Regulations 2004, SI 2004/293, reg 89(3); National Assembly for Wales (Representation of the People) Order 2007, SI 2007/236, art 87(5), (6).
5   As to the prescribed officer see PARA 770.
6   Representation of the People Act 1983 s 121(4); European Parliamentary Elections Regulations 2004, SI 2004/293, reg 89(4); National Assembly for Wales (Representation of the People) Order 2007, SI 2007/236, art 87(6).
7   As to the meaning of 'election petitions office' see PARA 768 note 12.
8   Election Petition Rules 1960, SI 1960/543, rr 2(5), 4(2); European Parliamentary Election Petition Rules 1979, SI 1979/521, rr 2(4), 4(2) (r 2(4) substituted, and r 4(2) amended, by SI 2004/1415). The Election Petition Rules 1960, SI 1960/543 have been applied for the purposes of Welsh Assembly election petitions and other petitions: see PARA 767.
9   As to returning officers for parliamentary elections see PARA 355 et seq. For the purposes of Welsh Assembly elections, the reference, in relation to a constituency election, is to a constituency returning officer and, in relation to a regional election, is to a regional returning officer (as to the meanings of which see PARA 18 note 2). As to the designation of returning officers at European parliamentary elections see PARA 365 et seq. As to the constituencies and electoral regions referred to in the text see notes 2, 3.
10 Representation of the People Act 1983 s 121(4); European Parliamentary Elections Regulations 2004, SI 2004/293, reg 89(4); National Assembly for Wales (Representation of the People) Order 2007, SI 2007/236, art 87(6). Where, by any provision of the Election Petition Rules 1960, SI 1960/543, or the European Parliamentary Election Petition Rules 1979, SI 1979/521, as the case may be, a petition or notice is required to be published by the returning officer, the cost of publication must be paid in the first instance by the petitioner or, as the case

may be, by the person by whom the notice was given, without prejudice to the manner in which such cost is ultimately to be borne by one or more of the parties to the petition: Election Petition Rules 1960, SI 1960/543, r 20; European Parliamentary Election Petition Rules 1979, SI 1979/521, r 19; and see note 8.

785. Time for presentation of election petition. In general, a parliamentary election petition[1] must be presented within 21 days[2] after the return of the member to whose election it relates has been made to the Clerk of the Crown[3]. The return of a member at a parliamentary election is not made until the writ with the returning officer's certificate indorsed on it reaches the Clerk of the Crown so that he may act on it[4], and the period of 21 days does not begin to run until then[5]. In general, a Welsh Assembly election petition[6] must be presented within 21 days after the day on which the name of any member to whose election or return the petition relates has been returned[7]. In general, a European parliamentary election petition[8] must be presented within 21 days after the day on which the relevant result was declared in accordance with the European parliamentary elections rules[9].

If, at a parliamentary or Welsh Assembly election, the return or the election is challenged on an allegation of corrupt practices[10], and the petition specifically alleges a payment of money or other reward[11] to have been made by the member or on his account or with his privity since the time of the return in pursuance or in furtherance of the alleged corrupt practice, it may be presented within 28 days after the date of such payment[12]. A parliamentary or Welsh Assembly election petition questioning a return or an election upon an allegation of an illegal practice may, so far as respects the illegal practice, be presented not later than the expiration of 21 days after the specified day[13]. The specified day for this purpose is the tenth day after the end of the time allowed for delivering to the returning officer returns as to election expenses at the election or, if later[14]: (1) that on which the returning officer receives the return and declarations as to election expenses by the member to whose election the petition relates and his election agent[15]; or, (2) where the return and declarations are received on different days, the last of those days[16]; or (3) where there is an authorised excuse for failing to make the return and declarations, the date of the allowance of the excuse or, if there was a failure as regards two or more of them and the excuse was allowed at different times, the date of the allowance of the last excuse[17]. Moreover, if the petition specifically alleges a payment of money to have been made or some other act to have been done since the specified day by the member or an agent of the member, or with the privity of the member or his election agent, in pursuance or in furtherance of the illegal practice alleged in the petition, the petition may be presented within 28 days after the date of the payment or other act[18].

1　As to parliamentary election petitions see PARA 761.
2　As to calculation of these time limits and as to the circumstances in which presentation might be deemed see PARA 768.
3　Representation of the People Act 1983 s 122(1). 'Clerk of the Crown' means Clerk of the Crown in Chancery: s 202(1). As to the Clerk of the Crown see CONSTITUTIONAL LAW AND HUMAN RIGHTS vol 8(2) (Reissue) PARA 921.
4　See PARAS 479–480.
5　*Re Poole Case, Hurdle v Waring* (1874) LR 9 CP 435.
6　As to Welsh Assembly election petitions see PARA 764.
7　National Assembly for Wales (Representation of the People) Order 2007, SI 2007/236, art 88(1). The text refers to an election or return at a Welsh Assembly election in accordance with Sch 5 (see PARA 490 et seq): see the National Assembly for Wales (Representation of the People) Order 2007, SI 2007/236, art 88(1).
8　As to European parliamentary election petitions see PARA 765.

9   European Parliamentary Elections Regulations 2004, SI 2004/293, reg 90. As to the meaning of 'European parliamentary elections rules' see PARA 383. The text refers to the day on which the result of the election was declared under reg 9(1), Sch 1 para 61 (see PARA 493): see reg 90. The Queen's Printers copy of reg 90 refers to the day on which the result of the election was declared under reg 9(1), Sch 1 para 56 but that refers to the citation that applied before Sch1 was substituted by SI 2009/186, and it is submitted that a reference to the European Parliamentary Elections Regulations 2004, SI 2004/293, Sch 1 para 61, should be preferred.

10 This includes a petition complaining that corrupt or illegal practices, or illegal payments, employments or hirings, have extensively prevailed even though the alleged offences are or include offences other than corrupt practices: Representation of the People Act 1983 s 122(7); National Assembly for Wales (Representation of the People) Order 2007, SI 2007/236, art 88(7). There is no equivalent provision for the purposes of European parliamentary election petitions because corrupt and illegal practices may be cited in such petitions only when they are related to personation and other voting offences: see PARA 765.

11 'Payment' includes any pecuniary or other reward; and 'pecuniary reward' and 'money' include any office, place or employment and any valuable security or equivalent of money and any valuable consideration: Representation of the People Act 1983 s 185; National Assembly for Wales (Representation of the People) Order 2007, SI 2007/236, art 137.

12 Representation of the People Act 1983 s 122(2); National Assembly for Wales (Representation of the People) Order 2007, SI 2007/236, art 88(2). As to European parliamentary election petitions see note 10. The payment, unlike a payment in furtherance of an illegal practice, may have been made at any time since the election. However, in *Kidderminster Case* (1874) 2 O'M & H 170 at 172, Mellor J (on the previous, but similar, statutory wording) expressed the opinion that the case must be confined to payments made within the 28 days and may not embrace those made within the 21 days after the return. There is nothing in the Representation of the People Act 1983 s 122(2) corresponding to the words 'so far as respects that illegal practice' in s 122(3) (see the text and note 13). It would seem, however, that the corresponding limitation is to be implied: see *Kidderminster Case* at 172 per Mellor J; *Brecon Borough Case, Watkins and Watkins v Holford* (1871) 2 O'M & H 43.

It would seem that extended time would not be allowed if another petition had already been heard and dismissed: see PARA 858; and cf PARAS 793, 861. This would seem to be the case where the petition was against a candidate first declared to be successful on the hearing of a petition against another candidate: cf *Taunton Case, Waygood v James* (1869) LR 4 CP 361.

13 Representation of the People Act 1983 s 122(3)(a); National Assembly for Wales (Representation of the People) Order 2007, SI 2007/236, art 88(3)(a). As to European parliamentary election petitions see note 10.

14 Representation of the People Act 1983 s 122(4) (amended by the Representation of the People Act 1985 s 24, Sch 4 para 44); National Assembly for Wales (Representation of the People) Order 2007, SI 2007/236, art 88(4). As to European parliamentary election petitions see note 10.

15 Representation of the People Act 1983 s 122(4)(a); National Assembly for Wales (Representation of the People) Order 2007, SI 2007/236, art 88(4)(a). As to European parliamentary election petitions see note 10. As to the time for delivering the return and the declaration to the returning officer see PARAS 280–281. In relation to a Welsh Assembly election, head (1) in the text refers to a member who was an individual candidate: art 88(4)(a). Where the member was a party list candidate, the day specified is that on which the Electoral Commission receives the return and declaration as to election expenses by the treasurer of the registered political party and the regional returning officer receives the declaration as to election expenses by that member: art 88(4)(b). As to references to a group of party list candidates and as to the meaning of 'individual candidate' for these purposes see PARA 230 notes 19, 23. As to the meaning of 'registered political party' for these purposes see PARA 256. As to the appointment of an election agent for parliamentary and local government elections see PARA 231; and as to the appointment of an election agent for Welsh Assembly elections see PARA 235. As to a registered political party's nominating officer see PARA 253.

16 Representation of the People Act 1983 s 122(4)(b); National Assembly for Wales (Representation of the People) Order 2007, SI 2007/236, art 88(4)(c). As to European parliamentary election petitions see note 10.

17 Representation of the People Act 1983 s 122(4)(c); National Assembly for Wales (Representation of the People) Order 2007, SI 2007/236, art 88(4)(d). As to European parliamentary election petitions see note 10. As to authorised excuses see PARA 688 et seq.

18 Representation of the People Act 1983 s 122(3)(b); National Assembly for Wales (Representation of the People) Order 2007, SI 2007/236, art 88(3)(b). As to European parliamentary election petitions see note 10.

786. Amendment of election petition. If a parliamentary or Welsh Assembly election petition[1] has been presented within the period of 21 days from the making of the return or, where the petition contains an allegation of corrupt practice and a specific allegation of payment, within 28 days after that payment[2], then, for the purpose of questioning the return or the election upon an allegation of an illegal practice, the petition may be amended with the leave of the High Court[3] within the time within which a petition questioning the election upon the allegation of that illegal practice could be presented[4]. The provisions as to the time of presentation of a petition alleging an illegal practice[5] or the amendment of such a petition[6] apply whether or not the act constituting the alleged illegal practice amounted to a corrupt practice, and they apply also to the corrupt practices of incurring or aiding, abetting, counselling or procuring the incurring of certain expenses not authorised by the election agent, or making a false declaration about such expenses[7], as if they were illegal practices[8]. An affidavit in support of the application is desirable[9].

The High Court has no jurisdiction to allow an amendment of a petition after the time prescribed by statute by the introduction of a fresh substantive charge[10]; nor to allow a petitioner to change the grounds on which he claims he has capacity to bring the petition[11]; nor to convert an offence charged under one statutory provision into an offence against another related provision, although the facts might support the latter offence[12]. It is submitted that there is no jurisdiction to allow an amendment introducing a fresh charge, whether the charge sought to be added is one of a fresh nature, or whether it is one only of a fresh instance not covered by the allegations in the petition as standing[13].

The objection to adding a charge after the time for presenting a petition has elapsed does not apply to withdrawing a charge, and it would seem that this may be done. The withdrawal of that portion of a petition which claims the seat cannot, however, be effected by way of amendment because the rights of the electors would be affected by their not having the opportunity of substituting another petitioner[14].

Allegations which disclose no offence or which are otherwise immaterial may be struck out[15].

1　As to parliamentary election petitions see PARA 761; and as to Welsh Assembly election petitions see PARA 764. There is no equivalent provision for the purposes of European parliamentary election petitions because corrupt and illegal practices may be cited in such petitions only when they are related to personation and other voting offences: see PARA 765.

2　As to the time limited for presentation of an election petition see PARA 785.

3　Leave ought not to be given on an application without notice: *Shaw v Reckitt (Pontefract Election Petition)* [1893] 2 QB 59, CA.

4　Representation of the People Act 1983 s 122(5); National Assembly for Wales (Representation of the People) Order 2007, SI 2007/236, art 88(5). The power of amendment given by this provision applies, it has been held, where it is sought to amend by alleging an illegal payment, employment, or hiring which is not an illegal practice: *York County, East Riding, Buckrose Division Case* (1886) 4 O'M & H 110 at 116. As to the withdrawal of petitions see PARA 813 et seq.

5　See PARA 785.

6　Ie, in relation to a parliamentary election, under the Representation of the People Act 1983 s 122(5) or, in relation to a Welsh Assembly election, under the National Assembly for Wales (Representation of the People) Order 2007, SI 2007/236, art 88(5) (see the text and notes 1–4).

7　Ie the matters which are corrupt practices, in relation to a parliamentary election, under the Representation of the People Act 1983 s 75 and, in relation to a Welsh Assembly election, under the National Assembly for Wales (Representation of the People) Order 2007, SI 2007/236, art 46 (see PARA 279).

8　Representation of the People Act 1983 s 122(6); National Assembly for Wales (Representation of the People) Order 2007, SI 2007/236, art 88(6).

9   *Great Yarmouth Borough Case* (1906) 5 O'M & H 176; *Cornwall, Bodmin Division Case* (1906) 5 O'M & H 225.
10 *Maude v Lowley* (1874) LR 9 CP 165 (municipal), which was followed in *Clark v Wallond* (1883) 52 LJQB 321 (municipal); *Norwich Case, Birbeck v Bullard* (1886) 2 TLR 273; *Cremer v Lowles* [1896] 1 QB 504, CA; *Lancaster County, Lancaster Division Case* (1896) 5 O'M & H 39 at 40. See also the doubt expressed as to the court having such jurisdiction in *Youghal Borough Case* (1869) 1 O'M & H 291 at 296 per O'Brien J. The peculiar nature of the jurisdiction and the importance in the public interest of securing an early determination of the matter are, it seems relevant considerations in regard to extensions of time: see *Senanayake v Navaratne* [1954] AC 640 at 851, [1954] 2 All ER 805 at 810, PC (Ceylon election).
11 *Hobson v Fishburn* (1988) Times, 21 November, DC. The petitioner had claimed capacity to bring the petition under the Representation of the People Act 1983 s 121(1)(b) (see PARA 781); he was refused leave to amend the petition out of time to claim capacity under s 121(1)(a) or (c) (see PARA 781); and he was also refused leave to withdraw the petition so that another petitioner could be substituted (see PARA 813 note 2).
12 See *Cork, Eastern Division Case* (1911) 6 O'M & H 318 at 337; *Manchester, Eastern Division Case* (1892) 4 O'M & H 120.
13 In *Cremer v Lowles* [1896] 1 QB 504, CA, there was a general allegation in the petition that the respondent had been guilty of 'other corrupt and illegal practices before, during, and after the election', but on his seeking to include in his particulars offences committed after the presentation of his petition and after the time limited for amendment, such particulars were struck out.
14 *Aldridge v Hurst* (1876) 1 CPD 410.
15 *Stevens v Tillett* (1870) LR 6 CP 147; *Brecon Borough Case* (1871) 2 O'M & H 170n; *Sheffield, Attercliffe Division Case* (1906) 5 O'M & H 218 at 220; *Northumberland, Berwick-upon-Tweed Division Case* (1923) 7 O'M & H 1 at 3.

787.   Supplemental petition. A supplemental petition, founded on new matter discovered since the original petition was presented, may be filed to cure some defect in the original petition[1] or to meet some difficulty as to the time at which the original petition was presented[2].

1   *Poole Case, Hurdle and Stark v Waring* (1874) 31 LT 171 at 177. Supplemental petitions which are founded on new matter discovered since the original petition was presented may be presented within the time within which the original petition could have been presented: see 2 Roe on Elections (2nd Edn) 148, 191.
2   *Poole Case, Hurdle and Stark v Waring* (1874) as reported in 2 O'M & H 123 at 127. However, the usual course is to amend the original petition as it avoids the necessity of giving security under the supplemental petition. As to the giving of security for costs see PARA 796 et seq.

788.   Service of petition. A parliamentary, Welsh Assembly or European parliamentary election petition[1] must be served in such manner as may be prescribed[2].

1   As to parliamentary election petitions see PARA 761; as to Welsh Assembly election petitions see PARA 764; and as to European parliamentary election petitions see PARA 765.
2   Representation of the People Act 1983 s 121(5) (amended by the Political Parties, Elections and Referendums Act 2000 s 138, Sch 18 paras 1, 19(3)); European Parliamentary Elections Regulations 2004, SI 2004/293, reg 89(5); National Assembly for Wales (Representation of the People) Order 2007, SI 2007/236, art 87(7). As to the service of documents for these purposes see PARA 804.

B. LOCAL GOVERNMENT ELECTIONS AND LOCAL AUTHORITY REFERENDUMS

789.   Form and contents of petition. A petition questioning a local authority referendum[1] or an election under the Local Government Act 1972[2] must be in the prescribed form[3]. The petition must state: (1) (except in the case of a local authority referendum petition) in which capacity the petitioner or each of the petitioners presents the petition[4]; (2) the date and result of the election or referendum (as the case may be) to which the petition relates[5]; (3) in the case of a petition alleging a corrupt or illegal practice at an election[6] or in the case of any referendum petition, the date from which the time for the presentation of the petition is to be calculated[7]; and (4) the grounds on which relief is sought, setting out with sufficient particularity the facts relied on but not the evidence by which they are to be proved[8].

The petition must conclude with a prayer setting out particulars of the relief claimed[9], and must be signed by the petitioner[10].

1 Ie a referendum held, in relation to Wales, under the Local Authorities (Conduct of Referendums) (Wales) Regulations 2008, SI 2008/1848, or, in relation to England, under the Local Authorities (Conduct of Referendums) (England) Regulations 2012, SI 2012/323. As to the meaning of 'referendum' for these purposes see PARA 574 note 2. The provision made for the questioning of an election under the Local Government Act 1972 is applied and modified for the purpose of questioning a local authority referendum: see PARA 766. As to the meaning of 'election under the Local Government Act 1972' see PARA 11 note 2. As to the application of the Representation of the People Act 1983 Pt III (ss 120–186) to other polls see PARA 763.

2 As to the questioning of an election in England and Wales under the Local Government Act 1972 see PARA 762.

3 Representation of the People Act 1983 s 128(3); and see note 1. The petition must be in the form set out in the Election Petition Rules 1960, SI 1960/543, Schedule (amended by SI 1985/1278), or a form to the like effect with such variations as the circumstances may require: Election Petition Rules 1960, SI 1960/543, r 4(1). The Election Petition Rules 1960, SI 1960/543 have been applied and modified for the purposes of a local authority referendum petition and other petitions: see PARA 767.

4 Election Petition Rules 1960, SI 1960/543, r 4(1)(a) (amended by SI 1985/1278). As to the persons who may present a petition see PARA 790.

5 Election Petition Rules 1960, SI 1960/543, r 4(1)(b); and see note 3.

6 Ie a petition mentioned in the Representation of the People Act 1983 s 129(2), (3) or (4): see PARA 793.

7 Election Petition Rules 1960, SI 1960/543, r 4(1)(c) (amended by SI 1985/1278); and see note 3. As to the time for presentation in such a case see PARA 793.

8 Election Petition Rules 1960, SI 1960/543, r 4(1)(d); and see note 3. As to allegations in the petition see further PARA 780.

9 Election Petition Rules 1960, SI 1960/543, r 4(1); and see note 3.

10 Representation of the People Act 1983 s 128(3); and see note 1.

790. Who may present a petition. A petition questioning a local authority referendum[1] or an election under the Local Government Act 1972[2] may be presented by four or more persons who voted or had a right to vote[3] as electors at the election or referendum (as the case may be)[4]. A petition questioning an election under the Local Government Act 1972 may be presented alternatively by a person alleging himself to have been a candidate at the election[5].

1 Ie a referendum held, in relation to Wales, under the Local Authorities (Conduct of Referendums) (Wales) Regulations 2008, SI 2008/1848, or, in relation to England, under the Local Authorities (Conduct of Referendums) (England) Regulations 2012, SI 2012/323. As to the meaning of 'referendum' for these purposes see PARA 574 note 2. The provision made for the questioning of an election under the Local Government Act 1972 is applied and modified for the purpose of questioning a local authority referendum: see PARA 766. As to the meaning of 'election under the Local Government Act 1972' see PARA 11 note 2. As to the application of the Representation of the People Act 1983 Pt III (ss 120–186) to other polls see PARA 763.

2 As to the questioning of an election in England and Wales under the Local Government Act 1972 see PARA 762.

3 As to the meaning of 'persons who voted or had a right to vote' see PARA 781 note 2.

4 Representation of the People Act 1983 s 128(1); and see note 1. The reference in s 128(1) to a person who voted as an elector at an election or who had the right so to vote does not include a person who had an anonymous entry in the register of electors: s 128(1A) (added by the Electoral Administration Act 2006 s 10(2), Sch 1 paras 2, 12). As to the meaning of 'anonymous entry' in relation to a register of electors see PARA 148.

5   Representation of the People Act 1983 s 128(1). As to the meaning of 'candidate' generally see PARA 230. See also *Re Cambridge County Council Election Petition, Fordham v Webber* [1925] 2 KB 740, DC.

791. Who may be respondent. A person whose election under the Local Government Act 1972[1] is questioned by a petition may be made a respondent to it[2]. Additionally, in the case of such an election, or in the case of any local authority referendum[3], any returning officer of whose conduct a petition complains may be made a respondent to the petition[4]. Two or more candidates (in the case of an election) or two or more persons (in the case of a referendum) may be made respondents to the same petition, but the petition is deemed to be a separate petition against each respondent[5]. A petition may be presented complaining of the election of a person who has since died[6].

Where the ground on which a petition seeks to avoid the respondent's election applies equally to another candidate elected at the same election (but who is not a respondent to the petition), it is not a necessary condition to the hearing and determining of the respondent's petition that the other candidate should be joined as a respondent[7], the underlying premise being that a petition is not competent for the purpose of obtaining relief whose effect would be to unseat an elected candidate unless the person whose election is being questioned has been joined as a respondent to the election petition[8].

1   As to the meaning of 'election under the Local Government Act 1972' see PARA 11 note 2. As to the questioning of an election in England and Wales under the Local Government Act 1972 see PARA 762.

2   Representation of the People Act 1983 s 128(2). However, an unsuccessful candidate cannot be made a respondent to an election petition against his will: *Maidenhead Case, Lovering v Dawson* (1875) LR 10 CP 711; *Yates v Leach* (1874) LR 9 CP 605.

3   Ie a referendum held, in relation to Wales, under the Local Authorities (Conduct of Referendums) (Wales) Regulations 2008, SI 2008/1848, or, in relation to England, under the Local Authorities (Conduct of Referendums) (England) Regulations 2012, SI 2012/323. As to the meaning of 'referendum' for these purposes see PARA 574 note 2. The provision made for the questioning of an election under the Local Government Act 1972 is applied and modified for the purpose of questioning a local authority referendum: see PARA 766. As to the application of the Representation of the People Act 1983 Pt III (ss 120–186) to other polls see PARA 763.

4   Representation of the People Act 1983 s 128(2); and see note 3. In *Absalom v Gillett* [1995] 2 All ER 661, [1995] 1 WLR 128, it was held that the presiding officer may be presumed to be the returning officer for the purposes of the Representation of the People Act 1983 s 128(2) in relation to an uncontested election. However, this case may have application only to City of London elections (within which context the point arose), as such elections are governed by local Acts which do not provide an equivalent remedy to that contained in the Representation of the People Act 1983 s 35 (returning officers for local elections in England and Wales: see PARA 354).

5   Representation of the People Act 1983 s 138(3); and see note 3. The petitions are tried together: see PARA 805. The court in *Pease v Norwood* (1869) LR 4 CP 235 seemed to doubt whether the provision by which the petition is deemed to be a separate petition against each respondent had any substantial effect. As to security for costs in such cases see PARA 796.

6   See PARA 782.

7   *Line v Warren* (1884) 14 QBD 73; on appeal (1885) 14 QBD 548, CA.

8   *Absalom v Gillett* [1995] 2 All ER 661 at 671, [1995] 1 WLR 128 at 138 per Laws J, in the context of a petition questioning a City of London election, applying *Line v Warren* (1885) 14 QBD 548 at 552–554, CA, per Brett MR. Common justice dictates that a successful candidate whose election and status as a democratic representative is impugned by litigation ought to be heard; because the Representation of the People Act 1983 s 128(2) defines the potential respondents to a petition under s 128(1), the subjunctive 'may' is a word of limitation rather than permission and the requirement to serve a petition is mandatory: *Absalom v Gillett*. In *Absalom v Gillett* at 670–671 and 137, Laws J noted that *Copeland v Jackson* (July 1933, unreported) supported the view that a successful candidate cannot be unseated without his being a party to the petition.

792. Mode of presentation of petition. The presentation of a petition questioning a local authority referendum[1] or an election under the Local Government Act 1972[2] is made to the High Court in the Queen's Bench Division in a similar manner to that in which the presentation of a parliamentary election petition is made[3]. The master who is for the time being nominated as the prescribed officer in relation to parliamentary election petitions[4] is also the prescribed officer in relation to petitions questioning elections under the Local Government Act 1972[5] or local authority referendums[6]. The master must send a copy of the petition to the proper officer[7] of the authority for which the election or referendum (as the case may be) was held, who must forthwith publish it in that authority's area[8].

1 Ie a referendum held, in relation to Wales, under the Local Authorities (Conduct of Referendums) (Wales) Regulations 2008, SI 2008/1848, or, in relation to England, under the Local Authorities (Conduct of Referendums) (England) Regulations 2012, SI 2012/323. As to the meaning of 'referendum' for these purposes see PARA 574 note 2. The provision made for the questioning of an election under the Local Government Act 1972 is applied and modified for the purpose of questioning a local authority referendum: see PARA 766. As to the meaning of 'election under the Local Government Act 1972' see PARA 11 note 2. As to the application of the Representation of the People Act 1983 Pt III (ss 120–186) to other polls see PARA 763.
2 As to the questioning of an election in England and Wales under the Local Government Act 1972 see PARA 762.
3 As to the presentation of parliamentary election petitions see PARA 784.
4 See PARA 770.
5 Ie under the Representation of the People Act 1983 Pt III.
6 Representation of the People Act 1983 s 157(6); Election Petition Rules 1960, SI 1960/543, r 2(3) (amended by SI 1985/1278); and see note 1. The Election Petition Rules 1960, SI 1960/543 have been applied and modified for the purposes of a local authority referendum petition and other petitions: see PARA 767.
7 Ie the officer appointed by the local authority for the purpose or, at a parish or community council election, the returning officer: see PARA 777.
8 Representation of the People Act 1983 s 128(4); and see note 1. As to the costs of publication by the returning officer see PARA 784 note 10.

793. Time for presentation of petition. In general, a petition questioning a local authority referendum[1] or an election under the Local Government Act 1972[2] must be presented within 21 days[3] after the day on which the election or referendum (as the case may be) was held[4].

If the petition complains of the election or referendum (as the case may be) on the ground of a corrupt practice[5] and specifically alleges that a payment of money or other reward[6] has been made or promised either since the election by a candidate elected at the election or since the referendum by any person (as the case may be), or on his account or with his privity, in pursuance or furtherance of that corrupt practice, it may be presented within 28 days[7] after the date of the alleged payment or promise, whether or not any other petition against that person has been previously presented or tried[8].

A petition complaining of the election or referendum (as the case may be) on the ground of an illegal practice and specifically alleging a payment of money or other act made or done either since the election by the candidate elected at the election (or by the candidate's agent or with the privity of the candidate or his election agent[9]) or since the referendum by any person (as the case may be), in pursuance or in furtherance of that illegal practice, may be presented at any time within 28 days[10] after the date of that payment or act, whether or not any other petition against that person has been previously presented or tried[11].

A petition complaining of an election where election expenses are allowed on the ground of an illegal practice may be presented at any time before the expiration of 14 days[12] after a specified day[13], this day being: (1) that on which the appropriate officer[14] receives the return and declarations as to election expenses by the candidate to whose election the petition relates and his election agent[15]; or (2) where the return and declarations are received on different days, the last of those days[16]; or (3) where there is an authorised excuse for failing to make the return and declarations, the date of the allowance of the excuse, or, if there was a failure as regards two or more of them and the excuse was allowed at different times, the date of the allowance of the last excuse[17].

The provisions as to the time within which an election petition alleging, either originally[18] or by amendment[19], an illegal practice may be presented apply whether or not the act constituting the alleged illegal practice amounted to a corrupt practice, and they apply also to the corrupt practices of incurring certain election expenses not authorised by the election agent or making a false declaration about such expenses[20] as if they were illegal practices[21]. Similarly, the provisions as to the time within which a referendum petition alleging, either originally[22] or by amendment[23], an illegal practice may be presented apply whether or not the act constituting the alleged illegal practice amounted to a corrupt practice[24].

1   Ie a referendum held, in relation to Wales, under the Local Authorities (Conduct of Referendums) (Wales) Regulations 2008, SI 2008/1848, or, in relation to England, under the Local Authorities (Conduct of Referendums) (England) Regulations 2012, SI 2012/323. As to the meaning of 'referendum' for these purposes see PARA 574 note 2. The provision made for the questioning of an election under the Local Government Act 1972 is applied and modified for the purpose of questioning a local authority referendum: see PARA 766. As to the meaning of 'election under the Local Government Act 1972' see PARA 11 note 2. As to the application of the Representation of the People Act 1983 Pt III (ss 120–186) to other polls see PARA 763.

2   As to the questioning of an election in England and Wales under the Local Government Act 1972 see PARA 762.

3   As to calculation of these times limits and as to the circumstances in which presentation might be deemed see PARA 768.

4   Representation of the People Act 1983 s 129(1); Local Authorities (Conduct of Referendums) (Wales) Regulations 2008, SI 2008/1848, reg 11(2); Local Authorities (Conduct of Referendums) (England) Regulations 2012, SI 2012/323, reg 15(2); and see note 1. For a case where an election petition was presented before the day of election because the petitioner's nomination was rejected by the returning officer see *Re Grangemellon Case* [1909] 2 IR 90 at 103.

5   This includes a petition complaining that corrupt or illegal practices or illegal payments, employments or hirings have extensively prevailed, notwithstanding that the offences alleged are or include offences other than corrupt practices: Representation of the People Act 1983 s 129(8); and see note 1.

6   This includes any office, place or employment and any valuable security or equivalent for money and any valuable consideration: Representation of the People Act 1983 s 185; and see note 1. In the case of a local authority referendum, the reference is to the ground mentioned, in relation to Wales, in the Local Authorities (Conduct of Referendums) (Wales) Regulations 2008, SI 2008/1848, reg 11(1)(d), and, in relation to England, in the Local Authorities (Conduct of Referendums) (England) Regulations 2012, SI 2012/323, reg 15(1)(d) (see PARA 766).

7   As to calculation of time for these purposes see note 3. A local authority referendum petition, on the ground that a payment of money or other reward has been made or promised since the referendum in pursuance of a corrupt or illegal practice, may be presented only with the leave of the High Court: Local Authorities (Conduct of Referendums) (Wales) Regulations 2008, SI 2008/1848, reg 11(3); Local Authorities (Conduct of Referendums) (England) Regulations 2012, SI 2012/323, reg 15(3). An application for leave must be made, not later than 28 days after the date of the alleged payment or promise, by application notice to the court at such time and place as the court may appoint: Local Authorities (Conduct of Referendums) (Wales) Regulations 2008, SI 2008/1848, reg 11(4); Local Authorities (Conduct of Referendums) (England) Regulations 2012, SI 2012/323, reg 15(4). Not less than seven days before the day so appointed, the applicant must serve the application notice, stating the grounds on which the application is made, on the respondent and the Director of Public Prosecutions and

lodge a copy in the election petitions office and publish notice of the intended application in at least one newspaper circulating in the voting area for the referendum to which the application relates: Local Authorities (Conduct of Referendums) (Wales) Regulations 2008, SI 2008/1848, reg 11(5), (6); Local Authorities (Conduct of Referendums) (England) Regulations 2012, SI 2012/323, reg 15(5), (6). As to the meaning of 'voting area' see PARA 580 note 2. As to the meaning of 'election petitions office' see PARA 768 note 12.

8   Representation of the People Act 1983 s 129(2); Local Authorities (Conduct of Referendums) (Wales) Regulations 2008, SI 2008/1848, reg 11(3), (4); Local Authorities (Conduct of Referendums) (England) Regulations 2012, SI 2012/323, reg 15(3), (4); and see note 1.

9   As to the appointment of an election agent for local government elections see PARA 231. In relation to an election where candidates are not required to have election agents (see PARA 231 note 3), the reference to an election agent is to be omitted: Representation of the People Act 1983 s 129(9).

10 See note 7.

11 Representation of the People Act 1983 s 129(3); Local Authorities (Conduct of Referendums) (Wales) Regulations 2008, SI 2008/1848, reg 11(3), (4); Local Authorities (Conduct of Referendums) (England) Regulations 2012, SI 2012/323, reg 15(3), (4); and see note 1.

12 See note 3.

13 Representation of the People Act 1983 s 129(4).

14 As to the meaning of 'appropriate officer' see PARA 231 note 5.

15 Representation of the People Act 1983 s 129(5)(a). As to the reference to an election agent see note 9. As to the return and declarations as to expenses see PARA 279 et seq.

16 Representation of the People Act 1983 s 129(5)(b); and see note 17.

17 Representation of the People Act 1983 s 129(5)(c). As to authorised excuses see PARA 688 et seq. Heads (2) and (3) in the text do not apply in relation to an election where candidates are not required to have an election agent (see PARA 231 note 3): s 129(9).

18 Ie the Representation of the People Act 1983 s 129(3)–(5) (see the text and notes 9–17).

19 Ie the Representation of the People Act 1983 s 129(6) (see PARA 792).

20 Ie the matters which are corrupt practices, in relation to an election, under the Representation of the People Act 1983 s 75 (see PARA 279).

21 Representation of the People Act 1983 s 129(7).

22 Ie the Representation of the People Act 1983 s 129(3) (see the text and notes 9–11).

23 Ie the Representation of the People Act 1983 s 129(6) (see PARA 794).

24 Representation of the People Act 1983 s 129(7); and see note 1.

794. Amendment of petition. If a petition questioning a local authority referendum[1] or an election under the Local Government Act 1972[2] has been presented within the period of 21 days from the day of election or referendum (as the case may be)[3], or within 28 days after the payment where there is an allegation of a corrupt practice and a specific allegation of payment[4], then, for the purpose of complaining of the election or referendum (as the case may be) on an allegation of an illegal practice, the petition may be amended with the leave of the High Court within the time within which a petition complaining of the election or referendum (as the case may be) on the ground of that illegal practice could be presented[5].

1   Ie a referendum held, in relation to Wales, under the Local Authorities (Conduct of Referendums) (Wales) Regulations 2008, SI 2008/1848, or, in relation to England, under the Local Authorities (Conduct of Referendums) (England) Regulations 2012, SI 2012/323. As to the meaning of 'referendum' for these purposes see PARA 574 note 2. The provision made for the questioning of an election under the Local Government Act 1972 is applied and modified for the purpose of questioning a local authority referendum: see PARA 766. As to the meaning of 'election under the Local Government Act 1972' see PARA 11 note 2. As to the application of the Representation of the People Act 1983 Pt III (ss 120–186) to other polls see PARA 763.

2   As to the questioning of an election in England and Wales under the Local Government Act 1972 see PARA 762.

3   Ie within the time limited by the Representation of the People Act 1983 s 129(1) (including that provision as applied and modified: see note 1): see PARA 793.

4   Ie within the time limited by the Representation of the People Act 1983 s 129(2) (including that provision as applied and modified: see note 1): see PARA 793.

5 Representation of the People Act 1983 s 129(6); and see note 1. It will be noticed that the High Court's jurisdiction does not have to be exercised by a judge on the rota for the trial of parliamentary election petitions. The statute in this respect follows *Ex p Haseldine* (1895) 59 JP 71, DC; and *Nichol v Fearby* [1923] 1 KB 480. As to the time for presenting a petition complaining of illegal practices see PARA 793. As to case law regarding the amendment of an election petition see PARA 786.

(iv) Service of Notices and Security for Costs

795. Service of notices on respondent etc. Any notice required to be served on a respondent to a petition[1] may be served by delivering it or sending it by post to any solicitor who has given notice of his appointment to act for the respondent[2]. A solicitor who has been so appointed must forthwith give notice of his appointment to the petitioner and lodge a copy of the notice in the elections petition office[3]. If no such notice has been given, any notice required to be served on the respondent may be served in the manner provided[4].

Any notice required to be served on the returning officer or the Director of Public Prosecutions in election petition proceedings may be served by delivering it or sending it by post to him[5].

1 Ie a parliamentary election petition or a petition questioning an election under the Local Government Act 1972 (Election Petition Rules 1960, SI 1960/543, r 2(2)), a Welsh Assembly election petition (Election Petition Rules 1960, SI 1960/543, r 2(2) (as applied: see PARA 767 note 1)), a petition questioning an election under the European Parliamentary Elections Act 2002 (European Parliamentary Election Petition Rules 1979, SI 1979/521, r 2(1) (amended by the European Communities (Amendment) Act 1986 s 3; and by SI 2004/1415)) or a local authority referendum petition (Election Petition Rules 1960, SI 1960/543, r 2(2) (as applied: see PARA 767 note 1)). As to parliamentary election petitions see PARA 761; as to the questioning of an election under the Local Government Act 1972 see PARA 762; as to Welsh Assembly election petitions see PARA 764; as to European parliamentary election petitions see PARA 765; and as to the questioning of a local authority referendum see PARA 766. As to the application and modification of the Election Petition Rules 1960, SI 1960/543 for the purposes of Welsh Assembly election petitions and for the purposes of a local authority referendum petition see PARA 767 note 1. The Election Petition Rules 1960, SI 1960/543, are also applied for the purposes of other petitions: see PARA 767. As to respondents see PARAS 782, 791.
2 Election Petition Rules 1960, SI 1960/543, r 21(2)(a); European Parliamentary Election Petition Rules 1979, SI 1979/521, r 20(2)(a); and see note 1.
3 Election Petition Rules 1960, SI 1960/543, r 21(1); European Parliamentary Election Petition Rules 1979, SI 1979/521, r 20(1); and see note 1. As to the meaning of 'election petitions office' see PARA 768 note 12.
4 Election Petition Rules 1960, SI 1960/543, r 21(2)(b) (amended by SI 1985/1278); European Parliamentary Election Petition Rules 1979, SI 1979/521, r 20(2)(b) (amended by SI 2004/1415); and see note 1. As to the manner of service see PARA 804.
5 Election Petition Rules 1960, SI 1960/543, r 21(3); European Parliamentary Election Petition Rules 1979, SI 1979/521, r 20(3); and see note 1.

796. Amount and form of security for costs. At the time of presenting an election[1] or referendum petition[2], or within three days[3] afterwards, the petitioner must give security for all costs that may become payable by him to any witness summoned on his behalf or to any respondent[4]. Within three days after the presentation of the petition, the petitioner must apply without notice being served on any respondent to a master to fix the amount of security for costs which he is to give[5]. In the case of a parliamentary, Welsh Assembly or European parliamentary election petition, the security must be such amount not exceeding £5,000 as the High Court or a judge of the High Court directs on an application made by the petitioner[6]. In the case of a petition questioning a local authority referendum[7] or an election under the Local Government Act 1972[8], other than a parish or community council election, it must be such amount not exceeding

£2,500 as is directed on such an application made by the petitioner[9]; in the case of a parish or community council election or a poll consequent on a parish or community meeting, it must be such amount not exceeding £1,500 as is so directed[10]. The security must be given in the prescribed[11] manner by recognisance or by a deposit of money, or partly in one way and partly in the other[12]. Deposit by way of security is made by payment into court in accordance with the general rules relating to security for costs[13].

If Parliament is dissolved after a parliamentary election petition has been lodged but before it is heard, the High Court will order the security deposited by the petitioner to be returned to him[14].

1   As to parliamentary election petitions see PARA 761; as to the questioning of an election under the Local Government Act 1972 see PARA 762; as to Welsh Assembly election petitions see PARA 764; and as to European parliamentary election petitions see PARA 765.

2   Provision is made for questioning a local authority referendum by applying and modifying the provision made for questioning an election under the Local Government Act 1972: see PARA 766.

3   As to the calculation of time limits for these purposes see PARA 768.

4   Representation of the People Act 1983 s 136(1); European Parliamentary Elections Regulations 2004, SI 2004/293, reg 94(1); National Assembly for Wales (Representation of the People) Order 2007, SI 2007/236, art 92(1); and see note 2. As to respondents see PARAS 782, 791. The time for giving security cannot be extended: see PARA 768.

5   Election Petition Rules 1960, SI 1960/543, r 5(1) (substituted by SI 1985/1278; and amended by SI 1999/1352); European Parliamentary Election Petition Rules 1979, SI 1979/521, r 5(1) (substituted by SI 1988/557; and amended by SI 1999/1398; SI 2004/1415). As to the application and modification of the Election Petition Rules 1960, SI 1960/543 for the purposes of Welsh Assembly election petitions and for the purposes of a local authority referendum petition see PARA 767 note 1. The Election Petition Rules 1960, SI 1960/543, are also applied for the purposes of other petitions: see PARA 767.

The text refers to the giving of security pursuant to the Representation of the People Act 1983 s 136 or, in relation to a European parliamentary election, under the European Parliamentary Elections Regulations 2004, SI 2004/293, reg 94. Although such provision is not made in the applied provisions as currently modified, it is submitted that it should be understood that, in relation to a Welsh Assembly election petition, security is given pursuant to the National Assembly for Wales (Representation of the People) Order 2007, SI 2007/236, art 92.

6   Representation of the People Act 1983 s 136(2)(a) (amended by the Representation of the People Act 1985 s 24, Sch 4 para 48(a); and the Political Parties, Elections and Referendums Act 2000 s 138, Sch 18 paras 1, 19(4)); European Parliamentary Elections Regulations 2004, SI 2004/293, reg 94(2); National Assembly for Wales (Representation of the People) Order 2007, SI 2007/236, art 92(2); and see note 2.

7   Ie a referendum held, in relation to Wales, under the Local Authorities (Conduct of Referendums) (Wales) Regulations 2008, SI 2008/1848, or, in relation to England, under the Local Authorities (Conduct of Referendums) (England) Regulations 2012, SI 2012/323.

8   As to the meaning of 'election under the Local Government Act 1972' see PARA 11 note 2.

9   Representation of the People Act 1983 s 136(2)(b) (amended by the Representation of the People Act 1985 Sch 4 para 48(b); and the Political Parties, Elections and Referendums Act 2000 Sch 18 paras 1, 19(4)).

10 Representation of the People Act 1983 s 136(2)(b) (as amended: see note 9) (applied with modifications by the Local Elections (Parishes and Communities) (England and Wales) Rules 2006, SI 2006/3305, r 6(b); and by the Parish and Community Meetings (Polls) Rules 1987, SI 1987/1, r 6(f)).

11 Ie prescribed by rules of court: Representation of the People Act 1983 s 185 (including that provision as applied see note 2); European Parliamentary Elections Regulations 2004, SI 2004/293, reg 86; National Assembly for Wales (Representation of the People) Order 2007, SI 2007/236, art 137(1). See the rules referred to in note 5; and PARAS 797–800.

12 Representation of the People Act 1983 s 136(2); European Parliamentary Elections Regulations 2004, SI 2004/293, reg 94(2); National Assembly for Wales (Representation of the People) Order 2007, SI 2007/236, art 92(2); and see note 2. As to recognisances as security for costs see further PARA 797.

13 See the Election Petition Rules 1960, SI 1960/543, r 2(4), the European Parliamentary Election Petition Rules 1979, SI 1979/521, r 2(3); note 5; and PARA 767. As to the general rules of court relating to security for costs see CPR 25.12–25.13; and CIVIL PROCEDURE vol 11 (2009) PARAS 745–748. In relation to a European parliamentary election petition and without prejudice to the rule that is set out in the text and note 5, a petitioner when making a payment into court on account of his security for costs may do so (if a petition relates to an electoral region other than the combined region) at the election petitions office: European Parliamentary Election Petition Rules 1979, SI 1979/521, r 5(4)(a) (r 5(4) added by SI 2004/1415). As to European parliamentary election petitions which relate to the combined region see the European Parliamentary Election Petition Rules 1979, SI 1979/521, r 5(4)(b) (as so added). As to the meaning of 'election petitions office' see PARA 768 note 12. As to the combined region see PARA 77.

14 *Carter v Mills* (1874) LR 9 CP 117.

797. Recognisances as security for costs. In the case of an election[1] or referendum petition[2], a recognisance as security for costs may be entered into by any number of sureties not exceeding four[3]. A recognisance must be acknowledged before a person authorised to take affidavits under the Commissioners for Oaths Acts 1889 to 1891 or the Solicitors Act 1974[4], and must be filed forthwith after being acknowledged[5]. The recognisance must be accompanied by an affidavit sworn by each surety, stating that after payment of all his debts he is worth a sum not less than that for which he is bound by his recognisance[6].

1 As to parliamentary election petitions see PARA 761; as to the questioning of an election under the Local Government Act 1972 see PARA 762; as to Welsh Assembly election petitions see PARA 764; and as to European parliamentary election petitions see PARA 765.

2 Provision is made for questioning a local authority referendum by applying and modifying the provision made for questioning an election under the Local Government Act 1972: see PARA 766.

3 Representation of the People Act 1983 s 136(2); European Parliamentary Elections Regulations 2004, SI 2004/293, reg 94(2); National Assembly for Wales (Representation of the People) Order 2007, SI 2007/236, art 92(2); and see note 2. As to the amount and form of security for costs generally see PARA 796. A security given by a petitioner may be liable to objection as insufficient: see PARA 799.

4 As to the powers referred to in the text under the Commissioners for Oaths Acts 1889 and 1891 see CIVIL PROCEDURE vol 11 (2009) PARAS 1026–1027.

5 Election Petition Rules 1960, SI 1960/543, r 5(2) (substituted by SI 1985/1278); European Parliamentary Election Petition Rules 1979, SI 1979/521, r 5(2) (substituted by SI 2004/1415; and amended by SI 2009/1118). As to European parliamentary election petitions which relate to the combined region see the European Parliamentary Election Petition Rules 1979, SI 1979/521, r 5(2) (as so substituted). As to the combined region see PARA 77. As to the application and modification of the Election Petition Rules 1960, SI 1960/543 for the purposes of Welsh Assembly election petitions and for the purposes of a local authority referendum petition see PARA 767 note 1. The Election Petition Rules 1960, SI 1960/543, are also applied for the purposes of other petitions: see PARA 767.

6 Election Petition Rules 1960, SI 1960/543, r 5(3) (substituted by SI 1985/1278); European Parliamentary Election Petition Rules 1979, SI 1979/521, r 5(3) (substituted by SI 1988/557); and see note 5.

798. Notice of presentation of petition and of security. Within five days[1] after giving the security for costs pursuant to an election or referendum petition[2], the petitioner must serve on the respondent[3] and the Director of Public Prosecutions a notice of the presentation of the petition and of the nature and amount of the security he has given, together with a copy of the petition and of the affidavit[4] accompanying any recognisance[5]. Service must be effected in the manner in which a claim form is served and a certificate of service must be filed as soon as practicable after service has been effected[6].

1   As to the calculation of time limits for these purposes see PARA 768. See also note 5.
2   As to security for costs see PARAS 796–797. As to parliamentary election petitions see PARA 761;
    as to the questioning of an election under the Local Government Act 1972 see PARA 762; as to
    Welsh Assembly election petitions see PARA 764; and as to European parliamentary election
    petitions see PARA 765. Provision is made for questioning a local authority referendum by
    applying and modifying the provision made for questioning an election under the Local
    Government Act 1972: see PARA 766.
3   As to respondents see PARAS 782, 791.
4   As to the affidavit see PARA 797.
5   Representation of the People Act 1983 s 136(3) (substituted by the Representation of the People
    Act 1985 s 24, Sch 4 para 48(d)); Election Petition Rules 1960, SI 1960/543, r 6(1) (substituted
    by SI 1985/1278); European Parliamentary Election Petition Rules 1979, SI 1979/521, r 6(1)
    (substituted by SI 1988/557; and amended by SI 2004/1415); European Parliamentary Elections
    Regulations 2004, SI 2004/293, reg 94(3); National Assembly for Wales (Representation of the
    People) Order 2007, SI 2007/236, art 92(3); and see note 2. As to the application and
    modification of the Election Petition Rules 1960, SI 1960/543 for the purposes of Welsh
    Assembly election petitions and for the purposes of a local authority referendum petition see
    PARA 767 note 1. The Election Petition Rules 1960, SI 1960/543, are also applied for the
    purposes of other petitions: see PARA 767. As to the application of the Representation of the
    People Act 1983 Pt III (ss 120–186) to other polls see PARA 763.
        Any enlargement of the time limit prescribed for the purposes set out in the text is absolutely
    prohibited under the rules relating to election petitions, which have primacy over the Civil
    Procedure Rules in this respect: *Ahmed v Kennedy, Ullah v Pagel* [2002] EWCA Civ 1793,
    [2003] 2 All ER 440, [2003] 1 WLR 1820, applying *Williams v Tenby Corpn* (1879) 5 CPD 135
    (service of notice within the prescribed time was a condition precedent to the trial of an election
    petition) and approving *Absalom v Gillett* [1995] 2 All ER 661, [1995] 1 WLR 128
    (incompetent petition served in relation to a City of London election could not be amended and
    served again out of time, despite the draconian effect). In the latter case, Laws J at 670 and
    136–137 cited *Carter v Griffiths* (28 July 1981, unreported) as being to like effect (rejecting a
    submission that the similar provisions that preceded the Representation of the People Act 1983
    s 136 were directory only), and noted that Ralph Gibson J in so holding cited *Devan Nair v
    Yong Kuan Teik* [1967] 2 AC 31 at 44, [1967] 2 All ER 34 at 40, PC (a case concerning similar
    rules in respect of election petitions in Malaysia, where *Williams v Tenby Corpn* was stated to
    be 'plainly rightly decided'). *Devan Nair v Yong Kuan Teik* was considered to be highly
    persuasive in *Ahmed v Kennedy, Ullah v Pagel*, which also overruled *Young v Figgins, The
    Shrewsbury Petition* (1869) 19 LT 499 (in which a failure to serve a respondent had been
    characterised as a 'formal objection' which could be ignored under a rule in the Election Petition
    Rules 1868, no equivalent of which survives in the Election Petition Rules 1960, SI 1960/543).
    See *Saghir v Najib* [2005] EWHC 417 (QB), [2005] All ER (D) 353 (Mar) (the petitioners, in
    leaving an unamended copy of the petition on the court's files and in purporting to serve
    amended copies to the respondents, had failed within the prescribed time to serve notice of the
    presentation of the petition or to serve a copy of the petition, and their failure to state, in the
    notice as to the nature and amount of security, the date on which security had actually been
    given constituted a failure to serve, within the time prescribed, any notice of the nature and
    amount of the security which they had given). See also *Ali v Haques* [2006] All ER (D) 113
    (Oct) (regarding the interaction between the Election Petition Rules 1960, SI 1960/543, r 6 and
    the European Parliamentary Election Petition Rules 1979, SI 1979/521, r 6 and the more
    generalised provisions of the Representation of the People Act 1983 s 184 (see PARA 804)). See
    further PARA 768. The right to free elections under the Convention for the Protection of Human
    Rights and Fundamental Freedoms (Rome, 4 November 1950; TS 71 (1953); Cmd 8969) ('the
    European Convention on Human Rights') First Protocol art 3 (see RIGHTS AND FREEDOMS
    vol 88A (2013) PARA 243), requires the Election Petition Rules 1960, SI 1960/543, to be read
    down, so as to allow the court to extend the time limit: *Miller v Bull* [2009] EWHC 2640 (QB),
    [2010] 1 WLR 1861, [2010] PTSR 1737 (cited in PARA 768 note 14).
6   Election Petition Rules 1960, SI 1960/543, r 6(2) (substituted by SI 1985/1278; and amended by
    SI 1999/1352); European Parliamentary Election Petition Rules 1979, SI 1979/521, r 6(2)
    (substituted by SI 1988/557; and amended by SI 1999/1398); and see note 5.

799.   Objections to recognisances.   A respondent to an election or referendum
petition[1] may object in writing to any recognisance as security for costs[2] on the
ground that any surety is insufficient[3] or is dead or cannot be found or
ascertained for want of a sufficient description in the recognisance, or that a

person named in the recognisance has not duly acknowledged it[4]. Within 14 days[5] after service on him of the notice of presentation of the petition and of the nature of the proposed security[6], a respondent who intends to object to a recognisance on any of those grounds must serve on the petitioner notice of his objection, stating his grounds, and issue and serve on the petitioner an application notice to determine the validity or otherwise of the objection[7].

1   As to respondents see PARAS 782, 791. As to parliamentary election petitions see PARA 761; as to the questioning of an election under the Local Government Act 1972 see PARA 762; as to Welsh Assembly election petitions see PARA 764; and as to European parliamentary election petitions see PARA 765. Provision is made for questioning a local authority referendum by applying and modifying the provision made for questioning an election under the Local Government Act 1972: see PARA 766. As to the application of the Representation of the People Act 1983 Pt III (ss 120–186) to other polls see PARA 763.

2   As to recognisances as security for costs see PARAS 797–798.

3   A security given by a petitioner is not invalid in itself, but is liable to rejection as insufficient: *Pease v Norwood* (1869) LR 4 CP 235.

4   Representation of the People Act 1983 s 136(4) (amended by the Representation of the People Act 1985 s 24, Sch 4 para 48(e)(i)); European Parliamentary Elections Regulations 2004, SI 2004/293, reg 94(4); National Assembly for Wales (Representation of the People) Order 2007, SI 2007/236, art 92(4); and see note 1.

5   As to the calculation of time limits for these purposes see PARA 768.

6   As to this notice see PARA 798.

7   Election Petition Rules 1960, SI 1960/543, r 7(1) (amended by SI 1985/1278; SI 1999/1352); European Parliamentary Election Petition Rules 1979, SI 1979/521, r 7(1) (amended by SI 1988/557; SI 1999/1398; SI 2004/1415). As to the application and modification of the Election Petition Rules 1960, SI 1960/543 for the purposes of Welsh Assembly election petitions and for the purposes of a local authority referendum petition see PARA 767 note 1. The Election Petition Rules 1960, SI 1960/543, are also applied for the purposes of other petitions: see PARA 767.

   As to the possibility of objecting to a recognisance on grounds other than those set out in the text see *Cobett v Hibbert* (1868) 19 LT 501; however, the contrary view is that the Representation of the People Act 1983 s 136(4) is exhaustive as to the grounds of objection.

800.   Hearing of objections.   An application notice to determine the validity, or otherwise, of an objection to a recognisance as security for costs pursuant to an election or referendum petition[1] must be heard in chambers by a master, subject to an appeal to a judge within five days[2] after the master's decision[3]. If the objection is allowed, the master or judge having cognisance of the matter must at the same time determine what sum of money will make the security sufficient, and the petitioner may within five days thereafter remove the objection by deposit of that sum[4].

The costs of and incidental to hearing and deciding objections made to the security given on the presentation of an election petition are in the court's discretion[5].

1   As to recognisances as security for costs and the application notice referred to in the text see PARAS 797–798. As to parliamentary election petitions see PARA 761; as to the questioning of an election under the Local Government Act 1972 see PARA 762; as to Welsh Assembly election petitions see PARA 764; and as to European parliamentary election petitions see PARA 765. Provision is made for questioning a local authority referendum by applying and modifying the provision made for questioning an election under the Local Government Act 1972: see PARA 766.

2   As to the calculation of time limits for these purposes see PARA 768.

3   Representation of the People Act 1983 ss 136(6), 185; Election Petition Rules 1960, SI 1960/543, r 7(2) (amended by SI 1999/1352); European Parliamentary Election Petition Rules 1979, SI 1979/521, r 7(2) (amended by SI 1999/1398); European Parliamentary Elections Regulations 2004, SI 2004/293, regs 86, 94(5); National Assembly for Wales (Representation of the People) Order 2007, SI 2007/236, art 92(5), 137(1); and see note 1. As to the application

and modification of the Election Petition Rules 1960, SI 1960/543 for the purposes of Welsh Assembly election petitions and for the purposes of a local authority referendum petition see PARA 767 note 1. The Election Petition Rules 1960, SI 1960/543, are also applied for the purposes of other petitions: see PARA 767. As to the application of the Representation of the People Act 1983 Pt III (ss 120–186) to other polls see PARA 763.

4   Representation of the People Act 1983 s 136(7) (amended by the Representation of the People Act 1985 s 24, Sch 4 para 48(e)(iii)); Election Petition Rules 1960, SI 1960/543, r 7(3); European Parliamentary Election Petition Rules 1979, SI 1979/521, r 7(3); European Parliamentary Elections Regulations 2004, SI 2004/293, reg 94(6); National Assembly for Wales (Representation of the People) Order 2007, SI 2007/236, art 92(6); and see notes 1, 3.

5   See the Senior Courts Act 1981 s 51(1); and CIVIL PROCEDURE vol 12 (2009) PARA 1732. See also PARA 767; and see *R (on the application of the Conservative and Unionist Party) v Election Comr* [2010] EWCA Civ 1332, [2011] PTSR 416, [2010] All ER (D) 241 (Nov) (cited in PARA 875 note 3).

801. Time when petition is at issue. An election or referendum petition[1] is at issue[2]: (1) where the petitioner gives the security for costs as required[3] by a deposit of money equal to the amount of the security so required, at the time when the security is so given[4]; and (2) in any other case, on the expiry of the time limited for objections to a recognisance as security for costs[5] or, if an objection is made, on that objection being disallowed or removed[6], whichever happens last[7].

1   As to parliamentary election petitions see PARA 761; as to the questioning of an election under the Local Government Act 1972 see PARA 762; as to Welsh Assembly election petitions see PARA 764; and as to European parliamentary election petitions see PARA 765. Provision is made for questioning a local authority referendum by applying and modifying the provision made for questioning an election under the Local Government Act 1972: see PARA 766. As to the application of the Representation of the People Act 1983 Pt III (ss 120–186) to other polls see PARA 763.

2   Representation of the People Act 1983 s 137(1) (s 137 substituted by the Political Parties, Elections and Referendums Act 2000 s 137(a), Sch 17 paras 1, 3); European Parliamentary Elections Regulations 2004, SI 2004/293, reg 95(1); National Assembly for Wales (Representation of the People) Order 2007, SI 2007/236, art 93(1); and see note 1.

3   As to the requirement to give security for costs see PARAS 796–797.

4   Representation of the People Act 1983 s 137(2)(a) (as substituted: see note 2); European Parliamentary Elections Regulations 2004, SI 2004/293, reg 95(2)(a); National Assembly for Wales (Representation of the People) Order 2007, SI 2007/236, art 93(2)(a); and see note 1.

5   As to objections to a recognisance see PARA 799.

6   See PARA 800.

7   Representation of the People Act 1983 s 137(2)(b) (as substituted: see note 2); European Parliamentary Elections Regulations 2004, SI 2004/293, reg 95(2)(b); National Assembly for Wales (Representation of the People) Order 2007, SI 2007/236, art 93(2)(b); and see note 1.

(v) Matters Preliminary to Hearing

A. JURISDICTION AND SERVICE

802. In general. With respect to an election or referendum petition[1] and the proceedings on it, and subject to the provisions which regulate the conduct of elections and referendums[2], the High Court has the same powers, jurisdiction and authority as if the petition were an ordinary claim within its jurisdiction[3].

1   As to parliamentary election petitions see PARA 761; as to the questioning of an election under the Local Government Act 1972 see PARA 762; as to Welsh Assembly election petitions see PARA 764; and as to European parliamentary election petitions see PARA 765. Provision is made for questioning a local authority referendum by applying and modifying the provision made for questioning an election under the Local Government Act 1972: see PARA 766. As to the application of the Representation of the People Act 1983 Pt III (ss 120–186) to other polls see PARA 763.

2   Ie, in relation to a parliamentary election or election under the Local Government Act 1972, the Representation of the People Act 1983 (including those provisions as applied and modified for the purposes of a local authority referendum: see note 1), in relation to a European parliamentary election, the European Parliamentary Elections Regulations 2004, SI 2004/293, or in relation to a Welsh Assembly election, the National Assembly for Wales (Representation of the People) Order 2007, SI 2007/236.

3   Representation of the People Act 1983 s 157(3); European Parliamentary Elections Regulations 2004, SI 2004/293, reg 106(2); National Assembly for Wales (Representation of the People) Order 2007, SI 2007/236, art 107(3); and see note 1. See also *R (on the application of the Conservative and Unionist Party) v Election Comr* [2010] EWCA Civ 1332, [2011] PTSR 416, [2010] All ER (D) 241 (Nov) (cited in PARA 875 note 3).

803. Notice of interim application. At least two clear days before the making of any interim application to the High Court, notice of it should be given at the election petitions office[1] and to the other side[2].

1   As to the meaning of 'election petitions office' see PARA 768 note 12.
2   This is the practice. See also Day's Election Cases 23.

804. Service of documents. Any notice, legal process or other document required to be served on any person with reference to any proceeding respecting an election[1] or referendum[2] for the purpose of causing him to appear before the High Court, the county court or any election court, or otherwise, or of giving him an opportunity of making a statement, or showing cause, or being heard by himself before any court for any purpose of the provisions governing legal proceedings in relation to election or referendums[3], may be served[4]: (1) by delivering it to that person or by leaving it at, or sending it by post by a registered letter or the recorded delivery service to, his last known place of abode in the parliamentary[5] or Welsh Assembly constituency[6], the area of the authority[7], the voting area[8], or the Welsh Assembly[9] or European parliamentary electoral region[10] (as the case may be) for which the election or referendum was held[11]; or (2) if the proceeding is one before any court, in such other manner as the court may direct[12]. In proving such service by post it is sufficient to prove that the letter was pre-paid, properly addressed, and registered or recorded with the postal operator concerned[13].

1   Ie a parliamentary election, election under the Local Government Act 1972, Welsh Assembly election or European parliamentary election. As to the meaning of 'Assembly election' in the context of Welsh Assembly elections see PARA 3 note 2; as to the meaning of 'parliamentary election' see PARA 9; and as to the meaning of 'election under the Local Government Act 1972' see PARA 11 note 2. As to European parliamentary elections see PARA 217 et seq. As to the application of the Representation of the People Act 1983 Pt III (ss 120–186) to other polls see PARA 763.

2   Ie a referendum held, in relation to Wales, under the Local Authorities (Conduct of Referendums) (Wales) Regulations 2008, SI 2008/1848, or, in relation to England, under the Local Authorities (Conduct of Referendums) (England) Regulations 2012, SI 2012/323. As to the meaning of 'referendum' for these purposes see PARA 574 note 2. The provision made for the questioning of an election under the Local Government Act 1972 is applied and modified for the purpose of questioning a local authority referendum: see PARA 766. As to the application of the Representation of the People Act 1983 Pt III (ss 120–186) to other polls see PARA 763.

3   Ie, in relation to a parliamentary election or election under the Local Government Act 1972, the Representation of the People Act 1983 Pt III (ss 120–186) (including that Part as applied and modified for the purposes of a local authority referendum: see note 2), in relation to a European parliamentary election, the European Parliamentary Elections Regulations 2004, SI 2004/293, Pt 4 (regs 86–122), and, in relation to a Welsh Assembly election, the National Assembly for Wales (Representation of the People) Order 2007, SI 2007/236, Pt 4 (arts 86–138) (see PARA 761 et seq).

4   Representation of the People Act 1983 s 184(1) (amended by the Political Parties, Elections and Referendums Act 2000 s 138, Sch 18 paras 1, 19(5)); European Parliamentary Elections

Regulations 2004, SI 2004/293, reg 122(1); National Assembly for Wales (Representation of the People) Order 2007, SI 2007/236, art 136(1); and see note 2. The appropriate procedure for the service of the petition, the notice of presentation of the petition and of the amount of the security for costs is that laid down by the Election Petition Rules 1960, SI 1960/543, r 6 or, in relation to a European parliamentary election, the European Parliamentary Election Petition Rules 1979, SI 1979/521, r 6 (see PARAS 768, 798), and thus they prevail over the more generalised provisions of the Representation of the People Act 1983 s 184 regarding the service of those particular documents: see *Ali v Haques* [2006] All ER (D) 113 (Oct). See *Scarth v Amin* [2008] EWHC 2886 (QB), [2009] PTSR 827, [2008] All ER (D) 265 (Nov) (personal service of a petition on the returning officer (including service on the officer's usual or last known residence) was not necessary for the purposes of the Representation of the People Act 1983 s 184; to require otherwise of a petitioner might defeat the public interest in respect of having an effective means to question elections under s 128; also a returning officer was necessarily an individual, but was not acting in his personal capacity in performing that office, or when he was served with a petition; election petitions were public law proceedings, not claims in private law).

5   As to the meaning of 'parliamentary constituency' see PARA 9.
6   As to the meaning of 'Assembly constituency' in the context of Welsh Assembly elections see PARA 3 note 2.
7   As to the area of the authority for which a local government election is held see PARA 11.
8   As to the meaning of 'voting area' see PARA 580 note 2.
9   As to the meaning of 'Assembly electoral region' in the context of Welsh Assembly elections see PARA 3 note 2.
10   As to the establishment of electoral regions for the purpose of elections to the European Parliament see PARA 77. As to service in the combined region see the European Parliamentary Elections Regulations 2004, SI 2004/293, reg 122(3), (4).
11   Representation of the People Act 1983 s 184(1)(a); European Parliamentary Elections Regulations 2004, SI 2004/293, reg 122(1)(a); National Assembly for Wales (Representation of the People) Order 2007, SI 2007/236, art 136(1)(a); and see note 2.
12   Representation of the People Act 1983 s 184(1)(b); European Parliamentary Elections Regulations 2004, SI 2004/293, reg 122(1)(b); National Assembly for Wales (Representation of the People) Order 2007, SI 2007/236, art 136(1)(b); and see note 2.
13   Representation of the People Act 1983 s 184(2) (amended by SI 2001/1149; and the Postal Services Act 2011 s 91(1), (2), Sch 12 paras 116, 118); European Parliamentary Elections Regulations 2004, SI 2004/293, reg 122(2) (amended by SI 2011/2085); National Assembly for Wales (Representation of the People) Order 2007, SI 2007/236, art 136(2) (amended by SI 2011/2085); and see note 2. The text refers to the postal operator within the meaning of the Postal Services Act 2011 Pt 3 (ss 27–67) (see POSTAL SERVICES vol 85 (2012) PARA 243).

B. ORDER, PLACE AND TIME OF TRIAL

805. List of petitions. The prescribed officer[1] must, as soon as may be, make out a list of all parliamentary[2] or Welsh Assembly election petitions[3] or all referendum petitions[4] (as the case may be) at issue in the order of their presentation[5]; the petitions questioning elections under the Local Government Act 1972 must be in a separate list[6]. The list of petitions at issue must be conspicuously displayed in the election petitions office[7] and be available for inspection by the public during office hours[8]. Where there are two or more petitions relating to the same parliamentary election or to elections under the Local Government Act 1972 or to the same Assembly election or the return in respect of the same electoral region, or to the same referendum or to referendums (as the case may be) held at the same time for more than one electoral area in the same local government area[9], they are to be bracketed together in the list of petitions and dealt with as one petition, but they are to take their place in the list where the last of them would have stood if it had been the only petition, unless the High Court directs otherwise[10].

1   See PARA 770.
2   As to parliamentary election petitions see PARA 761.
3   As to Welsh Assembly election petitions see PARA 764.

4   Provision is made for questioning a local authority referendum by applying and modifying the provision made for questioning an election under the Local Government Act 1972: see PARA 766. As to the questioning of an election under the Local Government Act 1972 see PARA 762. As to the meaning of 'election under the Local Government Act 1972' see PARA 11 note 2. As to the application of the Representation of the People Act 1983 Pt III (ss 120–186) to other polls see PARA 763.

5   Representation of the People Act 1983 s 138(1)(a); National Assembly for Wales (Representation of the People) Order 2007, SI 2007/236, art 94(1)(a); and see note 4. There is no equivalent provision under the European Parliamentary Elections Regulations 2004, SI 2004/293.

6   Representation of the People Act 1983 s 138(1) (amended by the Political Parties, Elections and Referendums Act 2000 ss 137, 158(2), Sch 17 paras 1, 4, Sch 22).

7   As to the meaning of 'election petitions office' see PARA 768 note 12.

8   Representation of the People Act 1983 ss 138(1)(b), 185; Election Petition Rules 1960, SI 1960/543, r 8 (amended by SI 1985/1278); National Assembly for Wales (Representation of the People) Order 2007, SI 2007/236, art 94(1)(b), 137(1); and see note 4.

9   As to the meaning of 'electoral area' see PARA 11; and as to the meaning of 'local government area' see PARA 33 note 7.

10 Representation of the People Act 1983 s 138(4); National Assembly for Wales (Representation of the People) Order 2007, SI 2007/236, art 94(3); and see note 4. Two or more candidates (in the case of an election) or two or more persons (in the case of a referendum) may be made respondents to the same petition, but the petition is deemed to be a separate petition against each respondent although the petitions may be tried together: see the Representation of the People Act 1983 s 138(3) (including that provision as applied and modified for the purposes of a local authority referendum: see note 4); and PARA 791. Whether two election petitions, of which one claims the seat while the other does not, may properly be tried together seems doubtful (*Maldon Case* (1853) 2 Pow R & D 143); but in *Cashel Borough Case* (1869) 1 O'M & H 286, where there were two petitions against the same respondent, of which one claimed the seat, Fitzgerald B decided that he would allow them to be opened together, but reserved his decision as to the further course. In *York County West Riding, Southern Division Case* (1869) 1 O'M & H 213, there were two petitions, one against two respondents, which also claimed the seat, and the other claiming the seat against one of these two respondents; they appear to have been treated as two separate cases. In *Stafford Borough Case* (1869) 21 LT 210, 1 O'M & H 228, there were two petitions, in each of which the petitioner and the respondent were different; they were treated as two different cases, although at 232 Blackburn J said that he would treat the evidence in the one case as applicable to both, except where application was made to examine or re-examine witnesses. In *Poole Case, Hurdle and Stark v Waring* (1874) 2 O'M & H 123, two petitions against the same respondent were heard together.

806.   Time and place of trial.   So far as convenient, election and referendum petitions[1] are to be tried in the order in which they stand in the list of petitions[2]. Within 28 days[3] after the first day on which a petition is at issue[4] the petitioner must apply by application notice to a rota judge to fix the time and place of trial and if the petitioner fails to do so, any respondent may, within a further period of 28 days, apply in the same manner as the petitioner could have done[5]. If no application is made in accordance with these provisions, the prescribed officer[6] must refer the matter to a rota judge who must thereupon fix such a time and place[7].

In general, the place of trial must be within the parliamentary[8] or Assembly constituency[9], the area of the authority[10], or the Welsh Assembly electoral region[11] (as the case may be) for which the election or referendum was held[12]. If, however, the High Court is satisfied that special circumstances exist which render it desirable that the trial should be held elsewhere, the court may appoint some other convenient place for the trial[13].

The special circumstances which must exist in order that the court may exercise its power of changing the venue of the trial must be such as to render the trial of the petition elsewhere not merely more convenient but more conducive to the ends of justice, and convenience or inconvenience is not in itself a special circumstance[14]. Without such special circumstances the High Court has no power to change the place of trial[15]. Applications for a change of venue should be made to the High Court and not to a judge in chambers[16]. If the petition is tried outside the constituency, area or region for which the election was held without the High Court's consent, the proceedings may be void[17].

1   As to parliamentary election petitions see PARA 761; as to the questioning of an election under the Local Government Act 1972 see PARA 762; as to Welsh Assembly election petitions see PARA 764; and as to European parliamentary election petitions see PARA 765. Provision is made for questioning a local authority referendum by applying and modifying the provision made for questioning an election under the Local Government Act 1972: see PARA 766. As to the meaning of 'election under the Local Government Act 1972' see PARA 11 note 2. As to the application of the Representation of the People Act 1983 Pt III (ss 120–186) to other polls see PARA 763.

2   Representation of the People Act 1983 s 138(2); National Assembly for Wales (Representation of the People) Order 2007, SI 2007/236, art 94(2); and see note 1. There is no equivalent provision under the European Parliamentary Elections Regulations 2004, SI 2004/293. As to the list of petitions see PARA 805.

3   As to the calculation of time limits for these purposes see PARA 768.

4   As to when the petition is at issue see PARA 801.

5   Election Petition Rules 1960, SI 1960/543, r 9(1) (amended by SI 1999/1352); European Parliamentary Election Petition Rules 1979, SI 1979/521, r 9(1) (amended by SI 1999/1398). 'Rota judge' means a judge on the rota for the trial of parliamentary election petitions (see PARA 769): Election Petition Rules 1960, SI 1960/543, r 2(2); European Parliamentary Election Petition Rules 1979, SI 1979/521, r 2(1). As to the application and modification of the Election Petition Rules 1960, SI 1960/543 for the purposes of Welsh Assembly election petitions and for the purposes of a local authority referendum petition see PARA 767 note 1. The Election Petition Rules 1960, SI 1960/543, are also applied for the purposes of other petitions: see PARA 767.

6   See PARA 770.

7   Election Petition Rules 1960, SI 1960/543, r 9(2); European Parliamentary Election Petition Rules 1979, SI 1979/521, r 9(2); and see note 5.

8   As to the meaning of 'parliamentary constituency' see PARA 9.

9   As to the meaning of 'Assembly constituency' in the context of Welsh Assembly elections see PARA 3 note 2.

10 As to the area of the authority for which a local government election is held see PARA 11. In the application of the Representation of the People Act 1983 s 130(6) to the election of a chairman of a parish meeting or to a poll consequent on a parish or community meeting on the question of appointment to any office, for the words the 'area of the authority for which the election was held' there is substituted a reference to the 'district in which the parish is situate': Parish and Community Meetings (Polls) Rules 1987, SI 1987/1, r 6(c).

11 As to the meaning of 'Assembly electoral region' in the context of Welsh Assembly elections see PARA 3 note 2. Where an Assembly election petition is presented, by virtue of the National Assembly for Wales (Representation of the People) Order 2007, SI 2007/236, art 87(1)(d) (see PARA 781 note 3), by a person claiming to have had a right to be returned to fill an electoral region vacancy (see PARA 215), the reference is to the Assembly electoral region for which a person claims to have had a right to be so returned: see art 89(3).

12 Representation of the People Act 1983 ss 123(3), 130(6); National Assembly for Wales (Representation of the People) Order 2007, SI 2007/236, art 89(3); and see note 1. Although the European Parliamentary Elections Regulations 2004, SI 2004/293, reg 91 is headed 'constitution of election court and place of trial', explicit provision for the place of the trial is not made therein. As to the power to adjourn the trial of a petition from one place to another see PARA 819.

13 Representation of the People Act 1983 ss 123(3)(a), 130(6); National Assembly for Wales (Representation of the People) Order 2007, SI 2007/236, art 89(3); and see note 1. If a parliamentary election petition relates to a constituency wholly or partly in Greater London, it may be heard at such place within Greater London as the High Court may appoint: Representation of the People Act 1983 s 123(3)(b).

14 *Tewkesbury Case, Collins v Price* (1880) 5 CPD 544, DC. In *Sligo Borough Case* (1869) 1 O'M & H 300, the venue was changed because a system of intimidation and violence was organised and carried out for months before and during the election, and down to and during the trial.

15 *Lawson v Chester Master, Cirencester Election Petition* [1893] 1 QB 245, in which it was held that the fact that the point in dispute would not necessitate the calling of any witnesses and that it would be more convenient and cheaper to have the petition tried in London did not constitute

special circumstances. See also *Tewkesbury Case, Collins v Price* (1880) 5 CPD 544, DC, where the court expressed grave doubts as to whether the absence of accommodation at the place for which the election was held constituted special circumstances; but see *Re Hexham Election Petition* (1892) Times, 8 November; *Cork, Eastern Division Case* (1911) 6 O'M & H 318 at 319; *West Ham, North Division Case* (1911) 6 O'M & H 392; *Arch v Bentinck* (1887) 18 QBD 548.

16　*Tewkesbury Case, Collins v Price* (1880) 5 CPD 544, DC.

17　*Hudson v Tooth* (1877) 3 QBD 46.

807. Notice of time and place of trial. Notice of the time and place of trial of election and referendum petitions[1] must be given in the prescribed manner, in the case of a parliamentary, Welsh Assembly or European parliamentary election petition, not less than 14 days before the day fixed for the trial[2] and, in any other case, not less than seven days before the day fixed for the trial[3]. The prescribed officer[4] must cause notice of the appointed time and place of the trial to be displayed in a conspicuous place in the election petitions office[5] and sent by post to the petitioner, the respondent[6], the Director of Public Prosecutions and, except in the case of a European parliamentary election petition, the returning officer[7].

On receipt of the notice, the returning officer must forthwith publish it in his constituency, the electoral region or, as the case may be, the local government area to which the petition relates[8].

1　As to parliamentary election petitions see PARA 761; as to the questioning of an election under the Local Government Act 1972 see PARA 762; as to Welsh Assembly election petitions see PARA 764; and as to European parliamentary election petitions see PARA 765. Provision is made for questioning a local authority referendum by applying and modifying the provision made for questioning an election under the Local Government Act 1972: see PARA 766. As to the meaning of 'election under the Local Government Act 1972' see PARA 11 note 2. As to the application of the Representation of the People Act 1983 Pt III (ss 120–186) to other polls see PARA 763. As to the time and place of trial see PARA 806.

2　As to the calculation of time limits for these purposes see PARA 768.

3　Representation of the People Act 1983 ss 139(1), 185; Election Petition Rules 1960, SI 1960/543, r 9(3); European Parliamentary Election Petition Rules 1979, SI 1979/521, r 9(3); European Parliamentary Elections Regulations 2004, SI 2004/293, regs 86, 96(1); National Assembly for Wales (Representation of the People) Order 2007, SI 2007/236, arts 95(1), 138(1); and see note 1. As to the application and modification of the Election Petition Rules 1960, SI 1960/543 for the purposes of Welsh Assembly election petitions and for the purposes of a local authority referendum petition see PARA 767 note 1. The Election Petition Rules 1960, SI 1960/543, are also applied for the purposes of other petitions: see PARA 767.

4　See PARA 770.

5　As to the meaning of 'election petitions office' see PARA 768 note 12.

6　As to respondents see PARAS 782, 791.

7　Election Petition Rules 1960, SI 1960/543, r 9(3) (amended by SI 1985/1278); European Parliamentary Election Petition Rules 1979, SI 1979/521, r 9(3); and see note 3.

8　Election Petition Rules 1960, SI 1960/543, rr 2(2), 9(4) (r 9(4) amended by SI 1985/1278); and see note 3. As to the costs of publication by the returning officer see PARA 784 note 10. As to the meanings of 'Assembly constituency' and 'Assembly electoral region' in the context of Welsh Assembly elections see PARA 3 note 2; as to the meaning of 'parliamentary constituency' see PARA 9; and as to the meaning of 'local government area' see PARA 33 note 7. As to the establishment of electoral regions for the purpose of elections to the European Parliament see PARA 77.

C. PARTICULARS

808. Particulars of petition. Where the allegations in the petition itself are quite general it is the practice to order immediately particulars of the nature of the alleged offences[1]. Further particulars will be ordered of the circumstances of each charge, the order usually directing the petitioner to furnish particulars of the names of the different persons[2] in regard to whom the offences are alleged to have been committed, together with their addresses and numbers on the register, or, failing that, their occupation. Similarly, particulars will be ordered of the persons[3] by whom the offences are alleged to have been committed, of the time and place of the commission of each offence and of its precise character, and, in the case of charges of bribery or treating, of its degree[4].

The question of the length of time before trial in which particulars will be ordered depends on the circumstances of each case, such as the character, area and population of the electoral area and the number of witnesses whom it is proposed to call[5], and also on the number of charges alleged in the petition[6]. The fact that witnesses may be tampered with is not a ground for diminishing the time for giving particulars[7].

If the particulars are not served within the time ordered, they may be struck out at the trial[8]. If the particulars do not comply with the order in respect of which they were given, an order for further and better particulars may be obtained, or the particulars may be struck out. Previous notice of the intention to strike out the particulars should be given to the other side; but the proper course is to make objection during the trial as and when evidence is tendered which is not covered by the particulars[9].

A party giving particulars in pursuance of an order or otherwise must file a copy within 24 hours after serving the particulars to the party requiring them[10].

1   *Anderson v Cawley* (1868) 19 LT 500; *Beverley Case* (1869) 1 O'M & H 143; and see the cases mentioned in Day's Election Cases 11, 12. See also *Lancaster County, Lancaster Division Case* (1896) 5 O'M & H 39; *Shoreditch, Haggerston Division Case, Cremer v Lowles* (1896) 5 O'M & H 68. Application is usually made by summons to a judge on the rota (see PARA 769); as a general rule the exercise of the judge's discretion will not be interfered with: *Barrow-in-Furness Case* (1886) 4 O'M & H 76, DC.

2   In *Maude v Lowley* (1874) LR 9 CP 165 at 167 (a municipal case), the court added the words 'so far as known'. In *Lenham v Barber* (1883) 10 QBD 293, DC (also a municipal case), the court refused to order the words to be added, Pollock B stating that it was his practice to omit them on the ground that they might be taken to warrant undue limitation; but in *Willes v Horniman* (1898) 14 TLR 343, CA, Grantham J inserted in his order the words 'if known', and the Court of Appeal refused to strike them out, A L Smith LJ stating that if omitted in this particular case they would probably have to be read in. The practice now is to leave them out on the ground that the person who gives the particulars can only give them so far as is known and the words are therefore implied: see *Cork, Eastern Division Case* (1911) 6 O'M & H 318 at 320.

3   *Londonderry Case* (1868) 19 LT 573; *Bristol Case, Brett v Robinson* (1870) 22 LT 487 at 488 (in the latter case, the Christian names not having been given in the particulars as delivered, an order was made for giving them); *Hastings Case, Stafford Case* (1869) 20 LT 180. In *Hexham Case* (1892) cited in Day 14, per Cave J, it was held to be insufficient to give the name of a political association as being that of the person by whom the offence charged was alleged to have been committed: the particulars should specify the name of the guilty member or members. In *Bradford Case* (1869) 19 LT 661, particulars of persons bribed and treated lumped together, not saying which was which, were held sufficient; but in *Horsham Case* (1869) 20 LT 180, Willes J considered that there should be separate lists of the persons bribed, treated, and unduly influenced.

4   For examples of particulars which have been ordered by judges in chambers, otherwise unreported see Parker's Election Agent and Returning Officer (3rd Edn).

5   *Rushmere v Isaacson* [1893] 1 QB 118, DC, where an order for delivery of particulars within seven days was, on appeal, enlarged to ten days.

6   *Cirencester Case* (1893) (cited in Day 12). In the early cases of election petitions the time allowed was generally three days: *Anderson v Cawley* (1868) 19 LT 500; *Tamworth Case, Hill v Peel* (1868) 19 LT 527; *Hereford Borough Case* (1869) 1 O'M & H 194 at 196; *Beal v Smith* (1869) LR 4 CP 145. Later the time ordered was longer, usually seven days: see *Furness v Beresford, York City Case* [1898] 1 QB 495 at 498, CA, per A L Smith LJ; *Oxford Borough Case, Green v Hall* [1889] WN 146, DC; *Clark v Wallond* (1883) 52 LJQB 321; *Lenham v*

Barber (1883) 10 QBD 293, DC (a municipal case). If there are special circumstances, an affidavit setting them forth ought to be filed. In *East Manchester Case, Munro v Balfour* [1893] 1 QB 113 the time ordered was 10 days. In *Cirencester Case* the following sliding scale was adopted by Cave J: 10 days if charges under 80, 15 days if charges under 160, 20 days if charges above 160. In *St George's Division, Tower Hamlets, Case* (1896) 5 O'M & H 89, and *Southampton Borough Case* (1895) 5 O'M & H 17, a sliding scale of 10 days if charges under 80, and 12 days if over 80 was adopted. In *Grimsby Case* (1903) cited in 2 Rogers on Elections (18th Edn) p 225, and in *Shrewsbury Case* (1903) cited in 3 Rogers on Elections (18th Edn) p 304, the scale was 5 days if the charges were not over 50; but if they were over 50, 7 days; and if they were over 80, 10 days. In *Shoreditch, Haggerston Division Case, Cremer v Lowles* (1896) 5 O'M & H 68, particulars of the general charges were ordered within seven days of the order and particulars of the specific charges within ten days of the trial. Where a charge was made against a returning officer of misconduct both personal and through his deputy, stringent particulars were ordered to be delivered within six days of the order: *Warrington Case, Crozier v Rylands and Neild* (1869) 19 LT 572. In *Clark v Wallond* (a municipal case), the Divisional Court considered seven days the usually proper time, and refused to alter an order prescribing that time.

7   *Drogheda Borough Case* (1869) 19 LT 528.

8   *York County West Riding, Southern Division Case* (1869) 1 O'M & H 213; but cf *Brecon Borough Case* (1869) 1 O'M & H 212, where an objection made to the admission of particulars on this ground was overruled by Martin B. The first-named case was one alleging a majority of legal votes and claiming the seat on a scrutiny.

9   *Cork, Eastern Division Case* (1911) 6 O'M & H 318 at 319–320.

10 Election Petition Rules 1960, SI 1960/543, r 17; European Parliamentary Election Petition Rules 1979, SI 1979/521, r 17. The copy must be filed in the election petitions office: Election Petition Rules 1960, SI 1960/543, r 2(5); European Parliamentary Election Petition Rules 1979, SI 1979/521, r 2(4) (substituted by SI 2004/1415). As to the meaning of 'election petitions office' see PARA 768 note 12. As to the application and modification of the Election Petition Rules 1960, SI 1960/543 for the purposes of Welsh Assembly election petitions and for the purposes of a local authority referendum petition see PARA 767 note 1. The Election Petition Rules 1960, SI 1960/543, are also applied for the purposes of other petitions: see PARA 767.

809.   Particulars where general corruption charged.   Where a charge of general corruption is made[1], the particulars which are ordered are necessarily wider than usual[2], and the names of particular persons alleged to have been bribed or treated will not be ordered[3]. A petitioner will, however, be ordered to specify the character and extent of the corruption alleged[4].

1   See PARA 895.

2   As to the usual particulars see PARA 808.

3   *Beverley Case* (1869) 1 O'M & H 143; *Taunton Borough Case* (1874) 2 O'M & H 66; *Wigan Case, Spencer and Prestt v Powell* (1881) 4 O'M & H 1. As to a distinction made between bribing and treating see *Wigan Case, Spencer and Prestt v Powell* at 2 per Grove J, where he said that the particulars of bribery must be more specific than those of treating, as one did not bribe hosts of people generally. See also *Manchester, Eastern Division Case* (1892) 4 O'M & H 120, where under a charge of general corruption the court refused to admit evidence of treating at a public house which had not been mentioned in the particulars. In *Hexham Case* (1892) cited in Day 14, and in *Worcester Borough Case, Glazzard v Allsopp* (1892) cited in Day 12, the particulars ordered were those only of time and of place; but see, contra, *King's Lynn Case, Armes and Holditch v Bourke* (1869) 1 O'M & H 206 at 207 per Martin B, in which he objected to receive evidence of general treating from a person who had been treated whose name was not in the particulars, although he did not think that it was necessary to give the name of the public house involved.

4   *Walsall Case* (1892) cited in Day 12; *Pontefract Case, Shaw v Reckitt* (1893) cited in Day 11.

810.   Amendment of particulars.   If a party wishes to give evidence of any circumstances not mentioned, or insufficiently mentioned, in his particulars[1], leave to amend the particulars may be asked for before or at the trial[2]. The court's practice in dealing with such an application has not been absolutely uniform, but the course generally pursued has been to allow instances not mentioned or insufficiently mentioned in the particulars to be given in evidence if the matter is substantial and if it appears that the failure to furnish the particulars or the sufficient particulars in due time was in good faith[3]. An affidavit to that effect should be filed[4].

In granting leave for the petitioner to amend his particulars, the court will consider whether the respondent will be prejudiced by such leave, and if it is of opinion that the respondent ought to have time to be enabled to meet such evidence the court will grant an adjournment for that purpose[5], and may also in its discretion award the respondent the costs entailed by such evidence in any event[6]. Particulars which are fishing or grossly insufficient will be struck out at the trial[7]. It is not usual to order particulars to be struck out before the trial merely on the ground of being insufficient. If the petitioner obtains further information by the time of the trial, he may, with leave, supply the deficiencies in the particulars served; if not, the insufficient particulars will be struck out at the trial[8].

The court will not allow an amendment of particulars at the trial where such amendment really amounts to an amendment of the petition[9]. On the other hand, a count which discloses no valid ground of objection may be struck out[10] and clerical errors in the wording of the count may be amended[11].

1   As to the particulars generally see PARAS 808–809.

2   See, however, *St George's Division, Tower Hamlets, Case* (1896) 5 O'M & H 89, where the application for leave to amend had been made to a judge in chambers and had been referred by him to be made to the judges at the trial; Pollock B considered the course a very inconvenient one, pointing out that an appeal would have lain from the judge at chambers to the Court of Appeal.

3   This seems to be the position which may be deduced from the various cases where the point has arisen. In *Wigan Case, Spencer and Prestt v Powell* (1881) 4 O'M & H 1 at 4 per Bowen J, an order for particulars drawn up in a form that the petitioners could be precluded at the trial from going into any case of which particulars have not been delivered 'can be modified at any time, and I confess I should not hesitate myself at any moment to disregard that prohibition, and to amend the order by stating that further cases might be gone into if the justice of the case required it, and if there was no danger of surprise upon the sitting member'. This statement was approved in *Cork, Eastern Division Case* (1911) 6 O'M & H 318 at 320. See also *Belfast Borough Petition* (1869) 19 LT 574, where Keogh J said that parties would not be excluded from giving evidence of instances coming to light before the trial, as had, likewise, been the custom of the House of Commons, and the court should investigate all such cases; *Bewdley Case* (1869) 1 O'M & H 16; *Carrickfergus Borough Case* (1869) 1 O'M & H 264; *Coventry Case, Berry v Eaton and Hill* (1869) 1 O'M & H 97; *Dublin City Case* (1869) 1 O'M & H 270, where Keogh J said he would allow the utmost latitude to amend unless it were evident that the party had kept back information available at the time of delivery of the particulars; *Longford Case* (1870) 2 O'M & H 6; *Harwich Borough Case* (1880) 3 O'M & H 61; *Evesham Borough Case* (1880) 3 O'M & H 94 at 95, where Hawkins J drew attention to the fact that the court could, in its discretion, after the close of the hearing, call and examine any witness, and he said that the respondent might exercise his option, subject to such power in the court, of having the evidence of charges not included in the particulars excluded during the hearing. To the contrary see *Bodmin Case* (1869) 1 O'M & H 117; *King's Lynn Case, Armes and Holditch v Bourke* (1869) 1 O'M & H 206 at 207; *Manchester, Eastern Division Case* (1892) 4 O'M & H 120 (where evidence was refused); and as to these cases see also PARA 850.

4   *Londonderry Borough Case* (1869) 1 O'M & H 274, where the respondent's counsel was allowed to cross-examine the petitioner's agent on his affidavit. See also *Cheltenham Case* (1869) 1 O'M & H 62; *Wigan Case* (1869) 1 O'M & H 188 (in each of which cases, the petition being part heard, Martin B said he could only allow the particulars to be amended by the addition of a name on an application by summons supported by affidavit). For a form of affidavit see *Longford Case* (1870) 2 O'M & H 6 at 10n; *Manchester, Eastern Division Case* (1892) cited in Day 153.

5   As to adjournment see PARA 819.

6   *Stafford Borough Case* (1869) 21 LT 210 at 212–213, 1 O'M & H 228 at 232; *Bristol Case, George's Case* (1870) 22 LT 731, 2 O'M & H 27; *Longford Case* (1870) 2 O'M & H 6;

Durham County, Northern Division Case (No 2) (1874) 2 O'M & H 152; *Bewdley Case* (1869) 1 O'M & H 16; *Hereford Borough Case* (1869) 1 O'M & H 194; *Penryn Case* (1869) 1 O'M & H 127; *Bodmin Case* (1869) 1 O'M & H 117 at 119 (where, however, Willes J discriminated between a charge implicating a sitting member personally and a charge against his agent, saying that, in the former case, he would allow the charge to be added to the particulars, giving the respondent, if necessary, time to answer it; but, in the latter case, he would only allow the charge to be added if the fact were shown to have come to the petitioner's knowledge since the delivery of the particulars); and see *Belfast Borough, Western Division Case* (1886) 4 O'M & H 105 at 106 per Dowse B; *Waterford Borough Case* (1870) 2 O'M & H 24 (where notice to amend the particulars by the addition of a name during the hearing was required to be served for the following morning, when the petitioner's agent was examined on oath as to when he had first heard it).

7   *Belfast Borough, Western Division Case* (1886) 4 O'M & H 105; *Worcester Borough Case, Glaszard and Turner v Allsopp* (1892) cited in Day 85 at 87.

8   *Worcester Borough Case* (1892) cited in Day 15; *Pontefract Case* (1892) cited in Day 15; *Walsall Case* (1900) cited in Day 15.

9   *Manchester, Eastern Division Case* (1892) 4 O'M & H 120; *Montgomery Boroughs Case, George v Pryce-Jones* (1892) cited in Day 14; *Cork, Eastern Division Case* (1911) 6 O'M & H 318 at 320, 337; and see *Cremer v Lowles* [1896] 1 QB 504, CA (where no amendment of the petition having been made, particulars of offences in connection with the return of election expenses, occurring after the presentation of the petition, were struck out).

10   *Shrewsbury Case* (1903) (a municipal petition case) cited in 2 Rogers on Elections (20th Edn) 172.

11   *Northumberland, Berwick-upon-Tweed Division Case* (1923) 7 O'M & H 1.

D. DISCLOSURE OF DOCUMENTS

811.   Disclosure and inspection of documents.   The rules of court relating to the disclosure and inspection of documents[1] apply to an election or referendum petition as if it were an ordinary claim within the High Court's jurisdiction[2].

1   As to these rules see CIVIL PROCEDURE vol 11 (2009) PARA 538 et seq.

2   Election Petition Rules 1960, SI 1960/543, r 2(4) (amended by SI 1999/1352); European Parliamentary Election Petition Rules 1979, SI 1979/521, r 2(3) (amended by SI 1999/1398; SI 2004/1415). As to the application and modification of the Election Petition Rules 1960, SI 1960/543 for the purposes of Welsh Assembly election petitions and for the purposes of a local authority referendum petition see PARA 767 note 1. The Election Petition Rules 1960, SI 1960/543, are also applied for the purposes of other petitions: see PARA 767.

812.   Production and admittance of documents at trial.   Notices to produce and admit documents at the trial of a petition are in the ordinary form[1]. If a notice to produce merely asks generally for the production of all documents relating to the matter in question, it will entitle the party giving it to the production of every document which ought to be filed and ought to be delivered to the returning officer, but it will not entitle him to the production of other specific documents unless he has named them in his notice to produce[2].

1   As to the general rules as to the production of documents at trial see CIVIL PROCEDURE vol 11 (2009) PARAS 538 et seq, 876 et seq. The practice of the election committees appears to have regarded a general notice as sufficient, if it indicated clearly to the party on whom it was served the particular document it called for: see *Rogers v Custance* (1839) 2 Mood & R 179; *Jacob v Lee* (1837) 3 Mood & R 33. A notice to produce 'all public books, documents etc relating to voters of the borough' was held to include the charter of the borough in *Youghal Case, Brown's Case* (1838) Falc & Fitz 385. See also *Bradford Borough Case* (1869) 1 O'M & H 30 at 31 per Martin B (the petitioner may call for any document in the respondent's possession, and on being produced it becomes evidence as being a document in the respondent's possession produced by him; notice to produce must be served so as to allow the party on whom it is served reasonable time to comply with it).

2   *Westminster Borough Case* (1869) 1 O'M & H 89 at 93 per Martin B (where the petitioner called for the production of certain canvassing returns, his notice to produce saying 'all

documents, books, and papers whatsoever and in anywise relating to the matters in question in this case' was held to be too general to entitle him to the production of the documents asked for). In the same case it was held (at 94) that a party was not entitled to call for and look generally at the canvassing sheets of the other party; but in *Northallerton Case* (1869) 1 O'M & H 167 at 168–169, Willes J held that a petitioner was entitled to ask for any particular entry in the respondent's canvass book.

E. WITHDRAWAL OF PETITION

813. Application for permission to withdraw petition. A petitioner may not withdraw an election or referendum petition[1] without the permission of the election court or the High Court[2] on application made by application notice to the election court or a Divisional Court at such time and place as the court may appoint[3]. If there is more than one petitioner, all must consent to the making of the application[4]. Not less than seven days[5] before the day so appointed, the petitioner must serve the application notice on the respondent, the returning officer and the Director of Public Prosecutions and lodge a copy in the election petitions office[6], and must also publish notice of the intended application in at least one newspaper circulating in the parliamentary[7] or Welsh Assembly constituency[8], local government area[9], or Welsh Assembly[10] or European parliamentary electoral region[11] (as the case may be) to which the petition relates[12]. The application notice must state the grounds on which the application to withdraw is made and contain a statement to the effect that on the hearing of the application any person who might have been a petitioner in respect of the election or referendum may apply to the court to be substituted as a petitioner[13]. The application to withdraw a petition must not be made until notice has been given in (as the case may be) the parliamentary or Welsh Assembly constituency, local government area or Welsh Assembly or European parliamentary electoral region to which the petition relates[14]. On receipt of the notice the returning officer must forthwith publish it in his constituency, the electoral region or, as the case may be, the local government area[15].

1 As to parliamentary election petitions see PARA 761; as to the questioning of an election under the Local Government Act 1972 see PARA 762; as to Welsh Assembly election petitions see PARA 764; and as to European parliamentary election petitions see PARA 765. Provision is made for questioning a local authority referendum by applying and modifying the provision made for questioning an election under the Local Government Act 1972: see PARA 766. As to the meaning of 'election under the Local Government Act 1972' see PARA 11 note 2.

2 Leave to withdraw so that another petitioner could be substituted was refused in circumstances when the petitioner who withdrew did not have capacity to bring an election petition (see PARA 781) and the petitioner who would be substituted would have such capacity: *Hobson v Fishburn* (1988) Times, 21 November, DC. In that case, a candidate who was too young to be duly elected was refused leave to amend the petition (see PARA 786 note 11) and was refused leave to withdraw since that would allow him (and a substitute petitioner) to achieve what the court had refused by way of amendment. As to other circumstances when leave might be refused see *Halifax Case* (1893) 4 O'M & H 203; *North Meath Case* (1892) Day 141. Since corrupt and illegal practices cannot now be prosecuted before an election court (see the Representation of the People Act 1985 s 24, Sch 4 para 58), the Director of Public Prosecutions would no longer appear to have any interest in whether or not the petition is withdrawn: cf *Shoreditch, Haggerston Division Case, Cremer v Lowles* (1886) 5 O'M & H 68 at 88.

3 Representation of the People Act 1983 ss 147(1), 185; Election Petition Rules 1960, SI 1960/543, r 12(1) (amended by SI 1999/1352); European Parliamentary Election Petition Rules 1979, SI 1979/521, r 12(1) (amended by SI 1999/1398); European Parliamentary Elections Regulations 2004, SI 2004/293, regs 86, 102(1); National Assembly for Wales (Representation of the People) Order 2007, SI 2007/236, arts 103(1), 137(1); and see note 1. As to the application and modification of the Election Petition Rules 1960, SI 1960/543 for the purposes of Welsh Assembly election petitions and for the purposes of a local authority

referendum petition see PARA 767 note 1. As to the application of the Representation of the People Act 1983 Pt III (ss 120–186) to other polls see PARA 763.

Where on the opening of the trial of an election petition it was announced that the petitioner had decided to withdraw, the hearing was adjourned in order that the statutory notice should be given: *Hartlepool Election Petition* (1869) 19 LT 821. In *Devonport Case* (1886) 54 LT 733, 2 TLR 345, an application for permission to withdraw the petition was made to a Divisional Court consisting of two judges neither of whom was on the rota. See also *Nichol v Fearby* [1923] 1 KB 480 at 493–494 per McCardie J; *Shaw v Reckitt (Pontefract Election Petition)* [1893] 2 QB 59, CA.

If it is sought to withdraw a parliamentary election petition, not in the prescribed manner, but by offering no evidence at the hearing, the court will make a special report to that effect to the Speaker of the House of Commons: *Hartlepool Election Petition* at 822 per Blackburn J. If the withdrawal of a petition is effected by fraud or collusion between the parties, or if material facts are withheld and there is any deception of the court, it is possible that the court might be able to recall its permission to withdraw or the House of Commons might be petitioned to direct a fresh trial: see *Taunton Case, Waygood v James* (1869) LR 4 CP 361 at 369, 372–373; *Nottingham Case* (1879) (reported in Cunningham on Elections (3rd Edn) p 644); and see *Dungarvan Borough Case* (1854) 2 Pow R & D 300 at 318; but in *Norwich Case* (1853) 108 Commons Journals 282, 364, and in *Pontefract Case* (1859) 114 Commons Journals 357, the point was left undecided. Cf PARA 858 note 6.

4   Representation of the People Act 1983 s 147(3); European Parliamentary Elections Regulations 2004, SI 2004/293, reg 102(3); National Assembly for Wales (Representation of the People) Order 2007, SI 2007/236, art 103(3).

5   As to the calculation of time limits for these purposes see PARA 768.

6   Election Petition Rules 1960, SI 1960/543, r 12(2)(a) (amended by SI 1999/1352); European Parliamentary Election Petition Rules 1979, SI 1979/521, r 12(2)(a), (b) (substituted by SI 2004/1415); and see note 3. As to the meaning of 'election petitions office' see PARA 768 note 12. As to respondents see PARAS 782, 791.

7   As to the meaning of 'parliamentary constituency' see PARA 9.

8   As to the meaning of 'Assembly constituency' in the context of Welsh Assembly elections see PARA 3 note 2.

9   As to the meaning of 'local government area' see PARA 33 note 7.

10 As to the meaning of 'Assembly electoral region' in the context of Welsh Assembly elections see PARA 3 note 2.

11 As to the establishment of electoral regions for the purpose of elections to the European Parliament see PARA 76.

12 Election Petition Rules 1960, SI 1960/543, rr 2(2), 12(2)(b) (amended by SI 1999/1352); European Parliamentary Election Petition Rules 1979, SI 1979/521, r 12(2)(c) (substituted by SI 2004/1415); and see note 3.

13 Election Petition Rules 1960, SI 1960/543, r 12(3) (amended by SI 1999/1352); European Parliamentary Election Petition Rules 1979, SI 1979/521, r 12(3) (amended by SI 1999/1398); and see note 3. The majority of withdrawals follow on an adverse recount: see eg *York City Case, Furness v Beresford* (1898) 5 O'M & H 118; *Christchurch Case* (1901) 5 O'M & H 147; *Denbighshire Boroughs Case* (1910) 6 O'M & H 57; *Wiltshire, North Western Chippenham, Case* (1911) 6 O'M & H 99; *Mile End Division, Tower Hamlets, Case* (1911) 6 O'M & H 100; *Gloucester Borough Case, Lynch v Terrell* (1911) 6 O'M & H 101; *St Pancras, West Division Case* (1911) 6 O'M & H 102.

The right to apply to be substituted as a petitioner on an application to withdraw a petition contained in the Representation of the People Act 1983 s 150 was repealed by the Political Parties Elections and Referendums Act 2000 Sch 17. However, no consequential amendment has been made to the Election Petition Rules 1960, SI 1960/543, r 12(3), or to the Representation of the People Act 1983 s 147(2) which continue to contain a requirement to include a statement as to substitution. This problem was addressed in *Re Appleby Ward of North West Leicestershire District Council, Roberts v Blunt* [2012] EWHC 481 (QB), where it was held that the obsolete provisions were to be disregarded.

14 Representation of the People Act 1983 s 147(2); European Parliamentary Elections Regulations 2004, SI 2004/293, reg 102(2); National Assembly for Wales (Representation of the People) Order 2007, SI 2007/236, art 103(2); and see note 1. Notwithstanding the statutory provision and the rules relating to the withdrawal of a petition, cases are reported to have been 'withdrawn' on an application made on or during the hearing without apparently complying with the statutory and prescribed requirements, but it seems that the procedure described as a withdrawal was, in fact, a dismissal of the petition on the petitioner's application: see eg *Pembroke Boroughs Case* (1901) 5 O'M & H 135 (application for leave to withdraw

granted by the court after the court had decided a question of the conclusiveness of the register against the petitioner); *Christchurch Case* (1901) 5 O'M & H 147 (application after recount and after filing of affidavits and after giving notice to Director of Public Prosecutions). See also *York City Case, Furness v Beresford* (1898) 5 O'M & H 118. Cf *Halifax Case* (1893) 4 O'M & H 203 (application to withdraw refused on the ground of insufficiency of affidavits); *St George's Division, Tower Hamlets, Case* (1896) 5 O'M & H 89 at 116 (after the result of the hearing of the petition and recriminatory case was determined, the parties agreed to drop further proceedings in the prayer for recount and scrutiny; the court consented to the agreement and the petition stood dismissed).

15   Election Petition Rules 1960, SI 1960/543, rr 2(2), 12(4) (r 12(4) amended by SI 1999/1352); European Parliamentary Election Rules 1979, SI 1979/521, r 12(4) (substituted by SI 2004/1415); and see note 3. As to the costs of publication by the returning officer see PARA 784 note 10.

F.   CONTINUATION, STAY OR DISMISSAL OF PETITION

814.   Continuation of trial despite the occurrence of certain events.   A petitioner who, after the presentation of his parliamentary election petition[1], becomes a member of the House of Lords, may apparently proceed with the petition[2]. The death of a respondent does not abate the petition[3]. A parliamentary election petition drops by the fact that Parliament is dissolved while the petition is pending[4], but it proceeds notwithstanding a prorogation of Parliament or the acceptance by the respondent of an office vacating his seat in Parliament[5]. The trial of a Welsh Assembly election petition[6] proceeds notwithstanding a respondent having resigned his seat or if he becomes disqualified from being an Assembly member[7] so that his seat is vacant[8]; and the trial of a European parliamentary election petition[9] is to be proceeded with notwithstanding that one (or more) of the respondents is no longer a member of the European Parliament ('MEP')[10]. The trial of a petition questioning an election under the Local Government Act 1972[11] proceeds notwithstanding that the respondent has ceased to hold the office his election to which is questioned by the petition[12].

1   As to parliamentary election petitions see PARA 761.

2   *Belfast Borough Case* (1842) Bar & Aust 553 at 554, where a motion before the House of Commons for the dismissal of a petition on this ground was, after argument, dropped. It seems that a person who has been returned for one place is not for that reason debarred from petitioning in another (see Orme's Election Laws p 261); and a person petitioning in one place is capable of being elected and returned for another, although apparently he must make his choice for which of the places he will sit if and as soon as the controverted return is altered in his favour (21 Commons Journals (1728) 135).

3   *Tipperary County Case* (1875) 3 O'M & H 19; *Ludgershall Case* (1791) 1 Peck 377n; *Dublin City Case* (1836) 91 Commons Journals 363 at 364.

4   *Carter v Mills* (1874) LR 9 CP 117; *Marshall v James* (1874) LR 9 CP 702.

5   Representation of the People Act 1983 s 139(3). As to disqualification for membership of the House of Commons see PARA 224. As to the application of the Representation of the People Act 1983 Pt III (ss 120–186) to other polls see PARA 763.

6   As to Welsh Assembly election petitions see PARA 764.

7   As to the meaning of 'Assembly member' see PARA 12.

8   National Assembly for Wales (Representation of the People) Order 2007, SI 2007/236, art 95(3).

9   As to European parliamentary election petitions see PARA 765.

10   European Parliamentary Elections Regulations 2004, SI 2004/293, reg 96(3).

11   As to the questioning of an election under the Local Government Act 1972 see PARA 762. As to the meaning of 'election under the Local Government Act 1972' see PARA 11 note 2.

12   Representation of the People Act 1983 s 139(3).

815. Application for stay or dismissal of petition. Before the day fixed for the trial[1], a respondent[2] may apply for the stay or dismissal of an election or referendum petition[3]. The application must be made by application notice to the election court or a Divisional Court at such time and place as the court may appoint[4]. Not less than seven days[5] before the date so appointed the respondent must serve the application notice, stating his grounds, on the petitioner, any other respondent, the returning officer and the Director of Public Prosecutions[6], and he must lodge a copy at the election petitions office[7]. An application may similarly be made to the High Court to take off the file a petition that is bad on the face of it[8].

1 As to the time and place of trial see PARA 806.
2 As to respondents see PARAS 782, 791.
3 Election Petition Rules 1960, SI 1960/543, r 13(1); European Parliamentary Election Petition Rules 1979, SI 1979/521, r 13(1). As to parliamentary election petitions see PARA 761; as to the questioning of an election under the Local Government Act 1972 see PARA 762; as to Welsh Assembly election petitions see PARA 764; and as to European parliamentary election petitions see PARA 765. Provision is made for questioning a local authority referendum by applying and modifying the provision made for questioning an election under the Local Government Act 1972: see PARA 766. As to the meaning of 'election under the Local Government Act 1972' see PARA 11 note 2. As to the application and modification of the Election Petition Rules 1960, SI 1960/543 for the purposes of Welsh Assembly election petitions and for the purposes of a local authority referendum petition see PARA 767 note 1. The Election Petition Rules 1960, SI 1960/543, are also applied for the purposes of other petitions: see PARA 767.
   As to cases where application has been made for relief in respect of an election, after a petition relating to it has been presented, see PARA 695. In *Hackney Case* (1874) 2 O'M & H 77, a summons to have the petition dismissed was taken out, but was, after argument, dismissed. In *Halifax Case* (1893) 4 O'M & H 203, a recount having already been granted, and having shown a majority of votes for the respondent, the petitioner, on the petition coming on for hearing, applied to the election court for leave to withdraw it, which was refused, and the respondent applied for a certificate that he had been duly elected, but his application was refused; Hawkins J said the court could not dismiss the petition without hearing it, and he differentiated the case from the *Renfrew County Case* (1874) 2 O'M & H 213 on the ground that in the latter case the petitioner had been heard, inasmuch as the recount had taken place in open court.
4 Election Petition Rules 1960, SI 1960/543, r 13(1) (amended by SI 1999/1352); European Parliamentary Election Petition Rules 1979, SI 1979/521, r 13(1) (amended by SI 1999/1398); and see note 3.
5 As to the calculation of time limits for these purposes see PARA 768.
6 Election Petition Rules 1960, SI 1960/543, r 13(2) (amended by SI 1999/1352); European Parliamentary Election Petition Rules 1979, SI 1979/521, r 13(2)(a) (substituted by SI 2004/1415); and see note 3.
7 Election Petition Rules 1960, SI 1960/543, r 13(2); European Parliamentary Election Petition Rules 1979, SI 1979/521, r 13(2)(b) (substituted by SI 2004/1415); and see note 3. As to the meaning of 'election petitions office' see PARA 768 note 12.
8 *Pope v Bruton* (1900) 17 TLR 182, DC, where the ground was that a petition did not lie; *Cox v Davies* [1898] 2 QB 202, DC, where the ground was that the petition did not disclose a valid ground of objection. In *Re Counter's Petition, Buckingham v Counter* as reported in [1938] 2 KB 90, CA, an application was made to strike out a petition on the ground that it was presented out of time.

G. PROCEEDING BY WAY OF SPECIAL CASE STATED

816. Petition proceeding by way of special case stated rather than by trial. If it appears to the High Court, on the application made in the prescribed manner of any party to an election or referendum petition[1], that the case raised by the petition can be conveniently stated as a special case, it may direct the case to be stated accordingly and the special case will be heard before the High Court[2]. The only additional material that should be appended to a special case should be material which the parties are agreed that the court should take full account of[3]. Only one counsel has a right to be heard on either side, although as a matter of exceptional indulgence the court may hear two[4]. The Divisional Court's decision on a case thus stated to it is final unless that court gives special leave to appeal on a question of law[5]. The Divisional Court may give special leave to appeal on any question of law[6], and if, accordingly, an appeal is made, the Court of Appeal's decision is final and conclusive[7].

In the case of a parliamentary election petition, the High Court's decision on the special case must be certified by it to the Speaker of the House of Commons[8]. In the case of a petition questioning either an election under the Local Government Act 1972 or a local authority referendum, a statement of the decision on the special case must be sent by the High Court to the Secretary of State[9] and must also be certified by the High Court by the signature of two or more of its judges to the proper officer of the authority for which the election or referendum (as the case may be) was held[10]. In the case of a Welsh Assembly election petition, the High Court must certify to the presiding officer of the Assembly[11] its decision on the special case[12]; and, in the case of a European parliamentary election petition, the court's decision must be certified by it to the Secretary of State[13].

1   The application must be made by application notice to a Divisional Court: Election Petition Rules 1960, SI 1960/543, r 11 (amended by SI 1985/1278; SI 1999/1352); European Parliamentary Election Petition Rules 1979, SI 1979/521, r 11 (amended by SI 1999/1398; SI 2004/1415). As to parliamentary election petitions see PARA 761; as to the questioning of an election under the Local Government Act 1972 see PARA 762; as to Welsh Assembly election petitions see PARA 764; and as to European parliamentary election petitions see PARA 765. Provision is made for questioning a local authority referendum by applying and modifying the provision made for questioning an election under the Local Government Act 1972: see PARA 766. As to the meaning of 'election under the Local Government Act 1972' see PARA 11 note 2. As to the application and modification of the Election Petition Rules 1960, SI 1960/543 for the purposes of Welsh Assembly election petitions and for the purposes of a local authority referendum petition see PARA 767 note 1. The Election Petition Rules 1960, SI 1960/543, are also applied for the purposes of other petitions: see PARA 767.

2   Representation of the People Act 1983 s 146(1); European Parliamentary Elections Regulations 2004, SI 2004/293, reg 101(1); National Assembly for Wales (Representation of the People) Order 2007, SI 2007/236, art 102(1); and see note 1. As to the application of the Representation of the People Act 1983 Pt III (ss 120–186) to other polls see PARA 763. Proceeding by way of special case stated means that the petition must be determined on the basis of the facts set out in the special case, rather than on the basis of facts as they might be found by the court: see *Considine v Didrichsen* [2004] EWHC 2711 (QB) at [2], [2004] All ER (D) 365 (Nov) at [2]. In *Re West Suffolk County Council (East Ward) Election* (1964) 108 Sol Jo 604, DC, where a candidate was disqualified and admitted it, the court did not order the case to be stated but decided to hear the case and declared the election void, notwithstanding that there was no provision for this more direct course in the election petition rules. It seems that it is not open to respondents in such proceedings, as it is open to them in appeals by way of case stated by justices, to seek to uphold the decision given in their favour on grounds not relied on when it was made: *Evans v Thomas* [1962] 2 QB 350 at 370, [1962] 3 All ER 108 at 118, DC, per Winn J. See also *R (on the application of Woolas) v Parliamentary Election Court* [2010] EWHC 3169 (Admin), [2012] QB 1, [2010] NLJR 1756.

3   See *Considine v Didrichsen* [2004] EWHC 2711 (QB) at [2], [2004] All ER (D) 365 (Nov) at [2], where it was agreed that the court should take account of contemporaneous documents appended to the case, but should not take account of other factual material which has been appended to it.

4   *Re Gloucestershire, Thornbury Division, Election Petition* (1886) 16 QBD 739 at 746.

5   Representation of the People Act 1983 s 157(1); European Parliamentary Elections Regulations 2004, SI 2004/293, reg 106(1); National Assembly for Wales (Representation of the People) Order 2007, SI 2007/236, art 107(1); and see note 1. See *Unwin v McMullen* [1891] 1 QB 694, 699, CA; *Shaw v Reckitt (Pontefract Election Petition)* [1893] 2 QB 59, CA; *Everett v Griffiths (No 3)* [1923] 1 KB 138, CA.

6   *Line v Warren* (1885) 14 QBD 548, CA; *Beresford-Hope v Lady Sandhurst* (1889) 23 QBD 79, CA.
7   Representation of the People Act 1983 s 157(1); European Parliamentary Elections Regulations 2004, SI 2004/293, reg 106(1); National Assembly for Wales (Representation of the People) Order 2007, SI 2007/236, art 107(1); and see note 1.
8   Representation of the People Act 1983 s 146(2). 'Speaker' includes Deputy Speaker and, where the office of Speaker is vacant, Clerk of the House of Commons, or any other officer for the time being performing the duties of Clerk of the House of Commons: s 185. The granting of a certificate may be postponed on reference of a question of law, a much less common procedure: see PARA 857.
9   As to the Secretary of State see PARA 2.
10 Representation of the People Act 1983 s 146(3); and see note 1. As to the meaning of 'proper officer' generally see PARA 140 note 2; but for these purposes in relation to parish and community elections see PARA 763.
11 As to the presiding officer of the National Assembly for Wales see CONSTITUTIONAL LAW AND HUMAN RIGHTS.
12 National Assembly for Wales (Representation of the People) Order 2007, SI 2007/236, art 102(2).
13 European Parliamentary Elections Regulations 2004, SI 2004/293, reg 101(2).

(vi) The Hearing

A. IN GENERAL

817.   Mode of trial and procedure and practice in general.   An election or referendum petition[1] must be tried in open court and without a jury[2]. Subject to the provisions of the Representation of the People Act 1983[3] (and, in relation to a Welsh Assembly election, the rules provided as to the conduct of elections for the return of Assembly members[4]) and subject to the rules governing the procedure for petitions[5], the principles, practice and rules on which committees of the House of Commons used to act in dealing with election petitions must be observed, so far as may be, by the High Court and election court in the case of parliamentary and Welsh Assembly election petitions or referendum petitions[6]. In particular, the principles and rules with regard to agency[7] and evidence[8], and to scrutiny[9], and to declaring any person elected in place of any other person declared not to have been duly elected[10], must be observed, so far as may be, in the case of a petition questioning an election under the Local Government Act 1972 as in the case of a petition questioning a parliamentary election or return[11]. It is provided by election petition rules[12], however, that subject to those rules and subject to the provisions of the Representation of the People Act 1983[13] (and, in relation to a Welsh Assembly election, the rules provided as to the conduct of elections for the return of Assembly members[14] and, in relation to a European parliamentary election, the European parliamentary elections rules[15]), the practice and procedure of the High Court are to apply to an election or referendum petition as if it were an ordinary claim within the High Court's jurisdiction notwithstanding any different practice, principle or rule on which the committees of the House of Commons used to act in dealing with election petitions[16].

1   As to parliamentary election petitions see PARA 761; as to the questioning of an election under the Local Government Act 1972 see PARA 762; as to Welsh Assembly election petitions see PARA 764; and as to European parliamentary election petitions see PARA 765. Provision is made for questioning a local authority referendum by applying and modifying the provision made for questioning an election under the Local Government Act 1972: see PARA 766. As to the meaning of 'election under the Local Government Act 1972' see PARA 11 note 2. As to the application of the Representation of the People Act 1983 Pt III (ss 120–186) to other polls see PARA 763.

2   Representation of the People Act 1983 s 139(1); European Parliamentary Elections
     Regulations 2004, SI 2004/293, reg 96(1); National Assembly for Wales (Representation of the
     People) Order 2007, SI 2007/236, art 95(1); and see note 1.

3   Ie including those provisions as applied and modified for the purposes of a local authority
     referendum (see note 1).

4   Ie the National Assembly for Wales (Representation of the People) Order 2007, SI 2007/236 (see
     PARA 383).

5   Ie the Election Petition Rules 1960, SI 1960/543, including those rules as applied and modified
     for the purposes of Welsh Assembly election petitions and local authority referendum petitions
     (see PARA 767).

6   Representation of the People Act 1983 s 157(2); National Assembly for Wales (Representation
     of the People) Order 2007, SI 2007/236, art 107(2); and see note 1. There is no equivalent
     provision under the European Parliamentary Elections Regulations 2004, SI 2004/293. As to the
     relevance of the principles, practice and rules on which committees of the House of Commons
     used to act see PARAS 771, 779.

7   As to evidence of agency see PARA 245 et seq.

8   As to evidence generally see PARA 831 et seq.

9   As to scrutiny see PARA 839 et seq.

10   As to the effect of any judgment see PARA 858 et seq.

11   Representation of the People Act 1983 s 157(2).

12   Ie the Election Petition Rules 1960, SI 1960/543 (including those rules as applied and modified
     for the purposes of Welsh Assembly election petitions and local authority referendum petitions
     (see note 5)) and, in relation to a European parliamentary election petition, the European
     Parliamentary Election Petition Rules 1979, SI 1979/521 (see PARA 767). The Election Petition
     Rules 1960, SI 1960/543, are also applied for the purposes of other petitions: see PARA 767.

13   See note 3.

14   See note 4.

15   As to the meaning of 'European parliamentary elections rules' see PARA 383.

16   Election Petition Rules 1960, SI 1960/543, r 2(4) (amended by SI 1999/1352); European
     Parliamentary Election Petition Rules 1979, SI 1979/521, r 2(3) (amended by SI 1999/1398;
     SI 2004/1415); and see note 5. This provision has the effect of limiting the scope of the other
     provisions set out in the text and notes 1–11.

818.   Attendance of shorthand writers. The shorthand writer of the House of
Commons or his deputy must attend the trial of a parliamentary election
petition[1] and the National Assembly for Wales requires a shorthand writer to
attend the trial of an Assembly election petition[2]. The shorthand writer that so
attends must be sworn by one of the judges of the election court faithfully and
truly to take down the evidence given at the trial and from time to time, as
occasion requires, to transcribe that evidence or cause it to be transcribed[3].
Accordingly, the shorthand writer must take down the evidence and from time to
time transcribe it or cause it to be transcribed, and a copy of the evidence must
accompany the certificate given by the election court (at the trial of a
parliamentary election petition) to the Speaker of the House of Commons or (at
the trial of an Assembly election petition) to the presiding officer of the
Assembly[4].

In the case of the trial of a petition questioning an election under the Local
Government Act 1972[5] or a local authority referendum[6], the shorthand writer
who is to attend the trial must be appointed by the commissioner to whom the
trial is assigned and must be sworn by the election court faithfully and truly to
take down the evidence given at the trial[7]. He must take down the evidence at
length and, if the election court so directs, a transcript of the notes of the
evidence taken down by him must accompany the court's certificate[8].

1   Representation of the People Act 1983 s 126(1). As to parliamentary election petitions see PARA
     761. As to the application of the Representation of the People Act 1983 Pt III (ss 120–186) to
     other polls see PARA 763.

2   National Assembly for Wales (Representation of the People) Order 2007, SI 2007/236, art 91(1). As to Welsh Assembly election petitions see PARA 764.

3   Representation of the People Act 1983 s 126(1); National Assembly for Wales (Representation of the People) Order 2007, SI 2007/236, art 91(1). There is no equivalent provision under the European Parliamentary Elections Regulations 2004, SI 2004/293.

4   Representation of the People Act 1983 s 126(2); National Assembly for Wales (Representation of the People) Order 2007, SI 2007/236, art 91(2). As to the Speaker see PARA 816 note 8. As to the presiding officer of the National Assembly for Wales see CONSTITUTIONAL LAW AND HUMAN RIGHTS. As to the certificate given by the court see PARA 858.

5   As to the questioning of an election under the Local Government Act 1972 see PARA 762. As to the meaning of 'election under the Local Government Act 1972' see PARA 11 note 2.

6   Provision is made for questioning a local authority referendum by applying and modifying the provision made for questioning an election under the Local Government Act 1972: see PARA 766.

7   Representation of the People Act 1983 s 131(3)(a); Election Petition Rules 1960, SI 1960/543, r 18(1) (amended by SI 1985/1278); and see note 6. As to the application and modification of the Election Petition Rules 1960, SI 1960/543 for the purposes of a local authority referendum petition see PARA 767 note 1. The Election Petition Rules 1960, SI 1960/543, are also applied for the purposes of other petitions: see PARA 767.

8   Representation of the People Act 1983 s 131(3); and see note 6. As to the shorthand writer's expenses see PARA 778. As to the certificate given by the court on the determination of a local government election petition see PARA 861; and as to the certificate so given on the determination of a local authority referendum petition see PARA 866.

B. ADJOURNMENT OF TRIAL OF PETITION

819.   Power to adjourn.   The election court for the trial of a parliamentary election petition[1] may adjourn the trial from one place to any other place within the constituency[2]. The election court for the trial of a petition questioning an election under the Local Government Act 1972[3] or local authority referendum[4] may in its discretion adjourn the trial from any one place to any other place within the local government area or place where it is held[5]. At the trial of a Welsh Assembly election petition[6], the election court may adjourn the trial from one place to another within the Assembly constituency or electoral region[7].

The election court for the trial of any election petition[8] may in its discretion adjourn the trial from time to time, but the trial must, so far as is practicable consistently with the interests of justice in respect of the trial, be continued from day to day on every lawful day until its conclusion[9].

1   As to parliamentary election petitions see PARA 761.

2   Representation of the People Act 1983 s 123(4). As to the meaning of 'parliamentary constituency' see PARA 9.

3   As to the meaning of 'election under the Local Government Act 1972' see PARA 11 note 2. As to the questioning of an election under the Local Government Act 1972 see PARA 762.

4   Provision is made for questioning a local authority referendum by applying and modifying the provision made for questioning an election under the Local Government Act 1972: see PARA 766. As to the application of the Representation of the People Act 1983 Pt III (ss 120–186) to other polls see PARA 763.

5   Representation of the People Act 1983 s 130(7); and see note 4. As to the meaning of 'local government area' see PARA 33 note 7.

6   As to Welsh Assembly election petitions see PARA 764.

7   National Assembly for Wales (Representation of the People) Order 2007, SI 2007/236, art 89(4). As to the meanings of 'Assembly constituency' and 'Assembly electoral region' in the context of Welsh Assembly elections see PARA 3 note 2.

8   Ie including European parliamentary election petitions (see PARA 765). However, there is no equivalent provision under the European Parliamentary Elections Regulations 2004, SI 2004/293, to that set out in relation to other election or referendum petitions in the text and notes 1–7.

9   Representation of the People Act 1983 s 139(2); European Parliamentary Elections
     Regulations 2004, SI 2004/293, reg 96(2); National Assembly for Wales (Representation of the
     People) Order 2007, SI 2007/236, art 95(2).

C. DUTIES OF PARTIES AND OF THE DIRECTOR OF PUBLIC PROSECUTIONS

820.   Duty of parties and court.   There is no obligation on the petitioner's
counsel to pursue charges, even though there may be good foundation for them,
if by the establishment or admission of other charges he has already attained the
avoidance of the election[1].

When the issue between the parties has been decided, there is no duty cast on
either of them to continue the inquiry in the public interest for the purposes of
ascertaining to what, if any, extent corrupt or illegal practices have prevailed; the
object of the petition being gained, there is an end of the inquiry so far as the
parties are concerned[2].

The court will only require such further evidence to be called as is necessary to
enable it to report whether corrupt or illegal practices have extensively prevailed
or not and also to see whether, in respect of offences with which particular
individuals have been charged, it ought to report those individuals[3].

1   *Durham County, Northern Division Case (No 2)* (1874) 2 O'M & H 152 at 156 per
     Bramwell B.
2   See *Wakefield Case* (1874) 2 O'M & H 100 per Grove J, cited in the *Barnstaple Case* (1874) 2
     O'M & H 105 at 109.
3   *Cheltenham Case, Smythies and Claridge v Mathias, Davies' Case* (1911) 6 O'M & H 194 at
     209. As to the items that must be stated in the report of an election court (including whether
     corrupt or illegal practices have extensively prevailed at the election) see PARA 859 et seq. It has
     been suggested that the election court has a duty to investigate any allegation of corrupt or
     illegal practices brought to its notice and that the trial cannot be shortened by concessions made
     by the parties: see *Ipswich Case, Packard v Collings and West* (1886) 54 LT 619, 4 O'M & H
     70; *Louth, Northern Division Case* (1911) 6 O'M & H 103; *Monmouth Boroughs Case* (1901)
     5 O'M & H 166; *Maidstone Borough Case, Cornwallis v Barker* (1901) 5 O'M & H 149 at
     151; *Worcester Borough Case, Harben and Cadbury v Williamson, Olds' Case* (1906) 5
     O'M & H 212 at 215. However, it is for consideration whether these views remain correct since
     persons can no longer be prosecuted for corrupt and illegal practices before election courts: see
     the Representation of the People Act 1985 s 24, Sch 4 para 58 (repealing the Representation of
     the People Act 1983 s 171 (prosecution of election petition offences in England and Wales and
     Northern Ireland)).

**821.   Duty of the Director of Public Prosecutions in relation to trial of election
petition.**   The Director of Public Prosecutions[1] may, and if the election court so
requests must, attend the trial of every election petition[2] by himself or by his
assistant or by a representative, who must be a barrister, a solicitor or (except in
the case of European parliamentary elections) an authorised person[3] nominated
by him to be his representative for this purpose[4].

If it appears to the Director that any person is able to give material evidence as
to the subject of the trial, it becomes his duty, without any direction from the
election court, to cause that person to attend the trial, and, with the court's
permission, to examine that person as a witness[5]. The Director has no right to
cross-examine witnesses called by either party on the hearing, although he may
call witnesses[6]. With the court's leave he may examine witnesses called by the
parties at the trial, but he ought not to ask for leave to do so without substantial
cause[7]. It is no part of his duties to call evidence with respect to matters at issue
between the parties, although if there should be, in his opinion, a collusive
withholding of evidence it would be his duty to call that evidence himself[8]. He is
not concerned with the proof of agency as affecting a party to an election

petition, and the court will not give him leave to cross-examine witnesses for that purpose, but he is concerned with proving to the court that the witnesses themselves have been guilty of offences[9].

Where information is given to the Director of Public Prosecutions that any offence has been committed in relation to an election, it is his duty to make such inquiries and institute such prosecutions as the circumstances appear to him to require[10].

1   As to the Director of Public Prosecutions see CRIMINAL PROCEDURE vol 27 (2010) PARAS 23, 33 et seq.

2   As to parliamentary election petitions see PARA 761; as to the questioning of an election under the Local Government Act 1972 see PARA 762; as to Welsh Assembly election petitions see PARA 764; and as to European parliamentary election petitions see PARA 765. As to the meaning of 'election under the Local Government Act 1972' see PARA 11 note 2.

3   'Authorised person' means a person, other than a barrister or solicitor, who, for the purposes of the Legal Services Act 2007, is an authorised person in relation to an activity which constitutes the exercise of a right of audience within the meaning of that Act (see LEGAL PROFESSIONS vol 65 (2008) PARA 512): Representation of the People Act 1983 s 181(3A) (added by the Legal Services Act 2007 s 208(1), Sch 21 paras 48, 52(b)); National Assembly for Wales (Representation of the People) Order 2007, SI 2007/236, art 133(3A) (added by SI 2010/2931).

4   Representation of the People Act 1983 s 181(2), (3) (s 181(2), (3) amended by the Representation of the People Act 1985 s 24, Sch 4 para 63; the Representation of the People Act 1983 s 181(3) further amended by the Legal Services Act 2007 s 208(1), Sch 21 paras 48, 52(a)); European Parliamentary Elections Regulations 2004, SI 2004/293, reg 119(2), (3); National Assembly for Wales (Representation of the People) Order 2007, SI 2007/236, art 133(2), (3) (art 133(3) amended by SI 2010/2931. In the application of the European Parliamentary Elections Regulations 2004, SI 2004/293, reg 119(2), (3) to elections that have taken place in the combined region (see PARA 77), the reference to the Director of Public Prosecutions is to be construed as a reference to the Attorney General for Gibraltar: reg 119(7). As to the payment of the expenses of the Director of Public Prosecutions or his representative see PARA 877.

5   Representation of the People Act 1983 s 140(6); European Parliamentary Elections Regulations 2004, SI 2004/293, reg 119(1); National Assembly for Wales (Representation of the People) Order 2007, SI 2007/236, art 96(5). See also PARA 824 note 3. This provision is applied also for the purposes of trying a petition questioning a local authority referendum: see PARA 766. As to the application of the Representation of the People Act 1983 Pt III (ss 120–186) to other polls see PARA 763. The Director is bound to obey the court's directions as to the examination of such a person: *Stepney Division, Tower Hamlets Case* (1886) 4 O'M & H 34 at 37 per Denman J.

6   *Stepney Division, Tower Hamlets Case* (1886) 4 O'M & H 34 at 37 per Denman J; *York County East Riding, Buckrose Division Case* (1886) 4 O'M & H 110 at 115. Generally speaking, the Director's duties are confined to assisting the court at the conclusion of the hearing of the petition in considering whether any particular individual has been guilty of corrupt or illegal practices: *Rochester Borough Case* (1892) 4 O'M & H 156 at 158.

7   See note 6.

8   The court ought, however, to be very cautious in allowing such evidence to be called by him: *Rochester Borough Case* (1892) 4 O'M & H 156 at 158 per Cave J.

    Where, after the hearing was closed and before judgment was delivered, the Director, under the court's direction, called a person who was said to have been bribed, and the petitioner claimed the right to cross-examine that person, he was not allowed to do so, on the ground that if he had wanted to ask the witness questions he should himself have called him: *Maidstone Borough Case, Evans v Viscount Castlereagh* (1906) 5 O'M & H 200 at 211 per Grantham J; but see *Worcester Borough Case, Harben and Cadbury v Williamson, Olds' Case* (1906) 5 O'M & H 212, where, after the respondent had abandoned his opposition to the petition, the petitioner was allowed to cross-examine a witness called to show cause why he should not be reported. In *Northumberland, Hexham Division Case* (1892) cited in Day 29, both the petitioner and the respondent were allowed to cross-examine a witness called by the Director on matters gone into by the court; the question of the right to cross-examine on other matters which were in the particulars was raised but not decided. As to cross-examination on behalf of the parties after a witness has been examined by the court see also PARA 824.

9 *Northumberland, Hexham Division Case, Hudspeth and Lyal v Clayton* (1892) 4 O'M & H 143 at 144 per Cave J. See also *Worcester Borough Case, Harben and Cadbury v Williamson, Olds' Case* (1906) 5 O'M & H 212.

10 As to the duty of the Director of Public Prosecutions in relation to election offences see PARA 882.

822. Member of House of Commons may not appear at trial of parliamentary election petition. A barrister who is also a member of the House of Commons may not appear as counsel on the trial of a parliamentary election petition[1].

1 See *Re Lord Kinross* [1905] AC 468 at 471–472, HL, per Lord James. The objection appears to be founded on the fact that a court trying a parliamentary election petition has the duty of reporting to the House of Commons, and therefore a barrister practising before it would be practising before a tribunal of which he is a member: *Re Lord Kinross*; and see LEGAL PROFESSIONS vol 66 (2009) PARA 1113. As to parliamentary election petitions see PARA 761.

D. WITNESSES AT ELECTION COURT

823. Attendance and swearing of witnesses at election court. At the trial of an election or referendum petition[1], witnesses are summoned and sworn in the same manner as nearly as circumstances admit as in a claim tried in the High Court[2]. On the trial, a member of the election court may, by order signed by him, require the attendance of any person, as a witness, who appears to him to have been concerned in the election[3] or referendum in question, and any person who refuses to obey the order is guilty of contempt of court[4].

It is not illegal to offer a reward for evidence[5].

1 As to parliamentary election petitions see PARA 761; as to the questioning of an election under the Local Government Act 1972 see PARA 762; as to Welsh Assembly election petitions see PARA 764; and as to European parliamentary election petitions see PARA 765. Provision is made for questioning a local authority referendum by applying and modifying the provision made for questioning an election under the Local Government Act 1972: see PARA 766. As to the meaning of 'election under the Local Government Act 1972' see PARA 11 note 2. As to the application of the Representation of the People Act 1983 Pt III (ss 120–186) to other polls see PARA 763.

2 Representation of the People Act 1983 s 140(1); European Parliamentary Elections Regulations 2004, SI 2004/293, reg 97(1); National Assembly for Wales (Representation of the People) Order 2007, SI 2007/236, art 96(1); and see note 1. As to the attendance of witnesses generally and the giving of evidence on oath see CIVIL PROCEDURE vol 11 (2009) PARA 1003 et seq.

3 Ie, in the case of a Welsh Assembly election, including a return to a vacancy in an electoral region (see PARA 215): see the National Assembly for Wales (Representation of the People) Order 2007, SI 2007/236, art 96(2).

4 Representation of the People Act 1983 s 140(2); European Parliamentary Elections Regulations 2004, SI 2004/293, reg 97(2); National Assembly for Wales (Representation of the People) Order 2007, SI 2007/236, art 96(2); and see note 1. This power has been exercised where witnesses have failed to attend on subpoena (*Norwich Case, Tillett v Stracey* (1869) 1 O'M & H 8 at 9 per Martin B; *Galway County Case* (1872) 2 O'M & H 46 at 50–51); and an order has also been granted where a witness was stated to be evading the service of a subpoena (*Waterford Borough Case* (1870) 2 O'M & H 1 at 3). In *Stroud Case, Baynes v Stanton and Dickinson* (1874) 2 O'M & H 107, the court was adjourned in order that a witness should be compelled to attend.

5 *Mallow Borough Case* (1870) 2 O'M & H 18 at 19. The offering of large sums in small constituencies, however, has been said to be objectionable: *Mallow Borough Case* at 19 per Morris J.

824. Examination of witnesses by election court. The election court may examine any person required to attend the trial of an election or referendum petition[1] as a witness[2] or who is in court, even though he is not called and examined by any party to the petition[3]. After any witness has been examined by the court he may be cross-examined by or on behalf of the petitioner and the respondent[4], or either of them[5]. Except in so far as the common law rules of evidence, practice and procedure have been applied to election petitions in pursuance of statute or by rule[6], they are not, as such, binding on judges presiding at the trial of an election petition[7].

1　As to parliamentary election petitions see PARA 761; as to the questioning of an election under the Local Government Act 1972 see PARA 762; as to Welsh Assembly election petitions see PARA 764; and as to European parliamentary election petitions see PARA 765. Provision is made for questioning a local authority referendum by applying and modifying the provision made for questioning an election under the Local Government Act 1972: see PARA 766. As to the meaning of 'election under the Local Government Act 1972' see PARA 11 note 2. As to the application of the Representation of the People Act 1983 Pt III (ss 120–186) to other polls see PARA 763.

2　As to the attendance of witnesses at an election court see PARA 823.

3　Representation of the People Act 1983 s 140(3); European Parliamentary Elections Regulations 2004, SI 2004/293, reg 97(3); National Assembly for Wales (Representation of the People) Order 2007, SI 2007/236, art 96(3); and see note 1. See *Evesham Borough Case* (1880) 3 O'M & H 94 at 95–96; *Montgomery Boroughs Case* (1892) 4 O'M & H 167 at 169–170 (in which case Pollock B cited *Northumberland, Hexham Division Case, Hudspeth and Lyal v Clayton* (1892) 4 O'M & H 143 as an authority for a statement which he made that the court had power to call witnesses to clear up any matter that had arisen in the course of the trial; but in *Northumberland, Hexham Division Case, Hudspeth and Lyal v Clayton* the court seems to have directed counsel for the Director of Public Prosecutions to call the witnesses, and in *Montgomery Boroughs Case*, Wills J said, where witnesses were not cross-examined, that the court might call on the public prosecutor to cross-examine). The common law does not admit of this being done except by the parties' consent: see *Re Enoch and Zaretzky, Bock & Co* [1910] 1 KB 327, CA. The court appears to have discretion in the matter. As long as the parties are at arm's length it does not seem usual for the court to call (as between petitioner and respondent) a witness whom both sides have abstained from calling, although after the conclusion of the parties' cases this is often done: see *Hartlepool Case* (1910) Times, 4 May; and cf *Montgomery Boroughs Case*.

4　As to respondents see PARAS 782, 791.

5　Representation of the People Act 1983 s 140(4); European Parliamentary Elections Regulations 2004, SI 2004/293, reg 97(4); National Assembly for Wales (Representation of the People) Order 2007, SI 2007/236, art 96(4); and see note 1.

6　As to the application of rules of practice and procedure in the case of election or referendum petitions see PARA 817.

7　See *North Norfolk Case* (1869) 1 O'M & H 236 at 239 per Blackburn J; *Wells v Wren, Wallingford Case* (1880) 5 CPD 546; but see contra *Cheltenham Case, Gardner v Samuelson* (1869) 1 O'M & H 62 at 63; *Bradford Borough Case (No 1)* (1869) 1 O'M & H 30 at 31. Election courts are required to observe the principles, practice and rules on which the committees of the House of Commons used to act on dealing with election petitions: see PARA 817. The common law rules of evidence were, in general, observed by committees of the House of Commons in trying election petitions, but it was stated that election committees had greater latitude in questions of evidence than courts of law: see *Bedford Case* (1838) Falc & Fitz 429 at 436. See also *Galway County Case* (1872) 2 O'M & H 46 at 51–52, where Keogh J, admitting, on a charge of spiritual intimidation, evidence of references made outside the trial of the petition since its opening, observed that in *Mayo County Case* (1857) Wolf & D 1 the election committee had received evidence of what was passing in the county pending the very hearing of the petition, and that, except where a special alteration had been made by statute, the election court must be guided, as far as possible, by the practice of Parliament; but see the cases dealing with the cross-examination by a party of his own witnesses cited in PARA 828. As to the production of documents see PARA 812 note 1; as to statements and admissions by parties see PARA 833; and as to statements by voters to third parties see PARA 834 note 2. In *Maidstone Borough Case, Evans v Viscount Castlereagh* (1906) 5 O'M & H 200 at 202, Lawrance J said: 'It is true that in election cases we have to throw overboard the rules which regulate ordinary cases, because we have to deal with peculiar circumstances'. Hearsay evidence is not normally admissible: see *Dover Case* (1869) 1 O'M & H 210; *Northumberland, Berwick-upon-Tweed Division Case* (1923) 7 O'M & H 1 at 8. Cf *Bridgewater Case* (1869) 1 O'M & H 112; *Durham County, Northern Division Case (No 2)* (1874) 2 O'M & H 152; *Taunton Borough Case* (1874) 2 O'M & H 66 at 69.

825. Evidence on commission. There is power to order a commission for the examination of a witness at an election court who is dangerously ill[1]. Evidence on commission has also been taken in the case of a witness about to leave the country[2]. If the order is made at the trial, the practice is to have the examination taken before the court registrar[3]. The shorthand writer must attend, and counsel may attend[4].

1　*Staleybridge Case* (1869) 19 LT 703; *Wells v Wren, Wallingford Case* (1880) 5 CPD 546 at 550 per Lord Coleridge CJ; *R v Maidenhead Corpn* (1882) 9 QBD 494 at 500, CA, per Jessell MR. As to the examination of witnesses at an election court see PARA 824.
2　*Exeter Case* (1911) 6 O'M & H 228, where the evidence was taken before a commissioner.
3　*Wallingford Case* (1869) 1 O'M & H 57; *Montgomery Boroughs Case* (1892) 4 O'M & H 167 (not reported on this point).
4　See *Wallingford Case* (1869) 1 O'M & H 57 at 58. As to the attendance of shorthand writers at the trial see PARA 818.

826. Perjury. A witness at an election court may be proceeded against for perjury committed at the trial of an election petition[1].

1　See the Perjury Act 1911 s 1(1), (2); and CRIMINAL LAW vol 26 (2010) PARA 668 et seq.

827. Ordering witnesses to withdraw. It seems that the election court may order witnesses to remain outside, even though the petition may contain charges against them[1].

1　*Montgomery Boroughs Case* (1892) 4 O'M & H 167. Where, however, other witnesses against whom charges are made are ordered out of court, the respondent's election agent may be allowed to remain: *Knaresborough Case* (1880) 3 O'M & H 141 at 142, where the respondent's counsel had asked that the election agent might be allowed to remain in court in order that he might receive instructions from him for cross-examination, and Lush J, in granting leave, likened the position of the election agent to that of a solicitor. As to the attendance of witnesses at an election court see PARA 823.

828. Cross-examination. The election court will allow a party to cross-examine his own witness if, in the court's opinion, the witness is hostile[1], and where the witness may be cross-examined, the party may also call evidence to contradict him[2].

1　*Coventry Case, Berry v Eaton and Hill* (1869) 1 O'M & H 97 at 104 per Willes J. As to the examination of witnesses at an election court see PARA 824.
2　*Coventry Case, Berry v Eaton and Hill* (1869) 1 O'M & H 97 at 104; *Lichfield Case, Anson v Dyott* (1869) 1 O'M & H 22 at 24 per Willes J; but see contra *Bridgewater Case* (1869) 1 O'M & H 112 at 114 per Blackburn J. In *Bewdley Case* (1869) 1 O'M & H 16 at 17, the same judge allowed a leading question to be put to a witness by the party calling him, observing that the rule was that a previous statement by a witness differing from what he stated on oath in court might be proved to shake his evidence, but could not be used as evidence in chief; in that case the previous statement by the witness had been taken down in writing, and he stated in court that he did not remember the substance of it. As to whether the hostility which occasions the leave must be shown on the trial itself, or may be deduced from inconsistency with a previous statement by means of the consideration by the court of such previous statement see *Bradford Case* (1869) 1 O'M & H 30 at 31, where Martin B disallowed a question as to the making of such previous statement, put by a party to his own witness, with a view to supplying evidence on which the court might consider the witness to be hostile, and the judge ruled that when he saw that the witness was hostile he would deal with him accordingly but, meanwhile, he saw nothing adverse in him. As to the examination of witnesses see generally CIVIL PROCEDURE vol 11 (2009) PARA 1036 et seq.
　　As to the practice followed by election committees see *Nottingham Case (No 2)* (1843) Bar & Arn 192 at 196–197, where, on a witness failing to give the evidence expected by the party calling him, that party was allowed to ask him if he had been intimidated. In *Leicester Borough Case* (1853) Report of Select Committee, Minutes of Evidence 52, the petitioner's counsel, on

objection having been taken to his calling evidence contradicting that of one of his own witnesses, asked the chairman if the committee had ruled that petitioners might not call a witness to contradict another whom they had called to prove their case. The chairman intimated to him that in the peculiar circumstances of that particular case he could not see how the inquiry could proceed without an opportunity being given of testing the character of the witnesses who had been called; accordingly he was allowed to call such evidence. See, however, *Cockermouth Case* (1853) Report of Select Committee, Minutes of Evidence 100, where it was resolved that evidence which the petitioners sought to obtain from one of their witnesses of an admission by a previous witness called by them that he had been bribed was not admissible; but where the evidence which a party sought to call in contradiction of one of his own witnesses was on a point in itself material and he sought to call such evidence in order to establish that point, the evidence was admitted (*Bury Case* (1859) Wolf & B 40 at 41; *Kingston-upon-Hull Case* (1859) Wolf & B 84 at 85).

829. Witness evidence and secrecy of vote. A witness at an election court[1] may not be required to disclose for whom he has voted[2], and it is only in those cases where he has publicly held himself out as belonging to some political party that he may be asked to which party he belongs[3].

The court may not discover how a person has voted until it has been proved that he voted and his vote has been declared to be void[4].

1 As to the attendance of witnesses at an election court see PARA 823.

2 No person who has voted may, in any legal proceeding to question an election, be required to state for whom he has voted: see PARA 385.

3 *North Durham County Case* (1874) 3 O'M & H 1 per Grove J; followed in *Harwich Borough Case* (1880) 3 O'M & H 61 at 63–64.

4 *Stepney Division, Tower Hamlets Case* (1886) 4 O'M & H 34 at 36. Where, however, on a scrutiny, the vote of a certain person had been declared bad, but, two ballot papers being found to have the same number, it was impossible to say which was the one that had been marked by that person, it was decided that both might be shown to him so that he might say which was his: *Finsbury, Central Division Case* (1892) 4 O'M & H 171 at 176.

830. Duty to answer questions. A person who is called as a witness respecting an election or referendum before any election court[1] is not excused from answering any question relating to any offence at, or connected with, the election on the ground that the answer may incriminate, or may tend to incriminate, that person or that person's spouse or civil partner[2]. Furthermore, he may not refuse to answer any such question on the ground of privilege[3]. Whether a witness may be asked or will be bound to answer questions seeking to show that he has been guilty of an offence at a previous election or referendum seems never to have been directly decided[4].

An answer by a person to a question put by or before an election court is not, except in any criminal proceedings for perjury in respect of the evidence, admissible in evidence against that person or that person's spouse or civil partner in any civil or criminal proceedings[5].

1 As to parliamentary election petitions see PARA 761; as to the questioning of an election under the Local Government Act 1972 see PARA 762; as to Welsh Assembly election petitions see PARA 764; and as to European parliamentary election petitions see PARA 765. Provision is made for questioning a local authority referendum by applying and modifying the provision made for questioning an election under the Local Government Act 1972: see PARA 766. As to the meaning of 'election under the Local Government Act 1972' see PARA 11 note 2. As to the application of the Representation of the People Act 1983 Pt III (ss 120–186) to other polls see PARA 763.

    In the case of a Welsh Assembly election petition, the reference in the text to an election includes a return to a vacancy in an electoral region (see PARA 215): see the National Assembly for Wales (Representation of the People) Order 2007, SI 2007/236, art 97(1).

2 Representation of the People Act 1983 s 141(1)(a) (amended by the Civil Partnership Act 2004 s 261(1), Sch 27 para 84); European Parliamentary Elections Regulations 2004, SI 2004/293,

reg 98(1)(a) (amended by SI 2005/2114); National Assembly for Wales (Representation of the People) Order 2007, SI 2007/236, art 97(1)(a); and see note 1.

3   Representation of the People Act 1983 s 141(1)(b); European Parliamentary Elections Regulations 2004, SI 2004/293, reg 98(1)(b); National Assembly for Wales (Representation of the People) Order 2007, SI 2007/236, art 97(1)(b); and see note 1.

4   Authority seems to be against the admission of evidence of corrupt practices at previous elections (*Windsor Case, Richardson-Gardner v Eykyn* (1869) 19 LT 613 at 615 per Willes J; *Taunton Borough Case* (1874) 2 O'M & H 66 at 70–71 per Grove J), unless such practices are connected with the election actually in question (*Galway Borough Case* (1869) 22 LT 75 at 76, 1 O'M & H 303 at 304; *Windsor Case, Herbert v Gardiner* (1874) 31 LT 133 at 135–136, 2 O'M & H 88 at 90–91; *Poole Case* (1874) 2 O'M & H 123 at 124–125). See also the Corrupt and Illegal Practices Prevention Act 1883 s 49 (repealed) which provided that questions about elections before 1883 were forbidden; and see the Election Commissioners Act 1949 s 4(2) (repealed).

5   Representation of the People Act 1983 s 141(2) (amended by the Civil Partnership Act 2004 Sch 27 para 84); European Parliamentary Elections Regulations 2004, SI 2004/293, reg 98(2) (amended by SI 2005/2114); National Assembly for Wales (Representation of the People) Order 2007, SI 2007/236, art 97(2); and see note 1.

E. EVIDENCE

831.   Proof of corrupt practices before agency proved.   On the trial of an election petition[1], unless the election court otherwise directs, any charge of a corrupt practice[2] (and, in the case of a petition questioning an election under the Local Government Act 1972, any charge of an illegal practice[3]) may be gone into, and evidence in relation to it may be received, before any proof has been given of agency on behalf of any candidate in respect of the corrupt or illegal practice[4]. The court has a discretion to admit evidence of a corrupt practice before proof of agency has been given or to insist on agency first being proved. If a case of agency has been opened by the party seeking so to give such evidence, the court will generally admit evidence of a corrupt practice before proof of agency[5], but the evidence should not be given unless the party calling it has a reasonable expectation of being able to prove agency[6].

Although an election court is a civil court not a criminal court, it is settled law that the court must apply the criminal standard of proof to charges of corrupt and illegal practices, and the burden of proof must necessarily rest on the petitioner[7].

1   As to parliamentary election petitions see PARA 761; as to the questioning of an election under the Local Government Act 1972 see PARA 762; as to Welsh Assembly election petitions see PARA 764. As to the meaning of 'election under the Local Government Act 1972' see PARA 11 note 2. As to the application of the Representation of the People Act 1983 Pt III (ss 120–186) to other polls see PARA 763. There is no equivalent provision for the purposes of European parliamentary election petitions because corrupt and illegal practices may be cited in such petitions only when they are related to personation and other voting offences: see PARA 765.

2   As to corrupt practices see generally PARA 704 et seq.

3   As to illegal practices see generally PARA 671 et seq.

4   Representation of the People Act 1983 s 139(4); National Assembly for Wales (Representation of the People) Order 2007, SI 2007/236, art 95(4). As to proof of agency see PARA 832. The court will need to ascertain whether illegal practices have extensively prevailed for the purposes of its report: see PARA 859.

5   *Guildford Case* (1869) 1 O'M & H 13 at 14 per Willes J.

6   *Bristol Case, Brett v Robinson* (1870) 2 O'M & H 27 at 29 per Bramwell B.

7   See *R v Rowe, ex p Mainwaring* [1992] 4 All ER 821, [1992] 1 WLR 1059, CA, at 829 and 1068 per Farquharson LJ, at 830 and 1069 per Nolan LJ and at 831 and 1070 per Parker LJ (reference to a person being 'guilty' of corrupt practice connotes a criminal offence and, accordingly, a criminal standard of proof is to be applied in a civil court no less than in a criminal court). See also *Akhtar v Jahan, Iqbal v Islam* [2005] All ER (D) 15 (Apr) at [536]–[548], Election Ct (decision revsd in part, on a point of evidence, sub nom *R (on the*

application of Afzal) v Election Court [2005] EWCA Civ 647, [2005] LGR 823); and *Re Central Ward, Slough Election Petition, Simmons v Khan* [2008] EWHC B4 (QB), Election Ct, at [60]–[69] per Commissioner Mawrey QC.

832.　Proof of agency. What constitutes agency on the trial of a petition[1] is a question to be decided on the circumstances of each case[2]. However, the concept of agency is much wider in election law than in other areas of the law, such as contract[3], and a candidate is responsible generally for the deeds of those who, to his knowledge, do such acts as may tend to promote his election, provided the candidate or his authorised agents have reasonable knowledge that those persons are so acting with that object[4]. It follows accordingly that, in order to give in evidence the commission of such acts by an agent, it is not necessary to prove that they were authorised or sanctioned; it is merely necessary to prove at some stage of the trial that the person committing them was an agent[5].

Statements, as distinguished from acts, by an agent are not prima facie evidence on the hearing of an election petition against a party for whom he had acted as agent at the election in question[6]. It may, however, be proved that a person is such an agent as to make his statements evidence against the party for whom he has acted, and directions given by an agent may be evidence[7].

Evidence should be confined to the charges alleged in the petition[8].

1　As to parliamentary election petitions see PARA 761; as to the questioning of an election under the Local Government Act 1972 see PARA 762; as to Welsh Assembly election petitions see PARA 764; and as to European parliamentary election petitions see PARA 765. Provision is made for questioning a local authority referendum by applying and modifying the provision made for questioning an election under the Local Government Act 1972: see PARA 766. As to the meaning of 'election under the Local Government Act 1972' see PARA 11 note 2.

2　As to evidence of agency see PARA 245 et seq.

3　*Re Central Ward, Slough Election Petition, Simmons v Khan* [2008] EWHC B4 (QB), Election Ct, at [56] per Commissioner Mawrey QC.

4　See *Wakefield Case* (1874) 2 O'M & H 100 per Grove J, cited in *Re Central Ward, Slough Election Petition, Simmons v Khan* [2008] EWHC B4 (QB), Election Ct, at [57] per Commissioner Mawrey QC. 'Agent' is thus not by any means restricted for these purposes to the candidate's official 'party agent' but covers a wide range of canvassers, committees and supporters, whether or not a candidate may have appointed them as agents, and knowledge of what they are doing does not need to be proved against a candidate for him to be fixed with their actions: *Re Central Ward, Slough Election Petition, Simmons v Khan*, Election Ct, at [58] per Commissioner Mawrey QC.

5　*Norwich Case, Tillett v Stracey* (1869) 1 O'M & H 8 at 10 per Martin B; *Westbury Case, Laverton v Phipps, Harrop's Case* (1869) 1 O'M & H 47 at 52 per Willes J; *Staleybridge Case, Ogden, Woolley and Buckley v Sidebottom, Gilbert's Case* (1869) 1 O'M & H 66 at 68 per Blackburn J; *Tamworth Case, Hill and Walton v Peel and Bulwer* (1869) 1 O'M & H 75 at 81 per Willes J; *Taunton Case, Williams and Mellor v Cox* (1869) 1 O'M & H 181 at 182 per Blackburn J; *Taunton Borough Case* (1874) 2 O'M & H 66 at 73–74 per Grove J. A candidate may have expressly forbidden the corrupt acts of his agent and still be held liable for them, to the extent of his election being avoided: see PARA 244.

6　*King's Lynn Case, Armes and Holditch v Bourke* (1869) 1 O'M & H 206 at 207–208 per Martin B; *Dover Case* (1869) 1 O'M & H 210 at 211.

7　*Dover Case* (1869) 1 O'M & H 210.

8　*Dudley Case* (1874) 2 O'M & H 115 at 119 per Grove J; *Greenock Case* (1869) 1 O'M & H 247 at 248. A petitioner, however, has been allowed to go into a ground of objection stated in the particulars but not specifically raised in the petition: *Londonderry City Case* (1886) 4 O'M & H 96. As to the amendment of a parliamentary or Welsh Assembly election petition see PARA 786; and as to the amendment of a petition questioning a local authority referendum or an election under the Local Government Act 1972 see PARA 794.

833.　Statements by parties. Statements and admissions by parties to the petition[1] are admissible in evidence against them, and the admissions of an original respondent may be given in evidence by the petitioner where the petition is being proceeded with against a substituted respondent[2].

1	As to parliamentary election petitions see PARA 761; as to the questioning of an election under the Local Government Act 1972 see PARA 762; as to Welsh Assembly election petitions see PARA 764; and as to European parliamentary election petitions see PARA 765. Provision is made for questioning a local authority referendum by applying and modifying the provision made for questioning an election under the Local Government Act 1972: see PARA 766. As to the meaning of 'election under the Local Government Act 1972' see PARA 11 note 2.

2	*Tipperary County Case* (1875) 3 O'M & H 19 at 34. It was there argued for the respondent that the admission by the deceased respondent as to his nationality was not admissible, on the ground that the authority of the cases decided before the election committees was against the reception of such evidence, and that questions of evidence arising in election petitions should be decided according to such authority and not according to the ordinary law of evidence, and Keogh J decided the point in favour of the petitioner entirely on the authority of the cases decided before the election committees. As to the court's duty to observe the rules on which the committees of the House of Commons used to act see PARA 817.

834. Statements by voters. Statements by voters to third parties may be given in evidence before an election court for the purpose of invalidating their votes in the event of a scrutiny; but, unless agency is proved or admitted[1], they do not constitute evidence against the opposite party[2]. Where the question of personation is raised[3], declarations and admissions of the person who voted that he is not the person on the register[4], or of the person on the register that he is not the person who voted, are admissible[5].

1	As to proof of agency see PARA 832.

2	*Windsor Case, Richardson-Gardner v Eykyn* (1869) 1 O'M & H 1 at 5–6 per Willes J; *King's Lynn Case, Armes and Holditch v Bourke* (1869) 1 O'M & H 206 at 208 per Martin B, where he laid down, with regard to statements to third parties by a voter as to his having been bribed, that in order to affect the respondent's seat it would be necessary to show that the voter had actually been bribed, not merely that he had said so; *Worcester Borough Case, Harben and Cadbury v Williamson, Olds' Case* (1906) 5 O'M & H 212. The balance of authority under the decisions of the old election committees is in favour of the admissibility in evidence of such statements by voters: see *Ipswich Case* (1835) Kn & Omb 332 at 387; *Leominster Case, Weaver's Case* (1796) 2 Peck 391 at 395; *Sudbury Case, Black Boy Case* (1842) Bar & Aust 237 at 245. See also *Bridgewater Case* (1869) 1 O'M & H 112 (admissibility of statements to and by the landlady of a public house for proving treating, and of conversations after the poll); *Londonderry Borough Case* (1869) 1 O'M & H 274 at 276–277 per O'Brien J (admissibility of statements of deceased person for establishing agency); *Stroud Case, Baynes v Stanton and Dickinson* (1874) 2 O'M & H 107 at 108 (admissibility of statement by a person, who had since disappeared, of the commission of bribery); *Durham County, Northern Division Case (No 2)* (1874) 2 O'M & H 152 at 153 (admissibility of statements made to canvasser). A book embodying the reports of the regular canvassers kept by the witness to whom the reports have been made is not strictly admissible; the canvassers should first be called to prove their returns: *King's Lynn Case, Armes and Holditch v Bourke* (1869) 1 O'M & H 206. See also *Westminster Borough Case* (1869) 1 O'M & H 89 at 94, where a question to a witness called on behalf of the respondent, who had been employed by a canvassing association, as to the total number of promises received, which was asked with the object of showing that it was such that he, acting as respondent's agent, would have been less likely to resort to bribery, was allowed. Where, on behalf of a petitioner, evidence was tendered of a conversation between a witness and certain voters with regard to their votes, on the petitioner's counsel stating that he was prepared to prove a criminal transaction between the respondent's agents and certain parties whom he had named in his opening as having been bribed, and that this evidence was tendered for the purpose of establishing such allegation, the evidence was admitted: *Nottingham Town Case, Hutchinson's Case* (1843) Bar & Arn 192 at 195–196.

3	As to personation see PARA 730.

4	*Westbury Case* (1869) 1 O'M & H 47 at 49 per Willes J. See also *Tipperary County Case* (1875) 3 O'M & H 19 at 34 per Keogh J.

5	*Finsbury, Central Division Case* (1892) 4 O'M & H 171 at 173, 175.

835. Contradiction by witness. The election court will not necessarily discard the evidence of a witness who has signed a statement to the opposite side contrary to what he had originally said, as his evidence may be corroborated by circumstances so as to lead the court to believe it, or his demeanour may give credibility to his evidence[1].

1   *Wigan Case, Spencer and Prestt v Powell* (1881) 4 O'M & H 1 at 5 per Grove J. That persons who have been, or are likely to be, subpoenaed by one side should be persuaded by the other side to make statements, or to sign already prepared statements, is most reprehensible: *Wigan Case*; *Montgomery Boroughs Case* (1892) Day 148 at 150; *Maidstone Borough Case, Evans v Viscount Castlereagh* (1906) 5 O'M & H 200 at 201–202; *Worcester Borough Case, Harben and Cadbury v Williamson, Olds' Case* (1906) 5 O'M & H 212 at 214.

836. Election documents produced following an order. Where an order is made[1] for the production by the relevant officer[2] (or by the National Assembly for Wales in the case of a Welsh Assembly election[3]) of any document in his (or its) possession (or, in the case of the Greater London returning officer, under his control) relating to any specified election, referendum or poll, the production by him or by his agent (or by the Assembly, as the case may be) of the document ordered, in such manner as may be directed by the order, is conclusive evidence that the document relates to the specified election, referendum or poll; and any endorsement on any packet of ballot papers so produced is prima facie evidence that the ballot papers are what they are stated to be by the endorsement[4].

1   As to the making of such an order see PARA 851.

2   Ie by the relevant registration officer at a parliamentary election or local government election for a principal area, parish or community council, by the proper officer of the appropriate local authority at a local authority mayoral election and a local authority referendum, by the Greater London returning officer at a London Authority election, or by the local returning officer at a European parliamentary election. As to the retention of parliamentary election documents by the relevant registration officer see PARA 503; as to the retention of local government and local authority mayoral election documents (including those relating to London Authority elections) by the proper officer of the appropriate local authority see PARA 505; and as to the retention of European parliamentary election documents by the local returning officer see PARA 510. As to the retention of documents relating to a local authority referendum or poll consequent on a parish or community meeting by the proper officer of the council see PARA 659. As to the meaning of 'Greater London returning officer' see PARA 211 note 8; as to the meaning of 'relevant registration officer' for these purposes see PARA 496 note 3; and as to the meaning of 'proper officer' for these purposes see PARA 851 note 2. As to local returning officers appointed for the purposes of European parliamentary elections see PARA 360 et seq.

3   As to the retention of documents relating to elections to the National Assembly for Wales see PARA 508. As to the National Assembly for Wales see CONSTITUTIONAL LAW AND HUMAN RIGHTS.

4   Representation of the People Act 1983 s 23(1), Sch 1 r 56(6) (amended by the Electoral Administration Act 2006 s 41(1), (4)(a)); Parish and Community Meetings (Polls) Rules 1987, SI 1987/1, r 5, Schedule r 35(6); European Parliamentary Elections Regulations 2004, SI 2004/293, reg 9(1), Sch 1 para 65(7); Local Elections (Principal Areas) (England and Wales) Rules 2006, SI 2006/3304, r 3, Sch 2 r 53(6); Local Elections (Parishes and Communities) (England and Wales) Rules 2006, SI 2006/3305, r 3, Sch 2 r 53(6); National Assembly for Wales (Representation of the People) Order 2007, SI 2007/236, Sch 5 para 68(6); Local Authorities (Mayoral Elections) (England and Wales) Regulations 2007, SI 2007/1024, reg 3(1), Sch 1 r 58(7); Greater London Authority Elections Rules 2007, SI 2007/3541, r 3(2), Sch 1 r 58(6), Sch 2 r 61(6), Sch 3 r 61(6); Local Authorities (Conduct of Referendums) (Wales) Regulations 2008, SI 2008/1848, reg 8, Sch 3 r 44(7); Local Authorities (Conduct of Referendums) (England) Regulations 2012, SI 2012/323, reg 8, Sch 3 r 44(7). As to the inspection of returns and declarations as to election expenses see PARA 284. As to the inspection of ballot papers see PARA 851.

F. RECRIMINATORY CASES

837. When recriminatory evidence may be offered. On the trial of a petition[1] complaining of an undue election and claiming the seat or office for some person, the respondent may give evidence to prove that that person was not duly elected, in the same manner as if he had presented a petition against the election of that person[2]. Such a case is called a 'recriminatory case' and the evidence given by the respondent is called 'recriminatory evidence'. If the respondent intends to give recriminatory evidence, not less than seven days[3] before the day fixed for the trial of the petition he must file[4] a list of the objections to the election of that person on which he intends to rely, and serve a copy of the list on the petitioner and the Director of Public Prosecutions[5]. Any party to the petition may inspect and obtain an office copy of any list so filed[6]. Except by the election court's leave, no evidence may be given by a respondent of any objection to a person's election which is not specified in such a list[7].

If the seat at an election is not claimed, the respondent may not call recriminatory evidence[8]. In such cases, the respondent may not give evidence as to the election expenses of an unsuccessful candidate, and may not set up such evidence by cross-examination[9]. It seems that where the petition claims the seat, recriminatory evidence may be offered notwithstanding that the prayer for the seat is abandoned at the trial[10].

On the trial of a referendum petition[11], the respondent may give evidence in the same manner as if he had presented a petition against the referendum[12].

1 As to parliamentary election petitions see PARA 761; as to the questioning of an election under the Local Government Act 1972 see PARA 762; as to Welsh Assembly election petitions see PARA 764; and as to European parliamentary election petitions see PARA 765. As to the meaning of 'election under the Local Government Act 1972' see PARA 11 note 2. As to the application of the Representation of the People Act 1983 Pt III (ss 120–186) to other polls see PARA 763.

2 Representation of the People Act 1983 s 139(5); European Parliamentary Elections Regulations 2004, SI 2004/293, reg 96(4); National Assembly for Wales (Representation of the People) Order 2007, SI 2007/236, art 95(5). In the case of a Welsh Assembly election, the reference to an election includes a return (see PARA 215): see art 95(5).

3 As to the calculation of time limits for these purposes see PARA 768.

4 Any document required to be filed in proceedings under the Election Petition Rules 1960, SI 1960/543 or, in relation to a European parliamentary election petition, under the European Parliamentary Election Petition Rules 1979, SI 1979/521 must be filed in the election petitions office: Election Petition Rules 1960, SI 1960/543, r 2(5); European Parliamentary Election Petition Rules 1979, SI 1979/521, r 2(4) (substituted by SI 2004/1415). As to the meaning of 'election petitions office' see PARA 768 note 12. As to the application and modification of the Election Petition Rules 1960, SI 1960/543 for the purposes of Welsh Assembly election petitions see PARA 767 note 1. The Election Petition Rules 1960, SI 1960/543, are also applied for the purposes of other petitions: see PARA 767.

5 Election Petition Rules 1960, SI 1960/543, r 10(2) (amended by SI 1985/1278); European Parliamentary Election Petition Rules 1979, SI 1979/521, r 10(2) (amended by SI 2004/1415); and see note 4.

6 Election Petition Rules 1960, SI 1960/543, r 10(3); European Parliamentary Election Petition Rules 1979, SI 1979/521, r 10(3); and see note 4.

7 Election Petition Rules 1960, SI 1960/543, r 10(4)(b); European Parliamentary Election Petition Rules 1979, SI 1979/521, r 10(4)(b); and see note 4.

8 *Blackburn Case* (1869) 1 O'M & H 198 at 199; *Gravesend Case* (1880) 3 O'M & H 81 at 82–83 per Denman J and Lopes J.

9 *Durham County, Northern Division Case (No 2)* (1874) 2 O'M & H 152 at 154 per Bramwell B; *Thirsk Borough Case* (1880) 3 O'M & H 113 per Denman J.

10 The authority of the cases before the election committees supports this view: *Coventry Case* (1803) 1 Peck 93 at 99; *New Windsor Case* (1804) 2 Peck 187 (where the point was argued at considerable length on either side); *Clare County Case* (1860) Wolf & B 138 at 143; and see also *Aldridge v Hurst* (1876) 1 CPD 410 at 416 (where these cases were reviewed by the Court

of Common Pleas in its judgment, given by Grove J). In the last-named case the court refused to allow a petitioner to amend his petition by striking out the prayer for the seat, one of the reasons for so refusing being that, otherwise, the right of giving recriminatory evidence would be lost to the respondent. The court pointed out that the petitioner might give notice to the respondent of his intention not to claim the seat, so as to enable the respondent to avoid the costs of meeting such a claim without, on the other hand, preventing the possibility of recriminatory evidence being given. Thus it would appear that in the court's opinion the abandonment of the claim at the trial would not preclude the offering of such evidence; but see *Gravesend Case* (1880) 44 LT 64, 3 O'M & H 81, where a grave doubt was expressed by Denman J and Lopes J as to whether, when the claim for the seat had been abandoned, with the consent of the respondent and of the court, the respondent might proceed with the recriminatory case.

11   Provision is made for questioning a local authority referendum by applying and modifying the provision made for questioning an election under the Local Government Act 1972: see PARA 766.

12   Representation of the People Act 1983 s 139(5) (substituted, in relation to England, by the Local Authorities (Conduct of Referendums) (England) Regulations 2012, SI 2012/323, reg 15(8), Sch 6 and, in relation to Wales, by the Local Authorities (Conduct of Referendums) (Wales) Regulations 2008, SI 2008/1848, reg 11(8), Sch 5). As to the application and modification of the provision made for questioning an election for the purposes of a local authority referendum petition see note 11.

838.   Allegation of charges against subsequent election.   If a recriminatory case[1] is abandoned owing to the petitioner abandoning his claim to the seat, and if the matters alleged in the recriminatory case are such as would disqualify the petitioner on a subsequent election, but, owing to the abandonment of the claim for the seat, they are not tried and there is no adjudication on them by the election court, these matters may be alleged in a petition against such subsequent election[2].

1   As to the meaning of 'recriminatory case' see PARA 837.
2   *Stevens v Tillett* (1870) LR 6 CP 147; *Gravesend Case* (1880) 44 LT 64 at 65, 3 O'M & H 81 at 82–83 per Lopes J and Denman J. See, however, the doubt expressed in *Stevens v Tillett* at 171 per Willes J as to whether, if such matters were known to the respondent in the former petition, so as to have been capable of being offered in evidence on the recriminatory case, and were not so offered, they might be alleged in the petition against the subsequent election. In that case, however, the recriminatory case had been opened and, three of the charges made in it having failed, it was abandoned before the claim to the seat was abandoned.

G.   SCRUTINY

839.   Object of and provisions as to scrutiny generally.   On a petition complaining of an undue election, the petitioner may claim that the successful candidate was not elected by a majority of lawful votes and demand a scrutiny[1]. The object of a scrutiny is to ascertain by striking off votes or adding votes which candidate had the majority of lawful votes[2].

The statutory provisions which govern the conduct of elections do not expressly state that a scrutiny may be demanded nor, if it can be demanded, the grounds on which votes allowed or disallowed at an election may be disallowed or allowed at the scrutiny. Those provisions do, however, provide for certain votes being struck off on a scrutiny for bribery, treating or undue influence[3], and they contain a provision which contemplates, although it does not expressly authorise, the rejection of votes on a scrutiny on the ground of the voters being disqualified from voting[4]. There is also statutory authority for the inspection of ballot papers for the purposes of an election petition[5]. It is also provided that, subject to the statutory provisions and the rules made thereunder, the principles and rules on which committees of the House of Commons used to act with regard to a scrutiny must be observed, so far as may be, by the High Court and election court, and that such principles and rules apply equally to all petitions[6].

1   *Taunton Case, Williams and Mellor v Cox* (1869) 21 LT 169 at 173, 1 O'M & H 181 at 186; *York County West Riding, Southern Division Case* (1869) 1 O'M & H 213 at 215.
2   As to the striking off of votes see PARA 841 et seq. At a local election in 1974 a scrutiny was held so as to enable votes which had been lawfully cast, but overlooked at the count, to be counted: see the Times (2 July 1974), concerning the local election at Barnet.
3   See PARA 842.
4   See PARA 149.
5   As to the inspection of ballot papers see PARA 851.
6   See PARA 817.

840.   History of scrutiny. To understand the scope of scrutinies it is necessary briefly to relate the previous law on this subject. Before the Reform Act of 1832[1] there was no system of registration for voters and the returning officer from the very necessity of the case was obliged to hold a scrutiny of the voters at the time of the poll[2], but committees of the House of Commons subsequently considered the validity of votes given at the election[3]. That Act established a register of voters[4] and restricted the inquiry at the time of polling to the right of any person to vote to the asking of three questions relating to the identifying of the voter with the person named in the register, to whether that person had already voted and to whether he still possessed the same qualification which had entitled him to be registered[5]. The correctness of the register could be questioned after the election on an election petition[6]. By the Parliamentary Voters' Registration Act 1843 the register of voters was made conclusive evidence, for the purpose of inquiry at the time of polling, of the voter's retaining the same qualification as that with which he was registered, and the inquiry was restricted to the remaining two questions[7]. Owing to doubts as to how far the qualifications of voters could be inquired into by a committee of the House of Commons appointed to hear an election petition, the register of voters was declared to be conclusive evidence of the right to vote except when an objection had been raised before the revising barrister appointed to revise the register and he had given an express decision, and except where there was at the time of voting either a legal incapacity which arose subsequent to registration or a legal incapacity under an Act of Parliament[8].

The provision declaring the powers of inquiry on the hearing of an election petition was repealed by the Ballot Act 1872[9], which in turn provided that every person whose name was on the register was entitled to be given a ballot paper, although this did not entitle any person to vote who was prohibited from voting by any statute or by the common law of Parliament[10]. The effect of this provision of the Ballot Act 1872[11], and the unrepealed provision of the Parliamentary Voters' Registration Act 1843[12] as to the inquiry at the time of polling, was held to make the register conclusive as regards the returning officer and the election court except in the case of persons who were prohibited from voting[13]. This did not mean persons who from failure in the incidents or elements of the franchise could be successfully objected to on the revision of the register, but persons who from some inherent or for the time being irremovable quality in themselves had not the status of parliamentary electors either by prohibition of statutes or at common law[14]. Examples of such persons were peers, aliens, minors and persons holding certain offices[15]. These provisions of the Parliamentary Voters' Registration Act 1843[16] and the Ballot Act 1872[17] have been repealed and are now replaced by similar provisions[18]. Although there is no longer any direct mention of the grounds on which a vote may be struck off on a scrutiny, it is assumed that an election court would follow the principles previously established except in so far as the present statutory provisions as to persons entitled to vote or disqualified from voting differ from the previous provisions[19]. Accordingly it would appear that the votes of persons who were not entitled to be registered because they did not have a residence, service or other[20] qualification would not be questioned on a scrutiny[21].

1   Ie the Representation of the People Act 1832.
2   *Petersfield Case, Stowe v Jolliffe* (1874) LR 9 CP 734.
3   *Erskine May's Parliamentary Practice* (21st Edn) p 36.
4   Representation of the People Act 1832 ss 37–57 (repealed).
5   Representation of the People Act 1832 s 58 (repealed).
6   Representation of the People Act 1832 s 60 (repealed).
7   Parliamentary Voters' Registration Act 1843 ss 79–82 (repealed).
8   Parliamentary Voters' Registration Act 1843 s 98 (repealed). As to these grounds see *New Sarum Case, Ryder v Hamilton* (1869) LR 4 CP 559. Where a minor was placed on the register but was of full age at the date of the poll, it was held that the committee of the House of Commons had no right to question the vote as no objection had been taken before the revising barrister: see *Aylesbury Case* (1848) 1 Pow R & D 82.
9   In 1868 the procedure for trying election petitions by election courts instead of by committees of the House of Commons had been established by the Parliamentary Elections Act 1868, and subject to rules of court under that Act the court was required to observe the principles, practice and rules on which those committees used to act in dealing with election petitions (see s 26 (repealed)).
10   Ballot Act 1872 s 7 (repealed).
11   Ie the Ballot Act 1872 s 7 (repealed).
12   Ie the Parliamentary Voters' Registration Act 1843 s 79 (repealed).
13   *Petersfield Case, Stowe v Jolliffe* (1874) LR 9 CP 734; *Pembroke Boroughs Case* (1901) 5 O'M & H 135.
14   *Petersfield Case, Stowe v Jolliffe* (1874) LR 9 CP 734. The requirement of being a British citizen in order to be registered as an overseas elector (see PARA 96) is presumably also a fundamental requirement because, whilst a person who is registered as an overseas elector but is not such a citizen is entitled to vote, this does not prevent the rejection of his vote on a scrutiny: see PARA 149.
15   *Petersfield Case, Stowe v Jolliffe* (1874) LR 9 CP 734; *Londonderry City Case* (1886) 4 O'M & H 96 at 101; *Oldham Case* (1869) 1 O'M & H 151 at 159.
16   See note 12.
17   See note 11.
18   As to the saving made in the statutory provisions for rejections on scrutiny see the Representation of the People Act 1983 s 49(5); the European Parliamentary Elections Regulations 2004, SI 2004/293, reg 17(2); the National Assembly for Wales (Representation of the People) Order 2007, SI 2007/236, art 26(2); and PARA 149.
19   As to the obligation of election courts to follow the principles and rules on which committees of the House of Commons used to act with regard to a scrutiny see PARA 817.
20   Ie if registered in pursuance of a voter's declaration: see PARA 125 et seq.
21   *Petersfield Case, Stowe v Jolliffe* (1874) LR 9 CP 734; *New Sarum Case, Ryder v Hamilton* (1869) LR 4 CP 559; *Pembroke Boroughs Case* (1901) 5 O'M & H 135.

841. Votes by persons under legal incapacity to vote. It would appear that any person who, being subject to a legal incapacity[1] to vote, votes at an election will have his vote struck off on a scrutiny[2].

A vote given by an alien may be struck off on a scrutiny[3]. In order to prove the validity of a vote given by a person who states that he has now ceased to be an alien by having been naturalised, the certificate of his naturalisation or a certified copy of it must be produced, and his own mere statement in evidence that he has been naturalised is insufficient[4].

A person not of voting age[5] on the date of the poll is not entitled to vote[6]. It would appear that, if such a person votes, his vote may be struck off on a scrutiny[7].

1   As to the meaning of 'legal incapacity' see PARA 95 note 8.

2   As to the saving made in the statutory provisions for rejections on scrutiny see the Representation of the People Act 1983 s 49(5); the European Parliamentary Elections Regulations 2004, SI 2004/293, reg 17(2); the National Assembly for Wales (Representation of the People) Order 2007, SI 2007/236, art 26(2); and PARA 149.

3   *Stepney Division, Tower Hamlets Case* (1886) 54 LT 684. This case appears to overrule the doubts expressed in *Berwick Case* (1880) 44 LT 289 at 290, in view of *Oldham Case* (1869) 1 O'M & H 151 at 159, although the latter case was decided on different wording.

4   *Finsbury, Central Division Case* (1892) 4 O'M & H 171 at 172. Presumably the same principle would apply to a person who claimed to be a Commonwealth citizen by virtue of his registration as such.

5   Voting age is 18 years or over: see PARAS 95 note 2, 97 note 14, 102 note 10.

6   See PARA 95 et seq.

7   See the savings for rejection on scrutiny mentioned in note 2. It is submitted that *Oldham Case* (1869) 1 O'M & H 151 at 159, which decided that a minor who voted could not have his vote questioned on a petition because no objection had been taken before the revising barrister, would not be followed in view of the implication in the Representation of the People Act 1983 s 49(5) that such a vote could be struck off on a scrutiny: cf *Petersfield Case, Stowe v Jolliffe* (1874) LR 9 CP 734; and see PARA 840.

842.   Votes struck off for bribery, treating and undue influence.   Where, on a parliamentary[1] or Welsh Assembly election petition[2] claiming the seat for any person, a candidate is proved to have been guilty by himself, or by any person on his behalf, of bribery, treating or undue influence in respect of any person who voted at the election, one vote for every person who voted at the election and is proved to have been so bribed[3], treated or unduly influenced must, on a scrutiny, be struck off from the number of votes appearing to have been given to the candidate[4]. It is not necessary for this purpose to go into the question of how the person bribed had actually voted[5]. If, however, on a scrutiny, it is proved that, although the voter entered the polling station and received a ballot paper, he did not vote but deliberately spoilt his ballot paper, the election court may order the ballot paper to be produced and examine it and, if it appears that no vote was in fact given, may refuse to strike off a vote on a scrutiny[6]. In a case of bribery it appears necessary to prove not only the giving of the bribe with a corrupt motive, but also that the person receiving the bribe acted corruptly[7].

1   As to parliamentary election petitions see PARA 761. The wording of the provision impliedly excludes petitions questioning an election under the Local Government Act 1972. As to the questioning of an election under the Local Government Act 1972 see PARA 762. As to the meaning of 'election under the Local Government Act 1972' see PARA 11 note 2.

2   As to Welsh Assembly election petitions see PARA 764.

3   'So bribed' means bribed by the candidate or any person on his behalf: *Boston Borough Case, Malcolm v Parry* (1874) LR 9 CP 610.

4   Representation of the People Act 1983 s 166(1); National Assembly for Wales (Representation of the People) Order 2007, SI 2007/236, art 118(1). On the trial of a Welsh Assembly election petition, the reference is to votes given to the candidate, where he is an individual candidate, or to the registered political party for which he is such a candidate, where he is a party list candidate: see art 118(1). As to the meanings of 'individual candidate' and 'party list candidate' in relation to a Welsh Assembly regional election see PARA 230 notes 19, 23. As to the meaning of 'registered political party' for these purposes see PARA 256. There is no equivalent provision for the purposes of European parliamentary election petitions because corrupt and illegal practices may be cited in such petitions only when they are related to personation and other voting offences: see PARA 765. As to the application of the Representation of the People Act 1983 Pt III (ss 120–186) to other polls see PARA 763.

    There is no power to add a vote for the candidate for whom the voter would have voted but for intimidation: *Oldham Case* (1869) 1 O'M & H 151 at 161.

5   *Boston Borough Case, Malcolm v Parry* (1874) LR 9 CP 610; *Down County Case* (1880) 3 O'M & H 115; *West Bromwich Case* (1911) 6 O'M & H 256 at 266. See also PARA 843 note 6.

6   *West Bromwich Case* (1911) 6 O'M & H 256 at 266.

7 *Boston Borough Case, Malcolm v Parry* (1874) LR 9 CP 610 (Grove J doubting); *Down County Case* (1880) 3 O'M & H 115. As to what constitutes bribery see PARA 709 et seq.

843. Votes struck off for corrupt and illegal practices. If any person who is guilty of a corrupt[1] or illegal practice[2] (or of illegal payment, employment or hiring at an election[3]) votes at a parliamentary[4] or Welsh Assembly election[5], his vote[6] is void[7], and accordingly may be struck off on a scrutiny[8]. If any person who is subject, under any enactment relating to corrupt or illegal practices, to an incapacity to vote at a parliamentary or Welsh Assembly election or an election to any public office votes at that election, his vote is void[9], and accordingly may be struck off on a scrutiny[10].

1 As to corrupt practices see generally PARA 704 et seq.
2 As to illegal practices see generally PARA 671 et seq.
3 As to illegal payment, employment and hiring at an election see PARA 682 et seq.
4 As to the meaning of 'parliamentary election' see PARA 9.
5 As to the meaning of 'Assembly election' in the context of Welsh Assembly elections see PARA 3 note 2.
6 The vote struck off is that of the particular person who is guilty and for this purpose there must be inspection of the ballot papers: *West Bromwich Case* (1911) 6 O'M & H 256 at 267; and see also PARA 842. Before the Ballot Act 1872 s 25 (repealed) and the Corrupt and Illegal Practices Prevention Act 1883 s 36 (repealed), which were the predecessors of the Representation of the People Act 1983 s 166(1), (2), the vote of the person bribed and that of the person bribing were both struck off: see *Southampton Case* (1869) 1 O'M & H 222 at 224; and see also the notes to *St Ives Case* (1775) 2 Doug El Cas 391 at 416.
7 Representation of the People Act 1983 s 166(2); National Assembly for Wales (Representation of the People) Order 2007, SI 2007/236, art 118(2). There is no equivalent provision for the purposes of European parliamentary election petitions because corrupt and illegal practices may be cited in such petitions only when they are related to personation and other voting offences: see PARA 765. As to the application of the Representation of the People Act 1983 Pt III (ss 120–186) to other polls see PARA 763.
8 As to scrutiny see PARA 839 et seq.
9 Representation of the People Act 1983 s 166(3); National Assembly for Wales (Representation of the People) Order 2007, SI 2007/236, art 118(3); and see note 7. As to incapacities for voting see PARA 905.
10 It is doubtful if counsel may be heard on behalf of voters whose votes are struck off: *Boston Borough Case, Malcolm v Parry* (1874) LR 9 CP 610 at 614.

844. Votes of persons guilty of personation and of persons impersonated. If a person whose name appears on the register proves that he has not voted at an election but a vote has been given in his name, the vote so given must be disallowed[1]. If, however, the person impersonated has voted on a tendered ballot paper[2], then on a scrutiny[3] the tendered ballot paper is substituted for the ballot paper originally issued[4]. The tendered ballot paper will be counted even if the presiding officer does not comply with all the statutory provisions regarding tendered ballot papers[5]; but, if the voter commits a breach of the statutory provisions by putting the tendered ballot paper into the ballot box instead of handing it to the presiding officer, the vote will not be counted[6]. A vote recorded by one person in the name of another who is on the register will be struck off whether the actual offence of personation is committed or not[7]. If, however, a voter was entered on the register under a wrong name and he, having a right to vote, voted in the wrong name, the vote is good[8].

In order for a vote to be avoided for personation, it has to be proved beyond a reasonable doubt that an offence of personation had taken place because, although the proceedings under a election petition are civil proceedings, the standard of proof that an election offence has been committed is set to the criminal standard[9].

1 *Finsbury, Central Division Case* (1892) 4 O'M & H 171 at 175; and see *Gloucester Borough Case, Guise v Wait* (1873) 2 O'M & H 59 at 64.
2 As to tendered ballot papers see PARA 403.
3 As to scrutiny see PARA 839 et seq.
4 See *Cirencester Case* (1893) (cited in Day 48), where the first voter had used the ballot paper of the second through an error of the polling clerk. Both votes were allowed, however, the court saying that if the respondent wished to strike off the first vote it should have been included in the particulars of votes objected to. If the presiding officer had erroneously marked the register thinking that the voter had previously voted, but at the scrutiny it is proved that in fact nobody had voted in the name of the person who voted on the tendered ballot paper, the tendered ballot paper will be allowed without a vote being struck off: *Berwick Case, McLaren v Home* (1880) 44 LT 289 at 290.
5 *Stepney Division, Tower Hamlets Case* (1886) 4 O'M & H 34, 37 at 43.
6 *York County, East Riding, Buckrose Division Case* (1886) 4 O'M & H 110 at 115.
7 *Berwick Case, McLaren v Home* (1880) 44 LT 289 at 290; *Oldham Case* (1869) 1 O'M & H 151 at 152.
8 *Oldham Case* (1869) 1 O'M & H 151 at 152; *Exeter Case* (1911) 6 O'M & H 228 at 233; *Athlone Borough Case* (1880) 3 O'M & H 57 at 59.
9 *Re Local Government Election for Eel Brook Electoral Division Hammersmith and Fulham Council*, sub nom *Thompson v Dann* (1994) 138 Sol Jo LB 221 (it was not possible to infer that personation must have taken place merely from a presumption of regularity and from the fact that the register had been marked against an elector's name before that elector's proxy had attended to vote; it was probable in this case that a mistake had been made in the marking of the register and the vote should have been counted). A criminal standard of proof has been applied also to find a person guilty of undue influence (which is a corrupt practice): see PARA 723.

845. Votes given to a disqualified candidate at an election. Votes given for a candidate who is disqualified[1] may in certain circumstances be regarded as not given at all or thrown away, and to decide this a scrutiny is not necessary[2]. The disqualification must be founded on some positive and definite fact existing and established at the time of the poll so as to lead to the fair inference of wilful perverseness on the part of the electors voting for the disqualified person[3]. Examples of the sort of disqualification that will cause votes to be thrown away are being a peer, an alien or a minor[4]. For the votes given for a candidate to be thrown away, the voters must, before voting, either have had or be deemed to have had notice of the facts creating the candidate's disqualification[5], and it is not necessary to show that the elector was aware of the legal result that such a fact entailed disqualification[6].

1 As to disqualifications for being a candidate see PARA 224 et seq.
2 *Fermanagh and South Tyrone Division Case* (1955) (cited in 105 L Jo 594). As to scrutiny see PARA 839 et seq.
3 *Clitheroe Borough (No 2) Case* (1853) 2 Pow R & D 276; *Re Launceston Case, Drinkwater v Deakin* (1874) LR 9 CP 626; *Gosling v Veley* (1847) 7 QB 406 (revsd on another point (1853) 4 HL Cas 679); *Claridge v Evelyn* (1821) 5 B & Ald 81.
4 *Re Bristol South East, Parliamentary Election* [1964] 2 QB 257, [1961] 3 All ER 354, DC; *Re Launceston Case, Drinkwater v Deakin* (1874) LR 9 CP 626; *Tipperary County Case* (1875) 3 O'M & H 19 at 42–49; *Trench v Nolan* (1872) IR 6 CL 464.
5 *Re Bristol South East, Parliamentary Election* [1964] 2 QB 257, [1961] 3 All ER 354, DC; *Re Launceston Case, Drinkwater v Deakin* (1874) LR 9 CP 626; *Beresford-Hope v Lady Sandhurst* (1889) 23 QBD 79, CA; *R v Bester* (1861) 3 LT 667; *Cork, Eastern Division Case* (1911) 6 O'M & H 318; *Mid-Ulster Division Case* (1955) Times, 8 October; *Fermanagh and South Tyrone Division Case* (1955) (cited in 105 L Jo 594). In *Re Bristol South East, Parliamentary Election*, it was held, inter alia, that where the facts which give rise to the incapacity or disqualification by status of a candidate exist and are made known to the electorate before their votes are cast, and the voters are also made aware that the legal consequence of those facts might be disqualification, votes given to such a candidate are given at the electors' peril, and, where disqualification in law is established, such votes are thrown away and are null and void, the court being bound to declare that the candidate for whom the next highest number of votes was cast has been duly elected. See also *Cox v Ambrose* (1890) 7 TLR 59 at 60, DC;

Etherington v Wilson (1875) LR 20 Eq 606 at 618, cited with approval in *Re Bristol South East, Parliamentary Election* [1964] 2 QB 257 at 295, [1961] 3 All ER 354 at 376, DC. Earlier cases appear to indicate that, where the disqualification is not notorious and depends on legal argument or on complicated facts, votes given for a candidate (even though he might be unseated by reason of his disqualification) would not be thrown away so as to give the seat to the candidate with the next highest number of votes: see *Abingdon Case* (1775) 1 Doug El Cas 419; *Penryn Case* (1819) Corb & D 55; *Cheltenham (No 2) Case* (1848) 1 Pow R & D 224; *Clitheroe Borough (No 2) Case* (1853) 2 Pow R & D 276; notes to *St Ives Case* (1775) 2 Doug El Cas 391 at 415; and the note to *Radnor Case* (1803) 1 Peck 496; but cf *Wakefield Case, Blakeley's Case* (1842) Bar & Aust 270 at 317; *Belfast Case* (1838) Falc & Fitz 595; *Cork Case* (1835) Kn & Omb 274; *Tavistock Borough Case* (1853) 2 Pow R & D 5; *Horsham Case (No 2)* (1848) 1 Pow R & D 240 at 258; *Leominster Case* (1819) Corb & D 1. For a discussion of early cases see the notes to *Leominster Case*. Express notice of disqualification is almost invariably given: see PARA 268.

6   *Fermanagh and South Tyrone Division Case* (1955) cited in 105 L Jo 594.

846.   Votes improperly recorded.   A scrutiny[1] may be demanded on the ground that votes at the count have been improperly accepted or rejected[2].

1   As to scrutiny see PARA 839 et seq.
2   *Re South Newington, Kingston-upon-Hull, Municipal Election Petition, Lewis v Shepperdson* [1948] 2 All ER 503. As to the count see PARA 424 et seq. Where a cross on a ballot paper is not put firmly into the correct box, the effect on its validity is a question of fact and not a question of law; each voting paper must be looked at on its merits and it is a matter of first impression whether the vote was clearly cast for one candidate or not: *Cornwell v Marshall* (1976) 75 LGR 676, DC; *Petition of Rowe* [2001] All ER (D) 329 (Dec), DC.

847.   Scrutiny and recriminatory case.   Where the election petition makes charges of corrupt or illegal practices and recriminatory evidence[1] is offered, the practice is to take the recriminatory case before the scrutiny[2]. The reason is that if both the petitioner and respondent are disqualified it would be a waste of time to go into a scrutiny. Where, however, the petition only claims the seat without alleging any corrupt or illegal practices on the respondent's part, the practice has been to take the scrutiny first[3].

1   As to recriminatory evidence see PARA 837.
2   *York County West Riding, Southern Division Case* (1869) 1 O'M & H 213 at 214; *Southampton Case* (1869) 1 O'M & H 222 at 225; *Northallerton Case* (1869) 1 O'M & H 167. As to scrutiny see PARA 839 et seq.
3   *Stepney Division, Tower Hamlets Case* (1886) 4 O'M & H 34 at 35; *York County East Riding, Buckrose Division Case* (1886) 4 O'M & H 110; *Finsbury, Central Division Case* (1892) 4 O'M & H 171 at 172; *Exeter Case* (1911) 6 O'M & H 228 at 229; *Petersfield Case, Stowe v Jolliffe, Aylward's Case* (1874) 2 O'M & H 94 at 95; *St George's Division, Tower Hamlets, Case* (1896) 5 O'M & H 89.

848.   Who may demand a scrutiny.   A respondent[1] whose election is proved to be void may still continue the scrutiny[2] with the object of showing that the person for whom the seat is claimed has not obtained a majority of lawful votes[3]. Similarly, if a petitioner is proved on the hearing of an election petition not to be qualified for election, he may still proceed with the scrutiny in order to show that the respondent had not received a majority of lawful votes and so was not duly elected[4].

1   As to respondents see PARAS 782, 791.
2   As to scrutiny see PARA 839 et seq.
3   *Norwich Case* (1869) 19 LT 615 at 620–621 per Martin B.
4   *Southampton Case* (1869) 1 O'M & H 222 at 225–226 per Willes J; *York County West Riding, Southern Division Case* (1869) 1 O'M & H 213 at 215–216 per Martin B; *Taunton Case, Williams and Mellor v Cox* (1869) 1 O'M & H 181 at 186. It seems that, if a respondent fails

on the principal case and succeeds on the recriminatory case (see PARA 837), he may still proceed with the scrutiny: *Southampton Case* (1869) 1 O'M & H 222 at 225–226 per Willes J.

849. List of objections to votes. Where the election petition[1] claims a seat or office for an unsuccessful candidate on the ground that he had a majority of lawful votes, every party must, not less than seven days[2] before the day fixed for the trial, file[3] a list of the votes which he contends were wrongly admitted or rejected, stating in respect of each such vote the grounds for his contention, and serve a copy of the list on every other party and on the Director of Public Prosecutions[4]. Any party to the petition may inspect and obtain an office copy of any list so filed[5]. Except by leave of the election court, no evidence may be given by a party against the admission or rejection of any vote, or as to any ground of contention, which is not specified in a list filed by him[6].

1 As to parliamentary election petitions see PARA 761; as to the questioning of an election under the Local Government Act 1972 see PARA 762; as to Welsh Assembly election petitions see PARA 764; and as to European parliamentary election petitions see PARA 765. As to the meaning of 'election under the Local Government Act 1972' see PARA 11 note 2.
2 As to the calculation of time limits for these purposes see PARA 768.
3 As to filing for these purposes see PARA 837 note 4.
4 Election Petition Rules 1960, SI 1960/543, r 10(1); European Parliamentary Election Petition Rules 1979, SI 1979/521, r 10(1). As to the application and modification of the Election Petition Rules 1960, SI 1960/543 for the purposes of Welsh Assembly election petitions see PARA 767 note 1. The Election Petition Rules 1960, SI 1960/543, are also applied for the purposes of other petitions: see PARA 767. As to the Director of Public Prosecutions see CRIMINAL PROCEDURE vol 27 (2010) PARAS 23, 33 et seq.
5 Election Petition Rules 1960, SI 1960/543, r 10(3); European Parliamentary Election Petition Rules 1979, SI 1979/521, r 10(3); and see note 4.
6 Election Petition Rules 1960, SI 1960/543, r 10(4)(a); European Parliamentary Election Petition Rules 1979, SI 1979/521, r 10(4)(a); and see note 4.

850. Particulars on a scrutiny. Where a petitioner claims the seat for an unsuccessful candidate, alleging that he had a majority of lawful votes, the court has no jurisdiction to order any particulars except those specified[1]. Where, however, a petition contains allegations upon which it claims to have the election invalidated and goes on, further, to request a scrutiny and to claim the seat, the ordinary particulars may be ordered[2] as to the former part of the petition, while as to the latter part of it no further particulars than those contained in the list of objections to votes[3] may be ordered[4]. Similar particulars are ordered of votes which are sought to be added[5]. Where no list of the votes to which it is intended to take objection has been delivered within the time specified, the court has no power to allow evidence of the votes objected to or of the objections to them to be given at the trial[6].

A party to a scrutiny is bound by his particulars[7]. He may not attack votes set out in the other party's particulars which are not set out in his own particulars, and with the objection to which the other party does not proceed[8]. Leave to give evidence as to those votes may, however, be given by the court on good grounds being shown by affidavit, the court making such terms as it thinks right to meet such a case[9].

1 *East Manchester Case, Munro v Balfour* [1893] 1 QB 113, DC; *Furness v Beresford, York City Case* [1898] 1 QB 495, CA.
2 As to the ordering of particulars in the case of these claims see PARAS 808–810.
3 As to the list of objections to votes see PARA 849.
4 *East Manchester Case, Munro v Balfour* [1893] 1 QB 113, DC. See also *Elkins v Onslow* (1868) 19 LT 528.

5   *Horsham Case* (1869) 20 LT 180; *Finsbury Case* (1892) (cited in Day 16); *Cirencester Case* (1893) (cited in Day 16). In *Horsham Case* (1869) 20 LT 180, particulars of such votes were ordered to be given three days before the trial.
6   *Neild v Batty* (1874) LR 9 CP 104.
7   *Finsbury, Central Division Case* (1892) 4 O'M & H 171 at 173–174.
8   See note 7.
9   See note 7.

851. Inspection of ballot papers and orders for production of election or referendum documents. Documents which relate to a parliamentary election or to a local government election for a principal area, parish or community council are kept in the custody of the relevant registration officer[1]; documents which relate to a local authority mayoral election or a local authority referendum or poll consequent on a parish or community meeting are kept in the custody of the proper officer of the appropriate local authority[2]; documents which relate to a London Authority election are kept under the control of the Greater London returning officer[3]; documents which relate to Welsh Assembly elections are kept in the custody of the National Assembly for Wales[4]; and documents relating to European parliamentary elections are retained by the local returning officer[5]. An order may be made for the inspection or production of any rejected ballot papers[6] or for the opening of a sealed packet of the completed corresponding number lists (in the case of a parliamentary election or local government election for a principal area, parish or community council) or a sealed packet of counterfoils (in the case of any other election) and certificates as to employment on duty on the day of the poll[7] or for the inspection of counted ballot papers which are kept in such custody or control[8]; and no person is allowed to inspect any rejected or counted ballot papers, or to open any sealed packets of completed corresponding number lists (or counterfoils, as the case may be) and certificates which are kept in such custody or control, otherwise than in accordance with such an order[9]. If satisfied by evidence on oath that the order is required for the purpose of instituting or maintaining a prosecution for an offence in relation to ballot papers or for the purpose of an election or referendum petition, the order may be made by a county court or, in the case of a parliamentary, Welsh Assembly or European parliamentary election petition, by the High Court or a county court[10]. In the case of a parliamentary election petition, the order may also be made by the House of Commons[11]. An order for the opening of a sealed packet of completed corresponding number lists (or counterfoils, as the case may be) and certificates[12] or for the inspection of any counted ballot papers kept in such custody or control may be made by an election court[13]. The order may be made subject to such conditions as to persons, time, place and mode of inspection, production or opening as the court making the order (or, as the case may be, the House of Commons) may think expedient[14]. However, in making and carrying into effect an order for the opening of a sealed packet of completed corresponding number lists (or counterfoils, as the case may be) and certificates or for the inspection of counted ballot papers which are kept in custody, care must be taken that the way in which the vote of any particular elector has been given is not disclosed until it has been proved that his vote was given and that the vote has been declared by a competent court to be invalid[15].

Strong grounds for making an order must be shown, and the court must be satisfied that the application for it is made in good faith, and will rarely, if ever, grant it unless a petition or prosecution has been instituted or is about to be instituted[16] and it is shown to be really required[17].

The power to make an order which is given to a county court (or, in the case of a parliamentary, Welsh Assembly or European parliamentary election petition, the High Court) may be exercised by any judge of the court otherwise than in open court[18]. An appeal lies to the High Court from an order of a county court[19].

1   As to the meaning of 'relevant registration officer' for these purposes see PARA 496 note 3. As to the retention of parliamentary election documents by the relevant registration officer see PARA 503; and as to the retention of local government documents by the relevant registration officer see PARA 505.

2   As to the retention of local authority mayoral election documents by the proper officer of the appropriate local authority see PARA 505; and as to the retention of documents relating to a local authority referendum or poll consequent on a parish or community meeting by the proper officer of the council see PARA 659. As to the meaning of 'proper officer' generally see PARA 140 note 2. As to the meaning of 'local authority' for the purposes of a local authority mayoral election see LOCAL GOVERNMENT vol 69 (2009) PARA 23. For the purposes of a poll consequent on a parish meeting involving an appointment to office, the proper officer is specified as being the proper officer of the council of the district in which the parish is situate or the county or county borough in which the community is situate: see the Parish and Community Meetings (Polls) Rules 1987, SI 1987/1, r 5, Schedule r 35(1)(a). For the purposes of a poll consequent on a parish or community meeting, any references to a proper officer of a council means any officer appointed for the purpose by that council: Schedule r 38(3).

3   As to the retention of documents relating to London Authority elections by the Greater London returning officer see PARA 505. As to the meaning of 'Greater London returning officer' see PARA 211 note 8.

4   As to the retention of documents relating to the election of members to the National Assembly for Wales see PARA 508. As to the National Assembly for Wales see CONSTITUTIONAL LAW AND HUMAN RIGHTS.

5   As to the retention of European parliamentary election documents by the local returning officer see PARA 510. As to local returning officers appointed for the purposes of European parliamentary elections see PARA 360 et seq.

6   Representation of the People Act 1983 s 23(1), Sch 1 r 56(1)(a) (amended by the Electoral Administration Act 2006 s 41(1), (4)(a)); Parish and Community Meetings (Polls) Rules 1987, SI 1987/1, Schedule r 35(1)(a); European Parliamentary Elections Regulations 2004, SI 2004/293, Sch 1 para 65(1)(a) (substituted by SI 2009/186); Local Elections (Principal Areas) (England and Wales) Rules 2006, SI 2006/3304, r 3, Sch 2 r 53(1)(a); Local Elections (Parishes and Communities) (England and Wales) Rules 2006, SI 2006/3305, r 3, Sch 2 r 53(1)(a); National Assembly for Wales (Representation of the People) Order 2007, SI 2007/236, Sch 5 para 68(1)(a); Local Authorities (Mayoral Elections) (England and Wales) Regulations 2007, SI 2007/1024, reg 3(1), Sch 1 r 58(1)(a); Greater London Authority Elections Rules 2007, SI 2007/3541, Sch 1 r 58(1)(a), Sch 2 r 61(1)(a), Sch 3 r 61(1)(a); Local Authorities (Conduct of Referendums) (Wales) Regulations 2008, SI 2008/1848, reg 8, Sch 3 r 44; Local Authorities (Conduct of Referendums) (England) Regulations 2012, SI 2012/323, reg 8, Sch 3 r 44. At a local government election or at a poll consequent on a parish or community meeting, 'rejected ballot papers' includes ballot papers rejected in part: see the Parish and Community Meetings (Polls) Rules 1987, SI 1987/1, Schedule r 35(1)(a); the Local Elections (Principal Areas) (England and Wales) Rules 2006, SI 2006/3304, Sch 2 r 53(1)(a); and the Local Elections (Parishes and Communities) (England and Wales) Rules 2006, SI 2006/3305, Sch 2 r 53(1)(a). There is no provision in any context to an order in respect of tendered ballot papers (see PARA 403); however, such ballot papers must be available to the election court so as to indicate how the voter who was entitled to vote would have voted if someone had not voted in his name before him.

7   As to certificates of employment on duty on the day of the poll see PARA 395. There are no such certificates at a poll consequent on a parish or community meeting.

8   Representation of the People Act 1983 Sch 1 r 56(1)(b) (amended by the Electoral Administration Act 2006 s 31(1), (7)(a)); Parish and Community Meetings (Polls) Rules 1987, SI 1987/1, Schedule r 35(1)(b); European Parliamentary Elections Regulations 2004, SI 2004/293, Sch 1 para 65(1)(b) (substituted by SI 2009/186); Local Elections (Principal Areas) (England and Wales) Rules 2006, SI 2006/3304, Sch 2 r 53(1)(b); Local Elections (Parishes and Communities) (England and Wales) Rules 2006, SI 2006/3305, Sch 2 r 53(1)(b); National Assembly for Wales (Representation of the People) Order 2007, SI 2007/236, Sch 5 para 68(1)(b); Local Authorities (Mayoral Elections) (England and Wales) Regulations 2007,

SI 2007/1024, reg 3(1), Sch 1 r 58(1)(b); Greater London Authority Elections Rules 2007, SI 2007/3541, Sch 1 r 58(1)(b), Sch 2 r 61(1)(b), Sch 3 r 61(1)(b). As to the completed corresponding number lists see PARA 410.

9 Representation of the People Act 1983 Sch 1 r 56(8) (amended by the Electoral Administration Act 2006 ss 31(1), (7)(e), 41(1), (4)(a)); Parish and Community Meetings (Polls) Rules 1987, SI 1987/1, Schedule r 35(8); European Parliamentary Elections Regulations 2004, SI 2004/293, Sch 1 para 65(9) (substituted by SI 2009/186); Local Elections (Principal Areas) (England and Wales) Rules 2006, SI 2006/3304, Sch 2 r 53(8); Local Elections (Parishes and Communities) (England and Wales) Rules 2006, SI 2006/3305, Sch 2 r 53(8); National Assembly for Wales (Representation of the People) Order 2007, SI 2007/236, Sch 5 para 68(8); Local Authorities (Mayoral Elections) (England and Wales) Regulations 2007, SI 2007/1024, Sch 1 r 58(9); Greater London Authority Elections Rules 2007, SI 2007/3541, Sch 1 r 58(8), Sch 2 r 61(8), Sch 3 r 61(8); and see note 6. As to documents which have been produced by order for the purposes of the trial of a petition see PARA 834.

10 Representation of the People Act 1983 Sch 1 r 56(1)(ii); Parish and Community Meetings (Polls) Rules 1987, SI 1987/1, Schedule r 35(1); European Parliamentary Elections Regulations 2004, SI 2004/293, Sch 1 para 65(1) (substituted by SI 2009/186); Local Elections (Principal Areas) (England and Wales) Rules 2006, SI 2006/3304, Sch 2 r 53(1); Local Elections (Parishes and Communities) (England and Wales) Rules 2006, SI 2006/3305, Sch 2 r 53(1); National Assembly for Wales (Representation of the People) Order 2007, SI 2007/236, Sch 5 para 68(1); Local Authorities (Mayoral Elections) (England and Wales) Regulations 2007, SI 2007/1024, Sch 1 r 58(1); Greater London Authority Elections Rules 2007, SI 2007/3541, Sch 1 r 58(1), Sch 2 r 61(1), Sch 3 r 61(1); and see note 6. As to parliamentary election petitions see PARA 761; as to Welsh Assembly election petitions see PARA 764; and as to European parliamentary election petitions see PARA 765. As from a day to be appointed the reference to 'a county court' in the text to notes 10, 18 and 19 is substituted with a reference to 'the county court' by the Crime and Courts Act 2013 s 17(5), Sch 9 paras 11, 52(1)(b), (2). At the date at which this volume states the law no such day had been appointed.

Dereliction of duty in counting ballot papers is an offence in relation to ballot papers: *McWhirter v Platten* [1970] 1 QB 508, [1969] 1 All ER 172, DC. On its true construction, what is now the Local Elections (Principal Areas) (England and Wales) Rules 2006, SI 2006/3304, Sch 2 r 53(1) permits an application to be made before any final decision was taken whether or not to present an election petition provided only and always that: (1) its purpose was to resolve a real doubt as to the correctness of the declared result; and (2) there was a real likelihood that, were the inspection to show the result incorrect, an election petition would follow; an application for a production and inspection order might also be made to establish whether it was worthwhile to present a petition: *Gough v Local Sunday Newspapers (North) Ltd* [2003] EWCA Civ 297, [2003] 2 All ER 456, [2003] 1 WLR 1836, which also cites *Re Three Rivers District Council Elections* (26 July 1991, unreported) (consent order made by county court for purpose of formal recount; election petition followed).

11 Representation of the People Act 1983 Sch 1 r 56(1)(i). The requirement about being satisfied as to the purpose of the order does not apply to an order made by the House of Commons.

12 There are no certificates as to employment at a poll consequent on a parish or community meeting.

13 Representation of the People Act 1983 Sch 1 r 56(2) (amended by the Electoral Administration Act 2006 ss 31(1), (7)(b), 41(1), (4)(b)); Parish and Community Meetings (Polls) Rules 1987, SI 1987/1, Schedule r 35(2); European Parliamentary Elections Regulations 2004, SI 2004/293, Sch 1 para 65(2) (substituted by SI 2009/186); Local Elections (Principal Areas) (England and Wales) Rules 2006, SI 2006/3304, Sch 2 r 53(2); Local Elections (Parishes and Communities) (England and Wales) Rules 2006, SI 2006/3305, Sch 2 r 53(2); National Assembly for Wales (Representation of the People) Order 2007, SI 2007/236, Sch 5 para 68(2); Local Authorities (Mayoral Elections) (England and Wales) Regulations 2007, SI 2007/1024, Sch 1 r 58(2); Greater London Authority Elections Rules 2007, SI 2007/3541, Sch 1 r 58(2), Sch 2 r 61(2), Sch 3 r 61(2); and see note 6. As to the effect of amendments effected by the Electoral Administration Act 2006 s 41(4) see note 6; and as to those effected by s 31 see note 8.

14 Representation of the People Act 1983 Sch 1 r 56(3); Parish and Community Meetings (Polls) Rules 1987, SI 1987/1, Schedule r 35(3); European Parliamentary Elections Regulations 2004, SI 2004/293, Sch 1 para 65(3) (substituted by SI 2009/186); Local Elections (Principal Areas) (England and Wales) Rules 2006, SI 2006/3304, Sch 2 r 53(3); Local Elections (Parishes and Communities) (England and Wales) Rules 2006, SI 2006/3305, Sch 2 r 53(3); National Assembly for Wales (Representation of the People) Order 2007, SI 2007/236, Sch 5 para 68(3);

Local Authorities (Mayoral Elections) (England and Wales) Regulations 2007, SI 2007/1024, Sch 1 r 58(3); Greater London Authority Elections Rules 2007, SI 2007/3541, Sch 1 r 58(3), Sch 2 r 61(3), Sch 3 r 61(3); and see note 6.

15 Representation of the People Act 1983 Sch 1 r 56(3) (amended by the Electoral Administration Act 2006 s 31(1), (7)(c)); Parish and Community Meetings (Polls) Rules 1987, SI 1987/1, Schedule r 35(3); European Parliamentary Elections Regulations 2004, SI 2004/293, Sch 1 para 65(4) (substituted by SI 2009/186); Local Elections (Principal Areas) (England and Wales) Rules 2006, SI 2006/3304, Sch 2 r 53(3); Local Elections (Parishes and Communities) (England and Wales) Rules 2006, SI 2006/3305, Sch 2 r 53(3); National Assembly for Wales (Representation of the People) Order 2007, SI 2007/236, Sch 5 para 68(3); Local Authorities (Mayoral Elections) (England and Wales) Regulations 2007, SI 2007/1024, Sch 1 r 58(4); Greater London Authority Elections Rules 2007, SI 2007/3541, Sch 1 r 58(3), Sch 2 r 61(3), Sch 3 r 61(3); and see note 6. As to the effect of the Electoral Administration Act 2006 s 31 see note 8.

16 In *Re Lancashire, Darwin Division Case* (1885) 2 TLR 220, DC, the court refused to allow an inspection of the ballot papers in the absence of a petition, and doubted whether it had jurisdiction to make such an order unless on a petition; but cf *McWhirter v Platten* [1970] 1 QB 508, [1969] 1 All ER 172, DC, where an order was made before the institution of a prosecution on the ground that the offenders and the nature of offences could not be ascertained until the ballot papers had been inspected. Where such an order has been made, the court at the trial of an indictment for an offence respecting the ballot papers may allow inspection of them: see *R v Beardsall* (1876) 1 QBD 452, CCR; *R v Quinlan* [1908] 2 IR 155.

17 *Re Lancashire, Darwin Division Case* (1885) 2 TLR 220, DC (cited in note 16); and see *R v Beardsall* (1876)1 QBD 452, CCR; *R v Quinlan* [1908] 2 IR 155.

18 Representation of the People Act 1983 Sch 1 r 56(5)(a); Parish and Community Meetings (Polls) Rules 1987, SI 1987/1, Schedule r 35(5); European Parliamentary Elections Regulations 2004, SI 2004/293, Sch 1 para 65(6) (substituted by SI 2009/186); Local Elections (Principal Areas) (England and Wales) Rules 2006, SI 2006/3304, Sch 2 r 53(5); Local Elections (Parishes and Communities) (England and Wales) Rules 2006, SI 2006/3305, Sch 2 r 53(5); National Assembly for Wales (Representation of the People) Order 2007, SI 2007/236, Sch 5 para 68(5); Local Authorities (Mayoral Elections) (England and Wales) Regulations 2007, SI 2007/1024, Sch 1 r 58(6); Greater London Authority Elections Rules 2007, SI 2007/3541, Sch 1 r 58(5), Sch 2 r 61(5), Sch 3 r 61(5); and see notes 6, 10.

19 Representation of the People Act 1983 Sch 1 r 56(4); Parish and Community Meetings (Polls) Rules 1987, SI 1987/1, Schedule r 35(4); European Parliamentary Elections Regulations 2004, SI 2004/293, Sch 1 para 65(5) (substituted by SI 2009/186); Local Elections (Principal Areas) (England and Wales) Rules 2006, SI 2006/3304, Sch 2 r 53(4); Local Elections (Parishes and Communities) (England and Wales) Rules 2006, SI 2006/3305, Sch 2 r 53(4); National Assembly for Wales (Representation of the People) Order 2007, SI 2007/236, Sch 5 para 68(4); Local Authorities (Mayoral Elections) (England and Wales) Regulations 2007, SI 2007/1024, Sch 1 r 58(5); Greater London Authority Elections Rules 2007, SI 2007/3541, Sch 1 r 58(4), Sch 2 r 61(4), Sch 3 r 61(4); and see notes 6, 10.

852. Evidence of vote at election, referendum or poll. In relation to a parliamentary election petition, a petition questioning a local government election for a principal area, parish or community council[1] or a referendum, the production from proper custody of: (1) a ballot paper purporting to have been used at any such election[2]; and (2) a completed corresponding number list with a number marked in writing beside the number of the ballot paper[3], is prima facie evidence that the elector whose vote was given by that ballot paper was the person whose entry in the register of electors[4] contained the same number as the number written as mentioned in head (2) above[5].

In relation to any other election or poll, the production from proper custody or control[6] of a ballot paper purporting to have been used at any such election or poll, and of a counterfoil marked with the same printed number and having a number marked on it in writing[7], is prima facie evidence that the elector whose vote was given by that ballot paper was the person who, at the time of the election or poll, had affixed to his name in the register of electors the same number as that written on the counterfoil[8].

1 As to parliamentary election petitions see PARA 761; and as to petitions questioning a local government election see PARA 762.

2 Representation of the People Act 1983 s 23(1), Sch 1 r 56(7)(a) (Sch 1 r 56(7) substituted by the Electoral Administration Act 2006 s 31(1), (7)(d)); Local Elections (Principal Areas) (England and Wales) Rules 2006, SI 2006/3304, r 3, Sch 2 r 53(7)(a); Local Elections (Parishes and Communities) (England and Wales) Rules 2006, SI 2006/3305, r 3, Sch 2 r 53(7)(a); Local Authorities (Conduct of Referendums) (Wales) Regulations 2008, SI 2008/1848, reg 8, Sch 3 r 44(8)(a); Local Authorities (Conduct of Referendums) (England) Regulations 2012, SI 2012/323, reg 8, Sch 3 r 44(8)(a).

3 Representation of the People Act 1983 Sch 1 r 56(7)(b) (as substituted: see note 2); Local Elections (Principal Areas) (England and Wales) Rules 2006, SI 2006/3304, Sch 2 r 53(7)(b); Local Elections (Parishes and Communities) (England and Wales) Rules 2006, SI 2006/3305, Sch 2 r 53(7)(b); Local Authorities (Conduct of Referendums) (Wales) Regulations 2008, SI 2008/1848, reg 8, Sch 3 r 44(8)(b); Local Authorities (Conduct of Referendums) (England) Regulations 2012, SI 2012/323, reg 8, Sch 3 r 44(8)(b). As to the completed corresponding number lists see PARA 405 note 11.

4 Ie or on a notice issued under the Representation of the People Act 1983 s 13B(3B) or s 13(3D) (notices specifying appropriate alterations to the register: see PARA 168) at the time of the election.

5 Representation of the People Act 1983 Sch 1 r 56(7) (as substituted: see note 2); Local Elections (Principal Areas) (England and Wales) Rules 2006, SI 2006/3304, Sch 2 r 53(7); Local Elections (Parishes and Communities) (England and Wales) Rules 2006, SI 2006/3305, Sch 2 r 53(7); Local Authorities (Conduct of Referendums) (Wales) Regulations 2008, SI 2008/1848, reg 8, Sch 3 r 44(8); Local Authorities (Conduct of Referendums) (England) Regulations 2012, SI 2012/323, reg 8, Sch 3 r 44(8).

6 As to proper custody or control for these purposes see PARA 851.

7 As to the ballot paper and security measures associated with the ballot paper see PARAS 386–387.

8 Parish and Community Meetings (Polls) Rules 1987, SI 1987/1, r 5, Schedule r 35(7); European Parliamentary Elections Regulations 2004, SI 2004/293, reg 9(1), Sch 1 para 65(8); National Assembly for Wales (Representation of the People) Order 2007, SI 2007/236, Sch 5 para 68(7); Local Authorities (Mayoral Elections) (England and Wales) Regulations 2007, SI 2007/1024, reg 3(1), Sch 1 r 58(8); Greater London Authority Elections Rules 2007, SI 2007/3541, Sch 1 r 58(7), Sch 2 r 61(7), Sch 3 r 61(7).

853. Petitions following equality of votes at election or referendum. If it appears that there is an equality of votes between any candidates at a parliamentary election[1] or election under the local government Act[2] and that the addition of a vote would entitle any of these candidates to be declared elected, any decision by a returning officer at the election, in so far as it determines the question between those candidates, is effective also for the purposes of the petition[3]. In so far as that question is not determined by such a decision, the court must decide between them by lot and proceed as if the one on whom the lot then falls had received an additional vote[4].

If, in relation to a Welsh Assembly election petition[5], it appears that there is an equality of votes between any candidates at a constituency election[6] or two or more individual candidates or registered political parties at a regional election have the same electoral region figure[7], and that the addition of a vote would entitle any of those individual candidates or any party list candidate of those parties to be declared elected, any decision in the case of a constituency election[8] or in the case of a regional election[9], is, in so far as it determines the question as to who is elected, effective also for the purposes of the petition[10]. In so far as that question is not determined by such a decision, the court must decide between them by lot and proceed as if the one on whom the lot then falls had received an additional vote[11].

If the petition relates to an election conducted under the European parliamentary elections rules[12] and it appears that there is an equality of votes between any registered parties or individual candidates at the election[13], and that the addition of a vote would entitle any of those registered parties or individual candidates to be declared elected then any decision as to equality of votes in the European parliamentary elections rules[14], as the case may be, is in so far as it determines the question between those registered parties or individual candidates, effective also for the purposes of the petition[15]. In so far as that question is not determined by such a decision, the court must decide between them by lot and proceed as if the one on whom the lot then falls had received an additional vote[16].

Where the petition relates to a referendum[17] as regards which, by reason of an equality of votes found at the count, the result was determined by lot, that determination is effective also for the purposes of the petition[18]. However, where the court disallows any vote cast in the referendum, such a determination has no effect and the court must declare the result of the referendum[19]. Where the petition relates to a referendum at which no equality of votes was found at the count and the court disallows any vote cast in the referendum and determines that an equality of votes was cast in the referendum, the result of the referendum must be determined by the court by lot[20].

1　As to the meaning of 'parliamentary election' see PARA 9. As to parliamentary election petitions see PARA 761.

2　As to the meaning of 'election under the local government Act' see PARA 11 note 2. As to the questioning of an election under the Local Government Act 1972 see PARA 762.

3　Representation of the People Act 1983 s 139(6)(a). As to the decision by lot by the returning officer in the case of equality of votes at parliamentary and local government elections see PARA 434; and in the case of equality of votes at a London Authority election see PARA 448. As to the application of the Representation of the People Act 1983 Pt III (ss 120–186) to other polls see PARA 763.

4　Representation of the People Act 1983 s 139(6)(b). For a decision by lot by the court see *Levers v Morris* [1972] 1 QB 221, [1971] 3 All ER 1300, DC.

5　As to Welsh Assembly election petitions see PARA 764.

6　National Assembly for Wales (Representation of the People) Order 2007, SI 2007/236, art 95(6)(a). As to the meaning of 'constituency election' in the context of Welsh Assembly elections see PARA 3 note 2. In the case of equality of votes at a Welsh Assembly constituency election see PARA 463.

7　National Assembly for Wales (Representation of the People) Order 2007, SI 2007/236, art 95(6)(b). In the case of equality of votes at a Welsh Assembly regional election see PARA 464. As to the meaning of 'Assembly regional election' in the context of Welsh Assembly elections see PARA 3 note 2; and as to the meanings of 'individual candidate' and 'party list candidate' in relation to such elections see PARA 230 notes 19, 23. As to the meaning of 'electoral region figure' see PARA 340.

8　Ie any decision between the candidates by lot under the provisions in the National Assembly for Wales (Representation of the People) Order 2007, SI 2007/236, art 17(1), Sch 5 r 60 (see PARA 463).

9　Ie any decision between the parties or individual candidates by lot under the National Assembly for Wales (Representation of the People) Order 2007, SI 2007/236, Sch 5 r 63 (see PARA 464).

10　National Assembly for Wales (Representation of the People) Order 2007, SI 2007/236, art 95(7)(a).

11　National Assembly for Wales (Representation of the People) Order 2007, SI 2007/236, art 95(7)(b).

12　As to the meaning of 'European parliamentary elections rules' see PARA 383. As to European parliamentary election petitions see PARA 765.

13　As to the meaning of 'registered party' in relation to a European parliamentary election see PARA 230 note 29; and as to the meaning of 'individual candidate' in relation to such an election see PARA 230 note 19.

14　As to the case of equality of votes at a European parliamentary election see PARA 340.

15　European Parliamentary Elections Regulations 2004, SI 2004/293, reg 96(5)(a).

16　European Parliamentary Elections Regulations 2004, SI 2004/293, reg 96(5)(b).

17 Ie a referendum held, in relation to Wales, under the Local Authorities (Conduct of Referendums) (Wales) Regulations 2008, SI 2008/1848, or, in relation to England, under the Local Authorities (Conduct of Referendums) (England) Regulations 2012, SI 2012/323. As to the meaning of 'referendum' for these purposes see PARA 574 note 2. The provision made for the questioning of an election under the Local Government Act 1972 is applied and modified for the purpose of questioning a local authority referendum: see PARA 766.
18 Representation of the People Act 1983 s 139(6) (s 139 as applied and modified: see note 17).
19 Representation of the People Act 1983 s 139(6A) (as applied and modified: see note 17).
20 Representation of the People Act 1983 s 139(6B) (as applied and modified: see note 17).

854.   Effect of judges' disagreement as to votes at a parliamentary election. If, on a parliamentary election petition[1], the judges constituting the court differ as to whether a vote should be added, it is not added[2]; if they differ as to whether a vote should be struck off, it is not struck off[3].

1 As to parliamentary election petitions see PARA 761.
2 *Berwick-on-Tweed Case* (1880) 3 O'M & H 178 at 182.
3 *Stepney Division, Tower Hamlets Case* (1886) 4 O'M & H 34, 37 at 40.

H. RECOUNT

855.   Application for recount at election. A petition which asks for a recount and claims the seat is a good petition even if it asks for nothing more[1]. The usual practice is for an application for a recount to be made by summons to a judge on the rota for the trial of parliamentary election petitions before the trial on an affidavit showing the grounds on which the application is based[2]. A recount is not granted as of right, but on evidence of good grounds for believing that there has been a mistake on the part of the returning officer[3]. If there are more than two candidates for more than one seat and a petition is presented against one, claiming as against him a recount and the seat, it is not necessary for the petitioner to claim a general recount, that is as regards the other candidate or candidates as well; on the recount against the respondent resulting in the petitioner's favour, he becomes entitled to the respondent's seat[4].

1 See PARA 761 et seq; and Day's Election Cases 4.
2 As to the manner of making interim applications see PARAS 802–803; and Day's Election Cases 16. In *Stepney Division, Tower Hamlets Case* (1886) 4 O'M & H 34, 37 at 50, however, the application was not made until the trial.
3 *Stepney Division, Tower Hamlets Case* (1886) 4 O'M & H 34, 37 at 50–51.
4 *Lord Monkswell v Thompson* [1898] 1 QB 479 (a municipal election case). It is not clear whether in such a case it is open to the respondent, except by petition against the other successful candidate or candidates, to claim a recount against him or them. See the judgment of Hawkins J and Channell J in *Lord Monkswell v Thompson* at 484–486. It is submitted that it is not open to the respondent to do so, on the ground that it would be a questioning of the election or return of such candidate or candidates and so could only be effected by petition.

856.   Procedure for recount. If an application for a recount is granted[1], the usual practice is to order the recount to be taken before the trial by an officer appointed for the purpose[2]. The order directing it generally directs that it is to be taken at the Royal Courts of Justice[3]. The respondent's ballot papers are counted by the petitioner and are then handed to the respondent to be checked by him, and those for the petitioner are similarly dealt with by the respondent. If any are disputed, the officer's opinion is sometimes asked and given, and if any paper remains disputed by either party, the officer reserves it for the decision of the election court, setting it out in his report[4]. After the counted ballot papers have been thus disposed of, the rejected ballot papers are dealt with in the same way.

1   As to applications for a recount at an election see PARA 855.
2   *Halifax Case* (1893) 4 O'M & H 203; but see note 4. The officer appointed is normally the
     Senior Master.
3   This is the usual practice, but in *Stepney Division, Tower Hamlets Case* (1886) 4 O'M & H 34,
     37 at 51, Denman J himself counted the ballot papers, the parties desiring that he might do so in
     order to save time and expense, but he stated that this was not to be a precedent. In *Renfrew
     County Case* (1874) 2 O'M & H 213, the recount took place in open court. As to the procedure
     to be followed when, the result of an election having been declared by the returning officer, a
     parcel of ballot papers is discovered uncounted see *Gough v Local Sunday Newspapers
     (North) Ltd* [2003] EWCA Civ 297, [2003] 2 All ER 456, [2003] 1 WLR 1836 (informal count
     of uncounted ballot papers made in absence of parties). See also *Macmanomy v Westley* (4 July
     1986, unreported) (formal count of votes in overlooked ballot box in presence of parties
     followed by recount of all the ballot papers cast); *Marshall v Gibson* (14 December 1995,
     unreported) (informal recount carried out in absence of parties followed by formal petition).
4   If the statutory requirements regarding the marking of a ballot paper are not substantially
     fulfilled, the ballot paper is void, and should not be counted; and, if it is counted, it should be
     struck out on a scrutiny. The decision in each case is upon a point of fact, to be decided first by
     the returning officer, and afterwards by the election tribunal, on petition: *Woodward v Sarsons*
     (1875) LR 10 CP 733. Each voting paper must be looked at on its merits and it is a matter of
     first impression whether the vote was clearly cast for one candidate or not: *Cornwell v Marshall*
     (1976) 75 LGR 676, DC; *Petition of Rowe* [2001] All ER (D) 329 (Dec), DC.

I. REFERENCE OF QUESTION OF LAW

857.   Reference of question of law by statement of case. If it appears to the
election court, on the trial of an election or referendum petition[1], that any
question of law as to the admissibility of evidence or otherwise requires further
consideration by the High Court, the election court may postpone the granting of
a certificate[2] until the question has been determined by the High Court, and for
this purpose may reserve the question by stating a case for the decision of the
High Court[3]. The case is heard by a Divisional Court[4].

The election court will not reserve a point about which the court entertains no
doubt, even though application is made to reserve it[5]. A point of law may not be
reserved unless it is one which would affect the whole result of the trial of the
petition[6].

1   As to parliamentary election petitions see PARA 761; as to the questioning of an election under
     the Local Government Act 1972 see PARA 762; as to Welsh Assembly election petitions see PARA
     764; and as to European parliamentary election petitions see PARA 765. Provision is made for
     questioning a local authority referendum by applying and modifying the provision made for
     questioning an election under the Local Government Act 1972: see PARA 766. As to the meaning
     of 'election under the Local Government Act 1972' see PARA 11 note 2.
2   Ie a certificate of determination on the petition. In relation to a parliamentary election petition
     see PARA 858; in relation to a local government election petition see PARA 861; in relation to a
     Welsh Assembly election petition see PARA 863; in relation to a European parliamentary election
     petition see PARA 865; and in relation to a local authority referendum petition see PARA 866.
3   Representation of the People Act 1983 s 146(4); European Parliamentary Elections
     Regulations 2004, SI 2004/293, reg 101(3); National Assembly for Wales (Representation of the
     People) Order 2007, SI 2007/236, art 102(3). The application to reserve a question should be
     made before the question is decided: *Londonderry City Case* (1886) 4 O'M & H 96 at 103.
     Where the election court decides a point, the fact of its being a difficult one does not make it a
     necessary practice that it should, on the application of one of the parties, reserve it for the
     Divisional Court: *Re Gloucestershire, Thornbury Division, Election Petition* (1886) 16 QBD
     739 at 740 per Lord Coleridge CJ. Where, on the argument before the Divisional Court of a
     question of law reserved by a commissioner on the trial of a municipal election petition, the
     respondent claimed the right to begin on the ground that he was in the position of one appealing
     from the commissioner's decision, and the petitioner opposed the claim, the court was of
     opinion that the respondent should begin: *Re Gloucester Municipal Election Petition 1900,
     Ford v Newth* [1901] 1 KB 683 at 686, DC. In *Re Stepney Election Petition, Isaacson v Durant*
     (1886) 17 QBD 54, on the argument of a question of law reserved by judges trying a

parliamentary election petition without deciding the question reserved, the point as to the right to begin was not raised, but the petitioner in fact began. In *Re Gloucestershire, Thornbury Division, Election Petition* (1886) 16 QBD 739 where also this point seems not to have been in dispute, the petitioner, who was in the position of an appellant from the decision, began. See *R (on the application of Woolas) v Parliamentary Election Court* [2010] EWHC 3169 (Admin), [2012] QB 1, [2010] NLJR 1756, [2010] All ER (D) 60 (Dec) (the provisions in the Representation of the People Act 1983 s 146 were consistent only with a clear acknowledgement by Parliament of the constitutional principle that it was the role of the High Court and appellate courts to interpret the law enacted by Parliament, and did not have the effect that the High Court could only determine a question of law arising on a parliamentary election petition if it were referred by way of case stated; a parliamentary election court is an inferior tribunal the actions of which can be the subject of judicial review; the scope of such review is not confined to an excess of jurisdiction in the narrow sense, but extended to correcting errors of law; failure to follow the procedure laid down by s 146(4) would ordinarily afford very strong reasons for the High Court to decline as a matter of discretion to exercise its judicial review jurisdiction). As to proceeding on a petition by way of special case stated (a much more common procedure than reference of a question of law by statement of case) see PARA 816.

4   See *Practice Direction—Alternative Procedure for Claims* PD 8A para 17A; and PARA 772 note 9. See also *Nichol v Fearby* [1923] 1 KB 480 at 493 per McCardie J. It is the practice, however, for cases to be heard by judges on the rota.

5   *Horsham Case, Aldridge v Hurst* (1876) 3 O'M & H 52 at 56; *Down County Case* (1880) 3 O'M & H 115 at 120; *York County East Riding, Buckrose Division Case* (1886) 4 O'M & H 110 at 114.

6   *Taunton Borough Case* (1874) 2 O'M & H 66 at 71 per Grove J; *Re Stepney Election Petition, Isaacson v Durant* (1886) 17 QBD 54 at 55 per Lord Coleridge CJ.

(vii) The Judgment and its Effect

A. PARLIAMENTARY ELECTION PETITION

858. Determination of parliamentary election petition. At the conclusion of the trial of a parliamentary election petition[1], the election court has to determine whether the member whose return or election is complained of (or any and what other person) was duly returned or elected, or whether the election was void[2]. If the judges constituting the election court differ on the question whether the member whose election or return is complained of was duly elected or returned, they must certify that difference, and the member or representative is deemed to be duly elected or returned[3]. If the judges determine that the member was not duly elected or returned, but differ as to the rest of the determination, they must certify that difference and the election is deemed to be void[4]. The court must forthwith certify the determination in writing to the Speaker of the House of Commons[5]. On such certificate being given, the determination is final to all intents and purposes[6].

1   As to parliamentary election petitions see PARA 761.
2   Representation of the People Act 1983 s 144(1). It has been stated that, before upsetting an election, the court ought to be satisfied beyond all doubt that the election is void: *Warrington Case* (1869) 1 O'M & H 42 at 44 per Martin B. As to the application of the Representation of the People Act 1983 Pt III (ss 120–186) to other polls see PARA 763.
3   Representation of the People Act 1983 s 144(3)(a).
4   Representation of the People Act 1983 s 144(3)(b).
5   Representation of the People Act 1983 s 144(2). See PARA 816 note 8.
6   Representation of the People Act 1983 s 144(1). Thus where an election petition claims the seat for an unsuccessful candidate, and the judges at the trial decide that the candidate was duly elected, a petition against that candidate's return cannot be presented subsequently: *Taunton Case, Waygood v James* (1869) LR 4 CP 361. If, however, collusion between the respondent and such a successful petitioner was shown, it might be competent for the House of Commons to order a second investigation, even though it might not be within the competency of the court to do so: *Taunton Case, Waygood v James* at 369 per Willes J and at 373 per Brett J (but Brett J

thought that the judgment, being a judgment in rem, might not be final if obtained by fraud and deception of the court). See *R (on the application of Woolas) v Parliamentary Election Court* [2010] EWHC 3169 (Admin), [2012] QB 1, [2010] NLJR 1756 (the provision in the Representation of the People Act 1983 s 144(1) for the certified determination of a parliamentary election court to be final to all intents as to the matters at issue on the petition did not evince a legislative intention to provide that a decision made on the basis of a wrong interpretation of the law could not be challenged, or as excluding judicial review; the statutory scheme was such that a parliamentary election court was intended to be the final arbiter on issues of fact, but not on issues of law).

859. Matters to be reported by court hearing parliamentary election petition. Where a charge is made in a parliamentary election petition[1] of any corrupt or illegal practice having been committed at the election in question, the election court must, in addition to giving a certificate[2] and at the same time, make a report to the Speaker of the House of Commons[3], stating: (1) whether any corrupt or illegal practice has or has not been proved to have been committed by or with any candidate's knowledge and consent at that election, and the nature of such corrupt or illegal practice[4]; (2) whether any of the candidates has been guilty by his agents of any corrupt or illegal practice in reference to the election[5]; (3) the names of all persons, if any, who have been proved at the trial to have been guilty of any corrupt or illegal practice[6]; (4) whether corrupt or illegal practices have extensively prevailed at the election, or whether there is reason to believe that corrupt or illegal practices have so prevailed[7]. However, before any person who is neither a party to an election petition nor a candidate on whose behalf the seat or office is claimed by the petition is reported by an election court to have been guilty of any corrupt or illegal practice, the court must cause notice to be given to him[8], and, if he appears in pursuance of the notice, the court must give him an opportunity of being heard by himself[9] and of calling evidence in his defence to show why he should not be so reported[10]. At the time of making its report, the election court may also make a special report as to any matters arising in the course of the trial, an account of which in the court's judgment ought to be submitted to the House of Commons[11].

Every report sent to the Speaker must be signed by both judges of the election court for it to become effective as the basis for future action; if the judges differ as to the subject of the report, they must certify that difference and make no report on the subject on which they so differ[12]. The report of the election court also must be laid before the Director of Public Prosecutions[13]. In order that any person should become subject to any incapacities or disabilities in consequence of the report of an election court[14], the report must contain, or must be equivalent to, a definite finding that he is guilty of the offence or offences entailing such incapacities or disabilities; he does not become subject to them by reason only of a report stating facts from which his guilt may be inferred[15]. Unlike its certificate of determination, the election court's report is not final and conclusive as to the matters contained in it[16].

1   As to parliamentary election petitions see PARA 761.
2   Ie a certificate of determination on the petition: see PARA 858.
3   See PARA 816 note 8.
4   Representation of the People Act 1983 ss 144(4), 158(1). As to the consequences of a candidate being reported guilty of a corrupt or illegal practice see PARA 894 et seq. As to the application of the Representation of the People Act 1983 Pt III (ss 120–186) to other polls see PARA 763.
5   Representation of the People Act 1983 ss 144(4), 158(3).
6   Representation of the People Act 1983 ss 144(4), 160(1) (s 160(1) amended by the Representation of the People Act 1985 s 28(1), Sch 5).

7   Representation of the People Act 1983 s 144(4). As to the meaning of 'extensively prevailed' see *Maidstone Borough Case, Cornwallis v Barker* (1901) 5 O'M & H 149 at 152–153.

8   Such notice should give the recipient sufficient detail to know the basis on which the court is seeking to name him in its report; there is no requirement for the notice to be in writing, but it would be easier to prove if it is in writing: *R (on the application of Khan) v Election Comr* [2005] EWHC 2365 (Admin), [2005] All ER (D) 203 (Oct) (applicant had not been named in the election petition and the opportunity afforded him to give evidence on behalf of some of the respondents did not constitute the statutory notice to the claimant required under the Representation of the People Act 1983 s 160(1)).

9   If the person on whom the notice is served is desirous of appearing and showing cause against being reported, he can only be heard in person; counsel or solicitor may not be heard on his behalf: *R v Mansel Jones* (1889) 23 QBD 29, DC. This case must be taken to overrule the decision of Denman J and Cave J in *Ipswich Election Petition* (1886) cited in the argument on the trial of *R v Mansel Jones*. Blackburn J, in *Bewdley Case* (1869) 1 O'M & H 174 at 176, was of opinion that a person who had received notice in consequence of charges of bribery being proved against him was entitled to be heard by counsel; but this opinion was given on the wording of the Parliamentary Elections Act 1868 s 45 (repealed), which did not contain the words 'by himself'. It was decided by all three judges in *R v Mansell Jones* at 34–35 that the election court had no discretion to hear counsel on behalf of persons showing cause against being reported.

10   Representation of the People Act 1983 s 160(1). Section 160(1) is a procedural provision and no finding akin to a criminal finding of guilt should be arrived at without the subject of that finding having had an opportunity to address the allegations against him: *R (on the application of Khan) v Election Comr* [2005] EWHC 2365 (Admin), [2005] All ER (D) 203 (Oct).

11   Representation of the People Act 1983 s 144(5).

12   Representation of the People Act 1983 s 144(6).

13   Representation of the People Act 1983 s 160(3) (substituted by the Representation of the People Act 1985 s 24, Sch 4 para 52(b)). As to prosecutions by the Director of Public Prosecutions see PARA 882.

14   As to these incapacities and disabilities see PARA 901 et seq.

15   *Grant v Pagham Overseers* (1877) 3 CPD 80. See also *Re Launceston Case, Drinkwater v Deakin* (1874) LR 9 CP 626 at 636–637 per Lord Coleridge CJ.

16   *Stevens v Tillett* (1870) LR 6 CP 147. In this case, where the judge, on the trial of a previous election petition, had reported that, in his opinion, the election had been properly conducted on the part of the then petitioner, it was held that, notwithstanding the report, on a petition against him in respect of a subsequent election, charges of corruption connected with the former election which had since become known might be gone into.

860. Subsequent action by House of Commons. On being informed by the Speaker of the House of Commons[1] of a certificate[2] and any report of an election court[3] trying a parliamentary election petition[4], the House of Commons must order the certificate and report, if any, to be entered in its Journals and give the necessary directions for confirming or altering the return, or for issuing a writ for a new election, or for carrying the determination into execution as the circumstances may require[5]. Where the judges make a special report[6], the House of Commons may make such order in respect of that report as it thinks proper[7].

1   See PARA 816 note 8.

2   Ie a certificate of determination on the petition: see PARA 858.

3   As to matters reported by an election court see PARA 859.

4   As to parliamentary election petitions see PARA 761.

5   Representation of the People Act 1983 s 144(7). The House of Commons Disqualification Act 1975 s 6(2) (relief for persons who are otherwise disqualified from membership of the House of Commons) has effect subject to these provisions: see s 6(3); and PARLIAMENT vol 78 (2010) PARA 910. As to the application of the Representation of the People Act 1983 Pt III (ss 120–186) to other polls see PARA 763.

6   See PARA 859.

7   Representation of the People Act 1983 s 144(7).

861. Determination of local government election petition and subsequent procedures. At the conclusion of the trial of a petition questioning an election under the Local Government Act 1972[1], the election court must determine whether the person whose election is complained of (or any and what other person) was duly elected, or whether the election was void[2]. The election court must forthwith certify the determination in writing to the High Court[3]; and the determination so certified is final to all intents as to the matters at issue on the petition[4]. A copy of any certificate made to the High Court must be sent by the High Court to the Secretary of State[5]; and the High Court must by the signatures of two or more of its judges certify such a copy of the certificate to the proper officer of the authority for which the election was held[6].

Where, on a petition questioning an election under the Local Government Act 1972[7], the election of any person has been declared void[8], and no other person has been declared elected in his place[9], a new election must be held to fill the vacancy in the same manner as on a casual vacancy[10].

Where the election court makes a determination in respect of the election of the Mayor of London[11] or in respect of the election of a constituency member of the London Assembly[12] and where: (1) the determination of the election court is that the person whose election is complained of was not duly elected[13] or that the election was void[14]; and (2) the return of that person at that election was taken into account for the purpose of deciding which persons were to be returned as London members of the London Assembly[15], the validity of the return of the London members of the London Assembly is affected neither by the determination of the election court[16] nor, in a case of the election of a constituency member of the London Assembly, by the subsequent return of a person as the constituency member for the Assembly constituency concerned[17]. Where the election court has made a determination at the conclusion of the trial of a petition questioning the election of the London members of the London Assembly at an ordinary election[18] and where[19] the proper officer of the Greater London Authority receives the copy of the certificate of the election court's determination in relation to the election which was questioned, he must send notice of the determination to the Greater London returning officer[20]. If the election is not declared void but the return of a candidate at the election is declared void[21], and no other person has been declared returned in his place[22], the vacancy must be filled (or, as the case may be, remain unfilled) as if it were a casual vacancy[23]. If the election is declared void, a new election must be held in the same manner as at an ordinary election[24], with the date of the poll at the new election being fixed by the Greater London returning officer[25] but falling no later than three months after the receipt by the Greater London returning officer of the notice of the determination[26]. If the determination of the election court is that the election is void, the Greater London returning officer must inform the returning officer for each Assembly constituency[27] of the contents of the notice of the determination[28] and of the date fixed for the poll at the new election[29]. The results of the elections of the constituency members of the London Assembly at the last ordinary election have effect for the purposes of ascertaining the results of the new election[30].

1   As to the questioning of an election under the Local Government Act 1972 see PARA 762. As to the meaning of 'election under the Local Government Act 1972' see PARA 11 note 2. As to the application of the Representation of the People Act 1983 Pt III (ss 120–186) to other polls see PARA 763.

2 Representation of the People Act 1983 s 145(1). Where the petition relates to an election of the London members of the London Assembly at an ordinary election, the election court must determine whether: (1) the person or persons whose return is complained of were duly returned; (2) some other person or persons should have been declared to be returned; or (3) the election was void: s 145(1A) (added by the Greater London Authority Act 1999 s 17, Sch 3 paras 1, 33). As to the meaning of 'London member' see PARA 11 note 5. As to ordinary elections of London members of the London Assembly see PARA 199 et seq.

3 Representation of the People Act 1983 s 145(2). In giving judgment, it is the practice for the court to give the reasons on which the judgment is based: see PARA 868.

4 Representation of the People Act 1983 s 145(1). As to the possibility of judicial review in respect of the election court's determination see PARA 771 note 3. See also *Taunton Case, Waygood v James* (1869) LR 4 CP 361. However, in *Goole Case, Marsland v Hickman* (1886) 2 TLR 398, DC, where it was argued on a municipal election petition that the election commissioner had in his report exceeded his powers, Grove J thought that as the commissioner's decision was final the High Court had no jurisdiction, and Stephens J said he entertained considerable doubt on the question of the High Court's jurisdiction and that at any rate the jurisdiction, if it existed, ought only to be exercised under extraordinary circumstances and where it was required in order that justice might be done.

5 Representation of the People Act 1983 s 145(5). As to the Secretary of State see PARA 2.

6 Representation of the People Act 1983 s 145(6). As to the meaning of 'proper officer' see PARA 140 note 2.

7 Ie except in the case of an election of the London members of the London Assembly at an ordinary election (for which separate provision is made: see the text and notes 18–30): Representation of the People Act 1983 s 135(1A) (added by the Greater London Authority Act 1999 Sch 3 paras 1, 32(1)).

8 Representation of the People Act 1983 s 135(1)(a).

9 Representation of the People Act 1983 s 135(1)(b).

10 Representation of the People Act 1983 s 135(1). As to the filling of casual vacancies in local government offices see PARAS 202–205. For the purposes of such an election, any duties to be performed by any officer are, if he has been declared not elected, to be performed by a deputy or other person who might have acted for him if he had been incapacitated by illness: s 135(2). As to elections in the City of London see PARA 33.

11 Representation of the People Act 1983 s 145A(1)(a) (s 145A added by the Greater London Authority Act 1999 Sch 3 paras 1, 34). As to the meaning of 'election of the Mayor of London' see PARA 11 note 4. As to elections for the return of an elected Mayor of London see PARA 199.

12 Representation of the People Act 1983 s 145A(1)(b) (as added: see note 11). As to the meanings of 'constituency member' and 'election of a constituency member of the London Assembly' see PARA 11. As to ordinary elections of constituency members of the London Assembly see PARA 199 et seq.

13 Representation of the People Act 1983 s 145A(2)(a) (as added: see note 11).

14 Representation of the People Act 1983 s 145A(2)(b) (as added: see note 11).

15 Representation of the People Act 1983 s 145A(3) (as added: see note 11).

16 Representation of the People Act 1983 s 145A(4)(a) (as added: see note 11).

17 Representation of the People Act 1983 s 145A(4)(b) (as added: see note 11).

18 Representation of the People Act 1983 s 135A(1) (s 135A added by the Greater London Authority Act 1999 Sch 3 paras 1, 32(2)).

19 Ie pursuant to the Representation of the People Act 1983 s 145(6) (see the text and note 6).

20 Representation of the People Act 1983 s 135A(2) (as added: see note 18). As to the meaning of 'Greater London returning officer' see PARA 211 note 8.

21 Representation of the People Act 1983 s 135A(3)(a) (as added: see note 18).

22 Representation of the People Act 1983 s 135A(3)(b) (as added: see note 18).

23 Representation of the People Act 1983 s 135A(3) (as added: see note 18). The text refers to the filling of a casual vacancy under the Greater London Authority Act 1999 s 11 (see PARA 204).

24 Representation of the People Act 1983 s 135A(4) (as added: see note 18).

25 Representation of the People Act 1983 s 135A(5) (as added: see note 18).

26 Representation of the People Act 1983 s 135A(6) (as added: see note 18). A new election is not to be held if the latest date which may be fixed for the poll falls within the period of three months preceding an ordinary election: s 135A(7) (as so added). As to London Assembly ordinary elections see PARA 199.

27 As to the meaning of 'Assembly constituency' in the context of elections to the London Assembly see PARA 11; and as to the meaning of 'constituency returning officer' see PARA 211 note 8.

28 Representation of the People Act 1983 s 135A(8)(a) (as added: see note 18).

29 Representation of the People Act 1983 s 135A(8)(b) (as added: see note 18).
30 Representation of the People Act 1983 s 135A(9) (as added: see note 18).

862. Matters to be reported by court hearing local election petition. Where a charge is made in a petition questioning an election under the Local Government Act 1972[1] of any corrupt or illegal practice having been committed at the election, the election court must, in addition to its certificate[2] and at the same time, make a report in writing to the High Court stating: (1) whether any corrupt or illegal practice has or has not been proved to have been committed by or with any candidate's knowledge and consent at the election, and the nature of such corrupt or illegal practice[3]; (2) whether any of the candidates has been guilty by his agents of any corrupt or illegal practice in reference to the election[4]; (3) the names of all persons, if any, who have been proved at the trial to have been guilty of any corrupt or illegal practice[5]; (4) whether any corrupt practices have, or whether there is reason to believe that any corrupt practices have, extensively prevailed at the election in the area of the authority for which the election was held or in any electoral area of it[6]. However, before any person who is neither a party to an election petition nor a candidate on whose behalf the seat or office is claimed by the petition is reported by an election court to have been guilty of any corrupt or illegal practice, the court must cause notice to be given to him, and, if he appears in pursuance of the notice, the court must give him an opportunity of being heard by himself and of calling evidence in his defence to show why he should not be so reported[7]. At the time of making its report, the election court may also make a special report as to any matters arising in the course of the trial, an account of which in the court's judgment ought to be submitted to the High Court[8].

A copy of any report made to the High Court by the election court trying a local election petition must be sent by the High Court to the Secretary of State[9]. The report of the election court must also be laid before the Director of Public Prosecutions[10].

1   As to the questioning of an election under the Local Government Act 1972 see PARA 762. As to the meaning of 'election under the Local Government Act 1972' see PARA 11 note 2. As to the application of the Representation of the People Act 1983 Pt III (ss 120–186) to other polls see PARA 763.
2   Ie its certificate of determination on the local government election petition: see PARA 861.
3   Representation of the People Act 1983 ss 145(3), 158(1). As to the consequences of a candidate being reported guilty of a corrupt or illegal practice see PARA 894 et seq.
4   Representation of the People Act 1983 ss 145(3), 158(3).
5   Representation of the People Act 1983 ss 145(3), 160(1) (s 160(1) amended by the Representation of the People Act 1985 s 28(1), Sch 5).
6   Representation of the People Act 1983 s 145(3). As to the meaning of 'electoral area' see PARA 11. As to the meaning of 'extensively prevailed' see *Maidstone Borough Case, Cornwallis v Barker* (1901) 5 O'M & H 149 at 152–153.
7   Representation of the People Act 1983 s 160(1). See also the cases cited in PARA 859 notes 8–10.
8   Representation of the People Act 1983 s 145(4). See *R (on the application of Khan) v Election Comr for the Aston Ward of Birmingham City Council* [2009] EWHC 1757 (Admin), [2009] All ER (D) 262 (Jul) (there is nothing in the legislation or any authority which purports to limit the scope of the Representation of the People Act 1983 s 145(4) so that the special report should only be about the election; the legislation is quite clear that the report can be about any matter arising in the course of the election court proceedings, which inevitably includes the way in which those proceedings are conducted by the parties concerned as well as the substance of the issues to be considered; further, there is, having regard to established authority, no requirement for the law to require notice that a special report is to be made, or to afford an opportunity to make representations in anticipation of such report coming to fruition, simply because a commissioner chose to deal with points he wished to make by placing them in a report rather than expressing them in the narrative of his judgment).

9   Representation of the People Act 1983 s 145(5). As to the Secretary of State see PARA 2.
10 Representation of the People Act 1983 s 160(3) (substituted by the Representation of the People
     Act 1985 s 24, Sch 4 para 52(b)). As to prosecutions by the Director of Public Prosecutions see
     PARA 882. As to the report's effect see also the cases cited in PARA 859 notes 14–16.

C. WELSH ASSEMBLY ELECTION PETITION

863.   Determination of Welsh Assembly election petition and subsequent procedures. At the conclusion of the trial of an Assembly election petition[1], the election court must determine whether the Assembly member[2] whose election or return is complained of (or any and what other person) was duly elected or returned or, if applicable, whether the election was void[3]. Where, at a constituency election[4], the election court determines that at a constituency election an Assembly member was not duly elected or returned[5] or that the election was void[6], and where the return of the member at that election was taken into account for the purposes of deciding which members were to be returned for the Assembly electoral region[7] in which the Assembly constituency is situated[8], neither the determination by the election court[9] nor the subsequent return of an Assembly member for that constituency[10] affects the validity of the return of those members for that electoral region[11]. Where the election court determines that at a regional election[12] an Assembly member for an Assembly electoral region was not duly elected or returned, the court in addition must determine that the regional election was void[13]. If the judges constituting the election court differ as to whether any Assembly member whose election or return is complained of was duly elected or returned[14], they must certify that difference and the member is deemed to be duly elected or returned, or some other person or persons are declared to be elected or returned or the election of all members for that electoral region is void[15]. Where the petition relates to a constituency election, if the judges determine that an Assembly member whose election or return is complained of was not duly elected or returned but differ as to the rest of the determination, they must certify that difference and the election is deemed to be void[16]. The election court must forthwith certify in writing the determination to the presiding officer of the Assembly[17]; and the presiding officer must publish any such certificate received by him in this way[18]. The determination so certified is final to all intents as to the matters at issue on the petition[19].

Where the election court so determines that a regional election was void, the presiding officer of the Assembly must forthwith after receipt of the certificate from the election court[20]: (1) fix a date, which must be no later than three months after receipt of the certificate, for a poll to be held at another election in the Assembly electoral region for which the regional election is determined to be void[21]; and (2) send a notice to the returning officer for the Assembly electoral region in which the election was held[22], stating that the election has been determined to be void[23], requiring that the election is held again for the purpose of returning the members for that Assembly electoral region[24], and stating the date fixed for the poll at the election[25]. The regional returning officer must, on receipt of notice under head (2) above, inform each constituency returning officer[26] for an Assembly constituency in the Assembly electoral region as to the contents of that notice[27]. The results of the constituency elections in the Assembly electoral region for which the election is held at the last Assembly general election have effect for the purposes of ascertaining the results of the regional election[28].

1 As to Welsh Assembly election petitions see PARA 764.

2 As to the meaning of 'Assembly member' see PARA 12.

3 National Assembly for Wales (Representation of the People) Order 2007, SI 2007/236, art 99(1).

4 As to the meaning of 'constituency election' in the context of Welsh Assembly elections see PARA 3 note 2.

5 National Assembly for Wales (Representation of the People) Order 2007, SI 2007/236, art 100(1)(a).

6 National Assembly for Wales (Representation of the People) Order 2007, SI 2007/236, art 100(1)(b). Where a constituency election is deemed to be void by virtue of art 99(4)(b) (see the text and note 16), the election court is treated as having determined that election to be void for the purposes of art 100(1)(b): art 100(2).

7 As to the meaning of 'Assembly electoral region' in the context of Welsh Assembly elections see PARA 3 note 2.

8 National Assembly for Wales (Representation of the People) Order 2007, SI 2007/236, art 100(1).

9 National Assembly for Wales (Representation of the People) Order 2007, SI 2007/236, art 100(1)(i).

10 National Assembly for Wales (Representation of the People) Order 2007, SI 2007/236, art 100(1)(ii).

11 National Assembly for Wales (Representation of the People) Order 2007, SI 2007/236, art 100(1).

12 As to the meaning of 'regional election' in the context of Welsh Assembly elections see PARA 3 note 2.

13 National Assembly for Wales (Representation of the People) Order 2007, SI 2007/236, art 99(2).

14 Ie subject to the National Assembly for Wales (Representation of the People) Order 2007, SI 2007/236, art 99(2) (see the text and notes 12–13).

15 National Assembly for Wales (Representation of the People) Order 2007, SI 2007/236, art 99(4)(a).

16 National Assembly for Wales (Representation of the People) Order 2007, SI 2007/236, art 99(4)(b).

17 National Assembly for Wales (Representation of the People) Order 2007, SI 2007/236, art 99(3). As to the presiding officer of the National Assembly for Wales see CONSTITUTIONAL LAW AND HUMAN RIGHTS.

18 National Assembly for Wales (Representation of the People) Order 2007, SI 2007/236, art 99(8).

19 National Assembly for Wales (Representation of the People) Order 2007, SI 2007/236, art 99(1).

20 Ie under the National Assembly for Wales (Representation of the People) Order 2007, SI 2007/236, art 99(3) (see the text and note 17).

21 National Assembly for Wales (Representation of the People) Order 2007, SI 2007/236, art 101(1)(a), (2). However, an election is not to be held if it appears to the presiding officer of the Assembly that the latest date which may be fixed for the poll would fall within the period of three months preceding an ordinary election: art 101(3). As to fixing the date of an ordinary Assembly election see PARA 213.

22 National Assembly for Wales (Representation of the People) Order 2007, SI 2007/236, art 101(1)(b). As to the meaning of 'regional returning officer' see PARA 18 note 2.

23 National Assembly for Wales (Representation of the People) Order 2007, SI 2007/236, art 101(4)(a).

24 National Assembly for Wales (Representation of the People) Order 2007, SI 2007/236, art 101(4)(b).

25 National Assembly for Wales (Representation of the People) Order 2007, SI 2007/236, art 101(4)(c).

26 As to the meaning of 'constituency returning officer' see PARA 18 note 2.

27 National Assembly for Wales (Representation of the People) Order 2007, SI 2007/236, art 101(5).

28 National Assembly for Wales (Representation of the People) Order 2007, SI 2007/236, art 101(6).

864. Matters to be reported by court hearing Welsh Assembly election petition. Where a charge is made in a Welsh Assembly election petition[1] of any corrupt or illegal practice having been committed at the election in question, the election court must, in addition to giving a certificate[2] and at the same time, make a report to the presiding officer of the Assembly[3], stating: (1) whether any corrupt or illegal practice has or has not been proved to have been committed by or with any candidate's knowledge and consent at that election, and the nature of such corrupt or illegal practice[4]; (2) whether any of the candidates has been guilty by his agents of any corrupt or illegal practice in reference to the election[5]; (3) the names of all persons, if any, who have been proved at the trial to have been guilty of any corrupt or illegal practice[6]; (4) whether corrupt or illegal practices have extensively prevailed at the election, or whether there is reason to believe that corrupt or illegal practices have so prevailed[7]. However, before any person who is neither a party to an election petition nor a candidate on whose behalf the seat is claimed by the petition is reported by an election court to have been guilty of any corrupt or illegal practice, the court must cause notice to be given to him, and, if he appears in pursuance of the notice, the court must give him an opportunity of being heard by himself and of calling evidence in his defence to show why he should not be so reported[8]. At the time of making its report, the election court may also make a special report to the presiding officer of the Assembly as to any matters arising in the course of the trial, an account of which in the court's judgment ought to be submitted to the Assembly[9].

Every report sent to the presiding officer of the Assembly must be signed by both judges of the election court and if the judges differ as to the subject of the report, they must certify that difference and make no report on the subject on which they so differ[10]. The presiding officer of the Assembly must publish any report of an election court so received by him[11] and the report also must be laid before the Director of Public Prosecutions[12].

1 As to Welsh Assembly election petitions see PARA 764.
2 Ie a certificate of determination on the petition: see PARA 863.
3 As to the presiding officer of the National Assembly for Wales see CONSTITUTIONAL LAW AND HUMAN RIGHTS.
4 National Assembly for Wales (Representation of the People) Order 2007, SI 2007/236, arts 99(5), 108(1). As to the consequences of a candidate being reported guilty of a corrupt or illegal practice see PARA 894 et seq.
5 National Assembly for Wales (Representation of the People) Order 2007, SI 2007/236, arts 99(5), 108(3).
6 National Assembly for Wales (Representation of the People) Order 2007, SI 2007/236, arts 99(5), 110(1).
7 National Assembly for Wales (Representation of the People) Order 2007, SI 2007/236, art 99(5).
8 National Assembly for Wales (Representation of the People) Order 2007, SI 2007/236, art 110(1). See also the cases cited in PARA 859 notes 8–10.
9 National Assembly for Wales (Representation of the People) Order 2007, SI 2007/236, art 99(6).
10 National Assembly for Wales (Representation of the People) Order 2007, SI 2007/236, art 99(7).
11 National Assembly for Wales (Representation of the People) Order 2007, SI 2007/236, art 99(8).
12 National Assembly for Wales (Representation of the People) Order 2007, SI 2007/236, art 110(2). As to prosecutions by the Director of Public Prosecutions see PARA 882. As to the report's effect see also the cases cited in PARA 859 notes 14–16.

D. EUROPEAN PARLIAMENTARY ELECTION PETITION

865. Determination of European parliamentary election petition. At the conclusion of the trial of a European parliamentary election petition[1], the election court must determine whether: (1) the member or members whose election is complained of were duly elected[2]; (2) some other person or persons should have been declared to be elected[3]; or (3) the election of all members for that electoral region was void[4]. If the judges constituting the election court differ as to any matter which they are required to determine, they must certify that difference and, to the extent that there is such a difference, the result of the election stands[5].

The election court must forthwith certify in writing the determination to the Secretary of State[6]; and the determination so certified is final to all intents as to the matters at issue on the petition[7].

1   As to European parliamentary election petitions see PARA 765.
2   European Parliamentary Elections Regulations 2004, SI 2004/293, reg 100(1)(a).
3   European Parliamentary Elections Regulations 2004, SI 2004/293, reg 100(1)(b).
4   European Parliamentary Elections Regulations 2004, SI 2004/293, reg 100(1)(c). As to the establishment of electoral regions for the purpose of elections to the European Parliament see PARA 77.
5   European Parliamentary Elections Regulations 2004, SI 2004/293, reg 100(3).
6   European Parliamentary Elections Regulations 2004, SI 2004/293, reg 100(2). As to the Secretary of State see PARA 2.
7   European Parliamentary Elections Regulations 2004, SI 2004/293, reg 100(1).

E. LOCAL AUTHORITY REFERENDUM PETITION

866. Determination of local authority referendum petition and subsequent procedures. At the conclusion of the trial of a petition questioning a local authority referendum[1], the election court must determine:

(1)   in the case of a petition presented on the ground that the result of the referendum was not in accordance with the votes cast[2], whether the result of the referendum was, or was not, in accordance with the votes cast in the referendum[3]; and

(2)   in the case of a petition presented on the ground that the referendum should be avoided either on account of corrupt or illegal practices[4] or on the grounds that corrupt or illegal practices or illegal payments, employments or hirings, committed with reference to the referendum for the purpose of promoting or procuring a particular result in the referendum have so extensively prevailed that they may be reasonably supposed to have affected the result[5], whether the referendum was void[6].

The election court must forthwith certify the determination in writing to the High Court[7]. A copy of any certificate made to the High Court must be sent by the High Court to the Secretary of State[8]; and the High Court must by the signatures of two or more of its judges certify such a copy of the certificate to the proper officer of the authority by which or in respect of which the referendum was held[9].

Where the election court makes such a determination under head (1) above, it must, as the circumstances require, either confirm the result of the referendum or reverse the result of the referendum[10]; and any reference (in whatever terms) in the timetable[11] to the date of the result of the referendum[12] must be construed as a reference to the date on which the election court certifies its determination[13].

Where an election court certifies, as its determination of a referendum petition specifying any of the grounds involving corrupt or illegal practices[14], that the referendum was avoided, the local authority concerned must hold another referendum, not earlier than two months and not later than three months after the election court has certified its determination in the matter of the referendum petition[15].

On the hearing of a referendum petition for which leave has been granted for the presentation of a referendum petition on the ground that a payment of money or other reward has been made or promised since the referendum in pursuance of a corrupt or illegal practice[16] at which the question asked relates to proposals involving either a mayor or elected councillors[17] and in which the majority of the votes cast are in favour of the authority operating arrangements which differ from its existing arrangements and after an election for the return of an elected mayor has taken place in consequence of the referendum[18], the court must dismiss the petition or allow the petition, and, where the court allows the petition, it must declare the referendum to be tainted, and order that a further referendum be held[19]. Where the court makes an order for a further referendum, the local authority must hold the further referendum as soon as reasonably practicable after the expiration of the period of five years beginning with the date on which the tainted referendum was held[20].

In relation to England, if the majority of the votes cast in a further referendum are in favour of the authority continuing to operate a mayor and cabinet executive, the authority must continue to operate those arrangements[21]. If the majority of the votes cast in a further referendum are in favour of the authority changing its governance arrangements to those which it operated at the time of the tainted referendum, as soon as practicable the authority must publish in one or more newspapers circulating in its area a notice which states that in consequence of the rejection in a further referendum of the authority's existing mayor and cabinet executive, the authority has resolved to operate the arrangements it operated at the time of the tainted referendum instead[22].

In relation to Wales, if the majority of the votes cast in a further referendum are 'yes' votes then, where the local authority is operating executive arrangements, it must continue to operate those arrangements unless and until it is authorised or required to operate different executive arrangements or authorised to operate alternative arrangements in place of its existing executive arrangements[23]. Where the authority is operating alternative arrangements, it must continue to operate those arrangements unless and until it is authorised to operate different alternative arrangements or authorised or required to operate executive arrangements in place of its existing alternative arrangements[24]. If the majority of the votes cast in the further referendum are 'no' votes, the local authority must implement the proposals that were its outline fall-back proposals[25] at the time of the tainted referendum[26]. The further referendum must be conducted in accordance with the provisions which regulate the conduct of local authority referendums generally, with minor modifications[27].

On the substantive hearing of a referendum petition for which leave has been granted on any other ground[28], the election court must either dismiss the petition or allow the petition[29]. Where the court allows the petition, it must declare the referendum avoided[30].

1   Ie a referendum held, in relation to Wales, under the Local Authorities (Conduct of Referendums) (Wales) Regulations 2008, SI 2008/1848, or, in relation to England, under the Local Authorities (Conduct of Referendums) (England) Regulations 2012, SI 2012/323. As to the meaning of 'referendum' for these purposes see PARA 574 note 2. Provision is made for

questioning a local authority referendum by applying and modifying the provision made for questioning an election under the Local Government Act 1972: see PARA 766. As to the meaning of 'election under the Local Government Act 1972' see PARA 11 note 2.

2 Ie on the ground mentioned, in relation to Wales, in the Local Authorities (Conduct of Referendums) (Wales) Regulations 2008, SI 2008/1848, reg 11(1)(a), and, in relation to England, in the Local Authorities (Conduct of Referendums) (England) Regulations 2012, SI 2012/323, reg 15(1)(a) (see PARA 766).

3 Representation of the People Act 1983 s 145(1)(a) (s 145(1) substituted, in relation to Wales, by the Local Authorities (Conduct of Referendums) (Wales) Regulations 2008, SI 2008/1848, reg 11(8), Sch 5, and, in relation to England, by the Local Authorities (Conduct of Referendums) (England) Regulations 2012, SI 2012/323, reg 15(8), Sch 6).

4 Ie on the ground mentioned, in relation to Wales, in the Local Authorities (Conduct of Referendums) (Wales) Regulations 2008, SI 2008/1848, reg 11(1)(b), and, in relation to England, in the Local Authorities (Conduct of Referendums) (England) Regulations 2012, SI 2012/323, reg 15(1)(b) (see PARA 766). The text refers to such corrupt or illegal practices within the meaning of the Representation of the People Act 1983, as are relevant to referendums by virtue of, in relation to Wales, the Local Authorities (Conduct of Referendums) (Wales) Regulations 2008, SI 2008/1848, regs 8, 11(8), and, in relation to England, the Local Authorities (Conduct of Referendums) (England) Regulations 2012, SI 2012/323, regs 8, 11, 13, 15(8) (see PARA 766).

5 Ie on the grounds mentioned, in relation to Wales, in the Local Authorities (Conduct of Referendums) (Wales) Regulations 2008, SI 2008/1848, reg 11(1)(c), and, in relation to England, in the Local Authorities (Conduct of Referendums) (England) Regulations 2012, SI 2012/323, reg 15(1)(c) (see PARA 766). The text refers to the grounds provided by the Representation of the People Act 1983 s 164 (avoidance of election for corruption etc: see PARA 895), as applied for these purposes, in relation to Wales, by the Local Authorities (Conduct of Referendums) (Wales) Regulations 2008, SI 2008/1848, reg 11(8), and, in relation to England, by the Local Authorities (Conduct of Referendums) (England) Regulations 2012, SI 2012/323, reg 15(8) (see PARA 766).

6 Representation of the People Act 1983 s 145(1)(b) (as substituted: see note 3).

7 Representation of the People Act 1983 s 145(2); and see note 1.

8 Representation of the People Act 1983 s 145(5); and see note 1. As to the Secretary of State see PARA 2.

9 Representation of the People Act 1983 s 145(6); and see note 1. As to the meaning of 'proper officer' see PARA 140 note 2.

10 Representation of the People Act 1983 s 145(1A) (added, in relation to Wales, by the Local Authorities (Conduct of Referendums) (Wales) Regulations 2008, SI 2008/1848, Sch 5, and, in relation to England, by the Local Authorities (Conduct of Referendums) (England) Regulations 2012, SI 2012/323, Sch 6).

11 Ie (1) (in relation to England only) the timetable included in the authority's proposals under the Local Government Act 2000 s 9MA (see LOCAL GOVERNMENT); or (2) the timetable included in the proposals that are drawn up, in relation to Wales, under the Local Authorities (Referendums) (Petitions and Directions) (Wales) Regulations 2001, SI 2001/2292, reg 17(3)(a), and, in relation to England, under the Local Authorities (Referendums) (Petitions) (England) Regulations 2011, SI 2011/2914, reg 17(2) (see PARA 568) or, as the case may be, reg 19(1)(c) (see PARA 571); or (3) the timetable prepared in pursuance of any other regulations or an order made, in relation to England, under any provision of the Local Government Act 2000 Pt 1A (ss 9B–9R) (arrangements with respect to local authority governance in England) (see LOCAL GOVERNMENT) and, in relation to Wales, under any provision of the Local Government Act 2000 Pt II (ss 12–27) (arrangements with respect to executives etc: see LOCAL GOVERNMENT vol 69 (2009) PARA 327 et seq); or (4) (in relation to Wales only) the timetable included in the proposals pursuant to the Local Authorities (Referendums) (Petitions and Directions) (Wales) Regulations 2001, SI 2001/2292, reg 17(7)(a)(ii) (see PARA 568) or, as the case may be, reg 20(3)(a)(iii) (see PARA 571).

12 Ie the result originally declared, in relation to Wales, under the Local Authorities (Conduct of Referendums) (Wales) Regulations 2008, SI 2008/1848, reg 10, and, in relation to England, under the Local Authorities (Conduct of Referendums) (England) Regulations 2012, SI 2012/323, reg 14 (see PARA 652).

13 Local Authorities (Conduct of Referendums) (Wales) Regulations 2008, SI 2008/1848, reg 13(1); Local Authorities (Conduct of Referendums) (England) Regulations 2012, SI 2012/323, reg 17(1).

14 Ie any of the grounds mentioned, in relation to Wales, in the Local Authorities (Conduct of Referendums) (Wales) Regulations 2008, SI 2008/1848, reg 11(1), and, in relation to England, in the Local Authorities (Conduct of Referendums) (England) Regulations 2012, SI 2012/323, reg 15(1) (see PARA 766).

15 Local Authorities (Conduct of Referendums) (Wales) Regulations 2008, SI 2008/1848, reg 13(2); Local Authorities (Conduct of Referendums) (England) Regulations 2012, SI 2012/323, reg 17(3). In relation to England, where another referendum is held in the circumstances referred to in reg 17(3), those regulations apply to the conduct of that referendum as they apply to the conduct of the avoided referendum subject to the omission of reg 4(1)(a), (b), (c)(vii), (viii) and the insertion of reg 4(1)(c)(x) which provides that another referendum is being held in consequence of the determination of an election court that the referendum last held in the authority's area was avoided: reg 17(4).

16 Ie under the ground mentioned, in relation to Wales, in the Local Authorities (Conduct of Referendums) (Wales) Regulations 2008, SI 2008/1848, reg 11(1)(d), and, in relation to England, in the Local Authorities (Conduct of Referendums) (England) Regulations 2012, SI 2012/323, reg 15(1)(d) (see PARA 766).

17 Ie if the question was in the form set out, in relation to Wales, if the question asked relates to proposals involving either a mayor and cabinet executive or a mayor and council manager executive, in the form set out in the Local Authorities (Conduct of Referendums) (Wales) Regulations 2008, SI 2008/1848, Sch 1 para 1, 2, or, in relation to England, in the Local Authorities (Conduct of Referendums) (England) Regulations 2012, SI 2012/323, Sch 1 para 1 or 2 (see PARA 575). As to the meaning of 'mayor and cabinet executive' see LOCAL GOVERNMENT vol 69 (2009) PARA 327.

18 Ie where the circumstances are as mentioned, in relation to Wales, in the Local Authorities (Conduct of Referendums) (Wales) Regulations 2008, SI 2008/1848, reg 12(8)(a), (b), or, in relation to England, in the Local Authorities (Conduct of Referendums) (England) Regulations 2012, SI 2012/323, reg 16(5)(a), (b) (see PARA 766).

19 Local Authorities (Conduct of Referendums) (Wales) Regulations 2008, SI 2008/1848, reg 13(3); Local Authorities (Conduct of Referendums) (England) Regulations 2012, SI 2012/323, reg 17(5).

20 Local Authorities (Conduct of Referendums) (Wales) Regulations 2008, SI 2008/1848, reg 13(4); Local Authorities (Conduct of Referendums) (England) Regulations 2012, SI 2012/323, reg 17(6). In the case of an order made in relation to England, this provision is subject to any arrangements which are made to combine the poll with that at another election or referendum (see the Local Authorities (Conduct of Referendums) (England) Regulations 2012, SI 2012/323, reg 10(1); and PARA 27): see reg 17(6).

21 Local Authorities (Conduct of Referendums) (England) Regulations 2012, SI 2012/323, reg 17(7).

22 Local Government Act 2000 s 9KC(2)(b)(i); substituted for this purpose by the Local Authorities (Conduct of Referendums) (England) Regulations 2012, SI 2012/323, reg 17(8).

23 Local Authorities (Conduct of Referendums) (Wales) Regulations 2008, SI 2008/1848, reg 13(5)(a). As to the meaning of 'existing executive arrangements' see PARA 561 note 10. As to alternative arrangements see LOCAL GOVERNMENT vol 69 (2009) PARA 364.

24 Local Authorities (Conduct of Referendums) (Wales) Regulations 2008, SI 2008/1848, reg 13(5)(b).

25 As to the meaning of 'outline fall-back proposals' see PARA 574 note 16.

26 Local Authorities (Conduct of Referendums) (Wales) Regulations 2008, SI 2008/1848, reg 13(6)(a). The Local Government Act 2000 s 27(13) (referendum in case of proposals involving elected mayor: see LOCAL GOVERNMENT vol 69 (2009) PARA 314) applies to the implementation of detailed fall-back proposals as if those outline fall-back proposals were outline fall-back proposals in the event that proposals under s 25 (see LOCAL GOVERNMENT vol 69 (2009) PARA 312) are rejected in a referendum under s 27 (see LOCAL GOVERNMENT vol 69 (2009) PARA 314): see the Local Authorities (Conduct of Referendums) (Wales) Regulations 2008, SI 2008/1848, reg 13(6)(b). Where the authority's outline fall-back proposals are the executive or alternative arrangements which it was operating at the date of the tainted referendum, the Local Government Act 2000 s 27(13) applies as if, for 'in accordance with the timetable mentioned in s 27(4)' (see LOCAL GOVERNMENT vol 69 (2009) PARA 315), there were substituted the words 'as soon as practicable': Local Authorities (Conduct of Referendums) (Wales) Regulations 2008, SI 2008/1848, reg 13(7). Where the authority's outline fall-back proposals are executive arrangements which involve a form of executive for which a referendum is not required, the Local Government Act 2000 s 29(1) (operation of, and publicity for, executive arrangements: see LOCAL GOVERNMENT vol 69 (2009) PARA 309) applies for the purpose of enabling the authority to operate executive arrangements in other circumstances; and

s 29(2) (see LOCAL GOVERNMENT vol 69 (2009) PARA 309) applies as if, for s 29(2)(b)(i), there were substituted the words 'states that, in consequence of the rejection in a further referendum of the authority's existing executive arrangements, the authority has resolved to operate the different executive arrangements that were described in its outline fall-back proposals at the time of the referendum': Local Authorities (Conduct of Referendums) (Wales) Regulations 2008, SI 2008/1848, reg 13(8). Where the local authority's outline fall-back proposals are alternative arrangements, the Local Government Act 2000 s 33(2) (operation of alternative arrangements: see LOCAL GOVERNMENT vol 69 (2009) PARA 366) applies for the purpose of enabling the local authority to operate the alternative arrangements set out in its detailed fall-back proposals as it applies for the purpose of enabling a local authority to operate alternative arrangements in other circumstances; and s 29(2) applies as if, for s 29(2)(b)(i) there were substituted the words 'states that, in consequence of the rejection in a further referendum of the local authority's existing executive arrangements the local authority has resolved to operate the alternative arrangements that were described in its outline fall-back proposals at the time of the referendum': Local Authorities (Conduct of Referendums) (Wales) Regulations 2008, SI 2008/1848, reg 13(9).

27 See the Local Authorities (Conduct of Referendums) (Wales) Regulations 2008, SI 2008/1848, reg 13(10); and the Local Authorities (Conduct of Referendums) (England) Regulations 2012, SI 2012/323, reg 17(9).

28 Ie where leave is granted in circumstances which are as mentioned, in relation to Wales, in the Local Authorities (Conduct of Referendums) (Wales) Regulations 2008, SI 2008/1848, reg 12 (other than reg 12(8)), or, in relation to England, in the Local Authorities (Conduct of Referendums) (England) Regulations 2012, SI 2012/323, reg 16 (other than reg 16(5)) (see PARA 766).

29 Local Authorities (Conduct of Referendums) (Wales) Regulations 2008, SI 2008/1848, reg 13(11); Local Authorities (Conduct of Referendums) (England) Regulations 2012, SI 2012/323, reg 17(2).

30 Local Authorities (Conduct of Referendums) (Wales) Regulations 2008, SI 2008/1848, reg 13(11); Local Authorities (Conduct of Referendums) (England) Regulations 2012, SI 2012/323, reg 17(2).

867. Matters to be reported by court hearing local authority referendum petition. Where a charge is made in a petition questioning a local authority referendum[1] of any corrupt or illegal practice having been committed at the referendum, the election court must, in addition to its certificate[2] and at the same time, make a report in writing to the High Court stating: (1) the names of all persons, if any, who have been proved at the trial to have been guilty of any corrupt or illegal practice[3]; (2) whether any corrupt practices have, or whether there is reason to believe that any corrupt practices have, extensively prevailed at the referendum in the area of the authority by which or in respect of which the referendum was held[4]. However, before any person who is not a party to a referendum petition is reported by an election court to have been guilty of any corrupt or illegal practice, the court must cause notice to be given to him, and, if he appears in pursuance of the notice, the court must give him an opportunity of being heard by himself and of calling evidence in his defence to show why he should not be so reported[5]. At the time of making its report, the election court may also make a special report as to any matters arising in the course of the trial, an account of which in the court's judgment ought to be submitted to the High Court[6].

A copy of any report made to the High Court by the election court trying a local authority referendum must be sent by the High Court to the Secretary of State[7]. The report of the election court also must be laid before the Director of Public Prosecutions[8].

1 Ie a referendum held, in relation to Wales, under the Local Authorities (Conduct of Referendums) (Wales) Regulations 2008, SI 2008/1848, or, in relation to England, under the Local Authorities (Conduct of Referendums) (England) Regulations 2012, SI 2012/323. As to the meaning of 'referendum' for these purposes see PARA 574 note 2. Provision is made for questioning a local authority referendum by applying and modifying the provision made for

questioning an election under the Local Government Act 1972: see PARA 766. As to the application of the Representation of the People Act 1983 Pt III (ss 120–186) to other polls see PARA 763.

2   Ie its certificate of determination on the local authority referendum petition: see PARA 866.

3   Representation of the People Act 1983 ss 145(3), 160(1) (s 160(1) amended by the Representation of the People Act 1985 s 28(1), Sch 5); and see note 1.

4   Representation of the People Act 1983 s 145(3); and see note 1. As to the meaning of 'extensively prevailed' see *Maidstone Borough Case, Cornwallis v Barker* (1901) 5 O'M & H 149 at 152–153.

5   Representation of the People Act 1983 s 160(1); and see note 1. See also the cases cited in PARA 859 notes 8–10.

6   Representation of the People Act 1983 s 145(4); and see note 1. See also *R (on the application of Khan) v Election Comr for the Aston Ward of Birmingham City Council* [2009] EWHC 1757 (Admin), [2009] All ER (D) 262 (Jul) (cited in PARA 862 note 8).

7   Representation of the People Act 1983 s 145(5); and see note 1. As to the Secretary of State see PARA 2.

8   Representation of the People Act 1983 s 160(3) (substituted by the Representation of the People Act 1985 s 24, Sch 4 para 52(b)); and see note 1. As to prosecutions by the Director of Public Prosecutions see PARA 882. As to the report's effect see also the cases cited in PARA 859 notes 14–16.

F. REASONS; CONCLUSION OF PETITION

868.   Grounds for judgment. On the hearing of election petitions it is the practice for the judges, in giving judgment, to give the reasons on which the judgment is founded[1].

1   *Ipswich Case, Packard v Collings and West* (1886) 54 LT 619, 4 O'M & H 70 at 71 per Denman J; *Norwich Case, Birbeck v Bullard* (1886) 4 O'M & H 84 at 90. If the judges differ in their judgment upon the issue, it is the practice for the junior judge to give his judgment first: *Great Yarmouth Borough Case* (1906) 5 O'M & H 176 at 178.

869.   Conclusion of petition. When the election court has given its judgment and has sent the certificate of its determination, the petition is concluded, and is, therefore, no longer affected by any event which may happen during the time which intervenes between the moment the court has finally parted with the certificate and the moment it reaches the hands of the recipient, even if that event is one which, if it had happened earlier, would have caused the petition to abate or drop[1].

1   *Marshall v James* (1874) LR 9 CP 702.

(viii) Costs

870.   Application of High Court principles with regard to costs. The rules of the Senior Courts with regard to costs to be allowed in actions, causes and matters in the High Court are in principle and so far as practicable to apply to the costs of election petitions and other proceedings under the relevant provisions[1]. The taxing officer must not allow any costs higher than would be allowed in any action, cause or matter in the High Court on the standard basis[2].

1   Representation of the People Act 1983 s 183(1) (amended by the Constitutional Reform Act 2005 s 59(5), Sch 11 para 28(1), (3)(b)); European Parliamentary Elections Regulations 2004, SI 2004/293, reg 121(1); National Assembly for Wales (Representation of the People) Order 2007, SI 2007/236, art 135(1). Provision is made for questioning a local authority referendum by applying and modifying the provision made for questioning an election under the Local Government Act 1972: see PARA 766. As to the application of the Representation of the People Act 1983 Pt III (ss 120–186) to other polls see PARA 763.

The text refers to the costs of proceedings arising from the provisions contained, in relation to parliamentary and local government elections, in the Representation of the People Act 1983 Pt II (ss 67–119) and Pt III (ss 120–186), in relation to European parliamentary elections, in the European Parliamentary Elections Regulations 2004, SI 2004/293, Pt 2 (regs 31–81) and Pt 4 (regs 86–122), and, in relation to Welsh Assembly elections, in the National Assembly for Wales (Representation of the People) Order 2007, SI 2007/236, Pt 3 (arts 37–85). As to costs of proceedings before the High Court see generally CPR Pts 43–48; and CIVIL PROCEDURE vol 12 (2009) PARA 1737 et seq. As to European parliamentary elections held in the combined region see the European Parliamentary Elections Regulations 2004, SI 2004/293, reg 121(4). As to the combined region see PARA 77.

2   Representation of the People Act 1983 s 183(1); European Parliamentary Elections Regulations 2004, SI 2004/293, reg 121(1); National Assembly for Wales (Representation of the People) Order 2007, SI 2007/236, art 135(1); and see note 1. The standard basis was previously known as the common fund basis. As to the basis of assessment see CPR 44.3; and CIVIL PROCEDURE vol 12 (2009) PARA 1729 et seq.

871. How costs are defrayed. All costs of and incidental to the presentation of an election or referendum petition[1] and the proceedings consequent on it, except such as are otherwise provided for[2], are to be defrayed by the parties to the petition in such manner and in such proportions as the election court or High Court may determine[3]. In particular, any costs which in the court's opinion have been caused by vexatious conduct, unfounded allegations or unfounded objections on the part either of the petitioner or of the respondent, and any needless expense incurred or caused on the part of the petitioner or respondent, may be ordered to be defrayed by the parties by whom it has been incurred or caused whether or not they are on the whole successful[4].

Where a petition or notice is required to be published by the returning officer, the cost of publication must be paid in the first instance by the petitioner, or, as the case may be, by the person by whom the notice was given, without prejudice to the manner in which such cost must ultimately be borne by one or more of the parties to the petition[5].

If a petition is withdrawn the petitioner is liable to pay the respondent's costs[6].

1   As to parliamentary election petitions see PARA 761; as to the questioning of an election under the Local Government Act 1972 see PARA 762; as to Welsh Assembly election petitions see PARA 764; and as to European parliamentary election petitions see PARA 765. Provision is made for questioning a local authority referendum by applying and modifying the provision made for questioning an election under the Local Government Act 1972: see PARA 766. As to the meaning of 'election under the Local Government Act 1972' see PARA 11 note 2. As to the application of the Representation of the People Act 1983 Pt III (ss 120–186) to other polls see PARA 763.

2   Ie, in relation to a parliamentary or local government election, the Representation of the People Act 1983 (including those provisions as applied for the purposes of questioning a local authority referendum: see note 1), in relation to a European parliamentary election, the European Parliamentary Elections Regulations 2004, SI 2004/293, and, in relation to a Welsh Assembly election, the National Assembly for Wales (Representation of the People) Order 2007, SI 2007/236.

3   Representation of the People Act 1983 s 154(1); European Parliamentary Elections Regulations 2004, SI 2004/293, reg 104(1); National Assembly for Wales (Representation of the People) Order 2007, SI 2007/236, art 104(1); and see note 1.
    It has been suggested that the discretion of the election court in dealing with costs is absolute and cannot be reviewed by the High Court: *Maidenhead Case, Lovering v Dawson (No 2)* (1875) LR 10 CP 726. But this view would no longer apply if the election court was subject to judicial review by the High Court; it is not settled whether the election court dealing with petitions under the Local Government Act 1972 is so subject: see PARA 779 note 3. See also PARA 771 note 3 (election court dealing with parliamentary election petitions). As respects the local election court, the High Court has jurisdiction to declare and order that its own taxing master should tax the costs in accordance with the formal order of the election court: *R v Cripps, ex p Muldoon* [1984] QB 686 at 698, [1984] 2 All ER 705 at 712, CA, per Sir John Donaldson MR.

In *Conservative and Unionist Party v Election Comr* [2010] EWCA Civ 1332, [2011] PTSR 416, [2010] All ER (D) 241 (Nov), it was held that the scheme in relation to costs under the Representation of the People Act 1983 s 154 was clear and, when legislated, was both intended to be and in fact was far more extensive than that which prevailed under predecessor legislation; those wider powers were far more than procedural: they extended the jurisdiction and the fact that the High Court recognised that it had a wider jurisdiction in relation to ordering costs against third parties than hitherto had been appreciated did not affect the position (or the governing principles of law) in any way; the authority of an election commissioner in the election court extended to making an order for costs and to making the ancillary orders to which the defendant referred, even if that arose after his judgment and certificate (which did not need to identify the order for costs). See also PARA 875 note 3. Accordingly, the Election Commissioner did not have jurisdiction to make an order joining a political party and a local political association as parties to election petition proceedings, with a view to making an order for costs of the petition against them, after the proceedings on the petition were concluded. The Commissioner was 'functus officio' when he purported to make the orders he did. The decision in *R v Cripps, ex p Muldoon* [1984] QB 68, [1983] 3 All ER 72 (affd [1984] QB 686, [1984] 2 All ER 705, CA) was applied, in the first recent example of the Court of Appeal indorsing its previous decision in *R v Cripps, ex p Muldoon*).

4   Representation of the People Act 1983 s 154(2); European Parliamentary Elections Regulations 2004, SI 2004/293, reg 104(2); National Assembly for Wales (Representation of the People) Order 2007, SI 2007/236, art 104(2);and see note 1. As to other provisions whereby neglect etc is penalised in costs see PARA 870.

5   See the Election Petition Rules 1960, SI 1960/543, r 20 (including that provision as applied and modified); the European Parliamentary Election Petition Rules 1979, SI 1979/521, r 19; and PARA 784 note 10. As to the returning officer's costs see PARA 878.

6   Representation of the People Act 1983 s 147(4); European Parliamentary Elections Regulations 2004, SI 2004/293, reg 102(4); National Assembly for Wales (Representation of the People) Order 2007, SI 2007/236, art 103(4); and see note 1. As to the withdrawal of a petition see PARA 813 et seq.

872.   General rule as to costs.   The general rule is that costs follow the event[1], but the rule may be displaced by special circumstances[2], in which case the court will make a special order[3]. The practice is that if the petitioner is successful and is awarded costs the respondent will nevertheless be awarded costs in respect of charges in which the petitioner was not successful and which involved the respondent in extra expense. The practice used to be to leave the question as to what extra expense has been so caused to be decided by the taxing master, but this practice no longer obtains[4], and the court settles the question of what costs should be allowed[5].

1   *Bolton Case* (1874) 2 O'M & H 138; *Louth County Case* (1880) 3 O'M & H 161 at 177; *Oxford Borough Case* (1880) 3 O'M & H 155.

2   *Carrickfergus Borough Case* (1869) 1 O'M & H 264 at 268–269 per O'Brien J.

3   *Stroud Case, Holloway v Brand* (1874) 3 O'M & H 7 at 12 per Pigott B.

4   See *Bush v Rogers* [1915] 1 KB 707. The taxing master had discretion to disallow expenses which the registrar had ascertained to be reasonable: *McLaren v Home* (1881) 7 QBD 477, DC.

5   *Northumberland, Berwick-upon-Tweed Division Case* (1923) 7 O'M & H 1 at 46. In this case the court apportioned the costs on a fractional basis: *Northumberland, Berwick-upon-Tweed Division Case* at 47. As to detailed assessment see CPR Pt 47; and CIVIL PROCEDURE vol 12 (2009) PARA 1779 et seq.

873.   Grounds for special orders.   There are many grounds of departure from the general rule that costs follow the event[1] on which the court, in its discretion, will award the bulk of costs to a party who has failed on a main issue, or make no order as to costs, or apportion the costs as the court sees fit. These grounds include failure of the party on the case mainly and primarily relied on, even though he gains his object[2]; failure of a party on an important charge against the other party, even though he gains his object[3]; divided success on the main issues[4]; abandonment of a main issue by either side[5]; failure by a party on some of the charges alleged by him[6]; the success of a party on some charge or charges although he fails on the main issue[7]; the judges' disagreement on a main issue[8] or disagreement on some of the charges[9]; the fact that, although the petition fails, the court is of opinion that an inquiry was called for[10], or that it has been occasioned by the opposite party's conduct[11]; if there is a scrutiny, the fact that the party who has requested it, although he has not succeeded in establishing a majority of lawful votes, has reduced the number of the opposite party's votes to an equality[12]; the fact that, considering the small majority of votes polled proportionately to the number of voters, the prayer for a scrutiny was reasonable[13]; the fact that a party has made charges recklessly[14], or that his particulars are oppressive[15], or unnecessarily voluminous[16], or that he has not attempted[17] or has failed[18] to substantiate them; the blamable conduct of a party with regard to an election[19]; the fact that the petitioners are people of no means, against whom, if defeated, no costs could be recovered beyond those covered by the statutory security[20].

Where grounds for making some special order as to costs are afforded by the conduct of one of the parties, the court may still, if dissatisfied with the opposite party's conduct, decline to depart from the ordinary rule[21].

1   See PARA 872.
2   *Plymouth Case* (1880) 3 O'M & H 107 at 112, where the court made no order; *Southampton Borough Case* (1895) 5 O'M & H 17 at 24–25, where, the election being avoided on the ground of an illegal payment and the petition failing on all other charges, the petitioners were allowed only such costs as would have been incurred had the petition been presented alone on the issue of that illegal payment, and the respondent was awarded the rest of the costs, with one exception (see note 19).
3   *Sandwich Case* (1880) 3 O'M & H 158 at 160, where, moreover, offences by the successful party having been proved, the court made no order.
4   *Stafford Borough Case* (1869) 21 LT 210 at 214, 1 O'M & H 228 at 234 per Blackburn J. In that case there were two petitions, but the court, as it stated, treated them as one.
5   *Horsham Case, Aldridge v Hurst* (1876) 3 O'M & H 52 at 56, where, the prayer for the seat and the recriminatory case respectively being abandoned, no order was made as to costs on these issues; *Gravesend Case* (1880) 3 O'M & H 81 at 82–84.
6   *Stroud Case, Holloway v Brand* (1874) 3 O'M & H 7, where the successful party was allowed no costs on such charges; *Lichfield Borough Case* (1880) 3 O'M & H 136 at 139–140.
7   *Bolton Case* (1874) 2 O'M & H 138 at 151; *Gloucestershire, Thornbury Division, Election Petition* (1886) 4 O'M & H 65 at 69, where a successful respondent was awarded no costs as to a charge of rioting and intimidation alleged in the petition, of which, although there was not enough evidence to avoid the election, there was, in the court's opinion, enough evidence to justify its being brought before the court.
8   *Down County Case* (1880) 3 O'M & H 115 at 129.
9   *Shoreditch, Haggerston Division Case, Cremer v Lowles* (1896) 5 O'M & H 68 at 88, where the respondent was awarded costs except on those issues as to which the judges differed, although they had differed on one issue which went to the validity of the election.
10 *Westminster Borough Case* (1869) 1 O'M & H 89 at 96 (no order made); *Guildford Case* (1869) 1 O'M & H 13 at 15 (no order made); *Warrington Case, Crozier v Rylands* (1869) 1 O'M & H 42 at 44 (no order made); *Coventry Case, Berry v Eaton and Hill* (1869) 1 O'M & H 97 at 111 (no order made); *Stepney Division, Tower Hamlets Case* (1886) 4 O'M & H 34, 37 at 58 (where, although the petitioner failed, the scrutiny showing that 200 persons had voted who had no right to vote, no costs were allowed); *Salisbury Case, Moore v Kennard* (1883) 4 O'M & H 21 at 29–30; *Islington, West Division Case* (1901) 5 O'M & H 120 at 132 (where, on a certain part of the case which, in the court's opinion, it was fair to investigate, no order was made); *Cornwall, Bodmin Division Case* (1906) 5 O'M & H 225 at 235 (where the petitioners were awarded costs on charges which, in the court's opinion, they were justified in bringing forward, even though the judges disagreed on those charges).
11 *York County East Riding, Buckrose Division Case* (1886) 4 O'M & H 110 at 119 (where a recriminatory case was founded principally on charges of omissions by the petitioner in his return of election expenses, which were admitted; although the court granted the petitioner relief, he was ordered to pay the costs of the recriminatory case).

12 *Gloucester County, Cirencester Division Case* (1893) 4 O'M & H 194 at 199; but see *Oldham Case* (1869) 1 O'M & H 151 at 166.

13 *York County West Riding, Southern Division Case* (1869) 1 O'M & H 213 at 216 per Martin B.

14 *Youghal Borough Case* (1869) 1 O'M & H 291 at 295, 299 per O'Brien J, where the successful petitioner was, on this ground, not awarded the general costs; *Pontefract Case, Shaw v Reckitt* (1893) 4 O'M & H 200 at 201–202.

15 *Norwich Case, Birbeck v Bullard* (1886) 4 O'M & H 84 at 91.

16 *Norwich Case, Birbeck v Bullard* (1886) 4 O'M & H 84 at 92.

17 *Lichfield Borough Case* (1880) 3 O'M & H 136 at 140 (where the respondent was awarded the costs of such charges); *Chester City Case* (1880) 3 O'M & H 148 at 149; *Carrickfergus Borough Case* (1880) 3 O'M & H 90 at 93 (where the successful respondent was awarded no costs except on those charges, contained in particulars recklessly prepared by the petitioner, which the petitioner had not attempted to prove); *Canterbury Borough Case* (1880) 3 O'M & H 103 at 105 (where the successful petitioner was awarded no costs on personal charges against the respondent, which he had withdrawn at the hearing); *Ipswich Case, Packard v Collings and West* (1886) 4 O'M & H 70 at 75; *Cornwall, Bodmin Division Case* (1906) 5 O'M & H 225 at 235.

18 *Bewdley Case, Spencer v Harrison* (1880) 3 O'M & H 145 at 147 (where the petitioner was ordered to pay the costs of charges of treating, which he had failed to establish, but was awarded the costs of the charges of bribery, two of which he had proved); *Berwick-on-Tweed Case* (1880) 3 O'M & H 178 at 183 (where the respondent, although successful on the scrutiny which was the prayer of the petition, was awarded only two-thirds of the costs on the ground that several of the charges raised by him in his objections had entirely failed); *Ipswich Case, Packard v Collings and West* (1886) 4 O'M & H 70 at 75; *Meath, Southern Division Case* (1892) 4 O'M & H 130 at 142 (where the seat was avoided on the ground of undue influence, but the respondent was awarded the costs of charges of bribery and corruption, which the petitioner had failed to prove); *Rochester Borough Case* (1892) 4 O'M & H 156 at 161; *Meath, Northern Division Case* (1892) 4 O'M & H 185 at 193.

19 *Carrickfergus Borough Case* (1880) 3 O'M & H 90 at 93 (following *Carrickfergus Borough Case* (1869) 1 O'M & H 264 at 268–269, and not following *Limerick Borough Case* (1869) 1 O'M & H 260 at 263, where Fitzgerald B stated that, according to parliamentary practice, unless the petition is held to be frivolous and vexatious, the petitioner cannot be ordered to pay the costs of it); *Windsor Case, Herbert v Gardiner* (1874) 2 O'M & H 88 at 93 (where the successful respondent was awarded no costs); *Dudley Case* (1874) 2 O'M & H 115 at 122 (where neither party was awarded any costs, on the ground that there had been blamable conduct on either side); *Londonderry Borough Case* (1869) 1 O'M & H 274 at 279–280 (where, on a scrutiny, time was spent in establishing the employment of certain voters by the respondent, he was disallowed the costs of the time so spent); *Southampton Borough Case* (1895) 5 O'M & H 17 at 24, where, in awarding costs to an unsuccessful respondent, the court excepted costs of evidence touching an indiscreet speech which respondent had made.

20 *Poole Case, Hurdle and Stark v Waring* (1874) 2 O'M & H 123 at 127–128; *Stepney Borough Case, Rushmere v Isaacson* (1892) 4 O'M & H 178 at 184; but see *Yellow v Meredith* (1903) 67 JP 111 (a municipal election petition), where the respondent was ordered to pay the costs, for although it was proved that the petitioners had not found any of the security, it was not proved that they had not the means of paying the costs of the petition. Cf *Re Long Sutton School Board Election Petition* (1898) 62 JP 565.

21 *Evesham Case, Hartland v Lehmann* (1880) 3 O'M & H 192 at 195 per Grove J.

874.   Disagreement over costs by judges on trial of petition. Where the judges trying a parliamentary election petition disagree as to the awarding of costs, no order is made as to them[1]. Where, however, the judges, although disagreeing on the issue as to the election being avoided or not, do not disagree as to all the charges made in the petition, they may award costs to the respondent on those charges on which they agree, making no order as to the others[2].

1 *Great Yarmouth Borough Case* (1906) 5 O'M & H 176 at 199. This principle would presumably also apply in the case of trying other election petitions: see PARA 817. In *Down County Case* (1880) 3 O'M & H 115 at 129, where the judges disagreed as to avoidance of the election, they declined, on that ground, to make any order as to costs. See also *Ipswich Case, Packard v Collings and West* (1886) 4 O'M & H 70 at 75 per Denman J.

2 *Shoreditch, Haggerston Division Case, Cremer v Lowles* (1896) 5 O'M & H 68 at 88 (following *Montgomery Boroughs Case* (1892) 4 O'M & H 167 at 170).

875. Costs against person engaged in corrupt practices. On the trial of an election or referendum petition[1], where it appears to the election court that a corrupt practice[2] has not been proved to have been committed, in reference to the election or referendum, by or with the respondent's knowledge and consent, and that the respondent took all reasonable means to prevent corrupt practices being committed on his behalf or in behalf of a particular result in a referendum, the election court may make an order with respect to the payment of the whole or part of the costs of the petition[3]. Accordingly, if it appears to the court that any person or persons is or are proved, whether by providing money or otherwise, to have been extensively engaged in corrupt practices, or to have encouraged or promoted extensive corrupt practices, in reference to the election or referendum, then, after giving such person or persons an opportunity of being heard by counsel, a solicitor or an authorised person[4] and examining and cross-examining witnesses to show cause why the order should not be made, the court may order the whole or part of the costs to be paid by such person or persons or any of them, and may order that, if the costs cannot be recovered from one or more of such persons, they are to be paid by some other of such persons or by either of the parties to the petition[5]. Where any person appears to the court to have been guilty of a corrupt or illegal practice[6], then, after giving that person an opportunity of making a statement to show why the order should not be made, the court may order the whole or any part of the costs of or incidental to any proceeding before the court in relation to that offence or to that person to be paid by him to such person or persons as the court may direct[7].

1   As to parliamentary election petitions see PARA 761; as to the questioning of an election under the Local Government Act 1972 see PARA 762; as to Welsh Assembly election petitions see PARA 764. Provision is made for questioning a local authority referendum by applying and modifying the provision made for questioning an election under the Local Government Act 1972: see PARA 766. As to the meaning of 'election under the Local Government Act 1972' see PARA 11 note 2. As to the application of the Representation of the People Act 1983 Pt III (ss 120–186) to other polls see PARA 763.

2   As to corrupt practices see generally PARA 704 et seq.

3   Representation of the People Act 1983 s 156(1) (amended by the Representation of the People Act 1985 s 24, Sch 4 para 51); National Assembly for Wales (Representation of the People) Order 2007, SI 2007/236, art 106(1); and see note 1. There is no equivalent provision for the purposes of European parliamentary election petitions because corrupt and illegal practices may be cited in such petitions only when they are related to personation and other voting offences: see PARA 765.

   The extent to which third party orders for the costs of an election petition can be made are limited to the circumstances set out in the Representation of the People Act 1983 s 156: *R (on the application of the Conservative and Unionist Party) v Election Comr* [2010] EWCA Civ 1332, [2011] PTSR 416, [2010] All ER (D) 241 (Nov) (the fact that the Representation of the People Act 1983 ss 154–156 did not expressly prohibit orders for costs against non-parties being made otherwise than in the circumstances set out in s 156 did not change the analysis of the scheme of the 1983 Act; the effect of the words 'except such as are by this Act otherwise provided for' in s 154(1) (see PARA 871) was to limit the circumstances in which non-parties could be responsible for costs to the circumstances set out in any provision in the Act, and the only provision in the Act which did that was s 156; considerations of statutory construction simply could not overcome the plain words of the exception in s 154(1), to say nothing of the words 'subject to the provisions of this or any other enactment' in the Senior Courts Act 1981 s 51(1) (see CIVIL PROCEDURE vol 12 (2009) PARA 1732), and the words 'subject to the provisions of this Act' in the Representation of the People Act 1983 ss 123(2) and 157(3) (see PARA 802)).

4   'Authorised person' means a person (other than counsel or a solicitor) who, for the purposes of the Legal Services Act 2007, is an authorised person in relation to an activity which constitutes the exercise of a right of audience within the meaning of that Act (see LEGAL PROFESSIONS vol 65 (2008) PARA 512): Representation of the People Act 1983 s 156(5A) (added by the Legal Services Act 2007 Sch 21 paras 48, 50(b)).

5   Representation of the People Act 1983 s 156(5) (amended by the Legal Services Act 2007 Sch 21 paras 48, 50(a)); National Assembly for Wales (Representation of the People) Order 2007, SI 2007/236, art 106(2); and see note 1.
6   As to illegal practices see generally PARA 671 et seq.
7   Representation of the People Act 1983 s 156(6); National Assembly for Wales (Representation of the People) Order 2007, SI 2007/236, art 106(3); and see note 1.

876. Repayment of expenses of election court for local election or local authority referendum petition. The election court appointed for the trial of a petition questioning a local authority referendum or an election under the Local Government Act 1972[1] may, in its discretion, order that the remuneration and allowances payable to the commissioner in respect of the trial of an election petition, and to any officers, clerks or shorthand writers, or the expenses incurred by the proper officer of the authority in receiving the election court[2], be repaid wholly or in part to the Treasury or to the proper officer, as the case may be[3].

1   As to the meaning of 'referendum' for these purposes see PARA 574 note 2. Provision is made for questioning a local authority referendum by applying and modifying the provision made for questioning an election under the Local Government Act 1972: see PARA 766. As to the meaning of 'election under the Local Government Act 1972' see PARA 11 note 2. As to the questioning of an election in England and Wales under the Local Government Act 1972 see PARA 762. As to the application of the Representation of the People Act 1983 Pt III (ss 120–186) to other polls see PARA 763.
2   As to these expenses see PARAS 777–778.
3   See the Representation of the People Act 1983 s 133 (including those provisions as applied for the purposes of questioning a local authority referendum: see note 1); and PARAS 777–778. As to the meaning of 'proper officer' see PARA 140 note 2. As to the Treasury see CONSTITUTIONAL LAW AND HUMAN RIGHTS vol 8(2) (Reissue) PARAS 512–517. As to the making of deposits or the giving of security for costs see PARAS 796–798; and as to the recovery of costs see PARA 880.

877. Expenses of the Director of Public Prosecutions. The Director of Public Prosecutions and his assistant or representative are to be paid such allowances as the Treasury may approve for expenses for the purposes of legal proceedings relating to elections[1], other than his general duties of making inquiries into the commission of any offence[2] which he is informed has been committed and of instituting prosecutions which appear to be required[3]. The costs incurred in defraying the Director's expenses incurred for those purposes[4], including the remuneration of his representative, are, in the first instance, to be paid by the Treasury, and they are to be deemed to be expenses of the election court[5]. If, for any reasonable cause, the court thinks it just to do so it must, however, order all or part of those costs to be repaid to the Treasury by the parties to the petition, or such of them as the court may direct[6].

1   Ie for the purposes of, in relation to parliamentary and local government elections, the Representation of the People Act 1983 Pt III (ss 120–186), in relation to European parliamentary elections, the European Parliamentary Elections Regulations 2004, SI 2004/293, Pt 4 (regs 86–122), or, in relation to Welsh Assembly elections, the National Assembly for Wales (Representation of the People) Order 2007, SI 2007/236, Pt 4 (arts 86–138). As to the application of the Representation of the People Act 1983 Pt III (ss 120–186) to other polls see PARA 763.
2   These general duties are specified, in relation to parliamentary and local government elections, in the Representation of the People Act 1983 s 181(1), in relation to European parliamentary elections, in the European Parliamentary Elections Regulations 2004, SI 2004/293, reg 119(1), and, in relation to Welsh Assembly elections, in the National Assembly for Wales (Representation of the People) Order 2007, SI 2007/236, art 133(1) (see PARA 882).
3   Representation of the People Act 1983 s 181(5); European Parliamentary Elections Regulations 2004, SI 2004/293, reg 119(4); National Assembly for Wales (Representation of the People) Order 2007, SI 2007/236, art 133(4).

4   It is submitted that 'those purposes' refer to the purposes referred to in note 1. This would include purposes in connection with relief (see PARA 690) and the withdrawal of petitions (see PARA 813), in addition to attendance at the trial of election petitions. The provision under which *Devonport Case, Pascoe v Puleston* (1886) 54 LT 733 and *Re Lichfield Case* (1892) 9 TLR 92 were decided was differently worded and, it is submitted, the decisions no longer apply.

5   Representation of the People Act 1983 s 181(6) (amended by the Representation of the People Act 1985 s 28(1), Sch 5); European Parliamentary Elections Regulations 2004, SI 2004/293, reg 119(5); National Assembly for Wales (Representation of the People) Order 2007, SI 2007/236, art 133(5). The previous practice which is apparent in the cases cited below has been for the court to refuse to make an order for the payment by a party to the petition of the Director's costs, even though an application for such an order is generally made. However, those cases were decided at a time when the Director was required to attend the trial of every election petition. That requirement no longer applies: see the amendment made by the Representation of the People Act 1985 s 24, Sch 4 para 63; and PARA 821. In *Norwich Case, Birbeck v Bullard* (1886) 4 O'M & H 84 at 91–92, Denman J and Cave J stated that the court will not make an order for the payment of the Director's costs by a petitioner unless a strong case of misconduct is made out, even though the court considered his case to be so terribly overloaded with charges which he failed to prove that, though successful, he was not awarded costs; but see *Worcester Borough Case, Glaszard and Turner v Allsopp* (1892) 4 O'M & H 153 at 155 where the court made such an order against the petitioner, stating that the petition and particulars contained many charges which, if proved, would have justified the Director of Public Prosecutions in taking steps. Where, however, a petition is utterly unfounded the court will make the order: *Lambeth, Kennington Division Case* (1886) 4 O'M & H 93 at 95. Where, also, an election is declared void on the ground of bribery by an agent and the court is of the opinion that, although there has not been bad faith on the respondent's part, there has been much carelessness bringing about the result which has caused the election to be avoided, and the court has derived valuable assistance from the attendance of the Director of Public Prosecutions, it may think it right to make an order for the payment of his costs by the respondent on the ground that the respondent has occasioned them: *Northumberland, Hexham Division Case, Hudspeth and Lyal v Clayton* (1892) 4 O'M & H 143 at 152.

6   See note 5.

878.   Returning officer's costs.

The general practice as to the costs of a returning officer who has been made a respondent to a petition[1] is that the election court exercises its discretion according to the nature of the reason for his having been made a respondent; he has no general immunity from liability to pay costs occasioned by his negligence in connection with an election[2]. Where the petition claims of an irregularity on the part of a returning officer, he may be ordered to pay the costs occasioned by the irregularity even though there may not have been any actual misconduct on his part[3], and in the same way he may be held liable in costs for his deputy's conduct[4]. Although irregularity affecting the result of the election may be proved against the returning officer by the petition, if he has not been made a party to the petition the court cannot order him to pay the costs of the petition[5]. The court may exercise its discretion by leaving the returning officer to bear his own costs[6].

1   As to respondents generally see PARAS 782, 791.

2   *Wilson v Ingham* (1895) 64 LJQB 775, DC, per Day J (note that Wright J, the other member of the Divisional Court which decided the case, wished to express no opinion as to the class of cases or kind of misconduct for which a returning officer might be liable in costs).

3   *Re Ennis Case, O'Loughlin v Scanlan* [1900] 2 IR 384; *Islington, West Division Case* (1901) 5 O'M & H 120 at 132–134.

4   *Islington, West Division Case* (1901) 5 O'M & H 120. In *Rainham Parish Council Case* (1919) 83 JP 267, where the returning officer had appointed an experienced deputy who had made a mistake in the counting, the court ordered the deputy to pay costs and made no order against the returning officer.

5   *Re Long Sutton Board Election Petition* (1898) 62 JP 565 at 566 per Wright J.

6   *Haverfordwest Case, Davies v Lord Kensington* (1874) LR 9 CP 720, following *Hackney Case* (1874) 2 O'M & H 77 at 87; *Re Athlone Borough, Election Petition* (1874) IR 8 CL 240;

Drogheda Borough Case (1874) 2 O'M & H 201 at 211; *Wigtown District Burgh Case* (1874) 2 O'M & H 215 at 230–231; *Clare, Eastern Division Case* (1892) 4 O'M & H 162 at 166.

879. Witnesses' expenses. The reasonable expenses incurred by any person in appearing to give evidence[1] at the trial of an election or referendum petition[2], according to the scale allowed to witnesses on the trial of civil actions[3], may be allowed to him by a certificate of the election court or of the prescribed officer[4].

Where witnesses are called and examined by the election court[5], their expenses are deemed part of the expenses of providing a court; otherwise they are deemed costs of the petition[6].

1   It would appear that these words are wide enough to include a witness who was summoned to attend but did not give evidence. It was assumed in *Trench v Nolan* (1873) IR 7 CL 445, and in *McLaren v Home* (1881) 7 QBD 477, DC, that the words were wide enough. Support for this view is also given by the wording of the provisions cited in PARA 880. On the other hand, it was thought necessary in *King's Lynn Case, Flanders v Ingleby* (1911) 6 O'M & H 179, and in *Cheltenham Case, Smythies and Claridge v Mathias, Davies' Case* (1911) 6 O'M & H 194 at 227, for the election court to make a special order that the registrar should have the same discretion as the master to allow the costs of witnesses who had not actually been called on the ground that the Parliamentary Election Petition Rules (Additional Rules dated 27 January 1875) r 5 (revoked and not replaced by the Election Petition Rules 1960, SI 1960/543), did not give the registrar such power. In the latter case, Channell J said that the registrar was to be given the 'usual discretion'.

2   As to parliamentary election petitions see PARA 761; as to the questioning of an election under the Local Government Act 1972 see PARA 762; as to Welsh Assembly election petitions see PARA 764; and as to European parliamentary election petitions see PARA 765. Provision is made for questioning a local authority referendum by applying and modifying the provision made for questioning an election under the Local Government Act 1972: see PARA 766. As to the meaning of 'election under the Local Government Act 1972' see PARA 11 note 2. As to the application of the Representation of the People Act 1983 Pt III (ss 120–186) to other polls see PARA 763.

3   As to this scale see CIVIL PROCEDURE vol 11 (2009) PARAS 1013–1015.

4   Representation of the People Act 1983 s 143(1); European Parliamentary Elections Regulations 2004, SI 2004/293, reg 99(1); National Assembly for Wales (Representation of the People) Order 2007, SI 2007/236, art 98(1); and see note 2. As to the certificate of the election court, in relation to a parliamentary election petition see PARA 858; in relation to a local government election petition see PARA 861; in relation to a Welsh Assembly election petition see PARA 863; in relation to a European parliamentary election petition see PARA 865; and in relation to a local authority referendum petition see PARA 866. As to the prescribed officer see PARA 770.

5   Ie by virtue of the Representation of the People Act 1983 s 140(2) (including that provision as applied for the purposes of questioning a Welsh Assembly election or local authority referendum), the European Parliamentary Elections Regulations 2004, SI 2004/293, reg 97(2), or the National Assembly for Wales (Representation of the People) Order 2007, SI 2007/236, art 96(2), as the case may be (see PARA 823).

6   Representation of the People Act 1983 s 143(2); European Parliamentary Elections Regulations 2004, SI 2004/293, reg 99(2); National Assembly for Wales (Representation of the People) Order 2007, SI 2007/236, art 98(2); and see note 2. This provision is for the protection of witnesses to enable them to recover their expenses from the party summoning them: *McLaren v Home* (1881) 7 QBD 477, DC. As to the recovery of costs see PARA 880. As to the expenses of providing an election court, in relation to a parliamentary, Welsh Assembly or European parliamentary election petition, see PARA 774; and, in relation to a local government election petition or a local authority referendum petition, see PARAS 777–778.

880. Recovery of costs. Where any costs or other sums, under the order of an election court or otherwise under the provisions which govern legal proceedings relating to elections and referendums[1], are to be paid by any person, those costs or sums are due from that person to the person or persons to whom they are to be paid; if payable to the Treasury, they are a debt due to Her Majesty[2]. In either case, they may be recovered accordingly[3].

If a petitioner neglects or refuses: (1) in the case of a parliamentary[4], Welsh Assembly[5] or European parliamentary election petition[6], for six months after demand[7]; and (2) in the case of a petition questioning a local authority referendum or an election under the Local Government Act 1972[8], for three months after demand[9], to pay to any person summoned as a witness[10] on his behalf or to the respondent any sum certified to be due to him for his costs[11], and the neglect or refusal is, within one year after the demand, proved to the High Court's satisfaction[12], every person who entered into a recognisance relating to the petition[13] is held to have made default in the recognisance and the prescribed officer[14] must thereupon certify the recognisance to be forfeited[15]. The recognisance is dealt with as if forfeited by the Crown Court[16].

1   Ie, in relation to parliamentary and local government elections, for the purposes of the Representation of the People Act 1983 Pt III (ss 120–186) (including those provisions as applied for the purposes of questioning a local authority referendum: see note 8), in relation to European parliamentary elections, for the purposes of the European Parliamentary Elections Regulations 2004, SI 2004/293, Pt 4 (regs 86–122), and, in relation to Welsh Assembly elections, for the purposes of the National Assembly for Wales (Representation of the People) Order 2007, SI 2007/236, Pt 4 (arts 86–138).

2   Representation of the People Act 1983 s 183(2); European Parliamentary Elections Regulations 2004, SI 2004/293, reg 121(2); National Assembly for Wales (Representation of the People) Order 2007, SI 2007/236, art 135(2); and see note 8.

3   Representation of the People Act 1983 s 183(2); European Parliamentary Elections Regulations 2004, SI 2004/293, reg 121(2); National Assembly for Wales (Representation of the People) Order 2007, SI 2007/236, art 135(2); and see note 8. As to the Treasury see CONSTITUTIONAL LAW AND HUMAN RIGHTS vol 8(2) (Reissue) PARAS 512–517.

4   As to parliamentary election petitions see PARA 761.

5   As to Welsh Assembly election petitions see PARA 764.

6   As to European parliamentary election petitions see PARA 765.

7   Representation of the People Act 1983 s 155(1)(a); European Parliamentary Elections Regulations 2004, SI 2004/293, reg 105(1); National Assembly for Wales (Representation of the People) Order 2007, SI 2007/236, art 105(1).

8   As to the questioning of an election in England and Wales under the Local Government Act 1972 see PARA 762. Provision is made for questioning a local authority referendum by applying and modifying the provision made for questioning an election under the Local Government Act 1972: see PARA 766. As to the meaning of 'election under the Local Government Act 1972' see PARA 11 note 2; and as to the meaning of 'referendum' for these purposes see PARA 574 note 2. As to the application of the Representation of the People Act 1983 Pt III (ss 120–186) to other polls see PARA 763.

9   Representation of the People Act 1983 s 155(1)(b); and see note 8.

10 As to the position where a witness is summoned but does not give evidence see PARA 879 note 1.

11 The only costs of the respondent that are certified are those that have been assessed by the master. It would appear that the certified costs of a witness refer to his certified expenses (see PARA 879) and not to certified costs of witnesses that have been assessed by the master.

12 Representation of the People Act 1983 s 155(1); European Parliamentary Elections Regulations 2004, SI 2004/293, reg 105(1); National Assembly for Wales (Representation of the People) Order 2007, SI 2007/236, art 105(1); and see note 8.

13 As to recognisances see PARA 797.

14 See PARA 770.

15 Representation of the People Act 1983 s 155(2); European Parliamentary Elections Regulations 2004, SI 2004/293, reg 105(2); National Assembly for Wales (Representation of the People) Order 2007, SI 2007/236, art 105(2); and see note 8.

16 Representation of the People Act 1983 s 155(2); European Parliamentary Elections Regulations 2004, SI 2004/293, reg 105(2); National Assembly for Wales (Representation of the People) Order 2007, SI 2007/236, art 105(2); and see note 8. As to the powers and duties of the Crown Court in relation to forfeited recognisances see SENTENCING AND DISPOSITION OF OFFENDERS vol 92 (2010) PARA 159.

(ix) Appeals

881.   Right of appeal.   No appeal lies without the special leave of the High Court from the High Court's decision in the trial of any election or referendum petition[1] on any question of law, whether on appeal or otherwise, under the provisions which govern legal proceedings relating to elections and referendums[2]. If leave to appeal is granted, the decision of the Court of Appeal in the case is final and conclusive[3].

1   As to parliamentary election petitions see PARA 761; as to the questioning of an election under the Local Government Act 1972 see PARA 762; as to Welsh Assembly election petitions see PARA 764; and as to European parliamentary election petitions see PARA 765. Provision is made for questioning a local authority referendum by applying and modifying the provision made for questioning an election under the Local Government Act 1972: see PARA 766. As to the meaning of 'election under the Local Government Act 1972' see PARA 11 note 2. As to the application of the Representation of the People Act 1983 Pt III (ss 120–186) to other polls see PARA 763.

2   Representation of the People Act 1983 s 157(1); European Parliamentary Elections Regulations 2004, SI 2004/293, reg 106(1); National Assembly for Wales (Representation of the People) Order 2007, SI 2007/236, art 107(1); and see note 1. The text refers, in relation to parliamentary and local government elections, to the provisions of the Representation of the People Act 1983 Pt III (ss 120–186) (including those provisions as applied for the purposes of questioning a local authority referendum: see note 1), in relation to European parliamentary elections, to the provisions of the European Parliamentary Elections Regulations 2004, SI 2004/293, Pt 4 (regs 86–122), and, in relation to Welsh Assembly elections, to the provisions of the National Assembly for Wales (Representation of the People) Order 2007, SI 2007/236, Pt 4 (arts 86–138).

   The provision set out in the text applies whether the decision sought to be challenged is of a final or of an interim nature: *Everett v Griffiths (No 3)* [1923] 1 KB 138, CA.

   As to application for mitigation and remission of incapacities see PARA 910.

3   Representation of the People Act 1983 s 157(1); European Parliamentary Elections Regulations 2004, SI 2004/293, reg 106(1); National Assembly for Wales (Representation of the People) Order 2007, SI 2007/236, art 107(1); and see note 1. See also *McHarg v Universal Stock Exchange* [1895] 2 QB 81 at 83; *Wynne-Finch v Chaytor* [1903] 2 Ch 475 at 485, CA; *Unwin v McMullen* [1891] 1 QB 694 at 699, CA; *Shaw v Reckitt (Pontefract Election Petition)* [1893] 2 QB 59, CA.

(4) PUNISHMENT OF OFFENCES

(i) In general

882.   Duty of the Director of Public Prosecutions in relation to offences. Where information is given to the Director of Public Prosecutions that any offence has been committed under the provisions which govern the conduct of elections or referendums[1], it is his duty to make such inquiries and institute such prosecutions as the circumstances appear to him to require[2].

1   Ie, in relation to a parliamentary or local government election, the Representation of the People Act 1983, or, in relation to a European parliamentary election, the European Parliamentary elections rules, or, in relation to a Welsh Assembly election, the National Assembly for Wales (Representation of the People) Order 2007, SI 2007/236 (see PARA 383) or, in relation to local authority referendums in Wales, the Local Authorities (Conduct of Referendums) (Wales) Regulations 2008, SI 2008/1848, or, in relation to local authority referendums in England, the Local Authorities (Conduct of Referendums) (England) Regulations 2012, SI 2012/323. As to the meaning of 'European parliamentary elections rules' see PARA 383. As to the meaning of 'referendum' for these purposes see PARA 574 note 2.

   The Representation of the People Act 1985 s 12 (offences as to declarations etc: see PARA 735) has effect as if contained in the Representation of the People Act 1983 Pt I (ss 1–66B): Representation of the People Act 1985 s 27(2).

2   Representation of the People Act 1983 s 181(1) (amended by the Representation of the People
     Act 1985 s 24, Sch 4 para 63); European Parliamentary Elections Regulations 2004,
     SI 2004/293, reg 119(1); National Assembly for Wales (Representation of the People)
     Order 2007, SI 2007/236, art 133(1). In the application of the European Parliamentary
     Elections Regulations 2004, SI 2004/293, reg 119(1) to elections that have taken place in the
     combined region (see PARA 77), the reference to the Director of Public Prosecutions is to be
     construed as a reference to the Attorney General for Gibraltar: reg 119(7). The Representation
     of the People Act 1983 s 181(1) has been applied and modified for the purposes of local
     authority referendums, in relation to Wales, by the Local Authorities (Conduct of Referendums)
     (Wales) Regulations 2008, SI 2008/1848, Sch 4 Table 1, and, in relation to England, by the
     Local Authorities (Conduct of Referendums) (England) Regulations 2012, SI 2012/323, Sch 4
     Table 1. As to the application of the Representation of the People Act 1983 Pt III (ss 120–186)
     to other polls see PARA 763.

883. General time limits relating to punishment of offences. A proceeding
against a person in respect of any offence under any provision contained in or
made under the provisions which govern the conduct of elections or
referendums[1] must be commenced[2] within one year after the offence was
committed[3].

In the case of summary proceedings[4] for any such offence, this time limit is
substituted for the general time limit that usually applies[5] for the trial of offences
summarily[6]. However, in relation to the prosecution of offences under any
provision contained in or made under the Representation of the People Act 1983,
a magistrates' court may extend the time within which proceedings must be
commenced to not more than 24 months after the offence was committed[7]. The
court may so act only if it is satisfied on an application by a constable or Crown
prosecutor that there are exceptional circumstances which justify the granting of
the application[8] and that there has been no undue delay in the investigation of
the offence to which the application relates[9]. If the magistrates' court so acts, it
may also make an order directing the relevant registration officer[10] not to cause
the documents retained by him to be destroyed at the expiry of the period of one
year[11] and extending the period for which he is required to retain them[12] by such
further period not exceeding 12 months as is specified in the order[13]. Such an
order may be made by the magistrates' court if it is satisfied, on an application
by a constable or Crown prosecutor, that documents retained by the relevant
registration officer[14] may provide evidence relating to the offence[15]. An
application for an extension of time either in relation to the commencement of
proceedings[16] or in relation to the period for which election documents are
required to be retained[17] must be made not more than one year after the offence
was committed[18]. Any party to such an application who is aggrieved by the
refusal of the magistrates' court to extend the time within which proceedings
must be commenced[19] or to make an order extending the period for which
election documents are required to be retained[20] (as the case may be) may appeal
to the Crown Court[21].

1   Ie, in relation to a parliamentary or local government election, the Representation of the People
     Act 1983, or, in relation to a European parliamentary election, the European Parliamentary
     elections rules, or, in relation to a Welsh Assembly election, the National Assembly for Wales
     (Representation of the People) Order 2007, SI 2007/236 (see PARA 383) or, in relation to local
     authority referendums in Wales, the Local Authorities (Conduct of Referendums) (Wales)
     Regulations 2008, SI 2008/1848, or, in relation to local authority referendums in England, the
     Local Authorities (Conduct of Referendums) (England) Regulations 2012, SI 2012/323. As to
     the meaning of 'European parliamentary elections rules' see PARA 383. As to the meaning of
     'referendum' for these purposes see PARA 574 note 2.
        The Representation of the People Act 1985 s 12 (offences as to declarations etc: see PARA
     735) has effect as if contained in the Representation of the People Act 1983 Pt I (ss 1–66B):
     Representation of the People Act 1985 s 27(2).

2   For these purposes, the laying of an information is deemed to be the commencement of a proceeding: Representation of the People Act 1983 s 176(2)(a) (substituted by the Representation of the People Act 1985 s 24, Sch 4 para 61); European Parliamentary Elections Regulations 2004, SI 2004/293, reg 114(9)(a) (substituted by SI 2009/186); National Assembly for Wales (Representation of the People) Order 2007, SI 2007/236, art 128(2). The Representation of the People Act 1983 s 176 has been applied and modified for the purposes of local authority referendums, in relation to Wales, by the Local Authorities (Conduct of Referendums) (Wales) Regulations 2008, SI 2008/1848, Sch 4 Table 1, and, in relation to England, by the Local Authorities (Conduct of Referendums) (England) Regulations 2012, SI 2012/323, Sch 4 Table 1. As to the application of the Representation of the People Act 1983 Pt III (ss 120–186) to other polls see PARA 763.

3   Representation of the People Act 1983 s 176(1) (amended by the Representation of the People Act 1985 s 28, Sch 4 para 61, Sch 5); European Parliamentary Elections Regulations 2004, SI 2004/293, reg 114(1) (substituted by SI 2009/186); National Assembly for Wales (Representation of the People) Order 2007, SI 2007/236, art 128(1); and see note 2.

4   Ie proceedings under the Magistrates' Courts Act 1980.

5   Ie the limit of six months set by the Magistrates' Courts Act 1980 s 127(1) (limitation of time: see MAGISTRATES vol 71 (2013) PARA 526).

6   Representation of the People Act 1983 s 176(1) (amended by the Representation of the People Act 1985 Sch 4 para 61, Sch 5); National Assembly for Wales (Representation of the People) Order 2007, SI 2007/236, art 128(1); European Parliamentary Elections Regulations 2004, SI 2004/293, reg 114(1) (substituted by SI 2009/186); and see note 2.

7   Representation of the People Act 1983 s 176(2B) (s 176(2A)–(2G) added by the Electoral Administration Act 2006 s 70(1)).

8   Representation of the People Act 1983 s 176(2A)(a) (as added: see note 7).

9   Representation of the People Act 1983 s 176(2A)(b) (as added: see note 7).

10   As to the meaning of references to the relevant registration officer for these purposes see PARA 496 note 3.

11   Representation of the People Act 1983 s 176(2D)(a) (as added: see note 7). The text refers to the period of one year mentioned in s 23(1), Sch 1 r 57 (retention and inspection of documents relating to parliamentary elections: see PARA 503). The making of an order under s 176(2D) does not affect any other power to require the retention of the documents: s 176(2E) (as so added).

12   Ie under the Representation of the People Act 1983 Sch 1 r 57 (see PARA 503). See also note 11.

13   Representation of the People Act 1983 s 176(2D)(b) (as added: see note 7). See also note 11.

14   Ie in pursuance of the Representation of the People Act 1983 Sch 1 r 57 (see PARA 503).

15   Representation of the People Act 1983 s 176(2C) (as added: see note 7).

16   Ie an application under the Representation of the People Act 1983 s 176(2A) (see the text and notes 8–9).

17   Ie an application under the Representation of the People Act 1983 s 176(2C) (see the text and notes 14–15).

18   Representation of the People Act 1983 s 176(2F) (as added: see note 7).

19   Ie an application under the Representation of the People Act 1983 s 176(2B) (see the text and note 7).

20   Ie an application under the Representation of the People Act 1983 s 176(2D) (see the text and notes 10–13).

21   Representation of the People Act 1983 s 176(2G) (as added: see note 7).

884. Prosecution of local election and local authority referendum offences punishable summarily. A prosecution for any offence punishable summarily committed in reference to an election under the Local Government Act 1972[1] may be instituted before any magistrates' court in the county in which the local government area[2] for which the election was held is situate or to which it adjoins, and the offence is deemed for all purposes to have been committed within that court's jurisdiction[3].

A prosecution for any offence punishable summarily committed in reference to a local authority referendum[4] may be instituted before any magistrates' court for the voting area[5] in which the offence is alleged to have been committed, and the offence is deemed for all purposes to have been committed within that court's jurisdiction[6].

1   As to the meaning of 'election under the Local Government Act 1972' see PARA 11 note 2.
2   As to the meaning of 'local government area' see PARA 33 note 7.
3   Representation of the People Act 1983 s 177(1) (renumbered by the Local Government (Wales)
     Act 1994 s 1(3), Sch 2 para 12(1)).
4   Ie, in relation to local authority referendums in Wales, under the Local Authorities (Conduct of
     Referendums) (Wales) Regulations 2008, SI 2008/1848, and, in relation to local authority
     referendums in England, under the Local Authorities (Conduct of Referendums) (England)
     Regulations 2012, SI 2012/323. As to the meaning of 'referendum' for these purposes see PARA
     574 note 2.
5   As to the meaning of 'voting area' see PARA 580 note 2.
6   Representation of the People Act 1983 s 177(1) (as renumbered: see note 3). Section 177 has
     been applied and modified for the purposes of local authority referendums, in relation to Wales,
     by the Local Authorities (Conduct of Referendums) (Wales) Regulations 2008, SI 2008/1848,
     Sch 4 Table 1, and, in relation to England, by the Local Authorities (Conduct of Referendums)
     (England) Regulations 2012, SI 2012/323, Sch 4 Table 1. As to the application of the
     Representation of the People Act 1983 Pt III (ss 120–186) to other polls see PARA 763.

885.   Offences committed outside the United Kingdom.   Proceedings in respect
of an offence under the provisions which govern the conduct of elections or
referendums[1] which is alleged to have been committed outside the United
Kingdom[2]: (1) in relation to the Representation of the People Act 1983, by a
Commonwealth citizen[3] or citizen of the Republic of Ireland[4]; (2) in relation to a
Welsh Assembly election, by a Commonwealth citizen, a citizen of the Republic
of Ireland or a relevant citizen of the Union[5]; or (3) in relation to a European
parliamentary election, by a Commonwealth citizen or citizen of the Union[6],
may be taken, and the offence may for all incidental purposes be treated as
having been committed, in any place in the United Kingdom[7].

1   Ie, in relation to a parliamentary or local government election, the Representation of the People
     Act 1983, or, in relation to a European parliamentary election, the European Parliamentary
     elections rules, or, in relation to a Welsh Assembly election, the National Assembly for Wales
     (Representation of the People) Order 2007, SI 2007/236 (see PARA 383) or, in relation to local
     authority referendums in Wales, the Local Authorities (Conduct of Referendums) (Wales)
     Regulations 2008, SI 2008/1848, or, in relation to local authority referendums in England, the
     Local Authorities (Conduct of Referendums) (England) Regulations 2012, SI 2012/323. As to
     the meaning of 'European parliamentary elections rules' see PARA 383. As to the meaning of
     'referendum' for these purposes see PARA 574 note 2.
         The Representation of the People Act 1985 s 12 (offences as to declarations etc: see PARA
     735) has effect as if contained in the Representation of the People Act 1983 Pt I (ss 1–66B):
     Representation of the People Act 1985 s 27(2).
2   As to the meaning of 'United Kingdom' see PARA 1 note 1.
3   As to who are Commonwealth citizens see BRITISH NATIONALITY vol 4 (2011) PARA 409.
4   See the Representation of the People Act 1983 s 178 (substituted by the Representation of the
     People Act 1985 s 24, Sch 4 para 62). The reference to the Representation of the People
     Act 1983 includes that Act as it is applied and modified for the purposes of local authority
     referendums (see note 7). As to who are citizens of the Republic of Ireland see BRITISH
     NATIONALITY vol 4 (2011) PARA 410.
5   See the National Assembly for Wales (Representation of the People) Order 2007, SI 2007/236,
     art 129. As to the meaning of 'relevant citizen of the Union' for these purposes see PARA 149
     note 16.
6   See the European Parliamentary Elections Regulations 2004, SI 2004/293, reg 115. As to the
     meaning of 'citizen of the Union' for these purposes see PARA 149 note 17.
7   Representation of the People Act 1983 s 178 (substituted by the Representation of the People
     Act 1985 s 24, Sch 4 para 62); European Parliamentary Elections Regulations 2004,
     SI 2004/293, reg 115; National Assembly for Wales (Representation of the People) Order 2007,
     SI 2007/236, art 129. The Representation of the People Act 1983 s 178 has been applied and
     modified for the purposes of local authority referendums, in relation to Wales, by the Local
     Authorities (Conduct of Referendums) (Wales) Regulations 2008, SI 2008/1848, Sch 4 Table 1,
     and, in relation to England, by the Local Authorities (Conduct of Referendums) (England)
     Regulations 2012, SI 2012/323, Sch 4 Table 1. As to the application of the Representation of the
     People Act 1983 Pt III (ss 120–186) to other polls see PARA 763.

The provision set out in the text would appear to apply to offences committed within the United Kingdom by any person irrespective of nationality and to offences committed outside the jurisdiction by those specified. In addition to the offence set out in relation to overseas elector's declarations in the Representation of the People Act 1985 s 12 (see note 1), the offence described in PARA 331 (broadcasting from outside the United Kingdom with the intent to influence elections) may be especially relevant in this context.

886. Evidence by certificate of holding of election or referendum and of electoral registration. On any prosecution for a corrupt[1] or illegal practice[2], or for any illegal payment, employment or hiring[3], and (except in relation to a European parliamentary election) on any proceedings for a penalty for sitting or voting after failure to deliver the return and declarations as to election expenses[4], the returning officer's certificate that the election mentioned in the certificate was duly held and that the person named in the certificate was a candidate at the election is sufficient evidence of the facts stated in it[5].

On any prosecution for a corrupt or illegal practice, or for any illegal payment, employment or hiring, the counting officer's certificate that the referendum mentioned in the certificate was duly held is sufficient evidence of the facts stated in it[6].

The certificate of a registration officer that any person is or is not, or was or was not at any particular time, duly registered in one of the officer's registers in respect of any address is sufficient evidence of the facts stated in it; and a document purporting to be such a certificate must be received in evidence and is presumed to be such a certificate unless the contrary is proved[7].

1   As to corrupt practices see generally PARA 704 et seq; and as to the punishment of corrupt practices see PARA 887 et seq.
2   As to illegal practices see generally PARA 671 et seq; and as to the punishment of illegal practices see PARA 888 et seq.
3   As to the circumstances in which relief is available see PARA 687 et seq; and as to the consequences of illegal payment, employment or hiring see PARA 889.
4   As to the financial penalty imposed for sitting or voting in office where no financial returns or declarations are transmitted see PARA 755.
5   Representation of the People Act 1983 s 180; European Parliamentary Elections Regulations 2004, SI 2004/293, reg 117; National Assembly for Wales (Representation of the People) Order 2007, SI 2007/236, art 131. In relation to a European parliamentary election, the returning officer may certify also that a registered party named in the certificate submitted a list at the election: see the European Parliamentary Elections Regulations 2004, SI 2004/293, reg 117. As to the meanings of 'list' and 'registered party' in relation to European parliamentary elections see PARA 230 note 29; and as to the meaning of 'individual candidate' in relation to such elections see PARA 230 note 32. The court has taken judicial notice of the holding of a general parliamentary election: *Coventry Case, Berry v Eaton and Hill* (1869) 1 O'M & H 97.
6   Representation of the People Act 1983 s 180 (applied and modified, in relation to Wales, by the Local Authorities (Conduct of Referendums) (Wales) Regulations 2008, SI 2008/1848, Sch 5, and, in relation to England, by the Local Authorities (Conduct of Referendums) (England) Regulations 2012, SI 2012/323, Sch 6). As to the application of the Representation of the People Act 1983 Pt III (ss 120–186) to other polls see PARA 763.
7   Representation of the People Act 1983 s 180A (added by the Representation of the People Act 2000 s 8, Sch 1 paras 1, 20); European Parliamentary Elections Regulations 2004, SI 2004/293, reg 118; National Assembly for Wales (Representation of the People) Order 2007, SI 2007/236, art 132.

(ii) Punishment of Corrupt and Illegal Practices etc

887. Punishment of corrupt practices. A person who is guilty of a corrupt practice is liable on conviction on indictment[1] to a penalty, the nature of which depends on whether it is a case of committing (or aiding, abetting, counselling or procuring the commission of) the offence of personation[2] or an offence at a parliamentary or local government election relating to an application for a postal or proxy vote[3], or whether it is a case of any other corrupt practice[4]. On summary conviction, a person who is guilty of a corrupt practice is also liable to a penalty[5].

If the circumstances warrant such a finding, any person charged with a corrupt practice may be found guilty of an illegal practice (which is for that purpose to be an indictable offence)[6].

1   Representation of the People Act 1983 s 168(1) (s 168(1) substituted by the Representation of the People Act 1985 s 23, Sch 3 para 8); European Parliamentary Elections Regulations 2004, SI 2004/293, reg 109(1); National Assembly for Wales (Representation of the People) Order 2007, SI 2007/236, art 120(1). As to elections in the City of London see PARA 33. As to corrupt practices see generally PARA 704 et seq; and as to the striking off of a vote of a person found guilty of a corrupt practice see PARA 843.

   The Representation of the People Act 1983 s 168 has been applied and modified for the purposes of local authority referendums, in relation to Wales, by the Local Authorities (Conduct of Referendums) (Wales) Regulations 2008, SI 2008/1848, Sch 4 Table 1, and, in relation to England, by the Local Authorities (Conduct of Referendums) (England) Regulations 2012, SI 2012/323, Sch 4 Table 1. As to the meaning of 'referendum' for these purposes see PARA 574 note 2. As to the application of the Representation of the People Act 1983 Pt III (ss 120–186) to other polls see PARA 763.

2   Representation of the People Act 1983 s 168(1)(a)(i) (as substituted (see note 1); and amended by the Electoral Administration Act 2006 s 74(1), Sch 1 paras 104, 121); European Parliamentary Elections Regulations 2004, SI 2004/293, reg 109(1)(a)(i) (amended by SI 2009/186); National Assembly for Wales (Representation of the People) Order 2007, SI 2007/236, art 120(1)(a)(i); and see note 1. The text refers to an offence, in relation to a parliamentary or local government election, under the Representation of the People Act 1983 s 60, in relation to a European parliamentary election, under the European Parliamentary Elections Regulations 2004, SI 2004/293, reg 23, and, in relation to a Welsh Assembly election, under the National Assembly for Wales (Representation of the People) Order 2007, SI 2007/236, art 30 (see PARA 730). The penalty is imprisonment for a term not exceeding two years or a fine, or both: see the Representation of the People Act 1983 s 168(1)(a)(i) (as so substituted and amended); the European Parliamentary Elections Regulations 2004, SI 2004/293, reg 109(1)(a)(i); the National Assembly for Wales (Representation of the People) Order 2007, SI 2007/236, art 120(1)(a)(i); and see note 1. In *R v Brindley* [1997] 2 Cr App Rep (S) 353, CA, an offence of personation which was planned and persisted in over a number of days drew a custodial sentence of eight months, one element of which was to serve as a deterrent to those who would interfere with the electoral process, being conduct which was held to be analogous to interference with the course of justice.

3   Representation of the People Act 1983 s 168(1)(a)(i) (as substituted and amended: see note 2); the European Parliamentary Elections Regulations 2004, SI 2004/293, reg 109(1)(a)(i); the National Assembly for Wales (Representation of the People) Order 2007, SI 2007/236, art 120(1)(a)(i); and see note 1. The text refers to an offence, in relation to a parliamentary or local government election, under s 62A, in relation to a European parliamentary election, under the European Parliamentary Elections Regulations 2004, SI 2004/293, Sch 2 para 11, and, in relation to a Welsh Assembly election, under the National Assembly for Wales (Representation of the People) Order 2007, SI 2007/236, art 14(11) (see PARA 731). The penalty is imprisonment for a term not exceeding two years or a fine, or both: see the Representation of the People Act 1983 s 168(1)(a)(i) (as so substituted and amended); the European Parliamentary Elections Regulations 2004, SI 2004/293, reg 109(1)(a)(i); the National Assembly for Wales (Representation of the People) Order 2007, SI 2007/236, art 120(1)(a)(i); and see note 1. In *R v Hussain* [2005] EWCA Crim 1866, [2006] 1 Cr App Rep (S) 336, a case which pre-dated the offence under the Representation of the People Act 1983 s 62A, a concerted course of action whereby incomplete documents for postal voting in a local election were obtained by deception and completed by, or on behalf of the defendant, had attracted a sentence of three years and seven months' imprisonment on conviction of a charge of conspiracy to defraud; in upholding the sentence, the Court of Appeal approved the deterrent element, having regard to the nature of the offence, and stressed the courts' responsibility in a democratic society to protect the country's electoral system from corruption or fraud, which in the instant case was said to have more dangerous consequences than those which sought to undermine the administration of justice.

4   Representation of the People Act 1983 s 168(1)(a)(ii) (as substituted: see note 1); European
    Parliamentary Elections Regulations 2004, SI 2004/293, reg 109(1)(a)(ii); National Assembly
    for Wales (Representation of the People) Order 2007, SI 2007/236, art 120(1)(a)(ii); and see
    note 1. The penalty is imprisonment for a term not exceeding one year or a fine or both: see the
    Representation of the People Act 1983 s 168(1)(a)(ii) (as substituted: see note 1); the European
    Parliamentary Elections Regulations 2004, SI 2004/293, reg 109(1)(a)(ii); the National
    Assembly for Wales (Representation of the People) Order 2007, SI 2007/236, art 120(1)(a)(ii);
    and see note 1.
5   Representation of the People Act 1983 s 168(1)(b) (as substituted: see note 1); European
    Parliamentary Elections Regulations 2004, SI 2004/293, reg 109(1)(b); National Assembly for
    Wales (Representation of the People) Order 2007, SI 2007/236, art 120(1)(b); and see note 1.
    The penalty is imprisonment for a term not exceeding six months or a fine not exceeding the
    statutory maximum or both: see the Representation of the People Act 1983 s 168(1)(b) (as
    substituted: see note 1); the European Parliamentary Elections Regulations 2004, SI 2004/293,
    reg 109(1)(b); the National Assembly for Wales (Representation of the People) Order 2007,
    SI 2007/236, art 120(1)(b); and see note 1. As to the statutory maximum see SENTENCING AND
    DISPOSITION OF OFFENDERS vol 92 (2010) PARA 140.
6   Representation of the People Act 1983 s 170; European Parliamentary Elections
    Regulations 2004, SI 2004/293, reg 111; National Assembly for Wales (Representation of the
    People) Order 2007, SI 2007/236, art 122; and see note 1. As to the punishment of illegal
    practices see PARA 888.

888. Punishment of illegal practices. A person guilty of an illegal practice[1] is
on summary conviction liable to a penalty[2]. A person charged with an illegal
practice may be found guilty of that offence notwithstanding that the act
constituting the offence amounted to a corrupt practice[3].

1   As to illegal practices see generally PARA 671 et seq.
2   Representation of the People Act 1983 s 169 (amended by the Representation of the People
    Act 1985 s 23, Sch 3 para 9); European Parliamentary Elections Regulations 2004, SI 2004/293,
    reg 110; National Assembly for Wales (Representation of the People) Order 2007, SI 2007/236,
    art 121. The penalty is a fine not exceeding level 5 on the standard scale: see the Representation
    of the People Act 1983 s 169 (as so amended); the European Parliamentary Elections
    Regulations 2004, SI 2004/293, reg 110; and the National Assembly for Wales (Representation
    of the People) Order 2007, SI 2007/236, art 121. As to the standard scale see SENTENCING AND
    DISPOSITION OF OFFENDERS vol 92 (2010) PARA 142. As to the drafting of such a charge see
    PARA 890. As to striking off the vote of a person found guilty of an illegal practice see PARA 843.
        The Representation of the People Act 1983 s 169 has been applied and modified for the
    purposes of local authority referendums, in relation to Wales, by the Local Authorities (Conduct
    of Referendums) (Wales) Regulations 2008, SI 2008/1848, Sch 4 Table 1, and, in relation to
    England, by the Local Authorities (Conduct of Referendums) (England) Regulations 2012,
    SI 2012/323, Sch 4 Table 1. As to the meaning of 'referendum' for these purposes see PARA 574
    note 2. As to the application of the Representation of the People Act 1983 Pt III (ss 120–186) to
    other polls see PARA 763. As to elections in the City of London see PARA 33.
3   Representation of the People Act 1983 s 170; European Parliamentary Elections
    Regulations 2004, SI 2004/293, reg 111; National Assembly for Wales (Representation of the
    People) Order 2007, SI 2007/236, art 122. As to the punishment of corrupt practices see PARA
    887.
        The Representation of the People Act 1983 s 170 has been applied and modified for the
    purposes of local authority referendums, in relation to Wales, by the Local Authorities (Conduct
    of Referendums) (Wales) Regulations 2008, SI 2008/1848, Sch 4 Table 1, and, in relation to
    England, by the Local Authorities (Conduct of Referendums) (England) Regulations 2012,
    SI 2012/323, Sch 4 Table 1.

889. Punishment of illegal payments or employments. A person guilty of an
offence of illegal payment or employment[1] is liable, on summary conviction, to a
penalty[2]; and any person charged with an offence of illegal payment or
employment may be found guilty of that offence, notwithstanding that the act
constituting the offence amounted to a corrupt or illegal practice[3].

1   See PARA 682 et seq.

2　Representation of the People Act 1983 s 175(1) (amended by the Representation of the People Act 1985 s 23, Sch 3 para 10; and the Political Parties, Elections and Referendums Act 2000 s 158(1), Sch 21 para 6(1), (6)); European Parliamentary Elections Regulations 2004, SI 2004/293, reg 113(1); National Assembly for Wales (Representation of the People) Order 2007, SI 2007/236, art 127(1). The penalty is a fine not exceeding level 5 on the standard scale: see the Representation of the People Act 1983 s 175(1); the European Parliamentary Elections Regulations 2004, SI 2004/293, reg 113(1); and the National Assembly for Wales (Representation of the People) Order 2007, SI 2007/236, art 127(1). As to the standard scale see SENTENCING AND DISPOSITION OF OFFENDERS vol 92 (2010) PARA 142. As to the drafting of such a charge see PARA 890.

　　The Representation of the People Act 1983 s 175(1), (3) has been applied and modified for the purposes of local authority referendums, in relation to Wales, by the Local Authorities (Conduct of Referendums) (Wales) Regulations 2008, SI 2008/1848, Sch 4 Table 1, and, in relation to England, by the Local Authorities (Conduct of Referendums) (England) Regulations 2012, SI 2012/323, Sch 4 Table 1. As to the meaning of 'referendum' for these purposes see PARA 574 note 2. As to the application of the Representation of the People Act 1983 Pt III (ss 120–186) to other polls see PARA 763.

3　Representation of the People Act 1983 s 175(3) (amended by the Political Parties, Elections and Referendums Act 2000 Sch 21 para 6(1), (6)); European Parliamentary Elections Regulations 2004, SI 2004/293, reg 113(3); National Assembly for Wales (Representation of the People) Order 2007, SI 2007/236, art 127(3); and see note 2.

890.　Drafting of charges on prosecution for corrupt or illegal practice or for illegal payments or employments.　On a prosecution for an illegal practice[1] it is sufficient to allege that the person charged was guilty of an illegal practice[2]. There is no similar provision in relation to corrupt practices[3] and it would appear necessary, therefore, for the charge to state the particular corrupt practice of which the person is alleged to have been guilty[4]. It is not essential that the date of the election should be stated[5].

　On a prosecution for an offence of illegal payment or employment[6] it is sufficient to allege that the person charged was guilty of an illegal payment or employment, as the case may be[7].

1　As to illegal practices see generally PARA 671 et seq.
2　Representation of the People Act 1983 s 169; European Parliamentary Elections Regulations 2004, SI 2004/293, reg 110; National Assembly for Wales (Representation of the People) Order 2007, SI 2007/236, art 121. Corrupt and illegal practices may be cited in European parliamentary election petitions only when they are related to personation and other voting offences: see PARA 765.
3　As to corrupt practices see generally PARA 704 et seq.
4　*R v Stroulger* (1886) 17 QBD 327; *R v Norton* (1886) 16 Cox CC 59.
5　*R v Yeoman* (1904) 20 TLR 266.
6　As to the offence of illegal payment or employment see PARA 682.
7　Representation of the People Act 1983 s 175(1) (amended by the Representation of the People Act 1985 s 23, Sch 3 para 10; and the Political Parties, Elections and Referendums Act 2000 s 158(1), Sch 21 para 6(1), (6)); European Parliamentary Elections Regulations 2004, SI 2004/293, reg 113(1); National Assembly for Wales (Representation of the People) Order 2007, SI 2007/236, art 127(1).

891.　Offences, corrupt or illegal practices etc committed by associations.
Where any corrupt[1] or illegal practice[2] or any illegal payment, employment or hiring[3] or any offence of not providing the required details on election documents[4] is committed by any association or body of persons, corporate or unincorporate, the members of the association or body who have taken part in the commission of the offence are liable to any fine or punishment[5] imposed for that offence under the provisions which govern the conduct of elections or referendums[6].

1　As to corrupt practices see generally PARA 704 et seq.

2   As to illegal practices see generally PARA 671 et seq.
3   As to the offence of illegal payment or employment see PARA 682.
4   As to this offence see PARA 748.
5   This would appear to mean any fine or imprisonment but not to include any incapacities to which an individual might be liable for the offence of which the corporation is guilty.
6   Representation of the People Act 1983 s 179; European Parliamentary Elections Regulations 2004, SI 2004/293, reg 116; National Assembly for Wales (Representation of the People) Order 2007, SI 2007/236, art 130. The Representation of the People Act 1983 s 179 has been applied and modified for the purposes of local authority referendums, in relation to Wales, by the Local Authorities (Conduct of Referendums) (Wales) Regulations 2008, SI 2008/1848, Sch 4 Table 1, and, in relation to England, by the Local Authorities (Conduct of Referendums) (England) Regulations 2012, SI 2012/323, Sch 4 Table 1. As to the meaning of 'referendum' for these purposes see PARA 574 note 2. As to the application of the Representation of the People Act 1983 Pt III (ss 120–186) to other polls see PARA 763. The text refers to offences, in relation to a parliamentary or local government election, under the Representation of the People Act 1983 (and including that Act as it is applied and modified for the purposes of local authority referendums) or, in relation to a European parliamentary election, under the European parliamentary elections rules, or, in relation to a Welsh Assembly election, under the National Assembly for Wales (Representation of the People) Order 2007, SI 2007/236 (see PARA 383). As to the meaning of 'European parliamentary elections rules' see PARA 383 note 2. As to elections in the City of London see PARA 33.

(iii) Punishment of Offences under the Political Parties, Elections and Referendums Act 2000

892.   Summary proceedings for offences under the Political Parties, Elections and Referendums Act 2000. Summary proceedings for any offence under the Political Parties, Elections and Referendums Act 2000[1] may, without prejudice to any jurisdiction otherwise exercisable[2], be taken against any body, including an unincorporated association, at any place at which it has a place of business, and against an individual at any place at which he is for the time being[3]. Despite the general time limit that usually applies[4] for the trial of offences summarily, any information relating to an offence under the Political Parties, Elections and Referendums Act 2000 which is triable by a magistrates' court in England and Wales may be so tried if it is laid at any time within three years after the commission of the offence and within six months after the relevant date[5].

1   As to offences generally see PARA 732 et seq.
2   Ie exercisable apart from the Political Parties, Elections and Referendums Act 2000 s 151(1).
3   Political Parties, Elections and Referendums Act 2000 s 151(1).
4   Ie despite anything in the Magistrates' Courts Act 1980 s 127(1) (limitation of time: see MAGISTRATES vol 71 (2013) PARA 526).
5   Political Parties, Elections and Referendums Act 2000 s 151(2). For these purposes, the 'relevant date' means the date on which evidence sufficient in the opinion of the prosecutor to justify proceedings comes to his knowledge (s 151(5)); and a certificate of any prosecutor as to the date on which such evidence as is there mentioned came to his knowledge is conclusive evidence of that fact (s 151(6)). As to offences relating to a European parliamentary election held in the combined region (see PARA 77) which are triable by a magistrates' court in Gibraltar see s 151(4A) (added by SI 2004/366).

893.   Offences committed by bodies corporate or unincorporated associations. Where an offence under the Political Parties, Elections and Referendums Act 2000[1] committed by a body corporate is proved to have been committed with the consent or connivance of, or to be attributable to any neglect on the part of any director, manager, secretary or other similar officer of the body corporate or any person who was purporting to act in any such capacity, he, as well as the body corporate, is guilty of that offence and is liable to be proceeded against and punished accordingly[2].

Proceedings for an offence alleged to have been committed under the Political Parties, Elections and Referendums Act 2000 by an unincorporated association is to be brought against the association in its own name (and not in that of any of its members) and, for the purposes of any such proceedings, any rules of court relating to the service of documents have effect as if the association were a corporation[3]. A fine imposed on an unincorporated association on its conviction of such an offence must be paid out of the funds of the association[4]. The statutory provisions which deal with the procedure on charges of offences against corporations[5] have effect in a case in which an unincorporated association is charged in England or Wales with an offence under the Political Parties, Elections and Referendums Act 2000 in like manner as they have effect in the case of a corporation so charged[6].

Where a partnership is guilty of an offence under the Political Parties, Elections and Referendums Act 2000 and the offence is proved to have been committed with the consent or connivance of, or to be attributable to any neglect on the part of, any partner, he as well as the partnership is guilty of that offence and is liable to be proceeded against and punished accordingly[7].

Where any other unincorporated association is guilty of an offence under the Political Parties, Elections and Referendums Act 2000 and the offence is proved to have been committed with the consent or connivance of, or to be attributable to any neglect on the part of any officer of the association or any member of the committee or other similar governing body of the association, he, as well as the association, is guilty of that offence and is liable to be proceeded against and punished accordingly[8].

1 As to offences generally see PARA 732 et seq.
2 Political Parties, Elections and Referendums Act 2000 s 152(1). Where the affairs of a body corporate are managed by its members, s 152(1) applies in relation to the acts and defaults of a member in connection with his functions of management as if he were a director of the body corporate: s 152(2).
3 Political Parties, Elections and Referendums Act 2000 s 153(1).
4 Political Parties, Elections and Referendums Act 2000 s 153(2).
5 Ie the Criminal Justice Act 1925 s 33 and the Magistrates' Courts Act 1980 s 46, Sch 3: see MAGISTRATES vol 71 (2013) PARA 513.
6 Political Parties, Elections and Referendums Act 2000 s 153(3). As to the procedure where an unincorporated association is charged in Gibraltar with an offence relating to a European parliamentary election held in the combined region (see PARA 77) see s 153(5A) (added by SI 2004/366).
7 Political Parties, Elections and Referendums Act 2000 s 153(6).
8 Political Parties, Elections and Referendums Act 2000 s 153(7).

(5) CONSEQUENCES OF LEGAL PROCEEDINGS

(i) Avoidance of Election or Referendum

894. Avoidance of election of candidate reported guilty of corrupt or illegal practice. If a candidate who has been elected is reported by an election court personally guilty or guilty by his agents of any corrupt or illegal practice[1], his election is void[2].

1 As to when a candidate is to be treated as having been reported personally guilty or guilty by his agents see PARA 901.
2 Representation of the People Act 1983 s 159(1); National Assembly for Wales (Representation of the People) Order 2007, SI 2007/236, art 109. There is no provision in relation to European parliamentary elections because corrupt and illegal practices relate only to personation and

other voting offences in that context: see PARA 765. As to elections in the City of London see PARA 33. As to the application of the Representation of the People Act 1983 Pt III (ss 120–186) to other polls see PARA 763.

895.   Avoidance of election by reason of general corruption, bribery, treating or intimidation.   Where, on an election petition[1], it is shown that corrupt[2] or illegal practices[3] or illegal payments, employments or hirings[4] committed in reference to the election for the purpose of promoting or procuring the election of any person have so extensively prevailed that they may be reasonably supposed to have affected the result, the election of that person, if he has been elected, is void, and he is incapable of being elected to fill the vacancy or any of the vacancies for which the election was held[5]. An election under the Local Government Act 1972[6] may be questioned on the ground that it is avoided under this provision[7]. An election is not liable to be avoided, otherwise than under this provision, by reason of general corruption, bribery, treating or intimidation[8].

1   As to parliamentary election petitions see PARA 761; as to the questioning of an election under the Local Government Act 1972 see PARA 762; and as to Welsh Assembly election petitions see PARA 764. As to the meaning of 'election under the Local Government Act 1972' see PARA 11 note 2. There is no provision for the purposes of European parliamentary election petitions because corrupt and illegal practices may be cited in such petitions only when they are related to personation and other voting offences: see PARA 765. As to the application of the Representation of the People Act 1983 Pt III (ss 120–186) to other polls see PARA 763.
2   As to corrupt practices see generally PARA 704 et seq.
3   As to illegal practices see generally PARA 671 et seq.
4   As to the offence of illegal payment, employment or hiring see PARA 682.
5   Representation of the People Act 1983 s 164(1); National Assembly for Wales (Representation of the People) Order 2007, SI 2007/236, art 116(1). As to elections in the City of London see PARA 33. Where, on a Welsh Assembly election petition, it is shown that corrupt or illegal practices or illegal payments or employments have prevailed in relation to a regional election for the purpose of promoting or procuring the giving of votes for a registered political party at the election, such acts, for the purposes of art 116(1), are treated as having prevailed for the purpose of promoting or procuring the election of each candidate on that party's list: art 116(2). As to the meaning of 'regional election' in the context of Welsh Assembly elections see PARA 3 note 2; as to the meaning of 'registered political party' for these purposes see PARA 256; and as to the meaning of 'party list candidate' in relation to a Welsh Assembly election see PARA 230 note 23. As to evidence given by certificate when the matters set out in the text are prosecuted see PARA 886.
6   As to elections under the Local Government Act 1972 see PARA 10.
7   Representation of the People Act 1983 s 164(3). See *Akhtar v Jahan, Iqbal v Islam* [2005] All ER (D) 15 (Apr), in which the elections for two wards were declared void on the grounds of widespread corrupt and illegal practices under the Representation of the People Act 1983 s 164 (as well as on the grounds of corrupt and illegal practices by the successful candidates), the Commissioner having found on the evidence that: (1) fraudulent applications for postal votes were made and electors' names improperly entered without their knowledge or consent on the absent voters' list; (2) unused ballot packages were improperly diverted by a wide variety of means; (3) the improperly diverted ballot packages were fraudulently used by completing the ballot papers and declarations of identity (now the postal voting statement) and despatching them to the Elections Office; (4) completed ballot packages were improperly diverted; and (5) improperly diverted ballot packages were opened and the contents fraudulently altered. On appeal, the finding against one councillor was quashed on evidential grounds but the other findings of personal corruption and general corruption were not affected: see *R (on the application of Afzal) v Election Court* [2005] EWCA Civ 647, [2005] LGR 823, Election Ct. See also *Re Central Borough Ward of Slough Election Petition, Simmons v Khan* [2008] EWHC B4 (QB), Election Ct.
8   Representation of the People Act 1983 s 164(2); National Assembly for Wales (Representation of the People) Order 2007, SI 2007/236, art 116(3). The provision set out in the text supersedes the common law by which an election might be avoided for general bribery or treating in favour of the successful candidate or general intimidation, whether or not the successful candidate or his agents were responsible for the bribery, treating or intimidation: *Bradford Case (No 2)*

(1869) 19 LT 723, 1 O'M & H 35; and see eg *Beverley Case* (1869) 20 LT 792, 1 O'M & H 143; *Lichfield Case, Anson v Dyott* (1869) 20 LT 11 at 14, 1 O'M & H 22 at 26; *Guildford Case* (1869) 19 LT 729 at 731, 1 O'M & H 13 at 14–15; *Bridgewater Case* (1869) 1 O'M & H 112 at 115 (bribery); *Ipswich Case, Packard v Collings and West* (1886) 54 LT 619, 4 O'M & H 70 (bribery and treating); *Tamworth Case, Hill and Walter v Peel and Bulwer* (1869) 20 LT 181, 1 O'M & H 75; *Pontefract Case, Shaw v Reckitt* (1893) 4 O'M & H 200 at 201, Day 125 at 129 (treating); *Drogheda Borough Case* (1869) 21 LT 402, 1 O'M & H 252; *Stafford Borough Case* (1869) 21 LT 210 at 211, 1 O'M & H 228 at 229; *Staleybridge Case, Ogden, Woolley and Buckley v Sidebottom* (1869) 20 LT 75 at 78, 1 O'M & H 66 at 72; *Dudley Case* (1874) 2 O'M & H 115; *Durham County, Northern Division Case (No 2)* (1874) 2 O'M & H 152; *Re Gloucestershire, Thornbury Division, Election Petition* (1886) 4 O'M & H 65 at 67; *South Meath Case* (1892) Day 132 at 140; *East Kerry Case* (1910) 6 O'M & H 58 (intimidation); *Hartlepools Case* (1910) 6 O'M & H 1 at 8. The provision does not refer to general personation, and at common law general personation, in the absence of evidence that the candidate or his agent was implicated, does not avoid the election (*Belfast Borough, Western Division Case* (1886) 4 O'M & H 105), although if a candidate's agent had arranged for voters to be personated, the election would, it seems, be avoided at common law (*Coventry Case, Berry v Eaton and Hill* (1869) 1 O'M & H 97 at 105). As to the statutory provisions by which personation is a corrupt practice see PARA 730; and as to the avoidance of an election on this ground where an elected candidate has been found guilty see PARA 894.

896. Avoidance of election for employing corrupt agent. If, at a parliamentary, Welsh Assembly or local government election[1], a candidate or his election agent[2] personally engages[3], as a canvasser or agent for the conduct or management of the election[4], any person whom he knows or has reasonable grounds for supposing to be subject to an incapacity to vote at the election[5] by reason of his having been convicted or reported of any corrupt or illegal practice[6], the candidate is incapable of being elected to fill the vacancy or any of the vacancies for which the election is held[7]. A local government election may be questioned[8] on the ground that the person whose election is questioned was, at the time of the election, by virtue of these provisions incapable of being elected[9].

A vote given at a parliamentary or local government election, or at a Welsh Assembly constituency election[10] or regional election, for a person who was, at the time of the election, incapable of being elected by virtue of these provisions, is not, by reason of his incapacity on this ground, deemed to be thrown away so as to entitle another candidate to be declared elected, unless given at a poll consequent on an election court's decision that he was so incapable[11]. Similarly, a vote given at a Welsh Assembly regional election for a registered political party[12] where at the time of the election each candidate included on the party's list was by virtue of these provisions incapable of being elected, is not, by reason of that incapacity, deemed to be thrown away so as to entitle another candidate to be declared elected, unless given at a poll consequent on the decision of an election court that he was so incapable[13].

1   As to the meaning of 'Assembly election' in the context of Welsh Assembly elections see PARA 3 note 2; as to the meaning of 'parliamentary election' see PARA 9; and as to the meaning of 'local government election' see PARA 11. As to elections in the City of London see PARA 33. There is no provision in relation to European parliamentary elections because corrupt and illegal practices relate only to personation and other voting offences in that context: see PARA 765. As to the application of the Representation of the People Act 1983 Pt III (ss 120–186) to other polls see PARA 763.

2   As to the appointment of an election agent for parliamentary and local government elections see PARA 231; and as to the appointment of an election agent for elections to the National Assembly for Wales see PARA 235. At a Welsh Assembly election, the reference is to a constituency or an individual candidate for an Assembly constituency or a regional election or his election agent (see the National Assembly for Wales (Representation of the People) Order 2007, SI 2007/236, art 117(1)(a)) or to a party list candidate or the election agent of the registered political party on whose list he is a candidate (see art 117(1)(b)). As to the meaning of 'Assembly regional election'

    in this context see PARA 3 note 2; and as to the meanings of 'individual candidate' and 'party list candidate', and as to the meaning of references to groups of party list candidates, see PARA 230 notes 19, 23.

3   For the canvasser or agent to be personally engaged, it is sufficient for him to be engaged with the knowledge and consent of the candidate or election agent: *North Norfolk Case* (1869) 1 O'M & H 236 at 238; *Norwich Case* (1871) 23 LT 701 at 702, 2 O'M & H 38 at 40–41.

4   It is not necessary that the agent should be an agent for the management of the whole election; it is sufficient if he is agent for part of the election. He must be not simply an agent who might be employed to such an extent as might make the candidate answerable for corrupt or illegal practices committed by him, but employed in the way of managing a portion of the election: *North Norfolk Case, Burton's Case* (1869) 1 O'M & H 236 at 239.

5   Representation of the People Act 1983 s 165(1); National Assembly for Wales (Representation of the People) Order 2007, SI 2007/236, art 117(1).

6   Representation of the People Act 1983 s 165(1)(a) (amended by the Bribery Act 2010 s 17(3), Sch 2); National Assembly for Wales (Representation of the People) Order 2007, SI 2007/236, art 117(2)(a) (amended by SI 2011/1441). The text refers to any corrupt or illegal practice within the meaning of the Representation of the People Act 1983 or the law relating to elections for the Northern Ireland Assembly, in relation to a parliamentary or local government election, and within the meaning of the Representation of the People Act 1983, the National Assembly for Wales (Representation of the People) Order 2007, SI 2007/236 (see PARA 383) or the law relating to elections to the European Parliament, the Northern Ireland Assembly or the Scottish Parliament, in relation to a Welsh Assembly election. As to European parliamentary elections see PARA 217 et seq. As to the law relating to elections for the Scottish Parliament see CONSTITUTIONAL LAW AND HUMAN RIGHTS vol 8(2) (Reissue) PARA 51 et seq; and as to the law relating to elections for the Northern Ireland Assembly see CONSTITUTIONAL LAW AND HUMAN RIGHTS vol 8(2) (Reissue) PARA 67 et seq. As to the imposition of incapacities in relation to candidates and others see PARA 905.

7   Representation of the People Act 1983 s 165(1) (amended by the Bribery Act 2010 s 17(3), Sch 2); National Assembly for Wales (Representation of the People) Order 2007, SI 2007/236, art 117(1). In relation to party list candidates at a regional election, the incapacity imposed by art 117(1) applies: (1) where the election agent engages such a person, to each candidate on the list; or (2) where the election agent does not engage such a person, only to that candidate who engages, or those candidates who engage, that person: art 117(3).

8   As to the questioning of local government elections generally see PARA 762.

9   Representation of the People Act 1983 s 165(2).

10 As to the meaning of 'constituency election' in this context see PARA 3 note 2.

11 Representation of the People Act 1983 s 165(3); National Assembly for Wales (Representation of the People) Order 2007, SI 2007/236, art 117(4)(a). In the case of an election of the Mayor of London, a vote deemed in accordance with the Representation of the People Act 1983 s 165(3) to be thrown away is to be so deemed only to the extent that it is a vote given so as to indicate that the person who was under the incapacity is the voter's first or second preference from among the candidates: s 165(4) (added by the Greater London Authority Act 1999 s 17, Sch 3 paras 1, 36). As to the meaning of 'election of the Mayor of London' see PARA 11 note 4. As to elections for the return of an elected Mayor of London see PARA 199.

12 As to the meaning of 'registered political party' for these purposes see PARA 256.

13 National Assembly for Wales (Representation of the People) Order 2007, SI 2007/236, art 117(4)(b).

897. Avoidance of local authority referendum by reason of general corruption, bribery, treating or intimidation. Where, on a referendum petition[1], it is shown that corrupt[2] or illegal practices[3] or illegal payments, employments or hirings[4] committed in reference to the referendum[5] for the purpose of promoting or procuring a particular outcome in relation to the question asked in the referendum have so extensively prevailed that they may be reasonably supposed to have affected the result, the referendum, if that outcome was achieved, is void[6]. A referendum is not liable to be avoided, otherwise than under this provision, by reason of general corruption, bribery, treating or intimidation[7].

1   Provision is made for questioning a local authority referendum by applying and modifying the provision made for questioning an election under the Local Government Act 1972: see PARA

766. As to the meaning of 'election under the Local Government Act 1972' see PARA 11 note 2. As to the application of the Representation of the People Act 1983 Pt III (ss 120–186) to other polls see PARA 763.

2   As to corrupt practices see generally PARA 704 et seq.

3   As to illegal practices see generally PARA 671 et seq.

4   As to the offence of illegal payment, employment or hiring see PARA 682.

5   Ie a referendum held, in relation to Wales, under the Local Authorities (Conduct of Referendums) (Wales) Regulations 2008, SI 2008/1848, or, in relation to England, under the Local Authorities (Conduct of Referendums) (England) Regulations 2012, SI 2012/323. As to the meaning of 'referendum' for these purposes see PARA 574 note 2.

6   Representation of the People Act 1983 s 164(1); and see note 1. See also the cases cited in PARA 895.

7   Representation of the People Act 1983 s 164(2); and see note 1.

898. Other circumstances in which a fresh election or referendum can be ordered. An election may be overturned, and a new election held, following an irregularity in the way the original election was conducted[1], or following a prosecution for election offences[2] or where a successful candidate is found to lack one of the qualifications for office[3]. An election or referendum may be avoided at the conclusion of the trial of a petition questioning such an election or referendum on any of the grounds so allowed[4].

A fresh local government election can also be ordered in certain circumstances by the High Court if such an election fails either wholly or in part or becomes void[5] and in other circumstances by the returning officer[6] or, in the case of parish or community elections, by the district council[7]. Proceedings may be instituted[8] against any person, on the ground that he acted or claims to be entitled to act as a member of a local authority while disqualified for so acting, even though the time for the presentation of an election petition has passed and the validity of the election itself cannot be challenged by that procedure[9], and the office in which he acted or claims to be entitled to act may be declared vacant[10].

1   See PARA 667 et seq.

2   See PARA 699 et seq.

3   See PARA 224 et seq.

4   As to parliamentary election petitions see PARA 761; as to the questioning of an election under the Local Government Act 1972 see PARA 762; as to Welsh Assembly election petitions see PARA 764; and as to European parliamentary election petitions see PARA 765. Provision is made for questioning a local authority referendum by applying and modifying the provision made for questioning an election under the Local Government Act 1972: see PARA 766. As to the meaning of 'election under the Local Government Act 1972' see PARA 11 note 2.

5   See PARA 209. In 1955 an order was made under the Local Government Act 1933 s 72(2) (repealed) for the holding of a fresh election of the mayor of Hastings because due notice of the holding of the annual meeting at which he was elected had not been given. In a case decided under the Municipal Corporations Act 1882 s 87 (repealed), concerning an election of aldermen which had been so conducted as not to be a lawful election, it was held that the proper remedy was by mandamus and not by an election petition: *Re Barnes Corpn, ex p Hutter* [1933] 1 KB 668, DC.

6   See PARA 209. As to the procedure on the countermand or abandonment of the poll because of the death of a candidate see PARA 513 et seq.

7   See PARA 210. The district council can still intervene although the time has passed for the presentation of an election petition: see *R v Miles, ex p Cole* (1895) 64 LJQB 420, DC (poll demanded by unauthorised person).

8   Ie under the Local Government Act 1972 s 92 (see LOCAL GOVERNMENT vol 69 (2009) PARA 301).

9   *Bishop v Deakin* [1936] Ch 409, [1936] 1 All ER 255.

10   See the Local Government Act 1972 s 92(2)(a)(i), (4); and LOCAL GOVERNMENT vol 69 (2009) PARA 301.

(ii) Votes Struck Off

899. **Votes struck off following a scrutiny.** Votes may be struck off following a scrutiny of original election documents in circumstances where a petitioner has claimed that the successful candidate was not elected by a majority of lawful votes[1].

1   As to scrutiny see PARA 839 et seq.

(iii) Recount

900. **Recount following application.** A petition may ask for a recount of the votes given (either to the petitioner alone or to all candidates at the election) and the request may be granted on a successful application claiming grounds for believing that there has been a mistake on the part of the returning officer[1].

1   As to the application and procedure relating to a recount on application see PARAS 855–856.

(iv) Report of Corrupt or Illegal Practices

901. **Court's duty to report election candidate or agent personally guilty of a corrupt or illegal practice.** At the conclusion of the trial of a parliamentary election petition[1], or a Welsh Assembly election petition[2] or a local government election petition[3], the election court must in certain circumstances make a report[4], which must state whether any corrupt or illegal practice has or has not been proved to have been committed by or with the knowledge and consent of any candidate at the election, and the nature of the corrupt or illegal practice[5]. For the purposes of the provisions which impose civil incapacities on candidates personally guilty of such a practice[6], if it is reported that a corrupt practice, other than treating or undue influence, was committed with a candidate's knowledge and consent, he is to be treated as having been reported personally guilty of that corrupt practice[7]; and if it is reported that an illegal practice was committed with a candidate's knowledge and consent at a parliamentary election, he is to be treated as having been reported personally guilty of that illegal practice[8].

The report must also state whether any of the candidates has been guilty by his agents of any corrupt or illegal practice in reference to the election[9]. If, however, a candidate is reported guilty by his agents of treating, undue influence or any illegal practice, he is not to be treated, for the purposes of the provisions avoiding an election or imposing civil incapacities[10], as having been reported guilty by his agents of the offences mentioned in the report if the court also reports that the candidate has proved[11] to the court: (1) that no corrupt or illegal practice was committed at the election by the candidate or his election agent[12] and the offences mentioned in the report were committed contrary to the orders and without the sanction or connivance of the candidate or his election agent[13]; and (2) that the candidate and his election agent[14] took all reasonable means for preventing the commission of corrupt and illegal practices at the election[15]; and (3) that the offences mentioned in the report were of a trivial, unimportant and limited character[16]; and (4) that in all other respects the election was free from any corrupt or illegal practice on the part of the candidate and of his agents[17].

The general statutory provisions[18] as to the consequences of the report that a candidate was guilty by his agents of a corrupt or illegal practice have effect subject to the express provisions[19] relating to particular acts which are declared to be corrupt or illegal practices[20].

1   As to parliamentary election petitions see PARA 761.
2   Ie other than where the petition relates to a vacancy return (see PARA 215). As to Welsh Assembly election petitions see PARA 764.
3   As to the questioning of an election under the Local Government Act 1972 see PARA 762. As to the meaning of 'election under the Local Government Act 1972' see PARA 11 note 2. As to elections in the City of London see PARA 33. As to the application of the Representation of the People Act 1983 Pt III (ss 120–186) to other polls see PARA 763.
4   As to when a report is to be made, and as to the procedure, in relation to a parliamentary election petition, see PARA 859; in relation to a local government election petition, see PARA 862; and, in relation to a Welsh Assembly election petition, see PARA 864.
5   Representation of the People Act 1983 s 158(1); National Assembly for Wales (Representation of the People) Order 2007, SI 2007/236, art 108(1). There is no provision in relation to European parliamentary elections because corrupt and illegal practices relate only to personation and other voting offences in that context: see PARA 765. As to illegal practices (including those which are also offences) see PARA 671 et seq; and as to corrupt practices (including those which are also offences) see PARA 704 et seq.
6   See PARA 905 et seq.
7   Representation of the People Act 1983 s 158(2)(a); National Assembly for Wales (Representation of the People) Order 2007, SI 2007/236, art 108(2)(a).
8   Representation of the People Act 1983 s 158(2)(b); National Assembly for Wales (Representation of the People) Order 2007, SI 2007/236, art 108(2)(b).
9   Representation of the People Act 1983 s 158(3); National Assembly for Wales (Representation of the People) Order 2007, SI 2007/236, art 108(3). References in art 108 to a candidate and his agent, or as the case may be, his election agent apply as appropriate to a party list candidate and the agent or, as the case may be, the election agent of the registered political party in relation to the list submitted by that party and on which that party list candidate is included: art 108(4). As to the meaning of 'party list candidate' see PARA 230 note 23.
10 See PARAS 894, 905.
11 The onus of proof lies on the candidate: *Rochester Borough Case* (1892) 4 O'M & H 156.
12 As to the appointment of an election agent for parliamentary and local government elections see PARA 231; and as to the appointment of an election agent for elections to the National Assembly for Wales see PARA 235. In the case of an election where candidates are not required to have election agents (see PARA 231 note 3), the matters to be proved under head (1) in the text are that no corrupt or illegal practice was committed at the election by the candidate or with his knowledge or consent and the offences mentioned in the report were committed without the sanction or connivance of the candidate: Representation of the People Act 1983 s 158(3).
13 Representation of the People Act 1983 s 158(3)(a); National Assembly for Wales (Representation of the People) Order 2007, SI 2007/236, art 108(3)(a). For a case where the candidate was held to have failed to satisfy the court on this point see *Walsall Borough Case* (1892) as reported in Day 106 at 114.
14 In the case of an election where candidates are not required to have election agents (see PARA 231 note 3), the matters to be proved under head (2) in the text are that all reasonable means for preventing the commission of corrupt and illegal practices at the election were taken by and on behalf of the candidate: Representation of the People Act 1983 s 158(3).
15 Representation of the People Act 1983 s 158(3)(b); National Assembly for Wales (Representation of the People) Order 2007, SI 2007/236, art 108(3)(b). In *Rochester Borough Case* (1892) 4 O'M & H 156 and in *Southampton Borough Case* (1895) 5 O'M & H 17, the court refused relief to a candidate because he had not satisfied the court on this point.
16 Representation of the People Act 1983 s 158(3)(c); National Assembly for Wales (Representation of the People) Order 2007, SI 2007/236, art 108(3)(c). In *Southampton Borough Case* (1895) 5 O'M & H 17, the illegal payment of a voter's railway fare was held to come within these words.
17 Representation of the People Act 1983 s 158(3)(d); National Assembly for Wales (Representation of the People) Order 2007, SI 2007/236, art 108(3)(d). In *Southampton Borough Case* (1895) 5 O'M & H 17, it was held that if there were a joint candidature, as may be the case at a local government election, relief could be granted to one candidate and refused to the other. If the candidate fails to obtain relief under this provision, he can still apply for relief on the ground of inadvertence (see PARA 691): *Cork, Eastern Division Case* (1911) 6 O'M & H 318 at 359.
18 See PARA 905.
19 See eg PARAS 276, 279, 671 et seq.
20 Representation of the People Act 1983 ss 159(4), 160(7); National Assembly for Wales (Representation of the People) Order 2007, SI 2007/236, art 110(6).

902.   Court's duty to report justice of the peace found guilty of a corrupt practice.   Where a justice of the peace is reported by an election court to have been guilty of any corrupt practice in reference to an election or referendum[1], the court must report the case to the Lord Chancellor and the Lord Chief Justice with such evidence as may have been given of the corrupt practice[2].

1   Ie in reference to a parliamentary, Welsh Assembly, or local government election (or any other election under the Local Government Act 1972), or a referendum held, in relation to Wales, under the Local Authorities (Conduct of Referendums) (Wales) Regulations 2008, SI 2008/1848, or, in relation to England, under the Local Authorities (Conduct of Referendums) (England) Regulations 2012, SI 2012/323. As to the meaning of 'Assembly election' in the context of Welsh Assembly elections see PARA 3 note 2; as to the meaning of 'parliamentary election' see PARA 9; as to the meaning of 'local government election' see PARA 11; and as to the meaning of 'election under the Local Government Act 1972' see PARA 11 note 2. As to elections in the City of London see PARA 33. As to the meaning of 'referendum' for these purposes see PARA 574 note 2. There is no provision in relation to European parliamentary elections because no petition may be brought in that context on the grounds of the commission of corrupt or illegal practices, except on grounds of personation or other voting offences: see PARA 765. As to when such a report as is mentioned in the text is to be made, and as to the procedure in relation to a parliamentary election petition, see PARA 859; in relation to a local government election petition, see PARA 862; in relation to a Welsh Assembly election petition, see PARA 864; and, in relation to a local authority referendum petition, see PARA 867.
2   Representation of the People Act 1983 s 161 (amended by the Representation of the People Act 1985 ss 24, 28(1), Sch 4 para 53, Sch 5; and the Constitutional Reform Act 2005 s 15(1), Sch 4 para 149); National Assembly for Wales (Representation of the People) Order 2007, SI 2007/236, art 113. The Representation of the People Act 1983 s 161 has been applied and modified for the purposes of local authority referendums, in relation to Wales, by the Local Authorities (Conduct of Referendums) (Wales) Regulations 2008, SI 2008/1848, Sch 5 Table, and, in relation to England, by the Local Authorities (Conduct of Referendums) (England) Regulations 2012, SI 2012/323, Sch 6 Table. As to the application of the Representation of the People Act 1983 Pt III (ss 120–186) to other polls see PARA 763.

903.   Court's duty to report barrister, solicitor, etc found guilty of a corrupt practice.   Where a barrister, advocate, solicitor, authorised person[1] or any person belonging to any profession the admission to which is regulated by law is reported by an election court to have been guilty of any corrupt practice in reference to an election or referendum[2], the court must bring the matter before the Inn of Court, Faculty of Advocates, High Court, tribunal or other body having power to take cognisance of any misconduct of the person in his profession, and the Inn of Court, Faculty of Advocates, High Court, tribunal or other body may deal with him as if the corrupt practice were misconduct by him in his profession[3].

1   'Authorised person' means a person (other than a barrister or solicitor) who, for the purposes of the Legal Services Act 2007, is an authorised person in relation to an activity which constitutes a reserved legal activity within the meaning of that Act (see LEGAL PROFESSIONS vol 65 (2008) PARA 512): Representation of the People Act 1983 s 156(5A) (added by the Legal Services Act 2007 Sch 21 paras 48, 50(b)).
2   Ie in reference to a parliamentary, Welsh Assembly, or local government election (or any other election under the Local Government Act 1972), or a referendum held, in relation to Wales, under the Local Authorities (Conduct of Referendums) (Wales) Regulations 2008, SI 2008/1848, or, in relation to England, under the Local Authorities (Conduct of Referendums) (England) Regulations 2012, SI 2012/323. As to the meaning of 'Assembly election' in the context of Welsh Assembly elections see PARA 3 note 2; as to the meaning of 'parliamentary election' see PARA 9; as to the meaning of 'local government election' see PARA 11; and as to the meaning of 'election under the Local Government Act 1972' see PARA 11 note 2. As to elections in the City of London see PARA 33. As to the meaning of 'referendum' for these purposes see PARA 574 note 2. There is no provision in relation to European parliamentary elections because no petition may be brought in that context on the grounds of the commission of corrupt or illegal practices, except on grounds of personation or other voting offences: see PARA 765. As to when such a

report as is mentioned in the text is to be made, and as to the procedure in relation to a parliamentary election petition, see PARA 859; in relation to a local government election petition, see PARA 862; in relation to a Welsh Assembly election petition, see PARA 864; and, in relation to a local authority referendum petition, see PARA 867.

3 Representation of the People Act 1983 s 162 (amended by the Representation of the People Act 1985 ss 24, 28(1), Sch 4 para 54, Sch 5; and the Legal Services Act 2007 Sch 21 para 51); National Assembly for Wales (Representation of the People) Order 2007, SI 2007/236, art 114 (amended by SI 2010/2931). The Representation of the People Act 1983 s 162 has been applied and modified for the purposes of local authority referendums, in relation to Wales, by the Local Authorities (Conduct of Referendums) (Wales) Regulations 2008, SI 2008/1848, Sch 5 Table, and, in relation to England, by the Local Authorities (Conduct of Referendums) (England) Regulations 2012, SI 2012/323, Sch 6 Table. As to the application of the Representation of the People Act 1983 Pt III (ss 120–186) to other polls see PARA 763.

904.   Court's duty to report conviction of certain offences to Electoral Commission.   The court by or before which a person is convicted of an offence under the Political Parties, Elections and Referendums Act 2000[1] or an offence committed in connection with a relevant election[2] must notify the Electoral Commission[3] of that person's conviction as soon as is practicable[4].

1 Political Parties, Elections and Referendums Act 2000 s 154(a). As to offences generally see PARA 732 et seq.
2 Political Parties, Elections and Referendums Act 2000 s 154(b). The text refers to a relevant election within the meaning of Pt II (ss 22–40) (see PARA 253).
3 As to the Electoral Commission see PARA 34 et seq.
4 Political Parties, Elections and Referendums Act 2000 s 154.

(v) Personal Incapacities

905.   Personal incapacity incurred on proof of corrupt or illegal voting practices at a parliamentary, local government election or local authority referendum.   A candidate or other person reported by an election court personally guilty of a corrupt or illegal practice[1], or a person who is convicted of a corrupt or illegal practice[2], in relation to a parliamentary or local government election[3] or local authority referendum[4], is during the relevant period[5] incapable[6]: (1) of being registered as an elector or voting[7] at any parliamentary election in the United Kingdom[8] or at any local government election in Great Britain or at any referendum[9]; or (2) of being elected to the House of Commons[10]; or (3) of holding any elective office[11].

If a candidate or other person so reported is already elected to a seat in the House of Commons, or holds any such office, he must vacate the seat or office as from the date of the report[12].

If a person so convicted is already elected to a seat in the House of Commons or holds any such office, he must vacate the seat or office[13] in question at the appropriate time for these purposes[14], namely the end of the period which is the period prescribed by law within which notice of appeal may be given, or an application for leave to appeal may be made, by him in respect of the conviction[15] or if (at any time within that period) that period is extended the end of the period as so extended or the end of the period of three months beginning with the date of the conviction, whichever is the earlier[16]. If, before the appropriate time, notice of appeal is given, or an application for leave to appeal is made, by such a person in respect of the conviction, he must vacate the seat or office in question at the end of the period of three months beginning with the date of the conviction unless[17]: (a) such an appeal is dismissed or abandoned at any earlier time (in which case he must vacate the seat or office at that time)[18]; or

(b) at any time within that period of three months the court determines on such an appeal that the conviction should not be upheld (in which case the seat or office is not to be vacated by him)[19]. Where such a person vacates a seat or office in this way, no subsequent determination of a court that his conviction should not be upheld entitles him to resume the seat or office[20].

If a person convicted of a corrupt or illegal practice has already been elected to a seat in the House of Commons or to any elective office, he must, in addition to being subject to the incapacities mentioned in heads (1) to (3) above, be suspended from performing any of his functions as a member of Parliament, or (as the case may be) any of the functions of that office, during the period of suspension[21], being the period beginning with the date of the conviction and ending with the date on which the seat or office is vacated or, where head (b) above applies, the date on which the court determines that the conviction should not be upheld[22].

Any incapacities or other requirements applying to a person who is convicted of a corrupt or illegal practice apply in addition to any other statutory punishment that is imposed upon conviction, but they are subject to the court's power to mitigate or remit them in cases where such power is given to the court[23].

1   As to illegal practices (including those which are also offences) see PARA 671 et seq; and as to corrupt practices (including those which are also offences) see PARA 704 et seq. As to the circumstances in which a candidate is treated as having been reported personally guilty of such practices see PARA 901. The incapacity does not apply where the person is guilty by an agent: *Morris v Shrewsbury Town Clerk* [1909] 1 KB 342, DC.

2   As to the prosecution of corrupt practices see PARA 887; and as to the prosecution of illegal practices see PARA 888.

3   As to the meaning of 'parliamentary election' see PARA 9; and as to the meaning of 'local government election' see PARA 11. As to elections in the City of London see PARA 33.

4   As to the meaning of 'referendum' for these purposes see PARA 574 note 2. Provision is made for questioning a local authority referendum by applying and modifying the provision made for questioning an election under the Local Government Act 1972: see PARA 766. The Representation of the People Act 1983 s 173(1)(a)(i), (2), (3) has been applied and modified for the purposes of local authority referendums, in relation to Wales, by the Local Authorities (Conduct of Referendums) (Wales) Regulations 2008, SI 2008/1848, Sch 4 Table 1, and, in relation to England, by the Local Authorities (Conduct of Referendums) (England) Regulations 2012, SI 2012/323, Sch 4 Table 1. As to the application of the Representation of the People Act 1983 Pt III (ss 120–186) to other polls see PARA 763.

5   For these purposes, the relevant period is the period beginning with the date of the report or the date of the conviction (as the case may be) and ending, in the case of a person reported personally guilty or convicted (as the case may be) of a corrupt practice, five years after that date or, in the case of a person reported personally guilty or convicted (as the case may be) of an illegal practice, three years after that date: Representation of the People Act 1983 s 160(5) (substituted by the Political Parties, Elections and Referendums Act 2000 s 137, Sch 17 paras 1, 8); Representation of the People Act 1983 s 173(3) (s 173 substituted by the Political Parties, Elections and Referendums Act 2000 s 136); and see note 4. However, if at any time within that period of five or three years a court determines on an appeal by that person against such a conviction that it should not be upheld, the relevant period ends at that time instead: Representation of the People Act 1983 s 173(3) (as so substituted).

6   Ie subject to the Representation of the People Act 1983 s 174 (mitigation and remission of incapacities: see PARA 910).

7   As to the striking off of votes given by persons under an incapacity see PARA 841.

8   As to the meaning of 'United Kingdom' see PARA 1 note 1.

9   Representation of the People Act 1983 s 160(4)(a)(i) (s 160(4) substituted by the Political Parties, Elections and Referendums Act 2000 Sch 17 paras 1, 8); Representation of the People Act 1983 s 173(1)(a)(i) (as substituted: see note 5); and see note 4. As to the meaning of 'Great Britain' see PARA 1 note 1. The incapacity imposed under head (1) in the text applies only to a candidate or person reported personally guilty or convicted (as the case may be) of a corrupt practice under s 60 (see PARA 730) or s 62A (see PARA 731) or an illegal practice under s 61 (see

PARA 700): s 160(4A) (added by the Political Parties, Elections and Referendums Act 2000 Sch 17 paras 1, 8; and amended by SI 2007/931); Representation of the People Act 1983 s 173(2) (as substituted (see note 5); and amended by SI 2007/931); and see note 4.

10 Representation of the People Act 1983 ss 160(4)(a)(ii), 173(1)(a)(ii) (both as substituted: see note 5).

11 Representation of the People Act 1983 ss 160(4)(a)(iii), 173(1)(a)(iii) (both as substituted: see note 5).

12 Representation of the People Act 1983 s 160(4)(b) (as substituted: see note 5).

13 Representation of the People Act 1983 s 173(1)(b) (as substituted: see note 5).

14 Representation of the People Act 1983 s 173(4) (as substituted: see note 5).

15 Representation of the People Act 1983 s 173(4)(a) (as substituted: see note 5).

16 Representation of the People Act 1983 s 173(4)(b) (as substituted: see note 5).

17 Representation of the People Act 1983 s 173(5) (as substituted: see note 5).

18 Representation of the People Act 1983 s 173(5)(a) (as substituted: see note 5).

19 Representation of the People Act 1983 s 173(5)(b) (as substituted: see note 5). As to a consideration of the situation that applied before s 173 was substituted see *A-G v Jones* [2000] QB 66, [1999] 3 All ER 436, in which the court, explaining the statutory regime, held that vacation of the seat is mere machinery consequent on the candidate's incapacity which is consequent on the conviction and that, if the conviction is overturned, the candidate's capacity to sit is restored and the seat, if not already filled by an election taking place between conviction and appeal, ceases to be vacant.

20 Representation of the People Act 1983 s 173(6) (as substituted: see note 5).

21 Representation of the People Act 1983 s 173(7) (as substituted: see note 5).

22 Representation of the People Act 1983 s 173(8) (as substituted: see note 5).

23 Representation of the People Act 1983 s 173(9) (as substituted: see note 5). As to the court's power to mitigate or remit see s 174; and PARA 910.

906. Disqualification from being the Mayor of London for failure to make returns as to election expenses. If, in the case of any candidate at an election of the Mayor of London[1], the return[2] and declarations as to election expenses[3] are not delivered before the expiry of the time limited for the purpose, the candidate must, as respects that election, be disqualified from being elected or being the Mayor of London[4].

Any application[5] by such a candidate for relief in respect of a failure to deliver the return and declarations as to election expenses must be made within the period of six weeks following the day on which the time limited for their delivery expires[6].

The disqualification from being elected or being the Mayor of London does not take effect unless or until the period specified for making an application for relief expires without such an application having been made[7] or, if such an application is made, unless or until the application is finally disposed of without relief being granted[8] or is abandoned or fails by reason of non-prosecution[9].

These provisions have been applied and modified for the purposes of local authority mayoral elections[10].

1 As to the meaning of 'election of the Mayor of London' for these purposes see PARA 11 note 4. As to elections for the return of an elected Mayor of London see PARA 199.

2 As to the meaning of 'return as to election expenses' see PARA 281 note 1.

3 As to the meaning of 'declaration as to election expenses' see PARA 281 note 3.

4 Representation of the People Act 1983 s 85A(1) (s 85A added by the Greater London Authority Act 1999 s 17, Sch 3 paras 1, 26). As to the application of the Representation of the People Act 1983 Pt III (ss 120–186) to other polls see PARA 763.

5 Ie under the Representation of the People Act 1983 s 86 (see PARA 688).

6 Representation of the People Act 1983 s 85A(2) (as added: see note 4).

7 Representation of the People Act 1983 s 85A(3)(a) (as added: see note 4).

8 Representation of the People Act 1983 s 85A(3)(b)(i) (as added: see note 4).

9 Representation of the People Act 1983 s 85A(3)(b)(ii) (as added: see note 4).

10 See the Local Authorities (Mayoral Elections) (England and Wales) Regulations 2007, SI 2007/1024, reg 3(2)–(5), Sch 2 Table 1.

907.   Personal incapacity incurred on proof of corrupt or illegal voting practices at a Welsh Assembly election.   A candidate or other person reported by an election court personally guilty of a corrupt practice[1] in relation to a Welsh Assembly election[2] is for five years from the date of the report, and a person reported by an election court personally guilty of an illegal practice[3] is for three years from the date of the report, incapable[4]: (1) of being registered as an elector or voting at any Assembly election, election to the House of Commons, election to the European Parliament[5] or local government election[6]; or (2) of being elected to the Assembly, the House of Commons, the European Parliament or as a member of a local authority[7]. If already elected to a seat in the Assembly or holding another elective office, such a candidate or other person so reported must from that date vacate the seat or office[8].

The incapacities imposed by head (1) above apply only to a candidate or other person reported personally guilty of a corrupt[9] or illegal[10] practice[11]. The provisions as to the consequences of the report that a candidate was guilty by his agents of a corrupt or illegal practice have effect subject to the express provisions relating to particular acts which are declared to be corrupt or illegal practices[12].

If a person is reported by an election court personally guilty of a corrupt or illegal practice under the Representation of the People Act 1983, in addition to being subject to the incapacities set out therein[13], he is for five years (in the case of corrupt practice) or for three years (in the case of illegal practice) from the date of that report incapable of being elected to and sitting in the Assembly, and if already elected to the Assembly, he must from that date vacate the seat[14].

A person convicted of a corrupt or illegal practice[15] is also subject to the incapacities set out in heads (1) and (2) above[16]. In addition to being subject to these incapacities, a person convicted of a corrupt or illegal practice who has already been elected to a seat in the Assembly or is holding an elected office must vacate the seat or office in question[17]. The incapacities imposed by head (1) above apply only to a candidate or other person reported personally guilty of a corrupt or illegal practice[18]. These incapacities are in addition to any other statutory punishment[19], but are subject to the court's power to mitigate or remit them in cases where such power is given to the court[20].

A person convicted of a corrupt or illegal practice under the Representation of the People Act 1983 is subject to like incapacities[21] as if at the date of the conviction he had been reported personally guilty of that corrupt or illegal practice[22].

A person convicted of a corrupt or illegal practice under the European parliamentary elections rules[23], in addition to the incapacities set out in those rules, is for five years (in the case of corrupt practice) or for three years (in the case of illegal practice) incapable of being elected to or sitting in the Assembly, and if already elected to the Assembly, he must vacate the seat as from the date of conviction[24].

1   As to corrupt practices see generally PARA 704 et seq. As to the circumstances in which a candidate is treated as having been reported personally guilty of such practices see PARA 901.
2   As to the meaning of 'Assembly election' see PARA 3 note 2.
3   As to illegal practices see generally PARA 671 et seq. As to the circumstances in which a candidate is treated as having been reported personally guilty of such practices see PARA 901.
4   National Assembly for Wales (Representation of the People) Order 2007, SI 2007/236, art 110(3), (5). As to savings and transitional provisions as to incapacities see art 149.
5   As to European parliamentary elections see PARA 217 et seq.

6 National Assembly for Wales (Representation of the People) Order 2007, SI 2007/236, art 110(3)(a). The incapacities imposed by head (1) in the text apply only to a candidate or other person reported personally guilty of a corrupt practice in relation to personation (ie under art 30: see PARA 730): art 110(4).

7 National Assembly for Wales (Representation of the People) Order 2007, SI 2007/236, art 110(3)(b).

8 National Assembly for Wales (Representation of the People) Order 2007, SI 2007/236, art 110(3)(b).

9 Ie under the National Assembly for Wales (Representation of the People) Order 2007, SI 2007/236, art 14(11) (see PARA 731) or art 30 see PARA 730).

10 Ie under the National Assembly for Wales (Representation of the People) Order 2007, SI 2007/236, art 31 (see PARA 700).

11 National Assembly for Wales (Representation of the People) Order 2007, SI 2007/236, art 110(4).

12 National Assembly for Wales (Representation of the People) Order 2007, SI 2007/236, art 110(6).

13 Ie subject to the incapacities set out in the Representation of the People Act 1983 s 160 (see PARA 905).

14 National Assembly for Wales (Representation of the People) Order 2007, SI 2007/236, art 111. This provision is subject to the provisions of the Representation of the People Act 1983 s 174 (mitigation and remission of incapacities: see PARA 910): National Assembly for Wales (Representation of the People) Order 2007, SI 2007/236, art 111. A person reported by an election court personally guilty of a corrupt or illegal practice under the European Parliamentary Elections Regulations 2004, SI 2004/293, in addition to being subject to the incapacities set out in reg 107 (see PARA 909), for five years (in the case of corrupt practice) or for three years (in the case of illegal practice), from the date of that report is to be incapable of being elected to and sitting in the Assembly and, if already elected to the Assembly, he must from that date vacate the seat: National Assembly for Wales (Representation of the People) Order 2007, SI 2007/236, art 112.

15 As to the prosecution of corrupt and illegal practices see PARAS 887, 888.

16 See the National Assembly for Wales (Representation of the People) Order 2007, SI 2007/236, art 123(1).

17 National Assembly for Wales (Representation of the People) Order 2007, SI 2007/236, art 123(2). The person must vacate the seat or office in question at the appropriate time for the purposes of this section, namely: (1) the end of the period which is the period prescribed by law within which notice of appeal may be given, or an application for leave to appeal may be made, by him in respect of the conviction; or (2) if at any time within that period that period is extended, the end of the period as so extended or the end of the period of three months beginning with the date of the conviction, whichever is the earlier: art 123(5). If, before the appropriate time mentioned in art 123(5), notice of appeal is given, or an application for leave to appeal is made, by such a person in respect of the conviction, he must vacate the seat or office in question at the end of the period of three months beginning with the date of conviction unless: (a) such an appeal is dismissed or abandoned at any earlier time (in which case he must vacate the seat or office at that time); or (b) at any time within that period of three months the court determines on such an appeal that the conviction should not be upheld (in which case the seat or office is not to be vacated by him): art 123(6). Where such a person vacates a seat or office in accordance with art 123(5) or (6), no subsequent determination of a court that his conviction should not be upheld entitles him to resume his seat or office: art 123(7).

18 National Assembly for Wales (Representation of the People) Order 2007, SI 2007/236, art 123(3).

19 Ie any punishment imposed under the National Assembly for Wales (Representation of the People) Order 2007, SI 2007/236, art 120 (see PARA 887) or art 121 (see PARA 888).

20 National Assembly for Wales (Representation of the People) Order 2007, SI 2007/236, art 123(10). The text refers to the mitigation and remission of incapacities under art 126 (see PARA 910).

21 Ie the incapacities imposed by the National Assembly for Wales (Representation of the People) Order 2007, SI 2007/236, art 111 (see the text and notes 13–14).

22 National Assembly for Wales (Representation of the People) Order 2007, SI 2007/236, art 124(1). The Representation of the People Act 1983 s 174 applies to any incapacity imposed under the National Assembly for Wales (Representation of the People) Order 2007, SI 2007/236, art 124 as if the incapacity was imposed under the Representation of the People Act 1983 s 160 (see PARA 905): National Assembly for Wales (Representation of the People) Order 2007, SI 2007/236, art 124(2).

23   As to the meaning of 'European parliamentary elections rules' see PARA 383; definition applied by virtue of the Interpretation Act 1978 s 17(2).

24   National Assembly for Wales (Representation of the People) Order 2007, SI 2007/236, arts 123(4), 125.

908.   Effect of person holding a licence or certificate under the Licensing Act 2003 reported as being personally guilty of corrupt or illegal practices. If it appears to an election court[1] that a person holding a licence or certificate under the Licensing Act 2003[2] has knowingly permitted any bribery or treating in relation to any parliamentary, European parliamentary or Assembly election to take place upon his licensed premises[3], the court must direct the conviction to be entered in the proper register of licences[4]. The entry of the report in that register must be taken into consideration by the licensing authority in determining whether it will or will not grant a renewal of the licence or certificate of the person reported, and it may be a ground, if the authority thinks fit, for refusing renewal[5].

1   As to the meaning of 'election court' for these purposes see PARA 769.
2   See LICENSING AND GAMBLING vol 67 (2008) PARA 26 et seq.
3   See the Representation of the People Act 1983 s 168(7); the European Parliamentary Elections Regulations 2004, SI 2004/293, reg 109(2); and the National Assembly for Wales (Representation of the People) Order 2007, SI 2007/236, art 115(1). As to the meaning of 'Assembly election' see PARA 3 note 2; and as to the meaning of 'parliamentary election' see PARA 9. As to European parliamentary elections see PARA 217 et seq. As to bribery see PARA 709 et seq; and as to treating see PARA 721 et seq. As to the Court's duty to report persons personally guilty of a corrupt or illegal practice see PARA 901.
     The Representation of the People Act 1983 s 168 is applied and modified for the purposes of local authority referendums, subject to the modifications specified, in relation to Wales, by the Local Authorities (Conduct of Referendums) (Wales) Regulations 2008, SI 2008/1848, reg 8(2), Sch 4 Table 1, and, in relation to England, by the Local Authorities (Conduct of Referendums) (England) Regulations 2012, SI 2012/323, regs 8(2), 11–13, Sch 4 Table 1: see PARA 15 note 2. As to the meaning of 'referendum' see PARA 574 note 2.
4   Representation of the People Act 1983 s 168(7)(a); European Parliamentary Elections Regulations 2004, SI 2004/293, reg 109(2)(a); National Assembly for Wales (Representation of the People) Order 2007, SI 2007/236, art 115(1)(b). In the case of an Assembly election, the court must:
    (1)   after affording the person such rights are as conferred on those about to be reported under art 110(1) (see PARA 864), report the fact that the person has knowingly permitted any bribery or treating in relation to an Assembly election to take place upon his licensed premises (see art 115(1)(a)); and
    (2)   bring the report before the licensing authority from whom, or on whose certificate, that person obtained his licence, and the licensing authority must cause the report to be entered in the proper register of licences (art 115(1)(b)).
     As to the register of operating licences maintained by the Gambling Commission see LICENSING AND GAMBLING vol 67 (2008) PARA 380.
5   Representation of the People Act 1983 s 168(7)(b); European Parliamentary Elections Regulations 2004, SI 2004/293, reg 109(2)(b); National Assembly for Wales (Representation of the People) Order 2007, SI 2007/236, art 115(2).

909.   Personal incapacity incurred on conviction of corrupt or illegal voting practices at a European parliamentary election. A candidate or other person convicted of a corrupt or illegal practice[1], in relation to a European parliamentary election[2], is during the relevant period[3] incapable[4]: (1) of being registered as an elector or voting[5] at any parliamentary[6] or European parliamentary election in the United Kingdom[7] or at any local government election[8] in Great Britain[9]; or (2) of being elected to the House of Commons or the European Parliament[10]; or (3) of holding any elective office[11].

If a person so convicted is already elected to a seat in the House of Commons or the European Parliament or if he holds any such office, he must vacate the seat or office as from the date of the conviction[12] or at the appropriate time for these purposes[13], being the end of the period which is the period prescribed by law within which notice of appeal may be given or an application for leave to appeal may be made by him in respect of the conviction[14] or, if (at any time within that period) that period is extended, the end of the period as so extended or the end of the period of three months beginning with the date of the conviction[15], whichever is the earlier[16]. If, before the appropriate time, notice of appeal is given or an application for leave to appeal is made by such a person in respect of the conviction, he must vacate the seat or office in question at the end of the period of three months beginning with the date of the conviction unless[17]: (a) such an appeal is dismissed or abandoned at any earlier time (in which case he must vacate the seat or office at that time)[18]; or (b) at any time within that period of three months the court determines on such an appeal that the conviction should not be upheld (in which case the seat or office is not to be vacated by him)[19]. Where such a person vacates a seat or office in this way, no subsequent determination of a court that his conviction should not be upheld entitles him to resume the seat or office[20].

If a person convicted of a corrupt or illegal practice has already been elected to a seat in the House of Commons or the European Parliament or to any elective office, he must, in addition to being subject to the incapacities mentioned in heads (1) to (3) above, be suspended from performing any of his functions as a member of Parliament or member of the European Parliament ('MEP'), or (as the case may be) any of the functions of that office, during the period of suspension[21], being the period beginning with the date of the conviction and ending with the date on which the seat or office is vacated or, where head (b) above applies, the date on which the court determines that the conviction should not be upheld[22].

Any incapacities or other requirements applying to a person who is convicted of a corrupt or illegal practice apply in addition to any other statutory punishment that is imposed upon conviction[23], but they are subject to the court's power to mitigate or remit them in cases where such power is given to the court[24].

1   As to the prosecution of corrupt practices see PARA 887; and as to the prosecution of illegal practices see PARA 888.

2   As to European parliamentary elections see PARA 217 et seq.

3   For these purposes, the relevant period is the period beginning with the date of the conviction and ending, in the case of a person convicted of a corrupt practice, five years after that date or, in the case of a person convicted of an illegal practice, three years after that date, except that if (at any time within that period of five or three years) a court determines on an appeal by that person against the conviction that it should not be upheld, the relevant period ends at that time instead: European Parliamentary Elections Regulations 2004, SI 2004/293, reg 107(3).

4   Ie subject to the European Parliamentary Elections Regulations 2004, SI 2004/293, reg 112 (mitigation and remission of incapacities: see PARA 910).

5   As to the striking off of votes given by persons under incapacity see PARA 841.

6   As to the meaning of 'parliamentary election' see PARA 9.

7   As to the meaning of 'United Kingdom' see PARA 1 note 1.

8   As to the meaning of 'local government election' see PARA 11.

9   European Parliamentary Elections Regulations 2004, SI 2004/293, reg 107(1)(a)(i). As to the meaning of 'Great Britain' see PARA 1 note 1. The incapacity imposed under head (1) in the text applies only to a candidate or person convicted of a corrupt practice under reg 23 (personation: see PARA 730) or of an illegal practice under reg 24 (other voting offences: see PARA 700): reg 107(2). As to the incapacity imposed in relation to European parliamentary elections held in

the combined region (see PARA 77) preventing a person from being registered as a European parliamentary elector or from voting at any European parliamentary election in Gibraltar see reg 107(1)(a)(ii).

10 European Parliamentary Elections Regulations 2004, SI 2004/293, reg 107(1)(a)(iii).
11 European Parliamentary Elections Regulations 2004, SI 2004/293, reg 107(1)(a)(iv).
12 European Parliamentary Elections Regulations 2004, SI 2004/293, reg 107(1)(b).
13 European Parliamentary Elections Regulations 2004, SI 2004/293, reg 107(4).
14 European Parliamentary Elections Regulations 2004, SI 2004/293, reg 107(4)(a).
15 European Parliamentary Elections Regulations 2004, SI 2004/293, reg 107(4)(b).
16 European Parliamentary Elections Regulations 2004, SI 2004/293, reg 107(4).
17 European Parliamentary Elections Regulations 2004, SI 2004/293, reg 107(5).
18 European Parliamentary Elections Regulations 2004, SI 2004/293, reg 107(5)(a).
19 European Parliamentary Elections Regulations 2004, SI 2004/293, reg 107(5)(b).
20 European Parliamentary Elections Regulations 2004, SI 2004/293, reg 107(6).
21 European Parliamentary Elections Regulations 2004, SI 2004/293, reg 107(7).
22 European Parliamentary Elections Regulations 2004, SI 2004/293, reg 107(8).
23 Ie punishment imposed under the European Parliamentary Elections Regulations 2004, SI 2004/293, reg 109 (punishment of corrupt practices: see PARA 887) or reg 110 (punishment of illegal practices: see PARA 888).
24 European Parliamentary Elections Regulations 2004, SI 2004/293, reg 107(9). The text refers to the court's power under reg 112 (mitigation and remission of incapacities: see PARA 910).

910. Mitigation and remission of incapacities imposed on proof of corrupt or illegal voting practices at elections. Where any person is subject to any incapacity by virtue of the report of an election court[1] and on a prosecution he or some other person in respect of whose acts the incapacity was imposed is acquitted of any of the matters in respect of which the incapacity was imposed, the court may order that the incapacity is thenceforth to cease so far as it is imposed in respect of those matters[2]. Where on a prosecution any person who is subject to any such incapacity is convicted of any such matters, no further incapacity is to be taken to be imposed by reason of the conviction, and the court has the like power, if any, to mitigate or remit for the future certain incapacities[3] imposed by virtue of a report of an election court as if they had been imposed by reason of the conviction[4]. A court exercising any of these powers must make an order declaring how far, if at all, the incapacities imposed by virtue of the report remain unaffected by virtue of the exercise of the power, and that order is conclusive for all purposes[5].

Where a person convicted of a corrupt or illegal practice is subsequently reported by an election court to have been guilty of such a practice, no further incapacity is to be imposed on him[6], by reason of the report[7].

Where any person is subject to an incapacity by virtue of a conviction[8] or (alternatively, in relation to a parliamentary, local government or Welsh Assembly election or local authority referendum) by virtue of the report of an election court, and any witness who gave evidence against him on the proceeding for the conviction or report (as the case may be) is convicted of perjury in respect of that evidence, the incapacitated person may apply to the High Court, and the court, if satisfied that the conviction or report (as the case may be) so far as respects that person was based on perjury, may order that the incapacity is thenceforth to cease[9].

1 Ie by virtue of reports following the trial of a parliamentary or local election petition (see PARA 905) or by virtue of reports following the trial of a Welsh Assembly election petition (see PARA 907). As to the meaning of 'Assembly election' in the context of Welsh Assembly elections see PARA 3 note 2; as to the meaning of 'parliamentary election' see PARA 9; and as to the meaning of 'local government election' see PARA 11. As to elections in the City of London see PARA 33. There is no provision in relation to the trial of a European parliamentary election petition because in that context corrupt and illegal practices relate only to personation and other voting

offences: see PARA 765; and cf, in relation to prosecutions pursuant to personation and other voting offences, the text and notes 8–9. Provision is made for questioning a local authority referendum by applying and modifying the provision made for questioning an election under the Local Government Act 1972: see PARA 766. As to the meaning of 'election under the Local Government Act 1972' see PARA 11 note 2. The Representation of the People Act 1983 s 174 has been applied and modified for the purposes of local authority referendums, in relation to Wales, by the Local Authorities (Conduct of Referendums) (Wales) Regulations 2008, SI 2008/1848, Sch 4 Table 1, and, in relation to England, by the Local Authorities (Conduct of Referendums) (England) Regulations 2012, SI 2012/323, Sch 4 Table 1. As to the meaning of 'referendum' for these purposes see PARA 574 note 2. As to the application of the Representation of the People Act 1983 Pt III (ss 120–186) to other polls see PARA 763.

2 Representation of the People Act 1983 s 174(1); National Assembly for Wales (Representation of the People) Order 2007, SI 2007/236, art 126(1); and see note 1.

3 Ie the incapacities imposed, in relation to a parliamentary or local election, by the Representation of the People Act 1983 s 160 (including that provision as applied and modified for the purposes of local authority referendums: see note 1) (see PARA 905) and, in relation to a Welsh Assembly election, by the National Assembly for Wales (Representation of the People) Order 2007, SI 2007/236, art 110 (see PARA 907).

4 Representation of the People Act 1983 s 174(2); National Assembly for Wales (Representation of the People) Order 2007, SI 2007/236, art 126(2); and see note 1.

5 Representation of the People Act 1983 s 174(3); National Assembly for Wales (Representation of the People) Order 2007, SI 2007/236, art 126(3); and see note 1.

6 Ie imposed, in relation to a parliamentary or local election, under the Representation of the People Act 1983 s 160 (see PARA 905) and, in relation to a Welsh Assembly election, under the National Assembly for Wales (Representation of the People) Order 2007, SI 2007/236, art 110 (see PARA 907).

7 Representation of the People Act 1983 s 174(4); National Assembly for Wales (Representation of the People) Order 2007, SI 2007/236, art 126(4); and see note 1.

8 Ie including, in this context, convictions following the prosecution of personation and other voting offences at a European parliamentary election (see note 1).

9 Representation of the People Act 1983 s 174(5); European Parliamentary Elections Regulations 2004, SI 2004/293, reg 112(1); National Assembly for Wales (Representation of the People) Order 2007, SI 2007/236, art 126(5); and see note 1. As to the application of the provision set out in the text in relation to European parliamentary elections held in the combined region (see PARA 77) see the European Parliamentary Elections Regulations 2004, SI 2004/293, reg 112(2).

INDEX

Elections and Referendums

BALLOT PAPER—*continued*
  replacement ballot paper, 404
  scrutiny. *See* SCRUTINY
  sealing of—
    completion of counting, on, 495
    electronic record, 495n[4]
    poll consequent on parish meeting, on
      close of, 495
    rejected papers, 495
  security measures associated with, 387
  spoilt, replacing, 404
  tampering with, offence, 738
  tendered ballot paper, 403
  transfer following election—
    European parliamentary election, 501
    local government election, 498
    parliamentary election, 496
    poll consequent on parish meeting,
      498
    Welsh Assembly election, 499
  voting procedure, 399
BARRISTER
  corrupt or illegal practice, court's duty
    to report where guilty of, 903
  member of House of Commons,
    restriction on appearance at trial,
    822
BILL OF RIGHTS
  parliamentary elections, and, 5
BLIND VOTER. *See* DISABLED VOTER
BOUNDARY COMMISSION
  electoral records, right to be supplied
    with, 184
  local government commissions—
    England. *See* LOCAL GOVERNMENT
      BOUNDARY COMMISSION FOR
      ENGLAND
    Wales. *See* LOCAL DEMOCRACY AND
      BOUNDARY COMMISSION FOR
      WALES
  parliamentary commissions—
    assistant commissioners, 69
    constitution, 69
    expenses, 69
    generally, 68
    joint meetings, 70n[4]
    permanent nature of, 68
    procedure, 70
    proposals, publicity and
      consultation, 82
    purpose, 68
    reports, 78
    review of constituency boundaries.
      See under ELECTORAL
      BOUNDARIES (review)
  procedure, 70

BRIBERY
  meaning, 709
  avoidance of election, 895
  charitable gift constituting, 714
  consideration for bribe, 710
  corrupt motive, 720
  corrupt practice, as, 709
  examples, 715
  excessive payments, 710
  giving money, 709n[5]
  legitimate expenses not constituting,
    718
  loans, 710
  local authority referendum, avoidance
    of, 897
  offer to bribe, 710, 720
  outstanding account, payment of, 713
  past services, payment for, 713
  payments for expenditure in bribes, 717
  procuring an office, 709n[6]
  proof of, 720
  receiving bribe, offence, 719
  rent, agreement to forgo, 715
  striking off of vote, 842
  time of bribe, 716
  time off work to allow for voting, 712
  travelling expenses, payment of, 711
  treating distinguished, 710
  vote, after, 716
BRITISH BROADCASTING
    CORPORATION
  Electoral Commission's views, need to
    consider, 59
BRITISH LIBRARY
  electoral records, supply to, 180
BROADCASTING
  election campaign. *See* CAMPAIGN
    BROADCASTING
  referendum period, during, 534
BROADCASTING AUTHORITY
  Electoral Commission's views, need to
    consider, 59
BY-ELECTION
  parliamentary. *See under*
    PARLIAMENTARY ELECTION
  Welsh Assembly. *See under* WELSH
    ASSEMBLY
CAMPAIGN BROADCASTING
  candidate's election expenses, 272
  code of practice, 332
  Electoral Commission's views, 59
  local items, during parliamentary or
    local government election period,
    332
  outside UK, with intent to influence—
    election, 331

CAMPAIGN
BROADCASTING—*continued*
outside UK, with intent to
influence—*continued*
illegal practice, as, 701
party's expenditure, 299
referendum. *See under* REFERENDUM
registration of party, need for, 253

CAMPAIGN DONATION
candidates, to. *See under* CANDIDATE
(ELECTION)
offences, 752
political party, to, weekly reporting,
311
recognised third party, to—
acceptance—
application of registered party
provisions, 327
restrictions on, 326
agent, through or by, 326
amounts to be disregarded, 325
anonymous donation, 326
donation: meaning, 325
evasion of restrictions, 328
forfeiture of prohibited donation, 327
gift: meaning, 325n[5]
identification of donor, 327
impermissible donor, 329
non-commercial terms—
money lent on, 325n[10]
property, goods or facilities,
provision of at, 325n[11]
permissible donor: meaning, 326n[6]
principal donation, treatment as
separate donation, 326
recognised third party: meaning,
313n[15]
restrictions on acceptance, 326
return, 327
sponsorship: meaning, 325
statement of relevant donations, 329
unidentifiable donor, 327
referendum participant, to. *See*
REFERENDUM (donation)

CAMPAIGN EXPENDITURE. *See also*
ELECTION EXPENSES
meaning, 299
advertising, 299
application for leave to pay claim, 304
authorisation, need for, 301
claims against registered party, 303
code of practice, 299
contravention of controls, offences, 751
declarations—
delivery to Electoral Commission,
308

CAMPAIGN EXPENDITURE—*continued*
declarations—*continued*
failure to comply with requirements,
civil liability, 755
false statement, 309
treasurer, by, 309
deputy treasurer, appointment, 300
disputed claim, 303
excluded items, 299
for election purposes: meaning, 299n[3]
leave to pay claim, 304
limitation—
combined polls, 306
European parliamentary election, 305
generally, 305
parliamentary general election, 305
Welsh Assembly election, 305
manifesto etc, 299
market research etc, 299
officers of registered party with
responsibility for—
addresses, 303n[9]
generally, 300
party political broadcast, 299
public meetings etc, 299
restrictions—
financial limits, 305, 306
payments, as to, 302
statute-bared claim, 303
unauthorised expenditure, 301, 302
returns—
auditor's report, 307
contents, 307
delivery to Electoral Commission,
308
documents to accompany, 307
failure to comply with requirements,
civil liability, 755
generally, 307
matters dealt with in earlier return,
307
public inspection, 310
treasurer's duty to prepare, 307
time for claim, 303
transport, 299
unsolicited material, 299

CANDIDATE (ELECTION)
meaning, 230
agency. *See* ELECTION AGENT;
ELECTORAL AGENCY
attendance at receipt of postal ballot
papers, 416
consent to being, where not given, 230
constituency candidate (Welsh Assembly
election), 230n[19]

References are to paragraph numbers; superior figures refer to notes

CANDIDATE (ELECTION)—*continued*
  Mayor of London. *See under* MAYOR OF
    LONDON (election)
  nomination—
    consent to, 258
    deposit, requirement for, 259
    party's nominating officer's
      functions, 253
    person not representing any party,
      where, 253n[9]
    proceedings, 261
    publication of statement of persons
      nominated, 267
    registration of party and officials as
      condition precedent, 253
    selection of candidate by political
      party, 254
    validity, 262
    wrongful rejection, effect on election,
      667
    See also NOMINATION PAPER
  party list candidate, 230n[23]
  polling agent, right to appoint, 394
  supply of electoral records to, 185
  time at which one becomes, 230
  Welsh Assembly election—
    by-election, inclusion on political
      party's list, 215n[10]
    generally, 227
    time at which one becomes
      candidate, 230
  withdrawal—
    corrupt inducement of, 266, 683
    false statement withdrawal, 266
    procedure, 266
    returning officer's duty on, 262
CANVASSER
  meaning, 247
  candidate's agent, as, 247
  police officer, by, 252, 747
CHARITABLE GIFT
  bribe, as, 714
CLERK OF THE CROWN
  breach of duty at parliamentary
    election, penalty for, 737
CODE OF PRACTICE
  campaign broadcasting, 332
  campaign expenditure, 299
  election expenses, as to, 269
  Electoral Commission's power to
    prepare, 53, 269
COMMUNITY COUNCIL ELECTION.
  See also LOCAL GOVERNMENT
    ELECTION
  abortive election, 210
  combined poll, where not permitted, 25

COMMUNITY COUNCIL
  ELECTION—*continued*
  declaration of result, 482
  election agent, 231n[3]
  electoral areas—
    establishment, 74
    review of electoral arrangements, 88,
      89
  election expenses—
    claim as to expenses, 294
    declaration as to, failure to make,
      676
    disapplication of statutory
      provisions, 293
    financial return as to, failure to
      make, 676
    illegal payment, 675
    public inspection of returns and
      declarations, 296
    return and declaration as to—
      duty to make, 295
      relief in respect of, 689
    time for making, 294
  frequency and term of office, 200
  notice of, 211
  official poll cards, prescribed form,
    389n[7]
  ordinary election—
    generally, 200
    insufficient nominations, 201
  questioning, 763
  vacancy in office, 205
COMMUNITY MEETING
  poll consequent on. *See* POLL
    CONSEQUENT ON PARISH ETC
    MEETING
CONSTITUENCY
  meaning, 9
  Boundary Commission. *See* BOUNDARY
    COMMISSION
  county and borough, 73
  establishment, for purpose of
    parliamentary elections, 73
  London Assembly. *See under* LONDON
    ASSEMBLY
  numbers in UK, 79
  parliamentary, division into districts,
    343
  reduction, plans for, 79
  Welsh Assembly, 76
CONTROLLED EXPENDITURE
  (NATIONAL ELECTION)
  meaning, 313
  application for leave to pay claim, 318
  appropriate amount, determining, 313
  authorisation, need for, 315

References are to paragraph numbers; superior figures refer to notes

ELECTION—*continued*
  financial controls—
    candidate's election expenses. *See*
      ELECTION EXPENSES
    contravention, offence, 751
    donations. *See* CAMPAIGN DONATION
    recognised third parties, on. *See*
      CONTROLLED EXPENDITURE
      (NATIONAL ELECTION)
    registered party's campaign
      expenditure. *See* CAMPAIGN
      EXPENDITURE
    regulated transactions involving
      registered party, 312
    third party expenditure in national
      parliamentary campaign. *See*
      CONTROLLED EXPENDITURE
      (NATIONAL ELECTION)
  freedom of expression, right to, 7
  generally, 1
  holding of, evidence by certificate, 886
  human rights—
    European Convention, 7
    international conventions, 8
  illegal practices. *See* ILLEGAL PRACTICES
  legislation—
    European elections, $3n^3$
    generally, 3
    local government elections, $3n^1$
    parliamentary elections, $3n^1$
    purpose, 3
    Representation of the People Acts,
      $3n^1$
    Welsh Assembly elections, as to, $3n^2$
  local government election. *See* LOCAL
    GOVERNMENT ELECTION
  London Assembly election. *See* LONDON
    ASSEMBLY ELECTION
  mayoral election. *See* MAYORAL
    ELECTION
  meeting. *See* ELECTION MEETING
  offences. *See* ELECTION OFFENCES
  parish council election. *See* PARISH
    COUNCIL ELECTION
  parliamentary election. *See*
    PARLIAMENTARY ELECTION
  petition. *See* ELECTION PETITION
  poll. *See* POLLING; POLLING DISTRICT;
    POLLING PLACE; POLLING STATION
  postal vote. *See* POSTAL VOTE
  principal area election. *See* PRINCIPAL
    AREA ELECTION
  proxy vote. *See* PROXY VOTE
  publicity at—
    advertisements, control of, 333

ELECTION—*continued*
  publicity at—*continued*
    broadcasting. *See* CAMPAIGN
      BROADCASTING
    defamatory statement, $330n^{18}$
    election booklet, $330n^{15}$
    free postal communications,
      candidate's right to, 330
  questioning—
    application of provisions to other
      polls, 763
    election court. *See* ELECTION COURT
    election petition. *See* ELECTION
      PETITION
    European parliamentary election, 765
    local election, 762
    parliamentary election, 761
    time limits, 768
    Welsh Assembly elections, 764
  recount following application, 900
  registration of electors. *See* ELECTORAL
    REGISTER; REGISTRATION OF
    ELECTORS
  returning officer. *See* RETURNING
    OFFICER
  right to vote. *See* RIGHT TO VOTE
  rules for conduct, 383, 556
  scrutiny. *See* SCRUTINY
  secret ballot—
    poll to be taken by, 385
    right to, 7
  supply of electoral records. *See under*
    ELECTORAL REGISTER
  uncontested—
    European parliamentary election, at,
      477
    local government election, at, 475
    parliamentary election, at, 474
    poll consequent on parish meeting
      etc, 478
    Welsh Assembly election, at, 476
  undue influence. *See* UNDUE INFLUENCE
    (VOTING)
  void, following breach of rules, 667
  voting. *See* VOTING
  Welsh Assembly election. *See* WELSH
    ASSEMBLY ELECTION

ELECTION AGENCY. *See also* ELECTION
  AGENT
  candidate's liability for corrupt or illegal
    practices, 244
  canvasser as agent, 247
  corrupt or illegal practice, court's duty
    to report where agent guilty of,
    901

ELECTION AGENCY—*continued*
    election committee member as agent,
        248
    election official forbidden to act as
        agent, 252
    employment or authorisation test, 245
    evidence of, 245, 832
    examples of agents, 250
    official acting as, prohibition, 746
    one act of corruption only, where, 246
    police officer prohibited from
        canvassing, 252
    political association as agent, 249
    proof of, 245, 832
    statutory prohibition, 252
    termination, 251

ELECTION AGENT. *See also* ELECTION
    AGENCY
    appointment—
        European parliamentary elections,
            239
        local government election, 231
        parliamentary election, 231
        Welsh Assembly elections, 235
    attendance at receipt of postal ballot
        papers, 416
    candidate as—
        European parliamentary elections,
            239
        parliamentary and local government
            elections, $231n^8$
        Welsh Assembly elections, 235
    candidate's liability for corrupt or illegal
        practices, 244
    community council election, $231n^3$
    corrupt, avoidance of election for
        employment of, 896
    counting agent, appointment of, 394
    death of—
        European parliamentary elections,
            239, 240
        parliamentary or local election, 231,
            232
        Welsh Assembly election, 235, 236
    default in appointment, effect—
        European parliamentary elections,
            240
        parliamentary and local government
            elections, 232
        Welsh Assembly elections, 236
    duties, 243
    election expenses, payment of—
        declaration accompanying return, 279
        generally, 270
        illegal practice, 675
        return as to, 279

ELECTION AGENT—*continued*
    election expenses, payment
        of—*continued*
        statutory bar on claims against, 276
    illegal payment or employment by, 682
    local government election. *See under*
        LOCAL GOVERNMENT ELECTION
    name and address, public notice of—
        European parliamentary elections,
            $239n^{23}$
        parliamentary or local elections,
            $231n^{12}$
        Welsh Assembly elections, $235n^{27}$
    office of—
        European parliamentary elections,
            242
        parliamentary and local elections,
            234
        Welsh Assembly elections, 238
    parish council election, $231n^3$
    parliamentary election. *See under*
        PARLIAMENTARY ELECTION
    polling agent, appointment of, 394
    sub-agent—
        nomination—
            European parliamentary elections,
                241
            parliamentary or local elections,
                233
            Welsh Assembly elections, 237
        office, 234, 238, 242
    transfer of donation to, 290
    Welsh Assembly election. *See under*
        WELSH ASSEMBLY ELECTION

ELECTION COURT
    adjournment of trial, 819
    amendment of parliamentary election
        petition, 772
    constitution—
        European parliamentary election
            petition, 769
        local election or referendum, 775
        parliamentary election petition, 769
        Welsh Assembly election petition, 769
    continuation of trial despite occurrence
        of certain events, 814
    costs—
        corrupt practices, where, 875
        Director of Public Prosecution's
            expenses, 877
        disagreement between judges, 874
        general rule, 872
        High Court principles, application
            of, 870
        manner of defrayal, 871
        publication costs, 871

ELECTION COURT—*continued*
  costs—*continued*
    recovery of, 880
    repayment of election court expenses
      as to local petition, 876
    returning officer's costs, 878
    security for. *See* ELECTION PETITION
      (security for costs)
    special order, grounds for, 873
    withdrawal of petition, on, 871
    witness expenses, 879
  counsel, restriction as to member of
    House of Commons, 822
  court of record, as, 771
  Director of Public Prosecutions—
    duties, 821
    expenses, 877
  disclosure and inspection of
    documents, 811
  dismissal of petition, application for,
    815
  documents—
    disclosure and inspection, 811
    production and admittance, 812
    production following order, 836
  duty of parties and court, 820
  election expenses—
    failure to make return and
      declaration, 772
    sent in late, leave to pay, 772
  European parliamentary election—
    appointment of masters, 770
    constitution, 769
    determination of petition, 865
    expenses, payment of, 774
    jurisdiction of court, 771
    jurisdiction of judges on rota and
      master, 772
    practice and procedure of court, 771
    registrar, 773
    status of court, 771
  evidence—
    agency, proof of, 832
    commission, on, 825
    contradictory, 835
    corrupt practice, proof before agency
      proved, 831
    election documents produced
      following order, 836
    oral evidence. *See* witness *below*
    party's statement or admission, 833
    recriminatory evidence, 837
    voter's statement, 834
  expenses, payment of—
    local election or referendum, 777
    parliamentary etc election, 774

ELECTION COURT—*continued*
  false statements, injunction to restrain,
    772
  hearing—
    adjournment, 819
    barrister member of House of
      Commons, restriction on acting,
      822
    duties—
      Director of Public Prosecutions,
        of, 821
      parties and court, of, 820
    evidence. *See* evidence *above*
    mode of trial, 817
    question of law, reference by
      statement of case, 857
    recriminatory case. *See* recriminatory
      case *below*
    shorthand writers, attendance of, 818
    witnesses. *See* witness *below*
  innocent act, excepting, 772
  judges—
    jurisdiction, 772
    rota judge: meaning, 806n[5]
    selection, 769
  judgment, reasons for, 868
  judicial review of decisions, 779n[3]
  jurisdiction—
    generally, 771
    judges on rota and master, 772
    local election or authority, 779
    parliamentary etc election, 771
    rules of court, subject to, 772
  listing of petitions, 805
  local authority referendum—
    accommodation and attendance, 777
    commissioners, appointment and
      qualification, 775
    constitution of court, 775
    determination of petition, 866
    expenses, repayment of—
      commissioner and staff, 778
      court accommodation and
        attendance, 777
      power to order, 876
    jurisdiction, 779
    matters to be reported by election
      court, 867
    officers and clerks, 776
    registrar, 776
    remuneration of commissioner and
      staff, 778
    shorthand writer, 776, 818
    subsequent procedures, 866
  local government election—
    accommodation and attendance, 777

ELECTION COURT—*continued*
  local government election—*continued*
    commissioners, appointment and
        qualification, 775
    constitution of court, 775
    determination of petition, 861
    expenses, repayment of—
      commissioner and staff, 778
      court accommodation and
          attendance, 777
      power to order, 876
    jurisdiction, 779
    matters to be reported by court, 862
    officers and clerks, 776
    registrar, 776
    remuneration of commissioner and
        staff, 778
    shorthand writer, 776, 818
    subsequent procedures, 861
  master—
    appointment, 770
    jurisdiction, 772
  member of House of Commons,
      restriction on appearance at trial,
      822
  mode of trial, 817
  parliamentary election—
    appointment of masters, 770
    constitution, 769
    determination of petition, 858
    expenses, payment of, 774
    jurisdiction of court, 771
    jurisdiction of judges on rota and
        master, 772
    matters to be reported by election
        court, 859
    practice and procedure of court, 771
    registrar, 773
    status of court, 771
    subsequent action by House of
        Commons, 860
  particulars of petition—
    amendment, 810
    application to rota judge, 808n[1]
    filing copy, 808
    further particulars, ordering, 808
    general corruption charged, where,
        809
    generally, 808
    judge in chambers ordering, 808n[4]
    time for giving, 808
  place of trial. *See* time and place of trial
      below
  practice and procedure, 771, 817
  quasi-inquisitorial nature, 771

ELECTION COURT—*continued*
  question of law, reference by statement
      of case, 857
  recount—
    application for, 855, 900
    procedure, 856
  recriminatory case—
    meaning, 837
    allegation of charges against
        subsequent election, 838
    evidence, right to give, 837
    list of objections, filing, 837
    prayer for seat abandoned at trial,
        837
    referendum petition, 837
    scrutiny, and, 847
  registrar—
    European parliamentary election, 773
    parliamentary election, 773
    Welsh Assembly election, 773
    local election or referendum, 776
  remission of incapacities, application
      for, 772
  rota judge—
    meaning, 806n[5]
    jurisdiction, 772
    selection, 769
  scrutiny of votes. *See* SCRUTINY
  shorthand writers, attendance of, 818
  special case stated, 816
  status, 771
  stay of petition, application for, 815
  time and place of trial—
    application to fix, 806
    change of venue, 806
    generally, 806
    notice requirements, 807
  Welsh Assembly election—
    appointment of masters, 770
    constitution, 769
    determination of petition, 863
    expenses, payment of, 774
    jurisdiction of court, 771
    jurisdiction of judges on rota and
        master, 772
    matters to be reported, 864
    practice and procedure of court, 771
    registrar, 773
    status of court, 771
    subsequent procedures, 863
  withdrawal of petition—
    application for permission, 813
    costs, 871
  witness—
    attendance, 823
    contradictory evidence, 835

ELECTION COURT—*continued*
witness—*continued*
cross-examination, 828
duty to answer questions, 830
evidence on commission, 825
examination by court, 824
exclusion from court, 827
expenses, 879
hostile witness, 828
incrimination of self, spouse or civil
partner, 830
perjury, 826
secrecy of vote, 829
swearing of, 823

ELECTION EXPENSES
meaning, 269
accommodation costs, 269
administrative costs, 269
advertising, 269, 272, 299
broadcasting, 272
candidate, statutory bar on claims
against, 276
circulars, 272
code of practice, 269
community council election. *See* parish
or community council election
below
concerted plan of action, incurred as
part of, 272n[16]
creditors' rights, 278
declaration—
failure to comply with requirements,
civil liability, 755
free or discounted goods, services
etc, 269
return, accompanying—
meaning, 281n[3]
appropriate form for, 281n[3, 7]
authorised expenses, 279
circumstances where not required,
282
delivery to Electoral Commission,
285
failure to comply with
requirements, offence, 281
forms, 279n[12]
generally, 279, 281
inspection, 283, 284
late delivery where candidate
temporarily outside UK, 281
parish or community council
election, 295, 296
disapplication of provisions in case of
non-local government election, 297
election agent, 269, 276
excluded items, 269

ELECTION EXPENSES—*continued*
goods, services and facilities etc, 269
illegal practice—
election under 1972 Act not being a
local government election,
where, 297
parish or community election
expenses, payment of, 294
individual candidates, limit in case of,
273
joint candidates at local government
elections, 275
limitation—
individual or party list candidates,
273
joint candidates, 275
Mayor of London's disqualification for
failure to make returns as to, 906
newspaper advertisement, 272
outsider's expenses, restriction, 272
parish or community council election—
claim as to expenses, 294
disapplication of statutory
provisions, 293
public inspection of returns and
declarations, 296
return and declaration as to, 295
time for making, 294
party list candidates, limit in case of,
273
party political broadcast, 272
payment—
meaning, 270n[1]
creditors' rights, 278
declarations. *See* declarations *above*
election agent, by, 270
generally, 270
less than £20, where, 270
offence, 270
otherwise than through an agent, 271
restrictions on. *See* restrictions on
payment *below*
returns. *See* returns *below*
statutory time limit, after, 277
permitted sum, 272n[15]
pre-candidacy expenses, Parliament
dissolved after more than 55
months, 274
public meetings, 269, 272
publications, 272
restrictions on payment—
exceptions to general rule, 270
generally, 270
offence, 270
Parliament dissolved after more than
55 months, 274

References are to paragraph numbers; superior figures refer to notes

ELECTORAL BOUNDARIES—*continued*
review—*continued*
England, local government electoral
areas—*continued*
London Assembly constituencies,
86
principal councils and parish
councils within principal area,
83–85
procedure on review and
recommendations for change,
84
European parliamentary electoral
regions—
implementation of recommendation
following periodic review, 93
order giving effect to change in
number of UK MEPs to be
elected, 94
periodic review of the distribution
of MEPs between electoral
regions, 92
recommendations as to distribution
of UK MEPs, 91
generally, 73
local government electoral areas—
England, in. *See* England, local
government electoral areas
above
Wales, in. *See* Wales, local
government electoral areas
below
parliamentary constituencies—
allocation to parts of UK, 81
Boundary Commission reports, 78
consultation over proposals, 82
electoral quota and geographical
area, relevance, 80
parity principle, 80
planned reduction, 79
publicity as to proposals, 82
qualifying party's right to make
representations, 82n^{15}
rules for distribution of seats, 79,
80
United Kingdom electoral quota,
80n^3
Wales, local government electoral
areas—
communities, review of electoral
arrangements for, 88
electoral area: meaning, 87n^3
electoral arrangements: meaning,
87n^3
fixing identifiable boundaries,
desirability of, 89n^8

ELECTORAL BOUNDARIES—*continued*
review—*continued*
Wales, local government electoral
areas—*continued*
multi-member electoral division,
89n$^{8, 12}$
principal areas in, 87
statutory rules to be observed, 89
Welsh Assembly electoral regions, 90

ELECTORAL COMMISSION
accounts, 45
advice and assistance—
power to charge for, 58
provision of, 58
relevant body's request for, 58n^2
secondment of members, 58n^3
annual report, 46
campaign broadcasts, power to express
views on, 59
chairman—
appointment of, 35
re-appointment, 35
removal from office, 36
tenure, 36
chief executive—
appointment, 38
political restrictions on, 39
power to designate a post on staff,
39n^{16}
termination of appointment, grounds
for, 39
code of practice—
campaign expenditure, as to, 299
election expenses, as to, 269
power to prepare, 53
referendum expenses, 535
committees—
delegation to, 42
establishment, 41
compliance with controls, duty to
monitor and regulate, 62
constitution, 34
consultation on electoral law
instruments, 54
disclosure notice—
meaning, 64
admissibility of statements in
evidence, 64n^{11}
documents, production of, 64n^8
power to give, 64
relevant individual, 64n^2
discretionary requirements, power to
impose, 758
document-disclosure order—
copies of documents, power to
make, 65n^{21}

ELECTORAL COMMISSION—*continued*
  document-disclosure order—*continued*
    documents under a person's control,
      65n[20]
    information-disclosure order, court's
      power to make, 65
    power to apply for, 65
    retention of documents, 65n[24]
  education function, 61
  Electoral Commissioner—
    meaning, 183n[7]
    appointment—
      generally, 35
      motion for address from House of
        Commons, 35n[3]
      nominating party, put forward by,
        35n[16]
    Assistant Electoral Commissioner—
      appointment, 40
      tenure etc, 40
      termination of appointment,
        grounds for, 40
    cessation of office, reasons for, 36
    disqualification for post, 35
    eligibility, 35
    expenses etc, 37
    pension, 37
    re-appointment, 35
    removal from office, 36
    remuneration, 37
    tenure, 36
  electoral records, right of access to, 183
  electoral systems etc, duty to promote
    public awareness of, 61
  enforcement undertaking, power to
    accept, 760
  establishment, 3n[6], 34
  European parliamentary electoral
    regions, review of. *See under*
    ELECTORAL BOUNDARIES (review)
  exercise of election powers,
    Commission's recommendation
    required, 56
  financial provisions, 44
  financial year: meaning, 44n[4]
  five-year plan, 44
  fixed monetary penalties, power to
    impose, 757
  inspection warrant—
    meaning, 64
    documents in electronic form, 64n[19]
    issue of, 64
    relevant organisation or individual,
      premises occupied by, 64n[13]
    restriction on use, 64n[16]
  investigation of, 34n[2]

ELECTORAL COMMISSION—*continued*
  investigatory powers—
    additional powers, 63n[4]
    annual report, information in, 63
    disclosure notice. *See* disclosure notice
      above
    document-disclosure order. *See*
      document-disclosure order *above*
    generally, 63
    guidance etc, power to issue, 63
    inspection warrant. *See* inspection
      warrant *above*
    offences and penalties, 66
    scope, 63
    suspected offences or contraventions,
      65
  local authority referendum, evaluation
    of pilot schemes, 661
  local elections in England and Wales,
    involvement in changes to electoral
    procedures, 55
  Local Government Boundary
    Commission for England, transfer
    of property, rights and liabilities
    to, 67
  monitoring and regulation function, 62
  Neill Report, following, 34n[1]
  obstruction, offence and penalty, 753
  performance standards for electoral
    officers, setting of, 57
  pilot scheme—
    local authority referendum,
      evaluation, 661
    local government election—
      evaluation, 522, 525
      participation in, 55
  policy development grant—
    meaning, 60n[3]
    conditions, imposition of, 60n[15]
    limit on, 60n[16]
    power to recommend, 60
    represented registered party, to, 60n[3]
    review of, 60
  powers, 34n[2]
  procedure, regulation of, 43
  proceedings, validity of, 43
  proof of instruments, 48
  public awareness of electoral systems
    etc, duty to promote, 61
  referendum—
    expenses, delivery of return, 543
    views etc on wording of question,
      528
  register of third party notifications, duty
    to keep, 314
  regulations made by, 47

References are to paragraph numbers; superior figures refer to notes

ELECTORAL COMMISSION—*continued*
report on elections and referendums, 51
representatives' power to attend
electoral proceedings and observe
working practices, 53
returns and declarations delivered to,
285, 308, 309, 322
review of electoral and political
matters, 52
review of polling districts and places,
representations to Commission,
346
staff—
appointment etc, 38
delegation to, 42
disqualification from membership of
House of Commons, 38n[4]
political restrictions on, 39
stop notice, power to impose, 759
transfer of property, rights and
liabilities—
from, to Local Government Boundary
Commission for England, 67
to, from Secretary of State, 34n[2]
views expressed on broadcasts, 59

ELECTORAL FRAUD
meaning, 754
corrupt or illegal practice, 754
effect, 754
generally, 754
postal voting, 754
scope of term, 754

ELECTORAL REGIONS
European parliamentary electoral
regions—
generally, 13, 77
review—
implementation of recommendation
following periodic review, 93
order giving effect to change in
number of UK MEPs to be
elected, 94
periodic review of the distribution
of MEPs between electoral
regions, 92
recommendations as to distribution
of UK MEPs, 91
Welsh Assembly election—
establishment, 76
review, 90

ELECTORAL REGISTER
alterations—
annual canvass, following, 151
appeal, following, 178

ELECTORAL REGISTER—*continued*
alterations—*continued*
notice of—
address in relevant election area,
168n[31]
appropriate publication date,
168n[28, 55]
clerical error, register containing,
168n[11]
determination of right to
registration, where, 168n[5, 6]
duty to issue, 168
effective date of, 168
interim publication dates, 168n[55]
prescribed manner for issue,
168n[12]
prescribed time on day of poll,
168n[36]
removal from register, 168n[8]
representation, person making,
168n[47]
time for issue, calculating, 168n[14,
15]
anonymous entry—
meaning, 145
application for, 147
certificate of anonymous registration,
145n[12]
declaration, offence, 735
omission from edited register, 167
police etc, supply to, 186
procedure for determining
application, 148
record of, 145n[12], 148n[12]
restriction on supply of record, 179
safety test, 147, 148
termination of entitlement to, 171
application for entry derived from
annual canvass—
determination of applications for
registration and alteration, 157
European parliamentary elector, EU
citizen's application for
registration, 159
form of objection to registration, 161
local government elector, form of
application for registration as,
158
objections to registration,
determining, 160, 162
parliamentary elector, form of
application for registration as,
158
procedural requirements, 162
registration, procedure for
determining applications for, 162

ELECTORAL REGISTER—*continued*
  application for entry derived from
    annual canvass—*continued*
    supply of forms, 157n[6], 160n[6]
  application for entry derived from
    individual registration—
    alterations to entries on register, 164
    determination by registration officer,
      163
    guidance, regard to, 164n[9]
  clerical error in, 168n[11]
  content, 145
  data matching to check entries, use of,
    152
  disclosure of information, restriction
    on, 179
  edited version—
    omitted information, 167
    publication of, 167
    sale, 188
  effect of register entries, 149
  electoral number—
    meaning, 145
    allocation, 145
  entry derived from annual canvass,
    application for. *See* application for
    entry derived from annual canvass
    above
  failure to comply with registration
    requirements, civil liability, 756
  form, 145
  full register—
    meaning, 167n[2, 9]
    inspection, restrictions on copying
      etc, 167n[9]
    sale, 188
    supply and inspection offences, 734
  inspection, election offences, 734
  list of proxies—
    meaning, 373n[14]
    effect of entry in, 149
    qualifying Commonwealth citizen,
      149n[17]
    relevant citizen of the Union, 149n[17]
  misdescription of person or place, 150,
    385
  overseas electors, list of—
    meaning, 143n[9]
    form and content, 146
    publication, 165
  parts, division into, 145
  peers, 145
  proxies, list of. *See* list of proxies *above*
  publication—
    duty to publish, 165
    edited version, 167

ELECTORAL REGISTER—*continued*
  publication—*continued*
    latest date for, 165n[4]
    list of overseas electors, 165
    manner of publication, 165n[3]
    notice of alteration of published
      register, 168
    relevant registers, 165n[3]
    revised version of register—
      generally, 165
      supply of information following
        publication, 166
  qualifying address, 145n[5]
  reforms to improve accuracy etc,
    proposed, 152
  revision of register, duty to publish, 165
  sale—
    direct marketing purposes, for, 7n[6],
      179n[18]
    edited register, 188
    entitlement to purchase, 188
    fee, 188n[3, 9]
    full register, 188
    procedural requirements, 188
    restrictions, 188
  supply of records—
    Boundary Commissions, to, 184
    candidates, to, 185
    community council, to, 185
    elected officials, to, 185
    election agent, to, 185
    election offences, 734
    Electoral Commission, to, 183
    general restriction on, 179
    generally, 185
    holders of electoral office, to, 182,
      185
    local authority, to, 185
    local authority archives service, 181
    national libraries, to, 180
    offence and penalty, 179n[18], 180n[6]
    parish council, to, 185
    persons who must not supply
      information, 179n[20]
    police etc, to, 186
    political party, to, 185
    processing of information, 181n[32]
    public libraries, to, 181
    research purposes, relevant
      conditions, 180n[11]
    security and intelligence forces etc,
      to, 186
    Statistics Board, to, 187
  Welsh Assembly constituency, details as
    to, 145n[15]

References are to paragraph numbers; superior figures refer to notes

ELECTORAL REGISTRATION
OFFICER. *See* REGISTRATION OFFICER

ENFORCEMENT UNDERTAKING
meaning, 760n[5]
certificate—
appeal against decision not to issue,
760n[18]
application, 760n[18]
revocation, 760n[18]
cessation, 760n[18]
compliance with, 760
Electoral Commission's power to
impose, 760
reasons for imposing, 760

ENVIRONMENT AGENCY
sale of electoral records to, 188

EUROPEAN PARLIAMENT
election to. *See* EUROPEAN
PARLIAMENTARY ELECTION
seats allocated to member states, limits
on, 6n[2]
total number of representatives, 6n[2]

EUROPEAN PARLIAMENTARY
ELECTION
meaning, 1n[4], 21n[2]
ballot paper. *See* BALLOT PAPER
by-election—
day of, 218
general election intervening, 221
generally, 13, 221
maximum delay in holding, 219n[11]
nominating officer: meaning, 220n[6]
See also vacancy, filling *below*
candidacy—
competent administrative authorities,
certificate made by, 228n[8]
court's power to make declaration,
228
disqualification for office of MEP,
228
generally, 228
House of Commons, member of,
228n[5]
nomination paper. *See* NOMINATION
PAPER
regulations, power to make, 228
relevant citizen of the Union, 229
time at which one becomes
candidate, 230
citizen of the European Union, 92n[6]
combined polls—
generally, 13
local government election, 16
parliamentary general election, 16
See also POLLING (combined polls)

EUROPEAN PARLIAMENTARY
ELECTION—*continued*
combined region, Gibraltar as part of,
13n[3, 12], 77n[4]
conduct of, rules for, 383
consent to nomination, 258
contested election. *See* ELECTION
(contested)
date for holding, 6n[5], 222
declaration of result at, 493
deposit—
requirement for, 259
return or forfeiture, 494
See also CANDIDATE (ELECTION)
deposit)
documents—
access to or control of, offence and
penalty, 745
order for production or inspection,
512
retention after postal voting, 502
retention and supply, 510
supply and inspection, 511
transfer after sealing up of ballot
papers, 501
election agent—
appointment, 239
candidate as, 239
death of, 239, 240
default in appointment, 240
name and address—
provided to appropriate officer,
239n[16]
public notice of, 239n[23]
national election agent—
meaning, 239n[5]
nominating officer deemed to be,
240
office, 242
revocation of appointment, 239
sub-agent—
illegal practice and offence, 241n[26]
nomination of, 241
office, 242
See also ELECTION AGENT
election expenses. *See* ELECTION
EXPENSES
election meeting. *See* ELECTION MEETING
elector—
meaning, 92n[6]
calculating number for electoral
region, 92n[6]
electoral regions—
generally, 13, 77
review. *See under* ELECTORAL
BOUNDARIES (review)

ILLEGAL PRACTICES—*continued*
  offences also constituting—*continued*
    examples, 699
    election publication, failure to comply
      with requirements as to, 703
    generally, 699
    issue of imitation poll card, 702
    summary offences, 671, 699
    voting offences, 700
  penalties, 888
  relief—
    affidavit supporting application, 697
    contravention of statutory
      requirements as to election
      expense returns or declarations,
      688
    costs of application, 698
    examples, 693
    failure to deliver or send returns or
      declarations of expenses
      authorised by election agent, 687
    grant of, 693
    illegal practice, payment, employment
      or hiring, 690
    inadvertence as ground for, 691
    notice of application, 696
    other reasonable cause as ground
      for, 692
    parish or community council election
      expense returns or declarations,
      689
    parties to proceedings, 698
    refusal, 694
    supporting affidavit, 697
    time of application, 695
  report by election court, 901
  striking off on vote on scrutiny, 843
  voting offences, 700

INJUNCTION
  court's power to grant, 665
  false statement about candidate,
    restraining, 665, 666

INTIMIDATION
  avoidance of election, 895
  local authority referendum, avoidance
    of, 897

JURISDICTION
  election court, 771

JURY
  electoral register as basis of selection,
    142n[2]

JUSTICE OF THE PEACE
  corrupt or illegal practice, court's duty
    to report where guilty of, 902

JUSTICE OF THE PEACE—*continued*
  inspection warrant on behalf of
    Electoral Commission, power to
    issue, 64

LOCAL AUTHORITY
  archives service, supply of electoral
    records to, 181
  elections. *See* LOCAL GOVERNMENT
    ELECTION
  poll, power to conduct, 15, 557
  referendum. *See* LOCAL AUTHORITY
    REFERENDUM

LOCAL AUTHORITY REFERENDUM
  absent voter—
    absent voters list, 596
    application for absent vote—
      indefinite period, for, 592
      particular period, for, 592
      particular referendum, at, 594–596
    different address, ballot paper sent
      to, 594
    postal vote. *See* postal vote *below*
    proxy vote. *See* proxy vote *below*
    record of entitlement, 593
    removal from record, 593
  advertisements, control of, 580
  approval of proposals, 654
  avoidance by reason of corruption,
    bribery, treating or intimidation,
    897
  ballot paper—
    false answers to questions put,
      offence, 619
    form of, 607
    inadvertently spoilt, 625
    marked by presiding officer, 622
    official mark, 607
    postal ballot paper. *See* postal ballot
      paper *below*
    procedure after receiving, 620
    questions to be put to voters, 619
    sealing up of papers, 656
    stamping of, 620
    tendered ballot paper, 624
  campaigning etc, pilot schemes. *See* pilot
    scheme *below*
  challenging voter, on suspicion of
    personation, 621
  close of poll, procedure on, 626
  conduct—
    pilot schemes. *See* pilot scheme *below*
    relevant legislation, 555
  counting of votes—
    appointment of persons for, 614
    arrangements for, 646
    attendance at, 646

LOCAL AUTHORITY
REFERENDUM—*continued*
counting of votes—*continued*
conclusiveness of decision as to ballot
paper, 649
counting and recording number of
ballot papers, 647
counting observer, 614
duly returned postal ballot paper,
647n[10]
equality of votes, 651
facilities for overseeing proceedings,
provision of, 646
recount, 650
refreshments etc during, 647
rejected ballot papers, 648
time provisions, 647
verification of ballot paper account,
647, 740
counting officer—
meaning, 576n[1]
assistance for, 586
declaration of result by, 652
documents—
duty to deliver, 657
duty to forward after postal
voting, 658
envelopes, duty to issue, 627
expenses, 587
functions, 586
information, duty to provide, 627
issue of poll cards by, 609
postal ballot papers, duty to issue,
627
postal voting statement, duty to
issue, 627
date of poll, notice of, 576
declaration of result, 652
direction requiring—
circumstances for, 570
contents, 570
petition received before or after, 571
procedure on receipt, 571
publicity for referendum, 573
time for holding referendum, 572
Welsh Ministers, from, 570
disabled voter, 623
documents—
delivery to registration officer, 657,
658
retention and public inspection of,
659
expenses—
meaning, 577
advertising, 577
excluded amounts, 577

LOCAL AUTHORITY
REFERENDUM—*continued*
expenses—*continued*
for referendum purposes: meaning,
577n[3]
free or discounted goods etc, 577
general restriction, 578
limit, 578
market research or canvassing, 577
media, dealing with, 577
promotional material, 577
public meetings, 577
publicity material, restriction as to,
569
rallies etc, 577
transport, 577
unsolicited material, 577
fall-back proposals—
detailed proposals following rejection
of referendum proposals, 654
outline proposals. *See* outline
fall-back proposals *below*
generally, 15
holding of, evidence by certificate, 886
hours of polling, 615
interfering with voter, offence, 620
keeping of order at, 617
legislation, relevant, 555
manner of voting at, 590
notice of referendum, 574
notice of date etc of, 576, 608
official poll cards, issue of, 609
outline fall-back proposals—
meaning, 568n[15], 574n[16]
inspection, 574n[18]
personation, offence, 621
petition calling for—
amalgamation—
generally, 562
order of amalgamation, 562n[3]
notification requirements
following, 564
procedural requirements, 563
restriction on amalgamation, 562
constituent petitions, 562
constitutional change, proposal for,
561n[10], 562n[14]
contents, 563
formalities, 563
notice period, 564n[9]
notice requirements, 566
petition date: meaning, 563n[11]
petition organiser, 561n[6]
post-announcement petition, 561
post-direction petition, 561
presentation to local authority, 559

References are to paragraph numbers; superior figures refer to notes

PARISH COUNCIL
ELECTION—*continued*
election expenses—*continued*
  illegal payment, 675
  public inspection of returns and
      declarations, 296
  return and declaration as to—
      duty to make, 295
      relief in respect of, 689
      time for making, 294
frequency and term of office, 200
notice of, 211
official poll cards, prescribed form,
    389n[7]
ordinary election—
  generally, 200
  insufficient nominations, 201
questioning, 763
relevant electoral arrangements, 74n[24]
vacancy in office, 205

PARISH MEETING
chairman, election of, 200
poll consequent on. *See* POLL
    CONSEQUENT ON PARISH OR
    COMMUNITY MEETING

PARLIAMENT
dissolution, procedure for, 189
election. *See* PARLIAMENTARY ELECTION
fixed term, introduction of, 189
prorogation, power of, 189n[14]
summoning new parliament, 189

PARLIAMENTARY ELECTION
meaning, 9
ballot paper. *See* BALLOT PAPER
Bill of Rights, and, 5
British citizen overseas, right to vote, 96
by-election—
  polling day, 195
  procedure for ordering, 191
  writ, issue of. *See* writ *below*
candidacy—
  death of candidate. *See* death of
      candidate *below*
  disqualification for membership of
      House of Commons, 224
  nomination paper. *See* NOMINATION
      PAPER
  time for becoming candidate, 230
  See also CANDIDATE (ELECTION)
combined polls—
  European parliamentary general
      election, 16
  generally, 9
  local government election, 16
  See also POLLING (combined polls)

PARLIAMENTARY
ELECTION—*continued*
commanding of elections for new
    parliament, 189
conduct of, rules for, 383
consent to nomination, 258
contested election. *See* ELECTION
    (contested)
date of. *See* polling day *below*
death of candidate—
  combined poll, 513, 515
  countermand or abandonment of
      poll, 513
  fresh election following abandonment
      etc, 515
  postal ballot papers issued, after, 514
  speaker of House of Commons, 513,
      515
declaration of result, 479
demise of Crown after proclamation
    summoning new Parliament, 190
deposit—
  requirement for, 259
  return or forfeiture, 481
  See also CANDIDATE (ELECTION)
      deposit)
documents—
  forwarding after postal voting, 497
  marked register, supply and
      inspection, 504
  order for production or inspection,
      512
  public inspection of retained
      documents, 503
  retention and supply, 503
  supply and inspection, 504
  transfer following election, 496
election agent—
  appointment, 231
  appropriate officer, provision of
      details to, 231n[5]
  death of, 231, 232
  default in appointment, 232
  details, provision of, 231
  office of, 234
  revocation of appointment, 231, 232
  sub-agent, nomination of, 233
  See also ELECTION AGENT
election expenses. *See* ELECTION
    EXPENSES
election meeting. *See* ELECTION MEETING
electoral areas, establishment, 74
European parliamentary election. *See*
    EUROPEAN PARLIAMENTARY
    ELECTION

References are to paragraph numbers; superior figures refer to notes

PARLIAMENTARY
    ELECTION—*continued*
  financial controls. *See* ELECTION
    (financial controls)
  generally, 9
  integrity of, 5
  legal incapacity, person subject to, 95n[8],
    109
  lists, right to inspect, 504
  marked register etc, right to inspect,
    504
  material, failure to display details on,
    749
  meeting. *See* ELECTION MEETING
  new Parliament—
    commanding of election for, 189
    demise of Crown after proclamation
      summoning, 190
    first meeting of, 190
  nomination—
    nomination paper. *See* NOMINATION
      PAPER
    proceedings, 261
    validity, 262, 263
    See also under CANDIDATE (ELECTION)
  notice of election at, 196
  notice of poll, 388
  official poll cards, 389
  petition questioning. *See* ELECTION
    PETITION (parliamentary election
    petition)
  polling day—
    by-election, 195
    demise of Crown, effect, 190
    early election, in case of, 195
    fixed nature of, 189, 195
  polling district at. *See under* POLLING
    DISTRICT
  polling place at. *See under* POLLING
    PLACE
  polling station. *See* POLLING STATION
  questioning—
    application of provisions to other
      polls, 763
    grounds for, 761
    petition. *See* ELECTION PETITION
      (parliamentary election petition)
    time limits, 768
  record of returns, 480
  registration of electors—
    deemed residence of person in
      custody, 120
    determination of residence, 117
    entitlement to be registered, 113
    mental hospital, patient in, 119, 121
    merchant seaman, 118

PARLIAMENTARY
    ELECTION—*continued*
  registration of electors—*continued*
    notional residence by way of
      declaration of local connection—
      cancellation of declaration, 121
      deemed residence, 121
      effect, 124
      formalities associated with, 122
      invalid declaration, 123
      offence as to, 138, 735
    overseas parliamentary elector, 114
    qualifying Commonwealth citizen,
      113n[9]
    rolling registration, 117n[3]
    temporary absence, 117
    See also REGISTRATION OF ELECTORS
  registration officer. *See* REGISTRATION
    OFFICER
  return book, 480
  return to writ, 480
  returning officer. *See under* RETURNING
    OFFICER
  right to vote at—
    generally, 95, 96
    See also RIGHT TO VOTE
  summoning new Parliament, procedure
    for, 189
  third party expenditure. *See*
    CONTROLLED EXPENDITURE
    (NATIONAL ELECTION)
  uncontested, procedure at, 474, 479
  voting age, 95n[2], 149n[2], 157n[15], 160n[9]
  voting at—
    absent voter, 363
    manner of, 363
    voting system, 339
  writ for—
    by-election, 192n[2]
    conveyance—
      address for, 193
      generally, 194
      method of, 192n[5]
      receipt for, 194
    deputy returning officer, delivery to,
      192
    issue and conveyance of, 192
    notice, form of, 192n[10]
    notice revoking notice of
      conveyance, 192n[12]
    parliamentary writs list, 193
    prescribed form, 192n[3]
    returning officer, directed to, 192

PARLIAMENTARY PARTIES PANEL
  constitution and functions, 50

References are to paragraph numbers; superior figures refer to notes

PEER

right to vote—
European parliamentary election,
where resident outside UK, 101,
115
parliamentary election, 95n[8]
registration provisions, 112

PERJURY

election petition proceedings, 826

PERSONATION

corrupt practice, as, 729, 730
striking off on vote on scrutiny, 844
voter challenged on suspicion of, 400

POLICE

canvassing by officer, 252, 747
electoral records, right to be supplied
with, 185
police area: meaning, 18n[2]

POLITICAL ASSOCIATION

candidate's agent, as, 249

POLITICAL PARTY

accounting requirements—
financial year: meaning, 298n[3]
generally, 298
qualified auditor: meaning, 298n[5]
campaign expenditure. See CAMPAIGN
EXPENDITURE
candidate—
selection of, 254
See also CANDIDATE (ELECTION)
donation to—
recognised third party. See under
CAMPAIGN DONATION
registered party—
acceptance or return, 289
exemption declaration, 311
weekly reporting during election
period. See weekly reporting
during election period below
electoral records, right to be supplied
with, 185
financial year: meaning, 298n[3]
funding, report on, 3n[6]
registered political party: meaning,
215n[19]
registration as condition precedent to
participation in election, 253
regulated transactions, weekly reporting
during election period—
anonymous participant in
transaction, 312n[17]
contents of report, 312
generally, 312
reporting period: meaning, 312
Secretary of State's powers, 312
weekly report: meaning, 312

POLITICAL PARTY—continued

weekly reporting during election
period—
anonymous donation, 311n[15]
content of weekly report, 311
declaration signed by responsible
officers, 311n[26]
donations, 311
exemption from requirement, 311
regulated transactions. See regulated
transactions, weekly reporting
during election period above
reporting period: meaning, 311
Secretary of State's powers, 311
specified election period: meaning,
311n[44]
weekly report: meaning, 311

POLL

parish or community meeting,
consequent on. See POLL
CONSEQUENT ON PARISH OR
COMMUNITY MEETING
right to vote in—
parish or community meeting,
consequent on, 106
Welsh Ministers' function, as to
exercise of, 105
Welsh Ministers, as to functions. See
WELSH MINISTERS (poll as to
functions)

POLL CONSEQUENT ON PARISH OR
COMMUNITY MEETING

meaning, 581
appointment to office, on question of—
public notice, duty to give, 212
uncontested poll, procedure at, 478
ballot paper—
false answers to questions put,
offence, 619
form of, 607n[3]
inadvertently spoilt, 625
marked by presiding officer, 622
official mark, 607
procedure after receiving, 620
questions to be put to voters, 619
sealing up of papers, 656
stamping of, 620
tendered ballot paper, 624
See also BALLOT PAPER
candidate's withdrawal, 265
challenging voter, on suspicion of
personation, 400, 621
circumstances for, 581
close of poll—
procedure on, 405, 626
sealing up of ballot papers, 495, 626

POLL CONSEQUENT ON PARISH OR
  COMMUNITY
  MEETING—*continued*
conduct of, rules for, 383n[6], 556
counting agent, 394n[7]
counting of votes—
  appointment of persons for, 614
  arrangements for, 424, 646
  attendance at, 646
  ballot paper void for uncertainty, 430
  casting of lots in event of tie, 434
  conclusiveness of counting officer's
    decision, 649
  conclusiveness of returning officer's
    decision, 432, 649
  counting and recording number of
    ballot papers, 647
  counting observer, 614
  duly returned postal ballot paper,
    647n[10]
  equality of votes, 651
  facilities for overseeing proceedings,
    provision of, 646
  generally, 425
  recount, 433, 650
  refreshments etc during, 647
  rejected ballot papers, grounds for—
    generally, 648
    lack of official mark, 427
    mark identifying voter, 429
    uncertainty, paper void for, 430
    unmarked paper, 430
    voting for too many candidates,
      428
  time provisions, 647
  verification of ballot paper accounts,
    425, 647, 740
day of—
  abortive poll, where, 210
  power to fix, 582
  timing, 582
death of candidate, effect, 210, 516,
  520
declaration of result, 483, 655
disabled voter, assistance from
  companion, 402, 623
documents relating to—
  delivery of documents to registration
    officer, 657
  order for production or inspection,
    512, 659
  retention and public inspection, 659
  retention and supply, 507
  transfer, 498
expenses incurred, 589
extent of, 585

POLL CONSEQUENT ON PARISH OR
  COMMUNITY
  MEETING—*continued*
hours of polling, 615
illiterate voter, assistance from
  companion, 402
interfering with voter, offence, 620
keeping of order at, 617
manner of voting at, 591
notice of, 212, 388, 583, 608
personation, offence, 621
polling agent, 394n[8]
polling station—
  admission to, 618
  allotment of electors to, 610
  counting observers, appointment, 614
  equipment, 611, 612
  exclusion of persons from, 618
  hours of polling, 615
  keeping of order at, 617
  loan of equipment, 612
  misconduct in, 617
  notice for guidance of voters, 611
  polling observers, appointment, 614
  presiding officers, appointment of,
    613
  provision of sufficient numbers, 610
  removal of person from, 617
  rooms, use of, 610
  See also POLLING STATION
power to demand, 15
proxy voter, requiring assistance due to
  incapacity, 623
questioning, 763
returning officer—
  appointment, 356, 588
  duty to deliver documents, 657
  notice given by, 356, 588
right to demand, 581
right to vote in, 106
sealing of ballot boxes, 616, 626
secret ballot, 606
transfer of documents relating to, 498
vote counting. *See* counting of votes
  above
voting procedure, 620
voting system, 342

POLLING
combined polls—
  costs, apportionment of, 17
  counting agent, 394
  elections and local authority
    referendum in England, 31
  elections for related areas, 30
  examples, 16
  expenses at, 17

POSTAL BALLOT PAPER—*continued*

counting of votes. *See* VOTE COUNTING

covering envelope—

meaning, 410n[6]

counting and recording, 421

mis-match between numbers, opened where, 421

notice of opening, 419

received before close of poll, 418

delivery to voter, acceptable methods, 411

free of charge, return to be, 406

information to accompany, 406

issue—

contravention of secrecy requirement, offence and penalty, 742

duty to issue, 406

envelopes etc, 406

information to accompany, 406

procedure on, 408

refusal to issue more than one to each elector, 409

time of issue, 407

list of rejected papers, 423

list of spoilt postal ballot papers, 414

local authority referendum. *See* LOCAL AUTHORITY REFERENDUM (postal ballot paper)

lost postal ballot paper, 415

opening of ballot paper envelopes, 422

opening of covering envelopes, 421

personal identifier, verification, 420

postage, 411

postal voting statement. *See under* POSTAL VOTE

receipt of—

agents in attendance, 416

contravention of secrecy requirement, offence and penalty, 742

notice of opening of ballot boxes and covering envelopes, 419

opening of ballot boxes, 420

opening of ballot paper envelopes, 422

opening of covering envelopes, 421

persons entitled to be present at, 416

rejected papers, 417

return of papers to returning officer, 418

recording of vote on, 413

rejected papers—

lists of rejected papers, 423

opening of ballot paper envelopes, on, 422

opening of covering envelopes, on, 421

POSTAL BALLOT PAPER—*continued*

rejected papers—*continued*

procedure as to, 423

receptacle for receipt of, 417

replacement ballot paper, 414, 415

sealing up of completed corresponding number lists, 412

security of special lists, 412

spoilt, 414

undelivered, effect on election, 411n[11]

POSTAL VOTE

application for—

appeal against registration officer's decision, 367

contents of application, 367

definite or indefinite period, 367

offences, 735

particular election, 371

ballot box—

notice of opening of, 419

opening of, 420, 421

provision of, 417

ballot paper. *See* POSTAL BALLOT PAPER

cancelled paper, retrieval, 420

conclusion of procedure, 423

corrupt practices, offences constituting, 731

counting of votes. *See* VOTE COUNTING

covering envelopes. *See under* POSTAL BALLOT PAPER

electoral fraud, involving, 754

envelopes to be issued to postal voter, 410

forwarding of documents after postal voting—

parliamentary election, after, 497

Welsh Assembly election, 500

instructions for voting by post, 413

local authority referendum. *See* LOCAL AUTHORITY REFERENDUM (postal vote)

marked copy of postal voters list, security precautions, 412

marked packet of lists, making up and sealing, 421

offences as to application or declaration, 735

personal identifier, verification, 420

postal voters list, 373n[7], 412

postal voting statement—

duty to issue, 406

no ballot paper envelope, 421

prescribed form, 406n[5]

procedures on opening of ballot box, 421

receptacle for, 417

References are to paragraph numbers; superior figures refer to notes

REGISTRATION OF
  ELECTORS—*continued*
annual canvass—*continued*
  generally, 151
  historical background, 152
  house to house inquiries, 151
  individual registration. *See* individual
    registration *below*
  power to amend or abolish, 153
  prescribed form, 151n[16]
  reform of registration system based
    on, 152
  registration officer's duty, 151
anonymous entry. *See under* ELECTORAL
  REGISTER
appeals—
  alteration of register following, 178
  appealable decisions, 172
  consolidation of appeals, 174
  costs, 175
  county court jurisdiction, 172
  Court of Appeal, to, 176
  documents to be forwarded to county
    court, 173
  Gibraltar, in, 172n[1]
  hearing of, 175
  notice of, 173
  notification of decision to registration
    officer, 178
  peers, rights of, 172n[1]
  pending, when notice of election
    given, 177
  proxy or post, right to vote by,
    172n[20]
  relevant EU citizens, rights of, 172n[1]
  respondents to appeal, 173n[12, 13]
  restriction on making, 172
  separate hearing after hearing of
    selected appeal, 175
  test-case appeal, 174, 175
entitlement to be registered—
  EU citizen as European parliamentary
    elector, 116
  local government elections, 113
  overseas parliamentary elector, 114
  parliamentary elections, 113, 114
  peer as overseas European
    parliamentary elector, 115
EU citizens, 112
European parliamentary election. *See*
  under EUROPEAN PARLIAMENTARY
  ELECTION
generally, 112

REGISTRATION OF
  ELECTORS—*continued*
individual registration—
  application for entry on register. *See*
    ELECTORAL REGISTER (application
    for entry derived from individual
    registration)
  canvass compatible with system of,
    duty to conduct, 154
  confirmation of entitlement to remain
    registered, 156n[3]
  new application for registration,
    156n[5]
  third new canvass: meaning, 156n[4]
  transitional arrangements, 156
  unregistered persons, invitation to
    apply for registration, 155
National Assembly for Wales, 112
offences associated with voters'
  declarations, 138
overseas elector's declaration—
  additional information, where
    required, 133
  attestation, 134
  cancellation, 132
  effect, 137
  formalities associated with, 132
  invalid declaration, 136
  offence as to, 138, 735
  transmission, 135
peers, 112, 115
register of electors. *See* ELECTORAL
  REGISTER
registration officer. *See* REGISTRATION
  OFFICER
regulations as to, power to make, 112
residence requirement—
  custody, person remanded in, 120
  determining non-residence, 169n[5]
  local government elector, 117
  mental hospital, patient in, 119
  merchant seaman, 118
  Northern Ireland, address in, 169n[4]
  notional residence by way of
    declaration of local connection—
    cancellation of declaration, 121
    deemed residence, 121
    effect, 124
    formalities associated with, 122
    invalid declaration, 123
    offence as to, 138, 735
  parliamentary elector, 117
  temporary absence, 117
  termination of entitlement to be
    registered, 169, 170
rolling registration, 117n[3]

RETURNING OFFICER—*continued*
conduct of election, duty to ensure
　compliance with rules, 383
constituency returning officer—
　European parliamentary election,
　　18n^2
　London Assembly elections, 211n^9
costs, 878
counting of votes. *See* VOTE COUNTING
declaration of election result. *See* VOTE
　COUNTING (declaration of result)
defect in title, 668
electoral records, right to, 182
European parliamentary election, for—
　deputies, appointment, 360
　designation, 360
　detailed assessment of account at,
　　362
　duties, 360
　encouragement of electoral
　　participation, 360, 361
　expenses, recovery, 361n$^{5,\ 18}$
　functions, 360
　local returning officer, designation,
　　360
　payments by and to, 361
list of lost postal ballot papers, duty to
　keep, 415
list of spoilt postal ballot papers, duty
　to keep, 414
local government election, for—
　designation of, 354
　discharge of functions, 354
　encouragement of electoral
　　participation, 354, 355
　expenses incurred by, reimbursement
　　etc, 355
　voting by, 354
　Wales, in, 354
nomination paper—
　decisions as to validity of, 264
　duties generally, 255
　errors, correction of, 265
　grounds for holding paper invalid,
　　263
　See also NOMINATION PAPER
notice of election, duty to publish—
　European parliamentary election, 223
　local government election, 211
　parliamentary election, 196
notice of poll, duties, 388
official poll cards, issue of, 389
parliamentary election, for—
　meaning, 350
　act or omission by, effect on election,
　　350

RETURNING OFFICER—*continued*
parliamentary election, for—*continued*
　advance on account of charges, 352
　detailed assessment etc of account,
　　353
　discharge of functions, 351
　duties, 350
　encouragement of electoral
　　participation, 350, 352
　execution of writ for, 350
　expenses, recovery of, 352n^9
　payments by and to, 352
　persons who can be, 350
　recovery of charges, 352
　sheriff as, death of, 350n^5
performance standards, 57
poll consequent on parish etc meeting,
　356
polling stations—
　duty to provide, 390
　presiding at, 393
　presiding officer and clerk at, duty to
　　appoint, 393
　See also POLLING STATION
postal voting—
　ballot boxes etc, duty to provide, 417
　postal ballot paper, duty to issue, 406
　receptacles, duty to provide, 417
　security and secrecy, duty to ensure,
　　417
secret ballot, duty to ensure, 385, 395
statement of persons nominated, duty to
　publish, 267
Welsh Assembly election, for—
　designation, 357
　detailed assessment etc of account,
　　359
　duties, 357
　encouragement of electoral
　　participation, 357, 358
　expenses, recovery of, 358n$^{5,\ 6,\ 19}$
　payments by and to, 358
working practices, observation by
　Electoral Commission, 53

RIGHT TO VOTE
British citizens overseas, extension of
　franchise to, 96
elector: meaning, 95n^2
European parliamentary election. *See
　under* EUROPEAN PARLIAMENTARY
　ELECTION
generally, 385
legal incapacity, person subject to, 95n^8
local government election, 97
mayoral election, 98
parliamentary election, at, 95, 96

RIGHT TO VOTE—*continued*
  peer. *See under* PEER
  poll—
    parish or community meeting,
      consequent on, 106
    Welsh Ministers' function, as to
      exercise of, 105
  prohibition on voting more than once
    etc, 95
  proxy vote. *See* PROXY VOTE
  referendum—
    local authority referendum, 104
    European Union Act 2011, under,
      103n^2
    Political Parties, Elections and
      Referendums Act 2000, under,
      103
  registration requirement. *See*
    REGISTRATION OF ELECTORS
  restrictions on—
    detained offenders, 107
    incapacity for offences, 109–111
    mental hospital, person detained in,
      108
    serving prisoners, 107
  secret ballot, by, 385
  voter: meaning, 95n^2
  voting age: meaning, 95n^2, 97n^{14},
    149n^2, 157n^{15}, 160n^9
  Welsh Assembly election, 99
RIOT
  polling station at, 396
SALE
  electoral register. *See under* ELECTORAL
    REGISTER
SCOTTISH PARLIAMENT
  Fixed-term Parliaments Act 2011, and,
    189n^4
SCRUTINY
  alien's vote, striking off, 841
  ballot papers, inspection of, 851
  bribery, striking off of vote, 842
  corrupt practice, striking off of vote,
    843
  disagreement between judges, effect,
    854
  disqualified candidate's votes, striking
    off, 845
  equality of votes, following, 853
  evidence of vote, 852
  generally, 839
  history, 840
  illegal practice, striking off of vote, 843
  impersonated person's vote, striking
    off, 844
  improperly recorded votes, 846

SCRUTINY—*continued*
  legal incapacity, striking off of vote,
    841
  list of objections to votes, 849
  object of, 839
  order for production of election or
    referendum documents, 851
  particulars, 850
  person not of voting age, striking off of
    vote, 841
  personation, striking off of guilty
    person's vote, 844
  persons entitled to demand, 848
  recriminatory case, and, 847
  striking off of votes, 899
  treating, striking off of vote, 842
  undue influence, striking off of vote,
    842
SECRETARY OF STATE
  meaning, 2n^1
  functions, 2
  mayoral election, power to make
    regulations as to, 198
  MEPs—
    power to make order as to change in
      number to be elected, 94
    power to make order revising
      distribution of, 93
  policy development grant, power to
    provide scheme for, 60
SECURITY FOR COSTS
  election petition. *See* ELECTION PETITION
    (security for costs)
SERVICE (DOCUMENTS)
  election petition, 795, 804
SERVICE VOTER
  declaration by. *See* REGISTRATION OF
    ELECTORS (service declaration)
  guidance for, 131
SHERIFF
  returning officer, as, 350
SOLICITOR
  corrupt or illegal practice, court's duty
    to report where guilty of, 903
SPEAKER OF HOUSE OF COMMONS
  death of, effect on parliamentary
    election, 513
SPEAKER'S COMMITTEE
  appointed member of, 49n^8
  constitution and functions, 49
SPECIAL CASE STATED
  election petition proceedings as, 816
STATISTICS BOARD
  electoral records, right to be supplied
    with, 187

VOTE COUNTING—*continued*
parliamentary or local government
election—*continued*
postal vote, notification of rejection,
426
recounts, 433
refreshments at count, 425
rejected ballot papers—
grounds for. *See* grounds for
rejecting ballot paper *above*
treatment of, 431
returning officer forbidden from
counting tendered ballot paper,
425
secrecy requirements, notification of,
424
time for counting, 425
time for starting count, 425
verification of ballot paper accounts,
425.
poll consequent on parish or community
meeting. *See* POLL CONSEQUENT ON
PARISH OR COMMUNITY MEETING
(counting of votes)
recount—
application, following, 900
European parliamentary election, 471
London Authority election, 447
Mayor of London election, 454
mayoral election, 439
parliamentary or local government
election, 433
Welsh Assembly election, 462
scrutiny. *See* SCRUTINY
Welsh Assembly election—
attendance at arrangements made
for, 458
combined poll, 458
conclusiveness of returning officer's
decision, 461
constituency election—
constituency returning officer, $18n^2$
polls at, 458
regional poll held on same day,
459
resolution in case of tie, 463
counting of ballot papers, 459
duly returned postal ballot paper,
$459n^{12}$
equality of votes, resolution in case
of, 463
facilities for overseeing proceedings,
provision of, 458
procedure at conclusion of count,
463
recount, 462

VOTE COUNTING—*continued*
Welsh Assembly election—*continued*
regional and constituency polls held
on same day, 459
regional election—
constituency poll held on same
day, 459
contested, ascertainment of results
at, 464
polls at, 458
regional returning officer, $18n^2$
rejected ballot papers, 460
time of count and verification, 458
verification of ballot paper accounts,
459, 740

VOTER
meaning, $95n^2$, $110n^7$, $399n^1$
absent. *See* ABSENT VOTER
attendance at polling station, 395
challenging, on suspicion of
personation, 400
disabled. *See* DISABLED VOTER
interference with, offence, 399, 741
legal incapacity, $95n^8$
personation, challenging on suspicion
of, 400
registration. *See* ELECTORAL REGISTER;
REGISTRATION OF VOTERS
right to vote. *See* RIGHT TO VOTE
service voter—
declaration by. *See* REGISTRATION OF
ELECTORS (service declaration)
guidance for, 131
undue delay, need to vote without, 399
voting by. *See* VOTING

VOTING
absent voting—
generally, 366
methods of, 366
personal identifiers record, 366
postal vote. *See* POSTAL VOTE
proxy, by. *See* PROXY VOTE
registration requirements, 366
See also ABSENT VOTER
age: meaning, $95n^2$
counting of votes. *See* VOTE COUNTING
hours of, 385
manner of—
absent voting. *See* absent voting
above
European parliamentary election, 365
local government election, at, 363
parliamentary election, at, 363
Welsh Assembly election, at, 364
parliamentary election, in, 95

References are to paragraph numbers; superior figures refer to notes

Words and Phrases

Words in parentheses indicate the context in which the word or phrase is used

absent voters list (local authority referendum), 596
Act annexed to Council Decision 76/787 . . . 92n[1]
additional member system (proportional representation), 340n[5]
administration function, 38n[8], 71n[7]
affected principal council, 85n[3]
amalgamated petition—
  (local authority referendum held in England), 562n[12]
  (local authority referendum held in Wales), 560n[17]
anonymous entry (electoral register), 145
application for credit, 188n[34]
appropriate returning officer (National Assembly for Wales), 18n[2]
Assembly general election, 17n[4]
authorised person (DPP's representative), 821n[3]
authority election, 11
available for inspection, 142n[18]
ballot, 3n[4]
ballot paper account, 405
ballot paper envelope—
  (election), 410n[8]
  (local authority referendum), 632
bank holiday—
  (absent voting), 367n[6]
  (claim for referendum expenses), 538n[9]
  (controlled expenditure by third parties), 317n[9]
  (election campaign), 230n[11, 31]
  (European parliamentary election), 223n[1]
  (parliamentary election polling day), 195n[27]
  (registration officer's duty), 141n[5]
bribery, 709
British Council employee, 127n[9]
broadcasting authority, 332n[1]
business, 303n[9], 538n[9]
campaign expenditure, 299
candidate, 230
canvasser, 247
certificate of anonymous registration, 145n[12]
change under EU law, 91n[8]
citizen of the Union, 92n[6], 102n[5], 149n[16]
close of the poll (European parliamentary election), 744n[3]

combined region, 77n[4]
committee room, 275n[8]
compliance period (referendum), 529n[29]
constituency, 9
constituency candidate (Welsh Assembly election), 230n[19]
constituency returning officer—
  (European parliamentary election), 18n[2]
  (London Assembly elections), 211n[9]
constituency vote, 406n[4]
constituent petitions—
  (local authority referendum held in England), 562n[12]
  (local authority referendum held in Wales), 560n[17]
constitutional change (local authority referendum), 561n[10], 562n[14]
controlled expenditure, 313
convicted person, 107n[1]
councillors of the community council, 74
councillors of the neighbourhood council, 74
councillors of the village council, 74
counting observer, 614
counting officer, 179n[20]
county council election, 18n[2]
county court (registration appeal), 172n[1]
covering envelope—
  (election), 410n[6]
  (local authority referendum), 632
criminal law or civil law decision, 228n[12]
declaration as to election expenses, 281n[3]
defined expenses, 287n[20], 546n[25]
delegate, 42n[2]
demise of the Crown, 190n[1]
designated organisation, 531n[5]
disclosure notice, 64
discretionary requirement (Electoral Commission imposing), 758n[2]
disputed claim, 276n[11]
document, 48n[1], 64n[8], 65n[7, 24]
document-disclosure order, 65
donation—
  (to candidate at election), 287
  (to permitted participant at referendum), 546
dual candidate, 204n[30]
dwelling (referendum meeting), 533n[5]
elected mayor, 998n[2], 198n[4]